Kosova 3: From Occupation to International Protectorate

Series Editors

Jason L. Frazer
Besa Pinchotti
Diane Tafilaj
Ramadan Musliu

Series translated by:

Avni Spahiu
Getoar M. Mjeku
Faton Bislimi

Originally issued 2012 in Albanian
by Jalifat Publishing in Houston and Faik Konica in Prishtina as
Kosova 3: Nga Konferenca e Londrës te Protektorati Ndërkombëtar

Published by Jalifat Publishing
Houston, Texas

JUSUF BUXHOVI

KOSOVA

Volume 3

From Occupation to International Protectorate

JALIFAT PUBLISHING
Houston USA
2013

*To my wife, Luljeta,
and children: Arsim, Njomëza, and Arta*

CONTENTS

FOREWORD

The UN Security Council Resolution 1244 of 10 June 1999 annulled two states: the Republic of Kosova declared by the Kacanik Congress of 7 September 1990 and the Belgrade-directed military occupation of Kosova since 23 March 1989 when Serbia had forcefully removed the autonomous status of Kosova as stipulated by the 1974 constitution. Rightly so, this occupation was deemed to be the fourth Serbian occupation of Kosova in the nineteenth century (the first one happened in 1912, the second one in 1918, and the third one in 1944).

This resolution put Kosova under an international protectorate, which would only end on 17 February 2008 when the elected bodies of Kosova, under the provisions of the Constitutional Framework, and in close cooperation with the international community, namely the West, declared Kosova an independent state. Needless to say, the declaration of independence marked an historic achievement – the fulfillment of the Albanian right for self-determination, which they always had, but could never enjoy until it was also supported by the West. And, the Western support was earned thanks to the policies of the 1980s and 1990s and especially thanks to the work of the Democratic League of Kosova that was established on 23 December 1989. In this context, the role of Dr. Ibrahim Rugova remains historic.

Viewed from a political vantage point, the international protectorate of Kosova was not only beneficial but it was also necessary because it removed a conquerer from Kosova – one that was about to use all of the available means to commit genocide against Albanians in Kosova. However, this development does not exclude the historic processes that Kosova underwent since the Serbian occupation of 1912, the social realities that faced the Albanians in Kosova and in other Yugoslav territories, especially during the last stage of the disintegration of Yugoslavia when after the abolishment of Kosova's autonomy and the reoccupation of Kosova by Serbia (which was

13

taking place in the name of "Serbian unity"), the deputies of Kosova's Parliament on 2 July 1990 had separated Kosova from Serbia through the Constitutional Declaration whereas the Parliament of Kosova during its historic meeting of 7 September 1990 had declared Kosova a sovereign republic able to decide on its ties with other republics on its own. The Kacanik Constitution had opened the way for other statebuilding steps, such as the independence referendum of September 1991 and the free parliamentary and presidential elections of April 1992 which resulted in the formation of the Government of Kosova and its respective ministries, including the Ministry of Defense and the Ministry of Internal Affairs.

This state, which would later be called a "parallel" state (although it was not a parallel state, rather a state that was created based on the democratic will of the people) and which would operate for the following six years, despite all of the difficulties and barriers it faced, managed to direct the efforts and activities of all aspects of life – economic, social, cultural, and political – towards survivial under the Serbian occupation and in line with the Kacanik Constitution. Therefore, there were two constitutional states of affairs in Kosova since the Kacanik Constitution up until the beginning of NATO's air strikes against Serbia on 24 March 1999:

- one which was established by the Kacanik Constitution upon which Kosova was an independent republic, a sovereign state with self-determination rights, in favor of which some 97% of Albanians or 87% of all Kosova peoples had voted;and,
- the other one, which represented the classic military occupation of Kosova by Belgrade.

So, these constitutional states of affairs were not parallel, but rather they were exclusive: the state produced by the Kacanik Constitution represented the free will of the Albanians for their own democratic and independent state, which had started to function and which was considered legitimate and legal by all Albanians. This situation would prevent Belgrade from organizing the life of Albanians in Kosova under its direction since the abolishment of Kosova's autonomy after which Kosova Albanians had organized into their own state – a state that Belgrade always wrongly portrayed as a "separatist farce" of some "nationalist extremists and terrorists." On the other hand, the Belgrade constitution that was brought upon Albanians by force on 23 March 1989 was overwhelmingly rejected by Kosova Albanians both formally and practically. This constitution, therefore, had no followers in Kosova as it was strongly rejected by Kosova Albanians in all ways and forms which ultimately included the armed resistance as the only way of fighting against the genocidial regime of Serbia which was using all means possible to destroy the Albanians in Kosova, their state, and their state institutions that were born in accordance with the Kacanik constitution.

Regardless of the fact that the Declaration of 2 July 1990 had formally separated Kosova from the Serbian occupation, in reality, the process of state building in Kosova could not be completed while Kosova was practically under military occupation.

However, understanding this historical process takes one back to the declaration of the Albanian independence of 1912, which resulted from the strong movement for an Albanian autonomous state of the summer of 1908 and 1912, during which times Kosova would pay the highest price (as was discussed in Book Two – Kososo During the Ottoman Empire) especially when the London Conference of Ambassadors of 1913 accepted the Serbian occupation of Kosova, and when the Paris Peace Conference of 1918 reconfirmed this occupation of Kosova then under the kingdom of three Slavic nations (Croats, Slovenes, Serbs) which would later turn into Yugoslavia, a country that would appear in three different versions (first as a kingdom, second under Tito, and third under Milosevic). But, even Yugoslavia would not stand the historic test of Kosova's independence because Yugoslavia itself was built on the basis of Serbian hegemonic ambitions and the political will of Albanians in their own right would one day prevail.

It is here and in this context that the formula of "point zero" of Kosova's statebuilding history starts with the international protectorate being disputed. Accepting the international protectorate as point zero in Kosova's state building history would leave aside, incorrectly, many historic processes of Kosova such as the Kosova liberation movement that would rise right after Kosova's occupation by Serbia, the national unification movement that took many victims, and the Kosova independence movement – first in the form of the Republic of Kosova in the 1960s (which culminated with the historic demonstrations in Prishtina on 27 November 1968 and in many other major towns across Kosova, marking the most massive Albanian demonstrations since World War II). These demonstrations, apart from carrying the call for a Republic of Kosova, did show the pro-western attitude of Kosova Albanians that was reiterated even during the 1981 demonstrations despite the fact that attempts were made to change their ideological

15

character. But, as will be seen, the pro-western commitment and ideology would turn into the basis of the political program of Albanians with the establishment of the Democratic League of Kosova in 1989 as a national movement, which would take on the task of the institutional resistance against the reoccupation of Kosova of 23 March 1989 – the resistance that would enable the establishment of the Republic of Kosova and later the declaration of independence of Kosova together with the armed resistance, regardless of the political nuances that distinguished them during the last phase of this development.

However, the state of Kosova, had historically been a reality fought by Serbia, just like the military occupation of Kosova by Serbia was a reality that the Albanians in Kosova continuously fought through their state and later their armed resistance. This occupation would not spare any means to destroy the people of Kosova and commit genocide against them. This regime had to be stopped and the way in which it was done included NATO's military intervention against Serbia, led by the US and its key European allies (Germany, Great Britain, France, etc).

PART ONE
THE PARTITIONING OF ALBANIA

CHAPTER 1
THE LONDON CONFERENCE AND INDEPENDENCE OF ALBANIA

A Partitioned Albania

The declaration of Albania's independence would find it in a desolate condition. The Albanian state, who delivered messages from Vlora, not only was clamped in only a few hundred square miles packed full of Albanian refugees from areas already occupied by neighboring countries, and Ottoman soldiers who had deserted battlefields and sought refuge, but it was also surrounded from all sides by the foreign occupying armies which were anxiously awaiting its collapse. It may sound absurd, but more people living abroad heard the news of independence (from the newspapers), than the ones living in Albania. It is important, however, that the news of the declaration of Albania's independence reached those, which were many, who wished it the least and would do anything to prevent it from prospering. Many foreign chancellorships and governments also knew about the declaration of independence and were well aware that the weight of resolving the Ottoman heritage in the Balkans would necessarily fall upon them. The issue was complex, and a possible resolution entailed in itself a vast number of political, social, and even cultural and spiritual factors which had mingled with one another throughout history; a history, which in its essence was not only a history of conquests and wars, but more so a clash between civilizations, whose imprints were rooted deep in every aspect of life. The new circumstances could bring about a political resolution only, for a social and cultural one that would satisfy everybody was impossible.

The political and diplomatic response that the Ottoman legacy in the Balkans required was not only the closure of the issue of redrawing maps, which was brought about by the emergence of the state of Albania, but rather quelling the appetites of the neighboring countries (i.e. Serbia, Montenegro, Greece, and Bulgaria). Such appetites, if satisfied, would not only endanger the existence of the newly established state of Albania, but would give rise to many other problems, which would soon appear.

Additionally, the interests of the Great Powers, which in principle had agreed with the existence of Albania, were in play as well, for it was impossible to exclude them from the conjunctures and interests of the Entente Powers and Triple Entente. While one party (Austria-Hungary) was in favor of an ethnic Albania, the others (Russia and France) envisioned the creation of a weak Albania, which would gradually become prey to the neighboring countries. This way, the Albanian issue would cease existing once and for all, allegedly as a result of its incompetence to prove itself a country.

With these concerns at hand, on December 17, 1912, shortly after the declaration of Albania's independence in Vlore, the Conference of the Ambassadors in London started to resolve certain issues in the Balkans. The fate of Albania was to be decided at this conference as well, despite the fact that the country was invaded from all sides: in the North by Montenegrin armies, in the Northeast by Serbians, and in the South by the Greeks; Shkodra in the North and Janina in the South were the only cities that had yet to fall; the Ottomans had joined forces with Albanians and were conducting a joint resistance, however, it would soon turn to be problematic, at least in the South, and serve well the predatory intentions of Greeks towards Albania.

Although occupied by the neighboring countries and still fighting for survival, Albania now had entered the European political scene, where it would remain forever despite its role in it and the difficulties that it would face. Under these circumstances, however, it was clear that the fate of Albanians was exclusively in the hands of the Great Powers. At the time, it was necessary to argue that the perpetual endeavors during the past thirty years (from the Congress of Berlin and onwards) for autonomy within the Ottoman Empire, were not in service of preserving and maintaining this empire but rather were in accordance with the provisions of the Great Powers. That is, that the status quo be used in such a way that the emergence of the state of Albania would come naturally as the next step in the evolution. A responsible behavior towards Albania was necessary at this point; it was important that it was not assessed from a dialectical point of view, namely 'liberators' and 'invaders', as many countries within the

Balkan Alliance sought. By doing so, Albanians and the Albanian issue would be categorized as 'losers', more specifically they would be classified as 'invaders', which inevitably would require punishment by others.

In its first address to the Great Powers, the government of Vlora would attempt to emphasize this element, but due to the fear of being misunderstood it only mentioned the role that Albanians and their recent uprisings played in weakening the Ottoman Empire. However, not addressing the real problem would not help them much. Rather, it would only reinforce the "excuses" of the Balkan Alliance countries to take over Albanian territories arguing that 'they are fighting against the Ottoman invaders'.

Nevertheless, it was the Albanians who declared Albania an independent and sovereign country, regardless of the fact that it was invaded from all sides by the armies of the Balkan Alliance. Now was the time that Albanians demand equal rights with other European countries, and respond firmly to the "excuses" with which the invading neighboring countries were abusing them, proclaiming that they were here "because they had fought the historical invaders." However, it was important that deeds committed during the war not take a political nature, even less be used as triumphs and prizes; on the contrary, it was necessary to clarify that if the requests of Albanians would continue to be disregarded, then the "liberators" would necessarily be seen as the new "invaders." This presented a good opportunity to argue with political, diplomatic and civilized facts, even more so, knowing that Albania had supporters among the Great Powers as well. Austria-Hungary, as one of the most determined supporters, was completely involved in the declaration of independence, not only politically (by conducting it) but also technically (by creating favorable circumstances).

Luckily, the Albanians' existential concern in those moments corresponded well with the preoccupation of the Great Powers, which would ensure that this along with other matters be brought to discussion. Rightfully, the nature of the resolution of the Albanian issue would determine the peace and stability of the region and beyond. Albania had now turned into a node on which depended the future political map of the Balkans. This issue, in turn, was closely related to the interests of the Entente countries (France, England, and Russia) on one hand, and the countries in the Tripartite Pact (Austria-Hungary, Germany, and Italy) on the other, in this region. Even among them, they had different interests and intentions in regard to the Albanian issue and more, now already revealed by the new circumstances in the region, so a mutual solution was inevitable.

It was exactly this clash of interests that would, on one hand, help Albania emerge as an independent state, while on the other hurt it, for it would be subdivided. Albania at this time was trapped between a maximalist treatment, in accordance with its natural ethnic spreading, and a minimalist treatment, which would try to shrink its territory to the point where it would no longer be able to survive on its own.

It was expected that the war for Albania would, on one hand, turn into a war for the Balkans aiming to maintain the current European appearance, while on the other hand, for a Balkan with Slavic-Orthodox domination. It was apparent that the current of events would take this direction ever since the war between the Balkan Allies and the Ottoman Empire reached its peak, since Vienna made sure to immediately let Russia know that it firmly stood behind the integrity of the newly established state of Albania, however, the modalities of the form of the government and its acceptance were to remain open at this time. This was one of the most important testimonies in favor of the new state of Albania that needed to be assessed fairly and in accordance with the circumstances, because it removed the doubts and ambiguities about its existence as a sovereign country, an issue that was still part of the agenda and was being discussed in some European centers.

At this time, even Russia, which had administered the war scenario of the Slavic-Orthodox states of the Balkans against the Ottoman Empire and which stood firmly behind their demands to share among them the areas "they would liberate", agreed that Albania should have its own place among the Balkan states. However, Russia foresaw it as a small principality, just for show, that would quickly fall into the hands of Serbs and Montenegrins, or would depend on them permanently. The recognition of Albania as a new state in the Balkans by Russia, came as a result of the tremendous pressures that came from Italy, Germany, and especially its most loyal ally, Austria-Hungary, which was determined to go to war not only with Serbia and Montenegro, but with Russia as well, despite its reluctance to do so. Austria-Hungary's willingness to go to war turned, indeed, into its most powerful diplomatic weapon in the days to come, especially when the arrogance of Montenegro and Serbia against Albania would hinder the work during the Conference of Ambassadors.

Despite the fact that the Entente countries, France and England, did not have special interests in Albania, Russia knew that they too supported the emergence of Albania and its place in the Balkans. France and England considered Albania a key factor in maintaining the balance and harmony in the Balkans, regardless of the fact that the former supported Greece's claims to the south of Albania, and the latter remained neutral on this issue. On a larger scale, Albania was also considered a sensitive point of contiguity between East and West. After the removal of the Ottoman Empire, Albania, on one hand, was seen by London as a bridge between the two, while Russia and its allies saw it as a danger to the western Christian civilization, arguing that Albanians with their largely Muslim affiliation would enter Europe as a "foreign body," dangerous for its well-being. This in turn would make them the main conspirators on the grounds of the war of civilizations.

The Conference of the Ambassadors in London, though with no prior preparations and arrangements that are customary in such cases, began its work with two previously constructed positions that were largely imposed by Austria-Hungary's diplomacy and politics, which were also consistent with the interests of the League Tripartite. These positions were:

a) Recognition of the existence of Albania, without the status that it should be assigned, and

b) With the agreement that Balkan countries that won the war against the Ottoman Empire should be rewarded with territories, but not on par with their full demands, since this would interfere with the interests of the Great European Powers, and the Tripartite League, especially with those of Vienna and Rome. They were aware that fulfilling the appetites of the Slavic Balkan countries would hurt their interests, since it would strengthen Russian influence in the Balkans, hence by making Albania an independent state they would in turn prevent such influence from further propagation in the Balkans.

Albania in this situation appeared to be a convenient tool; the only dilemma was how and to what extent this strategy would work. Here, indeed, were the chances for its survival.

For Albania the recognition of its independence was important from the very beginning, however it would be achieved, since there laid the resolution of many other issues directly related to the normalization of the current situation; this, however, could not be achieved until the invading armies which were holding the majority of the country hostage were removed. It was also important that Albania break all her ties with the Ottoman Empire, so that the latter's influence would not risk her place within the European countries. There were those who wished that Albania still keep its old ties, which were already unnatural, with the Ottoman Empire; these ties if kept, however, would endanger and hinder Albania's shift from East to West. Russia even claimed that "it was in the interest of European countries and the Albanian people to maintain their links with the Ottoman Empire because of their mass acceptance of Islam, which influenced and changed their mentality as a nation!"[1]

Even France was not all that far from this view, although its reasoning was not of a "civilization" nature, but rather of a practical one. According to some estimates, made by its diplomats in Istanbul "Albania's state organization and its administration should necessarily preserve something from the tradition of the Ottoman state, since they had played an important role in it."[2]

However, the anathema of the Ottoman heritage, which would be introduced mainly for tactical reasons in the green table in London, continued to function in different ways and take the form in accordance with the difficulties that the state of Albania would face during its painful consolidation period. Soon enough, Albania would go through a period of new developments; not only would there be many pro-Turkish uprisings led by the Islamic fanatic movement, but from July 1914 to October 1915, the Turkish flag would rise instead of the Albanian one exactly at the place where the independence of Albania was declared, namely Vlore. From this place, it would be demanded that Albania be returned to the Ottoman Empire, and that the sharia be restored as well.

Thus, in the first session of the Conference of Ambassadors, on December 17, 1912, under the chairmanship of Sir Edward Grey, it was decided that Albania was to become an autonomous part under the sovereignty of the Sultan, and under the exclusive supervision and guarantee of the six major powers. The Conference put Austria-Hungary and Italy in charge of studying and presenting to the Great Powers a project proposal concerning the organization of the autonomous state of Albania.

---

[1] Zavalani, Tajar: "*Histori e Shqipnis*," Tiranë, 1998. p. 241.
[2] *Ibid.,*. p. 237.

Regarding the borders, the Conference decided in principle that the autonomous Albania be bordered with Montenegro to the North, and with Greece to the South. By deciding that Montenegro be the Northern neighbor of Albania, the Great Powers shut out Serbia's road to the Adriatic Sea through the annexation of the territories in Northern Albania. Austria-Hungary played a crucial role here, since with its help the possibility that Serbia have access to the sea through the annexation of northern territories as it had happened before when its army conquered territories from Shengjin to Durres, was ruled out. But, on the other hand, Serbia was given the right to have a commercial outlet to the sea through a neutral and free Albanian "scaffold." Under the European control and the supervision of a special international force, a railroad would be built through these territories, which would enable the transportation of all goods including war ammunitions. The next day, December 18, the government of Serbia was subject to this decision as well.[3]

The decision of the Conference of Ambassadors about the recognition was that an autonomous Albania under the sovereignty and rule of the Sultan and under the exclusive guarantee and control of the six European powers was expected at that stage of the Conference and would rightly be regarded as a tactical step of the Great Powers. By doing so, on one hand, they would give more time to their other plans, as they should have done with other issues pertaining to the complex nature of the Ottoman heritage, and on the other hand, they would send a clear message to the countries of the Balkan Alliance, that they had no choice but to agree with Albania as an independent country and a new factor in the Balkans, regardless of how much they had fought against its emergence.

However, if the sovereignty of the Sultan had remained, Albania would yet again find itself the apple of discord amidst the Balkans, which would mostly favor those who had fought against its occurrence, and who in the future would continue to fight against it arguing that they were fighting the "last bastion of Islamic-Ottomans" in Southeastern Europe. This would even turn into a new Christian missionary supposedly in defense of western civilization, just as the hegemonism of the Great Serbian war against Albanians had claimed, from the appearance of the Grarashanin Serbia onward.

---

[3] *"Historia e Popullit Shqiptar,"* Volume 2, Prishtinë, 1969, p. 365.

Although we cannot say that the government of Vlora had not considered and even had in accordance with the ration of forces and fields of interest among the Great Powers, and in a way it had expected to at least enter the game as a testing instrument and shock absorber. A little later, it would be Ismail Qemali himself who was placed in some shady dealings with the Young Turks about their role in the uprising against the invading Serbs, that if failed, they would be placed back in the game to continue later with the implication of their consequences for the country and its destiny.

But, when speaking of the initial formulation of the Conference of Ambassadors in London, on December 18, 1912, when Albania would be declared an autonomy, the interest in this particular stage of Albania was the emphasis on the guarantees and the exclusive control of the six Great Powers in the country, which was also important that it be in favor of the Government of Vlora. Four Great Powers were charged with direct responsibility for the oversight of the situation in the country, as the government of Vlora was not capable of it even if it was given the mandate of the government, since it would be burdened with the responsibility of removing invading armies, no matter how many, out of the lines that the Conference would appoint as the Albanian border.

This began the era of Albania under international supervision, with several phases, which would not bring the country out of its crisis, but would at once abolish the risk of its decomposition as a state, which is what its neighboring countries wanted and acted upon. This therapy would later continue in various forms from time to time, making known, on one hand the importance of Albania's large international regional configuration, and on the other, pointing out the weaknesses, but also the incapability, of Albanians to take over the destiny of their country.

However, the recognition of Albania, whether it be autonomous, under the SOV, or under the sovereignty of the Sultan, would not interfere with their attempts and concern for the country. Rather, it would be seen that for two months it would be considered as a sovereignty of the Sultan, and as such, its problems not only would not be helped but would return as a great handicap. On one hand, from the inside, among the Albanians there would revive a spirit of pro-Turk Islamist confrontation, while on the other hand, on the outside, the neighboring countries (Serbia, Montenegro and Greece), the sovereignty of the Sultan could be used in various forms for destabilization and thus with the inability to consolidate, would adapt to expand with the Albanian territories and thereby further increase Russia's influence in the Balkans, while an autonomous Albania under the sovereignty of Sultan, could not have the seal of impact of Austria-Hungary and the League Tripartite countries, as would an autonomous Albania without ties to the Ottoman Empire.

Overlooking the sovereignty of the Sultan, as it was completely abrogated by the London Conference decision on July 29, 1913, finally, there would be an acceptance of the project for organization of the Albanian state, under which Albania would be proclaimed a principal autonomy, a hereditary sovereign, where any connection with the Ottoman Empire was omitted, but would not mean the removal of the Ottoman shadow. As it would be seen, she would continue to follow continuously and there would come a time when Albania would be dominated by an anti-European uprising that would take place requiring her to join Turkey, where it now appeared as Ottoman Albania, at least temporarily with an historic mortgage, fighting a life-or-death battle against the European Albania, a war which included Albanians, but whose brakes were held by its opponents, then Slavic and Greek led by the Orthodox Russia, who had many reasons for Albania to fall prey to self-destruction from within.

Two of the three hot spots around which would focus all the attention of the Conference of Ambassadors, namely, the crisis of Shkodra, Janina, and the issue of Kosova, were directly related to the aftermath of the Ottoman presence in defending them. While, on the other hand, Kosova and the Albanian rebellion against the Serbian occupation during and after the Conference of Ambassadors in London, would not be exempt from the implication of the Young Turks and their efforts to use in their interests the Albanian tragedy, which they had helped to create.

The crisis of Shkodra and Janina, which initially appeared to be matters of a military nature— where in the former, the fighting between the Montenegrin forces on one hand and the joint Ottoman and Albanian forces on the other would continue, and on the latter, the Ottoman forces aided by Albanian volunteers and patriots upon the calling of the government of Vlora would continue to fight against Greek forces — assuming the character of a struggle between "the liberators" and "invaders," where "liberators" were rewarded and "invaders" punished.

Of course, the relation between the "liberators," in this case the Serbian, Montenegrin, and Greek armies, and the "invaders," the Ottoman armies, would be easily explained if it were not for the Albanians who had joined the Ottoman forces in defending their country from the "libera-tors." In doing so, they had immediately assumed the status of the new invaders, which in turn made them allies of the ones who had been labeled as conquerors!

This "complication," at times incomprehensible from the outside and deliberately made confusing even more by the opponents of Albania, intended to use the war against the last remnants of the Ottoman Empire in Europe, specifically in territories mostly inhabited by ethnic Albanians, as a double alibi against Albanians and their interests: on one hand, their territories would be conquered under the pretext that they were conduct-ing a liberating war against the Ottomans, which in theory was correct but not in practice, and on the other hand, Albanians would practically be anatomized as participants and collaborators of the Ottomans!

Janina and especially Shkodra present the most typical example of this issue and this complexity. It is suspected that this whole situation could have been part of a larger scenario from outside, intending to use it as a "backup plan," and especially shift the focus away from certain issues, as was the case with Kosova, where the invading Serbian and Montenegrin armies were exercising a terrible genocide against the innocent Albanian population there.

There is no doubt that the issue of Shkodra was of such nature, for there are many indicators that point in that direction. The fact that the situation was aggravated when the Conference of Ambassadors on March 22, 1913, under the pressure of Austria-Hungary and Italy would categor-ically reject Russia's proposal that Shkodra be given to Montenegro, is the best testimony. Russia and Serbia would be the ones to directly encourage King Nikola to begin a blockade of Shkodra under the euphoria of nation-alistic slogans: "Shkodra or death." The purpose of these blockades was to protect the Serbian conquests in Kosova and Macedonia, while at the same time to create opportunities for gaps and conflicts among Albanians (here they were counting on the factorization of Esad Pashe Toptanit and his role in Shkoder). This in turn would create other problems and difficulties for Vienna and Rome and their supporters who were to take on the responsibility of governing Albania. It was clear that this intended fragmentation among Albanians was well thought and planned out by Belgrade and Cetinje in collaboration with Russia, especially as Esad Pashe Toptani would become part of their game both in relation to the international community and with Albanians as well.

Esad Pashe Toptani appeared "on stage" as an "autonomous Albanian factor" the moment that the commander of the garrison of Shkodra, Hasan Riza Pasha, was assassinated. Even more, it was suspected that Esad Pashe Toptani might have played a role in his death, since he was determined along with many other Albanian fighters not to surrender Shkodra, whose defense was also in the interest of Austria-Hungary who was also fighting not to give it up. For as long as it did not capitulate, but instead was defended by Albanians and not by medieval ghosts, the thesis that we were dealing with an Albanian region and not an imagined Montenegrin metropolis was confirmed. Witnessing that Montenegro assisted by Serbian forces had no intention of stopping the blockade of Shkodra and that the Conference risked losing its authority to become an instrument that would serve the Serbian-Montenegrin goals, Austria-Hungary threatened Russia to send its troops towards Sandzak in Northern Albania and Kosova to ensure the protection of Albanians from the Serbian-Montenegrin attacks, if the latter would not stop their violence against Shkodra.

Afraid from the Austro-Hungarian threats and the consequences that could follow risking everything that had been achieved hitherto in the Conference in favor of its Slavic allies, Russia allowed a fleet demonstration by the European powers on the Montenegrin coast. On April 5, the international marine squad under the command of the British Vice Admiral Sir Cecil Burney arrived at the coast of Tivari, and after a few days completely blocked the sea from Tivari to the Drin delta. Even after this marine squad demonstration Montenegrins did not agree to unblock Shkodra. But since Austria-Hungary had already mobilized its forces and was in a war state ready to deploy for Sanxhak, on April 12 Serbia finally agreed to withdraw its troops. With no Serbian forces in the area, it was clear that the Montenegrin army would not be able to take over Shkodra on its own. However, in order to achieve this, they took advantage of Esad Pashe Toptani's ambition to become the "king" of Albania, who agreed to enter into an agreement with the countries of the Entente and hand them over the city. It became known that previously he had requested the establishment of contacts with the representatives of the League Tripartite, but he was rejected by them on the grounds that he could no longer be trusted since he was already affiliated with Serbs and Russians. So, in order to still remain a "key" player, on April 22, 1913, Toptani signed an agreement with the Montenegrins to hand them over the city. He, along with Ottoman troops and Albanian fighters took what was left of the ammunition and fled toward Middle Albania, where he would establish his principality and work for his personal interests.

After seven months of fighting, the Montenegrin army entered Shkodra where it celebrated "the historic victory," which cost the city many victims, among which were many common citizens and patriots of Shkodra. As expected, on April 28, without the consent of the Great Powers, Vienna threatened that if Montenegro were not to withdraw its troops from Shkodra within a week, Austria-Hungary together with Italy would intervene by military means to take over the entire Albania. A similar threat was made to the Ottoman Empire as well; since, after April 19 it had signed a peace treaty with the Balkan countries and had practically given up any connections with Albania; it was required not to interfere with Albania's internal affairs and withdraw all its troops from there.

The threat of Austria-Hungary, and its preparations to march across Albania with Italy, seriously troubled Russia, which realized that an undesirable war with the Tripartite League was at the verge of breaking. This situation would deeply bother France and England as well, which would require a prompt response from Russia to relax the situation. So, two days before Vienna's ultimatum passed, Russia obliged Montenegro to accept the withdrawal of troops from Shkodra, and furthermore do it publicly.

Montenegro's army left Shkodra on May 14, 1913, after a three week stay and after it looted everything valuable and burned the old bazaar down. Shortly after, international forces entered the city. The city administration passed into the hands of a military commission headed by Cecil Burney and was composed of the officers of the fleet that had blocked the coast. The international commission disregarded the government of Vlora, and did not allow the Albanian flag to rise in Shkodra. A cantonal[4] administration was established in the city, which opened the doors for occasional international interventions in Albania. As it would soon be seen, the Northern city, governed by the International Commission of Control, would be spared form many difficulties with which other parts of Albania had to deal before the beginning of the World War I.

---

[4] *Ibid.*, p. 375.

The international intervention in Shkoder to end the Montenegrin occupation marked the first military demonstration of the West, in the history of Albania, which sided with Albania in its conflict with Montenegro.

The situation of Shkodra and its salvation from the foreign invasion (Montenegrin in this case), unfortunately was not to be repeated in Janine. It too had a similar scenario, but in this case not only were there different actors involved and different roles, but also the interests of the Great Powers varied. Just as before, we are dealing with the protection of an Albanian city now located in the South of the country. However, in this situation in addition to the Albanians who were already fighting alongside Ottoman forces, upon a decision made by the Government of Vlora on January 28, 1913, many other Albanians volunteered as well.

This decision, however, would appear to be questionable both from a political and military standpoint. Consequently, Greece would seize Janina and other surrounding regions more because it had "conducted a liberating war against the Ottoman invaders" rather than based on ethnic rights, since the population of Janina and the regions around it were largely inhabited by ethnic Albanians, a fact that was never questioned by its supporters either.

Although Greece's claims to the South of Albania were well known, the decision of the Government of Vlora to get involved in the war, even a defensive one, alongside the Ottoman Empire and against Greece, automatically made its intentions biased as well. Furthermore, despite the fact shortly after its involvement in the war it had also declared its neutrality, limiting itself exclusively to the protection of Albanians in case of an imminent threat by the Balkan armies; this would inevitably position it on the side of the losers as was the Ottoman Empire at that time.

Needless to say, the decision of the Government of Vlora was driven by patriotic sentiments to defend its own lands. However, the dilemma arises as to how much this act helped in maintaining the Albanian territories, such as Janina and the Preveza Bay, rather than resolving it by any other strategy.

If the attitudes of the Government of Vlora about the participation in the war alongside Ottoman forces to protect Janina and other Albanian territories appeared questionable, not morally but by the consequences that they brought about, towards the issue of Kosova and its protection it appeared helpless. Furthermore, it would become a permanent black mark in its conscience, bearing in mind that from the time of the League of Prizren and on, Kosova was the center of any Albanian movement. Many revolutions that preceded the declaration of independence were organized in Kosova, nevertheless, it was the first to fall prey to the Serbian and Montenegrin conquest, unable to prevent it. Even worse, unaccountable towards Kosova and its defense in these crucial moments of history, were not only the leaders of the National Movement, who did not fulfill their commitments arising from the Taxation Agreement, February, 1912, but the First and the Third Ottoman Army (Shkup and Manastir) who were responsible for its protection, behaved in exactly the same way: they did nothing to protect it.

Data show that the military command of Shkup and Manastir, upon regrouping their forces towards Shkodra and Janina, could have acted according to secret scenarios made between the Sultan and the Russian Czar. Part of this scenario was that the Balkan territories be surrendered to Russia's allies without much trouble, while the Ottoman Empire, on the other hand, would be guaranteed both by Russia and the Entente countries its interests in Aegean and the Black sea as well as in the Middle East. Ultimately, such a scenario was also used in the Russian-Turkish war of 1877/78, where Ottoman's defeat by Russia was prearranged by some Russian-Ottoman agreements to strengthen the Ottoman Empire in the East, Aegean, and Africa, while allowing the creation of a Great Bulgaria in the Balkans under the Russian influence. The Treaty of Saint Stefano had in some way blessed this arrangement, such that the Europeans needed the Congress of Berlin to correct it, and to keep the Ottoman Empire alive through the means of a status quo.

Reports coming from the line of fighting between the Ottoman forces on one hand and the Balkan Allies on the other hand, which took place on the border between Kosova and Serbia and on the part of Macedonia, testify that the Balkan forces did not encounter any serious resistance, as had been expected. Ottoman forces which were in larger numbers and possessed better artillery, under the withdrawal orders for "regrouping" (The Eastern Army in the direction of Istanbul, and the one bordering Serbia, Montenegro, and Greece departed in the direction of Shkodra and Janina) after a few initial symbolic fights would leave the first line of fire and abandon the Albanian militiamen. Despite the willingness of the Albanian militiamen to resist the Serbian and Montenegrin armies determined to regain "the Serbian medieval cradle" and avenge the lost battle five centuries ago, they would not be able to hold their grounds for long.

Even though Kosova and its protection would not return into an Albanian inclusive front to establish the Albanian state, in the political and diplomatic sphere, during the Conference of Ambassadors in London, it would turn into an open battle between, on the one side, the "historical right," that was fabricated by Serbs a long time ago and used by them to represent it as a "return to the medieval Serbian spiritual cradle," and on the other side, that of ethnic rights as a right to life that Albanians possessed. The first one was defended by the Russians while the second one was defended by the Austro-Hungarians. The latter however, were left to understand that they were not in favor of the absolute enforcement of this principle, since the results of the Balkan Alliance war against the Ottoman Empire appeared as evidence carried out by force, which could not be ignored a hundred percent. Vienna's representative in London said in one of the sessions of the Conference at the end of December, that the "land [that is] entirely inhabited by Albanian population should not be separated from Albania," while regions where Albanians constituted the majority of the population, could be subject to compromise between the Great Powers and could be used to meet the aspirations of neighboring states. Therefore, it was natural that this compromise would bring the recognition of Albania.

However, these attitudes extremely polarized Austria-Hungary with Russia, when they, based on these principles, presented their maps regarding the Albanian borders. On one hand was the ethnic principle, the one that largely guided Vienna's attitude, based on which Albania was proposed to include most of the territories in which the Albanian population comprised the majority (with the exception of a part from Central Kosova and the East, which however, left Prishtina and Shkup outside of the Albanian state). This idea was defended by Austria-Hungary from the beginning. On the other hand, Russia appeared with its opinion that Albania, without Kosova and other regions in Macedonia should be restricted to a small principality with no options for survival. Thus, the map of Austria-Hungary, which was presented to the Conference, was a draft under discussion, which if accepted, from the Albanian standpoint appeared to be optimal. This way, the boundary line in the North passed along Buna, following the old direction of the Montenegrin border with the Ottoman Empire until near Razhanicë and from there it continued in the form of a semi-circle passing south of Gucia and Plave, taking the direction near Peje, Gjakove, and Prizren that were included in Albania. From Prizren the border went down to the South and arrived in the mountains between Lake Ohrid and Prespa, including the towns of Diber and Ohrid within the Albanian lands. Further to the South of the Southeast, the border included Korça and Janina on the Albanian side and in the end it followed the line of the Kalamar River to the Ionian Sea, to the South of the island of Corfu.

Relying on the "historical right" and arguing that it was "the Serbian medieval center," out of which Serbian kings and Serbian church history had originated, and with similar slogans that were fabricated a long time ago by Serbian hegemonism, Russia proposed that Kosova and Macedonia should belong to Serbia, while the border line in the North to cross the Adriatic Sea near Drin's flow, then proceed toward the East until the union of White Drin with Black Drin. From there, it should continue over the course of the Black Drin, to the lake of Ohrid. The border then passed to the South and back to the West to go out to the Ionian Sea at the Qafali Cape, leaving Korça, Delvina and Saranda out of Albania. Compared with the map of Austria-Hungary, viewed by Albanian interests, the Russian map appeared minimal.

There was also a third map, that of the Balkan countries, that narrowed Albania to a size of a coastal province without Lezha, which went up to Vlora.

The fourth map was that of the Government of Vlora, which included all ethnic Albanian lands and was justified on this principle and was considered as maximal. This map was not discussed at all at the conference.

The history of maps that was presented to the Conference of Ambassadors in London and one that was selected on July 29, 1913 and became official, in fact, represents the history of the birth of the Albanian state cut with scissors on the green desk of the Great Powers and their conformants who helped them to halve the Albanian state. Though one should not forget that if Albania did not have the support of Austria-Hungary aided by Italy and Germany, it could have been erased from the map. In this manner, the Albanian issue would have remained unresolved, as a major potential for a crisis, as will be noted, which would continue to be part of the vibrations in the Balkans. Great European Powers, despite the fact that they would accept the Albanian state in its known size, would not do this based on the principles of ethnic rights and those of life, but on those of "historical rights." On these principles and in particular on the "right to the fruits of war," Serbia was given Kosova and part of Macedonia. In a similar fashion was dealt the case of Janina and other Albanian territories to the South, without caring to know why exactly on these "principles" the ethnic Albanian population remained outside the borders of the Albanian state in the Northwest and South, although in many parts as a majority, returned to a minority, where they were subject to the worst forms of forced assimilation, ethnic cleansing and other actions, which would lead even to state terror and genocide. One of these cases used by the Serb regime against Albanians is the terror that took place in Kosova in the last decade of the last century, to which, in the end, the countries of the West, among them Britain, France, Germany, and Italy, that in London had decided to halve Albania and enlarge Serbia by giving them Kosova and other occupied Albanian territories, led by the United States of America, had to use military intervention from the air, thus, separating Serbia from Kosova and putting it under the protectorate of the World Organization. Thus, a part of the injustices of the Conference of Ambassadors in London in 1913 were fixed.

Before this historical twist happened in Kosova, which took over seven decades of suffering and superhuman survival efforts, along with many disasters and calamities which Albanians that remained outside ethnic Albania went through, Albanian patriots, mainly from Kosova, who had led major Kosovar insurrections in 1908 when Young Turks came in power, and in 1911 and the summer of 1912, rose up against them and with the Memorandum of Shkup of 24 July consisting of 14 points, they forced the High Gate to accept their demands. As they drew lessons from the tragic suffering that resulted from their frivolity and actions though which they distributed the nationwide uprising and emptied a part of their accumulated energy when they should not have, they tried for another uprising, but this time against the Serbian and Montenegrin occupation forces, which after the decision in July by the Conference of London, held the right over Kosova.

It was a more desperate effort and with mutual threats rather than an action that promised any success. Hasan Prishtina, Bajram Curri, Isa Buletini and others from the National Movement, after the Conference of Ambassadors in London made the already known decisions, gathered in some parts of Albania to organize an uprising. They counted on those who were already forced to leave their territories, but also on the Albanian volunteers within and outside the country, and especially on those who had remained in their homes and had many reasons not to accept the new invaders. They would not accept the decisions of the Conference of Ambassadors nor would they respect the obligations of the Government of Vlora to remain neutral to any military action outside the borders recognized by the major European powers.

By trying not to give the impression of involvement in Kosova's uprising, the Government of Vlora in September 1913 appointed Hasan Prishtina as minister, even though it may have created yet another belief that Ismail Qemail had done this deliberately to give the irredentist movement, at least from the inside, some legitimacy. However, the Government of Vienna also showed interest in the Kosova uprising. Thus, it indirectly provided support to the Kosovars since the Albanian uprising in the Albanian occupied areas by Serbia would weaken the position of Belgrade so it would not be equally oriented in supporting irredentist movements in Bosnia and Herzegovina, which were becoming increasingly belligerent against the Austrian presence in this country, and as would be seen a year later with the assassination attempt of Serbian nationalists against Prince Franz Ferdinand in Sarajevo, paving the way toward World War I, which began with the entry of Austria in the war with Serbia.

There is likelihood that Serbia had an interest in this uprising. Some archival sources indicate that some of its agents infiltrated along the Albanian insurgents distributing money and weapons in parts of Diber and Gjakova and took orders from Belgrade as to which areas must necessarily be involved in the uprising. This was because, as will be seen, Serbia needed a cause to achieve three goals simultaneously:

First – that the uprising of the people of Kosova and Macedonian territories, which territories it had already won in London, would be used as an excuse for another terror to the rest and remaining part of Albania, an action which would be taken in the name of protecting its state borders, to trigger another wave of displacement of Albanians towards the Albanian State; in this way the occupied areas would continue to be ethnically cleansed to such an extent as to be ready for a rapid colonization as was envisaged by Belgrade;

Second – it intended to correct the legitimate conquests and add several other strategic points in regards to Albania, which would be declared as a "safety zone" and

Third – to bring down the government of Vlora and instead bring Esad Pashe Toptani, with whom it had very good relations and with whom it seemed that some deals were already made, even though, in the meantime, he would be introduced in the Government of Vlora as the Minister of Defense, whose main purpose was to stop such 'tricks.'

Without taking into account deals regarding who needed it (the uprising) more and who had put his/her fingers in it to achieve certain purposes, the uprising of the Albanians against Serbian occupation forces started from the second half of September in Diber, then proceeded to Struga and Ohrid and finally spread to Tetovo and Kosova, which included Prizren and Gjakova. Of course, Serbia after some initial losses that seemed to be projected, and which she quickly used for large scale internal nationalist mobilization, would soon recover and in early October begin a major counterattack in three directions with strengthened and numerous artillery units, including large caliber weapons that would relentlessly bombard and destroy settlements from Pollog in Macedonia to the far territories of Dukagjin, this way creating great terror to target points from the prior year in the war against Turkish forces. After a while Serb troops would access the inner parts of Albania and enter Tirana and Durres, leading to justified doubts that it had expected such a motive.

After all this, Vienna would again appear, this way preventing Serbia from achieving what it sought after the bloody oppression of the uprising in Macedonia and Kosova. On October 18, the Austrian Foreign Minister Berthold, for the second time in six months, would send an ultimatum to Belgrade to withdraw its troops from Albania within eight days or face war with Austria-Hungary.

Advised by France and Russia, Serbia quickly withdrew its military forces from Albania, but they were further strengthened in Kosova to carry out terror against the defenseless population. Now they could do this without any difficulty or risk of being faced with any possible ultimatums from Vienna, considering that they had the 'land patent' from the Conference of Ambassadors in London, based on which they could rage war whenever they wanted in the name of protecting the sovereignty and state integrity from Albanian separatist forces.

However, leaders from Kosova who had led this uprising continued to remain in Albania and developed other plans for rebellion against the Serb and Montenegrin invaders. They also included other external factors, especially Bulgarians and Turks, who after the Second Balkan War, when Serbia and Greece benefited even more, sought to join forces on a new Albanian-Ottoman-Bulgarian alliance. As would be seen, the "Ottoman shadow" would damage Albania from the outside as well as from the inside carrying it through other disasters. From the outside – it would put Albania into an early scenario of a new war that was being prepared between the forces of the Entente and the Triple Alliance; while from the inside – due to the illusion of a supposedly hidden connection with the Young Turks, which was intercepted by all sides, returned Kosova and Cameria to Albania – after a Muslim Prince was accepted in advance as the leader of Albania, mobilizing Albania even more around a division in favor or against a European Albania than resolving the issue itself.

The reason for this would be the appointment of a German named Wilhelm von Wied to take the crown of Albania, who was proposed by Romania and accepted by the Great Powers after having previously obtained the approval of Italy and Austria-Hungary.

Plans for Kosova to return to Albania with the support of the Young Turks (precisely those who were responsible and mainly at fault as to why Albanians did not gain their autonomy as part of the Ottoman Empire and thus avoiding the disaster and tragedy that would bring subsequent events) would be more part of plans that Albania, even as it is now, to fall from within, rather than return the lost territories when it had neither power nor the government, except for the internal chaos that was present.

This was the main reason that most of the Kosovars, who knew from where the disaster happening to them came and who could help them, aligned with Prince Wied, convinced that under a German prince and alignment on the side of the West, chances of returning to Albania were greater than with a Turkish prince and alignment with the East; even though this would lead them into another internal and fratricidal war like the one that later started between supporters and opponents of Prince Wied. This in fact highlighted the power of those who still thought of Albania as covered with green kerchieves (scarves), already an anti-historic creature on the European soil, that not incidentally was sought by Russia, Serbia and Greece, because they knew that in this way Albania and Albanians were judged to be eventually expelled from the Western family with violence and accused of deserving this despite the fact that they had been helped to break away.

With these concerns, Kosovars would be included in a barely unforeseen development, when concerns about the removal of the Serbian occupation would return into a priority to make Albania a state, without which there was no return of Kosova.

But before German Wilhelm von Wied was set as the leader of the Albanian state, there was initially the appearance of a war for the imaginary throne of Albania with various contenders, which turned into a virtual arena that moment when the Conference of Ambassadors made the decision that yesterday's imaginary throne of Albania would be filled by a prince from overseas.

The Struggle for the Albanian Throne

Who were the contestants for the throne of Albania and why would some of them, despite their failures, help the affirmation of the Albanian cause in international dimensions?

In a letter that Abdyl Frashëri directed to the Italo-Arbëresh Francesco Crispi in 1890, he informed him regarding the Albanians' plans to create an autonomous province or a small kingdom in accordance with the new organization of the Balkans. Among others, he would make known that the Albanians would accept a prince who would be their blood, hence an Albanian, who was familiar with their habits and able to lead to progress. On behalf of the Albanians of Istanbul, he proposed as the next king of Albania, Fuad Pasha, Prince of Egypt and the nephew of the famous Mehmed Ali, the organizer of the sub-kingdom of Egypt. Abdyl believed that the "European education of Fuad and his military skills gained in the Italian army had connected him with the West."[5]

Abdyl's proposal, although premature, was however significant for many reasons. Among them were those of a political nature that deserved attention because Albania's independence could be natural and probable as a development that went through the autonomy within the Ottoman

---

[5] Skëndi, Stavro: *"Zgjimi kombëtar shqiptar,"* Tiranë, 2000, p. 290.

Empire, so, that it appeared as a form of Ottoman Albania, which as such definitely should have a prince or king from abroad, as was the case with almost all other countries that gained their independence from the Ottoman Empire (Serbia, Greece, Romania and lastly Bulgaria) and went through the test of autonomy and princes or kings coming from abroad (usually Germans). However, because of the unique position of the Albanians in the Ottoman Empire as well as their role as a bridge between civilizations, it was preferred to be from the East.

This way the prejudice of the prince with "Albanian blood," coming from the East, but with European education, would not cause an immediate break with the Ottoman past much less impede the Western future of Albanians. This would make it more acceptable to Western nations, especially to Italy, which had its interests in Albania. England, too, because of its interests in Egypt, could hold a friendly attitude towards the small Albanian kingdom.[6]

A little later, always in the context of thinking about "the throne of Albania," initiated by Abdyl Frashëri, regardless of the level that he would have (a Prince or a King), in Europe candidates began emerging to fill the future Albanian throne and this marked an important stage of the intensification of the Albanian national awakening, which touched on important issues related to the special role that it should play as a state.

First among them was Don Juan de Aladro y Perez de Valsco who adopted the Albanian name Prince Gjin Aladro Kastrioti. He was born in 1845 in Spain and in 1867 he entered the diplomatic service of the country. While there, he was raised from the rank of the person charged with common duties to that of the foreign minister of that country. In 1886 he moved to Paris where he became the chairman of the International Committee of the Spanish Railways in Pyrenees.

Aladro claimed to be a successor of Skenderbeg, as the sister of the national hero was married to one of his predecessors. On the basis of what Aladro said and what is published in "Dicionnariw des contemporains," this ancestor was his great-grandfather, Prince de Aladro who followed King Karl from Naples to Spain. However, these statements said by Aladro could not be verified, even though the story seemed believable as Spain, via Naples, had been in contact with Skenderbeg.[7] In 1899 he issued

---

[6] *Ibid.*, p. 291.
[7] *"Albania,"* VII (1902), 70 and IX (1904), 114.

a manifesto where he made allusion regarding "his royal blood" and put himself at the top of the Albanian National Movement. Since that time and on, he was seen working for the liberation of Albania from the Ottoman Empire and was committed to its independence, directing towards Paris and other European countries the actions taken by his Albanian friends, among whom were also Faik Konica and Shahin Kolonja.[8] Some of the important Albanian intellectuals of the time, not only supported him, but they dedicated poems to him, as was the case of Luigj Gurakuqi and his poetry "A New Star," published under the pseudonym Geg Postripa.[9]

Besides the reference to the past that was related to Skenderbeg, Aladro drew attention to his projects regarding the future of Albanians and Albania, projects which most of the time were in line with those of the leaders of the Albanian National Movement. He requested for Albanians to be known as a nation and to legitimize the right to an independent state based on ethnic grounds, a state which had to be created in collaboration with the European powers and the Ottomans. He called for brotherhood amongst Albanians, as stated in the Qur'an and the Gospel, as well as for the integration of their homeland. By calling himself a "humble servant of Albania" and by signing as "Prince Gjin Aladro Kastrioti," he tried to create a cult around his persona by using the press, letters and other announcements.[10] In achieving this he was helped by newspapers "La Nazione Albanese," "Perlindja Shqiptare," authority of the Albanian society "Shpresa (eng. Hope)" in Bucharest and in the beginning, "Albania" of Konica. Konica later ceased support for Aladro because "there was no sufficient evidence that he came from the roots of Skenderbeg," and thus he called Aladro a "crazy braggart." Nikola Naco acted likewise, who in the newspaper "Shqiptari (eng. Albanian) called him"Russia's tool."[11]

Aladro, however, began to lose faith in part of Albanians when he returned to the exposure of the revolutionary spirit and its transfer to Albania from abroad. For this purpose he went about creating relation-

---

[8] See the report of Pasettit directed to Goluchowskit, Rome, February 12, 1902, no. 7 J, HHStA, PA XIV/12, Albanien, VIII/1.

[9] "*Albania,*" VI (1901), 105; "*Drita*" 1, November 14, 1901.

[10] See the texts of the announcements issued in 1902 and 1903 at A. Lorecchio, Rome, 1904, Note the document, page: CCCIXX-CCCIXXVII, quoted by S. Stavro: "*Zgjimi kombëtar shqiptar,*" Tiranë, 2000, p. 292.

[11] "*Albania,*" VIII (1905), 157; "*Shqiptari,*" June 8, 1903.

ships with revolutionary leaders of other nationalities such as those with the Macedonian B. Sarafov and the Italian Riccioti Garibaldi. The latter was known as an adventurer, whom the Italians wanted to send (introduce) to Albania so that they could find a cause to intervene and disembark on the Albanian coast. Because of this, Garibaldi was not supported even by the Italian-Arberesh, especially De Rada, who demanded that the Albanian National Movement be supervised by the leaders of the movement in Istanbul and Albania and be conducted in accordance with the already known national program. Aladro spent his capital for good, when in July 1902 he visited Vienna and there, in conversation with Count Lützov, one of the heads of the divisions of the Austro-Hungarian foreign ministry, required him to make himself and Albania unconditionally available to the Austrian Empire.[12] Vienna, which had special interests in Albania, followed these movements from the outside, but still focused on the relations with the Albanians in Albania, and specifically with the leaders of the Albanian National Movement in Istanbul.

After Aladro, Giovanni Castriota Skenderbeg of Auletta appeared on stage as the contender for the Albanian throne, for whom specifically Zef Skiroi was comomitted, who by objecting to the origin of Aladro, highlighted the Marquis of Aleutta, who lived in Naples as a "far more pure seed of the Albania's Lion." The Marquis that Skiroi supported, that is D. Giovanni Castriota Skenderbeg of Auletta, was called a "great god, noble and notorious," and had certain nobility titles. The King of Italy, on April 4, 1897, after a study conducted by the Council of Heraldry, decreed that he could use the name and carry the weapons of Gjergj Kastriot Skenderbeg.[13]

Marquis of Auletta, despite the support from Italo-Arberesh people, did not succeed in becoming a contender for the Albanian throne, since he was unknown in Albania and also to the leaders of the national movement.

Another active contender for the imagined throne of Albania was Prince Albert Ghika (alb Gjika) from Romania. He was a descendant of a Romanian royal family of Albanian descent. Its founder was George I Ghika, Prince of Moldavia (1658-1659) and of Wallachia (1659-1660) who was named by Prince Albert Ghika "Shqiptari (eng. the Albanian)." The

---

[12] Report of Count Lützov, July 8, 1902, HHStA, PA XIV/12, Albanien VIII/1.
[13] *"Albania,"* XII (1906), 6-7.

contender was the great-grandson of Prince Gregor III Ghika of Moldavia and Wallachia who was killed in 1777 in Jassy.[14]

It is noted that Albert Ghika, since the beginning appeared as an opponent of Aladro and his efforts to lead the Albanian movement, by projecting it on the side of Austria-Hungary. Albert Ghika, since the beginning represented the interests of Romania and Italy. Since Bucharest was interested in a Romanian-Albanian link and even came up with a project for a Vlach-Albanian federation, Prince Albert Ghika behaved along this framework, although he would always declare that his goal was an independent Albania. For this, he established himself as the Albanian "mandate" through a Congress that was held in Bucharest, which called in 15 Albanian delegates, although it was clear that they could have been from the Albanian diaspora in Romania but by no means from the "Albanian lands," as he said. In the newspaper "Neue Frei Presse" of Vienna, in November 1904, with the slogan *"Albania for Albanians,"* he unveiled his program, stating that *"the Albanian people should be prepared to defend their independence against any annexation effort."* In an interview with the Italian newspaper *"Il Giornale d'Italia"* Prince Ghika later stated that *"the true enemies of Albanians were neither Bulgaria, nor Serbia nor Montenegro, but Austria,"* by calling himself the supreme leader of the Albanian movement, he also said he would lead the Albanian revolution that would be strengthened by more than 12,000 European volunteers, mostly Vlachs, who, according to him "have a common cause with the Albanians."[15]

Obviously he would be called by Vienna a "vulgar adventurer,"[16] and as such could not be admitted as partner from Italy, either. This way, Prince Ghika did not find support for his plans from Rome, even though he adopted the revolutionary program of General Riccioti Garibaldi.

Ghika continued to seek support even in those places where it was the most difficult. He went to Montenegro and there he met with Prince Nicholas. In Podgorica he met with some of the leaders of the Albanian

---

[14] Report of Pavllacini directed to Goluchowski, Bucharest, March 21, 1905, No. 10D, HHStA, PA XIV/13, Albanien VIII/2.

[15] *"La Grande Albanian – Intervista col principe Alberto Gjika,"* "Il Giornale d'Italia," Roma, February 7, 1905, nr. 9G, HHStA, PA XIV/13, Albanien VIII/2.

[16] Skëndi, Satavro: *"Zgjimi kombëtar shqiptar,"* Tiranë, 2000, p. 297.

tribes. In this visit he was accompanied by the Albanian priest Gaspër Jakova Mërturi, who was the editor of "Herald of Albania" in Rome.[17]

But, as it would be seen, Prince Ghika lost support even from the "base," i.e. from Bucharest, when the Central Committee of the Congress of Bucharest excluded him as a member.[18] Desperate because everybody turned their backs on him, Ghika wrote a letter to Ismail Qemali, and complained about the Albanians and the Albanian movement by saying that this movement according to him had fallen into the hands of traitors and multiple beneficiaries.[19]

Even after this despair and the promise that he would give up the Albanian movement, Prince Ghika did not waive claim to the throne of Albania. Nevertheless, he and Alandro were not taken seriously by Albanians. Gjergj Fishta, the great Albanian writer, by taking as an example two comic figures among the people of Shkodra, the antagonists Jaha Begu and Palok Cuca, ridiculed at the *"Anzat e Parnasit"* the fantastic aspiration of Aladro Castriota and Prince Ghika as well as the illusory patriotism of their followers, that in order to pay their debts, they needed a society full of adventurous riders.[20]

What the writer Gjergj Fishta lashed as a *"fantastic adventurous riders' aspiration,"* in fact, would become a reality when the Conference of Ambassadors in London decided that the independent Albania shall be led by a foreign prince, who would be determined within six months. Responsibility for the "competition" that would deal with the selection of the prince who would lead Albania was left to Austria-Hungary and Italy.[21] However, the competition for the Albanian prince, where 17 candidates participated would be closed as early as November 1913, when

---

[17] *Ibid.*, p. 299.

[18] See the text of the notification by the Central Committee that was published in *"Laimtari of Shyqpenies,"* Rome, 1-14 August, 1905; as well as the copy that follows the delivery of Callenberg Goluchowski, Bucharest, April 27, 1905, no. 17 HHStA, PA XIV/13, Albanian VIII/."

[19] A copy of the letter of Prince Albert Ghika directed to Ismail Qemali from Charteau de Totamiresci (Romania), August 20, 1905, was found as an addition to the delivery of Kral directed to Goluchowski, September 2, 1905, nr. 73 HHStA, PA XIV/13, Albanian VIII/2. For more information, see Skëndi, Stavro: *"Zgjimi kombëtar shqiptar,"* Tirana, 2000, p. 299.

[20] Skëndi, Stavro: *"Zgjimi kombëtar shqiptar,"* Tirana, 2000, p. 300.

[21] Buxhovi, Jusuf: *"Kthesa historike 3,"* Prishtinë, 2010, p. 229.

the decision was made to appoint Colonel Wilhelm von Wied from the Wied royal family from Neuwied near Cologne as Prince of Albania.

Alongside the self-declared candidates like Don Aladro, Prince Ghika and Marquis Skenderbeg from Naples, whom for years behaved like contenders to the imaginary Albanian throne and the first two were included in the track record of several important events related to the independence of Albania, while the others remained in the framework of the competition, which in some cases transcended into a farce.

However, of the 17 contenders in the competing scene remained Prince Montpensier, feudal Prince of Egypt (later King Fuad the First), Prince of Urach, Prince Burhanedin from the Ottomans and the Turkish Marshal Izet Pasha (born in Naseliç of Macedonia) and Prince Wied from Germany who was proposed by Romania.

At first it would seem that Prince Montpensier, who had great wealth and a lot of energy for sports, had good chances of taking the throne of Albania, but was quickly eliminated because Austria-Hungary and Italy could not accept a French prince, because it contradicted their common interests. Prince Wilhem von Urach (from the family of Württemberg in Germany), a German general supported by Austria-Hungary, was certainly an important personality and gave the impression that he could play an important role in the throne of the Albanian state if he would be given the crown. But since Austria and personally Prince Franz Ferdinand and his stepmother Maria Teresa stood behind him, the rivalry between Vienna and Rome turned into an overwhelming obstacle for the German general. The Italian Ambassador in Vienna, von Avarno, had openly stated that Italy in no way could approve an Austrian candidate,[22] the same as Vienna would not accept an Italian candidate. In competition remained the German prince, Wilhelm von Wied, a Protestant, otherwise great-grandson in the paternal line of German Emperor Wilhelm I, therefore cousin of Wilhelm II, Prince Burhanedin of the Ottomans and Izet Pasha (of Albanian origin), proposed by the Young Turks and a major part of the Albanian representatives in Istanbul, who had addressed the Turkish government with a request that Marshal Izet Pasha be their candidate.

Although it was clear that Austria-Hungary and Italy, as well as other European powers, with the exception of Russia, would not support a Muslim prince in Albania, regardless of the expressed will of a good part

---

[22] Vlora, Eqrem bej: *"Kujtime,"* the second volume, Tirana, 2001, p. 56.

of Muslim Albanians, as this had to do with the determination that Albania abandon its political ties with the Ottoman Empire (and this was a request by the majority of Albanian Renaissance), the candidacy of Prince Burhanedin and that of Marshal Izet Pasha gave the Ottoman internal aspirations a special power (push), though not realistic ones, to test their strength in Albania in circumstances where it was already declared independent and the Conference of Ambassadors in London had known it. So Prince Burhanedin, who was the third son of Sultan Hamid, who had many supporters in Albania and especially in Kosova, tested and simultaneously encouraged conservatives from the ranks of fanatical Islamist forces. While General Izet Pasha, of Albanian descent, proposed by Young Turks and the majority of Albanians in Istanbul, tried restoring the Young Turks in power through illusory plans such as those to turn the Ottoman Empire in Europe by means of Ottoman Albania, which they would fight for years, while after the loss of the war with the Balkan countries and Albania's declaration as an independent state when it was also accepted, though shrunk by half by the Great Powers, they would try to return it under their control. As will be seen, the candidacy of the son of Sultan Hamid and Young Turk's general, Izet Pasha had a significant impact on future developments in Albania, because they encouraged on the one hand the Islamist fundamentalists to begin their renowned anti-historic movement to turn Albania under the Ottoman rule and on the other hand affected at a critical moment, the Interim Government of Vlora to lose its orientation and enter into an adventurous alliance with Young Turks, allowing their troops to secretly enter into Albania and organize an uprising in the occupied areas of Kosova and Macedonia in order thence to connect with Bulgaria and finally to create the Albania-Bulgaria-Turkey alliance. The events that took place in January 1914 in Albania with Major Beqir Grebena, who was deployed in Vlore as the commander of an operating group consisting of 420 soldiers who came on this "rescue mission" to Albania, show that the Young Turks were among the first to act and as such tried to destabilize the independence of Albania and further to continue with powerful movements of the Islamist funda-mentalists, mostly helped by Serbia and Greece, that would explode after the arrival of Prince Wied in Albania in March 1914, which would be as dire for the Albanians and Albania that for a moment it seemed that Albania was self-destructing when it had to prove itself.

Both of these developments, even though anti-historic and without any likelihood of success, actually found fertile ground , not because they had a chance – since Sultan Hamid's concept of *"Islamist stronghold"* for Albania, which he had been using for over thirty-four years, and the concept Young Turks had about the Ottoman centralism which would integrate the Albanians had failed precisely because of the issue of Albanians and fighting them (both had refused Albanian autonomy within the Ottoman Empire, when it was seen as the only option that would help make the evolutionary Albanian state in the ethnic dimension and contribute to the survival of the Ottoman Empire in the European part). But the circumstances through which the Albanians passed were extremely difficult circumstances while occupied by Serbian, Montenegrin, Greek and Bulgarian armies, which gave rise to hope that they could be saviors. Therefore, for the Islamic fanatics and numerous turkophiles, but also for numerous Young Turk emissaries who were scattered in large numbers in all parts of the country, it was not that difficult for them to persuade certain social classes about the request for an Ottoman Albania, which if nothing else, may have succeeded to unite the Albanians and their territories under a shared roof when they were already threatened to extinction by Slavic-Orthodox absorption.

This illusion was initially spread by the supporters of Prince Burhanedin, who used the most fanatical Albanian society from the ranks of the middle class, who in mosques and among the congregations (jama'at) propagated in favor of the son of the Sultan as the savior of Albania and as the protector of the Islamic faith. Furthermore, how far their fanaticism would go in regards to this is portrayed best by the example when Muslim fanatics in Middle Albania rose against Prince Wied in the summer of 1914 and later against Esad Pasha Toptani (because, according to them, he deceived them with false promises that Albania would be ruled by a Muslim prince) and surrounded Durres, their leaders, Haxhi Qamili and others, set up a pavilion in their camp, in Shijak, where, as they said, lived Prince Burhanedini, so that after the take-over of Durres he would take the Albanian throne![23]

The candidacy of Turkish Marshal Izet Pasha (of Albanian origin), had even more serious consequences, as it was directly related to the Young Turks' ambitions to return the lost "brilliance" since in August

---

[23] *Ibid.*, p. 57.

1912 the Albanians would be required to accept Shkup's Memorandum of Fourteen Points and in this case they would lose the government and the newly elected parliament dominated by them. After the Balkan War ended with severe consequences, the Young Turks in Istanbul raised their heads again and the first job they undertook was their attempt to some-what restore the Ottoman influence in Albania regardless of the price they had to pay for this to be done. Not even the decision of the Conference of Ambassadors of 29 July 1913 not to allow by any means, a possible Ottoman intervention in Albania, seemed to bother them. "Competition" for the prince of Albania came as generous and they nominated as candidate for the throne of Albania this unknown old Marshal. To give this issue a nuance of a popular movement, they hired propagandists from among the members of the linguistic institution *"Aksaray mahfili"* (Department of Aksa-Raji), an institute which wanted to introduce the Turkish alphabet in the writing of Albanian and under the direction of Arif Hikmetit, they sent them to Albania to propagate in favor of the Ottoman Albania.[24] So they named Major Beqir Grebena as commander of an operating group comprised of 420 experienced soldiers who would be sent to Vlore and there take control of the Provisional Government, and little by little, rely on the Muslim fanatic element and on that of pro-Turks to prepare the country for Young Turks plans.[25]

Austria-Hungary and Italy, which had the mandate from the Conference of Ambassadors to choose the prince who would take over the leadership of Albania, ignoring Turkey's candidates and their great noise, was finally determined to be Prince Wilhelm von Wied, born on March 26, 1876 in Neuwied, proposed by King Carol of Romania. Prince was the grandson of the Queen of Romania (from Wied family) and this explained the interest of Romania in his candidacy. Since he was Protestant and came from a royal family from the Upper Westphalia, which during the last three hundred years had given refuge to various liberal-minded individuals, this made him even more acceptable to govern a country such as Albania , where the coexistence of religions had always been what had distinguished this old European populaiton. Wied's castle in Neuwied on the Rhine near Cologne, had served as a cultural and intellectual center that had reconciled different antagonist streams, not only between Catho-

---

[24] *Ibid.*, p. 58.
[25] *Ibid.*, p. 58.

lics and Protestants, but also between the Germans and Dutch. Thus, Prince of Wied, who had a military occupation (the rank of colonel in the army of Prussia), was married to Princess Sophie Shönburg-Valdenbug from the royal family of Wartenberg in Saxony, appeared to be the most suitable person to take over the destiny of Albania, precisely because he was not Catholic, he was not the candidate of Vienna or Rome, and because he was proposed by a country (Romania) that did not belong to the corporation of the Great Powers. On November 8, 1913, the Great Powers agreed with this proposal, knowing very well that the extension of talks regarding the election of the prince would further aggravate the situation in Albania, which already appeared with many difficulties that came from the invading armies, which did their best to sabotage the Ambassadors Conference decisions. Difficulties also came from the dissatisfaction of Albanians regarding the severe situation, dissatisfaction which continued to increase.

Although the Prince Wied candidacy came from Romania and was accepted by the Great Powers, rightly it opened the issue regarding how and how much the appearance of a German prince as its leader would affect the newly created Albanian state, as it may open the question of how Germany would react to factors, which for various reasons, may impede the international deal surrounding the consolidation of the Albanian state.

Viewed in principle, the appointment of the German Prince as the leader of Albania versus the obligations that Great Powers had taken (control over the civil administration and finance in a period of ten years by an international commission consisting of delegates from six powers, then the organization of the administration, gendarmerie and other protective guarantees), the youngest state in Europe would have to turn in favor, as had happened with Greece, Bulgaria and Romania, which were consolidated as states when German princes were appointed to them in the same way. Nevertheless, this did not happen as will be seen, for two reasons. First – because of the neighboring states, primarily Serbia, Montenegro and Greece, which had taken more than half of Albanian lands – that although the Conference of London gave them the most part-they feared a German prince, who was the nephew of the German Emperor Wilhelm II, by having the support of Germany, could quickly consolidate Albania, which in turn would encourage Albanian irredentism. And secondly – because with the beginning of the First World War, which broke out six months after the German prince took over the helm of the Albanian state, the guarantor countries of Albania went to war against one another turning Albania into a war polygon, while after the war ended, once again was set on the green table, but now without Austria-Hungary and Germany as their traditional defenders. They lost the war and would be severely punished.

Prince Wied and the Fight against a European Albania

The Government of Vlora and the unbearable difficulties of the start – Ismail Qemali's departure from Albania on charges of preparing the conspiracy with the Young Turks – Delegation's departure to Germany under the chairmanship of Esad Pashe Toptani, along with Hasan Prishtina, to hand over to the German Prince Skenderbeg's Crown and displaying German sympathy regarding their relations with Albanians – The arrival of Prince Wied in Albania, the establishment of the Albanian government led by Turhan Pasha and the beginnings of the Islamist movement and the pro-Ottoman one organized by the Young Turks' emissaries but also by the agents of Serbia, Greece and Russia, with whom the Northern Epirus would join and behind whom stood Greece sometimes masked and sometimes openly – Conspiracy of Esad Pashe Toptani against Prince Wied and his departure to Italy – "Corfu's Protocol" and the early fragmentation of the Albanian state – In early June, Islamist forces led by Haxhi Qamili, with calls "love your father," removed the Albanian national flag and returned the Ottoman one, in Shijak. There was held an assembly where Albania was requested to be returned to the Ottoman Empire and be ruled by Shariah laws, while the Albanian language be written in Arabic letters – Alignment of the Albanian patriots, especially the Kosovar ones in protection of Prince Wied's government and of the European Albania.

In addition to the decision that: *1. Albania be declared an autonomous principality, sovereign, and heriditary; 2. Any connection with Turkey be removed; 3. Self-declared neutral under the guarantee of the Great*

Powers, the Albanian state was put under international control of six major powers (section four)[26].

The major powers exercised control over civil administration and finance for a period of 10 years, by an international commission that involved delegates of the six powers and a delegate from Albania (Articles 4 and 5). This committee was charged to work a detailed project on the organization of all branches of the administration of Albania (Article 6). A prince would be placed on top of this principality, who would be determined by the major powers (Article 1) within a period of 6 months (Article 7). Until the appointment of the prince and the formation of a final national government, local authorities and gendarmerie that existed at that time would be subject to control by the international commission (Article 7). A gendarmerie would be charged with providing and maintaining public order whose organization and direction would be entrusted to foreign officers (Article 8), who were elected from the Swedish army (Article 9).[27]

The Conference of Ambassadors did not wait six months, but in November made the decision that German Colonel Wilhelm Wied, from the royal family Wied from Neuwied near Cologne, was to be appointed as the Prince of Albania. The haste of the Great Powers to decide on the German Prince and to start the preparations for him to take the difficult duty as soon as possible, had also to do with the campaign that started in Albania and also abroad, especially in Turkey, about a Muslim ruler, possibly of Albanian descent, who was believed would be able to lead the country towards stability, but in one way to maintain its ties with the Ottoman Empire. Furthermore, at the request of a large number of Albanians in Turkey, mostly originating from Kosova, in August the Young Turks cabinet appointed Izet Pasha, Turkish Minister of War and of Albanian origin, candidate for the throne of Albania.

Before Izet Pasha was appointed candidate for Prince of Albania, the Young Turks, who had come to power and had ambitions to return again some of the past power, after the Second Balkan War in which Bulgaria lost a good portion of its territories that were occupied during the First Balkan War, launched a mobilization campaign (war) against the new expansion of the Serbs and Greeks, with the initiation of a Triple Alliance

---

[26] *"Historia e Popullit Shqiptar,"* the second volume, Prishtinë, 1969, p. 379.
[27] *Ibid.*, p. 380.

between Albani Turkey and Bulgaria, that meant none other than the inclusion of Albanians in a new Balkan war to serve the interests of the Young Turks and from which could hardly emerge anything except an even greater loss, since its eventual success caused trouble not only to those who did not want and did not allow it (Entente powers), but also those who counted on it (Austria-Hungary), and the latter, which in this respect also cared for Russia's interests in this area.

Regardless of this illusive pact made by the losers of the Balkan wars, initially this idea would seem attractive to a portion of Albanians who had lost their homes after the chaos that reigned in the country resulting from the presence of invading armies and who had begun to lose confidence even in the European salvation. It would attract especially the layer of Islamist fanatics, who after calling for a Muslim prince, would not delay their requirement of "we want the father," which after six months turned into the motto of the broader Islamist movement, bringing together middle class and peasants, who were keen to acquire fertile land that was promised to them and whose receipt of it depended on what Haxhi Qamili and other leaders that led the movement on the creation of an Ottoman Albania based on Shariah laws said.

Despite these retrograde developments, it would be a good part of the Albanians who accepted neither the dubious alliance with the Young Turks, nor the Muslim Prince and not even the formula for an Ottoman Albania, which to a large extent and in different ways was encouraged and aided by the enemies of the Albanians, that is, Slavic-Orthodox countries, which with this movement wanted to turn back the wheel of history, primarily at the expense of the Albanians and then use it as an excuse to exclude but also to eliminate once and for all the Albanian factor from the Balkan political and social scene. Albanian nationalists as social and intellectual elite knew that any political liaison with the past, that had to be left behind, would mean betraying the ideals of the Renaissance for a European Albania and what is worse, this endangered even that semi-Albania that was admitted (accepted) in London.

Albania, thus, was preparing to return to a new polygon accompanied with the confusion that was left behind during the getaway of the Ottoman Empire along with its distortion, and where the Young Turks wanted to exploit the discontent of the Albanians, for which they held a large portion of the guilt, and in this way return to the European space from behind the scenes.

The Young Turks' "surprise" that was preferred by the Albanian Is-lamists was even more desired by those who were interested in ending the Albanian state without having the chance to recover, and this would be done in the name of removing any possibility of the return of the Otto-mans in Europe. This was best demonstrated by the loose behavior of numerous Young Turks' emissaries, who had penetrated on all sides without encountering any obstacle, even in areas that Serbia and Greece occupied, calling for a new war against "Kaurs" rather than the liberation of the occupied territories by Serbs, Montenegrins and Greeks.[28]

However, the main concern in this development, that Albania in-creasingly kept turning into a test between its Ottoman past and the European future, seemed to be the involvement of the Government of Vlora and directly Ismail Qemali, especially when after the declaration of independence it was declared detached from the Ottoman Empire and thus acting rightly in such a way that their anathema would not turn into a barrier to the Albanian state. Of course, circumstances could have been beyond expectations and disappointing, especially the disregards by the Conference of London of Ismail Qemali as the leader of the Provisional Government. But also the International Control Commission, which would have forced him to look back, but not the political reasoning of a diplomat and politician who knows very well the role of anti-historic actions, as to make a deal as he would do with Major Beqir Grebenja, as a representative of the Young Turks in November 1913.[29] This deal allowed

---

[28] See the book *"Gjashtë muaj mbretëri 1914,"* Tirana, 2001. Secretary of Prince Wied, Captain Hearton Armstrong, describes in more detail the time when Prince was staying in Albania, from 7 March, 1914 until September of the same year, as well as those that he and Albania faced, which plunged into total chaos thanks to the activity of the Young Turks and their agents who were helped by Serbia, Greece, and Russia. (See pages 72-79).

[29] Ismail Qemali's agreement with Major Beqir Grebenja provided for the military units of the Young Turks to enter masked in Albania and along with their arms be sent to Lumë, Dibër and territories near the border towards Kosovo. The special Turk and Bulgarian units took over the uprisings, which were exercised for this type of actions. In advance, I. Qemali had another similar agreement with Bulgaria's consul in Vlora, Pavlov, to allow the entry of Bulgarian military agents into the border areas of Macedo-nia, who disguised with Albanian clothes took over the organization of the insurgencies against Serbs in Diber and its surroundings. Plans started to be implemented but they would be discovered through a denunciation by the Serbian consul in Vlora, P. Gavrilovic and submitted to the International Control Commission. This happened even

the Ottoman Empire to secretly introduce weapons and military forces into Albania on the grounds that it would enter into a war with Serbia – which did not exclude the possibility that in the hatch Russians and Serbs were involved, as they were interested in the further destabilization of Albania especially when the new German Prince was expected to come to the throne. The discovery of this "trick" does not seem to have been difficult at all; nevertheless, it served as a trigger for Ismail Qemali, to pass the power to the International Control Commission and be forced to leave Albania, in January 1914, and thus leave space to dubious actors that were inclined to different games, such as Esad Pashe Toptani and a few others, who would not delay in bringing Albania before a bend, that gave the impression to the uninformed or misinformed that its main opponents might have been right – Serbs and Greeks with those statements that Albanians do not deserve a state because they are not fit to govern, but should be governed by using violence.[30]

Nevertheless, the withdrawal of Ismail Qemali from the Albanian political scene with the anthem "of participation in a conspiracy against the country," did not relieve Albania from real conspiracies with which it would be faced after the arrival of the German Prince during those six months that he was in charge of the government, when the country would become an open arena for the destroyers from inside and outside, Albanians and foreigners who worked with zeal to make Albania appear lacking

---

though based on some sources it appeared that the Serbian consul, six months later, had sent Serbian and Russian weaponry to the units of Haxhi Qamili in the war against Prince Wied. In 7-8 January, 1914, Dutch officers from the Albanian gendarmerie, while checking the Austrian ships anchored in Vlore, found 11 officers and more than 200 soldiers, mostly Albanians, who came from Turkey. These officers were arrested, while the majority of the soldiers were sent to Trieste. In Vlorë, 20 people were arrested and Major Beqir Grebenja was one of them. In the seized documents, the links between the emissaries of Young Turks and Albanian personalities were discovered. A military court headed by Dutchman De Veer, sentenced Colonel Grebenja to death (which was changed into life in prison), and his 23 associates were convicted to various sentences. (See "*Historia e Popullit Shqiptar,*" second column, Prishtinë, 1969, p. 398-400.)

[30] See the book of the author Vladan Georgevic: "*Shqiptarët dhe fuqitë e mëdha,*" published in Leipzig in the German language in the beginning of the year 1913, which was filled with such defamations.

in governing skills and without any features of a civilization that should have found itself in the European society.

Before this development took place, which is in some way related with the end of the plot of the Young Turks, costing Ismail Qemali his departure from Albania, many of those who in one way or another took part in this from behind the scenes and even remained in the network of similar actions in various forms against the Albanian state and its stabilization efforts, participated in favor of the Albanian "demonstration" to the German King, which took place on February 21, 1914 in Neuwied, Germany, when he was formally handed the crown of the throne of Albania.

The Albanian delegation of 18 people, led by Esad Pashe Toptani, among which was also Hasan Prishtina in the capacity of the second man of the delegation, was received with great honor by the Prince of Wied, but also by the city of Wied.[31]

Albanian representatives, along with Prince Wied, carried the crown of the Albanian throne, with the expected special honors by the major of the municipality of the city of Cologne and where the top military and political representatives of the King Wilhelm resided along with his adjuntant Forster in charge, who in the great hotel "Victoria" of Cologne read the German king's wishes for Albania and Prince Wied. In this way he wished him good luck and promised Albania assistance from all sides so it would be able to take its place among the European states, where it said it had its place. And on this occasion, Skenderbeg's heroic struggle against the Ottomans was commemorated, which was one of the first and among the most glorious in the old continent.

In the evening, the Albanian delegation with Prince Wied attended a ballet performance in the theater of the city of Cologne, and the next day made a boat trip across the Rhine, which was followed by state honors from the fleet of the German kingdom and other units honoring the German army. This indicated that excluding the German diplomacy,

---

[31] The Albanian delegation that went to Germany, led by Esad Pashë Toptani, had representatives from all regions and had the following composition: *Durrës* - Milton Shovari and dom Nikollë Kaçorri, *Vlorë* - Xhemil Bej Vlora, dr. Spiro Koleka and Jusuf Hamzaraj, *Elbasan* - Shefqet Bej Vërlaci, Lef Nosi and Ahmet Hastpolari, *Shkodra* - Gjon Çoba, Berat - Sami Bej Vrioni, Hysen Bej Vrioni and Iliaz Bej Vrioni, *Korçë* - Abdyl Ypi and Dr. Turtull, Gjirokastra - Eqrem Bej Libohova, *Tirana* - Eqrem Bej Vlora and for all the provinces occupied by Slavs, the representative was Hasan Prishtina.

which was trying to give "inferior" impressions toward the appointment of a German Prince as the head of the Albanian state, even though the German policy and military structures supported the German prince, it was in their interest that Prince Wied succeed there.[32]

German press also paid attention to the arrival of the Albanian delegation in Neuwied as well as to the warm atmosphere with which they were confronted everywhere. Major newspapers dedicated their front pages to this event, reiterating the roots of the freiendhsip between Germans and Albanians dating since the time of Knight Arnold von Harff, i.e. from the fifteenth century, and who also came from the same province as Prince Wied. Their castles on the Rhine were separated by only a few kilometers. Also, the contribution of German historians and linguists in the cultural antiquity of the Albanians proved among the first, their links with Illyrians and Illyrian language.

The newspaper *"Reihnischer Zeitung"* brought another study conducted by the great linguist, Gustav Meyer, about the Western cultural identity of the Albanians, written and published during the Eastern Crisis, when Serb chauvinist propaganda made every effort to portray Albanians as unemancipated, with no history and no culture. The local newspaper *"Neu Wieder Zeitung"* of 21 February 1914, published a poem by poet, P. Schpielman, dedicated to the king of Albania and Albanian-German friendship with the wish that Albanians, with the help of the Germans, find their way to Europe as soon as possible, the same as the Greeks, Romanians, and Bulgarians when they were ruled by Germans after winning their autonomy (Romania and Bulgaria) and independence (Greeks) from the Ottoman Empire.

It would be seen that Schpielman's wish regarding Albania and Prince Wied to succeed in the creation of a common European Albania, would not be realized. After six months of governing, Prince Wied failed and Albania failed as well in its first test of proving itself as a European country. Even its sponsor, six major European powers, failed, so the trial of making the Albanian state was not used for the benefit of peace and European interests, as stated in the final statement issued at the end of the Conference Ambassadors in London on July 29, 1913, but Albania and its problems were used for their own interests, which led up to World War I,

---

[32] For more information regarding the German interests in Albania see the manuscript of Prince Wied *"Denkschrift über Albanien,"* 1917, in the documents part.

paving the way for other disasters that would continue to pave the road for World War II.

However, the German prince went to Albania convinced that he would succeed in fulfilling his mission that for him meant more than a task he had been given to benefit the new Albanian state and the Albanians, for whom he says that he always had positive opinions and for whom once coming in contact with them, he would never forget.[33]

He left Neuwied with applauses by the whole city. In Cologne too, he was admitted and congratulated by the city's Great Senate where senior officials of the German state were present. Before he hailed his fellow citizens, Prince Wied visited the major European Powers that had chosen him Prince of Albania. Prince Wied's first visit was to Rome, where he was accepted with a lot of respect. Nevertheless, Prince Wied's highest honors took place in Vienna. He was accepted with high honors as a statesman. In Schönbrun he was admitted by the Emperor Franz Joseph with whom he had a joint dinner that was also attended by Vienna's diplomatic elite. After he came back to Berlin, Prince Wied went to London and Buckingham Palace where he had lunch with Lord Hamilton. The next day, Prince Wied went to Paris where he was admitted by the President of the Republic, but according to his secretary, Captain Heaton Armstrong, the visit was "poor."[34]

The last visit to the countries that had appointed him Prince of Albania, Prince Wied had in St. Petersburg, where he was admitted with honors by the Czar of Russia and had lunch with him in the Winter Palace. Once he ended these protocol visits to the capitals of the major powers, the Prince headed to Albania, along with Princess Sophie and the modest suite, consisting of several consultants, an adjutant and two chefs.

Prince of Wied arrived in Albania on 7 March 1914, accompanied during the cruise in the Adriatic by several warships of Austria-Hungary, England, France and Italy. He departed from Trieste with the Yacht "Taurus" made available to him by Austria-Hungary. He was accompanied by von Trott, Courtyard Overseer, Irish Captain, Heaton Astrong, First Secretary, two of the princess' maids, Mrs. von Oidman and Mrs. von Fuel, the latter was the sister-in-law of the German Chancellor, von Bethmann-Hollveg. In addition, there were two members of a Private

---

[33] "Wilhelm, Fürst von Albanien: *"Denkschrift über Albanien,"* manuscript, 1917, p. 13.

[34] See *"Gjashtë muaj mbretëri 1914,"* memories, Tirana, 2001, p. 21

Council, who, however, currently did not belong but were accompanying him. These were Captain Kastoldi and Vice (Sub) Consul Buhberger, representing the interests of Italy and Austria in the courtyard.

In Durres, he was welcomed by thousands of people coming from different parts of the country, who welcomed him and wished him good luck. The first one to welcome the Prince was Esad Pasha Toptani, who was introduced in the yacht and from there, wearing General's clothes that the Prince brought from Postdam especially for this occasion, accompanied him and the princess during the overtaking in port and to the courtyard.

Prince Wied was impressed with his first meeting with the Albanians and from the heartfelt wishes that he received from them. There also were the nobles of the country, Bajraktars coming from all parts of Albania and other patriots, who held their hopes on the German prince.

After ten days, based on the suggestions of the Great Powers that had appointed him, Prince Wied formed the Albanian government. Turhan Pasha Permeti, former ambassador to the Ottoman Empire in Petersburg, one of the most successful diplomats of the Empire and whose career was very clean, was placed in charge. For his honesty, he was respected by all and was strongly recommended to the king. Although he was retired and old (75 years old) and made a quiet life in Istanbul, Turhan Pasha, as he declared, for patriotic purposes, accepted this post, even though he was aware that there would be trouble. In the government was also included Esad Pasha Toptani, who took two of the most important positions: Ministry of Internal Affairs and that of War.[35]

In his memoirs, Prince said that he had heard a lot about the Albanian general and his virtual power and for others that connected with his ambitions for power. However, he should keep him close so that, as far as it was possible, he could be used for the benefit of Albania.[36]

What Prince Wied does not openly say about Esad Pashe Toptani and his role in the government, is highlighted by his secretary, Irish Captain Hearton Armstrong, stating that the role that Toptani played in the government of Prince Wied was determined in advance by means of an agreement between him and the representatives of the Great Powers; that

---

[35] *Albanian Government was supposed to include the bajraktar of Mirdita, Prenk Bib Doda, who was offered the Ministry of Public Affairs, which he did not accept.*

[36] Wilhelm, Fürst von Albanien *"Denkschrift über Albanien,"* 1917, manuscript, p. 37.

he supported him, even though he promised the Islamist fanatics from Middle Albania that he would fight for Albania to be ruled by a Muslim prince. This issue would serve as another reason for their rebellion after the arrival of Prince Wied in Albania, which led to an armed movement against him.[37]

On 18 March, the first cabinet took the oath. Besides the Prime Minister, *Turhan Pasha*, who also held the post of Minister of Foreign Affairs, and Esad Pasha Toptani as the Minister of Interior Affairs and War, these ministers also belonged in the cabinet: *Aziz Pashe Vrioni* – Minister of Agriculture and Commerce (Trade), *Myfit Bej Libohova* – Minister of Religion and Justice, *Hasan Prishtina* – Minister of Post and Telegraph, Dr. *Mihail Turtulli* – Minister of Education and Dr. *Mehdi Frashëri* – Minister of Finance.

As can be seen, in the Cabinet of the Government of Turhan Pasha were included three ministers, that more or less, had taken part in the Provisional Government of Vlore, led by Ismail Qemali. They were: Esad Pashe Toptani, Myfit Bej Libohova and Hasan Prishtina. The first one had been the Minister of Interior Affairs; the second one had been Minister of Foreign Affairs, and the third one had been Minister in the composition of the government. The involvement of Toptani, Libohova and Hasan Prishtina in the cabinet of Turhan Pasha, which was made with the consent of the internationals, aimed to amortize three different social streams: the landowners, the Beys and the Kosovars, who were able to destabilize Albania at any time and this they proved during the one year that passed from the Declaration of Independence to the taking over of the government's competencies by the International Commission of Control. In fact, these social streams, each in its own way, had shown their potential to be disruptive rather than beneficial to the Albanian state, during the Government of Vlora, headed by Ismail Qemali, and that had serious consequences for the country, because, among other things, on the one hand they would undermine the authority of the Provisional Government, and on the other hand, would open the road to outside interferences.

In this regard, the activity of Esad Pashe Toptani would be the most influential, because as a large landowner, he oversaw almost all of the

---

[37] For more details see Armstrong, Hearton: *"Gjashtë muaj mbretëri 1914,"* memories, Tirana, 2001.

territory of Middle Albania and had the opportunity at any time to put into motion his numerous subordinates. If we add the armed forces that he had "inherited" from the withdrawal from Shkodra, saving them for personal needs, then his power was more clearly reflected, and came out best when he transferred his activity of creating the Albanian gendarmerie in Durres and Tirana. A little later, for the same purpose, that is to weaken the government of Vlora, in early October, 1913, in Durres, he established *"Presbytery of Middle Albania,"* in charge of which he put himself, in which case, he would cut relations with it and fought it as an opposing force. The power of "Presbytery" lay in an area, which included Durrës, Shijak, Peqin, Kavaje and Tirana, exactly there, where the Islamist movement started, and which diligently fought Prince Wied and the European Albania.

Even the Beys, represented by Myfit Bej Libohova, during the Government of Vlora, quickly turned their backs on Ismail Qemali. Myfit Bej Libohova, as Foreign Minister, departed from the Government of Vlora justifying his leave with excuses that *"Ismail Qemali interfered in his competences,"* but the truth has more to do with the *"redeployment"* of feudal entities toward the "conservative bloc" in circumstances when the Great Powers would not claim to protect the Government of Vlora, but *"to respect the existing local authorities."*[38]

This statement, along with the rejection of the Government of Vlora, legitimized the internal Albanian rivalries as well as acknowledged the power of the International Military Commission in Shkodra, led by the British. The introduction of the Myfit Bej Libohova in Turhan Pasha's cabinet was thought to capture (persuade) the feudal-conservative bloc.

Hasan Prishtina's entry in the cabinet was intended to "calm" the powerful irredentist stream of Kosovars and other Albanian parts that were left outside of the Albanian state, which were left to Serbia, Montenegro and Greece, by the Conference of Ambassadors. The irredentist movement had shown that it was ready to be put into action at any time during the uprising in September 1913, when it exploded in Diber and then was extended to most of Dukagjin, which would have as a consequence not only its oppression by Serbia, but also because it provided "excuses" for Serbian forces to enter the Albanian territories and reach the Adriatic so that they came with the demand *"for a new territorial*

---

[38] *"Historia e Popullit Shqiptar," third volume,* Tirana, 2007, p. 29.

compensation" , which was necessary "to protect themselves against the new Albanian attacks."[39]

With the allegations that with the inclusion of these three streams would succeed in the attempt to stabilize the Albanian state, Wied's regime was sanctioned by the Organic Statute of Albania, the fundamental law of the Albanian state, which was prepared by the International Control Commission (ICC) and was approved by him in Vlora on 10 April 1914.

The statute contains basic decisions taken by the Conference of Ambassadors in London on July 29, 1913. Under this statute, *Albania is declared constitutional, sovereign and hereditary principality under the guarantee of the Great Powers* (Article 1), which also guaranteed the totality of Albanian land and its neutrality (Article 2 and 3). Prince Wilhelm Wied was appointed to the throne of Albania (Article 7), who was the chairman of the civil and military administration (Article 14) and had the right to appoint the council of ministers. The principality's legislative body was the *National Assembly* which was composed of members elected by indirect vote – three representatives for each region (Articles 40 and 44). The representatives of religion, the Albanian High Commission in the "*Albanian National Bank*" and ten members who were appointed by the prince (Article 41.42 and 47) also belonged in the National Assembly. Albania was divided administratively into 7 Seljuks (prefectures); these were divided into kazas (subprefectures) and kazas were divided in nahiyas (municipalities) (Articles 95-97). The country's military forces were gendarmerie and militia (article 149). The official language and the compulsory language in schools was Albanian (Articles 26 and 279). The statute sanctioned private property, including landowners' property, and guaranteed the free exercise of economic, social and political activity. The positive significance of this statute was that the independent Albanian state was recognized de jure and de facto in the international arena.[40]

The beginning of the work of Prince Wied's government, not only was discouraging, but appeared to give the green light to all the opponents and enemies of the country to start attacking it as much as they could and from different sides.

---

[39] *Ibid.,* p. 49.

[40] "*Historia e Popullit Shqiptar,*" second volume, Prishtinë, 1969, p. 405.

Although six major European powers were already divided into two blocs: the Entente (Britain, France and Russia) and the Triple Alliance (Austria-Hungary, Germany and Italy), they appeared as guarantees for Albania and for the next ten years they took on this obligation to perform it together, as was said to help the establishment of peace and stability in Europe, even though some of them proved to the contrary. The concept of the European six that during the preparation of Prince Wied to take the throne demonstrated agreement. And with the arrival of the Prince in Albania, they began putting into action instruments that worked in their own interests, where it was noticeable that not all of the Entente countries and especially Russia were interested in constituting an Albanian state that would survive. While the Triple Alliance, which supported Albania and wanted to have it as an independent state had its differences and often times contradicted each other. Shortly thereafter, on one side Vienna required a much stronger Albania so that it would appear as one of the supporters of the interest of the Danuabian Monarchy (Habsburg Monarchy), in particular in the fight to prevent the domination of Orthodox Slavs in the Balkans, behind which stood Russia with its hegemonic claims and on the other side was Italy, which was also interested in the creation of the Albanian state, but not that strong, and even less that it was modeled on the Viennese model and under its influence.

While Vienna sought partners from nationalist forces and from broad classes, Italy required support from the elements with disruptive tendencies, as in that case of putting into play Esad Pashe Toptani and the likes who were shown to put their interests above those of Albania. When we add to this the Ottoman Empire factor, that after losing the war with the countries of the Balkan Alliance, in June 1913 it signed a peace deal and accepted to eventually depart from Europe and withdraw from Albania, leaving it under the supervision of the International Control Commission. After the return of the Young Turks in power, they had the illusion that they could still control the areas where they were previously – it was more than clear that the failure of making Albania was pre-programmed because it was too small and too weak to resist antagonism among supporters, who wanted Albania for their own benefits. The powerful destroyers and extremely perfidious for whom types of populations like Albanians were convenient prey were willing to put themselves at the service of one or the other party without any big price with the conviction that in turn certain social ambitions could be realized not in accordance with natural processes, but with political games of any order, even though they could harm the state.

However, conspiracies against Wied contributed to the creation of Albania as an independent state. As such, they started from inside and later outside. Their demonstrations had to be prevented at all costs and by all means to stop neighbors from making slanders about Albanians' inability to govern an independent state.

Conspiracies from inside initially came from those who were in the government, who had begun to mobilize their followers among the Turkomans, Islamists and other fanatics, whose number increased day by day and reached the degree of rejection based in Central Albania. One of them was Esad Pashe Toptani whose intrigues were in the service of the Italians, Serbs, Russians, and even the Young Turks and then were transferred to Muslim clergy. Even the conspirators from abroad contacted those from inside. This way the vortex of the International Control Commission (ICC) emerged, which included many faces, different interests, and different perfidious scenarios that destabilized the Albanian Government.

But one must not forget that in addition to the difficulties that the Albanian Government had with the International Control Commission, its bigger troubles came from the Greeks and Serbs. The International Control Commission, which spoke and decided on behalf of the six international powers and guaranteed the Albanian country, had the responsibility of eliminating these two groups. Nevertheless, at this time Serbia and Greece did not constantly work and operate against Albania. ICC had commitments to liberate Albania from the oppression of the Serbs and Greeks as well as from the problems that these countries caused. Internationals not only would not do anything in this regard, but they allowed Greece, along with the occupation of the territories and ongoing terror against the Albanians, to use the Greek minority in Albania and Orthodox fanatics among the Albanians that were still supervised by the Greek Orthodox Church and its propaganda to cause internal instability in Albania.

Thus, the first card to be activated against the government of Prince Wied and the Albanian state in general, during the early days, was the movement of Northern Epirus, behind which stood Greece, sometimes disguised and sometimes openly. Greece supported this movement by sending soldiers and arms and by intervening directly at the border, where the border issue between Albania and Greece was not yet resolved. Along with the Orthodox clergy that was its right hand, Greeks greatly agitated because they had to use this opportunity to break away from the country that soon would be joining the Ottoman Empire. Athens, which had the support of France and Russia, craftily used the alleged claims of the Greek minority regarding the outstanding issues in the south border, to bring difficulties to the Government of Durres, costing them a lot of work and lost authority and its ultimate deterioration.

"Northern Epirus" came into play during the time when the Border Commission with the Florence Protocol, in December 1913 ended the work regarding the definition of the border with Greece. But even after the appointment of Prince Wied as the head of the Albanian state, Athens did not end the crawling tactics to withdraw its troops in accordance with the Protocol of Florence, which was expected. Even though it could not openly contradict the decisions of the Great Powers, Greece did not give up its plans to cut off the southern provinces from Albania. So it did change tactics but not the purpose. Thus, on March 1, 1914, in accordance with the request of the Great Powers to empty the regions of the South, the Greek army left Korça. Nevertheless, Greece also left behind thousands of *andars*,[41] who ruthlessly suppressed any free expression of will on the part of the population. The same terror also happened in Korçë when Greek troops withdrew in early March where they left in the city hospital a number of "sick" soldiers and doctors who actually were Greek officers. They were also joined by the Greek Bishop Gjermanos. Secret "Northern Epirus" gangs the next day attacked the Albanian administration and tried to remove it, but gendarmes, under the command of the Dutch Major Snellen, who was joined by Albanian volunteers led by Th. Gërmenji, drew out the aggressors within a few days.[42]

The Greek plan, however, did not result in a withdrawal. Greek *andars* and Albanian Greekomans began to act in accordance with the artificial creation of the autonomy of "Northern Epirus," forcing Albanian people to flee their lands. To achieve this they used terror and even slaughtered the population. Such was the case in Manastirin e Kodres

---

[41] Committee armed groups, allegedly independent, fighting for "Northern Epirus," but that were actually regular Greek army units disguised to take actions in South Albania. In these units were included Orthodox Albanians, who were recruited by Jorgji Zografi, son of a Greekoman banker, Kristaq Zografi, from Qestorati.

[42] *"Historia e Popullit Shqiptar,"* third volume, Tirana, 2007, p. 60.

(Monastery of Kodra), near Tepelena, where on April 29, 1914, Greek gangs massacred 218 people, among them several women. During that time, more than 250 villages were destroyed and thousands of inhabitants killed.[43]

Greek authorities tried to give "legal" support to the "Northern Epirus" movement. They organized in Gjirokastra an "Epirote Congress" under the chairmanship of the former Foreign Minister of Greece, Jorgi Zografi. On March 2, 1914, this "Congress" announced the *autonomy of Northern Epirus* and formed an "interim government" under the chairmanship of Zografi.[44] A few days later, following the example of Zografi, the Major of the Greek Army, Spiro Spiromilo, also declared the *"Autonomy of Himara"* in an area that included seven coastal villages inhabited by Albanians.[45]

With the declaration of the "Autonomy of Northern Epirus," Zografi declared that neither the Great Powers nor "Greece" had the right to interfere in his internal affairs. He urged the International Control Commission (ICC) to order the commanders of Albanian forces not to enter within the borders "of his country," since the entrance into the territory of the "Northern Epirus" would be considered as "an aggressive act."[46]

In these circumstances, when the problem of "Northern Epirus" came out as an open intervention of Athens in Albania, and this definitely had consequences for Greece, the Greek Prime Minister Venizelos and Zograf changed their strategy. They stated that they did not require the separation of Korça and Gjirokastra from the Albanian territory, but these two provinces, without being separated from Albania had to be administered by a governor of foreign origin as a representative of the prince. Gendarmerie was recruited from among the local population and put under the command of Greek officers originating from "Epirus." Official languages in these regions were to be Albanian and Greek.[47]

Despite the opposition from the national circles and the readiness of patriotic forces to fight to eliminate this Greek construct, Prince Wied thought that they should act wisely regarding this matter. Therefore, he

---

[43] *Ibid.*, p. 61.

[44] *Ibid.*, p. 61.

[45] *Ibid.*, p. 61.

[46] *Ibid.*, p. 61.

[47] *Ibid.*, p. 62.

appointed Dutch Major Thompson of the gendarmerie, as the "extraordinary commissioner." His role was to take part in the talks that would be held in Corfu with the representative of *"Northern Epirus,"* Karapanos. Major Thompson went too far with the concessions and accepted the autonomy of the two regions, which kept formal connection with the country. The Government of Durres did not accept this agreement and they removed Thomson from his duty as "commissioner." The government decided to go themselves into the talks with the Greek representatives. However, this was not allowed by the International Control Commission which took over the talks with "Northern Epirus" representatives. In the first week of May, the International Control Commission went to Corfu and there, on May 17, signed an agreement, which was named the *"Protocol of Corfu."*[48]

With the imposition of the *"Protocol of Corfu,"* wherein the "Autonomous Northern Epirus" included Korça, Gjirokastra, Delvina, Himara Përmeti and Saranda – and the South was practically seceded from Albania – Athens would achieve two goals:

a) to bring the Government of Prince Wied to his first test of losing authority and failing, and

b) to directly put into action the movement of Islamist fanatics and other forces that required the removal of Prince Wied and gave as an alternative the option of a Muslim prince that practically opened the way for the involvement of Young Turks in the anti-Albanian conspiracies. These forces gained the "legitimacy" to appear on stage as defenders of Albania from the destruction that came from Greeks and Serbs.

---

[48] According to the *"Protocol of Corfu,"* two southern prefectures of Albania enjoyed a semi-autonomous administration, the organization of which was left in the hands of the International Control Commission. The Albanian government had the right to appoint or dismiss only with the consent of ICC high officials who would be from Albania. The two provinces had a local gendarmerie composed of local residents, which would go outside of these provinces only when the ICC saw it as necessary. The Albanian army did not have the right, except in the case of war, to enter into these regions. Orthodox communities had special rights. In schools with Orthodox students, the learning was in Greek language. In administration both languages, Albanian and Greek, were used. The protocol would enter into force when ratified by the Albanian government and that of "Northern Eprius"and adopted by the six Great Powers. (See: *"Historia e Popullit Shqiptar,"* third volume, Tirana, 2007, p. 63).

This way, Athens had chosen the best card to insert into the game against Prince Wied's government and destabilize it. As would be seen, Greece included various Albanian political streams, sometimes consciously and sometimes unconsciously, sometimes by despair and sometimes by anger, which did not appear linked to the "successes" of protecting Albania but with the failure of Prince Wied.

At this point, surprisingly and unfortunately for Albania, its "friends" and enemies joined together.

Prince Wied initially acted as if the difficulties they were facing were inevitable and would pass thanks to the successes that would be achieved little by little. As a German who believed in sincerity and commitment to the job and in the given word, from time to time he forgot that this was a place where you find in a common log the Orthodox Byzantism, Oriental impudence and Balkan ignorance, which can change everything. In fact, this would be his biggest problem, though Albania did not escape from the worst – since in the First World War the guarantor powers got into a war against one another and it was natural that the consequences would hit Albania first – even though it would save Albania from domestic disasters which took the form of the first fratricidal war among Albanians that would be encouraged on the basis of religion and regional divisions, and then, as usual, would be used by the Greeks and Serbs for their known intentions.

The first problems of this nature, for the German prince and to the detriment of the Albanian state started from his own government, namely from Esad Pashe Toptani. He represented the most typical example of the Oriental impudent behavior and the Albanian small-minded selfishness. Esad Pashe Toptani was known previously for his ambition to balance his economic power at any cost as one of the largest land owners in central Albania. With its politics in the highest structures of the Albanian state and without hesitation to think that he should be the first, despite his behavior in Shkodër and the damage that he would bring to the country, he was required to surrender the crown of Albania to the German Prince, promising that he would bow to his authority. However, it would be seen that this "offer for loyalty to the Prince" was part of Toptani's game and his agreements with Rome and Belgrade to keep the power so that one day he would sit on the Albanian throne, according to the plans of Italy or those of Belgrade. His appointment would be brought as an unavoidable task of Albanian politicians, since, according to him and the Greeks,

Albania could not survive without external support, and that was its destiny. In accordance with this maxim, that gained general legitimacy, keeping his private property together with his political power was important for Toptani, who used that in creating the aureole of "the first man" that was impassable. This concern was present also in Shkodra, when he handed the province over to the Montenegrins exactly at the time when the Conference of Ambassadors in London decided that it should not be separated from Albania as Montenegro and Serbia required. However, he took this action since he knew that this way he was playing the game of Entente, which was also a powerful card, where the Italians "secretly" had begun to flirt with them and, as it will be seen, later would join them. Thus, it is no wonder why the Italians, after having been removed from Shkodra, took Toptani and his units under their protection, along with the weaponry that he would take with him and use to strengthen his position in Central Albania as an insurmountable authority.

Prince Wied admitted that he knew about Toptani's properties and his penchant for power at any cost, but he also knew about his important role in the Albanian National Movement and knew his virtual power and the impact he had in Albania. That is why Prince Wied thought that he could be used for the benefit of Albania rather than the opposite. Prince Wied may have received this advice from the Albanians with whom he exchanged opinions before coming to Albania. They suggested that he work toward the sincere commitment to unite all of Albania's energy and direct it for its own benefit. He might have been also advised about this from abroad, especially from the representatives of the guarantor countries of Albania, which were interested to use the crown of the German prince as a tactic to include in one roof all the Albanian streams and social classes, especially the influential ones where Toptani was overwhelming. This was supported by the fact that the International Control Commission fulfilled Esad Pashe Toptani's desire to go to Germany and hand over the Albanian Crown to the German Prince, which raised him in Albania into a position that could not be ignored. Therefore, it is clear that there were also "suggestions" of the International Control Commission that convinced Prince Wied to include Esad Pashe Toptani in the government and charge him with the most important resources: internal affairs and war.

Despite this great "trust," Prince Wied kept Toptani under his observation and quickly noticed his goals and let the representatives of Austria-

Hungary, the main supporters, know about them. The prince received an answer from them where it was said that they were informed about all this and made sure to act when the right time came. However, it was Colonel Thompson the first to talk about this and break the news to the Albanian Pasha when he revealed the conspiracy that Toptani had staged with some of the emissaries of the Young Turks near Durres. Along with the emissaries, he was detained unilaterally by the international gendarmes. Nevertheless, Esad Pashe Toptani was taken under the protection of Italy and as such avoided the trial. In this case, he signed a declaration stating that he would permanently leave Albania and Albanian politics, a promise which he would not be able to keep. Colonel Tompson paid for his courage by having his head chopped, thus, being the first foreigner to be killed by Albanians because with honesty he put himself in the service of the creation of the Albanian state at a time when many Albanians were against it and fought it at all costs.

The temporary removal of Esad Pashe Toptani from Albania did not deter the spirit, his people, or its ghastly impact on Albanian politics. Rather, even that which was initially looked upon as an anti-feudal movement and maybe thought to have been a social revolt had to do with political issues. This way, it quickly became apparent that the rebels by mid-June, when they departed from the suburbs of Shijak and soon took it and Tirana over to get closer to Durres and threaten it, were not organized to resolve the social problems abound, but to show their clear political demands for the removal of the Prince Wied and the return of the Ottoman Empire. So, their goal was to create an "Ottoman Feud" or something similar that Esad Pashe Toptani had promised not only to his numerous followers but also to the representatives of the Islamist clergy in Albania, vowing that he would do his best after getting in, to change the course of the Government of Wied.

One should look here for the reasons behind the double revolt of the Islamist fanatics and pro-Ottoman forces towards Esad Pasha Toptani as well as the Government of Wied. This happened because the first one deceived and betrayed them while the Albanian state was not established as they imagined it. It did not have an Ottoman orientation but, according to them, was more of a tool to turn Albanians toward Christianity.[49]

---

[49] For more details see Eqrem Bej Vlora *"Kujtime,"* second volume 1912-1925, Tirana, 2001, p. 51-109.

Initially the rebellion would seem like a revolt against Esad Pashe Toptani and the non-fulfillment of promises. During the first attack against Durres he lost the protection provided by government forces. Many of the insurgents would say that they wanted Esad Pashe Toptani's head that they called "Esad kauri." Soon after the first failed attack in Durres and after they returned to Tirana, their main organizers and their inspirers united with the Young Turks and their agents with those of Serbia, Greece and Russia and that represented the engine of the movement.[50]

After they assessed that they already had the sufficient support of the people as well as from those abroad who led them, on June 3, 1914, the leaders of the Islamist movement in Shijak removed the Albanian national flag and put (returned) the flag of the Ottoman Empire and organized an assembly where they came out openly with their requirements designed into a program, which was profoundly anti-national and it compromised Albanians precisely on those grounds on which the hegemonic anti-Albanian propaganda by Serbs and Greeks had worked for about a century. The program included the following:

a) Removal (departure) of Prince Wied,

b) Introduction of Albania under the Ottoman administration or bringing an Ottoman ruler under the authority of Sultan

c) Declaration of Turkish as the official language, and if unable to achieve this, force the usage of Albanian in Arabic letters,

d) Replacement of the national flag with the Turkish crescent, and

e) Selection of Grand Mufti of Albania by Shaykh al-Islam of Istanbul[51]

The main forces coming from Islamist fanatics and pro-Ottoman ones were united to be led by the Mufti of Tirana, Musa Qazimi. There were also Mustafa Ndroqi, as the chairman of the general center, which included the Major of the Ottoman Army Xhenabi Adili, Vice President and members Musa Qazimi – Mufti of Tirana, Arif Hikmeti and Haxhi

---

[50] Amstrong, Heaton: *"Gjashtë muaj mbretëri 1914,"* Tiranë, 2001, p. 61-64. In the manuscript *"Kujtimet nga Shqipëria,"* Prince Wied talks about the infiltration of Serb, Greek, Russian, and other agents in the ranks of Islamist insurgents and their huge impact. He accuses the Italians, especially Ambassador Alioti, in Durres, who kept contacts with the rebels of Haxhi Qamili.

[51] *"Historia e Popullit Shqiptar,"* second volume, Prishtinë, 1969, p. 412; Wilhel, von Wied: *"Denkschrift über Albanien,"* manuscript, p. 26; Amstrong, Heaton: *"Gjashtë muaj mbretëri 1914,"* Tirana, 2001, p. 63.

Adil (known for returning the crown of Albania to the Sultan in exchange for being accepted back into its bosom) and others like him, whose general commander was chosen Musa Haxhi Feza or Haxhi Qamili.[52]

All of these were known as Islamist fanatics having pro-Ottoman stances. They announced that anyone who would go against their program would be punished. All those who housed supporters of Prince Wied or opposed the insurgency, would have their homes burned and would be punished with death. Mustafa Ndroqi, in an order he sent to the Presidency of the Council of the Uprising in Elbasan, wrote:

"Our main goal is the declaration of Ottoman convertibility and the unification with the Ottoman Kingdom."[53]

In an interview he gave to the Italian newspaper *"Il Messaggero"* on September 3, 1914, he stated:

"The Turkish flag is a symbol of the General Council."[54]

In addition to their leading headquarters and their political platform, the rebels organized armed units, built their government bodies and carried out a range of activities that gave a heavy punch to the institution of the new state and to the Albanian National Movement.[55]

After taking over Shijak and Tirana, the pro-Ottoman movement expanded. It included most of the former Albanian soldiers who had served in the Turkish garrisons under the command of Esad Pashe Toptani, who

---

[52] *Musa Haxhi Feza,* or *Haxhi Qamili* as he was called, who was elected commander of the general forces of the Islamist insurgents and that were required to return Albania to Turkey, was a supporter of a the melamin sect, which preached the renunciation of property, by using some sentences from the Qur'an. Indeed Haxhi Qamili, who was called a "proponent of social democratic ideas" by the Albanian ideological historiography and his movement was qualified as "anti-feudal" and given a positive note in history because it protected peasants from feudal lords and "put peasants revolutionary spirit in motion," to a large extent "his military headquarters," along with fanatic dervishes and Young Turks officers, was directed by Serb, Greek and Russian agents, disguised as dervishes that were incorporated in its ranks. (See *"Denkschrift über Albanien,"* p. 37; *"Diplomatische Aktenstücke betrefend die Eereingnise auf dem Balkan,"* herausgegeben von Österreichisch-Ungarischen Ministerium des Äußen 1914 „Aktet diplomatike rreth ngjarjeve ballkanike,"* published by the Ministry of Foreign Affairs of Austria-Hungary" – 1914).

[53] *"Historia e Popullit Shqiptar,"* third volume, Tiranë, 2007, p. 65.

[54] *Ibid.,* p. 65.

[55] *Ibid.,* p. 65.

were mobilized with money and promises from the leaders of the uprising. Further, it included Serbian intelligence services, as well as Greek and Russian ones, which were prevalent in many parts of Albania and did their best to make the Islamist movement massive so it would give the final and decisive coup to Prince Wied and his supporters, who were Albanian patriots from all parts of Albania and particularly Kosovars, who associated the fight for the return of Kosova with the establishment of the Albanian state and its strengthening under the German prince.

In these circumstances the pro-Ottoman Islamist movement tried to get Durres, the center of the Albanian government, which was protected by government forces from the units of Gjon Markagjoni, and above all, it was protected by about two thousand Kosovars that were led by Isa Boletini. There were other volunteers from among the citizens, led by Luigj Gurakuqi and Romanian, Austrian, German, and Italian-Arbëresh volunteers as well as a group that came from the U.S.

The attack on Durres began on June 15, but it failed due to the fight (war) of the guardians for life or death. However, on the same day, Colonel Thompson, the Dutch officer, was killed. He came in Albania in 1913 and was invited to organize the Albanian gendarmerie. The defeat of Durres did not repel the rebels. They turned to Fier and took it over on 12 July and then marched to Berat and occupied it on July 13 and, although governmental powers resumed it, on August 19 it again fell into the hands of rebels. At the end of August they surrounded (besieged) Vlora, but its inhabitants, in consultation with Ismail Qemali, after talks with the rebels, managed to avoid war, but with a price, and that was to remove the branch of the Government of Durres from this city. On 1 September 1914, the rebels entered Vlora and after they took down the national flag, they raised the Turkish one. This way they cleared the way for the coup against the Albanian state which was carried out after four days in Durres.

Under these circumstances where all cities were occupied and the Government of Durres had begun to extend its influence and fragile administration, it was noted that the activity of the Ottoman rebel movement against the state became increasingly insistent in its demands to make Albania backward in compliance with the successes that Northern Epirus would have in South, that represented a primary and existential challenge for the Government of Prince Wied. It was thought of as a priority that should be resolved since its source was the hypocritical behavior of the International Control Commission, which under the influence of French and Russians did not treat any of the problems of the South as a Greek conspiracy for territorial claims but as *"part of the unresolved problems regarding the border between Albania and Greece,"* which had been left open and sought answers in the same light as the decisions of the Conference of Ambassadors in London.

This would take a lot of energy and even suppress the government. This suppression was also admitted by Prince Wied after he left Albania and saw the behavior of Italy and Greece, which, during the First World War, after a supposedly neutral position, did not delay in taking the side of the Entente powers and captured the best parts of Albania, which were promised by Entente to them if they joined this alliance.[56]

Furthermore, after the First World War started and Albania again endured invasions from all sides, where in addition to the Serb, Montenegrin, and Greek invasions, Italian and French ones (the first in the South and the latter in Korça and its surroundings) were also added. Haxhi Qamili and his fanatics, rather than showing *"great love for their homeland in the fight against Kaur,"* as they said, concluded a peace agreement with "Northern Epirus" – on one side with the Ottoman flag and the other with the Greek one – so that after the war they signed an agreement regarding their feudal lands.[57]

---

[56] Wilhelm von Wied: *"Denkschrift über Albanien,"* manuscript, 1917, p. 47.

[57] Agreement to maintain the status quo with Greeks was reached by Haxhi Qamili on July 11 in Pogradec. It was declared to the correspondent of *"Die Presse"* in Vienna on July 15, 1914 that he did this to "focus toward the liquidation of the Government of Durres and Prince Wied." With this he cursed anyone who helped Prince Wied keep the throne by threatening them that he would deal with them ruthlessly. In the remark of the correspondent that most of the defenders of Prince Wied were Kosovars, who fought for Albania because this way they fought the return of their territory occupied by Serbs, he responded by saying that "who is on the side of the German Prince is enemy of God and Albania."

The Ottoman Coup against Albania

The occupation of Albania by Serbian, Montenegrin and Greek armies and the siege of the Government of Durres by the movement of Haxhi Qamili – Prince Wied leaves Albania while Islamist forces in Durres take over the Government and raise the Ottoman flag and urge the Sultan to restore Albania as part of the Ottoman Empire – The return of Esad Pashe Toptani with the help of Serbs and his struggle to topple the Islamist government of Haxhi Qamili –Toppling of the Serbian and Montenegrin invading armies by Austria-Hungary and their departure from Albania. – Setting the administration and the opening of Albanian schools in Kosova – Creation of Albanian autonomy in 1917 by Austria-Hungary, as well as the creation of Albanian autonomy in areas occupied by the Italians – The emergence of the National Committee for the Protection of Kosova in Shkodra and efforts to preserve national unity.

The beginning of the First World War found Albania, with the exception of Durres and Vlora, divided into three parts: the Middle (central) part – in the hands of pro-Ottoman Islamist movement led by agents of Young Turks; Eastern and Northeastern parts in the hands of Serbs; South in the hands of Greeks; while Shkodra in the hands of the International Control Commission.

It was clear that the outbreak of the First World War hit Albania in particular because it was protected by the six Great Powers as decided in the Conference of London, which were already at war with one other: Austria-Hungary and Germany on one side, and the countries of the Entente (Britain, France and Russia) on the other side. Italy was an exception, which had declared neutrality. However, it did not go too far and joined the Entente, after receiving promises to expand on the Albanian coast and in the eastern Adriatic as it turned out later from the secret Treaty of London of 26 April 1915.[58] This caused the International Com-

---

[58] The Secret Treaty of London of April 1915 is an agreement that was reached by the representatives of Great Britain, France and Russia on one side and Italy on the other. It consisted of concessions that Entente Powers had to give to Italy so it would pass in their side in the war against the Axis Powers (Austria-Hungary and Germany, joined by Bulgaria and the Ottoman Empire). Out of 16 provisions of this Treaty, 3 of them (5,6, and 7) had to do with Italy's expansionist claims in Albania and plans of the Entente

mission of Control to be paralyzed and within a few days before they left submitted their competences to the Commission of Consuls in Shkoder chaired by the "neutral" Italy.

Prince Wied, however, continued to stand, seeking direct support from Austria-Hungary and Germany, but without forgetting to ask the same from the Entente countries that were signatories to the London Conference. At this time, the London government and that of France promised to support the Government of Durres, as if they were not in the war with Germans and Austrians, and even would be very supportive to the decisions of London, stating that "the international obligations towards Albania will be carried out jointly,"[59] while Vienna pledged full support, but would suggest that in accordance with the new circumstances, Albania should act against Serbia, even if it was required to enter the war. This was required by Foreign Minister Bertchold to Prince Wied.[60]

Powers (excluding U.S., which joined this bloc in the second half of 1917; then it went to war alongside them and won), which wanted, through Albanian territories, to satisfy the greed of three Balkan states: Serbia and Montenegro who were fighting for a few months now on their side, and neutral Greece that hoped to draw on their side. According to section 5 of the Treaty, the Albanian coast from Buna in the North to Lezha would be given to Serbia and Montenegro, including the port of Shëngjin. According to section 6, the representatives of London, Paris and Petersburg agreed to give it to Italy, under its full sovereignty, Vlora, the Island of Sazan as well as a wide triangle of land, whose boundaries were set only in general terms. This triangle in the North and East would have the Vjosa River as a border, while its southern border would go from Vjosa, near Tepelena, and would stop in Himarë. According to section 7 of the Treaty, Italy agreed to give the Northern and Southern parts of Albania to Montenegro, Serbia, and Greece. Italy requested to form an incomplete, autonomous, and neutral Albanian state in Central Albania, which would not have diplomatic relations with other countries and would be represented by Italy. This meant that the Albanian state after the war would be placed under the Italian protectorate. (For more details: *"Historia e Popullit Shqiptar,"* third volume, Tirana, 2007, p. 78-79).

[59] Armstrong, Hearton: *"Gjashtë muaj mbretëri 1914,"* Tirana, 2001, p. 157.

[60] There is no official document in Vienna and in Prince Wied's documentation that argues regarding the efforts of the Government of Durres to enter in the war against Serbia because the Government of Vienna required from them to do so (see *"Historia e Popullit Shqiptar,"* second volume, Prishtinë, 1969, p. 418). The Albanian Government, according to the statute, was obliged to remain neutral. Even though the possibility that

Vienna thought that the inclusion of Albanians in the war against Serbia would contribute to the weakening of its military power that in turn would make it easier for Austro-Hungarians to focus on other fronts.

The involvement in the war against Serbia was also required by many Kosovar nationalists and patriots who thought that the irredentist movement that was being created could be put into action with all its power, since it was believed that the Austro-Hungarian war against Serbia presented a good opportunity for Kosova to return to Albania, from which it was separated by force. Some of the leaders of the national movement that were in Albania, among them Hasan Prishtina and Isa Boletini, required the Government of Durres to formally take the side of Austria in the war against Belgrade, convinced that the Axis Powers would win the war and organize another international conference, as happens after every war, that would bring other decisions in line with the interests of Albanian people for a common state.

The Government of Durres, not only was unable to fight against the invaders on its borders, as the Albanian patriots, mostly Kosovars, required but it was also worried because of the suffocation coming from within, i.e. from insurgents of Haxhi Qamili and pro-Ottoman Islamist movement. These insurgents after signing the peace agreement with the movement of "Northern Epirus," swung from all sides and savagely, without caring that it was defended by patriots, most of them nationalists from all parts of the country and numerous volunteers from Kosova and Northern Albania, who came to help with the conviction that this way they also helped the salvation of Albania and generally the Albanian issue since the liberation of Kosova should represent the first goal of any Albanian who knew that without Albania there is no Kosova, and without Kosova there can be no Albania.

The issue of the last defenders of the Government of Durres, most of them who were Kosovars and almost the only ones who accompanied

---

Vienna required this from Prince Wied could be excluded, however, it was aware of the situation in which the Government of Durres was. Under those circumstances, the Government of Durres could not survive for too long. Nevertheless, the actions taken by Vienna to attract Kosovars to enter the war against Serbia would be secure. Kosovars had many reasons to enter the war. Even the irredentist movement required this and was ready for war.

Prince Wied when on 3 September 1914 he left Albania[61] along with members of the Government and many leaders of the Albanian patriotic movement, who settled partly in Shkodra and partly in various European countries. This presented the beginnings of a serious tragedy that followed Kosova and Kosovars, perhaps a more severe one than that of the Serbian occupation two years earlier. While protecting the Government of Durres, a just duty and honor that was worthy of their lives, they faced no Serbs or Greeks, who were conquering the Albanian lands and continued to commit atrocities to its population, but faced their brothers from East Albania, who did not care about Kosova's problems and those of other Albanian territories occupied by Serbs, Montenegrins and Greeks. Their only concern was the creation of an Islamist Feud where they could still dream about the caliphate and its further expansion.[62]

---

[61] After leaving Albania, Prince Wied returned to Germany and on October 14, 1914 joined the military service, from where he was sent, as a major in the cavalry division to the Front of Flanders. On April 18, 1918, Prince Wied left the German army. He lived in Bavaria (München) for a long period of time. In 1925 he went to his aunt in Romania, Queen Elizabeth, where he was killed by Soviet soldiers in 1945.

[62] The first Kosovar bands under the leadership of Isa Buletini and Hysni Curri, originally about 400 fighters who joined 400 others and their total number later exceeding two thousand, came to Durres in the beginning of June. A few hundred Catholic highlanders led by the grandson of Capitain Mark Gjonmarkaj joined them. These forces were promised to the Government of Durrës: from Berat 1500 people, from Vlora 700, from Mat 800 people that were led by Ahmet Zogu and 2,000 people from Miredita that were led by Prenk Bib Doda. It was estimated that the force of 7,000 people would be enough to quench the Islamist movement, which originally had 2500 people. However, these forces that were promised to Prince Wied, besides those of Kosovar volunteers and Captain Mark Gjonmarkaj, would never be completely under the control of the Government of Durres because the regional leaders kept them for tactical purposes. This, as it would be seen, would weaken the protective power of the Government of Durres and at the same time encourage Islamist and pro-Turkish forces as well as Greek ones in the South to destroy the Government of Durres (See Eqrem Bej Vlora: "*Kujtime*," second volume, Tirana, 2001, p. 84/5). Ahmet Zogu even marched towards Tirana, but there was stopped, despite the requests for help he received from the Government of Durres. He always promised that he would go, but always found a reason to remain outside the protection of Durres. Similarly some units of vulunteers led by Preng Bid Doda entered Lezhë but did not move from there even though the Government of Durres paid for their

In Shijak and Tirana, especially during the summer when they were protecting Durres, Albanian patriots, mostly Kosovars but also volunteers from Germany, Austria, Romania and Italian-Arbëresh, fought against the insurgent forces of Haxhi Qamili and against the pro-Ottoman movement of the Islamist fanatics, who were against the national flag that was raised in Vlore and recognized internationally. They fought with the flag of Islam and the Turkish crescent and would shout "we want (love) the father!"

That summer, adamant Albanian patriots who protected the Government of Durres until the last moment fought for an independent and European Albania while the pro-Ottoman movement fought for an Islamist Albania, which would be covered with a green kerchief (scarf) and governed by Sharia law.

That summer, unfortunately for Albania and to the delight of its many opponents, a good part of the Albanians, rather than fighting its invaders (Serbian, Montenegrin and Greek) and looking for ways to help the already accepted Albania state, they assumed the duty of turning the clash of civilization in their space in the most militant and bloody way, which would, at the same time, include them in a most brutal and bloody fratricidal war.

This fratricidal war among Albanians was never accepted by Albanian historians who had an ideological and nationalist pathetic burden (as they always asked for a class enemy from outside as "imperialist"). The fact that Kosovars and other Albanian patriots in protection of the Albanian government fought with the national flag and requested an independent and European Albania, while the insurgents belonging to Islamist forces fought with the green flag and the Ottoman one, made it even more tragic. On the one side people died shouting "Long live Albania" and on the other side calling for God and "we want (love) our father!"

These calls would become even more tragic and would have serious consequences for the fate of Albania, since the internal war would result in a coup against the internationally acknowledged Albanian state, conducted by the Islamist movement. Once they came to power, not only were they unable to protect and save the country as they proclaimed, but

---

necessities and ammunition that came from Austria. (See: Amsgtrong, Hearton: *"Gjashtë muaj mbretëri 1914,"* Tirana, 2001, p. 110.)

opened the door to the Greek, Serb, and Montenegrin occupiers, that chopped Albania on the grounds that this way they were protecting the Western civilization from the Ottoman and Islamist Albania, who had appeared as a scarecrow (hob), after the Great Powers had offered the chance to leave behind the Ottoman shade, which were fully in line with the century-long Serbian and Greek propaganda to prevent the formation of the Albanian state.

When it comes to this issue and the necessity of a thorough explanation of it in accordance with the truth, it is interesting to highlight some of the arguments that support the allegations that during the summer of 1914, Albanians, among other things, had been involved in a fratricidal war which took place because of different goals. On one hand the goal was to protect the independence of Albania – and it included most patriots from all classes of the Albanian society (especially Kosovars and Cams), and on the other hand were excuses by the Pro-Ottoman movement and other fanatics of this spectrum to fight the German Prince because he was not a Muslim like most of the Albanians and would be used to return Albania under the rule of the Ottoman Empire. This was an anti-Albanian and anti-historic act since the Ottoman Empire was in its final throe and in agony, thus its efforts to restore the Empire were impossible, except at the expense of Albanians.

Anti-historic and anti-national actions of the Islamist movement, led by Haxhi Qamili and other militants from the ranks of fanatics – mostly agents of Young Turks who had joined the movement, but also Serbian, Russian, and Greek agents, as well as other who helped greatly to return the pan-Muslim spirit even in their programs and their political demands – could not be considered as *"anti-feudal movement with social character, even though it will include masses of peasants as its main driving force."*[63]

Even the clergy's actions, who were on top of it and went to Esad Pashe Toptani's properties and those of other feudal lords and gave some of the land to peasants, would not reveal the anti-feudal character of the movement. Rather, the Islamist movement started to appear and marched with the Ottoman flag and once they came to power, they removed the national flag and replaced it with the Turkish one, canceled the Albanian language, and returned to using the Ottoman language with Arabic letters.

---

[63] *"Historia e Popullit Shqiptar,"* first volume, Prishtinë, 1969, p. 423-426.

They introduced Sharia law and returned the more militant spirit of fundamentalism against which the Young Turks themselves had fought.

Arguments regarding this are not found only in the Assembly of the Movement of 3 June 1914 in Shijak, when the program consisting of few points to turn Albania into a province of the Ottoman Caliphate (removal of the Albanian language and the introduction of the Ottoman one, removal of the national flag and replacement with the Turkish crescent, selection of the Grand Mufti of Albania by Shaykh-ul-Islam in Istanbul and others) was approved, but also during other actions, among which the most clear and significant of this nature was the Assembly of Kruja of 11 February 1914 where the Islamists under the leadership of Musa Qazimi came with *"itifak"* (Islamic covenant), whereby the previous claims about the unification of Albania with the Ottoman Empire, issued in mosques and other gatherings even before the German Prince came, were reconfirmed.[64]

If "Itifak" was occupied with the protection and rescue of Albania "from the swallowing of Kaurs," as it was stated in the mosques by imams and envoys of the Young Turks, then they, along with about thirty thousand Ottoman soldiers, mostly deserters and withdrawn from the front lines in the North and Northeast (from the front of Kosova, Macedonia and Janina), who had done nothing to protect the country from Serbian, Montenegrin and Greek invasions, and yet found shelter in parts of Vlora and Shijak instead of suffering from hunger and malaria, would have been sent to Kosova and Çamëri to fight their oppressors, Serbs, Montenegrins and Greeks, and to not shed all of their fanatic thrust to the Government of Durres.

Since, as would be seen, Albania would collapse in Durres and not be defended there.

To prove that it was a coup by the Pro-Ottoman movement against Albania, which did not have *"anti-feudal [wings with] social character in it"*- as it was that of Haxhi Qamili[65] and fundamentalists of Musa Qazimi and others that demanded the return of Albania under the rule of the Ottoman Empire, along with the return of the Sharia and other Islamic laws which even the Young Turks had given up – of course would suffice

---

[64] *Ibid.*, p. 425.
[65] *Ibid.*, p. 418.

what was said above, despite being drawn outside the thick lines and outside the detailed arguments that would never end.

This anti-national and anti-historic act found the strongest reflection after Prince Wied was forced to leave Albania. This way, on September 5 in Durres, under the flag of Islam and the Ottoman crescent, the insurgents entered led by Musa Qazimi and Haxhi Alia and under the command of Haxhi Qamili. As if it was not enough the desecration of the flag, that was set in Vlore two years earlier and for which was shed so much blood over the centuries, the forces of Haxhi Qamili and Haxhi Ali, on their way to occupy the ruined Albanian throne, massacred all those who in any way had been connected with the protection of the Government of Durres or supported it.

In the suburbs of Durres, many patriots were executed from Kosova and Mirdita, who did not want to leave towards the North or elsewhere.[66]

Some of the German, Austrian, Romanian, and even Italian-Arbëresh volunteers, who during the summer had fought in defense of the Government of Durres and convinced that they were helping in the formation of the Albanian state, found similar fate,.[67]

On the same day, the fundamentalist wing of the Rebel Movement, on behalf of the entire movement, after it announced the "[overthrow of Prince Wied] from the Albanian throne," in a meeting of the "General Council"[68] made the following decisions:

---

[66] See *"Diplomatische Aktenstücke betrefend die Eereingnise auf dem Balkan,"* edited by Österreichisch-Ungarischen Ministerium des Äußen 1914. *"Aktet diplomatike rreth ngjarjeve ballkanike,"* published by the Ministry of Foreign Affairs of Austria-Hungary – 1914).

[67] Even though there is no real source that would confirm the exact number of volunteers who came from European countries (Austria, Germany, Italy, and the United States of America) to fight on the side of Prince Wied and protect Albania, some indirect sources suggest that the number of volunteers from abroad was approximately 130 people, most of them from Austria but also from Germany. Volunteers from the outside, some of whom were agents of special intelligence services of certain individuals that were very interested in exploring the situation in the country, were, most of them, intellectuals. Most famous among them was the architect from Vienna, Garsher, who opened an agency for sending volunteers to Albania and even he himself would be one of the defenders of Durres. (See Armstrong, Hearton: *"Gjashtë muaj mbretëri 1914,"* Tirana, 2001.)

[68] *"Historia e Popullit Shqiptar,"* second volume, Prishtinë, 1969, p. 420.

a) to return Albania to the Ottoman imperial crown,

b) on behalf of the Ottoman people in Albania, submit a request to accept Albania in the composition of the Ottoman Empire to the Sultan

c) to return to the usage of Turkish language, flag and other symbols of the Ottoman state, and

d) to immediately begin the implementation of Sharia law.

In this meeting it was decided to submit the requirements of the General Assembly to the Sultan personally by a delegation led by Haxhi Adili, where they wouuld also solemnly return the Albanian Crown.[69]

By applying faithfully the guidelines of the Young Turk Committee of Istanbul, they promised to the representatives of Austria-Hungary that they would cooperate closely with them and they would not make any important decision without their advice.[70]

So, the announcement of the "[overthrow] of Prince from the throne" and the requests by the General Council of the Islamist insurgent movement, emerging from the meeting of September 5, presented nothing but a coup against the first internationally recognized Government of Albania led by Prince Wied and against the independence of Albania.

Ironically to the history and to show that Albania would be an absurdity that often would define the direction of certain developments, even with internal contradictions, would be taken care of by one of the initiators of the conspiracies against the government of Prince Wied, Esad Pashe Toptani. Even this time, the man who was forced to leave Albania with the promise that he never return again and would not participate in any political activity, after World War started, left Italy, and after a short stay in Athens arrived in Nis, where there the Serbian government was at that time. After he agreed with Pasic on many points, and with him devised other plans through which the "Albanian throne" was promised to him, of course now in a different position and circumstances from those during the time of Prince Wied, when the Great Powers, at least formally, had common stances regarding Albania, formulated at the Conference of London, he went to Debar where he recruited many mercenaries. On October 2, 1914, he suddenly reached the "center" of the self-proclaimed "Ottoman Government of Albania" in Durres. Here he forced the General Council to pass the power to his hands and declared

---

[69] *Ibid.*

[70] "*Historia e Popullit Shqiptar*," third volume, Tirana, 2007, p. 68.

himself president of the "Provisional Government of Albania" (taking away the attribute "Ottoman" put by Haxhi Qamili) and General Commander of the Army.[71]

Thus, the coup of September 5 by the Islamist movement would suffer another coup, this time a "pro-Western" one conducted by Esad Pashe Toptani who just took over the direction of the "Provisional Government of Albania" and the position of the "General Commander." He restored the national flag and all acts and decisions which the Government of Prince Wied had brought through the International Control Commission, as well as his spirit.

The return of Esad Pasha Toptani, even though it seemed that somehow it had "softened" the spirit of the pro-Turkish campaign, and even gave the impression that he oversaw it due to some concessions that he made with the extreme groups from the ranks of the Islamist fanatics, by keeping them near with offices and property from those he had returned immediately after a month, since the Ottoman Empire, on November 2, 1915, he entered the war on the side of the Central Powers (Germany and Austria -Hungary). Things would be returned to its boiling point. They arrived to that point where they were on 5 September 1914 when the coup against the Government of Durres took place. The introduction of the Ottoman Empire at war and calls addressed to all the Muslims of the Empire, "to return to the holy war," would change for better the condition of those who had long ago been removed from power by Esad Pasha Toptani. Thus, without delay on November 23, 1915 in the village Sharrë in Tirana, the Pro-Ottoman Islamist movement led by Haxhi Qamil, came out of the woodwork, where it had crouched for awhile. The first thing they did was to raid Esad Pashe Toptani's compounds and properties, which were burned down. The same happened in Tirana to the compounds and property of other feudal lords, where the fire that was put to them, at the same time announced the return of their destructive power.[72]

After two days, the pro-Ottoman Islamist movement was able again through a "coup," but this time against Esad Pashe Toptani, to come in "power" and resume where it had left a month earlier. Thus, it continued to provide direct evidence for the return of that bit of Albania as if it were left deliberately cut off from foreign invasions, into an Ottoman "for-

---

[71] *Ibid.*, p. 68.
[72] *Ibid.*, p. 68.

tress," giving reason to the enemies of Albania to ruthlessly attack from all sides to undo it and this even to be seen as merit for protecting the Western civilization from the danger of Islam and its fanatic militants!

In fact, after Haxhi Qamili gained power in the meeting of the General Council held in Tirana on May 9, he started a vicious campaign not only against the supporters of Prince Wied, who hoped that the circumstances of war again would provide the opportunity to fight for Albania, but his campaign expanded against the Albanian feudal lords and others who did not join his movement. Within a short time, in Tirana and its region, he killed well-known patriots such as Ismail Klosi, Hajredin Fratari, Baki Gjebrea, Hysen Gjirokastra and others.[73]

When they saw what had been achieved and where they were going, the double putchist tried to change tactics. Thus, it would mean that those who had fought the most against Prince Wied and against the hopes of the Albanian intellectuals and patriots, convinced that with his help they could stabilize Albania, immediately returned into his supporters. On January 15, 1915, the leaders of the fundamentalist movement, in an assembly of delegates of ten sub prefectures, "on behalf of the Albanian people," sent a statement to the Great Powers, more to test the legitimacy towards the international community than to ensure the neutrality of Albania, which according to them *"had been ruined by Esad Pashe Toptani and his government."* On this occasion, the leaders of the Pro-Ottoman Islamist Movement required that the Great Powers return Prince Wied, against whom they had fought with so much dedication and willpower, and now they wanted him![74]

Years later, Prince Wied explained that it was a fraud, which came *"from those who had reduced my Kingdom Albania and my Albanian people, now sought to use my name for evil purposes. They sought to deceive any patriot among the intellectuals that were loyal to the Kingdom and bring them to their service."*[75]

This trick by the pro-Ottoman Islamist Movement would not be trusted, even though some of the activists of the patriotic and nationalist movement that were persecuted many times, who were gathered in Shkodra after they left Durres, were interested in finding a common

---

[73] Wilhelm, Wied: *"Denkschift über Albanien,"* manuscript, 1917, p. 49.

[74] *"Historia e Popullit Shqiptar,"* second volume, Prishtinë, 1969, p. 424.

[75] Note no. 23/1917 from the personal archive of Prince Wied, in Neuwied.

language with anyone for the salvation of Albania. But they quickly saw that all this was a tactic of Musa Qazimi and Haxhi Ali, who wanted to fit the war circumstances for already known purposes, especially when for such behavior they had received instructions from the Young Turks, who already appeared in the war as allies of the Axis Powers (Germany and Austro-Hungarians). It was natural that Vienna and Berlin were interested in Turkey's position in the Balkans, and Albania was seen as a good opportunity for this. Therefore, they would be adamantly rejected unless Musa Qazimi and Haxhi Alia were removed, and not until they returned the whole program of the Government of Durres, which was approved at the time of Prince Wied for a European Albania.

In response, Musa Qazimi, on 11 February in Krujë, repeated the demand for the unification of Albania with the Ottoman Empire and declared the covenant "itifikat" to achieve this goal. With Ottoman and Islamic slogans he began to exert a wild terror not only against the followers of Esad Pashe Toptani (which included, regardless of any difference, all Albanian feudalists and their property), but also against all Albanian patriots, whether they were young citizens or villagers, who had been partisans of Ismail Qemali or Prince Wied or that did not agree with the idea of a union between Albania and Turkey.

This was the second wave of fratricidal war among Albanians and among the wildest when compared in terms of masses that participated, and one with the most tragic consequences because of the persecution that took place in all parts of the country, leaving people with no other solution but to look for protection in areas occupied by Serbs, Montenegrins and Greeks.

In these circumstances, Haxhi Qamili as *"General Commander of the insurgent forces,"* raised the the fight against Albanian Beys and feudalists to a level of a holy war! Here is what Juristovski, an Austrian charged with duties in Durres, said about this:

> ...even at this stage, the movement led by Haxhi Qamili retained the Islamist slogans and the Turkish flag, that was considered by villagers a symbol of Islam and under whose shadow they hoped to achieve social liberation. Therefore, by being unable to separate from the propaganda of the Turkoman Priests, peasant rebels continued to consider the red and black flag as the symbol of the Beys, while the Albanian patriots who fought under this flag saw it as tools of feudal lords and foreign powers. Moreover, this view that took place due to the general backwardness that pertained among

the peasant masses pushed them to continue their aggressive acts against Albanian patriots and Albanian schools.[76]

The "Holy War" against the Albanian Beys and patriots, which was declared by the movement of Haxhi Qamili, and crimes that were made to the concept of the Albanian national state outside the Ottoman shadow, however, did not help in saving their unnatural creation – the Ottoman Albania. After the coup against Esad Pashe Toptani and the unprecedented terror that was exercised against any national core that has remained scattered in the area that was supervised by them, Serbs appeared again, giving the lethal hit to what was already declared as "Ottoman Albania" and to its stakeholders.

Serbia, which had been interested in such a creature, i.e. for a volatile Albanian Muslim Feud, so that they could fight against it with all their tools and do this in the name of Christian mission, relinquished the construct in which it had invested because the Ottoman Empire entered the war on the side of the Axis powers. Therefore, the liquidation of the "Ottoman waste" on the European part for Belgrade was a dual (double) "investment": against Entente affiliation, in whose name it was fighting and the obligation of European civilization to be released from the "seed" of fundamentalism.

Although days before, Haxhi Qamili sent an order to Serbs to distance themselves from possible provocations of Albanian bands and groups and took the responsibility to prevent any irredentist activity in the border area – without any reason – on June 2, 1915, Serbian military units, coming from Struga and Diber, under the command of Colonel Milutin Miskovic, began to march towards Middle Albania. The Serb commander addressed the nation with a demagogic proclamation that they were there to fight the "foreigners who worked on behalf of Turkey and Austria." In this communication, the Serb soldier, among other things, promised that once the work was finished, they would return the government led by Esad Pashe Toptani to Albanians.[77]

In order that their chosen one, Esad Pashe Toptani, to feel "more powerful," the Serbian army took care, which after taking over Tirana and most of central Albania and after pressing the Pro-Ottoman movement

---

[76] Cited according to *"Historia e Popullit Shqiptar,"* second volume, Prishtinë, 1969, p. 426.

[77] *Ibid.,* p. 432.

led by Islamist fanatics, without trying hard and by cruelly offending and humiliating those who with dedication and swank during that summer had ruined the seedlings of the Albanian state, unlocked Esad Pashe Toptani in Durres from where he would regain his "power" that a month ago they had taken from him.

In this case Esad Pasha Toptani, as expected, liquidated many of his opponents, while Haxhi Qamili and the most important leaders of the fanatic pro-Ottoman Islamic movement were jailed and had a court in Durres, where Haxhi Qamil and his closest associates were sentenced to death and later shot. This way they tried to stop such elements from entering the Albanian political scene again.

The end of the Islamist Pro-Ottoman movement as well as the bloody tragedy that would follow Albania from its declaration of the national independence until the second year of the First World War would not relinquish Albania from numerous other disasters through which it would pass for as long as the First World War lasted. The fact that the failing Ottoman mentality did not attempt to naturally keep its past through natural adaptations to circumstances and developments but worked to oppose future projects in the opposite direction of the historical processes that were happening, seemed to be a curse.

Thus, with the return of the authority that was a "gift" by Serbs and the new allies from Entente, Esad Pashe Toptani, in its already furrowed "feud" in the Durres-Kavaja-Tirana triangle, started another wave of reprisals against multiple opponents, which based on the size and consequences, again featured the continuation of the fratricidal war, where those who were "persecuted" yesterday, today became prosecutors and did not spare them or their families.

But neither did the "rescuer" of Albania from the pro-Ottoman Islamist forces and their supporters from inside and outside, Esad Pashe Toptani, have much luck. Although with the return of "power" by Serbia, Albania practically was separated according to the Italian-Greek settlement out of the "Durres feud" – (Vlora was invaded by Italian troops with "humanitarian pretexts" and to prevent "distortions among Albanian rivalries," while the autonomous parts of "Northern Epirus" were occupied by the Greek regular army, also with excuses "that it was necessary to stop the terror of Muslim militants against the Christian population," while Serbia and Montenegro had carried out their projected invasions) – with the entry of Bulgaria and Turkey in the war on the side of the Axis

Powers, the main ally, Serbia, was found in a very difficult situation, where it would not think anymore of Albania as an "ally" but save Serbia from the destruction that threatened it. So, once they found themselves between two fronts: the Austro-Germans and Bulgarians, the Serbian and Montenegrin armies were broken badly. Without the help of the Entente powers, Serb forces shattered and withdrew from Albania towards Peja-Çakorr from where they were sent to Corfu.

During the harsh winter, a large part of the Serbian army, while withdrawing from the territories, died from difficult weather and Albanian ambushes, that served as revenge for the crimes they had done since 1912 and onwards, after they had occupied the Albanian lands. Even though they were not organized enough, because instead of using Kachak attacks – where Serbian and Montenegrin forces were incurring significant losses, they would, however, reach the Albanian coast and from there go to Thessaloniki – they should have obliged them to surrender and then hand it over to the Axis Powers. Thus, it prevented them from recovering and using the same forces against Albania, as they did three years later.

In coastal parts, forces of Esad Pashe Toptani protected the shattered Serbian military by enabling them to withdraw towards Corfu. In some cases, Esad Pashe Toptani's forces entered into armed conflicts with Albanian groups that attacked the Serbian army that was withdrawing.

It is estimated that the Serbian army while withdrawing from the Albanian territory lost more than half of its human strength. This heavy defeat of Serbian and Montenegrin armies removed the power of Esad Pashe Toptani in Albania. Since in January of 1916, he "declared" war on Austria-Hungary, Toptani left Durres and went to Italy.

The cunning Pasha, with this act, used the only possible and most appropriate move that enabled him to return again to Albanian politics, from the "position of the winner." What's more, the war ended in favor of the Entente, and as it would be seen, Pasha was not wrong, though, even this "storage" did not help him in accomplishing his ideal to become Prince of Albania. In line with this move, Esad Pashe Toptani left Italy and went to France, and in August 1916, with about five thousand Albanian mercenaries moved to Thessaloniki and there he placed his "government." His forces, led by Osman Bali and Nel Hoxha, were taken near the Albanian border to fight against the forces of the Central Bloc.

In this way, Esad Pasha Toptani turned itself into a war "ally" for Entente,[78] taking the side of the victorious powers of the World War, namely those that in the Conference of Paris decided the fate and the future of Albania. This "alliance" turned into a jinx for him, when in Paris, he was assassinated by the young Avni Rrustemi, who in the court accepted that he had done this act in "effect" to "save Albania," a reason that would help him escape punishment, but would not save Albania from the troubles that it faced for a long time.

Following the Serb armies, in January 1916, the Austro-Hungarian armies entered Albania from two directions: from Northeast and North and were welcomed with a lot of enthusiasm. Austro-Hungarian forces in January took over Shkodra, Tirana, and Elbasan, and in February they took over Durres. In Elbasan, Austro-Hungarian forces met with Allied forces (with Bulgarian forces), which came from Macedonia and entered the city in the middle of February. A part of the Austro-Hungarian troops, from Middle Albania landed in the southwestern part of the country and stayed on the right side of the Vjosa River, where the front line with the Italian army was set. Other units arrived in the South of Berat and in the Southeast in Pogradec. Here the border with Greek invaders was set, which continued to maintain a neutral stance toward the global conflict. Bulgarian forces were forced from their Austrian allies to withdraw from Elbasan and to limit their occupation zone in the provinces of Librazhd and Pogradec. The front between Italian and Austro-Hungarian forces, set at the beginning (in March-April 1916) in the course of Vjosa, continued to exist for nearly three years until the end of the war, in October 1918. Meanwhile, the border between Austro-Bulgarian and Greek forces lasted a few months, until the autumn of 1916. In October, Greek forces in the South were replaced by French and Italian ones. French, coming from Florina, swept through the region of Korça and Italian forces went down from Vlora to the provinces of Gjirokastra and arrived in Erseka.[79]

---

[78] *"Historia e Popullit Shqiptar,"* third volume, Tirana, 2007, p. 83-84.

[79] According to the report of the Special Commission of Hague International Court, published in 1923, in Gjakove and its surroundings, ten thousand people were missing as a result of the terror of Montenegrin armies. Regarding the crimes committed by Greek and Serb armies against the Albanian population in the territories occupied by them or during their expeditions in the Albanian areas, among others see: *"Report of the Dutch officers of the gendarmerie for the onslaught in Grare on April 2, 1914"* (alb: *"Raportin e oficerëve holandezë të xhandarmërisë për kasaphanën në Grare më 2 prill 1914);" "Report*

In Kosova, where Serbian and Montenegrin armies had exerted great terror over the past three years, Austro-Hungarians were welcomed by all the people as liberators and rightly so, because Kosova had experienced one of the largest tragedies by the Serbian invasion that cost them tens of thousands of lives and over one hundred and fifty thousand who were forced to leave their ancient homes and go to Albania, Macedonia and Turkey.

The introduction of the Austro-Hungarian armies in Albanian lands, according to the Albanian nationalists and patriots was a long-awaited act but perhaps a bit late. They had wished for this many years ago or at least since the opening of the case of Macedonia, when the circumstances for the division of spheres of interest between Vienna and Italy on the one side and Russia on the other side, a supporter of interests of the Orthodox Slavic countries in the Balkans, was created. But demand for the annexation of Albania by Austria-Hungary became an inclusive concern at the moment when the Balkan alliance against the Ottoman Empire emerged in the beginning of 1912, the result of which was tragic for the Albanians and their territories, since in that war Serbia, Montenegro, Greece and Bulgaria, among other things, aimed at sharing the Albanian lands and preventing the Albanian state from entering the European state, from which the Ottoman Empire had to leave.

Creation of specific alliances between Serbia and Montenegro, Serbia and Bulgaria, then Bulgaria and Greece on the one hand, and the joint Balkan alliance on the other hand, suggested to the leaders of the national movement, that even though they had managed during the uprising in the summer of 1912, with the penetration into Shkup, to build the highest level of internal unity of Albanians and to use it as a form of pressure to the High (Supreme) Gate in Shkup to accept twelve of the fourteen requirements – the Ottoman Empire was unable to defend them militarily, and this laid the necessity to ask for support from its only ally, Austria-Hungary, who was able to do this since it had an interest in it.

---

of the International Control Commision about the murder of 217 women and children in Hormovë by the Greek captain, Saqilari," brought by Hozek,Qinan; Bourcart, Jacques:"L'Albanie et les Alabanias," Paris,1921; "Daily Bulleting of the English Parliament, June 1914, on the atrocities committed by Greek bands (Northern Epirotic);" "Deux documentes sur le crime," Tiranë,1923 and "UNRRA's report for the deportation and murder of the Albanian people in Çameri."

In the Assembly of Gërçë, in the summer of 1911, the demands for the creation of an autonomous Albania within the Ottoman Empire were made public. In parallel with this, Ismail Qemali, Luigj Gurakuqi and other leaders of the movement who were in Montenegro and were closer at that time to the Viennese representatives than ever and that somehow appeared as their unavoidable advisors and protectors, let them know the Albanian request that was to prevent the Balkan Alliance from achieving its goals, through a military annexation of Albanian lands by Austria-Hungary, which would be done on the grounds that this was sought by Albanians themselves. Likewise, the representatives of Mirdita, Malesia e Gjakoves, and Dukagjin, as well as many other organizations and individuals from abroad, required the same.

Of course, Austria-Hungary, which had opened the front with Serbia after the annexation of Bosnia and Herzegovina that was at a boiling point, did not allow such a step to take place in Albania, because it was in contradiction to the concept of preserving the status quo, but also to the agreement of the Triple Alliance, that neither Vienna nor Rome will undertake any action regarding Albania without mutual consent. Nevertheless, the Austro-Hungarian Foreign Minister, Berchtold, in a meeting with Ismail Qemali in Budapest on 17 November, before heading to Vlore to declare the independence of Albania, after agreeing on technical details required to perform this historic act for Albania, ensured the Albanian leader that despite the direction the war took and what the Serbian, Montenegrin and Greek forces fabricated regarding the Albanian territories, they could not prevent the proclamation and recognition of the Albanian state because Austria-Hungary, if necessary, would use military force against those who would try to prevent the implementation of the Albanian state.

This stance was not enough to appease the Albanians or for them to wait for the developments to take place. Nonetheless, this was more of a firm political determination of Vienna, that as the Balkan War started – and was more than clear that the Serbian, Montenegrin and Greek armies would win against the Ottoman Empire – to let the Russians know that the "priority of the politics of Austria-Hungary in the Balkans was the Albanian state." Moreover, they would not exclude the possibility of talking regarding its appearance and organization but by no means would allow excluding or hindering it.[80]

The interest of Austria-Hungary regarding Albania and Albanians was neither delayed nor random, but related to the long time strategic determination of Vienna to keep Albanians as an important factor in its concept of expanding further the influence in the Balkans, especially when the Ottoman Empire would inevitably come to an end. After the East crisis, the Danube Monarchy developed a special program for the inclusion of Albanians in the so-called *kultursprotektorat* (cultural protectorate), which foresaw the creation of conditions for cultural and educational elevation through the opening of schools in Albanian, where Albanians would be assisted in the process of national awakening.

The new circumstances, not only were suitable for such a move, but now they allowed Vienna to decide unilaterally, since it was not restricted by the internal agreement with Italy or interested in maintaining balance with Russia. Now it was fighting against both of them in the war, where only special interests created individually and through the means of war such as "capital" were valid, even if it were a political maximalist that had to serve certain purposes.

For Albanians, especially for those who lived in Kosova and Macedonia and were occupied by Serbs and Montenegrins, who along with the expulsion of the invaders experienced their organic and spiritual union after the terrible turmoil they endured, the emergence of the Austrian-Hungarian army was more than a relief. Therefore, it was quite understandable why old and young people lined up behind them, considering that in those vague and highly uncertain circumstances they provided protection, hope, and a future for them.

National leaders, among them Hasan Prishtina, Luigj Gurakuqi, Bajram Curri, Ahmet Zogu and others directed calls to the Albanians to welcome Austro-Hungarians as "protectors and liberators," as they had "protected at all moments the being and sacred rights of our nationality," but also, many of them voluntarily joined them in the war against the Serbian and Montenegrin occupation forces.[81]

---

[80] Zavalani, Tajar: "*Histori e Shqipnisë,*" Tirana, 1998, p. 221-234.
[81] "*Historia e Popullit Shqiptar,*" third volume, Tiranë, 2007, p. 84

When the Austro-Hungarian forces crossed the border in January 1916, they announced that they came to "help Albanians get rid of their common enemies, Serbians and Italians."[82]

Vienna hoped to reap the fruits of the political capital that it had invested in Albania for a long time, and in particular the impact that it had as a supporter of the Albanian issue in the Conference of Ambassadors in London and as an opponent of the greed of Serbia and Montenegro to conquer Albanian territory. Nevertheless, one should not deny that Vienna had its special interests in the Albanian factor since having Albania on its side was important in the new circumstances. Besides the merit of expelling the invader, Vienna took specific actions that showed that their arrival was connected with the fulfillment of the national rights that were denied by the previous invaders. Thus, in the Albanian territory, the Albanian flag returned, new schools were opened, and the "Literary Commission" was created to help in the reformation of the Albanian language. In addition to these actions, the Albanian administration was developed and other measures were undertaken that were necessary for an autonomous operation. So, the arrival of the Austro-Hungarian army was followed by the announcement of measures through which Albanians regained their human and national rights in scales that had not been previously known to them, where the national freedoms intertwined with the internal organization of social life on an institutional basis and operated in accordance with the law. Hence, after some time, the administration center located in Shkodër created the general departments of finance, education and justice.

In Kosova and in other areas until recently occupied by Serbs and Montenegrins, along with the beginning of the establishment of local government and administration in Albanian language with Albanian officials, Albanian schools were opened, which were welcomed with great enthusiasm and appreciation from the local public, which in large numbers began to respond to Austrian calls for the mobilization of volunteers who would join their armies in the war against the Serbs and Greeks.

This mobilization became even more comprehensive when Austro-Hungarians forced their ally, Bulgaria, to withdraw from Albanian territories where it was situated after it had removed the Serbian invaders from these parts, such as those of the provinces of Middle and East Albania,

---

[82] *Ibid.*, p. 85.

where in three months they had installed an "Albanian Prince" called Basi Bej, who soon remained a burned card in the hands of Bulgarians, who had had territorial claims.

The withdrawal of the Serbian and Montenegrin invading armies from Kosova as well as the emergence of the Austro-Hungarian army in their country however brought a part of the Albanian lands once again under the rule of a different invader; that is Bulgaria. After Bulgaria signed a military convention with Germany and Austria-Hungary to enter the war on the side of the Axis Powers, they agreed with Bulgaria's territorial claims to expand its territory into Serbia, Macedonia and Kosova that created a territory larger than that determined by the Peace of San Stefano in 1878.[83]

Thus, the Bulgarian troops, on 22 October 1915, occupied Shkup, while Kumanova was invaded the day before and from there they took the District of Gjilan. Thereafter, the Bulgarian forces went toward Prishtina and then conquered Ferizaj. On 10 November 1915 together with German and Austro-Hungarian forces they entered Prishtina and penetrated in three directions simultaneously: Bulgarians from the South, the Germans from the northeast direction (going through Llap) and the Austro-Hungarians from the northern part in the direction of Mitrovica. During the next ten days, Prishtina was divided into three parts, until finally, with Llap, was left under the supervision of Bulgarians. Thus, the border between Austria-Hungary and Bulgaria went from the village Milloshevë through Llap River up to its discharge in Sitnica; then it steeped in the mountains of Çiçavica, through the heart of Drenica. It included Rahovec and its surrounding territories and went to the White Drin and finally to Prizren. Zhuri was part of the Albanian territory occupied by the Austro-Hungarians.

So, under the Bulgarian occupation remained: Llap, Prishtina, Gjilan, Kamenica, Viti, Kaçanik, Ferizaj, Lipljan, Gllogovc, Suhareka, Rahovec and Prizren.[84] Boundaries between Austria-Hungary and Bulgaria were determined with the agreement of 1 April 1916. It was expected that Austria-Hungary would use some communication lines in the Bulgarian occupation zone. Part of Kosova that was under the Bulgarian occupation

[83] Rushiti, Limon: *"Rrethanat politiko-shoqërore në Kosovë 1912-1918,"* Prishtinë, 1986, p. 173.
[84] *Ibid.*, p. 177.

was part of the so-called "Military Inspection Province of Macedonia," which included 7 regions in Macedonia, Prishtina, and Prizren regions in Kosova.[85]

Even though a good part of Kosova and Macedonia remained under the Bulgarian occupation zone, many Albanian leaders saw favorable conditions for the formation of an Albanian government and the return of Prince Wied to Albania as the head of state, who continued to be seen as a symbol of independence and state sovereignty.[86]

The political elite in Albania supported this claim on the basis that Prince Wied was internationally recognized and, what was most important in these circumstances, his tough opponents, the Ottomans and Islamists, agreed for him to return. That is why they sent the invitation to him in December 1915. For this purpose, some Albanian leaders made preparations to call a national congress in Elbasan, which was opened on March 18, 1916. Nevertheless, these efforts did not prove fruitful, since Vienna thought that the Albanian issue should be resolved after the Axis Powers had won the war. According to them, this should be done at an international conference that would analyze not only the Albanian issue but also those concerning the region. Until this happened, Vienna continued to defend the idea that a program that would enable social and cultural emancipation would be enough for the Albanians.

In addition to the requirements regarding the return of Prince Wied that were refused by Vienna, new requirements related to the creation of an ethnic Albanian state began to appear. To create this state, Serbs, Montenegrins, and Greeks would need to return the occupied territories. Proponents of this idea assessed that with the removal of the Serbs and Montenegrins from Albanian territories and the entry of the Austro-Hungarian armies, suitable conditions had already been created for the creation of an ethnic Albania, which would be useful for Vienna and the Axis Powers as solid support.

Faced with increasingly loaded demands of Albanians to solve the Albanian issue in accordance with their national interests, whose avoidance or ignorance had contributed to the loss of trust in the politics of

---

[85] Dr. Avramovski, Zhivko: *"Konflikti austro-hungarezo-bullgar rreth Kosovës dhe synimet e Bullgarisë për të dalë në detin Adriatik përmes Shqipërisë 1915-1916,"* published in *"Gjurmime Albanoligjike,"* III, Prishtinë, 1973, p. 102-181.

[86] *"Historia e Popullit Shqiptar,"* third volume, Tiranë, 2007, p. 85.

Austria-Hungary, Vienna was forced to come up with a political advertisement which would reflect the position of the monarchy for Albania's political future. Thus, on December 9, 1916, after a conversation about Albania, which was held at the Army headquarters in Teshen (Czech Republic), the Austro-Hungarian Ministry of Foreign Affairs took a stand on the future of Albania, which became known in Shkodra on January 23, 1917, on the first anniversary of the entry of the Austro-Hungarian army into this city. Its content constituted in essence a compromise among different views that its compilers, militaries and diplomats had for the future of Albania.[87]

The proclamation was read by the commander of the Austro-Hungarian troops in Albania, General Ignaz Trollmann, who called on Albanians to have confidence in the military administration of the Empire, whose mission, according to Vienna, was to pull the Albanian people from backwardness, support its economic and cultural progress, and make it politically "fit" for the autonomous regime.[88]

The cultural autonomy that Vienna brought, which on January 23, 1917 was pronounced as "the autonomy of Albania," contributed to the national emancipation and civilizational consciousness. However, it was not enough for Albanians. Their savior and ally was required to declare the independence of the state, the same as Vienna had requested in the Congress of Ambassadors in London in the Spring of 1913. This time it came up with the project of the Albanian state on the basis of ethnic principles. Although it would not be accepted, however, it helped in the war against the Minimalism required by Russia to reach the compromise solution, where half of the Albanian territories were not included in the map of the new Albanian state. Nonetheless, without the efforts of Vienna, it would be impossible to make it.

The spirit of these requirements affected the demonstrations of 7 March, 1918, thus marking the fourth anniversary of the arrival of Prince Wied in Albania. This was transformed, across the country, into a broad political manifestation in support of an independent Albanian state. Through this manifestation, Albanians attracted the attention of the Great Powers regarding their cause and the answer to which they were looking forward.

---

[87] *Ibid.*, p. 87.
[88] *Ibid.*, p. 87.

Albania's autonomous administration idea, which initially was used by Vienna in circumstances when the outcome of the First World War was not clear, once again became important to the Albanian scene which caused rivalry between the former allies, Austria-Hungary and Italy, but also the Entente Powers, primarily France, who, each in their own way, was trying in this manner to present their positions in the Balkans.

Thus, almost parallel to the Austro-Hungarian initiative, the French decided to prepare a document for their zone on 9 December 1916. They announced it publicly in Shkodra on January 23, 1917. In the province of Korça, where the French military units of "Eastern Army" were settled, Albanian political forces and the command of the French army reached an agreement to create an "Autonomous Region." This agreement was signed on December 10, 1917 and it had a special significance because it reflected situations that the Great Powers used in Albania during the First World War (those of Axis or Entente) so that they could benefit for themselves the Balkan countries relying on an equalization with Albanians.[89]

The French-Albanian protocol of 10 December 1917 was also of this nature, which presented the French readiness to cooperate with Albanians in circumstances where the Constantinian Greeks, as opponents of the Entente Powers were forced to flee from Korça, while the Greek Venizelos as French allies pretended to replace them. Nevertheless, the French prevented them from doing so and removed the Greeks from Korça and its sorroundings.

Under this protocol, Korça with the districts of Blinisht, Cologne, Gora and Opar, formed "an autonomous province," which was administered by Albanians under the "protection" of French military authorities. Civil administration was entrusted to an administrative council, called a "governing council" consisting of those 14 people who had signed the document of 10 December 1916. In addition to the local gendarmerie,[90]

---

[89] Albanian-French Protocol of 10 December 1916 was signed, on the one hand by the commander of French forces of Korça, Colonel Hanri Dekuan, and on the other hand, by a delegation from Korca, consisting of 14 people (7 Orthodox and 7 Muslim): Elfim Cali, Emin Rakipi, Haki Shemsedini, Hysen Dishnica, Konstandin Nocka, Llambro Mbroja, Nikolla Evangjeli, Qani Dishnica, Rafail Avrami, Sali Babani, Tefik Rushiti, Vasil Kondi and Vasil Singjello.

[90] Themistokli Gërmenji, in the administration of the "autonomous" province, had the duty of the police manager.

the official language of administration was Albanian, and the official flag of the autonomous province was the Albanian flag.

The "autonomous" province of Korça did not live long because Paris changed the course when the king of Greece, Constantine abdicated. With the return to power of Venizelos, in June 1917, the new prime minister revoked the neutrality status of Greece and entered it into war on the Entente side. In this case the "Army of the East," which had signed a protocol with the Albanians was forced to rescind it. In order to do this, based on false charges, they arrested the chief leader of the patriotic movement of Korça, Themistokli Gërmenji. After a few days, he was taken before a military court in Thessaloniki, which relying on perjury, accused him "as an agent of the central powers" and sentenced him to death. Th. Gërmenji was executed on November 9, 1917 in Thessaloniki.[91]

Similar to Austro-Hungary that announced the "Albanian Autonomy", and the French military authorities announced in Korça the "autonomous province"; Italy, which controlled some areas in the South, reacted in the same way a few months after Vienna announced the autonomy of Albania.

On 3 June 1917, on the anniversary of the Italian constitution, the general commander of Italian forces in Albania, General Xh. Ferrero (Gaciani Ferrero), through a proclamation, addressing all Albanians inside and outside the country, declared independence throughout Albania, but "under the shade and protection of the Kingdom of Italy."[92] This "shadow" would keep the status of the Albanian state connected to Italy during the next two or three years in that it was faced with many different challenges.

Indeed Italy's interest to come up with a political project for Albania was prompted by the rivalry with Vienna and its territorial claims as well as from the French actions in the South, where they already oversaw Korça and its surroundings and emerged as a factor with "some unknowns" and as "a challenge coming from Paris to pursue Albanians," even though they would be signing the secret Treaty of London of 1915. What added to this concern was also a telegram sent by Italian soldiers in Albania to Rome, on December 17, 1916, where it was stated that *"the establishment of the Albanian flag in Korçë is a political event of great*

---

[91] *"Historia e Popullit Shqiptar,"* third volume, Tiranë, 2007, p. 91.
[92] *Ibid.,* p. 92.

importance. France is taking the only possible road toward positive re-sults—that is to favor Albanian nationalism without taking Esad and Venizelos into account."[93]

In this case, Rome was required to take into account the proposals made earlier to raise the national Albanian flag in Gjirokastër and establish an autonomous local administration. Thus, in January 1917 the Italian command publicly announced that henceforth the province of Gjirokastra would be known as "South Albania" and not "Northern Epirus." They also organized a six-member administrative council consisting of Muslim and Orthodox members (50-50), and on March 1, 1917, where they were allowed to raise the Albanian flag throughout the province of Gjirokastra. Italians continued with further measures such as the removal of Greek elements and Greekomans from the administration and replaced them with pro-Italian people, and closed schools in the Greek language and opened them in the Albanian language.[94]

In areas held by the Austro-Hungarians, the Italians and French offered their options regarding the autonomy and other movements that led toward developments to benefit the Albanian state. Nevertheless, in the Bulgarian occupation zone (a large part of Kosova and Macedonia), not only were there no signs of improving the situation for Albanians, but the situation was only worsening. Bulgarian invaders and their military used repressive measures against the Albanians in the same way as the previous invaders, the Serbians, had done. This contributed to the creation of a resistance movement in these regions, which after a while turned into a Kachak movement, where numerous Albanian and Serb bands were found in the same front -struggling against Bulgarian occupation.[95]

The resistance movement was more pronounced in Drenica, but also in Llap and Karadak. Kosova's Kachaks appeared early in the spring of 1916, among them the most prominent ones were: Iliaz Racaku, Jetish Behluli, Rexhe Bardhi and others.[96]

At this time in Kosova, people started talking about the appearance of Azem Bejta's regiment, whose attacks were mainly in the Austro-Hungarian region, from Mitrovica in the North to Peja and Gjakova. In

---

[93] *Ibid.*, p. 92.

[94] *Ibid.*, p. 93.

[95] Popović, Janićije: *"Kosovo u roptsvu pod bugarima 1915-1918,"* Leskovac, 1921, p. 87-88.

[96] Perović, Milivoje: *"Toplićki ustanak,"* Belgrade, 1956, p. 103-109.

the summer of 1918, regiments of Azem Bejta were seen cooperating closely with the "Chetniks" of Kosta Peçancit, where Azem Bejta's Kachaks and Serbian "Chetniks" agreed on a common fight against the Austro-Hungarians and to a lesser extent against the Bulgarians,[97] although it was known that the Bulgarians were those who practiced terror against the Albanian population. In accordance with this agreement was the military action of Azem Bejta near Runik, at "Perroi i Keq," where they attacked the Austro-Hungarian army and captured many soldiers and officers as hostages. After the French army arrived in Mitrovica with its leader commander Balsha, Azem Bejta Galica hosted a dinner in his honor and thanked them for fighting the Austro-Hungarians. He later surrendered the hostages to them. [98]

But, as it will be seen, the Kachak movement that was organized in Kosova against Austro-Hungary as well as its coordination with Serbian Chetniks did not save Kosova from Serbia's new occupation. This occupation took place after the arrival of French forces and did not save Azem Bejta and other Albanian Kachaks from the Serbian servitude and did not avoid the war between these two. However, Albanians (especially Kosovars) would not scratch the option of an ethnic Albania, an option supported by patriots and intellectuals from the Albanian National Movement, which had led to the independence of Albania. Nonetheless, this option became feebler and more distant when the World War was approaching its end, since the victory of the Entente and the defeat of the Axis Powers created the circumstances for a different Albania, a more adverse one than that coming from the Conference of London.

Although it can be said that the rivalry regarding the autonomy in Albania was becoming stronger – the Austro-Hungarian autonomy was weakening – and that of Korça after after six months was nullified. The Italian autonomy took the form of protectorate. This made clear that three of the Great Powers, guarantors of Albania from the Conference of London (Austria-Hungary from the battalion of Axis) and two from the battalion of Entente (Italy and France) had made their interest known, that even though it appeared "in defense of Albanians and Albania," they were important for the Albanian cause and its further treatment, regard-

---

[97] *Ibid.*, p. 199.

[98] Limoni, Rushit: *"Rrethanat politiko-shoqërore në Kosovë 1912-1918,"* Prishtinë, 1986, p. 198.

less of how the Albanian state looked. With the implication of Rome and Paris as Entente powers in the Albanian issue, it was clear that the secret Treaty of London of April 1915 had started to reveal itself. It was not necessary to comply with what was achieved with this treaty because the existence of the Albanian state, no matter who would be the winner of the World War, was not put into question but was only passed under the jurisdiction of the winners. This meant that the status of Albania could move from the maximalist point (if Vienna would win) to the middle point that is to return to the Albanian state as determined by the Conference of London or less (if the Entente powers would win). What was more important, it seems that even the option of Entente was "promising" because Italy and France, after the withdrawal of Russia from the war and the reduction of pressure from its recognized claims to extend the impact in the Balkans through its allies (Orthodox Slavic countries), clearly indicated that the Albanian state should be accepted, regardless of its internal organization and the size it would have. Moreover, such movements in Rome and Paris claimed that neither Belgrade's nor Athens's appetites would be met at the expense of Albania, especially those of Serbia, which counted on the support of France if the war were to be won by the Entente, with which Serbia was already aligned and expected rewards. In this way, Serbia would be able to expand its territories more deeply into Albania.

The offers that Albania received, those for autonomous administrations (from Vienna and Paris) and those for formal recognition of the supervised state by the Italians, were connected to a very important development. In April 1917, the United States of America entered the war on the side of Entente against the Austro-German bloc. U.S. gave a turn to the developments and helped Entente win the war in the autumn of the next year. U.S. President Wilson justified the entry of U.S. into the war with the dedication of the U.S. to establish a just peace. He, among other things, stated that the United States would not recognize the secret treaties. This was a historical position and at that stage of the war requested the removal of the Albanian cause from the secret bargains, such as the Treaty of London of 1915 and other similar agreements that were made in large numbers among the European Great Powers, who were in a race to benefit the Balkan countries on their side, where Albania and the Albanian territory in general was seen as a commodity for an inevitable equalization.

The Paris Peace Conference Seals the Partitioning of Albania

Albania's situation after the First World War – the Italian invasion and Rome's claim to dictate Albania's new status according to the Secret Treaty of London in 1915. – The project of the "Focus" federate of the United States of America regarding the independent Albanian state and the emergence of two streams on the future of Albania. – The government of Durrës and the Albanian representation in the Peace Conference in Paris. – The Italian mandate for the future of Albania and the initial US acceptance that Italy together with neighboring countries expand their territories with the Albanian ones. – The war of Vlorë and the declaration of the US President Wilson that the issue of Albania gets separated from that of the Adriatic.

The entrance of the U.S. in the war and the switch in favor of the Entente, which as an epilogue ended on November 11, 1918 with the victory of the Entente Powers (Britain, France, Italy, and USA), did not free the political and diplomatic European scene from the trouble it had at the time of the rivalry with the Central Powers. On the contrary, the fall of the Austro-Hungarian monarchy and the Prussian Germany failure, together with the departure of the Ottoman Empire from the European area, charged the victorious states (Britain, France and Italy) with responsibility toward the national states. Even though the war was won it did not solve these issues, especially those of the neighboring European countries. On the contrary, the fall of Austro-Hungary together with the departure of the Ottoman Empire left the winning party with the responsibility of solving the issues of the old continent as well as all other open questions that arose from that.

France which did not have territorial aims on the Balkans, like Italy did, nevertheless was interested that its two primary supporters: the Serbs and the Greeks would turn to become important regional factors, but that this would not deteriorate the relationship with the Italians and Britain. Because Paris had an intent to balance the gratification of Italy's ambitions in the Adriatic with its own troubles in the Mediterranean, Africa and the Near and Middle East, an intention that Britain also had, whom after the victory of the Entente powers felt like a real imperial power interested in the expansion of its influence over the Near and Middle East where the main sources of world energy were located, also had this intent.

With these and similar preoccupations, on January 18, 1919, the Peace Conference began in Paris with the participation of the United States of America, Britain, France, Italy, and Japan.

Since World War I had changed the relationship not only among the Great Powers of Europe, from which the previous powers of Austria-Hungary and Germany were excluded, and Russia was self-excluded, after the October Revolution, Russia and its conquered territories were turned into the Union of the Soviet Socialist Republics. In these circumstances, with the appearance of the US and Japan, the European scene was turned into a world scene, a change which would have great importance for the future developments for the reason that the main voice would be given to the Americans, whom unaccustomed to the traditional diplomacy and politics of Europe, soon would be freed from the trap of its tiring intrigues to cut down the main issues with pragmatism so that priorities would not be mixed with the secondary or tertiary issues. Also, in the last phase of the Conference, it would be seen that the U.S. protected the principles of freedom, democracy and the right of peoples for self-determination, principles upon which the American society was built and precisely upon the principles which President Wilson delineated in his ideas on the fourteen points of January 1918, which echoed widely because they rose so many hopes, especially among the small populations of Europe, including the Albanians.

Of this nature, the American stance toward the Albanian issue was also established after the behind-the-scenes motives and games were understood. President Wilson ordered that the Albanian issue be separated from that of the Adriatic, with which it was made clear to Rome, Belgrade, Athens and others that Albania would not be linked with the issues that preoccupied the interests of Italy and France on the Adriatic, which were those of the establishment of the boundary line between Italy and Yugoslavia, where Rome would get a good piece of the Adriatic coastline which was part of Austria-Hungary. Meanwhile in this regard, the relationship between Greece and Italy would also have to be solved.

The American stance that the Albanian issue should be separated from the Adriatic issue, apart from protecting the Albanian state from becoming a prey of segregation, also brought back the option of the Conference of London – which weakened the irredentist movement in Kosova. This movement a year earlier, with the foundation of the "Committee for the Defense of Kosova" in Shkodër had won the support of the area and requested the option of the ethnic Albanian state, which would have to be reached even with an armed war if necessary. It would be supported by the majority of the ruling elite of the area and would even appear as a requirement of the Government of Durrës delegation in the Peace Conference in Paris.

This political realism was also reasonable, because the protection of the "Albania of London" was imposed as a painful but necessary variant upon all of the Albanian political groups of that time, (pro-Italian of the government of Durrës, Tiranë, or the government that came out of the National Congress of Luzhnjë). In order to protect the state from further division by Serbs and Greeks, whose armies already occupied some portion of Albanian territory, and since they knew that Austria-Hungary was no longer there to give them ultimatums, they had chosen the method of "spinning wheels", giving legitimacy to their violent acts.

Athens also followed this strategy in the South, but also Italy with the occupation of Vlorë and other areas, used its position to achieve the role of the first mediator in the Balkans. With the success of this strategy, at the beginning of 1919, the so-called *mandate* for the Albanian issue from Britain, France and the US, safeguarded the balance of their own interests in the Adriatic and Mediterranean. The fall of Austria-Hungary and the weakening of Germany, on one side, and the retreat of Russia after the October Revolution from the political European scene on the other side, had relieved Italy from its main rivals in the Balkans, which made Italy behave in accordance to this role. Meanwhile, Serbia together with Croatia and the separated Slovenia from Austria-Hungary all united with the common state of the South Slavs, the so-called Serbo-Croatian-Slovenian Kingdom (which after six years would be called Yugoslavia). Eventually to fulfill its desire for territorial correction, in principle it satisfied itself with the occupation of some Albanian territories that it occupied during the Balkan wars and to which the Conference of London had given legitimacy. Frightened that it would disturb Italy with further open territorial intentions toward Albania, the Serbo-Croatian-Slovenian Kingdom (SCS) chose behind-the-scenes tactics which were implemented toward Albania from the inside, not giving up Esad Pashë Toptani (now an Entente ally) and the role that he was to play in the new circumstances, going as far as the organization of the inner rebellion like the one of Markagjon of 1921, when he seized the opportunity to penetrate into some parts of Albania with his troops, in order to protect his "feud" in

Mirditë. As would be seen, Belgrade in some instances, with much success was able to enter the Albanian political scene, such that in the events of 1924 was also able to influence the arrival of Ahmet Zog to power, even though for this issue it had been speculated a lot for "Serbian merits," in reality outside factors contributed to it as well. In any case, it can be said that Belgrade succeeded with such actions to keep the Albanian political scene hostage, not only from the inside, but also from 1918 until the end of 1924, succeeded in turning it into a partner toward the elimination and liquidation of the Irredentist Movement of Kosova.

With the Conference of Paris and after the acceptance of Albania in the Nations League, the option of the European Albania fundamentally won against the Ottoman Albania and the intrigue that by the Secret Treaty of London of 1915 was projected as the *Muslim Albania.* As prelude to the end of World War II, the return of the Albanian issue for international analysis (1918-1921) in reality presented a tormenting attempt for the project of European Albania to be energized.

Different from 1913-1914, when after the recognition from the Ambassadors' Conference in London, Albania crossed to the therapy of international supervision and within those fourteen months faced war both internally and externally so that in many ways the Albanian state did not pass the first and most important historic test of self-proof. During the time following World War I Albania and the Albanians were faced with, on one hand – the inner attempts of survival as a state with its internationally accepted dimensions and boundaries from the Conference of London, and on the other hand – the attempts from the outside of handling the situation in accordance with the Secret Treaty of London of 1915, where it would fall prey to neighboring countries. With Italy's appetite to extend toward the east side of the Adriatic, and London leaving Albania only a small portion lying from Durrës to Mat, Albania would still maintain the "Muslim" feudal epithet and exist under the Italian protectorate.

The actions for the implementation of this scenario, of course through violence or in accordance with the circumstances created by the war epilogue and the change of relationships between the powers on the world plan (the loss of the Central Powers and the victory of the Entente Powers and allies), began during the months October-November 1918 when the defeated powers (Austro-Hungarian and Bulgarian) were taken over by the victorious ones, which in Albania created four different occupation zones. From these, two were created after the end of the war, while the other two, the Italian zone and the French zone, which were also present during the World War, experienced changes only in scope. Thus, November 1918 found the French not only in the area of Korçë, but also in that of Pogradec, which they took in their hands from September 1917. Later, from July-August 1918, in war with the Austrian powers, the French also jumped to the area of Gramsh and Skrapar, whereas at the beginning of October 1918, they entered the middle area of Albania. However, the diplomacy of Romes, which viewed Middle Albania as a zone where the Italian units would be settled, intervened immediately in Paris and forced the French troops to retreat to their previous positions.[99]

It should be mentioned, however, that in the new circumstances, the mission of the French troops which were in Korçë and Pogradec also changed. It is noted that in the circumstances of the French-Italian oppositions toward the separation of Albania, and the Italian-Greek ones for South Albania, France was assigned the role of "the guard", who would not allow the Greek troops to enter, and even less the Italian ones until the Peace Conference would decide upon the future of South Albania. In accordance to this stance, at the end of October 1918, the French named their zone in Albania "the French administration of Albanian boundaries."[100]

In the meantime, Rome attempted to go to the Peace Conference with the strongest possible position, taking advantage of the Austro-German defeat and moving its troops toward the North with the intention of taking in its hands as soon as possible all the Austrian zone of its occupation in South Albania, hoping to prevent the eventual French expansions and to possibly prevent the entrance of Serbian powers into the boundaries of the Albanian state.

Thus, the Italian troops which were in Vjosë at the beginning of September 1918 progressed toward the North and chased the Austrian forces, reaching Shkodër by the end of October. The Italian zone of occupancy ranged from Konispol to the North, close to the Northern boundaries. In the East, the Italian troops settled roughly around the Black Drin.[101]

---

[99] "*Historia e Popullit Shqiptar,*" third volume, Tiranë, 2007, p. 96.

[100] *Ibid.*, p. 96.

[101] *Ibid.*, p. 97.

Nevertheless, the Italians were not left free to enter Shkodër as their own occupied zone. The French and Britains would react and force Rome to act in accordance with the agreement of 1915 when they each were obligated to act collectively in the "contested" zones, in which Shkodër by the proposal was placed under a military garrison administration among allies. The French colonel, Bardi de Fourtou, was placed in charge. The placement of Shkodër under the inter-allied administration created possibilities for the Serbian invader forces which entered Shkodër first (on October 20), and were then chased immediately by the Italian troops and forced to leave the city after a few days.

But, if the allies in the North would be able to get rid of the Serbian army from Shkodër and the surroundings which it also sought to include in its hegemonic plans toward Albanian territories, nevertheless it would not impede Belgrade to exploit the end of the World War to create its *"strategic zone"* which from its own side was called *"necessary for the protection"* of Serbia and its interests. This approximately included the areas of Peshkopi and Kukës, and also the highlands of Kelmend and Gjakovë. The aim of the Serbian government was the inclusion of this zone in the boundaries of the Serbo-Croatian-Slovenian state, which was founded after the end of the war, in December 1918.

With the new military realities that would come out of the Second World War, the Albanian issue would reach the Peace Conference in Paris, which would open up on January 18, 1919. It was organized by the five victorious Grand Powers of the war: Britain, France, Italy, USA, and Japan. Albania, although it was not an ally of any side, neither victorious nor defeated, nevertheless was found occupied by the military forces of some of the victorious powers, which had their own interests regarding Albania. And they were:

- First of all – that Albania would not be recognized as a state with the dimensions and boundaries that the Ambassadors' Conference of London of 1913 determined (since it was evaluated that this was determined by the interests of Austria-Hungary who had lost the war and was defeated as an empire).
- Second – even if there should be something left of it, then the frames of the Secret Treaty of London of 1915 should be preserved, from which the result was only a *Small Muslim Albanian* state somewhere in the middle (from Durrës to Mat) and even as such, to be left under the Italian protectorate.

The definition of the *Muslim Albanian State* as defined by the Italians, did not correspond to the Ottoman Albania that the Ambassadors' Conference in London had initially determined under the sovereignty of the Sultan, but rather, a "specific" creation with the anathema of a "foreign and dangerous body," which had to be quickly removed in the name of the elimination mortgage of "the match of civilizations" in the European context.

In any case, in the Peace Conference in Paris, the Albanian issue reached the certain treatment also due to the fact that during the World War the Albanians did not succeed in creating a single administration center nor in composing a single political program of their own. Apart from being occupied from the forces of the neighboring regions, and apart from the fact that they turned into a polygon of matches between the Entente and the Central Powers, for a long time Albania was left under the pressure of the inner war, which evolved between the pro-Turkish and Islamic forces which desired the return of the Ottoman Albania and the patriotic forces, which in many thrones would fight for an independent and European Albania.

This fratricidal war, the first among Albanians, supported and in most cases also directed by Serbs, Greeks and Italians, expended all the energy of Albanians, whom for this reason were interested in the Central Powers winning, so that they could return to the option in maximum, meaning that of the ethnic Albania, which from Prince Wied, who although left Albania, was introduced to the German government as a project that would need help to be implemented if the War was won by the Central Powers[102]. But, the defeat of the Central Powers and the victory of the Entente allies, had altered not only the factual occupational situation, but also the political one of Albanians, because now they appeared as hostage to Italian actions, with which the established military position in Albania directed the fate of Albanians and Albania as a whole in the Peace Conference.

Nevertheless, even under these circumstances, the *"Vatra"* Society of the Albanian colony in the US, an organization directed by Fan Nol, which developed a wide range of political activity during the years 1914-

---

[102] See Prince Wied's project regarding the ethnic Albania in *"Denktschift über Albanien"* (the Memorandum for Albania), in the third part of the book, which he will introduce to the German government in 1917.

1918, created a national platform which sought to serve as a base for the Albanian community demands, which would be introduced to the Great Powers. In a resolution approved by this organization, on July 1917, it stated:

> Let us secure in any legitimate way from the Great Powers and from the Peace Congress an Albanian state with its ethnic boundaries, with full royal independence, an economic and political Albania for Albanians.[103]

The *Vatra* Federate, in the years 1916-1917, sent Mehmet Konica to London and Dr. Mihal Turtulli to Lausanne to get the Albanian issue recognized by diplomatic circuits and the foreign press.

However, as would be seen in the specification of the new status which was thought to be introduced at the Peace Conference, different stances appeared from the National Movement groups. Nevertheless, with the end of the First World War, two political streams were crystallized. The representatives of the first stream requested a fully independent state with ethnic dimensions. This stream was powerfully supported by the Albanian patriots, especially those from Kosova, whom in Shkodër founded the "National Defense of Kosova" Committee which acted legally and was directed by Muezzin Kadri Prishtina. Representatives of the other stream thought of requesting from the Peace Conference the return of the independent Albanian state, placing it under the "Defense" of any of the victorious powers. The "Defense" status from a foreign power was thought to be a temporary measure, which would continue as long as there would be Albanian state entities rising and until these entities would be able to handle any inner rebellion. [104]

Certainly, even the issue of an outside "Defense" for Albania emerged without a unified stance, since some thought that this issue should be left to Italy, while others thought it should be left to the US. The pro-Italians, as an argument for the Italian "umbrella" over Albania and possibly "protector", if interested, based its weight and importance on the concept of the Great Powers and Rome's ability to halt the Serbian and Greek appetite for Albanian territories.

Led by the ex-prime minister of Prince Weid's government, Turhan Pasha Përmeti, a group of Albanian personalities from Switzerland, who

---

[103] Cited from "*Historia e Popullit Shqiptar,*" third volume, Tiranë, 2007, p. 123.
[104] "*Historia e Popullit Shqiptar,*" third volume, Tiranë, 2007, p. 124.

were located in Geneva, introduced this idea during the Peace Conference in Paris, giving rise to Italy receiving the so-called "mandate" for Albania. On the other hand, the pro-Americans, led by the belief that Albania needed the presence of a foreign power geographically distant, were determined for the US since they were not the signers of the London Treaty of April 1915, and because the Americans did not have specific interests for the Balkans, which could possibly influence the stability of the Albanian state.[105]

However, the two streams and their proposals could have been left outside the political context if the Albanians did not have the legitimacy of their pavement, which could only be secured even temporarily by having the representative mandate. Thus, the divided Albanian political forces had the burden of establishing a representative body which could act toward this aim. After the US entrance in the war in 1917, the signs of the Entente's victory became apparent. When Italy was gaining more and more every day, many of the Albanians from both inside and outside Albania, started presenting to Rome the plan to form a national Albanian government.

Of course, Rome also needed such a representative mechanism, with the condition that it would not appear as a government, but as a "Council" or "National Committee," to act "as a supplement" of the Italian delegation for the Peace Conference and that it would be used by Italy against the claims of neighboring countries. The leader of the Italian diplomacy, S. Sonnino, expressed openly that for this organization he would need *"faithful"* Albanians toward Italy and that he *"would have authority all over Albania, excluding Vlorë and its highlands,"* which were considered parts of Italy.[106]

In order for this specter to seem *"as inclusive as possible,"* the Italian government called upon Rome to develop negotiations with Mehdi Frashëri, Mustafa Kruja, Luigj Gurakuqi and Mufit Libohova, who had gone to the Italian capital from Albania, along with Mehmet Konica, who happened to be in London as a representative of *Vatra*. Ismail Qemal was also set to go to Rome, from Spain; however, his worsening medical

---

[105] *"Historia e Popullit Shqiptar,"* third volume, Tiranë, 2007, p. 128.
[106] *Ibid.*, p. 126.

condition did not allow him to contribute to the development of the political events of that time. [107]

Nevertheless, the issue of holding a Congress had now turned into a preoccupation also of other patriotic forces, which were not previously part of the negotiations of Rome. Some political figures, such as Preng Bibë Doda, Ismail Ndroqi, Abdi Toptani and others, had taken the initiative to hold a congress in Lezhë or Tiranë. This led to the Congress being decided to be held in Durrës, the ex-capital of the region.

The Congress of Durrës opened on December 25th, 1918, under the direction of Mehmet Konica and over 50 delegates participated in the event. They represented all the regions of the Albanian state occupied by the Italians, excluding Vlorë, the representatives of which the Italian command forbade participation, since this city was considered part of Italy. In the Congress, the regions of Lumës and Peshkopi were not included either, since there the Serbian regime was present, and also the areas of Korçë and Pogradec, where the French forces were present.[108]

In the Congress of Durrës everythin proceeded according to the Italian predictions. The selected political forces objected to the Italian stream and decided that instead of the *"Council"* or *"Committee"* to establish a Temporary Government, which would be directed by Turhan Pasha Përmeti, whom although in Durrës, appeared with pro-Italian stances, nevertheless, was chosen for that position to present the continuation of the Albanian state. Preng Bibë Doda was chosen Deputy Prime Minister and the chosen ministers were: Lef Nosi, Luigj Gurakuqi, Mehdi Frashëri, Mehmet Konica, Mustafa Kruja, Myfit Libohova, Petro Poga and Sami Vrioni.

The Congress also selected the composition of the delegation that would go to the Conference. Apart from the prime minister who led the delegation, other members were: the Minister of Internal Affairs, Mehmet Konica, Luigj Bumçi, Dr. Mihal Turtulli and Mit'hat Frashëri.

The Albanian delegation arrived in Paris in February 1919. The delegation presented to the Conference two memorandums with their requests, approved by the Congress of Durrës. The Albanian memorandums had to do with the request that the international re-recognition of Albania's independence, established in 1913 be re-examined and the issue

---

[107] *Ibid.*, p. 126.
[108] *Ibid.*, pg127

(of Kosova and Çamëria) get solved in accordance with the principles of the right of peoples to self-determination. This was heavily discussed during the war, at which time request was made to place US military forces in Albanian regions left outside the 1913 boundaries, which would be administered for one or two years.

The proposal of the Albanian delegation, although it was not taken into consideration by the Conference of Paris, nevertheles brought forth different movements among the Albanian neighbors: Greeks and Serbs. Athens brought forth the case of dividing Albanian territories in accordance with the Secret Treaty of London of 1915, whereas Belgrade expressed favor for the independence of Albania of 1913. This stance was determined by the harsh Italian-Yugoslavian rivalry on the Adriatic and Albania, which brought to surface the Yugoslavian strategy that the acceptance of the Albanian state which came out of the Conference of London was much more accommodating than the Italian protectorate for it, or that Italy should hold Vlorë or other regions. Belgrade had also come to the stance now that an Albanian state the dimensions of London, under the lead of Esad Pashë Toptani, was in accordance with the Yugoslavian interests.

Toward this strategy, with the recognition of the London Albania, Belgrade would be "flexible" in case the Peace Conference made another decision. In the Yugoslavian memorandum, which was introduced to the Conference in February 1919, among others stated that *"in case any other state had recognized the right to occupy or claim protectorate over a certain area or the whole of the 1913 Albania, then Yugoslavia, in order to protect its interests, would have the right to claim the portion which belongs to it."*[109]

The Italian-Yugoslavian rivalry certainly was important when it came to the formulation of the stances regarding Albania, to which the Peace Conference was subject, according to which, the interest of Italians was to leave out of the game the decisions of the Ambassadors' Conference in London, with the reasoning that since the international recognition of the independence and sovereignty of Albania in London on 1913 was a precocious act, it should be re-made. With the formulation of the "re-

---

[109] *Ibid.*, p. 131.

making," with which the US, Britain and France would agree, the issue of the Albanian state was also included in the *mandate system*.[110]

After this decision, it wasn't difficult for Rome to receive the *"mandate"* over the after-war Albanian state from the three Great Powers (USA, Britain and France), which it would first officially request on August 1919 from the External Affairs Minister, T. Titton, and which it would receive on December 9, 1919. In the reasoning of the memorandum, among others it was stated that, *"from its geographical position and the economic capacities, Italy is the most appropriate state to fulfill this task."*[111]

The Italian "mandate" over Albania, would be turned into a difficulty not only for the re-making of Albania, but also for the general resolving of the open issues that had emerged after the end of the First World War, especially those which needed to be defined after the fall of the Austro-Hungarian Empire and the defeat of Germany, where Italy and Yugoslavia were supposed to receive the greatest portion of the loot. As would be seen, the eventual "likings" between Rome and Belgrade toward the division of the Albanian territory unavoidably brought the reactions of Athens, which turned the issues into other rivalries between the heretofore allies.

However, one of the greatest difficulties that would appear to the Italian "mandate" in Albania, would be the refusal of Albanians to accept a new division of their territories and also with the placement under the Italian protectorate of that area appearing as an Albanian "state" wrinkled under Middle Albania foreseen as a *"Muslim Albania,"* which would also require contesting those decisions which could get a definite form if approved.

In reality, the National Albanian Movement against the decisions of the Peace Conference of November 1919, even without any central impetus, began to create its nucleus, since the delegation of the Durrës Government (the majority of it) agreed with these decisions, which now brought to surface the lines of government that Italy requested in Albania: a wrinkled state creature which was allowed to be extended only into

---

[110] *"The mandate system,"* around which the Peace Conference would be specified, predicted to include only those places and people that had not yet earned their national independence and that needed the guarding and the helping hand of a "civilized" power, to lead them toward independence.

[111] *"Historia e Popullit Shqiptar,"* third volume, Tiranë, 2007, p. 132.

Middle Albania. Out of its boundaries were left Gjirokastër, Korçë, Vlorë and Shkodër, the future of which was foreseen to become a further object of discussion in the Peace Conference.

A reason for the revolt of Albanians against those that were occurring under the "mandate" of Italy on Albania, surely was the Italian-Greek agreement of July 1919, known as Titoni-Venizelos, with which Rome recognized the Greek intentions in the South of Albania, with which it secured the support of Athens for the Italian benefits on the Adriatic which were connected with the so-called "issue of Adriatic." After this, there was also another agreement between the two ministers of the Government of Durrës (Mufit Libohova and Fejzi Alizoti), which was signed on August 20 with the two representatives of the Italian government, according to which Rome, *de jure* would take over the role of the controller over the actions of the Albanian state government, while in the meantime the protectorate over Vlorë and its surroundings would be recognized by Italy.

Under these circumstances, the different political organizations launched the call *"Homeland at stake"* and called upon the people to get their weapons and repeat the *"Prizren League."*[112] In this case, the idea was also born about calling a National Congress to take the necessary actions for the rescue of the area from the risk it was subject to. This Congress would be the organization that would legally replace the pro-Italian Government of Durrës.[113]

Along with the difficulties from the Italians, the patriots engaged around the call. The organization of the National Congress also faced difficulties from the Durrës Government, who together with the Italians, called a meeting of the senate, which would neutralize the National Congress, in order to prevent a development that would put it at risk.

In the meanwhile, the Italian authorities, by deciding upon the frames of the new Albanian "senate," inhibited the representatives of Vlorë from participating, since this city and its surroundings were now parts of Italy. In Vlorë, the Albanian patriots, among them Beqir Sulo, Osman Haxhia, Aristidh Ruci and others, contested this act and they used this mostly in the case of celebrating Seven years of Independence, when they organized large protests, which although halted by the Italian occupiers, turned into

---

[112] *Ibid.*, p. 142.
[113] *Ibid.*, p. 142.

all-population protests which were only dispersed through the use of weapons. This is where the "Long Live Albania" and "long live the Albanian Vlorë" slogans were prepared, which showed the political and patriotic mood of Albanians towards the Italian occupation and their stunts with dummy governments, like the one of Durrës.

The large protests of November 1919 and the wide manifestation of the patriotic spirit of Albanians dispersed among different occupied regions, which were intended to turn into real divisions, gave the final impetus to the different political circuits of the area to call the National Congress. The initiative came out of Tirana and was dispersed quickly everywhere, gathering a lot of support. The initiators of the National Congress were Aqif Pasha Biçaku, Eshref Frashëri, Sotir Peci, Ahmet Zogu, Hasan Prishtina, Hoxha Kadri Prishtina, Osman Myderrizi and others. An organizational commission with its center in Lushnje, consisting of 22 members, among which were Besim Nuri, Halil Libohova, Eshref Frashëri, Llazar Boze and Taullah Sinani, began distributing calls for the meeting of the Congress on January 1, 1920.

The Government of Durrës tried to prevent the meeting of the Congress and for this the Italians even utilized armed units against the meeting. Nevertheless the National Congress opened in Lushnje on January 21, 1920. In the Congress, over 50 representatives participated from all regions of the Albanian state, including Vlorë and the other regions, which according to the Peace Conference were outside the boundaries of the state. Aqif Pasha Biçoku was selected President of the Congress and Sotir Peci became Vice-President..[114]

The Congress of Lushnje made important political decisions, among which three can be considered historical.

The first decision had to do with the non-acceptance of the Peace Conference projects which limited the territorial independence and integrity of the Albanian state and the specification against every foreign mandate or protectorate. This also included opposition to projects to empower an Italian prince over the Albanian state or to place it under the "Defense" of the League of Nations, as the Government of Durrës had proposed.

The second decision sanctioning full sovereignty of the Albanian state was also of great importance since it required the approval of a constitu-

---

[114] *Ibid.*, p. 145.

tional act, which also gave rise to a Congress, like the High Council consisting of 4 people, with its members Aqif Pasha Biçoku, Dr. Mihal Turtulli, Luigj Bumçi and Abdi Bej Toptani, followed by the selection of the National Council (which was named "the Senate") consisting of 37 members and playing the function of the parliament.

The third decision having to do with the fall of the Durrës Government whose activity was considered anti-national, was also of great importance and decisive in pulling Albania out of the trap of outside mandates, concretely – the Italian one. In this case, the Congress chose a new government, led by Sulejman Delvina. Eshref Frashëri was temporarily chosen Vice President of the government, Mehmet Konica was chosen head of foreign affairs, Ahmet Zogu was chosen for Internal Affairs, Sotir Peci for Education, Hoxha Kadriu for Justice and Ndoc Çorba for Finances.[115]

Thus, the Lushnjë Congress, replaced de facto Albania's independence. The National Albanian Movement formed a single administration center for which there was much need in these decisive circumstances.

The Government resulting from the decisions of the Congress of Lushnjë and due to the inability to enter Durrës – since this was not allowed by the pro-Italian government and the occupying Italian powers that were sure to prevent its activity – was placed in Tiranë on February 11, 1920 and greeted with enthusiasm by the people, who had the belief that the decisions of the Congress of Lushnjë were the only ones that in those circumstances could rescue Albania from further division. From that day Tirana became the capital of Albania.

The activity of the Government of Tirana noted its first success when Tirana got rid of the Italian officers that led the Albanian gendarmerie and when the Internal Affairs Minister, Ahmet Zogu, together with the Minister of Justice, Hoxha Kadri Prishtina, supported by the patriots of Shkodër, took the city in their own hands. On March 12, they forced the French contingent to give the municipality administration over to the local council. After having done this, the French general, Bardi dë Futu, left Shkodër together with the French contingency. The next day, Shkodër announced its union with the National Government of Tirana. Shkodër continued to have only one contingency of Italian militants of the inter-

---

[115] Bartl, Peter: "Albanien," Munchen, 1995, p. 191.

ally garrison, but they were prohibited from dealing with the administrative issues of the city.

The successes of the National Government of Tirana were not without consequences in the relationship with internationals. Although the Great Powers continued not to consider the decisions of the Congress of Lushnjë and the Tirana Government valid, nevertheless, the Albanian entrance into Shkodër and the decision to unite with the Tirana Government after it announced the end of the inter-ally military administration, resulted in the Anglo-French-Italian compromise of January 14, 1920 not being fulfilled, with which the exchange of Rijeka and Shkodër was foreseen. The readiness of Albanians to protect the sovereignty of their state even with weapons, as it was seen in Tirana and Shkodër, and also noting that the situation could worsen, at last made the American President, W. Wilson, on March 6, 1920 declare the separation of the Albanian issue from the Adriatic, leaving to be understood that *"it would not accept any plan that would give Yugoslavia any territorial compensation of North of Albania for the land that would be taken somewhere else."*[116]

Thus, seeing that the Italo-Yugoslavian agreements would result in the complete division of the Albanian state, which ultimately was in opposition to the American principles of the peoples' right to self-determination and the protection of places at risk, declared in the case of the US entrance into World War, Washington undertook a direct measure with which the National Albanian Movement would get motivated to continue fighting and further their inner attempts.

The Tirana Government, taking into account the circumstances and the relationship of the powers, especially the open issues which the Peace Conference had left as "discussable," made its first diplomatic and political attempts toward Italy, which had the "mandate" on Albania from the Peace Conference, but at the same time had the largest part of Albania under its occupation. At the beginning of March 1920, in the meeting of the National Council, it received the first messages from the High Council of London for reaching a compromise, where the national rights of the Albanian people would be respected:

> We hope that Italy, taking into consideration the common will of the Albanian nation, will change the political stance it had up to now regarding the

---

[116] Cited from *"Historia e Popullit Shqiptar,"* third volume, Tiranë, 2007, p. 149.

Albanian issue and it will become a member of the full integrity and independence of Albania.[117]

On April 1, the same message was sent to Italy from the National Council, stating:

> Let it be God's will, after the energetic patriotic measures that the Government has undertaken, that Albania will come out as a free and independent state with its territorial boundaries.[118]

Since in Paris and Rome the political requests of Albanians were not finding the necessary echo, in the Albanian political scene the idea raised in Lushnjë began to spread, which was the idea that the last tool to be used that was left to Albanians was an armed war. Giving an echo to this call, the newspaper "Drita" of Gjirokastër wrote on March 1920:

> Every door is closed for us, in every foreign doorstep that we knocked no one answered us. Now we are left to deal with our worries ourselves. This is our only rescue, the only power that we can brag about is power itself.[119]

Prior to starting the war to return the sovereignty of the Albanian state, the government of Durrës returned to the negotiations with Belgrade and Athens, in order for the throne foreseen with Italy in Vlorë not to be influenced by these places. In April 1920, Tirana sent Dr. Sejfi Vllamas (Deputy, Senator) to Belgrade to reach an agreement for the retreat of the Yugoslavian forces from the occupied Albanian areas. Since Belgrade had initially declared that it preferred an independent Albania of the 1913s compared to an Albania under the Italian mandate, it expressed willingness to negotiate for the retreat of their troops, but only conditioning it with the retreat of the occupying Italian troops. The foreign affairs minister, Popovic, greeted the Albanians readiness to start an armed war against the Italians and it even promised aid in weapons and ammunition. In this case, Belgrade did not accept giving up the support it was giving to Esad Pasha Toptani, viewing him as the *"President of the Albanian Government."*[120]

---

[117] *Ibid.*, p. 150.
[118] *Ibid.*, p. 150.
[119] Bartl, Peter: "Albanien," Munchen, 1995, p. 193.
[120] "Politics," Belgrade, April 23, 1920.

The Tirana Government directed to Korçë another attempt to return its sovereignty, when Eshref Ademi was sent there with a message from the Prime Minister Sulejman Delvina to the French command. The French command in Korçë who was willing to listen to the Albanian requests, with the view that the French troops would be replaced with Greek ones, even though this was not in accordance to the Peace Conference or the American stance, according to which Korça should remain under the borders of the Albanian state.

The start of the replacement of the French troops with the Greek ones, foreseen at the end of the month, was followed by the stance of Albanian patriots to not allow the entrance of the Greek troops under the command of General N. Trikupis, which were already getting close to the borders of Albania. Thus, on May 26, 1920, the Albanian patriots, after a big protest in Korçë raised the national Albanian flag, whereas the municipality of Korça and the Primacy Council which constituted the local power declared the union with the Government of Tirana and decided to protect it from possible Greek aggression.

In this case, it needs to be emphasized that the French troops did not even halt the Albanian protests of May 26, which culminated with the elevation of the national flag in Korçë, neither did they oppose the decisions of the Municipality of Korça to unite with the Government of Tirana, which showed a silent stance of Paris opposite to the American one, which regarding this issue asked for the will of the Albanian people to be respected.

However, here we must notice another movement, of a wider political and diplomatic nature of French-Britain against the Italians and their claim to dominate the Adriatic, which could interfere with London's and Paris' interests. Thus, the stances of these two countries had an influence over Athens, so that it would not use military forces against the Albanians in Korçë, which it accepted also because at a time when it continued the war with Small Asia, the avoidance of a clash with the Albanians would help it in the East, where it intended to expand. For this reason the French and Britain support was decisive. The Britain had much interest that the Greek army would concentrate in Anadoll against the Turkish National Liberator Movement (which was putting the Britain interests at risk) and that the Albanians would not be impeded in their attempts to expel the Italians from their place, where during the World War many petroleum reserves were discovered, after which the interested Britain circuits had begun looking. [121]

In accordance with these developments, when the Vlorë war against the Italians included not only Albanians, but also other factions, such as the Yugoslavs, the Greeks, the French and the British and it was turning into a new Balkan poker movement, which nevertheless suited the Albanians – since this way they would take a decisive step in returning their state sovereignty and getting freed from the Italian mandate – on May 28, in the bordering country Kapshticë, a very important protocol was signed between the Albanians and the Greeks,. The Kapshtica protocol apart from helping the preservation of the May 26 victory in Korçë, where the union with the Tirana Government was declared, at the same time avoided the conflict with Greece, at a time when the preparations for war against the Italian army in Vlorë were at an end.

These preparations had begun in March 1920, when according to the negotiations developed in Lushnjë, the "National Defense" Committees were founded, whose purpose was to oppose any other Greek aggression in Korçë or Gjirokastër, but especially to organize the armed fortitude against the Italians in Vlorë. In this preparation, the main role was played by the Committee of Vlorë, directed by Osman Haxhiu, in which the Youth organization was also included and directed by Halim Xhelo.[122]

Against these circumstances, the Italian occupiers undertook measures to prevent an armed conflict in Vlorë, by attempting to detach it from the rest of the region. For this purpose, on May 17, a curfew was announced during which many organizers of the fortitude were arrested.

The fact that the situation was moving towards a war with Italy, and this apart from the Albanians, who were dedicated to taking decisive action to return their state sovereignty, was also desired by other outside factors (Britain, France and Greece). This fact is best proven by the opening of multiple weapon transporting canals in Albania from many directions, where together with them, many volunteers and commanders expressed their willingness for war. The Tirana Government also had a hand in this, which, after it selected Bajram Curri as a minister without a portfolio, under his lead, a cleansing operation started against the gangs in Middle Albania under the lead of Esad Pashë Toptani. Under these

---

[121] "*Historia e Popullit Shqiptar,*" Third volume, Tiranë, 2007, p. 154.
[122] *Ibid.*, p. 155.

circumstances of a full national mobilization, the Government of Tirana, attempted to leave the impression that the conflict with Italians was not of the war character between the Albanian state and the Italian state, but rather between the patriots of Vlorë to unite with the Government of Vlorë constituting the Albanian state.

A diplomatic movement started when the member of the High Council, Luigj Bumçi, was sent to Rome to discuss with the Italian External Affairs Minister, Karlo Sforcën, about a way to reach an agreement, with which Vlora would be given back to Albania, and where some other concessions of a military nature were foreseen, which would be given to the Italians. The Italian minister in this case refused the Albanian offer with the words: *"Vlora constituted a fulcrum of the Italian politics."*

The failure of the last diplomatic attempts between Tirana and Rome, gave the last signal of the war of Vlorë. On May 29, the "National Defense" committee called the parliament representatives from the city and from the occupied villages surrounding Vlorë, which all gathered in Barçalla, on the South of Vlorë. The gathered ones approved the Committee's proposal to begin the liberating insurgency. The parliament selected a committee of 12 members, which were responsible for organizing and directing the rebellion. Osman Haxhiu was once again selected as chief, whereas members were Sali Bedini, Qazim Koculi, Hazbi Cano, Ahmet Lepenica, Murat Myftari, and others.[123]

Many armed volunteers from the people of the surrounding areas replied positively to the call of the Committee of Barçalla, which on June 2, 1920 gathered in Beun, near Vlorë. There were approximately four thousand people, who on the opposing side had the Italian divisions 13 and 36 together with the motorized units and a few military airplanes. The numbers of the Italian forces reached roughly twenty thousand and were commanded by a central command in Vlorë, directed by General S. Piaçenti.

After an ultimatum that the "National Defense" Committee gave to the occupying Italian troops to leave Vlorë, on the eve of June 5 war began with the attack against the surrounding Italian garrisons in Kotë, Drashovicë, Gjorm and Matohasanaj, in which case the Albanian soldiers achieved great and unpredicted success. During these combats more than a thousand Italian soldiers and officers were captured prisoners, and

---

[123] *Ibid.*, p. 157.

many cannons, machine-guns, rifles, ammunition and other warlike materials were confiscated. After six days, the Albanian soldiers began the attack for the liberation of Vlorë. In this heroic battle many Albanians fell, among them also the commander of the Salari troops of Tepelena, Selam Musai.

Apart from the military victories in Vlorë, the Tirana Government secured an important victory also against the separatist forces. The operation against the sadist gangs, which began at the same time as the liberating battle in Vlorë (June 4, 1920) and which was directed by Bajram Curri, ended with a success within a few days. On June 13, 1920, Avni Rrustemi killed Esad Pasha Toptani,[124] which rebounded in a big way for the continuous mobilization of the volunteer forces and for securing the logistics of the war of Vlorë. At the same time, it also strengthened the position of the National Government of Tirana, since in this way, the main actor of behind-the-scene plans that were weaved against the Albanian state were eliminated from the Albanian and international political scene. Many facts say that the attempted attack in Paris which was performed by Avni Rrustemi could only be made possible after an initial agreement from Paris, London and even Athens, so that he could not be exploited by Italy or Belgrade.

In any case, it was the heroic war in Vlorë and the victories against the Italians that changed for better the position of Albania from the inside and the outside. Italy, at last would be forced to acknowledge its failure and begin negotiations for retreating from the occupied Albanian areas, and in so doing, lose its mandate on Albania, which the Peace Conference had given to it in November 1919. The Albanians regained international recognition of their state sovereignty with the borders of the London Conference. Plans for the division of Albanian territories and other issues among the Great Powers that were harmful to the Albanians finally and definitely failed.

Thus, the Italian-Albanian negotiations to give an end to the war of Vlorë and its occupancy from Italy did not begin between the Italian representative and the Vlorë rebellions, as Rome claimed. Instead, the Albanians requested that they be held at a higher level between the representatives of the Italian Government and the Tirana government. The Albanians were represented by Prime Minister, Sulejman Delvina, the

---

[124] *Ibid.*, p. 160.

Internal Affairs Minister, Ahmet Zogu, the minister without a portfolio, Spiro G. Koleka and the External Affairs Minister, Mehmet Konica. The Italian side consisted of Karlo Aliot Baryon, who had been to Durrës before in 1914, first as a diplomatic representative of Rome next to Prince Wied and then as a supporter of Esad Pasha Toptani. This was the composition of the government that demonstrated the national character of the war of Vlorë and the readiness of Albanians to secure the sovereignty of their state with all necessary attributes. The agreement of the protocol was signed in Tirana on August 2, 1920. According to it, the Roman Government would respect the sovereignty of Vlorë and the territorial integrity of Albania. The Protocol was signed for the Albanian party by the Prime Minister Sulejman Delvina and for the Italians by Gaetano Manzoni.[125]

However, the signing of the Albano-Italian protocol was preceded by the denunciation of the government of Rome's July 29, 1919 agreement with Greece, according to which the two neighboring countries would mutually support each other's claims in the Peace Conference regarding Albania. This act of Rome had to do with preventing any possible benefits of Greeks and Yugoslavians in Albania after her own failure, which suited the Albanian state to behave toward these states with the right to return its state sovereignty which was further in danger by Athens and Belgrade.

Of course, the victory of Vlorë and the signing of the Protocol with Italy, created possibilities for the Government of Tirana to return to its problems with Greece and Yugoslavia, since both of these states kept Albanian territories occupied. Belgrade had conditioned its occupations with the staying of Italy, whereas Athens with the decisions of the Peace conference.

In any case, Albania had troubles in the North and South, but was aiming to solve them with negotiations and diplomatic means. However, as would be seen, Belgrade, after the retreat of the Italian troops from Albania, did not keep its word to retreat after the agreement with Tirana. On the contrary, Yugoslavs began reasoning the persistence of their military forces within the Albanian borders with the excuse of "protecting" Yugoslavia from the irredentist movement and the presence of the military forces in the island of Sazan. The government of Tirana, in the case of the conflict of North Kopliku in the borders with Montenegro,

---

[125] *Ibid.*, p. 165.

directed itself to the Great Powers with a note, where the objectives of Belgrade were known, but not even this would change anything. Belgrade opened a range of provocations even to other occupied areas, when the Yugoslavs tried to oppose the establishment of the Drin prefecture with its center in Peshkopi, which was risen by the Government of Tirana. This turned into an armed conflict of wide dimensions, since the Dibrans and other volunteers requested the removal of the occupying army. After the initial battles, the Yugoslav forces brought additional reinforcements and began another big offensive on the other part of Drini, where they massacred and then returned to the area which they called "strategic."

The new Yugoslav occupancies and the massacre motivated the revolt of the patriotic forces, especially the Kosovars gathered around the "National Defense of Kosova" Committee who requested that the Government of Tirana enter an open war with the Yugoslavs, and that this should be preceded by a rebellion in Kosova and other occupied areas which Yugoslavia kept from the Ambassadors' Conference of 1913, and which the Peace Conference had just confirmed. The Prime Minister, Sulejman Delvina, although he recognized Kosova as a part of Albania separated unjustly, did not allow entrance into such a conflict with the Yugoslavs, since this would risk the state's attempts to return the lost sovereignty. On the contrary, to prove once more that it desired the settlement of a good neighboring relationship and the solving of the conflict through negotiations, the Government of Tirana, at the end of September sent a delegation to Shkodër, who entered negotiations with the Yugoslav representative Neshiç. The conditions of Belgrade, to retreat from the "strategic line," according to Neshiç were a *secure guarantee of borders*" and the following of a pro-Yugoslav political view, which meant to give up the stance of protecting the national rights and interests of the Albanians in Yugoslavia.

The Government of Albania, after having requested the help of the Great Powers to influence Belgrade to halt the aggression against the Albanian state and seeing that in this direction there was no action taken, decided to request the acceptance of Albania into the League of Nations, since this would strengthen its international position and at the same time create the possibility to influence resolve of the armed conflict with the Northern neighbor.

This turned out to be a successful and useful decision. Although there were objections at the beginning by Yugoslavia, Greece and France, on

December 17, 1920, the General Asembly of the League of Nations accepted the membership of Albania in the League with full rights.

This was a great success of the Albanian Government, among the greatest up to then, because with it the recognition of the Albanian state independence was restated, and in addition, the acceptance into the League of Nations created possibilities for the assessment in the international forum of the suspended issues between Albania and the neighboring countries.[126]

Nevertheless it must be noted that the quick acceptance of Albania into the League of Nations was done due to the engagement of Great Britain, the stances of which were decisive and at that time had shown interest in the petroleum resources in Albania. The government of Iliaz Vrioni, which in November 1920 had replaced that of Sulejman Delvina, entered an agreement with the Britain in which exclusive right was given to the Anglo-Persian Petroleum Company to request and to exploit the petroleum in Albania.

The acceptance of Albania in the League of Nations did not free it immediately from the difficulties coming from Yugoslavia and Greece, who were attempting to hold on to something from the occupied areas, or to place them under political supervision, and also from Italy, who although recognized its sovereignty, still aimed at earning a special position in Albania, more privileged than the other powers, such was the request to be recognized the right to intervene for the Defense of the territorial integrity and the sovereignty of Albania, if they were threatened by others. Clamped with these writhing movements of diplomatic nature, the League of Nations, with the decision of June 26, 1921, passed for discussion the request of the Government of Albania to the Ambassadors' Conference.

The return of the Albanian issue in the Ambassadors' Conference and the Italian requests for a "special position" in Albania, caused a reaction from Belgrade, who was still frightened by the Italian penetration in Albania. This way, it activated the separatist movement in Albania through the Captain of Mirdita, Markagjon, as Athens had acted upon Himarë but without success. Markagjon, who was in Yugoslavia a long time and there he was considered a card against the Albanian state, jumped to action in April 1921, and together with the mercenaries and

---

[126] *Ibid.*, p. 172.

other Yugoslavian forces, achieved his entrance in Mirditë in June. There, together with some others from Mirditë, he initiated a rebellion against the Albanian Government, but quickly it was defeated and he was returned to Yugoslavia. Upon suggestions of the Belgrade authorities, on July 17, 1921, he announced the "Republic of Mirdita" and requested its recognition by Belgrade, Athens and Rome. These same days, with the help of Yugoslavians and other mercenaries he entered Mirdita. The Yugoslav aggression through Markagjon and Belgrade's attempts to destabilize Albania, motivated the Britain Government to go openly on Albania's side and to judge Belgrade. The Britain prime minister, Lloyd George, in a note sent to the General Secretary of the League on November 7, 1921, requested a meeting of the League Council and the undertaking of measures through which the Yugoslav Government would be forced to respect the Nations League Charter, or else penalty measures would be undertaken against it, under the 16th clause of the charter.

The harsh testimony of Britain had an influence also on the stances of the Ambassadors' Conference specified for the Albanian issues, which on November 9, 1921, announced its decisions, where two main problems were addressed: that of the borders with the two neighboring Balkans countries, and the legal international status of the Albanian state.

Thus, regarding the Albano-Greek borders, the Ambassadors' Conference decided to keep the ones that were already set by the Firence Protocol, in December 17, 1913, whereas regarding the North-East borders, it requested to make some changes in favor of Yugoslavia, giving them a part of Luma, Has and Gollobrdë. For the specification of these changes, it was foreseen that a commission with representatives of the four signing powers would be founded: Great Britain, France, Italy, and Japan.[127]

The Ambassadors' Conference sanctioned the Defense of Albania's sovereignty and independence, but *giving Italy a special position*, according to which, if Albania was not able to protect the territorial integrity, the Albanian Government could ask for help from the League of Nations. In this case, Italy would be the one that would be authorized by the League of Nations to replace Albania's borders.

The decision of the League of Nations to recognize "a special position" for Italy, nevertheless, impacted Yugoslavia to retreat its troops out

---

[127] *Ibid.*, p. 174.

of the borders of Albania. This retreat was done at the beginning of 1922 and forced Belgrade to enter the negotiations for composing inter-state agreements with the Albanian state which would last until 1926, when they would finally be ratified by both states.

CHAPTER 2
KOSOVA AND THE SERBIAN-YUGOSLAVIAN REOCCUPATION OF ALBANIAN TERRITORIES

The Armed Resistance against Reoccupation

The Serbian occupier began placing civil administration immediately after the military occupancy in accordance with the decree of "regulating the liberated areas," which was based upon "the law of uniting the Old Serbia, Serbian Kingdom and its governance."- In accordance to these laws, two secret actions were performed: one was the disarming of the people and the other was the registering of the people by the military entities in Kosova and Macedonia, with mournful consequences for the Albanians. – The military terror as an ethnic cleansing tool of Albanians from Kosova. – The complementary measures for the administrative division of Kosova and the dispersing of its territories in Montenegro's and Serbia's direction, and the establishment of the preconditions for the quick colonization of Kosova with the Slavic people.

The invasion of Kosova (including the Albanian areas in Macedonia, from Shkup, Tetova, Dibra, and up to Manastir) by the Montenegro and Serbian military in December 1912 and the invasion of parts of Albania, were part of the agreements between Orthodox-Slavic Balkan states during their alliances to completely liquidate the Albanian issue through invasions and subsequent division of its territories amongst themselves. Even though politically this seemed impossible – since, as it is known, Albania and Albanians for a large part of the great European Powers (especially for Austria-Hungary and Italy, but also Britain) were turned into a factor that needed the altering of the Slavo-Orthodox dominions in the Balkans, and with it also the expansion of the Russian influence over this very strategic area. Nevertheless, the Balkans states sought to bring politics before finished acts through war, which in any case had to be considered, even if not in whole, then at least because Albanians and their territory could be turned to remnants, so that in time, the issue would lose its importance or would rest altogether.

This way, apart from exploiting the war with the empire forces among the front battle lines, so those that appeared as borders between Balkan states (Serbia, Montenegro and Greece) penetrated towards the parts that were said to be "in need of liberating them from the Ottoman invasion," the armies of these places had detailed instructions as to how to act in order to destroy the Albanian ethnicity as much as possible. Since it was very natural that the Albanians would resist the invading armies, but also prevent them from terrorizing the unprotected population, the invading armies had to act unmercifully and this had to be done under the excuse of "pro-Turkish armed resistance."[128] In accordance to this aim, the military commands had with them also the "special units" which were supposed to deal with the "selective genocide" against the Albanian people. This was brought forth also by a section of the Serbian press, citing the newspaper "Reich Post," in which case the murder of over 2500 Albanians in the regions of Gjakova and its surroundings were made clear.[129] For this massacre and other similar ones that were occurring those days, *"The Times"* stated that in the city of Gjakova, the military and power entities had killed 300 people.[130]

Similar alarming notifications also came from the Luma area, when the Serbian military massacred hundreds of inhabitants of this area even after a portion of the insurgents had surrendered their weapons. This had to do with the murdering of over 500 people and the mistreatment of their families who were forced to take flight toward the mountainous areas.[131]

Under these circumstances, came the emergence of the first administrative bodies, which were established by the invaders. They began to be placed as they were functioning in Serbia, in circuits, districts and munic-

---

[128] See the order of Division I of Shumadi directed to the operative units in the Prizren area in "Prvi Balkanski rat 1912-1913," Book II, p. 261; Hrabak, Bogumil: "Albaski ustanak 1912 godine," p. 207.

[129] "Srbske Novine," 10.01.1913

[130] Rushiti, Limon: *"Lëvizja Kaçake në Kosovë 1918-1928,"* Prishtinë, 1981, p. 11.

[131] *"Radničke Novine,"* 22.II.1913

ipalities in the first months of 1913, in accordance with the decision nr. 18714 of November 1912.[132]

Of course, these decrees and orders, like the one for *"regulating the liberated areas"* were based upon the law of *"uniting the Old Serbia, the Serbian Kingdom and its governance."*[133]

Conforming to these laws, two quick actions were performed: one - disarming the population and one - registering the population by the military bodies in Kosova and Macedonia,[134] which had mournful consequences for the Albanians.

The disarming of the Albanian population, which was done under the excuse that the hidden weapons would be used when needed, [135] was part of the organized state terror against the Albanian population which was done through military means, but which was rationalized with "measured for normalizing life" and "eliminating the factors that would inhibit this." In this case, the Serbian military bodies utilized brutal methods, not only demonstrating force, but also using humiliating and offensive methods toward their human dignity, after which the Albanians were forced to get their weapons and ask for revenge, or to migrate toward Turkey or Albania. When the first action was taken, it was followed by military campaigns of large dimensions, where villages and surrounding areas were besieged, and then "cleansed of the Albanian rebels." In the village of Nishor of Suhareka, on February 19, 1913, with the explanation that "the rebels were being sought," all the men of adult age were murdered, altogether 42. They were murdered in the eyes of their wives and children, and then, as a "penalty", it was said, a Serbian soldier was injured, although the villagers all claimed that no one had shot in the soldiers' direction; all their wealth was plundered. With this act, the village of Nishor, which had around 60 houses, was leveled to the ground.[136] With the same excuses and in the same manner such actions were carried out in Kabash of Prizren, where the Serbian military, from March 19 to April 1, 1913, killed 17 people, in Korishë 8 people, in Lubizhdë 1 person and

---

[132] Rushiti, Limon: *"Lëvizja Kaçake në Kosovë 1918-1928,"* Prishtinë, 1981, p. 13

[133] Guzina, Ružica: *"Opština u Srbiji 1839-1918,"* Belgrade, 1976, p. 447.

[134] *Ibid.*, p. 447.

[135] "Archive of the Military History in Belgrade," a report of the General Headquarters, case-53, p. 2, nr. 2/23, cited in Rushti, Limon: *"Lëvizja Kaçake në Kosovë 1918-1928,"* Prishtinë, 1981, p. 12.

[136] *Ibid.*, case 53, nr. 2/23.

Lugollavë another person.[137] The local sources claimed that twice as many people were killed.[138]

The order for the population registration was also part of this scenario, since it was done by the military bodies in Kosova and Macedonia and was conducted through military and violent methods. The population registration did not have such a civil character, as much as it had a military and strategic one for Serbia, since with the gathering of information about the current population, the civil and military regime, at the same time created an "alibi" for two anti-Albanian actions: on the one side, to declare as enemies those that for the reasons of terror had been hiding, and this it could now do in compliance with the law of "catching and eliminating the thieves" and on the other hand, to prevent the return of the migrated Albanians in different areas according to the Peace Agreement which it signed with the Ottoman Empire in April 1913, in which it formally promised that this would fall upon those who returned prior to April 1, 1915.[139]

Thus, in accordance to this decree, any five people who gathered at night could be declared "thieves," and the military regime interfered in the random gatherings of people in villages and in their celebrations. Based on this law, the military organizations had the right to kill without a court decision. It sufficed to say that it was about "thieves," or "enemies" and the issue would be closed.[140]

Conforming to this practice, which had taken troubling dimensions, the police commander of the Kosova District, with act nr. 7260 of October 21, 1913, declared as "thieves" all Albanians that were not at their homes and did not present themselves to the governing powers. The same act, in order to put disorder to everything normal in the Albanian peoples' lives, proposed the exile of the "rebel" families in the Serbian villages of Mitrovica, wherein whose homes were placed the Serbians brought by Serbian villages, giving them the rights to own unlimited amounts of land with the only condition that they be able to work it.

Although these drastic measures continued as long as the Ambassadors' Conference in London lasted, but then intensified after it ended

---

[137] *Ibid.*.
[138] Rushiti, Limon: "Lëvizja *Kaçake në Kosovë 1918-1928*," Prishtinë, 1981, p. 12.
[139] Guzina, Ružica: "*Opština u Srbiji 1839-1918*," Belgrade, 1976, p. 448, and "Uredba o javnoj bezbednosti u oslobodenim oblastima," Belgrade, 1913.
[140] *Ibid.*.

when Serbia's invasion of Kosova (and the Albanian areas in Macedonia) was justified, apart from the classic military occupation, neither Serbia nor Montenegro was able to assemble any civil power in the occupied areas. On the contrary, the nomination of police commanders in districts, seldom a highlight of the military power, which rushed to complete tasks so that the International Commission for Borders, selected by the London Conference, would be positioned to finishe acts, so as to define the borders exactly the way Serbia and Montenegro desired, but also the Greek ones in the South, to the avail of these regions.

At this time, a wide movement of resistance against the placement of any sort of Serbian power emerged, which was presented by individual actions, but also with the establishment of platoons in different areas, which would fight the invaders. Even though this fortitude lacked any internal connection or administrative center, the majority of the leaders of the National Albanian Movement that had organized the unsuccessful Defense of Kosova during the invading war of the neighboring countries against the Ottoman Empire, were located in Serbia in internment or detached from their homeland. While the region was under a harsh military regime, it nevertheless made the invader's plans more difficult to install the civil administration and create any conditions for the quick colonization of Kosova.

This was mostly hampered also by the worsening relationships between Belgrade and Austria-Hungary, on the eve of World War I, which were deteriorating because of the situation in Bosnia-Herzegovina, where Serbia had put Serbs to destabilize the area in accordance with its intention to unite the Serbs over there with Serbia.

Of course, under these circumstances, when the world was on the eve of a new crisis, which resulted in the unjust decisions of the Ambassador's Conference in London, which although had satisfied a large part of the Slavic-Orthodox requests (the Russian allies), had left the big bomb of Bosnia-Herzegovina wound up, waiting to explode. Belgrade would appear attentive in order not to destroy all the bridges with the Great Powers, which it took as allies, and which had also decided for a –semi-autonomous Albania. The Great Powers would not approve that the rest of the Albanians remaining under Serbia, Montenegro or Greece be subject to an unmerciful liquidation as these regions had foreseen.

Belgrade would also see, with the outbreak of the Dibër revolt in winter of 1913, which although provoked and aided by the Serbian military forces and their reporting services, that they were interested in ending their troubles with the remaining Albanian population in the Serbian state, when the Great Powers react harshly and request that Serbia behave in accordance with the international norms of respecting human and religious rights of all citizens. After the outbreak of World War I, Austria-Hungary entered a war with Serbia, which in the meanwhile Germany joined, creating this way the Central Powers. On the other side, Britain, France and Russia created the Entente Powers, so, being in a different situation, where the relationships could change, Belgrade not only diminished the military pressure against Albanians, but also tried to find allies among them, or nominate common governing committees in different districts and cities in which it had good relationships, where the elites would get many competences even during the Ottoman empire. In this way, Serbia succeeded in its concept of opposing the presence of Austro-Hungarian forces, which entered Kosova in 1916, after having defeated the Serbian army, which had escaped through Albania to Korfu. It even included a good portion of the Albanian Kachak Movement, among whom included Azem Bejta and others, who together with the Serbians fought against the presence of Austria-Hungary in Kosova, even though it was Austria-Hungary who had removed the Serbian occupation in the area which it supervised and had returned to Albanians all their national rights, from administration, education in Albanian and up to the announcement of an inner autonomy.

In any case, in September 1918, when it was understood that Bulgaria was going to surrender soon (on September 29 the act of surrender was signed), the Serbian government once again returned to the Albanians, mainly to those with whom it had had previous relationships and through which it had sought to utilize the Albanian issue for its own needs, so that it would win the title of its main supervisor. Esad Pasha Toptani, once again was inescapable since, he, together with his forces of over five thousand people, two years earlier had joined the Entente Powers while fleeing from Durrës. Serbia had rushed these last months to take over the financing of Toptani's army, which for Belgrade was known as "an ally army of the Albanian state."

This Serbian act was carefully planned and calculated because, with the support of Toptani's "Albanian army" it not only protected its right to define its future benefits from Albania, but prevented any sort of resistance that could be raised against the Serbian troops as soon as they would enter Kosova and the other regions, after the French ones. Through a proclamation in Serbian and Turkish (with Arabian letters) dispersed to the people in the regions of Kumanova, Prishtina, Lebana, Kaçanik, Mitrovicë, and Jeni Pazarit, the Serbian government called upon the Albanians "for collaboration against the Bulgarian and Austro-Hungarian invaders" and it promised that "we will become good friends again," leaving to note that "your fate is up to you."[141]

Although the French army entered Kosova first, followed later by Serbian military units, the Serbian Government, nevertheless, had done all the necessary preparations to organize the Serbian powers in the largest administrative centers, so that this time, the presence of the French army would be exploited for this purpose. Since the French army entered Kosova at the end of September 1918, the representatives of the Serbian Internal Affairs Ministry began the nominations of police commanders by the middle of October. The first to be nominated was Marko Despotovic from the Nerodime region; the municipality chiefs were then selected. At the same time, Zivko Popovic was nominated as police commander of the Gjilan region. In October the police for the regions of Llap and Graçanicë were also selected. After the organizing-nomination of the leaders of the police powers in the district of Kosova – the organizing for the powers in the district of Zveçan began followed by the regions of Vuçiterrnë and Drenicë. In the latter, Agjelko Neshic from Mitrovica was nominated, known for the violence which the Serbian army had imposed upon this region.[142]

In the Prizren and Gjakova districts the situation appeared "differently," since there, after the surrender of Bulgaria (September 29, 1918) and up to October 7, 1918 the French army appeared, having entered through the mountainous route of Tetova. For a week the elite of the area had taken power, consisting of some Serbians and some Albanians. The mixed elite had decided that both flags would be kept: the Albanian and the Serbian ones. An order for the recess of the rivalry was given following an incident that occurred (the murder of a Serbian from an Albanian, following a squabble in a cafeteria for a "political issue") and ended with the death penalty for the Albanian from the "judging body" directed by an Albanian. The Albanian "judge" which had announced the death penalty

---

[141] Hrabak, Bogumil – Janković, Dragoslav: "Srbija, 1918," Belgrade, 1968, p. 180-181.
[142] Rushiti, Limon: "Lëvizja Kaçake në Kosovë 1918-1928," Prishtinë, 1981, p. 24.

for the Serb's murderer, had gone out with an Albanian flag to await the French and Serbian troops, but had quickly found out that the same old invader was coming back, the one that three years earlier had been expelled by the Austro-Hungarian powers who now had lost the war. [143]

The organization of powers even in Gjakovë was based on the model of Prizren. A delegation of the elite of Gjakovë, consisting of Albanians and Serbians, went to Prizren, to the French troops' commander to ask for help in preventing Montenegrin troops from organizing the powers, since they had committed many crimes during the time they had stayed there. It is known that the Gjakovë elite requested the promotion of the union with the Serbian Kingdom if they wanted to get rid of Montenegro, which is what actually happened. Some of the elite had even taken upon themselves the responsibility for gathering signatures which were meant to "prove the Albanian peoples' willingness to unite with Serbia," [144] signatures that Belgrade later sent to the Peace Conference of Paris.

Independently from these actions, with the establishment of the above-mentioned powers, temporarily and with the help of the French army, the Serbian army, in accordance with the agreement with its allies, immediately penetrated the area and dispersed all its troops. Thus, the Supreme Serbian Command ordered the Timoku Division to re-occupy Kosova. The Serbian army entered Kaçanik on October 16, 1918, Ferizaj on October 18, and Lipjan on October 19. Another division, the Yugoslav one which was established in the Selanik area penetrated to Prishtina on October 20, from where its regiments would then be directed to Peja and the other regions of Kosova. During October they were placed under full supervision in accordance with the foreseen plans of the ally powers.[145] During the placement of the military units, nominations were made for various positions, returning much the same apparatus that had operated in Kosova from 1913 to that time.

Initially, Belgrade was loyal even to the territorial segregation of districts, circuits and other units, according to the segregation of 1913, expanding it to Has and Lumë too, regions that the Serbian army had occupied and kept under harsh military supervision. Thus, Kosova was divided into three districts: Kosova, Zveçan, and Prizren.

---

[143] *Ibid.*, p. 25.

[144] *Ibid.*, p. 25.

[145] *Ibid.*, p. 26.

The District of Kosova had these circuits: Nerodime (Ferizaj), Gjilan, Graçanicë (Prishtina), and that of Llapi (Podujeva).

The District of Zveçan had these circuits: Mitrovica, Vuçitërrna and Drenica (Devic).

The District of Prizren had these cicuits: Sharr (Prizren), Gora (Vranishta), Podgora (Suhareka), Rahovec and Gjakova.[146]

Two years later, the territory of Kosova was divided into 5 districts:

I. *The District of Zveçan* with its center in Mitrovica and police commander M. Banici, had three circuits, 25 municipalities with 302 habitats and 81,733 inhabitants. In the District of Zveçan were three circuits: Mitrovica with 8 municipalities, 130 habitats, 16,107 inhabitants and Police Commander Karojqic. In the Vuçiterrnë circuit with Police Commander Z. Mitic were 9 municipalities with 97 habitats and 32,405 inhabitants. The circuit of Drenica (center in Llaushë) with Police Commander L. Maric, included 7 municipalities with 75 habitats and 23,821 inhabitants.

II. *The District of Kosova* with its center in Prishtina and police commander J. Krasojevic, consisted of 55 municipalities and 506 habitats with 251,821 inhabitants.

III. *The District of Metohie (Dukagjin)* with its center in Peja and police commander R. Vasilevic had 21 municipalities with 267 habitats and 27,800 inhabitants; Istog with Police Commander J. Samarxhic, had 6 municipalities, 70 habitats and 18,947 inhabitants; the Peja circuit with Police Commander L. Protic, with 7 municipalities, 99 habitats and 30,900 inhabitants.

IV. *The District of Prizren* with Police Commander S. Todorovic, had 75 municipalities with 326 habitats and 114,402 inhabitants. This district included these circuits: Gora (Vranishte) with Police Commander Zh. Jevtic, with 16 municipalities, 52 habitats and 15,677 inhabitants; Luma (Bicaj) with Police Commander S. Dajic, with 10 municipalities, 31 habitats and 10,349 ihabitants; Podgora (Suhareka) with Police Commander M. Parlic, with 10 municipalities, 35 habitats and 13,229

---

[146] Hrabak, Bogumil: *"Reokupacija Srbske i Crnogorske države arbanaskom većinom stanovništva u jesen 1918, i držanje Arbanasa prema uspostavljenoj vlasti," in "Gjurmime Albanologjike,"* nr. 1, Prishtina, 1969, p. 258.

ihabitants; Podrimja (Rahovec) with Police Commander M. Protic, with 15 municipalities and 100 habitats, and 25,026 inhabitants; Prizren which formed a municipality with 16,370 inhabitants; Hasi (Krumë) with Police Commander M. Stojanovic, with 7 municipalities, 50 habitats and 12,033 inhabitants.

V. *The District of Shkup:* in which from the territory of Kosova included the circuit of Kaçanik with Police Commander J. Djordjevic, with 4 municipalities and 38 habitats and 10,193 inhabitants. [147]

As it can be seen, the territory of Kosova was divided into five districts with 18 circuits, 180 municipalities, 1,439 habitats, and over 549,871 inhabitants. Two other circuits were also included here: that of Lumë and Has, under the temporary occupation of the Serbo-Croatian-Slovenian Kingdom, with 17 municipalities, 81 habitats and 22,382 inhabitants.

This territorial division did not last long, since the Serbian Kingdom, united in a new state of the South Slavs after the end of World War I, under the pressure of the Serbian authorities which had began to show its claims that the new state would have to return to the Great Serbia, changed the administrative division in accordance to its well-known schemes for Serbianizing the occupied regions, especially the Albanian ones, by breaking the solidarity of the people that constituted an ethnicity. A trigger was also given to these administrative changes by the "Vidovdan" constitution of June 18, 1921, which had foreseen the new administrative division of the regions in accordance to the aims of the Serbian bourgeoisie. [148]

According to the law decree of April 22, 1922, the territory of Kosova was divided into these regions:

1. The Kosova Region with its center in Prishtina, which included these districts from the previous division: the district of Kosova without the circuit of Gjilan, the District of Prizren with all its circuits – excluding Lumë and Has (Albanian territories), the circuit of Vuçitërrnë, whereas from the territories outside of Kosova, the circuits of Toplica and Jabllanica were also included, which were parts of the district of Vranjë.

---

[147] *Allmanah Kraljevine* SHS, (First Part) 1921-22, Belgrade, 1922, p. 123-126.
[148] Čukinović, Ferdo: "Jugoslavija izmedu dva rata," Zagreb, 1961, p. 371.

2. The Vranjë Region from the territory of Kosova which included the circuit of Gjilan.
3. The Rashë Region, with its center in Çaçak, from the territory in Kosova included the circuit of Zveçan.
4. The Zeta Region, with its center in Cetinë, included the circuit of Dukagjin from the territory of Kosova, together with all the circuits that it included prior to this division.
5. The Shkup Region which from the territory of Kosova included the circuit of Kaçanik.[149]

This territorial and administrative division, which stayed in power for seven years, whose purpose was firstly to divide the ethnic Albanian area between Serbia and Montenegro, conforming to the Serbia-Montenegro pact, agreed upon on the eve of the Balkan wars. The invasion schemes to divide the Albanian ethnicity included Montenegro taking over Dukagjin and Serbia taking over the other part of Kosova together with Macedonia. Although the Serbo-Croatian-Slovenian Kingdom, established after the end of World War I, had taken over Montenegro and its identity, turning it into an "internal Serbian issue," nevertheless, the chauvinist circuits of Belgrade and Cetina had protected the agreement reached earlier on, so that the Albanian ethnicity of Kosova would be split into two parts, which conformed to the plans for its destruction. Thus, Dukagjin, by joining the region of Zeta, was detached completely from the social, economic and political link with the rest of Kosova, which was itself split into three other parts, where the Albanian municipalities of Gjilan and Prizren had been taken away from the district of Prishtina, and had been linked to some parts of the Toplica district. These regions were habituated by the Serbians which were economically linked to Nish and other parts of East Serbia. Similarly, Gjilan was joined with the Vranjë Region, and the Zveçan region (with Mitrovica, Vuçitërrna and Drenica) was given to the Rashë region, with a center in Çaçak. Shkup, which was previously split into a separate region, would continue to keep the region of Kaçanik.

So, this administrative division represented the most appropriate scenario with which, through economic, political and administrative methods, the Albanian ethnicity of Kosova and the other Albanian regions that had remained under Belgrade's invasion would be destroyed. Apart from the economical, political and administrative dispersing of Albanians in

---

[149] *"Službene Novine,"* nr. 92, April 28, 1922.

three different directions (toward Montenegro, Central Serbia and South Serbia), which was technically already unbearable for this population (lacking the infrastructure that linked Kosova with the centers necessary), the Belgrade regime had prepared the terrain and infrastructure for bringing the settlers in the Albanian territories according to the known laws for colonization and Agrarian reform, and also, for creating the conditions necessary to displace Albanians towards Turkey and other places in compliance with the conventions that were signed with Turkey for "re-settling the Muslim population."

In accordance to this administrative division, and the goals that would be pursued as a result, the military division of the territories of Kosova was also initiated. After the occupying wars of 1912, Armada II settled in Kosova with its center in Shkup. This lasted up until 1915. On August 19, 1919, with the decree of Regent A. Karadjordjevic, in the name of King Peter I, and with the proposal of the Army Ministry, the law decree regarding the military territorial division was established. The Serbo-Croatian-Slovenian Kingdom was split into four military zones, 15 regional divisions, 45 district regiments and 180 circuit battalions. [150]

Kosova was included in the Command of Armada II in Shkup under the framework of the Division of Kosova, whereas the Division of Kosova, with its center in Prishtina, was split into three district divisions: The Prizren Regiment Circuit, The Prishtina Regiment Circuit and the Novi Pazar Regiment Circuit.

The Novi Pazar Regiment Circuit linked militarily Mitrovica, Vuçitërrna, Drenica, Istog and Peja with Novi Pazar, Sjenica, Tutin and the other areas of Sanxhak. From this perspective also, the northwest areas of Kosova were detached from the center and were linked to those of Sanxhak, which, as would be seen, in the case of the law for "disarming" and that of "thieves," was exposed to a fierce military terror which tied a good portion of these areas into being declared as "muslim" so that they won the right to get "re-homed" in Turkey and thus, also flee there. The other region which did not surrender to being "re-homed," was left as a continuous target of military action undertaken in these areas with the excuse of sometimes "catching the thieves," sometimes "chasing the kachaks" (as much as this movement was present in this area from where it also operated). Usually the unprotected population suffered the conse-

---

[150] Rushiti, Limon: *"Lëvizja e Kaçakëve në Kosovë 1918-1928,"* Prishtina, 1981, p. 30.

quences, which, in the name of "cleansing," experienced the destruction of their homes, land and every existing thing they had, resulting in forced and violent displacement.

The Reemergence of the Kachak Movement and the Committee for the National Defense of Kosova

The Kachak movement appeared as a form of national resistance against the occupying Serbian and Montenegrin forces as soon as they appeared. – During World War I a part of the movement acted against the Bulgarian forces, whereas some others fought together with the Serbian Chetniks and, often under their supervision, against the Austro-Hungarian forces which defeated the Serbian occupiers. – Hasan Prishtina and other national leaders requested that Albanian Kachaks not be included in the battles against Austria-Hungary and not collaborate with the Serbians and the Chetniks of Kosta Peçanci in this direction. – Some Kachak units, like those of Azem Bejta, helped in liberating a part of Kosova from the Austro-Hungarian forces, but they were quickly forced to leave their place to the French units, which then gave those areas to the Serbian army, which then re-occupied Kosova. – Belgrade did not keep its promise which it made to the Albanian Kachaks that their aspirations for freedom and independence would be respected, while Azem Bejta's platoons began turning their weapons to their recent allies in the war against Austria-Hungary. – The foundation of the "National Defense of Kosova" Committee, in 1918 in Shkodër and the attempts for Kosova to join the Albanian trunk. – The irredentist leaders require from the Great Powers that Kosova gets returned to Albania. – Many letters and petitions were sent to the Peace Conference of Paris. – The National Defense got concentrated in Albania, whereas the Kachak platoons began acting in the central part of Kosova, attempting to prevent the colonization of Kosova. – The Belgrade regime began the wide police and military operations against the Albanian Kachaks in Drenicë and other areas. – In search of Kachaks, many villages were burned and the existential base of the rural population was ruined, beginning their migration to Turkey.

The Kachak movement is the first and most noted form of national resistance initially staged against the occupying Serbian and Montenegrin forces, which entered the Albanian territories during the Balkan Wars to continue opposing the Austro-Hungarian and Bulgarian forces. In order to interlink this activity again after the return of the Serbian occupier at the end of the World War, in autumn 1918, the movement continued retaliation for another few years with varying intensities, until the state convention between Yugoslavia and Albania was signed in 1926, when this activity faded almost completely.

This movement, however, up until the rise of the National Defense of Kosova Committee, remained in most cases without an internal link and without a directing center which would connect its activity to its political goals. These coincided with the international developments and especially those that had to do with the future fate of Albanians in the new circumstances when the relationships would be altered, in most cases to their detriment. This was also understandable since it was based upon a home-love stance of patriarchal factors (local, tribal feudal lord) who were willing to defend their home land at any cost. But this was not sufficient in those circumstances when they faced invaders with strong and organized police and armies, which were also backed by states with strong and prepared diplomacy and institutions to handle any sort of actions or maneuvers. Unprepared to act in accordance with the extremely difficult circumstances and even tragic ones which the majority of the Albanian population faced, the situation of the resistance that sprang from this patriarchal layer which believed in the common state as the only salvation worsened, when after the Peace Conference, Albania as a state was recognized according to the decisions which the Ambassadors' Conference of 1913 had made. In this case, after its acceptance in the League of Nations (1921), it took over the responsibility of accepting and ratifying the borders with Yugoslavia, without concern that its separated regions (Kosova and Macedonia) would be recognized by the new state, the Serbo-Croatian-Slovenian Kingdom. Thus, the state interest obligated Albania to let go of any kind of support given to the Kachak movement outside its borders, as it also took over the responsibility of fading out the irredentist movement within Albania, a movement which was very strong and active in the internal developments from the Congress of Lushnjë up until 1924. At that time, this movement was unable to act outside state borders, especially in Kosova, where the SKS Kingdom had now begun the process of de-nationalizing the occupied areas through colonization, agrarian reform, and other administrative and political measures. These difficulties were implicated in the internal political scene with fatal consequences resulting in its tragic end.

In any case, the national resistance against the new occupiers appeared from the time when the Serbian, Montenegrin, Bulgarian and Greek armies entered the Albanian territory and each began inititating its own regime with the intention of making it permanent. The revolt of Dibër of 1913 is well known, which also included a good portion of the northeast areas, resulted in bloodshed and the further penetration of the occupying Serbian army toward Albania. Well known are also the actions of a few armed groups in the regions of Dukagjin, Drenicë and Karadak against the placement of the first police-military units at the second half of 1913 and beyond. These actions increased in frequency following the decisions of the Ambassadors' Conference in London, where it was learned that Kosova and half of the Albanian ethnicity would be left under the occupation of the neighboring countries, occupied during the last war.

Nevertheless, after the Ambassadors' Conference of London and up to the time the First World War began, the occupying army purposely provoked the unprotected population rather than any organized movement such as those that appeared later on. Among these measures, the decree for "disarming" the Albanian population and the law for recruitment are known, which were preceded by the registration of the population by the military units. Many violent military provocations followed, not excluding those that violated the dignity of the Albanian population.

The start of the First World War and the year that followed marked the start of Serbian losses in the war with the Central Powers (Austro-Hungary and Germany which were also joined by Bulgaria and later on by Turkey). The situation in Kosova changed completely, since on the one side the Austro-Hungarians and Bulgarians appeared, who chased out the Serbian and Montenegrin occupiers while recognizing the Albanian people's national rights from the right to self-determination, education in the Albanian language, and free economic activity, rights that in 1917 would lead to the recognition of Albanian autonomy. On the other hand, the Bulgarians appeared, who would begin where the Serbian occupiers left off: with terror, violence, further de-nationalization, forced labor of men to build the Kërçovë-Manastir road, and the forced mobilization of Albanians to different battle scenes, where many of them lost their tracks forever. This in turn caused the revolting energy rallied to that day against the Serbs to turn against the Bulgarians themselves.[151]

Faced with these "double realities," the Kachak Movement and the armed resistance in general now needed to deal with a new set of perpetrators, although enemies of the Serbians and who in reality had gotten rid of the Serbians, but were now behaving differently. This was true for the Bulgarians and the regions that they held, which as seen from the troubles, were not significantly different from the Serbians. It was therefore reasonable that the first Kachak groups appeared in the Karadak area against the Bulgarian occupiers and their terror. This is where the activity of Iliaz Reçaku's groups is noted, where the names of Jetish Behluli, Rexhë Bardhi and others are also mentioned.[152]

Since the Bulgarian region included a good portion of Kosova (the East part of Kosova from Prishtina to Prizren, Shkup and Pollog), the Serbians took the opportunity to further their own intentions, by appearing "friendly" and requesting "a common and brotherly war against the German and Bulgarian occupiers" in opposition to their previous occupiers, who had exercised so much violence and military terror against the Albanians. For this purpose, on January 1917, the commander of Jabllanica e Epërme, Milenko Vllahovic, was seen in Prishtina in a meeting with Bajram Govor, to whom he had promised material and weaponry aid against the Bulgarians, with the condition that they would collaborate with each other. The Serbian soldiers had also penetrated to other parts of Kosova, where small Kachak groups appeared so that they could make agreements together.[153]

Such meetings and negotiations occurred also in Serbian areas occupied by the Bulgarians, such as Kurshumli and Prokupe, where some Albanian Kachaks participated in many negotiations with the Serbian soldiers that led the movement against the Bulgarians. Albanian Kachaks, with Serbian weapons and other aid, then tried to free Prishtina, Mitrovica and Peja, while the Serbian units acted towards Nish. It is known that in March 1917, a few Albanian Kachak groups participated in a battle in Kurshumli against the Bulgarians.[154]

---

[151] *Ibid.*, p. 18.
[152] *Ibid.*, p. 19.
[153] Perović, Milivoje: *"Toplički Ustanak,"* Belgrade, 1959, p. 103-109
[154] *Ibid.*, p. 112-113.

This activity which continued until the end of the First World War, nevertheless, in an indirect manner, put a good portion of the Kachaks from Kosova in an allied position of the Entente Powers where the Serbians and Montenegrins also stood. At the same time the main rivals of Albanians, such as Esad Pasha Toptani, whose forces were directly involved in the Entente side from 1916 until the end, participating even in the battle of Selanik, created a unique situation which merits special treatment, despite the fact that it rightfully ruins some ideological and folkloric stereotypes, through which these events and their whole complexity is viewed and explained as black and white.

However, regardless of this interpretation, which deserves to be given its own place, a special chapter in the collaboration between the Albanian Kachaks and the Serbian movement directed by Serbian soldiers, where sometimes the reserve military units of the resistance were also involved, was that of the war against Austria-Hungary. Although it was known that the Austro-Hungarians were the only ones that helped and supported the announcement of Albania's independence and helped in the London Conference so that Albania would be recognized, even partly, as a state, and that after the start of the World War it was they who had gotten rid of the Serbs and Montenegrins, it was also they that massacred the Albanian population during the invasion of Kosova and other regions and due to that occupying war, left Albania as a semi-state.

Even though the Austro-Hungarians had for the Albanians gotten rid of the invaders and had returned to them their national rights to education, administration, self-determination and autonomy which was later announced, a portion of the Albanian Kachaks operating in the zone occupied by Bulgarians, extended their activity in the Austro-Hungarian parts, where the Albanian leaders from Hasan Prishtina to others continuously made calls for the creation of an alliance with Austria-Hungary, Germans and fought against Serbia, unwilling to collaborate with them for their benefits.

Here, a decisive role was played by the active politics of Serbia, that the Albanian Kachak Movement, which in the Bulgarian occupied areas was openly supported and largely directed by Serbs, was directed to act in the area which was under Austria-Hungary, so that in this way, two goals would be accomplished at the same time. Firstly, the Kachak Movement lacked a directing center compatible with the positions of the Albanian National Movement. Secondly, the Albanian Kachaks while fighting against the Austro-Hungarians, would alienate the Albanians from the Entente Powers, their greatest supporters, the only ones that offered Albania and the Albanians any defense and further guarantee. In the meantime, Belgrade not only failed to guarantee anything, but failed to introduce them to the Entente Powers, but further attempted to introduce the Albanians as vowed enemies of the Entente and friends of the Central Powers, even though this, according to Kosova, was not conforming to reality, since a good portion of the Albanian Kachaks acted under Serbian supervision.

The Serbian influence over a few Kachak groups operating in the Drenica and East Kosova zones, based on Astro-Hungarian as well as Serbian information and French reports, increased even more during the Spring of 1918 leading up to the entrance of the French army into Kosova in September that year, followed by Serbian military units, to whom Kosova would surrender, and Albanian Kachaks faced a tragic reality as the Serbian invasion returned more powerful than ever. Even though it cannot be said that the Albanian Kachaks, who rightfully took to the mountains against the Bulgarian invaders, did this for the return of the Serbian invaders, but on the contrary, so that they would get rid of any foreign invasion, no matter where it came from. Nevertheless, with or without will, in the end, many of them fell into the Serbian trap, where they were left as tragic losers.

This was also done during the last phase of the National Albanian Movement when a portion of the feudal Albanians entered negotiations with Serbia and Montenegro, with the promise of "brotherly support" and "common liberation," though they quickly came to understand the deception from which harsh consequences would follow.

With such promises, the head Serbian Chetnik, Kosta Pecanac, had started negotiations with Azem Bejta too, the best known Albanian Kachak, who was involved in a war against the Central Powers. They met in the summer of 1918 somewhere in the village of Pridvoricë of Kollashin of Ibër, in the house of Olimpie Bozhovic. They discussed the "common war" against "the invaders." The discussions continued also in the village of Varage,[155] where similar actions, which had begun more than a year ago, were not left unnoticed and without reaction from the Austro-Hungarians, who declared Azem and his Kachaks as enemies. The Aus-

---

[155] Perović, Milivoje: *"Toplički Ustanak,"* Belgrade, 1956, p. 356.

146

tro-Hungarians and which they later fought in a few battles that resulted in the repressive measures against Bejta's people in the areas of Drenicë, which for "security reasons" resulted also in the deportation of a few Albanians to Austria.

The enmity with the Austro-Hungarians and the collaboration with Kosta Peçanci's Chetniks continued until the end at the benefit of the Serbians. Thus, near the end of the war, when a portion of the Austro-Hungarian forces were retreating at the place called "Prroni i keq," they faced an ambush from the Albanian Kachaks, in which they surrendered to Azem Bejta, believing they would be left free to go and leave. They believed that conforming to the agreement that they had reached with some of the leaders of the National Albanian Movement in Shkodër, who continued to view the Germans and Austrians as their only ally, and did not take into consideration the fate of the war, which ultimately harmed them.[156]

However, taken prisoners, together with all the warlike material, they would be surrendered to the French army, which, after it got the news, arrived in Mitrovica and took the Austro-Hungarian officers and soldiers from the Albanian Kachaks. The French commander Balshe, in this case, in honor of Azem Bejta and his merits in the war against Austro-Hungaria, held a dinner, where he was decorated with a medal for war merits and was given a sword as a trophy.[157]

The Albanian Kachaks and their leaders were quickly convinced that the "friendship" and the "common liberating war" with the Serbians was coming to an end and that it was being replaced with what was already seen in these areas in 1912, when the invading armies of Montenegro and Serbia had appeared and had started the unseen before terror against the Albanian population.

In reality, after the Serbian army got hold of the "liberated" regions from the French army and put in place the military-civil administration, the same one that was destroyed in 1915 from the Austro-Hungarian and German forces, they continued with the same attitude, but now it was more masked, by focusing on those that would not surrender their

---

[156] More information about the agreement between the leaders of the Albanian National Movement in Shkodër and the Austro-Hungarian military command in this city in HHStA – Haus-Hof-und Staatsarchiv, Politisches Archiv, Wien: Albanien: III-XXXVIII (1878-1918), doc. nr. 26/73

[157] Rushiti, Limon: *"Lëvizja Kaçake e Kosovës 1918-1928,"* Prishtinë, 1981, p. 22.

weapons, meaning the Kachaks, those whom they had supported until now against the Bulgarians, and even more against the Austro-Hungarians. In the meantime it also allured some of the local leaders from the elite for collaboration, by giving them some sort of role just for the sake of having it. The head Chetnik Kosta Peçanac, who, from Peja, where he had mobilized many masked soldiers, set out for Shkodër, "to rescue it from the Italian invasion," sending a message to the Albanian Kachaks to "return to the fruits of peace" so that they could "enjoy them together."

Since they did not stay long in Shkodër, because after the pressure from the Great Powers, who made the invasion of Shkodër from Serbia an issue and gave them an ultimatum to leave, Kosta Peçanci again returned to Kosova. However, on his way back from Shkodër, through Plavë and Guci, and Rugovë up to Peja, he began to exercise terror over the Albanian population, which he forced to take the avenues of "salvation toward Shkodra, so as to evacuate them from Kosova. A revolt, though not an insurgency, ensued in Peja, and especially in Rugova, in February 1919, but not an insurgency, which resulted in the burning down of many villages from Rugova up to Plavë and Guci and the murdering of 83 people, while the other part fled to Shkodër.[158]

Regarding the difficult situation resulting from the re-occupation of Kosova by the Serbian military forces, especially the Chetnik units of Kosta Peçanci which operated in the Pejë-Rugovë-Plavë-Guci region forcing the inhabitants of these areas to go toward Shkodër, as precisely as these forces until now had requested from the Albanian Kachaks to "fight the invader as brothers" (Austro-German), the National Defense Committee also reacted with a message directed to President Wilson, requesting his intervention as soon as possible so that Belgrade would stop the military terror. In this message it was noted that only in Shkodër were there now over five thousand refugees who were threatened to death by hunger.[159]

---

[158] See: *"Populli i Plavës, Gusinjës dhe Rugovës muhaxhir në Shkodër,"* published in the "Populli" newspaper, 25.II.1919, cited in Rushiti, Limon: *"Lëvizja kaçake në Kosovë 1918-1928,"* Prishtinë, 1981, p. 46.

[159] See: AQSH, of PEOPLE'S REPUBLIC OF ALBANIA, fund KMKK, file 23/3, nr. 708705, 28.II.1919, the protest against the actions of the Yugoslav government toward Albanians, sent to American president Wilson, and: *"Tragjedia e Kosovës, Ç'vajtojnë gërmadhat e Rugovës,"* published in the "Kosova" newspaper.

Of course, under these circumstances, the elite of the endangered population of Kosova also headed for help from the commander of Armada III of the Division of Kosova. The Prizren delegation (of five people), that of Gjakova, and other bordering areas presented substantial evidence of murders, raids, imprisoning, and prosecution that were done by the police, acting in the name of "the search for Austria-Hungary's allies."

However, troubling for this population were two other measures: the search for weapons, which was followed by brutal measures and the mobilization for an army, which began in the summer of 1919, where young men of 20-25 were forcibly involved. To escape such measures, many young men would head for the mountains and many others would find shelter in Albania or elsewhere, which gave the recently placed military entities even more reasons for massive prosecutions of the Albanian population. Under these circumstances, some of them would request to join the Kachak groups.[160]

However, even though the Kachak groups of Azem Bejta and others had managed to survive this terror by operating from Albania in Kosova and vice-versa, their activity was now greatly impeded since the military authorities of Belgrade had included them in their enemies' list (if they would not surrender their weapons) and had also expanded their presence in the regions of Drenicë and Llap, which for some time had been spared of their presence.

Nevertheless, in Spring and Summer of 1919, at the time when the work of the Peace Conference in Paris continued, after reports of increased military violence against the undefended population, the attention of the international factor was focused on the behavior of the state authorities of Belgrade in Kosova and the other regions inhabited by Albanians, which were now given to the SKS Kingdom. An increase was noticed in the attempts of the police-military forces to contact the Kachaks and make them surrender. These actions were carried out in the Drenica and Llap regions and had to do with Sadik Rama of Gjurgjevik and Azem Bejta, whose groups would sometimes act in these areas, in which case it was

---

[160] Habrak, Bogumil: "Jedan radikalski izveštaj o stanju na Kosovu 1921 godine," in "Vjetari i Arkivit të Kosovës," Prishtinë, IV-V (1968-1969) and 1971, p. 215, 217, 223.

reported that they succeeded in keeping prisoner some whole gendarme units, as occurred in the Orllat municipality.[161]

It is noted that the police commander of the Drenica area, in September of that year had called Azem Bejta for a discussion, as was Ramë Vllasa with friends also called by the Podujevë police commander, Cerovic, both of whom were promised posts in return for surrendering their weapons. Cerovic had met Azem Bejta in Zhabar of Mitrovica, where they had discussed other issues too, but no agreement was reached between them.[162]

Of course, the time of the one-sided agreements that went to the benefit of Belgrade, such as the one for "the joint war against the Austro-Hungarian invader," had now gone and the Serbians were the least interested in them. On the contrary, they were looking for reasons to continue the terror against the Albanian population, so that by blaming it for continuing to keep the "revolt and separatist movement" it would be continuously forced to flee its own land. This was now the official politics of Belgrade and to this end many different methods were used, all whose purpose was the creation of such circumstances that the Albanians would, first of all, feel economically insecure, de-possessed from their land and their ownings, then feeling provoked and in continuous conflict with the law and power. This was true when their youth needed to mobilize and escaped from this, when weapons were requested from them, when they continued their links to the Kachak movement, for which anyone could get prosecuted and accused, even though it was known that among the Albanians whoever requested shelter also found it. In one word, the Albanians had to believe that Kosova and the other regions left outside the borders of the Albanian state were not Albanian any longer, but a "sacred Serbian land," "stolen and occupied from them during the Ottoman regime," which had now turned to its "middle ages cradle," and which meant that for them it was now a foreigner. The latter was even demonstrated through the military, but also with the large campaign that the state undertook so that Kosova would appear as the "Serbian sanctity," by building orthodox monasteries in every location so that the Albanians

---

[161] Rushiti, Limon: *"Lëvizja e Kaçake në Kosovë 1918-1928,"* Prishtinë, 1981, p. 101.
[162] Bajram, Hakif: *"Rrethanat shoqërore dhe politike në Kosovë 1918-1941,"* Prishtinë, 1981, p. 101.

would be subject to the circumstances, so they would accept that they were on "Serbian land," or they would flee to Turkey.

Under these circumstances, the state terror in Kosova and other Albanian regions that had been left to Belgrade continued in the name of "returning the law and order" and "fighting the criminal gangs" as the Kachaks were called, who still continued their activity in different parts of Kosova, although detached, and in most cases with revenge actions against the police and military units that exercised terror. Also targeted were the Albanians that had begun to become involved in the state apparatus or to be nominated prefects, whom Belgrade usually chose from the families it previously had links with from the time of the Ottoman Empire. Some of these Albanians were now even involved in the elite of some cities and some other municipality councils, which were presented to foreign delegations that visited these areas or even diplomats who moved in and out of these areas to see the real situation, always focusing on the "protection of the minorities" and "the protection of their religious and ownership rights," which were conforming to the League of Nations Charter, while Belgrade in the meantime portrayed them as an enemy which was fighting to destroy the newly created and internationally recognized state of the South Slavs so that it could join another state – Albania.

At this time, after the acceptance of Albania into the Leauge of Nations and the obligations it had to ratify all the agreements with its neighboring countries, first of all with Belgrade, Tirana had accepted the reality of the Peace Conference of Paris, which meant the existence of the SKS Kingdom as a state which now also included Kosova and the other Albanian regions occupied by Belgrade during the Balkan wars. As such, the situation of the Kachak movement also radically changed, since now it was being considered unlawful and was being chased after not only by Belgrade, but Albania as well. Thus, Albania as a state would have only to consider the issue of the freedom and rights of the Albanian "minorities" outside its borders, which meant in the constitution of the SKS Kingdom, and never should it mention the issue of national unity, or the liberation of Albanians from Belgrade, ideas stayed fixed in the minds of the Albanians in Kosova and their movement which still which still involved connection to the common Albanian state.

Actually, here and with this issue, Belgrade found the permanent reasoning to exercise terror through police and military instruments against the Albanians, always reasoning that the Albanians do not accept the realities which the Peace Conference and the League of Nations had decided upon, but rather act toward the opposite, so as to destroy it, making them double enemies. Here it can be said that the Kachak Movement and its specification to not accept the Serbian powers but rather to fight them with all means possible, not taking into consideration the consequences, remained the most appropriate "weapon" for Serbia to realize the anti-Albanian objectives, from destroying their ethnicity up to creating the conditions for their permanent displacement, a process which, as would be seen, was put on open tracks and moved in the direction Belgrade specified for it. There are even many sources which say that the Kachak activity in Kosova, of a low intensity, even though it brought damage (such as the murder of any police or soldier), was needed by Belgrade for its premeditated intentions, and that its government continuously attempted to infiltrate many collaborators within the movement, who would radicalize its actions and behavior based to its needs, and above all, where the Kachak movement was at risk of fading, the Serbian police and military services would inject masked units of "Kachaks," who operated by killing leaders from the Albanian groups and "collaborators" of Belgrade and these were then charged over the real Kachaks and utilized as a reason for revenge against the undefended population.[163]

On the basis of this, during 1920/21, many murders and attempted attacks were conducted, while the cleansing of whole Albanian villages took place for the colonization of Kosova with Serbians and other Slavic peoples which had to be placed in these areas according to the laws for colonizing and the other measures which Belgrade had foreseen so that this process would be two-way: to bring and settle as many Serbians and Montenegrins as possible in Kosova, and alternatively, to displace as many Albanians as possible from Ksoova, all which would balance the ethnic structure in Kosova to the detriment of the Albanian population and to the benefit of the Serbian one.

Nevertheless, when Belgrade was using all the state and diplomatic mechanisms it could to achieve its targets against the Albanian population, such as ethnic cleansing with war tools, the Albanian state was in a

---

[163] For more details about this, see: Rushiti, Limon: "Lëvizja Kaçake në Kosovë 1918-1928," Prishtinë, 1981; Obradovič, Milovan: "Agrarna reforma i kolonizacija Kosova 1918-1941," Prishtinë, 1981, Hakif: "Rrethanat shoqërore dhe politike në Kosovë më 1918-1941," Prishtinë, 1981; Abdyli, Tahir: "Hasan Prishtina," Prishtinë, 2003.

very difficult situation since it was under many pressures that came from its neighbors; the national resistance of Kosova was also faced with the challenge of detachment from within and the return to an open problem for the Albanian state itself.

The first issue, that of the detachment from the inside, was almost a finished fact, since after the Peace Conference and its decisions, two groupings appeared: that of the Kachak movement in Kosova, dispersed in many areas and without an internal link or a single leadership, and then the National Defense of Kosova Committee with its center in Shkodër and its bases in Krumë, Tropojë and somewhere in the North, which would be forced to be subject to some external interests, such as the acceptance of the "protectionist" role of Italy. Although around 1921 and up to 1923, as a possible meeting place they had the so-called "The Free Zone of Junik" and also the area that connected these regions of Albania with Kosova, and where you could enter or leave, nevertheless, from 1922 and on, this would become more difficult due to the placement of the border line and its supervision, which Tirana had as a condition from the decisions of the Peace Conference, as well as from the League of Nations where it had accepted and had to ratify the state agreements with Greece and the SKS Kingdom.

This is where the second issue was also raised, having to do with Albania's obligations not to allow any irredentist movement within its borders and not to support the Kachak movement in Kosova and other Albanian regions that were under Belgrade. It even had obligations that, if necessary, together with Belgrade, would harmonize the activities for their elimination, as would occur later on.

Viewing it from this point, the national resistance appeared as an irredentist movement within the Albanian state and as a Liberating movement, within the Yugoslav state. The first consisted of a considerable intellectual and human potential, with around twenty thousand militants that could possibly be put into action and for this was seen with suspicion and high mistrust. The second one was in Kosova, also with a considerable potential of patriots, mainly from the feudal ranks and the rural population, who were ready for sacrifices and war, but opposite to them had a very prepared opponent with a very powerful police-military apparatus, which was in a mobile state and in the name of "terror" had the green light to clear its troubles with anyone who entered the Movement List. However, side by side with the lack of internal links and different political concepts, this movement had common opponents: the Albanian state and the Yugoslav one, also the international factor. The first one because it was acting with the state logic, and the second because it acted based on the hegemonic concepts for the destruction of the Albanian issue, whereas the third factor was an opponent because it just caused trouble.

In any case, the Irredentist Movement in Albania, in its most organized form, came to surface directly in the Spring of 1918, when in Shkodër, some Albanian patriots from the national movement of 1911/12, which had prepared the independence of Albania in November 1912, but that due to the known circumstances were deprived of announcing it and the content of the Declaration of Independence, among them Hasan Prishtina, Bajram Curri, Hoxhë Kadria and others, declared their intentions to join Albania with all its tools, without excluding a liberating war. These stances and this patriotic spirit of Albanians which would give so much to the independence of Albania, were present, even earlier on, but why it will culminate precisely at this time, the reasons have to be searched for in the latest developments. These developments were linked with the end of the First World War, when it was known that the Great Powers would hold a new conference in which they would determine the new borders in the Balkans, which left the understanding that the initiators of the irredentist movement were prepared to present the Albanian issue as open in all senses, which needed to be handled in whole and not with violent discrimination. Thus, facing these developments, when it was expected that new charters would jump into the game, the Albanian factor was forced to come out with clear requests, which had to conform to its right for their joint state on the bases of the ethnic outreach, a principle which had also served during the foundation of the other Balkan states, in the area where the Ottoman Empire had exercised its power. In this case, it had to be made clear that the violent separation of them, not only had not brought peace to the region, as was proclaimed, but it had made it even more insecure, since the Albanians did not accept these realities, which they also opposed with weapons.

Of course, to the avail of this specification was also the almost three-year Austro-Hungarian administration of the regions occupied by Serbia in 1912 and of a large part of Albania, which had returned to the Albanians their common national identity from administration, education and up to the institutions, those being even autonomous. The new situation had now even created pre-conditions to not allow the return of the Serbian and Montenegrin regime, even though the Peace Conference had legitimized these invasions in the state aspect. In Shkodër, the organizational structure of the movement began forming, whereas the branches of the Committee began to form even outside the region and around the world, giving the whole activity an overall engagement, so that the movement would appear as a rightful issue for the defense of the Albanian territories from the Slavic re-occupation. This right was also reasoned with the new circumstances that were created by the First World War as well as the giving up of the Great Powers from the guarantees that were given to the Albanian State, which should have been the same for the other decisions made in the Ambassadors' Conference in London in 1913.

The Irredentist Movement leaders had the belief that Vienna and Rome, although in opposite blocs of war, in principle were for the protection of the Albanian state on their ethnic basis, which they had also expressed in a way: Austria-Hungary by installing the Albanian administrative autonomy in the regions they had, and Rome, by declaring even Albania as independent under Italy's supervision, as much as it was outside the Greek and French occupations. Thus, the Albanian peoples' stance should also have been based on these factors, by not excluding even direct agreements with these states. What was important was that the idea of an independent Albanian state, be that even dispersed, existed somewhere and it was not just one-way. Hasan Prishtina, who was among the most noted from the National Defense of Kosova Committee, rightfully declared that *"the issue of the protection of Albanian territories and their return to their trunk, was not only a task for those whom had lost their home land due to neighboring occupations, but it was a task for every Albanian who loved Albania."*[164]

Hasan Prishtina in this case also commemorated the blood that Kosovar Albanians had spilled during the defense of their territories in war with the Serbian and Montenegrin occupiers, but also the blood that had been spilt in defense of Prince Wied in Durrës and other regions where Albanian kingdoms lay, contested and fought with by others, but mostly from its own Albanians and this would be emphasized later as a fratricidal war which could not occur ever again.

---

[164] See Hasan Prishtina: *"Nji shkurtim kujtimesh,"* second edition, Bari, 1925

From the developments that came to surface, not even the first obligation – that the war for the defense of Kosova and its return to the Albanian trunk should become a preoccupation of all Albanians – was not to be fulfilled, as the risk remained that 1914 would repeat itself as a bad year, where the defense of the Albanian state would turn into a fratricidal war also on a religious basis.

In fact, the first aspect, like the second one of the stance of Albanians toward the irredentist movement, appeared as outside characteristics with inside influences. Because the Peace Conference in Paris, even though it had problems in recognizing the Albanian state with the London borders – and this meant after more than two years of work – would firstly recognize the SKS Kingdom, who would after a while return to Yugoslavia, accepting beforehand to Serbia those that the Ambassadors' Conference in London in 1913 had given to her. Thus, Serbia had no need to think that it could lose the Albanian territories that it had occupied during the first Balkan War. On the contrary, after the First World War ended, as an Entente ally, Belgrade awaited its many rewards, as would occur with the taking over of Vojvodina, Baçka and Banat from Hungary, and it also waited for any Albanian portion, which was now considered requests in the name of "correcting the state security from the irredentist movements."

The international stance toward Serbia and the same one toward the SKS Kingdom, which as a joint state of the South Yugoslavs appeared with the importance of a regional force, from the start, made the Albanian state face the fact that it had lost Kosova and the other regions that London had left outside the Albanian borders, whereas the Albanian national movement for unity named it as internationally dangerous. The SKS Kingdom in its strategy to impede the stabilization of the Albanian state, combined external pressures with internal ones, which it used in doses, in order to avoid an international crisis, since this way it would risk an unnecessary match with Italy, but that like this it would hold Albania in the loop.

Even though the representatives of the Government of Durrës in Paris emphasized the importance of the forcefully separated territories from the Albanian state for its existence, in fact, they focused on the request for recognition of the Albanian state as specified by London and expressed their happiness if this would occur. The same was done by the government that resulted from the Congress of Lushnjë, meaning that of Tirana, and other governments to come would behave in the same way, which for the following two years switched back and forth in most cases violently and under the direction of the other states, especially the neighboring ones who were not at all interested in the stabilization of the Albanian state.

The irredentist movement for the liberation and union of Albanian territories which was led by the National Defense of Kosova Committee, although potentially powerful, lost much of its legitimacy from the outside as well as within its own land, especially in the occupied areas when the war against the Serbian occupiers dwindled down to some detached Kachak groups, who acted in the Drenica, Drin and Dukagjin triangle, until they faded completely.[165] Thus, the movement turned into an internal Albanian issue, which reflected in its political scene, got involved in some developments, which in time, returned as a boomerang to completely get liquidated, as occurred before and after the insurgence of June 1924. Since the National Defense of Kosova Committee took on the side of the Albanian left against the right, in which its fate was sealed in such a manner that even if the left won, its result would be the same, but not through blood because it was the logic of the state interest which determined this fate, whether it would agree with it or not.

Although these developments occurred, it should be said that the National Defense of Kosova – with its center in Shkodër, established under the circumstances when the First World War was entering its final phase, while the French forces now had entered in Kosova and the other Albanian regions and had begun returning them to the Serbians. – Since it was expected that in an international conference which was supposed to be held, the whole issue of the Ambassadors' Conference in London decisions were to be reassessed conforming to the new report of the powers resulting from the epilogue of the World War, and also the interests that had surfaced as a result. So from the Albanians' side it was required that the international decisive factor be given its response beforehand, especially where it would include the fate of Kosova and the other regions detached from its base during the Balkan Wars from the Serbians and the Montenegrins. This request should have been nothing more than the

---

[165] For more details around the Kachak Movement in Kosova, see Rushiti, Limon: *"Lëvizja kaçake në Kosovë 1818-1828,"* Prishtinë, 1981; Haxhiu, Ajet: *"Shote dhe Azem Galica,"* Tiranë, 1976; Haxhiu, Ajet: *"Hasan Prishtina dhe lëvizja patriotike e Kosovës,"* Tiranë, 1964, Çami, A: *"Lufta çlirimtare antiimperialiste e popullit shqiptar 1918-1920,"* Tiranë, 1969; Cana, Zekeria: *"Shpalime historike,"* Prishtinë, 1982.

request for a joint Albanian state conforming to the ethnic, historic and human rights, which the others whom also had just come out of the centuries' long Ottoman slavery already enjoyed.

These aspirations were also expressed by the Committee program, which requested that the territories from Sanxhak to Jeni Pazar, Kosova, Dukagjin, and then the territories in Macedonia, from Kumanova, Shkup, Gostivar in the direction of the Greek borders be included in the ethnic Albanian state.

When the Entente powers entered the Albanian territories, and with this the Central Powers declared as defeated in the war, the Committee directed the Great Powers with the request that the national program be realized.

So, apart from these requests, the Committee will also directed the Entente Powers to protest against the Slavic desolation in Kosova and the other regions re-occupied by them. Such is the request the Committee gave to the Peace Conference in Paris, on December 4, 1918. There, among others, it is stated:

"The Serbians, by achieving resettlement in 1918 within their political borders, through the Great Powers of the Entente, began to execute once more the methods of desolation; they bombarded and leveled to the ground seven villages of Pogur (the region of Peja), detained many of the members of the Prishtina elite, plundered the market in Peja and, after all of this, forced ten people from Peja and Gjakova to participate in the Serbo-Montenegrin national congress in Podgoricë."[166]

However, conforming to the changing circumstances, which now appeared very different from the ones of the Ambassadors' Conference in London in 1912 where the Central Powers (Austria-Hungary, Germany and Italy) had the main say and defended the interests of Albania, be that even partly the case, when on the side of the Entente Powers, the neighboring countries (Serbia and Greece) appeared as allies, though they had open intentions to destroy the London Albania, the Committee tried to accommodate to these realities, viewing Italy as the only supporter. Since Italy, although initially a member of the Central Powers, had abstained from the war, later on it joined the Entente Powers and, based on some secret agreements with the Britain and French, was promised that it

---

[166] Pushkolli, Fehmi: "Mbrojtja Kombëtare Shqiptare e Kosovës 1878-1990," Prishtinë, 1901, p. 80.

would have the main say regarding the Albanian issue. It was then expected that the Committee would seek support from Italy, whom appeared as the main impediment to the hegemonic claims of Belgrade and Greece toward the Albanian territories. The Committee even supported the penetration of Italy toward the North, especially to prevent Shkodër from laying on the hands of the Serbians, and made a call for Albanians to align themselves with the Italians. Thus, in January 1919, considering the role of Italy in the Peace Conference, the National Defense Committee declared its own outlook toward the Italian and French government thoughts. In this regard, it was said that the main purpose of the National Defense Committee was to have an independent Albania excluded from any possibility of a protectorate, and to have Kosovarescued and united with Albania. The Committee refused any conditions contrary to the ones stated above.

In this case, the specification to follow the Italian politics was justified with the fact that the Italian government wanted to chase the Yugoslav government from the North. Since this issue was in the interests of the Committee, the support of Italy was promoted.

Also, the Committee emphasized that no releases would be given to Italy regarding its territorial claims in Albania, nor would a protectorate be placed over Albania. "This has to be done carefully because it is necessary that Kosova be rescued."[167]

However, as would be seen from what occurred in the Peace Conference in Paris, the requests of the National Defense Committee were not taken into consideration by the Great Powers. The SKS Kingdom now was a new reality in the Balkans, as a very important factor which filled the emptiness created by the fall of the largest empires of time, the Austro-Hungarian and the Ottoman ones. This new reality not only left out any option for factorizing Albanians in regional dimensions, but also opened up the issue of further de-factorization of the Albanian state itself, so that it could have no possibility of returning to the aspirations for an Albanian union. As it will be seen, Belgrade will even attempt to make the whole Albanian issue turn to the Secret Agreement Treaty of London of 1915, where Albania was anticipated to shrivel down to the dimensions of a "Muslim Princedom" (with Esad Pasha Toptani on the lead), if it were not for the intervention of the American President Wilson, of February-

---

[167] *Ibid.*, p. 81.

March 1920, where it would first put down the Anglo-French-Italian compromise of 13-14 January 1920 which forecasted the exchange of Fium (Rijeka) with Shkodër and then will request that the Albanian issue be separated from "the Adriatic issue," so that there would no be any division between Rome and Belgrade. From this moment on, Belgrade will attempt, that with any minor correction, to support the concept of the London Albania, so that the influence of Italians on this area would be impeded. Since the rivalry between Belgrade and Rome for Albania and the Albanians in general did not appear any longer simply as an internal issue between these two countries, but also of the rivalry between the Entente Powers (the French for a smaller Entente consisting of the countries coming out of the fallen Austro-Hungarian Empire, and that of the Britain , whom sought a larger Entente according to the Americans' interest, where Italy and Greece appeared as decisive factors), it will help Albania and the Albanians in general to have a better situation from the one that was foreseen after the fall of the Central Powers (Austria-Hungary and Germany), her main supporters.

Conforming to this development, Albania as a state will earn good opportunities for survival and strengthening, provided that it not obstruct itself as occurred on the eve of the World War. The issue of Kosova and, in general, the areas remaining under the SKS Kingdom and Greece, turned into a minority issue which had to be defended according to the international covenants and the packet of cultural and religious rights which had come to power with the Covenant of the League of Nations.

The Albanian State and the Challenge of Kosova

From the Government of Ismail Qemali, that of Prince Wied and here-on, the Albanians of Kosova did anything they could to advance the Albanian state since it was clear for them that without an Albania there would be no Kosova. – The Albanian state, although it recognized the role of Kosova and the Kosovars for the independence of Albania, in its attempts for survival, such as the ones during and after the Peace Conference in Paris, did not make the issue of returning Kosova as a priority, neither did its defense. – The Government of Sulejman Delvina impeded the shipment of weapons from Italy to Kosova, as did

many that came after them. – After the decisions of the Peace Confer-
ence all of the Albanian governments pulled back from supporting the
Irredentist Movement. – In the inability to hold its activity in Kosova,
a portion of the Irredentist Movement began to get implicated in the
Albanian political scene.

Regarding the state aspect, the Parisian Albania did not differ all
that much compared to the London Albania. With a minor territorial
change, like the one in Shën Naumi and Vermosh in the North, which
was made in the last phase of the ratification process of the inter-
state agreements between Tirana and Belgrade, Albania held the po-
sition that it had from the time it was recognized as an independent
state. However, from the political and strategic perspective, the Pa-
risian Albania differed a lot from the London one. Although it did not
have the ten-year long guarantees of the six great powers nor their
direct presence, it nevertheless had the Italian mandate, which linked
it to Italian interests. These interests were at the same time interests
of Britain-America, which opened Albania to the Yugoslav risk which
was permanent, and would also take care of the issue of Kosova.

However, since it was separated the way it was, the Albanian state for
many years would not regain normalcy because it would precisely be the
problematic Kosova which would create discord both internally and
externally. Albania would be forced to confront the situation on multiple
levels since it was known that the role of Kosova was as an epicenter of the
National Albanian Movement, which had resulted in the independent
Albanian state, and whose fate meant conforming to the state logic that
was in opposition to that of the nation. This disturbance would become
even greater due to the fact that the Irredentist Movement had accumulated great energy in Albania, not only among Kosovars mostly from the
political elites who had found shelter in Albania and there had based
hopes of returning to their lost homeland and realizing their national
aspirations. This National Albanian Movement concept, which had been
put to action from the East Crisis and thereon, was also held by the
majority of the Albanians who had the belief that without a Kosova there
could not be a natural Albania, as there could not be a Kosova without an
Albania. This relationship would become stronger and more troubling
when taken into consideration that precisely this link could turn into an
impediment for the Albanian state, as it could also turn into mourning for

Kosova itself and its people if they would collide from within as did actually occur in reality.

However, it was apparent that in the first phase of Albania's confrontations with the Peace Conference in Paris and the actions undertaken so that the Albanian requests were as inclusive as possible, always for internal needs, the political elite in Albania tried some energy from the Irredentist Movement into the government structures of the Albanian state so as to keep it as close as possible to the condition that Albania fulfill the national interest which required Albania to first form and strengthen itself, in order for it to be able to tackle the Kosova issue. "The Patriotic Pragmatism" of the state-forming of Albania, as it appeared, had begun to turn into a general political position of Albanians, which had caused the Kosovar Albanians to fight with such commitment for Prince Wied.

In fact, the Albanians of Kosova and their Irredentist Movement focused in Albania would do anything they could so Albania would become a state, providing help during the most difficult times. This would be seen, especially during the Peace Conference in Paris, where chaos had begun to form, not only around the issue of the Albanian representation there, but also from the circumstances that held Albania captive from the inside, from the end of World War I and thereon. Italy on one side had occupied Vlorë and a part of the Albanian coastline and was attempting to turn this into its own permanent base all in the name of the mandate from this Conference. The French in in the South on the other hand, in the name of "preventing destabilization from the vor-epirote factor" had the Autonomy of Korça under its control. Then there was also the Belgrade presence in the North (Shkodër, Lumë, Mirditë and other regions which were destabilized according to their needs), which received a deserved response from the National Congress of Lushnjë in January of 1920. The Irredentist leaders, which presided over the National Defense Committee with its center in Shkodër, Hoxhë Kadri Prishtina, Hasan Prishtina, Bajram Curri and others, made many attempts to prepare for this historical congress regarding the fates of Albania and the Albanians, and after it ended in success, they took part in the Government of Tirana of Sulejman Delvina, and in all the following activities that led to the liberation of Vlorë and the return of the Albanian state dignity.

Thus, in the cabinet of Delvina's government, Hoxha Kadriu, who was at the same time president of the National Defense Committee, took the post of Justice Minister, a post which was very important since it carried the responsibility of preparing legal acts and other documents through which not only the legitimacy of the state of Albania would be brought back, but also the legal and political platform for the requests that would be presented to the Peace Conference in Paris. The first successes of the Tirana Government toward the return of Albania's sovereignty, such as the taking over of Shkodra from the French troops on March 12, 1920, and the next day the announcement of the Municipality decision for the city to join the National Government of Tirana, were linked closely to the activity and role of the National Defense Committee in Shkodër. Hoxha Kadriu, the Justice Minister, and Ahmet Zogu, Minister for Internal Affairs were backed by some thousands of armed militants of this Committee, who were ready to fight for Albania until the end. They demonstrated this in all of the events that were linked with the return of Albania's sovereignty in all of its regions, especially in the liquidation of the last people of Esad Pasha Toptani by forces led by Bajram Curri. These militants also participated in the war of Vlorë, where the Kosovars were among the first who crossed the Italian line in Pasha Liman and some of them lost their lives there too.

The military forces of the National Defense Committee, which infrequently were led by Bajram Curri, continued to remain the most faithful forces of the Sulejman Delvina government and the Minister of Defense, Ahmet Zogu. These troops acted in almost all emergency cases where the security of the Albanian Government was at risk. They had many internal enemies and rivals, but also external, among which the Yugoslavs were the most unpredictable because they continuously used the Kachak Movement of Kosova card to destabilize it, just like they also used defense as the excuse for the presence of their military forces in the area of Peshkopi, which had entered at the end of the First World War to "secure Albania from the presence of Italy." After the liberation of Vlorë and the retreat of the Italian troops, as well as the signing of the agreement between Rome and the Delvina Government, the Yugoslav forces had to leave the Albanian territory. In order to prevent this, Belgrade staged a conflict in Kopili (on the border with Montenegro), but in these fights, however, the forces of Bajram Curri and other volunteers from Kosova protected Shkodra from the Yugoslav occupation.

The attempts for stabilizing the Albanian society by the National Defense Committee during 1920, as well as the large contribution given by the Kosovars during that decisive year of the Congress of Lushnjë - the liberation of Vlorë and the liquidation of sadist forces, gave an end to the expansion of the Irredentist Movement in Albania, precisely because the excessive power of the movement was in opposition with the interests of the Albanian state. This absurdity can only be understood if the situation of the Albanian state is considered, with its attempts to win the necessary international support in the Peace Conference in Paris, which, according to it, was completely dependent upon the behavior of Belgrade. Thus, the first friction with the Irredentists on the basis of the state logic and its interests was between Sulejman Delvina and the National Defense Committee in August 1920 when the Government of Tirana was forced to prevent the landing of weapons on the Albanian coastline, dedicated for the armed movement in Kosova, led by Azem Galica and friends. In this case, the Prime Minister Delvina personally intervened, so that the weapons commenced from G. D'Ancunio would not land in any port of Albania.[168]

That these frictions between the Irredentist movement led by the National Defense Committee and the Albanian state, which was going through many troubles to get on a secure ground for international recognition, could turn into big troubles and oppositions, as occurred in reality, when the Albanian state even used force against the movement (in 1923 and 1924). This was also shown in the case of preventing the landing of weapons for the Kosova resistance, when Sulejman Delvina, at the beginning of September, sent a delegation to Shkodër to enter negotiations with the Yugoslavs, when it was noted to its representative Neshic that the Albanian government was not supporting any activity of the resistance movement in Kosova, and that it would not even allow activities which could lead to the supplying of Kosova with weapons. [169]

The same promises had to be given also by the government of Iljaz Vrion, which in November 1920 replaced that of Sulejman Delvina. By getting closer to Britain, who had a decisive role in accepting Albania in the League of Nations, done in December 17, 1920, Vrion and the Albanian government accepted further obligations in preventing the influence of Italy on the National Defense of Kosova Committee, which according to them, could destabilize the Albanian government for their own gain.

---

[168] "Historia e Popullit Shqiptar," third volume, Tiranë, 2007, p. 170.
[169] *Ibid.*, p. 170.

This measure, according to Britain, would show Belgrade that it had no valid "reasons" for holding on to a portion of North Albania for "security purposes".

Conforming to this, the government of Vrion requested that the Irredentist Movement rest its activities in Albania and at the same time interrupt any activity that could make the Kachak movement in Kosova rise, since according to Britain, this would prevent Yugoslavia from any legitimacy in preventing the stabilization of Albania from the inside and from practicing terror against the Albanian population in Kosova.

Of course, in these circumstances, opposing the behavior of the Irredentist Movement, as the international and the state logic requested, presented every Albanian government with great difficulties. In this case, the compromise formula would also be used, so the Albanian irredentists' power initially would be used for the needs of the state instead of leaving them in opposition.

Conforming to this, Hasan Prishtina, who was among the most noted of the National Albanian Movement and had lead the revolt of 1912, had succeeded in Shkup with the Fourteen Points to open the way to the establishment of the Ottoman Albania, which would be a transitory ethnic state, on December 1921 was given the post of the Prime Minister of the Albanian Government. Hasan Prishtina determined that in his cabinet he would adhere to "the democratic patriots' bloc." This group consisted of Fan Noli, Foreign Affairs Minister, Luigj Gurakuqi, Internal Affairs Minister, Ahmet Dakli, Finance Minister, and Zija Dibra, World Affairs Minister.

However, after seven days Hasan Prishtina was forced to give up the Prime Minister's post, since having led the irredentist movement, he was viewe as an impediment for the normalization of relationships with the neighbors, especially the Yugoslavs. After a week, Ahmet Zogu took power after entering Tirana with his many supporters, to begin the legitimization of experience through which, in the Albanian political scene, in the upcoming three years, the rules will be determined by power and its use, and also the consideration toward the external factors and their interests, to which the internal factors had to accommodate.

Under these circumstances, the Albanian Irredentist Movement and its power, on the one hand, in the name of the state logic and its interests, was forced to give up the concept of an ethnic Albanian state, to which the segregated regions would unite. In the first place, Kosova went through a liberating war and its perpetrators were then forced to get implicated in the internal politics of Albania, as occurred in the developments of 1922, 1923 and 1924 when it would get complicated in the Albanian political scene, where in some cases it would even have the main role (in the revolt of the left against the right), which as a result would lead to its tragic end, not only in Albania but also in Kosova.

Ahmet Zogu and the Irredentist Movement

Ahmet Zogu was pragmatic regarding irredentism, which was led by the committee "National Defence of Kosova," and this attitude was connected with state-leading rationality. However, Ahmet Zogu had a personal attitude toward the leaders of this committee – Bajram Curri and Hasan Prishtina, of the left wing, because of the thought that they would be involved in the coup d'etat of June, 1924, where Zogu would fall from the throne. Resolving those political issues with irredentist leaders would present an enormous problem for irredentism, which, instead of collaborating with "Kachak Movement of Kosova," started the activity against the Albanian government in the North region of Albania. Was Zogu involved in the segregation of "Kachak Movement of Kosova," which would start with the suppression of the "Free Zone of Junik" in 1923? Was the segregation of "Kachak Movement of Kosova" the sole condition for Yugoslavia to be conciliated?

The rapid progress of Irredentism and the resistance movement of Kosova, which was expressed in the Kachak fight and presented a crucial role in its fortunes, are related with the period of 1922-1924. This period is connected with Ahmet Zogu's governance, starting from the time of Sulejman Delvina's government (Minister of Defense), to his return as Prime Minister in 1924, continuing later as President of Albania, and finally the King of Albania.

This relation is not only formal, but essential, because it highlights the tragic circumstances through which Albanians and their concerns passed continually from the declaration of independence of the Albanian state toward other issues. During this time, Albanians entered into the major national issues such as unity and the right to make decisions for their state, issues that were denied from them for many years. Ahmet

Zogu is one of the most emblematic examples of individuals whose behavior during these development years was of great interest, as the highs and lows of his political life, as well as his general concept of the Albanian state, passed through Serbian-Albanian relations and later Yugoslavian-Albanian. In this vortex, which presented a challenge for each Albanian statesman during that time period and circumstances, it can be said that Ahmet Zogu appeared a bit more special. Ahmet Zogu was firstly charged with the responsibility of a vessel of Belgrade, another Esad Pasha Toptani, in the role of a puppet that had a very low price (to be back in power) and that for this he had "betrayed" the Kosova issue, to end up in Rome's hand, where he was recognized for the "merit" of taking Albania from the Yugoslav grip with the purpose "to protect" it with those of Italy.

Whatever surface evaluation can be conducted of Zogu's governance, which in Albanian history is known as Zogu's time and appears insurmountable and relates highly with foreign political policies, which impacted the stability of Albania and the way it passed through fifteen years of leadership, starting from Prime Minister, continuing to President, and ending as King. Irredentism and Kosova's resistance to Yugoslavian-Serbian occupation issues were also used and even sacrificed for internal interests. Their complexity and tragedy became even greater when they related to Yugoslavia, who caused these issues, but they never left the interests of the Albanian political internal scene, where it would be used and misused for various purposes until its brutal segregation.

Though, different circumstances imposed foreign policies to adapt to internal stability and this was inevitable for every person that would occupy that position; however, Zogu managed the foreign political factor in the way that it would strengthen its personal power and go up to that of an autocrat, but at the same time put it as a function of Albanian state to the extent where Zogu, himself, would appear as a stability factor. This would make him benefit directly; on the one side, he would benefit from the rivalries between Yugoslavia and Italy, and, on the other side, taking advantage of the regional rivalry between the great powers themselves, namely France and Italy. The purpose was for Albania to be upgraded from the remnant position, which was established from the secret Treaty of London, 1915, to state entity that to some extent determined the areas of interest, which increased the value of Albania as a state but at the same time enlarged the external threats.

Seen from this historical angle, it can be said that Zogu's regime improved, for a short-time period, the affairs with neighboring countries, which was a pre-condition for the internal stability of Albania. This would not happen taking into consideration the political and diplomatic circumstances, the emergence of fascism in the scene, whose upgrade led to the World War II, and which used Albania as its first victim.

The most noticeable thing from the fifteen years of Zogu's governance, including also two previous years when he worked as a minister in others' government, is that he should fight for the internal stability of the state, and secure it for a good portion of the time with the external factor established inside the state. Because, as it is known, Italy and Serbia, those two countries from the beginning of the World War I, each on its own way and with their tools, was present in Albania in order to influence its development in accordance with specific goals, which, as will be seen, do not only seek military presence in these areas, but also require for Albania to be adopted to their circumstances. Rome and Belgrade also had the same imperialist policy toward Albania and Albanians, with the only difference that Rome planned its expansion considering the monitoring of Albania as a state, unlike Belgrade that aimed for the separation of Albania, because in this way Belgrade felt safe. Also, Rome wanted for Albania to be fully monitored by them; however, they never intended to wipe Albanians from their ethnicity, as Belgrade wanted, which returned this issue with the purpose of hegemonic policy from the creation of the Serbian state and beyond.

Regardless of the political approach, both countries in order to achieve their goals used military means, while, each in its own way, tried to use the Albanian internal factor as a means of achieving their goals. Regarding this case, Belgrade had more "benefits," because they occupied more than half the Albanian ethnicity and were always able to destabilize from within the Albanian state, in the same way as they were able to seduce Kosova's Albanians and other areas through wise policies, in case they needed them for their interests.

Exactly here is highlighted the role and the position of Ahment Zogu to direct Albania to furious waves, not only to save her from being sunk, but also to achieve his goal - survival and stability of Albanian state. Furthermore, his advancement and approach to power, regardless of the methods and tools used, is closely related with the Italian as well as the Serb-Yugoslavian factor, who invested with the purpose to buy him. At this time, the Englishmen's role is crucial, which, in many places, would be considered as "crucial assistance to Belgrade." This assistance was given to Ahmet Zogu in December, 1924, and helped him to be back to power; otherwise, he would be inverted in the coup d'état of June and would have needed to be back to Serbia to prepare for power again.

Aware of the role and importance of Italy and Yugoslavia in the Albanian case, as well as the impact of these states in Albania, but also conscious that for maintenance and protection he had the strong English 'joker' attained by the concessions that he had given to British firms in oil and important natural resources of the country, Ahmet Zogu behaving as a skilled Pelhivan, who walks the tightrope, would determine, through walking, the side where his stick would touch.

It was not an easy task for Zogu to ensure this "choice." Choosing Rome or Yugoslavia, was not only related with Albanian's narrow interests with one country or the other, nor were they defined within a certain mutual range; instead, they passed through parallel tracks: in that of inevitable rivalry between Italy and Yugoslavia in Albania, and that of enormous rivalry among the great powers in the Balkans. This was divided into the Italian sphere of interests, which included England by its side and also Greece, and France's sphere of interest together with Balkan Slavic countries, Rumania, Czechoslovakia and the formation of "Small Atlanta." The second one pretended to be returned to power in the center and southeast side of the continent; the place that in ancient times was governed by the Danubian monarchy.

The United States of America, which in 1917 was involved in World War I, determining as such her fate in the benefit of "Entente" and in the detriment of "Axis powers," initially did not take sides. Later, USA tilted toward Italian interests, because of England, which wanted to support Italians and oppose France in its efforts to obtain the European power. What is more, USA was connected with England through common interest in the Middle and Far East, where a severe battle was being held to secure future energy resources, as well as trans-national lines of circulating goods.

Zog investigated very well the outline of these rivalries, and it was the USA component that favored the Italian side, especially, considering the role of the United States of America toward the Albanian case in the Peace Conference in Paris, in the most critical moments of Albanian future. In this conference, USA President, Woodrow Wilson, imposed the view that the issue of Albania should be separated from "the issue of the Adriatic." This decision was taken with the purpose of being equal with Yugoslavia and Italy in the case of the distribution of Adriatic's space.

Although there was rivalry among the great European powers, Albania already has its supporter, Austria-Hungary, who would help Albania to find her best way toward the national independence in the most difficult times. However, this did not mean that Albania was released from the difficulties that would come her way until it reached the solution of "Rubicon."

Here, in fact, began what were called Zogu's maneuvers, used to be released from Belgrade influence, which inevitably had to go through connections with Rome, determining in this way the side where Albania would be. This side was not a matter of inherent power of action, which should be obedient; rather it represented the skill of not only being in accordance with physical laws, but also evaluating the usage of political capital. With the Albanian-born tendency to smell the right side at the right time, and equipped with the dodge trend, Zogu was aware of the significance of the double-game in a narrow space. His purpose was to attain as much as he could, without making the impression that what he was really looking for was victory. Based on this attitude, there are three phases observed:

The first one: relating mainly to Yugoslavia

The second one: relating to Yugoslavia and Italy and their rivalry for Albania

The third one: relating directly with Italy and its role toward Albania

The first phase, which starts from 1920, when Zogu started to impact the Albanian unstable political scene, to be upgraded within it after two years as Prime Minister, rounded up by the end of 1924, when after the coup d'état of June of the left wing, Zogu, as it is usually said, with Belgrade's help – in the backstage of which the English and their economic and strategic interests for an Albanian monarchy in the Balkan actually stayed – returned to power to remain there for the next fifteen years.

The second phase relates to further efforts to normalize the relations with Yugoslavia, with the purpose of Yugoslavia giving up its country's intention of instability and rising to the signing of agreements for international recognition of the Albanian state on the borders of Versailles.

The third phase involves the time since 1927, when first treaty was signed with Italy, until 1939, when Albania fell prey to fascism.

Characteristic for the first stage was the Zogu's attentive behavior toward the Yugoslav factor, which had great advantages for Albania at the international level as an ally of the Entente and would mostly benefit from the collapse of the Austro-Hungarian monarchy. In this way, Yugoslavia would take advantage to be present militarily not only in the lands that it occupied in the First Balkan War and the occupations legitimized by the London Conference, but also in the interior parts of Albania, which the Paris Peace Conference determined as lands of the Albanian state.

In 1921, Zogu started to be involved in Albanian fights against Yugoslav occupation troops, continuing against those that would come to help the Mirdita Markagjon leader in the declaration of "Republic of Mirdita." After defining Albanian's borders in the Peace Conference of Paris, Zogu tried to solve all pending issues that Yugoslavia was using to destabilize Albania according to their needs. This match was unequal, since Yugoslavia had both the military force and international circumstances, which put them in advance. Moreover, Albania's inner problems regarding political and economic instability made her even weaker.

At this point, Zogu's aim was to convince Belgrade that Albania's stability and neutrality was also in Belgrade's interest. The core question was what that interest would be and whether Yugoslavia wanted it or not. However, after American intervention in favor of the Albanian state and the Peace Conference of Paris having recognized it in London's borders, together with the intervention of Italy to keep Albania for its own interests, for Yugoslavia there was nothing left but to accept the reality of the Albanian state existence that at least would not fall under Italian power. This specific option was unacceptable for Belgrade.

This reality, actually, is the one that Zogu would benefit from and supported the most. But the rivalry between Yugoslavia and Italy would be very carefully used, which is known as the Zogu's second phase. What would obtain the major attention from the Albanian government, was the relation that it kept with Yugoslavia until the beginning of 1926.

Because Yugoslavia and Italy were two important countries, Zogu would ensure that this "two-way fortitude" was done quietly and discreetly under the power of the Albanian state and would establish partnership with Italy with the purpose of creating multilateral cooperation with countries, especially those in neighborhood. This would have happened until March, 1926, where the first Pact with Italy was signed, although it claimed to be "part of bilateral cooperation." According to it, Italian doors were opened to Albania, which, as it is known, marked the end of Italian fascism. This opened a new chapter in Albanian history, extracting Albania out of the state frame and deriving it into a new, wider plan, some of which will be discussed later.

Regarding the first phase, it can be said that Zogu, as Interior Minister during the government of Xhafer Ypi, and, as Prime Minister from December 1922, made every effort to make Belgrade understand the obligations that arose from the decisions taken in the Peace Conference, regardless of the fact the Serb-Croat-Slovene Kingdom constantly tried to keep Albania under its collision, either through sabotaging international decisions, or through direct military intervention, always creating excuses. Since Albania did not have military forces, which would oppose Yugoslavian forces, it was looking to avoid such actions through political and diplomatic ways, as far as they were possible in the existing unequal situation.

One of the most difficult issues for the Albania state, which Belgrade used always as an excuse for intervention, was irredentism and its activity expressed in the committee "National Defense of Kosova," which had its leaders in Albania and they were very influential in the inner policy of the state (Hasan Prishtina, Bajram Curri, Hoxhë Kadria etc) and also included enormous human potential. Irredentism rightfully expected help from the Albanian state to fight Serbian and Montenegrin occupation and also to be an active part of it. Because the Peace Conference of Paris recognized Albania as a state in 1913, Albania was obliged to respect the international decision in order to ensure its existence; this meant a change in the attitude toward the irredentist movement, at least in the diplomatic or political plan level.

Actually, in this stage Zogu's governance problems started that as such, without exception, would have any Albanian government of that time, considering the fact that it was a case of a nation divided not by its will, where half of it remained excluded from the formation of national state. This half wanted to be all part of the "big state," which in turn affected the existence of the Albanian state itself. Therefore, each government that was looking for its interest would have decided from the state logic perspective, even if that was very painful. That is what Zogu actually did.

According to the state interests, at least in the first phase, Zogu tried to be attentive with Irredentism from within the country, with the purpose of not letting it be a problem for the internal issues of the state, especially for political rivalries, as would happen, and also was trying to secure that Yugoslavia would not have a reason to intervene in Albania, as they were always using Irredentism as an excuse. Because of this, Zogu would completely exclude Kosova's resistance movement, such as the Kacak movement, which was also physically connected the North side of Albania. Furthermore, Zogu was trying to separate those two places. This was a hard play for Zogu, who inevitably confronted the Irredentism movement, which was a Yugoslavian request, as well as international. From April 10, 1920, the time when the Peace Conference had finished the procedures, until November 9, 1921, when it approved Albanian's borders, continuing for ten more days for these border to be recognized by the League of Nations, the Peace Conference monitored every single attitude of Albania, especially that of the Irredentism movement. Yugoslavia, as will be seen, along with international pressure against the Irredentist movement, since Paris had confirmed its 1913 invasions and those that the Conference of London had given Belgrade, also utilized its separator power, not only to destabilize Tirana, but also to force her to act vigorously against the Irredentist movement from within, with the purpose separating it physically, politically, and spiritually.

One of these choices that was used by Belgrade in various ways from June 1921 until January 1923 was the one of the Markagjoni separatist movement in Mirdita.[170]

As was known, the separatist insurgency of Mirdita was organized by Yugoslav agents to make pressure on the Conference of Ambassadors in Paris in the beginning process of the Albanian borders approval, scheduled for November of that year. Markagjoni, with several hundred supporters, including Serb agents and Belarus, announced the "Mirdita Republic" and required it to be accepted internationally. So Mirdita's game and "its Catholic identity," which will be discussed in the Congress of Berlin by the French, to be separated from the Albanian issue in order

---

[170] More readings regarding this issue: "Yugoslavia and Albania 1918-1927," Tirana, 1991.

to deal in terms of its Western affiliation,[171] was introduced again from Belgrade for its usage, but this time for internal division purposes among Albanians on the religious basis.

This plan, however, was not so acceptable neither in Paris nor elsewhere, since neither the Italians nor the Americans had interest for Belgrade to understate the decisions of the Paris Conference, which were already being settled. Therefore, noticing that this plan was not being successful, Belgrade would take its forces that had been established inside the country; however, the main actor remained inside the country. After many lost battles that came mostly by the irredentist movement governed by Bajram Curri, including Ahmet Zogu as a member, Markagjoni and its supporters were back in Yugoslavia. By sheltering them, Belgrade started the process of destabilization of Albania. As will be seen, Pasic used and trained Markagjon in accordance with the neutralization of irredentist forces in Albania, which were settled at the border side, especially in the vicinity of Kruma, but also in the "Neutral Zone" of Junik.

In accordance with international commitments, after the Conference of Ambassadors in early January 1923 completed the work of defining Albanian-Yugoslavia, Belgrade sought from Tirana to attend the "irredentist nests clearance," such as "Neutral Zone" of Junik, which was meant to be part of Yugoslavian countries.

"Neutral Zone" of Junik, "Free Zone" of Drenica, and the End of the Armed Resistance

"The Neutral Zone," created in 1921 as a temporary democratic zone of the Yugoslav-Albanian border lines, with a "local self-government" of tribal nature, where issues were solved by "wise judgments" under the supervision of one leader, was a temporary shelter of the Kacak movement of Kosova, of those that performed any action against the Serbian regime, that mostly would be turned into a "logistics" of the Committee "National Protection of Kosova." As such, it was a barrier both for Belgrade and Tirana. On the one side, Ahmet Zogu sought to manage the irredentist movement and block it in this place of the coun-

---

[171] More on Buxhovi, Jusuf: "Berlin Congress 1878," Prishtine, 2008, p. 143-147

try; on the other side, Belgrade sought to bring the irredentist move-ment into an internal conflict. -Suppressing the "Neutral Zone" of Junik in 1923, as it would be given to Yugoslavia according to the Peace Conference, was the first step toward the extinction of the irre-dentist movement in Albania and the Kacak movement in Kosova. - The common interests of Tirana and Belgrade to extinguish the Kachak Movement in Kosova. – The creation of the "Free Zone" of Drenica as a trap against the Kacak movement and armed resistance of Kosova.

The "Neutral zone" of Junik was created in late 1921 by the Confer-ence of Ambassadors in Paris on the border between Albania and Yugo-slavia and was positioned from Qafa Morines to the Bistrica River in the Decan throat. This territory contained these villages: Junik, Mullic, Batushë, Brovina, Ponoshec, Shishman, Babaj the Boka, Popoc, and Koshare. After defining the north border of Albania and Yugoslavia, in early 1923, the neutral zone of Junik was abrogated.

Geographically, the area was twenty miles long, and from three to six miles wide, therefore it did not provide any opportunity for any inde-pendent neutral government, which could in turn be a "coalition of resistance." Even what is said in some non-critical texts of Albanian historiography and folk songs "about the accumulation of large insurgent Albanian forces operating with the purpose of making freedom plans," according to this aspect were non-stable, because the area had been bound by the Serb army from Erenik and Bistrica side, which made easier the monitoring of the situation and any movement that was done toward it or vice versa.

But before resolving the problems related with this area, which at the same time meant for the Albanian state to be directly involved along with the Yugoslav attack by military means, which consequently induced the migration of Albanians toward Turkey, one should understand the situation and the objectives pursued by this area.

First, it must be said that from the time when Albania was acknowl-edged in the League of Nations, and the Peace Conference assigned the expert group consisting of Britain, France, Italy and Japan, on October 17, 1921, a period of one month long to separate the boundary between Albania and Yugoslavia, the Belgrade regime launched a vicious military campaign against "Albanian terrorists," which appointed residents of border areas, with the purpose of eradicating them from the Albanian population. Bearing in mind this tragic reality, the Nations Association, asked the SKS Kingdom to stop all military and destruction operations. In order to provide protection to those who were involved in these fights, the Nations Association created the "Neutral Zone" for humanitarian purposes, from which all the military units had to be taken, while its local administration was done by local bodies in the country.

According to legal terms, "Neutral Zone" was a demarcation of Yugoslav-Albanian border lines, with a "local self-government" of tribal nature, where the issues were basically resolved by a "wise judgement"under the supervision of one leader. As such, it served as a temporary shelter of the Kacak Movement of Kosova fulfilling, as such, basic conditions for survival, and mostly of the people that were fighting against the occupation regime. However this place was more known as the "logistics"of the "National Defense of Kosova" Committee, which was settled in Krumë, Tropojë and some other parts of the north. Although they did not have any support from external forces, their basic intention was to impact the internal policies of the Albanian state.

This intention would even become the reason for the Irredentist movement to become biased, that is, starting to support the left wing and its revolutionary logic, which, considering the circumstances of that time, immediately turned Irredentism against the right wing. This hostility of Irredentism, especially of its leaders Hasan Prishtina and Bajram Curri, with the right wing, were directly related to Ahmet Zogu and his governance, where its ancient collaborators, who had great merits in the Lushnja Congress regarding the Albanian state sovereignty, and also played a crucial role in the extinction of Marka Gjoni's separatist movement in Mirdita, from March 1911and beyond, would return to permanent enemies. Hostility was related with the inclusion of Kosovars in the fight against Zogu and his governance, in the events of January and February of that year. The basic reason this resistance turned into an obvious revolt was due to the Jafar Ypit governance, who in early January of 1922, created "the Supreme Court of the State" and decided to disarm the population around the Yugoslavian borders. This decision was closely linked with Kosovars sheltered in these areas, but also the Albanian population, which was closely linked to Kosova's fate and which supported the irredentist movement. People of those areas supported Irredentism because the border and separation situation had ruined their life perspectives. People involved in this movement were also Bajram Curri, Hasan

Prishtina and others, who took the side of the democratic and leftist wing. After the failure of the March movement and the taking of state power from Zogu, a campaign against Kosovars, who were involved in these issues, began. Thus, Zogu's governance sentenced to death, in absence of other leaders, some of the main leaders of the movement.

In order to find protection from the prosecution, which had already targeted all irredentist members along with the Kacak people, who until then moved freely in northern areas, some of them switched to the "Neutral Zone" of Junik to find temporary accommodation and from there continued to other areas. Within a short period of time, this area was inhibited with around two thousand members of the Kosova's Irredentist movement and the members of the Kacak fighting unit, together with Azem Bejta, having a two-sided hostility: Tirana and Belgrade.

"Crowds" of most of the Kacak people in this area, would, for sure, save Belgrade for awhile from the Kacak people's actions, which in that year were highly reduced. However, it seemed that this did not suit Belgrade, whose interest was not for the Kacak people to be quiet, because this would mean there was no reason for them to destroy Albanian ethnicity. In order for the purpose to be achieved, they should have had a reason to make Albanians migrate and this reason was offered only through armed response from Kacak soldiers, who usually affected the undefended population and not the Kacak soldiers who could easily be sheltered in the mountains.

Therefore, despite international commitments that they would not intervene in those parts until the Peace Conference brought its decision, Army III ordered the Border Command of the Area, based in Prizren, to find excuses to get within that Zone and imprison the zone leaders. Nevertheless, the Belgrade army, after being well-prepared for military action, authorized invasion by the Chetnik forces led by Milic Krstic and Dimitrije Bracevic (two reserve colonels), which were accompanied by ranged gendarmerie forces along with artillery. There were two invasions during June in the Neutral Zone, where in 17-19 of that month, Yugoslav forces stayed in Junik for three days continually, where in the absence of Kacak soldiers, who moved in the mountains along with the Kacak population, destroyed a good part of the villages and their properties, achieving, as such, their main goal.[172]

---

[172] *Ibid.*, p.190

A similar attack during that month was also directed toward Decan, Batushe village, where Kacak people had settled, but there they would not find anything because the Kacak people moved earlier toward Tropoja.

If during that summer there were not any translucent confrontations between Kacak soldiers and the Yugoslav military and police forces, there, for sure, were Kacak hidden fighting units in different parts of Kosova against Belgrade "collaborators" and "spies." A large number of killings among Albanians were reported, which were accompanied with raids and similar actions by gendarmerie toward those that helped the Kacak people, where usually a large number of villages were suffering and being extremely punished.

It is very likely that this way of introducing the fratricidal war among Albanians was part of the special war that the Belgrade regime had planned in order to achieve its goal of making Albanians against each other as much as possible. According to this, Belgrade had also created the so-called "Government Council" of Junik in the "Neutral Zone," members of which were some rich family representatives whose obligation was to keep the order in this area . They also administered a local gendarme of 53 people, whose job was inevitably to fall into conflict with Kacak soldiers. In order for this enmity to increase, the Belgrade regime sometimes killed members of the "Government Council" and blamed the Kacak people for doing it, and then things were left in the hands of Albanian revenge and its laws, which satisfied Belgrade's objective.

On the other side of the border, toward Kruma and Tropoja, Kosova's Kacak people and irredentist movement leaders generally, were persecuted by Zogu's people among the Albanian police force, who, after the March proceedings, had declared Irredentism as an enmity movement. As the Belgrade regime had infiltrated people within the Kacak movement and through this action determined many of the Kacak movement decisions, similarly, Zogu had put some of his people inside the state police force and some others in the duty of closely observing Irredentism with the purpose of causing feuds with each other, which often ended up in murder. One of them was what Azem Bejta did to "Zef i Vogel" in Golaj Mountain in Albania.

This and similar murders that took place in Kruma, served as a pretext to the Tirana government to act against the Irredentist movement in these places, who had started from the beginning of August to keep order and harmony in these places. It was demanded for the local and Kacak population to be disarmed, which led to an armed conflict between government forces of Tirana and Kosova's Kacak people led by Bajram Curri along with local population which, as noted, were extremely connected with Kosova due to economic reasons. Bajram Curri forces together with highlanders of these areas, attacked government forces in Geghysen to continue then into Luma and the Malesi villages. This served as an excuse for Zogu to militarily retaliate against the Bajram Curri forces in some villages of the district of Dragobia which were highly destroyed. In Nikaj and Mertur, government forces arrested many people as "collaborators" of Bajram Curri.

Obviously Bajram Curri and his fighters did not suffer in this case because they left toward the "Neutral Zone" of Junik, where Azem Bejta's forces had also settled. After being grouped, the Kacak people switched their attention toward Kruma with the purpose of fighting Tirana's government forces. It seemed that for the Irredentism leaders, it was more important to fight against Tirana's forces than against Belgrade's forces, which had already surrounded the "Neutral Zone," not allowing, as such, anyone to be moved from there.

During October and November of that year, the Irredentist movement from the "Neutral Zone" of Junik again and for the last time addressed Kruma and other parts, where there was no military presence to ignite an anti-government uprising. As will be seen, this would be a troll, because as soon as Bajram Curri's insurgents settled in Krumë, the Albanian army marched to those parts. On January 27, from Kruma, the Albanian army commanded by Major Prenk Jaku, entered the "Neutral Zone." After some fighting, Kacak fighting units and their leaders left Junik towards the Highland and Rugova.[173]

The Albanian army remained in this section until February 21, 1923, when the Serb-Croat-Slovene Kingdom military marched into this part. It marched with the right given by the Peace Conference, which ruled this place, too.

The Yugoslavian military action against the population of this area was harsh because of the logic of fighting Albanian ethnicity as a war against Irredentism. Some sources suggest that part of this "cleaning"

---

[173] Research among AQSH, PEOPLE'S REPUBLIC OF ALBANIA from Kruma, MPB Tirana, Janary 29, 1923.

operation was also Albanian's state forces,[174] in order to serve as proof for international unity that Albania was unconditionally meeting its international obligations. Also, there are data that talk about how Zogu asked Belgrade to extinct the Markagjoni separatist forces settled in Yugoslavia as a "return" for Junik, which forces posed a threat to the Albanian state and its safety.[175] Although by that time they were not used for direct destabilization of Albanian the state, Markagjoni still remained a subject between Tirana and Belgrade opponents, but without any particular value.

The end of "Neutral Zone" of Junik and its placement under Yugoslav occupations marked the physical and political end of the Irredentist movement. The part that remained within Albanian state borders, as will be seen, was subject to the Albanian internal policy where it experienced its end, while the part that remained in Kosova and other Albanian areas of the Yugoslavian state, continued their armed resistance for another three –four years, but always at a loss, always more disparate of reaching their goal, for what they fought from the beginning of the time. The Kacak movement leaders, firstly Azem Bejta with his fighting unit, knew that they were facing a tragic situation, where one the one side Albania had not supported them because of the state interest and its personal interest, and from the other side, Belgrade was constantly trying to extinct them. Of course, those actions were interrelated and always wanted the extinction of the movement and the extinction of the Albanian case through violence.

This scenario, that according to Belgrade was taking the right direction, required that the extinction of the Albanian National Resistance Movement in Kosova be made to appear as if it had fallen from within, from its powerlessness. The purpose behind this was to make Albanians migrate from Kosova to Turkey and other places, and also to stimulate the colonization of Kosova with Serbs and Montenegrins, which would lead to the entire change of Albania ethnicity into Serbian ethnicity.

Belgrade had chosen the model of the "Neutral Zone" of Junik as part of this action, continuing to Drenica, exactly to the point where the Kacak movement had its strongest base from the time of its exposure during World War I, where its actions were enormously related to those of Serbian Chetinks, who were also fighting against Austro-Hungarian and

---

[174] Rushiti, Limon: "Kacak Movement in Kosova 1918-1928," Prishtine, 1981, p.191.
[175] Milo, Paskal: "Yugoslavia and Albania 1918-27," Tirana, 1991, p.156

Bulgarian forces with the purpose of returning the occupancy of Belgrade in Kosova, as actually happened, while the Albanian Kacaks were fighting against their "new" occupant.

After the extinction of the "Neutral Zone" of Junik, some of the soldiers had gone to Albania, while the majority (Azem Bejta and Mehmet Konjuhi fighting units) were going toward Kosova (Drenica and Llapi) where they had their shelters. Belgrade was interested in isolating the remaining Kacak population and their leaders, and supervising them according to their internal plans. Isolations not only meant to take them from other places, but also to differentiate them and their influence and then invalidate them through the various topics that spread everywhere through gossip, which could present a psychological victory for Belgrade towards the whole issue.

Thus, in order for Belgrade to show the world that they never had the intention of using war against Albanians, but they wanted to negotiate with them in order to "politically and socially integrate them," Belgrade asked to talk with Azem Bejta and other Kacak leaders. Negotiations were held in Drenica, firstly with some Albanian mediators that were part of Belgrade state structures, and later on with representatives of the Belgrade state and military and police forces. Belgrade's side in negotiations consisted of Ceroviz, Commissioner for Kosova and Macedonia, Police Commander of Zvecan County, the one of Drenica, Martinovic, as well as other officials from Shkup. Final negotiations were held in Oshlan, Drenica's village, in June, 1923. In this meeting, an agreement was reached for the "Neutral Zone" in Prekaz. Belgrade's press pompously informed about the declaration of public security chief at the Ministry of Internal Affairs, Zika Lazic that "Azem Bejta has capitulated, but he will remain free until the necessary investigations are done."[176] In this case, it was said that Lazic had some personal meetings with Azem Galica, where they arranged the entire deal.[177]

The "Free Zone" of Drenica, formed on July 1, 1923, remained until July 14, 1924, in the Prekaz municipality. At the beginning it included approximately all the villages of this municipality, but after some time it narrowed to only three villages: Galice, Mikushince, and Lubovc. This

---

176 More on this issue: Jelic, Milosav: "Letopis Juga," Belgrade, 1930, where is published the newspaper article "Politics" of Belgrade 22.VIII. 1923
177 *Ibid.*, p.207

deal called "vow-to-vow," which was never made public by Belgrade's government, but at the same time was not hidden, being used even to show the "tolerance" of Belgrade toward Albanian "insurgents." In the meantime, all state mechanisms to move Albanians and colonize Kosova had been settled, and were approximately as follows:

1. Azem and his fighting unit remained armed and free in a certain territory.
2. The population of these villages was free of any state obligation.
3. State authorities were not allowed to send any authority as gendarmerie, military, etc, with the condition that Azem and his fighting unit were to remain within their zone. Also, Azem was obligated to keep the order in his zone.[178]

After this "covenant," Azem Galica raised his compound in Galica.

In addition to the isolation of Azem Galica, furrowing his movement in three small villages, the Belgrade regime started negotiations with the other Kacak leaders with the purpose of isolating them, but not in the form of Azem Bejta, that seemed "more privileged," in his compound, but through ensuring "free movement" in their villages, where gendarmerie would not bother them and they would be free of taxes. In such an agreement with police commander of Vuciterna, Mehmet Konjuhi, and permission was given to construct a house in the Zagorth neighborhood of Dumnica village. With this verbal agreement, Mehmet, was allowed to keep ten armed friends provided they did not appear in the city.[179]

Similar verbal agreements were also reached with other Kacak leaders of Drenica. The Minister of Internal Affairs, Vujacic, had authorized Priest Angjelko Neshic from Mitrovica to contact the Kacak people and take them under his "protection." In this way, he reached agreements with Ahmet Delia and Fazli Berani.[180]

Such "peacemaking" of the Kacak movement along with the isolation of its leaders, led to its extinction, even though it resulted in an attack against gendarmes or police posts, but they were rare, divided, and most of the time with serious consequences for the innocent population, because of the severe results as arrests, raids, murders, and even forced deportation of Kacak leaders to different places, including Serbia.

178 Rushiti, Limon: "Kacak Movement of Kosova 1918-1928," Prishtine, 1981, p.207
179 "Politics," Belgrade, 22.VII. 1923.
[180] Jelic, M: "Letopis Juga," Belgrade, 1939, (Među Drenićkim kačacima), p.61-65

However, as it will be seen, verbal agreements and "covenants" did not endure for long, because for the Kacak leaders to have permanent "protection" Belgrade had no interest, because this carried the risk of them being an inspirational Albanian resistance; even though it resembled a farce. Belgrade thought that with the "peacemaking" with Kacak leaders and the "civil" behavior, through "forgiving their crimes," increased its political powers. Meanwhile, the severe surveillance toward Albanians was needed to make them migrate and also to accelerate the process of colonization of Kosova with Serbs, Montenegrins, and others, which was turned again to the Kacak people that through provocation made them act and then blamed them for "breach of vow." Of course, this scenario was not meant to start with Azem Bejta, even though it was meant to end with him, but with others outside "Free Zone" of Prekaz, which had a shelter but not a fortress.

So, in February of the following year, when Mehmet Konjuhi was constructing his new small house in the village of Zagorth, Dumnice, he was surrounded by gendarmeries, who asked him to surrender. Feeling deceived, but also underestimated by the siege, Mehmet killed a Serbian sergeant and three other gendarmeries. This was enough for Dumnica to be a clear target for a severe military campaign, where 23 people of the Konjuhi family were killed, but also others from Bajqinovci, Zeka, Mulaku, and Hajdini families. Mehmet Konjuhi, even though wounded, survived, and went to Azem Bejta's compound in Galica. There he was protected with the "immunity" of the "Free Zone," which, as will be seen, did not endure for a long time, until the middle of June.

In fact, the decision to extinct the "Free Zone" of Prekaz and the symbol of the Kacak movement, Azem Bejta, were held in Tirana and not in Belgrade. The reason for that was the overthrow of Zogu's governance by a leftist wing coup d'état. The leftist wing had brought Fan Noli to power, where the Irredentist movement and its leaders had played a major role, firstly Bajram Curri, Hasan Prishtina, and others, who had been the leaders of that movement, which was called by the leftist wing as the Democratic Revolution of June. This movement had brought the people of Soviet Bolshevism to head of Albanian state, a statement that was also reveled in the Albanian parliament, where a moment of silence was asked to grieve for the death of Levin.

Ahmet Zogu on his way to the Czech Republic had passed through the former Yugoslavia, where he had been talking with top executives of

Belgrade and he understood and enjoyed the support of Yugoslavia for him to be returned to power, which really happened six months later. It was so obvious that "preliminary" Yugoslavian actions for Zogu to be back to power were related with the extinction of its enemies, which were Kosova's Irredentists who at that time governed Tirana as well as the defense and security forces.

If the obligations that Belgrade had with internationals were to be added to this matter, especially to Great Britain and the right wing which would never tolerate the Balkans going toward Bolshevik Moscow, such was the case of Tirana, then it would be clear that SKS Kingdom would use the will of the international factor to make the leftist government of Tirana collapse for personal benefits with isolated leaders of the Kacak movement of Kosova, who should have been phisically extinct as soon as possible.

What happened in July, 1924, in Drenica surrounding Azem Bejta's compound when he and his "guest" were killed in the harshest police and military means, was just the beginning of this folder, which Belgrade used without being responsible to the international factor for these massacres. Azem Bejta fell heroically in the fight with a large number of Belgrade's military and police forces. Being injured, he died on July 26, 1924, and was buried in the cave of Quku, where he was"hidden" for half a century. The majority of the leaders of the Albanian National Movement followed Azem Bejta's fate, starting with Bajram Curri and continuing with Hasan Prishtina, who had done so much to merit the national independence along with Kosova's population. They were left without a homeland, and later developments took from them the right to fight for it, but not the ideals of liberation and national unity.

During this summer, there were revengeful acts against the Yugoslavian forces, but there was more state repression toward Kacak leaders and those that Belgrade government considered potential "actors." This made "suspicious" murders to happen to patriots, which were dismissed by the regime as "revenge" among Albanians for different cases. There were raids and murders, which were dismissed as "resistance" toward the state during the act of disarmament and Belgrade knew very well how to tell the story in their favor to the internationals.

Through late December of that year, Ahmet Zogu took his power back that has been taken from him in June by the leftist coup, and he started the revenge with the leaders of the Irredentist movement in

Albania, which ended tragically the activity of the "National Defense of Kosova" Committee and the Kacak Movement, as a crucial part of the National Resistance of Kosova against Yugoslavian occupation.

However, to understand the outcomes of this tragic end, it is necessary that current developments be related with those that happened in "Free Zone" of Junik and the end of this zone by Belgrade in 1923.

Regardless of the involvement of Zogu's government in the suppression of the Albanian resistance positioned in the neutral zone of Junik, which according to the Peace Conference of Paris was part of Yugoslavia, Albanians that migrated to Albania became nearer to the Irredentist forces, which believed that Ahmet Zogu and its government has betrayed them and they should do everything they could for this government to collapse. This division connected them with the left wing, which also tended to be revolutionary and aimed to use the enormous energy and power of the Irredentist movement as a tool to come to power at any cost.

In this phase in Albania, more than ever started the [miss] use of the Irredentism power for internal political interests, which reflected the situation when the election campaign for the Constitutional Assembly started, from September 30, 1923, until February 2, 1924. The leftist opposition, which lost those elections, consisted of two Irredentist representatives: Hasan Prishtina and Bajram Curri, whose role in the Albanian political sector was crucial and their determination was not only leftist, but also anti-Zogist. Many Kosovars that were against Zogu, cooperating with Albanian forces with those of Belgrade during the "cleaning" operations of the neutral zone of Junik associated with Zogu's attitude during the summer of 1924, when Zogu not only did not support Prince Wied, as he agreed with Bajram Curri and Hasan Prishtina, but was also involved in the fighting against the defensive positions of Durres, which represented the genesis of his suspicious behavior.

The transfer of an Irredentist part to the left wing and its usage for personal arrangements in the unstable Albanian political scene motivated Zogu to act against Irredentist leaders with "state logic." Through this logic, he was released from his strong political opponents, but at the same time he resolved the problems with Yugoslavia and met international requests stated in the Peace Conference of Paris and the National League, of which Albania was a member and expected new international recognition.

Progress that will be achieved during next two months, starting with the attempted attack against Avni Rrustemi (well-known revolutionary, who created the association "Atdheu" and later on "Bashkimi," and through these associations kept Albanians under revolutionary threat) on April 20 and ending on June 10, when rebellious forces entered Tirana and made the democratic government fall through the organized coup d'état – Irredentist leaders Bajram Curri,Hasan Prishtina, and others, making them as such, the basic players in the situation. The first one, Bajram Curri, headed the military forces and attacked the legitimate government of Shefqet Verlaci, whose minister was also Zogu, and brought to power rebellious forces. The second one, Hasan Prishtina, extremely supported the rebellious movement, which was in power through revolutionary violence. Thus, the right wing in Albania, which was defeated by red revolutionaries, who at Azem Rrustemi's burial swore revenge against any conservative assessment in Albania - and they realized that promise as long as they were in power - to the extent attributed to the Irredentist movement. This opened a new tragic chapter of Albanians killing each other and a deeper rift between Albania and Kosova, based on the left-right division, or based on the proponents/opponents of communism, which led to the East or West determination. The Albanian king tried to give an answer to this situation through the next fifteen years, but was not so influential because the Albanian people of the middle class had not only been isolated in the left grip using revolutionary methods to come to power, but they were also devoted to destroying the right wing of the Albanian monarchy, which in the end resulted in Albania being an East-communist country.

Before approaching the Albanian monarchy, Albania went through careful stages of Zogu's measurements in choosing between Italy and Yugoslavia, which ended with the first cooperation Treaty between Albania and Italy signed on November 27, 1927, ending as such, the Albanian rapture amid Rome or Belgrade. Of course, this phase came after Albania had solved all disputes with Yugoslavia regarding its acceptance of Albanian integrity of territories as well as the establishment of full diplomatic relations, where the two border disputes played a crucial role: that of South with Saint Naum, and that of the North with Vermosh. Those two borders were tasked to the Ambassador Conference and the Hague Court for two years, in order for both countries to be satisfied through a mutual agreement where Saint Naum became part of Yugoslavia, while Vermosh and other northern parts became part of Albania.

The left wing of Albania blamed Zogu for this exchange of territories, and related it to the alleged debt that Zogu had to Pashic for the assistance he had given Zogu at the time when he was back to power after six months of loss. This marked the end of the struggles through which Albania passed, starting from the Belgrade dictate, whose intention was to completely occupy Albania, similarly to that of the Albanian communists, who as soon as they came to the power, their political party and the Albanian state became part of Yugoslavian countries.

Conscious that he left an unresolved issue, which could jeopardize the Albanian state from East, Zogu finally determined to be strongly related with Italy, through which he would attain two favors: enormous economic help and a more favorable position toward Italy, which together with England were against France and its collaborators of the Small Entrant. From the strategic view, Italy was positioned on the winner's side, as Italy inside the Entrant favored England, and behind England was the United States of America, while Yugoslavia favored the French side and was positioned as "Small Entrant", presented as the French sphere of interest or the Middle-European interest.

Yugoslavia's deterioration was expected and planned well ahead. As this would not have any consequences for the Albanian state, Zogu tried to benefit as much as he could from the Belgrade situation and favor Italian agreements. Even at the time when Belgrade used the press to remind Zogu of his "debts," Zogu responded with calmness and diplomatic sense, as nothing extraordinary would happen, except that as a sovereign state, Albania had made agreements with another sovereign state for mutual benefits. Belgrade was reminded that even Italy was a Yugoslavian ally, and that the Treaty made between them, enlarged the opportunity for European states to proceed in peace. According to these statements, Zogu built a "deceptive" myth toward Yugoslavia, which could be ended by estimating Ahmet Zogu, who used the best alternative of the circumstances for the well-being of the Albanian state.

Regarding this issue, it must be stated that in addition to international obligations toward the Irredentist movement and its neutralization not only from within the state, but also outside the borders, with the purpose for Albanians to work out new realities, Zogu constantly tried to make Yugoslavia fulfill some of the basic civil rights of Albanians who remained in its areas in accordance with international standards for national minorities of that time. In interstate agreements of 1925 where borders were accepted from both states, three additional agreements on civil rights were included: One for Gjakova and Gjakova highlands, one for Plava and Gucia, and one for Dibra. According to this agreement, the population that lived across the border had entire free movement, free trade, free use of the property, and free use of natural resources (water, forests, and other resources). Gjakova's population used the right of free movement and free trade also for basic education in Kruma, and for those that wanted to continue higher education, in Elbasan or Shkoder. Through these agreements, the border that separated Albanians, even the fact that it was legitimized, was highly mitigated; therefore, its consequences were not as those of the communist regimes of Tirana and Belgrade, where the border between those two countries was non-patent, even though communist campaigns against fascism would say "here will be no border between communists."

CHAPTER 3
THE BEGINNING OF KOSOVA'S COLONIZATION

Agricultural Reform and Colonization

Kosova's colonization went through three phases and aimed at the migration of Albanians from their home. The first phase is connected with the occupation time until the end of 1915. The second phase starts from 1921 until 1931. The third phase lasts until 1941. – Agricultural reform as a colonization tool, along with the discrimination of Albanians, had to create power to stimulate the Albanian migration.- Violence and state repression toward Albanians through military and police forces was part of the big Serb national hegemony plan.- State administration and Agricultural Commission's duty was to create different obstacles to Albanians in order for them not to be able to prove the ownership of the land.-According to official statistics, between 1021-1942, 11,383 colonized families with 53,884 members were settled in Kosova; 49,244 of them were Serbs, 5,148 Croats, and 126 Slovenes. Those data are not accurate, since the military forces, police, and administrators had the right to remove colonies from the official statistic estimation. It is estimated that this number could be 20% higher or more.

The colonization of Kosova and other Albanian territories during the Balkan wars was the core intention of the Serb national hegemony plan. This plan was highly connected with the migration of Albanians from their home. This project started from the summer of 1913, when the London Conference had decided that Albanian occupied territories should be included in the Serbian and Montenegro state, and continued after World War II in 1941.

The colonization consisted of three phases: the first one starting from the occupation period until the end of 1915; the second one starting from

1921 until 1931; and the third one starting from 1931 until 1941. The first phase was based on individual actions, of colonies (naselenici) that used the laws to unify "liberated" territories of the so-called Old Serbia, which included Kosova, Macedonia, the Serbian kingdom, and Montenegro. At this stage, until the time when the law for inhabitation of the South area would be published in 1921, colonies had occupied land as much as they were able to work on it with their families. All of the colonies that had accepted living in Kosova, regardless of being farmers or not, were rewarded with land.

The second phase included the colonization from 1921 until 1932, supervised by the state, which used agricultural reform to violently change Kosova's national structure to the detriment of the Albanians and to the benefit of the Serbs. In this phase, the thought that agricultural reform would change the feudal ownership of farmers, where the state was the owner of the land was usually manipulated, while its users were temporary owners defined by state laws. Barren lands, forests, and those expropriated from the state were given to the colonies. Also there, colonies had the right to choose the best lands, because those "barren" lands which had been owned by Albanians that were expelled by force, those that migrated toward Albania and Turkey during the Balkan wars and World Wars.

In the third phase, from 1931 until 1942, even farmland was given to the colonies, land which belonged to Albanians.

In all phases, the land separation was done through agricultural reform laws, which had been in power from August 27, 1920.

However, when talking for the first phase, that of Serbian-Montenegro occupation, it must be stated that a "different" situation had existed, because Kosova and other Albanian territories were divided into two parts. Dukagjin was occupied by Montenegro, while the other part of Kosova along with Macedonia was occupied by Serbia. The border in Dukagjin was defined by the Drin and Bistrica rivers, while Gjakova was separated into two parts; the east side of Krena River was part of Montenegro and the west side was part of Serbia.

In the Serbian controlled areas, from the invasion and on, each Serb was free to take as much land as he wanted, without regard to whether the land was "state property" or Albanian's property. Albanians were not considered as citizens of the "New Serbia," but "violent" people from whom Serbia must be protected through military force. This also applied for their taken land, which was "legitimized" with "historical and spiritual Serb rights" where Albanians lost any right toward their own land.[181]

This situation continued until February 20, 1914, when Serbia published the "Ordinance for the colonization of liberated and annexed land by the Serbian Kingdom," and its amendments which were established on May 5th of that year.[182] In fact, after publishing this law, supposedly to create the circumstances for agricultural reform to begin and also to keep order in the state property, Belgrade started to legitimize all land occupations done by local Serbs but also those "vulnerable" colonies, that appeared interested in the Albanian land as soon as Serbia had started supervising that land. A special directorate, which was part of the Ministry of Forest and National Economy, had started to supervise this process and deliver property rights to Serbs, while Albanians were charged with too many, rigid and unbearable formalities.

In Monetengro's controlled areas (Dukagjin and a portion of Drenica), colonization had started immediately after the establishment of the occupying power. Monetengro had established the Agriciltural Commission, which started to work in December 1913. The Agricultural Commission had started the registration of property, land, and homes that belonged to the state and monasteries. For any disputes by Albanians, the Agricultural Commission required ownership proof in excess of 50 years. Most of the Albanians could not prove this, because the Ottoman Empire had taken all the cadastral registers and they could have been obtained only by going to Turkey (which was impossible); therefore, the Montenegro state declared each property that could not prove its ownership as "state property," as defined by the Agricultural Reform.[183]

---

[181] Obradović, Milovan: *"Agrarna reforma i kolonizacija na Kosovu 1918-1941,"* Prishtinë, 1981, p 134.

[182] More on that issue: Krsitć, Đorđe: "Kolonicacija Južne Srbije," Sarajevo, 1928; Urošević, Atanasije: „Agrarna reforma i naseljavanje," Skopje, 1937, p 826-833: Novaković, Kosta: „Kolonizimi dhe serbizimi i Kosovës"; Erić, Milivoje: " Agrarna refoma u Jugoslaviji 1918-1941," Sarajevo, 1958, p. 107; Hadri, Ali: "Marrëdhëniet agrare dhe lufta e PKJ në Kosovë dhe Metohi kundër Reformës Agrare të padrejtë të Jugosllavisë borgjeze," "Përparimi," 1964, nr. 9, p 589-599; Obradović, Milovan: "Agrarna Reforma i kolonizacija na Kosovu 1918-1941," Prishtinë, 1981.

[183] More on this issue: Pejović, Đoko: "Agrarna politika crnogorske vlade u krajevima oslobođenim u balkanskom ratu 1912," Istorijsi zapisi, 1-2, 1955, p 216.

In order for "Agricultural Reform" to be "legally supported," which was basically a violent occupation of Albanian land distributed to the colonies, as the Serbian Kingdom had also done, Montenegro on February 27, 1914, had published the law for inhabitation of the liberated areas of Montenegro. According to this law, the state declared all properties whose ownership could not be proven as state property. With this law, in Gjakova, the Agricultural Commission took twenty-six thousand ral of land (one ral was equal to 40 hectares), where 500 family colonies were meant to be settled. [184]As such, one simple family took 5 hectares of land for free, and for each addional member, a half hectar more. In addition, the colonies took another 50 acres to build their house and their garden. Colonies were exempt from paying land, livestock and state taxes, except those of church and education, for three years.

In Montenegro's areas, the Agricultural Commission work was supervised by General Vesovic, who had absolute authority for everything. General Vesovic who was known for his massacres toward the Dukagjin people, had utilized all military forces in the protection of the colonies. He also had been forcing Albanians to be transformed from Muslim and Catholic into Serbian Orthodox, accelerating the Albanian migration to Turkey, as well as the migration of others in Albania, through various repressive measures. He was focused in Peja and areas surrounding the Albanian border to achieve his goals. Those two areas, because of the national security, but also because of the protection of Orthodox monasteries (those of Decan and Peja), were meant to be "purely Serbian areas."

This process was stopped by World War I. As soon as the Austro-Hungarian and German military forces settled in the Dukagjin region, the colonies, together with Montenegro's occupation forces left toward Cakorri and Montenegro, and then the Albanians took their properties and their national rights (education in Albanian language, local autonomy, self-governance etc), that were absent until that time; therefore, the Albanians considered the Austro-Hungarian and German forces as their liberators.

The end of World War I, brought back the same invaders, Serbia, Montenegro, and Greece to the Albanians, with the only change being that Serbia and Montenegro had joined Croatia and Slovenia, which had declared their Serb-Croatia-Slovene Kingdom on December 1, 1918, right

---

[184] *Ibid.*, p.217

after the suspension of the Austro-Hungarian state. This new state, which was the most powerful state in the region, was recognized by the Peace Conference of Paris.

The creation of this strong state, created better circumstances for the Great Serbian hegemonic bourgeoisie in their purpose of denationalizing Kosova and other areas populated by Albanians (Macedonia, Montenegro, Sanxhak), with their primary instrument being the agricultural reform.

The second colonization phase (1921-1931) and the third one (1931-1942) belonged to this epoch and situation.

The colonization of Kosova and other territories populated by the Albanians, which were under the surveillance of the SKS Kingdom, started immediately after the formation of the common state, which was ruled from Belgrade's bourgeoisie.

The return process of the "expelled" families from Kosova from 1915 and on started urgently and extraordinarily at the time when in these areas the Austro-Hungarian and German military forces arrived, which ended the Serbian and Montenegrin occupation. Their return continued from 1919, immediately after the Regent Alexander Karageorgovic declared the kingdom of the three states (Serbia, Croatia, and Slovenia) and where he promised to the population of these states that they would be owners of their properties.[185] This process was meant to be the end of feudalism in favor of the new principle that the land belonged to the one who worked it. This meant that earlier landowners were expropriated (by state compensation), whereas people that were working on the land were made landowners through the Agricultural Reform laws that changed for specific areas, due to the changing of social relations in places where the Austro-Hungarian monarchy had ruled.

Although the termination of feudalism and the return of property rights to those that worked the land, according to agricultural reforms, was meant to be a modernized approach and should have been a positive thing also for the Albanians, because even for them it meant no more landlords, beys, and other feudal structures, this would not happen. Because those new processes created new owners, which were state owners, the Albanians were expropriated not to be owners of the new agricultural reform, even though they should have been valid for all

---

[185] See E. Šišić: *"Dokumenti o postanku Kraljevine SHS 1914-1919,"* Zagreb, 1920, p. 180.

peoples equally, but rather, created a new layer of ownership that was considered invasive. On the other side, Serbian occupation rights were given from the unity of the liberated land law created in 1914 and on, where every Serb colony could occupy as much land as they could, without regard as to whether it was Albanian's land, or lands that remained without ownership because of the migration and thus claimed to be state-owned.

Therefore, in Kosova from 1919 until 1921, colonization took three different directions, but all with one unique purpose - the invasion of Kosova's land. According to Belgrade's government, this process was called "inhabitation" of Kosova.

The first method was called "internal colonization" and aimed for the movement of Serbian population from the mountain areas, such as those from Sharri toward Lepenci and Sitnica rivers where Kosova's fertile plains were settled, those from Sredska toward Prizren; and those from Kollashini of Ibri toward Drenica and Mitrovica.[186]

The second method was Kosova's colonization with the Montenegrins' colonization, who asked to be settled in Peja, Drenica, and Kosova.[187] Montenegrins were also volunteers in Dukagjin and the Drenica regions. They marked the land and asked for help in constructing their homes. Even though they were armed, they also required the presence of a military force.[188]

The third method of colonization was that of volunteer colonies from Herzegovina and Dalmatia. Their demands were greater than those of the Montenegrins, because, in addition to farmland, they also demanded new houses near roads supplied with communication and protection. They also demanded farm animals and the presence of a military force.

However, despite the enormous opportunities of invading fertile land and gaining "state ownership" during 1919 and 1920, a large colonization did not take place. According to official statistics, during 1919 in Kosova 33 families were settled, 28 of them in Nerodime; whereas, in the following year this number multiplied tenfold. Most families were settled in Peja

---

[186] See Raportin e të ngarkuarit kryesor të Ministrisë së Reformës Agrare në Shkup, Sreten Vukosavljevic, nr. 235, of 28. VIII .1919, from Yugoslavian archive, Agrarian reform fond 1918-1941.

[187] *Ibid.*

[188] *Ibid.*

(125), while 77 families were settled in Istog, and 28 in Podujeve. For those colonies 130 houses were constructed. [189]

The fact that colonies in Kosova took as much land as they could, even though according to Agricultural reform one family could take 5 hectares at most, some took more, as was evidenced in the case of an active Major in the armed forces, Medenica, who took 18 hectares of land in Vitomirce, and Klajic, a teacher in Malisheve, who took 27 hectares of land.[190] Among those that appeared as large landowners in Kosova was Prime Minister Nikol Pasic, who had 300 hectares of land in Fushe Kosova which he had taken from the state with the excuse that he would build a monument in honor of the "heroes" of Kosova's Battle of 1389.[191]

From 1920 when the Colonization Law for the South areas was published, until 1931, when some formal, "regulations" were added to it, the discrimination of Albanians continued in the legal and administrative plan. This discrimination was well-known and was justified with "measures that had to be taken for the Serbians to be returned in their homes" in "extraordinary" circumstances created by the "Kachak terrorist movement" and also was justified by the "national interest" which in political language meant the denationalization of Kosova's population through the Serbian hegemonic project of increasing the Serbian population through the colonization and migration of Albanians to Turkey and other places. In this way, the first discrimination was one of ownership, where Serbs and Montenegrins took five hectares land per family, including half a hectare for every child, and half a hectare for the house and garden along with loans received from the state, whereas Albanians took a maximum of two hectares per family without the right of taking more for each child and other family member. When Albanian families were large, this two-hectares-per-family rule turned them into poor families. Also, in order for them to have these two hectares, they had to pass enormous administrative barriers, from the acceptance and loyalty toward the Yugoslav state (which meant citizenship) to other formalities that were secured only through corruption and the most they could get was then half of the land. Unable to face all these problems, Albanians were forced

---

[189] Obradović, Milovan: *"Agrarna reforma na Kosovu 1918-1941,"* Prishtinë, 1981, p. 136.
[190] *Ibid.* p.137
[191] Krstić, Đorđe: „*Kolonizacija Južne Srbije,*" Skopje, 1928, p. 5

to migrate toward Turkey, escaping as such from persecution, humiliation and state terror.

Another form of discrimination toward Albanians, which made them migrate to Turkey, was "Kachak property," which turned into state's property and later was given to colonies.

According to the amendment of 1926, which supported that of 1922, the state had the right to take the land and the property of Kachaks and their supporters, as it had the right to do the same with jailed families and other families they claimed to be "hostile."

With this amendment, Belgrade not only punished the Albanian national resistance, who was still fighting in some areas, confiscating their property, but also punishing their kinship and even their villages, if by any chance a gendarmerie was murdered or a police station was attacked there.

One of the most severe punishments, however, was the movement of Kachak families outside Kosova, mainly into Serbia. Like this, after the proclamation of the amnesty law of 1921, to which a small number of Kacaks responded, Belgrade started the implementation of this form of punishment to those that did not "obey" and were considered as outside the law. In the district of Prishtina, in March 1921, Ibush and Esad Vuciterna's mother and brothers, five Bajram Ternava's family members, and Latif Bajrami's wife, son and brother-in-law were incarcerated.[192] Also in that year, these families were incarcerated in Nish:

1. From the Metohia district, 27 families with 74 family members
2. From the Zvecan district, 22 families with 60 family members
3. From the Kosova district, 16 families with 81 family members
4. From the Prizren district, 11 families with 44 family members
5. From the Kumanova district, 3 families with 14 family members
6. From the Tetova district, 12 families with 58 family members
7. From the Raska district (Tutin, Jeni Pazar), 13 families with 69 family members
8. From the Manastir (Bitola) district, 6 families with 20 family members
9. From the Ohrid district, 1 family with 5 family members[193]

---

[192] Rushiti, Limon: *"Lëvizja kaçake në Kosovë 1918-1928,"* Prishtinë, 1981, p. 158.
[193] *Ibid.,* p.158

Who should have been involved in the "close" Kachak list or in the "wide" list, was decided by military and police institutions and their services in Shkup. According to the 27th provision of the South colonization law, the police and military forces were the institutions which decided for every situation in the border areas, as well as in places that were identified as "Kachak shelters," which should have been cleaned from Albanians because they were meant to be colonized by Serbs. There were many cases in which military and police forces were dressed as Albanian citizens and they staged Kachak actions, preparing the area, as such, for colonization. Police and military forces "pursued" masked "Kachaks" who randomly escaped from them, and the police then falsely published news of murderous actions toward police officers, and attacked a large number of villages with the purpose of disseminating Albanians. After their villages were destroyed, there was nothing left for the Albanian population, so they had to migrate toward Turkey or other countries. [194]

An example of such is one of the Prapashtica village, which was destroyed by police in their quest for the "Kachaks," where, as a punishment brought 22 Serbian families as colonies, who were settled on the properties of Albanians that were declared "enemies." Ten years later, a court announced as "unfair" the expulsion of Albanians from their territories, but this would be too late because many of the Albanians had migrated to Turkey.[195] Similarly, other villages of Kosova (Arilace, Kabash, and Jablanice) were colonized from colonizers of Krajina, Montenegro, and Dalmatia.

According to a flawed statistic (because the data for Kachaks and their leaders were kept by the Ministry of Internal Affairs and the Military Command of the 3rd Zone in Shkup), 295.5 hectares of land was confiscated from the Kachaks and given to the agrarian sector in Prizren. 2,761.3 hectares of land was confiscated from Kacaks and given to the agrarian sector of Peja (including Gjakova too). 500 hectares of Kacak land was given to the Serbian and Dalmatian colonizers of Llapi and Drenica. So

---

[194] More on this see: Krstić, Đorđe:"*Kolonizacija u Južnoj Srbiji,*" Sarajevo, 1928; Lazarević, Tihomir: „*Naš kolonizacioni problem,*" Srpsko Kosovo, nr. 7, Kosovska Mitrovica, 1921; Novaković, Kosta: „*Kolonizacija i srbizacija,*" Balkanska federacia, Vjenë, 1931; Albin, Prepeluh: "*Agrarna reforma naš veliki problem,*" Lubljana, 1933; Davidović, Jaša: „*Agrarni problem,*" Belgrade, 1928.

[195] Krstić, Đorđe: „*Kolonicaziaj u Južnoj Srbiji,*" Sarajevë, 1928, p.61.

this case included four thousand hectares of land that was confiscated from Kacaks and given to colonizers.[196]

In the same way, land was confiscated by the state from escaped "foreign people," "enemies," of Turkey during Balkan Wars, which was distributed to colonizers without any legal procedure.

In addition to the process of taking Albanian lands through occupation and illegal means, and giving it to colonizers in order to increase the number of Serbs in Kosova as was the aim of the Serbian hegemonic plan that started from "Nacertanja" and continued even to the creation of SKS Kingdom, Belgrade also tried to convert Kosova into a big Catholic feudal ownership, where the Orthodox monastery would be the largest landowner. From 1922 and on, medieval Orthodox churches, despite the fact that they were a common property of Catholics, where Albanians from the 4th century and on had invested in them because they were the first who accepted Christianity, were announced as Serbian Orthodox churches and spiritual property. They were considered "national property," therefore the monastery's properties of Gracanica, Peja, Decan, Levishka, Saint Arhangjel in Prizren, and Devic in Drenica would be eliminated. In this situation, there were one thousand and more hectares of land taken from Albanians and given to churches. In this way, the highest portion of land was given to Gracanica's monastery and to that of Decan, which were meant to be the centers of Serb and Montenegrin colonizers. In Gracanica and Decan the expulsion of Albanians from their land was done through military and police forces with the excuse that they did not have their property rights and they could not secure them within 48 hours. Because only some of them had the property rights, while the majority did not and they could not secure them because they were part of the Ottoman Empire and cadastral registers that came from the Ottoman time, was not of interest to the SKS Kingdom. The only possibility left for them was to migrate toward the mountain areas where government was renting the land out under very difficult conditions. In order for Gracanica to be the strongest Serbian place, until December 1932, 7625 hectares out of 11,391.41 hectares of farmland (more than the half) was given to family colonizers. 64.5 hectares of land were given to14 Cetnik families. In this area, 15 self-colonizers settled and were given 69 hectares of land.

---

[196] Obradović, Milovan: „*Agrarna reforma i kolonizacija na Kosovu 1918-1941*," Prishtinë, 1981, p. 146.

Through Agriculture Reform enormous efforts were made to increase the number of colonies in some places inhabited by Albanians, such as Gjakova and Podrima; through stimulation methods, these included loans, construction of houses, livestock endowment, and creation of infrastructure. Until 1932 in this municipality, fifty-three thousand hectares were prepared farmland out of the total seventy-seven thousand hectares this municipality had for colonizers. The Albanian population in that area numbered forty-three thousand. Also in Podrime, seventeen thousand hectares of land were prepared for the colonizers. Until 1932, 2153 family colonizers had been settled in the Gjakova municipality, mostly Montenegrins, who were supplied with 15613 hectares of land. 24 families with 235 hectares of land were settled in Podrime. Through agrarian intervention, 23 self-colonizers had been settled in Gjakova with 198 hectares of land. In Gjakova until 1932, 1995 houses had been constructed for colonizers, 560 out of those had been constructed from the government, and the others from colonizers themselves with loans and other assistance that they got from the state.[197]

Even in the region of Drenica, where the center of the Kacak movement was, enormous efforts were made to make Albanias migrate and to bring colonizers instead. Belgrade used the situation created, supposedly from Kachak movement, to ruin the basis of Albanian family life, or prohibit them from living there by law, even because of their support toward the Kachak movement, or because they lived in the same places where Kachak leaders lived. In Drenica, which was called Serbice, 406 family colonies were settled and supplied with the most fertile three thousand hectares of land. 44 self-colonized families were supplied with 330 hectares of land. In this area, the state constructed 414 houses for colonizers, as well as schools, clinics, and police stations. According to official statistics, until 1939 the construction of colonizer houses, which surpassed twelve thousand, was as follows: Istog with 1,027 houses, Peja with 1,229 houses, Gjakova with 1,955 houses, Podrimja with 596 houses, Mitrovica with 85 houses, Decan with 497 houses, Llapi with 1307 houses, Sharri with 808 houses, Podgori with 73 houses, Gracanica with 1,010

---

[197] Yugoslavia archives, S, 96, Box. 12/48

houses, Gilan with 688 houses, Nerodimja with 281 houses, Kacanik with 64 houses, and Ferizaj together with Nerodime 3621 houses.[198]

Yugoslav official data reveal that from 1920 until 1940 in Kosova the land had been distributed to 11,714 colonized families, 248 volunteer families, 80 Cetnik families, and 508 self-colonized families. The data reveal that in Mitrovica colonizers took 4.89 hectare per family, in Vucitern 7.29 hectare per family, in Decan 9.10 hectares per family, in Istog 8.9 hectares per family, in Peja 8.1 hectare per family, in Gjakova 8.1 hectare per family, in Podrimje 12.3 hectares, in Prizren 9.1 hectares, in Llap 8.5 hectares, in Gracanica 7.9 hectares, in Kacanik 8.1 hectares, and in Podgor 5.08 hectares per family. In Kosova, on average, one colonized family took 8.5 hectares of land per family. [199]

11,383 colonized families with 53,884 family members were settled in Kosova; 49,244 of them were Serbs, 5,148 Croats, 126 Slovenes. Those data are not accurate, because military and police forces, and administrators eliminated colonies from the official statistic measures. Therefore, it is estimated that this number is 20% greater.

Agricultural reform, as a tool to colonize Kosova with Serbs, Monenegrins and others, was not able to satisfy the expectations of its planners, who had planned to change the structure of Kosova's population for the next 20 years, to the detriment of Kosova's population. The purpose was to decrease the Albanian population from 86% (as it was during Balkan Wars) to 30% and increase the Slavic population (Serbs and Montenegrins) from 8% as it was in 1912 to 60%. Mathematically, in order for this estimation to be achieved, other methods were used to stimulate the migration of another 400 Albanians, and attract another 300 colonies.

Despite all favorable living conditions that Belgrade had offered to colonizers in Kosova, it did not achieve in bringing more than sixty thousand colonizers to Kosova. In this way, Belgrade achieved only 1/5 of its estimations; however, through various methods it succeeded in expelling more than two hundred thousand Albanians, or 1/3 of its estimation.[200] Regardless of the estimation, this was a big success for Belgrade,

---

[198] Yugoslavian achieves, 671-28-263, Raport i Drejtoratit Qendror të Agrarit, nr. 344 , 12 December 40.

[199] *Ibid.*

[200] There is no exact number of Albanians that migrated to Albania, or Turkey, neither in Yugoslavian archives, nor in those of Albanians and Turkey. Different sources speculate

which had achieved firstly through military and police forces against Albanian population, but also through other means, such as discrimination by agricultural reform, when their properties were occupied and the possibility of them securing property rights from the Ottoman Empire was by all means denied, and discrimination from feudal order, where the land workers won their land through constantly working it. Discriminated and pursued as such, denied from the land ownership, and also from ownership due to resistance against the state (the example of Kachak movement who were to be praised for curbing the colonization process of Kosova in accordance with Belgrade's purpose), the majority of the Albanian population left Kosova toward Turkey seeking a better life.

The Albanian Migration to Turkey and the Yugoslav-Turkish Convention

The process of forceful migration of Albanians to Turkey were a result of two big genocides against Albanians by Serbian forces: that of 1876-1878 wars, when the Toplica district was evacuated and that of 1912-1913 during the First Balkan War when Serbian and Montenegrin mil-

a number of 200-400 thousand. Albania does not have any information that tells the number of refugees sheltered permanently or temporarily during the Balkan war and on, because the Albanian state started to make the state archive from the forties; however, it does not include the data that would describe this problem. The Yugoslav Kingdom has been excused except for the Covenant, which was made with Turkey in 1938, which was not authorized therefore was not implemented, there had not been a large number of people who migrated toward Turkey; however, it accepts that this was an illegal process, which was done through temporary visas delivered by the Turkish consul in Skopje. This process included the Muslim population, recognized as "Turkish." Tito's Yugoslavia confirms that between the fifties and sixties, along with Turkish agreements, an expulsion of the Turkish had occurred, mostly from Macedonia and Kosova, Sanxhaku, but also from Vosnia, without ever giving an exact number of those that that migrated. The only credible source that talks about the Turkish and Muslim migrations is the Turkish archives that talk only for the migration of the Turkish without stating the exact nationality of those people that migrated. The Berlin Congress accepts, not officially, that in Turkey during the fifties, there were more than two thousand Turkish people re-nationalized.

itary forces conquered Kosova.- The return of Serbian military in Kosova in 1918 and the confirmation of Kosova remaining within Serb-Croatia-Slovene borders by the Peace Conference of Paris, initiated the third phase of Albanian migration from their homes through state violence. – The biggest wave f Albanian migration toward Turkey and Albania occurred during 1920-1931.- Kosova's colonization and Agricultural Reform represented the basic tools for Albanian migrations.-The beginning of negotiations between Serbia and Turkey for four hundred thousand Albanians within six years and the constituted agreement between Belgrade and Ankara.

Deportation of Albanians from their ethnic territories and the colonization of those territories with Serbs and Montenegrins, were all part of the Serbian national program. The implementation of this project started from the Balkan Wars, where the Belgrade war against the remnants of the Ottoman Empire in Albania's areas should have turned into a "liberation war" to "restore the old Serbia" against the Albanian population and its sole existence. As will be seen, during the First Balkan War, the founders of this program started its implementation. The founders were Serbian and Montenegrin military forces, as well as their ancillary services that switched the war against the Ottoman forces into a war against Albanians. Similarly this happened also in the 1877/78 war where the Serbian military forces penetrated into the Toplica district and destroyed 400 Albanian villages and settlements, which contributed to the migration of the entire population from that area.

The penetration and occupation of the Albanian areas during the First Balkan War, in autumn and winter of 1912/13, was done with the same program. Serbian and Montenegrin military forces, one from north and the other from three directions (from Ibri River, Nis, and Vardari River) attacked the undefended Albanian population, which during those invasions, in order to escape from the tragic massacre, left in two directions: toward Albania and Turkey. Those two directions were planned well ahead by the military forces and the plan was to pursue Albanians until the massive migration occurred in those two directions. In this way, according to some data, during the murders by Serbian and Montenegrin military forces, thirty thousand people were killed, around one hundred thousand Albanians had migrated as refugees to Albania, and more than fifty thousand migrated to Turkey. Most of them had migrated first into

Macedonia and Selanik, and from there they continued to Turkey. Many of them that had tried to go to Turkey through Bulgaria, Sofia (it is estimated to be twenty thousand people) were not able to do it. Many of them died in the streets, while a small portion of them had been taken under the protection of the Albanian Colony in Sofia, where, through humanitarian and religious organizations, they were directed to Turkey.

This process, which had not remained unnoticed by Europe, but also by Serbian Social Democrats,[201] still continued even after the decision by the Ambassadors Conference of London that those conquered areas by Serbian and Montenegrin military forces, would be part of these states. What is more, by late 1913 until August 1914, when World War I started, these two countries, systematically tried to use the state's tools, primarily those of the military and police forces, to continue the Albanian genocide. Well-known are Belgrade and Cetina's actions that severely provoked Albanians, such as in Dibra and Dukagjin during the autumn and winter of 1913, started a wide uprising and ended with tragic consequences, because the Serbian military force considered this as a "separatist movement" and took severe actions to actually destroy it. Similar actions took place in other areas of Kosova, where even the smallest resistance movement was followed by military response against the undefended population and its villages.

Among those harsh provocations, were also disarmament actions, mobilization actions, and particularly, religious humiliation, where religious objects were destroyed or sent into warehouses and horse barns, for military and gendarmerie comfort. Furthermore, according to note, The Third Army Command had proclaimed that they would keep all the mosques and other religious objects for war purposes.[202]

Well aware of social circumstances and also Albanian tradition, Serbian and Montenegrin military forces settled in some villages and violently built their headquarters in Albanian strongholds and removed their owners. Besides those severe actions, that ended up in the removal of their owners permanently, or in resistance (which was known how it would end), Serbian military authorities, always acting from orders to insult and

---

[201] For more information See Kosta Novakovic: *"Nacionalizacija i srbizacija Kosova,"* "La federatione balcanique," Vjenë 1931, then the newspapers *"Proleter," "Rad", "Socialistička zora," "Pravda," "Hak,"* etc.

[202] See Arhiv Jugoslavije (Yugoslavian archive), note 63, box 135, documents: 471, 14827, and 28.

humiliate the undefended Albanian population, put many of them in drudgery services for the army and at the same time continued the expulsion of large families, not taking into consideration whether they were young people, men, women, or children.

After World War I, with the formation of Serb-Croatia-Slovene Kingdom not only did this situation not change, but as it is known, with the declaration of agrarian reform in August 1920, the colonization process of Kosova and other Albanian territories that were under the surveillance of Yugoslavian Kingdom was started. In 1919-1941, Serbian bourgeoisie used the Yugoslavian state and its potential power to achieve its purpose anti-Albanian purpose. Agriculture Reform as a tool of colonization proceeded in other national discriminative forms, aimed at the destruction of Albanian ethnicity to the extent of creating a new report which was in favor of Slavic populations.

This report was well studied and its main purpose was the violent expulsion of Albanians from their territories toward Turkey and elsewhere, where on the one side Serbia used the Albanian armed resistance in the fight of protecting their territories, and from the other side it used national, economic, and political methods of discrimination, in order to create the impression for Albanians that they were strangers and enemies of the Slavic state and should therefore plan their future in other states, such as Turkey or Albania.

So here were stationed military and police forces, and economic and political discriminative methods were implemented which were meant to produce frustration, despair, and capitulation for the Albanian people. Whereas in places where Albanians revolted through armed resistance, as in the case of the Kachak movement, then this situation was used for state violence against Albanians with the purpose of destroying them, two outcomes resulted: the violent migration of Albanians, of those that resisted and of those that were declared as state enemies, and the population of their territories with Serbian colonies.

Of course this situation would create realistic circumstances for Albanians to move from their homes toward Turkey or Albania.

However, after World War I, being unable to use the war and its outcomes for Albanian migrations, as Serbia had done with the First Balkan War and whose operations had continued for one year thereafter, the migration process toward Turkey, which in most cases became an illegal act, included different factors from the Serbian military and police forces, speculators, criminals, and other benefiters, in a form of coalition. Although it can be said that from 1924 when the Republic of Turkey was declared led by Kemal Atataturk (Mustafa Qemal of Albanian oriogion) this process, at least officially, would be stopped and clarification from Belgrade would be sought; however Belgrade still continued its activities in larger proportions.

The way manipulations were done with refugees and their moving toward Turkey illegally, was best described in newspaper "Hak," which reveals the relation between the Yugoslav police and the Turkish consulate in Shkup, as well as the captain of the "Turan" ship, which transported Albanian emigrants along with Greek emigrants that were carried to Turkey according to the state agreement between Turkey and Greece for population exchange. This newspaper reported that refugees had to pay extra taxes to enter the ship, from which they were thrown into any Turkish harbor undocumented. [203]In this way, theYugoslav government succeeded in transporting to Turkey a large number of Albanians as Bulgarians. Through this process, 240 Albanian families from Prizren, Gjakova, and Peja were sent to Turkey and were left without documents in Istanbul.[204]

In order for the migration to involve the "Turkish people who had the right to visit their country of origin," the Belgrade and Turkish governments, in 1926, set in place an agreement for the evacuation of three hundred to four hundred thousand people, mainly Albanians, which between those two countries, were identified as "Turkish." This project, which later gained official support, was stopped for a while because of the newspaper "Haqimijeti Milijet" and "Milijet" of April 1927, but this did not stop the illegal transportation of Albanians toward Turkey. For this case, the major of the Zvecan district wrote to the king that "while I was a major of my region from 1924 to 1927, thirty-two thousand dangerous Albanians were expelled toward Asia, and their territories were inhabited by Montenegrins." [205]

The same agreement also addressed the migration of 6000 Albanians to Albania. From 1918 to 1929 more than one hundred thirty thousand Albanians were expelled toward Turkey by various means. This was not

---

[203] See: Newspaper "Hak," January, 30, 1924 and February 13, 1924.

[204] See the document of e Arkivit Shtetëror të Sekretariatit të Punëve të Jashtme e Mbretërisë SKS (DASIP)," 831, p. 7.

[205] Same document, no. 15

accurate data, however, because many of those migrants had been illegally transported to Turkey, and in the absence of their personal documents. The Turkish officials marked them as war refugees; the number of people that migrated from Kosova and other areas was more than one hundred thousand. In the meantime, 3126 families migrated to Albania, mostly passing the border through the northern part. Actually, this migration was never stopped because the SKS Kingdom had created permanent migration channels for Albanians in order to expel them from Dukagjin toward Albania. The methods were quite "simple:" after the actions of the Kachaks, when they murdered a policemen or a Serbian official, raids, imprisonment, and deportation of the population started, who, during their escape, were directed toward Albania. Near the border they were helped by military forces and other people; for other things needed, Belgrade was not interested.

Since Turkey had reached an agreement with Rumania, Bulgaria, and Greece for the migration of the Turkish people into Turkey, Belgrade opened the case of the "Turkish people" migration to Turkey. The Balkan Council meeting in Ankara in February 25-27, 1938, was used for this purpose, where the Minister of External Affairs of Turkey, Ruzhdi Arasi, presented the case of "Turkish" migration from the Balkans and proposed the formation of a commission consisting of two Romans, two Yugoslavs, and two Turks. In April 1938 this commission was formed and started its work on the Albanian migration from Kosova, exclusively.[206]

Ministerial conferences were held in Belgrade, four of them, from the beginning of March until the middle of June of that year. The Yugoslavian government gave priority to people that migrated from Kosova's villages, in order for the area to be emptied and ready for colonization.[207]

After many discussions regarding the number and the dynamics of the migration, the compensation that would be given to Turkey from Yugoslavia was also identified. According to this agreement, Yugoslavia would pay to Turkey the maximal compensation of fifteen thousand Dinars per family, or two to five thousand Dinars per family member, and from this compensation 20% was to be paid to Turkey in their domestic

---

[206] See: Dokumentet e Arkivit Shtetëror të Jugosllavisë DASIP, DNŽ, p. 15, doc.1 and p. 9, doc. 4.

[207] Bajrami, Hakif: *"Rrethanat shoqërore dhe politike në Kosovë më 1918-1941,"* Prishtinë, 1981, p. 159.

currency, while 80% was put in the National Bank of the Turkish Government account for the the provision of goods in Yugoslavia.[208]

The agreement between the Turk and Yugoslav government was settled on July 11. In this highly secret document are given data that explain what the purpose of the Covenant was. It states that forty thousand Muslim families would be expelled from Yugoslavia toward Turkey, from the territories that Serbia and Montenegro conquered in 1912 and 1913. The migration, according to the Covenant, would occur for six years, with provisions of extending it for one more year after the deadline. Yugoslavia would pay Turkey 500 Turkish lira per family, 30% of them in foreign currency, while 70% would be deposited in the National Bank, in the Turkish government account. With this deposited money, the Turkish government could buy goods in the Yugoslav market.[209]

According to Provision 12 of the Covenant, those that would be evacuated during migration, which would be expelled according to an annual list, must provide written declaration before the Yugoslav authorities according to Provision 53 of Yugoslavian Citizens Law, to give up willingly their Yugoslav citizenship. Those people would have the rights of immigrants according to Turkish laws, from the moment that Turkish representatives, who were working specifically on this issue, signed the annual list of migration to Turkey.

According to the Covenant, refugees that were expelled violently from their territories had the right to keep a portion of their livestock, and also the right to use the railway to Selanik, as well as other expenses that would be paid by the Turkish government.

The expulsion included this process: on July 1939, 4000 families were expelled; in 1940, 6000 families were expelled; in 1941, 7000 were expelled; in 1942, 7000 were expelled; in 1943, 8000 were expelled; in 1944, 8000 families were expelled.

The agreement and the following migration process affected the Vardar, Zeta, and Morava inhabitants, which were the Albanian-populated areas. The Yugoslavgovernment was responsible for determining the region that would start the migration.

---

[208] See: Dokumentet e Arkivit Shtetëror të Jugosllavisë DASIP, DNŽ, p. 15, doc.1; AVII. P. Box 95 a, p. 2. Doc.1.

[209] Bajrami, Hakif: *"Rrethanat shoqërore dhe politike në Kosovë më 1918-1941,"* Prishtinë, 1981, p. 160.

The Turkish government demanded the immediate approval of the Covenvant by Belgrade and Ankara. It was preferable for the Covenant not to be published because of the external and internal political circumstances. It was preferable for it to be known as a government amendment in accordance with the Financial Law of theYugoslav Kingdom.[210]

Anti-Albanian Programs of Serbian Academics and Cubrilovic's Memorandum

> *"Nacertanja" of Garashanin (document written by Garashanin explaining the procedure of Albanian cleansing), was a starting point of the Serbian hegemonic programs against Albanians and other Balkan populations. – Serbian academics, formulators, and supporters of Serbian political programs.- Intellectual Serbian Club and its role in anti-Albanian propaganda.- Publication of Vasa Cubrilovic's "Albanian Migration" of 1937, the most austere document that justified the genocide against a population from the state and would also include the use of military forces.*

Different from national politics of the eleventh century, which, for the Balkan Slavic-Orthodox population rested on expansionist ideology, Serbian nationalism projected the Great Serbia, relying on a platform of an extreme hegemonic process, that in order to realize its purposes was able to functionalize its ethnic cleansing processes, which took many forms, including those of using the "liberation" fights against the Ottoman Empire through the use of state violence. Yet without becoming a state, under the circumstances of an autonomous patriarchy, in Belgrade in the 40s of the eleventh century, the Serbian politician and diplomatic Ilia Garashanin, in 1844 published "Nacertanja," predicting the great state of Serbia would be two to three times bigger than it would actually become.

Of course, that in addition to an expansion toward the West (Bosnia and Herzegovina and Dalmatia), where the Slavic people had created the "core" of their Illyrian influx, it also expanded to Albanian territories (Kosova District, Bitola District, and Shkodra District) including Selaniku,

---

[210] *Ibid*, p.60

where the   Slavic-Macedonians constituted the majority. In this way, Serbia was planning to obtain access to two seas through Albanian territories: the Adriatic and the Aegean. For the Serbian ideology of nationalism and its hegemonic process, Serbia was "naturally" excused with the "historic medieval right." It didn't matter that this "right," which was unrealistic, was only one plan constructed over Kosova, which had to be implemented using all methods, including also those of war, which Serbia always utilized until the end of the twentieth century.

Thus, during the Serb-Ottoman war of 1876/77, Serbia made the first penetration into Nish, continuing onto Kursumli, mostly at the expense of the Albanian population. Even though Serbia lost this war from Turkey, Serbian military forces, sophisticatedly attacked Albanian territories and destroyed them and in so doing, forced a large portion of the population to leave. This warned of severe impending behavior, which Serbia utilized the following year when it used the Russian-Ottoman war and the loss of the Ottoman Empire for the same purpose, but this time with fatal consequences for Albanians, because throughout this deportation, the Serbian military forces cleansed Toplica from the all non-Serb population. In addition to the severe terror against the undefended population (it was estimated that there were more than ten thousand Albanians killed and more than fifty thousand expelled toward Turkey), more than 400 settlements were ruined. In the Peace treaty of "Saint Stephan" of March 1878 Serbia recognized these territories along with some others as part of their state, and many of these territories were recognized also by Berlin's Congress of June 1878, where Serbia as an independent state ruled 60% more than it had before, most of which was inhabited by Albanians as acknowledged by Serbian sources. According to these sources, Serbia in 1875, with 37 square kilometers of space, had 1.3 million inhabitants, 59% of them Serbian, 20% Vlahs, 30% Muslim population, mostly Albanians. The entire Toplica province (from Prokupa and Kursumli with an area of approximately eight thousand square kilometers), which one year later, during the Serb-Russian war was conquered by Serbian military force, was mainly inhabited by Albanians.[211] During this war and after the return of

---

[211] For more on the ethnic territories of Albania in Toplica district and the ethnic side of Belgrade's Pashallek, and other Serbian territories in the beginning of the Berlin Congress, see those Serbian sources: Jagodić, Miloš: „Naselevanje kneževine Srbije 1861-1880," Beograd, 2004; Protić, Stojan (Balkanicus): "Albanski problem i Srbija i Ausgro-Ugarska," Belgrade, 1913.

Serbian military forces, while eleven thousand people were killed or missing, more than one hundred thousand people migrated toward Kosova and Turkey.[212]

Feeling courageous from the Berlin Congress decisions, Serbia planned the next step to conquer the biggest part of Albanian territory, so that in cooperation with its allies (Greece, Montenegro, and Bulgaria) marked the end of the Albanian case by the division of their ethnicity into four parts, which would accompany the ethnic extinction of Albanians. This step would be accomplished through war, but this time with the purpose of being "liberated" from the Ottoman Empire, which by this time was definitely out of the European space. Seeing that Albanians from the League of Prizren, especially from the Young Turks revolution and on, were becoming stronger based on national programs aimed an autonomous Albanian state, the agreement between Hasan Prishtina and Ibrahim Pasha through which the circumstances for an Ottoman Albania was created, would be used to enter war with the Ottoman Empire.

Thus, the First Balkan war of autumn 1912, was not meant to be "liberation" from the Ottoman Empire, but more to prevent the creation of Ottoman Albania, which one day was meant to be a European Albania.

In fact, this war, on the one side was hegemonic and on the other side, invasive. It was hegemonic in that its intention was not to be "nationally liberated" – because four of these states had already exceeded their sizes of ethnic spaces, mostly in the deterioration of Albanians and their ethnicity – and invasive because after the Ottoman departure, Albanians were at risk of being invaded again, which threatened their very existence.

Following this scenario was part of the 'hidden" investigations but also open to the Balkan states (Serbia, Montenegro, Greece, and Bulgaria) that agreed among each other in the beginning of 1912 until the June of that year to divide the Albanian territories among themselves. Whether or not things would proceed in this way, was seen as soon as the war started against the Ottoman Empire, in October of that year when Hasan Prishtina signed an agreement with Ibrahim Pasha in Shkup which opened the doors for the creation of an Ottoman Albania as a new factor

---

[212] See Čubrilović, Vasa: *"Iselevanje Arnauta,"* Srpski Kulturni Klub, Belgrade, 1937, edited in „Delo," Lubljana, 1986.

in the Balkans, through which new areas of European interests were created.

Thus, the military forces of Albania's neighbors, firstly those of Montenegro, Serbia, Greece, and Bulgaria, started fighting against the Albanian population, which together with the Ottoman military forces tried to protect their territories from the new conquerers, which did not mean the "liberation" from Ottoman conquerers, but the invasion of the Albanian people and its destruction. Various European sources, constrained from entering into these zones, soon saw their real purpose when the Albanian situation against Balkan military forces was revealed.[213] Those sources noted that during the war of winter 1912-1913, the Albanian population of Kosova was subjected to genocide. From the Serbian and Montenegrin military actions, more than thirty thousand people were killed, mostly women and children, and more than six thousand were taken captive and sent to Serbian prisons, while more than one hundred thousand migrated to Turkey or Albania. This process continued also during 1913 where the Ambassador Conference of London decided that Kosova and Macedonia would remain part of Serbia, while Cameria would remain part of Greece. Well-known are the actions of the Serbian, Montenegrin, and Greek military forces that in the name of "fighting Albanian gangs" continued their politics of destroying the Albanian ethnicity. As it was seen earlier, various methods were used to force Albanians to leave their territories. In this case, it was the state's responsibility to prepare the territory for Slavic colonizers with the purpose that for a short period of time, the entire ethnicity of Albania would be changed, always to the detriment of the Albanian ethnicity and in favor of the Slavic populations.

Because World War I stopped this process for a period of time, the years between 1920 and 1940 were used for this purpose, but this time the methods of open fighting, such as those of the Balkan Wars was substituted with war against "terrorists" (this term included the Kachaks and the members of the National Resistance Movement against the Serbian invasion), as well as the state program for colonization, that used Agricultural Reform and its opportunities to take land from the Albanians, which led Albanians to migrate to other countries such as Turkey or Albania.

---

[213] More on this issue see: Leo Freundlich *"Golgota e Ballkanit"*; Novaković, Kosta: *"Nacionalizacija i serbizacija Kosova,"* Vienna, 1913.

Under these circumstances, it would be the intellectual elite of Serbia gathered in the "Serbian Cultural Club," which would continue to constantly nurture Belgrade politics and its hegemonic process to make "Nacertanja" real.

But, unsatisfied with the colonization results, which in the middle of the thirties, according to them, were not going as they had planned (ten thousand colonized families with sixty thousand family members were settled in Kosova, instead of forty thousand that were previously colonized), and even more unsatisfied with the process of Albanian migration toward Turkey and Albania (not more than one hundred fifty thousand people were expelled, while it was estimated that for twenty years this number would be doubled), the Serbian intellectual elite started to doubt the national politics of Serbia toward Kosova, that according to them, had not achieved the destruction of the Albanian ethnicity, which posed a threat to Serbian national interests. Therefore, the only solution was the massive migration of Albanians to Turkey and Albania, which should have been done through agreements with those two countries, especially with Turkey, which had already reached a similar agreement with Greece, Bulgaria, and Rumania for the acceptance of the Turkish population and its "repatriation" in Turkey.

In order for these agreements to have "intellectual" support along with an internal political consensus, the "Serbian Cultural Club" would take care to open a wide public debate regarding this case, from which a national platform would be taken, which would be obligatory for the state and their actions toward this issue, especially when this policy was starting to be disobliging from the other countries: Slovenia and Croatia and from the leftist wing of Yugoslavia (Social Democrats and communists), which, based on the principles of proletarian internationalism and its ideologic concepts of the committee, had started to oppose this policy, calling it hegemonic and chauvinistic. Therefore, under these circumstances, the Serbian hegemonic program needed a great "defense" from "Albanian risk" and also from their "proliferation in the South" that according to Dr. Borivoje Panjevaci, Secretary of State's General Statistics, "that risk would always be higher and higher for the Serbian population."[214] Moreover, Panjevaci, opening this debate in the "Serbian Cultural Club," mentioned

---

[214] Hoxha, Hajredin: *"Politika e eliminimit të Shqiptarëve nga trualli i Jugosllavisë së vjetër,"* "Përparimi," Prishtinë, nr. 5, 1970, p. 433.

that for the issue "to Albanians it is awakening the national feeling," that according to him "this alert has supportive circumstances, because the Albanian population lived in compact areas, that instead of being assimilated, as Yugoslavia wanted, it was having the opposite effect."

In addition, for Panjevci, the increase of Albanian natality was also alarming, instead of being the opposite, when for the first time he mentions the case of "biological expansion" as an Albanian "arm" which found support in the publication of Vasa Cubrilovic "Albanian's migration," where the most racist theses were expressed, similar to those of German Nazis, after coming to power, which had started with Vasa Cubrilovic's publication "Albanian migration" (Iselevanje Arnauta) held in the "Serbian Cultural Club" of Belgrade in March 1937, with its statements, which seemed "depressing" and "critical" at the same time - because on the one side the Serbian national purposes were not met and on the other side, the Yugoslav state had not used all its opportunities – in fact it promoted a state policy even more hegemonic against Albanians, where state violence was combined with diplomatic and political methods in order to justify the Albanian expulsion not only as a national strategic Yugoslavian interest, but also as an international interest, because the "keeping of the Albanian wedge" put the Central Balkan at risk, especially the fate of the Balkan communication Morave-Vardar.[215]

'The problem of the Albanians is not current with our national and state life," said Cubrilovic, to add "the Albanian triangle divided our older lands of Rasha from Macedonia and the Vardar River" and "Serbia had started to divide the Albanian wedge from the first revolt, expelling as such northern Albanians from Jahorina" in which "understanding and implementing the broad state concepts of Jovan Rastici, Serbia divided Toplica and Kamenica. At that time, provinces between Jastrebac and South Morava were cleaned entirely of Albanians."[216]

Of course that for Cubrilovic, who recognized what Serbia had done to Albanians from the time of Obrenovic, always tried to hide it by saying that they "were returning their Serbian lands" occupied by "Ottomans," at the same time criticizing the Yugoslav state for not continuing with the same intensity as that of 1876-78, saying that "the other part of the

---

[215] More on: Čubrilović, Vasa: „*Iselavanje Arnauta,*" Belgrade, 1937, „Delo," Lubljana, 1986.
[216] *Ibid.*

triangle was our state's responsibility to divide from 1918 and on," Cubrilovic did not criticize colonization methods, that were incapable of doing more than that, but demanded a new behavior, that of the massive expulsion of Albanians, which should be done with a brutal force from the organized state. "It is impossible to expel Albanians through gradual colonization" because "Albanians are the only population that through the last one thousand years achieved not only to be protected but also to expand."

Therefore, observing those developments, that for Cubrilovic was alarming, because "if Yugoslavia will not get rid of them, for 20-30 years we will have a terrifying irredentism, whose tracks are already being seen and are inevitably questioning all our invasions in the South."[217] Because the colonization had failed, Cubrilovic asked for the massive Albanian expulsion.

"Turkey had agreed to initially accept two hundred thousand Albanian immigrants, and this is the most acceptable form for us. We should accept the Turkish will by all means and utilize the Covenant as soon as possible for Migration."[218]

Conscious that this might somehow raise international concern, Cubrilovic said that "from this side we should not be worried; migration of some hundred thousand Albanians will not lead to a World war." On the contrary, for Cubrilovic "the biggest risk is that our allies France and England can be involved in this situation." But, as he always had an answer just as in this case he said that "we should respond with determination to them, because the taking of Morava-Vardar is in their interest, which was also seen during the last war, and this would be safer for us, but also for them, only when we conquer all the areas around Sharri mountain in Kosova."[219]

According to Cubrilovic and his fellow Serbian political and intellectual elite, in order for the massive migration of Albanians to be successful, Yugoslavia would need to pay attention to the circumstances that should be created for this process. He felt that it was important to create a suitable obsession, which could be accomplished in many ways, and as always, cited the buying of clerics and other influential people, who would con-

---

[217] *Ibid.*

[218] *Ibid.*

[219] *Ibid.*

tribute to the migrations, and states that "our press can make colossal actions." Turkey would also be part of this propaganda, along with the constant praise of the happy life there, where religion and Albania's connection to it would also play a strong role.[220]

In addition to this prerequisite, for Cubrilovic, however, the state and the tools it used were important, "by making life harder for Alabnians as much as possible." Among these activities, he stated that all methods of law enforcement capable of being used should be implemented including but not limited to: fines, imprisonment, ruthless execution of all police orders, and forced work in sweatshops. Also, judicial and economic pressure should be added by failing to recognize their land ownership, taxing profusely, forcing the settlement of all public and private debts, taking concessions, revoking their working licenses, and firing them from public and private employment positions.

It was important to make Albanians' life difficult in order to make them migrate as soon as possible; "sanitary measures" were also applied to achieve this end such as the destruction of the walls inside of houses that affected the morale of the Albanians, the use of severe veterinary measures that would make it impossible for Albanians to conduct trade with their animals, the destruction of tombstones, the forbidding of marriages and many other offenses of daily life.

Another aspect of the state violence was the distribution of arms to colonizers in order to organize Cetnik attacks. With these measures, Cubrilovic demanded the constant provocation of Albanians by Montenegrin colonizers who created conflict with the Albanians of Dukagjin. This created the illusion that Albanians were revolting and that state intervention was needed to crush them.

The final resort to fulfill Cubrilovic's purpose, "was the tool that Serbia had effectively used during 1878, which was the burning of villages and Albanian cities."[221]

"Villages are compact places, therefore they present a risk," he said, and that "the middle class and the rich should also be expelled, not only the poor. Only in this way would the process of Albanian migration be created and our South completely depleted," because "by sparing neither

---

[220] *Ibid.*
[221] *Ibid.*

blood nor money, our state could create a new entity of Toplica from Kosova and Metohija."[222]

The creation of "a new Toplica" from Kosova and Metohija, has to do with the repetition of the ethnic "cleansing" as was done in the Serbian-Ottoman war of 1876/77, and that of Russian-Ottoman war of 1878, where Serbia entered Toplica militarily and eradicated all the Albanians living there. As would be seen, this scenario, Cubrilovic mentioned some years later, at the end of World War II when he published "Minorities' problems in new Yugoslavia," and submitted in November 1955 to the National-Liberation Anti-Fascist Movement of Yugoslavia (LANJQ) to resolve the problem of Albanians and Hungarian minorities by claiming that they were fascist.

In addition to the Cubrilovic publication "Albanian Migration" which was used as a very important reference for the Yugoslavian-Turkish Covenant for the movement of Albanians to Turkey, these arrangements continued until the World War II circumstances excluded it from being implemented. The "Serbian Cultural Club" continued to show different opinions on this topic, whose common denominator was a Yugoslav state that would utilize everything in its power to make the Albanians migrate to Turkey or Albania. Among many opinions, some proposed that in addition to expelling Albanians from their country, they were also considering the possibility of ethnically moving Albanians to Bosnia and Herzegovina and Croatia. Joko Perina, a member of the Serbian Cooperative League of Sarajevo, proposed the cyclic movement within the state. According to him, this switch of Albanian population did not require sophisticated tools, while Albanians would be assimilated into the Slavic culture.[223]

Of course, in this process, in addition to the external factors that played a crucial role, it was also the Albanian's resistance against Serbian hegemonic forces (using armed resistance and also commitment to the political issues of the country), which was noted by Cubrilovic when he wrote "the Albanian nationality that is increasing everywhere" on the one side and from the other side the "Albanian women's fertility which defeated our colonialism policy."

---

[222] *Ibid.*

[223] Hoxha, Hajredin: *"Politika e eliminimit të Shqiptarëve nga trualli i Jugosllavisë së vjetër,"* in *"Përparimi,"* nr.5, 1970, p. 434.

The Political Participation of Albanians

Despite continuous state violence and terror used to displace them from their homes, to which they were forced to respond with armed resistance, Albanians tried to use political and institutional tools to fight for their denied identity and their rights as citizens. The first Albanian congregation was the one of 1919 under "Xhemjet" and it dealt with the protection of freedoms and religious rights. – The first Albanian deputies in the elections of 1920 and Belgrade's efforts to prevent a political union. – The collapse of "Xhemjet" and the various forms of prosecution of Albanian leaders. – The Radical and Republican Party forced Albanians to vote for them, while in the meantime the election campaigns turn into anti-Albanian demonstrations. – The efforts of Albanians to benefit from the involvement in the Serbian political parties and Yugoslav democratic charade, which led to the destruction of the country.

Despite the armed resistance against Serbian occupations, such as those during 1912-1913, which were reflected by the Kachak movement and other forms of popular resistance which greatly slowed down the colonization process of Kosova to bring it close to failure, the involvement of Albanians in the politics of the country was also another form of resistance against their displacement to Turkey and other countries as foreseen with the grand Serbian hegemonic programs which were imposed on Yugoslavia by Belgrade.

Although the involvement of Albanians in the political sphere of the country was unique because of the extraordinary conditions which they experienced due to the state terror exercised on them with the aim of displacing them to other countries; at the same time, politically it turned into a tragic farce despite all the weaknesses and inevitable manipulations through which they passed, in the end it was seen as part of the institutional resistance of migrating to Turkey. Without this segment, the expulsion of Albanians to Turkey and other places not only would have reached its maximum, but in the meantime, it would represent the end of ethnic Albanians in this region, the remains of which would join a literary creation referred to as "Muslim" or a similar creation that would later on be represented as "Islamized Slavs" which "had the opportunity to express the identity of their roots!"

Nevertheless, despite these specific conditions which were experienced, the involvement of Albanians in the politics of the country would actually begin after 1920, when the Serb-Croat-Slovene Kingdom declared parliamentarism, which at least formally Albanians should have been subject to, although their national identity was not accepted, only their religious one (as Muslims, which on this premise could be declared as Turkish). Furthermore, it can be said that some symbolic participation of Albanians (obviously the Muslim population) was also interested in the SCS Kingdom, despite the hegemonic and chauvinistic policy imposed on them by Serbs as a state-forming population, which was the key to the Karageorgevic dynasty. By means of parliamentarism, the world impression of this country and all its citizens without distinction was that everyone was equal in the political and economic development plan. However, this was not the case since the internal plan separated a feudal group from the rest of the wide population while turning them into Serbian nationalistic party toys with which they would win future votes, stimulating even more the expulsion of Albanians to Turkey and other places.

However, Albanians, even as Turks, Muslims or others, present in Kosova and their territories included in the Kingdom of SCS, appeared as the electorate which turned them into subjects of political parties which needed their votes, where a good number of deputies could be obtained (up to 20, a number that was equal to approximately 9% of the total number of seats in the parliament), but in order to obtain that number they had to compromise based on the conditions presented to them. Thus, by 1919 along with the Nikola Pasic Radical Party, which had continued its operations from the time of the Serbian Kingdom, in the territory of Kosova the Democratic Party of Svetozar Pribicevic also appeared, which was founded in Sarajevo and whose program was mostly biased toward the bourgeoisie concepts of Western Europe. Then, there were the leftist socialists' parties which appeared with ideological programs, Social Democrats and Communists displaying class equality, while the Great Serbian hegemonic parties and royal dynasty were heavily criticized parties that together with "Obzana" would later be banned, so they would go underground.

In these circumstances, the Radicals and Democrats remained the leading contenders for the Kosova electorate. The Democratic Party, although Serb-nationalistic from their point of view, at least declaratively, in its program tried to affirm the idea of a common Yugoslav state on a centralized basis. This party, which felt like "state-building," tried to harmonize the national unilateralism with state interests, but greatly favoring the Serbian bourgeoisie.[224]

Viewed from this perspective the Democratic Party seemed far away from the Kosova Albanian electorate Pasic Radical Party, because the Radical Party, despite its nationalistic program, back in the Conference of 1920 brought some changes to its program making it thus adapt to the new circumstances created. On this occasion, the Radicals asserted that they were committed to the principle of self-government in the province, municipality, district and country, to the extent that it did not put to the test the state community. This party also provided the protection of private property, private capital as well as stimulated capitalism, which appeared captivating for the feudal layer, which were keen to preserve properties and capital as well.

Moreover, the party urged Albanians to join in its pioneering activities in Kosova, while promising equality in education, culture, economics, and all other areas without excluding the regional self-government and the municipal one, where state interests would prevail.[225]

These promises and similar ones made by some of the local Albanian leaders generated their interest in the party, with whom they were beginning to cooperate. In addition to this, the leader of this party, Pasic, was in power and kept the country's policy in check, causing it to turn into a party state.

However, for certain Albanian political forces among the few feudal or Islamic clergy, despite the difficult circumstances the Albanian population was found in such as constant discrimination and without excluding the state terror and violence used on them in the name of implementing the "Law for Protection of the State" and other similar decrees "against terrorism," the first political party was founded under the name of "Islamic Association Muhavazi Hukug" or "Xhemjet," in Shkup, which among the Albanians was referred to as "Union." Its founding assembly was held on December 18, 1919. The founding meeting was attended by 64 partici-

---

[224] More broadly about the Democratic Party see Gavrilović, Branislav: „Demokratska stranka," Beograd, 1970.

[225] More broadly about the Radical Party see Mitrović, Živan: "Srpske političke stranke," Beograd, 1939.

pants. The elected Chairman was Nexhip Draga, a worthy warrior of the Albanian National Movement (deputy in the Osman Parliament), the elected Deputy Chairman was Sheh Sadedini, while the Secretary was Aqif Blyta from Gjakova. The official politics of the SCS Kingdom praised the "Southern Congress of Muslims," composed of "Turks, Islamized Slavs, and Arnauts (Albanians)."[226]

In reality "Xhemjet" was masked religiously (Islam), had Turkish orientation (its newspaper "Hak" would be published in Turkish and Serbian), while it was known that it represented and protected the interests of Albanians. This was a necessary mask because the SCS Kingdom did not recognize the Albanian nationality, while it recognized the Turkish one and accepted the "Islamic identity," which was allowed in the social, cultural, and political plan.

It is obvious that inside this construct the interests of Albanians had to be protected, at least on the social and economic plan, where the defense against discrimination as well as expulsion from the country would be presented as main priorities.

This party failed to preserve its autonomy because it was in the middle of two fierce rival political parties in Kosova, the Radical and Democratic parties. These parties were interested in the Kosova electorate, but only to the extent that they were a servant assigned certain duties and given rewards for completing them. But even in this regard, 'Xhemjet" started to narrow its space, especially after the pronouncements against the displacement of Albanians and the Albanian Muhajirun return request made by the deputy Ferat Draga in the Yugoslav Parliament. He represented this statement to the Hague Conference, a statement that prompted Belgrade to work to destroy this party from within by establishing different factions, while also using external pressure which led to its destruction ["Xhemjet"] four years later, and even caused the imprisonment of Ferat Draga.[227]

As an effect of these pressures, when two - three factions came to the scene they demanded that the party return to the religious base at the Second Congress in 1921 in which the party changed its name to "Muslim Organization of South Serbia in the SCS Kingdom." This showed clearly that Belgrade did not want any political engagement of Albanians, despite

---

[226] See: "Arhiv Vojnog Insitutat Istorije Jugosllavije" (AVII), P. IV/3, Box 54, doc. 228/2.
[227] See: Newspaper "Pravda," 18.I.1925.

the religious one which suited them for two reasons. Firstly, they wanted to eliminate any element of national identity, and secondly, they wanted to impose upon them the religious and Turkish identity because in that way, the displacement of Albanians would be made much easier. Those that could not endure the discrimination and constant state violence used on them would then be inclined to leave the country.

In accordance with this orientation imposed by the state, the organizational structure of this party would be compiled in the Third Congress which would be held on April 4, 1992. This congress was already characterized as a broad society which would incorporate all political perspectives in which Albanians were a part without the possibility of identifying themselves as such. Therefore, there were 11 Albanian deputies that participated in this congress, deputies who were chosen in the Yugoslav parliament. The Congress selected as its leaders, President Qenan Zijanë from Manastir, Vice President Ismet Bej Kemalina, a deputy from Gjakova, and Treasurer Kemal Osman from Shkup. From Kosova, the representatives were: from Prishtina, Haxhi Xhemajl Efendija and Sylejman Haxhi Efendija; from Gjilan, Hysein Agë Okllani and Sherif Bajrami; from Peja, Nazif Bej; from Pazar, Aqif Haxhi Ahmeti. Sali Jusufi was also a participant in this congress as the representative of Llap. The congress decided that "Hak" would be published every day in Turkish, while twice a week in Serbian. The newspaper had to be edited and published in Belgrade.[228] These conditions were important for the Yugoslav regime through which they imposed on Albanians a Turkish identity along with the Serbian one.

However, before this happened, Kosova would have its first parliamentary elections: the municipality one in August of 1920, and the parliamentary one on the November 28, 1920. These elections were used as demonstrations of the hegemonic politics of Belgrade in this territory which in turn would benefit the already-present displacement of Albanians to other countries.

Four parties competed in the parliamentary elections in Kosova: the Radical Party, the Democratic Party, the Communist Party and "Xhemjet." The last one was in coalition with the Radical Party which came to win three deputies, one of them Albanian (Mehmet Ali Mahmuti). These four parties won 18 deputies, where 10 of them were

---

[228] See: *"Iz Istorije Jugoslavije,"* Beograd, 1958, p. 199.

Serbian and 8 Albanian. It is worth mentioning that in Kosova 85,159 people had the right to vote, of whom 46,561 exercised their right. The party that won the most deputies was the Democratic Party with a total of 9 (four Albanians: Sherif Bajrami, Ramush Osmani, Sefedin Mahmutbegu and Ismet Karabegu). Then, the Radical Party won three deputies (one Albanian: Musa Sheh Zade), while the Communist Party won three deputies as well (one Albanian: Ethem Bylbyli from Zveçan).[229]

The parliamentary elections of 1920, although they were supposed to follow an election framework, still managed to turn into a manifestation of hegemonic Serbian plans where an anti-Albanian spirit dominated. This atmosphere came to the surface especially after the final results were published when the Radicals of Pasic, who were disappointed that they did not win more than three deputies (they estimated to win around 12-13), returned to their well-known methods of dealing with Albanians. This time, in February of 1921, after demonstrations occurred in Prishtina and other places around Kosova under the many threats directed at them, the Belgrade police directed by the Radicals with the justification of cleaning the place from Kachaks, who happened to have killed a gendarme (although this was not confirmed from the Albanian population and there was not even talk of a "war" with Kachaks as it was announced from all sides), entered Llap and committed a true genocide by killing and massacring hundreds of Albanians. A similar approach was also taken in other places, cities, and Albanian villages where the actions of the gendarmerie accompanied with local Chetniks gathered around the "patriotic" society "Bela Ruka" founded by Radicals for "protection from terrorists," tried to justify themselves through the "terror" of the Kachaks.[230]

The first legislation which was gathered on December 8, 1920 brought the first changes which damaged the democracy, but benefited the Unitarian force, which was led by the Serbian political parties (Radical and Democratic ones). These parties enforced the new constitution which brought the law of "Protection of the State" which expelled the labor movement and the leftists from the Democrats. Through this law, minorities did not have the right to enter politics and for that matter, political

---

[229] See: "*Arhiv Jugoslavie*" (Yugoslav archive), sinjatura 14, fascikli 15/18, doc. 1129 and 27625.

[230] About the massacres that happened in Kosovo during the months of Feb-April 1921, see newspapers "*Pravda*," Feb. 1921,"*Hak*," Feb. 1921 and "*Samouprava*," 3 Feb. 1921.

parties. A discriminating platform was created for their political participation in "state-forming" parties which asked for signatures of state
loyalty, the declarations of readiness to enter the "anti-terrorism" war and
recognition of Serbian literacy. The last one made it impossible for the
majority of the Albanian population to participate in any political activity
and the right to be chosen since at that time only few people actually
could fulfill this requirement.

Under these circumstances, the Radical violence began in Kosova.
This political party, the party in power which consisted also of members
from "Xhemjet," undertook a broad demonstration campaign as a state
party which tried to be violently imposed on Albanians leaving them with
no other alternative. In accordance to this objective, the Radicals established party branches in each city of Kosova while putting in leading
positions, people with power and influence, as well as others who were
obliged to declare that they were "voluntarily" joining this party. The
"White Hand" or as it was known "Bela ruka" (a paramilitary Chetnik
unit related to the royal yard) brought citizens to the congregations
organized by this party and forced them to join. It even went as far as
forcing Albanians to conduct introductory speeches for this party. [231]

This contributed toward "Xhemjet" joining the coalition with the
Radicals in the elections of 1923, a "relationship" which was very unnatural and damaging to "Xhemjet," but imposed and foreseen to destroy it.
This destruction occurred two years later when the Radicals were not able
to supervise all the actions of its leaders, especially authorities such as
Ferat Draga, who would try to use the parliamentary space to bring to the
surface the terrible conditions of Albanians and the violence used against
them. His attitudes were already known to be against the Albanian
displacement to Turkey and the agrarian reform which was put in place to
colonize Kosova with Serbs, as well as, his declarations and protests
against the use of state violence against the Albanians by military radicals,
Democrats, and the "White Hand". This violence was justified on the
basis that it was used against "terrorism," but in this case terrorists were
considered the Albanians who did not support and comply with the
suppressing politics of Belgrade and those who opposed their displacement to Turkey. Although in a coalition with the Radicals, Ferat Draga,
who was considered by the Democrats and others as an "instrument of

---

[231] More broadly see the newspaper *"Samouprava"* Feb-March 1922.

radicals," began to display the mutual agreements between the two political parties considered as "enemies," which were actually working toward state terror in Kosova. As evidence for this, he brought the case of the municipal elections of August 1923 before the Yugoslav parliament, when the whole of Kosova, especially in Mitrovica, these parties organized state terror against Albanians:

> All those who use terror during municipal elections are considered neither Radicals nor Democrats because they are bloodsuckers, because the oppressor will always remain as such. It is shameful and foolish for so much blood to be shed in Prishtina and Mitrovica, and this to happen on the day of elections.[232]

On this occasion Draga also explained the reasons why he joined the Radicals, reasons that according to him where inevitable in order to achieve some objectives:

> We from the Radical Party have not requested anything else besides what is guaranteed by the Constitution and existing laws. From all this we have not obtained anything, even though the Constitution provides the guaranty. We cannot open schools to be conducted in the national [Albanian] language although the law permits us to do that.[233]

However, Ferat Draga, would become an enemy with his "allies" although he criticized and tried to halt the displacement of Albanians to Turkey, a very important objective of the hegemonic politics of Belgrade. Besides the denunciations he made toward state militants, who operated openly in terrorizing the Albanian population, as in the case of Milic Krste from the Istog district for whom he stated that he "was armed to the teeth and killed as he wanted," Draga would also denunciate the Agrarian Reform which was openly utilized as a tool of colonization of Kosova with Serbs and other Slavic populations:

> We are not against the agrarian reform. Let it be implemented in places with little population. We consider that firstly land should be provided to the domestic farmers who have insufficient land, and from what is left to be given to settlers, hardworking farmers if necessary. But among the settlers that are brought here, the majority of them are not farmers, as for example,

---

[232] See the newspaper *"Hak,"* 17 Oct 1923.
[233] *Ibid.*

in the Dukagjin region there are cases when the settler holds the rifle, the lute, and sits under the shade while Albanians work the land under the pressure of the "authority" of the rifle. There are cases when an Albanian sows, reaps, and makes bundles, then the settler comes and takes the sheaves and brings them to his place. All this is done with the primary purpose to appall the Albanian population and motivate them to evacuate.[234]

Draga would protest with the words that "the problem of the minorities, in this case Albanians, is bringing dire implications for them. The tendency to eliminate Albanians is impossible to be realized. Melting this population and migration will never become a reality."[235]

These and other similar declarations by Ferat Draga, as well as, constant articles in the "Hak" newspaper discussing the organized crimes against the Albanian population in Kosova conducted under the supervision of special military and police services were not left unheard in the internal opinion of the country, and also the outside. Such declarations made "Xhemjet" and its leaders, Ferat Draga and others, who did not agree to what was happening in Kosova and other places populated by Albanians, Radicals and Democrats (the first ones in particular controlled the state power), begin compiling the scenario for destroying "Xhemjet" and the political liquidation of Draga and other leaders, even though, they from the beginning were forced to join the party, won the synonym "associate of Radicals" something that lowered their authority to a number of Albanians who considered them as "their [Radicals'] tools."

The order for destruction of "Xhemjet" and its leaders, primarily Draga, came from Pasic, who was sent to Kosova by his emissary, Toma Popovic. The orders were that for a part of "Xhemjet" among the Muslim fanatics related to the clergy, they would try to win them over by connecting them directly to the Radicals. It is obvious that this connection had to be done by providing promises and some favors to them, while the split from the inside with accusations and counteraccusations among themselves would remain permanent for "Xhemjet." Since there were other factors present among the Albanians (despite Croats who were looking for allies against the increasing Serbian hegemonic tendency), Radicals of Pasic, but also Democrats, requesting to halt at any cost any authority among Albanians, which although not much, would certainly contribute

---

[234] "Hak," nr. 689.

[235] "Hak" nr. 693.

toward staining the Yugoslav political scene. In this direction the Serbian political parties agreed completely and as it would be seen, they would split certain tasks and responsibilities in order for it to happen faster and through brutal means. This was to be done by having two main objectives in mind: firstly, the elimination from the political scene of those who were not supervised by Serbs, and secondly, afflicting Albanians by making them lose hope that they would survive by joining the local alliances against the Serbian hegemony which would ultimately cause them to migrate to other places. Therefore, it emerges that which will later be proven that the Serbian hegemonic politics in the political scenes in Kosova and other parts of Yugoslavia did not have political objectives, or parliamentarism establishment, but they were rather conducted to demonstrate violence. It was the use of violence which would be utilized in fulfilling the national hegemonic programs, which were in the open since "Nacertanja" of Garasan and would later on become available to the morbid electorate compiled by the Serbian elite, as the one of Cubrilovic that would later on be manifested in the "Serbian Cultural Club."

In reality this determination that later on would cause the fall of the Yugoslav of Versailles, began to be tested in Kosova on Albanians with the aim of being used on others as well (Croats, Slovenes), as would be the case with the elimination of the Croatian political leader Stjepan Radic in the Yugoslav parliament. This "trial" would begin with "Xhemjet" and its main leaders even though during the entire time they would be used as coalition partners, but would fall because the Unitarian and hegemonic Serbian parties would understand quite well that even in circumstances of violent "collaboration" with these political parties, even in circumstance of their vassal behavior, this was not only unsuitable but caused the opposite, because to Albanians, as Cubrilovic would take notice in his known elaboration "The Displacement of Albanians" the conditions of survival and oppression would "increase the national awareness of Albanians and with it irredentism as an inevitable phenomenon."[236]

This depressing evaluation led the Serbian hegemonic politics toward more radical measures including state terror and the evacuation of Albanians in great numbers. Indeed, for Pasic and others this would involve several steps: starting from in 1925 using them [Albanians] for the interest of the Serbian political parties, then from 1925 to 1938, the

---

[236] More broadly see Čubrilović, Vasa: *"Iselavanje Arnauta,"* Belgrade, 1937.

elimination of their political parties and melting the Albanian electorate with the Serbian political parties, and lastly, 1938 to 1941, removing them from any political determination. The last phase would be the most radical one which would enforce the violent displacement and evacuation of Albanians to Turkey through the use of the national convention with this country, as it was harmonized with the Ankara government, but whose ratification was left due to the Second World War.

The state terror by the Radicals was also proven in a letter from the German Embassy in Belgrade sent to the German Ministry of Foreign Affairs. The letter revealed that before the elections the government had begun with terror and Pasic and Pribicevic were directly involved. It was further stated that severe terror was evident especially in the region of Kosova and Dukagjin.[237] The same source revealed that terror was even used in councils of "Xhemjet", in cities where the government destroyed them by forcing their leaders to migrate to Turkey. There were similar cases in Gjakova, Peja, Istog, Drenica and others where they would be declared Kachak.[238]

To destroy "Xhemjet" or as known among Albanians, "Union," Pasic decided to first imprison Ferat Draga. Draga was put into prison in January 21, 1925 by the order of the mayor of Mitrovica, who personally communicated the decision to him. He was given a quick trial, mainly political, declared "guilty" and sentenced to 20 years in prison. The charges were that he killed Serbs during the First World War, but was saved by the amnesty of the King together with Bedri Pejani. He was imprisoned in 1927, but again released from punishment "on pardon." Besides Draga, other individuals with authority were arrested and sentenced. The police undertook concise and broad measures against Albanian deputies, targeting key authorities at them.[239]

Even though judicial proceedings against Ferat Draga aimed at his removal from politics, the major changes in the country's political scene and its players caused Draga to return to politics, but not in the foreground like before. Since, being a reference for all political gatherings in the country which changed their form but not their content, Draga "from the shadow" influenced these reports and to some extent even shaped

---

[237] See Avramovski, Žarko: „*Diplomatski izveštaji,*" document 79, 85.

[238] *Ibid.*

[239] See the newspaper report *"Politika"* of 1 Feb, 1925.

their direction. In the last years, he would come to help the Stojadinovic government in having as many Albanian supporters as possible, as this dealt with his political course which differed from the traditional Belgrade one because it was directed toward France, and the Axis countries such as Germany and Italy.

In this atmosphere, the elections of February 1925 were held in which the government formed a coalition with "the national bloc" composed of the Radicals and Democrats whose motto was "the anti-terrorism war," which translated into the social and political reality meant a war "against Albanians." This contributed to the worsening of the situation in Kosova because on Election Day, the army and gendarmerie came into action which ensured the majority of votes for this governance. Therefore, during elections not only Albanian politicians were imprisoned, but also their families.[240]

The practical curfew conditions established in Kosova during the elections of 1925, where the winners were the most extreme Serbian forces: the Radicals and Republicans spread these conditions to other parts of the country as well. The Serbian national-hegemonic bloc already felt threatened by any type of democratization of the country; therefore, the model of Kosova started to be carried to other parts, especially Croatia, where the nucleus which could tear down the Serbian hegemonism was being created. Ultimately, it was natural that these developments led to the assassination attempt against Stjepan Radic, the Head of the "Croatian People's Peasant Party" in the Belgrade parliament. By making use of this situation to promote a monarchial dictatorship, the king dissolved the Assembly and on January 6, 1929 annulled the Constitution of 1921. It was therefore a coup that brought to power the king who turned into a dictator. In fact, the king with this act, did nothing more than realize the Serbian hegemonic bourgeoisie desire that instead of a hegemonic Yugoslavia, a hegemonic Serbia was created.[241]

Regarding Kosova, the January 6 dictatorship brought an even more serious situation where the political and social circumstances became more difficult since the Albanian population was experiencing strong denationalization politics, while the torture continued and increased in frequency, and the colonization and displacement continued like before

---

[240] Čulinović, Ferdo: „*Jugoslavija između dva rata,*" Zagreb, 1961.
[241] Novaković, Kosta: „*Nacionalizam i srbizacija Kosova,*" Vienna, 1931.

with the only difference being that the moving mass had become even greater.[242]

The monarchical dictatorship in some aspect, but under the cloak of parliamentarism, continued even after September 3 when the King formally proclaimed the Constitution. In accordance with it, on November 8, 1931 the parliamentary elections were announced for the Yugoslav assembly. By law, Kosova was separated in four voting regions and could provide 15 deputies/seats. Compared to previous elections when it could obtain 22 seats, this time the parliamentary representation had been considerably lowered.

Although the new Constitution led to many changes in the political scene, not as much in the quality aspect, but more on the formal one, the present actors of Radicals and Republicans would lose their influence and as a consequence their space was occupied by political parties which were directed by the royal court. Thus, the *"National Yugoslav Party"* (Jugoslovenska nacionalna stranka) emerged on the scene. Despite this governmental party, another party emerged, namely the *"Yugoslav Nationwide Party"* (Jugoslovenska narodna stranka) which was supposed to bring some opposition, but it remained a partner of the above-mentioned party as it was led by the Ministry of Internal Affairs, as such, by the police. However, this party gathered millionaires and capitalists who focused on economic plans.

After the parliamentary elections of November 1931 which brought to power the monarchist bloc, which continued the dictatorship under the guise of parliamentarism, the elections of 1935 had in total four lists. The first one was the royal bloc with the governmental list of the Prime Minister Jevtic; the second one was the united opposition which was represented by the Slovene Macek; the third list was represented by "pasica," the former radicals who lost the positions they had, but saved the influence they could exert on certain Serbian hegemonic counties because they were still militants of the politics favoring the displacement of Albanians to Turkey, the assassins of whom still operated in Kosova under the direction of Belgrade police and army. The last list was the one

---

[242] Bajrami, Hakif: *"Rrethanat shoqërore dhe politike në Kosovë më 1918-1941,"* Prishtina, 1981, p. 247.

229

of "Zbor" which was represented by the Croatian Lotic, with fascist ideas. All these lists were presented in all regions of Kosova.[243]

In these elections, as expected, the winner was the governmental party, therefore the royal one, which won the necessary number of deputies to dominate the parliament without any concern that could come from the assembly. In the new parliament there were three Albanian deputies from the governmental party (Xhemajl A. Limani from Prizren, Ramadan F. Ramadani from Podgur, Behlul A. Haliti from Gora, Shaqir Halili from Llap, Mustafa Dërguti from Podrimja, Mahmut Begu from Peja, Zeqir Zeqiri from Gjilan and Sherif Beqir Voca from Vuçitërna).

This legislation, although it will be remembered for the major changes in the course of traditional Yugoslav politics, was now directed toward France and the Axis countries of Germany and Italy. This change occurred as a result of the influence Knjaz Pavli had on Milan Stojadinovic to dissolve the government in the meeting of the Ministerial Council.

The Stojadinovic government decided that the next elections were going to be held in December of 1938. In the political plan nothing really changed. The governmental bloc was the one to connect the royal court, which was supported by Serbian politics, to the opposing bloc of Macek, who sought the change of the Constitution and federalism of the country, a movement supported by other populations who as united could win the majority, while the third force was "Zbori."

In this political constellation, it would be noticed that Albanians tried to maneuver around the party in power, namely Stojadinovic, from whom they would request as a requirement for his party to stop the displacement of Albanians to Turkey. Although with no political party, Ferat Draga's presence was again felt; he was by now the Head of Vakef of Shkup. He appeared with two memoranda, which were sent to Stojadinovic, who showed "understanding" for them, but the reviewing issue was delegated to the Bosnian, Mehmet Sparo, who was part of his cabinet. It is known that Draga together with other local authorities and Muslim clergy would support the Stojadinovic party, which would win the majority of votes in Kosova and other Albanian-inhabited parts. So his Kosova list won a total of 226,716 votes, while the Macek list won 74,977 votes. On this occasion, from Kosova the mandate of deputy was won by a total of 11 Albanians coming from the party of Stojadinovic.

---

[243] Čulinović, Ferdo: „Jugoslavija između dvar rata," Zagreb, 1961, p. 98.

The Stojadinovic party won convincingly, though with fraud, under the pressure of international events which led to the strengthening of fascism and the announcement of a new world crisis. Therefore to prevent a greater impact on the home front, the royal palace, the Belgrade Serbian politics turned to an agreement with the Croats, who sought internal federalism as a condition for continuing the preservation of the common country. The King brought to power Dragisa Cvetkovic who among the Croatian partner found Vladimir Maçekun, with whom it was agreed to federalism in the country, thus creating the province of Croatia. This action of Belgrade satisfied the Croatian bloc, but it did not weaken the positions of Serbs as expected, and as the Albanians and other people oppressed by the Serbian hegemonism had hoped.

The Albanian factor, although it did not have the right to establish its own political party after the annexation of Albania by Italy and the introduction of Germans in Poland, therefore, under the pressure of these events that had begun to change the European political scene, was liberated to some extent from the internal violence used continuously against it. Furthermore, Turkey's official withdrawal from the ratification of the Convention with Belgrade for the expulsion of Turks and Muslims (Albanians) from Kosova and other Albanian-inhabited places slowed the pace of this process, while in some parts, stopped it completely.

In these developments, Ferat Draga reappeared as the Head of the Vakuf of Shkup who tried to preserve the role of the principal around whom the entire Albanian political and cultural issues were revolving. Thus, under his direction, the Albanian political party tried to get organized, as the first of a kind, but it would do so under the umbrella of the governmental party (the Stojadinovic party), as it was concluded that in those circumstances it would be more useful to cooperate with Belgrade than with some federalist declarations of Croats, who were acting based on their own self-interest. During a meeting of Ferat Draga with Albanian leaders (Iliaz Agushi, Qerim Zena, Jusuf Imeri, Sherif Voca, Adem Marmellaku, Jahja Daci, Sadik Kurti and Asim Lush) in the second half of 1939 it was specifically discussed that the royal governmental bloc should accept the legitimacy of the Albanian group within it.

Yugoslavia, which from 1935 onwards entered secret talks with Italy about a possible bargain regarding the eventual division of Albania and the new division of spheres of interest in the Balkans, was now very close to a direct relationship with these countries, as Stojadinovic initially and after him the Cvetkovic-Macek government saw its interests reflected by the Axis powers. For Belgrade, the annexation of Albania by Italy represented a good opportunity for Serbia, but also represented a threat because it would have to join this bloc. The opportunity had to do with the agreement with Italy for a possible split of Albanian areas according to their own interests, while the threat had to do with the reluctance to accept the pact with the Allies which meant the creation of the Great Albania.

It is inevitable that this threat would force Belgrade formally from the beginning of 1941 to join the Tripartite Pact, which was signed by the Cvetkovic-Macek government in March of that year in Berlin.

The Serbian and Croatian bourgeoisie, the rightists, were forced to accept the fascist pressure, while the leftist of the country organized by the European rightists (primarily Great Britain), ruined the Tripartite. Thus, a different situation was brought in the country, which proceeded the destruction of Versailles Yugoslavia, which, following the German attack on April 6, 1941 resulted in the capitulation of Belgrade six days later.

Ironically, the rapid capitulation of Yugoslavia and the creation of new circumstances that caused the destruction of the artificial Yugoslavia that was created in Versailles, engaged the leftist Yugoslavs (primarily Communists). During the entire time, these leftists were called "the prison of people," "artificial creation," "creators of the Great Serbian hegemony" and other similar phrases. In this newly created situation of anti-fascism, they would undertake not only the responsibility of protecting it, but in the end, restoring it, although this time as a communist state in the Easter Bloc.

CHAPTER 4
FASCISM, COMMUNISM, AND THE REUNIFICATION OF ALBANIA

The Fascist Occupation and Creation of Greater Albania

Albania was the first victim of Italian fascism. – The Albanian leftists and the influence of the Yugoslav communists toward the creation of the Communist Party of Albania. – The Collapse of Versailles Yugoslavia in April 1941 and the unification of the majority of Kosova and Macedonia's valleys with Albania. – The welcoming of fascists in Kosova as liberators. – The beginnings of the anti-fascist front in Albania under the supervision of Yugoslavs. – The Mukaj agreement and its termination. – Italy's capitulation, the arrival of the German forces and the separation of Albania's royal "crown" from fascist Italy. – The Second League of Prizren as a necessary patriotic movement and the risk of quisling anathemas.

The Yugoslav-Albanian Agreements of 1925 and 1926 stabilizd the Albanian state in terms of Eastern and Northeastern borders. In the meantime the remaining Albanians in the Yugoslav state, detached from Albania since the First Balkan War, continued to be held under pressure by Belgrade. Indeed, Belgrade did its best in destroying their Albanian ethnic structure (through the colonization of Kosova with Serbs and Montenegrins as well as their displacement to Turkey). Neither the Albanian state nor the Yugoslav one as artificial entities resulting from the Peace Conference in Paris would create safety or long life for them. As it will be seen, the emergence of the European fascism, initially in Italy and then in Germany, destroyed the Versailles entities. Albania was swallowed by Italy as it tried to save the "royal crown" within the empire of Victor

Emmanuel III, while Yugoslavia was broken into pieces by Germany. Along with the creation of the Croatian state, the Serbian state Nedic, and a good portion of the Albanian lands occupied during the Balkan wars of the Serbs and Montenegrins, joined the so-called "Greater Albania," which was to be held under the Italian tutelage, while the other part (namely the Western Macedonia with Shkup and Kachanik) was given to Bulgaria which included them under its state under the claims of immediately making them Bulgarians.

This development for Albania was not unexpected but inevitable for the circumstances, regardless of the stance and criticism that was made toward King Zog. Due to King Zog's generosity in allowing Italian expansion, investment, and capital in the area, which went against the national interests of the Albanian state, Albania chose to turn to Italy rather than the Rome-Belgrade-Athens political triangle. Even at the last moments, after the Munich Agreement and the occupation of Czechoslavia by Germany in March of 1939, and the major European powers left Italy with open doors for expansion toward Albania and Greece, King Zog tried to avoid the worst by agreeing to a military pact with Italy. This pact turned out to be an unsuccessful maneuver since the Italians had already decided to bring down the King and the Kingdom of Albania, even though they helped create it. This decision for the fascist Italy and its expansion projects toward Albania had long since turned into a "triumphal march," similar to the one of twenty-one centuries ago with the Roman Empire and Illyria where the Roman Empire tried to expand its power and majesty into three continents. All the others knew this, and were left with the option of voluntarily joining the Italians in mitigating the damages while considering themselves puppets of the new Romans, or rather, avoiding it by leaving the road open to them, which at least would not mean that they had the historical responsibility of agreeing with them, unlike Zog did.

For the Albanian circumstances it could be said that the Italian landing on the 7th of April was followed by a "stroke of luck in the middle of a disaster." The pact between Italy and Yugoslavia was terminated, a pact that ensured cooperation between Rome and Belgrade according to which the split of Albania was foreseen. Yugoslavia would take the Northern part with Shkodra which would provide access to the Adriatic, while Belgrade in the South direction would obtain Thessaloniki. Moreover, the fall of the Yugoslav Prime Minister Stojadinovic, who fell from power from the

British, was a helping hand since it was known that there was even a more tragic scenario in store for the Albanians. In a short amount of time, the ethnic scene of northern Albania would be completely changed due to enforced colonization, but also, due to acts of revenge on the Albanian population, acts which were justified in the name of resistance to the occupation.

Despite these scenarios, Italian fascism was not welcomed by the Albanian population, but rather opposed with demonstrations and spontaneous armed resistance.[244] After Italy landed in Albania with the appropriate military arsenal, it took all the necessary steps to appear as though the Albanian population willingly joined the "new empire", rather than appearing as a military invasion of a sovereign country. After entering Tirana, the Italian fascists on April 9, created an Interim Administration Committee headed by Xhafer Ypi, the former Prime Minister of Albania in the twenties. He quickly gathered the so-called Constitutional Assembly composed of 159 representatives drawn from all the Albanian strata, where there were 68 beys and landowners, 25 Bayraktars, 46 merchants, 20 clergy and several officers and intellectuals.[245]

On April 12, in the presence of Mussolini's personal representative, Foreign Minister Count Ciano, the Assembly approved the draft decisions of the invaders by declaring a "personal union" between Albania and Italy and deciding "to beg" the Italian King Victor Emmanuel III to approve the crown of Albania "'for his Majesty and his heirs."

The Assembly also approved the creation of the Albanian government, led by the big landowner Shefqet Vërlaci. This government became entirely subject to the Italian dictates and only represented an instrument through which the duties coming from Rome were to be accomplished, in accordance with the basic status of the 'Kingdom of Albania." This kingdom had been defined by the status of the Empire according to which the King of Italy and his heirs would exercise their legislative and execu-

---

[244] Armed resistance against the fascist occupation occurred in Durres, in St.Gjin, in Vlora and some parts of the North. In Durres, Mujo Ulqinako along with a few volunteers from the ranks of the Albanian army anticipated Italians with arms, but died heroically with others two hours later. Also Colonel Abaz Kupi similarly resisted. In Tirana and some other areas there were demonstrations and protests, where arms were used against fascists. More broadly see *"Historia e Popullit Shqiptar,"* the second volume, Prishtina, 1969.

[245] *"Historia e Popullit Shqiptar,"* the second volume, Prishtina, 1969, p. 663.

tive power in Albania; where the King of Italy would be the highest governing power of the Albanian state and had the right to declare war, make peace and make agreements for various international treaties.

In accordance with this status, the right of the foreign minister and armed forces would be taken from Albania through which the so-called "Albanian Kingdom" equated with those of the internal Italians that were being formed in the Italian kingdom. The Albanian diplomatic representations of that time would merge with the Italian ones, as would happen with the Albanian Army, the command of which would be subject to the Italians. The Albanian flag was set with fascist signs – the Italian fascist emblem.

During the Italian invasion of Albania, from April 7, 1939 and continuing with the capitulation of Yugoslavia from Germany and its breakup in April of 1941, a large portion of the Albanian focus was set on the leftists. The only hope was that it represented the only force which would be able to get rid of fascism, and simultaneously through the victory of socialism as a system of broad masses, where equality and social freedom, which had been lost due to capitalism and imperialism, would return. Therefore, the leftist movement, which in Albania had early supporters since the victory of the Bolshevik Revolution in Russia – and in June of 1924, came to power by a coup. This movement represented the only force in the country that in those circumstances would prove to be more explosive against the fascist invasion, since through this it foresaw its historical chance to fight for its ideas.

The Albanian communist militants, who already had an experience in the proletarian movement, either by participating in the Spanish civil war among the internationalist brigades that fought Franco (Mehmet Shehu, Musa Fratari and others), even those from the ranks of the Albanian communist groups formed in Paris and Moscow from 1928 onwards where some of them had managed to enter even in the highest structures of Comintern (Ali Kelmendi, appeared as a representative, who in Lyon, France, in 1935 founded the "Association of Albanian Brotherhood"), then, such, would soon be returned to Albania to develop anti-fascist activities, from the communist platform. So it would not be long before the Albanian internationalists focused in Korce and a little later in Shkodra to open the communist councils which started to spread their ideas in accordance with the teachings of Marxism-Leninism, which were accepted by Albanians, especially the youth. This was, therefore, more than a favorable case that the anti-fascist war combined with ideological slogans, used for communist purposes.

The offensive against the leftist fascism somewhat neutralized the protests and revolts of the intellectual and patriotic forces, which from the beginning had a clear leftist strategy to dominate that which would later on be positioned as the anti-fascist democratic front and turned into a nationwide liberation war.

The reluctance of the patriotic intelligence encouraged even the most militant section of the left, the control of the Albanian political space beginning with its border cities: Korca and Shkodra so that from the South and North they would come closer to the middle. In these two characteristic Albanian cities characterized by a traditional cultural spirit and emancipation above the national average, the communists were positioned, but not ideologically unified as expected. People from Shkodra were seen to be a little more reserved toward the communist militancy and required anti-fascist directives and their concrete implementation. However, the militancy of the Korce Communist Group and the liberal course of Shkodra, produced the "colors" of the leftist movement, so that the anti-fascist war turned into a war against the feudal and domestic capitalists.

This ideological rhetoric did not change profoundly even after the capitulation of Yugoslavia. While under the redirection of the space provided by Versailles, the creation of countries like Croatia, quisling Serbia, while in the meantime, part of Kosova (without Mitrovica to Vuciterne held under Germany) and without Podujeva and part of Karadak of Shkup (which was taken by Bulgaria) joined the "Greater Albania." The dispersed Albanian communist groups and the rest from the leftist movement which were being prepared in accordance to the directive of the Comintern, finally came together under a joint organization. All these represented critical points in this development which were well received by most Albanians, especially those from the rural parts of Kosova and parts of the valley of Macedonia, which for more than twenty years had suffered under the Serb-Yugoslav invasion and thought of fascists as liberators because in addition to the removal of the occupation and its violence, they had also returned their national rights. These rights included the opening of schools in the Albanian language, the creation of an Albanian administration, the creation of the local government, and others that were denied during the Yugoslav occupation.

For Kosovar Albanians and those Albanians in parts of Macedonia who had suffered so much, the statements made about fascism and their war had no importance. The important aspect was that they had brought down the Versailles Yugoslavia, no matter how, because with the fascist arrival they had regained their national rights and most importantly – Albanians, more or less, were united. Whether or not it was a "fascist beast" that "hid great risks for the future" as was said by the communists, the broad masses did not seem to care much. This was also the reason that in Kosova and the Albanian parts of Macedonia there were anti-fascist manifestations as requested by some communist emissaries from Albania who wanted to turn the the 28th of November into an anti-fascist demonstration in Kosova. At least for the two first years, there was solidarity with the German war against Russia and Greece since they were perceived as contributors to the Albanian destruction in the Congress of Berlin, as well as the crushing of Albania and separation of Albania into three states. Further, even after the founding of the Communist Party of Albania in November, the Albanian communists came up with a "platform" as to why fascism should be fought in Albania, and why the "Greater Albania" was a dangerous creation created by fascists "for their own needs and the disruption of the population on a new basis."[246] The population of Kosova who had started to enjoy the benefits of the national unification, however, did not show any interest in such propaganda. The Communist agitators remained without influence even when they rightfully discussed the Northern Mitrovica case as it was left outside the Albanian state and under the supervision of Germany, as well as other Albanian parts left under Bulgarians (especially Shkup), because the destruction of Yugoslavia by the Germans anytime could find a common language for the unification of all Albanian territories.

Albanians, therefore, wanted to believe Germans that their war, even though against the entire world, was in their (Albanian) interest, and there was no interest in turning their back on them [Germans] just so they could join what communists would call "fascist mischief." Fighting on the German side meant they were fighting the killers of yesterday and the new international world without borders and other similar ones behind which the Soviet Union stood.

---

[246] See *"Fashizmi terrorizon Kosovën,"* in "Zëri i Popullit," nr 8-9 Nov. 1942.

This belief was widespread among the people, especially the intellectuals from Kosova, who were aware that the Albanian union was a result of circumstances and events. This meant that the national union should not be seen as a "fascist merit" that happened for "their interests," but rather as a right of Albanians that had to be used in turning it into reality regardless of the international circumstances and developments.

How did the destruction of the Versailles Yugoslavia happen, and what did the scenario for the split of the Albanian land among the allies look like? Were these realities that truly opened the road for Albania in ensuring an eternal unification? Or, were these developments for foreign interests from whom Albanians had to benefit as much as possible, without forgetting, that these interests once were aligned with the Albanian interest?

These dilemmas gained even more importance when it was known that the destruction of Versailles Yugoslavia was part of its punishment for removing itself from the Tripartite Pact, which was signed on the 27th of March with the Belgrade government.

However, it is known that Hitler in March of 1941 had made a plan for the occupation and the division of Yugoslavia. This plan contained temporary guidelines for the division of Yugoslavia, under which the Chief Staff of the Supreme Command of the German Army, General Keitel, on April 12, 1941, divided it into three zones: the German, the Italian, and the Bulgarian one. Despite the formation of the sovereign Croatian state, the territory of the "old" Serbia was put under the German military administration of the Land Army Supreme Command.[247]

Although in principle it was decided that a large part of the Albanian lands would join "Greater Albania," which were set to be led by Italy, some dilemmas began to occur between Berlin and Rome regarding the issue of borders. Consequently, an urgent meeting was held regarding this issue in Vienna on April 21 and 22 of 1941 between the German Minister of Foreign Affairs, von Ribentrop and the Italian one, Count Ciano. Count Ciano had opposed the territorial maximalist demands of Bulgarians in the direction of Macedonia and Kosova. Italians represented the attitude that the Bulgarians would obtain the least possible Albanian land, since only through the trust of Albanians would a significant feature for the future important partners in the region be gained. Since Bulgaria

---

[247] Čulinović, Ferdo: „*Okupatorska podjela Jugoslavije,*" Belgrade, 1970, p. 523.

joined the Pact, even their needs were to be considered, which resulted in a part of Kosova given to it (a part of the Gjilan Region, Vitia, a part of Zhup of Sirnic and the Kachanik region). Later, in January of 1942, the Bulgarian territory was expanded with Podujevo, and on January 17, 1943 with Mitrovica and Vuciterna. The remainder was divided between Italy and Germany. Thus, in Vienna the demarcation line was determined between Germany and Italy (from the direction of Vinci in Slovenia through Leskovien Plitiva through Udbione and Donji Lapac in Livo, Bjellashnicë) – Priboj Lim – Nova Varos – Sjenica – Novi Pazar – Mitrovica - Prishtina.

According to this division, the Dukagjin region and the majority of Kosova belonged to the Albanian Italian protectorate. Three districts: Mitrovica, Vuçitërna and Podujevo belonged to the German zone of occupation, namely Nedic's Serbia. Germans, therefore, were interested in keeping Kosova's mineral mines as well as the railways linking Belgrade to Thessaloniki, while for the other parts they were open to discussion with their allies.

For the Kosova part, the Dukagjin Region and Macedonia composed the Italian protectorate called "Greater Albania," and in the summer of 1941 the Civil Commission for Kosova, Dibra and Struga was founded. The head of it was Fejzi Alizoti who had the rank of Minister in the government of Tirana. The administration was constituted based on the one in Albania, which was namely like the one in Italy. In December of that year, the governing of these areas fell under the responsibility of the Ministry of Liberated Areas in Tirana, which was abrogated in February, 1943. In these parts, the prefectures of Prishtina, Prizren, Peja and Dibra were formed, while later the one of Tetova. The prefecture of Peja was joined by the regions of Plava and Gucia, Rozaje, Tutin, Istok and Drenice. The Dukagjin region and the part of Kosova under the Italian occupation zone had around 8,000 square km and approximately 500 thousands inhabitants. The Albanians of these areas, based on the Tirana government decision, on October 18, 1941, automatically became citizens of Albania.

After the unification, Italy wanted for Kosova and other areas to appear with fascist attire as soon as possible. Therefore, "the Albanian Fascist Party," formed on June 2, 1939 in Tirana, started to open its branches in Prishtina, Prizren, Peja, and other Albanian cities. The Albanian Ministry of Education gave certain guidelines to schools requiring the "spreading of the Albanian irredentism and education in the new spirit."[248]

Unlike the German and Bulgarian occupation zones, where the Albanians endured many difficulties and disagreements with the circumstances under which they were put, especially for the Bulgarian occupied zone in the Italian zone, a dynamic economic life was fostered: new jobs were offered, the use of the mineral mines continued, and there was a rise in trade of consumer goods. In order for beys to benefit, the Tirana authorities allowed the renewal of feudal relations (landowners).

The headquarters of the High Commissioner and the Italian forces moved to Prizren. This city, to which many other trade, economic, administrative and cultural representatives moved, experienced a dynamic level of development, and became one of the most developed Albanian cities.

However, the situation was not the same for the three districts of Kosova, which came under the German occupation zone, along with Novi Pazar, which composed the Kosova prefecture with Mitrovica in the center, which was formally part of the Nedic's Serbia and was included in the Banovina of Drina with headquarters in Uzice. The Albanian national group had its Trustee in Banovina of Drina in the rank of the helper who participated in decisions on all matters pertaining to Kosova.[249] According to the decree of the "Council of Commissioners," which Milan Acimovic drew on August 6, 1941, the Kosova region, in addition to its districts, had zones. Their members consisted of the majority (Albanians), while their deputies were members of "the minority of at least 25%" (meaning Serbs), and other officials were among the Albanians and Serbs in proportion to their numbers in the districts. This was also true for the gendarmerie. The appointments were made by the "Serbian administrative authorities in Belgrade," while the Albanian personnel were assigned "in accordance with the Albanian national group leader."[250]

Despite the financial income, which was administered in accordance to the needs of the Kosova district involved in the German occupation zone, Albanians had the right to school in the Albanian language, alt-

---

[248] Hadri, Ali: *"Kosovo i Metohija u Kraljevini Jugoslavije,"* Istorijski glasnik, Belgrade, 1967, pages 62-65.

[249] Rajović, Radošin: *"Autonomia e Kosovës,"* Prishtina, 1987, p. 198.

[250] *Ibid.*, p. 200.

hough learning Serbian was obligatory. The educational staff in the Albanian schools were appointed by the Ministry of Education with proposals submitted by the leaders of the Albanian national group.[251]

A regiment of the German army was stationed in the district of Kosova, a regiment from the Division 717 of Infantry which had its center in Mitrovica. However, in the district of Kosova the "Albanian gendarmerie," was also formed under the command of Colonel Bajazi Boletitni, a former Yugoslav Army officer. This gendarmerie consisted of approximately one thousand members, some of whom were also units of the "Serbian State Guard," from which more than two thirds were Albanians, and which for a certain time were under the command of Ali Bej Draga, son of Fergat Bej Draga, the leader of the "Albanian National Group." There were also military units of Kosta Pecanci, which were composed of units of "volunteers" and others scattered among the villages. [252]

In May of 1941, the Committee of the "Kosova Albanian National Defense" was created to fight for Kosova and other territories occupied by the former Yugoslavia, now dispersed into three occupation zones to join one unity as a whole (in this case the Greater Albania). The Committee was led by Bedri Pejani – President, Rexhep Mitrovica – Vice President, Jalal Mitrovica – Secretary, while other members - Ibrahim Gkajova, Tafil Boletini, Kareem Begolli, Shaqir Curri, Qemajl Prishtina, Rexhep Krasnici, Tahir Zajmi and others.[253] A number of Committee members stopped in Prizren, and the rest, headed by Bedri Pejani, went to Mitrovica, in order to campaign for this part of Kosova to be included in the "Greater Albania." In Mitrovica, the Committee began publishing the newspaper "Kosovari," which continuously called for this region to join the united Albanian state under the Italian protectorate.

Apparently, the theme of "Albanian unification," separated the Commitee into two, namely, the pro-Italians (Ferhat Draga and Begri Pejani, who were engaged in ensuring that this part of Kosova be split

---

[251] Miletić, Antun: *"Kosovo iz aspekta okupacione uprave Vermahta u Srbiji 1941-1944,"* Kosova - Kosovo, Prishtina, nr 4/1975, pages 163-168.

[252] Hadri, Ali: *"Kosovo i Metohija u Kraljevini Jugoslaviji,"* Belgrade, 1967, pages 54-57.

[253] The Committee of "Kosovo Albanian National Defense" renewed its work in the summer of 1939 with the permission of the government of Shefqet Verlaci. They were willing that in "the case of the Yugoslav crises," which was known to soon escalate the collapse of the forced state, enter Kosovo and other Albanian territories to restore them to Albania.

from the "state" of Nedic and join Albania) and the pro-Germans (Xhafer Deva, who seemed to want more the autonomy of Albanians under Germany). [254]

To reconcile these differences, the "Albanian National League" was established in Mitrovica headed by Ali Draga, who as the leader of the "Albanian Group" represented Albanians before the German occupation authorities. The Secretary of the League was Vehbi Frasheri, the son of Mehdi Frasheri, the former president of the Albanian royal government and the later chairman of the Council of Regency of Albania (after the capitulation of Italy).

Under these circumstances, political life developed in Kosova and other Albanian regions that joined the Italian Albania, along with the other German occupied zones, with the exception of the occupied Bulgarian zone, which underwent the process of Bulgarization and contributed toward the Albanian unification by acting against it. As would be seen, Bulgaria was not concerned about the anti-fascist war as it played out in Albania from the beginning, but, was rather preoccupied with the war of reaching national unification, which ultimately became reality despite some difficulties resulting from the split among the three occupying zones.

Unlike the Albanian communists with militant conviction, to some extent this concern was shared by a group of intellectuals with leftist views, coming from the Korca camp, the Elbasan camp, or the Shkodra camp, which were included in the National Liberation Movement in Kosova, and made efforts that the anti-fascist war in Kosova, despite its limitations, be used to win Kosova the right of self-determination and unification with Albania, as would be specified in the Boyana Conference.

This situation remained at least until the beginning of autumn of 1943 when the fascist Italy capitulated and in its place, German forces occupied the area, which, as soon as they entered the Albanian territory, declared that they were friends of Albanians and intended to provide the protection and continuity of the Albanian state.

---

[254] Miletić, Antun: „*Kosovo iz aspekta okupacione uprave Vermahta u Serbiji*," Prishtina, 1975, pages 163-198.

The End of Greater Albania, the Independent Albanian State, and the Communist Takeover

Capitulation of Fascism in Italy in fall of 1943 and the end of "Great Albania." - The Arrival of Germans and the declaration of independence of the Albanian country. - Minister of Foreign Affairs of Germany, Ribentrop, edified that the independent Albanian country would be one of Germany's allies. On 16th of October in Tirana, the National Assembly was held; the participants announced the separation of Albania from Italy and Mehdi Frashëri was chosen the leader of The High Regency Council. - On November 5, the Regency led by Rexhep Mitrovica appointed Xhafer Deva as Minister of Internal Affairs. - The deputies of "Balli Kombetar" and "Legaliteti." - The initiative of a nationalist group in Prizren led to The Second Albanian League of Prizren Assembly.- One of the most important goals of The Second Albanian League of Prizren was gathering all Albanians into one country, which consisted of Kosova, Dukagjin, Sanxhak, and the eastern parts of Montenegro, western parts of Macedonia, and parts of Novi Pazar in the South, which were occupied by Greece. - The case of national union, similar to the Mukje agreement, divided the Albanian political forces between the right and the left, so that the left could win, which would help the country on the Eastern bloc.

The capitulation of fascism in Italy was not unexpected. The Italian army was not going to be ready for war until World War II started. This was made clear by Wehrmacht, but she needed an ally, which would remain militarily strong together with other allies from the collaborating countries. At the end of 1942 and beginning of 1943, for Hitler's strategy, the main concern was filling the Italian vacuum, not Italy's capitulation. On this occasion, the Balkan region had an important role in "keeping the front" on southeastern and eastern sides, so the Germans decided that Albania had to be proclaimed an independent country. The Minister of Foreign Affairs of Germany, Ribentrop, presented to Hitler the plan of forming an Albanian national government, one that would be able to negotiate positively and serve as an ally to Germany.

Ribentrop's stand came after an analysis by the Operating Headquarters of Wehrmacht, which said that "Albanians demand their independence. Whoever helps them, is a friend of theirs. Anglo-Americans were expected to declare the independence of Albania at the first chance possible. Therefore, the Germans needed to take measures to declare the Albanian independence immediately, so that Albanians would not take an enemy standpoint toward them."[255] Ribentrop contacted the Ambassador in Rome and the General Council in Tirana, stating the need to make a political decision regarding their stance toward Albania, which would be beneficial from a military aspect, since an independent Albanian country would be able to ensure the Albanian coast, especially the roads of Otranto, for Germany. On the other side, Germany balanced the politics of Albania, and turned Albania into a strong ally, where the forces between Germany and Albania were small, but very secure.

These instructions were also provided to the authorized Minister of Foreign Affairs of Germany for the Balkans (in Belgrade) Herman Neubacher, who at the beginning of September made contacts with Albanian authorities such as Ibrahim Biçoku, Xhafer Deva, Vehbi Frashëri and other pro-German Albanians, so that the new Albanian government would be pro-German.

So, right after the capitulation of Italy, on September 9, 1943, German troops disarmed Italian troops everywhere in Albania. That day, the German troop Commander-in-Chief in Albania, von Besel communicated:

> When the German troops enter your land, the independence of Albania will be ensured, the Great German Reich will be present and will fight down, but they have no intentions towards the Albanian land. Your desire for independence will be realized through the help that you will provide to the German army.[256]

The German general forwarded this message to important personalities and intellectuals during a meeting that they had in Tirana. He also called attention to the cooperation between the Albanian left and the Slavic neighbors, since in that way they would join the Russian Bolsheviks.

In order not to create an institutional and national vacuum and in order to destroy the structues which were created by Italian fascism, on October 16 in Tirana, the National Assembly was called, whose partici-

---

[255] *Ibid.,* p. 119.
[256] *"Historia e Popullit Shqiptar,"* Volume 2, Prishtinë, 1969, p. 721.

pants announced the dissociation of Albania from Italy and Mehdi Frashëri was chosen the leader of the High Regency Council.

On November 5, the Regency led by Rexhep Mitrovica, appointed Xhafer Deva as Minister of Internal Affairs. Vehbi Frashëri, the son of Mehdi Frashëri, was appointed Minister of Foreign Affairs, and the Minister of Economy was Ago Agaj. Lef Nosi, Bahri Omari, Kolë Tomora, Anton Harpi and others also joined the Regency.

It can be said that the High Regency Council and its government, had supporters from all levels of the Albanian society, excluding the communists. Since it was led by intellectuals and patriots such as Mid'had Frashëri, many deputies from the *Balli Kombetar* and *Legaliteti* joined the Regency. This movement was created because they were planning to develop a monitored and balanced national political stance between two issues, where fighting against fascism and not cooperating with it, would afford freedom.

In this situation, Germany was paying careful attention to Kosova and other Albanian territory that had been conquered by Yugoslavs. Well aware of this were many intellectuals and political forces from the Albanian government and from other administrative and national structures.

Of course in these circumstances which could determine the future of the Albanian country, many intellectuals from Kosova, who were responsible for this, together with other Albanian patriots, who were interested that the first independent Albanian state should strengthen and stay secured inside and outside, brought a wide scale of consensus.

This goal could only be accomplished through a national convention. The Second Albanian League Convention continued the work and projects of the First Albanian League Convention in Prizren in 1878, which also led to the creation of the first Albanian Government after the government of Skenderbeg. So, from 16 to 20 September 1943, the initiative for a nationalist group in Prizren led to the Second Albanian League Convention.[257]

In this gathering in Prizren, besides many representatives from Kosova and Dukagjin, delegates came from Eastern Macedonia, Sanxhak, and all of Albania. The Central Committee of the League appointed Rexhep Mitrovica as President, Musa Shehu and Kolë Margjini as Vice Presidents, both from Prizren, and other members: Sheh Hasani from

---

[257] See Zajmi, Tahir: *"Lidhja e Dytë e Prizrenit,"* Bruksel, 1964.

Prizren, Bedri Pejani from Peja, Asllan Buletini from Mitrovica, Tahir Zajmi from Gjakova and Qazim Bllaca from Suhareka.

At this convention the delegates of Kosova, Dukagjin, and Sanjak were appointed to assemble the National Assembly on the 16th of October in Tirana. One of the most important goals of the Second National Albanian League in Prizren was gathering all Albanians into one country, which contained Kosova, Dukagjin, Sanxhak, and the eastern parts of Montenegro, the western parts of Macedonia, and the southern parts of Novi Pazar, parts which were once occupied by Greece. One of the most important duties of the League was forming military units which would support the fullfillment of these goals. Under the government of Rexhep Mitrovica and Xhafer Deva, the mobilization and formation of the "Skenderbeg" division was created, which supported the nation against communist forces.

In these circumstances, after the capitulation of Italy, the Germans allowed Albanians to create their own government with an intellectual and patriotic foundation. During these important circumstances which could shape the future of the Albanian country, they were facing two dilemmas: supporting the anti-fascist movement, which was not easy because they had to turn their back on their main supporter of the Albanian State – Germany; or opening relations with the Albanian communist movement, which exhibited interesting politics showing alliance with the Anglo-Americans and simultaneously also with Russian ideologists.

If the first dilemma maintained neutrality of the Albanian government, the second dilemma would introduce the concept of political "rivalry." So, in order to fight the Russian Bolshevism and the communist ideology which was fairly supported in Albania by the middle class and the left intellectuals, especially after the foundation of the Communist Party of Albania in November of 1941, with the direct help of the Yugoslav communists, which, as will be seen, controlled the anti-fascist movement in Albania, turning it into a branch of Yugoslav communists. The "Balli Kombetar" was created in 1942 from well known intellectuals, patriots, clergyman and the social class from the West.

In this direction, a very important role was played by the British and the Americans, which required the right also to fight against fascism in Albania, so that the communist influence would be minimized. The communists were always ready for war and they wanted to impose their ideologic views.

Later, *"Legaliteti"* was formed, a movement which gathered supporters of King Zog and the Albanian monarchy. Abaz Kupi played an important role in the democratic anti-fascist front, until it was put on the wardship of the communists. This movement with an anti-fascist character minimized the influence of communists in Albania, for which Kupi and his followers, this mission was very important, since these relations would determine the fate of Albania: East or West.

The opening of the political rivalry in Albania with the involvement of the Albanian right, allowed the Anglo-American allies to expand their Albanian anti-fascism spectrum on a democratic foundation, an issue which offered Albania the chance to determine its future based on democratic ideas instead of ideologic concepts.

The Albanian right, advised by Anglo-Americans made the decision for the Albanians, to consider negotiations with communists to create a democratic anti-fascist front in Albania. Communists showed that they were ready for a united war, but with the intention of leading the war, accepted this offer fearing that if they didn't they would be considered pro-Soviet, which would harm them in many ways.

The first meeting of both representatives for these groups was in Tapiz, close to Tirana, on July 25, 1943. Their second meeting, where they also made a decision, was from 1-2 August in Mukje of Kruja. The General Council delegation consisted of Ymer Dishnica, Mustafa Gjinishi and Abaz Kupi which signed the creation of the "Committee for the Survival of the Albanians." This committee consisted of 6 member representatives of the organization "Balli Kombetar" and 6 representatives of The National Liberal Front. In the agreement it was anticipated that the common war would defend the ethnic Albanian country. The second point of the agreement of Mukja was consiedered "the hottest" because it spoke about joining all the territories which were once Albania. Some of the territories were Kosova, and other parts of Albania, where they had to deal with Bulgarians and Germans. The importance of Ulqin, Tivar and other parts was discussed and agreed upon that they should belong to Albania.

"Ballists" (Balli Kombëtar) wanted to fight for the ethnic Albanian country, while the communists wanted to work hard for the Albanian country, without borders or ethnicity (Communist Albania). Gjinishi required that the case of Kosova not complicate the agreement, since the concentration had to be done at the borders which were accepted internationally. He also declared that it was important to have an agreement which saved Albania instead of harming it, alluding to the creators of fascism (non-Communist Albania), with which communists wouldn't agree. The representatives of Balli Kombëtar, led by Mid'had Frashëri, fought to show and convince the others that the Albanian standpoint of always staying together did not come from fascism or others, but from the right and will of the Albanian population to stay together, an ideal which was infringed upon in London and Paris. They were defending the idea that "if fascism did something good and was in the interest of Albanians, nobody had the right to prevent it, but, rather, should try to support it."[258]

After many compromises and conversations, but also the swiftness of Ymer Dishnica, who was the leader of the National Liberal Front delegation, this case would receive an historic answer without worrying what communists from Belgrade or Moscow thought. The operation said:*"We will be fighting for an independent Albania, and for applying the act known universally guaranteed by the Atlantic (Western) front that decided the movement of Albanians to an ethnic Albania."*[259]

This statement became a point of contention since the communists, influenced by Yugoslavs, quickly betrayed Mukje's agreement, which opened the door to the disruption of the anti-fascist front and civil war all over Albania; and in so doing, ensured that Albania would remain in the communist bloc.[260]

The failure of Mukje and the many divisions of the Albanians led to the civil war, the third in a row, after the one that happened through 1914-1915 and 1924 – first with the pro-Turkey and Islamic coup d'etat followed by the coup d'etat of June of the leftists against the government of Zogu – these two would be the factors, which would impact further divisions among Albanians, and which would cause Albania to remain in the Eastern bloc.

The Yugoslav communists at the Albanian Comunist Party influenced the decisions during the war, and later were transformed into affiliation with Belgrade, which would become their puppet.

Hence, the Albanian right and other divided Albanian patriotic forces were incapable of coming out in an active war against the anti-fascist front, to turn it into a democratic movement which would earn the full

---

[258] *Ibid.*, p. 54.

[259] *Ibid.*, p. 61.

[260] *Ibid.*, p. 54/55.

support of the Anglo-Americans. In lack of this, the National Liberal Front would win, led by communists, inserting its liberal and national character with the war and communist ideologies, which by the end of the war would allow the creation of the communist dictatorship in Albania, which would have tragic consequences for the future.

Their winning also had to do with the experience of Yugoslav communists and the role that they had in the internationalist movement and also in the high levels of "Kominterna", with which the Albanian communists were entrusted. This was best reflected, when Milladin Popovic (Alia) and Dusan Mugosa (Sala), two Montenegrins, served in the training camp of Albanian communists. Milladin Popovic was a representative of Tito and Dusan Mugosa was a representative of the Communist Party in Kosova – who tried their best to convince Enver Hoxha and other communists to forget about the idea of guarding the right to unite Albania and Kosova.

Yugoslav communists not only were part of the Albanian Communist Party, but in November 1941, they also were involved in organizing the National Liberation Army's staff. The Yugoslavs participated in founding all other structures of the Liberation Army's Council. Everything was implemented through the Communist Party and played an important role in the Albanian government. As such the Yugoslavs had the most important say in foreign and internal decisions of Albania. The also determined the limits and territories where Albanian communists should be involved. In regards to the political arena and throughout the war they would remain under the dictatorship of Yugoslavs. Albania would appear as a united country, but its leaders would have to follow Yugoslav ideologies. As far as that, the Albanian leadership, the Versailles agreement was still in power in regard to Yugoslavia. The National Liberals consisted of two groups - one that was governed by the Versailles agreement and the other that was led by the communists from Kosova, which was formally connected to the Yugoslav Communist Party.

Communist Albanians and Kosova were using the Albanian national flag in wars, and it was not always accompanied by the communist symbol. So, by the Mukje agreement, which was cancelled by the communists, who also destroyed some understandings they had with Anglo-Americans, tried to direct Albania's outcome to be tied to the Western rather than the Eastern bloc. The Eastern and Western blocs are the source as to why the Yugoslavs kept Enver Hoxha under strict advisory; in this way they could ensure that he would not be influenced by the Albanian nationalists. The Albanian nationalists that were advised for the pro-Western movement would have forced Enver Hoxha to come up with an explanation as to why Albanian unity, which under Tito's guidance, was a bad idea.[261]

Regarding the Mukje agreement, Enver Hoxha made a self-criticism and confessed to Miladin Popovic and Dusan Mugosa, to whom he said *"that they were some opportunist Albanians (Dishnica and Gjinishi) which would work towards accepting the idea of a united Albania and united leadership,"* an idea to which the Albanian Communists would never agree, since according to Enver *"it was a fascist idea and we should fight against it."*[262]

The problems between Albanian communists and communists in Kosova started as a result of the Mukje agreement, which, in turn, brought the new development and the Conference of Bujan, on December 31, 1943 and on January 1-2, 1944. In June 1945, the Assembly of Prizren sealed the loss of Kosova, which was robbed by the Yugoslavs, but now under the communist flag of ideology. Communist internationalism, under the "magic formula" would solve all the problems, *"which were inherited from the imperialist and chauvinist politics of the past."*

On the contrary, Yugoslav communists, under the mask of demagogic formulas, managed to not only bring back the state structure in Kosova, but at the same time, under the word of unity and fraternization, they brought back the hegemonic supremacy that Serbs had during the time of theYugoslav kingdom, as would be seen, only a half century later.

The Revolutionary Hoxha–Tito Agreement on Kosova

The effort of communists from Kosova to be freed from the patronage of communists in Albania and the Yugoslav guidelines. – The organization of the Bujan Conference and its decisions – an act of historic responsibilty and the "careful" reactions of Yugoslavs against it reasoning that "an anti-fascism win would create possibilities to bring a brotherly solution to all disagreements in the past." – Enver Hoxha

---

[261] See Spasoje Djaković: *"Sukobi na Kosovu,"* Beograd, 1984, p. 398.
[262] *Ibid.*, p. 207.

didn't allow the landing of Anglo-American forces in North Albania in 1944, leaving Albania in the Eastern bloc. – The integration of partisan Albanian and Yugoslav units in Kosova in September of 1944 staged Kosova for another conquest by partisan forces, which left Kosova in Serbia.

The conference of Bujan on December 31, 943 and January 1-2, 1944 were not unexpected and not "a rushed act," as was described by Yugoslav commisars who during the war tried to minimize the conference's effect so that during the Prizren Assembly, on June 10, 1945, it would be devalued completely which, in that way, would bring the resolution to annex Kosova to Serbia.

The National Liberal movement in Kosova was also an armed resistence against fascists; it was an attempt by a small group of intellectuals from Kosova to keep the balance between the Albanian and Yugoslav internationalist communists, and on the other side Kosova's interest was to guard the national Albanian union, forever the right of Albanians, which was turned around by fascists, first the Italians and then the Germans. This was constituted in the National Assembly of October 16, 1943 in Tirana, where Albania was detached from the Italian "crown" of April 1939 and declared an independent country by the free will of Albanians.

As would be seen, in Kosova, the space of this maneuver was extraordinarily tight and hard, since fascists, maybe not as a whole, corrected an historic injustice and brought a new reality which needed consistency, instead of fighting with ideologies disseminated by the left, saying that it would bring sovereignty among the countries.

In Albania, one could talk about fascism from a leftist viewpoint and from other illusions that spread equally around the world of proletarians and this would not introduce anything new to the political plan or to intellectuals, since the left and anti-fascism in European metropolises was turned into an intellectual point of view which gathered the middle class and forces with a social-democrat orientation.

In Kosova and other places which were free from Serb and Greek conquest, bringing up these cases, was similar to accepting a new national betrayal, because the reality was bitter and the consequences excluded any investigation from any viewpoint even when they needed to understand them in a social way in order to deal with the challenges of the time, based on their importance.

Intellectuals from Kosova who studied in Albania (Korçë, Shkodër, and Elbasan) accepted the left and comunist ideas, because Marxist and Leninist theories seemed appealing and appropriate to solve the national cause of self-determination of the people. The participants of the Antifascist Movement of Kosova had patriotic intentions, with only a few ideologic ideas.

When they saw that fascism would not win the war, but the antifascist bloc brought together the Anglo-Americans and the Soviets, both the leftists and the rightists, they called for a common war of all forces against fascism. A great chunk of Albanian intellectuals and patriots from Kosova saw that the anti-fascist front and the national liberals offered the only opportunity to bring together all sides, even if they had to work with Yugoslavs, who were not to be trusted at all, promised that "a common war against fascism" would make up for the mistakes of chauvinist forces.

Those in Kosova who supported the left on this viewpoint, from the beginning, dealt with two unbeatable obstacles which would produce the largest consequences for the future of Albania and Kosova. These obstacles were:

a) - excluding Kosova in the common anti-fascist Albanian movement upon creation of new social and state realities.

b) - including Kosova in the anti-fascist movement against the National Liberation War of Yugoslavia, which was led by Yugoslavian communists.

In the first case, excluding Kosova from the common anti-fascist Albanian movement upon new social and state realities represented alpha and omega of the new Albanian tragedy, because if it were to take place, Kosova would be on the road to being under the Yugoslav regime and also stuck in the Eastern bloc – in the Soviet region.

The one-sided ideologic historiography in Tirana and those in Prishtina who coordinated with Tirana had tried to exclude Kosova from the common anti-fascist Albanian group upon creation of the new social and state realities which came as a result of the disintegration of Yugoslavia of Versailles. A good chunk of Albanian land was under the regime of Yugoslavia, so Kosova and Greece joined Albania, led by communists, trying to save the guards of old realities, to not vindicate the changes made by fascism, which on the contrary, what appeared to be was not true.[263]

The Komintern requested that communists utilize the new realities to adapt to circumstances to try to turn the division of the Albanian land in their own favor. Since the beginning of 1942, a big chunk of the Soviet Union fell under German hands and triggered the national states such as Ukraine, Kazakistan, and others to be reorganized. The Komintern then instructed the return of communist parties and their organizations to the states that were being reorganized, pretending to fight fascism, and at the same time occupying them.[264]

There were Yugoslav communists and Albanian communists, both who did not follow the request of the Komintern. In the Local Conference in Zagreb in the summer of 1941, when Yugoslavia did not exist, and some of the republics were forming their own states, so did Kosova and Macedonia by joining Albania and Bulgaria. Even though separated in states, the Conference decided that they should be organized at the level of the Yugoslavia of Versailles. This decision was made under the pressure of national Serb communists which were influenced by the Communist Party of Yugoslavia. The agreement of Stalin and Tito in Moscow to enforce the position of the First Secretary of the Comunist Party of Yugoslavia to be Gorcic, he lost Moscow's support, while in the meantime, Tito won and remained in power for half a century.

In Zagreb's Conference, besides the decision that the Yugoslav Comunist Party would preserve the organizational structure based on Versailles Yugoslav decisions, the decision of the Fourth Local Conference Party was canceled, where Yugoslavia was described as "the jail of nations". In this way, they ensured that the countries would not seek self-determination, but remain in Yugoslavia. These decisions ended up favorable for Albanians because upon completion of the anti-fascist war, it gave them the opportunity to again unite in one country based on the right to choose and self-determination.

After all, not all the communist forces from the "common Yugoslav house" recognized the directives defined by Tito during the Local Conference in Zagreb. The Macedonians, which were together with Bulgaria

---

[263] See Vukmanovic - Tempo, Svetozar: *"Memoari I, II"* 1966-1969, Beograd-Zagreb, 1985.
[264] *Ibid.*.

would not join their party organization with the Yugoslav communist center like it used to be before Yugoslavia was destroyed. The anti-fascist Macedonian front was connected to Bulgaria in agreement with the new realities and it ignored the Yugoslav reality. Tito, skilled as he was, continued with the parallel structures of the communist organization inside Macedonia. Tito's missionary for Macedonia and Kosova, the great scandalmonger Svetozar Vukmanovic – Tempo was responsible for these parallel structures was, who in the Prohor Pçinski monastery, nearby Kumanovo, created the Macedonian communist party and later the National Liberation Macedonian Council, a large number of whose members were Serbs. This Council acted on the anti-fascist movement of that area, so that after the capitulation of the fascist Bulgaria, they could quickly get in the game by presenting themselves as an "authentic Macedonian movement" which had been active a long time ago, and was led by the Yugoslavian center.[265]

As a result of this parallel party organization and the anti-fascist front, Tito put Macedonia as an equal unit of the new Yugoslavian federation, in the second meeting of the Anti-fascist Council of Yugoslavia (AVNOJ), when the anouncement of the third Yugoslavia was made, even though there were not any participants from Macedonia. These efforts by Tito inhibited the possibility of Albanians to organize under this new reality and the war against fascism. The Yugoslav Communist Party would no longer talk to the communists from the Macedonian and Kosova regions as a separate party since they were now considered part of Yugoslavia. After the fascist conquest of Albania, Tito sent emisarries to Albania to "help" shape the Albanian communist thinking to be from the ideologic viewpoint, not the national one. From the Komintern, where Tito had a large influence, and in Moscow, Tito was given authority to "care for Albanian communists" which would be used as a paternalist cart not only during the war but for later too. With the Declaration of the Informbiro (Cominform) of 1948, the true intentions of Tito were realized and this triggered the full detachment between the Albanian and Serbo-Yugoslav communist parties, which continued for the next fifty years.

---

[265] See: Tito, Josip Broz: *"Izgradnja nove Jugsolavieje III,"* Beograd, 1950; *"Historia e Lidhjes së Komunistëve të Jugosllavisë,"* Group of Authors, Prishtinë, 1985; Kardel, Eduard: *"Lidhja e Komunistëve të Jugosllavisë,"* Prishtinë, 1980.

The first Yugoslavian communist contacts with Albanian communists started in the second half of 1939 and went in two directions: Montenegro and Kosova. From Montenegro, Blazo Jovanovic was the leader, who was later accompanied by Ivan Milutinovic, one of Tito's most trusted men. Meanwhile, from Kosova there was Miladin Popovic and Dusan Mugosa, both leaders of the communist organization of Kosova, which at that time in Kosova numbered approximately 150 members, only two who were Albanians: Ramiz Sadiku and Ali Shukriu – both recruited as students in Belgrade.[266] In order to show a larger Albanian membership in the party, the Yugoslavs falsified lists and names which were made up in Belgrade.

Even though without a party basis in Kosova, Yugoslavian missionaries in Albania managed to forge a "friendship and brotherhood connection." Yugoslav missionaries convinced the Albanian communist leaders not to include the Kosova communists in their own communist structure, in this way, insuring Kosova to be left out and up for grabs after the war. In the beginning it was under the Boka Regional Committee and Montenegro, which in the Fourth Local Conference of the Communist Party Congress in Zagreb was connected directly with the Central Committe of The Comunist Party of Yugoslavia (CPY). Milladin Popovic and Dusan Mugosa were represented as Kosova Albanians, as organizational secretaries of the Regional Committe of CPY in Kosova and at the same time as a member of the Central Committee (CC).

These facts were important for the determination of Kosova's state, because as seen after the war, they became the federal unit of the Yugoslav Federation instead of having the right to their own self-determination. In the National Liberation Council Assembly in Prizren from 6-10 July 1945, Kosova, was put under the seal of Serbia against its own will.

However, not even with the smallest contradiction, Albanian communists accepted "the instruction" of Yugoslavian communists which in turn split the party organization of Albanians in Albania and Kosova, an organization which led the same scheme in the Anti-fascist Front and the National Liberation Front.

Under the directives of Popovic and Mugosa, which directly influenced the organization and foundation of the Comunist Party of Albania, in November 1941 in Tirana was held the first formation of the Com-

---

[266] Vukmanovic - Tempo, Svetozar: *"Memoari"I,II*, Beograd-Zagreb, 1985.

munist Party of Albania. The first speaker was an Albanian from Kosova, who was brought there under the notion that he would only take notes.[267] Popovic and Mugosa made sure that the communist movement in Albania would operate with an open mind and not only for national interests. With this advice, the Serbian communist party insured that the Albanian communist party would not participate in any form in the interest of a united Albania. So, conservative leftist intellectuals approached the movement with the conviction that it would preserve the national union, which, on the contrary, they were eliminated by internal intrusion and elimination of these Albanians by the police who were controlled by the far leftist members.

They are known very well for many cases of intellectual elimination well-known from the anti-fascist movement through these denouncements, which happened later with the liquidation of Emin Duraku, on 28 November 1943, one of the most distinguished intellectuals from Kosova, who was always ready and prepared for politics and behind-the-scenes challenges against the Serbs. Many Albanian communist members were denounced by Serb communists to Albanian law enforcement as Yugoslavian communist agents, and this happened after the Conference of Vitomirica ended, where for the first time Albanian communists from Kosova, who with the directive of the Central Committe of the Comunist Party of Albania had to be incorporated into the party structure of the Regional Committee of the Comunist Party of Yugoslavia for Albania and Metohia. Emin Duraku was presented with the idea that the anti-fascist war in Kosova had to be conducted in the interest of the Albanian people of Kosova and to the right solution of the national interest, a fact which raised animosity between Albanian and Serb communists, with which Tito's special man for Kosova and Macedonia informed the Central Committee of the Comunist Party of Yugoslavia regarding "possible infiltration of irredentist streams among Albanian communists," and were influenced by the idea of "Great Albania". This leadership of communists in Kosova eventually would need to be dealt with.[268]

---

[267] See Mugosa, Dusan: *"Shënime nga puna në Shqipëri"* 1941 -1945.

[268] See Letter of the Central Committee of the Yugoslav Communist Party to the Provincial Committee in Kosovo. Cited in Spasoje Djaković: *"Sukobi na Kosovu,"* Beograd, 1984, p. 382-386.

And the other case, the one that had to do with including Kosova in the anti-fascist movement of the organizational structure of the National Liberation War of Yugoslavia, which was led by Yugoslav communists, directly impacted the development of an anti-fascist movement in Kosova as well.

Also here, Yugoslav communists helped by Albanians, manipulated the situation in their favor, which would be seen at the end of the war when Kosova again and violently was kept under the Yugoslavian conquest as a "democratic" province under Serbian tutelage. For those who did not easily accept this idea, especially for the communists in the Drenica and Dukagjin regions, Yugoslavia took measures to cleanse them from the system.

Party organization, indeed did not have an opportunity to be left free from the ideologic concepts of classes in the circumstances where the Yugoslav framework was approved. But since these were accepted by the Communist Party of Albania, who came to the aid of the Yugoslav communists to spread the communist agenda throughout Kosova, which was announed through internationalist catchwords *"the solution of all contesting cases and inherited problems from the past, adapted with the right of people for self-determination, but that will be discussed to be launched after the war is won."* Some leftist intellectuals coming from Kosova were included in this activity. Fadil Hoxha, Hajdar Dushi, Emin Duraku, Sabrije Vokshi (Bija), Xhevdet Doda, Xhavit Nimani, Xheladin Hana, Ismet Shaqiri, Hysni Zajmi, Meriman Braha, Elhami Nimani, Xhevdet Hamza, Mazllom Këpuska and other Kosovars followed studies in Albania where they were members of the communist groups of Korça and Shkodra and were directed to return on "party duty" to Kosova. They were quickly incorporated into Kosova's party base, which was dominated by Serbs and Montenegrins, and the National Liberation Front, which could hardly be seen active, thus creating small partisan groups such as "Zenel Hajdini," later "Emin Duraku," the "Shari Command," one from Shala, and the "Bajram Curri" battalion which operated in the Dukagjin and Tropoja regions.[269]

---

[269] See Dr. Ali Hadri: *"Lëvizja Nacionalçlirimtare në Kosovë,"* Prishtinë, 1971; Fadil Hoxha: *"Kur pranvera vonohet,"* Prishtinë; *"Një jetë në shërbim të atdheut,"* Prishtinë, 2007, Spasoje Djaković: *"Sukobi na Kosovu,"* 1984.

These partisan units, even though smaller in number, with roughly three hundred fighters total, however, played an important role, because they reflected and determined the Albanian fight against fascism as an ideology, but not as a war for ultimate Albanian unity.

The Albanian dilemma started here in regard to the stance toward fascism in general. Siding on the war against fascism, which would bring Albanian freedom though not unity, it would be brought in such a form that unification would eventually have to be dealt with. These decisions became even more imminent since in the war against fascism now even the United States of America was participating, who on this issue, was in line with the Soviet Union. Since the Serbs first invaded Albania in 1877/78, and on the verge of the Balkan War, they promised Albanians that "after the emancipation from the Ottomans" there would be peace, equality and happy life, but in fact, the opposite occurred. The memories of the last few wars were still fresh, and the pools of blood shed that Albania endured during the last three decades were still visible.

The reality was bitter; fascism was not opposed by Albanians in Kosova. With arrival of Germans, Italians were viewed as allies even though they destroyed the Albanian kingdom and the Albanian unity during King Savoja's and Victor Emanuel III's kingdoms. Yugoslavs profited from this and all they had to do was wait for the Germans to get weaker, which was inevitable, especially since they were fighting on two fronts – Elba, against the infiltration of the Red Soviet Army, and Normandy, against the Anglo-Americans.

After the capitulation of Italy, in the fall of 1943, Yugoslav communists started to show interest in developing the anti-fascist war in Kosova and tried to keep it under their control. Left without any connection with the party base, which was founded in 1939, with the exception of some emissaries who went to Albania, sent by Yugoslavs assigned to delegate duties to Enver, Miladin and Mugosa, asked Kosovars for the cooperation between partisans of Kosova and Albania. These emissaries reserved the "right" to talk to the Albanians in the name of the agreeement between Tito and Hoxha, this kept the party organization and the front anti-fascist in Kosova still in control of Yugoslav communists. Tito's special missionary for Kosova and Macedonia, Svetozar Vukmanovic – Tempo, only once from the beginning of 1943 stayed for two days, hidden in Prizren with the Nimani family during his journey to

Tirana. [270] Usually Serbian-Yugoslav missionaries used Albanian names. Among those that took part in the communist movement and the fights in Kosova were: Pavle Jovicevic (Paloka), Milan Mickovic (Shefqeti), Dragutin Georgevic (Dauti), Milan Zecari (Zeca). By masking themselves with Albanian names, they infiltrated deep into Kosova's society, and the end of the war, shaped the decisions for Kosovars as to who was a friend and who was an enemy. As a result, February 8, 1945 they assigned themselves as arbitraters, which fought the Ballists, intellectuals, nationalists, and all of of those who kept the idea of Albanian union alive.

Before coming to this situation, many Albanian communists and intellectuals of the National Liberation Movement in Albania were sent to Kosova. Some independently helped the cause for national unity, and eventually started fulfilling some leading positions amongst the commanding structure of the war in Kosova, but also in the National Liberation Councils, which were the core of the local power. In the Conference of the Regional Committe of CPY for Kosova and Metohija which was held in Sharr, from 3-5 November 1943, of the many issues discussed, one was the maintenance of the military and Communist Party unit independent of Yugoslav control. The Albanian communists of Kosova, who disagreed with the communists in Albania and the ones in Yugoslavia, would imbrace the decision of the Regional Committee and change the name from "Kosova and Metohija" to the "Regional Committee of CPY of Kosova and Dukagjin." Also, the name of the Military Headquarters of the National Liberation Army was changed to the "Military Headquarters of the National Liberation Army of Kosova and Dukagjin." Fadil Hoxha was elected as Commandant of the Military Headquarters of the National Liberation Army of Kosova and Dukagjin. The operational staff of the National Liberation Army of Kosova and Dukagjin was now independent, and directly reported to the Military Headquarters of the National Liberation Army of Yugoslavia and the Military Headquarters of the National Liberation Army of Albania.

This development was disturbing to Yugoslavian representatives, especially Svetozar Vukmanovic Tempo, who quickly notified Tito of "the nationalist development among the Albanian communists of Kosova and their one-sided decision for war.[271] The Yugoslavian representatives to

---

[270] Shih: Svetozar Vukmanović – Tempo: *"Memoari,"* I, II, 1985.
[271] Spasoje Djaković: *"Sukobi na Kosovu,"* Beograd, 1984

Albania, especially Dusan Mugosa, asserted his authority and made sure that "the national and irredentist movements which were continuously developing in Kosova would not spread."[272]

As would be seen, Enver Hoxha this time was not too enthusiastic to take advice from Dusan Mugosa in favor of his suggestion as he took his advice in the past and didn't support the Mukje agreement. Hoxha was interested in resolving the Kosova case now, although the Yugoslavs thought it should be resolved after the war. The Yugoslavs wanted to continue "the mutual sincere communist trust" and fight against the fascists, creating new circumstances for resolving the Kosova question after the war.[273]

Since the agreement of Mukje was broken, Yugoslav communists had gained a great concession because the idea of "Greater Albania" (Kosova and Albania) would be eliminated, in this way insuring that the land occupied by Greece and Yugoslavia would continue to remain as their own and any Kosova question would need to be discussed in the National Liberation Council. This way any possible unity of Kosova and Albania would be eliminated. Enver Hoxha was well aware of this loss for Albanians and constantly in meetings with Yugoslav missionaries wanted to discuss the issue. Each time he brought the issue up he was severely criticized and eventually was officially criticized by Tito's missionary, V. Stojnic in the Albanian Communist Party Congress of Permet. For these issues, many other Albanian communists from intellectual circles were aware and disagreed with theYugoslavs, putting them in direct conflict with the Orthodox Yugoslavs led by Koçi Xoxe. Many of these intellectuals became victims of the war as seen later through history. This action against the intellectuals continued and intensified with the Infobureau Resolution. The Albanian communists of Kosova during the AVNOJ Conference in Jajce in November of 1943, were totally overlooked and not included. Kosova was no longer mentioned in the formation of the Federal Yugoslavia. This stand on Kosova made it clear to the Albanian intellectuals that they would have to side with the people of Kosova and work to find a final solution together. The anti-fascist front and the

---

[272] Dusan Mugosa: *"Shënime nga puna në Shqipëri* 1941-1944,"Titanë, 2002.
[273] See Enver Hoxha, *"Titistët,"* Tiranë, 1982.

National Liberation Army now were looked upon as a good framework for solving the Kosova question in favor of the people of Kosova.[274]

In the meantime, the creation of a National Liberation Council of Kosova and its expansion based on the foundations of a local power, built the future independence of the state based on this reality.[275]

The Kosova communist decisions were based on the Komintern communist suggestions and the Atlantic Treaty, where each country and its people were given the right to self-determination. Based on the Sharr Conference, where the framework to operate independently had been formed, the Kosovar communists saw the opportunity to call for the First Conference of the National Liberation Council of Kosova meeting in which Kosova's fate was decided.

In preparing for this very important conference, contacts with the Central Headquarters of the National Liberation Army of Albania was important, as it was important to keep contacts with the Central Committee of the Communist Party of Albania.[276]

But, guarantee for self-determination concerning the union of Albanians was needed also from the representatives of the Anglo-American allies, which now were located in Albania working on the anti-fascist mission. So, the first concrete meetings for this case and others were done with the representatives of the English mission who now were located in the North. It was natural to discuss the guarantee with them, since they represented Anglo-American allies. Even though the missionaries did not want to decrease the influence of the Communist Party, they were very careful while discussing the Kosova issue. Albanian nationalists hesitated to go to war with Germans, and whenever they were forced to participate, they always found reasons not to be harsh.[277]

During the preparation phase, the communists of Kosova had no means of communicating with the Yugoslav communists, even though it was expected, the Yugoslavs would be informed by Serbs using Albanian names. These Serbs wandered around various partisan organizations and

---

[274] Hibbert, Reginald: "*Fitorja e hidhur*," Tiranë, 1991, p. 333/43

[275] See: Buxhovi, Jusuf: "*Kthesa historike – lufta e Perëndimit për Kosovën*," Prishtinë, 2009, p. 318-343.

[276] From the author's conversations with Fadil Hoxha in Pristina in 1994. Fadil Hoxha Enver Hoxha admits that he has been informed about Boyana, but there was no access to the preparations of the conference or text of the Resolution of the Conference.

[277] Hibert, Reginald: "*Fitorja e hidhur*," Tiranë, 1991, p. 322.

worked as informants. After preparation work, which was very important for the conference, the decision was made to call the First Conference of the National Liberation Council for Kosova and Dukagjin. This conference was held in Bujan of Tropoja, in the Bajraktari Sali Mani's compound.

The conference was held on December 31, 1943 and January 1-2, 1944. The time and place were also important factors for this event. Time was important because after the capitulation of Italy and the loss of Germans in Stalingrad, the withdrawal of Germans from all fronts started, which was a big turn toward the win against fascism. The place was important because the Mountains of Gjakova, provided not only a natural bond between Kosova and North Albania, but in that area were the only secure bases of the anti-fascist movement, which since the Italian capitulation, were considered free zones, where everybody operated easily and without interruption. There were also two representatives of the English mission which operated in that area of Kosova. The Germans operated on the Prizren-Kukës line, and it didn't seem that they were interested in any trouble with anti-fascist forces. The situation there would remain the same throughout the year until the end of October and beginning of November when the German forces pulled back. As would be seen, this conference became the reason for many disparities and contention between Albanian communists from Kosova and Yugoslavs. They were afraid that the Communists from Albania would take the Yugoslav Communist side, and in this way, bring a catastrophic outcome not only for the people of Kosova, but the people of Albania as well. The outcome of all this would be seen 50 years later when the disintegration of Yugoslavia would start and the outcome of this conference would help achieve the declaration of Kosova's independence.

Delegates from all over Kosova arrived in Bujan two days before the meeting started. They were situated in the family compound of Sali Mani from Tropoja and neighboring houses. Security for the Conference was provided by the Battalion "Perlat Rexhepi" and the soldiers of the Battalion "Bajram Curri" from Dukagjin, even though in reality there was no danger, since the German forces were not even interested in crossing that area.

The meeting opened on the morning of the last day of 1943 by Xhevded Doda. He proposed that the honorary committee consist of the Supreme Commandant of the Soviet Army, Stalin, the English Prime

Minister, Churchill, and the American President, Theodore Roosevelt. In addition, he proposed the Supreme Commandant of the National Liberation Army of Yugoslavia, the president of AVNOJ, Dr. Ivan Ribar, the President of the National Liberation Council of Albania, Sejfulla Malishova, Supreme Commandant of the Headquarters of the National Liberartion Army of Albania, Spiro Mojsiu, the Political Commissary of the Supreme Headquarters of the National Liberation Army of Albania, Enver Hoxha, the Commandant of the Second Corps of the National Liberation Army of Yugoslavia, Peko Dapcevic; also proposed were: Myslim Peza, Haxhi Lleshi and Baba Faja Martaneshi, The Supreme Headquarters of The National Liberation Army of Kosova and Dukagjin, The Communist Party of Kosova and Dukagjin, The Kosovar-Macedonian Brigade, and the battalions "Perlat Rexhepi" and "Bajram Curri."

The participants fully supported this proposal and saluted it with great applause. With this formal conference setting, the participating delegates wanted to give their acts historical importance, as well as international legitimacy, especially since the the anti-fascist alliance was led by Americans and Britains, and the Soviets were among the participants.

Xhevded Doda then read the names of the participating delgates and proposed a leadership committee of 8 delegates, two of which were Ali Shukriu and Milan Zeçar, who were not present due to travel difficulties, but accepted their positions and the decisions of the conference:

Mehmet Hoxha, President – ex-Mayor of Gjakova,
Rifat Berisha, Vice President – ex-officer of the Albanian army,
Pavle J. Jovicevic (Paloka), Vice President – worker from Peja,
Xhevdet Doda – school principal from Prizren,
Fadil Hoxha – teacher from Gjakova,
Ali Shukria, student from Mitrovica,
Milan Zeçar, farmer from Ratkoceri, a small village close to Ferizaj
Hajdar Dushi, banker from Gjakova.

Hajdar Dushi kept the minutes of the meeting.

Xhevded Doda announced the delegate names as well as their verification regarding the First National Liberation Council of Kosova and Dukagjin: *Ismail Xhinali, Tefik Canga, Qamil Luzha, Xheladin Rama, Ismet Shaqiri, Adem Miftari, Xhevat Tahiri, Ymer Pula, Et'hem*

Zurnaxhiu, N. Basha, Hajdin Bajraktari, Bejto Shahmanovic, Milan A. Mickovic, Zymer Halili, Mehmet Dermani, Qamil Brovina, Gani S. Çavdërbasha, Syle B. Alaj, Shaban Kajtazi, Ferid Perolli, Haxhi Morina, Ismajl Isufi, Sabrije Vokshi, Velisha Mickovic, Lubomir Canic, A. Qerim Ibrahimi, Spiro Velkovic, Xhavit S. Nimani, Reshad Isa, M. Bajraktari, Veli Niman Doci, Rasim Collaku, S. Bekteshi, Jaho Bajraktari, Shaban Haxhia, Alush Gashi, Beqir Ndou, Xhafer Vokshi, Sima T. Vasilevic, Enver Dajqi, and Maxhun Doçi Nimani.

The first leader of the meeting was Professor Zekeria Rexha, who started the meeting with a moment of silence in honor of the soldiers who died during the anti-fascist war. Since this meeting was considered an historic act, Fadil Hoxha, the Commander of Headquarters of the National Liberation Army of Kosova and Dukagjin stated:

> "I am really happy to be able to greet you at this historic gathering... We do not recognize any fascist power or their actions. The future of our country will be guaranteed only through the uncompromised war against the fascist occupiers and with the help of the big anti-fascist bloc and in cooperation with the National Liberation Army of Yugoslavia and the National Liberation Army of Albania which are fighting side-by-side, and with the winning bloc of our allies: England and America."[278]

After Fadil Hoxha, Pavle Jovicevic-Paloka spoke, saying that it was his pleasure to greet the Conference in the name of the Regional Committee of CPY for Kosova and Dukagjin. Further, Jovicevic stated:

> "The decisions of Bujan will be historic, since for the first time representatives of our occupied regions of Kosova and Dukagjin, with no prejudice toward faith, political stance, or ethnicity, will sit together to decide on our future destiny."[279]

The words of Pavle Jovicevic regarding the Bujan Conference were historic, which he would later repeat in the Conference, where he was chosen as the Vice President of the leading committee. It is important to explain the hypocritical standpoint of Serbian communists who participated in the war of the anti-fascist movement in Kosova. They would completely adjust to the

---

[278] See archive documents cited in Spasoje Djaković: *"Sukobi na Kosovu,"* Beograd, 1984, p. 225.

[279] *Ibid.*, Box VII, film 5/3-4, p. 228.

circumstances and standpoint of most Albanians, at the same time, as soon as the rapport between the forces changed, and when Kosova was re-occupied by partisan and Yugoslav forces, their words would change and the Conference decisions were invalidated and they considered it even a mistake to have been a part of it. Further, in the eighties, when the wild campaign of Serbia differentiated Albanians between "good" and "bad"; the "good" ones meaning those who denounced their culture and historic herit-age, and the "bad" ones were those who did not. The Serbians in 1980 then characterized the Bujani Conference and discussions as *"inspiration against the armed revolution in Kosova, which will break out as soon as fascists leave!"*[280]

Besides Pavle Jovicevic (Paloka), another Serb, Milan Miçkovic (Shefqeti) gave a speech at the Conference, who also, as his predecessors, called the conference historic, because the Albanian people, down-trodden by the inhumane regime of the Yugoslav monarchy, for the first time won the right to decide for their own fate.

All the greetings and discussions accentuated the historic importance of this meeting. The resolution was adopted, leading to the right of Albanians in Kosova to join Albania; this right would only be approved if the anti-fascist forces won the war in Kosova and Albania.[281]

To keep everyone informed, the resolution was sent three weeks later by Fadil Hoxha, who was in the role of Commander-in-Chief of the Headquarters of the National Liberation Army, to the Albanian and Yugoslav counterparts, as well as to the Headquarters of the Communist Parties of Albania and Yugoslavia. This would be the first communique that Tito received directly from the Kosova and Dukagjin region, and not through the Serbian Communist Party. Also, the guarantee for fulfillment of the resolution would be required from the allies of the anti-fascist bloc: England, The United States of America, and The Soviet Union.

Informing Tito and the CC of CPY until then was done through his emissaries in Albania, or Svetozar Vukmanovic – Tempo, his special representative for Macedonia and Kosova.

The Central Committee of the Comunist Party of Yugoslavia reacted quickly with a letter of warning, however, with prudence, since the

---

[280] See NIN, Beograd, September 1981.

[281] Cited in "Këshilli Nacionalçlirimtar i Krahinës Autonome të Kosovës dhe Metohisë 1943-1945," p. 10.

resolution content spoke about the Albanians' right to join Albania through a free declaration, which was not contestable. The Yugoslavs responded by saying it would be necessary to wait because this question would not have an answer until all other cases were resolved and the anti-fascist war was victorious. Disregarding diplomatic language, which in those circumstances could have been different, the CC of CPY criticized Kosova for taking steps toward the creation of independent party and military bases reporting directly to them rather than going through Serbia. The message said:

> "...The Regional Committee should not have been created and the name of Metohia should not have been changed to Dukagjin for a simple reason because Dukagjin includes the parts which pass the border beyond Yugoslavia."[282]

Continuing with this tone, the letter ends in this way:

> "The resolution does not clearly show the character of the National Liberation Council. That council can only be an initiative, it can be a political organ of the majority, but it cannot by any means get the character of a jurisdiction, because you do not have free territories..."[283]

The Regional Committee of Kosova and Dukagjin was warned, for the moment, their actions would not lead to consequences for the communists in Kosova and their behavior towards building an independent rapport with the Albanian and Yugoslav communists. The Yugoslav army did not have any presence in Kosova because their army units could not go into Kosova even though they had tried it on many occasions. One was the case with the Second Corps led by Peko Dapcevic, who was stationed in Sanxhak, and defeated by Albanian patriotic forces, which were formed after the Second Prizren League Conference in September of 1943. About the same time, the government of Rexhep Mitrovica was installed in Tirana.

Before the re-occupation of Kosova by Yugoslav partisans, Tito and other masked Serbian hegemonists with a communist face used Enver Hoxha and the partisan forces to create favorable circumstances for their intentions. They then started their well-known scripts for the destruction

---

[282] Spasoje Djaković: "*Sukobi na Kosovu,*" Beograd, 1984, p. 210.
[283] *Ibid.*, p. 211.

of the military and political subjectivity that Kosova created during the last two years with all the hard work, so that they could achieve two goals at once - pacifying Kosova from patriotic and intellectual forces and through a harsh military terror, shaping Kosovar ideas for the "declaration" of Kosova as a democratic country willing to join the democratic Serbia!

The Yugoslav plan to re-occupy Kosova started with an agreement between Tito and Hoxha for sending the Albanian partisans into Kosova to fight German forces, which were already on their way back toward the North of Albania and the North of Kosova towards the Ibri valley and then into Serbia. Because, in this way, Yugoslav partisans would avoid confrontation with Albanian patriotic forces, while including the partisans surely would not allow Yugoslavs to go in easily.

In October of 1944, Albanian communists entered Kosova upon Tito's request, in the name of the Command Headquarters of the National Liberation Army of Yugoslavia. The Albanian brigades 3 and 5 entered Kosova. The first conflict against the Germans started the same day in Dukagjin, on the southeastern side of Prizren. The goal was to free the zone between two rivers, Drin and Ribnik. On the 16th of October they attacked Germans in Gjakova and the surrounding areas. These battles continued until the 7th of November when Albanian partisans from Kosova celebrated their victory. It is important to note that in Gjakova, Albanian partisans entered with national Albanian flags. Then the movements of partisans continued in two directions: towards Prizren and Peja. Prizren was freed on the 16th of November, and Peja one day later. At the end of November, Dukagjin was freed from German forces, which started abandoning their base and heading north.

After the entrance of the brigades from Albania into Kosova and their success, the southern and eastern parts of Kosova, towards Podujeva, Shkup and Gjilan, in Kosova, the Yugoslav units started to enter inside Kosova proper. They entered with the Albanian and the Yugoslavian flag with the five-pointed star in the middle. As soon as they entered in the cities, they showed photos of Tito and Hoxha, followed by catchwords in Albanian and English for fraternity, unity and friendship between Albanians and Yugoslavs created through the war against fascism.

Only later did the population learn the true meaning of "the freedom triumph" which was brought by partisans from Albania and Yugoslavia throughout their demonstrations. As it was anticipated, in silence, they tried to manipulate the local jurisdiction, who started supervising the military, which was done in the name of the people. Ozna, the Yugoslav military intelligence, which was located in Shkup, began to prepare for entrance into Kosova. They came up with lists of undesirable intellectuals, patriots and other persons who were now included in the register of collaborators with the occupier. Balli Kombetar, Legaliteti and other political forces were included in these lists, especially since they cooperated with the Albanian National Democratic Movement, which was greatly spread in Kosova. For Yugoslavs it was of great importance to know who was in agreement with them and who was not.

Meanwhile the mobilization of "volunteer" Albanians was sent to the North front of Yugoslavia, mostly in the Srem region, where the main German forces were positioned, but also towards Montenegro so they could fight for the coastal region up to Rijeka. The mobilization of volunteers would be a very painful and tragic chapter for Kosova because it was done forcefully and would accomplish two strategic goals for the Yugoslavs:

a) Decreasing the human potential in Kosova, especially the youth who were being considered as potentially problematic for the new scenarios being prepared against Kosova and

b) Preparing the terrain for bringing more Yugoslav partisan units into Kosova who were assigned to performing ethnic cleansing so that every nationalist force and patriot would be eliminated.

It was estimated that in the next two months, more than twenty thousand young Albanians were mobilized by force and marched toward the North and the Adriatic fronts through Albania and Montenegro, many of whom never returned to Kosova. Many of them died before facing the Germans because they were sent through mined territories.

The most tragic example is the one of the Tivar massacre, in which more than two thousand Albanians were killed. This represented a true case of crime against humanity. In reality, the victims of Tivar were mostly mobilized through violence in the Eastern area and around Prizren.

Two partisan units from Albania were deployed to provide transportation for the young Albanians from Kukes to Shkodra and then to Tivar, where they were supposedly going to engage in battle at the Adriatic coast. The march appeared more like a march to a concentration camp, much like the ones that Jews were sent to, than the "anti-fascist volunteer drive," as it was called by the Albanian-Yugoslav communists. The stories of the few that survived the road of death revealed unprecedented genocide. The partisans, with the help of the outrageous winter, treated the Albanians inhumanly by letting them die in the snow, or if they got tired, executed them "as saboteurs"!

To make things worse, some of them that survived were later tortured when they arrived in Shkodra, or they stayed there because they didn't want to return to Albania where they had endured such a bad experience. Whenever they were handed over to the Montenegrin partisans, as soon as they approached Tivar, at the old castle, they would start shooting at them, claiming that some of the Albanian "rebels" wanted to go away! The Yugoslavian data, which was later accepted as their investigation, did not hold anyone responsible, showed two hundred to be the number of victims that were killed with some others found "tragically" dead in a warehouse in Shibernik, which was burned, when many of the Albanian volunteers were sleeping. It was estimated that there were around two thousand deaths in Tivar, not including more than four hundred others who died "accidentally" in the warehouse when it caught fire.

CONCLUSION

From the Ambassadors' Conference of London to the Peace Conference of Paris, Albania and the Albanians faced an existential struggle. In London, the Great Powers together recognized an independent Albania, albeit reduced in size, and undertook to oversee its government for the next ten years. With the outbreak of World War I, the European powers were split – Austria-Hungary and Germany as the Central Powers and Britain, Russia, France (and later Italy) as the Entente – and the front between the two blocs carried into Albania. The country was invaded by neighboring states, hoping to achieve their hegemonic goals in the war, which ended only after the decisive involvement of the United States.

The war between states also ignited an internal war in Albania. The most tragic among such conflicts is notably one that could be characterized as a war between Ottoman Albania and European Albania. Prince Wied landed on Albanian soil on March 7, 1914, to become the nation's new ruler, as decided by the ambassadors in London. But his brief reign was soon met with bloodshed, as fighting took place until the German prince finally departed in September 1914, leaving the country in the hands of an international body.

This tragic regression was not a coincidence, nor was it outside of the plans of those opposed to the new state of Albania. Pro-Ottoman forces and religious fanatics among the Albanians took a leading role. At a time when the country, despite the truncation of its territory by the London decision, hoped to assert its character as a nation-state of ethnic Albanians; the pro-Ottoman groups worked for the opposite. They sought to restore the Ottoman Empire, even by the means of innumerous killings in the name of religion – a phenomenon that had previously been absent among the religiously diverse Albanians.

In fact, the pro-Ottoman and religious fanatics, on one hand, and their political antagonists, mainly proponents of equality and social justice, on the other hand, were first moved by the Ambassadors' Conference of London. As the international meeting opened in late 1912, one if its first decisions was to recognize Albania's autonomy under the sovereignty of the Ottoman sultan. While the creation of an autonomous state had been an Albanian project since the 1870s and throughout the period of national revival, it was such under the circumstances of the time. Albanian leaders saw independence as their ultimate goal. And now that the Ottoman state was no longer present in Albania, the November 1912 declaration of independence became irreversible.

In April 1913, the London Conference revoked its decision, removing every right of the Ottomans over Albania. During the preceding months, the Ottoman Empire had negotiated a peace treaty with the Balkan League (Serbia, Montenegro, Greece, and Bulgaria), while leaving the fate of the former imperial dominions on the peninsula to the Ambassadors' Conference. This meant that the Porte (Ottoman Empire) itself had vested the Europeans with the power to appoint Albania's new ruler. But the possibility that a Western prince could obtain the throne of the new monarchy provoked the pro-Ottoman and Islamist forces. They formed a sizeable group, concentrated among the middle class and those who were disappointed with the declared Albanian state while the country was overrun by its neighbors. Under such circumstances, they fought not only to maintain ties with the Ottoman Empire, but to salvage Albania as Ottoman territory. This could be done, in their view, by anointing a Turkish prince for Albania.

The plans for an Ottoman prince were ushered by the Young Turk regime, which bore the ultimate responsibility for the occupation of Albania by its Balkan neighbors. As a first move, the Ottoman government employed an army general of Albanian descent, Izet Pasha, so that he could work on "bringing together" the Albanians and Ottomans on what they had, until then, been unable to agree. The efforts were claimed to have the support of the majority of Albanians living in Istanbul and other parts of the Ottoman Empire, who would join the campaign for an Ottoman prince. In reality, this was an endeavor of the Young Turks to restore the political influence on Albanians that they lost due to poor leadership and unsound policies, which stubbornly refused the demands for an autonomous state. The campaign made great advances in Albania. Pro-Ottomans increased in numbers, especially in territories under Serbian occupation. Islamist fanatics and Young Turk agents visited those areas under instruction to use religious sermons in mosques to rally for the Ottoman Empire. The pro-Ottoman movement, however, became formally organized after the European powers appointed a German prince as the new monarch of

Albania. Wilhelm von Wied (William of Wied), a Protestant Christian, was approved by the Great Powers after a joint proposal of Austria-Hungary and Italy.

The Albanian intellectuals and political leadership welcomed the appointment of a German prince. Most Albanians were in favor of the decision, and viewed it as an opportunity to provide for the stability of the country. But as the pro-Ottoman movement drew support from its Young Turk masterminds, opposition to Prince Wied became a troubling issue. The Ottoman campaign grew particularly strong in central Albania, the same region that included Durrës, the new capital and seat of Wied's government. As early as February 1914, weeks before the new prince's arrival, the Vlora-based Albanian government had handed its power to the International Control Commission, a body consisting of representatives of the Great Powers with a mandate to supervise the newly-created state.

Certain members of the International Control Commission, in pursuit of the interests and directives of their home countries, were a major influence in the downturn of the political situation. As internal politicking ensued, the Commission not only failed to stabilize the country, but added fuel to the burning fire. In particular, the Italian representative, Baron Alioti, cooperated closely with Esad Pashë Toptani, a cabinet minister who would become the architect of the plots against Wied's regime. Soon a revolt led by Haxhi Qamili and other fanatic Islamic clergymen would break out against the prince in central Albania. The mufti (mayor) of Tirana, Toptani's hometown, played a pivotal role. Many historical sources point out that Italian agents, along with the Serbs and Greeks, furnished most of the weapons and financial support needed for the rebellion.

In this tragedy, the Albanians would end up fighting one another: on the one hand, a national front fought to defend the Albanian state under the Albanian flag; on the other hand, rebels fought under the Ottoman flag to return Albania to the hands of the Ottoman Empire. Through the summer and autumn of 1914, the pro-Ottoman forces defeated the Albanian state. The rebels took over Vlora in the south, and Tirana, among other towns, in central Albania, and an Ottoman standard replaced the double-headed eagle of the Albanian flag. Supported by Serbia and Greece, Esad Pashë Toptani headed a central government well into mid-1915, when he formally renounced Albania's neutral status and entered World War I against the Central Powers. As Austria-Hungary was already pursuing

Serbian and Montenegrin troops that had occupied Kosova and Albania,
Toptani escaped to Italy.

Toptani sent around 4,000 of his troops to join the Entente front in
Thessaloniki, but himself lived in exile for the remainder of the Great
War. During his time in Italy, and later in France, the Albanian pasha
envisaged his future rule over a Muslim dominion in the Balkans. The
now defunct project of an Ottoman Albania that had sparked the 1914
rebellion led way to a plan for a Muslim Albania. In the 1915 Secret
Treaty of London, Great Britain, France, and Italy agreed to further
reduce the size of the troubled Balkan country. The agreement sought to
create a feudal dominion spanning between the Mat River and Tirana in
central Albania as a "Muslim relic of Europe." This entity would become
an Italian protectorate allegedly aiming to "reconcile" Christendom and
Islam there where they had fought the most. But in reality, the chances of
its survival would be nonexistent, for the neighboring countries would
soon conquer the Muslim Albanian state, using Islam as a pretext.

The signatory countries took action to implement the secret plan as soon
as the war was over. The parts of Albania that had been previously held
by Austria-Hungary were placed under Italian occupation. Albanian
territories that were left outside of the 1913 borders (i.e., Kosova and
western Macedonia) were re-occupied by Serbia, which used additional
pretexts, such as the "creation of a buffer zone" to defend "against
separatist movements," to march further into northern and central
Albania. In the meantime, southern Albania – with the exception of
Korça and Gjirokastër, which remained under French control – was
occupied by Greece. There, again, Athens laid claims over territories it
called Northern Epirus.

Such an arrangement of foreign military control, based on the spirit of the
1915 secret deal, was in place in Albania, when the victors of World War
I gathered at Versailles in Paris for the Peace Conference. In addition to
Britain, France, and Italy, the United States and Japan would also take
part in the conference.

As a victor, Italy demanded a mandate over Albania. For this reason, the
Italian government undertook to also "represent" the Albanians, relying
initially on representatives with a pro-Italian attitude. Later, Rome also
established ties with other Albanian leaders, especially those who sought
the support of a powerful nation in light of Serbia and Greece's
increasing power in the region. Belgrade, in particular, not only had won
the war, but emerged now as the capital of the united Serbo-Croato-

Slovene Kingdom (later Yugoslavia), signaling a much greater influence than what Serbia had previously enjoyed.

The fate of Albania lay at the mercy of the Italian-Yugoslav settlements on the Adriatic basin for about two years until January 1920, when Albanian leaders took the matter in their own hands. At the Congress of Lushnje, Albanian delegates decisively renounced the 1915 Secret Treaty of London and rejected the Italian mandate to decide on Albania. At the time, Italy had not only occupied parts of the country, but had formally declared its annexation of the city of Vlora and its hinterland.

The Congress of Lushnje established a new national government, consisting of an executive cabinet and a representative assembly, which worked on reclaiming Albania's sovereignty. The government was headed by Prime Minister Sulejman Delvina, while other cabinet members included Interior Minister Ahmet Zogu, whose military expertise – along with the patriotic movement that ensued – proved instrumental in asserting control over the country. The new state institutions took over pivotal towns such as Shkodër in the north and later Korça in the south, focusing finally on liberating the Italian-held city of Vlora.

Realizing no alternative to armed action, Sulejman Delvina's government undertook the necessary preparations to liberate the city. The successful war against Italy represented the most audacious action for the salvation and defense of Albania against the numerous enemies and hostile plans they devised against her. Throwing the occupying forces in the sea, Delvina's government not only restored that which rightfully belonged to Albania, but was also able to impact the decisions of the Paris Conference.

The Delvina government's agreement with Rome for the withdrawal of Italian troops from Vlora and its hinterland put an end not only to the possibility of an Italian protectorate, but also ruled out the risk of a further repartitioning of the country. As Italy had been defeated and could no longer receive its mandate over Albania, the Italian government objected to the claims of Greece and Serbia for territorial expansion. At the Paris Peace Conference, Rome demanded the right to defend Albania's territorial integrity, in the event of a threat from Belgrade or Athens. But while this largely guaranteed the borders set in 1913, Italy obtained an advantage that would later enable great influence that ultimately led to the Fascist occupation of Albania in 1939.

During the period before the Fascist takeover, nonetheless, an important segment of history is marked by the reoccupation of Kosova and other

Albanian-inhabited lands. The territory, occupied by Serbia and
Montenegro during the Balkan Wars and later granted to the Slavic
kingdoms by the European powers in 1913, was reconfirmed as part of
the new Serbo-Croato-Slovene (SKS)kingdom by the Paris Conference.
French troops that had captured Kosova from the retreating Austro-
Hungarian and Bulgarian armies handed it over to the Serbs, whose
return ensued a series of massacres against the civilian Albanian
population. The Kingdom of Serbs, Croats, and Slovenes, founded in
1918, and later renamed to Yugoslavia, continued where the previous
Serbian and Montenegrin kingdoms had left off – terrorizing the
Albanians and forcing their migration to Albania and Turkey.
In addition to the mass deportation, Belgrade also began to colonize
Kosova with Serbs and Montenegrins from other parts of the country,
notably Bosnia and Herzegovina and Montenegro. Between 1920 and
1924, the regime forcibly expelled over 100,000 Albanians from their
land, which was then transferred to roughly 30,000 colonists who
migrated to Kosova.
The colonization process would be assisted by the so-called agrarian
reform, whereby Albanians were expropriated and the best land given to
colonists. Initially, colonists received as much land as they desired.
From 1924 onward, the government awarded each family with a
minimum of five hectares and another half hectare for every member of
the household. Additionally, the state provided for the transportation,
work equipment, and housing in easily accessible locations along
railroads and highways.
It was during this period that the Kachak movement would resume in
Kosova. A number of Albanian kachaks, notably the chetas of Azem Bejta
(also known as Azem Galica), had sided with Serbs during World War I,
hoping that Kosova would be returned to Albania. As reoccupation
ensued, the Albanian kachaks rushed to their arms to fight against their
former allies, although under very difficult circumstances.
The Kachak movement spread rapidly throughout Kosova. The regions of
Drenica and Llap were particularly mobilized in an existential struggle
against the reoccupation. In the meantime, the police terror against
innocent civilians increased, while Belgrade continued its use of force to
deport the Albanian population.
Between 1920 and 1924, the Kachak movement was closely linked to the
National Committee for the Defense of Kosova (Alb.: Komiteti Kombëtar
për Mbrojtjen e Kosovës), an irredentist organization founded in Shkodër

in 1918. The Committee's work, however, was not welcomed in Albania, as the Kosovar leaders became involved in the country's troubled political scene, siding with the left against right-wing leader Ahmet Zogu. The irredentists hence faced problems on both ends, with Tirana and Belgrade, which resulted the Albanian-Yugoslav cooperation in quelling the "Neutral Zone" of Junik in 1923. The dissolution of the buffer area along the Albanian border delivered a heavy blow to the national resistance in Kosova. A year later, the Serbs took over "Free Zone" of Prekaz, in Drenica, and killed Azem Bejta. Notwithstanding sporadic impulses that continued in different areas, the Kachak movement collapsed tragically.

The end of the national resistance in Kosova in the form of the Kachak movement and the consolidation of Ahmet Zogu's leadership – accompanied by the ratification of treaties in 1926 that Albania and Yugoslavia signed in accordance with their obligations to the League of Nations – provided for political and economic stability in Albania, especially after closer ties with Italy were established. The collapse of the resistance, however, put the Albanian population of Kosova and other areas under Yugoslav rule in a critical situation. Mass deportation and colonization, followed by efforts to assimilate the remaining population, threatened the very existence of the ethnic group.

Nonetheless, Belgrade did not appear content as, in spite of all endeavors, it had failed to create the desired three-to-one majority of the Slavic people in the subject areas. The Kachak movement had played a part in undermining the comfort of the colonists and had prevented the regime from serving as a "factor for safety." While Belgrade had used all means to quell the guerrilla fighters, resorting as well to atrocities against the civilian population, the kachaks had slowed down the colonization process and, in certain areas, prevented it entirely.

As a consequence, Serbian academics blamed the state for not handling the situation harshly enough, suggesting further an elaborate plan for the mass expulsion of the Albanians. The scholars called in particular for a treaty with Ankara that would permit the repatriation of Albanians in Turkey. Academic Vaso Čubrilović proposed radical measures, ranging from state-induced economic hardship that would lead to self-deportation to the more racist calls for preventing births among the Albanians, which were viewed as a fatal threat to the Serbs!

The result of the proposals was a Yugoslav-Turkish convention that permitted the relocation of 400,000 Albanians to Turkey within the next

*six years. However, the Turkish government refused to ratify the treaty.
As World War II lay in the horizon, Ankara began to gravitate towards
the Axis powers, which viewed Yugoslavia as an unfavorable creation of
Versailles and hoped to partition it as actually occurred two years later.
The Axis invasion of Yugoslavia brought about a partial and temporary
unification of the Albanians: a large part of Kosova and Macedonia was
annexed to the Italian-held "Greater Albania," certain eastern areas
were handed to Bulgaria, while Germany held on to the rest of the
territory (included within Nedić's Serbia, but providing for an Albanian
autonomy). Nonetheless, the border changes did not bring the spiritual
unification of the Albanians. In fact, the left wing repudiated what it
viewed as the "Fascist unification." The right wing considered the
process incomplete, as large areas remained outside of Albania's border
(under Bulgarian or German control).*

*The Albanian communists, swayed by the Yugoslavs, embraced the
internationalist doctrine of the proletariat and, refusing to cooperate with
the nationalists in antifascist war, brought Albania under the Soviet
sphere of influence. The spiritual and social terror of the Eastern bloc
was particularly devastating to the Albanian people and to the fate of
Kosova. From December 31, 1943 to January 2, 1944, antifascist
delegates of Kosova convened at the Conference of Bujan to affirm their
will for reunification with Albania. But despite the will of the people,
Kosova and other areas reverted to Yugoslavia at the end of the war. To
add insult to injury, the Yugoslav occupation this time enjoyed the
blessing of the internationalist communists of Albania, who subjected the
the nation to an oppressive ideology.*

PART TWO
THE YUGOSLAV REOCCUPATION
OF KOSOVA

CHAPTER 1
THE SERBIAN ANNEXATION OF KOSOVA AND KOSOVA'S EARLY STRUGGLE FOR AUTONOMY

The Military Invasion and the Albanian Resistance

The liberation of Kosova by the Albanian partisans, assisted also by the Kosova brigades, and the hand-over of Kosova to the Yugoslav partisans. – The beginning of the communist terror against the Kosova population conforming to Cubrilovic's program that the National Liberation War be used for the resolution of issues with the Albanians. – The rise of the Albanian resistance in Gjilan and the Karadak area against the Slavic communist regim led by Mulla Idrizi. – The nationalist forces hoped that the Anglo-American forces would intervene in Kosova. – The refusal of Shaban Polluzha and Adem Voca to continue mobilizing people to the North and the outbreak of the Albanian insurgency at large. – The placement of Kosova under military administration and the destruction of all military structures and local institutions of Kosova. – The Prizren Convention and the decision that Kosova would "voluntarily" join Serbia – the violent reoccupation of Kosova by Belgrade.

In Kosova, apart from the anti-fascist reality and the spread of its organization through the National Liberation Committees, which spread into the urban areas and in most cases was illegal, the real regime also existed. It had been in place from September 1943, as a result of the National Assembly, in which, after the segregation of Albania from Italy was declared, the High Committee of Regents was selected with Mehdi Frashëri as its leader. On November 5th it also declared the Albanian government with Rexhep Mitrovica as its leader. The representatives of the "National Front" (Balli Kombetar) were also part of the government.

Therefore, it was natural that the political forces, which had governed for more than a year, even after Germany's retreat from Albania, would take over the responsibility of safeguarding the area, in order to prove their legitimacy, at a very difficult time, conforming to the promises they made.

However, as would be seen, this responsibility was not fulfilled because the military formations, which the Albanian government had established under its name or that of Wehrmacht, as was the SS Battalion "Skenderbeg," aligned with the fascist forces and with them also faced losses in Albania, Kosova and elsewhere.[284]

Without the retreat of the Germans, hoping that the Anglo-American forces would join, the National and Patriotic forces remained in Kosova and in Albania. These forces were not able to fight together a common war, other than a spontaneous one, even though they had experienced the same defeat from the communist partisans. In common for these national and patriotic forces was the fact that they did not have an organizational connection. Not even the Anglo-American missionaries were able to avoid this inability to connect, even though they were stationed in the North of Albania and other areas with the intention of uniting them, so that they would appear as an alternative to the communist forces.

With the beginning of the retreat of the Germans from Albania, also came the end of the Albanian government, which a year earlier had gained the approval of the German Wehrmacht, and even Hitler himself, who welcomed Xhafer Deva in Berlin in the name of the head of the Second League of Prizren[285]. With Xhafer Deva, they also discussed the possibility

---

[284] "*Historia e Popullit Shqiptar,*" second volume, Prishtinë, 1969, p. 775.

[285] *The Second League of Prizren* was held in Prizren on September 16th, after the Fascist Italy capitulated. Looking at it from the historical responsibility that the Albanian patriots and intellectuals had in those circumstances, it was right that the Albanians act according to this, which implied a nation-wide platform for action. Its organizer was Xhafer Deva. Representatives from all ethnic Albanian regions participated, where it was decided that Albania be declared independent with the borders it had during the Ottoman Empire. Since Mitrovica and its region were under the German administration and a portion of the Kosova region under the Bulgarian regime, Germany was asked to return those regions to Kosova. From the organizational perspective, the Second League of Prizren appeared almost analogous with the structures of the First League of 1878. Rexhep Mitrovica was chosen to head the Central Committee of the League, whereas its members were: Tahir Zajmi, Qazim Bllaca, Sheh Hasani, Kolë Margjini, Asllan Buletini, Musa Shehu, and others. The leaders of the League's Committee changed. After Rexhep

of "military training of Kosova for self-defense." He was promised assistance from the "Fuhrer", which commenced, but this would be conditional upon his remaining under the service of the German Wehrmacht and its concepts. With this act, with or without intention, the Albanian government was burdened with the obligation to collaborate,[286] as were some other leaders of the Second League of Prizren. This collaboration, in the face of the sincere intentions and the necessity for the responsibility of the Albanian political factor to act for the fate of its place, in those important circumstances, where a national-wide response was necessary, a response was required which would conform to the challenges of that time.

The insecure terrain, upon which the government of Rexhep Mitrovica and lastly that of Xhafer Deva relied upon, would be seen exactly at the moment when the Germans prepared to leave Albania, after having lost the war from the anti-fascist forces when the partisans came out as the only victors. These governments' abilities to act were very limited and dependent upon the relations of the world war, so after this, they were left with nothing but to call an end to all their activities worldwide on October 26th, and with the assistance of the Germans, leave through the sea toward Vienna and Berlin.

The retreat of the government of Xhafer Deva to the West resulted in the quick filling in of the gap left by the partisan forces with the entrance of the partisan forces from Albania (Divisions V and III). Shortly thereafter, the government was handed over to the Yugoslav partisans, who furthered penetration with their brigades (in most cases Chetniks converted to partisans) toward Podujeva, Shkup and then Cakorr and Peja. In

---

Mitrovica, came Bedri Pejani, and lastly, Xhafer Deva. With the arrival of Bedri Pejani as the leader of the League, the issue of establishing the League's units was also discussed, units which were under its command. The Second League of Prizren decided to establish its branches and to safeguard the prerogatives of the central military command, which led the war against the partisans and defended the area in all circumstances from the penetration of the Yugoslav and Greek forces, and other external attacks. Bedri Pejani, on March 29, 1944, sent a letter to Hitler, in which he notified Hitler about the League and its stance for the establishment of an SS division in Kosova together with a military force of approximately 120 thousand soldiers, which would be able to defend Kosova. In this case, he asked for equipment and assistance to achieve his goal.

[286] "Historia e Popullit Shqiptar," second volume, Prishtinë, 1969, p. 811

this way the region was reoccupied by over thirty thousand organized military forces, nevertheless, leaving behind the spirit of the "will" of safeguarding Kosova based on the promise made at the Assembly of the Second League of Prizren the year before. However, this spirit was spread in pieces, without an organizational head, and unsubstantiated by the optimistic promises of the Vienna Radio, which Xhafer Deva dedicated to the separated units of the "National Front" (Balli Kombetar). But these promises did not reach anyone's ears under these circumstances of information darkness placed by the partisan dictatorship and its propaganda. Nevertheless, it can be said that even in that difficult situation of the Yugoslav partisan regime in Kosova, which had been led by the Albanian partisans, the vow of protecting their homeland started to become functional in the form of an armed resistance. This resistance, even though it didn't have a widespread concept or a single operating center, nevertheless brought to the surface a different language of Kosova – that of a clash with the Slavic-communist regime, which apart from the widespread refusal, also articulated the armed resistance against the regime, as a just issue to defend itself from a warned genocide which was being prepared against the area by the communists. This regime became even more ominous as it related to the prior hegemonic programs of Belgrade against Albanians and their territory. Even though the Yugoslav propaganda immediately labeled the armed resistance as one of the "National Front" and other national and patriotic groups, which began in Ferizaj and then in Gjilan, it intensified from the beginning of December and on, as "the beginning of the Albanian counterrevolution in wide dimensions," led directly by the secret headquarters of Xhafer Deva[287]. The possibility cannot be ruled out that among these forces, had risen the hope that the Anglo-American forces had promised to intervene.

The wide-spread alarm sounded by the eruption of the "counterrevolution," was conveniently exploited by the Yugoslavs in order to achieve their goals as soon as possible. This conformed to the threats and scorns directed at Kosova from the Conference of Bujan and on, according to which the entrance of the Yugoslav partisan units in Kosova was supposed to result in:

a) The destruction of the local forces' structures, which had resulted from the National Liberation Conference in Bujan

---

[287] See Djaković, S: ""*Sukobi na Kosovu*," 1984, p. 236.

b) The destruction of the military structures of Albanians and the melting of their remains into the composition of the Yugoslav army

c) The cancellation of the decisions of the Conference of Bujan regarding the Albanians' self-determination to unite with Albania, as a right to which they were entitled according to the Atlantic Charter, and apart from this, the establishment of circumstances for another "voluntary declaration" for the unification of Kosova and Serbia, from the same forum.

Therefore, without the dimension of the "counterrevolution" and its alarm, the Yugoslavs would not have been able to declare the establishment of the military state, as would be put in place on February 8, 1945. Without this "alarm," the circumstances would not have been established for a factual reoccupation of Kosova and its annexation to Serbia, including the Prizren Convention, held from 8 to 10 July, 1945.

The Yugoslav reoccupation of Kosova by the partisans, which reached the dimensions of genocide four months later, was the third in a row (the first one in the winter of 1877/78, with the penetration of Serbs into Prokupe and Kursumli; the second one in 1912, with the occupation of Kosova and other regions by the Serbian military). The second Memorandum of Vasa Cubrilovic warned that the Yugoslav reoccupation would take this direction. He also authored the first anti-Albanian Memorandum of the Serbian academics from 1937, which was handed over to Tito in October, and cryptically reported "the issue of minorities in the new Yugoslavia," with a particular stress on liquidating the issues with the indigenous German population in Banat and Srem in the North, which included around 700,000 people. According to this, they were to be chased unmercifully from their land with the excuse that they were collaborators of the German fascists. According to Cubrilovic, in Kosova, there had been a collaborative government led by irredentist Kosovars, with Xhafer Deva at the helm, labeled as the top German agent. The Elaborate also foresaw that in Kosova, they had to declare the "eruption of the counterrevolution," as soon as the Albanians began reacting to their various provocations, which were supposed to lead them to outbreak.

"For us, the main problem is how to destroy the minority blocs in the important geopolitical territories" to highlight that: *"the state is the one that should support this with all its equipment and every method."*[288]

Among these methods, as the most convenient for the circumstances, he mentioned war as the one with which this lifelong problem would be solved. *"The army, during its war operations should cleanse in a planned manner and without mercy the ethnic minorities..."*[289]

Along with the cleansing of Kosova of Albanians, Cubrilovic also asked for the cleansing of Pollog of Macedonia as well as other Albanian regions in Montenegro:

> Kosova and Metohija were considered strategic centers of the Balkans. This zone separates Montenegro from Serbia and both of these from Macedonia. These territories of the Democratic Federation of Yugoslavia will not have a strong reciprocal relationship between them, until they are able to have direct ethnic borders. This issue is especially important for Macedonia. The territory of the Upper Stream of Vardar is under the Albanians; whereas, its lower stream is under the Greeks. We, the Slavs of the South have only the middle stream. Our positions, based on this perspective, are too weak... For us, the prolific fields of Pollog, Kosova and Metohija are very important economically...[290]

In order for the Elaborate to be successful, Cubrilovic asked for the position of Agrarian Minister in the federal government, with the promise that *"with all my heart, I will put at disposal all my knowledge and experience for the service of the Upper Command of the National Liberation Army and the Partisan Units for the composition of detailed plans."*

Tito accepted Cubrilovic's offer, even though he never admitted that his mandate in this position was related to the elaborate for the liquidation of issues with the German minority and the Albanians in the circumstances of war. The only thing he admitted is that the Serbian historian had made a place in the cabinet of the First Federal Government due to the proposal of Serbia.[291]

---

[288] See the Second Memorandum of Vasa Çubrilovic: *"The Issue of Minorities in the New Yugoslavia,"* of November 1944, handed to Marshal Tito, published in "Mladina" of Lubjana, 1990

[289] *Ibid.*

[290] *Ibid.*

[291] From the conversation between the author and Fadil Hoxha, in Prishtinë, 1994.

No matter what the reasoning, and the fact that the familiar historian, Sarajevo's attempted attacker against Prince Ferdinand, instead of the position of Minister of Culture or Science, took that of the Agrarian Minister, having at his disposal all the necessary police and military infrastructure to achieve the goals he had set. And as will be seen, the Srem offensive of December 1944 and January – April 1945, ended with full success according to Cubrilovic's program. What the Soviets did not achieve in this frontier, the Chetnik units did. These Chetnik units were converted to partisans in accordance with the familiar Tito-Shubashic agreement reached with the assistance of the English, and they cleansed one by one the German inhabitants of Slavonia and Banat from the indigenous German population, with the reasoning that they had been German servants. Two hundred thousand Germans killed and six hundred others chased from their territories and forced to migrate permanently to Germany, is the "brilliant" balance of Cubrilovic's Elaborate from November 1944.

In Kosova this Elaborate was also acted upon. The "eruption of the counterrevolution" was declared, the military campaign to cleanse the area of "the fascist collaborators" began, and after a while the military regime was positioned. Although it was not able to cleanse Kosova from the Albanians as Cubrilovic requested, this regime, nevertheless for six months, as long as the military state lasted, murdered over fifty thousand Albanians from the frontiers of Kosova to Srem and along the Adriatic, violently deported thousands of people, and initiated the secret liquidations which later on took the dimensions of genocide!

Apart from the victims, even harsher for the Albanian population would be the communist terror which was masked as a national regime of brotherhood and unity. As the first act of what turned into a genocidal tragedy against an unprotected population, was the violent mobilization of over twenty thousand young Albanians to the Srem frontier or the Adriatic, from which the majority of them never returned.

All this blood spilling began on November 30, 1944, with the directive that Miladin Popovic, who had returned from Albania in the position of General Secretary of the Party, in the name of the Regional Committee of the Communist Party of Yugoslavia for Kosova and Metohija (the name Dukagjin was replaced with Metohija as a reaction to what was called "the Albanianism" of the party base in Kosova to the detriment of Yugoslavia), would direct all local party committees in

Kosova, which had now already become part of the highly skilled revolutionary regime whose behavior included ruthless imprisonments, raids, and harsh military court decisions.

This directive called for:

1) The mobilization of young Albanians to Northern frontiers
2) The cleansing of the territory from the enemies, those that had served the occupier and the traitors of the area
3) The confiscation of weapons from the Albanian people
4) The destruction of all previous organizations of local forces (the National Liberation Committees) that were not in accordance with the CPY criteria, meaning those that were established in the First Conference of the National Liberation Committee in Bujan, and
5) The Party organizations to be formed in Albanian villages, those for the youth, sports and others according to the criteria for Brotherhood and Unity.

With the initial implementation of these actions as well as the harsh campaign for solving the issues with the Albanian intellectuals, the patriotic forces from the elite imposed resistance against the chauvinist rave of the Serbian Chetnik units. A more stressed resistance was later noticed against the violent mobilization and shipment of Albanians to the war frontiers in the North and through Montenegro toward the Adriatic.

In the beginning of December, after the decree had arrived for solving the issues with those that were not communist and were not part of the partisan movement, whom at the same time were labeled as anti-communist and reactionary (as were around 90 percent of the Albanians), precisely in the second day of this month, on December 2nd, the first battles between the Albanian resistance and the Serbian partisan forces occurred in Ferizaj and then also in Gjilan, on December 23rd, which was led by Mulla Idriz (Hajrullahu)[292]. Along with Mulla Idriz, in the insurgence of Anamorava, Hysen Terpeza also appeared in different groups as its leader, along with many others.[293] The Yugoslav information sources

---

[292] Djaković, Spasoje: "*Sukobi na Kosovu,*" Belgrade, 1984, p. 240; Pirraku, Muhamet: "*Mulla Idriz Gjilani dhe Mbrojtja Kombëtare e Kosovës Lindorre 1941-1951,*" Prishtinë, 1995.

[293] For more details regarding Hysen Tërpeza's role in the resistance that was against the reoccupation of Kosova from the Yugoslavian partisans, see Mustafë Xhemaili: "*Hysen Terpeza – një legjendë Kosove,*" (Journalism), Prishtinë.

were very interested in claiming higher than actual the number of imprisonments; since, as would be seen, they would need this in order to begin
the last offensive against Albanians in Kosova. This last offensive, in
accordance with the goals established by the newest Elaborate of
Cubrilovic, in the battles of Ferizaj up to Gjilan, lasted all through December. In these information sources, it mentioned that over four thousand Albanian "Ballists" from the Balli Kombetar (National Front)
participated in these battles, even though it was known that the main
forces of Balli, together with the remainders of the SS Division
"Skenderbeg" retreated with the German army group "E" North, or
toward the South to Greece,[294] meaning that there were no such organized units of these formations in Kosova.

In fact, in these combats – which preceded those that later appeared
in all parts of Kosova – only a few hundred Albanians participated; in
most cases they were deserters that had detached from the mobilized units
which were making preparations for the North frontiers. The possibility
can not be ruled out, however, that they were led by some Albanian
patriot who had detached from their file, or from the dispersed units of
"Balli Kombëtar," but maybe even from the SS division, among the groups
of those that could not stay still during the Serbian terror. Certainly, they
were joined by the voluntary forces of the Ferizaj and Gjilan regions
during the combats, since it was for a rightful defense against the occupiers who had entered after the German retreat and spared nothing that
crossed their path, especially in the mountainous villages. In those circumstances of terror, a single echo of a gun sufficed to make all others
join.

The resistance began at the start of December in Ferizaj and Gjilan,
and expanded towards Qyqavica and Vushtrri, where there was also a
confrontation of the Yugoslav partisan forces, but also a harsh revenge
against the undefended Albanian population. After this resistance was
suppressed with bloodshed, during the last days of December and the
beginning of January, when the violent mobilization of Kosova's youth to
the North and the Adriatic continued – from where the news started
coming regarding their bad fate in Tivar and poisoning in Shibnek – the
Albanian resistance forces tried to utilize the mobilization charter against
mobilization.

---

[294] See Djaković, Spasoje: "*Sukobi na Kosovu,*" Belgrade, 1984, p. 239-246.

Shaban Polluzha, who had initially participated in the mobilization of Albanians and the establishment of two units that would head north, began to create a new mobilization without the Operational Headquarters knowledge, apart from the one that was led by the Kosova VII Brigade which was responsible for these actions. After a few "explanations," Shaban Polluzha nevertheless accepted that the units he had mobilized in the Drenica area (around four thousand troops) were subject to the preparations of the VII Brigade and then sent north. The first group, consisting of two thousand and five hundred people, without Shaban Polluzha, set out toward Vushtrri and Podujeva on January 20, accompanied by the Serbian Division 46, and arrived in Kursumli from where it headed to Srem. On January 22, the second mobilized group, accompanied by the Serbian Division 46 and Kosova's VII Brigade, with approximately two thousand people, led by Shaban Polluzha, headed toward Podujeva. From Vushtrri, going through the villages of Banjë, Gllavnik and Lower Dumnicë, the group began to disperse little by little. The mobilized group left through the villages with the reasoning that they did not want to go to the North while Kosova was being infiltrated with Serbian partisan brigades that exercised terror upon the Albanians there. The next day, the mobilized group led by Shaban Polluzha reached Podujeva, but there it stopped. Their stance was clear: we will remain in Kosova and we will fight for it if there is a need to defend it. To convince them to continue to Srem, Fadil Hoxha, accompanied by Ismet Shaqiri, personally negotiated with Shaban Polluzha. Fadil Hoxha was the Commander of the General Headquarters of the National Liberation Army of Kosova.

The negotiations were not successful, since Fadil Hoxha's task was to convince the Albanians to head north, whereas Shaban Polluzha's intention was that with this refusal to create the circumstances for the establishment of a defense frontier for Kosova from the Serbian Chetniks and the gangs that entered through the North, this was something that did not depend on Fadil Hoxha. During the time negotiations were taking place, the Serbian Brigade 46 began military preparations in Lluzhan for blocking the return of the Albanian units, preparations which were made without notifying Fadil Hoxha, who was not interested in a conflict between the Albanians and the Yugoslav partisan units, since he knew what a tragic epilogue it would have for Kosova.[295]

Conflict seemed to be unavoidable in the moments when some of the units opposed the order to head north and began dispersing. Serbian forces had placed a barricade in Lluzhan, preventing small groups from passing Llap and then Sitnica. Serbian forces attacked them from behind and so, in defense of those attacks by the Serbian battalion, they began to regroup towards the villages of Nevolan, Resnik, Kulë and Shalicë. This action was sufficient reason for the next day the Operational Headquarters of the National Liberation Army of Kosova, under the directive of the Operational Headquarters of the National Liberation Army of Yugoslavia and the Operational Headquarters of the National Liberation Army of Albania, to give the green light for an armed war, as it was said, *"against a counterrevolution and internal reaction, which had erupted in Kosova."*[296]

---

[295] From the author's conversation with Fadil Hoxha in Prishtina, 1994.

[296] See Dr. Ali Hadri: *"Shqiptarët në Mbretërinë e Jugosllavisë prej vitit 1918 e deri më 1941 dhe pjesëmarrja e tyre në LNÇ të Jugosllavisë,"* a separation in *"Historinë e Popullit Shqiptar,"* second volume, Prishtinë, 1969, p. 811. It is interesting to say that the term "counterrevolution" for the eruption of resistance against the communist violence in Kosova and the term "counterrevolutionaries" toward all those that in different ways had confronted the communist dictatorship and become part of the revolt, was accepted by the Albanian ideological historiography in Tirana, but also by the historians in Prishtina, as Çubrilovic had anticipated and the Serbian chauvinists masked as "internationalists," whom, apart from solving "the issues" with Albanians, also sought to win the support of the allies from the anti-fascist frontier, so that the Albanians would be deprived of any kind of request for realizing the decisions that the Bujan Conference had made regarding their right to unite with Albania, something which could only be achieved after common victory against fascism was achieved. The Albanian ideological historiography did not change this approach even after the harsh communist dictatorship fell in Albania, neither did the majority of the historians from Prishtina, those historians that had studied the National Liberation War and in most cases had exaggerated it according to the requests of those that ordered them. In Prishtina, two scientific sessions were organized regarding the insurgence in Drenica and the role of Shaban Polluzha and the other nationalists, where many of the facts came to surface as to what really occurred in the winter of 1944, and spring and summer of 1945. The other extreme also occurred, however, that with pathetic and folkloric stances many epithets and merits were assigned that actually were not earned, and under those circumstances, were not even capable of being earned. This approach could free the Yugoslav leadership of the time from the responsibility it had for

The same war scenario was used with the mobilized groups of Adem Voca which had been gathering for a few days in the Vushtrri-Mitrovicë-Shalë triangle. Different from Shaban Polluzha, who had requested to negotiate with the Operational Headquarters of the National Liberation Army of Kosova, commanded by Fadil Hoxha, Voca had begun negotiations with the high officials of the party: Ali Shukria and Spasoje Djakovic. The latter at that time led the military information service OZNA, responsible for the cleansing of Kosova from "the reactionary and counterrevolutionaries," with its base in Shkup from where it prepared all the traps against the Albanians. During the negotiations, Voca requested that the division of power in Mitrovica be according to the forces he had (around four thousand volunteers), and also that the mobilized groups would not be taken to the North, but remain in Kosova to defend themselves from the Chetniks of Zika Markovic, who operated freely in the Shala and Llap areas. During the negotiations Djakovic refused all of Voca's requests and meanwhile the Serbian 26th Brigade had begun its attacks against Shaban Polluzha's units which were retreating toward Qyqavica. The same day, the 25th Serbian Brigade, stationed near Mitrovica, began its military operations against the forces of Adem Voca, and they retreated toward Staritergut, where the next day, on January 26th they faced a harsh battle with the Serbian partisans who were assisted by Division 46.

The next day, after Adem Voca's forces were surrounded in the Trepça area, cannons and artillery were used against them, which caused them large losses. However, a portion of them succeeded in retreating toward the village of Pantinë, where Adem Voca was from. There, at his house, together with his brothers and seven sons, he was barricaded and refused to surrender. On February 11, Adem Voca, together with those he had at home were killed.[297]

Ten days later, Shaban Polluzha faced the same fate in Tërstenik of Drenica, as would thousands of their fellow soldiers all over Kosova. They were murdered cruelly during the cleansing operations that continued during that whole sanguinary summer and autumn against "the remain-

---

performing genocide towards the undefended population, under the reasoning that it had fought a military movement organized and prepared from the outside, consisting of orderly units, external divergence, etc.

[297] See the PKS documents for Kosova and Metohija nr. 06-482, cited by Spasoje Djaković: *"Sukobi na Kosovu,"* Belgrade, 1984, p. 248.

ders of the quislings and the enemy's collaborators." Three days prior to Adem Voca and his family's murder, Josip Broz Tito placed Kosova under a military regime. With the decision number 31 of February 8, 1945, he ordered the establishment of the Military Directorate in Kosova, which took over all civil power, tasked with "eliminating the armed insurgence in the liberated Kosova." [298]

In its reasoning, it stated:

> The situation in Kosova and Metohija worsened even more by the end of January due to the appearance of the armed Ballist forces. Observing this situation in Kosova and Metohija, where there are around 10 thousand rebels who put the peaceful lives of the citizens and people's government to risk and have the intention of bringing back the fascist regime, the Supreme Headquarters of the National Liberation Army of Yugoslavia ordered the placement of a Military Directorate in Kosova and Metohija with the intention of eliminating as quickly as possible the enemies and creating the circumstances for an un-interrupted operation of the people's and citizens' government.[299]

With this same order, Sava Derlevic, the commander of the Operational Headquarters for Kosova and Metohija was now named commander of the Military Directorate. Colonel Gjuro Medenica was named Political Commissary. Colonel Nikolla Bozhanica was named Commander of the military zone of Kosova and Metohija.

The military directorate in Kosova had at its permanent disposal three divisions with 30,000 regular soldiers. They were then joined by another 12,000 reservist and local unit troops. [300]

With the placement of Kosova under military administration the whole infrastructure of the local government was ruined, which had begun its formation after the First Conference of the National Liberation Committee of Kosova. The whole General Operational Headquarters of the National Liberation Army in Kosova was led by Fadil Hoxha. The Military Directorate was commanded only by top officers sent from Belgrade, who were almost all Serbian and Montenegrin; while the partisan units in Kosova who had come out of the war, were even left out from

---

[298] *Ibid.*, p. 252

[299] *Ibid.*, p. 252

[300] *Ibid.*, p. 253.

the militant actions developed from February 8 up to the end of April. During these hostilities, after February 22, when in Tërstenik of Drenica, Shaban Polluzha was killed together with all his fellow soldiers – while the focus was mainly on "cleansing" the areas from "the remainders of the Ballists and the collaborators' servants." These murders were in fact all part of the terror previously planned for the Albanian population.

Those that prepared the scenario for placing Kosova under a military zone, from where they would then be free to cleanse everyone from the contagious disease of "counterrevolution," also took action to prevent any possible "surprises" from their own sides. The cleansing from counterrevolutionaries was done alongside the "temporary" removal of all Albanians from the leading structures responsible for setting down the "counterrevolution" that had erupted among the Albanians due to their "positions of ideological fascism" (with this qualification, any scenario of Britain arriving in Kosova for the sake of an anti-communist movement would be elminitated).

Thus, in Prishtina, on March 15, Miladin Popovic, the Political Secretary of the Regional Committee, was killed. Under the directive he signed on December 2, 1944, the partisan-communist terror began in Kosova, which was anticipated by the second Elaborate of Vasa Cubrilovic *"Regarding the ethnic minorities in the new Yugoslavia."* It was known that in that directive all the actions were initiated, from the forced mobilization of Albanians and their shipment to the North, the beginning of the campaign for solving the issues with the enemy's collaborators and the "Albanian reaction," and up to the other actions that created the conditions for state terror against Albanians, actions for which two months later the Military Administration in Kosova took responsibility, so that the conditions for war returned and war became an appropriate tool for their implementation. Hence, with full rightfulness the question arose: What was behind his murder? Was it Albanian revenge for the one that promised the most equality, brotherhood, and unity and above all even the just resolution of Kosova's issue according to the will of its people after the common victory against fascism was achieved? Or, was it a natural step of development – as was the anti-Albanian course which still had to be taken – which was supposed to eliminate in any way those that could impede it from within?

The formal version itself of Miladin Popovic's murder by the militants that supervised Kosova – and were at the peak of their grave crimes against the Albanian population in Drenica and in the name of "cleansing from the counterrevolutionaries," – was not only suspicious, but even fully conformed to the familiar scheme of blaming the Albanians and qualifying them as enemies of the people's revolution, and with that blame, gaining even more internal motivation through terror.

The declared attempted attacker, Haki Taha – was never fully proven since he was found murdered or had killed himself. In either case, it served as a typical example of those circumstances and those miserable developments, which satisfied even the real murderers, and satisfied even those that wanted to see this murder as their own and in their fantasy actually dreamed of it. The rancor of an Albanian nationalist, familiar to Miladin, worked from both sides, whether it was that of proving the murder was prompted by simple patriotic motives, because he had "betrayed", or that of proving the Serbian accusation that the whole Albanian anti-fascist movement was established to unite with Albania, and this was their revenge to the man that impeded it.

In any case, Miladin Popovic's murder gave cause to two extremes on the issue of Kosova that acted in parallel and fed on one another:

That of the Serbians – that the resolution of it with radical tools should be sought even in the circumstances of the communist ideology. These radical tools could even be extreme (through a counterrevolution, colonization and state covenants for massive displacement of the Albanian population into Turkey).

And that of the Albanians – that the reoccupation of Kosova by Serbia should never be accepted, and all possible tools should be used for liberation from Serbia, both legal and illegal, until the goal is achieved, because otherwise, history would repeat itself with all its miseries.

In the circumstances when Kosova was entirely subject to military terror, it was natural to see actions for the scenario of "volunteered unity of Kosova with Serbia," which was accomplished with the "democratic declaration of the representatives of the people of Kosova." In these circumstances, Kosova was experiencing terror from the three armed divisions of the National Liberation Army of Yugoslavia, with over 30,000 active soldiers and 12,000 from the reserve units who were also in active service, assisted by over 6,000 partisans from the Third and Fifth Battalions of the National Liberation Army of Albania, filled in by another four groups that had come to the assistance of the Yugoslav partisans.

The Convention of Prizren of the National Liberation Committee of Kosova and Metohija showed just how "democratic" the will of the population's representatives could be under the circumstances of a military state and military leadership, which for five months caused the whole population to bleed through the murder and massacre of over fifty thousand people, reasoning that this fight was "against the counterrevolutionaries" and "the fascist collaborators." The Convention of Prizren was held from July 8 to 10, 1945. There, 153 "delegates" gathered, of course "processed" from all parts of Kosova and they "unanimously" decided, that which was already agreed upon in Belgrade, where it was stated that *"the Albanian people of Kosova and Metohija would voluntarily unite with the Democratic Serbia, as an autonomous province, since there they saw better opportunities for social and socialist development."*

It is noted that among the delegates, the relationship between the Albanians and Serbians was in favor of the Serbs and Montenegrins, even though according to the official notes of Belgrade, Kosova's population was 63% Albanian, and this percentage was known to be even higher. Almost all of the participants of the Bujan Convention, who had voted for the familiar resolution giving the Albanians the right to self-determination, also participated in the Prizren Convention. Now, the same people, *"with full will"* were said determined to *"join Serbia"*! It was even said that the same people would express gratitude to the Military Directorate for *"the great merits they had for suppressing the counterrevolution in Kosova"* and *"returning peace and people's government to Kosova"*[301]

The squelching of the Albanians' armed resistance in Kosova, during the winter of 1944 and Spring 1945, as well as the Prizren Convention of the National Liberation Committee from July 8 to 10 – where the forced decision was made for the alleged *"free willingness of Albanians to join the Democratic Serbia as its autonomous province"* – could not simply be "a fixed internal issue of the democratic Yugoslavia," as was stated by the Belgrade propaganda and their supporters in Tirana. These propagandists and supporters had handed over Kosova to the Yugoslav partisans and then during the time that the partisans killed and slaughtered Albanians in Kosova during the sanguinary winter and spring, supported their call both ideologically and militarily. Despite the fact that the communist

---

[301] *Ibid.*, p. 261.

Comintern recognized the right for self-determination for peoples occupied by foreign powers and Roosevelt and Churchill agreed to the self-determination of all peoples based on the Atlantic Charter, this right of self-determination was denied to the people of Kosova.

If everything were to follow the logic of reconstructing Yugoslavia from within – based on "federal and democratic principles" which came from the Comintern, such as the ones that had been approved in the meeting of the Anti-fascist Committee of the Peoples of Yugoslavia (AVNOJ) in Jajce, when Yugoslavia was declared a federal state consisting of six equal republics – then even at the first chance, Kosova should have had an equal place in this composition, always conforming to the free will of the Albanians. The same would have been valid for the principles of the Atlantic Charter, where again, the Kosova Albanians had the right to self-determination. Thus, both principles were violated to the detriment of Albanians in Kosova.

Of course, the federal and "democratic" Yugoslavia that was being constructed tried to prevent the placement of Kosova under Military Administration – during January to June 1945 – from being viewed as the "decisive circumstances" that caused the delegates of the National Liberation Convention of Prizren to be forced to vote for joining with Serbia. Rather, they pretended that with the elimination of the counterrevolution, and the cleansing of Kosova from the reactionaries and their many masked servants, they had enabled precisely the "democratic declaration" of Albanians, conforming to their right for self-determination! Thus, the Albanians in Kosova, together with others, had utilized this right in Prizren – in the most marked and representative place of their state-building history which was linked with the Albanian League of Prizren of 1878 – and not in Bujan, because there, a year prior to this, not all of the "representatives of the people of Kosova" had participated, and also because citizens of Albania had also voted there! Hence, in order for this "declaration" to seem as "democratic" as possible, Belgrade had also utilized "the procedure of democratic anticipation" for three months, which was left at the disposal of the Albanians to realize this right, since the whole issue, meaning the Albanians' request resulting from the Prizren Convention "to join democratic Serbia" had to pass through the approval of the Yugoslav Federation to the Republic of Serbia.

The Resolution of the Prizren Convention of July 10, initially was approved by the Assembly of Kosova and Metohija which was constructed on July 8, in which case the 153 delegates of the Prizren Committee were automatically passed on to the New Regional Assembly of Kosova and Metohija, whereby they had an additional 17 others to become 170 altogether. Thus, on July 9, the so-called Regional Assembly of Kosova and Metohija accepted the decision of July 10 by giving full democratic "legitimacy" resulting from a "People's Assembly" to "The Resolution for the annexation of Kosova and Metohija within the Federal Serbia."[302]

On August 7, 1945, Kosova's "request" for joining Serbia was analyzed in the AVNOJ meeting in Belgrade. After the "request" that Kosova join the Federal Serbia was approved by the Federation and passed on to the Serbian Government for analysis, it was approved on September 2, in the meeting of the leaders of the Serbian People's Assembly. The Kosova representative, Mehmet Hoxha – President of the first Conference of the National Liberation Committee in Bujan, who also kept this position in the Prizren Convention – directed to the Serbian representatives the request that Kosova join Federal Serbia as an autonomous province. Dusan Mugosa, who was with him, translated his request into Serbian, which was approved, only after the President gave half an hour break to the representatives in order to think about Kosova's request! In this case, the law was also enacted for the construction and organization of the Kosova and Metohija region.

Thus, after the procedure of analyzing and approving Kosova's "request" to join Serbia with "free will," Kosova and Metohija's status as a province was finally sanctioned with the 1946 constitution of the Federal People's Republic of Yugoslavia.

From Bujan to Prizren

Even though Kosova as an "oblast (territory)" was annexed to Serbia after the military take-over and this made it a part of the Federal Yugoslavia, Serbia canceled this association with the Federation with its 1946 Constitution, forcing all decisions regarding Kosova to be made by Serbia. – With the Constitutional Law of 1953, the regions were further limited in their territory; thus, their jurisdiction was lowered to

---

[302] Salihu, Kurtesh: *"Lindja, zhvillimi, pozita dhe aspektet e autonomitetit të Krahinës Socialiste Autonome të Kosovës në Jugosllavinë Socialiste,"* Prishtinë, 1984. Page 31.

that of districts. – The Albanian disagreement with this situation was reflected with the organization of the Albanian National Democratic Movement (ANDM), which in 1946 illegally began its activities for liberation and national unity. – According to this definition, the ANDM was not only an enemy of the Yugoslav state, but also that of Albania, in which case Tirana and Belgrade acted unitedly to eliminate its units placed in different parts of Kosova and Macedonia. – Thus, in the continuous attempts for enlarging ANDM, a portion of its leaders were imprisoned and many of them were sentenced to death and executed (Gjon Serreçi, Ajet Gërguri, Ukë Sadiku, Hilmi Zarici and Osman Bunjaku), whereas another portion of them were convicted with harsh sentences. – Belgrade widened its repressive campaign against Albanians with the intention of displacing them to Turkey.

Kosova's autonomy was in fact ideological, even though it was violent and achieved through the military state after its reoccupation by the Yugoslav partisans, and with the Tito-Enver approval of September 1944 which placed it under the Serbian regime. It had to do with a familiar model that had begun to be used in the Soviet Union after the Bolshevik Revolution victory of October 1917, when the oppressed people occupied by the Russian Czar, instead of liberating themselves from the occupation, in new circumstances – meaning that of the Proletarian Revolution victory – replaced the national principle with the class one, where freedom and everything pertaining to its slogans were solved with ideological recipes.

Tito's Yugoslavia also passed across such recipes, which reformulated its familiar rhetoric about "Versailles Yugoslavia as a peoples' prison" which "has to be destroyed" in order for the "captive people to be liberated from its regime" and other such things that were said during the twenties, meaning from the First Party Congress in Dresden of Germany in 1924 and up to the Fifth Local Conference of the Communist Party of Yugoslavia in Zagreb in March 1940. It reformulated this rhetoric with "defending Yugoslavia, but as a Federation," a stance which it definitely confirmed in the Local Conference of June 1941, after Yugoslavia had been destroyed after its capitulation in April of that same year, when it was shattered into many pieces (Croatia had become independent, Quisling Serbia was under Nedic, and a good portion of the Kosova and

Macedonian regions joined the so-called Greater Albania under the Italian crown, whereas another portion joined Bulgaria).

Upon these bases – meaning that of formal defense of the state organization of Yugoslavia which no longer existed – the organization of the Communist Party of Yugoslavia continued, relying on the federal principles which were appropriate for its people. Upon this scheme, that of local committees (that of Serbia, Croatia, Slovenia, Bosnia and Herzegovina, Montenegro, Vojvodina, Kosova and Metohija), the party organization was also created and later on, that of the anti-fascist movement.

In fact, this form of "federalist" organization of the party had started to appear in 1937 when Josip Broz Tito, with the assistance of the Comintern and Stalin, returned from Moscow to take over the lead of this party. That same year, the Committee of the Communist Party of Yugoslavia for Kosova and Metohija (KOSMET) was also founded, which was linked to the Regional Committee for Montenegro, Sanxhak and Boke. In 1940, in the Fifth Conference of CPY in Zagreb, the Committee of the Communist Party of Yugoslavia for Kosova and Metohija was directly connected to the Central Committee of the Communist Party of Yugoslavia.[303]

The following party activity and that of the structures during the anti-fascist war – which represented the base of the local autonomy – also followed this route, but specifically, as would be seen in the first Meeting of the National Liberation Committee of Kosova on December 31, 1943 and January 1 and 2, 1944, in Bujan, the right for self-determination, as it would be in the Bujan Resolution, conformed to the ideological concepts of the Comintern, but also the Atlantic Charter of people's right to free and democratic self-determination.

The self-determination principle – which in the Bujan Resolution anticipated the Albanian's right to declare unity with Albania – circumvented the principles of the Atlantic Charter (free and democratic declaration) so that it all turned into an "internal" ideological principle, so that "Kosova joined Federal Serbia upon its own free will."

However, the formal, legal process of constructing Kosova's autonomy from the Meeting of the National Liberation Committee in Prizren on

---

[303] See the record from the Fifth Conference of PKJ, p. 8, cited by Kurtesh Salihu: *"Lindja, zhvillimi, pozita dhe aspektet e autonomitetit të krahinës socialiste autonome të Kosovës në Jugosllavinë socialiste,"* Prishtinë, 1984, p. 9.

July 8, 1945 – where the next days, on July 10, the same entity, by issuing a resolution, decided on "joining this region with Federal Serbia under the Democratic Federal Yugoslavia," required over four months and ended with the issuance of the First Constitution of the Federal People's Republic of Yugoslavia, on January 31, 1946.

With this Constitution, the ratification of power was approved, which had already been decided during the revolution, but then, apart from the federal units (six of them), the autonomous territories were not mentioned, a fact which denied the thesis of the Yugoslav ideological history, that of Kosova (up to 1989), but also Albania, regarding the "source" of Kosova's autonomy during the NLM (National Liberation Movement). As was seen, *the autonomy category*, appeared after the war, to legitimize the occupation of Kosova by Serbia, which, as opposed to this fact, at least formally, this process passed through the Federal Yugoslavian gate, in the first Constitution in which it stated, regarding the autonomy, that: "The Republic of Serbia has under its framework the Autonomous Province of Vojvodina and the Region (oblast) of Kosova and Metohija."[304]

Thus, observing it from the formal, legal aspect – outside of any "sources" of NLM and decisions of the Second Meeting of the Anti-fascist National Liberation Committee of Yugoslavia (AVNOJ) in Jajce on November 29, 1943 – Kosova's autonomy was placed in the day's agenda for the third meeting of AVNOJ, on August 7, 1945. Only after the third meeting of AVNOJ was held, the Assembly of the Republic of Serbia, on September 3, 1945, "analyzed" and implemented the request from the Regional National Liberation Committee that was previously decided at the Assembly of the Region resulting from its gathering in Prizren on July 10, 1945. During this period (prior to the Constitution), the Assembly of the Autonomous Region of Kosova and Metohija also enjoyed its judicial independence. During this period, the Autonomous Region of Kosova and Metohija was represented directly in AVNOJ by 15 representatives that the Regional Assembly had chosen for this higher entity of the Yugoslav government.[305]

The Autonomous Region of Kosova and Metohija formally kept this position also during the Serbian Constitution of 1947, since it conformed

---

[304] See: article 2, paragraph 2 of the Constitution of the Federal People's Republic of Yugoslavia, January 31st, 1946
[305] *Ibid.*

to the first Constitution of the Federal People's Republic of Yugoslavia (FPRY), approved on January 31, 1946. Even though this relation – the interconnection with the Federation – was watered down by Serbia, nevertheless, the Region sanctioned the state organization conforming to the Federal and Republic Constitution. Thus, the Autonomous Region issued its Statute, as its own highest act of law, which conformed to the Constitution of the FPRY (article 104).

The reasons for "tolerating" this situation – at least during the next two years – which was more a formality, had to be observed in the brotherhood relationships of Yugoslavia and Albania as well as Tito's and Hoxha's plans to add Albania as a seventh republic, a plan in which, Kosova and the other Albanian regions separated from 1912 and on – after the different occupations during the First Balkan War by the Serbian and Montenegrin armies – would also be included in the Albanian Republic. As stated before, Enver Hoxha especially supported this idea, and he wrote to Tito several times for joining the Yugoslavian Federation.[306]

However, even without this plan, from the entrance of the Yugoslav partisans in Kosova after the Tito-Enver Hoxha agreement of 1944 and up to the Informbiro (Cominform) Resolution of 1948, the Yugoslav-Albanian relationship had been the same since Albania had been previously placed politically, economically and even militarily under the Yugoslav tutelage. Thus, Belgrade – which hoped that this trend would continue up to the full engulfment of Albania – attempted to turn Kosova's autonomy – for which Bujan was sacrificed – into a model of "brotherly internationalist collaboration between two countries" where all of the issues of the past were melted down, even if they had been of a heavy nature, such as the genocide which Serbia had continuously performed against the Albanians from the Eastern bloc crisis onwards, which had resulted in the reoccupation of Kosova and the other Albanian regions in the First Balkan War.

After the Informbiro (Cominform) Resolution and the beginning of the breakdown in the relationship between Tirana and Belgrade – in 1949, after Enver Hoxha fully connected to the Soviet Union, turning into a renegade of Stalin – their full detachment occurred. Belgrade took advantage of the opportunity to replace Kosova even formally under the

---

[306] For more details, see: ""*Libri i bardhë*," Belgrade, 1953.

302

Serbian tutelage. Thus, during the next two years, even the few economic projects – such as the ones regarding road infrastructure, medicine, and other social issues which were supervised by the Federation – were temporarily interrupted. But even the few ties that remained were passed on to Serbia. If in addition, these defense and security provisions were added – which were "special" because in between Yugoslavia and Albania a great ideological campaign had begun – then it was more than clear that the spirit of political austerity between the two places which had up to then been "brotherly" relationships, turned the issue of Kosova's autonomy into a new instrument in the hands of Serbia. Through this instrument, Serbia could hold Kosova under its quarantine, so that on one side it would detach from development and on the other side it could utilize its ideology for a new oppression, which would enable the realization of its previous hegemonic plans for denationalization and displacement of Albanians, all of which would be camouflaged under the war against Stalinism and the irredentist ideologies, where police violence would be used and not military.

Thus, with Serbia's insistence, in 1953, there was a constitution, with which the autonomy of the regions no longer was a source of the Federation, but instead, the rights of the autonomous regions became the rights that the Republic had over these units. Hence, they no longer were a source of "the free will of the people to join Federal Serbia" as it was stated in the Prizren Resolution of July 10, 1945 – where as such they had passed through the Third Meeting of AVNOJ when Federal Yugoslavia had been established – but as "rights" that passed from the Republic to the units, meaning that the regions lost their original rights. Thus, in this spirit, the Constitutional Law of the FPRY was enacted with which a few provisions of the 1946 Constitution changed. The Constitutional Law superseded Chapter XI of the 1946 Constitution, precisely the one that had to do with the state power of the autonomous regions, replacing it with a new Head (IV) named "Principle dispositions upon the government organizations of the autonomous regions." According to this law, the rights of the autonomous regions were determined by the Constitution of the Republic of Serbia.[307]

With this Constitutional Law, even the dispositions of Article 44 of the 1946 Constitution were abrogated, with which the Federation was

---

[307] See: the FPRY Constitution of 1953, article 13, paragraphs 1 and 2.

authorized for accepting new Republics and attesting to the formation of new autonomous regions. This way, Belgrade succeeded, on one side, to erase the genuine federal character of the regions that were accorded to it, and on the other side, to impede their expansion to autonomous republics (as was requested a little later) or republics, as requested by the Albanians from 1968 onward.

Since the Federation no longer determined the autonomous region's right, not even in general, it authorized the Peoples Republic of Serbia (PRS) to do this with its Constitutional Law. Based on these authorizations, the Constitutional Law of the Peoples Republic of Serbia, after it assigned the form of the autonomous regions, assigned its duties and rights which had to conform to the laws and Constitution of the PRS. Starting from such an orientation, the Constitutional Law of PRS determined in detail the competencies, as well as the organization and the rights of the autonomous regions. In the dispositions of the Constitutional Law of PRS – with which the rights of the autonomous regions were determined – the base principle dominated, according to which the regions did not have original rights, but only the rights allowed by the PRS. This principle was widely eminent even in the Statute of the Autonomous Regions of Kosova and Metohija. Thus, based on those that were stated, it comes as a logical conclusion that the autonomy in Yugoslavia gradually began to lose its attributes determined during the NLM, as a Federal unit, and gradually turned itself into a unit under PRS, in which its autonomy greatly lost importance. [308]

The further shrinking of the regions' autonomies did not stop simply with the Constitutional Law of 1953. The Rebuplic of Serbia continued with its practical and political actions to work towards this direction, so that it lowered them to the level of a district, as an administrative community of that time. At the beginning of the sixties, the issue of the autonomies expanded to the highest party levels of Serbia, with the intention of establishing a political platform for such a change. Thus, the Executive Committee of the Central Committee (CC) of the Communist Party of Serbia (CPS) raised the issue of "autonomous tendencies" presented in the previous period, although according to the 1953 Constitution, the autonomies were deprived of the Federal status that they had with the 1946 Constitution. In this direction, it was requested that the

---

[308] See: the PRS Constitution, 1947, article 114

Federal Constitution not include any dispositions that dealt any more with the autonomies, but that this remain an issue of the Republic; that the autonomy would transform into a mediocre political-territorial community, which could be formed in any territories; that the regions would not be directly represented in the National Chamber of Federal Yugoslavia, but that this would be done by the Republic.[309]

The only positive thing in all of this revolution of autonomy values was the proposal according to which with the new Constitution of the PRS, the Autonomous Province of Vojvodina and the Region (oblast) of Kosova and Metohija would be identical based on designation, status, and organization.

In this case, it should be highlighted that with the 1946 Constitution of Yugoslavia and with the 1947 constitution of PRS, Vojvodina enjoyed a higher scale of autonomy than previously, while Kosova had a lower scale of autonomy than previously, which was noticed even in their naming, where the first one (Vojvodina) was an *autonomous province*, while the latter (Kosova) was an *autonomous region (oblast)*. Since the Albanian language does not make this distinction, it was marked as "an autonomous region," whereas in Serbo-croatian *"an autonomous oblast (oblast is viewed as its own territory with no privileges, while province is viewed as an external territory with many autonomous privileges)."*

This language characteristic, appears to have been to the political advantage of Serbia, where at least formally, Albanians would not understand the distinction in the scale of autonomy between what they had received (lower one) and that of Vojvodina (higher one). Nevertheless, after 17 years, this tie between autonomies in Serbia was achieved, but in these circumstances it meant nothing more than equity in devaluation.

Apart from these politics, the autonomous regions thoroughly lost their federal affiliation and the genesis of their autonomy. Since the Republic of Serbia according to the new Constitutional Law had won its right to form other regions if needed, it would mean that they would totally fall under Serbia's will. This was best reflected in the Federal Constitution when it stated that "in the Republic of Serbia the Autonomous Region of Vojvodina and that of Kosova and Metohija exist, *which*

---

[309] See: the record from the meeting of the Secretary of the Regional Committee of LK of Serbia for Kosova and Metohija, on September 2 and October 18, 1961 (from the Regional Committee's archive)

were formed in 1945 with the decisions of the People's Assembly of Serbia, based on the will of all the people of these territories."[310]

Apart from the shrinking in the social, organizational, and political plans, with the constitutional changes of 1963, the autonomous regions enjoyed neither financial autonomy nor judicial autonomy. In this direction, they seemed more like local forms of administration as opposed to political-territorial autonomies.

The continuous degradation of Kosova's autonomy was not only a judicial and constitutional issue – it found its direct expression in the two constitutional modifications that had been made: that of 1953 and 1963. Under those constitution modifications, Kosova was fully placed under Serbia's tutelage with the right that it could shrink even further down to the dimensions of a political community similar to that of districts or large municipalities. As such, it was also a political issue that had to do with the wide social definition, which was interlinked with the familiar hegemonic politics of greater Serbia developed from 1912 and onwards against the Albanians in Kosova. Such politics had the intention of physical and spiritual annihilation of this population from its own ethnic territories, which would result in the displacement of a quarter of the Albanians to Turkey, Albania and other regions. In the new circumstances, the proletarian internationalism and ideological propaganda was used, even the so-called socialist-development programs (cooperativism, collectivism, employment and others) and even the emancipist socialist processes of discriminating Albanians in "the name of progress."

Albanians felt doubly stricken in these circumstances because they were forcefully placed under the communist regime and violently deprived of their right to national unification which even fascism had provided to them, to live in a common country, a right which the Bujan Resolution had also guaranteed them. It was then expected that they would express their grievance against the violent communist system and against their remaining under Serbia. All of this would be reflected on the one hand with the anti-communist movement and on the other hand with the liberation movement for unification with Albania. The circumstances for them appeared to be too difficult and illusionary especially after the agreement of Yalta and the specification of the spheres of interest.

---

[310] The FPRY Constitution, 1963, article 111, paragraph 1 (the beginning of the sentence); article 112, paragraph 2

Nevertheless, the state terror which continued even after the war and the process of returning under Serbia's repressing tutelage, represented continuous cause for a resistance movement among the Albanians.

In fact, the first phase was the one from the reoccupation of Kosova by the Yugoslav partisans based on Tito's and Hoxha's agreement for inserting the Albanian partisan units in Kosova. The different patriotic forces, many of which had participated in the anti-fascist frontier, had united with one another to fight against Kosova's reoccupation. These patriotic forces knew that the internationalist flag that the Serbo-Yugoslav and Albanian partisans held against the German forces during their retreat – masked the new occupation of Kosova. This would quickly be noticed when the Yugoslavian partisans began to show their real intentions, which, as will be seen, conformed to the newest Elaborate of Cubrilovic. When this movement against the Serbo-Yugoslav reoccupation of Kosova under the communist mask was joined by the other forces of the resistance movement, such as those of Shaban Polluzha, Mehmet Gradica and many others who had refused to go to the Srem frontier – then it all turned into one great movement which was attributed as a counterrevolution. This attribution helped Belgrade declare a state of emergency and begin with the familiar state terror during winter and spring of 1945, which had tragic consequences (thousands killed), a tragedy, which as was seen, ended with the dissolution of the Bujan Resolution.

The sanguine extinction of Kosova's insurgency in Drenica did not put a halt to the resistance movement, even though the state terror and massacres continued in other ways. Different groups of patriots – left out of the anti-fascist movement which would be supervised by the communists (National Front, Legality and others) – started regrouping under the democratic platform. Thus, an ethnic Albania was required, a single united country of Albanians, which would be democratic, which at the same time meant a double war - to unite all Albanians into one country, that apart from changing the borders also meant a war against communism which was placed over Albania and Yugoslavia, as well as the war of extracting the countries that now belonged to the Eastern bloc, based on the division of spheres of interest.

The idea of a democratic ethnic Albania was not new. It had appeared even during the anti-fascist war among different patriotic forces. However, under the anti-fascist frontier they were not able to develop this idea as the Left had done for its own intentions. The anti-fascist war nevertheless had succeeded to turn the anti-fascist movement in Albania into a communist movement, which was supervised by the Yugoslav communists.

After they had practically lost the battle with the Albanian left which was linked to the Yugoslav left and the Comintern, these patriotic forces attempted to get activated when the events were nearing the familiar epilogue.

One of these forces was *"the Albanian National Democratic Movement" (ANDM)*[311], a conglomerate of a few groups, the majority of which were connected to the "National Front," but also "Legality", which had lost their organizational orientation during the last phase of the war, but not their determination for a democratic Albania. ANDM had made clear during the war its stance toward a single Albania, which would unite its ethnic territory into a single democratic country with the support of its West allies, especially the English, who at that time were seeking a political force that would be able to act. As it is known, these patriotic forces – among them the so-called "Irredentist Committee" of Gjakova, consisting of Selman Riza, Ejup Binaku, Skënder Shkupi, Rexhep Krasniqi, Haki Taha, Ibrahim Fehmiu and Halim Spahia – during the last phase of the war joined the British and their missions in different regions, especially in the North of Albania (the Dukagjin area). In December 1943, they spoke with the British observers about forming some groups which would not be under the communist impact but would act independently against the fascist forces. [312]

During Spring and Summer of 1944, when the Nazi fascist forces were experiencing losses in all of their frontiers and the western allies were at the final offensive to give the last fist, some of the intellectuals who saw the risk that Albanians would remain under the Eastern sphere, got

[311] For more details regarding *the Albanian National Democratic Movement" (NDSH)* see Çeku Ethem: *"Mendimi politik i lëvizjes ilegale në Kosovës 1945-1981"*; Basha-Keçmezi, Sabile: *"Lëvizja ilegale në Kosovë 1945-1948,"* Prishtina, 1996; Nasi, Lefter: *"Ripushtimi i Kosovës, shtator 1944-korrik 1945,"* Tirana, 1994; Pirraku, Muhamet: *"Ripushtimi jugosllav i Kosovës 1945,"* Prishtina, 1992; Gërguri, Mehmet: *"Ajet Gërguri dhe Lëvija NDSH 1945-1947*; Dobra, Ismet: *"Lufta e Drenicës 1941-1945 dhe LDNSH"*; Pushkolli, Fehmi: *"Mbrojtja Kombëte Shqiptare e Kosovës 1878-1990,"* Prishtina, 1991; Dermaku, Ismet: *"Gjon Serreçi dhe NDSH-ja,"* Prishtina, 1996; Grainca Ibrahim (Cërnilla): *"Deri në vdekje për atdhe,"* Prishtina, 2006.

[312] Hibber, Reginald: *"Fitorja e hidhur,"* Tirana, 1993.

determined to form an Albanian political force with a Western and democratic orientation. From a few dispersed notes and records of certain investigation conducted during the imprisonment of these activists by the judicial and police organizations in 1947, it can be understood that there were some meetings towards this, in which case it was decided that the *"Albanian Central Democratic National Committee"* be formed.[313]

The founding meeting was held in Prizren and the members of the Central Committee were chosen: Halim Spahia, Tahir Deda, Maliq Beu, and Ibrahim Fehmiu. Among the early activists were: Bislim Hajrizi, Bardhec Doda, Limon Jusufi, Marie Shllaku, Rexhep Mahmuti, Bardhyl Abdyli, Bernard Lupi, Ymer Berisha, Sulejman Lleshi, Ajet Gërguri, Hamdi Berisha, Ibrahim Grainca-Cërnilla and others.[314]

It is noted that many of these were active participants in the anti-fascist movement brigades in Kosova as well as the Albanian ones. Some of them were also members of the National Liberation Committee of Kosova as well as the *"Albanian National Committee"* (Hilmi Spahia, Ibrahim Cërnilla and others), which was legally formed in Prishtina and was supported by the Belgrade and Prishtina governments, being considered an adjunct of the governing and administrative organizations.

Direct steps were taken to organize a movement upon these bases. The Albanian Central Democratic National Committee decided to take on the Congress of Lypovic, on June 25, 1946, where it was also decided that its branches (one in Shkup and the other in Kosova) would unite and act, in which case a central leadership was chosen with Gjon Serreç at the lead, who was among the most noted activists of this organization. The program of five points was also approved in the Congress. The main point had to do with the decision that Albania would be formed as a democratic country over all the ethnic Albanian territories, and that in the external collaboration, the Committee would support England. ANDM also had its military headquarters, Commander of which was Ajet Gërguri.[315]

This organization acted under very difficult circumstances, such as those of the military administration, which in the winter and spring of 1945 in Drenica and other parts of Kosova, cruelly repressed the Albanian

---

[313] Dermaku, Ismet: *"Gjon Serreçi dhe NDSH-ja - dokumente arkivore,"* Prishtina, 1996, p. 223-231.

[314] Pushkolli, Fehmi: *"Mbrojtja Kombëtare Shqiptare e Kosovës 1878-1990,"* 1991, p. 140

[315] *Ibid.*, p. 142.

armed resistance. Its groups took responsibility for keeping the spirit of the movement alive in different parts of the area, always hoping that it would also gain Anglo-American support. However, as would be seen, in the circumstances where the communists had stabilized their government in Yugoslavia and Albania, the chances for allied forces landing in this area were very small, too little in fact that they were disappointing, also due to the fact that these areas were now under the Soviet zone of interest and that any Anglo-American implication in these areas would mean an interference with the Soviet sphere of interest.

Based on this specification, ANDM's enemy was not only the Yugoslav state, but also the Albanian one, who would act together towards the elimination of this organization and its units in different parts of Kosova and Macedonia. Thus, from 1945 until 1947, Belgrade and Tirana imprisoned and killed hundreds of activists and members of this organization. In the continuous attempts to expand the movement, a good portion of its leadership was imprisoned and many of them were sentenced to death and executed (Gjon Serreçi, Ajet Gërguri, Ukë Sadiku, Hilmi Zariqi and Osman Bunjaku) while another portion of them were convicted with harsh sentences. Thus, during 1947 two judicial processes were held, one in February in Gjilan, and the other in April in the Distrcit Court in Prishtina. In the Court of Gjilan, these activists of the ANDM were convicted: Maliq Sahiti, Ramadan Agushi, Jakup Malisheva, Rexhep Shema Dajkovci, Arif Salihu, Riza Osman Hoxha, Destan Budriga, Lazër Josipi, Rrustem Statovci, Sejfedin Shabani, Hysen Murteza Dalladaku, Ismail Rrahman Mema, Nijazi Çarkaxhiu, Hamdi Dalipi, Zija Ymer Shuku, Haki Zylfiqari, Salih Aliu, Iljaz Beqiri, Murat Zherka, Fehmi Ramadan Zherka, Hajredin Fazliu, Sylë Hajredin Fejza, Abas Rexhep Behluli, Xhemail Maksuti, Hajrush Jakup Halimi, Fahri Halimi, Hilmi Jakupi, Shefki Metushi, Ibrahim Grainca-Cërnilla, Asllan Buza and Raif Ejup Tasholli.[316]

In the Prishtina court process, held in April 1947, in the District Court, in addition to death penalties with which the leaders of this party were sentenced: Gjon Serreçi, Ajet Gërguri, Ukë Sadiku, Hilmi Zariqi, Osman Bunjaku; others were sentenced to ten years of prison: Zukë Haxhiu, Abedin Selman Braha, Abdullah Musliu and Hamid Emini.[317]

---

[316] Dermaku, Ismet: *"Gjon Serreçi dhe NDSH-ja,"* Prishtina, 1996, p. 140.
[317] *Ibid.*, p. 224.

Apart from these courts, in Prizren, in a similar process held in July 1946, Marie Shllaku, Father Bernard Llupi, Kolë Parubi and Gjergj Martini were also sentenced to death. Marie Shllaku was the first Albanian female to be found in the leadership of such a movement, which was among the most massive up to then. She, together with the others convicted in Prizren, was executed on November 14, 1946. [318]

Those that succeeded in getting out of the country were involved in various dispersed organizations, which had the intention of creating a democratic Albania, even though the chances that this would be achieved were very low. Some of them participated in different groups which time after time attempted to land in Albania through different operations, however, without any success, since in the circumstances of the cold war and the bloc division, such actions were doomed to fail without having fully started.

The Farce of "Brotherhood and Unity" and the State Terror

> *The continuous retention of Kosova under the state terror provisions, which were exerted through the police apparatus always with the reasoning that "the construction of the new world required the destruction of old mentalities," the return of colonialism and the continued displacement of Albanians to Turkey, which needed a new covenant, similar to the one between the Yugoslavian and Turkish governments of 1938 – three of the main tasks Belgrade sought to realize in the circumstances of the communist dictatorship. – the farce of Belgrade's regime with the formation of the "National Committee of Albanians" in Prishtina during the establishment of the military administration in Kosova as well as the requests of seven points that they presented to Tito during their meeting in Belgrade, which were labeled "from the positions of the Albanian nationalism" and for this, most of them were imprisoned or eliminated in various ways.*

After the reoccupation of Kosova in autumn and winter of 1944, enabled by the great assistance of the Albanian partisans, who after they had

---

[318] See: *"Dokumentet e Lëvizjes Nacional Demokratike Shqiptare"* by Hysen Azemi, "Vjetari" nr. XXV-XXVI, pages 254-256.

freed it from the Germans, handed Kosova over without any conditions, Belgrade focused on three issues:

1) the continued retention of Kosova under the state terror provisions, which were exerted through the police apparatus always with the reasoning that "the construction of the new world required the destruction of old mentalities,"
2) the return of colonialism
3) the continued displacement of Albanians to Turkey, which needed a new covenant, similar to the one between the Yugoslav and Turkish governments of 1938.

The first issue was supposed to keep the previously started actions going, from the entrance of the Yugoslav partisan units in Kosova in October 1944, where after a while the military administration was placed and the military actions began against the Albanian resistance towards the Yugoslav occupation and violence. This resistance was repressed with blood loss and approximately fifty thousand victims were left behind. The military presence could not be held for long because Yugoslavia's further plans for engulfing Albania through Kosova would be at risk (through the federal links with Belgrade or any other way). Also the concept of the Balkan Federation with which Tito would become the great regional communist leader would be endangered. Nevertheless, the option was left for the police, with their specialized violent tactics, to keep Kosova under continuous terror.

There were many "reasons" for this terror. And they could be even found in the opposition of Albanians to remain separated and under the communist regime, which was expressed especially with the armed resistance that erupted immediately after the war and continued in different forms. These reasons could also be found in the "brotherhood-unification" concept as a magic formula with which Albanians could continuously be provoked since it worked upon the principle of social elimination, where "the principle of the internationalist new" implied the "destruction of the reactionary old." But all of this appeared as an organized distraction which began with the destroying of family units, the environment, and all other social spheres of life. These tactics also included the confiscation of private property, the destruction of small economies and violent collectivism, under the framework of "accepting and constructing new socialism" and further "deepening" of "brotherhood-unification" – as was said was "destroyed by fascism".   All these activities contributed to colonialism, which was done in the "name of the right of those persecuted by the fascists to return to their century long territories," even though it was known that those left in 1941 were not locals but a colony that had settled in between the two wars, right after the Agrarian Reform had begun. The Reform was done to the detriment of Albanians and their property, which was taken away from them violently and was given to the settlers who were protected by the Serbian army and police.[319] Thus, this was the main factor that raised the scale of the state pressure towards Albanians from both sides - towards shrinking their living space, and towards taking away their prospect for the future. Hence, "as an alternative" was migration to Turkey, which was nothing new or unknown to the Albanians since it had functioned from the occupation of Kosova in autumn and winter of 1913 by Serbia and Montenegro, during which thousands of Albanian families, apart from finding shelter in Albania, were forced to find salvation in Turkey. The second occupation of Kosova by Serbia in 1918 had returned this process, which continued more intensely during the thirties, even prior to the signing of the Yugoslavian-Turkish Covenant of 1938 for displacing Albanians to Turkey.[320]

The option of re-colonization and that of massive displacement of Albanians to Turkey began after the breakdown between Albania and Yugoslavia in 1949, when the emergence of the ideological Iron Curtain and the impassable border between Albanians erased all hopes for future unity. In the meantime, some other factors also had an impact on the accelerated and increased displacement of Albanians to Turkey even under the mantra of "brotherhood-unification."

Two of these factors had a greater impact:

---

[319] For more details regarding colonization in Kosova during 1918-1941 see Obradovic, Dr. Milovan: *"Agrarna reforma i kolonizacija na Kosovu 1918-1941,"* Prishtina, 1981, a capital-documentary study, where detailed records are given regarding the structure of the colonizers and their allocation in different parts of Kosova together with the descriptions of the "granted" properties by the Yugoslavian state.

[320] See the magazine *"Arkivi Shqiptar,"* year 2, nr.1-2, Tirana 2000, where according to a confidential report which is kept in the Central Albanian Archive, Fund 251, year 1930, file 194, p. 402, there are details presented regarding the displacement of over 300 thousand Albanians from Kosova and other occupied areas by Yugoslavia to Turkey. During 1931 or 1932, around 26,450 Albanian families were registered in Turkey. (Cited by Marenglen Verlit *"Kosova – sfida shqiptare në historinë e një shekulli,"* Tirana, 2007).

1) the campaign against the Albanian intellectuals and the Albanian culture which began right after the war, where in the "name of solving the issues with the reactionaries and the quislings" the revolutionary courts, without any sort of process executed in mass the remainder of what had been the social and intellectual elite. The campaign gained its harsh dimensions in 1949 and up to the sixties, where even the few modifications that the educational emancipation had brought began to get ruined. The educational emancipation had resulted from the opening of primary schools in the Albanian language and the High School of Gjakova, which were mainly assisted by teachers and educators from Albania, and

2) the government-sponsored program for disarming the population, which began immediately after the war, as soon as the resistance movement in Drenica, Dukagjin, and other parts of Kosova got repressed, to continued further on with the reasoning of "continued hostile activity," but reached its peak during Winter 1955/56.

After the declaration of the Informbiro (Cominform) Resolution of 1948, Yugoslavia was criticized and later on also excluded from the Communist Bloc directed by Moscow. The breakdown of the relationship with Albania in the beginning of 1949, as would be seen, gave a good opportunity for the Serbs to quickly eliminate even the few achievements that had been reached with great effort in those very uncomfortable circumstances of military and police violence in Kosova in the area of primary education as well as literary and informative creativity in the Albanian language. These few achievements were only approved by Tito and the Yugoslav communists because apart from the Serbian issues – that Kosova remain with as few Albanians as possible, and possibly without any formed intelligence – was that of creating the conditions for engulfing Albania as the seventh Republic (with Kosova in it) or as a part of the Balkan Federation. These options were open and had conjunctions even with Stalin up to the time of the Informbiro (Cominform) Resolution, and they were inevitably required to be preceded by some other resolutions in the emancipation plan. After these plans failed and Enver Hoxha in Albania began to resolve the issues with the pro-Yugoslav militant draft of Koçi Xoxe and others, and Stalin created a political and economic blockade against Yugoslavia where he forced it to find supporters from the West, then Belgrade analyzed the vital chance to continue with the Albanians there where it had left off after the removal of the military state in Kosova, in June 1945. However, this time, the familiar propaganda calling Albanians "counterrevolutionaries" and "fascist collaborators" overused during the genocide in Drenica, and then against the Albanian National Democratic Movement, gained ideological connotations and they would be called "Stalinist" and "Enverist"!

The campaign was used to continue with the further elimination and destruction of cultural and intellectual values that the Albanians linked to the national spirit and the western civilization, which had begun to return during the years of national unification. From the forces that had participated in the anti-fascist war, attempts had been made to keep them, even in the circumstances of the communist reality. These attempts were supported in the platform of the *National Committee of Albanians of Kosova and the Dukagjin Plain,"* established at the Conference held in Prishtina, on March 27-28, 1945. In the program specification of this platform it was stated that "the Albanian people had to be helped in order to utilize the fruits of the National Liberation Movement for national affirmation, for social liberation, for political, cultural-educational elevation" where the learning of Albanian people's history and the affirmation of their cultural values were also included.

Even though the *"National Committee of Albanians"* was established at the time of the placement of the military administration – when Kosova was covered by blood in Drenica and other parts and continued to be so due to the communist terror, in those circumstances everything could appear as a farce, which the communist regime needed as a facade to cover up its crimes and to deceive Albanians. Nevertheless it was a part of the intellectual resistance which would continue to mobilize the general spiritual and social endurance in a wider plan, where the clear requests of the Albanians were expressed regarding their political and social future. These requests, from a delegation of the *"National Committee of Albanians,"* – where many activists and patriots were present, such as Rifat Berisha, Halim Spahia, Vesel Rexhepi, Mehmet Krileva, Qamil Luzha, Ibrahim Cërnilla-Grainca and others – were expressed to Josip Broz Tito, in April 1945, when they were greeted by him in Belgrade. In the name of this delegation, Qamil Luzha presented these requests to Tito, which was part of the *National Committee of Albanians*:

1. *That Albanians as a people would enjoy their national freedom and equal rights with the other peoples of Yugoslavia*
2. *That the usage of national Albanian symbols be allowed*
3. *That the territories would be returned to the Albanians from which they were unjustly taken with the agrarian reform and colonization by the old bourgeoise regime of Yugoslavia*
4. *That the Albanian schools continued to operate*
5. *That in the state organizations, Albanians would also be elected*
6. *That the relationships with Albania remained as close as possible and the borders remained only formally if it were not decided for Kosova and the Dukagjin plain to join Albania based on the Resolution approved in Bujan, and*
7. *That all the Serbians that had exercised violence against Albanians during the old Yugoslavia would be removed from the state organizations*

Even though Tito supported in principle the Albanian requests, promising that "the Albanian population will be offered all possibilities to develop and construct its own culture, to earn its own schools," he emphasized that "in order for the new Yugoslavia to form, which for the Albanians of Kosova and Metohija will be different fron the old Yugoslavia, today it is necessary that the Albanian people help." Nevertheless, most of the members of the delegation, during that meeting, were eliminated, some by being avoided politically, some by being imprisoned under the accusation of participating in "hostile activities," where among them there were also those that were sentenced with the death penalty, such as Halim Spahiu and others, and also those that were murdered, such as Rifat Berisha, who was a top official in Kosova.[321]

In Kosova, the infamous OZNA (the Informational Service for People's Defense) again had the main say, with its familiar apparatus of prosecution and eavesdropping. They began to look into the old files gathered from previous regimes as well as open new files on the people. Teachers, journalists, and the intellectuals were persecuted, even those from the communist families, who had completed their high schools in the Serbian language or had started studying in the University of Belgrade,

---

[321] Pushkolli, Fehmi: *"Mbrojtja Kombëtare Shqiptare e Kosovës 1878-1990,"* Prishtina, 1991, p. 131-133.

316

and by marrying with Serbian females had started giving the first testimonies for "the new life." In the absence of the "model" of Albania and Enver Hoxha, through general attacks against anything that represented value even in those circumstances, the middle and uneducated class which was the majority, would gain collective depression and this way would be determined for the alternative of displacement as the only solution. Enver Hoxha and his ideology, even with its negativity toward Kosova, in relation to the Serbo-Yugoslavian reality, in most cases had functioned for the better. According to this intention, the Albanian Language Institute in Prishtina was closed down, the High School of Gjakova was moved to Prishtina, where after a while it closed down, all of the names of organizations were changed to Serbian, and they were written in the Cyrillic alphabet. In other words, everything that was requested and achieved by the "Albanian National Committee" from the beginning was canceled due to the engagement of their activists.

These changes were supposed to be emphasized, especially in the Albanian environments, so that at least formally and administratively the visual identity of Kosova would be changed from that of the Albanians to that of the Serbs, a vision which had started with the entrance of fascism and partially retained even after the communist revolution. Of this nature would also be the orders for removing the national Albanian symbols from public and private usage, such as the national flag, which during the National Liberation War was used by the partisans, but accompanied with the communist and Yugoslavian flag, even after the war. According to these politics, in 1956, the "Prizren Process" was organized, which after 1966 was declared invalid and was evaluated as a part of the great Serbian campaign against the Albanian intelligence and politicians. This process also included almost all of what up to that day represented intellectual value to Albanians in Kosova.

The unpopular action of gathering the weapons, even prior to reaching its peak, was present in different forms from 1945 and onwards. Belgrade never gave up this idea for arms collection, since it always was a "reserve issue," not because the Albanians had some weapons left over from a long time ago (many of them not even usable) and this was known; it was also known that they could be gathered with a single order if this were to be desired, but because through them, the situation could always be kept tense. They could always then reason different actions such as: the persecution of "ballist gangs" and "remainders of the reactionaries," as well as different actions of "cleansing." These actions were always reasoned with "finding of hidden weapons" and other such accusations. Nevertheless, the unpopular action of gathering the weapons would peak precisely in that harsh winter against Albanians all over Kosova, in which case due to the heavy raid and maltreatment through which over thirty five thousand Albanians went, over 400 people died.[322] Although the ratification of the covenant by Ankara and Belgrade was interrupted by the beginning of the Second World War, it had to be reactivated. And as a result of all of this was the second great wave of displacement of Albanians to Turkey, from 1956 to 1966, which is estimated to encompass around a quarter million displaced people. This means that during ten years, a fourth of the population permanently left Kosova. For the Serbs, who would have liked for this digit to be two - three times larger, this represented a considerable success, which kept their hopes up to wait for another chance for similar actions. Nevertheless, this time, in Turkey, different from the displacement during the two world wars, or that of 1912/14, when mainly the rural border regions (that of Dukagjin and Pollog) migrated, in the years after the war and the fifties, the population from the cities migrated, which apart from craftsmen, the road of no return was also be taken by the emancipated citizens, which represented a great loss for Kosova.

The Revolutionary Movement for the Unification of Albania

After the melt-down of the "Albanian National Democratic Movement"(ANDM) in 1947, the spirit of national unification which it left behind would be kept alive by the Revolutionary Movements for unification with Albania which appeared at the end of the fifties and the be-

---

[322] Regarding the dimensions of the actions for gathering weapons, in 1955/56, see the testimonials of "Rilindja" newspaper in some feuilletons from October 1966 up to March 1967. There are also details regarding the processes that were held against the members of the Yugoslavian security service UDB in the court of Prishtina and that of Nish, who were involved in what were called "abuse" and found their judgment in the Plenum of Brioni, in June 1966, when the minister of the Yugoslavian police Aleksander Rankovic was removed, with what Tito finally got the opportunity to direct Yugoslavia toward the Yugoslavian self-governing course, which would bring him closer to the market economy and the Yugoslavian society towards political liberalization.

ginning of the sixties, by organizations such as "the Revolutionary Party for Unification of Albanian Territories" of Metush Krasniqi, "the Revolutionary Committee for Unification of Kosova with Albania" of Kadri Halimi and Ali Aliu and others, leading up to the "Revolutionary Movement for Unification with Albania" of Adem Demaçi.

The continued state terror against the "enemies" who in most cases were Albanian intellectuals or local authorities with impact on the Albanian population continued to be persecuted by police and the discrimination of Kosova by continuous exclusion from the economic and development programs of Serbia and Yugoslavia, in which case, the differences between Kosova and other regions and republics of Yugoslavia deepened, resulted in the loss of hope for the future of Kosova; however, the struggle kept the spirit of the resistance against Belgrade's regime alive.

During the first years after the war, the spirit of the anti-communist resistance was fed by the democratic ideas upon which the Albanian-wide future was supposed to be constructed under the framework of a common country linked with the West, such as the "Albanian National Democratic Movement" (ANDM) program, from 1945-1947. At the end of the fifties and the beginning of the sixties, a revolutionary movement for unification with Albania appeared which was influenced by the circumstances of the time, since it was conforming to the social and political realities of the Albanian state, which was known to be communist. Thus, in 1957 we also have the first organization of this nature, the *"Revolutionary Party for Unification of Albanian Territories"* led by Metush Krasniqi, where other activists were also involved, such as Sejdi Kryeziu, Mark Gashi, Metë Dërmaku, Qemal Kallaba, and Mehmet Ajeti.[323] It should be noted that Metush Krasniqi, in this spirit, continued even after he was released from prison, turning into an integral figure of the illegal movement, who viewed the idea for national unification as being closely linked with turning the Albanian world towards the West. In the continued activity for national unification, in 1960 the organization known as *"The revolutionary committee for unification with Albania"* led by Kadri Halimi, Ali Aliu, Ramadan Halimi and others emerged. [324]

---

[323] See: Çeku, Ethem: *"Shekulli i ilegales,"* Prishtina, 2004, p. 30 and Novosella, Selatin: *"Demonstratat e gjashtëdhjetetetës,"* Prishtina, 2008, p. 11.
[324] *Ibid.*, p. 48.

It is natural that the preconditions for such a change be sought initially in the breakdown of the relationship between Yugoslavia and Albania, which until then had been too "brotherly" because they had Moscow and Stalinism as a common denominator. Tito detached, however, while Enver Hoxha remained faithful and even in the most fanatic form, even after Stalin's death in 1953. Enver did not even agree with Krushchev, as was seen where Yugoslavia realized that there was no longer support anywere for Albania or Kosova. One should keep in mind the international factor and the new realities which appeared after the division of the bipolar spheres of interest, where on the one hand was the West, and on the other hand the East with the Soviet Union. In the latter (East) fell Albania, while Yugoslavia positioned itself in the middle, which enabled Yugoslavia a more favorable international position, whereas for Albania a greater isolation, especially when it left Moscow and approached China, which emerged with the version of the brutal communism of "the stone age."

State violence, discrimination, persecution and all the pressure which had the intention of chasing Albanians to Turkey, returned after the triple gentleman's agreement: Yugoslavia, Greece, Turkey, and with the Tito – Fuhad Kypril agreement of February 1953. It was natural that dissatisfaction would be expressed against challenges of existence, which would lead to necessary actions and concrete requests, such as that for detachment from Yugoslavia and unification with Albania. Not only did this clash with the invulnerability of the state borders, but also, it clashed with the politics of the Albanian state. Albania was worried about its inability to fight Yugoslavia but at the same time was threatened by Greece regarding the "vori-epir" issue of southern Albania."

The Albanian resistance returned to the irredentist logic which up to then had lost two battles (in 1918 and 1945), however, despite the reality of these losses, they still wanted to continue with the same logic, which became a preoccupation of the majority of Albanians. As was seen from Metush Krasniqi's activity and his *Revolutionary Party for the Unification of Albanian Territories"* of 1957 as well as *"The Revolutionary Committee for Unification of Kosova and Albania"* of 1960, at the beginning of the sixties and on, a continuous process towards Albanian unification would arise. Again through revolutionary methods, the activity of Adem Demaçi from 1958 and on gave special direction to it, since it softened the "revolution" with *the right to self-determination*, which was an ideological doctrine launched by the Comintern and accepted as a practice for "equality of people" even by the Soviet Union. In the "manifest" which emerged with the statute of the *Revolutionary Movement for the unification of Albanians,*" and with Demaçi's second imprisonment in 1964, where he said that "as a fifth grader in Prishtina, I started feeling dissatisfaction, because, in my opinion, at that time those in power had started raising the so-called issue of Turks in Kosova. Even later on, in 1955/6 when Kosova's hidden weapons were taken away, this moment had an impact on me and I began to express my dissatisfaction," which according to him for "stabilizing the situation in the Balkans it was best that Kosova join Albania, with *referendum* or with *war.*" In describing these intentions, Demaçi said "I got this idea about forming an illegal organization, based on strong principles where I would be at the top of this organization, while leaders of groups in different cities would be the young Albanian writers."[325]

Demaçi was detained on December 19, 1958, whereas in March, 1959, the District Court of Prishtina sentenced him to five harsh years in prison. The Supreme Court of Serbia, in June of that year, revised the decree of the District Court of Prishtina and lowered his sentence to three years.

Adem Demaçi was imprisoned two more times: in 1964 when he was sentenced to 15 years of prison and served 10 years, and also in 1975, when he was again sentenced with 15 years of prison. He came out of jail for the third time in 1990, precisely when Yugoslavia was in the process of disintegration, while Kosova, for which he had anticipated and desired unification with Albania, soon declared its Constitutional Declaration (on July 2) with which it detached from Serbia and on July 7 in Kaçanik, the Kosova Assembly declared Kosova as a Republic. From this point, Kosova's difficult but unstoppable journey toward an independent state continued.

Demaçi's three incarcerations, each in their own way, were emblematic for the Albanian resistance of that time and that form and the direction that it would take. These incarcerations were also symbolic for the fashion in which they were sanctioned by the Yugoslav laws, since the first (1958) had to do more with a *verbal delict*, "a hostile propaganda,"; the second time (1964) for direct organization which was intended for the revolutionary movement for unification of Albanians, but with its con-

---

[325] See: Bajrami, Hakif: *"Dosja Demaçi,"* Prishtina, 2004, p. 29.

crete actions (with the placement of a few communist Albania flags and the distribution of a few illegal pamphlets among students and teachers) remained at the propaganda level. The third incarceration (1976) was for the formation of the "National Liberation Movement of Kosova," where the possibility for unification with Albania could not be excluded.

The social and political processes in which Albanians were involved during the mid-sixties and on, did not go in the direction of Albanian unification, but rather that of the state building of Kosova, a process whose historical tracks would be irreversible from the moment that the request for the Republic of Kosova emerged in the 1968 rallies. These demonstrations were the first and largest of its kind after the war with Yugoslavia, where Albanians' request for equality with others, was neither realized nor sanctionable by law. Despite the fact that it was known from the formal politics of Belgrade under the impact of the Serbian politics, which refused the Albanians equality with others, different labels were attached to it too, such as that of the "counterrevolution," that of "irredentism" and lastly that of "separationism" based on which the Yugoslav prisons were filled with Albanians.

Nevertheless, Demaçi's actions as a new writer, who had rightfully caught the attention of the literary opinion with his book "the Blood Snakes" and other stories, was part of an intellectual and political concern which had to be expressed. This expression was important, especially after the state terror was exercised upon Albanians and their rights were openly violated, giving rise to the issue of migrations to Turkey, risking the destruction of the ethnic Albanian existence according to the familiar hegemonic plans of Belgrade, which continued from the East Crisis with tragic consequences for the Albanians. Of course, under these circumstances, the repressive powers, which continued to retain the coordinates of the Great Serbian hegemonism, masked under the communist ideology, had under its attacking target the intellectual conscience of Albanians, so that the uneducated population with the slandered Turkish-Islam identity would remain troubled from the spiritual, social and political perspective, so that then they could more easily be subject to the displacement process which was up and going, after the signing of the Tito-Kypril agreement of 1953, which reactivated the Yugoslav-Turkish interstate covenant of 1938.

The imprisonment and the judicial process conducted for Demaçi in 1959 was not, as it was stated by Belgrade's propaganda, simply "a retaliation that the state gave to the expanding irredentist attempts," which the new writer had manifested with the creation of an illegal organization and a program that he had defended for the whole time. It was also a part of an organized campaign of violence towards the Albanian intellectuals so that they could be eliminated from any possibility of raising the Albanian political awareness to stand up for their rights as much as they could in those circumstances and take responsibility for their future.

Belgrade's regime, from the breakdown of the relationships with Albania, had used the method of eviction of intellectuals "coming from" Albania to Kosova and their forced return to Albania, with the reasoning that "they practiced nationalist indoctrination" even though it had to with the educated Kosovars who after the occupation of Kosova had found shelter across the border, and who had the right to return to their homeland. This method had greatly weakened the intellectual base in Kosova, especially the part which had national and anti-communist awareness, since they were important figures of culture, creativity, science, and education, whom after the war had become active in the emancipation and cultural streams of the Albanians in Kosova, in those few cultural and educational institutions which were earned with great effort. With the imprisonment and persecution of Demaçi and other intellectuals from Kosova, Belgrade sought to initially "incriminate" with the anathema of the "destroyers" of Yugoslavia, the first generation of intellectuals in formation, which was not ready to give up their right for self-determination. Belgrade wanted these intellectuals to use their knowledge to advance "brotherhood and unity" propaganda rather than for unification with Albania.

Unlike the first time, when the whole judicial process was based upon "face to face conversation" and expressions of opinions for the heavy situation, which came under the framework of "hostile propaganda," the second time, so that of June 1964, Demaçi was imprisoned with the "corpus delict" as the founder of the *revolutionary movement for unification of Albanians*" under the accusation for penal activity by article 117, paragraphs 1 and 2 of the Penal Code. In this case, as a testimonial was the statute of the *revolutionary movement for unification of Albanians*" as well as the other documents, which Demaçi had composed and and with which he started the organization and the involvement of other people. Thus, together with Demaçi others were also imprisoned, who endured interrogation of various forms, and brought before the District Court of

Prishtina, on August 1964 the following: Sabit Ratkoceri, Hazir Shala, Salahudin Daci, Azem Beqiri, Abdyl Lahu, Ahmet Haxhia, Xhafer Mahmutxhiku, Dibran Bajraktari, Sabri Novosella, Tefik Sahiti and Njazi Saraçogull (a Turkish citizen with Albanian origin, from Istanbul). Adem Demaçi was sentenced to 15 years of prison, while the others were sentenced 5 and 10 years.[326] For this action, in Prishtina, Ilmi Rakovica, Shefqet Jashari, Vezir Ukaj, Selman Berisha and Enver Mehmeti[327] were also judged.

Alongside the Court of Prishtina, in the Court of Peja and that of Gjilan, similar processes were held against activists who in different forms were part of this organization or were linked to it through different cities of Kosova. Thus, in Peja, the activists from Gjakova were also convicted, such as: Professor Kadri Kusari (Dushi), poet Myrteza Nura (Xaja), Hyda Dobruana, writer Teki Dërvishi, Asim Vula and Professor Avni Lama.[328] The court in Peja convicted: Remzi Balaku, Shefqet Deçani, Sylë Shala, Ramadan Shala, Ahmet Zeka, Selajdin Daci, Nezir Gashi, Mehmet Krasniqi, Vesel Shala, Abdyl Shala and Nimon Podrimja.[329]

In Mitrovica the convicted were: Mustafa Vehnari, Hysen Daci, poet Zeçir Gërvalla, singer Ismet Koshutova and Arif Hoxha.[330]

In Gjilan the convicted were: writer Rexhep Elmazi, Fehmi Elmazi, Isa Bajrami and Abdyl Qerimi.[331]

It has been noted that during the investigations but also in the judgment process, the accused expressed their determination regarding their specification to be part of the *revolutionary movement for unification of Albanians*" organization and their loyalty toward this idea. With some small exception, all of them admitted their voluntary membership and their availability to act according to the program of the organization for achieving its goals, which started with the procurement of the right for self-determination up to detachment, with the intention of liberation and

---

[326] Bajrami, Hakif: "*Dosja Demaçi,*" Prishtina, 2004, p. 85.

[327] Judgment act K. Nr. 266/64 of 26.08.1964.

[328] Judgment act K. Nr. 68/64 of 08.08.1946.

[329] Judgment act K. nr. 74/64 of 21.08.1964.

[330] Judgment act K. nr. 258/64 of 22.08.1964

[331] Judgment act K. nr. 252/64 of 11.08.1964.

unification of Albanians, as stated in the documents of the organization *"the unification with Mother Albania."*[332]

Also, in this process, the determination for utilizing revolutionary tools in accordance with this goal – both peaceful and violent ones – was proven, where the armed war and the general people's insurgence was anticipated,[333] even though as it was anticipated, it remained only as an illusion of the revolutionary romanticism, which, under these circumstances was understandable and useful, but never implementable.

For "assistance" Lenin and his messages for "resolving the issue of borders between the socialist countries" were called, which according to Demaçi, the "Yugoslavian leaders" and some Albanian leaders, had forgotten."[334]

It is noted that, in the statute and program of the *"revolutionary movement for unification of Albanians"* organization – apart from the rightful criticism given to Kosova for falling behind in all fields as compared to other parts of Yugoslavia – are also appraisals for the economic and political situation in Albania and especially for its external course, for which:

> Albania is now following a more independent policy than it ever did throughout its history [and] is developing upon healthy bases, [and that] the events after the 22nd Congress of the Communist Party of the Soviet Union (CPSSR) gave the Albanian leadership the last lessons that the politics of relying mainly on its own powers are the most right and secure politics there are.[335]

Even with these issues which must viewed according to the spirit and complexity of the time, the *"revolutionary movement for unification of Albanians,"* lead by Adem Demaçi's organization and other similar ones,[336] remains historical, because no matter what it had in its program, it

---

[332] *"Dosja Demaçi,"* p. 86: *"Statuti i Lëvizjes Revolucionare të Bashkimit të Shqiptarëve,"* point I, p. 1.

[333] *Ibid.*, point II, p. 1.

[334] *Ibid.*, p. 96.

[335] *Ibid.*, p. 109.

[336] According to the data, in the period between 1958-1964, these organizations had also been formed and acted illegally:

1. In Anamorava in 1957, Metush Krasniqi formed the illegal organization named *"the Revolutionary Party for the unification of Ethnic Albanian Territories with Albania"*

represented the right but also the will of Albanians not to conform with the unjust segregation imposed upon them from 1912, and, in addition, brought to surface the determination of Albanians in Kosova and other parts of the ex-Yugoslavia, to fight for their right for *self-determination* even under the dire circumstances that the Yugoslav regime had brought. This was a right which the Albanians never gave up, through which they would win the right to determine their own fate and future according to their own will. In this case, the right for self-determination, which Demaçi emphasized and upon which he relied, represented an important change, which not only made relevant the "revolutionism" which Metush Krasniqi and his followers as rightists maintained permanently, but he turned it into a factor of the unavoidable rhetoric of the time conforming to the ideological realities in Albania and Yugoslavia, where such changes could take place even with agreements under the framework of "the internationalist family."

(PRBTSH). This organization emphasized the Western affiliation of Albanians and the National Unification, which at the same time represented liberation from the Eastern affiliation and the communist ideology.

2. In the Plane of Dukagjin, in Peja, in 1959, the illegal organization was formed named: *"The Organization for Unification of Albanian Territories"* (BTSH) and

3. In Anamorava, in 1960, Kadri Halimi together with Ali Aliu and Hyrije Hana formed the illegal organization named: *"The Committee for Unification of Albanian Territories"* (KBKSH).

CHAPTER 2
KOSOVA AS PART OF THE FEDERATION

Brioni Plenum and the Demand for a Republic of Kosova

The fourth assembly of the Central Committee of the Communist Party of Yugoslavia in June 1966, called the Plenum of Brioni, was a resolution of issues between the bureaucratic and reform groups, which was supposed to decide about the future of Yugoslavia in the direction of the centralist socialism, which would one day have to choose whether to unite with Moscow or remain closer to the West. – Tito's victory over Rankovic opened the way for great changes in the economic and political system but also for modifications in the Federation towards federal strengthening, which as a precondition had the removal of Kosova and Vojvodina from under Serbia's tutelage and their connection to the Federation. – The judgment of the heavy deformations against Albanians during the twenty-year period brought forth a liberal climate in Kosova, which was manifested with positive changes in education, culture, economy and the political life. – The 1967 modifications of amendments opened Kosova's way towards the Federation, upon which then the request for the Republic of Kosova was raised, a request which emerged into the debate for constitutional modifications and was supported by the intelligence of Kosova, which justified itself with the right for self-determination, a right which the Albanians had earned during the anti-fascist war and the Bujan Resolution, but which was violently denied from them in 1945 after the Serbian annexation.

The Constitution of 1963, not only totally canceled out the participation of Kososva regions in the Yugoslavian Federation, where their genesis was from the first Constitution of 1946, but it also created the possibilities for a bureaucratic centralism, which would give power to the unitary

327

forces as well as their attempts to dominate Yugoslavia, forces which came from Belgrade. However, the bureaucratic centralism and the expanding phenomena of unitarianism was negatively reflected in the economic and political plan, since they clashed with *self-governance*, a model which had already started to be proven successful, which had made the Yugoslavian socialism seem as a "liberal model" and to be affirmed into the so-called "Third World" (later on, the movement of the non-aligned nations from 137 countries, mainly Africa, Asia and Latin America, led by Tito until his death in 1980).

This made it possible for these counter-expressions to find place in the Eighth Congress of the Communists of Yugoslavia, of December 1964, where Tito and his closest collaborators (Kardelj, Bakaric, and Vlahovic) could create the political platform without any difficulties, since the party that they controlled held the monopoly and the last word.

In reality, the internationalist issues were not treated in a special manner in any of the party congresses after the war (the V, VI and VII), since it was evaluated that the class (communist) aspect further on had to remain the key to their solution. This made the followers of the central-bureaucratic practices emerge with the idea that in the field of international relations no problems existed any more, since the ones that had been important were solved, thus, requesting the removal of the national issue from the points of the day.[337]

Even with these evaluations – which to the opinion left the impression that Yugoslavia "had positively solved the national issues" and that self-governance marked another advanced chapter of social and political relations in place – the 1963 Constitution and the modifications that were made, showed that the top political leadership of the federation (Tito, Kardel, Bakaric) had accepted these changes under the pressure of the central-bureaucratic forces, in order for the formation of "arguments" to destroy them. This was best reflected in the first half of 1966, when the whole issue turned into an open conflict which gained its own epilogue, with the defeat of the central-bureaucratic forces in the Fourth Plenum of the Central Committee of the Communist League of Yugoslavia, known as the Plenum of the Brioni. This very important modification gave a

---

[337] Rajoviq, Radoshin: *"Autonomia e Kosovës,"* Prishtina, 1987, p. 404

new impulse to the further development of self-governance, as well the resolving of issues regarding international relations.[338]

Prior to this major change, these realities – meaning the central-bureaucratic ones, which were led by the Serbian political elite – seemed unacceptable for the Western Republics (Croatia and Slovenia), which knew that if this development was further allowed, Serbia and its natural allies in the Federation (Macedonia, Montenegro and Bosnia and Herzegovina) in the near future, could change the image of the Federation to the avail of the Serbian Unitarianism, who as a natural ally had the Soviet socialist model of "the strong hand." It must be understood, that Tito, unsatisfied with the strengthening of the Serbian central-bureaucratic leadership, in the Central Committee of the Communist Party of Yugoslavia (CPY), in March 1959, requested analysis of the issue regarding the position of the national minorities under the reasoning that "because of the central-bureaucratic practice, there were problems in this field which had to be analyzed and solved."[339]

In this case, the "Conclusions of the Central Committee of the CPY regarding the issue of national minorities" were approved, which without any explanation were not published. Three years later, in the "Communist" newspaper, a detached piece of them appeared; however, they only became fully known after five years, in the Eighth Congress of the CPY, in December 1964, after which they were also fully published together with other documents of the Congress.

As would be seen, the "reasons" why at that time these conclusions were not published and in fact no public debate in the party base was allowed, had to do precisely with the stance toward national minorities when the *"national minorities" terminology was* abandoned and replaced by *"nationality."*[340] Tito's confrontation with the bureaucratic forces from the Serbian communist routes was constructed and directed towards Rankovic.

This modification was not simply a terminological issue. On the contrary, it had to do with a more adequate definition for the position of the nationalities and their new role that they would have in Yugoslavia as equal subjects in the Federation. The real conditions were thus created for

---

[338] See Perunović, Branko: *"Istorija Jugoslavije 1918-1970,"* Belgrade, 1980, p. 517-572

[339] See *"Osmi Kongres SKJ,"* Belgrade, 1965

[340] *Ibid.*, p. 47.

the position of the regions (that of Kosova-Metohija and Vojvodina) to be removed from the tutelage of Serbia under which they had been placed with the Constitutional amendments of 1967, 1968, 1971 and the ones that were approved in the 1974 Constitution.

For this process, the platform was prepared by the Eighth Congress of CPY of 1964, which in 1965 put into action all its party mechanisms, so that by the end of that year and the second half of the next year, they were brought to surface, initially called "the differences," then "un-unity" and lastly the conflict of the highest levels, which had to be put to an end. Thus, on July 1, 1966, on the Fourth Plenum of the Central Committee of the CPY (Brion Plenum), it all ended with the defeat of the central-bureaucratic forces and their dogmatic-bureaucratic supporters, Alexander Rankovic, Svetislav Stefanovic and others, whom, after they were excluded from the party, also retreated from all social and political functions. With this, Yugoslavia entered an important phase of social, political and economic liberalization, the position of leaning towards equality with the others in the Federation, from which the Albanians also benefited. Their defeat at the same time opened a process of widespread differentiation within the party structures, but also the state ones which were burdened with "the phenomena of heavy distortions against Albanians," especially in Kosova and the Dukagjin plain where these distortions had huge consequences.

The Internal State Security (UDB) was accused of these distortions, as well as other judicial and police organizations, which had been part of this chain. Apart from the dismissal, pensioning or exclusion of a portion of the state apparatus of the UDB from Republican routes, they were also prosecuted and convicted. This was made possible, since Rankovic himself – who on July 1, 1966, resigned from the state functions (Federal Minister of Internal Affairs and Vice President of the Yugoslav Federation) – in September of that year, by the request of the Central Committee of Serbia's Communist Party, which requested of the the Central Committee of the CPY, that he be excluded from the Communist Party of Yugoslavia (CPY). In addition, a group of top Serbian political leaders, such as Svetislav Stefanovic (Assistant Minister of Internal Affairs), Vojin Lukic, Slobodan Kostic and Generals Milan Zezel, Miloje Milojevic and others were also excluded from the CPY.

Apart from the differentiation process and the opening of processes against the main supporters of the deformations, the rehabilitation of victims from the assembled processes organized by the Serbian State Security Service in 1950-1964 had also begun in Kosova, among which the court had also declared as invalid the *"Prizren Process"* of 1953 whereby some famous Albanian intellectuals and politicians had been imprisoned, while many others were prosecuted in different ways as "nationalists." The infamous action of 1955/56 of the gathering of weapons was also judged harshly, an action during which thousands of Albanians had been mal-treated and imprisoned, among which there were also victims. The displacement of Albanians to Turkey had not remained free from criti-cism either, together with other pressures that had followed this process involving around a quarter million Albanians.

Of course, under these circumstances, the Plenum of Brioni and the issues it raised – especially the concrete actions that were taken against the supporters of heavy deformations towards Albanians – was received in Kosova as an important event which could lead to positive turns, with the condition that apart from the punishment that these actors of such deformations would receive, other issues would also be raised which had to return the faith of Albanians. These issues had to do with a radical change of their constitutional position which was linked with regaining the right for self-determination, which in those circumstances could be realized by constitutional modifications, from where the Albanians would gain an equal status with the other federal units.

In fact, the Albanian political class of Kosova at that time, as well as the forming intelligence, quickly understood that the essence of these modifications and the surfacing of the deformations, which were ad-dressed towards Rankovic and his service, had the intention of creating the circumstances for changing the relationships within the Federation, which had to move from the destruction of the centralist-bureaucratic bloc (of the Serbian leadership of Belgrade) to the strengthening of the federalist-self-governance line. The elevation of Kosova's position to the range of federal units then appeared as a precondition for the success of this change, a change which to the Tito Yugoslavia presented new oppor-tunities to be positioned against the centralist and Unitarian logic, which in the future could turn it towards Moscow and its ideology. Thus, the political leadership of Kosova – up to that point demeaned and abused in various ways by Serbian politics – would not put all of its political concen-tration as much on the liability of those that had caused the deformations (since this was considered a matter of the judicial entities) as much as it created the conditions for that situation to be used to change its social, political and judicial position. Thus, from the Seventh Meeting of the Regional Committee of the Communist League of Serbia for Kosova and Metohia, held in the Summer of 1966, – where big changes would be made[341] – the communists of Kosova, without a dilemma under the impact and with the "directions" of the Yugoslav leadership interested in the victory of the new course, focused on two main issues, which would bring forward the processes for elevating Kosova to a federal factor:

- *The problem of economic development in Kosova and*
- *The acceleration of social and national emancipation as well the emancipation of the Albanian nationality through forced equality, which had to be expressed through constitutional modifications.*

The first issue – meaning the treatment of economic development in Kosova, by referring to the causes and factors that had brought it to that state, and which had to be overcome as quickly as possible – represented not only the discriminatory stance towards a portion of the more economically left behind regions, but also the intentions that hid behind it, which were linked with the creation of the conditions for displacing Albanians to Turkey, for which the way was opened after the gentlemen's agreement of 1953 between Yugoslavia and Turkey. In the analyses which came out at that time, reflecting the whole treachery of keeping Kosova behind, were supposed to discriminate the Albanians but without laying hands on the Serbians and the others, who had to be stimulated and

---

[341] In this Plenum, Dusan Mugosa was replaced by Veli Deva. Mugosa was the president of the Communists of Kosova from the war up to then, who during the war, as a delegate of the Communist Party in Albania, had impacted the decisions that Enver Hoxha took, by turning him into a servant of Tito. With this modification, the communists of Kosova were freed from the person that had in his hands most of the deformations in Kosova which had been done from 1945 on, especially those that were linked with the destruction of the intellectual structures of Albania. In this Plenum, the decision was also taken for the intellectuals of the period after the war to be put in the leadership of the Regional Committee, such as Mahmut Bakalli, who within a short period of time became a leader of the communists in Kosova, who was put in the leadership of the political processes with which Kosova's possibilities were opened to detach from Serbia and join the Yugoslav Federation as its constitutive element, as occurred with the Constitutional changes of 1968 up to 1974, which ended with the approval of the New Constitution of Yugoslavia.

would benefit from this. Thus, the most perfidious methods were brought to the surface, when the lack of developing Kosova was utilized, so that the Serbian and Montenegrin frameworks which entered Kosova (from the police, the armada, administration, education and other structures) took "special stimulating supplements" and special wages. The local Serbs were paid additional expenditures for medical and other services in Belgrade, while the Albanians were forced to accept the services of a very low level. It was ascertained that even those economic investments that had been made during the mid-fifties and on, the majority of them would go to the municipalities where there were Serbs, while even if a unit was opened outside of those municipalities, Serbians and Montenegrins received employment priorities.

However, even in the beginning of the sixties, when with the insistence of the Federation, investments were beginning to be made in some areas, they were made in such a way that these investments were tied to the Serbian organizations, which would open up their dependent units and not allow any independent development. It was ascertained, that in this way, many organizations from Serbia had exploited the specified funds that were designated for the economic development of Kosova and used them for their own needs, by masking this with the opening up of a non-functional unit there. The only exception here were the investments in the mineral and energy capacities, where Kosova had the largest reserves in area: lignite (63% of Yugoslav production), zinc (47% of the area reserves), Trepca's gold (unstated amounts but among the largest in area), silver with 37%, chrome with 51%, phosphate, and others.[342] However, even here, the investments were done for their extraction and not for internal processing. Even Kosova's electricity (the capacities of which were among the largest in the area) in most cases was exported to Macedonia, Montenegro and Serbia, and at very low prices. There were a few known agreements signed in 1964 with Macedonia with which the thermal power plants in Kosova were obliged to supply the Metallurgic Combine of Shkup with electricity and gas at very low prices, while Kosova did not have enough electricity even for its own needs. The same occurred with the "Trepca" mine in Mitrovica, where the minerals were melted there, while the processing departments were constructed in

---

[342] Gucia, Ismet: *"Burimet natyrore si faktor i zhvillimit ekonomik të Kosovës,"* Prishtina, 1982, p. 75.

Kraljevo, Uzica and other Serbian places. Trepca's minerals were processed all over, while the end products that were found in the Kosova market cost too much. In such a state was also agronomy, the products of which were collected in Kosova as raw material at very low prices, while they were processed in different parts of the country, from which much was earned by exporting them. This method of economic exploitation of Kosova and its raw materials commemorated the colonial behavior, which came to the surface after the Plenum of Brion, where even what was noted in the Yugoslavian statistics as economic investment in Kosova and by looking at it from the perspective of mere digits showed a sensible growth between 1955 and 1965, was nothing more than a colonial form of exploiting Kosova for Yugoslavia's economic purposes, initially the Serbian ones which supervised everything. This was best reflected with the national income per capital of 7,188 in Slovenia, while in Kosova only 730 dinars, which means it was ten times lower.[343] The formal statistical data left understood that Kosova in 1966 had 1,250,000 people, from which only 90 thousand workers were employed in the social sector or 8.3% of the population, which was the lowest percentage in the area. However, this percentage, when it was analyzed upon the basis of nationality, it lowered even further the number of Albanians employed to only 5.3%. Thus, by the mid-sixties, in Kosova, only 1 out of every 17 Albanians was employed, 1 out of every 7 Turks, 1 out of every 4 Serbs, and 1 out of every 3 Montenegrins. At the same time, the representation of Albanians in the regional organizations was at the minimum level, while the representation of them in the organizations of the Republic and the Federation was barely representative. In some services, such as the State Security Service, diplomacy, and military there were also very few Albanians.[344]

Relying on these parameters, the political leadership in Kosova requested that Yugoslavia come out with a stance regarding the economic position of Kosova, where a special development was anticipated, which would pass through a fund of the Federation for Kosova. In this case, the stance came out that Kosova would more easily solve its many economic, social and other problems and that it would be able to contribute more to realizing national equality as a federal unit, with the separation as a

---

[343] Bjelogrlić, Dušan: „*Dvadese godina ekonomskog razvitka Jugoslavije,*" Belgrade, 1973, p. 89-100.

[344] *Ibid.*, p. 332.

Republic. These requests were supported in the explanation of the right of nations for self-determination. [345]

The truth was that these opinions appeared, in most cases, in closed meetings and negotiations with the representatives of the Federation with most responsibility, but also through the work of the Regional Assembly Commission for the issues of the autonomous regions of Kosova and Metohija's statute.

Thus, in the meeting of the Board of the Central Committee of CPY for international and inter-republic issues, on February 20, 1967 – in the case of analyzing the thesis of "the character and role of the Federation in the conditions of the social self-governing system and the structure of the Federation's organizations regarding this role," – the Kosova representative on this Board, Asllan Fazlia, presented his opinion: "since the same factors that brought the creation of federal units – also brought the creation of autonomous regions, then the scale of the Republic's rights and that of autonomous regions should also be the same, respectively a further step has to be taken in comparison to the 1963 Constitution of the Federal Socialist Republic of Yugoslavia and the conveyance of rights and tasks of the Federation to that of a Republic should be followed also with the conveyance of rights and tasks of the Republic to that of the autonomous regions."[346]

Fazlia's proposal went in several directions: either a direct bonding between autonomous regions and the Federation, or the establishment of the Federal Serbia with some Federal (autonomous) republics. The maxim of his thoughts was that "the relationships within the Republic were not solved as they should have been."[347]

This stance was also held by the majority of the political class of Albanians in Kosova and this was important, since upon this the whole strategy would be constructed for the elevation of Kosova to the federal level, with which it could be removed from under Serbia's tutelage.

Since the pressure for constitutional modifications grew everyday and it usually came from Croatia and Kosova, where first the strengthening of

---

[345] Rajovic, Radoshin: *"Autonomia e Kosovës,"* Prishtina, 1987, p. 415.

[346] See *Stenogrami i mbledhjes së Komisionit të CC të CPY për marrëdhënie ndërnacionale dhe republikane,* on February 20nd, 1967, CC archive, III/144, p. 61-66, cited by Rajovic, Radoshin *"Autonomia e Kosovës,"* Prishtina, 1987, p. 416.

[347] *Ibid.*

the Rebublic's role in the Federation was requested, while Kosova wanted to gain the status of an equal unit in the federation by always mentioning the request for a Rebublic, the Central Committee of the CPY, at the end of 1967 and beginning of 1968, determined the ideo-political platform and the different constitutional directions on the evaluation that since Federalism is a process and not a formula, it was natural that, with the transformations in the society – the Federation would also transform, even in the sense that instead of leaning on a state basis, it would lean more everyday to a self-governing basis.

According to this platform, it could also be expected that the political leadership of Kosova, would determine its own platform, which attempted to retain the internal political equilibriums, but which for a motto had the right for self-determination. In this case, the references went to the Bujan Conference, but also to the decisions with which Yugoslavia was formed according to the self-determination principle which included also the right for detachment. Thus, in April 1968, Fadil Hoxha, President at that time of the Assembly of Kosova, speaking about the different directions of the constitutional modifications, said:

> We consider that we lack many things. Let us take one of the essential theses – Yugoslavia is a union of nations and nationalities of Yugoslavia, because, if it is not also a union of nationalities of Yugoslavia, then this nationality would be outside or a visitor or something else. Since it is a union of nations and nationalities, then this concept has to be expressed in a consequential manner in the Constitutional thesis, not only in the entry paragraph, but everywhere else where nations and nationalities of Yugoslavia are also mentioned, since they constitute this union as it is.[348]

According to Fadil Hoxha, since the status of the autonomous regions – as a wider social-political union, created on the basis of self-determination of the peoples of these regions under the framework of the Federation – had been changed, then it must be returned to its source state from where it was created. This means that Kosova had to earn its right to be a part of the Federation, independent from the way it would be defined, taking into consideration the fact that the autonomous regions in the new Yugoslavia were formed based on the decisions of the Second and

---

[348] *"Rilindja"* Newspaper, April 14th, 1968

Third Session of the AVNOJ, according to the principles of self-determination which included the right for detachment.[349]

That is what Fadil Hoxha prejudicated in April 1968 – when he raised the issue of Kosova's source right for self-determination, which he and his followers had expressed in the Bujan Conference Resolution, but which had been overlooked due to the agreement of Tito-Enver, which as a consequence resulted in the annexation of Kosova by Serbia and its violent placement under Serbia's tutelage – in a way was stated in August of that year, in the meeting of the Communist Party in Gjakova, from where the *"Kosova can become a Republic"* came out.[350]

The Communist Party of Gjakova came to the same conclusions as the Communist Party of Kosova, and these conclusions were widely made known to all the people of Kosova as well as to all of Yugoslavia.

In Gjakova, it was requested:

1. *In the Constitution of the Socialist Republic of Yugoslavia,* **the Albanian minority** *be elevated to the name* **the Albanian nationality,**
2. **The use of the Albanian national flag** *be guaranteed by law and the constitution*
3. *The region of Kosova be declared* **The Republic of Kosova**

During this meeting, these requests also came out:

a. *The right for* **self-determiantion**
b. *Instead of a statute, let Kosova have her own* **Constitution**
c. *Let* **Kosova have 20 representatives** *like all other republics, in the Nations Chamber of the Federal Assembly.*[351]

The stances of the Political Party of Gjakova were quickly supported by the political parties of all the cities of Kosova. Highly important in this direction was also the support of the Political Party of Prishtina. There also, after many discussions, some requests were raised:

- *The Constitution of the FSRY and that of Serbia should accept the right and the will of Albanians for self-determination*
- *The region should be turned to a federal unit*

---

[349] *Ibid.*

[350] See the report of the *"Rilindja"* newspaper in Prishtina, August 19th, 1968.

[351] *Ibid.*

- *The second article of the Constitution of the FSRY should be changed and it should be insisted that Yugoslavia consist of eight federal units*

At the end it was stated that it is the right of each nation and nationality for self-determination up to detachment. Thus, it should be requested that the region be turned into a Republic.[352]

The historical message of Gjakova was, for the first time, by a political party in which the highest political leadership of Kosova participated, and in a direct manner was requested that Kosova be declared a Republic – a request which later on was accepted in a referendum by the Albanian intelligence and its whole social spectrum and turned it into a motto of the Albanian political program. The Serbian leadership of Belgrade, although up to then, under the pressure of the changes that had occurred from the Brion Plenum, had expressed its willingness to accept the modifications that "were to the avail of deepening the self-governance and the political and social reforms," awaited with concern. Nevertheless, the Serbian leadership tried to camouflage it with the stance that "the position of autonomous regions, which is valid also for the other social-political communities, cannot be separated from the further process of de-centralization and position strengthening, of the independence and responsibility of municipalities and associate organizations as self-governing system, which constitute the base of the social-political system."[353]

However, the "maturity" of the Serbian leadership towards the request for the Republic of Kosova, which had come out of the Political Party of Gjakova as a legitimate request from the Albanians, which for the first time after World War II was expressed in that manner, together with other following requests, caused harsh reactions among the Serb intellectual and nationalist circuits, which had reacted in some meetings held by students at the University of Belgrade. In those gatherings, it was said that "the change of the constitutional position of the regions, especially that of Kosova, presented a betrayal of Serbism." There it was also said that "the

---

[352] Novosella, Selatin: *"Demonstratat e gjashtëdhjetetetës,"* the first book, Prishtina, 2008, p. 52.

[353] See the report of the newspaper *"Borba"* of Belgrade, August 22nd, 1968.

Republic of Kosova meant a cleansing of it by Serbians and a loss of the Serbian medieval cradle."[354]

The emergence of the request for the Republic of Kosova, independent of the reactions of Belgrade, in Kosova had found great support and had turned to an unseen atmosphere of intellectual and political mobilization in which almost all of the Albanian social layers were involved. Since the public discussions had begun regarding the constitutional changes, the Albanian intellectual circuits in Kosova (through universities, institutes and information instruments) were put at the head of these requests.

They echoed in the Kosova press, led by the newspaper "Rilindja" with its publications, but they also created a strong echo in Belgrade (which had started to call them "nationalist and separatist ideas"), but also in other centers, especially in Zagreb and Ljubljana, for which the elevation of Kosova's status to that of a Republic would give them the opportunities to finally be freed from the risk of Serbian Unitarianism.   In the Sixth Plenum of the Central Committee of Serbia, at an earlier time (during June of that year), Dobrica Qosic's declaration against the constitutional changes, especially those where Kosova would gain the status of a Federal affiliation, had given a clear messages that one day he and others like him would come in the open. The intellectuals of Kosova would not stop with the threats of the Serbian nationalists, but continued to support the request for the Republic of Kosova.   By requesting the status of Republic, they would also attain the right for self-determination up to detachment.

In this case, it was stated that Kosova as a Republic represented the interest of Albanians in Kosova, but also benefited the Yugoslavian Federation, as it was in the interest of Albania, as well as the international community, since this compromised resolution enabled the retaining of Yugoslavia as a union of equal nations and nationalities, as it also neutralized the claims of the unitary forces from the positions of the Serbian nationalism and hegemony, which sought to dominate the Yugoslavian Federation and to place it under Moscow's tutelage.   These attempts always remained active and as would be seen, they came to surface a little later on in different forms, even then when there were breezes which halted the Soviet ship and at some time even sent it toward destruction.

---

[354] Petranović, Branko: "*Istorija Jugsolavije,*" 1918-1970, Belgrade, 1980, p. 572.

During these discussions, the Albanian intellectuals used the Leninist principle of self-determination of people up to detachment and of choice, which the Comintern had also approved and were part of the political platform of the Yugoslavian communists for the resolution of national issues in the Versailles Yugoslavia, from the Founding Congress of Dresden in 1924. In this case, the Resolution of the Fifth Congress of the Communist Party of Yugoslavia of 1928 was also commemorated, which had come out according to the stance of the Comintern regarding the destruction of Yugoslavia as a creation of Versailles, which, according to the option for destroying such a Yugoslavia called a "prison of peoples," was about the unification of Kosova and Albania.[355]

The stance of the Yugoslav communists from the Fourth Congress was also supported in the Local Conference of the Communist Party of Yugoslavia held in 1934, in the documents of which it was stated that "the formation of the Versailles Yugoslavia as well as the entrance of Kosova into it, represented the occupation which the Serbian troops had created against it."[356] In the other party documents which originated from this Conference, the stance also came out that "the only rightful solution of the national issue in Yugoslavia and the Balkans would be to place the regime of the workers and villagers of each population, who would unite with their own will in a workers' and villagers' federation of the Balkans, which meant that "The Communist Party of Yugoslavia would help the movement of the repressed people: Croatians, Slovenians, Macedonians and Montenegrins, but also Albanians, to form their own independent states."[357]

It should be stated that the Central Committee of the Communist Party of Yugoslavia, which was elected in Ljubljana, on December 24,

---

[355] For more details regarding this issue, see Dedijer, Vladimir: *"Novi prilozi za biografiju Josipa Broza Tita,"* the third book, Belgrade, 1984, p. 167. Tito's biographer, in this case, for the first time also brought the record of the Resolution, where it said: "The Party often expresses its solidarity towards the revolutionary workers and villagers from the other people of Yugoslavia, and especially with the Albanian Revolutionary Movement from the Committee of Kosova. In this case he makes a call to the working class to support the war of the repressed and segregated Albanian people for independence and for unification with Albania."

[356] Dedijer, Vladimir: *"Novi prilozi za biografiju Josipa Broza Tita,"* the third book, Belgrade, 1984, p. 167.

[357] *Ibid.*, p. 167.

1934, and consisted of: Josip Broz Tito, Blagoje Parovic, Milan Gorkic, Miho Marinko and Vladimir Copic, took this stance.[358]

Although the stance of the Yugoslavian Communists from the first Congress, the Fourth in 1928, the Local Conference of Ljubljana in 1934, and up to the Local Conference of the Communist Party of Yugoslavia in 1941, had changed according to the circumstances as were those that the emergence of fascism had created. Nevertheless, in all its variants, the principle of self-determination of people up to detachment was retained, which had been emphasized as a platform also in the Second and Third Meeting of the Anti-fascist National Liberation Committee of Yugoslavia (AVNOJ) when Federal Yugoslavia was created.

Thus, based on these documents, the historian Ali Hadri would point out that "by using the rights for self-determination, the peoples of Kosova were contributors to the creation of the new Yugoslavia," although this "contribution" was made under scrutiny and in direct conflict with the ideological principles upon which the New Yugoslavia had been created. Supporting self-determination as an issue of factual circumstances, Professor Gazmend Zajmi, argued that "Nationalities as a collection had this right as nations also had it." Fehmi Agani made it known that "all requests that had been presented as requests from the majority of the people should be supported." He emphasized that "they should be our requests." While Rezak Shala, the regional prosecutor, insisted that "*The Republic of Kosova is an imperative of time and this right should not be given up.*"[359]

This specification, for the Albanian intellectuals, gained importance in new circumstances, since it would return them what they had been violently deprived of from the Prizren Resolution of July 1945 and on-wards, when the Bujan Resolution had been disregarded. In this case, the stance of the top Yugoslav leaders was also emphasized (that of Moshe Pijade, expressed in 1940 in the Local Conference of the Communist Party in Zagreb), their stance regarding the formation of "the Villager's and Worker's Republic of Kosovo," as he had mentioned, for the resolution of

---

[358] *Ibid.*, p. 167.

[359] For more details, see: Mišović, Miloš: "*Ko je tražio Republiku Kosova,*" Belgrade, 1987; Đaković, Spasoje: „*Događaji na Kosovu,*" Belgrade, 1981; Novosella, Selatin: „*Demonstatat e gjashtëdhjetetetës,*" Prishtina, 1981.

the issue of national rights of Albanians, which he also repeated in 1953 during an analysis in the Federation.[360]

Always conforming to the Leninist concept, the Albanian intellectuals, had also commemorated Enver Hoxha's conversations with Josip Broz Tito during 1946, regarding this issue, which it was said that they were left for later "due to the circumstances" which were linked "with the Serbian reaction," for which it was evaluated that after the strengthening of Yugoslavia's position as an un-integrated place, as well as the twenty-year repressive politics against the Albanians in Kosova which was judged in the Brioni Plenum in 1966, Belgrade was not able to oppose.

Of course, from the Albanian intellectuals' side, during the constitutional discussions, many more arguments of this nature resulted, but after a month, their zeal was put to a halt, even totally closed down with the stance that came from the highest party leadership of Kosova, where it was said that "the option of the Republic of Kosova was never a part of the requests of the communists of Kosova," but instead, "they were engaged for the enrichment of the constitutional position of Kosova on the Federal level, so that even at that level its rights would be realized."[361]

There was no doubt that the pullback from the request for the Republic of Kosova was done under pressure. Fadil Hoxha, President of the Board for Constitutional Changes, one of those that for the first time had initiated this issue in April of that year – an issue which in August was raised in the Political Party of Gjakova and the other political parties of Kosova – admitted that prior to the opening of the public discussions regarding the future constitutional changes, he had been invited to Brione by Tito. During the Brione visit, in the presence of Edward Kardel and

---

[360] For more details regarding this issue, see: Dedijer, Vladimir: *"Novi prilozi za biografiju Josipa Broza Tita,"* Belgrade, 1985; Đaković, Spasoje: *"Događaji na Kosovu,"* Belgrade, 1981; Kardelj, Eduard: *"Razgovori sa Staljinom,"* Belgrade, 1963; Çeku, Ethem: *"Kosova në sfondin e diplomacisë së Jugosllavisë dhe të Shqipërisë 1945-1981,"* Prishtina, 2009; Butka, Uran: *"Mukja shans i bashkimit peng i tradhtisë,"* Tirana, 2007; Pushkolli, Fehmi: *"Mbrojtja Kombëtare Shqiptare e Kosovës 1878-1990,"* Prishtina, 1991; Buxhovi, jusuf: *"Kthesa historike - Shteti paralel dhe rezistenca e armatosur,"* Prishtina, 2009.

[361] Buxhovi, Jusuf: *"Kthesa historike - shteti paralel dhe rezistenca e armatosur,"* Prishtina, 2009, p. 104.

Vladimir Bakarac (two of Tito's closest collaborators) and mediators of the 1974 Constitution, opened the discussion regarding the issue of the future status of Kosova, where the possibility had also been mentioned for the elevation of Kosova to the level of a Republic. According to Fadil Hoxha, Tito discussed the issue of Kosova with the understanding of it being somewhere in between his stance and one of a proposal. Interrelating to Tito's words, Kardel had expressed his opinion that before the definite outcome of Kosova was defined, it should also be discussed with the Serbian leadership. But, Tito had replied: "let this issue initially open and then we will see how it goes." Bakaric had intervened saying that the Serbian leadership should now know that Kosova couldn't be kept under the situation it had been under up until now. "The Serbian friends have a good chance to create new bridges of good faith with the Albanians."[362]

However, as would be seen, the Serbians still were not able to create new good faith bridges with the Albanians. The stance of the Serbian leadership now was clear: they could accept in-between solutions, so that Kosova would be represented in the Federation, but also linked with Serbia.

The Serbian stance would not remain without consequences for the top political leadership of Yugoslavia, which had its own doubts from the beginning, even though it was decided that Kosova and its status would be exploited for changing the relationships in the Federation to the avail of federalism, where regions would also become a part of it, no matter what they were called. It was more than clear that Tito and Kardel, after they had tested the Albanians' desires and the Serbians' stance, where the stance of the international factor regarding the issue was also tested, they had come to the conclusion that Kosova and Vojvodina had to be elevated to the scale of federal units. The Serbian reaction was to continue further with the Brezhnev doctrine regarding the ideological "right" which they had given themselves to intervene in the socialist camp in the case her interests were tested. The Serbs also did not want to provoke the West by giving Kosova the rights to be an equal federal unit.[363]

Fadil Hoxha best represented the essence of this compromise which came from above, with which, in the political level of Kosova, the opening of the issue of the Republic of Kosova began and ended:

---

[362] *Ibid.*, p. 104.

[363] See Meier, Viktor: *"Wie Jugoslawien verspielt wurde,"* München, 1995.

It does not mean that the issue of the Republic cannot be raised... but, we have to evaluate what is realistic, really realistic and possible in this direction of affiliation of the autonomy, the essence of which we know our desire but not what we will be able to achieve.[364]

No one in Kosova would agree with this compromise. The intellectual and social elite, which had participated in the constitutional discussions, after it got the signal from the political head to open the issue of the request for the Republic of Kosova – as a solution that was beneficial for all, and with which the Yugoslavian Federation could be defended from the Serbian challenges, which it would have to unavoidably face one day – rightfully felt disappointed, but also betrayed. Because, after the removal of the issue from public debate, the punishing actions had begun, which in most cases were political, such as the ideological differentiations, against the supporters that had raised the request for the Republic of Kosova, who were not left without consequences. Even though this time the request for the Republic in the public debates was not sanctioned with judicial prosecutions, as would occur later on against the protestors, nevertheless, some of the popular intellectuals were named as nationalists, in which case some of them were removed from the lead of institutions but not be left without a job. Similarly, some prosecutors and judges would lose their positions but not their jobs.

The Historic Demonstrations of 1968

The withdrawal by the political class of the request for the Republic of Kosova, which had gained referendum support from all social layers in Kosova and was unanimously supported, had not removed it from the opinions of the day. The request was acquired by the youth and students, which in October and November 1968 protested in some cities of Kosova, initially in Prizren, on October 6th and ending with those in Prishtina, on November 27th, which were the greatest and historically the most important. – The Request for the Republic of Kosova was associated with the right for self-determination gained during the antifascist war. – The peaceful protests of the Albanian students and youth were followed by police violence, which resulted with many victims and many wounded.

---

[364] Mišović, Miloš: „*Ko je tražio Republiku Kosova,*" Beograd, 1987.

Despite the closing of public debates where Kosova requested the status of Republic and the political leadership of Kosova retreated under Serbian pressure and the compromise of the Yugoslav leadership with that of Serbia, the issue for status of Republic did not disappear. On the contrary, it appeared to open the spirit of Pandora's Box, which, once out, would never return. Everyone knew this, but it was an issue of what form the discussion would take.

Nevertheless, for the Albanians in Kosova, encouraged by the intelligence and the confidence of the students and all other social layers, which had been interlinked with this development, it was clear that they could not stop the pursuit of this goal no matter how manipulative the politics were, and despite the actions Belgrade would take to fight them. Because the request for the Republic of Kosova was now a nation-wide request and had legal binding achieved by referendum, going back now would only mean returning to the scrutiny of Serbia. To avoid this, the issue needed to be internationalized as quickly as possible. Of this nature were also suggestions and advice, sometimes open (through the press), and sometimes through discussions which developed in federal forums. Even if these discussions were not public, they somehow leaked into the open, reaching Albanians through other centers (especially Zagreb and Ljubljana) which were now very interested in Kosova and its requests to turn into a promoter of change, where protests and other forms of collective pressure would be used.[365]

In fact, from spring of that year and onward the spirit of the students' protests, form Paris and up to Berlin had encompassed European metropolises and had also reached Belgrade. The students of Belgrade, even though they tried to act the "revolt of the youth against the objection of their fathers toward social changes," they appeared as "special," since they were not Pro-European, meaning for reforms, liberty, democracy and change, and they were not leftist in the meaning of "social and societal reforms," as they appeared in Paris and Berlin. Apart from any slogan against "the red bourgeoisie," their essence had to do with the revolt against the warned constitutional changes, which in essence were nationalist from the Serbian hegemony positions. In Belgrade in the students' gathering, mainly those that were against the Plenum of the Brioni spoke.

---

[365] See the writings of "Vjesnikut" of Zagreb, September 23, 1986

The emergence of this thesis was dangerous, since it mobilized the Serbian nationalism and the unitary forces to turn toward Moscow, which put Yugoslavia at risk of losing its position in the buffer zone, with which neither the West nor the East would agree.

However, the students' revolt and the youth one in general, in Kosova, was steered towards the request for the Republic of Kosova, since now it had the full intellectual, social and political consensus of all the Albanians, who supported it. Brought to the open by the intellectual Albanian elite, and approved unanimously from all the social layers, the move toward Kosova as a Republic had to continue, since any sort of halt would mean another historical defeat for the Albanians. Thus, it was natural that in accordance with this internal agreement, it had to pass on to the students and the youth, which was to be in line with the the intellectual concept which had appeared during the public discussions, where for the first time the request for the Republic of Kosova was associated with the right for self-determination that the Albanians enjoyed from the National Liberation war and on, which had also inspired the activity of the illegal groups, which up until then had defended the liberation war and national unification, in most cases through the use of the right for self-determination, be that even as an ideological blueprint.

And as such, these ideas were articulated in the protests that appeared during October in Prizren, beginning on the sixth day and ending on the November 27 in Prishtina, the strongest protests ever seen in Kosova since the World War II. Tens of thousands of peaceful protestors participated in these protests, which sought the Republic of Kosova under the framework of the Yugoslavian Federation.

Of course, the great protests in Prishtina on November 27, 1968, as well as the protests that preceded them (in Prizren on October 6, Theranda on October 8, Peja on October 19), along with those that were held on the same day in Besiana, Mitrovica, Gjilan, Ferizaj and other centers of Kosova, did not fall from the sky as "spontaneous gatherings." Their organizers were mainly students and other activists of the wide Movement of the Resistance, and almost the whole population of Kosova participated, but as a mentor, for the first time, they had the intellectual class of Kosova, from which the professors and lecturers of the universities and science collaborators of different institutions were determined to bring to life one of the most successful developments in the history of the state-development of Kosova. Belgrade, as a leader "in the shadows" of the protests of November directly accused professor Ali Hadri and Fehmi Agani from the Philosophical Faculty of Prishtina, Gazmend Zajmi from the Judicial Faculty, the regional prosecutor, Rezak Shala and a few journalists of "Rilindja" for whom it was said that "they were the moving head in those circumstances, which led all the activities."[366]

Thus, this process became one of the most successful ones, since it took a historical turn – the difficult transformation of the movement for national resistance from an illegal one to a legal one, in which all the social and political layers of Albanians would participate.

There was also another historical change that took place here. The request for the Republic of Kosova to be equal to others in the Yugoslavian Federation replaced the request for national unification with Albania, a request that appeared at the end of the fifties and beginning of the sixties and accompanied by many activities from the left and the right (although it would not exclude the idea totally, since it would further on remain a strategic option), even though it was known that Enver Hoxha, when this idea began to emerge among the illegal groups from 1958 and on, not only did not defend it, but he also opposed it and criticized it, despite the fact that a part of these organizations retained the ideological compass of the formal Tirana.

Nevertheless, these two requests, that of equality of the Republic of Kosova and the unification with Albania, in common shared the *principle for self-determination up to detachment,* a principle which had its source in Leninist theory, which was used also in the Program for *"The Revolutionary Movement for the Unification of Albanians,"* established by Adem Demaçi in 1964.[367], It was also used in the requests of the Albanian politicians during the opening of the debate for constitutional changes in the Political Party of Gjakova when this right was emphasized in order to find a place in the new constitutional changes, but also in the intellectual debates in all the meetings held in Kosova at all levels.

The change between *unification* with Albania to *equality,* meaning the elevation of the status of Kosova to that of a Republic equal with the others in the Yugoslavian Federation, was not non-confirming, nor opposing as it appeared, but it had to do with a strategic specification, which led to the same, meaning that the Albanian population could

---

[366] See: *"Buletini i kuq"* of Tanjug, of December 2, 1968, p. 3.
[367] See: *"Dosja Demaçi,"* Prishtina, 2004, pages 86-115.

realize its historical aspirations, such as the national unification, not any longer through revolutionary means including an armed war, which were launched to the air sometimes by Tirana and sometimes by Moscow for their own ideological needs, which served the Cold War, but with the achieving of social and political equality, which then provided also the final act in accordance with the general developments.

Thus, Kosova had to gain the status of a Republic and this, initially required the liberation from Serbia's tutelage where it had been placed after the partisan re-occupation in 1944 due to the internationalist agreement Tito-Enver Hoxha, so that after a while it could act according to its own interests, as an equal unit of the Federation.

Thus, the requests that up until that day were illegal had now started becoming legal. The revolutionary principles were replaced with democratic principles, which could not be punished and could not be classified as "counterrevolutionary," "irredentist," or "separatist," as Belgrade did when the rights of Albanians for liberty and equality were supposed to be activated. Hence, the request for "The Republic of Kosova" appeared as a formula that Belgrade could refuse and combat, as it would do in reality, but not in the fashion that the ideological hypotheses enabled illegal activity. As a legal and open request, the request for Kosova as a Republic, based on the right for equality with others, as a civilizing postulate and democratic standard, would tighten it like a rope around its throat, and would drown it the more it would try to take it off violently, until one day it would all end with the destruction of its hegemonic project – Yugoslavia.

The first protests requesting the Republic of Kosova, which during October and November were held in many cities of Kosova, but also Tetova and Ulqin, began in Prizren on October 6, 1968. The initiation in Prizren was not accidental, because this city was linked to the Albanian League of Prizren of 1878, the most important event in the history of Albanians regarding detachment from the Ottoman Empire. They were organized by the students: Meriman Braha, Pashk Laçi, Haxhi Maloku, Rafet Rama of Rahovec, Isa Demaj, Zymer Neziri and Gjergj Camaj of Tuz, as well as the many intellectuals who were active and led protests during the debate for constitutional changes when the request for the Republic of Kosova emerged.

The gathering of the protestors occurred next to the monument of the Albanian League of Prizren. After worshipping the leader of the

League, the mass of protestors directed themselves towards the center of the city, where at the popular Shatervan, the request for the Republic of Kosova, was made.

Thus, Prizren became the first place in which during a large protest the Republic of Kosova was publicly requested. These were the first protests of the Albanians after the Second World War where the Albanians were requesting equality, which would return to them their right for self-determination and the ability to enjoy their historical rights.

After the great notification given in Prizren and the echo it had everywhere, the spirit of the protests encompassed the whole area. Two days later, the same ones were held also in Suhareka (todays' Theranda), organized by Isa Demaj, Haxhi Bajraktari and Isa Morina.

In the protests of Suhareka, held on the afternoon of October 8, apart from the slogan *"Kosova Republic"* the requests were also made for the opening of the University of Prishtina and the allowance of the national flag.

Another important protest held during October was that of Peja. The students and intellectuals of this city and other cities of Dukagjin, who had been very active during the debate for constitutional changes where the request for the Republic of Kosova had been supported, decided to express through public protests the need for other national rights such as the opening of the University of Prishtina, the allowance of the national flag, and other civil and national rights from which the Albanians had been deprived for so long.

The protests held on October 19, organized by the young: Isa Demaj, Ramadan Blaka, Xhemajl Gashi and Zymer Neziri (the majority of whom had also participated in the first protests in Prizren), began with the gathering at the High School "Ali Kelmendi" and continued to the center of the city, where thousands of citizens of Peja and the nearby regions joined them, who were notified about the protest. There the slogan was "Kosova Republic" followed also by the requests for the flag and the University of Prishtina.

At the end of the protests, the police imprisoned the organizers; the regional court convicted Ramadan Blakaj to fifteen days of jail, while Xhemajl Gashi, Zymer Neziri and Riza Smakaj received thirty days of prison. [368] These were the first convictions for the organizers of the protests in Dukagjin.

The protests in Gjilan were organized by Irfan Shaqiri, Rexhep Mala, Xhamit Dermaku, Ahmet Hoti and Fatmir Salihu, and many other activists. They began from the yard of the High School. The protestors held photographs of Marx, Engels and Tito as well as the national flag together with the Yugoslavian one. The protestors also had charts with the slogans: *"We want self-determination," "We want a constitution." "We want a university,"* and others. [369]

With these slogans, the protestors passed through the main streets of the city up to the bus station, to return to the place from where they had begun.

For the organization of the protest in Gjilan, on November 27, the Court of Gjilan convicted Irfan Shaqiri with one year in prison, while for the same offense they convicted Rexhep Mala, Xhavit Dermaku, Ahmet Hoti and Fatmir Salihu.

In Podujeva, the protests were successful and massive, while in Mitrovica, they were interrupted by the police, which took actions to keep them limited. In these cities also the same slogans were used, such as the one for the Republic of Kosova, the Constitution, the University, liberation, and equality.

In Podujeva, some of the organizers: Hamit Abdullahu, Sabit Syla and Hakif Sheholli were imprisoned and convicted with a year and two months of prison, while Hasan Shala, Shaqir Shala, Selatin Vokrri, Bahri Shabani, Xhafer Ejupi, Abdullah Nishevci and Nezir Bunjaku were convicted by the Court of Offense with thirty days of prison. [370]

Compared to the protests in Gjilan and Podujeva, which proceeded without any incidents, those in Ferizaj were followed by the intervention of the police, which utilized force to prevent the marching of the protestors to the center of the city. The protestors, despite all the barriers the police had put before them and the violence that was used against them, managed to continue towards the center, to gather in front of the building of the Municipality Assembly, where speeches were made by the organiz-

[368] Neziri, Zymer: *"Isa Demaj – jeta dhe veprimtaria atdhetare,"* Prishtina, 2000, p. 112.

[369] Novosella, Selatin: *"Demonstratat e gjashtëdhjetetetës,"* 1, Prishtina, 2008, p. 116.

[370] *Ibid.*, p. 131.

ers, explaining the reasons for the request for the Republic of Kosova, the basis for this protest. The police intervened at around 3 pm to disperse the protestors, who in retreat continued the protest in other parts of the city, where there also were clashes with the police. In this case, the police arrested some of the organizers and the Offense Court convicted with thirty days of prison the following students: Mehmehet Emërllahu, Avdullah Zymberi, Muhamet Sylej-mani, Beqir Beqiri, Hasan Muhaxheri, Sylejman Bytyçi and Ekrem Beqiri. Hasan Abazi and Ismet Ramadani were also convicted and imprisoned for "hostile activity".[371]

The protests of October and November ended with those that were held in Prishtina in the afternoon and continued to the late hours of the evening of November 27, 1968.

As it was expected, these protests were substantial based on the requests they presented through the Albanian intelligence during the constitutional debates, massive based on the participation, and civilized based on behavior. Also, they had to reflect political maturity, since in those circumstances Prishtina was burdened with special communications, which had to conform to the historical requests (self-determination and the Republic of Kosova) which now had appeared and required additional approval for them to be put into action.

Since some of the main organizers were students and intellectuals, who had participated in the public discussions for the constitutional changes, but who at the same time patronized in the highest intellectual and creative circuits in Kosova, precisely of those which were at the top of these requests, it was expected that the protests of Prishtina would reflect the spirit of this relation. This concept was also seen in the speech of their main leader, Osman Dumoshi, which he made before many protestors (tens of thousands) who were positioned in front of the Regional Theatre.

After he stated that "we can not let our ideals go unrealized," Osman Dumoshi, in the name of the "Committee of the Protestors," read the seven points of request:

1. *The full realization of our national rights;*
2. *Our people have to enjoy all the rights the others enjoy;*
3. *The quick improvement of the social-economic conditions;*
4. *The full realization of the decisions of the Fourth Plenum. The full removal of all those individuals from the Bureau of Internal Affairs*

---

[371] *Ibid.*, p. 141.

(UDBA/SPB) and elsehere who took advantage of their positions to abuse Albanians;

5. The realization of the decisions of the Tenth Regional Plenum, specifically the improvement of the structure of the employees in the leading positions;

6. The improvement of the studying and living conditions of the students, as well the improvement of the social and national structure of the students, and;

7. The placement of control over the wealth of the people who had gained wealth by abusing their position in a questionable manner.[372]

Looking at it from the perspective as to when these requests were made, then, it is noted that they conformed to the political requests, which the political leadership of Kosova had presented from the Fourth Plenum and on, and they, in most cases had found place also in the party resolutions of all the levels resulting during 1966 and 1967, which had served the platform for social and constitutional changes with which also the relationships in the Federation were supposed to change, which were reasoned as necessary for the perfection of self-governance and its application in the social, economic and political life of the area.

Nevertheless, looking at it from the perspective of a process as well as the developments it brought, these requests appeared as a political platform for a great turn in history, since behind them was the request for the Republic of Kosova, with which, based on the others in the Federation, it would return to Albanians the right for self-determination. Thus, it is not an accident that the protests of Prishtina had as their head the large *"self-determination"* chart, since it was the common name of all the issues that opened all doors.

Also, it is not an accident that after the presentation of Osman Dumoshi's requests, from the mass emerged the request for the Republic of Kosova, which would be the most meaningful, precisely because it politically dismantled the essence of *self-determination*, which outside of this request could remain only as a simple slogan and nothing more.

---

[372] See the archive of Kosova, *Dosja e demonstrative te vitit 1968,* Prishtina, cited by Novosella, Selatin: *"Demonstratat e gjashtëdhjetetetës,"* 1, Prishtina, 2008, p. 161/2.

In reality, the beginning of the protests with the slogan for "self-determination," and the reading of the requests from seven points, summarized conceptually and substantially the protests of Prishtina under the framework of a program among the most realized up to then. Even the slogans for *"proletarian internationalism"* which followed the requests, and some similar ones which emerged from various corners, were not able to entangle the historical orientation of the protests of Prishtina, which this time were directed towards *equality*, where *self-determination* implied the *Republic of Kosova*, which was legally and openly requested, in an institutional and non-institutional way, as requested during the public discussions by the Albanian intelligence in Prishtina and other cities of Kosova, as it was requested also in the protests beginning in Prizren and ending in Prishtina, represented the greatest turn in history, which put the statehood of Kosova on irreversible tracks.

Of course, this political change that was produced by the protests of October and November of 1968, the stamp of which was given on November 27 in Prishtina, would not be convenient for those who did not want this behavior of Albanians, since they changed the stereotypes upon which the national movement was based. This movement, which in the circumstances of bloc bipolarity and the Cold War carried the great risk that it would return as another great historical boomerang to the Albanians, turned into an open war for national equality, which as its motto had the Republic of Kosova, which had to be achieved through institutional routes and democratic tools, a route which could be opposed and confronted by the East, but never the West, which had an interest in such a thing.

This was also seen by the use of violence towards the protestors, where there were also many injured and one killed from the bullets of the police (the youngster from Prishtina Murat Mehmeti, rightfully declared a hero of those protests that evening), who were provoked by the police units, which were interested with all their might for the protests of Prishtina to lose their civilized aspect, with which they had begun, in order for them to turn into a "nationalist and chauvinist vandal orgy" in which case the political requests, such as those that were presented before the protestors should not appear at all.

However, even with these heavy provocations and the infiltration of the many collaborators from among the protestors to say slogans with ideological and chauvinist contents, with which the Yugoslavian police had continuously tried to quell the rightful requests of the Albanians, the organizers of the protests succeeded in defending their concepts as rightful and democratic requests. Thus, they also showed themselves readily available to negotiate with the political representatives, such as Ismail Bajra, but above all, also with the intellectuals and professors of the faculties of Prishtina (Mark Krasniqi), with the condition that for this the violence against the protestors as well as the police provocations and their many collaborators must be stopped.

An agreement was even reached with Mark Krasniqi to create the "Committee of the Protestors" with whom they would meet the next day. After this agreement was reached, at some time around 10 pm, the organizers requested a quiet dispersing of the protestors, by asking them to continue the next day in support of the "Committee of the Protestors" which would present the requests that were declared before the protesters.[373]

The protests did not continue the next day as it was anticipated. There would also not be any talk with the Committee of the Protestors because, the next day, the streets of Prishtina awakened to many groups of Yugoslav police and army, who had practically established an undeclared police-military state.

The same day the imprisonment of the protest organizers had begun, in which case Osman Dumoshi, Adil Pireva, Selatin Novosella, Hasan Dërmaku, Xheladin Rekaliu, Skënder Muçolli, Iliaz Pireva, Skënder Kastrati and Afrim Loxha were found behind bars.[374]

The court process in Prishtina ended on April 7, 1969. In all the sessions, the accused declared that they had acted with premeditation and the full belief that the protests in Prishtina and other places were in full compliance with the right of Albanians for self-determination, which was also their right, a right from which they had been violently deprived. The Republic of Kosova was called a natural and unavoidable solution which was for the good of the Albanians, Yugoslavs, and Albania as well as for European peace and stability.

In the end, the District Court of Prishtina declared the protest organizers of Prishtina guilty and convicted them with heavy sentences: Osman Dumoshi, Selatin Novosella and Hasan Dermaku with five years in prison;

---

[373] *Ibid.*, p. 187.

[374] Pireva, Adil: *"Gjashtëdhjeteteta shqiptare,"* Prishtina, p. 79.

Skënder Kastrati and Xheladin Rekaliu with four years in prison, and Adil Pireva, Afrim Loxha Iliaz Pireva and Skënder Mucolli with three years of prison.

In addition to the main organizers of the Prishtina protests, another seventy or more people were also convicted with various sentences. Asllan Kastrati was convicted with six months in prison; Sylejman Kastrati with three months of prison, Bedri Novosella, Sylejman Pepshi and Halil Qosja, Ramadan Ramadani and Tefik Çeliku, with a month in prison. [375]

As it was expected, the protests of Prishtina were judged by the political leadership of Kosova and the highest one in place, but outside of any particular campaign, as would occur later on. Even though their content, was not reflected in the area press as it should have been, or they were circumvented with the random qualifications of "hostile activities," they nevertheless put into action an unstoppable process of positive changes for the Albanians, among which, of course the most important were those that had to do with the constitutional changes, which led up to the elevation of the status of Kosova to the level of a unit of the Federation as well as the opening of the University of Prishtina in Albanian. Yosip Broz Tito himself, in the Ninth Congress of the Communist League of Yugoslavia held five months later in Belgrade, spoke of the Albanian protests in Kosova, and in principle took a positive stance upon three requests from the seven which were laid down in the protests of Prishtina:

1. *The constitutional changes must be rushed, with which the state of the autonomous regions will change to the avail of their adequate representation in the federation according to the needs of the development of the socialist self-governance*

2. *It is an obligation of our community to enable in every aspect the development of the autonomous region of Kosova as quickly as possible*

3. *Regarding the flag, for which it has been spoken enough, the Albanians need to have their flag, but that flag has to in any case conform to the state sovereignty and integrity of Yugoslavia and for this a clear disposition has to be made.* [376]

---

[375] Novosella, Selatin: *"Demonstrata e gjashtëdhjetetetës,"* Prishtina, 2008, p. 202.

[376] See: *"Deveti Kongres SKJ,"* Belgrade, 1969, pages 86-87.

Constitutional Amendments and the Establishment of the University of Prishtina

> *The Federal Assembly of the Socialist Federal Republic of Yugoslavia on December 16 and 18, 1968, approved the completions and changes to the constitutional amendments VII-IX, where the main change was the VII amendments, according to which the autonomous regions, even though they were a part of SR of Serbia, were at the same time a constitutive element of the Yugoslav federation. – This formulation in the VII amendment was elaborated and solidified in the XVIII amendment, and up to a point on the VIII and IX. – The autonomous units, in the VII amendment, changed their name and since then appeared as – socialist autonomous regions, whereas Kosova and Metohija (Kosmet) changed their name to – Kosova. – The change in Kosova's name which took effect with the VII amendment of the Socialist Federal Republic of Yugoslavia, and later on also with the amendments of the Socialist Republic of Serbia, was done by the request of Kosova and expressed a new political reality to the benefit of Albanians. – On January 15, 1970, after the completion of all the faculties in Albanian, the University of Prishtina was established. – The first rector of the University of Prishtina was Professor Idriz Ajeti, a popular linguist and supporter of Albanian education in Kosova, who in his welcome speech, emphasized that the establishment of the University of Prishtina represented one of the greatest achievements of Albanians during this century, which opened the path for becoming equal with the others from the education, cultural, social, and political perspective.*

Alongside the historical merit which turned the self-determination conscience into a legitimate request by placing it on the open institutional tracks as a part of a common political credo of an unstoppable historical process, which after forty years resulted in the creation of the state of Kosova, the protests of the sixties through the eighties also enjoyed credit for the acceleration of the establishment of the University of Prishtina in the Albanian language as an Albanian national educational institution in ex-Yugoslavia, which deserved the most praise for its creation of an intellectual and state-forming conscience of the Albanians. However, apart from the acceleration of the establishment of the University of Prishtina, the protests of the sixties through the eighties also directly influenced the creation and consolidation of other national educational and cultural institutions in Kosova, including communications, publishing activities in Albanian, theatres, ballet, music, research institutions, and the establishment of the Sciences and Arts Academy in Kosova.

The establishment of the University of Prishtina was a pivotal development, among the most dynamic which Albanians had experienced in the ex-Yugoslavian arena since their violent entrance through occupation. It had a special importance, since it served to create the concept of an institutional infrastructure for which Kosova was in need for its elevation to the scale of a federal unit. With the university in the Albanian language, Kosova entered the queue of educational and scientific elite in the area through its national intelligence.

The truth is that the development of higher education had started to gain its place in Kosova since 1960 when the High School of Pedagogy had been opened in Prishtina as well as the Department for Albanian Language and Literature, as a branch of the University of Belgrade, which had taken over the responsibility for opening its branches in Prishtina according to the concept of that time emanating from Belgrade that the superior education of the Albanians, a process that could not be stopped, had to be supervised by Serbia and had to be based on their integration into the Serbian culture. However, apart from what Belgrade aimed, the higher education and the opening of faculties in Prishtina, was preceded by a sensitive development which occurred with the opening of high schools in Kosova (high schools in all cities and villages, normal schools – in addition to those of Prishtina and Prizren – also in Peja and Gjakova as well as other professional institutions of economy, medicine, geodesy and others). Thus, in the years 1960-61, the number of students in the high schools in Albanian language doubled from the 5600 that it had been. In the following two years, this number surpassed twenty thousand and in 1965/66 it reached thirty thousand.

Apart from the opening of the Department for Albanian Language and Literacy, at this time in Prishtina, always as a branch of the University if Belgrade, the Faculty of Philosophy opened, as well as the one of Law and Economics. In the Faculty of Philosophy, apart from the Department for Albanian Language and Literacy, the instruction in the Albanian language had started to develop partially, also in the Department for History, Geography, Sociology, and other departments. In 1964 the Technical Faculty also opened, that of Construction, and a while later also the branch of Architecture. There were also lessons held in Serbian, only where there was no possibility for them to be in Albanian. However, even this problem started to be solved with the engagement of the professors and lecturers from the University of Tirana, which occurred after the signature of the Protocol for Educational and Cultural collaboration with Albania in 1968.

To round out this process, and so to create the conditions for the establishment of the University of Prishtina, the Faculty of Medicine, Dentistry, and Pharmaceuticals also had to be opened.

The opening of this faculty in Prishtina was refused based on the reasoning that conditions were lacking (the existence of clinics and other hospital infrastructures in Kosova). In this case, specialized cadres in the Albanian language were also lacking in this field, even though this could be remedied by borrowing some from the University of Tirana, but also by the lecturing of a few courses in Serbo-croatian until the Albanian experts, a portion of whom were outside of the country for specialization and were expected to return within two - three years, were available.

The issue of the opening of this faculty was complicated when it was initially politicized in a few intellectual and nationalistic circuits of Belgrade, which initially criticized the opening of this faculty in Prishtina by reasoning that it lacked cadres, clinics and research institutes. Later, it was opposed based on political reasons, pretending that the political leadership of Kosova needed this to detach from Serbia.

Nevertheless, in 1969 the compromise was reached that the Faculty of Medicine in Prishtina would be opened as "bi-lingual", in Serbo-croatian and Albanian with parallel lessons, in cases where experts existed, while in cases that they did not, they would be loaned from Belgrade, Zagreb, and other centers. The exercises would also be conducted together, while the special ones would be conducted in the clinics of the University of Belgrade and other university centers of the country. Under these arrangements, The University of Tirana had also gained an important role, which had made important commitments to help the Faculty of Medicine, but, according to the agreement, other departments as well, especially those of the natural sciences.

Thus, in 1969/70 all the formal conditions were established for the foundation of the University of Prishtina. The University of Belgrade took over the responsibility of closing down this interim process in a professional and proper manner.

The University of Prishtina was solemnly declared open on January 15, 1970. A great solemn academy ceremony was held in Prishtina, which turned into a general celebration. The politics, but also the Albanian intelligence in Kosova, each in their own way, celebrated a great victory, even a historical one, and for this they had reasons. As an important achievement, it was also utilized by the state politics of Belgrade, which evaluated this act as "achievements of the Albanian nationality in Yugoslavia towards the realization of their full rights." This event did not remain without similar intonations by the Serbian leadership, which although it was not enthusiastic, such as the Kosova one was, admitted that "it had to do with an important victory of the Albanians, which had been achieved also with the engagement of Serbia." In this case, a great merit was also attributed to the University of Belgrade, which from the beginning of the sixties started opening several branches of faculties in Prishtina, but that apart from this, from after the war and onwards, it had been a host of many Albanian students, who had studied in Belgrade and there had gained professional and academic titles. This issue had also been emphasized during the solemn academic occasion in Prishtina, but also in other places when the University of Belgrade and other educational and pedagogic institutions were especially thanked for their role and contribution towards the elevation of Albanian cadres, where in the sixties, in Belgrade, more than one thousand Albanian students had continued their studies each year.

Idriz Ajeti, the popular linguist and supporter of the Albanian education in Kosova, was chosen the first rector of the University of Prishtina. In his welcome speech, he emphasized that the establishment of the University of Prishtina represented one of the greatest achievements of Albanians during that century, which opened their way to be equal with the others from an educational, cultural, social and political perspective.[377]

The establishment of the University of Kosova was followed also by the opening and establishment of Science and Research Institutes, which had begun immediately after the Plenum of the Brion. Under this spirit, it had begun with the re-opening of the Albanological Institute in Prishtina which had been closed down in 1953, to continue with the opening of the Institute for History in Kosova (which initially was called the Institute of

---

[377] "Rilindja," January 10, 1970.

History of the National Liberation Movement), and some other research institutes from the field of exact sciences.

This great educational and cultural development was followed by publication activities in the Albanian language, in which case the publication house *"Rilindja"* had started publishing its most important works of the Albanian writers, from the traditional ones, up to those politically forbidden on both sides of the border, and up to the modern ones created in Kosova, Albania and other Albanian regions. Thus, *"Rilindja"* had published during a year around two hundred titles with copies of every book from three to ten thousand copies. Between 1967 and 1969 alone, *"Rilindja"* published the classics of Albanian literacy, while later also published the studies of Professor Eqrem Çabej, which as such had never been published not even in Albania.

Alongside *"Rilindja"*, much work for the publishing of Albanian literature for all scales of Albanian education was also done by the Unit for Publishing Texts and School Tools, which in 1969 was detached from the Unit of Serbia, where it had published books for the primary education translated from those in Serbo-Croatian and conforming to the Serbian class program plans. This unit published for the first time school texts based on the Kosova class program plans, where the use of Albanian national literature, history, and music had also been included. These texts were composed by Albanian authors from Kosova, while some of the capital texts of this nature were imported or republished from Albania. This way, the republishing of *"the Albanian Peoples' History"* in 1965 by the authors of the University of Tirana, was the most important undertaking, where the Albanians, for the first time were joined by their history regardless of their ideological differences.

The specification of the Albanians in Kosova to remain loyal to the common history, was best shown by the 500th anniversary of the death of the national Albanian hero, George Kastrioti Skenderbeg, for which a scientific symposium was held in Prishtina, in which besides the scholars from Prishtina and other regions where Albanians lived, historians from Albania also participated, some from Yugoslavia and others from outside. In this symposium, for the first time the theses for the participation of Albanians in the War of Kosova were laid down, as well as that for Milesh Kopili's Albanian origin (Milosh Obilic according to the Serbian historiography), an interpretation although had not been accepted by the Serbian historiography also it could not be suppressed. Serbia was feeling paranoid about the closeness of Tirana with Prishtina, a relation that began after 20 years of estrangement. All this was because Serbia was afraid that her true intentions toward Kosova would be known, so they used "the irredentist and counterrevolutionary" movements in Kosova, which had begun from 1968, as an excuse to further punish Kosova. Despite this abomination, but in the opposite sense, the protests of Kosova not only failed to impede the further affirmation of Kosova's autonomy, as it was called with the judicial language that politics used, but the requests of the Albanians for more equality up to the level of a subject of the Federation accelerated the whole process of constitutional changes, which formally opened in 1967 with the approval of the platform of the Central Committee of the Communist Party of Yugoslavia for the "constitutional reform," but which had stumbled due to the Federal Assembly's strategy still dominated by the Serbs to shrink the issue down to one of corrections. With this strategy, the I-VI Amendments were supposed to have been made to the 1963 Constitution, which were limited only to a few cosmetic organizational corrections to a few authorizations of the federal units.

This made the members of the Kosova's Board for Constitutional Changes, in collaboration with those from Croatia and Slovenia, who were interested in essential changes with which the image of the Federation would change, and where Kosova would also find its place under its framework together with the others, to request an essential reform, which had to be done with the completion of the VII-XIX amendments of the 1963 Constitution of the Socialist Federal Republic of Serbia.

Thus, under the pressure of these three delegations and the directives which were given from the highest party leader of the country (Vladimir Bakaric, Tito's main collaborator, who said that this was done with Tito's insistence after the protests in Prishtina and the different international reactions that brought importance to this issue),[378] the Federal Assembly of the SFRY on December 16 and 18, 1968, approved the changes and modifications to these amendments.[379]

With the VII amendment (which replaced article 2, paragraph 1 of the SFRY Constitution) it was specified that the Federal Socialist Repub-

---

[378] For more details see: Buxhovi, Jusuf: *"Kthesa historike 3 – shteti paralel dhe rezistenca e armatosur,"* Prishtina, 2009, p. 97-119.

[379] Rajovic, Radoshin: *"Autonomia e Kosovës,"* Prishtina, 1987, p. 423.

lics of Yugoslavia consisted of six republics, but, when the turn came to the Republic of Serbia to be listed under the republics, this formulation was given:

> "The Socialist Republic of Serbia with the autonomous region of Vojvodina and the Socialist autonomous region of Kosova, which are parts of it."

However, the main change for the autonomous regions, which occurred with the VII amendment is – as it comes out clearly from the amendment – that now the autonomous regions, even though they are in the composition of the Socialist Republic of Serbia, they are *at the same time a constitutive element of the Yugoslav federalism.* This formulation of the VII amendment was processed and concretized in the XVIII amendment, and up to a point also in the VIII and IX amendments.[380]

The autonomous units, in the VII amendment, changed their name and since then they appear as – socialist autonomous regions, while Kosova and Metohija (Kosmet) changed its double name to a shorter one – Kosova.

The change in Kosova's name which was included in the VII amendment of the FSRY Constitution, and later on in the amendments of the SR of Serbia, was done by the request of Kosova. The insistence of Albanians in Kosova for this change was not formal, neither was it from a linguistic perspective, as it was attempted to be interpreted in some regions, by persons who were not interested in explaining their real reasons, which were historical, but also political and national. Because, for the Albanians, without exception, Kosova's specification as Kosova and Metohija (Kosmet – shortly), as it had been in the Yugoslavian Constitution of 1946 and that of Serbia in 1947 and as it was also repeated in those of 1953 and 1963, was conforming to the great Serbian hegemonic logic, where *Metohija* (Greek word: land of the church) specified Kosova as a medieval center of the Serbian church, while Kosova as interlinked with it was the spiritual Serbian cradle!

The removal of the name of Dukagjin – which Kosova had from the Party meeting in Shar, in 1943, and which had been legitimized also with the local governing structures established with the Anti-fascist National Liberation Committee of Kosova and the Dukagjin Plain in the first Conference of Bujan in 1943/44 – was supposed to deprive Kosova from

---

[380] *Ibid.*, p. 424.

its historical, centuries-long Albanian identity, which it had from the time of Dardania, Byzantine and the Ottoman Empire. Then it had appeared also as an independent "Vilayet" from 1886 and on, as it was also supposed to deprive it from the anti-fascist organization, when the structures of the local government were established based on this concept, which, as it was known in Bujan, was specified for self-determination, which, a year later was violently canceled in the Prizren Convention on July 10, 1945, after Kosova was reoccupied by the Yugoslavian partisans, who had placed military administration to resolve their issues with the nationalistic Albanians, who above all wanted to realize their right for self-determination with which they were allowed to unite with Albania.

Even though by the reasoning of the delegation from Kosova at the Federal Convention it was said that all the representatives from Kosova from all nationalities there agreed with this change, so with the naming of Kosova, the truth was different. Regarding this issue, the Serbian leadership of Belgrade had received a "recommendation" from Tito about the naming of Kosova, so that no trouble would be made but that it be accepted as the Albanians requested.[381]

This came to the surface after the events of 1981, when it was said that the change of the name of Kosova by Albanians had given courage to the Albanian nationalism and irredentism to request the Republic of Kosova, since that way, they had turned it into a slogan of their "nationalism."[382]

The most important changes in the relationships within the Federation and the federal structures of Yugoslavia were accomplished with the VII and VIII amendments, which recorded the beginning of the essential reform of the Federation. However, with the XVIII amendment (with which they were replaced, more specifically, articles 111 and 112 were removed from the FSRY Constitution) the constitutional position of the autonomous regions was essentially adjusted to make them constitutive elements of the Federation (which was specified now in the VII amendment). No further possibility for their removal was anticipated (which according to article 111 of the FSRY Constitution was possible).[383]

---

[381] See the interview of Pavle Joviçevicit in NiN nr. 32, Belgrade, September 1981.

[382] For more details, see: Đaković, Spasoje: *"Događaji na Kosovu,"* Belgrade, 1981; Mišović, Miloš: *„Ko je tražio republiku Kosova 1945-1985,"* Belgrade, 1985

[383] Rajovic, Radoshin: *"Autonomia e Kosovës,"* Belgrade, 1987, p. 425

The constitutional changes were approved by the Serbian Parliament in January 1969, when it approved the IV-VIII amendments of the Constitution of the SR of Serbia.

The parliament of Kosova approved the constitutional changes on February 24, 1969. This was an important step which would open its way to the new phase for constitutional changes, which would begin in 1971 and end in 1974 when the New Constitution of the SFRY would be approved.

According to the changes in the Federation, where its new image appeared consisting of 8 federal units, the Communist League of Yugoslavia also began to form which had both the political and state monopoly.

In the Ninth Congress important changes were made, which later on were also called the "federalization of the Communist League of Yugoslavia."

Thus, in this Congress, also the change of the name and the organization's status was made to the Communist League of Serbia for Kosova and Metohija, respectively Vojvodina. With the changes made, the organizations of the Communist League of the regions became independent as The *Communist League of Kosova*, respectively *the Communist League of Vojvodina*. With this change, the Communist League of Kosova was detached from the tutelage of the Communist League of Serbia and was directly linked with the *Communist League of Yugoslavia.*

As will be seen, "the party federalism" made Serbia even more dissatisfied, since in this way, it lost its monopoly, which it had now started to lose in the social and state plan with the constitutional reforms, through which Belgrade could not supervise the Federation. This led to the situation where a portion of the Serbian communists, dissatisfied with this course, turned to organizing a "genuine" communist party, which would be linked with Moscow. This was a disappointing Serbian act, which caused Tito to turn with even more insistence to the initial course of constitutional reforms and at the same time act against the so-called nationalist and liberal forces which were up and awakening, in order for him to remain in the driver's seat, which was not only between two antagonistic blocs, but was also on top of a great world-wide movement, that of the non-integrated.

The 1974 Constitution and the Elevation of Kosova's Status to that of the Other Yugoslav Republics

The 1974 Constitution had its way opened by the XX-XLII amendments of the SFRY Constitution, which were approved by the Yugoslavian Parliament on June 30, 1971. – In the XX amendment, Point 4, the autonomous regions essentially strengthened their constitutional position in the Federation by gaining the opportunity together with the other republics (and with the same rights as the republics) to decide about the Federation's affairs according to the conformity principle (consensus), to give their approval for changes in the SFRY Constitution and other issues. – With this, the autonomous regions, from the judicial-constitutional and factual perspective gained important elements of statehood (sovereignty), respectively the largest part of the attributes of a Republic. – The Federal Parliament, on February 21, 1974, approved the Republican and regional constitutions. – On February 28, 1974, the Parliament of the Socialist Region of Kosova approved its first Constitution. Thus, Kosova for the first time in 1974 earned its Constitution with which it independently settled its social, economic and political relations upon the basis of the unique social-economic and political system of Yugoslavia. – With these changes the real sovereignty of the Republics and autonomous regions was established upon the natural resources and income that was a product of the joint work of the specified Republic or the specified autonomous region, with which it can be said that the real conditions were established for the creation of the "eight national economies" which resulted in the reorganization of the Federation into "eight equal units" among which Kosova was also one.

The constitutional changes in the IV-XXIII amendments opened the door for major changes with which the Yugoslavian Federation image changed, but they were not sufficient to result in the concept of full independence of the republics and the regions to the federal scale. Other changes were also needed, especially those, which secured economic independence to the federal units, but also independent behavior on many other issues. Croatia and Slovenia started to lay down their requests regarding "the pure accounts" at the federal level as well as among the republics. Zagreb and Ljubljana had many reasons for such a thing, since

Belgrade further on, in a centralist manner supervised the national incomes of these republics, which did not want their effort to go to the "common kitty," where the others benefited without any effort.

Kosova also requested "pure accounts" and for this it had among the most persuasive reasons, since it was economically falling behind (even with a sensitive development which had been put to action the last two years), while the developed ones were moving forward very quickly, but that this development was accomplished based on the exploitation of the raw materials which were taken from Kosova at cheap prices, or upon the centralist agreement, which were to the detriment of Kosova and the benefit of others. These relationships were emphasized in the relations between Kosova and Serbia, but also Macedonia, which exploited the energy sources of Kosova (the electric energy of the power plants in Kosova as well the gas), according to a long-term agreement imposed with prices twice as low as the ones in the market. It was also at issue that the resources of Kosova were imported as raw material from Kosova, while their processing was done in the other centers of the federation. Kosova requested that under the framework of future constitutional changes, this issue also be resolved so that Kosova would decide itself regarding its own resources and their usage, according to an economic development policy. From this aspect, Croatia also – which secured over three billion dollars a year through its tourism, which constituted 40% of the income from the outside – requested that a good portion of this income would be supervised by Croatia itself and not the Federation, where Serbia further on retained the right to decide for them. Slovenia, on the other hand, had developed an export industry, but the currency was left to Belgrade. Vojvodina too, which was a granary of Yugoslavia, felt discriminated by the administrative prices which were put upon its grains, while Belgrade exported the agriculture products that it took from this region.

The "commotion" regarding "the pure accounts" led to the nationalist and centralist confrontations among the main centers especially between Zagreb and Belgrade; so in the period 1971-1973 there were two political "interventions" from above, the first one from Tito initially against the *"Croatian spring"* and then, a year later also against *"the Serbian liberals."* Political actions were taken against the "Croatian nationalist movement" as well as the "Serbian liberals" in which case, the party and republican state head in Croatia, Savka Dapçeviç-Kuçar was removed together with a group of supporters because they had requested the independence of Croatia "upon nationalist bases." Similar actions were also taken against the Serbian liberal from Belgrade, led by Latinka Perovic, actions which showed them that Tito acted according to "symmetry" by not allowing the course of reforms in the Federation, neither the concept of socialist self-governance to lose its balance from the dogmatic-centralist forces which were regrouping, nor from the liberal ones.

To remain the main patriarch of all developments as well as changes which were apparent from the sixties and onwards, with the "political broom," Tito gave clear signs to Moscow that he was not intending to concede to Brezhnev and his course to expand "the circle of natural ideological allies" from where the Soviets once were kicked out. Thus, in Serbia, judicial actions were taken against the so-called *Group of Tivar* (Serbian intellectuals, the majority of them university professors from Belgrade, but also some from Prishtina), in which case they were imprisoned under the accusation of attempting to organize hostile activities for destroying the constitutional run from the positions of Unitarianism and dogmatism, where their linkage with Moscow was mentioned and the plans that Yugoslavia would return again under the orbit of Soviet political influence.

In reality, *"The Group of Tivar"* was nothing more than a part of the project of Serbian communists, who were dissatisfied with the changes that had begun in the Plenum of Brion in the Summer of 1966 when Alexander Rankovic was eliminated and, as was called, the group of centralist-bureaucratic forces, were determined for the establishment of a "genuine" Communist Party, which would be linked with the Communist Party of the Soviet Union. In Tivar they had held the founding Congress, where over two hundred representatives had participated from different parts of Serbia, Montenegro, as well as representatives from Kosova, Serbs, which in most cases were professors from the University of Belgrade, who conducted lectures in Serbo-Croatian also in a few departments at the University of Prishtina. They were subject to a judgment, where they were convicted to many years in prison.

Different from the Serbian "Marxists," the nationalist Croatians and Serbian "liberals" received party punishments.

Tito behaved in a similar manner to some "opponents" in Slovenia and Macedonia with which he solved his issues without concern that many of those who would be judged and convicted politically were of the same opinion to change and shape the entire process.

Since now he was the uncontested leader of the Non-Aligned Movement with 137 countries and in the center of the world's attention, while his age would have its own consequence (he was approaching the eighties), rather than worrying about what was going to happen with his heritage when he died, Tito rushed to federalize the area as much as possible, giving Serbia every opportunity, unilaterally, to place it under its supervision.

Thus, Tito ordered the Federal Parliament to open the procedure for new changes to the FSRY Constitution.

The leadership of the Communist League of Yugoslavia in February 1971 analyzed and approved the "conclusions for the social-economic and political issues of the Socialist Autonomous Region of Kosova." With this, the results up to that day and the problems in developing this autonomous region were presented and some tasks were determined that had to do with the overall help of the Federation and the SR of Serbia as well as the other republics for the development of Kosova as soon as possible. These tasks related to the consequent application of equality and the strengthening of equal international relations, to further develop and enrich the autonomous region of Kosova.[384]

In the conclusions it also said that "it is necessary to take a further step in the direction of constructing the Federation as a function of statehood and sovereignty of each of the republics and the autonomy of the regions, as a support for the equality of nations and nationalities."[385]

The Federal Parliament created the Board for the Constitutional Changes, whose work was developed under great tension, since open clashes began to manifest between the representatives of the Republic of Serbia and those of the Region of Kosova, who requested that Kosova be equal in the Federation in every aspect with the Republics. In the meeting of the Parliament of the Republic of Serbia it was emphasized that the regions were not federal units and therefore their internal relations should be regulated by Serbia.

---

[384] Rajovic, Radoshin: *"Autonomia e Kosovës,"* Prishtina, 1978, p. 433.

[385] *Ibid.*, p. 433.

Under this atmosphere, the Federal Assembly, after six months of public discussion, approved the XX-XLII amendments of the FSRY Constitution on June 30, 1971.

In the XX amendment, Point 4, the regions essentially strengthened their constitutional position in the Federation, by gaining the opportunity, together with the republics (and with the same rights as the republics), to decide for the Federation's affairs according to the *principle of conformity (consensus)*, to give their approval for changing the Constitution of the FSRY and other issues.

With this, the autonomous regions, in the judicial-constitutional aspect, gained important elements of statehood (sovereignty), respectively, the major attributes of a Republic.[386]

The second group of amendments (XXV-XXVII) also included changes that had to do with the economic function of the Federation and the economic relations in the Federation. Here, among others, approval of the republics and regions was required for the signing of international treaties with which the obligations for the republics and regions were created.

The third group of changes involved the amendments with which the Leadership of the FSRY was created, as a collective unit which consisted of the presidents of the Republic and regional Parliaments based on their positions, as well as two members from each of the republics and one member from each of the autonomous regions.

The leadership of the FSRY, apart from the function of *the Chief of the State*, also took other rights and tasks which, for the realization of equality among nations and nationalities, would harmonize the common interests of the republics and regions.

After the approaches regarding the main amendment changes were reached, the Coordinating Board of the Federal Parliament under the direction of Edward Kardel, in spring of 1973, launched the Constitutional project for public discussion, which lasted half a year. The Federal Parliament, on February 21, 1974, approved the new Constitution of the FSRY. After this, the republican and regional parliaments approved the republican and regional constitutions.

---

[386] Ferović, Abedin: „*Autonomne porkrajine u savremenim ustavnim sistemima,*" Prishtina, 1985, pages 255-256.

On February 28, 1974 the Parliament of the Autonomous Socialist Region of Kosova approved its first constitution. Thus, Kosova for the first time, in 1974, gained its Constitution with which it regulated in an independent manner the social-economic relations and the political system, understandably, upon the basis of a unique social-economic and political system of Yugoslavia. In this way, Kosova earned the right to organize its regional units completely independently and to specify its rights and tasks along with their reciprocal relations.

According to the Constitution of the Socialist Autonomous Region of Kosova, the Parliament appeared as self-governing and the highest structure of the local government in Kosova based on its rights and tasks. The Parliament of Kosova consisted of 3 chambers: The Chamber for United Work (90 representatives), the Chamber of Municipalities (95 representatives), and the Social-political Chamber (50 representatives).

Another central structure in Kosova was the Headquarters of the Autonomous Socialist Region of Kosova, which was established as a new structure based on the Constitution of the Autonomous Socialist Region of Kosova (ASRK). The Headquarters of the Autonomous Socialist Region of Kosova consisted of 9 members.

Other structures of the region were the Executive Committee of the ASRK Parliament and the regional structures of administration: The Constitutional Court, the Supreme Court and other judiciary structures, which in essence had the same function as the respective republican and federal structures.[387]

Thus, with these changes the *real sovereignty of the republics and autonomous regions* was established based upon natural resources and the income gained by the united work of the specific republic or the specific autonomous region. In other words, the real conditions were created for the creation of *"eight national economies"* which consequently reorganized the Federation from *"eight equal units,"*[388] among which was also Kosova.

Tito came to Kosova to personally to inform the Albanians that Kosova would have its own place in the Federation as an equal unit with the others. Thus, from April 12-14, 1971, Tito visited Kosova for the third

---

[387] Salihu, Kurtesh: *"Lindja, zhvillimi, pozita dhe aspektet e autonomitetit të Krahinës Socialiste të Kosovës në Jugosllavinë socialiste,"* Prishtina, 1984, p. 67-77.

[388] Mirić, Jovan: *"Sistem u krizi,"* Zagreb, 1984, pages 14-32.

time, which marked his next-to-last visit (the last one would be in October 1979).

The first time Tito visited Kosova in 1950 at the time when the Albanian wounds were still open following the genocide imposed on them in the Winter and Spring of 1944/45, when the Serbo-Yugoslav partisan brigades reoccupied it, when approximately fifty thousand Albanians had died, mainly young ones, while the harsh repression by police and overall discrimination continued. In Prishtina, to those that gathered to wait for him, he spoke from the "Blue train," so without any contact with the citizens, for the "communist future," which one day would also come for them, while to the workers of Trepça he said that "socialism is not propaganda but a concrete act."[389]

When Tito visited Kosova in 1967, he was greeted differently than when he visited in 1950. After the destruction of the Rankovic group and his clique, which had been accused of the heavy deformation in Kosova against the Albanians that had occurred during the last twenty years, when they had been exposed to persecutions, murders and very harsh discriminations resulting in the displacement of a quarter of a million Albanians to Turkey from 1950 to 1965, Tito's conciliatory messages could only be persuasive if they were linked to further changes through which Kosova would be freed from the Serbian tutelage and linked directly to the Federation. The many important positive turns which had started to appear in all fields of social, economic, cultural and political life after the Plenum of Brion and on, especially the initiation for constitutional changes which had been given those days, resulted in Tito's visit being followed with a different attention from the Albanians. They were well aware that he kept the stone and the nut in his hand, and did nothing without the interest of other important issues, which were usually linked to international concerns. This time it was known that the changes in Kosova were not only an issue for the Albanians, as much as they had to do directly with the change in their position, but they also had to do with the issues that were linked with the future of Yugoslavia, where the Albanians' role and behavior could appear as a decisive factor for its fate. This had been shown by the resolving of issues with Rankovic and his clique, when his fall was linked to the heavy deformations that his police apparatus exercised toward Albanians, even though it was known that

---

[389] "*Tito në Kosovë,*" Prishtina, 1975, page 18.

Tito had used this as a "reason" to eliminate not only political opposition, but also a powerful rival, who appeared as the supporter of centralist-bureaucratic politics, which had the best chances of coming to power after him, and this posed the threat that Tito's inheritance would end with an unexpected turn towards Moscow, by which the Serbs could turn against Yugoslavian supervision, which they had done some time before. In order for this not to happen, Tito and his supporters could be defended only with constitutional changes that led towards its federalization, where Kosova and the Albanians appeared as decisive factors that would keep these balances.

These and other similar scores smelled good to the Albanians in Kosova, who saw Tito once again as the key person, as he had in fact been during the whole time, who could change things and lead them in a different direction compared to that of the years during the war and after the war, when he had decided about Albania's fate, to remain in the East, as he had also decided about Kosova's fate to remain under Serbia. Now the circumstances had changed in favor of the full return towards the West, where the Albanians and Kosova emerged as key to this return.

This meaningful development commemorated many aspects of the Eastern Crisis, when the four Albanian "vilayets" under the Ottoman Empire had put to action the spheres of interest among the great powers, but this time, its dimension one half the size and had shrunk to the size of Yugoslavia, to which Kosova's role in the Federation appeared as one of great political importance, since it could determine an even better position towards the West in the situations of great turns, which were expected, despite the fact that Tito was the leader of the non-aligned areas and as such he could stand without any trouble between the antagonist blocs and greatly benefit from them, and this could last forever.

Thus, conforming to this issue, in 1971, Tito was greeted with enough affection by the Albanians, since beside the positive changes that had penetrated into all facets of life – even though they further on were disproportionate to the scale of development of the country – nevertheless, with the constitutional amendments of 1968, Kosova had started to move away form Serbia and to move towards the Federation. This route was now open and it was expected to continue. It represented the test of faith and survival of Yugoslavia, which depended on Kosova's trial and its behavior. The establishment of the University of Prishtina in Albanian, the opening of research and science institutes as well as national Albanian institutions, the right of Albanians to use their national flag and other national symbols, which were regulated by law and the other changes, had raised the hope that Kosova could also earn the status of a Republic, as it was requested during the October and November protests in 1968 in Kosova, a request which had marked a change in the stance of Albanians regarding the future of Yugoslavia. The request up to that time for national unification with Albania through revolutionary means, expressed by the illegal movement, as well as those of ideological nature that "the victory of the Marxists-Leninist forces in Yugoslavia would make it possible for the resolving of the issue of Kosova to be done in an internationalist way," as a precondition had to have "the fall of modern revisionism and Titoism," as noted by the Tirana propaganda, which inspired a few Stalinist groups in Kosova and similar ones, was replaced with the legal request for full equality with the others at the Federal level, which did not represent anything other than a change in the strategy, since it was considered a part of the right for self-determination which could be secured in an institutional manner if Kosova would earn the status of Republic. Thus, as such, it was supported by all social layers of Albanians and as such turned into their political platform, from which there would be going back, despite the many different attempts to make Albanians steer away from this course.

In fact, the visit of 1967, which occurred after the fall of Rankovic, as well as that of 1971, which came after some of the requests of the 1968 protests were fulfilled, such as the establishment of the University of Prishtina, the allowing of the national Albanian flag and other national symbols, the placing of cultural and educational relations with Albania and other positive changes, apart from the need for "reconciliation" with the Albanians, which Tito needed for his internal needs, such as the federalization of Yugoslavia, which was also in their interest, so all of these changes he anticipated to create the preconditions to get closer to Albania, an issue which also the West desired and requested in different forms for geostrategic reasons. Albania, which had abandoned the Treaty of Warsaw, now represented a military vacuum of a strategic nature, which in a way was allowed to be filled by an Eastern military presence, which was possible, in case in Tirana the relations of the forces would change to the harm of Enver and to the advantage of any of his "unknown" rivals, who could abruptly come to the scene with the help of the Soviets even though it appeared that Enver in this aspect was quite secure.

Not only the sly Tito was nervous, who as would be seen had credible information about what was happening in Albania, but NATO and the West in general had it too, and were very interested for the formal Tirana to get closer to Yugoslavia, independent of the dogmatic-Stalinist course that Enver held and the propaganda he exercised upon these bases within and outside the country, so that the Adriatic and the Western Balkans in general would definitely close any doors to the Soviet presence in those parts.

There are many indications that the Western screenplay to get Tito closer to Enver Hoxha had started since Albania had been removed from the Warsaw Pact, and for this, Kosova and the issue of advancing the autonomy, as was said, did not accidently enter the game with a double role as it entered in 1968: on the one hand to change the relations in the Yugoslavian Federation to the benefit of federalism, which would strengthen Tito's course even after Tito, and on the other hand, to open the way for convergence and collaboration with Albania so that with the changes in Kosova, it could connect to the West through Yugoslavia.[390]

However, different from in 1967, when Tito during his visit to Kosova, had officially informed Tirana that Kosova would return to the Federal Yugoslavia in a suitable form – where this message from Tito was also understood as an attempt to prevent Moscow's possible penetration in this space through the Serbian allies, with which he had also accompanied a supporting message for Yugoslavia from Enver Hoxha in 1969 that "Albania would be on Yugoslavia's side if it were to be attacked by the Soviet Union,"[391] as had occurred to Czechoslovakia. This time, however, Albania was waiting for concrete actions for Kosova to really go to the Federation, as it also waited for other steps with which the Albanians would regain all their rights that they had been deprived of up until then, but outside of the request for the status of Kosova to be elevated to that of an equal Republic with the others. In fact, now there were many arguments that spoke about Enver Hoxha, at that phase, being against the Republic of Kosova up to that point where he called it "a trap from Tito in which the Albanians of Kosova should not fall," by making a call for "Albanians to fight this maneuver."[392] This will be discussed in the chapter

---

[390] See Tönnes, Bernhard: „Sonderfall Albanien," München, 1980.

[391] For more details see: Hoxha, Enver: "Titistët," Tirana, 1982.

[392] Hoxha, Enver: "Ditari politik për çështjet ndërkombëtare 1966-1967," Tirana, p. 147.

where the formal stance of Tirana would be analyzed regarding the Republic of Kosova in all its phases, a stance which will appear as variable: from one of denial – in 1966 and – and one of support, from 1981 and on, a change which in both cases, whether denied or approved, would be in common with the Stalinist ideology.

Of course, this time Tito, who had positively valued Tirana's feedback toward the "offer" he had made because Enver Hoxha also had his own issues in this game – which even though they continued to be of the internationalist nature and with ideological calculations, of which, as it will be seen, Tito had no fear at all – he did not come to Kosova with bare hands. In the Ninth Congress of the Party he created the platform for these changes, while prior to heading for Kosova he had held the highest meeting of the Party forum, where the definite stances were determined upon which the Constitutional Board of the Federal Parliament would compose the changes, with which Kosova would initially gain the status of a federal unit, as would occur with the Constitution that was approved three years later. Tito had anticipated this development, because the elevation of Kosova to a Federal entity, apart from changing the relations in the Federation to benefit strengthening of the Federation in accordance with the interests of the Western Republics (Croatia and Slovenia) and in general with Yugoslavia's stance of retaining its neutral position, between the two blocs from which it gained greatly, but which was to the benefit of the West, at the same time lowered the possibilities for the penetration of the Soviet influence, which was intended to be achieved through the strengthening of the dogmatic-bureaucratic forces, which had support in Serbia and its allies Montenegro and Macedonia, which had joined Serbia through "the fear" of equality with Albanians.

However, retaining the Soviet Union as far as possible from Albania, meaning as far as possible from Yugoslavia as well, which was judged useful by Enver Hoxha, was also the intention of Tito, as well as NATO and the West in general.

The "Blue Book" and the Serbian Warning against Kosova

Raising the status of Kosova to the subject of Federation augmented Serbian nationalism at all levels. – They would not allow the establishment of national institutions of Kosova, the expansion of Albanian-

language publishing activity, which was the most powerful activity in the country, and would not allow cultural and educational cooperation with Albania, in particular the adoption of a common literary language. –Intellectual, scientific, and political Serbian cliques started to oppose the "loss of Kosova without war." – After Cosic, even different groups of professors at the University of Belgrade, demanded from the Serbian politics the prevention of Kosova's seperation from Serbia. – Based on those "demands," in June 1976, the Serbian Presidency formed a working group led by professors from the University of Belgrade, Najdan Pašic and Ljubomir Tadić, whose task was to "inform" the Serbian presidency about constitutional changes of 1974 and their negative impact on Serbia. – At the beginning of the followinig year, those ratings which were summarized in a dossier called the "Blue Book" were reviewed and approved as material for internal use. – Tito, not happy with what was happening, reacted in the Karagjorgjeva meeting, prompting warnings of "national war" and seeking the preservation of the Constitution of 1974.

The constitution of 1974 and its changes paved the way for the separation of Kosova from Serbia and its connection with the Federation. The political situation and the general circumstances in the country prompted Kosova policy to behave in this spirit, as an equal federation, and Albanians to create the belief that they were being treated equal with others. This spirit began to spread and reflect the extent of awareness consensus in all areas and its use as part of Albanian identity. This was highly expressed in culture, education, creativity, and sports. In this way, cultural and educational institutions in Kosova, the University, the Academy of Sciences and Arts, Institute of Albanology, Institute of History, Archive of Kosova, Kosova's Library, Kosovafilm, Theatre of Kosova, Kosova Museum, and information tools along with the book publication headed by "Renaissance" were self-nominated as Albanian national institutions, and were considered the same by other republics, too. Except for Serbia and Macedonia, other Republican countries treated Kosova's cultural and educational achievements as representation of Albanian culture. Thus, in this way Prishtina was taking the epithet of a cultural, educational, and social Albanian center. Gradually, this started to happen also with politics. Although it can be said that this pleased the Albanian politicians, still, they were trying to guard themselves from this epithet because it was coming from those that opposed equality of Albanians as a people and opposed Kosova as being a part of the Yugoslav federation, and as would seen, Albanian politicians would be both publicly and privately declared against those achievements.

In this regard, it was Serbia that was increasingly dissatisfied with the changes that had occurred from 1966 and continued with changes to the constitutional amendments in 1967, 1968 and especially those from 1971 which led to the changing of Constitution in 1974.

Serbs were particularly unhappy with the celebration of the 100th anniversary of the "League of Prizren" in Kosova, even though its importance was given at the Yugoslav and international level (in this case the embassies in Bonn, Brussels, Paris and Washington had organized the reception of the activity). At this anniversary, Albanians highlighted historical analogies between equality requirements laid down by the Renaissance under the Ottoman Empire, which were linked with the creation of an autonomous "vilayet." This "vilayet" would open the path and create the conditions for national independence and the creation of the Republic of Kosova, giving Albanians the right of autonomy, which one day could also be used for national unity. [393]

Prishtina and Tirana had organized joint manifestations for the first time in honor of this important historical event. Also politicians from Kosova and Albania had started to talk about a national union; for that history had violently taken from Albanians and now was the time to take it back through political means. According to Serbia, this was already happening, and they should act to prevent it, but without losing the good relationship with Tito.

Developments that occurred after the adoption of the new Constitution of Yugoslavia in 1974 showed that the advancement of Kosova's constitutional position in the federation, where Kosova, with consensus right, would basically appear equal to the other republics, had begun to create trust between Albanians and Yugoslavs. This had also created an "undeclared conciliation" between Tito and Enver Hoxha about Prishtina being assisted twofold: from Belgrade to strengthen its position in the federation, and from Tirana to strengthen its social and cultural identity, which would help Prishtina to realize its rights. Enver Hoxha would not aban-

---

[393] For more details see: Hoxha, Enver: *"Titistët,"* Tirana, 1982.

don his ideological plans, which, as would be noted, were intended for internal needs.

This time Tito was not intending to trap Enver Hoxha (which was what Enver always thought) or Albanians. On the contrary, Tito was interested in Kosova and its case to be treated as a twofold strategic benefit, where both countries, mostly Kosova, would benefit. This would be shown with the actions taken for the development of cultural, educational, and economic (though modest) cooperation between Tirana and Prishtina, that is, between Albania and Kosova. Although this seemed to be a "tight" collaboration, in the Yugoslav-Albanian state context it was practical and beneficial mostly for Kosova. On one side, Tito wanted to create the spirit of good faith among Albanians firstly, which for twenty years were having bad relations among themselves; on the other side he wanted to renew his old, excellent relationship with Enver Hoxha when they cooperated in the creation of the "Balkan Federation" or Seventh Republic (Albanian-Kosova), which was intended to join the Yugoslavian Federation. However, those plans were broken by Stalin.

This cooperation, regardless of the intentions of its main actors, Tito and Enver, to achieve their strategic plans, opened the doors of cultural and educational development of Albanians, which was highly useful in the common literary language agreement approved in Tirana, in the Language Unification Congress in 1972 with the participation of the Albanian delegation formed by linguists from Prishtina, Shkup, and Montenegro - from all Albanian territories in Yugoslavia.

The Albanian delegation in Tirana was official and had the blessing of all political structures of Yugoslavia. This meant that the unification of the literary language and its standards identified by the Conference of Tirana obligated Yugoslavia to apply this agreement in all areas of official administration, public information, and schools. Yugoslavia accepted the common written language, which further paved the way for internal, cultural, and spiritual unity among Albanians. Thus, Albanians divided into two different states, started to face spiritual unity for more than two decades. This was a big victory for them, and also a good dividend policy for Tito and Enver Hoxha, Yugoslavia and Albania. This would be seen in the future political and social development that Albanians and Yugoslavs experienced. They would have different interpretations: one of them was that Yugoslavia's approval of the common language agreement (common standard approval), caused Albanians to be seen as a minority, depriving them as such from the right of citizenship, which would be reflected in the status of Kosova Republic, as required by Prishtina. The other one stated that this unified literary language and its standard approval would further strengthen the commitment of Albanians to fight for the right of autonomy and national union.

However, cultural and educational cooperation between Prishtina and Tirana, especially the Language Unification Congress, had increased even more the displeasure of Serbia for this "connection" between two countries (Albania and Kosova). Serbia did not approve of this connection, which presented the baseline for problems between Prishtina and Belgrade and also between the Serbian and Yugoslav leadership, in which, occasionally, would include Tito's "symmetrical" interventions.

Indeed Serbia had never agreed with what happened in the Fourth Plenum (Brion), where Rankovic and his group were accused of serious distortions to Albanians. This had opened the path of social and political changes, where Kosova was used as the epicenter of twofold changes: Kosova's extraction from Serbia, and Kosova's acceptance into the Federation, which changed its way of functioning, since its new position would also create the conditions for a better strategic position of Yugoslavia.

Dobrica Cosic, a famous Serbian writer, was the first to talk about these current developments in Serbia. In the Sixth Plenum of the Serbian Party in 1968, Dobrica Cosic came out with the thesis that "Serbia which had won the war, was now losing the peace," and "Kosova and Albanians appeared as a factor that was destroying and seriously threatening Serbian national policy and its identity," because "Albania national equality was leading to an increase of their irredentist awareness, and thus creating conditions for Kosova to secede from Serbia and Yugoslavia." In the debate forum with the senior Serb party, Cosic repeated the language that Cubrilovic spoke in both his anti-Albanian elaborations in 1937 and 1944, in order to increase the awareness "that Serbians were being threatened by the biological expansion (birthrate) of Albanians!"[394]

Cosic used offensive words, such as calling Albanian mothers "childbearing machines" and many other such names, in order to come to the conclusion that the violent secession of Kosova from Serbia, though it was under the slogan "weaker Serbia – stronger Yugoslavia," would end in the destruction of Yugoslavia.

---

[394] For more information see Cosic, Dobrica: "Stvarno I moguce," Belgrade 1987.

Dobrica Cosic would be suspended from the Central Committee of Serbia and a little later by the Communist Political Party, in which he had belonged since the war time and had been one of the Serbian intellectuals, who, with his voluminous writing "Vreme smrti" (time of death), had enjoyed the reputation of a Serb nationalist writer who had introduced the Serbian hegemony in literature. His conflict with the political party for the Kosova case, and with Tito and his style of ruling, that he consistently expressed, and his commitment to the "Memorandum" of the Serbian Academy of Sciences and Arts in 1986, would give him the epithet of "father of the nation." This in turn would bring him to the" throne" of the so-called "third Yugoslavia" of Zhablak, the throne that would not survive the test of time.

Although Dobrica Cosic tried sell out his epithet of "father of the nation" that he got from within because of his chauvinistic rage against Albanians, as an ideological dissent against "Tito and his communist rule," he was not successful. As will be seen, mainly nationalist intellectuals and Serbian Unitarians from "Francuska Number 7" (Belgrade address of the Serbian Writers Club) gathered around him, and began to fall into conflict with "Tito and his way of rule" not from the ideological point of view, because they wanted freedom and democracy, but because they required the opposite: unitarianism and hegemony. They sought to continue the oppression of Albanians because the advance in their rights "endangered national Serbs in Kosova," which they called the "foundation of Serbia;" because they demanded the Yugoslav Federation not to strengthen the role of the republics, but be further centralized to strengthen even more the Serbian unity, especially in the circumstances after Tito. Therefore, it is not by chance that those who had made Cosic a Serbian icon (mainly writers and university professors) started organizing for the establishment of a Marxist-Leninist communist movement with a Soviet orientation. Those people provocatively, in early 1971, organized the Founding Congress in Tivar, which was attended by many intellectuals, Serbian professors from Serbia, Montenegro, and Kosova.

Tito reacted harshly against this aggravation. He imprisoned the organizers and made a rapid trial to sentence them to long prison terms. Furthermore, he used this situation to refine the University of Belgrade from dogmatic advocates, who were increasingly raising their voice in this regard, using Kosova as an inspiration. Those developments in Serbia benefited Tito in the conclusion of his project of Federation reform toward dividing his federation into eight equal units where Kosova was also included.

In these circumstances, when the Serbian political leadership realized that Tito had no intention of stopping his mission that he had begun in the Plenum of Brion, nor did he intend to concede under the Serbian pressure, they made a tactical retreat but in return required the return of the head "Serbian liberal leaders." Serbian liberals, headed by Latinka Perovic, Ivan Stambolic, Marko Nikezic, and others who were against Serbian nationalism with a chauvinistic trend, primarily against Cosic and his intellectual club and against the Serbian bureaucratic group headed by Draža (Dragosav) Markovic and others who were waiting for Tito's death, which could come soon since Tito was getting old (at that time he was in his eighties).

Tito, who was already known for his dictatorial tendency and had to decide on everything by himself, without allowing for the credit of others, even if those decisions were in accordance with the processes that he, himself started, without any hesitation would sacrifice the "Liberal Serbian Movement." Moreover, as all these issues were left in the hands of Markovic and his cronies, Tito convinced himself that in this way he would win twice (by doing what he wanted to do and by making Markovic part of the decision).

But, as will be seen, after the death of Kardel and the first signs of the disease (gangrene), from which Tito would die in May 1980, Serbian Unitarian forces began to raise their voice. Everything started with the Serbian "disappointment" about "problems" that were brought from the dual position of the provinces (Kosova and Vojvodina) in republic-federation relations, which, according to the Serbs "had started to be abused" by provincial leaders, who had begun to bypass, but also to ignore the Republic of Serbia. This issue started in some political parties in Serbian cities (Nis, Uzice, and Kragujevac), continuing on toward Belgrade, from which "clarifications" were demanded as to what was going on in this situation. Based on these "demands" the Serbian Presidency in June 1976 would form a working group which would study and "inform" the body about changes in the constitution of 1974 and its negative impact on Serbia.

Serbian leadership, supervised by Draža Marković, who was among Tito's "loyalists" but waited for Tito's death, treated the issue as a "constituent concern" needing a solution. When Unitarian and political forces among the University of Belgrade and Serbian academics joined this case, among who were professors from renowned constitutional law, Najdan Pašic and Ratko Markoivic, this became an internal debate. This internal debate served the creation of a file which was called the "Blue Book " (Plava Knjiga), which took place in March 1977 and became part of the political platform for reviewing the legal position of the Serbian Republic and its regions, which at that time appearing as part of the Yugoslav federation and in accordance with their competences, were treated as Republics.

Serving as "top secret" and used only for internal use, the "Blue Book" reached up to the highest levels and even to Tito, who was informed about what was happening in Serbia and Belgrade regarding the "Blue Book", but was not reacting because at the same time, he was dealing with some military loyalists (generals) who were influenced by the dogmatic-centralized spirit and whose relations were reaching Moscow. Although the elimination of these generals would cause no public debate, it would be understood that Tito's wife, Jovanka Broz, was also involved. Jovanka Broz was a Serbian from Knin, with whom Tito would not divorce, but would remove from his private life. After finishing the job with the generals and his wife, Tito called on and made responsible the Serbian leadership headed by Draža Markovic. They apologized with the excuse that the "blue book" was only a "summary of the comments that were coming from the constituents "and it did not represent the Serbian leadership's political position. Serbians were more than willing to cooperate in order to clarify all "misunderstandings" and "misrepresentations" that were made in certain Serbian corners.

Tito did not execute the Serbian leaders, as expected, but he promised that "uncertainties" in Serbia regarding the republics/provinces would be removed in the first constitutional changes. Although Tito did not explain how those ambiguities will be clarified, that in turn had concerned the Serbs, according to Tito's closest collaborator, Vladimir Bakaric, there was no other form of correction but to declare Kosova as a Republic.[395]

Although Tito was not severe on the Serbian leadership, who had raised issues regarding the changes in Constitution of 1974, such issues

---

[395] More on this issue, See: Strohm, Carl Gustav: *"Jugoslawien ohne Tito,"* 1979; Meier, Viktor: *"Wie Jugoslawien verspielt wurde,"* 1995; Buxhovi, Jusuf: *"Kthesa historike,"* first book, Prishtinë, 2009.

that were seen to emerge soon after Tito's death, however, he had taken the necessary steps to announce that the Yugoslav federation with eight equal units should remain a "testament" that no one could change. Furthermore, some assessments that he would give at the "Karageorgev Meeting" in December of 1979, about the disputes among regions and republics, criticized the unilateral behavior of some political leadership of the republics and provinces to "the detriment of common interests," confirmed this determination. However, these statements would later be interpreted, as Tito had called the constitutional changes of 1974, in particular the strengthening of the provinces in the Federation, as "mistakes" and "to the detriment of the unity of the country."[396] On the contrary, Tito thought that Yugoslavia was protected by these eight equal units of the Federation (part of which also was Kosova) from nationalist and other separatist movements. Tito repeated this statement also during his visit to Kosova, a week before the Karageorgev meeting (on October 16, 1979, in Prishtina) when he highlighted the importance of Kosova winning the new constitutional changes (those of 1974), for which the Western bloc had openly expressed its interest in maintaining the political and economic stability of Yugoslavia.[397]

In accordance with this support that Tito had gained even outside of the country, along with the purpose of saving the integrity of Yugoslavia, he started to support the Kosova Movement for National Unity again. This movement was headed by Adem Demaci and his group of 19 individuals, who were imprisoned in 1975 and 1976 and sentenced by the District Court of Prishtina with 15 months to 4 years of prison. Along

---

[396] More on "Karagjorgjeva Meeting" See Cenčić, Vjećeslav:"*Titova poslednja ispovest,*" Belgrade, 2001, where it is said that there are presented the stenograms of Tito's speech, which were taken from Josip Kopinic (one of Tito's biographers). However, those speeches were contested by General Kosta Naxh, who attended this meeting and says that there was no stenogram (because Tito did not want it), as it was commented by some other historians that attented this meeting. Furthermore, Tito's main biographer, Vladimir Dadijer, („*Novi prilozi za biografiju Josipa Broza Tita,*" Belgrade, 1984) does not talk about any stenogram, which doubts the presence of „stenogram" in the Karagjotgjeva Meeting, as presented by Cencic, but was more of a construct that needed to be used in order to underestimate the concept of Tito for federalism.

[397] More on "Tito perseri ne Kosove," Prishtina 1980, (Tito's word in the common meeting of leadership of KK of LK of Kosova and KSA leadership of Kosova in December 16, in Prishtina).

with Adem Demaci who was sentenced to 15 years in prision, Skender Kastrati was sentenced to 12 years of prison, Hetem Bajrami, 7 years of prison, Hasan Dermaku, 10 years, Osman Dumoshi, 7 years, Fatmir Salihu, 7 years, Xhavit Dermaku, 9 years, Sherif Masurica, 7 years, Sami Dërmaku, 6 years, Zijadin Spahiu, 5 years, Isa Kastrati, 6 years, Ahmet Hoti, 6 years, Nijazi Korça, 6 years, Irfan Shaqiri, 7 years, Hilmi Ramadani, 5 years, and Nazim Shurdhani, 4 years of prison.[398]

Even though Demaci was considered to be the principal defendant of the movement and was already serving a sentence at the time the organization had started to operate, the Demaci group, monitored by a political process, was sentenced for "hostile activities" (unification and foundation of the organization).[399] This demonstrates that not the actions, but the ideas needed to be punished, in order to make sure that they would not continue to spread.

Albanians knew very well what this " continuation of spread" meant, which was not to ask national unity because this would bring the destruction of Yugoslavia, and they also knew what Enver Hoxha meant with his demand of finding an "ideological" solution to this problem. However, this never meant that Albanians would give up their mission of making Kosova a Republic. The position of the Yugoslavian Federation regarding the constitutional changes was certain with Tito alive. The federation should have cemented its intention for Kosova's position inside the federation prior to his death, in order to make Kosova strong enough to face Serbia if needed (the time when Tito would not be alive). If Kosova's place had been secured, it would have ensured that each place be inspired by "federal Yugoslavian identity," which would exclude Serbian presence.

Kosova from 1971 continued to operate in this direction of social, economical, cultural, and political development. Even the fact that Kosova was not as developed as other Yugoslavian regions, from the Brion Plenum continuing to the year 1968 when the first constitutional changes were approved by amendment VI-XIX, Kosova developed enormously in all aspects of life. This happened because starting from 1970, Kosova used the federation's fund for the underdeveloped regions at the height of 0.89% gross production of the country. The fund was approximately one hundred million dollars per year. In fact, the status of underdeveloped

---

[398] "Dosja Demaci," Prishtina 2004, p.428
[399] Ibid., p.429

country was given to Kosova in 1965. However, those funds were given to Kosova in exchange for its natural resources (gold, zinc, chromium, phosphorus, and coal), which were processed as raw materials in developed countries and from there they were exported, leaving Kosova as such without any benefits. From 1970 this fact would change, allowing Kosova to use 42.3% of the overall amount of the Federal Fund for underdeveloped countries. This percentage was increased in the eighties by 45%, which raised the contribution of the Fund in the economic development of the country by 72%, the contribution of banks by 10%, and those of workers' organizations by 9.9%.[400]

Those investments increased the number of employees in Kosova from 38 thousand employees that Kosova numbered in 1953, to 190 thousand in 1980.

This increase would also show up in the national structure, which was against Albanians. Thus, from the total 192 thousand employees that Kosova numbered in 1980, 129 were Albanians (67.2%) and 43 thousand were Serbian (23.6%).

Besides developments in investments, Kosova also achieved success in education and equal national treatment. Until 1945, Kosova numbered 250 schools in poor operating conditions. However, in 1980, Kosova numbered 899 primary schools. Along with schools, the number of students increased too. There were 35 thousand students in 1950; while in 1975, Kosova numbered 318 thousand students among whom 238 thousand were Albanians, 70 thousand Serbian, 1500 Turkish, 6 thousand Romanian and others. The number of Albanian students increased to 268 thousand in 1980. [401]

Success was achieved in the secondary/high school, too in the period of 1966-1980. The number of secondary/high schools was increased from 13 to 129. The number of students increased from 65 thousand to 84 thousand. The national composition of secondary/high school was improved the last fifteen years. In 1960, 44.5% were Albanians, 41% Serbian, 9.2% Montenegrins, and 2.5% Turkish. In 1980 this percentage changed, increasing the number of Albanian students to 68%, decreasing the number of Serbian students to 21%, and others to 8%.

---

[400] Salihu, Kurtesh, Vepra e Cituar, p.168
[401] See: Enti Statistikor I krahines Socialiste te Kosoves: te dhenat, 1976-1980, p.123-125

University and higher level schools were taking place in Serbo-Croatian. From 1968, Albanian started to be taught in schools. With the foundation of the University of Prishtina, the Albanian language strengthened its roots, engaging many Albanian students that came from secondary/high schools. According to the data, in the academic year 1960/61, 1500 Albanian students studied at the university. In 1980, the number of Albanian students increased in 39,707, 24,652 of whom were regular students. The national composition until 1960 was very unfavorable for Albanians. In 1980 this changed in favor of Albanians, whose percentage increased to 72%. In 1960, Kosova had only 38 Albanian graduated students; while in 1980, it numbered 3,222 graduated Albanian students.
402

---

402 *Ibid*

CHAPTER 3
THE REEMERGENCE OF SERBIAN CENTRALISM AND THE BEGINNING OF YUGOSLAVIA'S DISINTEGRATION

The Events of 1981 and the Increasing Demands for the Republic of Kosova

The death of Tito opened Pandora's Box for the destruction of Yugoslavia of AVNOJ, which was not ready to face the antagonisms and problems of that time, where the Kosova and Albania case remained the main problem – Student's protests in Prishtina that started on March 11 and continued on March 26, and April 2,3,4, with the request for the Republic of Kosova, mirrored the situation of that time where the equal position of Kosova in the Yugoslavian federation was being challenged and according to the "Blue Book," the invasion of Kosova by Serbia was expected to happen. -Brutal behavior toward peaceful protests in Prishtina and the usage of special federal forces on March 26 raised the revolt of Albanians in the April protests. - Evaluated as a "counterrevolutionary incident" coming from "Albanian nationality and irredentist movements" from the Yugoslavian Presidency and that of CC of Yugoslavia, the political leadership of the Federate was subject to Belgrade leadership. The political leadership of Kosova, in the XVII meeting of RC (Regional Committee) and CP (Communist Party), was forced to accept the qualification of "counterrevolutionary" in Kosova. The Kosova leadership betrayed the equality of Kosova in the federation, to which they had themselves contributed, but they also opened the doors for political differentiation that ended with the imprisonment of a hundred thousand youth, expulsion of students and professors from educational programs, and the worst, they targeted and named Albanian intelligence, national institutions, and other state entities that had been created with an enormous effort. – The political platform

387

for Kosova, approved in September by CC and CPY, were made co-conspirators of Serbia against Kosova,. The other republics of Yugoslavia were forced to act according to the Serbian standpoint.

On April 4, 1980, after a harsh illness (gangrene), 88 years old, Josip Broz Tito died. This anticipated death brought with it anticipated events, which after ten years would obliterate Yugoslavia; Tito's creature was not only governed by him for half a century as a sole powerful patriarch but he also achieved its separation from the Eastern bloc, the communist era, making as such Yugoslavia the leader of the "Non-Aligned Movement" (third world), which included 137 countries from Africa, Asia, Latin America, and Caribbean regions.

So Tito was an important political personality of national means, who had impacted the Albanian political scene and the Albanian situation, not only the direct cases that were related with the Albanian communist state but also those that were related with Kosova's fate, starting with the invasion of Kosova by Serb-Yugoslavia in autumn 1944, continuing with its violent union with Serbia, then Kosova's separation from Serbia (1966), and ending with the Yugoslav federation (1974 Constitution).

In all these developments, Josip Broz Tito had played a crucial and decisive role, a role that could be evaluated in various ways but could never be neglected.

The survival of Tito's image, even after his death, which was assembled with the slogan " After Tito Tito" formed by Belgrade leadership, was nothing but a resolution of issues with Tito and his development path in order to substitute this path with that of Serbian unitarianism.

This announced resolution of issues should have begun in Kosova, since according to Serbian nationalists and Unitarians that formed this dogma (starting with Cosic and ending with the creation of the Blue Book), Kosova had the formula to re-establish "normal Serbia." What is more, Kosova was used as a precondition for the Yugoslavian "rescue" from diffusion, but also for the Yugoslav strengthening in accordance with Serbian interests. Kosova had the key for solving Yugoslavian issues, which were internationally known and were predicted to fall into crises because of the Albanian issue and other issues that were related with it and its region. According to Serbs, Albanian issues dated from the Eastern crises, but the Yugoslavian model was never able to solve them.[403]

Of course this threatening environment would be mostly experienced in Kosova, which without Tito, who had supported her in all its cases (even if those were bad cases, or for good as that of 1966), was undefended. This was happening because the federation consensus along with others was put in doubt by the currently created political situation, which was intentionally provoked by Serbia in order to destroy Kosova, - and as will be seen, they achieved their goal. Therefore, it was expected that Albanians, being in touch with current developments, also would be creating their future plans that were related to their requirement of becoming Republic of Kosova. Albanians required Republic status due to three interests: that of Yugoslavia, Albania, and of Western countries, which wanted the continuation of Yugoslavia because of its middle position with Eastern countries, which had started to change their way of leadership even in Poland with the appearance of "Solidarnost" (Solidarity).

Kosova's interest - as a Republic within the Yugoslav Federation, and Serbia's interest - Yugoslavian unitarianism without federalization, did not only present "internal" disagreement in Belgrade-Prishtina relations, but it also represented an open opportunity for widespread confrontations. The Albanian interest for Republic status could not be realized anymore because Belgrade did not allow that; Serbian interest for state unitarianism and bureaucratic centralization was not accepted by other Republics such as Croatia and Slovenia and some Western countries because they knew that this Serbian interest would destroy the strategic stability of bipolarism.

Under those circumstances, where "status-quo" was clearly unstable and its destruction was a matter of time, it did not matter who would start first, but how activities would be developed and what side the forces would take: that of federalization, or that against federalization that included various scenarios from different western countries in accordance with their interests.

Since Albanians were interested in federalization, which had been undefined, it was natural that they would ask for Republic status. Their

[403] See Strohm, Carl Gustav: *"Jugoslawien ohne Tito,"* 1979; Horvat, Branko: *"Kosovsko pitanje,"* Zagreb, 1987; Buxhovi, Jusuf: *"Kthesa historike,"* first book, Prishtina, 2009.

request was presented on March 11, 1981, during student protests that took place in Prishtina, same as it was presented in 1968 and had made enormous changes in the development of Albanian issues, changes that were closed with the constitutional amendments of that year to continue with the 1974 Constitution where Kosova would gain the status of federal unit.

It was natural that the requests of students for Kosova Republic were provoked from Belgrade to be presented exactly at that time, in order to be used for Serbian planned scenarios for the destruction of the 1974 Constitution, as it was announced in the "Blue Book."[404]

Despite those speculations, which should be well-hidden in the secrete archives that for sure contained relevant information on leaders and their activities, those speculations were the product of an old situation, which had gone through Tito's Yugoslavia continuously for thirty-five years, in order to come to the point where it could not be continued anymore.

Thus, the March 11, 1981, protests that were developed late at night, started first in the Student Centers of Prishtina. "The reason," told "was the discontent for the poor cuisine," as one of the students had thrown the food and this had "provoked" the revolt that continued up to the Radio Prishtina building, where a group of students disturbed the public order.[405]

That this case was not about "the discontent for the poor cuisine" that had "spontaneously sparked" upset in the student center, would be understood the next day when semi-official information was spread about a similar movement of students in Prizren and some other regions that were followed by the Belgrade press present in Kosova at that time. This press also announced other student protests.[406]

The political leadership of Prishtina had not really announced any public decision, even though they had started their activity of "taking precautionary provisions" to stop those kinds of protests that according to this governance was a reason more for Serbian unitarians and nationalists to start their plan of destroying the self-governed Yugoslavia and remove it from this dialog. [407]

---

[404] For more on this issue, see: Meier, Victor: "Wie Jugoslawien verspiet wurde," 1995

[405] "Renaissance," 13 March, 1981

[406] See newspaper *"Večernje novosti"* and „*Politika-Expres*" 13 March 1981.

[407] See Mahmut Bakalli declaration for German agency of news DPA, on 22 March, 1981.

The "gossip" atmosphere, however, was stopped the day that Tito's relay was meant to come, which that year, for the first time after Tito's death, on March 26, post mortem, went from Prishtina to Belgrade. The political leadership of Kosova had been prepared to return this public manifestation of 11 o'clock into a "demonstration of determination to follow Tito's path." This implied that March 11 events in Prishtina's student center and in front of Radio Prishtina should have been minimized and forgotten forever. School youth were called to "honor Tito."

However, early in the morning, the news of the student meeting in the Students Center quickly spread. This place was usually used by students to pass free time and have fun.

At 10 o'clock, the Student Center was full of students and the number was increasing more and more. Police, not a large number, were settled in front of the canteen, at the crossroad to the center of the city and the university. It seemed that police knew very well the direction of demonstrators and their purpose was to not allow students to go to the center where Tito's ceremonial was being held.

Observing that the situation "was getting out of control," Kosova's political leadership ordered the University of Prishtina to calm the students and understand their requests through negotiations. A mixed group of executives, politicians, and professors were assigned to talk with the students in order for the case not to get any bigger. In this delegation, besides Rector Gazmend Zajmi and Pajazit Nushi (Vice President of Kosova's Executive Council), Azem Vllasi and Sanije Hyseni were also present. Vllasi and Hyseni were the presidents of the Youth Association and were considered to be part of the "new followers of Tito." From the student side, there were many other organizers working outside this common address, such as Riza Demaj (who read student's requests), Ali Lajci, Teuta Hadri and others that were determined to continue demonstrating until their requests were satisfied.

In fact, talking with professors, politicians, and executives, despite their requests for now known conditions, there was also talk about politics and Kosova becoming a Republic as the only acceptable solution. This was consistent with request of Albanians for autonomy. [408]

---

[408] Hajrizi, Mehmet: " Historia e nje organizate politike dhe demonstratat e viti 1981," Tirana, 2008, p.178

Negotiations among professors, politicians, executives, and students had not resulted in a solution, as soon as the officials asked to change the location and move into the sports hall that was located in the Student Center. Students did not accept this because they felt that they could be trapped, and besides, their intention was to protest in the center of the city, at the time when Tito's manifestation was being held.

At 12 o'clock, students had started to protest toward the center of the city. In their hand they held posters "Kosova Republic," "We Are Albanians, not Yugoslavians," "Trepca works, Belgrade is built from it." They were followed by ideological ovations with Marxist-Leninist content, known from Tirana's propaganda, whose explanation was related with ideologist incrimination of the Kosova Republic request with the anathema of "coming from outside" in order to destroy "state sovereignty," which is what happened in reality.

Police did not allow students to march in the direction of the center, but a group of students was separated and marched toward the Sports Hall and then continued toward "Kodra e Diellit" and to the center. However, even in this way, students were stopped by police who were determined to stop any kind of protest.

In the meantime, police had started to use force against the students. Smoke bombs and tear gas was used against students and the entire Student Center was filled with them.

During the night, special federal forces were brought from Belgrade that interfered with severity and caused many injuries to students and other demonstrators. Special units had entered the Student Center and beat the students leaving many of them seriously injured, and hundreds of them were sent to the police station to be tortured. This situation also included high school students that had joined the protest.

This brutal intervention of Serbian police toward students, their injuries, and their imprisonment threatened all Kosovars with this severe behavior toward students who had asked for social and political requests in a peaceful way.

But, exactly this silent protest of the students of Prishtina and their increased demands that were consistent with the overall political and social statement of Albanians bothered Belgrade's political leadership that was dominated by Serbs and their followers. They had done everything possible to bring the situation to this point, in order to create a reason for severe intervention.

Since inmate students were not released, while the units of special federal forces were settled in Ajvali (near Prishtina) and started to brutally expel people from their houses in different parts of Prishtina (looking for the organizers of the protest and demonstrators who had been filmed with cameras by the police), a big explosion was expected. The revolt had spread and even the fact that no organization claimed responsibility for organizing the revolt and demonstrators, there were many activists "without addresses" that time to time held some improvised speeches stressing the requirements of the students of the March 26 protest and those of April 1, 2, 3, 1981. Along with these students and pupils from high schools, workers had also joined the protests, knowing that they had started a case that could not be stopped anymore. [409]

Protests started in Prishtina from the early morning, continuing in other cities of Kosova. In Prishtina, workers of the construction enterprise "Ramiz Sadiku" started the protests in the neighborhood of Lakrishte and continued to the center of Prishtina. Later, workers from the Obilici plant along with those of the coal mine, who had come to Prishtina by walking from Mihja Siperfaqesore in Obilic, joined the protest. In the center of Prishtina, in front of the Provincial Committee, activist Hydajet Hyseni, member of the "Marxist-Leninist Organization in Kosova" talked to the demonstrators. He talked about the social problems of Kosova and he stressed the current colonial position of Kosova. Hyseni also mentioned the case for Kosova Republic, which was cheered by the large crowd.[410]

Protests continued on April 2 and 3. They spread to other regions of Kosova, but their starting center was Prishtina, where a thousand participants gathered and protested.

---

[409] In Kosova, at the time of the 1981 protests, many organizations were illegally active, such as: *"Organizata Marksiste Leniniste e Kosovës OMLK"* (Mehmet Hajrizi, Hydajet Hyseni, Azem Syla, and others), *"Lëvizja Nacionalçlirimtare e Kosovës dhe e Viseve Shqiptare në Jugosllavi"* (Metush Krasniqi), *"Lëvizja për Çlirimin Nacional dhe Social të Kosovës"* (Mustafë Xhemjli, Bajrush Xhemajli, Imer Grainca, Xhabir Morina and others), *"Partia Komuniste Marksiste-Leniniste e Shqiptarëve në Jugosllavi"* (Abdullah Prapashtica, and others), *"Fronti i Kuq Popullor"* (Ibrahim Kelmendi and others), *"Grupi Marksist-leninist i Kosovës-Llap"* (Bajram Ajeti and others) and also some organizations inside and outside Kosova. *(See: Hajrizi, Mehmet: "Histori e një organizate politike dhe Demonstatat e vitit 1981," Tirana, 2008, p. 172; Basha-Keçmezi, Sabile: "Organizatat dhe Grupet ilegale në Kosovës 1981-1989, Prishtinë, 2003).*

[410] Hajrizi, Mehmet: previously cited book, p.183

On April 2, Belgrade, after sending additional police forces that were not able to stop the protests, denounced the state of emergency in Kosova. Kosova was surrounded, while in Prishtina and other areas, tanks and military units emerged and assumed the responsibility of protecting the institutions, Radio and Television of Kosova. On the second and third day many victims were encountered. *Naser Hajrizi, Asllan Pireva and Xhelal Maliqi were murdered in Prishtina; Riza Matoshi and Sherif Frangu were murdered in Ferizaj on the third of April; Sali Zeka, Sali Abazi, and Ruzhdi Hyseni in Vushtrri, and Sokol Bajrami was murdered in Mitrovica.* During those three days many people were injured from bullets or from brutal interventions of special federal police units that were supplemented by police forces from Serbia also. Military airplanes of "Mig" aviation from Serbia started to attack Prishtina.

On the third day, protests had spread to most regions of Kosova. However, they were suppressed shortly before the state of emergency where many incarcerations happened. Yugoslav police and their coopera-tors, that had closely followed and filmed the protests, started imprisoning many of the activists and demonstrators that appeared to be the founders of the protests. However, in the absence of a document that would prove the common center of the organization, the real founders were never determined, not even in courts. Many activists from different illegal groups had been sentenced by courts, which had condemned the protests and their spread of propaganda for Kosova Republic and other banners such as those containing ideologist content (Marxist-Leninist).

The imprisoning of demonstrators and the court processing, from of-fense (30 days in jail) to prosecution continued the entire year and then transformed into various political forms, to which all the Kosova popula-tion would be subject, requesting a political platform from the political leadership of the country in order to serve as a reference point for future actions. This platform, as will be seen, was approved in the XXII Meeting of CC of Communist Party of Yugoslavia in Belgrade on November 17, 1981.

Before this, the CC and CPY leadership in Belgrade, on April 5 made the tough decision of qualifying protests as "hostile events with coun-terrevolutionary purpose." In this case, the banner "Kosova Republic" and requests for autonomy and equality were characterized as hostile and counterrevolutionary whose purpose was to destroy Yugoslavia.[411]

In this meeting, the main speech was presented by the Macedonian representative, Lazar Kolishevski, who had blamed Kosova's social and political leadership for the current situation, first of all, Mahmut Bakalli the leader of the Presidential party and then Fadil Hoxha, member of the state and political party leadership. Pointing out Bakalli and Hoxha was not by chance, because by pointing out the two strongest people, the ideals of Kosova Republic and autonomy would be suppressed. Beside Bakalli and Hoxha, Kolishevski had pointed the finger toward many political and social institutions that were recently established in Kosova, attacking mostly the educational system (particularly the university) that was charged with "inspiring the irredentist era", continuing on with other cultural institutions, media, and state institutions that had conducted discriminative politics against non-Albanians in Kosova (firstly against Serbians, Montenegrins, and Romans) who were obligated to migrate from Kosova. Kolishevski opened the case of "ethnic cleansing of non-Albanians" and that of the powerful impact of Albanian politics in the "creation of irredentist consciousness" that was created by the "cooperation of Tirana in education, culture, and sport development." Generally speaking, Kolishevski blamed all the participants and followers of Plenum of Brion, continuing with the statement that "the leadership of Kosova had deceived Tito and his cooperatives." This approach, more cynical and perfidious, emanated from Serbian politics that from war time and on had been used by Belgrade in the same fashion in 1944 to stop the anti-fascist struggle of Macedonians, who were then connected with Bulgaria on the Yugoslav side. [412]

Since, on April 5 the leadership of the political party accepted the evaluation of the protests as hostile and counterrevolutionary, it was known that all political centers of the country would adopt this evaluation, especially Kosova, and that in accordance with those evaluations other conclusions should be made and spread througout the entire country, according to which also the political party, courts, and police were to behave.

---

[411] See: "Politika," Belgrade, 6 April, 1981.
[412] *Ibid.*

Thus, during April (April 13 and 27) two meetings of the Presidency of the Provincial Committee of the League of Communists of Kosova were held in order to make the political leadership of Kosova accept their fault, which was a step toward preparing the country for the new political platform that was going to come. According to the transcripts of those two meetings, the political leadership of Belgrade led by that of Serbia, which, after the April 5 events, had started the implementation of its plan, sent to Kosova the "Albanian squad" "marginalized" by Tito: Ali Shukriu, Sinan Hasani, Kole Shiroka, who had the responsibility to widen their group with the other "people who were distanced" from "Albanian nationalists." Their purpose was to "take the matter in their hands" to support the thesis that "the counterrevolution explosion" was something "authentic" and was led from the base.

So, the thesis of the "counterrevolution explosion" in Kosova, that was planned well ahead by the Belgrade government also in order to resolve the issues with Yugoslav federalization and with Tito and his way of rule that, as would be seen from the Plenum of Brion, had mostly bothered Serbia, must have emanated from Kosova and Albanian politicians. Albanian politicians should have been "self-critical" and accept not only their "mistakes" but also their tenacity to continue the hostile activities, that of "Albanian reaction" and similar cases that had impacted the political state of the country in the last years, which contributed to the entrance of Serbian forces. Veli Deva was one of the people who declared that "this was a case of an undisciplined and counterrevolutionary people, not youngsters but adults who are leading." To Deva, this movement at the university was led by professors![413]

Ali Shukria was the first to claim the term for this movement as a "counterrevolution" and would support it by relating it with the antifascist war. The March and April 1981 case, evaluated as threatening from counterrevolutionary forces of national and irredentist character, was compared with the case of 1994 winter, that according to him, the counterrevolution had exploded. Shukria argued that "they were forced to fight again, but that was the time of revolution and war and we knew that we

---

[413] See: Mbledhja e Shtatëmbëdhjetë e Komitetit Krahinor të Lidhjes së Komunistëve të Kosovës, included in the publication "Komunistit"- *"Vlerësimi i shkaqeve, i rrethanave dhe i pasojave të demonstratave armiqësore dhe organizimi e veprimi i LK dhe i fuqive të tjera të organizuara socialiste në Kosovë,"* Prishtina, 1981, p. 269.

had to stop this" and that for this case it was the right reaction, because this was "a war that will continue for a long time."[414]

Since the two meetings of the Presidency of Provincial Committee, were given such evaluation similar to those that were given from CC and CPY Leadership on April 5, proposed by Lazar Kolisevski and accepted unanimously, nothing more was left but to start the cleansing of the Leadership Committee. Of course, according to the information that was presented by Kolisevski, those people were Mahmut Bakalli, the leader of the Presidency and the person who had the support of Tito and came from the "second" generation, that of after the war, without "revolutionary merits." Bakalli had the credibility of an emancipated political intellectual in the social leadership with two main opponents: in Kosova "the revolutionary generation" that Tito had started to abandon and Serbian politicians that were against the new generation that Tito supported and were seen as Tito's successors. Those successors were Mahmut Bakalli in Kosova, Josip Verhovec in Croatia, and Milan Kucan in Slovenia that were the candidates for leading the country. [415]

After those meetings, where CC and CPY decisions were accepted more because of the obligation rather than political accordance, under Belgrade's pressure to find "the culprit" of "national" and "counterrevolutionary indoctrination" that remained without leadership, since Bakalli had resigned from the post of Chairman of the Presidium of the Regional Committee of the League of Communists of Kosova. His resignation was consistent "with the effort to help the serious condition that had come from the protests and hostile position of Albanian nationalists and irredentists."[416]

The expected resignation of Bakalli had not pleased Belgrade, because it did not mirror the willingness and commitment of Bakalli and his followers "to solve the issues with the organizers who caused the Albanian national and irredentist movement." Furthermore, that started to be seen as an attempt to blame the "new course" for which Bakalli was considered to be at fault. "It made no sense to follow only the new demonstrators, while their aspirators would remain intact," was said in Belgrade.[417]

---

[414] *Ibid.*

[415] Buxhovi, Jusuf: "Kthesa historike," first book, Prishtina 2009, p.112-120

[416] See: "Renaissance," March 2, 1981.

[417] "Politika," Belgrade, April 22, 1981.

Under these circumstances, on April 5, 1981, the Seventeenth Meeting of the Provincial Committee of the League of Communists of Kosova was organized, where the assessment of the causes, circumstances, and consequences of the hostile demonstrations were evaluated. In this meeting, the resignation of Mahmut Bakalli from the position of Chairman of the Presidium of the Regional Committee, presented on May 1, was accepted. Veli Deva replaced him for a one-year term. He was the president of communists in Kosova in 1966, and 10 years earlier, in Tito's period, had been replaced by Bakalli.

As it was expected, the Provincial Committee of the League of Communists of Kosova, with orders given by Belgrade, introduced an official political document called "The assessment of causes, circumstances and consequences of the hostile demonstrations."[418] On this occasion, at the time when in Kosova the special federal units and Yugoslavian Army elite units were established, the political leadership was entirely subjected to the Belgrade plan. In this way, the anti-Albanian Serbian politics legally came back with the purpose of "deepening of socialist autonomy and the brotherhood and further affirmation of the nations and nationalities" and other issues relating to this topic, that were related to the national and homogenic Serbian politics of the nineteenth and twentieth centuries. This was the time of "Nacertanja" of Garasanini continuing with the elaborations of Vasa Cubrilovic (the first one in 1937 and the second one in November 1944), which aimed at:
- Collapse of political elite, that from 1966 and on was determined for equality in the Yugoslavian federal system,
- Collapse of the intellectual elite of Albanians, that saw the subject of political equality as Republic status, which was presented as a general request in the protests of 1968,
- Collapse of the educational system, from primary school to university, depriving the national spirit,
- Collapse of the Albanian scientific institutions (Albanian Institution and Historical Insitution),
- Collapse of cultural institutions, starting with those of publications, theaters, ballet, and music),

---

[418] "Assessment of causes, circumstances and consequences of the hostile demonstrations," published by "Komunisti" Kosova, May 1981.

-   Collapse of cultural values, starting with areas of spiritual stories and those historical.

Beside those, it attempted to destroy all cultural, educational, and spiritual relations between Kosova and Albania that were established in 1968 according to the state agreement of cultural and educational exchange, whose importance was crucial, especially for the unification of the common literary language and its rules.

This anti-Albanian program was to have the support of:

1) Political ideology differentiation (in line with Serbian ideology), which was announced as a long and continuous process that should have included all social structures, especially education and culture.
2) Legal process for national and irredentist forces and their followers. The irredentist forces were to be penalized according to the severest law.

With those provisions, the Serbian politics of Belgrade had created the pre-conditions for their two strategic purposes: (a) the collapse of the constitution of 1974 and (b) the return of Serbian control in the federation.

The first aim was to ruin Kosova's constitution by political means, so following the judicial changes that would start in 1986 and end in 1989 and Kosova's autonomy would be withdrawn and be forced to return to the status of 1945 when it was violently annexed to Serbia against her will. The statement of "counterrevolution" similar to that of 1944, gave Serbia the necessary legal tools to make it happen.

Once the "United Serbia" was created and strengthened, Belgrade took full control of the federation. This control was taken with the pretext of strengthening and stabilizing, which had full support from the internationals. According to Serbia, they would be better off allowing a Unitarian and centralized Yugoslavia that was stable rather than a non-stable federation full of internal problems that could easily become external problems, such as the case of Kosova, which could not remained isolated. It was assessed that the lesson that Kosova received, that it was an organic part of Serbia, would also be received by Vijvodina and Montenegro. Macedonia was also considered part of this group, since it had Albanians among its population that one day could outnumber the Macedonians. For this reason, Macedonia was to accept Serbian vassalage as the only means of protecting it from the "Albanian invasion." A similar scenario was planned for Bosnia and Herzegovina inhabited mostly by Serbs, where fabricated "Yugoslavians" (mostly Bosnians) were returned to support Serbia. Serbia's intention was to manage Serbia's interest from Belgrade, where Croatians and Slovenians would be minorities and the other republics would be supporting Serbia.

Of course the Serbian scenarios were to start in Kosova in order to continue to other places. Firstly, focusing on this case, referring to the past and "mistakes" they had made, so that the threatening "counterrevolution" was recognized in Kosova on behalf of the "future" and its construction, always in accordance with Serbian interest, and then to continue into Yugoslavia.

With this plan, the first battle started for the destruction of the political system in Kosova, as a pre-condition for the cultural, institutional, and spiritual collapse. The XVII meeting of the Provincial Committee of the League of Communists held on May 5 in Prishtina, with the imposed assessment of the protests as "hostile activity with counterrevolutionary character" coming from Belgrade, opened the doors for other activities, such as the destruction of the political elite of Kosova with Yugoslavian orientation (Mahmut Bakalli) and the return of old Serbian vassals (Ali Shukriu, Sinan Hasani and others). This in turn created the pre-conditions for the destruction of the Albanian intellectual elite and the destruction of the overall infrastructure of educational and culture institutions in Kosova. In this case, the political framework was formed with the political platform of the Yugoslavian level, approved in November of that year in the meeting of the Central Committee of Yugoslavia, whereby Serbia had the approval of the entire country and as it would be seen, would also have a free hand in Kosova.

The collapse of the political elite of Kosova with Yugoslavian orientation (resignation of Mahmut Bakalli) was part of a prepared scenario, since, as it was said, it was correlated with Kosova's concept for equality but also for that of Albanians in Yugoslavia at the federal level, returning Prishtina to the eighth center of Yugoslavia, but with social, cultural, and political epithet, which was not accepted by Serbs but also not accepted by Macedonians and Montenegrins where a good portion of Albanian ethnicity resided. Therefore, the declaration of equality as a "counterrevolutionary" idea by the Serbs was fueled with hatred and brought to the point of bearing arms against the entire population of Kosova. Even though historical circumstances were not the same as those of 1944, where Cubrilovic required the use of the "counterrevolution" formula for the revolution in order to solve the issues with Albanians, Germans, and Hungarian, Belgrade saw the option of war put into action, as happened in 1991 and so on.

In fact, in the XVII meeting of Provincial Committee of the Communist League of Kosova this political form was promoted, starting with political differentiation and ending with the use of arms, if required. The acceptance of the assessments served from the meeting of April 5 of CC and CPY Presidency from where the assessment of the protests began as "an Albanian hostile, counterrevolutionary activity with national, irredentist base," was to have had the support among Albanians in order for the situation to seem as Albanians were solving issues among themselves, something that would ease Belgrade's work even more. The resignation of Mahmut Bakalli had created the preconditions for starting the differentiation between the highest political leader of Kosova and three advanced politicians (Ali Shukriu, Veli Deva, and Kole Shiroka) who accepted counterrevolution as an assessment, with the purpose for it to be "worked" even more by "Junior" Azem Vllasi, who would say the "protests were a consequence of a hostile and counterrevolutionary activity." This opened the monstrous process of political differentiation that endured seven years and in the end would not save Vllasi either; it opened the path of imprisonment that had started on March 27 in Prishtina with the imprisonment of many young students that participated in the protests of March 11 and those of April 1, 2, and 3[419] continuing with many

---

[419] Tracing the organizers of the protest at the University of Kosova, police arrested many students from March 27, 1981; while on August 30, 1981, District Court of Prishtina sentenced: *Gani Koci, Ali Lajçi, Bajram Kosumi and Merxhan Avdyli* with 15 years of prison; *Murat Musliu, Hamdi Hajdini, Riza Deman, Hamdi Zymberi and Xun Çeta* with 13 years;, *Kadri Kryeziu, Jonuz Jonuzi, Sylë Muja, Muslim Kosumi, Halit Osmani* with 10 years; *Ramadan Gashi-Dobra, Gani Maxhuni and Gani Vllahia* with 8 years; *Selim Geci, Bedri Deliu, Ramë Demaj and Fahri Ymeri* with 6 years of prison. (*More on that See: Hajrizi, Mehmet:"Histori e një organizate politike dhe demonstratat e vitit 1981,"* Tirana, *2008, p. 248*). For participation in Prishtina's protests, County Prosecutor in Prishtina filed indictments against: Hydajet Hyseni, Mehmet Hajrizi, Gani Sylë, Fatmir Krasniqi, Ferid Çollkaku, Nezir Myrtaj, Berat Luzha, Sherafedin Berisha, Ismaijl Syla, Hysni Hoti, Kadri Luzha, Mustafë Ademi and Jashar Alijaj. County Prosecutor covicted: Ismajl Haradina, Hasan Ukëhaxha, Avdullah Hasanmeta, Jashar Salihu, Shkurte-Drita Kuçi,

thousands of others until 1999, where many people were murdered and tortured. [420]

What is obvious in these assessments is the sophisticated strategy targeted against the University of Kosova, against scientific institutions, against publishing houses in the Albanian language, especially its promoter "Rilindja," against textbooks of all levels, and against the cultural and educational cooperation with Albania.

These three fields, along with that of cultural and educational cooperation with Albania were not chosen by chance; the first ones were related to the national cultural identity of Albanians, which also formed their social and political identity, while the cooperation with Albania connected Albanians in the spirit of national unity.

The last one was not occasionally addressed by the Serbian leadership of Belgrade and Serbian intellectuals, because according to them, that one was the "place of the Albanian irredentist nest," which "was spiritually renewed on the basis of national unity," as it simulated the loss of Kosova for Serbs, who "in the circumstances of rapid developments for Albanians, left nothing but for Serbs to get out."[421]

However, in the XVII meeting of Regional Committee and CPY in Prishtina, the biggest attack was against the University of Kosova and the overall research activity in this institution since it presented the foundation for the national education for Albanians that had started to strengthen in Kosova after 1966. In the opening statements, as well in the Belgrade assessment of the situation that was to be accepted in its entirety, the University of Kosova was attacked the most. It was called the "inspiring center and center of hostile and counterrevolutionary activities by the

---

Xhavit Hoxha, Din Ahmetaj, Nazmi Selmanaj, Ali Dërvishaj, Muhamet Haklaj and Nimon Mustafaj.

[420] According to official documents, only in the first four years of protests, 4,000 people were sentenced. During 1981-1990, 183 citizens and 63 Albanian soldiers in the Yugoslavian army were murdered and 1,346 soldiers and 10,000 citizens were sentenced for political penalty. With an average sentence of 7.1 years, 3,500 individuals were sentenced. Every third Albanian was treated by police in this period, while in 1990 more than 7,000 students were poisoned with war toxins. (See: Sabile Keçmezi-Basha: "Diferencimet e dënimet ndaj shqiptarëve morën përmasa të mëdha," Epoka e Re, May 9, 2006, p. 10, cited from: Hajrizi, Mehmet "Historia e një organizate...," Tirana, 2008, p. 249.)

[421] See: Cosic, Dobrica: "Kosova 1956-1995," Belgrade, 2004.

Albanian national and irredentist movement," while professors and other staff were considered "militants of this idea." Those statements were made with the purpose of orienting the campaign against this institution, which would have the support of the political platform that the Central Committee of CPY would take four months later, a platform that would serve this harsh process of political ideology differentiation, whose victims were many professors and instructors of the university. Thus, in the XVII meeting of Regional Committee of CP of Kosova on May 5, 1981, all the participants (with the exception of Mahmut Bakalli, Pajazit Nushi, and Dervish Rozhaja) willfully accepted Belgrade's assessment of the "national and irredentist movement at the University of Kosova." Bakalli and Nushi, although in principle accepted those assessments, disagreed with many points, attempting not to fault the university but the inability of the society to meet the material requirements for this institution's "national and non-academic influence."[422]

Academic Dervish Rozhaja was the only one that refused to accept the assessments and reasons that were given for the University of Kosova, and therefore was severly attacked by Ali Shukriu, Xhavid Nimani, Dusan Ristic and others.[423]

Even after the explosion of the protests, the University of Kosova was targeted by Belgrade, because the demolishers of the 1974 Constitution had obviously seen that Serbia had lost its first and most important "battle" with the creation of this institution, which had rapidly turned into a nest of Albanian intellectual society in Kosova and in other regions of Yugoslavia. Reasonably, the university would be seen as "a center of Albanian nationality," not in a negative way, as it was taken by Belgrade, but in a positive one, as a nursery of intelligence of the Albanian national identity, one whose spirit was maintained even when faced with incessant attacks that were meant to destroy it. It would be this university, where the protests of 1968 and 1981 were initiated, whose motto was Kosova Republic, which survived the severe violence against its students from 1981 and on, but also that of the professor and academics during the harsh process of differentiation of political ideology that sought the

---

[422] See: Mbledhja XVII e KK të LK të Kosovës, May 5, 1981 - *"Vlerësimi i shkaqeve, i rrethanave dhe i pasojave armiqësore...,"* published in *"Komunist,"* Prishtinë, 1981, p. 188-193 and 164-169.

[423] *Ibid.,* p. 243-247.

destruction of this educational institution, without which the state-forming movement would not have had the force to continue this historical process.

In this long process, for about seven years, with which the XVII meeting of Regional Committee of CP in Kosova opened the way, it should be stated the position of activists that protected Kosova Republic starting with professors and educators of this university, headed by Ukshin Hoti, Professor of Philosophy Department, requested the rights of Albanians that had been taken away from them since Bujan until now. In protection of this statement, Ukshin Hoti together with Halil Alidema, Shemsi Recica (professors in the university), Ekrem Kryeziu (director), Ali Kryeziu (diplomat), and Mentor Kaqin (student) were imprisoned and sentenced in 1982 "for support of counterrevolution." Ukshin Hoti and others in the judicial process defended Kosova's request for Republic.[424]

Albania and the Demands for the Republic of Kosova

From the beginning to the end, regarding Kosova's case, Enver Hoxha had considered that a solution to all the problems would come from the ideological concepts according to Marxist-Leninist theory and that of proletarian internationalism. -Enver Hoxha opposed the Revolutionary Movement for Unification of Albanian territories, such as that of Metush Krasniqi in 1958 and later on the Revolutionary Movement for Unification of Adem Demaci, because according to him those movements were "revolutionaries."-Although he supported the Marxist-Leninist movement in the diaspora and among migration regions, Enver Hoxha strongly opposed the request for Kosova Republic that was announced in the protest of 1968 calling it "Tito's trap against Albanians," for which attention should be paid and caution should be taken to reject such traps under all circumstances. –Only after Tito's death, did Enver Hoxha change his mind to be pro Kosova Republic, which he supported and included in the VIII Congress Resolution of the Labor Party of Albania in 1981. However, he asked for the Republic to be under the Marxist-Leninist ideologic course, as would be reflected also in the activities of many illegal groups of Kosova, but also groups

---

[424] See Hoti, Ukshin: "Filozofia e ceshtjes shqiptare," Prishtina, 1997

From the Second World War and on, Albanian-Yugoslavian relations between Tito and Enver were basically influenced by their attitude toward Kosova, with the only difference being that Tito from the beginning to the end had treated those purposes for the benefit of Yugoslavia, so that Kosova would remain part of it (in accordance with the statement of Local Conference of the Communist Party of Yugoslavia in 1941, to save and protect Yugoslavian integrity, a statement that had changed from the Fourth Congress when Yugoslavia was called "the artificial creature of Versailles and oppressive force of nations," that should be destroyed in order for the suppressed nations to regain their liberty and right to autonomy). Enver, on the other hand, looked for the solution to the Kosova case in accordance with the ideologist concepts of Marxist-Leninist theory and proletarian nationalism, from which in his mind the solution for every case could be found. Furthermore, according to Enver, even the autonomy of the nations as a Leninist principle was closely related with communism and could be applied only under communism and no other system. Enver had never strayed from this ideologist concept, even in the cases when everything was going in the opposite direction, such as the separation of the Soviets with Stalinists during the Khrushchev time, or the "soothing" of Chinese toward Americans in the mid-seventies when they started the normalization of economic relationships with them, while Albania continued to remain "the only lantern of communism near the Adriatic!"

The case for Kosova Republic was also included in this context, which was required as a legal requirement in 1968 from all levels of the Albanian society, a case which was strongly protested in order to transform it into a political program that would open the path of state-formation for Kosova.

Before moving to Kosova Republic and its increase into a nationwide request of the Albanians of Kosova from 1968 and on, which Enver Hoxha did not support and called "Tito's trap against Albanians," while after the protests of 1981, when this case, influenced by many factors (known and unknown) started to move more quickly into an historical development, he supported the democratic right of Albanians and even included it in the resolution of the Eighth Congress of the Labor Party of Albania. However, well before the essence of this change would be seen, one should look at the time period from 1944 to 1949 as well as on to 1966, since these years were emblematic and played an important role in the Albanian movements in Kosova and their future which seemed to be connected with the fate of Albania. Complications resulted due to Enver Hoxha's ideological concepts and also with the state logic of not changing borders, as an international norm, upon which Tito also relied when he acted with severity against the patriotic movement of Albanians in Kosova.

As it was said earlier, especially for the developments that had impacted the abolition of Bujani's Resolution and the creation of the circumstances that had brought Kosova's annexation by Serbia and its violent unification in July 1945, Enver even in the case of those tragic developments for Kosova and for the overall Albanian cause, behaved according to his Marxist-Leninist ideology. According to facts, Enver was and still remained a supporter of proletarian internationalization and this doctrine that was used to solve every problem, even if those were tough cases such as that of Kosova and the Albanian fate from 1912 and so on when Albanians had been separated due to the Serbian-Montenegrin-Greeks aggression. Moreover, he defended his ideologic concepts fanatically and submitted them to the case of Kosova and the Albanians in general. He defended those concepts even when Albanian state's existence was in jeopardy during the "Balkan Federation" (Yugoslavia-Bulgaria-Albania) project. Enver spoke about those ideologies enthusiastically and wanted to implement them as soon as possible; however, he was stopped by Tito who had other opinions regarding that case, as he was commited to the project of "Albanian Republic in Yugoslavia," where Albania together with Kosova and the other regions occupied by Serbia would join Yugoslavia as the "Seventh Republic." [425]

This time, which could be called the most bizarre time of Enver Hoxha's love for Tito and Yugoslavia and for the communist ideology, held fatal consequences for Kosova and the Albanian fate. Of course, Albania would have been under the former Yugoslavia if it weren't for the

---

[425] More on this issue, See: *"Libri i Bardhë,"* SIP, Belgrade, 1953; Dedijer, Vladimir: *"Marrëdhëniet jugosllavo-shqiptare 1939-1948,"* Tirana, 2005; Đaković, Spasoje: *"Sukobi na Kosovu,"* Belgrade, 1984; Dizdarević, Njazi: *"Albanski dnevvnik,"* Belgrade,1984

international circumstances that firstly, would determine the interest between East and West, set in the Yalta Agreement of non-changeable borders, and secondly, the intervention of Stalin, who, fearing the Balkan ally headed by Tito as seen by the Resolution of 1949, started an open conflict with Tito, which ended with Stalin's defeat and Tito's victory. During those three years, Albania had been returned into a place of Yugoslavian vassals. Albania did not have sovereignty, neither from inside, nor from outside. Under those circumstances, Belgrade determined all the Albanian cases, starting with economical ones and continuing with those of internal security, while the external and diplomatic plan (without a Ministry of External Affairs) was entirely subject to Yugoslavian diplomacy, which "housed" some Albanian diplomats in some embassies in world centers that Yugoslavia owned at the time. To Enver, the Kosova case was seen only as a region under Serbia's sovereignty and never anything else. Albanians, as a minority, should make an attempt to realize their rights with their international behavior of deepening the further rapprochement between Yugoslavia and Albania without excluding the "union of Albanian Republic from it."

This was the historical frame of Enver Hoxha's behavior from the beginning phases of the Yugoslavian intervention in Albania (from 1941 until 1949), to which any detail could be added or removed, but it would never miss its base.

From 1948 and mostly 1949, after the appearance of the conflict between Stalin and Tito, resulting in the creation of the Informbiro (Cominform) Resolution, Enver Hoxha changed his mind, by disconnecting from Tito and uniting with Stalin and the Soviet Union, without considering the problems that this would cause for Albanians in Yugoslavia. As was known, from that time until the starting of the sixties, when the disconnection with the Soviets began, according to their orders, Enver started applying all his ideologies against Tito, firstly by calling him "an American agent" that should be reversed from power through revolutionary methods and war, then continuing with the attack against the Yugoslav socialist autonomy program, calling it a "revisionist road" that should also be reversed through revolutionary methods.

In fact, from the time of Albania's connection with the Soviet Union in 1949 until 1953, when Stalin died, Enver Hoxha had even requested military intervention against Yugoslavia, but that needed to be directed by the Soviet Union as "Tito's punishment" for his betrayal of the Marxist-

Leninist system. In one letter that Enver Hoxha had sent to the Central Committee of CP (Communist Party) of USSR on September 2, 1949, for "Kosova and Metohija,"[426] he stated that "Tito and his friends are imperialist agents and have connected Yugoslavia with imperialism" and he accused "them of making Yugoslavia into a prison of nations where Hitler's fascist terror reigns." He asked "the liberation of nations by Yugoslavia from this fascist and imperialist gang be treated as an urgent case," where according to him "the same should happen with the case of Kosova liberation," which should be joined with that of Yugoslavia for which Enver argues "that it should be made with war and blood because there is no other way. Tito and his way of rule should collapse," and this was a war "against the Yugoslavian proletariat, led by the New Communist Party, with the Marxist-Leninist and internationalist base," that presented "the national liberty of Yugoslavia." As a base, this war would be preceded by "an armed revolution against fascist imperialists and their internal followers headed by Tito." In this armed war Enver also saw the solution for Kosova's case. "We think that the Albanian nation of Kosova, Metohija, Macedonia, and Montenegro should fight in order to be free from the other nations of Yugoslavia."

And, according to Enver, the first thing that Albanians must do is "to enter in a severe war without compromise against Tito and continue to an armed revolution. They must win the war as soon as possible. If there were other nations that wanted to start the war that was even better, because in this way the isolation and suppression of the Kosova movement would be avoided."[427]

But, also with this case, as it happened with that of the National Liberation War, Enver Hoxha said that "Kosova should consider their war strongly related with the war of other nations against the Yugoslav context of Yugoslavia, because otherwise it will be isolated and suppressed."

So, also here, the formula that was given in 1944 when the Yugoslav partisans reinvaded Kosova in the "name of communist liberation" was repeated. In this case, it was said that "Kosova's population needs to understand that the liberation and gain of democratic and national rights

---

[426] See Dedijer, Vladimir: *"Novi prilozi za bografiju Josipa Broza Tita,"* Belgrade, 1953; Kaba, Hamit – Çeku, Ethem: *"Shqipëria dhe Kosova në arkivat ruse 1946-1962"* (documents), Tirana, 2011, p. 103-110.

[427] *Ibid.*

could be achieved only by merging their war with the struggles of other Yugoslav countries."

In this letter, Enver even gave the Soviet people instructions for leading the war when he said "Kosova and Metohija should have its own leadership outside the war, a National Liberation Committee, which should determine the line of war based on the Informbiro (Cominform) Resolution and Marxist-Leninist-Stalinist principles. In the war the International Communist Party for Kosova and Metohija inside the International Communist party of Yugoslavia should be organized and created." The tutelage of Yugoslavian communism was again essential, but this time under Soviet and Stalin control. In this case Enver said that "Albanians of Kosova and Meothija should build their confidence and commitment toward the USSR, toward the Bolshevik Party, and toward Stalin, and that Albanians should understand that without accepting this fact there would never be a united Albania," because "Kosova Albanians should understand that their ruthless enemy and the whole camp is American imperialism, their satellites and the Tito clique, which is nothing more than his intelligence services." [428]

At that time, Tirana's propaganda with great fanaticism followed Moscow's intentions to overthrow Tito. However, the costs were to turn Albania into a ghetto and ferocious concentration camp and also to suppress the Albanians in Kosova that Belgrade fought on the grounds that "Tirana's Stalinists" and their followers in Kosova were supported by Moscow and presented danger to the stability of the country.

Under these circumstances, in the fifties, the notorious arms collection started, that was nothing more than a state terror against Albanians in order to make them migrate toward Turkey since this road was already opened for them by the "gentleman's" agreement between Tito and Cyprus in 1953, which reactivated the Yugoslavian-Turkish covenant of 1938 for the migration of four hundred thousand Albanians to Turkey. Thus, the armed action relating to this migration resulted in the migration of about one quarter million Albanians to Turkey that took place between the years 1955 and 1965.

Even in these more modest circumstances, the Albanian diplomatic services outside (Albania had four representatives in the European countries: Brussels, Paris, Rome, and Vienna; one consulate in Belgrade

---

[428] *Ibid.*

and one embassy in Turkey together with a consulate in Istanbul), under the orders of the political apparatus and information service supervised by the Soviet KGB, tried to connect with Albanian political organizations in the diaspora on ideologic bases, Marxist-Leninist, and gave them instructions not to accept activities of any other nature. According to Enver Hoxha, who later had followed Kosova's case and its patriotic movement of the sixties,"[429] the cause of Marxist-Leninist ideological preparation of the Kosova Albanians and Yugoslavia was most important in the spirit of toppling Titoism and opening the road to return to Marxist and Leninist ideology within Yugoslavia and the Yugoslavian leadership[430] rather than giving importance to the national unity requested by illegal groups led by Metush Krasniqi and Adem Demaci and others that appeared at the end of the fifties and the beginning of sixties.[431]

And, as will be seen, Enver critiqued the National Movement of Kosova for Albanian Unity, saying that this movement "is politically and organizationally perverted" and that "it follows very little pre-war features, coming out with banners such as 'War to be united with Albanians,' and that it did not fight enough and properly to gain from Tito's purpose of opening Albanian schools." He also said that "the war was developed with a secret group that kept no secrets from the secret police (UDBA)." He also made other such statements in order to critically conclude that "there was a missing Marxist-Leninist leadership that would use the situation in the best way possible."[432]

In this case, Enver Hoxha critiqued the revolutionary platform for Albanian union with war, which would first be elaborated by Metush Krasniqi in 1958 and would become the platform of many illegal groups of the time. According to him "Kosova's case is not an easy case and it cannot be solved as fast as some Kosovars in good faith think," and that "the Kosova population should understand that under those circumstances, Albania could never attack Yugoslavia. The People's Republic of

---

[429] See Hoxha, Enver: *"Ditari politik për çështje ndërkombëtare 1968-1969,"* Tirana, cited by Çeku, Ethem: *"Kosova në sfondin e diplomacisë së Jugosllavisë dhe të Shqipërisë 1945-1981,"* Prishtina, 2009, p. 209

[430] *Ibid.,* p.209

[431] See: "Dosja Demaci," Prishtina, 2004

[432] AQSH, p.10/AP, year 1966, file no., 185, p.12, 13-15, 16-18, cited by Çeku, Ethem: "Kosova në sfondin e diplomacisë së Jugosllavisë dhe të Shqipërisë 1945-1981," Prishtina, 2009, p. 208-209.

Albania could never be aggressive. If Yugoslavia were to attack Albania, that would be another problem. In this case, Albania would defend itself, would fight, and would win, and Kosova's problem would be treated differently."[433]

So, Enver, who at the time that Stalin was alive, required war and blood in order to ruin "the imperialist ideology of Tito," in Yugoslavia which he called "American spy," with the change of Moscow's stance toward Belgrade and the abandonment of the Stalinist war logic by Khrushchev, saw the war case as a fatal mistake that would present a suicide. Aware that there would not be any Soviet intervention in Yugoslavia, as required by the Informbiro (Cominform) Resolution, and aware that Yugoslavia had strong international support because it was removed from the socialist camp, Enver Hoxha called for an ideologic revolution, in which Yugoslav nations together with Albanians were needed to ruin "Tito's revisionism."

Enver Hoxha continued to support those ideological concepts until 1966 when the Fourth Plenum of CC of the Yugoslav Communist Party (Brion Plenum) was presented. In this plenum, Tito ruined the bureaucratic dogma of Alexander Rankovic, who was responsible for all the terrors against Albanians from the post-war time and on, especially in the fifties and sixties, although it was known that in Yugoslavia nothing could happen without Tito's awareness.

Since the word was for a positive change, that regardless of the purposes it served and how it was reasoned, it opened the path to a new social and political development from which Albanians and Kosova would benefit the most. To Enver Hoxha and the Chinese people, this new path of "American imperialism" was highly dubious due to the thought that it would cause problems for them both internally and externally. This came together with Brezhnev's announcement of "limited sovereignty" for the Eastern countries, of which Albania was one, which had announced unanimously the removal of the Versailles Pact, removal that was never officially accepted by Moscow.

Under these circumstances of fear and isolation, when the country was being filled with work camps and internment centers, and the economic difficulty was deepening, Enver Hoxha had minimum interest in the improvement of Kosova's case, especially for such improvement that

---

[433] *Ibid.*

411

meant removing Albanians from Marxist-Leninist ideology, and bringing them into "Tito's autonomy" and "his fraud." This moved Enver Hoxha to write his pamphlet "Yugoslavian autonomy as modern revisionism" that became propaganda that spread through Radio Tirana and was transmitted to many countries in different languages, but also as a "special" publication for the diaspora and "immigrants" in the West, who should have been "attracted" by the "Albanian communist paradise" and revolted against "imperialism" to join the "world revolution!"

In this path, Enver Hoxha found himself in an even more difficult situation when in Prishtina and some other cities of Kosova, Macedonia, and Montenegro, in October and November 1968, big Albanian protests exploded with the first-time request for Kosova Republic. This request was inspired by the Albanian intelligence of Kosova, stemming from public discussions about future constitutional changes in Yugoslavia.

In those protests, which were the biggest protests presented by Albanians following World War II and presented the relationship between intellectual groups and youth momentum, where there was no ideological requirement but rather, democratic ones of equality and civilization (request for the opening of University of Prishtina in Albanian language), Enver Hoxha realized that Kosova was not under his rule anymore. What was happening in Kosova, from the Brioni Plenum and on, not only was not in accordance with Enver's internal propaganda and his messages toward Kosova regarding the "Marxist-Leninist revolutionary era" that was to be followed in Kosova and used "to ruin Tito and other revisionists," but it spoke of something quite different that revived fear in Enver Hoxha.

Therefore, it was predicted that the request for Kosova Republic, manifested in that way (with intellectual and social consensus) and expected with high attention even from outside countries, especially from the West, which had related Kosova's case to the internal stability of Yugoslavia even after Tito's death, in order for Yugoslavia to never be part of Eastern countries, as Serbs required, after Rankovic's fall and on, would not be supported by Albania, who reacted as unprepared for such a case. Furthermore, Enver Hoxha, some days after the protests in Kosova that were evaluated by some Yugoslavian resources as "hostile and inspired by outside countries," justified that "we are not involved in those protests" and we swear "that we are not going to develop any intelligence work either in Yugoslavia or in Kosova." [434]

In this case, Enver Hoxha did not even mention the Kosova Republic cause, which was the main request in those protests, but only stressed the solution of national rights inside Yugoslavia.

In fact, Enver Hoxha held an ungrateful and distrustful attitude toward Kosova Republic for two main reasons: because it endangered his internal position, but also his external one. His internal position was endangered because the request of Kosova Republic as part of the Yugoslav federation, as a representation of Albanian political will against revolution and the Marxist-Leninist ideology, was believed to have happened for many years by Albanian citizens, when "Tito and his followers will fall in Kosova" to the benefit of an International-Stalinist Yugoslavia, ruining the entire effort for ideologist propaganda made in Kosova with the purpose of strengthening the dictatorship supported by Marxist-Leninist propaganda. His external position was endangered because a reformed federation in accordance with western concepts, where Kosova had its own place within the eight equal units, could turn it into a "capitalist country" which would present danger for Albania, because this return of Yugoslavia toward capitalism would present a "pretext" for the Soviet Union to turn Albania into a Soviet conspiracy.

Therefore, it was not surprising the fact that Enver Hoxha stressed his doubt as to whom the Republic would serve, to which political specter it would belong and what its effect would be on his regime.

This so-called Albanian outside Republic, projected by Tito, could serve as an Albanian reaction center and center for Albanian fascist and war criminals, fugitives that lived in Europe and in the United States of America. Kosova's Albanians should not fall into this trap. They should fight this maneuver of Tito that would possibly be used to further his interests."[435]

The fear of Kosova Republic remained the same for Enver Hoxha even after it received a negative response from Tito. The constitutional amendments of 1968 and especially those of 1971 strengthened this fear of this continuing and unstoppable process that would result in Kosova being a Republic. At this time, there was some evidence that through

---

[434] *Ibid.*, p.216
[435] *Ibid.*, p.229-230

some channels, such as oral messages sent to Fadil Hoxha, a diplomatic representative of Albania in Belgrade in 1970, Enver Hoxha asked Tito to rigorously refuse the Republic, but to find a solution in accordance with autonomy related to national rights. [436]

Even though the evidence that was presented in Tirana's archives remained of a speculative nature because its validity could never be confirmed from the "other side", that of Fadil Hoxha, while Yugoslavian archives, now under Serbian surveillance, continued to hold protected many of those documents of a strategic nature of that time along with other documents that had to do with the solution of this case. However, the messages of Enver Hoxha remained opened as they were sent to Albanian immigrants and immigrant centers in Germany (clubs and associations) through his agents, and also to the Marxist-Leninist groups placed in Germany, Belgium, Sweden, and other European countries that supported the negative statement toward Kosova Republic, that was considered "Tito's trap." At the same time, it was required that Albanians fight for their national rights in accordance with the Marxist-Leninist ideology that for a starting point had the war against "Yugoslavian revisionism" and "Tito's autonomy."[437]

But, in the 1981 protests the Republic of Kosova was still sought, despite the orders that the ideologist propaganda of Enver Hoxha put into action. Regardless of the fact that in those protests were many pronounced ideologist voices of Tirana's propaganda that had found their way into some illegal organizations, their main request would remain for Kosova Republic. This returned into a general request saving its inspiration from the 1968 historical protests, when this request, highlighted from the intellectual and political class of Kosova and from its intelligence in the political platform, for the first time was accepted by Kosova's Albanians and other regions of Yugoslavia.

---

[436] See: AQSH, p. 10/ Ap, year 1970-1971, file no. 387/1, p. 1, cited by Çeku, Ethem: *"Kosova në sfondin e diplomacisë së Jugosllavisë dhe të Shqipërisë 1945-1981,"* Prishtinë, 2009, p. 233.

[437] More on this issue: *"Vefasungschutz"* 1977. Annual report of the Ministry of Internal Affairs of Germany around the activities of the extreme political right, the extreme political left from non-Germans and their organization, supported by the outside, where an important place was dedicated to Marxist-Leninist groups that were supported by Tirana, p. 60-111.

Under these circumstances, it would be seen that those protests had opened a new historical chapter, which was not only related with Kosova and its future but also with the Yugoslav future and its geopolitical and geostrategic problems that dated from World War II. Continuing with many international cases with high potential for crises, it would soon feel that in the Balkan region huge movements were taking place that would also bring huge changes that were not directed by ideological means, but on the contrary, were directed by equality, liberty, and democratic means that had started to show up in Eastern countries too. Enver Hoxha would stop a bit and support Kosova's request for Republic. This time, he started to protect what he had called "Tito's trap toward Albanians that should not be believed." Furthermore, in the Eighth Congress of Labor Political Party of Albania, in November 1981, in Tirana, Enver Hoxha included the request for Kosova Republic in the Congress Resolution, making it an official document.

"The requirement of Kosova to recognize its Republic within the federation is a right requirement that does not hurt the existence of the Federation."[438]

Before coming to the position when the requirement of Kosova for Republic would be included in the documents of the Labor Party, which were administered by Enver Hoxha, the Albanian government should have been strengthened inside and outside and for this it would need three weeks. Thus, the first pronunciation was on April 8, in the Party's newspaper "Voice of the People," where the protests were described, but at the same time support was given to them without mentioning the main request: Kosova Republic. In this case, huge attention was dedicated to Yugoslavian charges against Albania to which were attributed not only the support toward Stalinist ideology, but also the involvement in the protest organizations. "Voice of the People" refused this categorically as slander, refusing any kind of intervention from the Albanian state in the organization of protests or in their stimulation. The refusal was done continually even by Enver Hoxha's cooperators, such as Ramiz Alia, who led the propaganda apparatus of that time inside and outside Albania, especially the Maxist-Leninist groups in some western countries, part of whom were

---

[438] See Hoxha, Enver: "Titistët," Tiranë, 1982. Fjala e Enver Hoxhës në Kongresin e Tetë të PPSH-së.

some individuals from Kosova that had asked for political asylum in those countries, and some that had been present in the 1981 protests.[439]

Without taking into consideration the charges and counter-charges of this nature in Belgrade-Tirana relations, on April 17, 1981, The "Voice of the People" for the first time openly supported the main request of protests for Kosova Republic, without mentioning its starting point from 1968 when it had legally been presented and from that time it had turned into an active political platform of Albanians in Kosova, which served continuous developments, such as that of 1981, through which this request accelerated and reached huge proportions. This newspaper that presented the beliefs of the Labor Party of Albania and that of the communist state of Albania, clarified the demand of Kosova's request for Republic evaluating that "Kosova was requiring the status of republic under the Yugoslavian Federation" saying that this status "represents the aspiration of one big population that was asking for its right to 'sovereign status' and not that of a 'national minority' that had been unfairly assigned to Jajca."[440]

"Voice of the People" continued to support the requirements of the protests of 1981, always using the defense as attack, drawing arguments such as those for Kosova's right for autonomy that was gained through the participation of Albanians in the fascist war and was refused after the war, but without mentioning the role that Enver Hoxha had determined Kosova to be part of "Serbian chauvinism." Enver Hoxha and his way of rule was ruined by Yugoslavian-Albanian cooperation, which never had the intention of finding a solution for unsolved issues, but had the intention of a communist victory under the international flag, whose dogma Tirana made official and saved for many years, regardless of its support

---

[439] See Shala, Blerim/Halili, Llukman/Reka, Hazir: "Unë, Ramiz Alia dëshmoj për historinë," Prishtinë, 1992.Talking about the 1981 protests and about whether Albania knew or not, Ramiz Alia declared: "Not at all! One might even say that the events of 1981 were completely unexpected for us. Not only were they unexpected, but often, even later, i.e. in 1982-83, when we had entered in a very fierce controversy with the Yugoslavs, we wondered who would be interested in the events of 1981. Because of the fact that the development of relations between Albania and Kosova were so favorable to the Albanians, these events inconvenienced more someone other than the Albanians themselves. I have personally thought many times that those events brought more benefits to Serbs." (P. 89).

[440] "Voice of People," April 17, 1981, p.1-3

toward Kosova Republic, which it wanted to be oriented toward Marxist-Leninist ideology although that was impossible and absurd.

However, Enver Hoxha agreed with the Republic of Kosova that from 1968 and on, the first time that the request of Kosova being Republic with a political and intellectual consensus was presented, had called it "Tito's trap against Albanians" to "American imperialist construct against Albanians and Albania that was done in cooperation with Yugoslavian revisionism."

Of course in order to do that, Enver Hoxha was obliged by internal and external circumstances, where external circumstances were the most important, because Kosova Republic in the future relations with the Yugoslavian Federation led Albania toward a federal union that was not dominated by Serbs. In this case, it was not an ally of the Soviet Union, who represented an icon to Enver Hoxha, and he had lately warned them that the "danger was coming from East, from Moscow, who was asking for Yugoslavian destabilization along with that of Albanians, in order to turn back its hegemony into these parts." [441]

Although the danger for Albania and Yugoslavia was coming from the East, Enver Hoxha did not give up his ideology of seeing the West as "imperialists" that should be fought by all means. This applied especially for the United States of America and NATO. He continued to call NATO America's "instruments of imperialist aggression". It was noticed that even after he started to support Kosova's requirement for Republic, that was estimated as an Albanian right to be treated equally with other countries, a right that had been acquired during the fascist war, Enver Hoxha continued to call USA and western countries "imperialist," while in the immigrant clubs (Albanian workers from Kosova and other Yugo-slavian regions with temporary work in western countries, especially in Germany) and in the diaspora continued to spark Marxist-Leninist ideologies. He even started the creation of such organizations that acted in Germany, Belgium and other states. Those groups cooperated with Albanian-German, Albanian-Belgium, Albanian-Italy Friendship Associa-tions and others who were mostly left extremists with Maoist leaning that

---

[441] See Buxhovi, Jusuf: *"Kthesa historike,"* second book, Prishtina, 2009, p. 111; Shala, Blerim/Halili, Llukman? Reka, Hazir: *"Unë, Ramiz Alia dëshmoj për historinë,"* Prishtina, 1992, p. 91.

were part of the "Red Brigades." Those groups received instructions from Tirana to protect Kosova Republic, but under Marxist-Leninist ideology.

In some European centers (Brussels, Bonn, Paris, and Zurich) the bodies of these organizations had started to be published: "Voice of Kosova," "Freedom," "Union" and others that acted as transmitters of "Voice of the people" and "Union." Those flyers, which entered illegally in Kosova and other Yugoslavian regions, had the purpose of sparking Marxist-Leninist ideology.[442]

This ideologist activity of Tirana had no chance of mobilization toward Albanian intelligence, which had no reason to substitute a communist dogma that was responsible for every tragedy of Kosova and Albanians with another fanatic dogma, such as that of Stalinism, from which even Moscow had resigned. However, this was beneficial for Belgrade to discourage the request for Kosova Republic and other political requirements of Albanians, which were legally announced and were protected by Yugoslavian police. Even more, on this premise the state violence of 1981 toward Albanian youth, culture, and science was supported, when one small reason was enough for multiple imprisonments to occur, most of which ended with severe sentences.

The Serbian Campaign against Kosova's Autonomy and the Beginning of the Militarized "Peace"

> *Approval of the Political Platform for Kosova opened the path for a long and troublesome process of ideologist differentiation that included all Albanians for many years. Along with many imprisonments, punishments, and job dismissals of many known intellectuals and publishers, were isolation measures (holding them in unofficial imprisonment and without stated time because of "security reasons.") Along with those measures, the wide campaign of ideologist differentiation included also the University of Kosova and also other educational and cultural institutions, when many scientists and publishers were dismissed from their jobs for not accepting the political platform, nor the ideolo-*

---

[442] About Marxist-Leninist propaganda of Tirana to Marxist-Leninist groups in Germany and immigration clubs, See: *"Verfassungsschutz"* 1977-1987, Bonn, published by Bundesminister des Innern, Referat Öffentlichkeitsbarbeit.

gist differentiation.-Return of the Yugoslav military head of Serbia (General Lubicic) scores the beginning of the "quiet" military strategy toward Yugoslavian federation that was mirrored with the deprivation of Kosova from Territorial Defense, that was gained with the 1974 Constitution. - Start of the "Serbian National Movement" in Kosova and its use by Milosevic to impose constitutional changes. - Miners strike of Trepca and December's strikes of Albanians through Kosova in defense of Kosova Consitution.

After the approval of "Political Platform for Kosova" by the Central Committee of the Communist Party of Yugoslavia in November 1981, where the qualification of Kosova's protests as "hostile" and "counterrevolutionary" by "Albanian nationalists and irredentism positions," was accepted, a qualification that, as will be seen, was in accordance with Serbian requirements headed in Belgrade and its strategy that came from the "Blue Book" to return Yugoslavia into a Unitarian state led by Serbia. This qualification started the phase of political return of Serbia in Kosova, but now in the role of tireless prosecutor making investigations and raising charges against any action made for the benefit of Albanians being treated equally with the others. It had the purpose of preparing the preconditions for the future changes of the constitution through which in the name of "the creation of Serbian unity" along with "the strengthening of the federation on the principles of cohabitation and deepening of Serbian unity and brotherhood," would return Kosova to the constitutional position of 1953, to the level of "region."

With the approval of "Political Platform for Kosova" that Serbia had imposed on the political leader of Yugoslavia, but was also followed by harsh reactions such as those of Tito's cooperator, Vladimir Bakaric, who said that "the Platform" was unnecessary when the country already had the Constitution, laws, and political programs,[443] in reality pointed the beginning of the "quiet" military strategy against the Yugoslavian Federation. This was mostly noticed with the deprivation of Kosova from the Territorial Defense right as an autonomous segment, foreseen in the 1974 Constitution. According to this, Kosova and other country units had the autonomy system under the Territorial Defense, commanded and elected by Kosova, with military staff composed of Albanian officers and reserve

---

[443] "Vjesnik," Zagreb, December 2, 1981

units of thirty thousand individuals, separated into many battalions and three divisions. The Territorial Defense of Kosova, in accordance with the law, also had "defensive" arms from simple caliber weapons to 125 millimeter balls and some anti-aircraft systems of bacteriological defense along with those of infrastructure that could be supplied by another division in a critical situation.

Using the order of "extraordinary measures," which had come into force on April 2, 1981, when the Yugoslavian Leadership upon Serbian request, announced an extraordinary condition in Kosova on the grounds of being defended from the counterrevolution. This situation was saved for many years and under this order that allowed it "to behave in accordance with the situation," the General Staff of the Yugoslav Army asked the Socialist Federal Republic of Yugoslavia (SFRY) Leadership to pass the control of Territorial Defense to the General Staff of People's Army of Yugoslavia (YNA) for the security and defense of the country. This measure, considered as "temporary," even though it was counterconstitutional, was approved by the Socialist Federal Republic of Yugoslavia (SFRY) Leadership on December 11, 1981,[444] when the "instruction" for "concrete action" was published "in order not to endanger the country's capacity to be defended." This instruction supported the Territorial Defense of Kosova against autonomy rights that were guaranteed by the 1974 Constitution. This measure was taken without even warning the Kosova Leadership and its officials, that according to law were commanders of the Territorial Defense of Kosova. It was this state of emergency that allowed such actions.

Even though this action was taken after six months, in fact, the Territorial Defense of Kosova along with the Special Police Forces of Kosova were "neutralized" from April 3 when the implementation of the state of emergency started. The commander of the Territorial Defense of Kosova was deprived of all his competences, while the weaponry, storage, and organizational structures of the defense were passed into the hands of the Central Staff of People's Army of Yugoslavia (YNA), which put a part of the operational command in Prishtina. Also, on April 3, all arms of the Territorial Defense of Kosova were blocked from the special units of the People's Army of Yugoslavia (YNA) along with military objects. Similar events happened with the reserve units, that were intended to serve

---

[444] "Polititika," Belgrade, December 12, 1981

"temporarily," holding only a small number of them (2000 in all Kosova), but without arms and under the command of Serbian officers or locals that were assigned by Belgrade.

In fact, Serbian militaries of the political leadership of Belgrade were brought to "quiet" the military strategy toward the constitutional situation of Yugoslavia, led by Nikola Lubicic, a member of the Serbian Leadership, who was a Tito cooperator for many years and was a retired Minister of Defense (later replaced by Petar Gracani). The Serbian leadership of Belgrade did not occasionally determine Tito's military general as a leader of State Leadership. This was done because he had the military experience that Serbia needed in those circumstances to gain the Yugoslavian Army, which happened when its command performed according to Serbian requirements in the federation, especially to those that created conditions for the Belgrade politics to act unlawfully such as the extraordinary measures that were needed to hold Kosova and the Federation under pressure. Also, however, at those times the internal situation, "Serbian unity" within the Federation was a priority and it was also important for Serbia to remain an international partner and after the death of Tito, observe with attention any changes that might lead to a change in the course of Yugoslavia in relation to areas of interest. Since in that phase, Serbia was not interested in leaving the impression that it wanted to change "Tito's way," but on the contrary, in order to save the partnership with the West and especially with the Non-aligned Movement, which played the role of leaders, the Yugoslavian Army, influenced by Belgrade politics, entered in some new army arrangements with USA, Germany, France, and Great Britain. With the last one it reached an agreement for the production of a modern military helicopter; with France for the modernization of military airplanes (Orao, Soko, Jastreb) that Yugoslavia produced for their military purposes that in the future should be included in the army of some Arabian and African countries; with Germany for the production of "Leopard" tanks, through which the Non-aligned countries of Africa and Asia would be armed, while with Americans, the Yugoslavian Army signed an agreement for the production of some rackets with mid-action circle, which were sold to Arabian and Islamic countries (Iran and Pakistan). Yugoslavia played the main role in those productions.[445]

---

[445] More on this issue: "Der Spiegel;," no. 33/1982

With those arrangements with Western countries, that brought more than 3 - 4 billion dollars in 1983 from the sale of arms. Yugoslavia managed to be the fifth largest exporter of arms in the world (after USA, Soviet Union, Great Britain, and France). This created good opportunities for the Yugoslavian economy to handle the economic crises that followed immediately after Tito's death, when the trade deficit was more than 4 billion dollars, while debts were more than 17 billion dollars.[446]

As will be seen, the Yugoslavian Army and its military industry closely related with those of other NATO countries for the production of arms during the next 5 - 6 years, when the political situation in the country worsened, saved the economical stability of the country. This was considered by the Serbian politics of Belgrade as a continual support to surpass the Federation with military strengthening, which should also gain the support of Kosova in order to pass the test that should then go through the Federation. In this aspect, some of the main European countries, but also USA, should support Belgrade in order to continue to save the political situation. This means that the military position of the country had been strengthened[447] and as would be seen, would in turn support and strengthen the Serbian politics, and would be mirrored with the appearance of Milosevic and his known course of destroying the Yugoslavia that was created by Tito, a creature with which the Western countries had mostly benefited.

Of course, the "silent" military strategy toward the Yugoslav Federation that continued to affect the Yugoslavian politics toward being that of Serbia, would continue in that "silent" form until 1991, when the war against Slovenia and Croatia first appeared. Meanwhile, Serbian militarists that dominated the Yugoslavian Army, acted outside their duty in politics, such as the case of Lubicic in Serbia, but also within their duty, such as the garniture of Tito's "new generals" mainly educated in the American military academy (Kadijevic, Perisic, Hadjic, Ratko Mladic) and others that supported the hegemonic course of Belgrade politics and turned into the military commanders that ruined Yugoslavia and started their hegemonic programs of genocide against Bosnians and Croatians.

In the meantime, from the beginning of the Yugoslavian Army intervention in Kosova on April 2, 1981, when it participated in the oppression

---

[446] Meier, Victor: "*Wie Jugoslawien verspielt wurde,*" 1995.
[447] See Rulman, Hans in "Der Spiegel," 33/1983

of demonstrations (at that time, Ratko Mladic was the commander the Yugoslav army in Prishtina) that exploded with the request of Kosova Republic, and continued to April 23, 1989 (surpassed with tanks Kosova's Assembly in order to secure the constitutional changes that would ruin Kosova's right to autonomy) the Yugoslavian Army presence in Kosova secured the territory to Serbian politics. In this way, Lubicic, as an official of the Serbian Leadership, militarized the Serbian politics from 1981 to 1986, when instead of him, another of Tito's generals, Peter Gracan, came while the other generals (Kadijevic, Minister of Defense) held the political leader of Yugoslavia under constant surveillance so he would not impede the Serbian politics in Kosova, Vojvodina, and Montenegro, when Milosevic started the so-called "yogurt revolution" in order to bring his vassals into power.

In this aspect, the Yugoslavian Army and its generals' role to violently change the Serbian-Kosova reports from 1989, even those of the Federation, remained crucial. What is more important to see in this development, is that "silent" military strategy, ideologist differentiation of Albanians in Kosova, which cost the imprisonment of many activists of the movement for Kosova Republic and the cleansing of the educational system at all levels, including military schools.

Two such processes against Albanian army cadets and officers were held in Zagreb and Bjelina in 1986. Thus, from 1981 to 1989, 168 Albanian officers and 998 soldiers in Yugoslavian Army were imprisoned and sentenced by military courts. In the meantime, the safety of the Albanian soldiers in the Yugoslav army (Serving in the Yugoslav army at that time was mandatory and included all nationalities) was in jeopardy, and during this period, 63 Albanian soldiers were murdered.[448]

This pursuit culminated with the staged tragedy of Paraqin barracks, when Aziz Kelmendi was declared guilty for the murder of six officers,

---

[448] See the notes of *"Këshillit për Mbrotjen e të Drejtave dhe Lirive të Njeriut në Kosovës,"* and that of "Komitetit kosovar të Helsnikut" that present the Helsink Committee of 1989 when they visited Prishtina. The names of those that were imprisoned and murdered are presented in this file during the military service of YNA in the period 1981-1989 and other data of this nature, associated with the court processes and other documents. Those materials served to open the debate by the American Committee for Human Rights in the Council of American Congress for Human Rights in Washington on April 1990.

who were accused of carrying out this massacre with "irredentist and nationalist motives."

"Kelmendi shot Yugoslavia" was said in YNA's statement.[449]

In a predetermined process, all Albanian youth were sentenced with harsh prison for "participation in an organized crime with political motives."

In accordance with this statement, there were also other activities of the Yugoslavian Army Special Services and those of the Informative services (UDBA) against Albanian migration to the West, especially against the political prosecutors that had been sheltered in Western countries and continued their operations within the diaspora, and also against those in the European countries in the support of the request for Kosova Republic. This prosecution was subject to mysterious assassinations along with many others that tried to organize the Kosova Republic outside the Marxist-Leninist ideologist recipes, that were coming from different centers and that according to German sources were very active.[450]

So, at the time of those criminal and terrorist activities that were led by the Yugoslavian military politics, after the "silent" military strategy of spring 1981, the process of political differentiation was developed in Kosova called "collective psychoses toward an entire population," which took on different forms of prosecution and police "processing".[451] In 1986, Belgrade created the political base for the beginning phase of constitutional changes, through which, as it was said, Serbia aimed for "internal unity," while Yugoslavia aimed for "state stability." In this direction, after changes that had taken place in the Yugoslavian leadership, where Fadil Hoxha was replaced by Sinan Hasani and Ali Shukriu went into Party Leadership, the Yugoslav assembly approved a resolution to deploy Serbian-Yugoslavian controlling groups into Kosova that in fact would take care of the last "hostile centers" among the administrative and judicial systems of Kosova. By this resolution, these centers were entirely subject to Serbian surveillance and these Serbian groups were given authority to make changes in the courts, assign prosecutors, and assign

---

[449] See "Politika," Belgrade, 1987

[450] See the reports of the Ministry of Internal Affairs of Germany presented in "Verfassungsschutz," 1977-1987.

[451] See the German novelist Gynter Gras declaration given for the newspaper "Renaissance" May 22, 1995.

other people in the court and police system as well as all other administrative functions of Kosova. Those groups also had the "right" to dismiss even the leaders of municipal assemblies from their work if they were suspected of discrimination of Serbs and Montenegrins by Albanian nationalists.

Under these circumstances, the process of changing the constitution started, where Serbia started returning to its hegemonic strategy in Kosova and Vojvodina in order to then to continue on with the federation. Since the constitutional changes, according to the constitution in force (Article 49), Belgrade sought to eliminate with strong political means (as used in Kosova in the prior five years) any constitutional mechanism that affected the equality of the federation where Kosova and her right to autonomy was involved.

However, conscious that the second one did not find the support of other members of the federation (especially that of Slovenia and Croatia) that would not allow this because of their interests, the Serbian leadership of Belgrade concentrated on the constitutional changes internally, in order first to ruin the regions and then continue with the federation. In this direction, Belgrade's leaders took measures to make changes in Kosova which would stop Kosova from having autonomy. Thus, Sinan Hasani was sent as the leader of the state instead of Fadil Hoxha, who after the 1981 protests was passive for fear that he could be followed by the court, as happened later by the request of "insulted Serbian women." Sinan Hasani had published a book that critiqued Kosova's political leadership, firstly Bakalli and then those that had already been eliminated in 1981 for being Albanian "nationalists" and Tito's cooperators.[452] The current leader of political party was also replaced by Ali Shukriu who was one of the first people who had accepted the assessment of Kosova Republic as "counterrevolutionary." As such, he was the leader of the ideologist differentiation staff from where all the prison lists, cleansing of universities and educational, cultural, and state institutions from "counterrevolutionaries" had come. In Kosova, Azem Vllasi became the new party leader, who from 1981 as "an alternative" of previous leadership was active in the political life that Belgrade had defined in its content and

---

[452] Hasani, Sinan: *"Kosova – të vërtetat dhe mashtrimet,"* Prishtinë, 1986.

form. Belgrade had acted in that way to assign its vassals into Kosova's political life, who helped Belgrade during constitutional changes.

Despite the fact that Serbia had taken the political and state leadership of Kosova under its control, despite the numerous imprisonments, pursuit of Albanian educational staff from institutions and their replacement by Belgrade vassals, the moment that it opened the case for constitutional changes, Serbia encountered difficulties at all levels of Kosova. Thus, it encountered difficulties from the highest leaders of the political party, those leaders that had been chosen by many careful processes from the platform of political ideology for Kosova brought in 1981 continuing with the power institutions that were not ready to resign from the fundamental changes, as that of the federation consensus and its subjectivity. Furthermore, even Vllasi, who was shown to be too generous to Serbian nationalists, accepting separated schools, where Serbs were privileged, creating special departments where Serbs were employed in companies and also building Serbian shelters in Kosova, did not accept the change of Article 49 of the constitution which meant changes into different republic and regions.

All the political developments from spring 1987 to 1989 were connected with the paradigm of Article 49 of the Constitution, which included the overall Yugoslavian political factor, mostly supporting Serbia, where also the political leader of Kosova was separated into a "protector of autonomy", and "a protector of changes." This differentiation among Albanians was getting bigger and bigger and also included other social levels of Kosova, which, without any support, tried to be aligned with the strong people, although they did not share the same opinions with them.

Seeing that the case was getting difficult, Serbia started using the so-called "Council for Protection and Self-Existence of Serbs and Montenegrins in Kosova," known as the "Staff" of Fushe Kosova which was headed by Milovan Solovic, Bogdan Kecman, and Bosko Dimitrijevic. It also included many Serbian politicians of Kosova that started using this Council for political pressure. The Fushe Kosova "Staff", supervised by the Belgrade "Staff," headed by Dobrica Cosic and Serbia's academic writers gathered into "Francuska 7", where the Writers Association of Serbia started with meetings and protest marches toward Serbia and Belgrade requesting to make Kosova part of Serbia otherwise all of them would migrate from Kosova!

This "threat" was pressured by the political leadership of Kosova to accept the changes, without using the autonomy, and this was used for other parts of Yugoslavia too (Vojvodina and Montenegro), in order to make obvious what was going to happen.

This "movement" very quickly included the Serbian Orthodox Church (the first aspirator), the Writers Association of Serbia, and the Science Academy of Serbia that supported it by all means. The academy also created the "Serbian Memorandum," which had been taken over by the writer Dobrica Cosic. This Memorandum turned into the platform of this Movement and Serbian politics, and also an action plan for the Yugoslavian collapse.

The "Council for Protection and Self-Existence of Serbs and Montenegrins in Kosova" and many militants that were recruited on institutional bases were meant to create an atmosphere of fear around Kosova among Albanians but also among the political and intellectual levels in order for the constitutional changes to be accepted as Serbia had proposed them.

Those threats that went beyond Kosova to reach Croatia and Slovenia as well as other parts of the country, that hoped that even after "Tito's death, Tito would remain alive," were supported by the Yugoslavian Army, who had created the "silent" military strategy in the federation, while now they were openly stating their support for this movement whose purpose was the collapse of Yugoslavia under Serbian nationalists and hegemonic ideology.

Under these circumstances, Slobodan Milosevic came to state power as leader of the "Serbian Movement for Changes" that presented the will for the return of Yugoslavia to Serbia, which would be headed by Belgrade. The Serbian national interests were announced in the "Memorandum" of Serbian academics, where Tito was pronounced an enemy of the Serbian population, Yugoslavia of AVNOJ a construct against Serbian interests, and the 1974 constitution as the guilty factor for Serbia's destruction.

Even though at the beginning Milosevic was "distanced" from the "harsh language of the Memorandum" but not from its content, it was accepted because it had as supporters the Serbian intelligence and the Serbian Orthodox Church, and at the same time they were the first to raise the alarm for "losing Kosova" and "its invasion by Arnauts," who "with the problems that they were causing," "helped by Tito's communists" had ruined the Serbian medieval cradle.

As it will be seen, the language that Milosevic used in this direction did not differ much from that of Patrick Pavle, who blessed "the Serbian National Movement" gathered around the "Staff" of Fushe Kosova and all its actions that had been taken from the beginning of the Yugoslavian collapse whose purpose was genocide against Bosnians and Albanians.

Milocevic started to use the noticeable "Serbian patriotism momentum" to make changes to the constitution. He stated in his meeting in Fushe Kosova on April 24, 1987, organized by "Movement" for protests against "Albanian nationalists," and repeated it two years later on June 28, in Gazimestan, on the occasion of the commemoration of the 600th anniversary of the Battle of Kosova, when he proclaimed war if "Serbian interests will not be followed."

Milosevic started to carry the "patriotic momentum" into other places too, especially in Vojvodina and Montenegro, but also into Bosnia and Herzegovina. Those countries were threatened to "fight in order to protect Yugoslavia" and through this threat they spread the news of the formation of a new Yugoslavia in accordance to Serbian politics.

This threat was understood "right" in Montenegro and Macedonia, who joined Shkup and Titograd around the Milosevic platform for the creation of a united Serbia, and for the constitutional changes to be supported in Kosova, no matter how that would be achieved. Pro-Serbian politicians from Macedonia (Mojsov, Gligorov, Kolishevski and others) officially supported the Serbian request and said that they "understand the Serbian concern that was presented by the Serbian population".[453]

The arrival of Milosevic in Kosova on April 24, 1987 and his support for the Serbian nationalist requests increased even more the pressure toward the political leadership of Kosova and other structures, such that even though they were under complete submission, they were not ready to accept these changes. This was made clear in all the meetings that were held for constitutional changes, where it was made clear that Kosova's population would react in order to protect its case despite the threats and the military and police forces that were present in Kosova, which were

---

[453] See the declaration of Llazar Mojsovit in Yugoslavian Assembly on May 23, 1981, published in "Politika" of Belgrade

ready to start the war in order to be protected from the "counterrevolution."

But, when the population was used for political purposes, as Milosevic did, even Azem Vllasi returned to the mobilization of the Albanian labor class to oppose Milosevic. Thus, using the atmosphere at that time about the constitutional changes as a "base," whose changes were opposed even by Albanian politics, that were not ready to accept the role of betrayal, Azem Vllasi and his "group" decided to hit the streets with Trepca's miners and start the "protest march in defense of the constitution" and also start the protest against the political pressure by Belgrade in Kosova, that aimed for the collapse of Kosova's autonomy.

In fact, the return of Vllasi in defense of the Albanians presented not only his disconnection, but also the disconnection of a political group of Kosova (Kaqusha Jashari and others) that until then had supported the ideologist differentiation in Kosova. This differentiation for many years had brought great damage by supporting discriminative measures against Albanians and privileging Serbs in order for them to remain in Kosova or to make "the migrants pressured by Albanian nationalists" come back. However, lately the political group of Kosova had started not to follow those Yugoslavian political attitudes that pressured Albanians to accept the constitutional changes in accordance with Serbia. Some of them did not accept the violence toward historical events, such as that of the Federal Room of Yugoslavian Assembly of November 15, where the Bujan Resolution of 1943/44 was announced as a political not a judicial act. Thus, in the seventeenth meeting of CC and CPY, which had ended with a severe polarization among Kosova (Vllasi and Jashari) and Serbian representatives (Sokolovic, Angelkovic and others) that were supported by Macedonian representatives (Mojsovi, Kolishevski, Glikorovi, and others) had started the conflict among Kosova's "rebels" (Vllasi, Kaqusha, Jashari) with their Serbian supervisors that ended with Belgrade's victory because there was the risk of losing the constitution battle. With CC and CPY instructions, the Provincial Committee of CPY decided to discharge Vllasi from this forum with the justification that he could not be present in two forums at the same time, that of CPY and CC and Kosova. A similar thing happened with Kaqusha Jashari; she had a severe confrontation with the political leader of Serbia, and as a result was also discharged from the leadership of KK and CP of Kosova. Ramiz Kolgeci, who was an official of the Kosova Leadership, was now appointed as Party Leader.

429

Thus, Belgrade was discharging those people that for many years had served with confidence, but now had decided to confront Belgrade.

At the time that the Provincial Committee was in session, where those "cleanings" were taking place and Belgrade was planning its final attack that would note the collapse of Kosova's autonomy, late in the night, a thousand workers marched toward Prishtina to support and encourage the Provincial Committee of the Communist Party of Kosova to accept neither pressured, nor collective resignations.

On November 17, 1988, in the morning, after the miners of the third shift left the mine, they joined the miners of the first shift and decided to express their revolt against the political situation of Kosova with the organization of a protest march from the "Trepca" mine of Stari Tergu to Prishtina. Miners that were joined by other workers marched 52 kilometers on foot. In the Sports Hall of Kosova in Prishtina more than three thousand miners and workers arrived from "Trepca."[454]

The workers movement in Kosova from November 17 to 19 turned into a wide movement, joined by students, professors, and other social levels, that marched from many different centers on foot. On November 19, in Prishtina, more than a hundred thousand workers arrived from all parts of Kosova. It was one of the biggest movements of its kind that with the slogan "No to Serbia" had put all Kosova's population into action.

These protests that were full of pro-Yugoslavian slogans, such as "Long Live Tito," "Long live Brotherhood" and others, and where Vllasi, Kaqusha Jashari and some Yugoslavian leaders were cheered, had the aim of protecting the 1974 Constitution, for which, as it was said, only Kosova was fighting because others knew that this was already a done deal.

In response to 1974 Constitutional "defense," in the New Belgrade, in the Serbian center of the Yugoslavian capital, which politically was not considered as such anymore, a meeting called "Union and Brotherhood," was held that night, where a hundred thousand Serbs protested against the Albanian gatherings, calling them "counterrevolutionary acts." The next day, the Yugoslavian Leadership called for an immediate stop to Albanian "national gatherings" in Kosova. One day later, the Conference of the Communist Party of Serbia was held where Milosevic called the late situation in Kosova a "national and counterrevolutionary renaissance of Albanians" to stop the constitutional changes that were considered to be

---

[454] See Abrashi, Aziz/Kavaja, Burhan: "Epopeja e minatoreve," Prishtina, 1996, p.20-22

crucial for the Serbian and Yugoslavian fate. In this case, Milosevic threatened Albanians that Serbia was going to continue its plans and Kosova should accept them. He took the support of the CC and CPY Leadership, Macedonian Vasil Tupurkovski, for this ultimatum, who showed his "concern for the counterrevolutionary revival in Kosova." as it had happened in 1981. He even posed the question: "how can this happen?" It required yet another joint action against Kosova.

In this spirit it was also brought up in the chairmanship of the CC and CPY Leadership of November 23, led by Croatian Stipe Shuvar, who fully supported the highest political forum of Serbia and asked for this to happen at the state line, although it was known that the federation units, regarding Kosova, acted under the dictates of Serbs.

But, the late discussions of the CC of Serbia and the CC of Yugoslavia, announced the rapid deployment of the state of emergency in Kosova, even though, as such, with the exception of "special measures" as well as its management according to "administrative guidelines," was present from 1981.

In accordance with those guidelines, on November 23, 1988, the Executive Council of Kosova decided that the Provincial Secretariat of Internal Affairs order the prohibition of citizen circulation and entrance in public places in respective regions, especially those of massive gatherings. Entrance of large groups in public places in Prishtina and other cities of Kosova, and any organized arrival in Prishtina was prohibited.

Since, all the roads for public protests had been closed, though open for Serbs, "Trepca" miners again appeared on February 22, 1989 with their organized strike. Around two hundreds miners were closed in the eighth corridor, 800 meters beneath the ground. Thus, with the miners' hunger strike, the protest movement took a new form, that resulted in a severe response from Belgrade, in the spirit of that what Milosevic had declared in Fushe Kosova, that the changes would be made "with or without willingness."

The hunger strike of the "Trepca" miners endured eight days. One of the requests was the "guarantee of the Constitutional foundations of 1974" with the warning that the attitudes that were not in harmony with the constitutional amendments would not be accepted. Only those attitudes that were in accordance with 1974 Constitution would be accept-ed.[455]

Also, one of the miners' requests was the removal of Rrahman Morina from the leader position of the Provincial Committee of CP Leadership of Kosova, with the justification that he had not complied with miners' requests. Along with this, the resignations of Ali Shukriu and Hysamedin Azemi were also called for, Milosevic's most reliable individu-als who were committed to making the constitutional changes of Kosova's autonomy collapse.

The miners' strike ended on February 28, after they were promised that their requests would be taken into account, so the required people had already resigned. The language that was used in this case was deceiv-ing; euphemisms were used to disguise the real situation, where the next day the "resignations" were accepted neither by the CP and KK Leader-ship of Kosova, nor by Milosevic. On the contrary, as will be seen, the final protest of the miners was used by the Serbs to implement the final phase of their plan to violently destroy Kosova's autonomy.

Beside this awaited epilogue, the "Trepca" miners' strike was closely followed by the intellectuals of Kosova, who had supported the strike from the beginning, being in solidarity with the miners. The Writers Association, known until that time for their intellectual organization against the nationalist and hegemonic course of Serbian academics and writers toward Kosova, during all this time held literacy meetings, under the slogan "in the support of underground assembly," in which almost all Albanians writers of Kosova had participated.

As soon as the strike started, an intellectual group, with the academic initiative of Gazmend Zajmi and historian Zekeria Cena, started the development of an intellectual appeal "For the institutional support and affirmation of the constitutional position of Kosova on the basis of the fundamental principles of the FSRY constitution," which was signed by 125 Albanian intellectuals, starting with academic Idriz Ajeti, Mark Krasniqi, Rexhep Qosja, Gazmend Zajmi, Dëvish Rozhaja, Anton Çeta, Zekeria Cana, Fehmi Agani, Hajrullah Gorani and other well-known writers, by Dr. Ibrahim Rugova, and by the majority of the Writers Association members and other intellectuals from the University of Kosova, the Institute of Albanology, the Institute of History, "Rilindja,"

---

[455] *Ibid.*, p.34

and the Radio Television of Kosova. The 215 Appeal was made public on February 21, directed toward the Serbian Assembly and the opinions of Yugoslavia. [456]

Although the 215 Appeal was more a desperate plea for Serbia to protect something that had no chance of being protected, such as the 1974 Constitution, where the editors of this text took a step beyond the request for Kosova Republic that was requested by political and civilian identity in the 1968 and 1981 protests, for which the Albanian youth had shed blood and had been prosecuted for many years, and that many of them were still sentenced for the Kosova Republic request, Serbia started a follow-up campaign against the drafters and signatories by ideologically differentiating them from the Communist Party, continuing with the expulsion from their jobs. This was a "solving issues" case with those that tried to strengthen the 1974 Constitution, which formally was nearing its end.

The Violent Abolishment of Autonomy and the Fourth Serbian Occupation of Kosova

> *Vllasi and other leaders of the"Trepca" imprisonment and the determination of house arrest for many Albanian intellectuals and politicians opened the last phase of the violent collapse of Kosova's autonomy. Outside the political debate, in the last moments, the 47th amendment was introduced, according to which, Serbia had the opportunity to destroy Kosova's autonomy.- In the big protests in Ferizaj and Prishtina and other cities of Kosova against the collapse of autonomy by the Yugoslavian police and army, 13 persons along with hundreds others were murdered.- The isolation of 253 intellectuals and the severe violence exercised against those people that disturbed the European opinion.- The starting phase of Serbia's plan for Kosova with the imposition of violent measures in educational, cultural, and administrative institutions.- Court, police, and municipalities were "cleansed" of Albanian "nationalists" and were substituted with Serbs brought from Serbia.- The arrival of Milosevic in Gazimestan on July 28, 1989, and the arrival of one million Serbs to commemorate the 600th anniversary of the Kosova Battle.- Declaration of war for Kosova and Yugoslavia.*

---

[456] *Ibid.*, p.34

On March 1, 1989, Serbia finished its last preparation to bring Kosova to the state of emergency, in which the constitutional changes were imposed. The last night of February, on the 28th, when the news regarding the end of the Trepca miners' strike was announced and the "resignations" of Rrahman Morina, Ali Shukriu, and Husamedin Azemi occurred, the largest protests ever seen were held in theYugoslavian capital of Belgrade. More than one million protesters were united in Belgrade to call the students of Belgrade, the "Staff" of Fushe Kosova, the Serbian academics and writers, and those of the Orthodox Church of Serbia, which played the spiritual role of nationalist and hegemonic ideology that exploded for more than a year now. Protests started in the Student Center of New Belgrade and continued to the center of the Yugoslavian capital, before the Federal Assembly.

With the slogan "In protection of Yugoslavia" the protesters asked the Yugoslavian Leadership to react against "Albanian nationalists and chauvinists in Kosova" (even though the Leadership had ordered the placement of the state of emergency two days before) in order for Kosova to be part of Serbia, which would "bring back the confidence of long-suffering Serbs" to "remain in their historical and spiritual Albanian land that was taken from them by Albanians." The protest started with the request for imprisonment of Vllasi and "other nationalist leaders of Albania" and also set the state of emergency.

Students, as a condition to be separated, asked for the presence of the President of the Yugoslavian Leadership in the protest, the Bosnian Raif Dizadarevic, who had supported the illegal pressure of Serbian leadership in Belgrade.

At night, Dizadrevic showed up at the protest that was held before the Federal Assembly, where he said everything that the prompter whispered to him. Thus, he said that Serbia would be unique by the constitutional changes that should be accepted by Kosova and that in Kosova a state of emergency would be placed in order to overcome the Albanian nationalism and chauvinism.

Milosevic showed up there too, who, satisfied with what he had achieved there, told the protesters that Vllasi would be arrested. He ended his speech with the threat that "all Yugoslavian enemies will be imprisoned!"[457]

The protests dispersed only after accepting those promises from the President of the Federal Socialist Republic of Yugoslavia (FSRY) Leadership and from Milosevic about the "enemies" imprisonments. That night, Azem Vllasi, member of CC of CP of Yugoslavia, was imprisoned. Along with Vllasi, Trepca's directors and Stari Tergu's leaders were also imprisoned.

After the imprisonment of Vllasi and the others, that day an emergency meeting was held by the Yugoslavian Assembly, which also marked the end of the actions. In that meeting, delegates heard the Macedonian Lazar Mojsov's (member of Yugoslavian Leadership) speech, where he talked about the "discovery" of a "famous document" that was coming from the "Albanian staff for revolution," prepared by "an Albanian communist group" (with camouflaged names due to conspiracy reasons), which supposedly was made in February 1989 with three main action phases.

The starting phase included the organization of general passive strikes in companies, factories, schools, and universities. According to Mosjov, this phase was successfully realized and its main goal was to keep the miners on strike underground.

The second phase was to start on March 15, to coordinate with the day that the Kosova Assembly would debate on the Serbian Constitution, and was also symbolically related to the explosive anniversary of the counterrevolution of 1981.

The last phase included an armed revolt with the general request that "We Albanians can only talk with arms. There is no time for reconciliation. The time has come."[458]

After Mosjov's speech and the material provided to the debaters "for internal usage" by the Security Service of State, where "the organizers' names of the Albanian protest of November 1988 were indicated," the Yugoslavian Assembly concluded with an action plan not only to quickly prosecute the "counterrevolutionary staff" in Kosova, but also for the prevention of any further organized action. According to the Yugoslavian Assembly proposal, on March 8 the Yugoslavian Assembly started the

---

[457] See the News Agency "TANJUG," March 2, 1989

[458] Cana, Zekeria: *"Apeli 215 i intelektualëve shqiptarë,"* 2001, p. 166.

implementation of the state of emergency measures in Kosova, whose purpose was the "constitutional protection, law and public order maintenance, civilian and social property security, normalization of life and work, renewal of traditional faith." [459]

Kosova's Assembly accepted and supported the state of emergency measures of the FSRY Leadership. The setting of the state of emergency in Kosova, even though not officially declared, had continued its operations for many years already in accordance with its special decrees for "special cases" and also asked for the approval of amendments for the Serbian Constitutional changes. Regarding this case, it was said that "the approval of those amendments was of high importance, not only for the Province and Socialist Republic of Serbia, but also for Yugoslavian stability; therefore, those amendments should be approved on time."[460]

After the decision of the Executive Council of Kosova, whose leader was Nazmi Mustafa, who started the implementation of the state of emergency in Kosova, the overall action for the preparation of the political atmosphere for the implementation of the Serbian constitutional amendments was based on the Kosova Presidency and the Presidency of the Kosova Party and its leaders: Remzi Kolgeci and Rrahman Morina. After the imprisonment of Vllasi and the placement of the state of emergency, the confidants (Remzi Kolgeci and Rrahman Morina) of Milosevic, used their political and state "authority" to implement the constitutional amendments, through which Kosova lost its autonomy right and returned under Serbia, as it was violently placed from 1945 to 1967.

Thus, the two leaderships (that of Kosova and that of the Communist Party), headed by Remzi Kolegeci and Rrahman Morina, on March 14 emerged with a common statement, where it was said:

"Two leaderships fully supported the Constitutional amendments of the Republic of Serbia, which made it possible for the Republic of Serbia to exercise its functions and competences that were needed in its republic territory. With those changes, the fundamental principles of the 1974 Constitution will not be changed and a starting point was the realization of overall national equality of Serbian territories, where Kosova was included."[461]

---

[459] *Ibid.*, p.167
[460] *Ibid.*, p.167
[461] "Politika," Belgrade, March 15, 1981

After the decision of the two Kosova leaderships to support the constitutional changes, the same thing was asked of the municipalities, in order for them to have the approval of all levels.

Under the state of emergency, the municipalities supported the statement of the two Leaderships for Constitutional changes. Also the Leadership of the Working People's Socialist Party of Kosova supported this act.

The amendments were approved by two intellectuals (Academic Syrja Popovci, as President of the Leadership of the Constitutional Commission of the Assembly of Kosova and Professor Kurtesh Salihu, Kosova's Assembly delegate), which before the people of Kosova provided a "guarantee" that with these constitutional changes Kosova would not lose anything but gain![462]

Also the Provincial Executive Committee in the March 21 meeting proposed to the Kosova parliament to accept the amendments of the Serbian constitution. That same day, the meeting of the Commissioners of Kosova's Assembly was held, where clarifications were asked by some Albanian delegates for amendment number 47, which was not included in the project for public discussion, so it was included at the last minute and foresaw the procedure of Serbian Constitutional change. This amendment was changed requiring now the thought of autonomous provinces instead of their full compliance as was required in the 49th amendment of Federal Constitution. This change opened the path for the collapse of Kosova's autonomy from Serbia, because Serbia through this amendment could implement all the necessary constitutional changes without asking for provinces' thought. According to the 47th amendment Serbia was not obliged to take into consideration the thought of the provinces. Serbia could ask for the thought, but it did not need to follow it. The president of Kosova's Assembly, Vukashin Jokanovic, said that necessary clarification would be given in the Assembly meeting.

However, for this situation where the main changes led to the collapse of Kosova's autonomy, no clarification was given even on the day that the Kosova's Assembly meeting was held. Thus, the leader of Kosova's Assembly, Vukashin Jokanovic, as soon as he opened the "sol-

---

[462] See the declaration of academic Syrja Popovci of February 22, 1989 in Serbia's Assembly ("Renaissance" February 23) and that of Kurtesh Salihu in Kosova's Assembly meeting on March 23, 1989 ("Renaissance," March 24, 1989).

emn" meeting of the Assembly, where the highest representatives of the Federation and Serbia were present and many others, it was said that the proposed amendments did not change the basic principles of the Constitution. Through this change, the biggest differences would be avoided; the legislative authorizations of the Serbian republic would be more comprehensive, though the rights and obligations of the autonomous provinces as defined in the Yugoslavian constitution would not be changed.

However, even after taking the necessary precautions for this case not to be changed, some of the Albanian delegates, who did not approve the proposed amendments, asked for clarifications regarding those changes and the procedures that were used to include them in the Constitution. Jokanovic tried to interpret all this case as a political agreement among Kosova's representatives and those of Serbia and the Federation that came at the last moment. However, he said that the "thought" of the provinces was an obligation to Serbia that needed full respect, and even Serbia would not act outside this political agreement with the provinces.[463]

Statements against these changes to the amendment were made by Melihate Termkolli, Uke Bytyqy, Riza Lluka, Sadik Zuka, and Remzi Hasani. Professor Kurtesh Salihu repeated the statement that Kosova would not lose anything with those changes, but would gain. For this he used the "faith in the Communist League" as an "argument," which "did not allow regression."[464]

In this "faith" spirit, many other "guests" from Serbia and the Federation spoke, giving more promises than arguments for this case that clearly ruined Kosova's autonomy.

In this atmosphere, in which each discussion was becoming more and more threatening, while in the Assembly hall some armed individuals started roaming about, President Jokanovic put to vote the proposal of the Commission for Constitutional changes, in order to gain the consent for amendment texts from IX to XLIX in the Serbian Constitution.

Disregarding the Assembly rules for casting a secret ballot, for these changes a raise of hand was requested instead (so it would be known who was against it and could be later persecuted). The first question was about who supported the proposal. Without doing any count, it was said that the

---

[463] "Renaissance," March 24, 1989.
[464] *Ibid.*

majority supported it. Then the second question was about who opposed it and it was ghastly concluded that only 10 opposed the proposal. The ballot ended with the question of those that abstained, to conclude that only two of them did so.

Delegates that had voted against the proposal, those ten that had been counted were: "Ukë Bytyçi, Sadik Zuka, Shkëlzen Gusia, Remzi Hasani, Menduh Shoshi, Melihate Tërmkolli, Riza Lluka, Bajram Buqani, Mehdi Uka and Agim Kastrati." According to various evidence (film and photographs) that proved that the number of those that voted against the proposal was much higher, this was not allowed to be measured because this would mean that the forum of 2/3 votes for the approval of the proposal would not be possible.

However, the voting process was done in a non-democratic, illegal way and what is more important, it was done under the pressure of the state of emergency that was announced, in which case Kosova's Assembly building was surrounded by police forces and the Yugoslavian Army, while in all public places of Prishtina the Yugoslavian Army tanks were positioned.

This proposal was opposed by Albanians, who started the protests with the slogan "We give life, but we never give Kosova." The strongest protests were held in Ferizaj, where big clashes occurred between citizens and the police force, where the Yugoslavian Army intervened. The same happened in Prishtina, where thousands of students and civilians gathered in the center of Prishtina in order to oppose the proposal. Late in the night, police forces and Yugoslavian Army put their armored units into action, which, along with gases, used also arms against the protesters. In Prishtina 13 individuals were murdered and hundreds of them were injured. However, those numbers were hidden by the government, but not from world's media, which had their accredited journalists in Prishtina in order to follow the work of Kosova's Assembly and those around it.[465]

---

[465] See the newspaper *"Frankufter Allgemeine"* March 25, 1989, where the news of 13 murdered Albanians in the protest in Prishtina was published and also the comment *"Kushtetua e tankeve"* on March 27 written by known analyst Viktor Mayer, who had closely followed the situation and the developments that ended with the violent collapse of Kosova's autonomy along with collapse of Yugoslavia. This author talks about those things in his book *"Wie Jugoslawiern verspielt wurde"* (How did Yugoslavia collapse?) published in 1995, one of the richest publications on this theme.

The March 23, 1989 ballot was experienced by Albanians as the fourth conquer of Kosova by Serbia (the first one in 1912, the second one in 1918, the third one in 1944 by Yugoslavian partisans, that was made in compliance with those of Albania), an invasion that was solemnly celebrated on March 28 in Belgrade when the "Vidovdani" constitution was announced.

In fact, this was a reinvasion, similar to that of 1945 where in Prizren on July 10, the National Council of Kosova members, which in Bujan had approved the Resolution for unity with Albania, under the pressure of Yugoslavian partisan tanks were obliged to give their "conformity" for Kosova to join Serbia "willing-fully."

Also in March 1989, a state of emergency was announced, the same as in 1945, by telling national delegates, basically counselors, that they "were voting for their future" and they needed to do that for the benefit of the country.

These two situations had a common denominator – in both instances Kosova was invaded and in both instances Albanian blood was shed.

This reinvasion would show its real face and that it did not support Kosova's "equality" and the respect that Kosova had until then, would be seen when Belgrade started the imprisonment of those that had opposed the constitutional changes, starting with intellectuals where 253 of them were isolated and sent to Serbia to be brutally tortured there. This situation was widely known in the world media.[466]

During April, Serbia started to clean all the administrative and state offices of Albanian "nationalists" using the violent measures that were inherited from "the package for the revival of normalcy in Kosova" announced on the day that constitutional changes were made. Those changes implemented by the Serbian reinvasion in accordance with their immediate projects compiled by Cubrilovic and continued by Cosic together with Serbian academics and writers, had foreseen that for a short time Kosova was going to be under Serbian occupation. This meant the loss of Albanian identity that was first seen in 1966.

The establishment of violent measures was first done in a "selective" way, where "the order and security" was mostly disturbed, such as in the University of Kosova from where the "counterrevolutionary action" had started in 1981 continuing with the overall educational system. In this

---

[466] "*I izoluar – rrugtimet nga tunelet e tmerrit,*" Prishtina, 2009.

case, the Albanian rector of the University of Kosova was replaced by one from Serbia and similar replacements were made with other academics of the university. Serbian leaders were appointed as leaders of Kosova's high schools, and in places where it was impossible to do something like this (in high schools where no Serbian students were present), then cooperators of Serbia who had openly supported the constitutional changes were appointed as directors.

From May, when the differentiation process had continued, but now was more severe than the first time, the Albanian publication houses were held under the gun, starting with the newspaper "Rilindja", which was the biggest newspaper in the country, along with other publications in the Albanian language. This newspaper together with the Radio Television of Prishtina was declared "the nationalist and irredentist spirit." In "Rilindja" most of the journalists and editors had been differentiated, who, as it was said "for many years had refused the ideologist differentiation process" and "with their nationality had opposed the politics of the Communist Party" especially the politics that had to do with constitutional changes. During May, most of those journalists and editors had been expelled from the Communist Party and from their job, and some of them were penalized for "spreading international hate". This newspaper was censored by the staff that came from the Communist Party Committee who was now in charge of editing the newspaper. They had enormous authority to decide for each of the writings. Similar censorship proceeded for some well-known journalists of Radio Television of Kosova, who did not join the differentiation ideology.

The same ideology continued toward other cultural institutions of Kosova that ended with their expulsion from leadership positions and their replacement with those of Serbia.

The biggest campaign of this nature was done with the administrative and state entities, such as the police force and the courts. Thus, between May and June of that year, all the municipal and provincial prosecutors were temporarily or for a long time "expelled from their work" through early retirements. Similar action was taken with the leaders of courts. Also, all Albanian leaders and directors of municipalities were replaced by those of Serbia. This measure was justified not "with the improvement of the leadership in benefit of Serbia, which would replace Albanian nationalists" but as "professional help."

What presented the full collapse of Kosova's autonomy and was rightly called the fourth reinvasion, which, as such was historically presented, was the visit of Slobodan Milosevic to Gazimestan on July 28, 1989, on the occasion of the remembrance of the 600th anniversary of Kosova's battle, where one million Serbs that came from all the Yugoslav regions were gathered. This was a minor event in Serbian history, but mostly a demonstration of hegemonic-chauvinist ideology of Serbia, that was carried out in the name of Yugoslavia and with its help. As it would be seen, war was announced there in the most transparent and threatening way, when Milosevic said that "Serbia is faced with a movement where it should realize its national interests through peace, but if necessary, also through war."[467]

Milosevic's speech in Gazimestan, in front of one million people, but also in front of the political, social, and military Yugoslavian leaders, had to be like that; not only because it was felt to be victorious against Kosova, from which Serbia had taken the autonomy, and shed blood in Kosova without being stopped by others, but also because in that place, where the nationalist and hegemonic spirit of Serbia had started from the 19th century and on, Yugoslavia was informed that it was their turn to follow the Serbian dictate, if it wanted to continue to operate or suffer the same same fate as that of Kosova.

This was not only a message, but a threat, that was well understood by the others in the federation that did not prevent Serbia from arriving at that point, but was not understood by the international factor, which hoped that this situation would lead to "the strengthening of the federation of Yugoslavia." However, as will be seen, Serbia did not intend to stop there, but intended to implement its hegemonic plans to create the Greater Serbia, even if that needed to be called Yugoslavia.

---

[467] More on this issue: Milosevic speech in Gazimestan presented in *"Politika"* Belgrade, June 29, 1989.

CONCLUSION

Enver Hoxha's consent to Tito's request, made in September 1944, to have Albanian partisan brigades enter Kosova first, along with those of Kosova to fight the Nazi-fascist forces on their way north, with Yugoslav partisan (Serb and Montenegrin) groups following was rightly claimed to have established conditions for a Yugoslav re-conquest of Kosova, the third within two decades.

It will be clear that the so-called fraternal cooperation between the Albanian and Yugoslav partisans in Kosova and the war against the withdrawing German forces was rather an Albanian blood shedding that turned into a Calvary that forged internationalist cooperation, the consequence of which was the annexation of Kosova by Serbia and its placement under its tutelage.

Constantly under the slogan of "pursuing against fascist forces", Albanian partisans from among the ranks of the 5th Brigade of Albania with two small detachments of Kosova partisans, entered Dukagjin from where without difficulty they "liberated" Prizren, Gjakova, Peja and other parts of this area, although German forces had already withdrawn to the north leaving behind Albanian volunteers who would be fought, but at the same time, as soon as "people's power" was being set, in Anamorava and Kosova Plain, Yugoslav partisan brigades from Serbia and Macedonia entered. Using demagoguery that they were coming to join "Albanian partisan brothers to pursue the German occupier", after having taken over the main points of oversight and deployed heavy weaponry, they began "cleansing operations" against the "quisling forces" and "enemy collaborators", targeting Albanian patriotic forces of the anti-fascist front (detached groups of Balli, Legaliteti, and other anti-communist forces), awaiting the arrival of Anglo-American allies.

Realizing that this was a setting of tragic clockwork, Albanian patriotic forces, though without any common connections and mostly without a compass soon aligned around a joint front against Kosova's re-occupation that was taking place through a communist plot to hand over Kosova to Yugoslavia.

443

Mullah Idriz of Gjilan and other patriots of Karadak, who were joined by a large number of Albanian officers "in anticipation" of allies, remaining in that Albanian interior profusion outside the ranks, were among the foremost to counter Serbian partisan units, which were actually Chetnik units converted recently to partisans under the Tito-Subasic agreement. In November these forces regained Gjilan and parts of Anamorava from the Yugoslav partisans, moving toward Ferizaj and the rest of the Kosova Plain, where the "people's power" had begun a large-scale mobilization that by sending young people with no experience to the war fronts of Srem and the Adriatic, beside emptying Kosova of Albanians, brought in Yugoslav partisan units that would settle accounts with Albanians under the label of being "fascist collaborators" exactly as Cubrilovic had planned in his most recent Elaborate called "The Issue of Minorities in the New Yugoslavia ", submitted to Tito a few days before in Belgrade.

Thus, during that year's autumn and winter, Kosova turned into a slaughter-house, similar to that of autumn and winter of 1912/13, when Serbian and Montenegrin armies entered Kosova and occupied it, separating it forcefully from the Albanian trunk.

But this time, it was the partisans - Yugoslav and Albanian – that thanks to internationalist collusion under the oath of fighting "counterrevolution" that had allegedly broken out in Kosova, were jointly conducting this most tragic "mission". And, "counterrevolutionaries" were those who refused to leave Kosova in the hands of Chetniks converted into partisans and many other patriots betrayed in many ways, who were defending their own country from Yugoslav communist re-occupation. According to the scenario, to defeat "counterrevolution" in Kosova, Serbia and other parts of Yugoslavia sent in four divisions of partisans (with over 30 thousand men), including also partisan units from Albania, which at all times cooperated with the Yugoslavs.

How important was to Yugoslavia this vital chance to settle accounts with Albanians according to the Cubrilovic Elaborate, is best explained by the fact that the partisan forces sent to Kosova were separated from those who were to be sent to the Srem front against the Germans, who were barricaded in that part to prevent the infiltration of allies from the South and Soviets from the East. For Belgrade, Kosova's re-occupation appeared more important than the other fronts.

Therefore, the unequal war between Albanian patriots and Yugoslav partisans during January and February of 1945 that took place in Drenica and its vicinity (after a deliberate realignment before being deployed in that area), could not end without great Albanian bloodshed, with thousands killed, exactly as Cubrilovic would have in his Elaborate.

But Albanian patriots were not only killed in Drenica but in other parts of Kosova, where Chetnik-Partisan Brigades operated. They were already being killed in the Srem front too, where over six thousand young people, mobilized as "volunteers", were sent to meet the partisan brigades in the war against the Germans, who were used mostly in the role of vanguard units for cleaning mine fields.

And, they were also being killed on Albanian soil, as happened on their way to Bar, to where over three thousand young people were headed going from Prizren through Kukes to Shkoder (a hard journey) followed by Albanian partisan brigades, who even before handing them over to the Yugoslav partisans, massacred many of them at the Buna River, for refusing to become victims of Chetniks, as happened with the rest, who were cruelly slaughtered in Bar after staging an alleged escape attempt!

The Kosova tragedy became even greater after the deployment of the Military Administration in Kosova from March to June 1945 by a decree from Josip Broz Tito under the pretext of creating conditions for the establishment of people's power in the part where the "counterrevolution" occurred.

Setting up a military administration, which had begun to act even before it was officially announced, (from the date of entry of Yugoslav partisan detachments in September 1944, when the antifascist movement in Kosova and local government structures - National Liberation Committees were also denied legitimacy), had another more tragic purpose for Kosova: the cancellation of the Bujan Resolution on the right to self-determination of Albanians to unite and the passing of a new one by which Kosova "expressed its will" to join Serbia.

This "free will" was expressed in Prizren on July 10, 1945 under the pressure of arms and Albanian blood, which was shed anew. In these circumstances, the Assembly of Prizren "voted" in favor of a resolution for the annexation of Kosova by Serbia, which was then sent "as a request" to the Federal Assembly in August of that year, so as "to accept the Albanians' request", in September, to be approved by the Assembly of Serbia as well.

The consequences of Kosova's Serb annexation was felt promptly. Under the banner of proletarian internationalism and the Yugoslav-Albanian (Tirana and Belgrade) brotherhood and unity, repressive measures against the Albanians began to be applied, persecuting them as "accomplices of fascism" or "counterrevolutionaries". Most Albanians

445

faced similar qualifications, who unfortunately found no support in Albania, which in response to the slightest complaint handed them over to the Yugoslav security.

This policy became even more ferocious after Enver Hoxha severed his relations with Tito, as the latter removed himself from the clutches of Stalin and the Kremlin dictator abhorring him with the Informbiro (Cominform) Resolution, with Enver to be the first to join convinced that Tito was not able to accept orders from the Communist centert, by which the Tirana offspring would have open doors to get even closer to the Communist "Mecca" - Moscow.

These circumstances too were greatly used by Serbia to settle accounts with Albanians charging them as Stalinists, Enverists and similar.

With this charge on their back, the few existing intellectuals were persecuted, and the achievements created with great difficulties in the past two-three years utilizing the "internationalist" mood that engendered the Tirana-Belgrade cooperation in an emancipating plan under Socialist Realism frames (opening of primary schools in the Albanian language, publication of "Rilindja" newspaper) were gone.

This affected those who could not find comfort or hope in Enverist Stalinism or salvation from Serbian violence that used perfidious methods of "brotherhood and unity" to again turn to migration to Turkey, as the only salvation left. This road was significantly facilitated by the signing of a Gentlemen's Agreement between Tito and Cupruly on the migration of "Turks" to Turkey, starting a huge Albanian exodus. It is estimated that within ten years close to a quarter million Albanians from Kosova and Macedonia moved to Turkey. This time it was the urban population, encouraged by the Yugoslav authorities and some Islamic clergy by issuing title deeds of "Turkish ethnicity" to them, accelerated their displacement to Turkey. Their properties, at a very low price, were bought by Serbs and Montenegrins and other Slavic elements that filled their place.

Their displacement to Turkey was also accelerated by the "weapon collection" campaign of winter of 1955/56, where thousands of Albanians were imprisoned and tortured in most brutal ways by the Yugoslav police. Even the few abuses that were admitted after the Brioni Plenum, in 1966, with the fall of the Police Minister, the Serb Rankovic, made it plain that such a scenario was prepared by Belgrade in using state violence, which was justified by security reasons, to accelerate the removal of Albanians to Turkey.

446

In such circumstances of state terror, it was understandable for the Albanians, who never agreed with the invading Slavs, to show signs of resistance for their national liberation and unification.

Even though the Communist "liberation" had washed them in blood, while the beginnings of establishing a socialist system had exhausted them of their last energy, by the end of the fifties the emergence of the first illegal revolutionary organizations occurred (Metush Krasniqi's "Revolutionary Party for Unification of Albanian Lands" of rightist orientation and others), to come to the "Revolutionary Movement for Albanian Unity" of Adem Demaçi of 1964, which inspired the resistance against occupation, and at the same time fed the faded hopes for national unification, despite the fact that the revolutionary methods for liberation and unification in such circumstances were but a romantic illusion, while the communist ideology, set on both sides of the border as the main cause of the Albanian tragedy, appeared to be too inconceivable for Albanians.

But despite the Communist distrust, Albanians, lacking intellectuals and a civic elite, which had been terribly liquidated by the Communists, needed years to get back on their feet in order to be able to accept rebellion and armed struggle against the Belgrade regime, something that the latter wished for in the circumstances of the Cold War and Bloc bipolarity, in the name of "quenching a counterrevolution" and international "right" to state sovereignty to easy carry out its early projects against the Albanians.

By the mid-sixties, more specifically from the Brioni Plenum and on (held in June 1966) when Tito faced his main rival, Alexander Rankovic – his police minister, justifying it mostly with the abuse used by his service against the Albanians (even though behind the scenes there was an ongoing life or death war between two socialist concepts: on one side a bureaucratic-state one, backed by Serbian politics, which increasingly showed a tendency of approach to Moscow, and on the other, a self-governing model that was supported by Croatia, Slovenia, and behind which stood the troika: Tito-Kardelj-Bakaric), the position of the Albanians and Kosova changed for the better, paving the way for comprehensive social developments, which led toward national equality, opening the way for constitutional changes through which, within a short time, its status rose to the level of a Federal entity.

This major change was reflected in the opening of the University of Prishtina in January 1970, thus completing the national education infrastructure in Kosova, while changes in Amendments VII-IX to the Constitution of 1967 and 1971 led to the 1974 Constitution, which granted Kosova the status of a Federal entity, formally linked with Serbia, but with the right of veto in the Federation, with a formal duality and even to the detriment of Serbia.

Indeed this is what triggered Serbia's resistance against Kosova's relative equality in the Federation and its accelerated economic, educational and cultural development, which although continued to keep Kosova within the less developed parts of the country, in order to fill the gap a bit it needed years and fourfold greater investments than those of the rest of the country, it was still kept away from Serbia's tutelage as forcefully established from 1945 onwards, directing it towards the Federation instead, which for Serbia was unacceptable because, as Cosic said, "with the loss of Kosova, Serbs lost the spiritual cradle of their medieval history."

Thus, the beginning of the extraction of Kosova from Serbia and its alignment with the Federation was not just a matter of changing internal relations that supporters of "self-governance" took over the side of "dogmas" with their face turned towards Moscow. Although it could not be contested, this opened up a broader geostrategic and political configuration, with which Tito, in an undisclosed deal with Westerners argued by different sources, sought to prevent any possibility of Soviet penetration in the Balkans, especially in Albania, which although had severed ties with Moscow and had approached China, remained a problematic area for the West, which was somehow approached through Yugoslavia, in order to maintain its military neutrality.

Although Enver Hoxha intensified his ideological propaganda against Tito and self-governance, which he called a revisionist practice of imperialism, Soviet intervention in Czechoslovakia and the announcement of the Brezhnev doctrine of "limited socialist sovereignty" made him see a danger coming from the East and in no way from the imperialist West. Enver Hoxha both in 1968 and 1970 sent open messages to Yugoslavia that it would be on its side "in case it is attacked by the Soviet Union."[468]

In these circumstances, when Kosova and its status no longer represented only a domestic issue, being calculated under the carpet by the decision-making centers as a key regional factor, which, however, although this dimension was kept concealed and in some cases even if minimized as being at Belgrade's permanent hand, there was the emergence of the "Blue Book" (1977), which remained as a "frozen"

---

[468] For more see Meier, Viktor: *"Wie Jugoslawien verspielt wurde"*, 1995; Buxhovi, Jusuf: *"Kthesa historike"*, Book II, Prishtina, 2009.

threat against both Kosova and Yugoslavi. This book also mobilized the overall Serb potential from among the intellectual ranks, the Serbian Orthodox Church and other social and political layers, gaining strength in times after Tito that soon highlighted elaborates by the Serb academicians determining Belgrade's policy frameworks.

One should keep in mind that the pivot on which these projects mobilizing Serbian hegemony will be the Albanians' request for the Republic of Kosova within the Yugoslav Federation, legally declared by the Albanian political and intellectual class in the summer of 1968 with the opening of the debate on the future constitutional changes. In the autumn of that year, historical demonstrations held in the cities of Kosova, closing with that of Prishtina on November 27, turned into a political program that brought together all Albanian layers starting from illegal ones, which had originally fought for national liberation and unification under revolutionary slogans and ideological concepts, to legal ones, which first fought for equality with others in an institutional way considering it as a basic human, social and political right, for which an incessant struggle was needed. It was therefore a conceptual twist, where the demand for equality had to lead to self-determination and then to eventual union, an issue that had to be in overall agreement with Albania, and above all, in full compliance with the West and in no other way.

Thus, the awareness of equality turned into a political formula as a demand for the Kosova Republic, representing an all-Albanian consensus, to which, as would be seen shortly, Enver Hoxha too gave his consent, the one who had previously not only rejected it, calling it "fraud by Tito that Kosovars should not accept", but had fought it, pointing out to the Kosovars that the struggle against Titoite revisionism and his overthrow was advantageous to turn Marxism-Leninism into a priority and a prerequisite to resolving the issue of Kosova, in order to achieve it in cooperation with the Yugoslav internationalists, who would come to power after Tito!

This change of behavior and social and political consciousness of the Albanians, to have demands expressed openly and with arguments, not only was disliked by Serbia, who would rather have them stick to the Enverist doctrine on Kosova, as that would keep them out of the game, preventing the development of a democratic process, threatening Yugoslavia, as the "Blue Book" had even before Tito's death, while the Serbian determination made Albanians gather strongly around the demand for the Kosova Republic, as a democratic, legal and legitimate demand.

The positional barricade, however, came to an end with Tito's death, when it was more than clear to Kosova that Serbia would create a disarray to hinder this development, feeling it had more reason to "rush" into revealing its case for the Republic of Kosova, of course as a demand for democratic opening, as done during the summer and autumn of 1968 when it was debated and demonstrated in a very civilized manner. Belgrade retaliated with its own card, that of destroying what had been achieved so far (the 1974 constitutional position), in order not only to prevent the implementation of the Republic of Kosova as a legitimate and democratic demand, but to also destroy the social, political and legal basis on which it stood and could move further.

The breaking point of this development were demonstrations of 11 March 1981, which broke out in the students' cafeteria in Prishtina, where the complaint on the poor food represented only a reason to trigger protests, which, as expected, on March 26 turned into open demonstrations with social and political demands, among which was that of self-determination and Kosova Republic. The protest turned massive with demonstrations of 2, 3 and 4 of April throughout Kosova to turn to a broad and unstoppable political refrain of Albanians for years to come, which would be attributed to their relative silence in relation to the official policy asked to carry out ideological and political differentiation.

In this case, Belgrade's response was severe, as expected; it would use police force and the Yugoslav army, in the name of protecting the unity of Yugoslavia and protection from Albanian "counterrevolution." The entire former Yugoslavia was used against Kosova, even though it was obvious that Serbia had issued the "Blue Book", which relied strictly on bringing down the 1974 constitutional status and relations it had established, which had to commence in Kosova in order to then turn against the Federation in order to ensure supervision by Belgrade.

Of course such behavior needed a "counterrevolution" and a Yugoslav political platform, which would leave the entire issue in the hands of Serbia, as happened from April 5 onwards, when the two chairmanships of Yugoslavia (both state and party) in a joint meeting drew the conclusion that the Albanian demonstrations qualified as "hostile events from the positions of Albanian nationalism and irredentism" reaching the size of an eruption of a "counterrevolution."

These harshest qualifications, which Kosova faced in 1944, when it was bleeding to death while creating opportunities for Serbian annexation, opened the way once again to a similar re-occupation process that would include the destruction of autonomy.

This road, which took seven years, began with a military-police force in order to extinguish a "counterrevolution" resulting in many dead and wounded and hundreds of thousands of persons imprisoned (about 3500), sentenced under the indictment of "hostile activity" that included all those who showed support for the Republic of Kosova. This continued with a process of many years of ideological and political differentiation and the destruction of all educational, cultural and national institutions, and their overall activity.

The police and military violence also followed the very destruction of Kosova's autonomy, on March 3, 1989, when the Yugoslav Presidency just days before, forced by a million people gathered in Belgrade to protest against the "Trepca" miners' strike and their demands rejecting constitutional changes, ordered a state of emergency in Kosova, a situation which, with a break, continued in Kosova ever since April 1981, but this time it served the act of a "willful approval" of the Serbian Constitution, bringing down Kosova's autonomy.

From that day on, throughout Kosova, protests continued everywhere with unprecedented harshness and bitterness, as the destruction of autonomy was experienced as the fourth occupation of Kosova. Albanian protesters were met by the Yugoslav police and army with fire, killing many young people who cheered for the Republic of Kosova.

These murders were also a warning for the murder of Yugoslavia, which soon came from those who in March of '89 had condemned the Republic of Kosova to death. They failed, however, not only in doing so but also in its emergence and implementation, placing it on the proper tracks of an ongoing historical process.

PART THREE
THE STATE-BUILDING MOVEMENT

CHAPTER 1
THE DECLARATION OF THE REPUBLIC OF KOSOVA AND THE PARALLEL STATE

The Emergence of Albanian Intelligentsia and Acceptance of Political Responsibility

The "Memorandum" of Serbian academics and the issues it raised faced the Albanians with another reality, that "protection" through silence was not sufficient any more, but rather an active stance was required going as far as revealing political concepts, such as the right to self-determination, which others enjoyed, something that was used in the first confrontation of Serbian-Albanian writers in Belgrade, in April 1988. – In the Belgrade confrontation, Albanian writers were able through their civilized attitudes to score an intellectual and political victory against hegemonic Great Serbian concepts, after which the Serbs accepted an undeclared war, with which, as they said, "Serbs would restore Kosova conquered by Albanians with the help of Tito and the Catholic conspiracy against the Serbian people"! – Albanian writers called re-occupation the violent destruction of the autonomy of Kosova on March 23, 1989, clearing the way for the break-up of Yugoslavia, which could stand only as equal, provided Albanians too had a place in it.

Even prior to the formal suspension of Kosova's autonomy, especially since 1986, when Serbia with the help of the Yugoslav Federation succeeded in overseeing much of the political and social and economic situation in Kosova using the ideological-political platform for Kosova as its strongest weapon – through the process of ideological-political differentiation – the Albanian intelligentsia would not agree with the situation. First, with the rejection of this process, and later crossing from defense to attack, this change was reflected especially following the appearance of the "*Memorandum*" of Serbian academics and after the commencement of a debate on constitutional changes through which, Serbia sought to lay the groundwork for the domination over Yugoslavia in order to turn it into Serbo-Slavia.

The emergence of the "*Memorandum*" of Serbian academics in December 1986 and opening of issues, such as those declaring Tito's Yugoslavia a "creature against the interests of the Serbian people," created by "a Comintern entrapment against the Serbian people" of "losing in peace time what they had won in war," with Kosova being among the "losses," which according to the authors of the Memorandum "represented the Serbian soul since Middle Ages and on,[469] and other similar known claims of hegemonic Serb propaganda of the 19th century, which had inspired conquests and genocides against Albanians from the Eastern Crisis onwards, had made the Albanians face a reality that was equally an existential challenge. Naturally, Serbian academics exploited the turbulent situation that was created by Belgrade's Serb politics since 1981, when Serb nationalism, according to a known scenario of the "Blue Book" of 1979, emerged on Yugoslavia's political scene, in order for it to become operational turning eventually into a state program in the hands of the Serbs to be implemented in accordance with the program, which meant no other than the collapse of Tito's Yugoslavia, on the one hand, and re-occupation of Kosova on the other.

These two actions had to be combined with each other, serving the same purpose, that of the triumph of nationalism and Serbian hegemony. The calling on "historical rights" and "Serb spiritual and ethnic memory in Kosova" presented nothing but war against Yugoslavia for having allowed this to happen in the fight against Kosova as they had violated the Serbian sanctity. Serbian academics assessed that, in the circumstances, the international community would accept Yugoslavia as redefined by Serbian interests, no matter how it was called, with Kosova sacrificed to this change, which was a small price to pay for the benefit of an agreement between West and East, to which the Serbs always thought they were the key keepers.

This and all that stood behind such an estimate that had already come out openly, would capture well the Albanian intelligentsia, which until

---

[469] See "*Memorandum srpskih akademika,*" Delo, Ljubljana, 1987, p. 8.

then had carried the main burden of ideological-political differentiation, but which had not seen it appropriate to expose itself before the time came, though its silence for the Serbs had the equivalent of being committed for a Kosova Republic, simmering as a political concept in the demand for full equality with the others.

And time to contravene had already come. The emergence of the "Memorandum" of Serbian academics, although it was claimed that it represented an "intellectual concern," in fact, was a political concept, based on an expansionist platform of Great Serbian hegemony out of Garasanin's "Nacertanija" of 1844, targeting mostly Albanians and Kosova: as a people who allegedly "had prevented Serbian historical right to be carried out in accordance with their ethnic extension" and "Serbian Kosova" for turning into a victim of "Great Albanian hegemony at the time of Ottoman conquests," which allegedly was used by Albanians to conquer turning it into a "metastasis of Islamic fundamentalism," dangerous to Christianity and Western civilization in general.[470]

Although the Serbian political and state leadership would supposedly respond against this monstrous project with a certain "distance," which was more of a cosmetic nature, however, it would not distance itself from the two key "charges" which the document was raising: first – that Tito was referred to as Serb-eater," and the second – that AVNOJ Yugoslavia was "an ideological creature contrary to the Serbian national interests," although neither one was true knowing that it was exactly Tito who would prevent the fragmentation of the Kingdom of Yugoslavia in accordance with earlier demands presented by the Comintern that Yugoslavia, as a prison of peoples, should be dissolved and its peoples be granted self-determination. These claims were supported by Yugoslav communists at the Founding Congress of Dresden in 1928 and the Local Conference since 1941. It would be exactly Tito who would seek to defend Yugoslavia and the party organization and that the anti-fascist war be conducted in accordance with the structure of the state that did not exist any longer.

For the Albanian intellectuals the emergence of the "*Memorandum*" of Serbian academics and full solidarity with it of the Serbian Orthodox Church, writers and most of Serbian intellectuals was a clear omen to which needed an immediate response on an intellectual plain, but also on

---

[470] *Ibid.*

a political one, without excluding the possibility of accepting in certain circumstances political responsibility.

As the "*Memorandum*" would appear in the second half of December of that year, and publicly would appear in early spring, a time intertwined with the emergence of the "Serbian People's Movement," such as the so-called Kosova Polje "Headquarters," its activation for political purposes by Milosevic would accumulate power.

It would be put into operation in Kosova on the occasion of his famous visit on April 24, 1986, when he addressed the Serbs "that no one can beat you up any longer," promising to bring back to them the "hijacked Kosova by Albanian nationalists and chauvinists"[471] and similar, at a time when Albanian intellectuals, mostly gathered in the Kosova Writers' Association, which was led by Dr. Ibrahim Rugova, would begin to respond to the "*Memorandum*" of Serbian academicians. It was a very convenient opportunity to test how and how much the process of ideological and political differentiation had affected their intellectual courage, being mostly protected through silence, which for the Serbs was equivalent to the demand for the Republic of Kosova.

At first, responses were individual, mostly views and criticism published in the Zagreb and Ljubljana press, where Albanian intellectuals found space for expression and thence their voice spread out into the country, but also into the world. Later, this turned into a common opposition with the Kosova Writers Association becoming an address, in which for the first time began to unfold political and social interests of the Albanians. The latter, although being consistent with the slogan for the preservation of Tito's Yugoslavia, which had already begun to be heard more and more in the western parts of the country, showed clear outlines on which to maintain it, emphasizing full equality with others, implying in a political language – equal part of federalism, namely the Republic of Kosova, what had first appeared as a demand in 1968 in a legal manner by the Albanian political and intellectual class, later becoming an all-popular demand during historical demonstrations of October and November of that year, to be renewed in 1981 with wide-ranging power.

The slogan of equality, as an appropriate formula fermenting the demands of the Albanians for self-determination, without excluding the option of national unification accordingly, would dominate the overall

---

[471] See "*Politika,*" Beograd, 25 April 1987.

Albanian intellectual discourse on which political demands were being built. At the same time, they continued to oppose to the level of devaluation the views of the Serb *"Memorandum,"* by which Serbian politics were inadvertently receiving negative points, while Albanian attitudes were being positively evaluated, especially by the international community, with the latter seeing two different languages in all of this: the Serbian one, which was based on a historical right built on myths, and the Albanian one, based on the right to life beyond hegemonic claims justified from a scientific and civilization point of view.

However, the *"Memorandum"* and the attitude towards it revealed two different political and social concepts: that of yesterday and that of today, or that of hatred and that of understanding and tolerance, that of war and that of peace. In this context, the Albanians were double winners: on an intellectual and also political plain. In the first for being able without any difficulty to bring down the "argument" about Serbian "historical right" as a hegemonic construct manipulated from mythology and, in the second, for opting for equality, democracy, and values of Western civilization, which, with the emergence of the Polish "Solidarity," or even with the first signs of "Perestroika" in the Soviet Union were already demands sought in Eastern countries.

In this respect the views of intellectuals were equivalent with the developments and the spirit of reform, which would be expressed a year later, on the occasion of the founding of the Democratic League of Kosova, the first Albanian party, which quickly turned into a movement among the most powerful of the Albanian world after the war and beyond, setting on parallel tracks two historical developments:
- *Demise of communism, and*
- *Process of building the Kosova state.*

Before this historical development occurred, Albanian intellectuals, mostly gathered in the Kosova Writers Association and led by it, had two crucial showdowns with Serb "memorandumists," namely with the main mentor of Serbian hegemonic politics, and its leader Milosevic. The first took place on April 26 and 27, 1988, in the so-called "duel between Serbian and Albanian writers" in Belgrade. And, the second was at the Congress of Yugoslav Writers in Novi Sad in June of that year.

The duel of the Albanian-Serb writers in Belgrade was be "mediated" by both Belgrade and Prishtina politics, respectively Milosevic and Vllasi, leaders who, even though not equal (as the first held the second in his hand playing with him as he would, and the latter with a faint hope that at at last moment he could get some help either from within Yugoslavia or the international community in order to survive, even though he realized how hopeless that was), still wished to foist on their main alibis into the game: intellectuals, each one for his own purposes. Milosevic was convinced that the superiority of Serbian intellectuals was great opposite those of Prishtina, as the first enjoyed the support of the state and politics that backed their programs, as was the case with the "*Memorandum,*" while Vllasi was also convinced that, judging by recent reactions of Albanian intellectuals against the "Memorandum" of Serbian academics and pressure coming after the advent of Milosevic as Serbian party leader, they would get a good space to empty their little and long-held frustration. This would create an opportunity for a last breath of an exhausted and worn out class he was leading, and whose end he felt, to which he perhaps could "consent" with people tired of politics of continuous concessions without any counter value which served to their detriment.

Regardless the bids of Belgrade and Prishtina politics, which had been clearer in this case, Kosova writers had met with full approval the Serbian bid, even though it had been political, as it allowed for direct confrontation which they never had before.

Thus, the team of Kosova writers travelling to Belgrade was composed of the following: Dr. Ibrahim Rugova, Rexhep Qosja, Jusuf Buxhovi, Besim Bokshi, Sabri Hamiti, and Ali Aliu to face the following Serb writers and academicians: Aleksandar Petrov, Pavle Ivic, Radovan Samardjic, Rade Stojanovic, Milan Komnenic and Jovan Deretic. Serbian writers that planned to take part in the discussion were Zivorad Stojakovic, Petar Saric, Dusan Batakovic and Radosav Zelenovic, and from the Albanian writers side Hasan Mekuli and Azem Shkreli.

The debate opened with the speech of the President of Writers of Serbia, Alexander Petrov, who as was expected, briefly outlined the contents of the Memorandum of Serbian academics published recently in Belgrade. Petrov sued Albanians for racist behavior against Serbs, for alleged chauvinism and genocide against them, using, as he said, "weapons" provided to them by Tito and the Constitution of 1974. In this case he accused Albanian writers of turning a deaf ear to this crime happening in broad daylight and before the whole world, thus becoming part of it. On this occasion, he addressed the Albanian writers with the following accusation: "You stand deaf before reality and you scare us to death. You are masters of fog and smoke. You have made a mockery of justice, you have thrown values away, you plot against the culture, you have declared war on sound reason," going as far as to claim: "You are sick of historical aggression, while we are suffering from historical yearning...".[472]

As a host, Petrov closed his remarks with the threat that "the Serbian people felt lucky provided someone ridiculed it. But it too is not ready to suffer evil for the sake of the happiness of foreigners if disaster looms as the only reward."[473]

Petrov's euphemistic threat would turn quite transparent by poet Komnenic who began his pathetic speech with the following words: *"Gentlemen, we are at war! Once we realize this, then why hide it? Declared or not declared, war is but a matter of formality."*[474]

That this war was neither new nor unknown, but rather part of a conspiracy to "Catholic revival" in Eastern Europe against Serbs and their being, especially after 1622, when the Congregation of Religious Propaganda was founded, which included Albanians, historian Samardzic said without hesitation:

"This age-old battle continues today throughout the day, a battle that one day will bring to their ultimate historical defeat, where the West together with Albanians will be totally marginalized in the Balkans."[475]

Notably, the intoxication of Serb writers with hatred, going as far as declaring war, facilitated the work of Albanian writers in demonstrating a civilized attitude, an intellectual level, scientific competence when needed, and also political maturity. They never found it difficult to not only reject such theses, but also to win a most important intellectual victory, something that was increasingly bringing them closer to the point that they inevitably had to take over the responsibility for political leadership of the people in circumstances of a great historical turning point that was on the brink.

In these circumstances, namely of Serbs declaring war on Albanians, and serious accusations against the Europeans, who supposedly supported and incited Albanians against Serbs – defenders of Western Christianity – the first duel between Serbian and Albanian writers was concluded in

---

[472] For more see A. Petrov's speech in Buxhovi, Jusuf: *"Kthesa historike – Vitet e Gjermanisë dhe epoka e LDK-së,"* Prishtina, 2008, p. 136.

[473] *Ibid*, p. 136.

[474] *Ibid*, p. 127.

[475] *Ibid*, p. 136.

Belgrade, the first of its kind. Albanians, who, in Belgrade inflicted a hard blow against the Great Serbian hegemonic propaganda of Serbian intellectuals, being in the wake of what Garasanin had started and continued by Cubrilovic with his elaborates against Albanians, and ending up with that of Cosic and circle of "Francuska 7," had reason to comfortably expect the anticipated "retribution" in Prishtina two weeks later, realizing that by both the domestic and foreign public opinion, would be able to hear the Albanian truth, which until then had been banned and cursed as "hostile activity from the positions of Albanian nationalism and irredentism."

But what would rightly be called intellectual victory of the Albanian Writers in Belgrade would not be repeated in two weeks' time, as it had been agreed between the writers of Prishtina and Belgrade. In a press release, it was the Belgrade writers who threw the towel claiming there was no sense in giving Albanian writers an opportunity of exploiting public panels for their nationalistic and chauvinist propaganda![476]

In fact it was Belgrade politics that had prevented the holding of Prishtina's "revenge," under the conviction that evidently Albanian writers would not only refuse to follow the course of the Kosova political leadership, already known for years of wavering and recoiling in order to supposedly preserve what had to be preserved even at the cost of sacrifice, but for keeping an uncompromising intellectual attitude which ignored the dictate of daily politics and the language of slanders spread for years by the Serbian intellectual elite inclined to even incite a war in the name of an historic right, which already, by their elaborations, was turning into a state conception to be implemented by all means, including those of war. This was the motto of the so-called "yogurt revolution," already operating in Vojvodina and Montenegro to garnish belligerent power behavior. Therefore, it was totally meaningless that the spirit of triumph, which began to overcome and set in motion, as stated, the Serbian people everywhere it stretched and had its graves, should be harmed in Prishtina by Albanians and their propaganda.

Within this contemplation one should see the withdrawal of Serbian writers from "revenge of Kosova," hardly waiting to thus defend themselves from the defeat by Prishtina, realizing that nothing could change neither Albanians nor what was said. Even the word "revenge" that they used had something ominous in it, as it no longer meant natural conver-

---

[476] *"Politika,"* Beograd, 10 May 1988.

sations among intellectuals, whether or not on controversial issues on which they disagreed, but it rather warned of revenge, war, not of opinions, but literally.

Perhaps the Serb withdrawal made by Belgrade's politics had been encouraged by the foreign press response, especially the German, French, British and American, that almost uncensored assessed the performance of Albanian writers as a daring intellectual demonstration, at a time when even in circumstances as those existing at Kolarac University, described through multiple pressures, made the Serbian writers realize they had lost the battle in which they had mostly invested.

German newspapers of authority took note even before the duel was about to commence, calling it an important intellectual test. On the opening day, *"Frankfurter Allgemeine"* brought a piece on *"Historical Breaking,"* recalling that after seven years of pressing and unprecedented prosecution, Albanian intellectuals got the chance to say what they should have said long before. It commemorated Serbian Memorandum and its acquisition by the Serbian political class for purposes, which through constitutional changes would restore the situation prior to 1974, which meant nothing other than an obvious warning that Yugoslavia was falling prey to Serbian unitarianism, setting the conditions for unpredictable changes in the ratio of forces in the region and beyond.

"Kosova has to be the first scapegoat of this turning back to yesterday," the paper draws the assessment, as "Albanians will not accept this, and rightly so," then it should be expected that Tito's heritage resources will eventually fall precisely where they are unsure.

The newspaper had a similar response during the time of the Belgrade discussion, using the occasion to recall all those that years ago were seen as dilemmas and rightful concerns.[477]

Munich's *"Süddeutsche Zeitung"* dedicated a whole page to the writers' contest in Belgrade.

"Albanian writers said no to Serbian Memorandum and no to constitutional changes by which Serbia intended to turn Kosova into its tutelage."[478]

"Serbian writers received clear answers from Albanian writers," would assess *"Frankfurter Rundschau,"* regretting though why between

---

[477] *Ibid*, p.154.
[478] *Ibid*, p.154.

the two nations the last links were finally broken when already thought they could find common grounds.[479]

Magazine "*Der Spiegel*" was even clearer and direct when bringing to the forefront Komnenic's words directed to Albanians "We are at war; everyone knows this."

"Any time Serb writers mention war, it is not about a poetic metaphor, but about blood. So it always has been, and why should it not be so now..."[480]

Belgrade's newspaper "*Politika*" most clearly explained that "it was extremely biased reporting of some newspapers and western media from the Belgrade talks, granting space only to already known Albanian insinuations while ignoring or distorting Serbian arguments that created the impression that it could get worse in Prishtina."[481]

In any case, the failure of the writers' talks in Prishtina was perceived by the Albanian public opinion with the impression of an intellectual success achieved in highly unequal circumstances, but at the same time with the justified fear that Belgrade would respond by increasing the level of repression in Kosova. The latter had already become random and it could increase in order to prevent the intellectual model of opposition to be carried over to daily political level, where the Serb offensive was already focused on in its campaign for constitutional amendments in accordance with its project to bring down Kosova's autonomy and through promises and deception, or through threats, attracting any support it could get for its own purposes.

The Serbian-language newspaper "*Jedinstvo*" of Prishtina, which for years had turned into a militant pamphlet of Serb nationalism, whose writings were usually picked by Serbian prosecutors as sufficient proof for bringing lawsuits against Albanians, unequivocally stated that any display of nationalistic Albanian writers, such as the one in Belgrade, where they had used free debate and Serbian hospitality for known purposes, should be prevented from passing over to the constitutional debate.

The same newspaper demanded an initiation of investigation over the statement published in the newspaper "*Süddeutsche Zeitung*," coming from the ranks of Albanian writers that "Albanians consider Serbian

---

[479] *Ibid*, p.155.
[480] *Ibid*, p.156.
[481] See, "*Politika,*" Beograd, 30 April 1988.

Memorandum as an open threat of war," and to a similar statement by Ibrahim Rugova brought by "*Le Monde*" of Paris.[482]

A militant analyst, Mirko Cupic, one of the main militants in Milosevic's staff in Kosova, called for criminal accountability for Albanian writers for, what he called, anti-Serb propaganda exercised for a long time in the foreign media, especially German and French, spreading all sorts of lies, and going even as far as warning the West to be cautious against an aggression that Serbia was preparing against Kosova.

"How can someone prepare for an aggression against his own country and home when Kosova is Serbia's home, cradle and everything?!..."[483]

The spirit of intellectual opposition in Belgrade was more widespread than expected, and it had begun to revive some confidence in itself, even if for short-term domestic needs.

And, it was rightly so, because, used with a fierce propaganda that both electronic and written Serbian media exercised almost continuously, with slanders and insults against the Albanian culture and heritage of a most severe kind, the Albanians were politically suppressed and left at the mercy of ruthless prosecutors and Serbian investigators, going everywhere beyond the minimum of what was allowed and maximum of what was not against those who opposed clear and leading ideologues of what came from Belgrade.

Another intellectual victory, this time in the political plain, Albanian writers would mark at the Yugoslav Writers Congress, the last of its kind, held in June 1988 in Novi Sad. In this Congress Albanian writers would have a "slightly easier" contest with Serbian writers, as they were not alone as they were in Belgrade. Rather, in Novi Sad, on the same tune with Albanian writers were Slovenes and Croats, speaking out openly against the hegemonic policy of Belgrade, with Serb writers actively involved even as militants of Serb nationalism.

It was the "*Memorandum*" of Serbian academics, whose originator was the writer and academician Dobrica Cosic, who had opened these irreconcilable fronts, which as would be seen led to the destruction of Yugoslavia. Slovenian writers would forewarn of breaking their ties with the Union of Writers of Yugoslavia if there was no distancing stance from the Serb "Memorandum" and behavior of Serbian writers. Croats de-

---

[482] "*Jedinstvo,*" Prishtina, 2 May 1988.
[483] *Ibid.*

manded the same, while Albanian writers in addition to supporting this approach also revealed their concept of the right to self-determination to be activated at the moment that the common roof began to collapse from the dripping caused by the hegemonic behavior of Serbian politics.

In their presentations in Novi Sad, Albanian writers emphasized openly the Albanian position on the right to determine their own destiny and warned that, if necessary, they would assume political responsibility.

"We too know our way," was the message of Albanian writers at the Yugoslav Writers Congress, received as a message at home and abroad, announcing their direct involvement in the events that would follow after the collapse of the autonomy of Kosova on March 23 of the following year, coming at the forefront of political movements, beginning with the establishment of the first Albanian party after the end of World War II in all Albanian-inhabited areas: The Democratic League of Kosova on December 23, 1989.

The Establishment of the Democratic League of Kosova and the Beginning of the All-Popular State-founding Movement

An historic interview by Dr. Ibrahim Rugova published in the well-known German weekly Der Spiegel *describing Kosova as being re-occupied by Serbia on March 23, 1989, as war was declared on Tito's Yugoslavia on June 28 of that year by Milosevic in Gazimestan warned about the appearance of Albanian intelligence on the political scene taking responsibility for the fate of the country. – Germany and the United States of America began to encourage Kosova Albanian intellectuals to establish a political party as soon as possible. – The nucleus of the founders of the Democratic League of Kosova came from* Rilindja, *gaining the main support from the Kosova Writers Association and the Academy of Sciences and Arts. – The establishment of the Democratic League of Kosova, the first Albanian party of rightist and pro-western orientation took place in Prishtina on December 23, 1989, in an Assembly attended by 127 people. – Its staggering growth within three months turned the party into an all-popular movement mandated by all Albanians. – In addition to the collapse of the League of Communists of Yugoslavia in Kosova, within a short time, the Democratic League of Kosova initiated and led the process of Kosova's seces-*

sion from Serbia, done with the approval of the Constitutional Declaration on July 2, 1990 and the proclamation of the Republic of Kosova at the Kacanik Assembly on September 7, 1990.

After the violent destruction of the autonomy of Kosova on March 23, 1989, rightly experienced by Albanians as an occupation of Kosova by Serbia, Belgrade took over all social and institutional mechanisms in Kosova. Through the Yugoslav military-police apparatus it began a takeover of all structures of power in Kosova after having been blamed for the "Serb tragedy in Kosova." On this occasion it turned to harsh repression against all those who had prevented the adoption of constitutional amendments or in any form resisted the changes. So, a week later, the Serbian police took in isolation 256 intellectuals (politicians, journalists, university professors, and different professionals), sending them to prisons in Serbia using unprecedented violence against them. This, however, did not go unnoticed by the Slovenian and Croatian media, which alarmed the world and forced Belgrade to admit that "someone" had exceeded the powers during the isolation of Albanian intellectuals (imprisonment without trial under emergency law declared in Kosova by a decision of the Presidency of Yugoslavia in early March).

This irritated beyond measure the entire Kosova Albanian population, which by now clearly realized Serbia had launched a state terror campaign, similar to that of the years 1944/45 when it had been re-occupied by Yugoslav Partisan detachments with the consent and assistance of the Albanian ones, which, jointly, in the name of "cleansing out of reactionary forces" began a wild anti-Albanian campaign, as a consequence of which over 50 thousand Albanians were killed.

That this was part of planned violence, aimed at destroying any kind of institutional structure of Kosova would also be seen by the violent measures that the Serbian Parliament had enforced throughout Kosova, granting a free hand to Serbian commissioners brought in from Belgrade to act with complete arbitrariness in all areas of life, making arbitrary dismissals and appointments of directors, managers, and ordinary workers, who were completely defenseless by any law.

In the spirit of this violence a big rally was held on June 28, 1989, in Gazimestan, near Prishtina on the occasion of the commemoration of the 600th anniversary of the Battle of Kosova. To celebrate the triumph over Kosova, but also to threaten Yugoslavia, which already had a turn, Mi-

467

losevic brought about a million Serbs from all parts of Yugoslavia, led by militant hordes soon to be paramilitaries, who would start Serb aggression in Slovenia, Croatia, and Bosnia and Herzegovina. These units had already been on the move for over a year carrying Lazar's remains killed in the Battle of Kosova of 1389 all over "Serbian lands," from Knin, Croatia (where after two years the so-called "balvan revolution" – timber revolution would take place), to Bosnia and Herzegovina, Montenegro, and Kosova, taking place under the auspices of the Serbian Orthodox Church, which in this way, through incense, marked the places through which the Serbian hordes had to cross in order to massacre others, with the promise that they were "fulfilling Lazar's testament!"

The arrival of the Serbs and their behavior during the day of "*Vidovdan*" turned into a demonstration of the Serbian occupation, which was carried out three months earlier with the destruction of Kosova's autonomy in its Assembly. This demonstration was even worse for Albanians as it was taking place in the eyes of the highest political and state leadership of the country, who were present at Gazimestan, as Milosevic promised to the Serbs that "Serbia will achieve its goals through will or through force,"[484] creating the impression that, to protect their selfish interests, they did not bother to think about the fate of the Albanians, which seemed to be left in its own hands.

But, evidently, Yugoslavia settling accounts with Albanians through Milosevic would not protect the rest from Serbian hegemony. Because, in fact, from that day on, Milosevic's militant gangs turned to other parts of Yugoslavia to submit them to Belgrade's Serb dictates, as reflected in the fall during that summer of the leaderships of Vojvodina, and Montenegro, in order to continue later with the leaderships in Bosnia and Herzegovina, and a year later in Croatia, where they would kindle the wick of the war for the destruction of Yugoslavia, whose flame everyone would see, but no one would accept but Albanians, who would speak out loudly.

One of them depicting himself drastically in this regard, was Dr. Ibrahim Rugova, President of Kosova Writers' Association, who on the occasion of Gazimestan "celebration" had the courage to send the alarm through the famous German weekly "Der Spiegel" alerting the world about how in Gazimestan Milosevic had declared war on Yugoslavia, after

---

[484] See Milosevic's speech published in *"Politika,"* Beograd, 29 June 1989.

having destroyed the autonomy of Kosova by force, calling it "re-occupation by Serbia."[485]

With extraordinary intellectual courage, political clarity, and argued public language, Dr. Rugova called Milosevic's speech in Gazimestan and the behavior of over a million Serbs in Kosova as "declaration of war to both Albanians and Yugoslavia." On this occasion he had informed the international community, especially European countries, which stood watching Milosevic's actions, that he would never stop, as hoped, after strengthening the Federation, as his deception went, but would rather continue his hegemonic battle. "Serbia has turned back to its hegemonic programs and will never stop," Rugova said all concerned, recalling that Albanians had already been sacrificed, but that this was only the first step, which would end in bloodshed and spread throughout the Balkans. Albanians, though vulnerable, although left at the mercy of ruthlessness, as Rugova would disclose, would not sit idly by, but would act in accordance with their own interests.

Dr. Rugova's interview in the noted German weekly echoed largely in the European public, since it was also carried by many other noted European newspapers, which, in this case, promoted Rugova as the only Albanian leader, who was obliged to take up the task, as the Albanian political class was entirely torn down by force, while the people were seeking someone to take their fate in his hands before Belgrade could bring in a renegade of its own in Prishtina.

The interview greatly infuriated Belgrade as well. Serbian newspapers, staying watchful to any action or statement by Albanian intellectuals, demanded political and criminal liability against "enemy number one," as Belgrade's "Politika" called Dr. Rugova.[486]

In line with this campaign enkindled in the Belgrade press, the Socialist League of Working People of Kosova (a satellite organization of the party), demanded that the prosecution bodies undertake measures to arrest Dr. Rugova and his followers (meaning some of the writers of Kosova who, also, in those days and in the same spirit, had granted interviews to some European media expressing similar sentiments on the situation in Kosova after the violent collapse of its autonomy from Serbia).

---

[485] See Dr. Ibrahim Rugova's interview in *"Der Spiegel,"* 26 July 1989.
[486] See *"Politika,"* Beograd, 22 July 1989.

Certainly Dr. Ibrahim Rugova would have ended up in prison on that very same day or in an isolation regime as it happened with many intellectuals those days, following demands by "rally-goers" of "Kosova Polje" during a recent protest rally in Gracanicay, if it were not for an intervention by the United States of America and certain European countries, taking him under protection almost demonstratively, not only by means of statements, such as that of the U.S. State Department, dated July 26, 1989, and a letter by the Council of Europe, but also with the arrival of the U.S. Ambassador in Belgrade Zimmerman in Prishtina to meet Rugova, with whom he would take a walk on a Prishtina street and have lunch on the terrace of the "Grand" hotel, which had already turned into Milosevic's military headquarters.[487]

United States envoys of those days asked for different meetings with other Albanian intellectuals, who had recently been in the forefront of the confrontation with Belgrade's policy. They talked directly with some of them about the possibility of establishing an Albanian political party in Kosova, which would be able to take over a new political organization in circumstances when the Yugoslav government, following pressure from Western countries, passed a law on the organization of free citizens in political associations and parties, which supposedly would curb Serbian unitarianism on the march.[488]

Even before the international community showed an interest in engaging directly to encourage some Albanian intellectuals to establish a political party, the needs had already been felt and presented by a group of intellectuals (journalists of "Rilindja" and distinguished writers) who clearly felt that the time had come, especially after realizing that Belgrade had already stirred a movement to test the mood of some intellectuals outside Kosova Writers' Association to be involved in the Initiative for a United Democratic Yugoslavia (Udružena Jugoslovenska Demokratska Iniciativa – UJDI) of Prime Minister Ante Markovic, who had the support of some European Union countries under the illusion that such a move could somehow deter Milosevic, or at least create a balance against him. Furthermore, a meeting of the emissaries of Prime Minister Markovic

---

[487] For more see Buxhovi, Jusuf: *"Kthesa historike – Vitet e Gjermanisë dhe Epoka e LDK-së,"* Prishtina, 2008, pp. 177-179.

[488] For more on first contacts of Albanian intellectuals with German and American representatives interested on Albanian political organization, see Buxhovi, Jusuf: *"Kthesa historike - Vitet e Gjermanisë dhe Epoka e LDK-së,"* Prishtina, 2008, pp. 125-177.

with some of the intellectuals inclined towards an illusory Yugoslavism (some thirty persons attending), was held in early August in Prishtina, discussing the establishment of an UJDI branch for Kosova, giving consent to the initiative, which, however, would fail, together with some other similar projects, which Belgrade aimed at introducing into the game, in order to dissuade Albanians from coming out with an authentic national party, but rather with different constructs as determined by Belgrade in order to be able to manipulate their goals.

Of course its failure and the failure of the like on the shelves of Belgrade had to do with putting into action the Initiative Group for the Establishment of the Democratic League of Kosova from the "Rilindja" group,[489] on whose initiative the ARD German television had informed the public in July.[490]

Thus, the core, which would turn into an Initial Council on the Establishment of the Democratic League of Kosova, would be joined by Dr. Ibrahim Rugova by signing the list of initiators. After Dr. Rugova, the founders' list was signed by some of the best known writers and intellectuals, some of whom, however, for the circumstances bore special weight, such as the names of academics Idriz Ajeti, Dervish Rozhaja, Mark Krasniqi, Anton Çeta, and Fehmi Agani.[491]

In the background of the initiative there were many other intellectuals and academics, among whom the noted academic Gazmend Zajmi, who together with Professor Fehmi Agani contributed to the conception of the party program, presented at the Founding Assembly of the Democratic League, held on December 23, 1989 on the premises of the Association of Writers of Kosova, whose work 127 people attended, who, after having heard the material (party program and status),[492] from Jusuf Buxhovi, being their author, accepted by acclamation the Initiative

---

[489] "Rilindja" initial group was composed of writers and publicists: Jusuf Buxhovi (coordinator and author of all programs and party documents), Mehmet Kraja, Xhemail Mustafa and Ibrahim Berisha.

[490] DPA, 14 July 1989.

[491] For more on the List of Initiators of Founding the Democratic League of Kosova see: Buxhovi, Jusuf: "Kthesa historike – Vitet e Gjermanisë dhe Epoka e LDK-së," Prishtina, 2008, pp.125-177.

[492] See: Program of Democratic League of Kosova, original version, prepared by Jusuf Buxhovi, presented to the Founding Assembly, pp. 212-216.

Council's proposal for Dr. Ibrahim Rugova to be elected President and Jusuf Buxhovi as his Secretary General.[493]

It should be emphasized in this case that the drafting of the party documents, especially its program, had been subject to reviews among compilers, but also by German and American representatives (from the U.S. Embassy in Belgrade), who had shown interest in the points on which the program would be based, upon which several meetings took place with the American and German representatives in Prishtina, some of which were attended by Academic Gazmend Zajmi.

Everyone agreed that the program had to be simple and contain four demands:

1) Demand for equality in the Federation or Confederation, with Kosova emerging as an independent entity,

2) Demand for political pluralism,

3) Demand for democracy, and

4) Demand for free market economy.

An important one was the demand for full equality in the Yugoslav Federation or Confederation, as it enabled Kosova to come out of Serb re-occupation in which it found itself since March 23 of that year. Any other formulation would render party registration and its work difficult. Also important was the name "Democratic League of Kosova," as it fraught with the Albanian League of Prizren, the first political organization of Albanians to create an Albanian autonomous state within the Ottoman Empire, which would have preceded the independence process of Albania.

The U.S. Representative ensured that the work of the Founding Assembly of the Democratic League would take place unhindered by police, provided that it had been duly reported to state bodies in accordance with federal law, which would happen by the Coordinator of the Initiative Council on the Establishment of the Democratic League, presenting the documents in time to the police along with supporting documentation.

The establishment of the Democratic League of Kosova, on December 23, 1989, was an important event, because as will be seen, with it turning within a short time into an all-popular movement (with about 700 thousand members), it put into action two parallel historical processes:

---

[493] *Ibid*, p. 226.

a) The collapse of the League of Communists of Kosova and its satellites (the Socialist Alliance of Working People, Youth Alliance, etc.), and

b) Management of Kosova's secession originally from Serbia and then from Yugoslavia in a legal and legitimate manner.

Both of these processes took place within a short time (within half a year) and represented the foundation on which the future state of Kosova was built.

This road, through which the Democratic League of Kosova passed, was among the most successful through which an Albanian party had ever passed. It turned into an all-popular movement by including all the Albanian social and political forces of both the right and left and all illegal movements active since the war onwards, especially since 1958, as was the right-wing movement of Metush Krasniqi and Demaçi's *"Revolutionary Movement for the Union of Albanians"* and other broad spectrum organizations and illegal groups, which were included in the demonstrations of 1968 and 1981 demanding that Kosova become a Republic.

The nationwide movement led by the Democratic League of Kosova was joined by organizations operating abroad, such as the *"People's Movement of Kosova"* (LPK), known for its leftist determination, operating as its collective member for three years. Even as LPK left the LDK-run "umbrella" of the general movement, a large portion of its activists in the country still continued to be active in parallel state structures in the branches and sub-branches, providing valuable contributions, especially in the organization of armed resistance, installed within the parallel state structures.

The first and foremost test as a major political force, one of the largest that had ever appeared in general, the Democratic League of Kosova passed exactly with the complete destruction of the basis of the League of Communists of Kosova within three to four months. This development was expected for several reasons: from the fact that communism had been imposed by force on Albanians, after having paid a high price since 1944 onwards (with about 50 thousand dead and thousands imprisoned). As such they never trusted it (communism), up to the latest developments, when Serbia, under the political platform of the League of Communists of Yugoslavia over Kosova, approved in 1981 and onwards, systematically worked against the interest of the Albanians, reaching as far as the destruction of Kosova's autonomy in 1989. Therefore, the emergence of a legal Albanian party outside its dogma and ideological framework, driven

473

by intellectual elites with Western concepts, coming at the forefront of the political process, created for the first time an opportunity for Albanians to be able to gather for a union on a national platform, connecting with the West and its civilization, to which they had belonged but were separated by communism. The quick expansion and strengthening of the Democratic League of Kosova as a party with Western concepts had also rejected Belgrade's backstage efforts of many years, especially abroad, to portray Albanians as supporters of Stalinism and Enverism.

On this platform, Albanians joined LDK and at the same time in mass left the Communist League. While the number of Albanians in the ranks of the League of Communists crossed the figure of 40 thousand members (many of whom were not members out of conviction but rather because membership was a condition to move up in leadership positions in education, economics, administration, judiciary and police, which by the Plenum of Brioni and on were mainly led by Albanians), LDK mass membership (on the first days with a thousand a day, and from March to the end of April the number increased five-fold), affected the League of Communists within a short time to lose all Albanian membership and remain a Serbian party. Furthermore, the departure of Albanians from the League of Communists turned into an open and unstoppable demonstration against the regime in Belgrade, at the time when the "Rilindja" organization would give back party cards and collectively join the Democratic League of Kosova. It was therefore a joint action of a special significance not only for the circumstances, but also for further political developments.

In this scenario the whole satellite of the League of Communists, the Socialist Alliance of Working People of Kosova collapsed while its members collectively left and joined the Democratic League of Kosova.

This process was also accelerated by the public attitude of the Democratic League of Kosova behavior, taking over at the very beginning the role of Albanian political leader as well as the responsibility for the fate of the country. In late March, Dr. Ibrahim Rugova, with LDK attaining breathtaking proportions, with membership exceeding half a million, said in one of the press conferences of the kind he held regularly every Friday at 10 am at the Association of Writers of Kosova that "the Democratic

League of Kosova is the only legitimate representative of the Albanians of Kosova, taking responsibility for the fate of the country."[494]

Such a pronouncement by Dr. Rugova on legitimacy evoked great interest in both Yugoslav and international circles, realizing that the Democratic League of Kosova was not a simple party any more but rather a popular movement, which had gained full legitimacy among Albanians, regardless of their beliefs and current settings. This represented the greatest victory in this plain, as usually, in situations of historical turns with which they were faced in the last century, divisions of various currents, wings and the like, had prevented them from uniting around a common political program.

Serbia did not consent to the Albanian political internal unity about democracy, equality, freedom and Western affiliation, significant to the circumstances and upcoming events, and, unable to stop this development, tried to divide it from within, as it had planned and operated for years in this regard. It declared the Democratic League of Kosova as a "Great Albanian organization" fighting for the destruction of Yugoslavia under the "farce of democracy," with which accounts had to be settled as soon as possible, a threat that further strengthened the determination of Albanians to join the party.[495]

This threat became the slogan of the Kosova Polje "headquarters," which in meetings held there or in Gracanica demanded the government bodies to "arrest the leaders of the counterrevolution led by Rugova."[496]

These and similar threats directed against Dr. Rugova would not stop the "flow" of LDK's large Albanian membership. On the contrary, it increased further making this party exceed the boundaries of Kosova, extending to other areas inhabited by Albanians, especially in Croatia and Slovenia.

Although LDK's position was to appear as a party in Kosova, however, opposite that development, it inadvertently became a *"mother party"* for all Albanians. Advised by the Americans not to extend outside the boundaries of Kosova (with the exception of receiving branches in Croatia and Slovenia, not affecting administrative sensitive lines), the LDK

---

[494] See LDK press release, 26 March 1990, included in LDK materials at the Archive of Institute of History of Kosovo: "*Dosja Jusuf Buxhovi – materialet e LDK-së,*" Box I.

[495] See a statement by Zivorad Igic, high Serb official in Kosovo for "*Politika,*" Beograd, 28 March 1990.

[496] See: "*Jedinstvo,*" Prishtina, 1 April 1990.

presidency took over the formation of political parties of Albanians in the Presheva Valley, Macedonia, and Montenegro, as it was necessary to maintain internal social and political cohesion of the Albanian factor in order for this to be used in accordance with the upcoming circumstances and events. Thus, in Macedonia, the *"Party for Democratic Prosperity,"* in Presheva Valley, the *"Party for Democratic Action,"* and in Montenegro the *"Democratic League of Montenegro"* were established.

These parties, from the early 1990s when the destruction of Yugoslavia began as admitted by the Badinter Commission in late 1991, operated as branches of the Democratic League of Kosova, and under its full supervision, although since June of 1990 they would have a common framework within the *"Coordinating Council of Albanian Political Parties in Yugoslavia,"* led by Dr. Ibrahim Rugova. Thus, this made him the leader of all the Albanians of Yugoslavia, a post that further strengthened his position within Yugoslavia, but also in relation to the international community, which began to treat him as such.

However, his most powerful boost as leader of Kosova and leader of all the Albanians of Yugoslavia, Dr. Ibrahim Rugova and the political legitimacy of all-popular movement which he headed, was given by the United States of America on the occasion of his visit to the U.S. in April 1990. Dr. Ibrahim Rugova, accompanied by a broad spectrum of intellectuals from Kosova and other parts of Yugoslavia was invited by the Council for Human Rights of the United States Congress to give testimony to that forum. Dobrica Cosic from Belgrade, who was accompanied by a professor from Belgrade University, an expert on international law, Radosav Stefanovic, involved in the *"Serbian Renewal Movement"* (a pro-Chetnik Organization led by the Troika: Seselj-Draskovic-Kostunica), and a bishop of the Serbian Orthodox Church were also invited to testify.

After the testimony of Albanians in the U.S. Congress (with Dr. Rugova and others), presenting the familiar option of Albanians from the LDK program about full equality of Albanians in the Yugoslav Federation or Confederation, not excluding the possibility, in accordance with possible re-alignments in Yugoslavia, for Albanians from all areas of Yugoslavia to unite, and Cosic's testimony, which rejected any prior subjectivity of Albanians in the Federation or Confederation (as according to him it was in violation of Serbian national interests and, to prevent this even war was included), Dr. Ibrahim Rugova was received by Robert Dole, Congressman and Vice Chairman of the Republican Party.

In the meeting he was received with the high honors of a national leader. This treatment would be granted to him consistently by the U.S. officials the whole time.

On this occasion, Dr. Rugova was assured by the powerful U.S. Congressman, Robert Dole, and other senior U.S. officials, who received him, that he would enjoy the support of the U.S. if they maintained the course of civil resistance to avoid any provocation that could draw Kosova Albanians into war. Dr. Rugova pledged that he would follow the determination of Albanians to democratically fight for consensual commitment for an equal status in the Yugoslav Federation or Confederation. He introduced there the concept of the Democratic League of Kosova, which, through legitimate means, needed to create a democratic infrastructure.

Dr. Rugova revealed before Senator Dole and other senior U.S. officials his plans for Constitutional Declaration of Independence (which was being prepared), as a first step towards the creation of institutional subjectivity of Kosova in accordance with their determination to be equal, but independent. Dr. Rugova reiterated what he had said openly on March 23, 1989, when Serbia destroyed Kosova's autonomy and re-occupied Kosova that the first step to be done was the declaration of independence from Serbia through legitimate and democratic means.[497]

The Declaration of the Republic, Constitutional Convention, and Referendum on Independence

With the Constitutional Declaration of a political constitutive character, announced on July 2, 1990 by the Assembly of Kosova, Albanian delegates in Prishtina, among others, annulled the Prizren Resolution of 1945 on Kosova's union with "Federal Serbia." – The Constitutional Declaration and the Kacanik Constitution – the highest constitutional acts of Kosova after the Bujan Resolution which, de jure, began Kosova's constitutional building by the representatives of the people. – The act of the Constitutional Declaration of Kosova was accompanied by additional laws.- The Kacanik Assembly and referendum for independence – historical positions.- Kacanik Assembly set a referendum

---

[497] For more see Buxhovi, Jusuf: *"Kthesa historike – Vitet e Gjermanisë dhe epoka e LDK-së,"* Prishtina, 2008, pp. 272-279.

for independence and free parliamentary elections in Kosova within six months from which came the first Government of the Republic of Kosova.- The Referendum on Independence, held September 26 - 30, 1991, was attended by 87.01% of the Kosova population eligible to vote, with Kosova declared an independent and sovereign state by 99.87% of participants. – The announcement of these two important acts was followed by Serb terror and banning of Albanian media: Radio Television of Kosova on May 5 and "Rilindja" and all the other Albanian-language newspapers on September 8.

The Republic of Kosova, the promulgation and enforcement in both conceptual and strategic terms, was related to the political philosophy of the state-building movement derived from the program of the Democratic League of Kosova, whose initial starting point was reaching the status of an equal subject which provided the right to an independent path. This path was likely to follow in the direction of a regional-scale crisis and wider, because Yugoslavia, as Belgrade was acting against the climate and reform process that had begun in eastern countries, to quickly bring major changes in the world, was also acting against western interests. These acts of promulgation included the Constitution of Kacanik on September 7, 1990 and the holding of a referendum on independence on September 26 – 30, September 1991.

The Kacanik Assembly and declaration of the Constitution of Kosova was preceded by the Constitutional Declaration of July 2,[498] which also

---

[498] Complete text of the Constitutional Declaration on the Independence of Kosovo:
Given the resolutely expressed will throughout Kosovo, the majority of Kosovo's population, a will also summarized in the Declaration of the Academy of Sciences and Arts on the new constitutional status of Kosovo, as well as considering the role and position of the Assembly as a representative body and the highest constitutional authority and power in Kosovo, the Kosovo Assembly solemnly proclaims this:

CONSTITUTIONAL DECLARATION

For Kosovo as an independent and equal unit within the federation (confederation) of Yugoslavia and as an equal subject with other units in Yugoslavia.

l. This Declaration expresses and declares genuine constitutional position of Kosovo and this Assembly as an act of political self-determination within Yugoslavia;

represented an historical event, the most important of the state-building process, as members of the Assembly declared Kosova independent from Serbia, by which the status of Kosova was brought to a federal unit level, equal to the others. This was an important historical deposition not only in relation to internal developments, but also to external ones, no matter how and to what degree it would be accepted and no matter how it was treated under the circumstances.

This act ended once and for all the dual status of Kosova between the position of the subject of the Federation on the one hand, and remaining part of Serbia, as promulgated by the 1974 Constitution. This condition nurtured the next crisis and even preset it to the extent that it would be seen as part of those international conjunctures upon which future delimitations of specific areas of interest would be based viewing the Versailles Yugoslavia as a temporary creature. Therefore it was expected that over the speculation of the instability segment of Yugoslavia in the circumstances of the fall of bi-polarity of the blocs, or similarly, to those

---

2. The Assembly, by proclaiming by it and on its level Kosovo as an equal unit in Yugoslavia, based on the principles of authentic democracy to respect the will of the people and the human and national collectivities, awaits confirmation of this constitutive act in the Constitution of Yugoslavia with the full support of democratic public opinion in Yugoslavia and international public;

3. This Assembly confirms Kosovo and its new constitutional position as a politi-cal- constitutional community and as a common political-constitutional position of equal citizens and nationalities of Kosovo, where Albanians, as the majority of Kosovo's population and one of most numerical peoples of Yugoslavia, as well as Serbs and others in Kosovo, are considered a people-nation and not a nationality (national minority);

4. Meanwhile, until the legal final application of this Constitutional Declaration the Assembly and governing bodies of Kosovo support their relations in the Yugoslav constitutional order on the constitution of Yugoslavia and not on constitutional amend-ments of SR of Serbia of 1989, which annuls the Assembly's decision of 23 March 1990 on the granting of consent to these amendments;

5. The Assembly of Kosovo, until the issuance of the new Kosovo constitution, henceforth will publicly communicate under this name, simultaneously appointing it a social-political community, whose body is only as Kosovo.

Prishtina, 02. 07. 1990
(Signatures of each delegate follow, a total of 114).

that appeared after the collapse of the Berlin Wall, to focus on actions of both Albanians and Serbs in opposite and conflicting relations. The Albanians engaged in further changes towards full subjectivity of the Federation, and Serbs acted with all means in favor of a complete collapse of this subjectivity, which they achieved on March 23, 1989 through the use of force and state of emergency.

However, the bloody events of March, which in Albanians' view were experienced as a Serbian re-occupation, the fourth consecutive one since 1912, once and for all put an end to any illusion that with Belgrade a "common path" or "historic compromise in the context of democracy" could be found, as one could hear the skillful proponents of UJDI say in Kosova and elsewhere in the Yugoslav centers, as incited by Brussels and other European centers. Therefore, this experiment with many risks for Albanians and their future, needed a deserving answer as soon as possible, and, it could not find it from anywhere other than from the intellectual elite of Kosova, primarily by the Writers' Association, being among the first to understand the Serbian campaign for constitutional amendments as part of Belgrade's strategy to turn Yugoslavia into a Greater Serbia as already advertised in the final Memorandum of Serbian academics two years earlier.

These intellectual elite, many of whom had no prior interest for politics, had no choice but to assume the historical responsibility beginning with the debate (duel) with Serbian writers in the Belgrade meetings of April 1988 to the Congress of the Yugoslav Writers in Novi Sad, two months later. Thus, the result of this responsibility would first be the establishment of the Council for the Defense of Human Rights and Freedoms (CDHRF) and slightly later, on December 23, 1989, the establishment of the first Albanian party – the Democratic League of Kosova, which quickly became a greater movement carrier, which simultaneously streamlined two parallel historical developments: the parting from communism and its ideology and the detachment from Belgrade.

The first development, namely parting from communism, as noted above, would be so rapid, that in only three months in Kosova there would be no Albanian left with a red membership card except a handful of them that Milosevic held hostage to present to the foreign media "as loyal citizens of Serbia" who were no longer accepted by the Kosova Albanian political and social environment.

The process of detachment from communism had brought a state of internal mobilization similar to that of release from a heavy burden – while from the outside, the U.S., European countries and important decision-making centers, came praise and numerous acknowledgments, which became of great importance for gaining the credibility of Western affiliation and its civilization. This support was especially important following all the charges against Albanians issued continuously by Serbian propaganda as being Islamic fundamentalists threatening the West, and as Marxist-Leninists of the worst Stalinist type. This "breathing" could turn into a new choking if not followed by other steps, which would be in accordance with the declaration of Kosova Republic done through legal and legitimate means – by the Assembly and its mandated members.

After all, the declaration of Kosova Republic was not only necessary behavior as compelled by circumstances following the forced collapse of the autonomy of Kosova and what was expected to happen, but rather a duty towards the long sacrifice for national liberation and unification, as articulated in various forms since 1944 onwards by the *"Albanian National Democratic Party"* (NDSH) and other forces of the right and the left. These forces were led by Metush Krasniqi, Adem Demaçi and others in the late fifties, in order that in the sixties, after the Brioni Plenum they come out openly as a comprehensive and powerful demand of the political and social spectrum through historic demonstrations of 1968 and 1981, paving the way for irreversible processes leading to a comprehensive awareness of equality with others as a prerequisite for the realization of aspirations for an independent state, seen primarily as an evolutionary development, which in certain circumstances could necessarily change direction.

As the Democratic League of Kosova, in its role as a subject carrier supported by other political parties, took over the organization of these developments, it was only reasonable for this initiative to determine its dynamics, so that all actions were to some extent consistent with developments in Yugoslavia. By now already open confrontations were hammering increasingly between Serbian trends for hegemony on the one hand and Slovenia-Croatia breaking away through democratic determinations on the other.[499]

---

[499] Buxhovi, Jusuf: *"Kthesa historike – Vitet e Gjermanisë dhe Epoka e LDK-së,"* published by "Faik Konica," 2008, p. 243.

The "western" republics of Yugoslavia were very much interested that Albanians, after rapidly bringing down the entire infrastructure of the League of Communists of Kosova proving that they had been forcefully included into the Communist front paying too high a price for half a century, propped up as much as possible their will to secede from Serbia through democratic means. Kosova's status outside Serbia was seen not only as a fellow traveler but also as a safe ally who would harmonize interests against the same rival if not enemy. So, just as the news spread on the establishment of the Democratic League of Kosova, envoys from Zagreb and Ljubljana, mostly journalists and media reporters who followed with great attention the rapid spread of the party, hovered around in Prishtina in search of establishing connections with Dr. Ibrahim Rugova and other LDK senior executives.

In early January, the Albanian leader hosted the first messenger of Janez Drnovsek, an editor of "Delo" of Ljubljana, who after having talked about the newspaper, this being a mere pretext, passed in an eye to eye meeting the message of the President of the Yugoslav Presidency of that time (Janez Drnovsek).[500]

Various emissaries came to see Rugova from Croatia, Bosnia and Herzegovina, but also from Sanxhak and Vojvodina Hungarians, to be informed about what was happening in Kosova and learn about Albanians' views or to inform him about their own plans.

Croatians were more direct and more open in their demands. They suggested common steps and proposals such as the one for the opening of a branch of the Democratic League of Kosova in Zagreb to serve as a liaison office with Croatia. As will be seen shortly, Croats, among the first to be facing the aggression of the Yugoslav Army in the area of Knin and Eastern Slavonia, breakaway parts declaring themselves "independent Serbian provinces," had much interest to have countless Albanian recruits among the JNA (Yugoslav National Army) estimated at one third of those involved in the fighting in Croatia, and Albanian officers serving in various barracks in the country, sabotage their protection and desert or optionally cross over to the Croatian Army.[501]

Upon the establishment of the branch of the Democratic League of Kosova in Zagreb on January 13, 1990, the Secretary General of the

---

[500] *Ibid*, pp. 241-243.

[501] Author's conversation with Vladimir Seks in Zagreb, 22 May 1990.

Croatian Democratic Union (HDZ), Ivan Bobetko, son of Gen. Bobetko, defense minister in Tudjman's government and architect of the Croatian army in the liberation war against the Yugoslav Army, had a special meeting with Rugova. They discussed aspects of the status of Albanian recruits deserting as soon as Croatia would face an anticipated aggression from the Serb-led Yugoslav Army which had already announced it was not going to tolerate the establishment of "Pavelic's Croatia." [502]

The interest of the "western" parts of the country for Kosova and its commitments increased significantly after the declaration of the Constitutional Declaration of July 2 of that year, by which Kosova seceded from Serbia but waiting for the determination to be legitimized by declaring the Republic of Kosova with the right to decide independently on its relations in the Yugoslav Federation or Confederation.

Thus, in accordance with the position expressed in Washington during his talks with Vice President Robert Dole, Dr. Ibrahim Rugova, after receiving the approval of the Presidency of the LDK, would authorize a

---

[502] Based on various sources and on holdings of the Government of the Republic of Kosovo the number of Albanians recruits who deserted from the Yugoslav Army when it went to war with Croats, exceeded three thousand. Over two thousand were in Bosnia and Herzegovina and over a thousand in Slovenia. A large number of them, always under the agreement with the Albanian representatives, shall be submitted to the Croatian forces by whom they will be sent to military training camps, and some of them through various channels would leave Croatia for Austria, Hungary, Italy and Germany. A number of about four hundred Albanian soldiers will pass from Slovenia, optionally, to be sent to different countries to seek political asylum.

A number of Albanian officers from the ranks of the Yugoslav Army who served in Croatia surrendered to the Croatian forces together with barracks, as was the case with Djakovo of Slavonia barracks, while a few others, like officers Fehmi Ladrofci, Tomor Buza, Rame Cervadiku, Nevxhet Haziri, Bekim Berisha, together with 49 Albanian soldiers formed an Albanian unit with the Croatian Brigade 118 in Goscic. Many senior Albanian officers (Rrahim Ademi, Agim Ceku and others), along with many other soldiers who were in service in Croatia, Slovenia and Bosnia and Herzegovina, initially fought in Bosnia and Herzegovina against the Serb Army and then took the Croatia ranks of the Army elite units in the forefront of Croatian forces in the war against the Yugoslav Army. Many of these officers and soldiers were included in the ranks of the Armed Forces of the Government of Kosovo (FARK) and the Kosovo Liberation Army. Agim Ceku, on the eve and during the NATO intervention in Kosovo, was found in the position of Commander of Staff of the Kosovo Liberation Army.

Commission headed by Fehmi Agani to start work for the proclamation of the Republic of Kosova. Professor Agani, as he had done during the Constitutional Declaration, cooperated with the delegates of the Assembly as well as numerous other experts in drafting the Constitution and other acts to give the action full legitimacy.

Obviously these very important steps, which determined the future of Kosova, were not made without consultation with the Americans and Germans. The U.S. and German suggestions and some others coming from European centers were not something new and out of the concept of the Democratic League of Kosova and subjects keeping the same tune. Top LDK leaders and the national expert group were focused on the issue and were searching for a way to implement this action in a best way and in line with the common strategy.[503]

The Group considered to be competent, along with some of the members of the Presidency of the Assembly, would within a short time, at most in three months, carry out all the work, so that the MPs could decide to declare Kosova Republic and adopt its constitution. These preparations needed to be made despite any opinion, and especially protected by party and other groups' statements.[504]

Dr. Rugova had personally taken over the coordination of the Commission's work with the Americans and Germans, whose representatives on this issue were in constant contact with him, as was done with the preparation of the Constitutional Declaration of July 2. The concentration of the Democratic League of Kosova on doing the Kacanik Assembly preparation work, the weight of which was mainly carried by members of the Assembly, was focused on the concept of being in line with current developments, namely in declaring the Republic of Kosova as an independent unit, as part of Yugoslavia, but as noted in section two, enjoying the right to decide on its relation to the Federation as an equal subject.

The Americans also suggested Dr. Rugova for this position, which in the circumstances represented a significant step toward other solutions, without allowing Belgrade to blame Albanians as destroyers of Yugoslavia thus creating "excuses" for reckless repression against them and, as such dominant among the Albanians after the Constitutional Declaration of

---

[503] Buxhovi, Jusuf: *"Kthesa historike – Vitet e Gjermanisë dhe epoka e LDK-së,"* 2008, p. 248

[504] *Ibid*, p. 249.

July 2. Of the latter he received strategic guidance on the next steps, as well as guarantees that these decisions would be supported by the United States of America and Western countries if they were in accordance with the declared commitments of Albanians regarding their pro-western course.

Thus, on September 7, 1990, in Kaçanik, a clandestine meeting of the delegates of the Assembly was held declaring the Republic of Kosova and approving its first Constitution, which was called the Kacanik Constitution. This historic action was met with general approval of the Kosova Albanians and the rest of Albanians in their ethnic areas in Yugoslavia. Although the delegates to the historic Assembly of Kacanik would leave Kosova on that same night (with some leaving to Macedonia, Albania and western countries), they left behind certain historical tasks to be carried out by the Democratic League of Kosova and personally by Dr. Ibrahim Rugova, among which the most important were the following:

a) Proclamation of a referendum on independence,

b) Holding of free parliamentary elections within six months, and

c) The formation of the Government of the Republic of Kosova.

Accomplishing these tasks was important not only to round up the legitimate democratic infrastructure of the state of Kosova, but also to take over the organization of overall life in the circumstances of the Serbian occupation in which Kosova was already found.

However, the holding of a referendum on independence, which was in accordance with the documents of the Kacanik Assembly, would take a whole year, a time with possible curves and dynamic developments on the Albanian internal plain, with the deepening crisis of Yugoslavia evolving through war towards a violent dismemberment, and especially with developments on an international level with the unification of Germany marking a new chapter in postwar Europe.

The latter was of particular importance, as the beginning of the breakup of the Soviet empire and the disintegration of the Warsaw Pact, the collapse of bloc bi-polarity and the Cold War opened a new geopolitical and geostrategic chapter in the trial of which was expected to cross the Yugoslav crisis, as in the new circumstances it had lost its role and the place it had enjoyed over the past forty years as a buffer factor between the two superpowers.

This entire process, however, was moving on three parallel plains:

a) *that of legitimizing the will of the Albanians to self-determination;*
b) *continuation of the breakup of Yugoslavia through the secession of the federal units and use of Yugoslav Army by Serbia for hegemonic purposes, and*
c) *the start of international intervention in the crisis initially through uncertain mechanisms of crisis prevention, to avert (proven to be unsuccessful), or keep custody of its dissolution process, preventing it from becoming a regional disarray with unforeseen consequences, which also could not be held under control as Serbia was prepared to create new facts through violence, which prevented any initiative and concept for a global solution of the crisis and its complexity.*

This development, however, which deserves special attention, high-lighted two contrasting realities as well as parts of opposite concepts: on the one hand, the use of war and its tools for creating violent facts representing an imposed policy, and on the other, the use of peaceful means, primarily, those of democratic commitments even if lacking necessary infrastructure.

The first path was represented by Belgrade, who at first would not hesitate to hammer this determination to become part of the overall strategy to achieve the goals set from the time of the Memorandum of Serbian Academics.

The second path was followed by Kosova Albanians, unreservedly supported to the price of sacrifice by the Albanians in Macedonia, Presheva Valley, Montenegro, and elsewhere scattered in the former Yugoslavia, the result of which would be parallel state building, legitimized after the holding of a referendum on independence,[505] which opened the way to the establishment of the first government of Kosova with the consensus of the political parties.

However, the declaration of the Republic of Kosova in Kaçanik and the referendum on independence, by which Kosova Albanians were

---

[505] The decision on the Referendum for the Republic of Kosovo as a sovereign and independent state was taken by the Assembly of Kosovo in its meeting held on 22 September 1991. The Referendum was held from 26 to 30 September 1991. According to the Electoral Commission on Referendum, 450 electoral constituencies, spread across 1,500 polling stations, voted in favor of the Republic of Kosovo as a sovereign state 913.705 or 99.87%. 104 voted against, while 933 were invalid lists. For various reasons, 136.535 voters failed to appear at the polls. The total of those voting reached 87.1%.

declared independent, did not free Kosova from its care for the fate of Albanians in Macedonia, Presheva Valley and Montenegro. Even though the republics in which they were included had already begun to exploit the right of self-determination to be declared independent, which obliged Kosova to respect this fact if it wished the others to do the same towards it, this did not render it free from caring about Albanians, even more so when it was still not clear as to how Belgrade would behave in the process, what dimensions it would take and other issues rightly taken up not only by Albanians, who were pointing out the necessity for a joint Albanian consent in case the Yugoslav crisis deepened pursuant to the Serbian threat to intervene with force "to prevent the fragmentation of the Serbs."

Therefore, in these rather vague circumstances, Kosova had plenty of other reasons, especially of ethnic nature, to be concerned – about the developments in the republics with which it bordered (Serbia, Montenegro, and especially Macedonia), as they contained a stretch its ethnic continuity, which with their independence, the administrative borders of yesterday would become new state borders and with those borders what to some extent until yesterday breathed naturally with Kosova in a social, economic and cultural way, dispersed into three other states.

Since certain realities could not be changed unilaterally while waiting for further clarification of the circumstances, and wishing not to do anything to make the road difficult in the implementation of the Republic of Kosova, which for all Albanians in Yugoslavia represented a common reference, but also wishing to be ready for any rather unpredictable challenge in future developments, Albanians in Kosova, Macedonia, Montenegro and in the Presheva Valley, at a time when the flame of war had begun to spread over western Yugoslavia and was obviously spreading to other parts, the political parties of Kosova, Macedonia, the Presheva Valley and Montenegro established the Coordinating Council of Albanian political parties in Yugoslavia. The move had to do with the designing of a common platform with which the Albanian political parties appeared versus the crisis and its unpredictable developments, so as to store an Albanian position in accordance with the suggestions of important international factors such as Americans and Germans for joint actions and through civilized means. On October 11, 1991, only a few days after the referendum on independence in Kosova, the Coordinating Council of Albanian Political Parties in Yugoslavia expressed in a political statement the political will of the Albanian people for the resolution of the Albanian question in Yugoslavia with three open options. It was argued that the "political parties in Yugoslavia as legitimate representatives of the Albanian will" in this democratic and peaceful determination rely "on the basis of the right of peoples to self-determination, in accordance with the principles of the CSCE and the Paris Conference."[506]

---

[506] See publication *"Lidhja Demokratike e Kosovës – Documents, ngjarje, shënime,"* on the fifth anniversary of the foundation of the Party, Prishtina, 1994, pp. 77, 78.

The text signed by Dr. Ibrahim Rugova, Chairman of the Council, presented in its entirety below, shows the position of eleven Albanian political subjects: Democratic League of Kosova, Party of Democratic Prosperity, Democratic League in Montenegro, Democratic Action Party, Peasants' Party of Kosovo, Democratic Party of Albanians, Kosovo Parliamentary Party, Social Democratic Party of Kosovo, Albanian National Unity Party, Albanian People's Party and Albanian Democratic Party:

A) The unresolved Albanian national issue in Yugoslavia is a consequence of the division of the Albanian ethnic lands, which with the creation of the state of Albania in 1913, in compact ethnic territories outside it remained more than half of the Albanian people, who never enjoyed legitimate national rights, neither in the royal Yugoslavia, nor in the socialist Yugoslavia;

B) The partitioning of the Albanian territories that became contemptuous of ethnic principle in the delimitation of state and contemptuous of the will of the Albanian people, continued in Yugoslavia, by partitioning the Albanian people in political-administrative borders of Kosovo, Serbia, Macedonia and Montenegro. A certain political autonomy for the Albanian people existed only in Kosovo as guaranteed by the 1974 Constitution, which is still in force and according to which Kosovo is a constitutive element of the Yugoslav Federation;

C) Contrary to the Constitution of Yugoslavia, Serbia revoked in 1989 Kosovo's autonomy, abolished all national rights of Albanians, stripping Albanians of every right to sovereignty and subjectivity, removing them from all state institutions, with the Assembly the Government and all municipal assemblies suspended, revoking teaching in Albanian language at all levels, closing down the media in Albanian, applying Serbian and Cyrillic writing as the official language in public communication, warding off over eighty thousand Albanians;

D) Expressing disagreement with such a situation, the Albanian people organized peaceful protests, in which over half a million people took part, with workers holding general strikes. Serbian authorities responded with violence: over 100 Albanians were killed, 300 wounded, over 12 thousand persons imprisoned and sentenced, and over 600 thousand people passed through police procedure.

E) Realizing that Yugoslavia proved an unsuccessful model for solving the national question in the Balkans, Kosovo MPs on July 2, 1990 proclaimed the Declaration of

Under the first option: If the external and internal borders of Yugoslavia were not changed the Republic of Kosova should exist as a sovereign and independent state, with the right to union with sovereign states in Yugoslavia. The part of the Albanian people to remain living in Macedonia, Montenegro and Presheva Valley will have the status of a constituent state-forming people with all the rights arising from this.

Under the second option: If the external borders of Yugoslavia do not change, but the internal borders between the republics do, then the demand will be an Albanian Republic in Yugoslavia, built on the basis of ethnic principles and other principles that apply to Serbs, Slovenes and peoples of the rest of Yugoslavia.

Under the third option: If the external borders of Yugoslavia are to be changed, then the Albanians in Yugoslavia, through the declaration of a general plebiscite will decide on the unification of territories in which Albanians live thus creating an Albanian integral state in the Balkans in its ethnic boundaries.[507]

The declaration of the Coordination Council of Albanian Political Parties in Yugoslavia, both then and in subsequent developments, such as those of the bloody breakup of Yugoslavia, is of historical importance as it would not be limited only to issues of Kosova and its solution, but would include all the complexity of the Albanians in Yugoslavia interconnecting and raising it as the background of the Albanian unresolved issue in the Balkans. Its attentive consideration revealed the demand for the reconsideration of the Albanian question in accordance with the three options that were available, providing the answers to these options were realistic, optimal, and provided a legitimate base for solving the Albanian question.

In the first option, if the external and internal borders of Yugoslavia were not to be changed, the Republic of Kosova would emerge as an independent state with the right of sovereign relations in Yugoslavia, where the rest of the people remaining in Macedonia, Montenegro, and Presheva Valley would have the status of a constituent people with all the associated rights.

Independence and on September 7, 1990 proclaimed the Republic of Kosovo. This was a logical solution of state organization in Kosovo as a political territorial unit, in which lived 90% Albanians with 10% of the rest.

[507] Ibid, p. 78.

In the second option, if the external borders of Yugoslavia were not be changed but the internal ones were, the demand for an Albanian Republic in Yugoslavia remained, built on ethnic principles and other principles that applied to the Serbs, Croats, Slovenes, and others.

In the third option with changes of external and internal borders, the Albanian people, through a plebiscite, would decide to unite with Albania.

In all three variants, there are demands for radical changes in the situation of Albanians from optimum to maximum, representing a more advanced political platform of Albanian demands that kept the open options of resolving issues emerging as fundamental for the overall Albanian issue to be answered in accordance with their ethnic and historical right. The Albanian Republic in Yugoslavia and finally, the right of union with Albania would reject almost all speculation, whether from ignorance of the facts, or from other purposes charging the state-forming movement with the curse of "preserving Yugoslavia at any cost" and an alleged "autonomous feud in it" by all means. [508]

The third option does not only share in the spirit of the famous Bujan Conference Resolution of December 31, 1943 and January 1 – 2, 1944, on the right of the Albanian people of Kosova for unification with Albania, as pointed out,[509] but it goes even further, because this right is not limited only to Kosova Albanians, but also to those of Macedonia, Montenegro and Presheva Valley, who had rightful aspirations for a joint status with other parts of Albanian ethnicity from which they were forcefully detached.

And, evidently, this stigma, even when it appeared ignored and formally everything revolved around the so-called right of state sovereignty and its inviolability would cause more trouble to the international community and Serbia itself than making things easier for it. Because of Serbia's paranoia, Albanians would stand even more firm on their way, no matter that there would be situations when out of pressure from the international community they would show a willingness to compromise by which they would not gamble their way out of the game but would never give up their main goal, which seemed achievable because in this important historical twist the world as a whole, for the first time was able to reveal its options, and at the same time it was able to even act and fight

---

[508] *Ibid*, p. 78.
[509] *Ibid*, p. 79.

with all means, as would happen when it deemed it necessary. This determination, together with the determination to finally become part of Western civilization, would not be left without echo. The West, led by the U.S., finally, would be convinced that it would have to act as a sincere ally, which should be supported to the end, especially being in the interest of the West, which, along with the Slovenes and Croats, would find Albanians as their most trusted supporters.

Albania and the Kosova Events

July 2, 1990 marked two diverging events in two Albanian centers in Prishtina and Tirana: In Kosova, with its assertion of the Constitutional Declaration, broke away from half a century of Serb occupation, while in Albania, with the outbreak of violence, which was reflected by the orchestrated entrance of Albanian citizens into several Western embassies, Albania entered a nightmare leading to chaos. – Only after Tito's death did Enver Hoxha accept the demand for the Republic of Kosova, which Kosovars demanded as of 1968 onwards, but Enver had maintained the concept of solving it on an ideological basis. – Why did the Tirana regime do nothing when Kosova's autonomy was lost by Belgrade's use of tanks on 23 March?

To achieve further factoring of the Albanian element as a functional whole, regardless of the form of action, a state deposition was needed, as an unavoidable factor of these important designs. But time would show that the Albanian state, since the violent destruction of Kosova's autonomy by Serbia in March 1989, when in Prishtina and other Kosova towns blood was being spilled by many Albanian youth in clashes with Yugoslav police and military forces, even as this everyday violence was attaining unbearable proportions, kept silent. They kept silent because the the cruel communist regime feared the reforms that swept eastern countries and any pickup with the Kosova leadership scared the Albanian leadership of losing power, as the movement in Kosova was pro-Western and a democratic demand, which in both cases was contrary to the determination of the communist regime in Tirana. Therefore, the caution shown in at least noting any kind of formal objection to Belgrade or UN Security Council on the use of tanks by the Yugoslav Army in Kosova as well as the establishment of a state of emergency was part of this fear. This can even explain the unnecessary hesitation of officials in Tirana to show their readiness to at least formally welcome Albanian political organization displayed with the establishment of the Democratic League of Kosova in December of that year bringing to the political scene of Kosova a nation-wide movement that meant the declaration of an independent state of Kosova, initially being detached from Serbia, as was done with the Constitutional Declaration of July and later in the proclamation of the Republic of Kosova in Kacanik granting Kosova the right to self-determination, freedom to act in accordance with the upcoming circumstances anticipating the process of the disintegration of Yugoslavia.

Difficulties with the Albanian approach were expected and inevitable considering what had come in between Albania and Kosova for more than half a century, such as the harsh communist ideology, with Albania continuing even after the death of Enver Hoxha in 1985 to be one of the last bastions of Stalinism. It continued to care for nothing other than the "trust in the fulfillment of the ideals of communism," which had to be subject to all concerns, including those related to Kosova and its fate even in the circumstances of the eighties onwards when it was clear that Yugoslavia after Tito had no future and was rightly predicted that the crisis and its end would be linked to Kosova as an unresolved issue.[510]

The Albanian leadership continued with strong commitment its un-willingness to deal with this issue and with the lack of any political sense for the next crisis which included the Albanian world. Following Germany's approach in the early eighties as one of the rare cases that could be called historical, which compared to the time of Enver Hoxha and his statements during the demonstrations of 1981 when he seemed to support Kosova's demands, he officially withdrew from the previous position which appeared useful for both Kosova and Albania itself.

This unreasonable withdrawal related to the rejection of an offer by the conservative Bavarian politician Franz Josef Strauss, who, despite many difficulties and refusals coming from official Tirana, succeeded in

---

[510]See Karl Gustav Strom's book *"Jugoslawien ohne Tito,"* published in 1979, with the well-known German publicist and historian drawing the conclusion that Yugoslavia after Tito will not be able to resist the historic test as he failed to raise Kosovo to the level of an equal subject in the Federation, namely granting it a Republic status, besides the fact that it with the 1974 Consitution enjoyed an equal subject status, a status that was dual in nature, being within Serbia.

visiting Albania in 1984. On this occasion Albania was offered an important economic and cultural package, which to be carried out, as a prerequisite contained a German request for the establishment of diplomatic relations, while Albania demanded first payment of reparations from World War II estimated at several hundred million dollars. For the German side this sum would not pose any problem, but in turn it required that this be equated with agreements and various economic projects that Germany would implement in Albania within a short time. [511]

Although some foreign observers would blame Enver Hoxha for the refusal, there are assumptions that Enver, though ill and almost out of time, saw no "imperialist intentions in the German offer," as some of his followers claimed later, as he had requested that this be considered "cautiously" and "responsibly" and "without deviation from communist determination," and under these "messages" of leaving no space for any kind of trap one should look at Ramiz Alia's behavior for the refusal in the way it was made.

The West, after Reagan came to power, had begun its star wars doctrine, bringing the Soviet Union before capitulation in the arms race and having opened the first cracks in the East as reflected first in Poland with "*Solidarnost*" in various forms, continuing with other areas, that is, after concluding that Russian hegemony was before an unstoppable withdrawal from the West's interest. For Germany, entering Albania was a logical step of taking away from the Soviets one of the most important spots in the Balkans before it filled in some other form, especially since Albania began to cool down its relations with China, which had filled the Soviet gap.

But it would be the descendants of Enver Hoxha, those who refused Strauss ostensibly on behalf of their dictator due to their trust and loyalty to Stalinism. This made it clear that Albania's door to Germany was open and by that, those of the West, without having to warn or knock on them. Furthermore, the offer was repeated to Albania four years later, on the occasion of the visit of German Foreign Minister, Hans Dietrich Genscher to Tirana, on the occasion of the opening of the German Embassy. As Genscher's visit was also another first official visit of a minister of a country of the European Union, who was also a member of NATO, it was expected that it would present a good case for the official of Tirana to behave differently towards Genscher from how it behaved towards

---

[511] Buxhovi, Jusuf "*Kthesa historike: Vitet e Gjermanisë dhe Epoka e LDK-së*," 2008, p. 30.

Strauss. He (Strauss) might have been rejected under the pretext of being seen as too extreme right which could not be afforded in a Stalinist place, while Genscher came from among the liberals and belonged to the the the group of experienced diplomats, who were always willing to compromise.

This time too, Ramiz Alia, though without the tutelage of Enver Hoxha, would not show signs of "softening" towards the West, although years later he would try to explain it by claiming that these "measured steps were necessary in order to keep the internal balance of Albanian society," which, as he put it, was not yet ready for such radical changes, and similar excuses that he would manipulate.[512]

Through perfidious rhetoric he would evaluate the German interest for Albania, linking it with the tradition of good cultural relations between the two countries, without going beyond that.

Some German sources speculated that the inhibitor role was Enver's widow Nexhmije, who was rumored to have been standing on the alert with great attention so that Albania would keep the image of the "red castle on the shores of the Adriatic." Furthermore, it was said that she ran the proponents of this image, which continued to be "exported" to the West as well by keeping the Marxist-Leninist-Stalinist groups and financing their propaganda, though this cost the poor Albanian state dearly by losing the remaining hard currency it had collected by selling vegetables abroad.[513]

Even though Enver's widow might not have had any sympathy for the Germans and their offer, she and her role would be used precisely by Ramiz Alia and his numerous followers, who were very dogmatic, preferring not to ever do certain moves accordingly even at times when they seemed to manifest an interest.

---

[512] See the book "*Unë, Ramiz Alia – dëshmoj për historinë*," by Blerim Shala, Llukman Halili and Hazir Reka, published by "Zëri" in 1992. In a conversation with the authors, Ramiz Alia touches upon the issue of Straus' visit and the German offer, saying a working group had been formed on it existing until 1987 when Albania established diplomatic relations with Germany. Alia says that many of the discusiions and German instructions would be heeded but that it would be internal circumstaces that prevented "rough turns."

[513] Author's conversation with the German publicist Hans Waler Poll in Bonn, as member of the "German-Albanian Friendship Association", who had visited Albania on several occasions meeting and talking to Nexhmie Hoxha.

Instead, after the death of Enver Hoxha, the Albanian leadership in Tirana lost all the flexibility that Enver Hoxha at times indicated in his geopolitical and geostrategic plan when he gave clear signs that the greatest danger to Albania come from the East, Soviet hegemony and its inclination to intervene in the Balkans. This often caused him to pledge support to his sworn opponent, Josip Broz Tito, by seceding from the Informbiro (Cominform) from 1949 onwards, "if Yugoslavia would be attacked by the Soviet Union,"[514] as he did in 1968 when the Soviet Union entered Czechoslovakia quenching with tanks an anti-Soviet uprising in Prague, and the same was repeated in 1975.

This affected the German publicist Horst Wessler on a panel in "*Westdeutsche Rundfunk*" held in October 1990 in Cologne to assess that "Enver Hoxha, after having severed ties with Moscow and Beijing, will not see Albania and Albanians endangered by anyone other than Moscow and its allies in the Balkans," pointing his finger towards Bulgaria. ...This position was supported by passages of Enver Hoxha's speech at the Eighth Congress of the Party of Labor of Albania in Tirana, when after showing support for the Kosova Albanian demonstrations in March and April 1981 and for their demand for a Kosova republic within the Yugoslav Federation, which until then had not supported but rather abhorred as "a trap set by Tito against Kosova," shall disclose that for the "destabilization of Yugoslavia and the Balkans one should have in mind the Bulgarian-Russian factor, as well as their efforts to it, from where their dangerous game would start."[515]

The majority of Kosova's political class understood well this bitter reality. Therefore, even without the U.S. and German suggestions to be cautious with Albania, at least for as long as it showed no signs of opening toward reform movements similar to those in which the Eastern countries were already involved after the collapse of the Berlin Wall, Kosovars were very interested to see Albania engaged in democratic reforms, wishing them to be smooth and free of the complications that occurred in Romania. It was hoped that in this respect it could be Kosova and its extremely sensitive situation that would compel the official Tirana and its political

---

[514] Tonnes, Bernhard: "*Sonderfall Albanien,*" 1990.

[515] Buxhovi, Jusuf: "*Kthesa historike – Vitet e Gjermanisë dhe Epoka e LDK-së,*" Prishtina, 2008, p. 199.

class to adopt a responsible behavior, by which the solution of the Albanian issue in the region would open to a new perspective.

But exactly July 2 of that year was a day of a very significant event and development for Albanians on both sides of the border. Prishtina and Tirana would give the world diverging messages even proving that Albania and Kosova were not on the same page. For on that second day of July in Prishtina, Assembly delegates announced the Constitutional Declaration expecting it to be echoed across the entire Albanian world and abroad, while in Tirana, on that same day, an unexpected chaos occurred during an orchestrated assault of Albanians by certain segments of the state entering foreign embassies, followed by victims and scenes recalling the Romanian unrest, thus attracting the attention of all the world!

And, the justifiable enthusiasm and joy among the Albanians expected to erupt after an act such as the historic announcement of the Constitutional Declaration was mixed with concern and certain suspicion that this could be a case of contingency rather than deliberate behavior by someone so that Prishtina's July 2 would go unnoticed in the world replaced instead by the unrest in Albania and concerns coming from there.

However, what took place in Tirana on July 2 and the developments through which Albania would pass during those six months, with the ultimate dropping of the iron curtain, the heaviest one in the entire communist bloc, would support those who were suggesting to Prishtina to advise Albania to get rid of its communism or face serious consequences. This, before asking it to be fraught with the issue of Kosova and its resolution in accordance with the will of the people of Kosova, which with the announcement of the Constitutional Declaration of July 2, 1990 and the decision of the Assembly of Kaçanik of September 7 of that year, had already begun to legitimize and be concluded with the Referendum of Independence in September 1991.

This development had a massive move of people from various legal organizations throughout the world who believed that the independence of Kosova would come through the help of Albania and her ideology, to leave that and join the nationwide movement led by the Democratic League of Kosova and its state-forming concept by legitimate means and West-oriented institutional ways, such as the Constitutional Declaration of July 2, Kacanik Constitution and Referendum on Independence, to

496

become part of the historic project, which would lead to the separation from Serbia and Kosova.

Solidarity and the Beginnings of Parallel Institutions

The beginnings of apartheid measures by Belgrade after the strike of Independent Trade Unions of September 3, 1990 and the rejoinder of Albanians with parallel organization of solidarity and assumption of local government organization. – Democratic League of Kosova occupied the space of local governance through the extension of its branches and sub-branches. – First measures of demonstrating Serbianization in Kosova in administration and education by the Serbian government decree of January 2, 1991 which removed the Albanian language from official use and declared Cyrillic script for use not only in the administration and judiciary, but also in issuing personal documents.- The refusal to apply "common Serbian curricula" in Albanian education was used by Serbia as an opportunity to outlaw Albanian education, while granting Albanians an opportunity to organize their national education in accordance with the concept of the Constitution of Kacanik. – Albanian internal homogenization through internal solidarity, which included Albanians of Macedonia, those of Presheva Valley, Montenegro, and the Diaspora, represented the strongest weapon of the parallel state, which was formed soon after. – An all-Albanian solidarity continued even after the Government of Kosova declared a 3% tax on income to be used by the Funding Council for Kosova – the so-called Emergency Fund – which would fund education, health, and other state structures of Kosova, including those of armed resistance.

The behavior of Albanians since the Kacanik Assembly of September 7, 1990, when the Republic of Kosova was declared, to the time of the Referendum on Independence in September 1991, despite the appearance of a governance vacuum – because after the Kacanik Assembly both the current deputies and the government accepted the legitimacy of the new constitution after the declaration of the Republic of Kosova placing themselves in its service until the newly elected government, and

Kachaniks would leave Kosova,[516] – would be out of the supervision of the Serbian government, as the Belgrade propaganda claimed, or in accordance with the laws established by violence, which it called useful for the unity of Serbia without being reluctant to say they were suitable for the "minorities" as well. The Serbian authorities through the use of the police and emergency measures, starting from administration to economy, led the state apparatus but not the internal organization of the Albanians, who had begun to show clear signs of "parallel lives," turning soon into a parallel power and state, even to be called "a state within a state" at the moment it elected the Government of the Republic of Kosova by the end of 1991.

The main Albanian political entity, the Democratic League of Kosova, whose organizational infrastructure in some way had replaced almost all the previous local government mechanisms and called by certain analysts and European observers as a highly functional and extremely useful "pre-parallel state" for the circumstances,[517] was forced to turn its partisan base activity into direct social care activities for the layers of the population threatened by the Serb strategy which envisaged, in addition to state violence, social pressure and poverty to force Albanians to leave and migrate, encouraging a "quiet" ethnic cleansing of Kosova's ethnic Albanians. So, what was called a display of a "pre-parallel state," was closely related to the internal organization of the Democratic League of Kosova and its internal alignment across branches and sub-branches, from where its operational logistics were used in the entire country to put in motion the mechanisms that later would be based around the local governance infrastructure.

---

[516] It refers to the Government of Kosovo coming out of Serbian elections, organized by the Serb regime in Kosovo in September 1989 following the suspension of Kosovo's autonomy, which was headed by Jusuf Zejnullahu with the inclusion of several past government ministers. As this legislation's delegates would proclaim the Kacanik Constitution and leave Kosovo, the same was done by the "Government" led by Jusuf Zejnullahu, who accepted the legitimacy of the Republic of Kosovo by rejecting Serbia. Some of the ministers of this government joined the Bukoshi Government, which was appointed by the end of 1991 and began being active as of the beginning of 1992 and continuing until 23 March 1999.

[517] See various German authors: Viktor Meier, Matthias Rüb, Paul Lendwei, Rupert Neudeck, Andreas Zumach, Dieter S. Lutz, Mihael Stenger, etc., appearing with analyses and reviews in the German media between 1989 and 1992.

Although the party structure was initially seen as part of a political organization and a more complete alignment in the entire territory of Kosova, soon enough it would be necessary that those who gained leadership mandates through the branches and sub-branches at the same time would take over a lot of work related to the organization of local government outside official structures going as far as to become undisputed local authorities.

This "trend" emerged after the general strike of September 3, 1990, when due to total solidarity with the proclamation of Independent Trade Unions of Kosova, led by Professor Hajrullah Gorani,[518] the strike was joined by administration officials, those of education, health, media and the entire private sector. On that day, despite warnings from the Serbian regime that stringent measures would be taken against striking employees in the state administration, and public and health institutions, life was completely paralyzed in Kosova.

Many foreign journalists, diplomatic representatives and other international observers in Kosova saw Albanians' readiness for demonstration and discipline, but at the same time also faced the unity and strength of the undisputed nation-wide movement, which after the Constitutional Declaration of of July 2 and complete collapse of the monopoly of the communists in Kosova, the Democratic League of Kosova, appeared as an insurmountable factor enjoying the confidence of the whole Albanian population, whose mandate it had.

The party "mandate" burdened the Democratic League of Kosova and its local structures with taking the responsibility of organizing life wherever repercussions of Serbian repression and violence took place. The harshest consequences would be those caused by the Serbian government following July 2 and September 3, 1990 when all the municipalities in Kosova were suspended together with their managing staff and other municipal structures. They were replaced by managers coming mostly as "reinforcements" from among local Serbs entirely unprepared and unpro-

---

[518] Professor Hajrullah Gorani, a reknown economist and President of the Independent Trade Unions of Kosovo was also a member of LDK Presidency, successfully tying his actions betwen the trade unionists and an all-popular movement led by the LDK. Prior to the strike and upon its declaration, for this "political diversion with the workers" Professor Gorani was arrested and sentenced with 30 days in prison, giving the trade union protest a grand dimension, that of an all-popular demonstration, which it turned into.

fessional, or else from Serbia. On the other hand, strikes by Albanians were being used as an "alibi" for launching classical apartheid methods. With the start of the dismissal and exclusion of Albanians from their jobs, health care system, education, public administration and other institutions (the judiciary, police, and other services), full employment opportunities for local Serbs were created, with good preconditions to stimulate the arrival of the Serbs from Croatia and Bosnia. This measure by Belgrade had been announced in time as "restoring the balance spoiled in the ethnic Serbian cradle," which could be done through organized and even "illegal" removal of unemployed Albanians abroad with the help of state mafia, and by promoting their mass migration as a result of their lack of living perspective.

After September 3, 1990 this process initially started with the dismissal of all Albanian managers of public companies from managing positions, continuing with the suspension of judges, prosecutors and public and state administration staff. Similarly, directors of schools, kindergartens, and cultural institutions were suspended.

According to estimates of Independent Trade Unions of Kosova and the Council for the Defense of Human Rights and Freedoms, from September to December nearly the entire management and administrative structure of Kosova among the Albanians fell victim to these measures, namely over five thousand persons.[519]

With the aim of best identifying these violations, the Independent Trade Unions of Kosova in cooperation with CDHRF created a joint legal defense service, by which the decisions issued by the Serbian authorities and other systemized documentation was addressed to the international mechanisms dealing with human rights, and various world organizations, from humanitarian ones to the UN Security Council.

The second wave of the expulsion and dismissal of Albanians from work continued under the pretext of the strike of September 3 linked to violent measures that the Serbian government undertook in almost all public enterprises, and those of health, culture and education. Imposed administrators asked the remaining Albanian employees, who were not yet removed or dismissed, to sign a "necessary pledge of loyalty to the

---

[519] See periodical Human Right's report for the months of September-December 1990. It contains the data on various forms of pressure that the Serb police authorities exercised against trade union activists and certain structures of those employed in healthcare being threatened with the loss of their jobs.

state of Serbia" in the form of a particular document. Those who refused to sign it could not manage over the enterprises. This right was denied to judges, prosecutors, police officers and administrators resulting in the loss of the right to work.

By early 1991 imposed municipal governments began to implement the Decree of the Government of Serbia of January 2 of that year for the official use of the Serbian language and its script in administration, inscription, and public places.[520]

According to this decree, which came into effect immediately, and which stated "it was in line with the joint common constitution" adopted in March 1989, the Serbo-Croatian language with Cyrillic alphabet emerged as the official language for official use. This abrogated bilingualism in Kosova, as defined in the Kosova Constitution of 1974, which was seen by the authors of the Memorandum as one of the main factors that "had incited great Albanian ideas and an awareness of Kosova as Albanian," a development that allegedly discouraged Serbs by "seeing their cradle as being lost," and the like. As retaliation against the Albanian language was also the degradation of Albanian in the decree itself, ranking it among "local languages in use" the Turkish, Roman, and Egyptian languages![521]

The use of language as an open provocation, which the Serbian regime used for cleansing governance and health administration of Albanian doctors and other technical personnel, attained perturbing proportions when imposed Serbian managers and administrators of hospitals and clinics would order prescriptions written in Serbian language and in the Cyrillic alphabet for Albanian patients. This measure also applied to diagnostics and histories, going as far as prohibiting the use of the Albanian language in communicating with patients. Through this measure, the Faculty of Medicine clinics were soon cleansed of well-known Albanian specialists and doctors who refused to accept these discriminatory measures and the humiliation it caused them. Some left voluntarily while others were always excluded on the grounds of "refusing to abide by Serbian state laws."

---

[520] See the report by the newspaper "*Politika*" of Belgrade of 2 January 1991, with parts of the decree on the official use of the Serbian language in Kosovo.
[521] *Ibid.*

Both the public and state administration stopped using bilingualism, that is, equal use of the Albanian and Serbian language and their script in administration, official documents and the judiciary. From January 1991 all official documents had to bear the seal and emblem of Serbia. Birth and marriage certificates, and personal documents (ID cards, passports, driving licenses and others) were issued only in the Serbian Cyrillic alphabet.

Pursuant to the policy of demonstrating Kosova's Serbianization was the decree for public inscriptions, road and traffic signs, exclusively in the Serbian language and in the Cyrillic alphabet. Albanian café-shop owners, shop owners and artisans, were ordered, to inscribe their firms first in Serbian language and in the Cyrillic alphabet, while the company names, if they happened to be in Albanian, had to be written first in the Cyrillic alphabet. As the Albanian language alphabet has thirty-six characters, and the Serbo-Croatian language has less, then the words using letters lacking in Serbian were replaced by Serbian letters, deliberately demeaning the Albanian language!

Similar was true for the personal identities, which changed whenever written in Serbian, causing many problems in dealing with the Serbian authorities in the judiciary and civil administration, because a single letter could be the cause of opening different property contests.[522]

One of the measures that ultimately accelerated the establishment of a parallel system of Albanians in Kosova affecting final detachment of Albanians from the Serbian violent regime, was the treatment of education at all levels. Serbia wanted to Serbianize through implementation of curricula according to Serbian law, while Albanians would continue to use those approved by the Kosova curricula regardless of the difficulties they faced for years.

This bone of contention Serbia and its administrators had planned in the framework of the essential measures to restore the Serbian state in Kosova excluded by the 1974 Constitution. After all, it was not by accident that after the 1981 demonstrations Belgrade poured all the anger and venom against the University of Kosova, the scientific-educational personnel of this most important institution of Albanian identity, intellectual awareness and educational institution in Kosova, labeling it as "counterrevolutionary."

---

[522] *Ibid.*

And, it was not by accident that the notorious differentiation process started and continued with the University of Kosova and Albanian national institutions, such as the Academy of Sciences and Arts of Kosova, Institute of History, Institute of Albanian Studies in Prishtina, and news media "Rilindja," Radio Television Kosova, and theater and film.

If Serb academics from Belgrade abhorred Albanian education in Kosova and the Kosova University as a bastion of "counterrevolutionary ideology," if Serb writers, following the forced overthrow of Kosova's autonomy, demanded from the Serbian Government to urgently close down the Albanian University of Kosova and place under supervision the entire secondary education, then the decree to have all the levels of education in Kosova work by the Serbian curricula emerged as the best weapon and most effective way to achieve this goal. Albanians would make it clear that compromises could be made on some issues, but in no way on those concerning national identity and civilization in general, such as education, culture and information. This determination, even Belgrade had the opportunity to test three years earlier upon the project of the so-called "common cores" on a Yugoslav level on literature and history curricula, when Serbs tried in the name of "togetherness" to narrow the learning of language, national literature, and history. Kosova's opposition, along with that of Slovenia and Croatia, caused the Serb project of neo-Yugoslavism in education fail to get a green light as Belgrade had requested. The program of the Democratic League of Kosova, recognized by the majority of Albanians, but also other major documents about the fate of Kosova, such as the Kacanik Constitution, language, education and culture remained the foundations of cultural, educational and spiritual identity of Albanians.

The Kacanik Constitution provided also for the protection of others' cultures in Kosova according to the most advanced standards of the time.[523]

Since education in general for Albanians appeared as a fundamental issue requiring a common position and long-term concepts, it was clear that the protection Albanians were going to show for their curricula and their justifiable rejection of the Serb curriculum was to follow political competencies and mutual strategic positions which for years were deliber-

---

[523] *"Akte të Kuvendit të Republikës së Kosovës 2000 – 2002,"* Academy of Sciences and Arts of Kosovo, 2005, pp. 11-41.

ated with a final outcome on agreeing to disagree. But it would be the technical side, the location of the schools, the issue of textbooks, and insurance of the network of teachers and school staff that was transferred almost prematurely to the local infrastructure through the branches and sub-branches. And, being preoccupied with it for years, going through many extremely difficult trials and challenges, the parallel state of the Albanians passed one of the greatest historical tests, if not the greatest, that the state of Kosova brought to the degree of acceptance as part of the functional state-building and civic concept unprecedented so far as political philosophy and experience.

Forms of pre-parallel organization of the state, along with the local structures of the Democratic League of Kosova, extended to twenty-two municipalities in Kosova, were helped by Kosova unionists coming from the ranks of the trade unions with their experience and willingness to take over a lot of important work. This readiness emerged from the very concept of Independent Trade Unions and their determination to be an active and dynamic part of political organizations against the occupying state, whose primary goal was the destruction of the Kosova work force in order to break the main backbone of popular support. It should also be noted that the Independent Trade Unions of Kosova entered this historical process with an important experience of nearly two years of matching with the Serbian regime and its repressive apparatus, when workers were placed on top of major unrest, such as the "Trepca" miners' hunger strike in January and February of 1989, leading long marches of workers in defense of the Constitution and similar movements, making it clear to the Serbian regime that the workers were ready for any sacrifice. Therefore, the general strike of September 3, which was backed by the Democratic League of Kosova and supported by the entire Albanian population of Kosova, showed Albanian political unity in the fight against the Serbian regime and measures long exercised in Kosova. This was quite clear to Belgrade. In line with this demonstration was the behavior of the Serbian regime to start a general offensive to demolish all the "stubborn" structures of Kosova's Albanian society, in the belief that this would bring to their "smoothing" and kneeling down in acceptance of the Serbian state even through force and violence.

In the circumstances of a new Albanian organization coming after the emergence of the Democratic League of Kosova and its concept of a state-building movement through a parallel state – which began to be implemented accordingly once all democratic procedures of its election (refer-endum for independence and free parliamentary elections) were done – Kosova unionists, as an active part of the Albanian society, joined it accepting as bloc membership in the movement from the first moments of its foundation to continue later as a key ally in organizing all of its forms. This is best reflected when the leadership of branches and sub-branches of the Democratic League of Kosova municipalities were provided support by the local branches of the Independent Trade Unions of Kosova. This interaction rose to the level of a permanent joint agreement between the trade unions and the LDK, affecting the Independent Trade Unions of Kosova to play an important role in all stages of the establishment of the state-building movement in Kosova, mainly as its core institutions. Because, it would be parts of Independent Trade Unions of Kosova, education unions, health workers' unions, media trade unions, and lastly trade unions of Kosova police service,[524] that would directly submit loyalty to the Chairman of the Democratic League of Kosova, Dr. Ibrahim Rugova, as Kosova's main leader, even before he, by the free vote of the people in May 1992 was elected president of the Republic of Kosova, a

---

[524] The loyalty of branches of Trade Unions of Kosovo started with the involvement of trade unions in the education branch of the education council set up by the Democratic League of Kosovo, led by Professor Fehmi Agani, with joint actions linked to both concrete and strategic issues. Unionists were an important part of this Council. Similarly the branch of healthcare workers union, almost entirely involved in the direct operation of the Democratic League of Kosovo in the field of health, at a time when the Albanian population from day to day was being deprived of healthcare and its services, expressed the need for the branches and sub-branches to build fast a parallel organization of health services. The Union of the employees of the Kosovo Police was the last to submit loyalty to the Democratic League of Kosovo as carrier of the statehood movement. This also had its own reasons, as given the complexity of the service there was a close agreement between the leadership of the Democratic League of Kosovo and some party leaders from the Coordinating Council of Albanian Political Parties from Yugoslavia, that the police service of Kosovo had to first be constituted on a union level and then, in various forms of the service, pass successively to the ranks of adequate parallel state structures, which were formed after the election of the Government of the Republic of Kosovo. This agreement was harmonized with the U.S. embassy advisers on security issues, who from the beginning were monitoring many of the strategic actions of the Democratic League and later of the Government, maintaining the main say.

mandate granted to him by the Albanians once again in the circumstances of Serbian occupation.

This interaction not only enabled the first appearance of the nuclei of the Kosova Albanian parallel state but with successes reached in practice in many areas of life it affected the handling of the parallel life as a necessity in the struggle for liberation and independence.

The period from Kosova's declaration of a sovereign state at the Kacanik historic Assembly of September 7, 1990, the Independence Referendum of September 26, 1991, and the appointment of the Government of the Republic of Kosova emerging out of the deal of the spectrum of political parties at the end of October, along with the first successes achieved in the field of international affirmation of the Kosova issue – (the trip of Albanian representatives in the U.S. at the invitation of the U.S. Congress, the evidence provided there, the visit to Prishtina by U.S. congressmen and senators, headed by Robert Dole in August 1990, Senator Nickles' amendment on restoring and respecting the rights of the Albanians,[525] MEPs visits, frequent presence of international human rights monitors and others) – a great success represented the extraordinary homogeneity of the population through versatile solidarity. This solidarity reached a high level, rightly seen from the outside as an unprecedented shield of efforts to resist Serbian violence and pressure. It was regarded as a powerful weapon against the regime in Belgrade, by which Albanians achieved two important historic objectives: that of civilized behavior of a people organized in every respect and in all areas of life, so one that deserves a state, and that of narrowing and exposure of the Serbian government in Kosova solely to the extent of an occupier."[526]

In fact what would be called an unprecedented weapon against Serbian violence and plans to use all means to crush a whole nation in the face of the whole world, grew even more after the emergence of the real weapons that had already begun to cast fire on various fronts in Slovenia and Croatia while the Yugoslav Army, headed by Serbs positioned on

---

[525] Senator Nickles' Amendment was subtmitted to the Administration of President Bush for approval after Senator Dole's visit to Prishtina in August 1990 being a witness to the Serb violence in Kosovo against Albanians, whose both individual and collective rights were being violated. The U.S. Administration approved it on 5 May 1991.

[526] See Viktor Meier's assessment in his book „Wie Jugoslawien verspielt wurde," 1995, pp. 99-121.

their side, was reasoning with the alleged "protection of Yugoslavia from secessionists."

In these circumstances the homogenization represented the internal link from fear and uncertainty, and solidarity as the only and last resort of defense, which should be used without hesitation, especially if one had in mind that the international community, unable to do anything, had accepted the process of the dissolution of Yugoslavia.[527] The latter was already on the downfall but for Albanians it all represented another uncertainty and greater risk, because they were seen as scattered minorities in Serbia, Macedonia, and Montenegro. Faced with this difficult situation, the political structure that had taken the lead, on its way to do all the depositions concerning the determination and declaration of the political will of the Albanians – such as the Constitutional Declaration of July 2, Declaration of the Kosova Republic at Kaçanik Assembly and holding of the Referendum on Independence soon to follow, in the face of these actions, which were in line with the dynamics of the development of crisis of the country – no big effort was needed to put into action what would be seen as a "powerful weapon" against Serb violence and occupation.

But, the homogenization and sense of solidarity to be placed into effective action needed an orientation in order that the situation be kept under permanent supervision. And, this was accomplished through the slogan "help your neighbor first." The use of the slogan linking ethics with belief seemed to be the most convenient and simplest way, where each political philosophy could be based on the condition that it provided reliability. Since the concept of the state-constituent movement that the platform of the Democratic League of Kosova was promoting for the first time had created an internal unity out of ideological amalgam and other divisions that it had produced, in which all views and currents of both legal and illegal actions had found full expression. This was an opportunity for the first time for the so-called "internal fronts" to turn into a common front, that of institutional resistance against Serbian occupation, with the parallel state playing a crucial role. Thus, it was expected that the organizational focus rested on the premise of internal solidarity, as a

---

[527] See decision of the Hague Conference on arbitrariness of disintegration of former Yugoslavia through Badinter's Commission, declaring Yugoslavia in December 1991 in a process of disintegration and setting the criteria for the acceptance of new states to be met following secession from Yugoslavia in order to be accepted as legitimate.

starting point for further constructions, which without this segment would not go far.

As developments were taking place at an increasingly dramatic and even tragic pace, Serbia was showing that it would not stop to realize the threat of Milosevic issued in Gazimestan on the occasion of the commemoration of the 600th anniversary of the Kosova Battle that "Serbia would not spare even war as a means for the realization of its aspirations." They were being reflected by the escalation of violence in Kosova, where Albanians were exposed daily to pressures and provocations aimed at the expulsion of the population from its ethnic lands. It was expected that in anticipation of Kosova's state institutional configuration which its legitimacy needed to win the free elections to be held in April of the following year, the slogan "first help your neighbor" expanded with "helping hand for self-help" was attributed to the political movement to include the country's leading intellectual and creative powers. The Democratic League of Kosova, as carrier of the Movement, in its first Assembly, held on May 5, 1991, made concrete and very important steps when in its Central Council, it included 55 eminent intellectuals of Kosova, from academicians to the politically persecuted, such as Professor Kadri Halimi, who in 1960, at Anamorava, together with Ali Aliu and Hyrije Hana, led the illegal organization *"Committee for Unification of Kosova with Albania."*[528]

---

[528] The first Assembly of the Democratic League of Kosovo, held in Prishtina, in its new organizational structure, according to the Statute approved by the Assembly, defined the Central Council as the main body of the party. There were twelve central committees, in which those of the political system, education and culture, issues of social protection, health, the media, legal issues, self-defense, economy, foreign relations and ecology, formed the core of the parallel state. Noted intellectuals and experts of Kosovo were elected to lead the commissions. They came from the following composition of LDK Central Council: *Dr. Ibrahim Rugova, Jusuf Buxhovi, Dr. Idriz Ajeti, porf. Fehmi Agani, Dr. Bujar Bukoshi, Dr. Ali Aliu, Dr. Rexhep Ismaili, Dr. Sabri Hamiti, Dr. Gani Bobi, Dr. Ejup Statatovci, Dr. Nexhat Daci, Dr. Fatmir Sejdiu, Dr. Faik Brestovci, Ramë Buja, Edita Tahiri, Mehmet Hajrizi, Dr. Ismet Salihu, Dr. Fadil Raka, Anton Kolaj, Mujë Rugova, Edi Shukriu, Ibrahim Berisha, Rexhep Gjergji, Skender Blakaj, Dr.Binak Kastrati, Mehmet Kraja, Fadil Hysaj, Kadri Halimi, Dr. Zenel Kelmendi, Mensur Fejza, Dr. Shaqir Shaqiri, Adil Pireva, Mujë Krasniqi, Dr. Abdyl Krasniqi, Ibush Jonuzi, Engjëll Berisha, Agim Çavdërbasha, Selatin Novosella, Xhemail Mustafa, Isa Haxhiu, Myrvete Dreshaj, Shyhrete Malaj, Agron Dida, Milazim Krasniqi, Nexhat Krasniqi-Nekra, Basri Çaprici, Skënder Kastrati, Arif Bozaxhi, Naip Zeka, Irfan Pashoja, Fadil Kryeziu, Dr. Simë Dobreci, Idriz*

Inclusion of noted intellectuals in the Central Council and intellectuals from among the Women's Forum of the Democratic League of Kosova in the work of respective committees influenced for good at the grassroots level, as they were managing with certain portfolios, especially those dealing with social care, education, information and self-defense, by which they won the confidence of the people, convinced that there was something on which they could find support.

Social care did not coincidentally turn to a work priority, because violent measures undertaken by the Serbian occupying power in the economy, public administration and public services, had hit the middle class society which found itself at risk professionally and materially, because employees who lost their jobs, unable to obtain social assistance, were turned at once into social cases. Therefore, as such they would not only be helped financially, but something had to be done so that they would still feel useful to society and their neighborhood and this could be best achieved by finding a place for them in the activities related to the functioning of the parallel state, an activity which needed so many volunteers. In the field of health, the engagement of doctors and other staff and technical assistance, who left or were fired from work, went just fine, as the branches and sub-branches, almost spontaneously, began to operate the parallel health service. Discharged doctors soon joined the mobile teams in the field that already acted as portable ambulances. LDK Women's Forum in cooperation with the Union of Health Workers in many parts of Kosova had set up maternity checkpoints of respective teams reaching as far as the most remote areas of the country to assist nursing mothers and newborns. Similarly were treated pediatric services, dentists and others, spreading and moving widely into schools and wherever they were needed. Services were offered for free, while the health workers union solidarity fund, which kept funds established by donors and aid from abroad, saw to rewarding those in need. There were many cases when a certain layer of doctors who enjoyed better conditions, gave up any kind of payment for the benefit of their colleagues.

Thus, solidarity was the starting point of protection from the effects of Serbian violence, but at the same time it represented an internal coun-

---

Berani, Abdyl Rama, Paulina Lumezi and Milihate Shala. Committees included outside members, mainly professionals, who tended to the creation of certain policies.

terattack against programs intended to demolish the structure of civil resistance prior to its being well established in action. But the internal solidarity, which ran from close family to extended family and into the neighborhood, community and beyond to reach its highest point of expansion to where it was most needed, would not be successful without the participation of Albanians from Macedonia, the Presheva Valley, Montenegro, Croatia, and Slovenia, where many Albanians lived and worked. The concept of solidarity would also not be successful without the unreserved help of Albanians from the diaspora, those from the United States and various European countries, where they were already working as temporary workers or even as citizens of those countries.

Solidarity from within was primarily reflected through the collection of goods for home consumption, from food to clothing. While externally, solidarity was reflected by the depositing of funds into solidarity funds raised through the branches of the Democratic League of Kosova, which were submitted to the central committee of solidarity, which was then distributed through branches and subsidiaries in accordance with the requirements as presented by their representatives. So it was prior to the operating of the fund of the Government of the Republic of Kosova as specified by the contribution of 3% of personal income and profits mainly from the Diaspora.[529] The statement on asset specification managed by the Central Funding Council during the seven-year period shows that 81% of funds were spent on primary education needs, 0.5% to 3.3% on university and research institutes, 3.8% on Kosova institutions and municipalities, 0.3% to 0.2% on culture and sports, 0.4% for health, 1.2% for social assistance, 2.1% on assistance for vulnerable regions, 3.8% on assistance to

---

[529] For the period October 1991 – September 1999 the Government of the Republic of Kosovo raised through its Republic funds and other sources a total of 217,666,570.60 DM, 3,632,099.67 USD, 30,566,699.17 FRS and 24,120 Pounds. These sums were raised in 19 regular funds of the Republic of Kosovo: participation of the LDK Self-Defense Fund in Stutgart, Action on Kosovo Independence, Relief Action for Drenica, occasional help from the diaspora in Turkey, Slovakia, Spain, Canada, bank prime rates and other sources. The Fund of the Republic of Kosovo in Germany was most successful in fund collection. The fund collected a total of 116,394,647.41 DM or 43.75% of total assets. The Fund of the Republic of Kosovo in Switzerland came in second with 46,259,861.77 FRS, with a participation of 28.88% in the General Fund. (*See Report of the Government of Kosovo for the period October 1991 December 1999, submitted to the Assembly of Kosovo in January 2000*).

vulnerable families. If the percentages are broken down in the language of numbers, it appears that for education needs (including subsidizing the publication of textbooks) 76,340,613 DM was spent. In addition to these funds there were the supplementary ones such as 1.8 million DM for documentation and textbooks, 4.2 million DM for the Faculty of Mining and Metallurgy, 1.6 million DM for clothing and food for school children, 150 thousand DM for scientific activities, 35 thousand DM for publishing activities, 35 thousand DM to "Rilindja" and others.[530]

An important part of internal solidarity was also the care for artists, writers, scientists, and academics. Initially, the Democratic League of Kosova, and later the Government of the Republic of Kosova established a solidarity fund for artists, activated from the autumn of 1990 and running until March 1999. The fund initially provided monthly payments to 22 reporters and editors of "Rilindja," all of them dismissed after its foreclosure, as well as 13 journalists from Radio and Television of Prishtina. To this number were added 27 writers, 12 artists and 6 academics. Salaries for journalists, writers, artists and academics ranged from 200-400 DM per month, an amount significantly larger than that of Serbian and Russian academics.[531]

As the Government of the Republic of Kosova in March 1992 established its Central Council for Finance in Kosova, it took over management of the entire school system funding, but at the same time it took over the financing of the Albanological Institute, the Institute of History of Kosova, Kosova Archives, Theatre of Kosova, and also partially financed the publishing activity of "Rilindja," Office of textbook publications, transformed into "School Book" Publications, and the Pedagogical Institute of Kosova. Earlier, occasional assistance would go to Museum employees and other information institutions that were transferred to Tirana (Radio Television of Kosova – satellite program).

According to data from the documents of the Government of the Republic of Kosova, as well as the documentation of the Democratic League of Kosova from the period 1989-1992, submitted to the Institute of History of Kosova and being currently analyzed, the parallel state of

---

[530] See work Report of the Government of the Republic of Kosovo 1991-1999, submitted to the Assembly of Kosovo in January 2000, p. 36.

[531] Full documentation lists of solidarity with journalists, writers, artists and academics is found in the Documents Fund of the Democratic League of Kosovo, submitted to the Institute of History of Kosovo, processed as "LDK File," Box I-VI.

Kosova for eight years financed more than twenty-two thousand teachers, university professors, educators and education administrators, and financed more than twelve hundred employees of arts, culture and creativity as part of the Kosova institutions, even of those outside institutions for making efforts to keep them open.

The Challenge of Education – A Paramount Issue

School curricula – the "apple of discord" between Prishtina and Belgrade, and the first test for the protection of national identity which always tested the state-building loyalty. – Closing down of Albanian schools – part of the Serbian strategy for Kosova submission and creation of conditions for a "quiet" ethnic cleansing of Kosova. – Serbian vandalism of education and culture – retaliation for the refusal made against a pro-Serb orientation of Yugoslavism.

By September 1991, when it was clear that Serbia through perseverance in all levels of education in Kosova to work with the Belgrade-issued curricula had begun to put into action the strategy of the collapse of the Albanian education in Kosova – and doing so by blaming Albanians – an Albanian rejoinder was needed to this challenge. This response was proven to be one of the most difficult, but also a very important one for the preservation of the nucleus of the Albanian population in Kosova before any scattering that would be inevitable and even fatal if they had to give up on keeping the Albanian education alive even despite facing numerous difficulties and problems bearing consequences for years after the process of Kosova's secession from Serbia.

If things were to be regarded only in terms of numbers, excluding other factors over which strategic concepts are set, however, the language of figures indicates that a major enterprise with about twenty-two thousand teachers, educators of all levels and other associated services of the entire school infrastructure, together with over three hundred thousand pupils and students, and if behind every student stood only parents, it appears that the educational system, the one called the "basement education," involved more than half of the active population in Kosova to keep at home in more serious circumstances of pressure and Serbian state terror. And in the face of this fact it is needless to say what Kosova would have been after a few years and how it would look without this action and without this commitment in this area.

Given that the active civil resistance and parallel state as a form of institutional resistance would be almost meaningless without national education on which the future was projected, the leadership of the Democratic League of Kosova and the Trade Unions of Employees of Education, Albanian Teachers' Union (ADL) "Naim Frasheri" and the inherited infrastructure of the system (Institute for Publishing textbooks and school supplies and Pedagogical Institute) reached a common agreement. According to it Serbian curricula could not be accepted, even if Belgrade made good its threats that in the "schools of Serbia in Kosova," as stated, any teaching with separatist curricula would not be permitted, and that separatist teachers and professors would not be funded.

This persistence and determination would probably not make sense and would nullify any initiative without including as to where and how the Albanian teaching would take place when it was known that Serbia had already started to shut the doors to schools for Albanian students, and that they would eventually close down upon rejection of the Belgrade curricula. Apart from purely technical dilemmas, related to the provision of premises for hundreds of thousands of students, there emerged a dilemma of an additional nature: tables and chairs and, above all, the issue of financing a system of over twenty-two thousand employees.

Certainly many more other issues and dilemmas existed related to textbooks, their publication, distribution and everything else. But, the one that was more sensitive, more unpredictable, was concerned with the behavior of the Serbian occupying regime towards the parallel education, as it was known that it represented the foundations of Kosova's statehood. It was known that the doors of schools would shut down for Albanian students. What was not known was if the doors of schools for Albanian students in private homes and other premises to be used for the teaching could be kept open, or if they would be tolerated by Belgrade. One had also to account for the risk of occurrence of other internal unforeseen factors that could compromise the determination, which considering its time duration was accompanied with the potential risks of emerging confusion that could ensue from the validity of education in relation to society.

Dr. Fehmi Agani, responsible for education and the development of a national education strategy in the context of Serbian occupation, told U.S.

representatives that "there will be no compromise with national education with the Serbs even if we will be forced to keep our schools in the fields and mountains and through the snow and rain..."[532]

No doubt that Fehmi Agani's words expressed an Albanian consensus on the issue as well as those related to the determination that there should be no bargaining with the main segments of national and state identity even when related to a dilemma which was being whispered here and there whether children and the young generation could also fall prey to being sacrificed for a failed political project. These and other dilemmas were not only principled and political, but also vital as it was one thing to talk and another to fulfill it, especially considering the circumstances, which were both predictable in as much as with major risks.

Indeed, Serbian officials from the ranks of enforced structures running education, who had formally sought talks with representatives of the Albanian education, were rather made to demonstrate the well-known Serbian stance that for Belgrade "separatist education" in Kosova had come to an end rather than to find even a temporary compromise. Serbian officials would not even accept the Albanian side's proposal under which

---

[532] International representatives and diplomats accredited in Belgrade, especially on the American and German parts, more often showed concern about what was called "dispute" with Serbia about school curricula and irreconcilable positions between Belgrade and Prishtina. Many of them raised the issue of the simple humanitarian aspect that had to do with endangering children in private schools, even if it would not be disturbed by the Serbian authorities. Their curiosity was also connecte to where the Albanian schools were placed and how long it could take considering that opportunites for a normal learning process were very meager. Not infrequently the question was posed as to if all this posed an adventure which could backfire for the Albanian political factor if parents facing difficulties and dangers for the children suffering from Serbian violence would one day give up that form of education. Moreover, there was also criticism that the behavior of Albanians appeared as anti-educational and inhumane, precisely because the children were denied the right to education and emancipation, even when held in inappropriate circumstances or national discrimination being better than no education at all. American representatives also offered their good will of mediation to Professor Agani and representatives of the Education Workers Unions and the Teacher's Association through specific conversations, but they did not bring anything, as Serbia linked the issue of education in Kosovo with obligations arising from the new constitution, approved in March 1989, which was unacceptable to the Albanians, as it was approved by violence and against their will.

the school year would begin and continue with the current curricula, by excluding Serb students from this position, applying Serbian curricula instead, while in the future a joint commission could be set within a year, in line with political developments and circumstances that would arise, and other decisions could be taken. Moreover, Albanians were also able to accept what was already turning into reality, sharing and learning process of students by national origin, even though this would go to their detriment, because they were not in a position to choose on anything. Serbs, who had already begun to discriminate against Albanian students and teachers in every aspect, from September 1 were being encouraged to say no to Albanian education by blaming the latter, which among others, released Belgrade of its financial obligations towards the Albanian education from an income of salaries and other expenses for school infrastructure reaching a total of as much as 120 million dollars annually!

An uncompromising war against Albanian education, which followed the ruining of the autonomy of Kosova by force in March 1989 was underway not hiding its intentions as publicly manifested in the admission competition for new students to the university year 1991 / 1992 announced in June of that year, when the University of Prishtina, placed under the state of emergency measures a year before, announced vacancies for only two thousand new students from Kosova and as many for students from other parts of Serbia . The latter, for the first time, to study in Kosova were offered special working conditions and study, among the best in the country. The latter were offered special benefits for study the best of their kind. In addition, for the first time instruction in the Albanian language was being abolished.

The rector of the University of Prishtina at that time, Radivoje Papovic, a "brown-nosing" assistant to Albanian professors during the seventies, becoming a target five years later to an attempted assassination in Prishtina in an action of which Kosova Liberation Army (KLA) took responsibility, would boastfully rant: "There will be no more great Albanian indoctrination at the University of Prishtina!"[533]

---

[533] See *"Jedinstvo"* of Prishtina of 20 June 1991. In the article, Rector Papovic, spoke with anger about "settling scores with great Albanian chauvinist ideology that had grown up around the school with the help of Serbian money," an ideology that, according to him, "had produced killers of Serbia and Serbian being in Kosovo and Metohija." This pamphlet written by Rector Papovic was also published in the Belgrade press, where as usual, through letters to the editor and other forms, represented supportive feedback

The outburst of Rector Radivoje Papovic had to do not only with the exclusion of Albanian students from the University of Kosova, but it equally hit well over two thousand Albanian students from Macedonia and the Presheva Valley and Montenegro, who studied since the sixties in Kosova's various faculties becoming somehow despite Kosova's administrative division an educated and civilized part of Albanian ethnicity in Yugoslavia, which had begun breathing towards a common spiritual integration which in later years would be displayed as part of the collective identity. In the seventies the University of Prishtina, had been given a quota which was more or less maintained. This was done with the intention that Prishtina and Kosova be rightly considered by Albanians of other parts of Yugoslavia as a common herd of Albanian identity, which was not seen with favorable eyes by either Macedonia or Montenegro, who were blaming Prishtina for "Albanian paternalism," an issue that in 1981 formed the basis of the accusation condemning the University of Kosova as the "center of Albanian nationalism and irredentism." Even despite this accusation and significant consequences arising from it, especially in limiting the number of students, vacancies for Albanian students from Macedonia and Montenegro were always preserved.

But, in the new circumstances, Serbia was determined to ban an Albanian university in Prishtina extending its occupying power all over. This automatically meant the end for the research institutes and scientific institutions belonging to superior education infrastructure. Under the new Serbian measures, Kosova was to become a province of marginalized Albanians and their culture, while gaining for the Serbs an increased piety as a Serbian cultural, educational and spiritual center joined by religious

---

from all parts of Serbia, and especially from the Kosovo Serbs, who "with the ending of the irredentist university" in Kosovo saw the "beginning of the return of Kosovo to a Serb cradle."

Belgrade's "*Politika*," as an ultra nationalistic newspaper, had turned in the recent years into a drum of Great-Serb chauvinism, in which Albanians were always presented as "being sworn enemies of the Serbs," tried to turn Papovic's poison that had surpassed every measure and was beginning to be exploited by the foreign media to argue hegemonic policy toward Kosovo by Belgrade, into a reduced "clarification" that the "University of Prishtina would be neither Serbian nor Albanian, but rather a university in the true sense of the word - a center of knowledge and non-ideological and non-political emancipation. So it would be for all citizens who intend to study."

iconography to be reflected in the construction of a large Serbian Orthodox church on the University campus, close to the University Library from where after emergency measures Albanian books and everything else related to the Albanian cultural identity there were being removed. A new Serbian Orthodox Church was announced as one of the greatest and imposing temples of Serbian Orthodoxy in the Balkans,[534] with reportedly many others to come, which were allegedly destroyed during "Kosova's Albanianization by force" in which the spiritual monuments of the medieval Serbian Orthodox sites allegedly suffered the most, the restoration of which was related to the demagogy of the great Serbian indoctrination at all levels.[535]

---

[534] The Serbian Orthodox Church started building in the University area, without a permit and in violation of the city's urban plan approved in 1985. Groundbreaking work started in June 1991, on the day "Vidovdan" in the presence of the Serbian Patriarch Pavle of the Serbian Orthodox Church, which held a solemn mass from top to bottom chauvinistic, in which he eventually called for Kosovo's return to Serbia, regardless of the means to be used. Like Milosevic two years earlier at Gazimestan who had declared "the right of Serbian rule over Kosovo," which had to be restored by force and by means of war, the Serbian patriarch had declared the "Serb spiritual and historical right over Kosovo and Metohija," which according to him was occupied by "Albanian national-communists through the help of the antichrist and anti-Serb Tito.". The ultranationalist leader Vojislav Seselj, after blessing the foundations of the Orthodox Church in Prishtina promoted Serb volunteer units, who he said "will restore Tzar Lazar's fallen glory in this country in defense of Christianity." With such an orgy he was putting forward the gilded cross on the dome of the church in 1995. Besides Archbishop Pavle the ceremonial was also attended by the highest political leadership of Serbia (besides Milosevic), with the presence of Dobrica Cosic, author of the recent Memorandum of the Serbian Academy of Sciences, who though had failed as president of the rump Yugoslavia, elected in 1992, spoke on behalf of the Serbian people and its historic right over Kosovo with pathetic scenes, resembling that of Chetnik voyvodas in Bosnia, who had already stained their hands with the blood of Bosnians.

[535] According to the data of the *"Association of Protection of Endangered Peoples"* in Götingen of Germany, published by its leader, Timan Cylh, in Bulletin no. 33/98 of 1998, Serbia, increasingly through the use of violent measures and conditions of curfew placed from time to time in Kosovo from 1989 to 1998, built 34 churches in the name of rebuilding those ravaged by Albanians, though it could never provide proof for this. It staretd in Prishtina with the construction of a large church, the size of Saint Sava in Belgrade, while in Gjakova, a city with 99% Albanians, looking for traces of medieval

The Formation of the Kosova Government and Parallel State Institutions

> *Establishment of the Republic of Kosova – set the conditions for starting implementation of parallel state of Kosova. – In addition to other ministries, the Ministry of Defense and Ministry of Internal Affairs were established and care taking for Albanian recruits and officers in Croatia, Slovenia and Bosnia and Herzegovina resumed. – The truth about the first attempts to organize the defense and self-defense in Albania and Croatia and the shortcomings in this regard. – Many members of the Kosova Police Service from among "self-defense," who were "on hold," ended up in Serbian prisons without having been involved in any activity of the resistance movement.*

Since neither Albanians nor Serbs would give way – and it suited the Serbs, who had been expecting "Albanian stubbornness" – the Albanians had little left but to find alternative routes to schools outside of their school buildings, which took years to build with the labor of workers in Kosova, while Serbs even formally were proclaiming the schools as "Serb" and ultimately placing in them their nationalist iconography in line with the Serb medieval spirit dominated by the cross and the Serb state emblem. To complete the image serving their goal, school names were replaced with mainly names of figures and personalities from the Serbian Middle Ages or those from the past with sentiments against Albanians. This was a continuation of what a year before, on the occasion of the enforcement of emergency measures, began as a unilateral removal of school names of Albanian writers and historical figures, allegedly made "upon parents' request" who could not accept that their children endured "ideological pressure of Albanian separatism" and the like, thus opening the way for other acts of vandalism against Albanian schools with which the media was reporting always "in a positive spirit." Therefore, it was

---

churches, smacked in the central park of the city, after having ruined a monument against fascism, built a large church. In this city of about fifty thousand Albanians, with no more than over a thousand Serbs there was an Orthodox church. *"The Association for the Protection of Endangered Peoples"* from Götingen reported of similar actions of the Serbian Orthodox Church in Bosnia and Herzegovina and parts of Croatia, where in the early nineties Serb rebels, aided by the Yugoslav army, had proclaimed the Serb state of Krajina, which had also promoted medieval Serbian Orthodox iconography.

predictable that the final occupation of Albanian schools would be followed with demonstrations and vandalism of breaking busts of Albanian historical figures and dumping them in garbage sites and in the streets.

Such an act of vandalism was the ruin of the bust of Hasan Prishtina in front of the primary school in Prishtina bearing his name, an act marked with provocations, and Albanians responding against the destroyers although this would be hindered by the Serbian police intervening to protect rampant demolishers. In some places fierce clashes with Serbian police ensued in an attempt to prevent the desecration of monuments of Albanian culture that was taking place in public.

The stage of vandalism among the most barbaric ones, taking place upon the removal of busts and Albanian culture symbols from schools and generally against spiritual traces of Albanians, was replaced by the expulsion of Albanian parallel education outside school buildings, opening a chapter that would last many years of what would be called underground education, which represented both symbolism and reality. For, the Albanian education in its efforts for survival had to face very difficult conditions, on the one hand with the improvisation of private facilities and schools in most unsuitable conditions for minimum work activity, and on the other, to see it was not hampered by the Serbian police. The latter purged what it called "illegal schools" of Albanians, not equally to ban them in as much as to keep them and educational activities altogether in a broken state, in a state of internal fear and de-concentration in order to have education fail in the inside and lose any sense for both students and parents. The goal was to compromise from the beginning the main component of the parallel state, which in this segment was determined to behave in accordance with the Constitution of the Republic of Kosova approved at the Kaçanik Assembly, an implementation of the Kosova's state most important and susceptible sector.

Relying on this determination that was rather historic, Albanian education in Kosova would be burdened with the task and responsibility of being among the first to be put at the service of the sacred cause of the state of Kosova and its implementation. This major undertaking, involved directly and indirectly all the human potential of Kosova and its positive energy, which for the first time in history would fall as an investment among the most powerful ones of civilized proportions, as the survival and maintenance of Albanian education, from the first grades of primary school to university level, doing a good service not only to Albanians, who needed it mostly, but also to others, to civilization in general. Furthermore, it can be said that education, even in the way it was taking place, was good service for the Serb occupiers themselves, realizing they were not dealing with vandals but rather with civilized people.

With the establishment of the Government of the Republic of Kosova,[536] which following a referendum held on independence in which the absolute majority Albanians said yes to independence, in late October, preconditions were virtually created for pre-parallel forms of organization to have full supervision of the Government, although evidently their management and implementation continued to further remain a burden for local government, namely branches and sub-branches of the Democratic League of Kosova, which covered the entire territory of Kosova and were almost irreplaceable in all respects.

It should be noted that the first provisional government of the Republic of Kosova was elected by the Assembly of Kosova on October 19, 1991 and was a coalition government. Dr. Bujar Bukoshi was elected Prime Minister from the Democratic League of Kosova, a urologist by profession, distinguished activist of the party since its establishment.

The following ministries comprised the Government initially:
- Ministry of Economy and Finance,
- Ministry of Education, Science and Culture,
- Ministry of Justice,
- Ministry of Health, Labor and Social Welfare,
- Ministry of Defense,
- Ministry of Internal Affairs,
- Ministry of Information, and
- Ministry of Foreign Affairs.

Dr. Bukoshi and several of the ministers after spending six months in Slovenia moved to Germany, near Stuttgart. Later they moved to Bonn, where Dr. Bukoshi led other portfolios, with that of Information in Switzerland, and the Education, Interior and Defense Ministers in Tirana.

On the German part the Government of Kosova was never officially recognized, but it was tolerated as part of the Democratic League of

---

[536] On the activities of the Interim Government of the Republic of Kosovo see for more in Buxhovi, Jusuf: "*Kthesa hitorike – shteti paralel dhe rezistenca e armatosur,*" 2009, part on "Documents," pp. 431-522.

Kosova which had its branch representation in Germany. Unofficially, certain circles of the German Government helped the Government of Kosova in many ways, as Germany, along with two hundred thousand refugees it was hosting, with their number increasing day by day, and with over one hundred thousand Albanians who as guest workers or other forms had obtained German citizenship, had other interests as well even deeper for Kosova so that would in no way remain under Serbia, although one did not get such an impression from the political games used in diplomacy and German politics to keep to the tune of the main international player.

In Germany the Government installed at that time the three percent fund, to which for years Albanians from Kosova, Macedonia and the Presheva Valley and other places where they worked and stayed temporarily in the West deposited considerable amounts held at the German bank, in a Swiss bank and later in "Dardania" bank in Tirana. But before doing that, the Government took over all the funds theretofore abroad, among which the most important one was that of the LDK branch in Germany "In defense of the fatherland," in Aachen, that of Switzerland and donations in the USA. These funds were used to finance government activities, but also to maintain education, health, and culture and wide-scale social solidarity in Kosova, used by many families in need of financial assistance.

In order to institutionalize the issue of the distribution of assets and in accordance with domestic needs, the Government of the Republic of Kosova upon the proposal of the Central Council of the Democratic League of Kosova, which until then had been carrying all forms of organization of parallel power, on March 16, 1992, with Decision 01/32, established the *Central Financing Council*. Mehmet Hajziri was appointed Chairman of the Board, and the Central Council of the LDK was composed of the following members: Mustafë Blaka, Ismail Kastrati, Muharrem Ibrahimi, Ali Gagica, Skënder Dyla and Bajram Shatri.[537]

Regarding representation abroad, the Government succeeded in having a single office in Tirana, called the *Office of the Republic of Kosova*. During its work in Tirana the office faced difficulties and many problems,

---

[537] For more on the work of the Central Finance Council of Kosovo, see the book *"Central Finance Council of Kosovo"* by Mehmet Hajrizi, Ismail Kastrati and Bajram Shatri, Prishtina, 2007.

working in circumstances of pressure coming from different sides with which it was not capable of dealing, not properly prepared or authorized to deal with many issues, which in time turned into a burden and even an open problem.

As the Government of the Republic of Kosova, which was temporarily in exile (the Prime Minister in Germany, and several ministers in Tirana, Switzerland and elsewhere) needed another two to three months before it got itself on its knees, at a time when the school year had started, taking care over the education continued to remain under the jurisdiction of the *Central Council of Education* gathering representatives of all levels of education: Association of Albanian Teachers "Naim Frashëri" (LASH), the Department of Labor Unions of Education, Institute for Publishing Textbooks and Learning, a work body which had managed to successfully cope with many problems of finding school premises for all levels of education and carrying out preparations for the beginning of the learning process without delay. Here too the factor of homogenization and unprecedented solidarity was evident, involving a whole army of volunteers and activists, who had taken over the selection of school buildings and their adaptation to the extent possible as far as their supervision and physical maintenance. Since most classes were held in facilities that were normally found in suburban neighborhoods and settlements outside the city, as was the case with university teaching, the utmost was being done to ensure transportation for both students and teachers in a way not to be quite obvious to the eyes of the Serbian police and their agents, who often intervened in some facilities.

It was only in the second semester after the winter vacation that lasted over a month, that the Government of the Republic of Kosova, through the Ministry of Education, began to help and later guide the educational process in Kosova. This of course brought obvious improvements, among which, the most important was providing salaries for teachers and other personnel engaged in the learning process. Although initially symbolic, salaries were regular gradually reaching the level of the average teacher's salary received in Serbian schools.

Initially, the salaries for teachers were provided by the Government using the solidarity funds pouring from all sides, especially from abroad and donations that were indirectly provided by some European countries, which were very interested to have some kind of peace preserved in Kosova in circumstances of war, which had already broken out in the north of the country. With the establishment of the "three percent" fund,[538] the Government of the Republic of Kosova gained the opportunity of treating Kosova's education, through the Central Council of Finance and its funds not only in a consistency with the creation of basic conditions (improving teaching conditions in facilities and providing teachers' salaries), but also in doing something more for providing textbooks free of charge ("Alphabet Book" and other elementary school textbooks), so that on all levels of education texts were published in accordance with the curricula of the Republic of Kosova, which had already been approved.

In this regard, cooperation with relevant educational institutions of Albania was beneficial as well as the assistance from the Albanian state provided for the maintenance of education in Kosova. This was preceded by the cooperation agreement between the Ministry of Education of the Republic of Albania and the Republic of Kosova in August 1993. That marked the time when the first attempts of educational institutions of the Republic of Kosova and those of Albania worked together on drafting some common textbooks, especially in the field of language, literature, history, and other branches. Under this agreement activities in various fields such as education took place: setting up joint committees for all professional fields of education, establishing joint committees to develop common curricula, preparation of joint textbooks and authors, harmonization of pre-university and university education systems for the exchange of personnel and students in various fields as well as their engagement in joint research projects and the advancement of teaching through organizing various forms of vocational and scientific training. Experts from both Prishtina and Tirana soon signed an agreement through which criteria would be defined for the common textbooks for primary education.[539]

---

[538] The Government of the Republic of Kosovo on November 20, 1991 began the procedure for the establishment of the Foundation in Geneva on December 15, 1991 and approved by Decision 7/91 on fundraising for the Republic of Kosovo. The decision foresaw the setting up of funds of the Republic of Kosovo for each country, where the fundraising base would be workers' wages with a net average of 3%. (See Work Report of the Government of the Republic of Kosovo 1991-1999, p. 26).

[539] Work Report of the Government of the Republic of Kosovo 1991-1999, pp. 22, 23. According to the Association of Albanian Teachers "Naim Frashëri" (LASH), since 1993 onwards, along with the work done on the preparations for the design of textbooks in accordance with national education and their publication in very difficult circumstances,

With the formation of the Government of the Republic of Kosova, along with education, which remained the main pillar of the implementation of the state of Kosova, significant attention was paid to the surviving segments, such as social protection of the population at risk with the aid and its distribution remaining as the main factor.

Indeed, although the Government of the Republic of Kosova had established its Ministry of Labor and Social Affairs and the Ministry of Economy and Finance the main burden continued to fall on the organizational structures of the Democratic League of Kosova through its branches and subsidiaries. For more than a year, i.e. since the general strike of employees of Kosova declared by the Independent Trade Unions of Kosova, these structures took care of those who would be among the first to fall victim to violent measures of the Serbian emergency management that had begun to be enforced against the Albanian managers and health employees, dismissed for either rejecting loyalty to the Serbian state, or for showing solidarity with trade unionists and their demands, which Belgrade considered as political.

Besides the field of education and the priorities it rightfully enjoyed, the Government of the Republic of Kosova began to exert an influence and oversight in other areas: the health, information, and lastly defense and internal organizational issues.

These departments with independent ministers whose names would appear occasionally on papers with no other information on their specific activity,[540] would in time gain special importance, especially as they raised the demands for an active opposition to Serbian violence, even though their activity would be challenged by external and internal limitations and inconsistent developments as those of the 1997-1998 period, something

---

due attention was paid to the design and publication of a joint textbook with Albania. For this purpose several joint working groups were set up to develop common nuclei on language, literature, history and geography, the result of which would be compiling and publishing joint textbooks, such as History book IV, Albanian language textbooks II, III and V, Old Albanian Literature for high school with Theory of Literature and World Literature for secondary schools. This included Music Books V and VI, Literary Reading V and VI and Mathematics I for the first grade. The projects included 65 experts on relevant subjects, including professors, writers and teachers.

[540] *"Akte të Kuvendit të Republikës së Kosovës 2 korrik 1990 2 qershor 1992,"* AKSHA, 2005, Prishtina, pp. 136-138.

that deserves a special and thorough analysis as to why the Government of the Republic of Kosova was not able to carry out its constitutional obligations and what factors prevented action in this direction.

However, parallel institutions in Kosova, as a practical form of implementation of the Kosova state, could not be operating nor surviving without the necessary material support and necessary revenues paid from the solidarity funds, that of the "three percent" on the Albanian national level within and outside the country, a merit of those who contributed money, but also of the work and commitment of the Government of the Republic of Kosova and its Central Council of Finance in Kosova, which was responsible for the funds raised to reach their needed places.

As the Government of the Republic of Kosova from the beginning along with the establishment of the Ministry of Defense and Ministry of Internal Affairs had appointed ministers of Defense and Home Affairs,[541] it is interesting to see how they functioned and what their activities were. By clarifying their work or lack of it one may explain the dissatisfaction of the subjects who participated in the establishment of the Government, but also the demands of "opposition" groups and intellectuals outside the party for the institutional resistance or so-called "peaceful" movement to turn to an active resistance, whose scope could captivate all forms of active opposition up to armed resistance.

But, it can be said that these two ministries, at least until Dayton and a little beyond, by mid-1996, aimed rather at studying the situation, the overall Albanian police and military potential scattered across foreign and overseas fronts, namely holding under custody and mobility the Kosova police service rather than their operational functionality. Dr. Bujar Bukoshi, Prime Minister of the Republic of Kosova in exile, said the whole commitment of these two ministries had been "monitoring" and researching Kosova's defense and police resources, which speaks for a passive concept, or what would have been the period of "waiting" or "standby."

"From 1992 to 1997 there were no plans for war activities. Even the talks with the Government of Croatia about Albanian soldiers and officers who happened to be there during the outbreak of war, were of a "waiting"

---

[541] See *"Aktet e Kuvendit te Republikës së Kosovës 1990-1992,"* Documents part, with the presentation of decisions on setting up the Ministry of Defense and Ministry of Internal Affaris and appointment of respective ministers. See *"Work Report of the Government of the Republic of Kosovo 1991-199,"* discussed in the Assembly of Kosovo in January 2000.

nature, so that the conditions for them would be provided to exercise and keep ready, but in no way to create formations for a future army of Kosova in exile."

Dr. Bukoshi would like to declare the same about agreements with the Government of Albania on military training camps there since 1992, where there would be training of several hundred volunteers treated, however, as reserve units. The situation changed from 1997 onwards with the emergence of the armed resistance with the Kosova Liberation Army, which will be discussed extensively in Part Two.[542]

However, the facts show that although these ministries were of a "defensive" and "investigational" character, they would be targeted by the prosecuting bodies of the Serbian regime, to restrict their activation in accordance with the needs and developments. Thus, many from among former members of the Kosova Police Service and officers from the Territorial Defense of Kosova were imprisoned and sentenced to long prison terms, while others were forced to leave Kosova.[543]

---

[542] For more on the issue see: Buxhovi, Jusuf: "*Kthesa historike – shteti paralel dhe rezistenca e armatosur,*" Prishtina, 2009, pp. 223-234.

[543] According to the Work Report of the Government of the Republic of Kosovo submitted to the Assembly in January 2000 it appears that the basic structure of the Ministry of Internal Affairs included 3,324 Kosovo Albanians, who during 1989/90 refused to be in the service of Serb-installed institutions applying Serbian constitution and laws. Having abandoned jobs, Police Independent Trade Unions of Kosovo were organized maintaining their positions s such. According to the same report, but lacking details, members of the Kosovo Police Service in their situation of "waiting" were engaged in certain activities collecting important data on the activity of Serb police and military forces and other paramilitary units operating in Kosovo, forwarded later to "certain information services abroad." During such activities, 145 members of the Kosovo police force in 1994, were arrested by the repressive Serbian bodies and sentenced to 416 years in prison. The report also spoke of about 1,067 police officers mistreated, 125 of whom had their apartments arbitrarily taken away. For more, 37 members of the Kosovo police force were killed during the war for the liberation of Kosovo, two of them killed outside war operations, while 5 of them were wounded in battle.

CHAPTER 2
THE DISSOLUTION OF YUGOSLAVIA AND KOSOVA

Kosova Becomes a Global Issue

The decision-making international factor focused from the very beginning on the problem of Kosova as part of an initiating process that could lead to the disintegration of Yugoslavia, but it failed to respond to Belgrade's actions when the abrogation of autonomy set the preconditions for that development as there was no ready answer to be given to all open issues.- The UN Security Council reacted twice against Belgrade's actions in Kosova highlighting human rights violations, while Moscow sought to punish "provocations by Albanian separatists on Belgrade," such as those of the promulgation of the Kacanik Constitution. – While the Council of Europe and European Union were cooperating with Yugoslavia seeking for a quick status of membership candidate to be granted, the European Parliament in Strasburg issued two resolutions, which at first condemned Belgrade's actions of suspending Kosova's autonomy on March 23, 1989 and demanded that Kosova be restored to its constitutional position of 1974, while in the second, approved in March 1990 required that the "republics and autonomous provinces should be granted the same right of self-determination to be expressed by democratic means, as was consistent with the foundations of international law, where everyone is guaranteed the right to freely determine their own future.."- European parliamentarians visited Prishtina in 1991 reporting on apartheid against Albanians and seeking to halt talks with Belgrade for accession to the European Union. – The European Union, under pressure from MEPs (Members of the European Parliament) placed conditions on the accession talks with the European Union with a "democratic test" that Belgrade had to pass by holding free elections in December 1991, provided that Kosova Albani-

ans participated in them. – Kosova rejected the election on the grounds that it had already proclaimed its Republic of Kosova and that within a short time it would hold its own parliamentary elections. – The rejection by Albanians of the Serbian elections declined Belgrade's candidacy bid for membership status in the European Union. – This was the first victory for Kosova internationally.

From previous treatment it will be seen that the parallel Kosova state began to emerge even before it had the institutional support that it would gain after the formation of the Government of the Republic of Kosova and beginnings of its work in February 1992. So, it was part of emergency actions imposed by the circumstances following the expulsion from work of those remaining few Albanians after the strike of February 3, 1990 and the refusal of Serbian curricula in Albanian education, the burden of which fell on the organizational structures of the Democratic League of Kosova, through its branches and sub-branches throughout Kosova and its membership that included nearly the entire Albanian population of the country. As swift actions of solidarity with the passage of time turned into organized forms of behavior on the basis of an emerging local government, which the Government of the Republic of Kosova adopted turning them into long-term working systems upon which the whole edifice of a parallel system would rest eventually separating Albanians and Serbs in opposite directions thus opening the way to the development of an independent state of Kosova.

It should be noted that the intensification of building parallel organization was inevitably followed by the disintegration of Yugoslavia, reaching its point of no return by the time the Yugoslav army, controlled by Serbs, began its war march first in Slovenia in May 1991 (which they would shortly abandon as part of the Serbian strategy in order to allow the secession of Slovenia as a "concession" to achieving its goals of creating a different kind of Yugoslavia based on Belgrade's plans)[544] and later in

---

[544] See the statement by Dorbica Cosic, author of the last Memorandum of the Serbian Academy of Sciences and Arts in 1986 and the next President of the Federal Republic of Yugoslavia to the Italian newspaper "Il Tempo" of 27 June 1989, in which he calls Slovenia's secession from Yugoslavia a "natural" issue as it had never been part of the Yugoslav state homogeneity. "New Yugoslavia can live very well without Slovenia, which has a place in the West."

Croatia by creating Serb mini-states (in Knin and Eastern Slavonia). These violent creatures were used by Belgrade at various stages, but not always in accordance with the arrangements made in advance. As will be seen, in the end it lost them altogether, and this for Serbs represented a double loss, because, besides the deception many of them lost forever their places of birth and homeland to become refugees in their mother country or elsewhere.

But the edifice of the parallel system of Kosova with their institutions serving an entire organization obtaining the forms of state within the state, served both their internal and external needs. It was a dual and inseparable service provided, however, the results showed dissimilarities for the fact that the internal setting and operations were not equally reflected on the foreign side. This would probably be the reason why that parallel state as much as it would be strengthened, despite troubles with the Belgrade regime that was trying to prevent its every step, faced additional problems of its own during its horizontal expansion, due to the belief that all of this suited the international community well, not to deal equally with Kosova and its issue, rather devoting its attention to other areas with open conflicts with Serbia and its policies.

At first glance it looked on the surface that everything seemed subject to this logic. But, evidently, the very determination for civil resistance through the parallel state, i.e. institutional movement, presented a very good chance, first for itself by non-involvement in a conflict ahead of time, and second – it was a good chance for the international diplomacy so that it could handle the Yugoslav crisis in accordance with its internal symmetry and opposite the natural flow, i.e. from the top down, which means initially targeting the removal of the roof of what appeared to be a common house, in order to be dealing later with its foundations. And, a cause for it was certainly the very dynamics of the crisis and its direction that can be called oblique, that although the attack had begun targeting Albanians and their autonomy in March 1989 (implying a similar counter

---

Cosic shows his generosity also in regard to some Croatian coastal towns, such as Zadar and Sibenik, saying that "culturally and historically they have always been part of Italy, to where they can go."

A similar statement was given by Borisav Jovic, Milosevic's close associate and one of the architects of the destruction of Kosovo's autonomy by force. "Slovenia's leaving does not harm the concept of the Yugoslav state." See Belgrade's "Politika," May 27, 1991.

response), however, this did not happen thanks to the determination of Albanians to avoid a direct conflict with Belgrade, and thanks to their commitment to civil resistance through the parallel system, which was carried on the opposite side, i.e. in areas where Kosova and its troubles looked as a good alibi to break away from Belgrade and its unitarian-hegemonic trends which had turned into state policy. Furthermore, such flow was desired, and thereafter, some of the Yugoslav policy figures were included in the conflict with Serbia before the latter wished it, accepted this in time saying "it was a mistake for Croats not to do more so that war would be triggered in Kosova before it reached Knin."[545]

In certain observations and analyses, which despite claims of their all-inclusiveness appear to be one-sided, the Albanian institutional resistance phenomenon in Kosova with the parallel state, was rather seen as a deviation to avoid conflict than in the service of achieving a result toward accomplishment of goals. There is a reluctance in even admitting that it was a waste of time, for an excessive and harmful self-consumption of Albanians who may have helped the Belgrade regime to feel comfortable in its military campaigns in Croatia and Bosnia and Herzegovina without concern for Kosova, which, if it had taken active opposition, certainly its fate and the destiny of the entire issue would have been different.[546]

On this occasion it was forgotten that Albanians had submitted themselves to the concept of a political philosophy whose purpose was to build their state subjectivity in accordance with long-standing historical goals of freedom and independence on the precondition of secession from Bel-

---

[545] See statement by Stipe Suvar, member of the Party Presidium of Yugoslavia from Croatia, in "Nova Dalmacia" in May 1997. Shuvar, among other things, would accept that behavior of Rugova and his associates as much more perfect than it was thought, because it avoided a conflict with Serbia, which would be disastrous for Albanians, but very useful for the rest and by building a parallel state from within it became a factor to the extent that it would later become insurmountable, as Albanians would win for themselves a pattern of a civilized people who endured the fierce Serbian violence of which one day they had to be released, if not for another, then for the sake of moral cleaning of conscience that the Western society felt as a civil duty.

[546] See Rafael Biermann "Lehrjahre im Kosovo," 2006; Paskal Milo: "Kosova nga Rambuje në pavarësi," 2009. Of this nature are countless books of journalism, publicities and trivials of both Albanian and foreign authors, done obviously on errands, appearing as disconnected observations outside the process or as tendencies of Albanian internal rifts for various interests.

grade and its violence, a dissolution that needed international legitimacy. In those critical circumstances, civil resistance through the parallel state was deemed as the most appropriate form having been accepted without reservation by the Albanian population, clearly realizing that even so and they were entering into a historic showdown of settling accounts not only with a fierce occupying occupier, but also facing a prejudice created by the century-long propaganda against Albanians as a people who not only did not belong to the Western civilization, but who stood against it, as shown when they sided with the Ottoman conquerors who represented a danger to European civilization. Similarly this would seal its fate in remaining in the hands of Belgrade to solve this "historical problem" and even be rewarded for this.

Pursuant to this existential determination, Albanians, compared with other nations of the former Yugoslav Federation, were disadvantaged as they were forced to face the tempest of the dissolution of the common state on their own. The other republics enjoyed the status of an independent entity in the Federation with the formal right of self-determination through secession, something that was denied to Albanians because in the Yugoslav federation since 1974, Kosova was both a constitutive part and compositional part of Serbia, a dual position, which had brought about the Yugoslav crisis. Hence, to become an equal status factor in this process for both internal and external needs one had to act in that regard. Initially, the approval of the Constitutional Declaration of Independence of July 2 followed by the declaration of the Republic of Kosova, the Referendum on Independence and finally the legitimate election of the government completed the infrastructure of the state of Kosova, as an expression of a right based on the political will of a people, necessary in the circumstances of such developments, a process which had taken two full years.[547]

---

[547] See Ukshin Hoti *"Filozofia politike e çështjes Shqiptare,"* "Rozafa," Tirana 1995. Ukshin Hoti, a political scientist and intellectual and one of the architects and supporters of the implementation of the idea of the Republic of Kosovo, as early as 1981 demonstrations, showed support for the idea of the Declaration of Independence on July 2, 1990 and the declaration of the Republic of Kosovo at Kacanik Assembly on 7 September 1990. Even though he was rightly critical toward many weaknesses depicted in the civil resistance movement writing competently on them, among others he stated that "by opting for a Republic and unification of Albanian territories under European integration processes, without the reason of force, the Albanian people showed their political maturity." - Quotation p. 99.

Therefore, the time since the founding of the Democratic League of Kosova, as a carrier of the all-statehood movement, which related to the processes of major global changes after the fall of the Berlin Wall, was filled with all that was needed for this historical deposition among the most important ones in the last century.

Although from the outset, as compared with the flame of war that had included certain areas it would seem that Albanians, while the boiling and escalations in the rest of the country moved towards a breaking point, intimidated and silent were waiting for Godot, however by avoiding any conflict with Serbia, who liked conflicts, they followed a road of progress of internal construction, being very strategic, as mentioned, with which Kosova finally extricated itself from the position of a national minority and the trap that pursued them since World War II on in order to position themselves as a constituent people.

Setting themselves free from the snare of a minority, as will be seen, was not an easy job and not without problems, as besides the obvious concept already existing within the overall statehood movement, which began with the founding of the Democratic League of Kosova, required a mobilization of the existing democratic mechanisms to reflect their free will in accordance with the right of self-determination, such as a referendum. The declaration of the will that belongs to all people, as opposed to the circumstances of dissolution which Yugoslavia was currently experiencing as a country that was falling apart, was of a special significance. Because, no matter how an international conference of the level of emergency measures, such as that of The Hague, would react to this fact, the referendum remained an unavoidable instrument, constantly granting legitimacy to statehood demands of the people and this could not go on remaining permanently negligible regardless of the obstacles.

This very deposition and speed with which it would be achieved provided an opportunity for the international diplomacy and decision-making factor for Kosova and its problems, even when it seemed that it was being sidelined or neglected because as it surpassed adequate treatment, showing a strong alibi so that in certain circumstances and at the right time might take its rightful place, as it would happen eight years later in Rambouillet. This historic investment was long and should be viewed as such.[548]

Nevertheless, current developments in the Yugoslav political scene may have conditioned priorities, which have the behavior of the international settlement and European diplomacy and its mechanisms in accordance with it. However, it may in no way detract the behavior of the Kosova Albanian factor within this complexity in pursuing its own path and in showing a different behavior, rejecting stereotypes which were supposed to keep it under scrutiny or specific therapy, where the interests of Albanians did not appear consistent with certain plans and stances of a part of the international factor, as being partial and not always in line with the Western interest. That would have been both justified and expected, as Albanians were following their own political vision and in a certain way focused on building an independent state turning it into an interest of the West and its further positioning on this part of the world of great geopolitical importance. This was the outcome no matter the difficulties and its rejection from both inside and out and regardless of the war waged against it by the Serbian regime, which, in accordance with violence used for years against Albanians could have perhaps expected reactions being even submissive from a scared intellectual and social layer, which could use the possibility of forming parties as some kind of décor in the service of the trend without excluding "nervous and extreme" actions that could be conducted from somewhere that could also be called "irredentist and counterrevolutionary residue." It could never have expected such a response of organization by state within a state, which according to them, was not only doomed to failure from within, but also from without by being ignored, as it was believed that Serbia held the title-deeds over Kosova, and as such they were to remain permanent if not for anything other than being protected by the international law of state sovereignty, though to be untouchable, while Albanians would have not much left than

---

[548] See "*Der Kosovo – Krieg und das Völkerrecht,*" 2000 edited by Reinhard Merkel of noted authors of international law: Bruno Simma: "*Die NATO, die UN und militarische Gewalvendung: Rechliche Aspekte,*" Jurgen Habermas:"*Bestalität und Humanität: Ein Krieg an der Greze zwieschen Recht und Moral,*" Dietre Senghaas; "*Recht und Nothilfe,*" Ulrich K. Preuss: "*Der Kosovo-Krieg, das Volkerrecht und die Moral,*" Georg Megle: "*Ist dieser Krieg gut? Ein ethischer Kommentar,*" Ulrich Beck: "*Über den postnationalen Krieg.*"

be treated as a minority to which they could either consent or commit suicide.

Whenever mentioning the clear vision towards achieving a major goal moving in two parallel historical tracks: that of separation from totalitarian communist ideology and secession from Serbia, which also would be concluded successfully, one should keep in mind that the movement of the civil resistance of Kosova Albanians with the concept of the parallel state, as an institutional movement that would attain democratic legitimacy, since the Declaration of Independence of July 2, Kacanik Assembly and independence referendum at the end of September 1991 and the first parliamentary elections of 1992 would be the only movement in Europe and elsewhere, which after World War II, within a period of ten years, would succeed in reaching its goals with relatively little damage. This when compared with the negative scenarios that Serbia could have put into action if it were not convinced that the Kosova issue be treated as a minority issue transferred to that of secession no matter what the basis would be to support the conjuncture. In the world there are many problems that vegetate in various ways for decades on end, unlikely to approach solutions. Many of them, despite the tragedies they produce, seem to become daily routine unfortunately no longer posing special concern for the public to put pressure on politicians to respond with a solution.

However, this chosen road too does not seem to have been easy nor without numerous sacrifices going as far as those paid with bloodshed in all stages including that of open war. There were even moments when the very durability and dedication to the parallel state were seen from the outside as "problems" conditioning that which would subsequently lead to an active opposition. Lack of flexibility of the parallel state "to fit into the circumstances," i.e. to concede – and that meant abandoning the definition of an independent state – became cause for unjustly accusing it as an alleged unrealistic sense, "for cemented attitudes" and similar "that led to extremism and armed opposition."[549]

---

[549] See Rafael Biermann in "*My Lehrjahre Kosovo*," 2004, quoting Holbrooke, Hill and several U.S. politicians involved in recent negotiations with Milosevic, who tend to blame for the emergence of war "Rugova's long upholding of the parallel state and rejection of any compromise with Belgrade to reduce demands for independence turned into a refrain," namely to accept autonomy or any other form which would help the resolution of the Kosovo crisis!

What sometimes is called the Albanian "stubbornness," and sometimes even a weakness and going around a circle which reportedly may have suited Serbia and its regime, if viewed from the perspective of the international positioning, although resembling a self-excluding flaw as it could not be taken as a state issue but rather as one of autonomy, will indeed represent the strongest weapon and the most powerful argument of the Albanians. One day the "arguments" of the Serbs in treating Kosova as a minority rights issue would fall, rejected by Albanians, and all the fixations on a part of the international factor would also fall realizing that the issue of Kosova is not Serbia and its behavior in accordance with international law on state sovereignty, but rather the demand by Albanians stubbornly seeking to act through installation of a parallel state to break that convention.[550]

However, it was illusory to think that the decision-making international factor and the international community would accept unilateral independence of the state that Kosova Albanians, proclaiming by democratic means, since the proclamation of the Declaration of Independence by the members of the Assembly, declaration of independence by the Kosova Assembly in Kacanik and the referendum for Independence as the highest expression of the will of the people. Even if Albanians happened to have the power to do by force of arms, this determination would need internal legitimacy of international acceptance to become an equal part of the international community and its institutions outside of which there can be no independence or functional state. Thus, talks and diplomacy were inevitable for Kosova as well, regardless through what doors it would be introduced and how it would be treated. The important thing was that it was introduced, even if not properly heeded. This intake and this venture would, in fact, represent the main challenge of Albanians towards internationalization of the issue of Kosova as an open crisis and as part of an unresolved issue, such as was the Albanian issue generally, because it had to go first through the filter of international mechanisms for prevention of crises in order to be transferred to the jurisdiction of diplomacy and its treatments.

---

[550] See Matthias Kuntzel "*Der Weg in den Krieg,*" Fabian Schmidt "*In Griff der grossen Mächte,*" Paul J.J.Welfens "*Der Kosovo Krieg,*" Heinz Loquai "*Der Kosovo-Konflikt – Wege in einen vermeidbaren Krieg.*"

This development may not be understood unless one wants to see the inside of the issues but only their reflections in accordance with their wishes. But the truth is that the problem of Kosova and its treatment no matter how awkward it would appear by its indirect exclusion at the Hague Conference, would not remain excluded as a first impression would be, nor extremely ignored as many articles of the time assessed, reaching in that respect the level of great despair.

Kosova was not formally included in the Hague on the grounds that it was only dealing with Federation subjects and linked with the European Troika mission that presented the Yugoslav presidency two months before in Brion with an "ultimate package" of responsible behavior in crisis circumstances, like those that had already erupted. Kosova's political subjects, including both party and governing ones emerging from the Kacanik Assembly after the declaration of the Republic of Kosova, strongly submitted in its most important stage an application for international recognition in accordance with the criteria that the Badinter Commission had established by the Conference in order to facilitate its own work. This was done under the hope that since there was no desire or willingness for a common life, and this was already reflected in the hostilities that started in Slovenia and Croatia, the process and act of dissolution of a complex state with numerous unknowns and profound hostilities boiling from inside for a long time, it would end with an agreement reached at the green table to be followed by champagne toasts.

Although no official reply would come from the Badinter Commission to the request sent by the Government of the Republic of Kosova for international recognition,[551] it would, however, not be rejected, as a clear indication that it remained open as a future issue, which, as will be seen, would take years and even an international intervention to release it from the convention of being treated as a minority issue under Serbia in order to bring it to the position of interim international supervision, as set by Resolution 1244 of the UN Security Council on June 10, 1999.

The German expert of international law, Georg Brunner, Cologne University professor and author of several books dealing with interna-

---

[551] The Government of the Republic of Kosovo addressed the Badinter Commission with a request for recognition of Kosovo as an independent state. The argument was completed with the steps taken since the Declaration of Independence, Kacanik Assembly and Referendum on Independence, which concluded a democratic process in accordance with the people's right in such circumstances.

tional law, justified the application of the Republic of Kosova to the Badinter Commission to recognize the independence on the basis of the will of the people through the referendum held in September 1991, and as something that deserved a positive response. But, as to why this did not happen, he blamed the influence of political factors and international conjunctures. The fact that it was not rejected indicates the major dilemmas of the judges who by not rejecting it left it open, as an unresolved issue, although Belgrade interpreted this as an approval of its affiliation.[552]

Before being addressed in international forums, entering through the back door, as it would happen in the second half of the Hague Conference, remaining there as a general concern, regardless of the treatment it would receive, the Kosova issue would have to pass through deserving mechanisms of international institutions legitimizing it as a crisis issue separate from the package of the treatment of minorities, which usually discussed violations of human rights and freedoms, but not essential ones that concerned Kosova and its problem. For its treatment by the Council of Europe, being among the first to draw attention to violations of human and collective rights of Albanians in Kosova, and its complete bypassing by the European Union, which was concerned with drawing Yugoslavia to be admitted under the European roof provided that the reformist forces win the battle against Milosevic's nationalist course and to finally reach at the European Parliament, which had issued two resolutions against Serb violence in Kosova, the fact of its autonomy being brought down by force from Serbia on March 23, 1989 was not enough to indicate that this ruined the stability in the Federation. It made no difference seeing the footage on the tragic murder of the youth in the streets of Prishtina and other cities of Kosova by Yugoslav army tanks as they were protesting to defend their case as direct opposition of popular anger against Serbia's reoccupation policies toward Kosova in a new form. Dealing with the first instances of international institutions needed also concrete proof of the legitimacy and credibility of the Albanian factor in relation to themselves

---

[552] Author's conversation with Dr. Geogrd Bruner in Cologne, in February 2000. Professor Bruner said after Kosovo's placement under the UN protectorate based on Resolution 1244 of June 10, 1999, that it was legitimate and civilizing deposits of Albanians from the Constitutional Declaration of 2 July 1990 and the Kacanik Assembly of 7 September 1990, and in particular the Referendum on Independence of 1991 that helped take Serbia out of Kosovo and place it under an interim international protectorate.

and to others, especially to the outside one, in order to change the treatment in a crucial historical process.

This legitimacy was possible only if it was authentic and enjoyed support, which in the circumstances could be one of an institutional nature, known to have been ruined by violent measures of Belgrade and needed both time and infrastructure to be reorganized. Or, legitimacy could be obtained by a union of citizens in political parties, such as the Democratic League of Kosova as a political party of Albanians in Kosova with a membership of 700 thousand people, legitimized by the massive support coming from the entire population of Kosova, making at the same time a complete detachment from the League of Communists.

But even when the Albanians met at least "formal conditions" to knock somewhere else, chances to be rejected at the very beginning or be heard even formally were almost pre-programmed. The reason for this was the behavior of the Albanians before the international community, being entirely not based on the platform of complaints on violations of human rights and their severity, which could have gone to what qualifies as an alarming violation of collective rights (although that too was not lacking), but rather on their positioning on resolving the Kosova issue in accordance with the political will of Albanians expressed openly and by legitimate means, based on the concept of equality with the rest so it would gain equal status in the Yugoslav Federation or Confederation, namely to be treated not as an object, but as a political subject emerging with clear concepts and goals.

On this position, the demands of Kosova Albanians, initially completed both with the Declaration of Independence of July 2, 1990 and the decision of the Assembly in Kacanik of September 7, 1990 on Kosova's declaration of republic within the Yugoslav Federation with the right to negotiate further forms of its staying in it or not, always in accordance with the emerging circumstances and definitions, and the referendum results would be conceived as legitimate statehood demands. As such, and with an almost fanatical consistency it would be filed anywhere, despite the attitude of the international community, evidently most of the time repulsive based on the burden of a national minority issue and the stigma of it being an internal affair of Serbia, even when Belgrade with its behavior towards it had lost any entitlement to its "possession."[553]

But it must be said that it was precisely the general insistence by Albanian political parties and all layers of the people not to give in from this approach, which kept open the issue of Kosova, even when that was being ignored – and with it actually Serbia was encouraged to continue its repression of Albanians, even when kept in the drawer – as would happen when handling the demand of the Government of the Republic of Kosova to apply for recognition by the Badinter Commission, bringing it to the point where eventually it would be regarded in the well-known manner. However, this behavior too should be seen as an important and necessary introduction towards the internationalization of the Kosova issue. Therefore, stopping slightly on delineation of the Kosova issue in relation to the main international mechanisms for as much as the United Nations, the Organization for Security and Cooperation in Europe (OSCE), the Council of Europe, European Parliament, European Union and NATO were dealing with it, aims at bringing to light aspects of the internationalization and not its dimension of being ignored or rejected, although of course it could also be addressed in that respect being seen in disagreement or confrontation with the external factor, which would lead to the erroneous conclusion that the Albanians and their demands were not hostile to Serbia, but to the international decision-making factor and its relevant mechanisms. Although a part of the international community, for various reasons, by the fact that it had not been equally committed to taking compulsory actions against Serbia, or not expected to draw the resolution of the Kosova issue out of its minority treatment, the role of the international community was and remained crucial. The outcome would show this.

In accordance with this attitude one should see and distinguish the factors that the issue of Kosova and its problems edified on the level of generalized political principles and norms of international humanitarian

---

[553] See an essay by the noted German philosopher, Jürgen Habermas *"Bestialität und Humanität. Ein Krieg an der Grenze zwieschen Recht und Moral"* (*Cruelty and Humanity. A War bordering on law and moral*), published within the book „*Der Kosovo-Krieg und das Völkerrecht,*" editor Reinhard Merkel, 2000.

The noted German philosopher will be among the first who, in the context of the treatment of the issue of Kosovo in accordance with humanitarian law, justifed NATO's intervention calling for a change of the international law of state sovereignty.

law, but without helping in any way its solution. This is how one should look at those who were interested in considering it based on the condition that it followed certain steps in accordance with the internal layout of the development of the crisis by trying to find its solution through democratic means and mutual compromises and not out of the frames where the minority issue was sealed. And, one should equally look at those who were concerned with finding solutions in accordance with the new layout of the areas of interest emerging after the collapse of bloc bi-polarity, the Cold War and the collapse of the Soviet empire, but who had been waiting for the right moment for it to become an unprecedented case.

Factors maintaining political principles and norms of international law, among which the Organization of the United Nations, OSCE, Council of Europe and the European Parliament, were among the first to have access to the Kosova crisis obliging them necessarily, as initially with the violation of human rights and later with the magnitude of the violations of democratic rights it had already become an international concern.

It must be said that in the first stage, namely since March 1989, when Serbia violently destroyed the autonomy of Kosova and until June 1991, when Slovenia and Croatia declared independence and the Yugoslav Army supervised by Serbs launched an aggression in Slovenia and later Croatia, the interest in Kosova and its problem mainly focused on the violation of human rights. In the meantime only once and casually did the UN Security Council mention the violation of human rights in Kosova in reviewing the annual report of the Commission on Human Rights, and it was at the behest of the U.S. Representative, who criticized Belgrade for serious violations of human rights. Even in a closed debate of the world's highest forum, in October 1990, Kosova was mentioned when the Russian representative to the Commission in the additional report of human rights referring to the deterioration of human rights in Kosova tried to amputate Moscow's position that "Kosova Albanians clashed with the laws of the Serbian and Yugoslav state not because it denied them any of the rights guaranteed by the constitution, but due to separatist demands" (the case of Kacanik constitution was named a separatist act).[554]

Unlike the UN Security Council which at that period mentioned in only two cases aspects of violations of human rights in Kosova, without taking any position and without issuing any resolution – with this not

---

[554] Bierman, Rafael: *"Lehrjarhre im Kosovo,"* 2004, p. 291.

even being expected, as according to the rules of procedure was done upon a proposal by the UN Secretary General, any of the UN member countries or upon a proposal by a permanent representative of the Security Council – the main European mechanisms in this period, somehow turned its attention to the events in Kosova, but always with fear of spoiling internal Yugoslav balances already set in motion with the Europeans refusing to see it. This can best be illustrated by the behavior of the Council of Europe, which since June 1989, even after the forceful ruin of Kosova's autonomy by Serbia followed by bloodshed of Albanians opposing the re-occupation of Kosova by Serbs, Yugoslavia would be given a guest status in the assembly of the Council of Europe, while in February of the following year, as if nothing had happened, it received the candidate status for equal membership, giving Yugoslavia a favored treatment for admission to the European Union!

Spring and summer marked the first talks between Brussels and Belgrade for a *favored status*, but which, thanks to the commitment of the Council of Europe, was conditioned upon the autumn parliamentary elections to be free and democratic, meaning that their legitimacy would only be gained with the participation of Albanians in them.

Here, in fact, for the first time Kosova would enter its card in the game showing its strength, the same as Belgrade would show its determination to act against it no matter the cost.

As polls in Serbia in December of that year were boycotted by Albanians on the grounds that after the Constitutional Declaration of July 2 and the Kacanik Assembly declaring the Republic of Kosova, nothing connected them with Serbia, with the only possible connection being in the Federation or Confederation as equals, and that Kosova would soon hold its own parliamentary elections in accordance with the Constitution of Kacanik. This caused Serbia to lose its veneer of democratic legitimacy versus Europeans, who were willing to bring it under the roof of the European home, though Belgrade had given all the evidence in Kosova that did not agree with its spirit and principles upon which it stood. The Council of Europe, following a visit by its delegation to Kosova, the conversation it had with Albanian leaders, and on the basis of the situation it saw in the field sounded the alarm for the first signs of apartheid, and discontinued talks with Belgrade for Yugoslavia's accession to the association.[555]

This was the first victory of Kosova on the international plain in its long war against Serbia, which in the European public would not be equally stressed and exhausted by the fact that a significant part of its media, safeguarding the settings of certain European political centers around certain interests to be highlighted later, or under the impact of Belgrade propaganda continued to do their work as they would for so long, regardless that it was increasingly becoming a card burning by its own fault.

Although the Council of Europe would disclose that Kosova and its problem represented a condition for Yugoslavia's EU treatment, it would, however, be the pragmatic European politicians and interests of certain European countries, for the European Union to continue to be convinced that Milosevic's course towards its destabilization could possibly be absorbed, stopped or even won over for the European option, if Belgrade would still be offered admission to the European home in an expedited procedure and without conditioning the restoration of the status of Kosova to the position of the 1974 Constitution.

That it would not abandon this definition would be reflected in the European Union keeping silent to what was going on in Kosova and Serbia from March 1989 until the end of 1990 which provided much cause for concern exactly because of the great ideals and principles upon which the European edifice was built and supported. Jacques Delores, President of the Presidency of the EU Commission, during the visit of Budimir Loncar, Foreign Minister of Yugoslavia in April 1989 and the visit of Prime Minister Markovic in March 1990, stated that Brussels remained at the receiving position for Yugoslavia into the European Union with an accelerated procedure.[556]

To give credibility to Brussels' steps, Yugoslavia was admitted to PHARE (organization contributing to EU Eastern countries aspiring EU accession). With that Belgrade would get an immediate assistance of 35 million ECU. A third protocol, which would be signed once Yugoslavia officially gained a privileged candidate status, and this had to take place after the elections in Serbia announced for December of that year, in

---

[555] Report of the Council of Europe, 19 September 1991.
[556] TANJUG, 22 March 1990.

which Kosova did not participate and with which Belgrade's road to accession would be stopped, anticipated an aid of 730 million ECU.[557]

EU commitments and promises to Yugoslavia regardless of what was happening in Kosova, contested by the Council of Europe, would not be viewed favorably by the European Parliament as well. From Strasbourg, Brussels received clear conflicting messages about the stance toward Belgrade regardless of Serbian actions in Kosova.

A considerable number of MEPs, some of whom had visited Kosova,[558] and would continue to visit it despite the difficulties caused by Belgrade with some of them deserving for the outbreak of the truth in the European public and relevant international diplomatic and political circles had begun to voice concern over what the Serb regime was doing in Kosova, and against the silence kept by the European institutions and other stakeholders of its policy. European parliamentarians were the first and only who at that time responded openly against the abolition of Kosova's autonomy and Serbian politics of blood-shedding violence against Albanians. On April 13, 1989 the European Parliament adopted a

---

[557] *Ibid*, p. 293

[558] The first group of MEPs who visited Kosovo was chaired by German MEP Doris Pack, in early June 1990. The visit was organized by the then Prime Minister Ante Markovic, flirting with the West at large, urging him so that his neo-Yugoslav lines outweighed the Serbian nationalistic ones. Markovic, who would later establish a Yugoslav-oriented party UJD (Democratic Union Party of Yugoslavia) and tried to organize a branch in Prishtina at the end of August 1989, was forced to allow the visit by MEPs in Kosovo despite obstacles made by Serbia, as it was the only way for it to be established as a political factor in Yugoslavia that could be supported from outside. However, it was Belgrade's intervention that spoiled almost all the plans of the visit from the meeting with Albanian MPs who voted against the Serbian Constitution and intellectuals who were tortured in Serb prisons during the last isolation case when they were held in detention without legal support in accordance with the state of emergency decree. ... The meeting with Albanian MPs and intellectuals maltreated in Serbian jails failed due to a Serb blockade "angry of European intervention in defense of Albanian separatists", at the entry to the hotel "Grand," where talks were scheduled to take place. This exacerbated the Albanians to demonstrate against the Serb blockade of MEPs, which ended with harsh Serbian police force intervention against Albanian demonstrators. MEPs left Kosovo with a horrifying impression, while Belgrade propaganda threw all the blame for the failure of the visit on Albanians, as usual, who had planned the visit for a nationalist demonstration.

resolution showing deep concern for the explosive situation in Kosova, expressing indignation about violence and repressive measures used by the police.[559]

Belgrade was reminded of the commitments arising from the OSCE Charter. On this occasion, the European Parliament drew its attention to the consequences that may arise for European peace and stability if nationalist outbursts and destructive actions they caused continued to be tolerated in Yugoslavia. By mid-June 1990, the European parliamentarians once again passed a resolution in a strongly worded protest against the decision of the Serbian government in Belgrade to forcefully dissolve the Kosova Parliament and all its institutions as the Albanian MPs declared the Constitutional Declaration of Kosova's independence on July 2, which were replaced through emergency violent measures at all levels, including municipal assemblies and even local communities.

The European Parliament Resolution of June 1990 would ultimately bring out what the European politicians were trying to keep under the cover or bypass with generalized and concealed statements on allegedly minor violations of human rights. The resolution stated the violation of collective rights of Albanians, stressing that "the political and cultural rights of the Albanians are being violated" consequently with violent constitutional changes in Serbia made against the will of the Albanian people of Kosova. The resolution demanded that the 1974 constitutional position be restored to Albanians. It would further demand that all military and security forces be withdrawn from Kosova, all political prisoners held in prison since 1981 be released, conditions in the prisons be improved where Albanians were unjustly held based on political demands that the Yugoslav criminal code had penalized, censorship on the media be removed, and all Albanians expelled from March 1989 be returned to their places of work.[560]

To somewhat diminish the bad impression that the European parliamentarians created during the first visit, the Serb leadership invited MEPs to a fresh visit to Serbia and Kosova. Here it seemed for the first time that a harmonization of views occurred between Milosevic and Markovic, as for both of them a "positive" European test was needed for the actions to

---

[559] Cited by AFP, 20 April 1989.

[560] Full text of Resolution of European Parliament published in "Frankfurter Rundschau," on 5 September 1990.

follow during the next months. Officially Belgrade highlighted how much it valued the European willingness to offer membership to Yugoslavia in the European Union promising it would meet all the conditions relating to the respect of human rights and minorities.

However, the brief visit of a group of European parliamentarians in Prishtina in March 1991, though directed by Belgrade, did not bring the "positive" impression that the Serbian regime and the federal government of Markovic had hoped for. Back in Strasbourg, MEPs visiting Kosova not only saw no improvement of the situation, as Belgrade propagated, but rather, saw the opposite: deterioration. On March 13, 1991, the European Parliament presented a new draft resolution on Kosova, in which, besides describing the difficult situation in which the Albanian population in Kosova was found, being exposed to measures of apartheid by the state in many areas of life, from employment to education and health, a demand was made for the right of self-determination for Kosova and Vojvodina. Resolution ended with the following conclusion:

> Republics and autonomous provinces should be granted the same right of self-determination to express themselves democratically and by democratic means, because it is consistent with the foundations of international law, where everyone is guaranteed the right to decide freely on their own future.[561]

However, the issue of Kosova as related to the process of collapse of the former Yugoslavia, like the entire Yugoslav crisis, turned into an international concern with great confusion. The Yugoslav crisis would bring to the surface the lack of mechanisms dealing with the prevention of regional or global crises but also an unwillingness of coping with them in new circumstances, which a part of the decision-making factor, fed by the illusion that the cold war should be replaced with peace and understanding, saw as relics of a by-gone policy.

The collapse of bloc bipolarity and removal of the cold war, which had kept the world for half a century in the grip of bloc tensions, with the reform process that had brought great and very positive changes in the East, rid the world of the fear of apocalyptic-size confrontation, but not of the possibility of emerging different crises and problems which, as the

---

[561] See Resolution of European Parliament from the plenary meeting on 15 March 1991, cited according to Rafael Biermann „Lehrjahre im Kosovo," 2004. p. 295.

emergence of the crisis of former Yugoslavia, highlighted the problems facing the international community and the new world order in general, despite the expectation that the world was already on new tracks. And this issue brought to the surface the importance of new international mechanisms, which accordingly would be able to react in time in several respects – from crisis prevention, preventive measures, not excluding those for authorized use of force, which needed a new definition, mandate, and international credibility. So, it was in need of not only a unity of decision-making at the highest international forum, such as the UN Security Council, but also an instrument to implement it.

The effectiveness of the international community to use enforcement action against Iraq as Baghdad would not respect the resolutions of the UN Security Council for withdrawal from Kuwait, not only will not be repeated when the new crisis was spreading in the Balkans with the prospect of involving one of the most vulnerable regions, but there the limits of action would be shown in the new circumstances and with much of the old mentality of the past time remaining, creating opportunities for it to get out of control, as did happen.

In the case of the Iraq crisis, the UN Security Council was unique and had authorized the international coalition for the use of war and it had worked as it was being led by the United States of America and major countries of the West, agreeing on joint action. Their common agreement was on securing energy resources of strategic importance for the economy of the developed world of the West and the world to which even Russia and China could not remain disinterested.

The Yugoslav crisis showed another dimension of many different factors, over which stereotypes of international law and spheres of interest moved, held by bi-polarity in a static state, now being put into action in a direction that seemed unpredictable. This change was underway, and pending the historical unfolding crisis encompassing those from within, it was becoming a trigger for the main actor of the world political scene, now in the role of sole arbitrator, to have the last say.

This impression was certainly not without support, knowing that the U.S. was occupied with the Iraqi crisis and the commitment to keep international coalition forces around using the crisis for their profiling as the world's only superpower which had many reasons not to hurry and build step by step its strategy of the one responsible for the fate of the world in accordance with its own vision. American strategists of the Cold

War not only stayed in fashion, but they had been observing and detecting potential crises and their sizes which would serve them in further steps to be used to strengthen the role of the sole superpower of the world. The end of the Cold War implied a global affection and happiness without weapons and without areas of interest. America had a vision of remaining the only superpower in the world that could be achieved if those areas that until now were under Eastern influence, and were now under the euphoria of democratic transformations, steeped to the West. And, wherever these processes where not used for reform but their opposite, as happened in Yugoslavia, frustrations had to be allowed, development and behavior of internal and external players had to be seen.

Europeans, on the other hand, surprised for the better with the reform process in the countries of Eastern Europe and the first signs of disintegration of the Soviet empire, emerging after the fall of the Berlin Wall, and at the same time confused with the storm of changes with the German unification setting new circumstances in Europe and the world, were not ready for any other changes in the area of Yugoslavia, outside of internal arrangements, fearing they could not face the unpredictable consequences.

American global thinking and a lot of the compliance with it on the geopolitical and geostrategic level, even by Europeans of North Atlantic affiliation, seemed to be hovering in face of varied European realities, which in the absence of the Cold War, could throw into the game other behaviors from those of the "European identity" including the reaffirmation of anarchic pacifism and everything else, which, one day, could turn into an obstacle for the new world order and economic globalization that the West, led by the Americans, turned into the position of the world's only superpower.

From this perspective it was understandable why Belgrade was left free, not only to act to "restore internal constitutional unity," forcefully undermining Kosova's autonomy, but also would be offered economic aid and promises to speed up the path toward the European Union provided they were satisfied with that. Thus, the American abstinence and European fear seemed to have revealed the spirit of a new illusion related to the expectation that the overall prevalence of democratic processes that had incorporated Eastern countries would emerge as soothing therapy in Yugoslavia, which had many prerequisites for positive changes towards democracy possibly becoming their champion, opening the road to being the first for integration into the European Union. However, developments in Yugoslavia, although with no sign or warning of being democratic, but rather as part of Serbian hegemony that did not hesitate to show its teeth, were often interpreted as measures to strengthen the Federation, including those of centralized nature, provided they were efficient, unique and what was said "of a modern European state in line with the challenges," which really highlighted the fears of Europeans from opening the Pandora's box in the Balkans.[562] Even though it was clear that it had already begun to open, with its free spirit irreversible, which had to be met responsibly and with clear concepts in mind, initially realizing if it could be maintained within a single state creation whose time had already been consumed, and if that was impossible from both an internal erosion and the external environment, to find a way how to act further so that the process would not turn into a showground of crisis with many unexpected unknowns which were feared by most.

To prevent this, clear principles had to be applied on which a new model or models would support the new state in line with the goals and interests of everyone, with the criterion of self-determination as the sole basis of directing the issues towards solutions, but this too appeared with the dilemma as to for whom this right should be recognized: the subjects of the Federation or ethnicities?

Either one of the definitions could barely satisfy everyone, especially Serbia, which preferred a mixture of both, provided that it could decide how far they should follow up with one another, which for the others the Serbian arbitrariness was unacceptable.

Indeed, the lack of clear concepts and the response to the crisis would solidify international mechanisms on principles and adhering to them, something that was only encouraging the spread and deepening of the crisis. With the Americans being preoccupied with Iraq and the Middle and Far East generally in creating significant geostrategic favors, and not in a hurry for the reasons raised above, it was the Europeans who had to respond. The Washington officials had even suggested that the emerging crisis in the former Yugoslavia was seen by the Americans as a European problem that must be resolved in accordance with European interests and

---

[562] See Viktor Meier *"Wie Jugoslawien verspielt wurde"* with the author providing one of the profound anamneses reflecting the destruction of third Yugoslavia.

their sincere commitment, but without forgetting the North Atlantic interests and their complexity.[563]

Naturally, there was also mention of the recognized principles of international law, but on the other hand, along with the suggestion that the processes of dissolution of Yugoslavia should not be backed by anything.

It was more than obvious that the American behavior that was consistent with certain pragmatism and political interests saw Yugoslavia and her problems as no priority, although they expressed concern for them. So, the demand was that Europeans initially carried the responsibility for what was happening in their courtyard while considering their attention toward Western global interests. This approach was expected, but not the complete U.S. abstention from the development because, as it will be seen, Belgrade understood this as a clear signal that while the Americans would not show any great concern and as long as they would not be threatened with intervention, they could still follow the path they started. With the Europeans they could behave as they wished, rightly convinced that they had no clear concept of what the answer should be for the great challenges with which they were faced, but it was even more obvious that they did not even have internal political and diplomatic unity for the simplest action, let alone those implying different pressures reaching as far as the use of the means of enforcement. Rather, some of the European countries that still maintained the old compasses of Western unity were assessing it whenever necessary as a U.S. dictate and attempt for neo-imperialist hegemony. In the European Parliament, rhetoric of the Cold War was frequently repeated, targeting not the "other side" that no longer existed but rather an open propaganda against NATO, which certain groups at ecological parties, those of pacifist cover and neo-leftists were seeing it in the new circumstances on the grounds that Europe already appeared without enemies and without internal crises.

It was only when the flames of war began to be seen exploding in Slovenia and Croatia that the European mechanisms were alerted, however faced with consequences of inferiority or even misjudgment. Senior officials in Brussels deemed right a response by a group of MEPs who warned in time in the period from March 1989 to March 1991 by approving three resolutions on the situation in Kosova that, although not duly considered, served as a warning.

---

[563] *Ibid*, p. 133.

However, it would provide an opportunity for the Kosova crisis and its problems to appear not as a "secessionist isolated case within Serbia," as presented by Belgrade and somewhat even accepted as such, but rather as an extremely sensitive part of the whole Yugoslav crisis, which if it were to remain in the same frames it had been set, it would hardly come out on the surface with the dimensions provided by the Yugoslav complexity.

Therefore, with the Yugoslav army tanks displayed in Slovenia and Croatia, the European Union interfered with the delivery of an emergency Troika meeting in Brioni, which began an awakening of Europeans from the deception in which they had watchfully fallen, setting Kosova and its problems on the streamline of secession from Serbia and Yugoslavia. It appeared as the right and the only possible answer by Albanians, who saw more than clearly that there was no going back, although they would face rejection from the very beginning, being circumvented, and finally reaching a point of concern of an international global scale, finally stating the it had been created by the creature of Yugoslavia and pulled out of it by the crisis of Yugoslavia.

The Hague: The End of Yugoslavia and the Beginning of a New Crisis

The aggression of the Yugoslav army in Slovenia and Croatia would bring the international community before fait accompli. – The Hague Conference began with the concept of extinguishing fire in Yugoslavia and ending with the acceptance of its dissolution. – The Badinter Commission and its criteria under which only republics were recognized the right of secession triggered a greater crisis, as Belgrade could not agree with the profusion of Serbs in three other countries: Croatia and Macedonia – with minority status, while in Bosnia and Herzegovina marginalized by Bosnians and Croats. – Carrington's plan for "special statuses," which included Kosova and its rejection by Serbia on the grounds that it could not allow a repetition of the situation of the 1974 Constitution. – Serbia rejects Carrington's Plan and an ultimatum confronting it with international sanctions, while Kosova duly submits an application for recognition, which is neither examined nor denied.

The Hague Conference would show the very vulnerabilities that the Milosevic regime had expected from the European diplomacy and the European Union mission. Furthermore, with the removal of Kosova from the agenda and any consideration, and thinking that as compensation for the Serbian leadership Belgrade would obtain a constructive partner in the restructuring process of the remaining Yugoslavia through agreement and peaceful means. Milosevic positioned himself in the role of the one who would pull the international community by the nose for years turning it into an accomplice and abettor to prolonged crisis according to a Belgrade scenario during its most tragic stages, such as ethnic cleansing and crimes committed against humanity initially in Croatia and then in Bosnia and Herzegovina and finally in Kosova.

The chronology of the beginning of the Hague Conference, in September 1991 and its position on the Badinter Arbitration Committee about giving recognition or non-recognition to acceptance of states requesting it provided they met the criteria provided,[564] would bring out on one side the Europeans' powerlessness to influence the crisis prevention, or at least to stop the momentum and, on the other, the promotion of Milosevic as a "master" of diplomatic actions with a combination of military actions establishing fait accompli. On the day that at The Hague of the Netherlands began the International Conference on Yugoslavia (ECCY), the Yugoslav Army, which had already withdrawn from Slovenia and had severed all connections with other parts of Yugoslavia, continued its successful military operations in Slavonia (by Vukovar siege) and the Knin Krajina, where Serbs declared their own state, and three days later began the bombing of Dubrovnik. Its military successes in the war fronts helped Belgrade to further strengthen its arrogance towards the Conference and its leaders, setting a framework of behavior. This would be reflected especially since in early October Serbia and Montenegro took over the supervision of the State Presidency demanding to be recognized as heir to the Socialist Federal Republic of Yugoslavia, which had already started to collapse.

---

[564] The Badinter Commission, which was chaired by the President of the Constitutional Court of France, Robert Badinter, including in its composition heads of the Constitutional Courts of Belgium, Germany, Italy and Spain, determined the criteria for recognition. The Commission on December 7, 1991 came out with the position that "Yugoslavia is in the process of disintegration." The Commission determined the acceptance criteria for states separated from Yugoslavia, relying on Carrington's Plan.

Faced with these circumstances, Lord Carrington made persistent efforts. However, upon realizing that he had no other choice, he came out with the position on the Yugoslav crisis through a plan based on the breakup of Yugoslavia as a state.[565]

Before coming to this decision, contrary to the expectations of the organizers of the Conference, and the illusion that numerous concessions to Milosevic would change course, one needs to take note of Carrington's Plan about the *"special statuses,"* a formula that envisaged the solution of issues of national minorities and the rights of ethnic groups which in the former Yugoslavia enjoyed the status of administrative and political autonomies (Kosova and Vojvodina).

Initially, it must be said that the introduction of the category of *"special statuses"* for nationalities was not a matter of linguistic subtlety, as one can expect, but rather an essential treatment of the rights of nationalities towards their narrowing and being stripped of the political and administrative component containing substantial autonomy which Kosova and Vojvodina had enjoyed. This was actually the first concession to Milosevic to link him with the conference. Another concession made to Belgrade was that of the categorization of minority ethnic groups, to only be recognized by cultural features and language. Language could only be used in information and in local primary education, which according to Belgrade presented a standard in accordance with the international level.

Lord Carrington, however, had not initially been willing to strip Kosova and Vojvodina, within the special status, of their political and administrative autonomy, even though this categorization was already thought to include the Croatian Serbs, who had not been organized into an autonomous administrative unit but who had achieved that through the means of war and violence, which also stimulated war despite a statement of the Europeans that war would not be rewarded. But here will soon come Milosevic's interference with two footnotes, reflecting clearly Belgrade's calculations strategy. The first was the introduction of a clause stating that "this status will apply separately for the Serbs living in parts of

---

[565] Lord Carrington's Plan foresaw accepting federal republics as independent states in their administrative boundaries. They would be recognized internationally after addressing the Badinter Commission where conditions would be reviewed. Republics could enter into direct talks with each other for other forms of organization, provided that they were in accordance with the democratic will. The plan envisaged modalities that would regulate issues other than economic and cooperation ones.

Croatia and representing majority population," and also with the exception of Vojvodina from the special status even though with the 1974 Constitution it was treated as an autonomous unit within the Yugoslav Federation.[566]

Thus, in its first draft, based on the South Tyrol model, the Carrington Plan anticipated:

- *The right to national emblem, emblems, which could freely be used;*
- *The right to dual citizenship, which members of an ethnic group could enjoy in their mother republic as well;*
- *The right to an educational system of their own, which respects the values and needs of the ethnic group;*
- *The right to have a legislative body;*
- *The right to its own administrative structure and possession of local police;*
- – *The right to its own legal system, which will be responsible for regulating the internal affairs reflecting as a body the structure of the local population, and*
- *Have certain international supervision.* [567]

But Milosevic rejected the first draft on the grounds that "Kosova is Serbia's internal matter" and does not belong at The Hague. Milosevic said that "the special status should only include the regulation of Serb areas in Croatia." Serbian Krajina and Kosova cannot be compared in any way, because the Krajina is a case of protecting the rights of a constituent nation of Yugoslavia, while Kosova is a case of a nationality (national minority) whose country of origin is outside Yugoslavia.[568]

Likely, Lord Carrington after yielding to Milosevic in advance of the preparatory phase would not be shown equally blind to Milosevic's rejection and his justification that Kosova be excluded from the draft. He recalled the Badinter Commission's views and its criteria, according to which international recognition was conditional upon respect for minority rights and their protection under the special statuses. Since Serbia would neither accept the decisions of the Badinter Commission nor would

---

[566] See Gert Ahrens' conversation with Rafael Biermann in October 2002. *"Lehrjahre im Kosovo,"* 2004, p. 344.

[567] Carrington's draft-plan presented at the session of 18 October 1991, according to M. Weller *"The Crisis,"* 1999, p. 80.

[568] Bierman, Rafael: *"Lehrjahre im Kosovo,"* 2004, p. 346.

compete for recognition, Milosevic asserted that these did not oblige him, but under cover he would not give up seeking other concessions up to the last minute, which as will be seen, even though they too were not enough.

At the meeting of October 25, 1991, Lord Carrington came up with two versions of the same concept that Belgrade's requests would be refused because he thought that through this, no more concessions would be made to him. It specified the criteria of the special status units. According to the second draft, parts with special status should be permanently demilitarized, without any military units stationed in them, and without any military exercises on the ground and in the air.[569]

Evidently, the newest version of Carrington's plan for the permanent demilitarization of areas with special status created preconditions for the withdrawal of the Serb units from Knin and Eastern Slavonia and Croatia, as well as of units from the parts inhabited by a Serb majority. Perhaps Belgrade would agree that in the Serbian-inhabited parts of Croatia (Knin and Eastern Slavonia) there would not be a military presence but would not accept this in any way for Kosova, where military and police presence represented Serbia's main policy supporter there, which will be seen in later developments they would be reserved for the final action.

When it comes to Kosova, in the final wording of the text stood the following:

> Republics should in accordance with Article II, paragraph 6, restore the constitutional position of autonomous provinces, which they had before 1990, so that Kosova and Vojvodina would return to the situation before 1989.

This single paragraph had been deliberately stored to the last bid, that of November 4, 1991, the day before the handover of an ultimatum to Belgrade, which it would nevertheless not accept, despite the last-minute concessions made, such as those related to the expansion of the autonomous rights of Serbs outside Serbia, and especially with the removal of a paragraph stating an obligation to restore the status of the autonomous provinces to what they had before 1990, as this was inconsistent due to the fact that there was no former Yugoslavia and its Constitution.

---

[569] Carrington's draft-plan presented at the session of 18 October 1991, according to M. Weller "The Crisis," 1999, p. 80.

Obviously, Serbia would reject Carrington's Plan on the grounds that it left half of the Serb people outside the state, turning them into national minorities. This, then, was unacceptable to the Serbs, who considered that they had created Yugoslavia with their own blood and had to carry the responsibility of its preservation even with blood.[570]

This pledge of the Serbs would have the official support of Moscow, with the latter sending certain messages to Brussels not to accept "the logic of secessionism," but that of the preservation and protection of Yugoslavia from its destroyers.[571]

Milosevic declared that those who did not wish to remain in Yugoslavia could go, but not by taking away parts of Yugoslavia or Serbian ethnicity. This openly surfaced Serbian goals of creating a Greater Serbia disguised under the cover of what appeared as remnants of Yugoslavia.

The international decision-making factor, especially the Europeans, could now be convinced that it was not that Serbia wanted to be equal with others, when it justified so the violent destruction of Kosova's autonomy, but it was a determination set by the Serbian hegemony, wishing to control the others and behave according to Greater Serbian programs.

Faced with this bitter truth Lord Carrington had no choice but to present Serbia, on behalf of the European Union with an ultimatum, giving it until November 5, 1991 to accept his plan or face multiple sanctions. The ultimatum also let Serbia know that the rejection of the plan would force the EU to start talks with the cooperative republics on their international recognition.

Obviously, Milosevic rejected the ultimatum and the reformulated versions which included more concessions that were presented to him until November 5, 1991 by Lord Carrington. In the meantime, after the deadline of the ultimatum and its overcoming, Milosevic focused on the war. The Yugoslav army after a two-month siege took Vukovar, inflicting profound losses to Croatian defenders, without sparing the citizens and their property. Over two thousand Croatian defenders were killed, along with more than a thousand victims from among the citizens added to the "Serbian glory" and to the Europeans keeping silent, in the old city of

---

[570] See Memorandum of Serb Academy of Sciences and Arts of 1986, published by "Delo," Ljubljana, 1997.
[571] AFP news piece from Moscow of 20 September 1991.

Slavonia, which would soon be declared a political and administrative center of the Serbian province of Slavonia, from where violently the last Croatian citizens left replaced in their homes by families of war criminals from Serbia, Bosnia and Herzegovina and Croatia, as "reward" for "heroism and the blood they shed to unite the Serb lands."

The London Conference and Kosova's Memorandum

The appearance of the Federal Republic of Yugoslavia and its consequences for Kosova.- Kosova's counter response to Belgrade retaliating with free parliamentary elections, in which Dr. Ibrahim Rugova won the mandate of the Kosova people as the first President of the Republic of Kosova. – Following the election for the President of the Republic of Kosova, Dr. Rugova requested from the Security Council of the UN to have the blue helmets and international observers placed in order to prevent the inclusion of Kosova into the war. – Dr. Ibrahim Rugova's trip to the London Conference with the mandate of the President of the Republic of Kosova, although in an observer status, drew the attention with his clear "no" to the international community about the inclusion of Kosova within the Federal Republic of Yugoslavia and with his "yes" in favor of negotiations and compromises on the basis of this approach. – Kosova's Memorandum handed to the Conference, had as its motto the stance that "the Republic of Kosova is an independent state reality and irreversible, built upon the sovereignty of the people of Kosova and its freely expressed will, which represented the first international penetration of the Republic of Kosova. – The London Conference created a Group on Kosova, with headquarters in Geneva, which was directed by the German Gerd Ahrens.

After closing The Hague chapter, with the Badinter Commission estimates finally sealing off the third Yugoslavia, the international community, namely the European Union, began facing true troubles with Serbia. Belgrade would not only refuse to accept Carrington's plan to end the Yugoslav conflict peacefully, but would point its weapons of war against the decisions of the Hague Conference such as was the recognition of Croatia, initially recognized by Germany in a hurry, even though it did not control almost half of its territories, which had already fallen into the hands of Serbian rebels, who, aided by the Yugoslav army, had declared their independent feuds in Eastern Slavonia, Posavina and the Knin Krajina, dividing Croatian territory into three separate parts, unable to communicate with the center appearing as a dysfunctional state.

The hasty recognition of Croatia and Slovenia by Germany, although expected, caused some concern among European countries since the German action had begun to awaken fear that a united Germany would not cross over beyond the European integration projects of the measured package over eastern countries, of course after they had fulfilled conditions, toward establishing certain areas of interest. Such observations reached Bonn from Paris and London, while Belgrade accused Germany of retaliation against the Serbs for their alleged contribution against fascists during World War II. It seems that Belgrade was successful in playing with European divisions, which it had calculated from the beginning and, later would be supported, especially when trying to activate it to divide Americans and Europeans, including also NATO and other international mechanisms.

The Serbian Orthodox Church went even further when in a publication of its branch in Munich accused Germany "for retrieving the friendship with Pavelic's Ustasa and the Nazis." It also sounded the alarm about "concrete plans that Germans already had with the Albanians on the creation of a Greater Albania, similar to that of the Nazi-Fascists of 1941," in which initially Kosova as an independent state would take over, as stated "the major role of anti-Serb and anti-Western conspiracy," as "the Albanian state would represent nothing other than a basis for Islamic fundamentalism and similar."[572]

Evidently, the first German-European frictions on the hasty recognition of Croatia, although the Badinter Commission with a few remarks granted a passing grade to the Croatian request, would have consequences, initially reflected in the withdrawal of the German Foreign Minister

---

[572] "Bulletin of the Serb Orthodox Church in Munich" no. 3/1992. Serbian Orthodox Church in Germany with headquarters in Munich was one of the most extreme spokesmen for great Serbian hegemony in the West in general, sparing no means to use for propagating the alleged oppression of Albanians against Serbs and their spiritual monuments, as stated, in Kosovo and Metohija – the Serbian and Christian spiritual center, "threatened by Islamic fundamentalism" and "Albanian terrorists," who, according to this propaganda, were in a dual mission: against Serbia and against the Christian Europe!

Hans-Dietrich Genscher to be replaced by Klaus Kinkel, who would not always be able to maintain a consistent line of the German policy towards the Balkans drawn up by his predecessor. He would even be blamed in some stages of the crisis of former Yugoslavia for extending unnecessary compromises to Belgrade, trying to involve the European Union and the international community as well, which, if it were not for the consistent attitude of Christian Democrats as coalition partners in the Bonn Government, led by Chancellor Helmut Kohl, to turn on the proper rails provided, could have consequences for the rest as well.[573]

One is aware of open disagreements between the defense minister Volker Ruhe from the ranks of the Christian Democratic Union, and Klaus Kinkel from among the Liberals about the so-called *"sanitary corridor"* around Kosova, with NATO troops being stationed in northern Albania to eliminate any activity by Albanian armed groups entering Kosova in order to resist from there Serb military forces. Kinkel would be in favor of the "corridor," while Ruhe stood against a *"sanitary corridor"* around Kosova, as that, according to him, would suffocate Kosova, while the Westerners would thus provide enormous service to the Serb police and military forces against the vulnerable Albanian population giving the Serbs a free hand to carry out violent ethnic cleansing.[574]

In order to present the Serb "feuds" in Croatia, Knin Krajina, Eastern Slavonia and the Republika Srpska in Bosnia and Herzegovina as "independent Serbian entities fighting to preserve and protect the common Serb ethnicity, which would extend from anywhere there were Serbs who

---

[573] One of the biggest problems of the German foreign minister, Klaus Kinkel, who before becoming foreign minister was Interior Minister and the head of the German Intelligence Service (BND), who, with abhorrence, was charged with helping, in various ways, prepare the Croatian immigration to secede from Yugoslavia. Under pressure from the Left for a denial, in some cases he was shown to be cooperative with Milosevic, especially when in 1996 he entered into an agreement with him for the return of over one hundred thousand Albanian refugees who had found asylum in Germany. Content on accepting Croatia as an independent state and Zagreb's efforts to regain sovereignty over territories kept by the Serbs from 1991 to 1995, Kinkel did not show an equal interest in Kosovo seceding from Serbia, because in the future this could have consequences for Croatia and Bosnia and Herzegovina. Furthermore, keeping Kosovo under Serbia he viewed as relevant to the Serbian Krajina in Croatia, which after a Croatian offensive in the summer 1995, was returned to Croatia.

[574] Matthias Kuntzel: *"Der Weg in den Krieg,"* p. 142.

had to defend their treatment as a constituent people, the rump Yugoslavia, Serbia and Montenegro, on April 27, 1992 declared a joint federation called the Federal Republic of Yugoslavia. It included, without their consent, Kosova and Vojvodina as provinces, although the first by its Constitutional Declaration of July 2, 1990 and the Declaration of the Republic of Kosova at Kaçanik Assembly on September 7 of that year and the parallel state, being out of its political system and society long ago, and the latter completely extinguished as the Serbs there appeared as a majority in relation to other minorities dispersed and lacking ethnic connections.

The state of the Serbs and Montenegrins had proclaimed itself as heir to the Socialist Federal Republic of Yugoslavia, a country which Badinter Commission in December 1991 declared as falling apart. Although the UN Security Council, thanks to the U.S. veto would not automatically accept the creation of the new Serb-Montenegrin supplant replacing the former Yugoslavia in the global organization, with the support of Russia, China, and a great number of Arab and Islamic countries, it would sit in its seat as an observer without a voting right. This would have political and psychological effects for the continuation of fighting, as with the facts accomplished in the battlefield Milosevic could only keep the hands of the international community tied causing the Serbs to keep hostage states already internationally recognized such as Croatia and Bosnia and Herzegovina, which could not function as such, while Macedonia, which had declared its independence, with the constant threats made, was being forced not to act against the interests of Serbia, especially in relation to Kosova, Albania or the Western countries.

Kiro Gligorov was more careful not to upset Belgrade than tending to his own interests. So, the expected emergence of the Serb-Montenegrin state provided the Serbian political behavior with additional opportunities and numerous destructive variations against other parts, where it had started the fire making the local Serbs in Croatia and Bosnia and Herzegovina to "independently" fight to defend their ethnic being against the international community as well involved in the process of resolving the crisis. Milosevic conducted the war in Croatia and Bosnia and Herzegovina from Belgrade, this time not in direct form with the Yugoslav People's Army having the main say, but through local Serb military forces, such as the army of Republika Srpska in Bosnia, a subsidiary of the former Yugoslav People's Army, commanded by General Ratko Mladic and its infamous paramilitary formations and others being kept in Knin and Slavonia. With this, at least formally, he removed the responsibility of actions conducted by the Serbs in Bosnia and Herzegovina and Croatia, in the meantime keeping the hold tightly connected to Belgrade's plans on rearrangements of what had already been left behind from the space of the former Yugoslavia.

The announcement of the Federal Republic of Yugoslavia or the creation of Zabljak – a county on the border with Montenegro, where Serb lawyers and politicians gathered quickly allegedly having read the decision of a "common state" of Montenegrins in the meantime passing a constitution by that name would affect both Kosova and its further position.

Although Kosova had declared independence and with its parallel system continued to function as a state within a state, without being internationally recognized, however, it remained prey of Serbia. Indeed, it was in a position even more inappropriate than before when in the Yugoslav state it enjoyed the treatment of an autonomous entity within the Federation and could count on the support of those who shared the same troubles with Serbia. In the new circumstances it was defined as no more than a cultural province.

Although they proclaimed their own republic in Kacanik in September 1990, held a referendum for independence and formed the Government of the Republic of Kosova, and had for more than a year begun organizing and establishing a parallel state, which operated very successfully in almost all areas of life, the Kosova Albanians considered the announcement of the Federal Republic of Yugoslavia as invalid and non-binding for them, something outside their will, no matter what the de facto as an occupier state with army and police, kept under surveillance all corners of the country. Although the parallel state of Albanians on its own had lined Serbia within the police and military presence in a repressive occupying apparatus, it however was there forcefully and unilaterally appearing as a carrier of sovereignty over Kosova Albanians, who exercised it in the most possible uncivilized way, which even though criticized from abroad, the international community did not dispute, while abhorring Albanians as "separatists" turning them into an issue of the problem, rather than the opposite. The newest Serbian-Montenegrin state construct and the way it was created confirmed this best. Therefore, not without reason, in the Kosova press the declaration of the Federal Republic of

Yugoslavia would be called "fifth occupation of Kosova by Serbia from 1912 onwards."[575]

The Kosova Albanian leader, Dr. Ibrahim Rugova announced that "Albanians had nothing in common with the state of Serbs and Montenegrins, but were continuing to feel occupied by the Serb-Yugoslav Army and they would treat this as a military aggression against them."[576]

Ibrahim Rugova, being unrecognized internationally after a month in the first parliamentary elections in Kosova, elected as the first President of the Republic of Kosova, stated that the international community now had even more reason to see that Belgrade had annexed Kosova, a situation that could not in any way be acceptable, since that would mean becoming an accomplice to this act of occupation. He recalled that Kosova, in accordance with the will of its citizens expressed in the referendum, had opted for an independent state, which should be recognized and protected in accordance with international law from such aggressions. On this occasion, Rugova for the first time would require acceptance of international troops and UN observers in Kosova.

Indeed, in different variants, with an ultimate invitation of NATO troops, this request by Dr. Ibrahim Rugova now as President with a popular vote mandate, turned into a demand for the Albanians positioning of Kosova, turning its case into a part of important geostrategic interests of the West, which, as would be seen, was crucial to its fate.

Dr. Rugova and the entire political spectrum, in the context of continued fighting in Croatia and Bosnia and Herzegovina, turned the request for the deployment of international observers and later international troops into a solid alibi for the galvanizing of the Kosova issue with pretexts of protection from Serb repression, which would be called a police and military aggression by Belgrade. This focus would have effects not only in public but also in political circles first to be used as a threat for the protection of the people of Kosova, as would be the case with the U.S. Christmas warning in December of that year issued to Belgrade by President George Bush about "the red line," and later as an open option that would eventually be used seven years later with the air campaign of NATO forces against the Serbian army in Kosova and parts of Serbia to end the Kosova crisis.

---

[575] *"Bujku,"* Prishtina, 26 April 1992.
[576] In a long interview to *"Westdeutsche Rundfunk"* of Cologne, 28 April 1992.

Besides the call to the international community for protection from Serb-Montenegrin re-occupation, which the "new state" conducted with the approval of the Constitution of Zabljak, the Assembly of the Republic of Kosova and the Government of the Republic of Kosova, were already on the verge of the most powerful response to Belgrade, but also to the international factor with organizing the first multiparty elections in Kosova held on May 24, 1992.

In these elections, Kosova voted for a multiparty parliament and for the President of the Republic of Kosova, with Dr. Ibrahim Rugova as the single candidate. Rugova won the elections with over 90% of the vote. With this he won his first presidential term in the history of the state of Kosova.

With free elections for the Parliament of the Republic of Kosova and the mandate of the President of the Republic of Kosova, Dr. Ibrahim Rugova required participation in the International Conference in London, which began in the British capital on August 26, 1992. Lord Carrington, who as noted, had problems with the basic definitions of the concept of the conference, offering resignation on the first day of the Conference, giving his place to his deputy, Lord Owen, let Dr. Rugova know that he would be welcome to London but was not officially invited:

> If you intend to be in London during the holding of the Conference for this I will be happy. I want to let you know that there is a chance that you and your delegation will meet Queen Elizabeth II at the conference center facilities. But you will also meet with me, with Foreign Minister Vance and other participants. As for practical and other reasons you and your delegation will not be seated in the conference hall, the organizers will enable you to follow the work of the conference live from the "salle d'ecoute," on the screen.[577]

The warning about the treatment awaiting him in London would, however, not prevent Dr. Rugova from traveling there, parading around under those conditions, although the mandate as President of the Kosova people could have guessed his position to be somewhat different. But it

---

[577] Carrington's letter to Dr. Ibrahim Rugova on 17 August 1992. Cited according to M. Weller „The Crisis," 1999, p. 86 (back translation).

was that very mandate of the Albanians, and fear of it, that kept others even more reserved and rejecting of it.[578]

The London Conference, although seen as a continuation of the Hague conference, represented a higher degree of engagement and international presentation from the previous not limiting itself only to the commitment of the European Union, but engaging in the issue for the first time, the UN and OSCE mechanisms, remaining with the crisis until 1995, doing more damage than good, when what was originally launched as the International Conference on the Former Yugoslavia (ICFY) came to an end. This would be reflected by demonstrating the participation of 31 countries, along with those of the EU, neighboring countries of former Yugoslavia (attended also by Albania with a delegation headed by Foreign Minister Alfred Serreçi), attended by representatives of the Islamic Conference, the OSCE delegation and representatives of the five permanent UN Security Council countries. It should also be noted that the very circumstances in the former Yugoslavia were different from those of the Hague Conference, which gave cause for cautious optimism, at least to those who did not understand Serbian politics and its perfidy, or because they wished to see such a development.

But what were these different circumstances and what was to be expected of them when appearing as such?

First – as after the assessment of the Badinter Commission the former Yugoslavia was in the process of disintegration, and this was already reflected in the declaration of independence of Slovenia and Croatia as well as the recognition of Macedonia and Bosnia and Herzegovina, conditioned on the outcome of general referendums, which would eventually happen.

Even though these new realities were accompanied by the Yugoslav Army aggression against them (Slovenia and Croatia and then Bosnia and Herzegovina) – thus highlighting their by-products, such as the Republika Srpska in Bosnia and Herzegovina, the Croatian entity in Herzegovina and emergence of the Serb autonomous states in areas under their control in Croatia (Slavonia and Knin), seceding from it more than a year before – they, however, were fanning the crisis in several parts making it more

---

[578] The assessment was shared by the noted analyst Viktor Meier as expressed in Bonn in 1996, upon his receiving the "Honorary Member" Award of Kosovo's Journalists Association and promotion of his book *"Wie Jugoslawien verspielt wurde."*

unpredictable for the international factor and more treacherous for Belgrade.

But the fact that Bosnia and Herzegovina and Croatia emerged as independent states, regardless of the fact that they were not controlling key parts of their space, it would suffice for the international community to directly oversee and intervene in them, in certain circumstances, against the permission and influence of Belgrade, as needed before that time. Thus, in Bosnia and Herzegovina, with Serb aggression unable to be stopped, however, many international observers, humanitarian organizations, representatives of OSCE and finally UN missions were sent in UN protected areas (Srebrenica, Zepa, Bihac, Tuzla and Bosanski Brod), which although not protected at critical moments but would be handed over to Serbian criminals instead, were able if necessary and upon "ripe conditions" to impose upon the Serbian aggressors a duty through limited *ultima ratio (last resort)*, as indeed happened before going to Dayton.

Secondly – with the announcement of the Federal Republic of Yugoslavia, on April 24, 1992 by Serbia and Montenegro, although not formally, Belgrade accepted the new state configuration of the former Yugoslavia space as an inevitable reality, despite the way it would behave toward it. This was of importance for the further development and escalation of the crisis, as this made things clear in relation to Serbia's stance to the new state realities but also to Serbia itself in regard to its concepts of the crisis, by which Belgrade's hegemonic policies accepted the defeat of the projects on which it had begun the demolition of Tito's Yugoslavia, as a community of equal republics and provinces of the Federation to be replaced by a centralized state, supervised by Serbia in accordance with what was seen as its historic merit.

Third – with the emergence of these realities, Milosevic had begun to lose the aureole of "a modern Serbian messiah," as knitted by the Kosova Serb poets,[579] since it was quite clear that there would be no common state of all Serbs in the Balkans, a Greater Serbia, or similar, which would retain the keys of the region, as loudly stated by the great war propagandists fed by the idea of the last Memorandum of Serbian academicians after being put into circulation, mobilizing most of the Serbs. This curve could not

---

[579] See a poem by Rade Zlatanovic dedicated to Milosevic in *"Književne Novine,"* Belgrade, 15 July 1989 after his appearance at Gazimestan on the 600th Anniversary of the Battle of Kosovo.

remain without consequences for the Serbs themselves, cheated and frustrated and living for years with the illusion of all kinds of promises to one day become disappointed with the reality appearing completely different: with no Serbian Yugoslavia and without a great Slavic imperium. Milosevic had tried through new elections to achieve mobility by handing over the post of the Serbian-Montenegrin state president to Dobrica Cosic, author of the new version of the Serb Memorandum, who was solemnly sworn in on May 31, 1992 as the first president the Federal Republic of Yugoslavia, with Milan Panic, an American businessman of Serbian origin appointed as Prime Minister.

Milan Panic seemed to appear as counterpart to Milosevic, not only to the great Serbian hegemonic rhetoric setting the country on fire, but also towards economic and social concepts in general based on the spirit of a liberal course of market economy and free flow of capital. He therefore seemed a man of the West, even of an American model, and his introduction into politics could have meant that what had been achieved so far had to have its appropriate dividend policy and international support, with which Belgrade could not be equally pleased as it had not managed to achieve all it had intended, but not disappointed if it could keep what it had gained.

These expectations became even more accessible as it seemed that Milosevic, with the Serbian president's post seemed to be yielding to the "realists," namely the Cosic-Panic duo at the top of the new federation, which was to his merit. Moreover, it was believed that after the recent changes in Belgrade, the Serbian political circles had already understood the defeat of Milosevic's course, but that as much as possible had to take care that the destruction caused by the Serbs would not turn into a general Serb crush, which would hit precisely those who thought that through hegemonic nationalist euphoria the opposite would be reached.

Therefore, Panic's statements before and during the conference, such as those condemning the war, saying he was sorry for the victims in Croatia and Bosnia and Herzegovina, sorry for the troubles with which Kosova Albanians were facing, promising to engage in sincere conversations to restore education in the Albanian language, schools, hospitals, workplaces and others, would turn on the general mood inside and outside the London Conference. Especially, as he signed the 12-point document by which the Federal Republic of Yugoslavia assumed the recognition of all the states – former republics of former Yugoslavia and the restoration of the autonomy of Kosova and Vojvodina, of course, be made after talks with Albanians and others, a condition that would soon loop back against both Panic and the international community.

However, what soon followed was nothing short of a reality show rather than political reality culminating with a meeting with Dr. Ibrahim Rugova, in the face of TV cameras of the world reflecting mutual "courtesy," followed by great promises of the Prime Minister of the new Yugoslav state for Kosova Albanians. Besides expressing public pity, Panic offered Rugova three ministerial positions in his government and other governing "concessions."[580]

"Within two weeks Albanian students will return to university buildings," Panic stated echoing in the conference and outside of it, to be launched as the main media sensation news of the world! The media sensation also included a public feud between Panic and Milosevic during the conference as well as a piece of paper with the English words "Shut Up," which Panic held in his hand as Milosevic was addressing the conference using words entirely different from those heard by him before.[581]

Belgrade's policy, therefore, was emitting "different signals" and this was important for the moment, at least for a little diplomacy to drive it out of the depression in which it was falling, despite the risk that everything would turn into a fraud among many it would face for many years to come.

Aware of the new circumstances, which could change the mood for a while and this could have been part of Serbian tactics to adapt to new circumstances, without giving up their strategic course, Rugova accepted the challenge of the realities with the belief that the game required tireless players ready for different tactics. Outside the official part of the conference, however, he would try to get meetings with representatives of leading global mechanisms and important personalities and the world media. Apart from a brief meeting with Queen Elizabeth II, he met with Carrington, Lord Owen, the Secretary of State Vance, former Secretary of State James Baker, and other dignitaries.

---

[580] "*Rilindja,*" 24 September 1992.

[581] Bierman, Rafael: "*Lehrjahre im Kosovo,*" p. 385.

"The important thing is to be present," Rugova said to a BBC reporter, while his main adviser, Fehmi Agani, said that "the London Conference has met our expectations."[582]

But was it a realistic assessment of the situation in accordance with the circumstances that Fehmi Agani said about meeting the expectations of Albanians? Or everything was part of political marketing, which had become part of the operational behavior of Albanians in the function of waiting for "other" developments. These were necessary for the concept of the parallel state and for their fragile patience as to not fall prey to various provocations. Even though the situation was serious and dissatisfaction was reasonable, if someone wanted to see Kosova, with its concept of waiting and internal construction, be included in internal turmoil disrupting the civil resistance of Albanians as a model of a state within a state, which had started to yield results with positive resonance and was turning into an important fact of their civilized behavior, resulting in disarray and total chaos, then Serbia would have a free hand "to bring order" thus retaining an opportunity for an ethnic cleansing of Albanians, which was already at the time, as a result of violence and the Serb repression, silently taking place.

Although the London Conference was turning into a Panic show, either by his promises issued there or for his criticism related to Milosevic's policy and its aggressive course, it can be said that from the perspective of a long-term investment consistent with their state-constituting concept and its implementation, it would meet the expectations of Albanians in two aspects.

The first aspect concerns the demonstration of readiness for a comprehensive cooperation of Albanians with the international community as well as their willingness to talk and compromise with Belgrade on issues of life, from education, schools, employment, and other information related to everyday life and its problems, without linking it with the status issue.

The flexibility and willingness for talks related to problems in Kosova and not of its issue would enable the Kosova issue to be transferred to a "*Special Group*" for Kosova. It would be initiated by the Conference together with other groups, whose work would be located in Geneva turning for more than two years into a test and trial between Albanians

---

[582] AFP, 30 August 1992.

and Serbs, between Prishtina and Belgrade, which although with no results, enabled the Albanian side to succeed in bringing negotiations with Serbia on an international plain in accordance with the opinion that an international presence, even if not of a considerable size, would help the galvanization of the overall issue of Kosova and its only solution through international intervention.

Also, for domestic needs, any kind of international meeting had a positive reverberation, as it mobilized Albanians around the parallel state and civilian-institutional resistance course, which had guaranteed difficulties and perhaps even failures with the rest but promises, which, however, could not remain without political dividends that would come out some day. Its German chairman, Gert Ahrens explained this best praising the Albanians for clear concepts and diplomatic maturity whereby burning Belgrade's cards every day which it thought it could hold firmly in its hand to use them as a trump of its citizenship and its limits.[583]

The second aspect had to do with the demonstration of the determination of Kosova Albanians to protect their state, which they had declared in the Kacanik Assembly on September 7, 1990 and confirmed in the Referendum on Independence on September 26, 1991 and the free parliamentary elections of May 1992. The Kosova delegation submitted to the London Conference a *"Kosova Memorandum,"* declaring the Federal Republic of Yugoslavia a void state for the Republic of Kosova, and Kosova as a sovereign state, which retained the right to association with other states, but in no way swallowed by them. Any act outside the will of Albanians transferred to the Republic of Kosova was declared inadmissible. The memorandum made it clear to the decision-making international factor and international community in general that Kosova was ready for talks with anyone, even with Belgrade, but in no way outside its position of an independent state. In the text's motto stood that "the Republic of Kosova is an independent and irreversible state reality, built upon the sovereignty of the people of Kosova and its freely expressed will."[584]

At the London Conference the Albanian delegation headed by Dr. Ibrahim Rugova, with the mandate of the first President of the Republic of Kosova, although in its margins, while the problems of Kosova were placed in the context of a particular group seeing it mainly as substantial

---

[583] See Ahrens, Gert „*Containing Ethnic Conflict,*" 2005.
[584] See Weller, Marc "*The Kosovo Conflict,*" 1999.

autonomy attracted the attention with their clear *no* to the international community on its inclusion within the Federal Republic of Yugoslavia and a *yes* to negotiations and compromises on the basis of this stance. The London Conference, in accordance with its development and the issues to be taken into consideration, naturally, awakened associations with the Ambassadors Conference of 1913, held in the capital of the old monarchy, when the fate of Albanians and Albania as an independent state was decided, halved, while the other half (ethnic Kosova and ethnic parts of Macedonia and Montenegro occupied by the Serb and Montenegrin armies in the Balkan wars) were granted to those very states that even after 89 years of rule over them could not change their behavior as conquerors. But this time in the London Conference the Serbs could not expect gains any longer but were rather afraid they had to turn over what they once had unjustly and violently taken, because now it was getting out of hand. Historical similarity would probably be equally fateful if Kosova and Albanians would accept the role of a political object, as they were, and with all the attention focused on whether the Albanian declared state would survive even in its shrunken form.

This time, at the London Conference, at the negotiating table among the 31 countries involved in determining the fate of the remnant of the former Yugoslavia, not any longer as a regional factor as it was seen then, Albania too attended, having survived the historical challenge of the first London, to call it so.

Now those who caused its misfortune in the second London, Belgrade and Podgorica, united in a Federation which could not be other than temporary, were subject to a re-examination of their own selves and what they had once unjustly won. Kosova, which declared its independence two years earlier and had recently held free elections and elected a President, was in the wave of its final secession from them, a detachment that would nevertheless be achieved seven years later but with its genesis beginning with the London Conference. Although while the Conference was being held it was not noticeable by the shortsighted ones, but by far-sighted ones who saw more than clearly that the disintegration of the former Yugoslavia could not possibly be taken as a finished matter, as one condemned to historical failure with its mission carried out, if its main generator, Kosova, would remain under Belgrade.

The Geneva Marathon and Kosova's Interests

Efforts by Kosova Albanians not to be excluded from the process of establishing self-determination; different strategies in accordance with developments in Bosnia and Herzegovina. – The five points of the Government of the Republic of Kosova addressed to the Special Group for Kosova and their importance for taking Kosova out of the political blockade. – The first demand for the presence of international observers in Kosova on the border line separating Kosova with Serbia and Kosova's exclusion from the UN embargo imposed upon Belgrade, setting the first conditions to gradually release Kosova from Belgrade supervision and get Serbia out of Kosova. – The return of the idea of "substantial autonomies" and concerns of Europeans in the Geneva talks fearing that the issue of Kosova's status was getting in through a small door made Geneva talks fail, something that Milosevic too had demanded. – Former German Minister of Foreign Affairs, Genscher, criticized European diplomacy that the concessions being made to Belgrade to the detriment of Kosova would only deepen the crisis, while officially Bonn would blame Owen for sidelining Ahrens from leading the Geneva talks after he drafted a secret plan with Belgrade to partition Kosova.

At the London Conference, the delegation of the state of Kosova, headed by President-elect Dr. Ibrahim Rugova, now faced the already known fact that Kosova Albanians and their issue would remain outside the center of attention of the international community, which was focused on the war in Croatia and Bosnia and Herzegovina that had erupted and was following the direction of the Serbian plan, establishing facts through force. However, this did not mean that Kosova had to give up the road it had started from the state building and running the parallel state by all means. Any attempt to draw the attention away from this definition, meant accepting the challenge of war, for which in the circumstances Albanians had no interest nor were they ready for something like that, as it would only represent a suicide suiting Belgrade and its policy. Therefore, the establishment of the "Special Group" for Kosova within the group on minority issues, under the direction of Gert Ahrens – although part of the international makeup in the crisis of the former Yugoslavia, which obviously could not be resolved without addressing the wholeness of this segment (especially after accepting Slovenia and Croatia as independent states and announcement of the Bosnians and Croats in favor of an independent Bosnia, Serb entities in these parts had come up with their own states) – called for flexible behavior and fine political and diplomatic sense. And, above all, it wanted Kosova to appear with its own concept, not excluded from the process in the meantime, not undermining the determination for an independent state of Kosova, which was announced and began to function with the establishment of parallel institutions in Kosova, a fact that could be used for certain purposes.

Since the London Conference was officially presented with the *"Kosova Memorandum"* by the delegation of the Republic of Kosova justifying and defending the independent state of Kosova representing the most important document of this nature in general – with which the international community and deciding factor, as well as Belgrade, acknowledged the intentions of Albanians, making it plain that the federation between Serbia and Montenegro called the Federal Republic of Yugoslavia was not accepted by Albanians as not being in accordance with their will – their participation in the "Special Group" for Kosova represented a good opportunity for the Kosova issue to even in that way keep it on the agenda of international attention. In accordance with the circumstances and developments, in particular those in Bosnia and Herzegovina, the announcement of the Republika Srpska could represent a good trump for political and diplomatic maneuvers that could have a base case of comparability between the Serb state there and the state of the Albanians in Kosova versus the amalgamation that could be opened within the framework of the complexity of solving the Albanian and Serb issues in the Balkans, as basic issues, without which there could be no stability in the region or Europe. The actual conduct of the international setting, focusing on the problem of Bosnia and Herzegovina and Croatia, as a matter of priority, neglecting Kosova and its issue, did not mean that there were no other scenarios into the game different from the Hague concept on the recognition of the right of secession to the republics of Yugoslavia, or on having no right to it, especially as it was known that Belgrade opposed it, being concerned about the Serbian people dispersing in many states rather than living in a common one. The motto that anything was possible and nothing was impossible could also apply to Albanians.

Surely Albanians were not missing their own calculations and accounts of many options, from realistic ones to those pertaining to political fantasy. The collapse of the former Yugoslavia had opened Pandora's Box and its spirit appeared restless and at the same time unpredictable, because it opened numerous opportunities, and above all, because it lay the "Balkan loaf" at a table of areas of interest, as it had always been, however sidelined for a while by the bi-polarity and the cold war. Moreover, the Bosnian war and the behavior of the Serbs there, had forged the sense of Kosova Albanians for waiting and patience knowing that the outcome of the fate of Serbia and the overall restructuring in the former Yugoslavia would entirely depend on the outcome of the war and consequences it would have on the political and diplomatic plain.[585]

Speculations and calculations were one thing and the reality was another. Kosova Albanians were facing attitudes and decisions of the London Conference to which they had to respond responsibly and wisely, especially as the international community at the conference, even in the form of a show, was faced with the Serbian declaration of willingness to cooperate and solve many of the problems, for which Prime Minister Panic had blamed Milosevic and his policies, detaching himself and turning around in that way many of the issues that could be taken as a source of crisis. In this regard Albanians were facing the need to work out a tactic that would be flexible, cooperative with both the international community and Belgrade, whose platform would rely on what Milan Panic had promised in London, namely solving problems in Kosova starting from education, schools, employment, ending of repression and similar, but not touching at all upon the status issues.

---

[585] The German publicist, Horst Wesseler, at a symposium held at the "*Westdeutsche Rundfunk*" in Cologne in January 1995 on the topic "*Former Yugoslavia and its consequences for the region,*" brought some speculations and calculations of Albanians with the war Bosnia and Herzegovina, with the assessment that the war, although with serious consequences for Bosnians, had not damaged Kosovo and no harm was expected, but that its further extension could lead to a fatigue and Belgrade's compromise of international dimensions. While achieving the goals of Serbia in the war and its loss that could only come from international intervention would suit Kosovo and its case. In the first case, Serbia would be ready to enter a compromise with the international community on Kosovo. In the second case, Serbia would not be able to keep its hegemony over Kosovo. The author speculates on the possibility that the Bosnian conflict for both Albanians and Serbs could turn into a precedent for secession and union.

In this spirit of pragmatism, the Kosova delegation would show up in Geneva on September 15, 1992, headed by Dr. Fehmi Agani and composed of Dr. Ejup Statovci, rector of the University of Kosova, Dr. Hivzi Islami, Rexhep Osman and Halim Hyseni, presenting the position of the Republic of Kosova in five points. In this marathon, Dr. Agani, like in other trials, proved to be very skilled even when it seemed that the extremely cunning and vastly experienced Serbian diplomacy was in a position to dictate terms, set the pace of staying in the game to the end, convinced that it could win at the last moment by both the unforeseen and predictable that were part of the game. As would be seen the five points reflected a part of this strategy. Therefore, they deserve special attention as the inappropriate situations were sought to become appropriate.

First point – was connected with a rapid engagement by Cyrus Vance and Lord Owen to enable Albanian school children and students a continuation of the learning process in Albanian at all levels up to the university, along with research activities at the university. It also demanded allowing the Academy of Sciences and Arts of Kosova to function.

Second point - had to do with the demand to remove all the discriminatory laws and violent measures across all institutions and enterprises, enabling Albanians removed from management positions and work to get back to their jobs.

Third point – related to stopping colonization efforts in Kosova, which had begun to be introduced by the Belgrade government to bring the refugees from Croatia and Bosnia and Herzegovina to be settled in the properties of Albanians.

Fourth point – showed a demand for permanent stationing of observers of the European Union and the OSCE at the border separating Kosova from Serbia.

Fifth point – was connected with the exemption of Kosova from the UN Security Council sanctions imposed on Serbia and Montenegro.

This was justified by the view that since Kosova was not involved in the Yugoslav conflicts or military actions it was unfair to punish Kosova with both Serb repression and international sanctions.[586]

---

[586] Document of the Government of the Republic of Kosovo forwarded to the Geneva Conference, cited according to M. Weller: *"The Crisis,"* 1999, p. 89.

The five points and their reasoning seemed to have pulled Kosova's delegation out of barricades after the "we don't accept this" and "we don't accept that..." Now the hedge was put in place to counter that, although not affecting status issues, as the two sides had agreed during the Panic-Rugova meeting in London. And – as both sides were pointing to their own plans for solving the problem in Kosova – *points four* and *five*, directly, touched upon the issue that the Albanians saw as part of the implementation of the state of Kosova through the parallel system, which would provide further galvanizing of the Kosova issue that went in favor of accepting the new realities created such as that of the parallel state. Because, the demand for permanent stationing of international observers on the border separating Kosova with Serbia and Kosova's exclusion from the UN embargo imposed upon Belgrade, created first conditions to gradually release Kosova from Belgrade's supervision and extraction of Kosova from Serbia, a concept that would be a political conjuncture to gradually find its place in Rambouillet acts, which were drawn up on the strategic components leading Kosova to independence.

The perception of Kosova Albanians and the strategy to use Geneva for their purpose would bother the Serbs, while a part of the international community would also seek clarifications as to whether the talks on the issue of Kosova's status were being accessed from backdoor through the influence "of some external factor." So, in the meantime there would be more and more vigilance "against the diversion of Albanians" and their "hidden" supporters, thus breaking the principles of the Geneva Conference, as it seemed that these talks were only dedicated to suit Belgrade which could solely agree or disagree and not the others.

Regarding this issue, which had begun to turn into a larger concern, an associate of Lord Owen recalled the disappointment of the German Foreign Minister Hans-Dietrich Genscher after the submission of the second draft of the Carrington plan, when following the acceptance of the final version by the conference it underwent major changes to the benefit of the Serbs and to the detriment of established principles, and this occurred under the dictate of Milosevic, creating the impression that under the carpet specific games were being played with Belgrade against achieved provisions.

"This is not the way to solve problems, but rather to deepen them," said Genscher. These attitudes were explained by the German Foreign Minister four years later in his book "*Memoirs*" saying that at that stage both London and Paris were not sufficiently free from keeping Serbia at any cost as an important regional factor, even at the expense of others, which was unacceptable to the Germans.[587]

These and similar concerns, which for the first time highlighted certain differences between the internationals and attitudes related to the appearance of solving the Kosova issue outside set out principles, precisely because Belgrade was misusing them for its own purposes, caused Vance to send a letter to the UN Security Council on November 13, 1992, providing the world's highest body with assurances that in Geneva nothing else was being discussed but true autonomy, and in no way preparing the ground for secession or independence of Kosova.

"Both Kosova's independence and independence of the Knin Krajina posed no solution to the crisis because the existing borders should be respected. Solutions should be sought on the basis of substantial autonomy."[588]

Similarly, the UN Secretary General emphasizing "substantial autonomy" referred to Lord Carrington's formula from the Hague Conference, which was rejected by both Milosevic and by the Memorandum of Albanians of Kosova, who did not give up their demand for an independent state as they had declared two years before at the Kaçanik Assembly.

Opening the issue of substantial autonomy for Kosova at the UN Security Council not only spoke about protecting the principles of this issue, it also showed a clear disagreement among the international settings, in which at that stage of development of American abstinence, the British and French positions led to understand to some extent the advantage of maintaining Belgrade as a regional factor, while Germans saw the Albanian factor as a function of repositioning in favor of other linings, where the extraction of Kosova from Serbia as much as possible had a special significance, which should be paid attention to, but with no imposition, the way it had happened upon the hasty recognition of Slovenia and Croatia.[589]

As the London Conference, intending to holding the view of Belgrade as an important partner omitted the words "substantial autonomy" from

---

[587] Genscher, Hans-Dietrih *"Ereinnerungen,"* Berlin 1995.

[588] Letter by S. Vance sent to the UN SC on 13 November 1992. Cited according to *"The International Conference,"* Volume 2, 1997, p. 1213.

[589] Matthias Kuntzel *"Der weg in dern Krieg,"* 2000, pp. 79-83.

the treatment package of "special statuses" as something that won everyone's approval including permanent members of the Security Council,[590] could have compelled the UN Secretary General to reiterate the definition in order to strip the opportunity of speculation from those trying to introduce into the game factors of certain spheres of interest.

The next May, for fear of misinterpretation by the Kosova Albanians, but also in order to create clarity with the Milosevic regime about the issue of autonomies that could not fade away upon someone's wishes, the governments of France, Great Britain, Russia, Spain and the United States opted against the independence of Kosova.[591]

Should this be seen as an international consensus against the independence of Kosova coming from the most important countries of the world, or did this imply political pressure on the parties so that the Geneva talks focused on solving problems overloading the crisis and not status issues, which were sponsored by the international decision-making factor?

Of course there could be room for either one. It seems that the latter was the closest, being clear that the efforts of the international community should not disperse over issues reserved to be treated at the end but rather to follow the direction of preventing the war and its proportions. This however, would benefit neither the Geneva talks to obtain the desired direction nor the inability to reduce its crisis potential. Rather, the trends that seemed somewhat favorable with the changes in Belgrade's leadership with the arrival of Cosic and Panic at the head of the Federal Republic of Yugoslavia and Milosevic's "degradation" in Serbia, would soon fade away and ultimately come to an end.

Milosevic, who appeared in the London Conference as having lost power in relation to Cosic and Panic and this, for some time, would change the mood of the Conference, had just returned to Belgrade and had begun to take measures in order that Panic's promises given to the international community would fall into water. These were in particular those that anticipated excessive Serbian cooperativeness, especially on the acceptance of the republics that were already dismembered having been internationally recognized as independent states and the tirade on the

---

[590] Report of the Secretary General of UN, cited according to M. Weller: *"The Crisis,"* 1999, p. 90.

[591] Biermann, Rafael *"Lehrjahre im Kosvo,"* 2004, p. 396.

Albanians about normalization of education in Albanian language at all levels, promising that within two weeks Albanian students would return to the university premises, promises about the cancellation of the emergency measures in economy and administration, and finally the offer of three ministerial positions in the federal government.

The mood, though not equally open, would be investigated in the first round of the Geneva talks once the Federal Minister of Education, Ivic, demanded that the education issues with the Kosova side not be discussed abroad, but only in Belgrade, Prishtina, in Novi Sad or even in Shkup. This was justified with better technical possibilities and direct communication, showing that the Yugoslav Minister had received clear directives despite commitments made at the London Conference to continue its work in groups and other issues in Geneva under the supervision of Gert Ahrens, as a group leader for the specific issues which included the Kosova Group, Belgrade did not allow for their galvanization.

The Kosova delegation asked to work in accordance with the decisions of the London Conference, but as would be seen, Ahrens, the leader was forced to accept a compromise, allowing direct talks and meetings of the sub-groups, while keeping the main focus in Geneva, where heads of delegations would meet occasionally. Also, upon Belgrade's insistence, issues of education would be separated from the rest.

The Serbian Government then under the influence of Milosevic was takings things into its own hands, as seen with the anticipated meeting in Geneva in early November in which the Belgrade delegation did not show up. The Serbian Government barred its own representatives from travelling to Geneva on the grounds that it was intended for the internationalization of the Kosova issue. This affected the federal government delegation not to go to Geneva without the delegation of the Serbian government. This was the first but not the only sign, in which the international community would try its behavior limits with Belgrade, while Milosevic would see once again that he could return to the game continuing with the style that he had begun and with which he was having success.

The Albanian side, however, continued to be cooperative to the end. It agreed to continue negotiations under the new circumstances, namely those dictated by the Serbs, but without changing the position or commitment on the main points. Thus, it accepted that the first talks with the Serbian side be held in Prishtina on October 13 – 14, 1997. The Prishtina talks were held in terms of demonstrating students and thousands of Albanian citizens in defense of Albanian school, culture and national identity. The demonstrations were peaceful but did not affect much the change of positions. Albanians would hold to their position about education and their curricula, while Serbs would also defend their positions, appearing slightly "soft" on the issue of school premises, anticipating the possibility of Albanian school-children returning to school buildings, even as separated. Indicative in this respect was the joint communiqué issued from the meeting, stating, among other things that *"the two sides agreed that the situation had to be changed in terms of creating the conditions for normal maintenance of the learning process on all levels."*[592]

But what were those conditions "for normal maintenance of the learning process on all levels," and how were they assessed by one party and the other?

Here, in fact, the breaking point would come as early as the next meeting on October 22, 1992 in Belgrade, where the Albanian side presented a list of properties that should be returned to school education in the Albanian language from primary to university education proposing as a compromise to apply the curricula used based on the 1974 Constitution. This would be a temporary solution, before an acceptable solution was found, which needed at least a year's time labor, negotiations and reflection on the textbooks to be published so that everything would meet a prior requirement for assessing the duration of the crisis within two to three years, delaying though to suit Kosova in order to release itself of the Serb pressure and simultaneously be able to follow the developments elsewhere in order to be consistent with the final strategy to be created.

The first demand, although not openly challenged, remained almost impossible to realize as the Kosova Serbs had declared they would have no joint classes with Albanians in the same schools no matter what politics would decide. The mythical propaganda that was developed over the past few years over Kosova as the Serbian cradle and its alleged usurpation by Albanians had rendered them so arrogant that according to this logic they had usurped all the school buildings they found fit, even though in many places there was not a sufficient number of students even for a single class, not caring at all for Albanian students who were out in their private homes and basements. In order not to disrupt the comfort of Serb mili-

---

[592] *"Politika,"* Belgrade, 15 October 1992.

tants in Kosova and determined to keep them as sacred there where they could do what they pleased, the Serbian government introduced into the option the possibility of building alternate schools for Albanians, but this was just a bubble in the marketing service for the foreign market about the alleged readiness to solve the problems it had caused itself keeping them as such as they were intended for violence and repression against the Albanian population in order for it to succumb to the dictates of Serbian discriminatory dictate or take the road to exile, as was already happening with hundreds and thousands of families increasingly migrating to western countries in search of conditions for education of their children.

Regarding the compromise proposal for using the 1974 curricula during the following school year to be applied only for the Albanian side, this was rejected on the spot on the grounds that Serbia could not accept non-existing constitutional conditions, much less dualism which had brought about "Serbian discrimination." Albanians would be reminded of the new federation and the required behavior in accordance with the Zabljak Constitution passed by the end of April following the declaration of the joint Serb and Montenegrin state.

This caused the Kosova delegation not to show up at the next meeting in Novi Sad on November 11, which was scheduled to take place with Gert Ahrens' participation. The Yugoslav delegation showed retribution against Albanians by boycotting the Geneva meeting of November 17, called by Ahrens to discuss a compromise solution, with the anticipation that the international community, in the event of a settlement, would take over financing of Albanian schools through the construction of temporary facilities, similar to Africa and elsewhere, while the context of the curriculum would be neutralized simultaneously (within a year) if the Albanians would accept the implementation of the curricula of some European countries with similar problems (as one of South Tyrol). It was anticipated that, if agreed, to work hastily with international education experts, so that the school year for over three hundred thousand Albanians would take the right direction. The Yugoslav side would not appear in the announced meeting on December 3, despite giving its consent to attend. Again "technical reasons" would be found and again Albanians would remain in suspense regardless of the school year that had already started and the Ministry of Education of the Republic of Kosova, with a three week delay, ordered the commencement of work through private-owned facilities.

Under obvious international pressure being increasingly fed by the powerful world media with alarming pictures of discrimination against Albanian students as preschool children and those of the first primary classes being chased by Serbian police and alphabet books being torn up on the grounds that they belonged to the "separatist curricula," the Belgrade delegation showed up in Prishtina, but rather to demonstrate the static Serb position rather than to open a way out of the difficult situation with which Albanian schools were faced.

In fact this was expected. Because, in Serbia Milosevic's power was already being restored, a recovery confirmed by the outcome of the parliamentary elections in that country held in late December when he, competing against Panic, won 56% of the vote with his rival winning 34% of votes, despite the fact that the latter promised a turn towards the West, employment, rapid economic development, membership in the European Union and even friendship with Americans, by which according to him Serbia would not only be protecting its own threatened interests, but would also ensure the position of an important regional factor and everything else.

Against these circumstances, situated between a pro-western and extreme nationalist option amounting to racism between Panic and Milosevic, Serbs chose the latter. This would be depressing for those who were still trying to maintain the image of a supposedly pro-democratic and pro-European Serbia, but at the same time a significant issue in bringing it in its true light, with medieval logic and conscience, a weaving of Orthodox Byzantism and pan-Slavic ideology emerging as a substitute for the collapse of the red Soviet empire, seemingly an anachronistic development, but evidently part of the Serbian hegemonic model, which, in different variants, emerged from the Eastern Crisis and on.

Consequences of Serbian determination to stick to single-mindedness was seen as early as December 29 with the vote of confidence that Milosevic had asked for at the federal parliament, bringing about the demise of Panic as Prime Minister. The talkative politician would return to California to his affluent businesses, from where he came (he had U.S. citizenship), while the international community kept fresh in its memory his show at the London Conference, when he promised so many things causing a change of the mood in as much as it would affect some irremediable realists even saddened by him who almost believed that Serbia had left behind a bad nightmare and was returning to its soberness.

This marked the end of the "show politics" of Panic and the return of the Milosevic political scene, weakening the position of Kosova Albanians in relation to Belgrade, even though they never expected something important from the first.

Despite the circumstances that were not new to Albanians, but rather part of an overall Serb concept on the issue of Kosova, with education playing an important role in efforts to extinguish its national identity, the Kosova delegation would be cautious and as usual cooperative, at least not to lose the continuity of internationalization of the issue in that way.

The Serbian delegation too was tempted to continue playing various tricks, making efforts to blame Albanians and "their stubbornness" for their failures, as part of its strategy, connecting everything to "the idea of separatism," which they had turned into a political creed.

In the January 1993 meeting, Milosevic would send the Serbian Minister of Education to Geneva with his "surprise package" of Serb "concessions in favor of Albanian students and improvement of their situation," envisaging their return to school premises, although separated from the Serbs, paying of teachers, and allowing for the publication of textbooks and recognition of diplomas of the previous year, even though teaching was conducted outside the Serbian educational system.

As it is said that the devil hides in details, they would soon bear the *Serbian seal of conditioning* stamped on diplomas and other documents depicting "Serbian generosity" as a farce for external use and for extracting benefits from it wherever possible, especially where good words would do rather than their fulfillment.

Of course, the Albanian side did not accept this, seeing it as not such an important formality compared with the improvement of the situation for hundreds of thousands of students, but because, it would mean giving up the most important segment of national identity and education simultaneously meaning giving up the Constitution of the Republic of Kosova, which explicitly defined the insignia of the certificates and other documents that had to be in accordance with the decisions of the Republic of Kosova on their use.[593]

Insisting on status issues would have given a reason for the Serbian delegation to act against Gert Ahrens, who by Serbs, being a German,

---

[593] *"Acts of the Assembly of the Republic of Kosovo - 2 July 1990 – 2 May 1992,"* published by the Academy of Sciences and Arts of Kosovo, 2005, pp. 11-46.

could not as much enjoy equal support for the behavior of his anti-Serb government (supposedly because of the stance of Germany to recognize Croatia's independence on its own thus stimulating Croatian separatism), than the habit of considering the issues that had previously been seen as separated from those of the status and belonging to "minority problems," linking them to their main component, which according to Belgrade had made Albanians stick to their "separatist" positions, using them not for helping to solve problems, but rather to demonstrate separatism.

This and other observations would cost Ahrens his departure as the group leader, which Owen would justify by the division of labor, explaining the maneuvering to create *"a local Group for Kosova"* and his departure from it and the *"Working Group on Specific Issues"* to which it belonged so far, and the appointment of the French diplomat Masset as in charge of Kosova, by the efforts to reduce German influence in resolving the Kosova conflict, which strengthened Serbia's position, exactly in accordance with new Serbian demands after Milosevic's restoration to power.[594]

The official Bonn not only not supported Owen's decision, but he reprimanded him for his great flirtation with Milosevic to the detriment of Albanians and their determination for their independent state, which he saw as "part of the crisis and even as its motivation," while he would also call Dr. Ibrahim Rugova "an Albanian leader of nationalistic ideas expecting for Kosova to become a state and then unite it with Albania."[595]

The German high political and diplomatic circles, especially those of the Ministry of Foreign Affairs, raised serious doubts that Lord Owen and Milosevic were looking for a secret plan to partition Kosova.[596]

And here would be revealed what would be called the German direct interest on the Kosova crisis, which will be discussed later, from where the

---

[594] Biermann, Rafael: *"Lehrjahre im Kosovo,"* 2004, p. 407.

[595] Owen *"Balkan-Odysse,"* 1995, p. 66 – 106. In the book Lord Owen also provided further details of the functioning of the Albanian parallel state, calling it an extremely perfidious form, but extremely successful towards achieving profitability for Albanians for this project, and also beneficial from the part of international public, especially the U.S., who watched with fascination the Albanian civil resistance, and probably supported it, without being aware that another Albanian state in the Balkans was playing on the whole geopolitical and geostrategic concepts, clearing the way for other unknowns and contingencies.

[596] Bierman, Rafael: *"Lehrjahre im Kosovo,"* 2004, p. 409.

German position started to be built that as long as Serbia would pursue an anti-Albanian policy in Kosova, Albanians would be helped step by step in taking Serbia out of Kosova. Already there was a conviction that strengthening and functioning of the Albanian parallel state presented the best means to achieve this, thus more support for it would mean an evolutionary achievement of the purpose.

At the international level, the German position followed the U.S. and NATO line according to which for as long as Belgrade refused to handle the issue of Kosova in accordance with its importance, and using repression instead as a means of ethnic cleansing the Albanians. Efforts had to be made to prevent this repression by all means, including military intervention, as the German Defense Minister Volker Ruhe warned in 1993, implying Kosova's final pulling out from Serbia replacing it with an interim international presence.

Under the stigma of these positioning delineations, which will be played under the cover, appeared also the failure of the Special Group on Kosova working on education. This performance probably determined its outcome in an official letter which reached Geneva on April 21, 1993 from Belgrade, saying:

> Further talks can only take place on the basis of the Constitution of the Federal Republic of Yugoslavia, where Kosova and Metohija is part of Serbia and Yugoslavia, a reality which will be confirmed by the London conference as well.[597]

The Serbian deposition made the Albanians respond promptly to their own positioning on Albanian education and its right in accordance with the Constitution of the Republic of Kosova. The Albanian delegation, in this case, blamed Milosevic personally and the Serbian side for the obstruction, which had never been interested to solve the problems of education in Kosova, having created them in the first place and kept them as such part of its demolition strategy against Kosova.[598]

In a long conversation with "*Westdeutsche Rundfunk,*" Fehmi Agani, who had very successfully led the Kosova delegation at the Geneva talks

---

[597] "*Yugoslavia, Statement on Negotiations and Education Issues,*" 29 August 1993. Cited according to M. Weller: "*The Crisis,*"1999, p. 92.
[598] "*Rilindja,*" 27 September 1993.

583

and his long trips to Belgrade and Prishtina, positively set the experience of these negotiations, although they had given no results.

"We knew that Serbia would maneuver and manipulate as much as possible. This is what happened also with Panic's promises in London and with other cases. However, Kosova, having no illusions that Belgrade would change the color of their hair, had its own interests for such talks. Because, through them we kept the international community by our side and were also able to open many issues that otherwise would never have been opened..."

In the end, Dr. Agani recalled that the crisis in the former Yugoslavia and Kosova were not easy crises, as they had been produced by certain conjunctures of time and areas of interest, operating on regional and global levels and they could be solved only as such.

"Albanians are set for civil-institutional resistance. It will continue the resistance for as long as it will be possible. There is no turning back from the parallel state, because it would mean giving up the Republic of Kosova and its historic project..."[599]

The Beginning of American Engagement in Kosova and the Christmas Warning

The American watch helped deepen the crisis in the former Yugoslavia. – Three reasons for the U.S. threat to Serbia. – U.S., although occupied in Iraq, knew what Serbia was not allowed to do. Therefore it was warned not to spread the war into Kosova. – The American Christmas warning to Belgrade was preceded by the briefing that Senator Pressler made to the U.S. administration "it is to be believed that Serbs will sooner or later destroy the Albanian people through war, if this will not be prevented."- The State Department too had created the impression that Kosova could be the next target by the Belgrade military. – The powerful U.S. press loudly alerted about the possibility of Serbian aggression in Kosova, based on concrete scenarios as to how it would look and what purposes were to be followed, among which the most morbid one was that envisaged by the Seselj and Serb radicals of Kosova's ethnic cleansing of Albanians to take place following the staging of some

---

[599] "*Westdeutsche Rundfunk,*" broadcast in Albanian on 28 September 1993.

kind of Albanian uprising against Serbia, giving Belgrade a pretext for military intervention, although it was known that the Albanians had by plebiscite opted for civil-institutional resistance and its concept of the parallel state. -In addition to warning Belgrade, the Americans urged Albanians not to fall into the Serbian trap to destabilize Macedonia. – The great role of the Albanian-American lobby towards raising awareness among the U.S. public and U.S. politics in favor of the Kosova issue.

The failure of the Owen and Vance mission and of the whole concept of the London Conference, despite efforts to keep the former Yugoslav crisis under international scrutiny for some time even without clarity, had numerous reasons from those of a conceptual nature to those of areas of interest being underway and expected to be clarified, although initially new realities were being ignored, whereas Yugoslavia could not continue to exist. Even when this was evident, there was a rejection of the fact that a unitary Serbia could not replace it, being the main cause of the crisis that had ruined it and the concept on which the former Yugoslavia had stood. And finally, there was no comprehensive new strategy to analyze once again the regional factors in accordance with the new changes and what could already be expected, among which the Albanian question and its problems too would inevitably play a role in it. It was known that many open problems and even more so feared disagreements that everything could lead to an even greater regional and European crisis.

The main cause of the crisis in the former Yugoslavia as a European problem remaining in the tragic circle and vegetating in accordance with the direction determined by the Belgrade Serbian politics, should be sought in the U.S. abstinence, which since World War I and on was turned into a decisive factor of solutions of European and world problems in general, an issue that Belgrade knew very well and counted on it convinced that at the end this score would turn in its favor.

Factors that kept away the U.S. involvement in the early stages of development in the Yugoslav crisis have been mentioned earlier. These factors made it impossible to turn it into a priority of direct U.S. engagement, as it happened in early 1994 with the sending of its envoy Holbrooke to Bosnia and Herzegovina as far as Dayton and continuing with intensity in 1998 and 1999 with the Kosova crisis, when the U.S. would take over the whole process determining its outcome.

Seen through the prism of Albanian interests in general and that of Kosova and the regional one in particular, the Albanian issue since the Eastern Crisis and on smelled with all its complexity and weight, but without its adequate relevance as part of the West's sphere of interest. The U.S. commitment to the Albanian question and redefinition of the role of the U.S. in accordance with changes after the fall of the Berlin Wall and the collapse of bloc bipolarity gained weight only with the issue of Kosova and its opening as an important regional factor, where the West saw certain and even important interests.

In this context, Kosova and its problem would not only gain weight within the Yugoslav crisis and its unpredictable wing, but also within a regional one in general, because it raised and put into motion two issues at once that could not be seen as detached: its status – and no matter the outcome – the redefinition of the Albanian issue in general as an important regional and Western European problem.

This nonsense could no longer be ignored, as it had its own dynamics even outside its treatment, and things were already moving in the direction that could not be other than in accordance with Albanian interests and its growing awareness of being an important subject, able to behave in accordance with the potential it had which already felt like a willingness for the right changes.

Although official U.S. documents, at least in those of public access, carried little information about the treatment of this issue in accordance with the different views, being both logical and even expected, but which the opening of diplomatic and state intelligence archives (after the thirty year deadline) shed light on this, it was already possible to speak of clear signs of an overall viewing of the Albanian factor as a matter of interest for the West even before the beginning of reforms in Eastern countries, where the curves of significant changes were noted. Moreover, this focus also went back in the early years of the Cold War setting, when efforts of lining the West-East division were to win over the benefit of the first, trying it exactly on the Albanian territory, although without success and with consequences for the Albanians themselves.

It also had its own both historical and political reasons, which spoke in favor of having the new circumstances used for appropriate action in order that the Albanian factor, which, as noted, was never reconciled with the violent realities. Ever since the division of the churches in the 11th century and onwards, the Albanian factor had been transferred to the

East, to find its place in the future American and Euro Atlantic geopolitical and geostrategic planning as part of the Western world and its important supporter exactly where geopolitical and geostrategic fractures had always found ground and had been unpredictable.

Many global political analysts agree that what gave rise to the West (primarily the U.S., and also Germany and later major European countries) to draw attention towards what is now called a historic turn of Albanians towards the West and its placement on the agenda (although cautiously and in line with other regional developments) was the pace of the nationwide movement in Kosova. With the establishment of the Democratic League of Kosova, in December 1989, it set into motion, on the one hand the harsh process of Albanians secession from communist ideology and its remnants (Marxist-Leninist groups) which, directed by communist centers, had been constantly contaminating their persistent determination for the West, and on the other, the process of secession from Serbia, as a permanent occupier. And, also, in view of this historical storage was the separation of Albania from the grips of the communist ideology and its opening towards the democratic process that took place in December 1990, although this break in Albania would be followed by many difficulties of both the nature of the restoration of an ideological awareness under a pluralistic guise, and the emergence of anarchist and even destructive expectations promoted and supported from abroad.

It should also be said that although both the movements of Kosova and Albania started under different circumstances and with different purposes: first, as a result of the beginnings of the former Yugoslavia crisis leading to its dissolution, with Albanians declaring their secession from Serbia and later with the Declaration of the Republic of Kosova as an independent state, and the second aimed at bringing down the communist dictatorship in Albania and democratic reforms – they are both on a common historic course – the resolution of the unresolved Albanian issue that had been ongoing since the Eastern crisis and on. Albanians from Prishtina and Tirana would have the same historical path and Albanian leaders on both sides of the border would always try to protect themselves from what was used externally as an anathema against Albanians and their historical right to live together like other peoples of the region who have gone through almost the same historical circumstances (the time of Ottoman rule and later communist ideology). Though they achieved it by democratic means and in a peaceful way, it would function not only in the political consciousness of Albanians, but also in the international community although with other connotations. Therefore, even outside its active function, it would act powerfully in different ways in as far as influencing both politics and current conjunctures, affecting mostly the pragmatism needed for certain solutions, whether temporary or partial. Because, behind every stance and concept of solving the crisis in the former Yugoslavia, whether partial and inconsistent with certain developments, Albanian unification would turn into a metaphor of unprecedented political futurism, which would not only affect and nurture it, but would turn it against the very cause!

Of course, this nonsense traversed the confusion, the helplessness of the whole behavior of the international community, especially the EU, before, during and after the escalation of the crisis in the former Yugoslavia with consequences for both its stakeholders and others involved. Moreover, if the political slogan that "Europeans know what they don't want, but do not know what they want" would be analyzed through the language of political realities, it could best be illustrated by the Albanian issue and problems arising from it. Therefore, from both the perspective of political and diplomatic spheres of interest, the Albanian issue and factor, traditionally treated rather as a political object to be used for bargaining, was expected in a given moment to turn in its negation of what had been taken as "stabilization," where the new state realities in the Balkans since the Eastern crisis onwards (Greece and three Yugoslavias), including the halved Albanian state, would be shown bearing big problems, and the foremost of them, (Yugoslavia), historically unstable, would return after its dissolution to the starting point, almost back to the point of the Eastern crisis. In the light of new circumstances, it would turn into a rather political concern, because the political reality had to be seen accordingly with the circumstances opposing past solutions.

This political concern and its mist would roll over and make its way into to the Hague Conference. It can be said that although it was clear that the former Yugoslavia could not be maintained, which was the initial starting point of the conference and for which Europeans were able to pay a great tributet, behind it appeared the unpredictability of the Albanian factor, first with the issue of Kosova, which evidently could not be contained under Serbian supervision and with the consequences that this development could have for the other Balkan countries and its effects in the Balkan region, despite the fact that Kosova appeared to set a precedence.

Obviously even in the most improbable circumstances, such as those envisaging Albanians as willingly becoming part of the new Serb-Montenegrin state, even as a federal or confederal part, it would not work for long simply because the Albanians at the very start would outnumber Montenegrins, while soon becoming numerically equal to the Serb population, with clear demographic perspective to even surpass it, consequently breaking the ethnic balance, which in Balkan circumstances would inevitably bring about peaceful or violent changes. This quite realistic forecast was never intended by those who had set the background of the Balkan realities ignoring the Albanian factor, at least in a historical perspective. The European diplomacy and decision-making factor was held back not only in the London Conference and its aftermath, but until the time when the Americans would be involved, treating it outside the traditional European interests and outside the trap of their conventions, and above all, outside of graphic signs of mania demographic graphics in favor of Albanians, which had begun to blur their necessary political clarity to be tested in considering the new realities and in not accepting them!

Of course, the American involvement in the crisis in the former Yugoslavia and their leadership towards a solution no matter how and how much this would be stable and acceptable to others, would initially give the impression of political expediency and interests arising from the differences in views. This implied positioning on certain principles (respect for human rights, respect for existing borders, respect for international law and other related matters), relating to the principles of equality and freedom, on which the American state was built. So, the Americans did not join the dance only as firefighters to extinguish a crisis that was taking international proportions for the sake of certain political stability or to prevent the maintenance of an anti-historical status quo. Rather, the commitment of the United States of America towards resolving the Kosova issue appeared as a good opportunity in relating democratic and humanitarian aspects to the specific interests of the West towards the expansion of spheres of interest in this part of the world, where the Albanian factor – versus Serbs, Bulgarians and Greeks, who at least spiritually would never break the bonds of orthodoxy and the influence of

Moscow – appeared as a supporting element among the safest for the West and its presence in this area.

Indeed, this focus would be noticed by the end of the eighties, with the proximity of U.S. diplomats and politicians of this country, who would put themselves in search of finding bridges with Kosova Albanian intellectuals, mainly from the ranks of writers, who would be among the first to confront the hegemonic nationalist Serbian trends after the publication of the Memorandum of the Serbian Academy of Sciences and Arts from 1986 onwards doing so with intellectual responsibility and competence by demonstrating their clear pro-Western determination, aimed at their detachment from the East. The U.S. Administration followed with interest the civilized approach by the Kosova intellectuals in the face of continuous provocations against them coming from Serbian unitarian events, responding against them with a civilized request on an equal status with the rest in the federation, with the removal of the minority abomination turning into a democratic demand through democratic means. Therefore, it is not accidental that the U.S. diplomats would be the first to support Albanian intellectuals gathered around the Association of Writers of Kosova and their "Rilindja" core as they decided to establish the Democratic League of Kosova, the first Albanian party in the former Yugoslavia with western orientation with a concept standing, along with equality and democracy, for the return of Albanians towards the Western civilization and its values of which they were violently deprived after the Second World War.[600]

The American interest in the progress of the democratic movement in Kosova will be reflected in the great commitment that LDK together with other subjects of Kosova for rounding up as soon as possible the legitimacy of Kosova's will to detach itself from Serbia through the initiation of the Constitutional Declaration of July 2, 1990, Declaration of Kosova Republic at the historic Assembly of Kacanik on September 7, 1990, and Referendum on Independence in September the following year. In all these stages the Democratic League of Kosova and the turns it brought in Kosova would be supported without reservation by American diplomats in Belgrade, who sometimes, as would happen with Dr. Ibrahim Rugova when on the occasion of the publication of an interview in "*Der Spiegel*" and his being threatened with imprisonment by the Belgrade

---

[600] Buxhovi, Jusuf "*Kthesa historike – vitet e Gjermanisë dhe epoka e LDK-së,*" 2008, p. 179

regime, and the demand for his lynching by Serb militants in Kosova, would take the role of his direct protector. The U.S. ambassador in Belgrade, Zimmerman, accompanied Ibrahim Rugova for several days walking in the streets of Prishtina setting an American alibi for the Albanian leader in the face of the Serb regime and their militants! In April 1990, the Democratic League of Kosova succeeded within only three months to demolish the entire infrastructure of the communist party in Kosova, and for this great job the Albanian leaders earned an invitation by the U.S. Congress as guests in Washington. As stated earlier, there, along with bringing evidence in the Senate Council for Human Rights, Dr. Ibrahim Rugova would be met by the powerful Senator Robert Dole, and would have a joint meeting with Dobrica Cosic, but before that happened he was given the treatment of an Albanian leader similar to that of legitimate statesmen.[601]

But would the U.S. interest on developments in Kosova be only a matter of natural interest for democratic processes in different countries or something more than that? And what could have been the factors that influenced its turn into an American special interest that would be the case with the commitment of the U.S. administration in the late nineties when it turned into a promoter of what would bring about this historical curve?

Besides the Albanian factor in Kosova and its decisive movements as those of the late eighties that should never be seen separate from the earlier ones since after World War II and onwards constantly challenging the Serb-Yugoslav occupation demanding national unification, thus arousing the curiosity of the American administration, (especially those for Kosova Republic from 1968 onwards), it would be the Albanian factor in the United States of America, the Albanian lobby "Albanian-American Civic League" (AACL), and its huge commitment of a great historical dimension[602] that would place an important impetus throughout that

---

[601] *Ibid*, p. 253

[602] *"Albanian American Civic League"* (AACL) gathered U.S. citizens of Albanian descent. In the eighties at the top of the Albanian lobby came Former Congressman Joe DioGuardi, an Albanian-American of Arbëresh descent. The lobby succeeded in turning the Kosovo issue into a permanent interest of American politics thanks to the commitment of some well-known U.S. senators and congressmen, such as Robert Dole, Tom Lantos, Elliot Engel, Larry Persler and others, reaching as far up as Presidents Bush and Clinton. With its hard work, among other things, the Albanian lobby came to the House

process as interest for Kosova and its case turned into a U.S. interest as officially confirmed by the State Department on December 24,1998, just at the time when six years earlier the administration of President George Bush formulated its American threat addressed to Milosevic: *"In the event of conflict in Kosova caused by Serbian action, the U.S. will be prepared to employ military force against Serbs in Kosova and Serbia proper."*[603]

The truthfulness of the threat and the way it would be handed in writing to Milosevic, as an official record after he had solemnly declared victory over his rival Panic in the elections for the president of Serbia thus throwing into the water all the promises he had given to the London Conference on the alleged peaceful course that the newly-announced Federal Republic of Yugoslavia would attend towards the newly independent states that seceded from it, and especially towards Albanians, who had been promised to restore everything that the Serb regime in Belgrade had taken away from them by force from March 1989 onwards.

Was the Christmas Warning directed to Belgrade an accident, a moral gesture, a simple or true phrase? And, how should it be understood from the perspective of events and the future?

Surely, it was neither an accident nor merely a moral gesture, and it was no simple phrase – a smoke bomb, which is often used for political

---

and Senate to submit resolutions and many other complaints of particular importance with which U.S. policy toward Kosovo would be affected to the extent that in the late nineties the U.S. took upon themselvesto find a resolution to the Kosovo issue, and becoming the main supporter of independence. The first success of the Albanian-American lobby to raise its voice in defense of the Kosovo issue was the resolution that Congress approved in early 1986. It was entitled *"Expressing Concern over the Living Condition of Ethnic Albanians in Yugoslavia."* It was supported by Diana Johnston, Hawks and Eagels. Another success of the great Albanian lobby, without which others to come would not be achieved, is unequivocally the affinity and unity of the Albanian community on the basis of the a civilized determination on the ideals of American society, far from any ideological or regional affiliation. The Lobby succeeded in overcoming divisions and Albanians internal rifts turning instead to major national issues, such as Kosovo and the democratization of Albania, focusing all their energy and attention in this regard.

[603] Christmas Warning full text in English: *"In the event of conflict in Kosovo caused by Serbian action, the U.S. will be prepared to employ military force against Serbs in Kosovo and Serbia proper."* Cited according to Burton: *"The Path to Crisis."*

intimidation and the like. The word was to be an active threat, the truth-fulness of which would be seen partly in Bosnia and Herzegovina with the use of air strikes against Serb positions through which the Dayton Agreement was reached. But, in general its bluntness would be seen in the case of NATO military attacks against Belgrade's military and police forces in Kosova and in Serbia interior.

Of course the U.S. Christmas warning was not a response issued only because it was necessary in a certain situation for short-term effects. It was an expression of a position already taken in a most direct way, which sometimes gives the impression of a deliberate departure from the diplomatic sense and language to reach the level of a demonstration close to an ultimatum. This had its reasons among several which had to be expressed in such a way for others to be distinguished.

First – the U.S. saw the war in the Balkans and its dimensions differently from Europeans, where the risk of its further spreading and expanding would affect the U.S. and Western interests in general.

Secondly – in accordance with the size and potential of the war crisis in the Balkans and its developments implied it would turn into a sensitive part of the U.S. election campaign in November of that year.

And third – as there was fear that in the shadow of the war in Bosnia and Herzegovina Belgrade could take military actions in Kosova to bring about established facts, which then could be used to weaken the Euro-Atlantic position in this part, which would benefit the Russians. In short, this warning was also true for Moscow as supporter of Belgrade as to how far they could go.

Regarding the first issue, namely the American fear that the crisis could break into "dangerous" proportions that could be deemed "unpredictable," the U.S., although occupied with Iraq and the problems that opened in the Middle East and the region in general – though apparently not all that much concerned about the European managing of the crisis in the former Yugoslavia – would undertake a series of "undetectable" actions so that the crisis in the former Yugoslavia remained confined where the war had already erupted: in Croatia and Bosnia and Herzegovina vegetating there either dripping evil or producing the needed clarity for further action that would be consistent with U.S. interests in the region and beyond, which, of course, required time, especially as some of the processes of democratic reforms in Eastern countries were not yet rounded, while in some countries, different assumptions and internal clashes were continuing. As with or without war, the western parts of former Yugoslavia (Slovenia and Croatia) had declared independence and regardless of the difficulties arising with the Serbs were considered part of Euro-western conjunctures – while Bosnia and Herzegovina had turned into a war arena, but as sealed into a conflict that could be kept under scrutiny – other parts remained: Kosova and Macedonia, as dangerous, because the flames in them could automatically spread into other parts of the Balkans (Albania, Bulgaria, Greece and Turkey). This was impermissible for both Washington and NATO.

Therefore, the Bush administration focused on Macedonia, Kosova and Albania in particular. In the first, i.e. Macedonia, order was demanded and kept away from any conflict. Beforehand, Washington warned countries surrounding Macedonia (Albania, Bulgaria and Greece) to stay contained and not hinder in any way the constitution of Macedonia as a state. Even Tirana and Prishtina were asked to not promote anything against the Referendum on Independence of Macedonia or any action to destabilize from within. Belgrade propaganda, thinking it fit for its own ends, propagated its own media, warning with the "burning of Macedonia by great-Albanians and the like, not ruling out the possibility of introducing into the game its own players, naturally "Albanian fanatics" who it would secretly lead in to act in covert ways. The U.S. ambassador in Belgrade, Zimmerman, in late August met twice in Prishtina with Rugova and some other ethnic Albanian leaders, to let them know about the U.S. position on Macedonia and the role of the Albanians, especially those from Kosova, who for obvious reasons enjoyed great prestige among Albanians of Macedonia considering the positions of Prishtina leaders as fraternal.[604]

U.S. Ambassador to Macedonia (FYROM), Robert Frowik, would later speak about large-scale scenarios prepared for Macedonia by its neighbors (with the exception of Albania and Kosova) and by certain EU circles, that it could not have survived without direct U.S. involvement. Among them are mentioned the ongoing efforts of the Serbian Orthodox Church and Serbian hegemonic circles, which had demanded that Macedonia be divided among Serbia, Bulgaria and Greece, doing so under the

---

[604] See LDK Protocols from August-September 1991 at the Archive of the Institue of History of Kosovo in the Fund: Jusuf Buxhovi: Box I-VIII.

justification that allegedly "if that hadn't been done Macedonia in the near future would be part of Albania."![605]

That was not only a demand by the Serbian Church, but also by the Serb leaders at all levels and strains. Vuk Draskovic, well known for his great Serbian and pro-Chetnik party *"Serb Renewal Movement"* (Srpski pokret obnove), whose militants were among the first to kindle the war in Bosnia and Herzegovina, openly demanded the partitioning of Macedonia into three states seeing that as "a peacemaking factor for the region and beyond," as in that way "a deep wound" would be closed.[606]

Similar scenarios were staged against Macedonia from Greece as well, ostensibly to protect stability in the Balkans, pointing the finger against the Albanians, seeing them as incendiary, as according to the Greek Prime Minister Mitsotakis, Albanians everywhere "cherish the idea of the unification of all Albanians in a common state, which they had been working for since the League of Prizren." In a letter to Bush he urged for Macedonian protection from Albanian nationalists.[607] Washington received alarming information from its diplomats and missionaries in the Balkans as well. Lawrence Eagleburger, U.S. Secretary of State, in a report to his government, focused Kosova and Macedonia as potential countries for Belgrade's future military aggression.[608]

To prevent this and other dangerous scenarios in Macedonia and around it, the U.S. government took over the stationing contingent of U.S. troops as part of an international observation mission of the OSCE mandate, as demanded by President Kiro Gligorov. The UN Security Council's meeting on December 11, 1992 decided on the deployment of 500 blue helmets and later on doubling the contingent in Macedonia (UNPROFOR, and since 1995 UNPREDEP).

However, the second issue, that of the U.S. election campaign, and the third one – that of the fear that under the smoke of the war in Bosnia and Herzegovina, Serbia would be able to fait acompli in Kosova, which would then be used for other purposes that would surely not remain without subsequent responses, would excrete all the importance of the Kosova problem. On one hand, as a problem left open as compared to the

---

[605] Dukovski, Darko: *"Makedonien und Jugoslawien-Konflikt,"* 1999, p. 143.

[606] *Ibid*, p. 143

[607] Biermann, Rafael: *"Lehrjahre im Kosvo,"* 2004, p. 419.

[608] *Ibid*, p. 419.

rest of the former Yugoslavia issues, which although overlooked as a minority issue in the Hague and London Conferences, it was obvious that it could not be resolved in the framework of minorities, especially as Albanians had declared their own state and were implanting it through the parallel institutions. And on the other hand, it could be Serbia itself which, aware of the determination of Albanians for independence and long-term effects that the parallel state of the Albanians could create against it – given the circumstances that could be in favor of the Albanian project for the success of their state even in its current form – would use as a countermeasure a staging of a conflict for a final showdown to settle accounts with Kosova Albanians, which then would certainly include Albania and Albanians in Macedonia, thus creating a new Balkan crisis of European scale and broader.

About these scenarios, the U.S. administration did not need that much information from its intelligence services because they were already in the public option and came from all sides. The war in Bosnia and Herzegovina and the proportion of the Serb crimes were a clear indication of what the Serbs were ready to do. This made Washington bring the issue of Kosova and its crisis potential from a "third-rate issue," where it was initially found, to one of priority.

However, this change would also be supported by numerous testimonies of the time of U.S. senators and congressmen in the U.S. House of Representatives and the country's public opinion. In June of that year, Senator Pressler expressed his concern before the U.S. Senate with the following words: *"It is likely that the Serbs will sooner or later obliterate the Albanian people through war if this is not prevented."*

Senator Pressler's remark made headlines and also reached the State Department on which occasion its Representative Ralph Johnson confirmed: *"Kosova can be the next target of the Belgrade military.*[609]

This great concern echoed strongly in the American press, sounding the alarm for possible Serbian aggression in Kosova, including concrete scenarios on what that would look like and what purpose would be followed, with the most morbid being the one already announced by Seselj and Serb radicals envisioning the ethnic cleansing of Kosova Albanians to be done through the staging of an Albanian uprising against Serbia, which Belgrade would take as an excuse for military intervention,

---

[609] Yugoslavia: *The Question of Intervention*, Hearing, 11 June 1992, pp. 3,7 and 11.

although it was known that the Albanians in a plebiscite had opted in favor of a civil-institutional resistance and its concept of the parallel state.[610]

The powerful media campaign was joined by the American administration. Thomas Nile drew attention before the U.S. Senate: *"Kosova could be the next step of Serbian tactics of violence. Serbia's neighbors are concerned about the possibility of a war breaking out in Kosova."*[611]

In these circumstances, the Bush administration was left with no choice but to somewhat appease the Europeans through a press release issued by the foreign ministers of NATO Council of Ministers, whose author was Eagleburger, stating:

> The explosion of violence in Kosova will expand the size of the conflict in the region and this will pose a serious threat to international peace and security. Therefore, a measured response should be issued by the international community.[612]

On this occasion, the foreign ministers of NATO countries for the first time demanded a *preventive presence of a United Nations mission in Kosova*, although not clear as to what kind it could be, *civil* or *military*. However, the meeting also spoke of what could be called a pre-Christmas warning that President Bush addressed to Belgrade on December 24, 1992. In this case the Secretary of State Eagleburger explicitly warned Belgrade: *"Carrying the Bosnian conflict to Kosova will not be tolerated. The U.S.A. will not allow this."*[613]

It is interesting to note that the Secretary of State came to Europe with strong words after having met President Dr. Ibrahim Rugova two

---

[610] See some of the articles in the American media regarding possible war scenarios in Kosovo: *"The Serbian Death"* by Strobe Talbot in *"Time,"* 1 June 1991, Peter S. Green *"Yugoslavia's spreading war"* in *"US News & World Report,"* 29 June 1992, Janice A.Brown – *"The next exsplosion"* in *"Commonwealth,"* 17 June 1992, Karen Breslau – *"Will Kosovo be next?"* in *"Newsweek,"* 31 August 1992, J. F. O. McAllister *"Ever greater Serbia. Belgrade likely to turn its guns on Albanian Kosovo"* in *"Time,"* 28 September 1992

[611] Thomas Niles statement of 30 June in *"Europe,"* August 1992.

[612] Statement by NATO Council of Ministers issued on 17 October 1992, published in Auerswald/Auerswald *"Kosovo Conflict,"* 2000, p. 64.

[613] Statement by Eagleberger on 16 December 1992, cited according to *"The Kosovo Conflict,"* 2000, p. 64.

days before, with whom he had long conversations. First he met him in Stockholm on December 15, 1992, at a meeting of foreign ministers of the OSCE and secondly in Brussels on December 17. At NATO's Headquarters the Secretary of State held a joint press conference with Dr. Rugova, in which the leader of the Kosova Albanians thanked deeply the American people and its government for their attention and the support shown for the people of Kosova for, what he termed, "their way to independence."

The U.S. Secretary of State, in his turn, on behalf of the U.S. government, praised the "prudent and responsible way that the people of Kosova were behaving under the leadership of Dr. Ibrahim Rugova."[614]

In these circumstances, which seemed very dramatic, and from the point of a very gloomy view of the bloodshed in Bosnia when Milosevic had won the presidential election with a majority vote against Panic, who was thought to be "Washington's man in Belgrade," coming out this time stronger than before, it was quite expected that the Christmas Warning would be issued on December 24, 1992. It was being said that President Bush intended to send a warning to Milosevic personally through Eagleburger, former U.S. ambassador to Yugoslavia, who was known for his friendship with Milosevic and whose appointment to the post of Secretary of State had been followed with awe and opposition by American conservative circles, who knew the position of their former ambassador in Belgrade's support, even when Milosevic had declared war against Albanians and the rest and that Serbia, as he bluntly said, "was facing historical battles, which it had to win in both lawful and unlawful ways."

However, the American media on the same day the Christmas Warning was issued received and published it on their front pages, as a U.S. position against the expansion of Serbian aggression in Kosova, which at least from a formal point of view, meant no other than lifting Kosova and its problems to the level of U.S. priorities. It could even be said that the lining of Kosova from list C, in which it was with Rawanda, Somalia, and several other African countries, which needed no prevention and humanitarian aid, to be transferred to the so-called A list of strategic priorities, was aimed at keeping it under direct supervision,[615] the importance was enhanced even more keeping in mind that in Washington Kosova and its

[614] Statement by U.S. State Department on 17 December 1992. Published in *"The Kosovo Conflict,"* 1999 p. 63.

[615] Kuntzel, Matthias *"Der Weg in den Krieg,"* p. 141, etc.

problem had an entirely different treatment, similar to that of Europeans, being focused as a minority issue, which needed merely "democratic therapy" and nothing more.

The Americans defended this same approach after the London Conference and the Geneva talks, where the delegations of Kosova and Serbia were mainly dealing with education issues. Furthermore, in May 1993 the position of four European countries became known: France, Great Britain, Spain and Russia as opposed to Kosova's independence, joined by official Washington, arguing that they were doing it so that the talks in Geneva would not be burdened with statutory issues, but rather with specific ones of education, a differentiation that, as will be seen, did not suffice to take the direction of solutions, as Belgrade knew fully well what was hiding behind them.[616]

The Christmas Warning was accepted and reiterated by the new U.S. administration, headed by Bill Clinton, who had won the November elections. On January 10, 1993, the U.S. Secretary of State, Warren Christopher, repeated the threat to Belgrade issued by Bush. It was also repeated by the U.S. ambassador to the United Nations, Albright, on August 9, 1993 submitting the text of the warning to the UN Security Council as an American position.

So, in this case the Clinton administration would not be different from that of Bush, with the focus remaining on its supervision with efforts to prevent its explosion, but without any access to dealing with factors causing it and without introducing any initiative to resolve it, which in the eyes of the strategists would look, as Clark Howard would ascertain, as a priority without priority.[617]

But even if one could grant approval to the assessment that that kind of behavior was something that looked like a priority without priority, the Christmas Warning kept Albanians on the course of civil resistance within their parallel state.

It remains, however, to assess how and how much that had an impact on the Serbs. These opinions were divided. They range from those saying that the U.S. warning had an impact against their rushing into Kosova to assessments that it was precisely that which helped Belgrade to raise

---

[616] See the joint stance of the five countries against Kosovo's independence M. Weller "*The Crisis,*" p. 80.

[617] "*Civil Resistance,*" p. 89.

Albanians' illusion that "one day they would be rewarded for showing patience," which influenced them to calm down with promises, while Serbs in Bosnia and Croatia had their back protected from the South.

Certainly looking back at the assessments of the Christmas warning could move pro and against, and in accordance with the approach, could be interpreted in different ways if it were not for the year 1999 and NATO's air strikes against Serb forces in Kosova and other parts of Serbia, using the determination of the United States of America as a promoter in approaching the issue of Kosova with a determination to get Serbia out, which not only had plagued the autonomy of Albanians, but had not shown any interest in the Albanian democratic determination, the most civilized of the time, to respond in the same way. Rather, Belgrade had only considered ethnic cleansing of Kosova Albanians and in order to achieve that goal had also used means of war.

But, it became obvious that the American commitment, in addition to stimulating the interest of democracy and democratic reform in Eastern countries, and in addition to the protection of human and ethnic rights, also focused on the strategy of showing off as a world superpower, which had a responsibility for the new world order based on the principles of economic and political globalization with special attention to be paid to Western global interests, and that was more than expected of her, found in a very favorable situation to run in accordance with its historical interests.

The space of the former Yugoslavia in general and Kosova in particular, as a catalyst of crisis, showed a very good case for a new profiling of a sensitive European point, which offered opportunities for further realignment with U.S. and North-Atlantic interests of particular importance, as seen by the U.S. national security expert, Zbigniew Brzezinski. The latter saw it as essential for the U.S. strategy as a global superpower of the future demanding a U.S. presence in Europe, precisely in a very safe space, free of impact of political unrest and other movements that align the Old Continent with Asia.[618]

Opponents of the new world order and globalization, mostly from among the ranks of neo-leftists, Islamic fundamentalists, and various ecological groups, with the U.S. behaving after the collapse of bloc bipo-

---

[618] Brzezinski, Zbigniew *"Die Einzige Weltmacht,"* cited according to Matthias Kuntzel *"Der Weg in den Krieg,"* 2000, p. 145.

larity as the only superpower, would call this neo-hegemony and neo-imperialism, submitting everything to its own interests, including crises and disasters of others, which, even if not staged, were always used for such purposes. With this careful vocabulary and a magnifying glass would be seen and assessed the U.S. commitment to resolve the Kosova crisis, even though for years it had been treated as a "reserved matter" or solved by means of war.[619]

Germany and the Kosova Issue

Germany's major role to bring to light the historical truth about Albanians and their Western antiquity, one of the biggest supports given to the Albanian question since the Eastern Crisis and on to return to the European family from where they were violently forced out. – German efforts in favor of Albanian historical truth and its reflections on science must have had a great influence in politics. Deposits by German scientists are well known against the Serbian hegemony propaganda in the field of journalism and quasi-science with which Serbian politics bombarded the European public and the diplomacy of the Western countries. – Acceptance and accommodation of over three hundred thousand persecuted people and care for them would rank Germany among the strongest advocates of the Albanian people in their efforts to implement the state of Kosova. – The German press was one of the world's most engaged entities in its defense and presentation of the truth about Kosova.

Some of the first friction of German diplomacy with Lord Owen occurred when he by mid-1993 eliminated the German representative in the Geneva talks for the former Yugoslavia, Gert Ahrens, from his post as director of the Special Group for Kosova and replaced him with the Frenchman Masset. Although publicly it was said that this was a personal assessment of the British lord through personal changes in the team to better the negotiation process, it showed that the former Yugoslav crisis

---

[619] See authors Heinz Loquani, Elmar Altvater, Michael Kalman, Jurgen Scheffran, Norman Paech, Ralph Grabert, Stefan Gose and Paul Schafer comprised in the book „*Der Kosovo-Krieg,*" published by Albrecht/Shaefer, 1999.

would last as long as it would not only because of the Serbian strategy to play with all the cards, where that of accomplished acts and diplomatic skills were used, but also because Belgrade would greatly help certain international conjunctures from those of principled aspects (state sovereignty, minority standards, etc..) to the delimitations of the concealed areas of interest. Documents detached from reality, various diplomatic acts and those that could be reconstructed from the reality of conferences on the former Yugoslavia left the impression that the problem of the crisis of the former Yugoslavia and its size had been Milosevic alone and his known behavior and not any other factor affecting the negotiation process and the overall course of the crisis among the largest after the Second World War. Although since the beginning of the crisis and its explosion it was being said that Europeans might have had no clear concepts as to how to resolve the crisis, and could not have been united about the measures to be taken, in at least preventing it or holding it under fixed supervision without ever publicly acknowledging it, certain countries saw certain interests involved in the crisis and its developments including particular interests in the game, which in different ways contributed, with two of them in particular, having been determining ones.

This refers on one hand to the French-British tendency to hold Serbia as a regional factor even after the dissolution of the former Yugoslavia, and on the other to the German tendency to eliminate Belgrade as much as possible from that role.

Both these tendencies had their epicenter in treating Kosova and its issue in accordance with the Serbian factor. To make the absurd greater, it equally backfired against Belgrade even as it was held on to, and even when it was anticipated to secede from it.

After the secession of Croatia and Slovenia from the former Yugoslavia and their accelerated acceptance by Germany outside the European plan, Serbian dominance lost two of the important factors associated with the West which suited its treatment as a "strategic bridge between East and West." Since the London Conference determined the fate of an independent state to Bosnia and Herzegovina, regardless whether it could ever function as such, Kosova remained, which could have a twofold impact: on one hand, to shrink Belgrade's state space, and on the other with its secession from Serbia, the Albanian factor in the Balkans to win great geopolitical and geostrategic importance turning into an interest for the West, which would automatically lower the rating of the remnant of Yugoslavia.

It was more than obvious that this development had already been put on its tracks. It remained to slow it down or contain it as much as possible doing so by international principles, or those on which the international community would reach agreements, although they were mostly inconsistent and derided by those who devised them.

The Kosova crisis and its problem, and within these agreements, issues that could likely cause damage or be stumbled over, would either move toward "partial interests," or in the direction of strategic ones in order to one day reach the point where the geostrategic interests of the highest level would break with those of international conventions, such as that of state sovereignty and the inviolability of borders. In The Hague and London conferences, so-called "partial interests" dominated in a perfidious way, as the Europeans were not willing to approach global interests, although everyone knew that they were inevitable. Therefore, it was also expected that this limitation would deepen the crisis. But it must be said that even in The Hague and London, the Kosova crisis represented, if not a conflict, then the initial dysfunctions among Europe's interest of traditional conventions and the interest of Atlantic Europe, whose fate would be decided at Rambouillet benefiting the latter.

If it can be said that the United States of America viewed the crisis in the former Yugoslavia and within it that of Kosova, despite remaining outside of it (due to the Iraq war), from the beginning through the magnifying glass of global change and continuing so once engaged in its solution, it could also be said that in this whole process they had Germany by their side. This was expected, not only because the United States of America since the end of World War II helped Germany to survive as a state, as the Soviets, French and British had in mind seeking to punish it in a most severe way and destroy it entirely, but would also support it after its splitting into two parts and four military zones, to recover economically and later even politically (through the famous Marshall Plan) after its division in two parts. Americans would help Germany in crucial moments of its unification after the fall of the Berlin Wall with the faltering among European powers as to whether German unification could create an imbalance in the stability of the European continent. Although upon the signing of the merger agreement in 1990 Germany declared that it would preserve and protect the concept of a united Europe, on a political and strategic plain the European interest would be seen as closely related to that of the West in general, in which the North Atlantic Alliance and the United States of America play an important role, as guarantors of stability. Even when after fourteen years of dominance of conservative government the left would come to power, known for its familiar anti-American rhetoric, it would not only keep the course, but would rush to give Washington blank support for the preparation of the NATO military campaign against Yugoslav forces in Kosova.

Upon the outbreak of the Yugoslav crisis, Germany had its own accounts to settle with the union being not quite prepared to be involved in what would quickly be called a European trial, as was its engagement since June 1991 when the Yugoslav Army moved into Slovenia and later Croatia and the European Union was forced to intervene to prevent further escalation even with the imposition of its dissolution as a state on which only a few thought so far. But, surprisingly, the power of Germany with the strength of a phoenix to cope wonderfully with the merger process, eliminating all obstacles that could keep it hostage internationally because of concessions that the union demanded, would soon be included in the issue of developments in the former Yugoslavia, making use of the Serbian aggression against western republics in favor of promoting its dissolution as soon as possible by helping Croatia and Slovenia to gain international recognition outside the dynamics of the Hague Conference.

Belgrade and its supporters called it German revenge as the Serbs fought the Germans in two world wars and even, if someone read the Serbian version of history, they were the most deserving for their losses! In this case, it seemed to be forgotten that it was neither Germany nor the Americans who for years fueled the Serb nationalistic euphoria in their struggle for domination of Yugoslavia, rightly arousing the feeling of protection of the rest through secession to escape Serb unitarianism and hegemony, but it was rather the Serb hegemonic policy openly proclaimed with the Memorandum of Serbian academics, accepted by the Serbian political elite and its leader Milosevic, which began to destroy all the reasons for a common state.

Of course, after the beginning of Serb aggression against Slovenia and Croatia, following their declaration of independence, Germany was among the first that demanded support for the two former Yugoslav republics to help cope with aggression. Acceptance as independent states, always in accordance with the arbitrariness of the Badinter Commission, formed by the Hague Conference, was the best way possible in this regard.

Even though it seemed that what was labeled as Germany's "rush" to recognize Slovenia and Croatia would be a handicap for the German policy of not interfering in the other affairs of the breakup of former Yugoslavia rather turning into a mere observer, still, since 1993 onwards, Germany started to play an active role in this process. Initially it worked on the mitigation of the consequences of this crisis by accepting hundreds of thousands of refugees from Kosova, Croatia, and Bosnia and Herzegovina giving them temporary shelter. In the meantime it would bear the biggest burden of humanitarian aid to the displaced, for the refugees and people remaining for years in various war zones. It then proceeded with direct political engagement in several initiatives not at all that effective politically in a duo, as the one of Kinkel with the French Foreign Minister Vedrin and others such as those of the Contact Group.

On the premise of this commitment emerged that which can be seen as Germany's interest to resolve the Kosova issue following on a principled plain the framework of international agreements and in a strategic one that of the western sphere of interests as being paved by Washington. But it must be said that even when it adhered to the principles of international agreements and when fighting for western interests in accordance with the Northern Atlantic ones, Germany also had special reasons to see its own interests and engage accordingly regardless of well-known determinations and stances.

But, what were those reasons and German special interests over Kosova? And, how much and how were they reflected in the very flow and direction of the crisis and of the negotiating process? And, finally, what impact did they have on the outcome of taking Serbia out of Kosova as a precondition for its independence?

Among the special reasons and interests were certainly those of a pragmatic nature, but also of a political nature, without excluding certain social and historical society contexts, where century-old cultural relations between the two nations established certain congeniality.

Pragmatic reasons of course influenced the course of Germany in having an interest to resolve as soon as possible and as fair as possible the Kosova crisis. For it would be exactly Germany who would feel the effects of the first shocks, reflected in continuous flows of refugees toward this country, beginning by the end of the eighties to continue with the same intensity later in order to reach its peak in the years 1998/99. Official data showed that during the ten year period in Germany there were about 400 thousand Albanian refugees, most of who would never return home. If we add to this figure a number of about one hundred thousand Albanian migrant workers from the sixties and seventies, who in the meantime used the right to family reunification, it appears that Germany carried the burden of keeping and caring for about one fourth of the population of Kosova. These people not only found temporary housing, but many of them turned it into permanent residents, either by providing a work permit after gaining the right of political asylum (over two hundred thousand of them), or by finding other options (marriages with Germans) to become German citizens. This huge burden cost Germany a lot, as besides Albanian refugees it also received Bosnian refugees, Romans, Macedonians, Serbs, and others, spending for them over five billion German marks annually.

The first priority of German policy was to create circumstances to prevent the influx of refugees, whose numbers in the critical phase had reached several thousand per day, in order to then create conditions for the return of refugees. However, evidently, even if a political solution was found in Kosova on the basis of some kind of autonomy, as foreseen by the international community, it would be difficult to stop the flow of refugees to Germany, because Albanians did not trust the regime in Belgrade, and rightly so. For the past had shown clearly that Serbia had anti-Albanian purposes, having re-stated them and turned them into national policies, which it did not hesitate to defend.

Faced with this reality, the German official policy, after two or three failures to reach an agreement with Belgrade for the return of Albanian refugees, as many of them had been exposed to police repression as soon as they came back home and had to become refugees again, had reached a conclusion that only by finding a political solution of having Serbia leave Kosova, even as a temporary protectorate condition, could keep Albanians in Kosova, after which preconditions would be created for the return of refugees there.

As the international factor after the failure of the London Conference and the dragging of the Geneva talks was preoccupied with the problems of the war in Bosnia and Herzegovina and Croatia, it was clear that the issue of Kosova could not be dealt with but rather kept out of any provocation to war, because it would have fatal consequences for the West being faced with over a million Albanian refugees, many of whom had intended to head for Germany. Thus, from The Hague to the Dayton Conference, the German policy focused on supporting the parallel state of Albanians in Kosova and assisting its "logistics" in Germany – the Government of the Republic of Kosova, allowing for the collection of a solidarity fund and the "*Three Percent Fund.*"

Although at first skeptical of parallel institutions and their functioning in Kosova, German political authorities realized in time that the parallel government in Kosova represented an important and highly successful segment of civil resistance among the most special of the time, turning day by day into a political deposition of Albanians on their right to secession from Serbia. The Belgrade regime in Kosova, despite the assertion of being "in their own home" with the parallel state in place had turned into an ordinary repressive invader that controlled only its own military and police apparatus and nothing else.

Through frequent actions it had already begun to be targeted by Albanian illegal groups who were turning to forms of armed resistance, which were not inconsistent with the reality of their parallel state, which by keeping education in extremely difficult circumstances, organizing health care, internal solidarity and other segments, despite the fierce repression of the Serbian police, was turning into a civilized reality that could not remain without political effects. Albanians, with their behavior, had taken Serbia out of Kosova, reducing it to a mere police and military occupier whose end was anticipated. All the decision-making international factor had to do was to recognize and support it.[620]

And precisely here lie the reasons for the first friction of the German diplomacy with Lord Owen in Geneva in June 1993, when the German politician, Gert Ahrens, was eliminated from the special leadership group for Kosova and that, according to Hans-Dietrich Genscher, happened because Belgrade had understood quite well that Germany saw no other way of resolving the Kosova problem in the long term other than removing Serbia from there. It would be best expressed by its position that: "Germany, driven by the intense pressure of Albanian refugees and others from the area of former Yugoslavia would clearly see that it was not in its interest, nor in the interest of Europe, to keep such a Serbia with Kosova

---

[620] For more see evaluation by the German Chancellor Helmut Kohl in Jusuf Buxhovi's: "Kthesa historike – shteti paralel dhe rezisistenca e armatosur," Prishtina, 2009, p. 214.

in it, as it would be permanently unstable. Even if there were no other interests here, this would suffice to say it openly."[621]

But, even in the circumstances before and after Dayton, Germany was not be able to state plainly what it already knew to be the solution to the crisis. The official policy of the conservative Christian Democrats in coalition with the Liberals, which at the national level with German unification had reached its historical peaks, but which in addition with the recognition of Slovenia and Croatia as independent states had met some of the main policy coordinates of the traditional German politics even as a cultural sphere, was careful in regard to what were called internal European balances, facing the Balkans with a highly sensitive test. This however, did not detract it from building internal consent with Washington in which the future of Kosova was excluded from Serbia for both political reasons and reasons of areas of interest. Only the combination of these two within the North Atlantic options could work.

Besides the official German policy, which at least publicly acted pragmatically and in accordance with international positions, but in the humanitarian plain, by accepting over a million refugees from the region and spending great amounts of money for the care of the vulnerable populations in areas affected by war, it was the German public that played a crucial role in animating the Kosova crisis in terms of the broader social, cultural and historical aspects. It has been said that since the Eastern Crisis on, Albanians would be victims of hegemonic appetites of great Serbian policy in a continuum, as Serbia since the Congress of Berlin to the Balkan wars expanded steadily in favor of their ethnicity, using wars for ethnic cleansing and genocide against the Albanian people albeit that in the so-called peacetime would continue it for the same purposes using different means.

The powerful German press and electronic media from the beginning of the Kosova crisis, as Serbia launched its campaign ostensibly to improve its constitutional position, but acting rather to destroy Kosova's autonomy of 1974, and especially since it in March 1989 ruined it by the use of tanks and the state of emergency, alerted both the German public and politics into looking at the issues in their true light rather than becoming subject to European silence towards what the well-known publicist Viktor Meier called "a warning chronicle of an organized crime

---

[621] *Ibid*, p. 215.

against an entire people in the eyes of the whole world."[622] This assessment was enforced further by what the noted analyst and publisher of the newspaper *"Frankfurter Allgemeine,"* J. F. Reissmüler had to say about the Albanians "as a people of culture being subjected to an uncivilized people, such as Serbs, and subject to an anti-European state, such as Serbia, which does its best to entice Europe allegedly on being threatened by Albanians and the like. The Serbian tale about the wolf and the lamb should for once be rightly understood."[623]

The engagement of the German press and media to reflect the truth of Kosova from the perspective of social and historical complexity undoubtedly highlighted the cultural affinities and meeting points of the two peoples from antiquity and early Middle Ages and on especially in a light of friendship, where different and numerous German missionaries, consuls and finally scientists revealed the Albanian people and its history in a spirit of antiquity and autochthony among the oldest in Europe. German scientists from Leibniz, Xylander, and Hahn to Gustav Mayer were the first to speak of the Pelasgian-Illyrian origin of Albanians calling the Albanian language the daughter of the Illyrian, stands confirmed through further research by German scientists, who were rightly considered as founders of Albanological thought and science. German efforts regarding Albanian historical truth and its reflections on science must have had a great influence in politics. Contributions are known by Ger-

---

[622] See the book *"Wie Jugoslawien wespielt wurde"* and other writings by the author in the newspaper „*Frankurter Allegemeine*" of Frankfurt and „*Züricher Zeitung*" of Zürichut, with Meier bringing most professional evaluations and analyses in the German speaking press, providing the entire truth of a hegemonic behaviour against Albanians for a long period of time. This influential German author highlighted the truth that in Kosovo the rights of Serbs were threatened, as Belgrade's propaganda claimed, but rather a great clash between the right to life and ethnicity of Albanians with the so-called Serbian historic right over Kosovo was taking place, with the latter according to the author being part of great lies and speculations by the Serbs as they had never even been in the Middle Ages an ethnic majority there. Meyer disclosed that Albanians were indigenous, that they always presented a majority in Kosovo, and that even what the Serbian propaganda called „Serbian spiritual testimony" was Albanian, because Albanians were among the first in the Balkans to have accepted Christianity, since the third century, with Serbs, as well as all Slavs, receiving it in the tenth century.

[623] Johan Georg Reissmüller: *"Serbien in Schwierigkeiten,"* in "Frankfurte Allgemeine," 20 November 1991 and 24 December 1991.

man scientists against the Serb hegemonic propaganda in the field of journalism and quasi-science, with which Serb politics bombarded European politics and diplomacy of the Western countries. With the publication of the *"Etymological Dictionary of the Albanian Language"* in Paris, the great linguist Gustav Meier, presented the European public and politics with a major scientific and cultural monument, at a time when it was mainly informed about Albanians by the Serbian propaganda accompanied by the Greek and Russian ones portraying them in the worst possible ways not sparing insults and debarment from a civilizational point of view. Hahn's Albanological studies in several volumes, Bopp's collection of studies and publication of the first *Albanian-German Dictionary* by Arnold von Harff of 1496[624] were of great importance as the German public found a civilized people rather than a "rogue and dangerous one to European civilization."[625]

If these were added to the decision by the Conference of Ambassadors to have Prince Wied sent as Viceroy of the Albanian state and the reverberation that his appointment King of Albania had made, together with his impressions of Albanians and Albania during his six-month stay on top of a restless Albania still dismembered by its neighbors, who had already brought it to such a bad state, it is understandable why the Germans would create such a reflection of a civilized European people, existentially vulnerable in a space where Slavic-Orthodox invasion for centuries was turned into an anti-European policy, which not only affected the vital interests of the West, but also the cultural and historical identity of their ancient roots.

---

[624] *Arnold von Harff*, Knight of Cologne, was among the many of the time to take pilgrimage trips to the Holy Land. According to records kept at the Library of Cologne and those from Südostinstitut of Munich, von Harf, on his passage stopped in Albania, where he had spent several days. He stopped in Ulqin, Shkodra and Lezha. For his personal communication needs with the natives he marked down the words as they sounded in Albanian and translated them into German. There was a total of 52 words, which, after returning to Germany, he published together with some brief explanations of Albanian territories. Therefore, von Harff's *Albanian-German Dictionary* is very valuable linguistic evidence, but also historical, among the first of its kind to be known.

[625] Djordjević, Vladan *"Albanien und die Grossmächte,"* Leipzig, 1913.

This articulation was surely supported by the similarities of historical disasters of the last century that followed the two peoples, such as the violent divisions, regardless of motives (Albanians divided since the London Conference and the Germans separated after World War II). As the Berlin Wall – as a geopolitical division line on one side, and inter-Albanian wall – as a historical injustice to a people, on the other, would represent two major typical wounds of Europe for half a century, it was only natural for them to play a special role to sensitize the German public but also the German policy on the Kosova issue, especially after the fall of the Berlin Wall, when the Germans tasted the flavor of the union, while Kosova and its tragedy reminded them what it meant for a nation to be violently divided and unable to cope with it because of the spheres of interest and certain international conjunctures.

The flow of Albanian refugees into Germany following Serbian aggression in Bosnia and Herzegovina with all the terrible images of violence carried by TV cameras around the world, presented a good opportunity for Germans to link the bitter past with a tragic reality through which were still going those who continued to remain victims of Serbian hegemony even by justifying this based on "international principles" and various calculations in which certain interests appeared more important than the right solutions. This, even, for many politicians, turned into a matter of remorse, burdening them and also German politics for years.[626]

---

[626] Author's conversation with former Chancellor Helmut Kohl, Bonn, May 2000.

But this did not prevent some of them from expressing this publicly, asking that the treatment of the Kosova problem be not bypassed although it was in contradiction to the international positions, [627] so that one day and in certain circumstances, the German policy would be among the first to join the U.S. in favor of the use of force to draw Serbia out of Kosova justifying this by the moral argument of not allowing a new Auschwitz to happen.[628]

---

[627] MP Peter Gloz, after a visit to Kosovo in 1993, in a Bundestag debate on Kosovo would say that "trains are going in the opposite, towards a final separation, which must be taken into account, if one desired peace in the Balkans. Gloz will recall the Kosovo Albanian trunk as divided by force in 1912 as a historical fact that had to be considered, not to be used in any form of revanchism against the Serbs, but to improve an injustice, which has become a factor of crisis. Gloz will mention the parallel Albanian state and its function as one of the models of unprecedented civil resistance in Europe and in the world, which indicates a civilizational consciousness of Albanians, who even in circumstances of full occupation and repression were pursuing a peaceful way. See 127th session of the German Bundestag of 23 September 1993, minutes 15227.

[628] Fischer, Joschka: "*Vitet e koalicionit kuq-gjelbër,*" 2008. The slogan "*never again Auschwitz*" used for the first time by the German Foreign Minister Joschka Fischer in the book was justified because the Greens had to change the political course from that of peace to the definition of defending endangered peoples by air intervention or the use of war for humanitarian aims. In the German public opinion the question of the morality of international law was opened, which allowed a state to protect itself against "separatism" to use the tools of war against its own population, a "right," as would seen in the case of the Serbs against Albanians undermining their ethnic structure, that turned the international community complicit in the crime. Joschka Fischer demanded, in accordance with Kosovo and its case, that the Albanians are helped to escape Serb genocide through a humanitarian pretext under Chapter Five of the UN Charter for the use of military intervention in particular cases, and that international law be changed in favor of the protection of national minorities. Those who behaved like Serbia should be denied the right of minority ownership by all means.

CHAPTER 3
FROM GENEVA TO DAYTON

The Parallel State and Confrontations with Serbia

Dr. Rugova's argumentation for opting for institutional resistance, i.e. parallel state of the Albanians excluding the option for war prematurely. – First repressive measures of the Belgrade regime against members of the Ministry of Defense and Interior and the imprisonment of over two hundred Albanian officers and policemen and consequences for the parallel state. – Continuing efforts to keep members of the military and police units in Kosova on standby in Croatia, Slovenia and the West highlighted the difficulties these services faced lacking a clear concept of civil resistance aligned with an armed resistance institutionally led in accordance with the Constitution of the Republic of Kosova.

The Hague Conference neither distracted nor disappointed Albanians. Yugoslavia was proclaimed as breaking down and what would be left of it were only numerous problems affecting more or less everyone. The Versailles and AVNOJ creature,[629] which connected it with the multiple disasters through which they had passed for more than eight decades, no

---

[629] The First AVNOJ meeting (Anti-Fascist Council of the National Liberation of Yugoslavia) was held on 29 November 1943 in Jajce, where the decision was made to establish the Federal Yugoslavia of six republics: Serbia, Croatia, Slovenia, Macedonia and Bosnia and Herzegovina. It would be called the second or Tito's Yugoslavia. Delegates from Kosovo were not invited in the meeting, which opened a dilemma of them being intentionally left out, as Kosovo was supposed to join Albania, in accordance with the Bujan Resolution, which would be approved shortly (December 31, 1943 and 1, 2 January 1944) or that it remained "Serbia's internal matter," as actually happened following its annexation by Serbia with the Kosovo Assembly Resolution ACNLK held in Prizren on July 10, 1945.

longer existed. But for the Albanians who had never reconciled with its existence, this did not mean that by announcing its dismantling their troubles would finally end. Rather, as would be seen, they still had to fight against the legacy of their past in an almost unique way: to get Serbia out of Kosova, not for being an occupier, but for committing human rights violations which could not go unpunished! This actually best explains the international positions on the crisis, highlighting once again the fear of dealing with the complexity of the Albanian factor appearing as inevitable in such circumstances, where the issue of Kosova represented a key node, the treatment of which depended on the stability or instability of the region and beyond. The international factor saw it clearly from the foreplay of the Hague Conference and beyond. But it would be different conjunctures and areas of interest that deprived it of proper treatment, although it was obvious that Albanians would not consent to this.

Although according to the Badinter Commission the right to be recognized as independent states belonged to the republics, the Government of the Republic of Kosova rushed to complete formalities to compete in due time. Albanians had proclaimed the Republic of Kosova in a legitimate way and by democratic means. This was confirmed in a Referendum on Independence. Kosova's request was not considered on the grounds that the Commission had the mandate to deal only with the republics and not with the provinces, and that for the moment represented a concern but not an ultimate disappointment to give up or change the course, as it was obvious that the downfall that had already started would be surely followed up with a solution that it could not bypass Albanians, regardless of the difficulties they had to face and, obviously, they would be numerous. Therefore, they had a duty to act in accordance with their interests, as was done with the political organization and the decisions taken on July 2 and September 7 with the Declaration of Independence and the decision of the Kosova Assembly in Kaçanik on the declaration of the Republic of Kosova rounded up in a Referendum on Independence utilized by Albanians for their democratic right to make a statement about their future.

"We have declared our independence and are in its construction. We will do our best to place it on right tracks. We therefore with great devotion will do our jobs, and if we do well, then others will support us."[630]

---

[630] Interview by Dr. Ibrahim Rugova for the German TV ARD, broadcast on 23 June 1992 on "Tagestemen" program at 20:30.

So this was a typical statement among many similar ones by Dr. Ibrahim Rugova given to the foreign media, which after the closing down of "Rilindja," Radio and Television of Prishtina by the Belgrade regime represented almost the only source of information for Albanians. This seemingly reassuring statement by Dr. Rugova on "doing our own job" turned into a motto of the parallel state commitment to be accepted as a prerequisite for its implementation, thus creating the conditions for its recognition and acceptance. They both gave hope and optimism that mobilized all layers of Albanian society: totally ignoring the Serbian occupying state focusing instead on building the state through proving its replacement for the Serbian occupying one. Even if this took a while it represented a success.

Confidence in the parallel state and opportunities to realize it multiplied after the emergence of the initial forms of institutional state organization and its direct indication in its main segments, such as the organization of educational process with curricula of the Republic of Kosova in all levels of education, organization of health service and general solidarity, with an already operational system of social care for vulnerable families and the unemployed, similar to social abstinence.

Returning the attention to the parallel state and local institutions would be made even more diligent and attentive with the outbreak of war in Slovenia, Croatia and later in Bosnia and Herzegovina.

"Our work is our war," Rugova would say.[631]

This saying turned into a catchphrase of the civil-institutional resistance of Albanians, operating simultaneously in a double way: in establishing internal facts through building the parallel state, and in avoiding traps and provocations that would draw Kosova into an early conflict with tragic consequences for the Albanians, not only because they were vulnerable and entirely unprotected, but also because in those circumstances, they remained outside the concern of the international community, who saw with concern what was happening in Croatia and Bosnia and Herzegovina without being able to intervene, even though it would recognize Croatia's independence. But this did not prevent the fall of about one half of its territory into the hands of rebel Serbs, with the latter aided by the Yugoslav Army having announced their independent states and not caring a bit for Croatia's independence.

---

[631] Statement given to "*Westdeutsche Rundfunk*" of Cologne on 20 November 1992.

In this atmosphere of commitment to building parallel state institutions, Kosova waited for the London Conference in September 1992. Of course, as discussed earlier, Dr. Ibrahim Rugova, now with the mandate of the first President of the Republic of Kosova, which he achieved in the May elections, together with Prime Minister Dr. Bujar Bukoshi, flew to London, as an observer. However, this didn't bother him or the Kosova Albanians to be treated as a minority issue under Belgrade, as a conviction prevailed that the issues would remain open until the end of the war in Croatia and Bosnia and Herzegovina in particular, with many unknown scenarios and opening many opportunities including one for Kosova as well. This conviction would be considerably enforced with the creation of the *"Special Group"* for Kosova whose work would be transferred to Geneva producing nothing other than a waste of time, which the Belgrade regime used as double-faced tactics to conduct empty negotiations and promises while continuing with establishing fait d'accompli by force and war. But for Albanians, who were involved in the Geneva talks, despite the course they took, it had not been entirely a waste of time. Rather it was assessed that although nothing had changed, and this had been expected, the talks were used for the internationalization of the Kosova issue with contributions of a most civilized kind, countering violence and war, apartheid and most severe forms of discrimination with the alternatives of the parallel state by peaceful means, where education was the main pillar, including other segments, which also played an important role in the overall architecture of the parallel state and its historical testimony.

"It is important for us to stay out of war," Dr. Rugova would say to BBC in Albanian repeating that similarly in his meeting with Lord Carrington in London.[632]

---

[632] An interview for the Albanian BBC broadcast on 28 February 1992. In this talk Dr. Rugova unveiled the unknowns of the Bosnian war and its implications for resolving the Kosovo issue. "The Bosnian Serbs have proclaimed the Republika Srpska, but they did so through war. We have declared the Republic of Kosovo in a legitimate way and through democratic means. Republika Srpska is the fruit of bloody violence and Serbian aggression against Bosnia and Herzegovina, which had the right of self-determination to be used for the majority of its people, while Kosovo emerged as an expression of the democratic will of the Albanians as a majority people. I want to believe that the democratic world and especially the United States will show more understanding for democratic determination than for those with guns, which one day may not be accepted or

The policy of non-involvement in the war and of waiting for the Serbs in Croatia and Bosnia and Herzegovina to spend their ammunition, to their own detriment, was accepted by the vast majority of Kosova's population. Building the parallel state and patience were beginning to turn into a particular political philosophy, which did not express itself only by internal results, but also by the respect it gained from outside, especially by decision-making factors, such as the United States America, Germany and many other European countries. Some of them, along with the political and moral support they provided to the civil resistance of Kosova Albanians, were beginning to help Kosova by accepting a large number of workers for seasonal jobs. Such arrangements were made with Austria and Switzerland, where workers were employed in an organized way in the health sector and gastronomy. Serbia used its state influence against them, but it continued in various ways until this form of supervised employment, hindered by many formalities, often hard to deal with for the lack of administration, passed into the hands of various clandestine groups, a move that could be seen as part of the backstage activities against the internal organization of Albanians in order to have it fail as much as possible.

Since the beginning of the Albanian parallel organization imposed by conditions – such as those of mass dismissal from work and the closing down of institutions at all levels, which was institutionalized with the formation of the Government of the Republic of Kosova in late 1991 and the beginning of its work in January of the next year – its segments faced troubles with the Serbian government. The Belgrade regime did its best to prevent forms of solidarity that involved structures and sub-branches of the Democratic League of Kosova in all parts of Kosova. Activists involved in solidarity relief, being distributed based on social lists, were persecuted with many of them ending up in prison, just as Albanian school organizers were persecuted, not sparing those who opened their homes and property for the teachers and students who were seeking to pursue avenues of knowledge by any means. This however, did not prevent further expansion and organization of the parallel state. Evidently since autumn and winter 1992, namely after the London Conference, besides

---

corrected regardless of blood and sacrifice. In politics it is important to achieve something without damage and without destruction ... This is our aim..."

completing the technical infrastructure for all levels of education from primary to the university, including preschool children and kindergartens, along with the organization of a health network, which included a large portion of the medical staff dismissed from the Kosova health system, the Government of the Republic of Kosova started to organize two important departments: Defense and Interior.

Incorporation of these ministries came after the decision of the Assembly of the Republic of Kosova for the appointment of ministers,[633] the core of which would be made up mainly from the Albanian employees of the Kosova Police Service, mainly professionals and specialists from various police services dismissed from jobs or who left beforehand due to disagreements with the Serbian repressive apparatus and methods of violence against Albanians and army officers who had served previously in the Yugoslav People's Army, among them military officers and technicians who at the beginning of the war left the Yugoslav Army, or switched over in the service of the Croatian and Bosnian armies, fighting successfully with the intention of carrying their military experience and knowledge over to their service of Kosova and its issue.

Before starting this form of institutional organization, the branches and sub-branches of the Democratic League of Kosova, along with working groups and committees dealing with the solidarity issue, aid distribution and social care, with the directive of LDK Presidency had formed the Council for Self-defense and Information Council. Both of them included union workers from the ranks of the former Kosova police force and those working in self-defense, the institutions of territorial reserve units, including experts from the fields of defense and security. With the Constitution of 1974, territorial defense was part of military defense of the country possessing certain mechanisms of self-defense from weapons to the organization of reserve units, which were occasionally summoned for military exercises. Like other federal entities, the country had a territorial self-defense corps commander and military headquarters. This mecha-

---

[633] *"Acts of the Assembly of the Republic of Kosovo- 2 July 1990 to 2 May 1992,"* a publication of KASA, 2005, pp. 132,133. Assembly of the Republic of Kosovo with its decision KK no. 33/91 and KK no. 34/91 and based on Article 155 and 117 of the Constitution of the Republic of Kosovo appointed a Minister of Defense of the Republic and a Minister of Interior of the Republic. The decision makes no mention of names, but the initials N.N. Dr. Bukoshi explains this on grounds of keeping confidentiality that was very important for the circumstances.

nism actively included about a thousand military officers and others, who were responsible for more than forty thousand reservists. This potential was so great that, as will be seen, Croatia used it to create its own army, which, once declared an independent state, was placed under the command of the Croatian state, to be the first to take part in fighting against units of the Yugoslav Army in Croatia.

Kosova, however, was not able to carry out this transfer of the reserve structure for its own military needs because the Yugoslav People's Army, commanded by Serbs in 1986, in an unconstitutional way dispersed the Territorial Defense of Kosova, whose commander by Constitution was President of the Presidency of Kosova. This degradation dated back earlier, by mid-1981, when following the demonstrations in March and April, under pretexts of extraordinary measures, territorial defense of Kosova was released of all heavy and light weaponry, with the exception of firefighting and civil emergency equipment. After the forced abolition of Kosova's autonomy in March 1989 by a special decree of the Serbian Presidency the Territorial Defense of Kosova was dispersed. Demonstratively the Yugoslav Army would take over the premises, equipment and all other assets that belonged to it.

Albanian officers and other staff who lost their jobs in the service, organized in a trade union branch, had been among the first to volunteer to be included in local councils of self-defense. ...The aim was to keep close as many professionals from these units as possible doing so quietly and vigilantly. A team of Americans who occasionally visited Kosova had reached a "silent" agreement with Dr. Rugova to have the help of some of their "humanitarian" missionaries who came around in Kosova.[634]

Similar was the case with members of the Kosova Police Service, organized in their independent union. Their superiors were among the first to pledge their loyalty after September 7, 1990, when the declaration of the Republic of Kosova in Kaçanik recognized the legitimacy of Dr. Ibrahim Rugova as the President. Dr. Rugova received the officers of the Kosova Police Service (a delegation of three) and thanked them for their loyalty to the Republic of Kosova. While the Kosova government was being formed, it authorized a member of the LDK Presidency as responsible for the Kosova Police Service to hold regular meetings with representatives of this important service. As the branch of the Independent Union of Kosova

---

[634] Buxhovi, Jusuf: *"Kthesa historike: Vitet e Gjermanisë dhe epoka e LDK-së."*

Police Service had a membership of over three thousand people, mainly professionals from the ranks of police forces and other professional services, most of them, in various forms, were included in the work of municipal councils of self-defense and information. It was a rewarding job, because circumstances were being created for the very valuable police and military potential of Kosova to first prove themselves as part of the state of Kosova during its parallel functioning, and secondly – they had to be prepared for an active protection and self-defense, which, one day, could also reach the level of military confrontation with Serbia, as would occur when a large part of the Albanian military and police officers were successfully included in the ranks of the Kosova Liberation Army. After the formation of the Government, municipal councils became part of relevant ministries of the Government of the Republic of Kosova continuing to work in different organizational circumstances, outside the party organization and supervision of local government.

The Serbian state apparatus cracked down hard on all activists included in the composition of local councils of self-defense, being equally harsh against any form of active organization of the Police Service of Kosova Albanians. According to data provided by the Information Center of the Democratic League of Kosova of November 1991, the Serbian police and persecution authorities of the Yugoslav People's Army, within six months, many former police officers and staff from the police services had been taken under temporary custody among whom 57 persons involved in activities of parallel structures of the Democratic League of Kosova in municipalities were sentenced to prison. In addition, 13 former Albanian army officers, most of them from territorial defense reserve service in Kosova, were charged with "activities against the state." Some of them from Anamorava were prosecuted on charges of "organizing an illegal Albanian army."[635]

Following the formation of the Government of the Republic of Kosova and appointment of respective ministers, whose names were kept in conspiracy together with their other structures, action would be taken against them as soon as information was fabricated. However, if detentions and repressive measures used by the Belgrade regime against them

---

[635] See Bulletin of the Information Center of the Democratic League of Kosova no. 11/1991. It provides a list of the local structure of the arrested policemen sentenced in prison from one to six months.

including prison sentences (and they were draconian) stand as an indicator of the activity of these services,[636] then it could be said that they worked mostly without the public being aware. The heaviest blow was received in the case of the arrest of over one hundred members of the Police Service and the Kosova Protection, headed by the former commander of the Territorial Defense of Kosova, Gen Hajzer Hajzeri by the end of 1993, whose trial took place six months later in May 1994 in the great hall of the Assembly, where exactly four years earlier Serbia violently abolished the autonomy of Kosova.

Previously, a group of young people were imprisoned by the Yugoslav Army forces, under the charge of having committed military exercises in a camp in Albania as members of the armed forces of the Ministry of Defense of the Republic of Kosova. A military prosecutor in Nis, in a public statement, carried out by Belgrade media, said he would bring the names of two members of LDK Presidency involved in this activity, although they were not imprisoned, proving clearly that the Serbian regime aimed at targeting Dr. Ibrahim Rugova himself and his course of civil-institutional resistance, if not for any other reason than to have his "peaceful aureole" removed in the eyes of the international community.[637]

Rugova, in turn, considered the imprisoning of members of the Kosova Police Service and some army officers together with General Hajzeri, "a serious provocation of the Serbian repressive regime against the police and military forces of Kosova, involved in protecting the order and the right to self-defense from paramilitary units and their activists operating openly in all parts of Kosova terrorizing Albanians."[638]

---

[636] See the Report of the Government of the Republic of Kosovo 1991-1999 submitted to the Assembly of Kosovo in January 2000, p. 11.

[637] See newspapers *"Politika"* of Belgrade and *"Jedinstvo"* of Prishtina of 20 December 1993.

[638] See the Report of the Government of the Republic of Kosovo 1991-1999, p. 13. The report admits the existence of a "special" organization, where the emphasis was put on defensive concepts through reserve units. Thus, it says that the Defense Ministry in all municipalities of Kosovo (with the exception of Leposavic, Zubin Potok and Shterpce) would form supporting units of the cluster size to company-level of municipalities. The report says that by mid-1992 most municipalities would be covered by command leadership bodies and military formations. It claimed that in the municipality of Prishtina alone some 100 military company-size formations were set up.

As usual, Rugova this time too used the opportunity to highlight the need for the presence of international observers and extensive international presence in Kosova, which would be constantly repeated in every meeting with leaders of the great powers, as were those in 1994 with Bill Clinton in the U.S., Helmut Kohl in 1996, Pope John Paul in Rome and senior NATO officials to go so far as to openly seek in 1998 the presence and then intervention of NATO troops realized a year later. However, mass imprisonment of members of the Kosova Police Service and the troops of the former Territorial Defense included in the ranks of the Kosova Ministry of Defense together with their commander and heavy prison sentences would reveal the fear that the Serbian regime felt from the police and military potential displayed by Kosova, even though a good portion of them, because of both an inevitable profusion and lack of proper organization and other deficiencies accompanying these services stayed out of concrete activities. Severe sentences and constant persecution made a part of the members of the Kosova police service and military force leave Kosova. Some left to Albania with the hope of finding opportunities to get properly organized. Some moved to different countries of the West seeking temporary shelter. From Albania and abroad many of them were then mobilized for the war in Kosova as part of the Armed Forces of the Republic of Kosova (FARK) and within the Kosova Liberation Army (KLA).

Kosova and Albania: Understandings and Misunderstandings

After the declaration of pluralism in Albania, in fact, the two political blocs, left and right, rather than fighting for a mid-term and long-term strategy for Kosova to gain independence as soon as possible turning into an important factor of the Albanian issue and its comprehensive resolution began to play with open alliance with the political blocs in Kosova. – The anti-communist opposition of the time had an ally in Kosova – the Democratic League of Kosova and between them a solid friendship was created while former Albanian communists began to re-activate their connections with ideological groups from Kosova, mainly in the West creating an almost illegal nucleus of missionaries, who failed to recognize the new political reality in Kosova, although many of them, from the beginning of the nationwide movement were includ-

ed in the leadership structures of the Democratic League of Kosova and parallel state, particularly in the Emergency Fund.- Difficulties faced by official Tirana to set a balance between the demands of the international factor to view the Kosova issue as an internal issue of Serbia and those of Kosova for the recognition of the independent state. – Efforts of defactorization of Rugova and introduction into the game of his opponents, who had no democratic legitimacy and the disruptive consequences of this.

The social change in Albania that would eventually affect the country in December of 1990 was met in Kosova with great hope that the liberation of Albania from long isolation and communist ideology of the fiercest kind in the world would have a positive impact for it too. ... Kosova Albanians, who had already proclaimed the Republic of Kosova and were in the process of building the internal state of Kosova believed that the spirit of reform in Albania would take the prescribed direction, and the Albanian society would not only catch the right course it so badly needed but also because it would help Kosova and its issue that was regarded as part of the unresolved problems of Albanians in the Balkans, where the international community would gain the chance to see and treat Albanians as an important part of their geopolitical and geostrategic interests.

Although ever since the suspension of Kosova's autonomy by force, in 1989, Tirana proved to be very restrained against the Serbian vandal act that besides destroying the social and institutional infrastructure it followed by a bleeding of Albanians who had protested against what had been viewed as Serb reoccupation, the intellectual layer of Kosova, having assumed the Albanian political organization, together with the rest of Kosova intelligence showed an understanding of the "abstinence" of the Albanian state. This was a result of the belief that Albania found itself in a pre-storm phase of internal analyses and breakdowns towards an explosion that would occur over a year and a half later after Eastern countries removed communist dictatorships from their national political scenes, sometimes due to internal democratic reforms and sometimes through the use of revolutionary violence, as happened in Romania.

That caution came about after the events of July 2 of that year in Tirana filled with vandalism as embassies of several western countries were stormed. This turned into a world event, while in Prishtina, MPs of

Kosova Assembly declared the Constitutional Declaration of Independence opening the way to Kosova's secession from Serbia and its removal from the Albanian trunk, which was eventually realized after nine years, on June 10 with the signing of the Kumanovo Agreement between NATO and Serbian armed forces, confirmed by UN Security Council Resolution 1244. Despite the blow that Prishtina received from the events of July 2 in Albania, Kosova political forces still expected positive changes in the country. The conflicting messagae as coming from a meeting held in August of that year between the intellectuals and Ramiz Alia in which he said that there would not be pluralistic political parties but pluralism inside the socialist party. This suited the communist regime seeking in that way, too, to sabotage the spirit of political and social reforms and keep the socialist party in power even if the changes to the party were merely cosmetic. This doubt of pluralism would never be removed completely even after the last events in December of that year when finally students' demonstrations exploded in Tirana and the Political Bureau of the Party of Labor led by Ramiz Alia allowed for party-based organization, but without removing the monopoly of the Party of Labor. This monopoly, as would be seen, in March of the following year when the rusty ideological apparatus gave way to stormy pluralist elections, would win the first elections drawing Albania into the next stage of social and political unrest. Finally, victory was obtained a year later in early elections imposed by the Democratic Party of Sali Berisha.

But this victory, too, evidently did not draw the Albanian state out of the crisis, while the Albanian society would not be free of the totalitarian mentality and its legacy. The struggle for pluralism was not used equally for reform and social change as much as for revenge against itself.

However, even such an Albania with so much turbidity would be useful for Kosova, because the Iron Curtain had already fallen and everything was beginning to take a new turn. Moreover, the Albanian Parliament, despite domestic concerns which were boiling in June 1991 recognized the will of the Kosova Albanians for independence declaring that it would recognize the decision of Kosova's legitimate authorities, although this was not equal to the official recognition that Kosova needed in those circumstances. In this case, the Albanian state and diplomacy received instructions not to enter into any possible arrangements outside this commitment. The Government of Albania, in December of that year recognized the results of the referendum for independence in Kosova and welcomed the formation of the Government of the Republic of Kosova, which could be taken as some kind of compensation for the official non-recognition of Kosova's statehood. But, even without an official recognition of the state of Kosova, statements by both the Albanian Parliament and Albanian Government represented a significant support to Kosova coming from Tirana, since the border dividing Albanians, one of violent division, would finally be open.

First contacts showed romanticism supplanted in a difficult process of recognition, bearing both difficulties and misunderstandings. Politically, the Albanian opposition came up with the most advanced theses about the problem of Kosova, which, over time, it corrected, namely after coming to power (after a year) adopting them in its pro-Western foreign policy that Albania followed.[639]

But in the aftermath of pluralism in Albania, in fact, the two political blocs in Albania, left and right, rather than fight for a mid and long term strategy for Kosova to gain as soon as possible its proclaimed independence thus becoming an important factor towards a comprehensive resolution of the Albanian question, began to play with open alliances with the political blocs in Kosova. "Thus, the anticommunist opposition of the time had a willing ally in Kosova, the Democratic League of Kosova and between them solid friendship took shape." On the other hand, former Albanian communists began to reactivate their connections with ideological groups from Kosova, mainly in the West creating an almost illegal nucleus of missionaries who failed to recognize the new political reality in Kosova,"[640] although many of them from the beginning of the nationwide movement were included in the leadership structures of the Democratic League of Kosova and parallel state.

It must be said that the delimitations of these divisions and their schemes, sometimes more openly and sometimes secretly, followed the process of cooperation between Albania and Kosova granting new turns to affiliation, so that everything took a direction of polarization between the left and right.

Viewed from the perspective of the past, this cooperation could be divided into three phases, not only in time, but also in content, highlight-

---

[639] See: Buxhovi, Jusuf: "Kthesa historike – shteti paralel dhe rezistenca e armatosur," Prishtina, 2009, pp. 234-258.

[640] *Ibid*, pp. 234-258.

ing what may rightly be called the process of inter-Albanian understandings and misunderstandings.

The first phase marks the beginning of reforms in Albania, from December 1991 until mid-1992.

The second phase marks the arrival of the Democratic Party of Sali Berisha to power until the downfall of his government and collapse of the Albanian state in February-March 1997, a time that could be divided into two sub phases: before and after Dayton.

And the third phase, also with many upturns and extremely important for Albanians, is that from the second return of Fatos Nano to power up to the military intervention of NATO against Serb military forces in Kosova and Serbia in March 1999.

Regarding the first phase, that of the continuing occurrence of Ramiz Alia as Albania's president and Nano's Socialist government, successor of the former communists, which did not entirely cut its ideological links with the Party of Labor, keeping also some old methods of work, it can be said that Kosova had a reason to be cautious, even without it being suggested by the international factor, which greatly monitored the work of the Democratic League of Kosova as carrier of the statehood movement.

However, representatives of political parties and intellectuals began to move towards Tirana, to dually measure the pulse.

Dr. Rugova demanded a distancing from the turbulent interference in the Albanian political scene, even though this did not mean giving up support for the Democratic Party and the rest of the pro-Western wing whose short role of opposition was supported even through direct investments.[641]

At this time the first contacts with the Socialist Party were established with Ramiz Alia using a new rhetoric to show his care and concern over developments in Kosova and further in the former Yugoslavia that was involved in the first waves of perennial war, where the Albanian factor faced multiple dangers left without protection. On this issue, the President of Albania expressed caution asking the Kosovars and the rest of Albanians across the border to do the same, especially as the Albanian state was in a very unstable condition.

But one should keep in mind that this time produced some of the joint efforts of Albania and Kosova to attend preparations for Kosova's

---

[641] Buxhovi, Jusuf *"Kthesa historike: Vitet e Gjermanisë dhe epoka e LDK-së,"* 2008.

defense and self-defense, reflected in the opening of certain temporary drilling centers of volunteers from Kosova and the diaspora for the approaching war. Moving with caution as to not have Albania get involved in a conflict with Serbia and being accused by the international community for inflicting a regional crisis, consents were reached mostly verbally with no official statements. But even as such they would be interrupted after a short time, to be reopened after four years,[642] when the armed opposition began in Kosova as well against Serb military and police forces leading to NATO air intervention against the Yugoslav military and police forces in Kosova and Serbia.[643]

Unlike Kosova's political class and intellectuals, who did not seek anything from Albania but to overcome as soon as possible its own fever of changes and not slip into any unforeseen crisis, a part of the diaspora, from the early days of its opening, was present in Albania. Because of both the yearning for their country already present in every Albanian expressed in waiting with great enthusiasm for the changes and the desire to see the opportunities to invest there, but without excluding the naiveté, ignorance, and perhaps even some malice that the first encounters with

---

[642] For more see: Buxhovi, Jusuf: *"Kthesa historike – shteti paralel dhe rezistenca e armatosur,"* Prishtina, 2009, pp. 234-258.

[643] After the emergence of the Kosovo Liberation Army, Albania became an infrastructure base for the overall preparation of the Kosovo war with two "parallel lines": the institutional (by the Government of Kosovo) and the illegal. The latter came from abroad intoned by the "People's Movement of Kosovo" LPK, headquartered in Switzerland, which opened a problematic chapter of strife and numerous controversies about the "primacy" over conducting armed resistance in Kosovo, not without consequences if Dr. Rugova, as President of the Republic of Kosovo, and Dr. Bukoshi, Prime Minister of Kosovo would act in accordance with the Constitution of the Republic of Kosovo. In 1998, the Ministry of Defense of the Republic of Kosovo was transferred to Tirana, where Colonel Ahmet Krasniqi was appointed Minister of Defense, who, along with the Kosovo Liberation Army, which was already present in Albania, engaged in preparing the war in Kosovo. But in September of that year, Colonel Ahmet Krasniqi was assassinated in Tirana, which even though it was never legally resolved, does not relieve the Albanian state of responsibility together with the Albanian political spectrum, knowing that FARK was under the influence of Sali Berisha and the KLA was under the excessive influence of Fatos Nano, with clashes between the Albanian "right" and "left" being inevitable as reflected in the armed resistance movement in Kosovo, which was subject to relations of forces in Albania's political scene in accordance with their interests.

Albanian immigrants had brought more damage than benefit, thus paving the way to certain misunderstandings that would burden Albanian recognition and proximity imposing unnecessary difficulties and misunderstandings.

To make things worse, some of those who were among the first to rush into Albania, in fact, used their posture of patriotism, both successfully and unsuccessfully, for various fraud and deception from those dealing with dirty businesses to the creation of the first nests of crime, to which, as noted, an Albania in transition would not be immune with segments of the state mechanisms getting involved in them, thus attracting more attention to the risk that the opening of Albania to the region would carry rather than dealing with the major problems facing the Albanian world, particularly Kosova.

Indeed, the first phase of approach between Kosova and Albania was very critical, as it would mostly meet a frustrated Albanian part from among the Albanian diaspora with an explosive layer of Albanian society in Albania, being mainly a victim of the regime, but which was brought after the removal of the internal and external wall to a position of unprecedented spiritual delirium beyond values and rules. And the clash of these extremes highlighted what was not natural on either side from where many animosities stemmed unnecessarily in a great historic internal victory leaving it with a bad taste hardly removable for years to come.

The second phase, the one more packed with events and which was reflected in the first political, cultural activities and the true fall of the Albanian wall – revealing both successes and difficulties in internal Albanian communication and in relation to the international community – included the time from 1992 to 1997. But, this phase had its sub-stages, those of before and after Dayton, namely the deep crisis of the Albanian state which would fall from the chaos caused by the financial pyramid scheme.

This would be a time not only of political alliances between the blocs mentioned above, but also of other alloys with new emerging trends on other issues, whatever they may be, rather than the common fates in those circumstances too dramatic not only for Kosova but also for Albania and the Albanian world in general.

The time after Dayton will find special treatment in the next chapter, and within that treatment there will be room for a more detailed review of relations between Kosova and Albania from the pragmatic aspects to defense and security aspects associated also with the concept of active resistance. However the first part of the second phase of cooperation, from 1992-1995, would be the time after the passing of a declaration in the Parliament of Albania on Kosova in 1991, which did not mean an official recognition of the Republic of Kosova, and despite this "caution," Kosova would address Albania not only the first sanctuary for the necessary infrastructure of the parallel state, but also for diplomatic assistance and other services, not excluding those of a strategic nature. It was natural for the Albanian state to have special obligations and responsibilities not only to be ready to react in all circumstances, but also to have a strategy for action, which initially had to be harmonized between Tirana and Prishtina and then with other regional factors. Because the crisis caused by the fall of the former Yugoslavia, obliged the Albanian world in general and the Albanian state in particular to not see it as a regional crisis, but as a good opportunity for Albanians, upholding the right of Kosova for an independent state, creating preconditions for the unsettled Albanian question to place it on right tracks for its historical solution.

And, how would Albania respond in this direction but with political and economic stability and commitment to the course of democratic reforms from within and by working out how to become part of west-European integration as soon as possible. In the very first statement of the Albanian government of anti-communist coalition emerged some concepts accepted by the West as standards of Albania's integration in the Western world. Albania emerged with a new role in the region, something that would help Kosova and its problem a lot, so that the political reality could not be seen with suspicion but rather with understanding, especially when it came to the collapse of distrust loaded during a century of Belgrade and Russian-Orthodox propaganda in general.

Thus, the Western orientation of Albanian politics and its messages in this spirit stated on March 22, 1992 as its strategic interest towards integration into Western institutions, such as NATO, Council of Europe, European Union and others, would show Albania in a new light as a factor of stability in the region and aspiring for the common European family.[644]

Even its declaration on Kosova recognizing the will of the Albanians to self-determination and its commitment that in case of conflict in

---

[644] *Ibid*, p. 47.

Kosova, Albanians would resist as a nation, no matter that the state of Kosova was not being officially recognized by Tirana, in good measure, would be in accordance with the demands of Kosova and those of the Albanians in general. The latter, even, would echo inside and out, as Belgrade was warned it could not behave as if Kosova was its own ranch but that it would face an all-Albanian response while the international community too would be warned that the Kosova crisis is offline and it could not be viewed as such being an issue that concerned all Albanians being obliged to act jointly when the situation demanded. This was neither a threat to others nor behavior that could be seen as destabilizing the region. Rather, it was in line with the historical right of Albanians to be equal with others and in the interest of peace and stability in the Balkans and the region. For, what was required was in the democratic spirit, through democratic means and in accordance with international law.

Since Albanians did not cause the crisis, but rather were its victims with the risk of continuing to remain its victims unless they got involved to overcome it, this meant depositing their civilized contribution to cope with it through democratic means and in accordance with the spirit of European concepts and options for joining under the European roof. In fact, its solution within the context of European integration was the most important meaning for the Albanians, which could simultaneously be taken also as a token of their sense of European and Western belonging, precisely in line with the National Awakening program on the Albanian world returning to its historical, cultural and spiritual roots generally found in the West as foundations of its civilization.

This concept had been shared by both the Democratic League of Kosova and overall statehood movement and the Democratic Party in Albania, which a year later would be found on top of an anti-communist coalition in Albania.

In light of these commitments that the government of anti-communist coalition in Tirana stated, one should also see the first "land-ings" in Tirana of some of the segments of the parallel state of Kosova from the logistics management, as far as circumstances permitted, to the information system and other conditions that Kosova Albanians needed in their efforts towards the implementation of the state of Kosova. Thus, an Office of Kosova opened in Tirana, a kind of representation sometimes called a "liaison office" between Kosova and Albania and sometimes even

Kosova Embassy in Albania or the like, and this was also compatible with the very behavior of the Albanian state of (non) recognition of the state of Kosova, pursuant to the declaration of the Albanian Parliament, which fell short of a decree of recognition by the Albanian government and other recognition procedures. But regardless of the Albanian state calculations, the Kosova Office in Tirana presented the first segment of the declared state of Kosova in 1990 and confirmed by the September referendum for independence in 1991, a reality which although not recognized internationally, marked the establishment of the Kosova state as a historical fact, which for many years would be subject to such internal construction.

However, the work of the Office of Kosova in Tirana – along with its representative character and symbolism of the messages to be ambiguously understood in the Albanian world to act responsively and consistently with the historical importance of its political and social actors in general and the Albanian state in particular – would bring out the first weaknesses of such a nature in both those of Kosova's organization in this field, and those of the the Albanian state in relation to the first level of inter-Albanian representation of very great importance. And this would happen as a result of the fact that either party was at least concerned with the genuine work of the mission. Unfortunately, even those sent from Kosova to lead it, and even some of their partners in Tirana, were hardly aware of the mission or the importance of that representation.

Seemingly, the destiny of being in inevitable troubles without which Albanians constantly seem to face even when they have nothing to do, was shared by the part of information and the media, which the Government of the Republic of Kosova temporarily installed in Tirana. This referred to a daily half-hour TV program aired within the Albanian Television prepared by the editorial staff of reporters from Prishtina "installed" in Tirana (Mehmet Haziri and others).

The agreement between the Governments of Kosova and Albania on the satellite TV within the Albanian Television, was a right and beneficial one, especially under the circumstances in Kosova where there was a complete information blackout caused by Belgrade following its closing down of Albanian media in 1990. But, evidently, along with the Office of Kosova in Tirana there was also a TV program dedicated to Kosova. This program was a primary and very convenient outlet in which impacts and political interventions against Kosova based on bloc alliances were being tried, which would be referred to later, but now inconsistent with the

631

principles on which they were connected finding proper space in the initial inconsistencies within the political factor and that of the Government of Kosova in exile, which later turned into divisions with consequences among Kosovars, rather as a destruction than opposition against what would be called Rugova's "peaceful course" with its concept of the parallel state as a form of implementation of the state of Kosova from the inside according to the circumstances.

Indeed, the relationship between Dr. Ibrahim Rugova and Berisha, even when they first showed up embracing each other in Skenderbeg Square in Tirana depicting for the enthusiasts of national unity a lukewarm framework of their ideals had never been as cordial as it seemed for the simple reason that Dr. Ibrahim Rugova in no way and in no time before and after Sali Berisha's government accepted paternalism of Albania over Kosova, especially in circumstances when the Albanian state was not able to create stability from within, as was evident since the transition and on. Due to well-known historical circumstances and the complexity of the Albanian issue in the Balkans, the solution of which depended on external factors and conjunctures of spheres of interest, which had created the Albanian crisis in the first place and had led to the situation in which it was to be viewed as extremely dangerous, Dr. Rugova, as a recipe for solving the Albanian issue initially defended the concept of creating two stable states in the Balkans (Albania and Kosova). This was a precondition for national unification and any other conversation in this direction, which had to be an expression of democratic circumstances of the Albanian people, who both in Albania and Kosova would declare themselves on the form of a common state, in which the identity of Kosova on which a cultural and historical Albanianism stood, had to turn into the pillar of the union to keep it standing.

Historical fates had been cruel and tragic for Kosova, which during the last two centuries had been the center of political and cultural movements for the creation of the Albanian state and all other statehood movements, which on the verge of disintegration of the Ottoman Empire it had turned into a bad omen precisely because of the fact that Kosova, not only geographically, represented an historically strategic hub where interests met and civilizations clashed. But this did not mean that Kosova and its historical identity, the epicenter of the Albanian identity since antiquity (Dardania), Middle Ages and the Kosovar League of Prizren, where in the summer of 1880 it had set up its own government, the first after that of Skenderbeg in Kruja, a development that turned into a promoter of processes that led to the independence of Albania, had to be sacrificed for the sake of the idea of national unity, which, as admitted by its fanatics, beyond international relations and developments, not only hampered this process, but also endangered the existence of the Albanian state itself. Therefore, not only the history of the bitter separation of Kosova from the Albanian trunk and different realities that were created during eight decades of divisions with two short intermissions of joint living (three years at the time of the entry of Austria-Hungary from 1916-1918 and that of fascist occupation in 1941-1944), but historical continuities and spiritual processes as well forced the preservation of the component of Kosova within Albanian relations in any form. Because, in that way the power of Albanian historical memory in both its horizontal and vertical lines was preserved, without which there could be no present or future. The loss of spiritual identity of Kosova with roots going as deep as antiquity, and its sacrifice for the décor of national unity, meant the loss of the historic right to it, just as the Great-Serb propaganda claimed with its fixations on it as allegedly being the cradle of Serbian medieval soul and the like, which had even affected conjunctures of spheres of interest depriving the state of Kosova of the right to recognition as an ethnic and living fact of the Albanians.

Therefore, protecting Kosova's history meant protecting the history of a natural Albania, where the state of Kosova, alongside the Albanian state, appeared as a reality of one entity, which had to preserve the balances of Albanian ethnicity in a social, cultural and political aspect.

This observation that represented the platform of the Albanian future and displayed an intellectual, social and political reasoning as a majority in Kosova, confronted Dr. Ibrahim Rugova as bearer of this kind of thinking with that part of the Kosova Albanians who were convinced that in those circumstances the national unification of all Albanians rather than the state of Kosova should be the concern of Kosova and other Albanian territories separated by violence from their ethnic trunk in 1913. The state of Yugoslavia, with its Serbian embryo, was the one that had divided Kosova through occupation from the Albanian trunk and one had to use precisely its downfall to remedy this historical injustice. It was thought that this should be Albanians' major concern to be articulated in Albania, Kosova, Macedonia, Montenegro and even in Çameria and everywhere no matter what the response would be and no matter how much that would bring together all the possible conjunctures to stand in a new Balkan front, similar to that before the Balkan wars, against enemies and in inconsistency with the anticipation of those who were beginning to see within the Albanian factor in the Balkans, with one or two Albanian states, Western strategic interests, as opposed to the traditional or Russian-Slavic ones.

The reasoning of the Albanian unification by means of war, presented since the occupation of Kosova by Serbia and Montenegro in the fall and winter of 1912, continued even after the appearance of the wall of separation between Albanians. However, it would find its reflection in revolutionary ways and means in illegal activities during the fifties and sixties yielding to another form of struggle to achieve this goal, such as the one demanding equality to be articulated with Kosova Republic, as an interest of the Albanians, restoring them the right of self-determination, and the possibility to use it in a democratic way.

This demand did not mean abandoning Albanian unification and the right to it, which was a prerequisite for the appeasement of the Balkans. It appeared in the favor of unification, out of ideology and other burdens, in which the state of Kosova and its construction from within represented a pivotal force of an unstoppable development. Both the 1968 and 1981 demonstrations and general popular movement of 1989 initiated and led by the Democratic League of Kosova, is the best illustration. It provides the historical articulation of the component of freedom, democracy and equality and the demand for pro-western orientation, on which Albanian unification would be achieved on the basis of institutional and non-institutional, legal and illegal actions.

Frictions between Dr. Ibrahim Rugova and Sali Berisha were not of nationalistic nor of romantic nature, but rather of a pragmatic nature as the Albanian state had to accept the international formulas set for Kosova and its resolution no matter how it behaved from within, a conduct which initially left the impression that Berisha and his government accepted the political and state identity of Kosova in accordance with the expressed will of the Albanians in the September referendum for independence in 1991, supporting the government of the Republic of Kosova opting for a parallel state. On this occasion, Berisha and his government, as well as all Albanian nationals opened their doors wide to Kosovars in those evil times for them with many of them finding temporary shelter in Albania, as a consolation for the loss of Kosova.

634

However, this loving care and generosity had its limits as it had to be in accordance with the views of the international community providing the recipe for its solution. And, here is when the so-called "state reason" interfered having been so tragic for the patriotic elite of Kosova in the twenties and thirties, and also in the forties, even after unification done by the fascists or in the ideological and internationalist cooperation of the communists. In the first case, for Albania to survive as a country, it had to sacrifice its "National Committee for the Defense of Kosova," established in 1918 in Shkodra in dramatic circumstances for the fate of the Albanians. Whereas, in the second case, for the sake of proletarian internationalism and communism all "reactionaries" and "counterrevolutionaries" had to be sacrificed (with rightist intellectuals, patriots and nationalists) who even when trying to save their heads in Albania were being arrested and handed over to the Yugoslav security to be tried.

Thus, in the first case, the "state reason", being above all the rest, alienated former fighters for independence of Albania, including the founders of the movement and its leaders, Hasan Prishtina, Ismail Qemali, Esad Pasha Toptani, Nexhip Draga and others. These were the ones who met in Istanbul's Taksim district in the spring of 1912 to issue the call for an all-Albanian uprising, soon to find themselves on various fronts, not separating from Albania the fate of Kosova and avoiding Kosova's tragedy to affect Albania, aiming instead to raise Albania's awareness that there could be no Albanian state without Kosova, had to give up the cause of a common Albanian state and consent to partition! And their not consenting was dually condemned from two sides at once: from Albania – considering it risked losing the remaining half of the state, and Belgrade – for not giving their consent to their Kosova prey! More foolishy, it happened both in Tirana and Belgrade that Kosovar patriots would be condemned to death, such as Hasan Prishtina murdered in Thessaloniki with his assassin expecting to be rewarded by both Tirana and Belgrade!

The situation was similar after World War II, but this time the "reason of the state interest" was replaced by "ideological reason," whose victim would be both the nationalists and the major idea of unification of Kosova with Albania as approved in the Bujan Conference on December 31, 1943 and January 1-2, 1944. Those demanding unity would be fought relentlessly. Also, the anti-communist and anti-Yugoslav insurgency that had erupted in Kosova in November 1944 was quenched in a bloody and unprecedented terror carried out in addition to Serbian Chetnik brigades that had replaced their "sajkaca" hats with five-pointed red stars, by two brigades from Albania.

But Kosova, with the declaration of the Republic was already breaking the laws of this Albanian "dialectic" with so much misfortune and so tragic for the Albanians and their destiny. It appeared as a state, which had to be helped in order to prove itself from within and in particular under circumstances such as those of Serb occupation. While accepting outside help, regardless of how difficult this was for the Albanian state pressured by both the international factor continuing to align Kosova with the remaining Yugoslavia, the fear of jeopardizing processes in the way of European and Atlantic integration presented an important condition towards stabilization and return to the European family from which it was separated through ideology for half a century.

Here, in fact, appeared both understandings and misunderstandings between Prishtina and Tirana. Differences one day would become significant because on one hand, the will of the people of Kosova was non-negotiable by anyone, including Albania, and on the other hand, there were misunderstandings regarding the attitude in opposing such circumstances, which were neither easy nor simple for both parties upon which old clichés of international conjunctures leaned heavily.

Official Tirana would like to stay on its course of strategic commitments in relation to Kosova. She was also forced to behave in accordance with its national interests, so that the settlement of the Kosova issue should not fall into incongruity with the international community and international factor, which ignored the will of the its people, though declared in a legitimate way.

Evidently, in time, this dilemma of the official Tirana began to weigh down on relations of a natural rapprochement between Prishtina and Tirana. Dr. Rugova showed no sign of giving up the Republic of Kosova and determination to implement it through the parallel state, regardless of the difficulties that emerged and which in time began to disturb Albania in case that this stubborn attachment to it could become an obstacle for the Kosova issue to move towards finding a solution, which according to Tirana would come in the view of sensible compromises that kept the compass of the international factor.

That dilemma of Albanian leadership had even engendered a way of thinking as to whether the Kosovars should be more sensitive and slightly lower their demands in favor of what would be realistic and possible. As would be seen, Dr. Rugova refused to accept any sensitivity in this regard. For him, the independent state, which had already been declared, despite the difficulties, remained non-negotiable, even in the face of closed doors, as would happen in The Hague, or when doors were open for him only as an observer a year later at the London Conference, or when he accepted the Geneva talks within the Group for Kosova for solving problems in Kosova, such as education etc., but never gave up the key principles related to Kosova's status. Moreover, he kept the course after Dayton too and even when he was criticized that his parallel state had begun to turn into a negation of itself. The civil resistance, as perceived by many, especially by numerous opponents in Kosova, did not lead to its realization, as Rugova estimated, but turned against it instead. Thus, he had to stop becoming its inhibitor, but rather an actor on its own and for the set goal, and this could be done only by changing the course towards either realism or radicalization.

Indeed the issue of changing course would not bring to light the direct responsibility of the Albanian state for the emergence of other options, whether of pragmatic nature, since it contradicted its statement on recognizing the political will of the people of Kosova, which would be an anti-historical stance and extremely politically unacceptable, but that would bring out the rivalry between authority without a state, which Rugova had, and the state without authority which Berisha had. And, this would turn into an uncommon match between the power of authority and authority as power.

Of course, Dr. Ibrahim Rugova did not have the same cards and tools that Berisha had, who in this "duel" had another great advantage such as that of using the discontent of Rugova's opponents towards the course of the civil resistance with the parallel state, which were increasingly vocal as long as the peacefully promised state was lingering. With currents of national unity added, a part of which had already left the Democratic League of Kosova, where they belonged from the beginning and had established the National Unity Party (UMIKOMB), and various revolutionaries, it was not hard for other partners to join in the game. Since most such people "resided" in Tirana, with those among them using the aureole of "national unification" also for dirty businesses at the expense of the inexperienced Albanian state, Berisha did not have difficulty establishing links with Rugova's opponents doing so on the basis of an alleged care by the Albanian state about Kosova's overall political spectrum. These links would also have consequences, justified by what certain circles had already begun to promote as "a move towards dynamism of civil resistance" and return to the so-called "active civil resistance," turning in fact rather into an activism ensuring supervision over the political spectrum of Kosova from Tirana than a qualitative change of course, which, if diminished in relation to the international factor, it would only help it.

The two greatest divergences between Dr. Rugova and Sali Berisha, as stated, would clash not over an "activation of peaceful resistance" to become more persistent and combined with active forms of resistance, but rather to disable it, so as to concede before the so-called "democratic spirit in Serbia," which should be helped by Albanians to "democratize" Serbia!

For the first time this happened in 1993, and the second time in 1996, just when the Tirana regime was facing an internal explosion and it was expected that the Kosova card would be used to either bypass or face it, by hardening its crisis in relation to Serbia, for which there were many reasons.

In both times the government of Tirana supported the opposition in Serbia demanding the same from the Albanians of Kosova and Rugova personally, arguing that "democratization of Serbia would help Kosova to help solve its case too." This, despite the well-known fact that it was precisely the so-called democratic opposition in Serbia that in regard to Kosova and Albanians surpassed Milosevic and it was precisely the parties gathered around the Serbian "opposition" bloc that had sent their first volunteers into the Bosnian war and had promised to send similar ones to Kosova and Macedonia. Moreover, Rugova in an interview for "Rilindja," carried by the German news agency DPA, would not accidentally mention that "the Serbian opposition went beyond Milosevic in their stance against Kosova."[645]

Dr. Rugova explained this position in detail a few days later in a long interview for *"Westdeutsche Rundfunk"* of Cologne, exposing Milosevic and his fascist ideology against Kosova from the ideas of Serb "democrats," on whose stance Serb actionism had been built. ...On this occasion he recalled that Vuk Draskovic, one of the leaders of the Serbian opposition, was the main founder of the "Serbian Renewal Party" with a pro-Chetnik program, liaising with the principles of the Serbian Chetnik

---

[645] DPA (Deutsche Presse Agentur), 20 November 1993.

movement of World War II announced by its ideologue Molevic, with the Serb national priority to eradicate Bosnians and Albanians from what was called the "Serbian historical cradle." Therefore, not unfairly, he reminded those who called for solidarity with the Serbian opposition demands as being in solidarity with initiators and inspirers of the Serbian criminal policies.[646]

These relatively big discrepancies between Prishtina and Tirana on the basis of solidarity with opposition parties in Serbia and their efforts to remove Milosevic from power were not tactical in nature, but rather fundamental; no special diplomatic or political sense was needed. The hegemonic course that Milosevic had begun to implement was part of the Great Serbian strategy arising from the recent Memorandum of Serbian academics that had complete national consensus. So, the political struggle in Serbia was being waged in order to change actors rather than concepts. The fall of Milosevic was rather projected as an effect of vindication for certain doings, while "lamb skin reformists" would continue with their wolf habits. This was best reflected in the case of the "pressure" to which the Bosnian Serb leadership, Karadzic and Mladic were subjected to make them accept the Vance and Owen plan for Bosnia – in which tactically Milosevic and Cosic would also be engaged – while Draskovic, Djindjic, Kostunica and the rest of the "druzba" from among "oppositionists," would go to Palje to encourage Karadzic and Mladic not to give way before the international community and Milosevic, but to protect what had been achieved through criminal war against Bosnians and Croats in Bosnia!

Another misconception that would extend beyond the political relations between Prishtina and Tirana would be that of handling the Albanian political factors in Macedonia, the Presheva Valley, Montenegro, and the diaspora.

It was known that initially, after the establishment of the Democratic League of Kosova, this party, also, upon a suggestion by Americans and Germans, would take over the supervision of the Albanian political parties extending to other parts of former Yugoslavia ethnically related to Kosova with their intelligentsia mainly educated in Kosova's faculties and many of intellectuals coming from these areas living in Prishtina rightly considering Kosova as the spiritual and political center and as an Albanian pied-

---

[646] *"Westdeutsche Rundfunk"* - WDR, Albanian Broadcast, 29 November 1993.

mont. Albanian political parties in those parts were interconnected with Prishtina and in May 1990 joined the Political Coordination Council of Albanians in Yugoslavia, led by Dr. Ibrahim Rugova, who upon his return from a visit in the United States of America, between April 4 and 12, 1990, where he met Senator Robert Dole, was promoted by the American administration as the leader of all Albanians from Yugoslavia, thus becoming impassable and immovable. His image grew significantly wherever there were Albanians in the Yugoslav space.[647]

Furthermore, it would be obvious that the early dissolution of the former Yugoslavia through war would bring Albanians closer with each other after having been divided by administrative borders, with the risk of becoming state borders and them being subjected to further profusion. This union was best reflected in the authority that Dr. Ibrahim Rugova enjoyed, already having turned into an all-Albanian leader. He and his movement were expected to provide a comprehensive response, where Albanians outside Kosova's borders, but ethnically and spiritually con-nected, demanded to be treated jointly and not remain detached. There-fore, it was not by chance that in November 1991 the Albanian political parties from Yugoslavia sent a memorandum to both the Hague Confer-ence and international decision-making factor dealing with the crisis in the former Yugoslavia and its fate containing three options in which Albanians presented their views on their future in circumstances of the maintenance or the breakup of former Yugoslavia. In the first option, i.e. in case of a change of internal borders in the common state, maintaining the external ones, the Republic of Albanians emerged as the only solution, but on the contrary, if external borders changed, Albanians would decide by plebiscite on their own fate, not excluding the possibility of joining their national state. [648]

Dr. Rugova's role in conceiving this statement was great. And, obvi-ously, it would further strengthen his authority though from the outside that made him a likely target by all of those who feared that.

It seemed that in Tirana the latest formulation of the political state-ment, conditioned with the joining of the national state sounded good.

---

[647] Buxhovi, Jusuf: "*Kthesa historike – Vitetet e Gjermanisë dhe Epoka e LDK-së,*" 2008, p. 254

[648] See political declaration published in the brochure: *Lidhja Demokratike e Kosovës – Documents, ngjarje, shënime,* 1994, pp. 77-78.

Not that the matter could be taken into consideration by the Albanian state, perhaps rightly so, as both the Hague and London Conferences had accepted the fact of the dissolution of the former Yugoslavia and were working to turn the new realities into state facts without war. But this could be used in order to take away some of Dr. Rugova's integralist authority which he enjoyed among Albanians all over the former Yugoslavia, in order to carry it over to Tirana improperly with an inherent anticipation of solutions which had not yet reached a certain outcome to be accepted without returning to accomplished political facts.

Although it could be said that in the new circumstances Albania was obliged to engage directly in the issue of the dispersion of the Albanian factor in the former Yugoslavia and react to further fragmentation, even without being able to come up with their own attitude on this issue of great interest for Albanians and their subsequent fate in the circumstances of re-alignment in the Balkans, the official Tirana had accepted almost without any reaction what happened in the Hague and later London. It had blessed any proposal coming from the international community, while in relation to the Albanian political forces from different parts of former Yugoslavia, now detached from one another, it exercised its influence for accepting the new realities, but that the meaning of these "new realities" meant first of all detachment from the influence of Rugova's and Kosova's authority turning to Tirana's authority.

This scenario was tested in Macedonia in search of new partners who would respond appropriately to the new challenge of Macedonia, which was declared a state without the consent of the Albanians, but whose existence from the beginning was put under the supervision of the Americans and NATO being treated as a "high risk factor" that had to be kept free from any threat. Such a threat, especially coming from the Albanian and Serbian side, could destabilize it giving a regional dimension to the crisis in the former Yugoslavia with many risks that neither the U.S. nor, Europeans, but by all probability Moscow was unable to accept, although Russia would take Belgrade's side with the latter declaring Macedonia as its own interest with the risk of sooner or later introducing its card into the game.

If Albania had turned its eyes towards Macedonia in favor of the interests of ethnic Albanians living there, using the treatment that the Americans and NATO had been providing – and this did not happen, at least not formally, without Tirana being notified as well – to have the guarantees of the Albanian state in its defense be exchanged with the treatment of Albanians as a state constituent people of Macedonia, it could possibly make sense being in the spirit of the possible. But as this was not done, and in order not to turn it into a liability issue the game had been to introduce dethroning of political parties in Macedonia, initially with the demolition of the "monopoly" of the first Albanian party – the Party of Democratic Prosperity, founded in Tetovo in 1990. It had been considered a natural ally of the Democratic League of Kosova, not only because they were almost part of the same political concept, but also for the fact that this party, even after the recognition of Macedonia as a state, still maintained its inertia ties with Kosova. With the Albanian factor still sharing the same common development through which they had passed for more than half a century, the option of Albanian unification through integration or other forms saw it initially linked to Kosova, as a natural scale to continue further with Albanian unification.

Evidently, the Macedonian factor too was bothered more by the first option of the Party of Democratic Prosperity for maintaining ties with Kosova than the other option of a "radical" spirit, as was that of Illyria and dividing Macedonia, against which it knew it could well be defended, given the fact that there existed an American and international shield, which could be used as needed, especially against the Albanians demanding the status of a constituent people in Macedonia. With this abomination, even official Shkup, but also its reserve ally – Serbia, could benefit greatly, on one side to justify repressive measures against the Albanians and on the other to rebuff as much as possible Kosova's demand for statehood that could have a destabilizing impact for Macedonia.

However, in Macedonia, after many intricacies that would not pass without concern, a second political entity of Albanians emerged – the Democratic Party of Albanians (DPA), which paved the way for further developments of disintegration of the Albanian factor in many parts of Macedonia and far from any influence of Rugova and his concept of state building and proximity with Albania. As a minority, this party's relation, as noted, would not be useful either for Macedonian Albanians, or for Albania, which had weakened the Albanian factor in the former Yugoslavia, whose status continued to remain open, which disconnected between Shkup and Prishtina, appeared an easy target for those who settled scores at its expense.

First Signs of "Losing" Patience

First separations from the course of civil-institutional resistance in favor of armed resistance options of some political parties outside the Democratic League of Kosova, demanding ever more openly for a return to active resistance, which would include demonstrations and civil disobedience, while Rugova stated that Albanians had declared their independent state and did not need to turn into a Serb "opposition" through disobedience. – Second Assembly of the Democratic League of Kosova and support for Rugova by layers of sacrifice demanding "power of authority." – World leaders seek to strengthen Rugova's role and support for civil-institutional resistance.

With the formation of the Special Group for Kosova, for the sake of treating the minority issues in the former Yugoslavia, the London Conference faced two parallel developments: the establishment of facts through violence created by Serbs in Bosnia and Herzegovina and Croatia and the establishment of facts by means of civil-institutional resistance, as was the parallel state of Kosova Albanians in accordance with the Constitution of the Republic of Kosova. These developments revealed simultaneously the absurdities, on one hand, with facts created through force, such as those of the Bosnian and Croatian Serbs, dictating the terms and direction to the international factor, while using the established facts by peaceful means with the parallel state, such as that of Kosova Albanians, to establish specific arguments against a particular policy so that one day it would be abandoned.

Obviously the political conversion of one fact or another needed time to reach the level of change for the international factor to respond in favor or against such realities.

The long road of political conversion to acceptance of the reality of established facts such as the parallel state and its management through work and superhuman effort waiting for the day it would happen, did not rid Kosova of difficulties and concerns created since the London Conference. In a long struggle to establish facts through civil-institutional resistance it would have to face Serb occupation violence on one hand and risking one's patience from within on the other. When other options in the game are added, from changing the course of civil resistance to an armed resistance, creating frustrating circumstances out of the immense violence reaching to the demand to get into an immediate war against Serbia (as the thinking that was the only way for the issue to be considered by the international factor, etc.), then all the complexity of a political consequence emerges, which could rather be threatened from within, from loss of patience, than external violence and its escalation.

In fact the first signs of losing patience came after the London Conference. Despite the optimistic statements of Dr. Ibrahim Rugova and Professor Fehmi Agani that in London "Kosova's anticipation was met," the public would have realized that there were realities of violence that were being considered, while those of peace were entirely overlooked or ignored. The rights recognized for the Serb representatives of Bosnia and those of Croatia to present their views in informal sessions while Lord Carrington offered Dr. Rugova in a "gentlemanly" way a TV monitor to follow the Conference from a room beyond would also mobilize Rugova's opponents in Kosova seeking to change the course in favor of activating an organized opposition in various forms without excluding the most radical ones.

In these circumstances, there was an increasing number of political forces and groups that began to break away from the influence of the Democratic League of Kosova calling for the opening of the "Southern Front," as Croatia demanded, convinced that only war could bring the issue to the negotiating table and that everything else was a waste of time and pain that suited the Serbian regime.

The National Unity Party (UNIKOMB) had already withdrawn from the Coordinating Council of Albanian Political Parties and the support it had given so far to the parallel state. Its proponents, as will be seen, with the idea of national unification, were spread across dispersed Albanian areas from Montenegro, the Presheva Valley and Macedonia, in search of joining forces for this purpose. Across the suburbs of Prishtina more and more graffiti appeared calling for war with pamphlets distributed by numerous radical groups. Calls for war usually accompanied those against the "national betrayal," usually attributed to the Democratic League of Kosova and its founders as bearers of the parallel power, including calls to start war first from within under the motto of "clean your own home of evil before passing its doorstep," which showed that the civil resistance movement with its parallel state had begun to be fought against from within, perhaps less so from losing confidence in patience, and more so from the fear of the success of patience.

There were not only graffiti and pamphlets that were calling for war. Certain political forces, which continued to defend the institutions of Kosova attending in the formation of the Government of the Republic of Kosova, also demanded that the parallel state civil resistance should change course, as stated, to an active civil resistance. In this regard Veton Surroi's Parliamentary Party, who would later pass into the hands of Adem Demaçi, was always most "creative" to reflect dissatisfaction with the state of occupation and to manifest its opposition through various actions of daily protests at a set time, which included pot and skillet noise in the evening, igniting candles, carrying empty coffins through the streets of Kosova with the inscription "violence is buried here" and other slogans, with citizens proposing different ways to protest, including strikes and forms of civil disobedience. Although Dr. Rugova waived course over the parallel state and focused on key segments such as education, health and internal solidarity to function better, and that was going to happen as a result, he did not pay much attention to the "mutinies." They would be neither helped nor criticized, a known behavior of his used very successfully over the years of the parallel power succeeding in most cases to neutralize his opponents, who even when looking "radical" remained a few steps behind. Occasionally, during a regular press conference that he held every Friday on the premises of the Association of Writers of Kosova, he responded to questions about pot and skillet brandishing with irony as "we are a pluralistic society where everyone has the right to express their opinions and to demonstrate what they think is right."

But was Kosova really in a pluralistic state, where everyone was free to express his own opinion and demonstrate as one wished, as Rugova said? Or, was it merely a new form of dissatisfaction over the course of civil resistance that seemingly could change nothing, rather than with the violence of the Milosevic regime, with brandishing pots and skillets appearing as entertainment that would help the regime to convert the resistance in Kosova from a concept of the state and its implementation through parallel life to a civil discontent with the regime, which was natural and beginning to manifest itself in different ways in Serbia and by doing so have the abomination of being an oppressor of a people and their demands for freedom and independence lifted?

It seemed that the latter was closer to the truth.

By the middle of 1993 Geneva talks eventually failed realizing that for more than a year there had been nothing but delays, on one hand, with the Kosova delegation defending its positions on the Albanian education and curricula of the Republic of Kosova, and on the other Belgrade refusing to yield occasionally issuing proposals in as far as to give the impression of one wishing to solve the problem of education in Kosova but that it was being hampered by linking it to the status of Kosova and well-known positions of Albanians for their own state.

Lack of success in Geneva certainly presented a rather different cause for resentment, since in autumn the second school year held in private homes would start, in unsuitable buildings and basements, in much worse conditions despite the solidarity of the citizens, who spared nothing to keep up the Albanian school already identified as the main segment of overall resistance. Those who had hoped that not more than one single school year would go to waste, as provided to achieve victory, had reasons to be disappointed as the second school year was about to start in the same conditions seeming like an endless reality beyond imagination that it all could be part of short sprints rather than a long marathon with both the energy and timing playing a crucial role. Although one could say that the financial situation of education was not so bad, as the three percent fund and other donations provided the income for teachers, university professors and staff, however, it was clear that the quality of education had decreased significantly sometimes reaching critically low levels. This caused concern among both teachers and parents, who knew that further continuation of that situation could bring about a failure with multiple consequences severely testing the entire parallel system and civil resistance.

For one of the architects of this strategy, Professor Fehmi Agani, who led the Kosova delegation in Geneva showing great skills to counter Serbian delays by responding with the concept of the parallel state even when that was not deemed that necessary, it after all turned into a success for Kosova. It had been proven that the Kosova issue could not be resolved by means of solving some problems in Kosova, such as education, health care and others, as one part of the international factor and even Serbia believed, but rather by the resolution of Kosova's status in accordance with the will of its people that had already been expressed in the 1991 referendum – seeing the problems of education and generally the parallel system as an inseparable part of the state of Kosova with which one should get used not to despair but to further mobilize.

"Problems and difficulties show that we are on the right path."[649]

Professor Agani was in fact forewarning a marathon and this significantly changed the situation. Rugova and his associates were facing two very important challenges at the same time: maintaining the parallel state at all costs, regardless of the price to be paid, and keeping the patience to avoid an armed conflict with Serbia.

The conflict with Serbia in accordance with its scenarios to draw Albanians into it in order to settle accounts with them through a "flash Krieg," was not only disfavored by Rugova and Albanians who were following the course of civil-institutional resistance, but also by the international community, primarily the United States of America, which was engaged in Iraq expecting certain things to be clarified. And, NATO did not want that either, being still in the process of internal restructuring in accordance with the new circumstances of the collapse of bloc bipolarity in search of a new role as a factor of the only force in the world. Albania too could not afford a conflict with Serbia, facing major problems with the transition obviously needing a lot of time for that. Furthermore, in this respect, Albania's problems were multiplying instead of being reduced, increasingly weakening one of the strongest cards of Kosova that could be used to be introduced into the game in due time.

The first test was namely that of keeping up the parallel state, and the second, avoiding a conflict with Serbia, aimed at using the time factor towards achieving the ultimate goal outside a conflict with Serbia, or even controlling it when it could no longer be avoided. In case of the latter, it was being calculated first that Serbia would be neither a regional power factor, as it still was with the big military and fighting potential it inherited from the Yugoslav People's Army and continued to strengthen it with what it was getting from Moscow and some Arabic countries so that it was estimated as one of the powerful armies in Europe. Secondly – one counted on an all-Albanian response, turning it into a regional and international crisis that inevitably meant an overall alignment of the Albanian factor in a joint front of war against Serbian invaders in defense of the interests and values of the West.

The time factor as a calculated ally of political philosophy of civil-institutional resistance and its concept of nation building through patience, as will be seen, would not be easily manipulated. Because, patience

---

[649] "Rilindja," 20 September 1993.

as a virtue, which as early as in Plato's conception of the state, counted for one of the most important places of political morality, had begun to show signs of beating from within, exactly from where it should be implemented. This referred to the suggestion that something had to change in the way the concept started to put into action outside support and other dilemmas in regard to turning the civil-institutional resistance to an active resistance, activating all existing resources pending, such as those of defense and self-defense within the two ministries, that of Defense and Internal Affairs, which were formed long ago, but without any active function. In this internal squirm, there were some signs that led to understand that in the wake of Dayton, Prime Minister of the Republic of Kosova, Dr. Bukoshi had requested from President Dr. Rugova to dynamize the resistance doing so even despite international advice that sought civil-institutional resistance, ignoring on the other hand the facts of violence devoting attention to specific problems instead. But, Rugova accepted no dissonance with the international factor, especially with Americans, as he believed that all of those could entrap Kosova towards the Serbian or Russian bait with tragic consequences for the Albanians.

"Discrepancies" between the Presidency and the Government, whether or not as hatching from "somewhere," would be made public, but, although they would not pull down the edifice of the parallel state, they would bring about a "reshuffle" of tasks and transfer of more powers to Rugova and his staff in Kosova and partly in Tirana, while Bukoshi would be dealing with the collection of the three percent fund in the West and the use of the fund and other funds to be collected for Kosova in a way as to be protected from abuse.

In a word, Rugova demanded that the parallel state be managed from the "base" under his full supervision, something that turned towards the "party trust" as the starting point of everything.

Returning to the "party trust" and lack of coordination with the Government, particularly on fundamental issues of the state, such as those of security and defense when Kosova was occupied by Serbia, would be an additional reason for Dr. Rugova's opponents to look at the parallel state with greater mistrust. Some political parties, whose candidates had "participated" in the Kosova Government being called a grand coalition government, withdrew from the governing coalition with their ministers, without ending their activity, but rather taking it outside the LDK umbrella. Others withdrew entirely from political activity, on the grounds that this entire behavior resembled moving in a circle, an anemia that brought nothing but further vegetating, suggesting to past activists to join the course of an active resistance against the Serbian regime, no matter where that came from.

Returning to the "party trust," first tested in the diaspora at the expense of competences of the Government, becoming an internal model as well, turned into a problem for the Democratic League of Kosova itself. Its Second Convention, on July 14, 1994, brought to an end for good what had been evaluated from the very foundation of the party as a liberal and intellectual spirit. Beyond the statute and rules and with no requests from the base, Dr. Rugova appointed a Presidency in which there was no place for any of the founders (some had left in time having no ambitions in politics while others did not comply with Rugova's authoritarian tendencies). Instead, it gained great strength with the political prisoners "wing," many of whom were participants in the 1968 and 1981 demonstrations and prominent activists in the base where the parallel state was undergoing its main test. Among them there were those with ideological weight behind which they would not be unloaded, giving reason to suspicion that the nation building movement could slip from the right with its cohesion and popular support towards the left becoming once again hostage to some Eastern conjuncture.

The well-known analyst Viktor Meier, who had frequent meetings with Dr. Rugova and founders of the Democratic League of Kosova, serving at times as some kind of an adviser to Prime Minister Bukoshi, assessed Rugova's behavior at the Second LDK Convention as necessary pragmatic behavior. This behavior was imposed by both internal and external circumstances, lacking international support for an independent state of Kosova, but with the deciding factor, especially Americans being in favor of the parallel state of Kosova, Albanians, while carrying out the tasks in Croatia and Bosnia and Herzegovina, and with the parallel state marking the first signs of fatigue. Faced with such circumstances, considering the fact that Kosova had to wait, Rugova had no choice but to keep to the concept of implementation of the parallel state through authority and charisma, no matter how much it would vegetate and no matter how and to what degree it would estrange it from the intellectual part. His base, namely LDK, with devoted activists willing to make all kinds of sacrifices represented the strongest defense to which he could turn at any time using it to exercise unrestricted authority, preserving at the same time the parallel state from internal depravity, which would be fatal for Kosova at that time.

In this regard Rugova would use the patriarchal consciousness and legacy of monism, according to which the leader had authority over all social projects. Therefore, Rugova did not find it difficult to activate and use this tool in those very difficult and equally decisive circumstances.[650]

After all, Rugova realized that while the international community was preoccupied with the war in Bosnia and Herzegovina, and while the Americans did not engage as they should taking upon themselves to resolve the crisis in the former Yugoslavia, one had to wait, acting accordingly, based on circumstances and the commitment to preserve by all means what had been built.

It must be pointed out that Rugova's charisma to rise to an undisputed Albanian authority was enjoyed not only among Albanians in the former Yugoslavia but also in Albania and elsewhere in the world, as to be considered the greatest Albanian leader of the new era and not unreasonably supported by the most powerful political personalities of the world, from U.S. President Bill Clinton, with whom he met several times since 1994 and Pope John Paul II, who called him a politician with great intellectual credibility, and many others. And, his popularity in high international dimensions could be measured with that of Vaclav Havel and possibly surpassing it, as the authority of the Czech politician was linked to the phenomenon of dissidence, being of a temporary nature, while that of Rugova was linked with a major crisis in which he emerged victorious thanks to the fact that he opposed violence by civil resistance and a parallel state, turning it into a unique model of our time. The powerful world media, to which Rugova paid great attention, even when his project for an independent state of Kosova was circumvented or ignored by international conferences, contributed to this as well. Thus, any analysis of Dr. Rugova's presentation by the electronic media, among them the most powerful in the world, such as CNN, NBC, NTV, Euronews, BBC, ARD, ZDF, ORF and others, and the attention he received both in timing and terms, appeared similar to that of a major global statesman. In the electronic media, with the exception of Milosevic, who is an example for the worst, Dr. Rugova was considered more powerful than all the rest of

---

[650] Author's conversation with Viktor Meier in Bonn, November 1997.

the Balkan leaders and those of Eastern countries, leaving Sali Berisha behind more than twice.[651]

Similarly, the prominent European and world newspapers paid great attention to Rugova, raising him to the ranks of famous charismatic leaders, even at times when internally his authority seemed to fall. Renowned newspapers of the world found him always in their headlines. *"Le Monde," "The New York Times," "Washington Post," "Die Welt," "Frankfurter Allgemeine," "Züriher Zeitung"* and others, well-known magazines such as *"Time," "Der Spiegel," "Newsweek"* and others featured him as a frequent guest of honor. The German magazine *"Der Spiegel"* would be among the major European media at three crucial moments, promoting Rugova as a leader with clear visions and critical judgment about the crisis and its causes, calling them by name, and indicating without hesitation what it was about, speaking from various global decision-making centers. A few of them were of such a nature with three of them remaining most remarkable in highlighting their time and proving to be right.

The first time, in June 1989, when Milosevic showed up in Gazimestan to speak about "the right of the Serbian people to lawfully and unlawfully return what had been won in the war and taken away in peace"- Rugova warned the world that what it was dealing with here was a warmonger who had to be stopped in time. On this occasion, he was among the first to maintain that with the destruction of Kosova's autonomy, on March 23, 1989, Milosevic launched a military aggression in Kosova and was preparing to do the same against Croatia, Slovenia, Bosnia and Herzegovina, and other parts.

The second time in January 1996, after the Dayton accords – he called the "celebrating" of Milosevic as a partner for peace a major error by the West, equating it to his crimes, which could be corrected only if force was used against him, as would happen three years later.

The third time, in May 1999, when with the help of Western countries he was released from being hostage to Milosevic where he was kept by force – he spoke of the need to force Milosevic and his army to capitulate and not have him withdraw through agreements that would keep issues open between Albanians and Serbs and Serbia itself would be

---

[651] An analysis of the German Institute for International Media in Bonn for the years 1997 and 1998.

simultaneously deprived of proper democratization, proving to be rather true.

With media and political authority abroad Rugova must have found it easy to turn into an undisputed icon, which would work even at a time when it was clear that the parallel state was facing difficulties to survive.

However, there was something else too that kept Rugova on the throne, despite the difficulties that the parallel state was facing. It was the lack of alternatives in relation to the parallel state, on one side, as a state project through which Kosova would eventually drive out the Serb occupier and, one the other, the lack of a personality that could compete against him.

Regarding the first issue, the parallel state and the challenge of its implementation was part of the nation building political concept that arose from the strategy of the Democratic League of Kosova and related to the Republic of Kosova as an independent state, which had been declared in September 1990 and confirmed in a referendum for independence a year later. So, 99% of Albanians opted in favor of it. It gained the pledge of support of all Albanians without exception. While the determination for a parallel state and its building from within and according to circumstances was also a commitment of all Albanians, regardless of how much they were aware of the difficulty and duration they had to face. Moreover, the demand for *patience*, which turned into a slogan of that time, being used and also misused, represented a means towards achieving the goal. *Sacrifices* were also part of the *means to reach the goal* and a good part of the population, already accustomed to it, did not take it as a burden but rather as a task. Adding seductive rhetoric about "independence and democracy" and that "Kosova's independence has no alternative" and that the "independent state of Kosova, open towards Serbia and Albania, appears as a factor of peace in the Balkans" enabled Rugova to maintain and defend with his superior rhetoric the spirit of the historic designation of Albanians to neutralize even the biggest and toughest opponents for the simple reason that for the circumstances the independent state of Kosova was reduced to the parallel state and its institutions, no matter how they appeared, being more realistic, and accessible, and as such had no alternative.

Even when the signs of armed resistance against Serbian violence and later of war appeared, the state of Kosova lost neither its relevance nor its weight. Rather, it would remain as such, along with segments of the parallel state, with war being viewed as a means for its realization. Theories that the liberation war stood outside the state of Kosova, or something that ruled it out for purposes of national unification and similar, appeared unstable.

And, as it were, with the Republic of Kosova largely identifying with Rugova and his concept, rather than the opposite, it was not at all difficult for him to muster the domestic political scene in Kosova with ease. Even when the parallel state was being fairly scrutinized and criticized demanding a change of direction from civil resistance to an active civil resistance, as stated, concrete alternatives were also lacking. There was rumor about possible loss of patience, on the international factor ignoring the parallel state, there was talk about the fact that that kind of behavior could suit the Milosevic regime to keep Kosova in a state of repression and as an arena where his militants won votes and strengthened their positions in Belgrade and rumors went on, though hardly a single valuable suggestion came as to what to change and how to act in that direction. Strikes, clattering of pots, candles, protest marches and civil disobedience against the Belgrade regime posed nothing else but a decor which did not bother Rugova a bit, rather suiting him fine, as that was all a way of venting accumulated anger without consequences and which risked remaining closed and simultaneously showing the superiority of the determination for the independent state with a parallel system, where everyone participated, and which even provided space for radical action.

The question of a personality that would compete with Rugova definitely was linked with the state-building concept and parallel state as part of the implementation strategy of the Republic of Kosova. This project had raised Rugova up, and the project was protecting him from any shock, precisely because it was a plebiscite expression of Albanians, and as such remained intact under any circumstances, including those that could be imposed by the international factor, or what an eventual defeat in the conflict with Serbia could entail. The option of the independent state of Kosova could not be brought to question even by national unification to which the Albanians were rightly aligned with all their being as an issue enjoying general consensus, but not outside of Kosova's state identity, much less of its one-sided termination in its favor. Because this related to the common awareness that the common was created by the particulars and as such they built a sustainable entirety. In this historical pedestal

Rugova could not be jeopardized by any other personalities, no matter what their aureole could be.

Here indeed one should look for the causes of those numerous defeats of "battles" which Rugova's opponents of all kinds suffered, as a consequence of which he became rather more authoritarian, that made him turn a deaf ear on certain new realities, as those he would later face in Rambouillet.

Dayton's Foreplay and Flouting of the Serbian Myth

The beginnings of American involvement in Bosnia and Herzegovina and measures for destroying facts that Serbia had created through war. – Croatian offensive "Storm" and the return of Croatian sovereignty. – Serbian massacres in Srebrenica and other UN protected areas shocked the world setting in motion the international community to use force as a political tool. – The bombing of Serb positions around Sarajevo by NATO air forces and the military victories of the Bosnian-Croatian forces radically change the situation to the detriment of the Serb invaders. – Croatia's liberation from Serbian forces in Knin and Slavonia caused a displacement of the majority of Serbs from Croatia to Serbia. – Serbia threatened war if Banja Luka fell into the Bosnian hands, while Americans prevent complete defeat of Serbian military forces from Bosnian-Croat forces as it would create a regional chaos that everyone feared, especially the Europeans. – Dynamic developments in Croatia and Bosnia and Herzegovina forced Dr. Rugova to send a demand request to the UN Secretary General and Security Council for establishing an international protectorate in Kosova. It would last three years and then, under the supervision of the UN, a referendum would be held in which people would determine their future. – Rugova's request was also addressed to the Americans on the grounds that Belgrade, after its defeat in Croatia and Bosnia, planned a deployment of half a million Serb refugees to Kosova.

The crisis in the former Yugoslavia and its dissolution as a process in all its extent, had two crucial moments associated with significant curves leading to its outcome, although some open issues were left from which certain recidivisms could arise.

The first decisive moment had to do with the commitment of the United States of America to impose a solution, and it would happen by the middle of 1994, focusing on the war in Bosnia and Herzegovina and Croatia in order to change its direction to the detriment of Belgrade and in favor of Bosnian Croats thus releasing politics from being the Serb hostage as it had been kept for more than three years. U.S. intervention almost on its own made it plain that a solution had been determined according to the dictates of Washington that was also consistent with the interests of the West in general.

The second moment too had to do with the U.S. direct commitment to the solution of the Kosova problem since 1998 onwards, whose outcome would also be determined according to the dictates of Washington and Western interests in general. So one may say that the answer to be given to the problems of Bosnia and Herzegovina and Kosova would be exclusively the American commitments and concepts imposed upon the Europeans and generally upon the international community. The U.S. would be forced to act in this way from both the reason of its own strategic interests, and the fear that inaction could jeopardize the whole concept of reform in the Eastern countries to follow with other possible cracks in the new order world.

The tragedy of Bosnia and Herzegovina and all that occurred during the four years caused by Serbian aggression after the country had been granted the right to an independent state in accordance with the requirements of the Badinter Commission, in fact represented an inability of the European diplomacy to manage difficult crises such as that in the former Yugoslavia, and it also represented a defeat of the Europeans regarding such challenges, which were issues that they should solve. Experience had shown that Europeans were incapable of diplomacy or the use of coercion when needed, which is what in fact the crisis in former Yugoslavia required. Therefore, a U.S. intervention was expected to appear before the West had to face a political and moral bankruptcy among the most serious of recent times.

The solution by the Americans, no matter what it was, required the undertaking of certain actions beforehand to be put on the tracks of the movement and that meant changing fixed positions on establishing facts which were forcibly turned to realities. Among these facts created by force were Serb conquests in Croatia (creation of two mini-states: of Knin Krajina and Western Slavonia, without excluding the enclave of Baranja) and the reality of the Serb Republic (Republika Srpska) in Bosnia and Herzegovina, which oversaw the largest part of the country and had established virtually all conditions for Milosevic to use it as a trump card.

Faced with these realities, which not only posed political and military favors for Milosevic in his efforts to achieve the goals he had for himself, but for something more, the Americans would begin the demolition of Serbian alibis. Initially they put talks together with both Bosnian and Hercigovina Croats as well as Bosnians in order to reach a state agreement, with which Izetbegovic and Croat leaders of Herzegovina, who had long before proclaimed their state of Herzeg-Bosnia with West Mostar as its center thus helping a lot the strategy of Karadzic and Mladic to divide Bosnia and Herzegovina into two parts, united in a common federation. The Bosnian-Croat Federation was reached in March 1994 presenting the first actions of the Bosnian-Croatian bloc in Bosnia and Herzegovina for not losing more energy against each other, but to focus rather on joint military war against the Serbs and their hegemony over their country. The "reconciliation" between the Bosnians and Herzegovinian Croats, was evidently neither easy nor simple, because, besides the differences they had as people, it was the policy of Tudjman and the Croatian nationalist bloc which shared with Milosevic the partitioning of Bosnia and Herzegovina into two parts, with Bosnia belonging to the Serbs and Herzegovina to the Croats, thus marking the so-called "historic reconciliation" of Serbs and Croats, who had been in a way reached between Tudjman and Milosevic in Graz , in 1992. The tragic war against Bosnians seemed to have created this reality, and it was expected that one day, for the sake of "pacification of the Balkans" and "elimination of any residue of Islamic traces" for which the Europeans had allegedly great interest, it would be accepted. So, the "forging" of this alliance was neither a technical nor tactical issue, but rather a strategy which had to be built at the expense of breaking the conventions of traditional religions and even at that, with bloodshed and deep hostilities in between.

Another U.S. important step that conditioned the success of the alliance between Bosnians and Croats in Bosnia and linked directly to its implementation, which would break Belgrade's myth of the Yugoslav army as an invincible regional military force, would be the project of military preparations to restore Croatia's territorial sovereignty, which from 1991 onwards was kept under on-site inspection of Serb separatists, where "Serb rebel armies" represented nothing but a disguised Serbian occupation of the country by the Yugoslav Army directed from Belgrade.

There were many signs that indicate that, in addition to the weapons that the Bosnian-Croatian army received in Bosnia and Herzegovina from various semi-legal channels, numerous U.S. military specialists, members of the NATO Special Forces and other military experts from several western countries would be infiltrated in their ranks. Together, they would be engaged in one year of preparation of the military and professional army, which would be put into action at appropriate times. In parallel with the preparation of the Bosnian-Croat army, the Croatian army too would be prepared for war against Yugoslav military units in the Knin Krajina and Western Slavonia, where it was known that Belgrade had long focused all military logistics to protect the Serb "states" in those parts, but also to simultaneously maintain a political pressure on the international factor.

The United States of America had already clearly shown that force had to be used to show Serbia that it should abandon Great-Serbian projects and be forced to accept an imposed international solution, but that it should initially take place on the front where it had demonstrated its force through war.

It should be said that despite almost overt U.S. actions of this kind in Bosnia and Herzegovina and Croatia towards entering a new war, Belgrade did not emit signs that it was about to change course nor did it intend to take precautions to change the direction of developments, which as will be seen, would soon take a direction against the Serb aggression. Indeed, at the beginning of January and February, Serbian units began to provoke the so-called UN protected zones of Bosnian populated areas (five of them) surrounding them by additional forces, especially besieging Srebrenica where over thirty thousand Bosnians had been locked in with a number of refugees from eastern parts of Bosnia, who lived under appalling conditions and were facing a humanitarian disaster of enormous proportions.

But, how could one explain this behavior by Belgrade versus those circumstances knowing that a military conflict with the Americans could not be won? Was it an irrationality displayed by those who lost their ties with reality and its dimensions, or was it about the Serbs counting that it was all part of American pressure, without the backing of an unsettled West, seeking legitimacy for military intervention that it was not likely to get from the UN Security Council, where Russia and China maintained their right to veto, while the Arab-Islamic countries stood against U.S. military intervention? In those circumstances, speculation went so far as to claim an alleged secret agreement had been reached between the Americans and Milosevic on a comprehensive plan to resolve the crisis in accordance with Serbian interests, which did not exclude the division of Bosnia and Herzegovina, and a similar deal with the case of Kosova, before which a formal U.S. military action was needed, for the sake of the site, could U.S. military action even be used in order for things to fall into place and, even there, to bargain a solution?

These speculations were based on a great combination of facts also because between Serbs and Croats a principled agreement existed, as reached in Graz between Milosevic and Tudjman in 1992, and that everything that had happened on the battlefields of Bosnia and Herzegovina during the three last years, had been nothing but part of a disguised scenario where both Serbian and Croatian forces in Bosnia and Herzegovina were rather dividing the common Bosnian prey than fighting each other and this had been obvious to those observing the situation – Americans and NATO, regardless that it had never been said. Even the so-called Herzeg-Bosnia was part of this scenario, the same as it had been known about a corridor in Bosanski Brod and Bijeljina being part of the agreements of the same nature. It was also estimated that the European countries themselves, who had accepted Bosnia and Herzegovina as a state, would agree with a pragmatic solution, which would finally calm Serbs and Croats, even if the Bosnian factor was to somehow be sacrificed, but without making a public noise. If one added to this the fact that Belgrade, as compensation, would relinquish Kosova (of course keeping the North with monasteries for itself), doing so with elegance, through an interim protectorate there to be followed with a referendum the outcome of which was known, then the division of Bosnia, despite violating certain principles, seemed like "calming down the region," at least by forcefully eliminating one factor from the game (Bosnians), which could be said was in the interest of the Europeans as well.

In light of these speculations would be the introduction of the Croatian Army in Western Slavonia and its acquisition from local Serb forces there without much difficulty, although the Croatian Army feared it could experience a repetition of 1991 defeats when its territorial defense units were severely beaten by the Yugoslav People's Army. These speculations, at least through "overt" actions, got a somewhat satisfactory if not a final response from the American factor being now clear that neither the "tempering" of the Bosnian-Croat Federation in Bosnia and Herzegovina or the arming of the Croatian Army was done to intimidate Milosevic, to be later introduced in the game for a concession to Kosova or elsewhere, but rather to achieve three main goals, which, as noted, appeared as part of the American concept.

First – that the former Yugoslav space be redefined in line with Washington's geostrategic interests, representing also the West-European interests in general.

Second – Bosnians, being threatened with extinction, to be taken under protection.

And third – for Serbia to eventually collapse as a regional factor, not to be able to answer Russian interests in the Balkans.

The first goal, namely redefining the former Yugoslav space in accordance with the geostrategic interests of Washington and the West in general, implied the third one, namely that Serbia should not remain a regional factor, at least not in the size it once was, nor be able to present a possible core for restoring Russian influence in the Balkans.[652]

The second goal, namely the preservation of the Bosnian entity, related definitely to the maintenance of Bosnia and Herzegovina as an independent state, no matter how functional it would be, to first of all preserve a Bosnian-Muslim ethnicity not only from Serb-Croat ingestion but also from other factors wishing to exclude it from Balkan configurations fearing it could become a core for a future fundamentalist Islamic state in the region.[653]

Within this goal fell also the positive effects that the Americans wanted to achieve in relation to Islamic and Arab countries to make them appear that they were not anti-Islamist, as indicted not only by Al Qaida fundamentalists and other extremists with whom the Americans were already at war, but also by a good part of the Arab and Islamic world, which due to the functioning of the stereotype that "the enemy of my enemy is my friend" were continuing to support Serbia, with a part of them following this same course in relation to the Kosova issue as well!

---

[652] Kuntzel, Matthias *"Der weg in den Krieg,"* 2000, p. 50.

[653] Hofbauer, Hannes *"Neue Staaten, neue Kriege,"* Vienna, 1999, p. 61.

Rather, the U.S. intervention in Bosnia and Herzegovina to prevent Serbo-Croatian scenarios against its division and to impose the maintenance of the Bosnian factor in it as a state entity, turned into the only defender of Bosnians in this part of the world but also what might be called the European Islamic identity upon which began to build some of the stereotypes of international conjunctures in accordance with this factor, which historically had left its mark on the old continent's space despite the fact that since the Eastern Crisis and on everything had been done to invoke evil against it as dangerous!

The alignment of this element and its functionalizing for political purposes would also be noted in the U.S. policy towards Kosova, when President Bush Junior, on the occasion of his visit to Albania in the summer of 2007 pointed out in the Albanian Parliament "the U.S. commitment in the protection of Muslim Albanians" as a civil duty,[654] regardless that this assessment contradicted their stance since the National Awakening and on that no religious beliefs and identities, but rather nationality was determinant of their common identity.

Achieving these strategic goals would not be possible for the American factor in circumstances of the presence of the UN mandate and UNPROFOR, which had rather helped a justification of Serb conquests than protecting vulnerable populations.

Once again the incomprehensible behavior of Serbs would give rise to substantial amendments, which mandated the blue helmets to take over the Special Forces for rapid action in a contingent of 15 thousand infantrymen, who were supervised by the Americans and NATO. With the occupation of Srebrenica by the Serbs in June 1995 and the terrible massacre that they carried out against eight thousand Bosnians, mostly young and elderly, killing them in mass despite "assurances" by the Dutch to provide full protection during their deportation to Tuzla, all the preconditions had been created for the U.S. and NATO to begin applying an *ultima ratio* against Serb forces in Bosnia and Herzegovina.

Previously, the Serbs would underestimate the French blue helmets holding them tied up and kept as hostages to prevent NATO bombing against their targets and this would also affect their friends and protectors of yesterday to be irritated and turned away. Maybe this too speaks of

---

[654] See the speech of the U.S. President, George Bush before the Albanian Parliament, June 2007, as published in „Zëri," 11 June 2007.

Serbian calculations that by compromising blue helmets they were moving towards an unwritten deal with the Americans and out of the reach of the Europeans, as the UN presence prevented the Serbs and this had to yield to new realities.

Busy with the occupation and elimination of the Bosnian enclaves in their parts formally protected by blue helmets, Serbs could not have properly accounted for the scenarios coming from Croats and the Bosnian-Croat alliance, now facing the opening of two almost parallel fronts: in the Knin Krajina and the so-called "Herzegovina Pocket" from the combined units of the Bosnian-Croat Federation, which was activated against Serb Army positions in the length of a hundred kilometers from the Dinara Mountains to the Neretva gorge. The Croatian "Storm" would be so severe and so effective that the Serb units stationed for years in Knin and Krajina would be dismantled within four days, as the Croatian Army entered Knin raising there the Croatian flag. However, for the "Storm" to be really stormy this was ensured by Americans and NATO, when in a breathtaking action, extremely codified, they obliterated all the missile systems and bases in Knin and Ub (near Zagreb), where ground-to-air and ground-to-ground small and medium ray missiles had been deployed among the most modern that the Yugoslav army had, to which Russian but also Chinese ones were added. In this case, the Americans and NATO deactivated the entire military logistics system of the Serb Army in this part, leaving it separated from other parts of Bosnia and Serbia.

However, the great victory of the Croatian Army in Knin and other parts of the so-called Serb Knin Krajina stronghold forced the entire Serbian population to flee from these parts (over two hundred thousand of them). The fleet to Serbia was led through the northern Bosnian corridor. The Serb population from these areas, which for years had lived with the illusion of a "heroic people," protected also by a "heroic and invincible army," turned at once into refugees, to which were added tens of thousands of Serbs from the Neretva valley. Long lines of Serb refugees dragging across parts of Northern and Eastern Bosnia spoke of the ultimate defeat of the great dream of Serbia and the Serbian myth from where in the early part of 1987, under an unprecedented rasp of Orthodox liturgy, remains of Prince Lazar were rambling, as rumored, for "the holy journey through the Serbian lands of Kosova from Knin to Kosova."

Although the Croatian "Storm" and its successes almost immediately removed from the agenda the issue of "Serbian autonomous states" in

Croatia and the Americans left with having on the table only Bosnia and Herzegovina, needed another reason to begin air strikes against Serb targets in Sarajevo and its surrounding. It was necessary to show that the use of force had begun, the final instrument that could lead to their complete military defeat, which, as will be seen, was not something that the Americans would have liked not only because Serbs would appear willing for a political solution to the crisis in Bosnia and Herzegovina according to the plan already envisaged by Holbrooke, but also for other strategic and geopolitical reasons.

The shell that fell on the Markale Sarajevo market in late August, which killed 73 people and seriously wounded hundreds more, although the Serbs would deny it was fired from Palje or their position, but claimed it was an international staging against them, would suffice to blame the Serbs in order to commence from August 30 to September 14, 1995 a limited NATO air bombing campaign against Serb positions around Sarajevo and other strategic parts. This campaign was followed by ground offensive forces of a Bosnian-Croatian army, which had already started from the southeast and Bihac area towards Banja Luka achieving great successes against Serb forces, which attacked from the air were not able to use aviation, heavy armor, or receive logistical and other assistance, as usual, from Serbia.

The loss of about 70% of the territories they conquered and kept seriously threatened with further continuation of fighting under those circumstances would be perceived as a heavy loss with serious consequences for all of Serbia and the Serbian people, so that on October 5, 1995 Mladic's Serb Army would be forced to sign a cease-fire agreement.

And, for the absurd to be greater, it would be the U.S. intervention that brought about the twist to the detriment of the Serbian aggressor, which would force the Croatian forces not to penetrate into Bosnia and Herzegovina in pursuit of Serbs! Furthermore, it was the U.S. intervention that prevented the Bosnian-Croatian army from conquering Banja Luka, the Serbian "fortress," where there were already over two hundred thousand refugees from Croatia and many other parts of Herzegovina, who could be soon joined by over half a million Serbs from northern and northeastern parts of Bosnia where the Serbian Army deserted its positions and was retreating.

Faced with a large-scale potential collapse, which could destabilize the entire region, as Serbia had threatened to go to war directly if Banja

Luka would fall into the hands of Bosnians, or the Croats were to close the Posavina corridor (something that Milosevic would do just as well as the only way of saving himself from internal lynching), the Americans took all measures to turn the situation "into normality." This normality meant accepting Serb military defeat in Bosnia, but without capitulation, which was conditional upon the acceptance of a peace plan for resolving the crisis in Bosnia and Herzegovina according to American dictates. Serbs would accept U.S. conditions provided that they vis-à-vis Bosnian forces would be allowed to undertake a supervised "counter-offensive" to round up the territories in line with those that were already planned and as such were needed by the Dayton agreement in Dayton.

The use of force against the Serbs yielded expected results by accepting at once all the conditions submitted to them by the Americans. Moreover, it was believed that they would have accepted more, if the Americans would want to go further.

Thus, those who for years had terrorized the region holding the international community by its nose, being puffed up that they were militarily invincible, had come to a defensive position in only a few days defending themselves not with weapons but with the help of the threat of chaos and transfer of war to other parts of the region. But the Americans and NATO were more afraid of opening other problems in the region from the chaos in Bosnia and Herzegovina and the impact it would have in Serbia rather than by threats coming from its army. It was estimated that hundreds of thousands of Serb refugees from Bosnia to Serbia, who were on their way crossing the Drina, could open a civil war in Serbia and fold it into a chaos that would quickly spread to Albania, Macedonia, Montenegro, Bulgaria, Greece and Turkey to include the entire region and to become a great disarray, for which neither the Americans nor anyone else would have an interest or need.

The emergence of the U.S. factor in Bosnia and Herzegovina and its commitment in everything preceding the concept of the Dayton Conference would rightly awaken hopes it would come to an important twist. At least, the Serbian game with the international factor would end, together with numerous calculations feeding various political circles speculating on certain purposes. Therefore, it was expected that the United States of America would come up with the last word and it meant a lot.

Morbid scenes from the blockade of Sarajevo and the unrestrained Serbian Army versus their defenseless victims filling TV programs for more than three years had created dejection in the general public, which demanded by all means to see an end to such violence. Since the United Nations had proven unable to do so, even though it was present with its blue helmets in declared protected areas, it was the Americans alone who emerged as the Messiah, in the same way they had appeared in Europe during World War I when it was turning into a tragic stalemate position, and during World War II against fascism.

But, how would the Albanian factor see the U.S. involvement in Bosnia and Herzegovina? And what steps would it take to become an active part of American arrangements in this regard, which could be used to be treated as an important subject? Should they still stick to their civil resistance with the parallel state as Albanians' only option? Or, they had to introduce other cards into the game, unopened until then, without excluding radical steps, such as opposition leading to an armed resistance, serving in the function of implementation of the state of Kosova, as declared in Kaçanik, without excluding the possibility of this option expanding with demands affecting a redefinition of the Albanian question in the Balkans.

Here one could introduce into the game various calculations reaching as far as demands for national unification, to be overlaid in accordance with the interests of the overall Albanian factor, primarily in concert and cooperation with the Albanian state, but also with other concerned parties interested in raising the Albanian question as an unresolved issue, but not before it was properly measured before it could turn into a boomerang for Albanians.

These and similar dilemmas were of great importance, because this was about the warning of a significant turning point, when it was known that Americans did not come to Europe to become part of Serbian delays with which Europeans were accustomed and even agreed with for years being subjected to the behavior of Belgrade, but had come to impose solutions, regardless of whether they would be sustainable and on what principles they would be based. The American statement that they would establish peace in the region meant taking measures to really establish peace believing it could not be achieved by retreating to the Serbs and their empty promises and creation of established facts by force across the battlefields.

In addition, the Albanians found it in their own interest to know as to how far the American involvement would go in the crisis of former

Yugoslavia and what was Washington's strategy in the crisis as a whole and to its parts in particular to see what treatment it envisaged for Kosova so that, in accordance with these reports, act accordingly to ensure more favorable treatment in this package. This was necessary also due to the fact that Washington had warned that its commitment to the crisis in the former Yugoslavia began with stopping the war in Bosnia and Herzegovina and ending the Croatia crisis, but it did not remain so. So, one had to see the U.S. engagement as part of a larger package, which would include all the territory of the former Yugoslavia, but that could go further, affecting willingly or unwillingly other parts and touching upon other issues if interests were involved. If all this was compounded with a redefinition in terms of spheres of interest by major changes in the East, where the Americans had emerged as the main say appearing as the only world superpower, it could be contemplated that the U.S. commitment represented a good chance for Albanians to become part of the concept of these changes.

Looking for these dilemmas and responses, it appeared that the prelude to Dayton and Dayton itself was rather part of illusions by Albanians in waiting rather than on how to act in that direction. It would also be seen that Kosova and Albania, despite the fall of the inter-border that had divided them for years had not only never had a common strategy for the D Day, but were not even on the same wave-length. This perhaps would best be seen when Kosova remained rightly stuck to its commitment to the independent state in accordance with the decisions of the Kaçanik Assembly on the declaration of the Republic of Kosova as an independent state and referendum for independence in accordance with the free declaration of the will of the people. While the Albanian government would uphold this will in principle, it on the other hand, would also support the views of the international community to keep Kosova as autonomous within the remaining Yugoslavia, which was already declared as the Federal Republic of Yugoslavia. It would do so without ever being able to bring opposition, even in principle, when evidently the former Yugoslavia was torn inside and Albanians were entitled to decide upon their own future, as it happened, but which had to be noted from Tirana and supported by all means and at all times.

Albanian diplomacy, despite sincere willingness to assist Kosova, proving it in every given chance, was trapped into this confusion, because it missed both project and strategy for Kosova and its issue to be used for opening the Albanian issue in the region, where the declaration of maximalist positions without turning to definite demands could help achieve the optimum, which in this case was the recognition of Kosova as an independent state.

The Albanian state, rather, in a diplomatic and political plain was operating between an optimum and a minimum, a move that at most in this case could bring the Kosova status to an international protectorate position. The Albanian state could therefore be glad if Kosova would eventually be put on an international therapy with an interim status as demanded by the Kosova Albanians in the first place after having declared the Republic of Kosova as an independent state setting it at the center of their determination.

Speaking of the Albanian state and its anemia in relation to the international community in defending the issue of Kosova with greater tenacity one should seek the reasons for this behavior as constrained by domestic developments through which Albania passed, speaking clearly of a preceding severe crisis it would face in two years' time with Berisha's Government collapsing and the Albanian state, after an 84-year existence falling down and becoming a European concern. Signs of the negative emerged on the eve and during the Dayton talks, with on one side a pyramid system operating in Albania and on the other, the turning of Albania into a butt of international drug addiction and clandestine center of refugees from the Middle and Far East gathered and distributed to Italy and other parts of Europe by which the Albanian state had become a threat to the old continent. This negative development was also reflected in clandestine links that certain Albanian state structures were involved in the breach of the arms embargo against Serbia and Serbs of Bosnia and Herzegovina!

Notably, in these circumstances, Dr. Rugova, faced with challenges of implementation of the parallel state in Kosova, and on the other side of the crisis the Albanian state evolving towards imminent collapse, would turn to the party's strength and its full support for its base to take over the leadership of parallel institutions – but aware of the fact that Americans needed an offer of compromise for putting the issue of Kosova on the agenda – would come up with the proposal of an interim international protectorate, without giving up the independent state of Kosova and clinging to the refrain of the independent state even when he knew that a compromise was required. As the U.S. Congressman, Eliot Engel alerted the American Administration of Serbian intentions soon to colonize Kosova with Serbian colonists from Croatia and Bosnia, Dr. Rugova during a visit to the UN utilized the U.S. Congressman's report and his deep concern to inform the UN Secretary General on the serious situation of violence in Kosova by permanent Serbian state terror that could deteriorate if the Serbian plans to start its colonization with over two hundred thousand Serbs from Croatia and Bosnia went ahead. The demand for an international protectorate in Kosova would justify the necessary transitional time that both Albanians and Serbs needed so that after settling down they would turn to negotiations on the final solution of the Kosova issue, which should be done through democratic means.[655]

The demand for an international protectorate in Kosova and the presence of international forces, without mentioning the model of the blue helmets in Bosnia and Herzegovina, which had failed to fulfill its mission, but rather helped the Serbs legitimize their conquests, would be sent to the United States of America.[656]

Compared with the UN request, the request to the United States would be more detailed and the international protectorate would be limited to three years. After the expiration a referendum would take place, also under the UN supervision, deciding on the final status of Kosova in accordance with the free will of its citizens.

Noticeably, Dr. Rugova's commitment at a time of an ever greater American resolve in settling the crisis of the former Yugoslavia, more in line with possible options that could be in use, along with the request for recognition of Kosova and its fundamental determination, would also come up with a proposal for confederal links with Albania if this would be allowed for the Bosnian Serbs in relation to Serbia. During a meeting with U.S. Assistant Secretary of State Talbot, Dr. Rugova mentioned the option of Confederation Kosova and Albania as a real possibility, which would be in line with the Balkan realities.[657]

The analyst Viktor Meier was not equally understanding of the Kosova-Albania confederation option and its introduction as a model of balance similar to the state connections of Serbs on both sides of the Drina, being formally unacceptable because it needed first to go through

---

[655] Newspaper *"Kosova,"* 30 November 1994.

[656] *Ibid.*

[657] Baleta, Abdi *"Kosova nga Dejtoni në Rambuje,"* p. 29.

two scales of declarations: in Kosova and Albania, which could be trouble-some, and it also needed two international decisions, the first being recognition of Kosova as an independent state and then allowing for confederal association, which also appeared with difficulty, even of a technical nature. Instead, he suggested further support for the Republic of Kosova as an independent state, as declared at the Kaçanik Assembly, on condition it was placed under certain international supervision, the beginning and end of which would be determined through an interna-tional arbitrator. Meier asked the Albanians to base their request for the recognition of the Republic of Kosova on the 1974 Constitution, the Article defining it as an equal unit of the Federation, although its Para-graph One said also it was "within the Republic of Serbia." As the Federa-tion stood above the Republic, under international positive law, then, in case of dispute, the higher provision, such as that of the Federation, was more powerful than that of the Republic, to which the second was sub-ject.[658]

This assessment was also shared by the renowned expert in interna-tional law, Professor Georg Brunner from the University of Cologne, who said that the Badinter Commission should have relied on this provision and not on the arbitrariness of the dissolution of the former Yugoslavia. Instead it should have started with the constitutional position of 1989, which was changed by force from Serbia and was illegal with Albanians rejecting it, and even more so as on July 2, 1990, when they announced their Constitutional Declaration of Independence seceding from Serbia in legitimate and most deserving democratic means. Professor Brunner thought that the failure of response to the request of the Government of the Republic of Kosova by the Badinter Commission was due precisely because of this element, which its lawyers knew, and if they considered it they could not avoid it, something that was not in accordance with the provisions of the international political settlement to recognize and accept Kosova's right to secession at that stage.[659]

The open request for international protection that Dr. Rugova sent to the UN and presented to the United States, was preceded by one of those not at all rare attempts of Rugova's "secret diplomacy" of "eye to eye" communication with Belgrade, authorizing Professor Fehmi Agani, who

---

[658] Author's conversation with Viktor Mayer in Bonn, November 1997.
[659] Interview for *"Ekskluzive," no.* 3/2000.

would be present in almost all negotiations and mediations with the Serbian side from the Geneva ones to Rambouillet. The German press would be the one that for the first time would disclose several months of negotiations of a Kosova delegation, headed by Agani, with a Serbian high level delegation (it referred to a meeting with the Vice President of the Serbian Government and some of Milosevic's senior advisers), who held secret talks at the Swiss Embassy in Belgrade. The talks began in April 1994 and lasted until September of the same year.[660]

It became known that negotiations between Albanians and Serbs were based on a pattern similar to the Israeli-Palestinian talks in Oslo and in the center of its treatment was a subject matter defining "a three republic solution," under which the new Federation would rely on the principle of building upon three republics, interconnected according to Serbs and equal according to Albanians, with different variants and sub-alternatives, mentioning on one hand confederal powers, and on the other limited and republican sovereignty. This federal-confederal community would consist of Serbia, Montenegro and Kosova. Some sources said that Serbia had agreed in principle to have equality in the Federation, but that the Kosova's link with the Federation had to pass through Serbia, which meant to be somewhat distinct from that of Montenegro and the like. However, talks had failed as Kosova refused to accept any "dual position" in the Federation that would go through Serbia, because of its bitter experience with the 1974 Constitution in the Yugoslav Federation, and Serbia had not been able to accept Kosova's full equality in the tripartite relationship, as it concluded that it would be an inevitable step towards its secession from the Federation.

Tim Judah speculated on the reasons for the failure finding one of them not as much in Milosevic's rejection of the project as in his fear that this would have consequences for his future power. According to him, it was the opposition that stood on more radical positions than Milosevic regarding Kosova and was doing its best to utilize it as much as possible for both influence and the electorate, as it did in "accepting in principle" the Vance and Owen plan on Bosnia and Herzegovina a year before, but that it was the opposition representatives headed by Kostunica, Djindjic,

---

[660] "*Frankfurter Allgemeine Zeitung*" of 26 September 1994. The famous German newspaper cites well-informed German sources. The same will be mentioned by T. Judah in his book „*Kosovo,*" 1997, p. 95.

Draskovic and others who had encouraged Karadzic and Mladic not to acquiesce before the Milosevic-Cosic "betrayal"![661] Judah did not deal equally with the reasons of interests of Kosova for this project, as they seemed natural and in accordance with the open attitude of Dr. Rugova to discuss all issues related to the future of Kosova. Although the author, with a publicist's approach, would be inclined towards the concept of a civil resistance movement with the parallel state seeing it rather as a situation consuming too much time for Albanians at the expense of responsible action and confrontation, without which, he estimated there could be no change in the situation of moving Kosova out of Serbia. He too admits that the consequence to guard the demand for an independent state of Kosova in all variants and in all kinds of talks had been of an historical importance.[662]

A similar assessment was made by the German newspaper "TAZ," which was among the first to inform about these talks in order to point out that Albanians needed them regardless of what they brought and how they were interpreted, because this kept them in the game, an issue which was very important for Kosova and its issue.

The Albanian side also never mentioned the issue publicly, including Rugova who would avoid it whenever questioned by foreign journalists. Fehmi Agani would admit that such talks took place, arguing with the well-known position that "Albanians are always willing to talk with anyone about all issues but without giving up the determination for the state of Kosova. The state of Kosova can be built through different ways. The important thing is not to give it up."[663]

---

[661] See T. Judah *"Kosova, luftë dhe hakmarrje,"* 2002.

[662] *Ibid.*

[663] An interview for the Albanian broadcast of "Westeutsche Rundfunk" of Cologne, 30 September 1994. There, Fehmi Agani claimed that the international community was also interested that Albanians participate in them, seeing if such a status woild fit into a tripartite federation. According to Professor Agani conversations had no prospect because Serbs were not interested in such a state, joining it rather to show the international community that they supported the option of negotiating with Albanians allegedly offering a solution, but that it was their determination to an independent state that in the end threw everything into the water. To the hypothetical question of what would happen if Serbia agreed for Kosovo to become an equal part of the tripartite federation (three republics), Professor Agani answered that first one had to talk to the Americans for their opinion and then it would be a question for a referendum.

Dayton – Chapter of Incomplete Peace and Warning of a New War

Use of means of war for diplomatic purposes, such as those used during the NATO bombing against Serb positions around Sarajevo, an efficient measure to force Belgrade to accept the conditions of the international community. – The stand of the U.S. president "about open gates of peace" sounded more like a threat and a warning against both actors who had to sign it and to the Europeans themselves, who spent years dealing without success with the crisis in the former Yugoslavia, that henceforth it would be pressure and enforcement that would have the key say in the process of establishing peace. – In Dayton an enforced peace had to be signed and accepted, no matter how just it was. The important thing was to show that it was still possible. – The UN Secretary General was not present at Dayton, not invited intentionally by the Clinton administration after the debacle that the blue helmets experienced in Bosnia, especially at Srebrenica, blamed for one of the biggest massacres carried out after World War II against Bosnians by the Mladic army. In this way the United States had eliminated a theoretical possibility that the conference could be affected by the UN and behind the scene games of certain countries and permanent members of the Security Council, which had shown that they were not interested in a peaceful solution to the crisis of the former Yugoslavia, but rather its continuation in the hope that it would enlarge hanging as a rock around the West's neck. – Dr. Ibrahim Rugova's letter asking to include Kosova in the Dayton Conference and the response of President Clinton that Kosova and its problems remained for a special treatment. – Increasing Albanian demands to turn civil resistance into an active resistance, without excluding war.

International conferences since the Second World War arousing the attention of the world such as that of Dayton are rare. The reasons were numerous, from political, diplomatic, and humanitarian aspects. Expectations were also great because it was being organized under the leadership and direct dictates of the U.S., which was unavoidable in the circumstances when Europe and its diplomacy were facing political, but also moral and humanitarian collapse in general. In addition, further prolongation of the crisis risked involving the region and other factors, gaining wide-ranging and unpredictable proportions, which would fast invalidate all that had been achieved in the last three or four years after the collapse of détente and bloc bipolarity of which the West had benefited the most.

For the Conference, however, its urgency was not natural being subject to a dynamic model of unprecedented shuttle diplomacy. U.S. envoy Richard Holbrooke used a new method of working more effectively with Belgrade and the Contact Group operating directly and in a time interval of only one month, namely from September 8 to October 7, agreeing on issues that they could not agree for years. Thus, the first meeting of the Contact Group was held in Geneva on August 8, 1995, the second in New York on September 23 and the third in Moscow on October 7, when it would be decided to call the Dayton Conference on November 1 of that year.

This extraordinary efficiency did not come out of a blue sky. It was a direct result of the use of means of war for diplomatic and political purposes, just as it was long sought by different centers but prevented from the demagoguery of peace talks and exploits to the contrary. The long-standing dictum "better one hundred years of talking than a daylong of war" had been long compromised and the American intervention in this crisis showed the contrary, "a day of war was sometimes worth more than one hundred years of successful negotiations." As Holbrooke's shuttle diplomacy started right after the Croatian "Storm" in the Knin Krajina occupied by Serbs, succeeding fast, Serbs began to see that they were militarily vulnerable and therefore had their myth broken, after being able for years to continue to establish facts by the use of force even during the negotiations with the international community and even exploiting them for their own purposes, as it would happen with the presence of the UN mission and their troops.

The start of the NATO bombing against Serb army positions around Sarajevo and in other strategic parts of Bosnia accompanied by a ground offensive of Bosnian-Croatian troops and their big and fast successes in all lines of the front, would be used by Holbrook to pressure Milosevic to accept the American conditions and to do so as soon as possible before the situation on the fronts of the war would deteriorate forcing him to accept a deal that would be even more unfavorable for him. ... And lastly, it would be the signing of the ceasefire between the warring parties in Bosnia and Herzegovina on October 5, 1995, where General Mladic, who bragged so much about his weapons, accepted the dictates of weapons and war losses, that made Russia on September 7 of that year, at the meeting of the Contact Group in Moscow agree to eventually give its consent to both the Dayton conference and the concept of peace. Therefore, it was expected that the Dayton conference itself would abide by the rhythm and pace of the success of the American diplomacy. It even not accidentally opened with congratulations sent by President Clinton that "the gates of peace in the Balkans had been opened."

In Dayton an enforced peace had to be signed and accepted, no matter how just it was. The important thing was to show that it was still possible.

The stand of the U.S. president "about open gates of peace" sounded more like a threat and a warning against both actors who had to sign it and to the Europeans themselves, who spent years dealing without success with the crisis in the former Yugoslavia, that henceforth it would be pressure and enforcement that would have the key say in the process of establishing peace. Therefore, this was the mood in which the Dayton Conference started, bringing together for the first time members of the Contact Group, Chairman of the International Conference on the Former Yugoslavia, Carl Bildt, who had earlier replaced Lord Owen and actors of the Balkan: Milosevic on behalf of the Federal Republic of Yugoslavia, Tudjman on behalf of Croatia and Izetbegovic on behalf of the Presidency of Bosnia and Herzegovina. Americans, both as arbitrator and peacemaker, were represented by the Secretary of State Christopher, Defense Minister Perry, Homeland Security Secretary Lake, Deputy Secretary of State Talbot, with mediator Holbrooke and his associates Hill and Gelbar. Also present were General Clark and NATO General George Joulwan with their messages to remind the presence of power in the service of diplomacy.

The conference was noted for the absence of representatives of Kosova Albanians and this had rightly caused a surprise for the media and the public, after the promises that had come from all sides, especially the Americans, that one day they would be rewarded for their peaceful behavior and patience. The surprise became even greater as the presence of a Bosnian Serb delegation, headed by Momcilo Krajisnik (in his capacity as spokesman of the Serbian Parliament) and composed of Nikola Kolevic (vice president of the Serb Parliament) and the so-called foreign minister of Republika Srpska, Aleksa Buha, was noted in the Conference halls, who although officially ignored, were there to sign a peace accord with Izetbegovic, by which Bosnia and Herzegovina would be accepted even by them as a common state despite their swearing that it would never happen. Thus, the impression was that Dayton had considered or rewarded those who had waged war instead of following peaceful resistance, gratifying those who had killed rather than those who were being killed. This impression would not go away even though there were others who had used war for political purposes, such as Croatian Serbs, who had not been invited to Dayton, although evidently their advance had come to a halt prior to that by the Croatian "Storm" which destroyed within three or four days all the facts established by war for years. In this case their issue was removed from the agenda, affecting the Dayton conference in the way of "restructuring" the determination to deal with the problems of an overall treatment of the former Yugoslavia problem, as initially warned, turning it into a Conference on Bosnia and Herzegovina, as it actually ended up.

This will not unload the weight of speculation by those who were claiming it was Milosevic again that had prevented the introduction of Kosova on the agenda, as he had done in The Hague and London, [664] even threatening boycott, which would later prove to be a hoax, and going as far as spreading the rumor that it had been done by Holbrooke (which he later denied), as the American diplomacy needed such maneuvers against opening issues for which it had no interest in those circumstances to be treated. Eventually, they were proven to be something that Milosevic and his propaganda needed to prepare the public on the acceptance of the Dayton accords not by the Serbian will and its interests, as said, but rather upon American dictate, hiding behind the elimination of Kosova in the talks, creating the impression that it was and remained an internal matter of Serbia and nothing else. This was best shown by the response of the U.S. government to Dr. Ibrahim Rugova's letter that he sent to President Bill Clinton demanding the inclusion of Kosova in the Dayton Conference receiving a deserving treatment in line with the U.S. position that Kosova would one day be rewarded for its patience and peaceful path it followed for years without taking into account the difficulties it had encountered.

U.S. Ambassador in Belgrade Rudolf Perrina explained in person to Dr. Rugova Washington's position about not including Kosova in Dayton and the reasons why. According to the American ambassador, there had

---

[664] See Bierman, Rafael *"Lehrjahre im Kosovo,"* 2004, pp. 471-482 and other authors speculating on the thesis.

originally been a version of the conference to include Kosova, but "because of the special circumstances" Washington evaluated that it was better to leave it for later, to be treated in a complex manner.

"The success of the solution of the Kosova issue should not be threatened by other issues."[665] This was the American response in anticipation of special treatment of the Kosova issue.

The U.S. ambassador would also inform Dr. Rugova that Dayton would be reduced only to the issue of establishing peace in Bosnia and Herzegovina, which would inevitably include Bosnian Serbs as signatories to the peace accords while it would leave the door open to other issues.

So, Dr. Rugova had been well informed and first-hand about the direction of the Dayton Conference and the American position, as President Clinton had personally written that Kosova would have special attention on another occasion assessed as appropriate and that its inclusion in Dayton would not only marginalize it, but any decision taken that would suit the Serbs would ultimately keep it from treatment that would come later just as the U.S. President had written to Rugova.

As Dr. Ibrahim Rugova had never made this public, the right question would be why he never used President Clinton's promise in defusing his increasingly numerous opponents, who seemed to have had rejoiced on what they sounded the alarm as "an Albanian debacle in Dayton," to at least inform his numerous followers, those who carried the burden of the parallel state to stay on the course with the hope that behind them stood the greatest power of the world. The latter did not really forget them, and the issue of Kosova, although after three years of waiting, would be taken up the same as it had been done with Bosnia and Herzegovina through the

---

[665] From author's conversation with Dr. Ibrahim Rugova in Petersberg near Bonn in December 1995. Dr. Ibrahim Rugova admitted that he had been pleased with the reasoning of the U.S. Ambassador. The arguments raised were acceptable, though explaining them in the circumstances was quite difficult, because the Serb military losses in Bosnia and Herzegovina and Croatia left the impression that Serbia had capitulated militarily and that its military forces would be destroyed soon. For this very reason he once again addressed the U.S. President with another letter reminding him the commitments made, to which President Clinton responded back through Ambassador Perrina, pledging commitments that the United States of America would keep their promise to the Albanians, so that they were rewarded for patience and peacefulness, which had been in line with Western interests.

use of ultimatums against Serbs creating conditions to force them to the negotiating table.

Was there already a doubt in Dr. Rugova's mind about the Americans too on not keeping their word and leaving Albanians at the mercy of a ruthless and lonely fate, as had happened so many times in history? Or, was it all part of an agreement with the Americans not to make such promises too public, keeping them rather at closed political levels, something that could make sense? Besides these justified guesses, however, the reason why Rugova kept the issue to himself might have been of a "technical nature" as the letter of the U.S. President to Rugova was handed over personally by the U.S. Ambassador in Belgrade, Perrina, which could have intimidated Rugova to speak out about something that he did not have in possession, even though he had seen the letter from the U.S. Ambassador and was allowed to read it.

The reasons why Dr. Rugova kept silent about President Clinton's letter regarding special attention dedicated to Kosova to be treated on some other occasion may also be associated with the fact that if something like that was to be used in the circumstances when those who had committed crimes against humanity, among the worst after World War II, and their leaders (Karadzic and Mladic) on the eve of the Hague Conference were charged for these war crimes, it could be taken as an American game that could undermine U.S. credibility, the only and last remaining hope for Albanians. Rugova certainly did not want to shake in any way his faith in the Americans and their crucial role as savior for Kosova despite the fact that Dayton justifiably concerned him a lot. Because putting in doubt the reliability of the Americans, no matter how little it would be, would at no time undermine the whole edifice of the Albanian parallel state and everything that had been done so far. Rugova also knew that the loss of trust in the Americans would represent suicide for Albanians, and that should not be allowed.

However, Albanians had been informed from the highest U.S. levels about their goals, with the promise that they would be met and that was what mattered.

Nevertheless, Dayton for Albanians had functioned as a psychological factor of particular importance acting in two ways. On the one hand – towards further motivation of opponents of civil-institutional resistance and determination for the parallel state and, on the other – towards a sober kind of thinking that Dayton was concluding a chapter of the former Yugoslavia crisis, no matter how, by also opening the next chapter, the last one, which inevitably linked Kosova and its fate. Furthermore, evidently Dayton as a psychological factor would continue to function even later, after having closed some processes, where patience, prudence, and fulfilling of the American promise to Kosova were justified by the time.

The first, namely opponents of Dr. Rugova's course, did not hesitate to sue him for being a "rogue" and even a traitor – and as usual it would be a part of the intellectual spectrum politically scattered and always pathetically prating about the imagined national unions and vague wars – continuing to use Dayton rather to settle accounts with the civil resistance and the concept of parallel state than to provide any other way that would be acceptable in providing a new solution. But Rugova would not be less attacked by the representatives of those political parties from among the Albanian Party Coordinating Council, initially involved in the concept of the parallel state, that raised doubt on his success if it continued to remain without its active side of resistance by other means, with mostly protests, strikes and forms of civil disobedience against the occupier appearing, which Rugova neither joined nor rejected.

It must be said that among Dr. Rugova's opponents were also some of those dissatisfied who had been malcontent with Dayton and what it had brought, and who not only rejoiced but had been particularly motivated to call for war. This included the militants in favor of the war course. Compared with those pathetic chatterers with mouths full of war ideas speaking from their armchairs and political parties without any support among the people – who had initially supported the course of civil re-sistance, but who did not agree to "pacifism" – militants were the ones who were most loyal and willing to enter it regardless of its price. They would even be joined by many of those who sacrificed for the parallel state, turning into self-sacrificing who did not deny their yesterday's sacrifice, but rather continued to pursue the goal by other means. For, they, even when they found themselves on the front lines, even when they were bleeding, would always have in mind the state of Kosova as a goal.

The latter, those thinking sober, would not despair, but would have time to calmly think about the fact that after Dayton left out of the game one of the main segments of the great Serbian concept of dominance over the former Yugoslavia – swallowing Bosnia and Herzegovina, as it had planned in the last Memorandum of Serbian Academics – then they would still continue to think and draw conclusions about what had to be done to assist in this process and how Albanians should act to benefit from it as much as possible.

What had happened within three weeks in Dayton, from between 1 and 21 November had spectacularly revealed two things that seemed almost impossible before that.

First – it was the "consent" of Serbs and Bosnians to live in a common state, even with Federal-Confederal boundaries and realities for a long time appearing to be incompatible.

Second – Slobodan Milosevic appearing as a "peace-maker" and his rise as the main partner of the Americans!

The first issue, that of "consent to agreement" between the executioner and the victim, perhaps could somehow be swallowed given the circumstances. But declaring Milosevic "man of peace" and his rising to be the main partner of the Americans and the West in general, the architect of the greatest tragedy in the Balkans after World War II, was a question that no one thought possible, including Serbs themselves.

Of course, that too had its reasons, which could be explained only through the logic of political games. Milosevic's turning from the greatest enemy of the Americans and the West in general to their "partner," even if temporary, could not possibly have been a scenario without Milosevic's involvement and even enticing it. Although time would one day show (after having opened all relevant documents from the archives) it can be assumed that between the Americans and Milosevic, at least in global lines, there was an agreement. In the absence of deserving sources, there were various indications and speculations justifying the "twist." Among these indications, however, one should mention those that might have lured Milosevic to accept U.S. plans, since there he saw the opportunity to benefit from something they had promised, without being forced to turn out a complete loser. Certainly one of these "allurements" was precisely the federal-confederal division of Bosnia and Herzegovina into two sections, one Serb and one Bosnian-Croat, in which the first would in time join Serbia through a referendum or similarly, which could have been treated with Milosevic as such. This speculation could be thrown into the game due to the fact that a good part of Europeans would rather see Bosnia and Herzegovina divided between Serbs and Croats than in the hands of the Bosnian Muslims, who were considered an "Islamic fundamentalist enclave" in the vital part of Southeastern Europe. So, with such a separation two goals would be achieved simultaneously: that of removing from the agenda the risk of an Islamic state in the Balkans, which according to Serbian and Orthodox propaganda, with "Islamic Albanians would represent an anti-European reality," and also by dividing it between the two rival nations, good opportunities would be created for pacifying the area of former Yugoslavia, which was everyone's aim.

Later this "appeasement" would include Albanians for the same reasons to achieve an ideal level.

It was estimated that the Serb-Croat appeasement in Bosnia and Herzegovina would create preconditions for "pacifying" the Albanians, with the status of Kosova representing a good opportunity for the issue to gain a positive response, as Serbs would eventually agree that "their medieval cradle" be carried over to the western parts, across the river Drina, where in fact that which is called a Serbian state had its roots, artificially transferred later to Kosova.

Even without these speculations, Milosevic's temporary rise as "a man of peace" and leading "partner" of the Americans and the West can be understood if one considers Milosevic's "concessions" at Dayton to accept the U.S. demands, and it is important to see, as perhaps only through them one could understand the "impossible" politics in certain circumstances as well as its "miracles."

By all means, the first Serb "concession" relates to the preservation of Bosnia and Herzegovina as a common state and having the act of Serb consent carried out not by legitimate representatives of the Serbs, who had proclaimed Republika Srpska and had shed blood for it, but with Milosevic doing that for them. The precedence for Americans and those who were present at Dayton seemed to not matter at all, even though almost two years ago for that same reason and exactly because the Bosnian Serbs had refused to sign, Vance and Owen's plan on Bosnia and Herzegovina had failed, despite being at some points even more favorable than the current one that the Americans had imposed. Speaking and deciding constantly on behalf of the Bosnian Serbs, Milosevic had given up that part of Sarajevo, which Serbs had focused as inalienable and threatened to never give up because it would leave the Republika Srpska without a Serb identity. Without much intricacy he had signed the transfer of the entire vicinity of Sarajevo as far as Palje in the hands of the

Bosnian-Croat Federation, by canceling their "state" for which so much blood had been shed.[666]

In a gentleman's style, Milosevic accepted to leave open the "Gorazde corridor" with a "free status" for Brcko and Sava corridor to be monitored for a period of one year by the internationals to be later settled by mutual agreement.[667]

Similarly, he accepted agreements for the final return of Eastern Slavonia and Baranja to Croatia and signed two separate state-level agreements with Tudjman on issues dealing with the return of the Serb minority to the Knin Krajina, which until a month before had its own "autonomous state" in that part and whenever Milosevic was referred to in order to have an influence over them, at least to not hold Zagreb hostage by occasional grenade throwing from Ubi and vicinity of Karlovac, only twenty kilometers far from Zagreb, said "they are those who decide and a peace deal should be signed with them."

And, what is more surprising, the agreements on behalf of the Bosnian Serbs and those with Tudjman, Milosevic would connect and would not sign as President of the Federal Republic of Yugoslavia, but as President of Serbia, which was legally part of Yugoslavia, and had no right to sign in that capacity!

Such behavior by Milosevic at Dayton and "authorizations" he had taken over himself with the Americans appreciating them as "legitimate" would shock the world media, with some of them wondering if "the world politics had reached the highest degree of an incurable amnesia."[668]

---

[666] An internal evaluation of the German Representative in Dayton, Wolgang Ischinger, to the German Government as taken from *"Deutsche Aussenpolitik,"* 1998, p. 121. It said among other things: *"It was indescribable to see how Milosevic had joyfully turned into an impassable partner of all those who devoted their greatest attention to him... One got the impression that he would sign anything ..."*

[667] See newspaper *"Frankfurter Allgemeine Zeitung"* of 25 November 1995, with Milosevic being compared with the manners of a gentlemanly Clark Gable in the movie "Gone with the Wind."

[668] Laura Silber: *"The Hero of Dayton,"* in *"World Policy Journal,"* 1996. Silber further in the article asked a suprising question: *"..How is it possible that the man who for years treaded upon countless victims and brought so much suffering to innocent people recieved such a renaissance? ... How was it that President Bill Clinton, during the Ceremony of signing the agreement in Paris, shook the hand of the man, whom Eagelberger three years before portrayed as a war criminal? ..."*

Another "concession" made by Milosevic in Dayton was the one linked with the guarantees for an active implementation of the agreement with the international factor binding Belgrade with specific obligations, envisaging also an obligation for Belgrade to act against those who inhibited it therefore assuming a lot of hard work that could also lead to Serb-Serb confrontations and civil war, as had happened in the past.

The most problematic point for Bosnian Serbs and Belgrade in general, which was feared as turning into a blockade, was Milosevic's agreement at Dayton that allowed the stationing of NATO troops in the IFOR peace mission in the Republika Srpska.

"Something like that could hardly be contemplated until recently," the German diplomat and publicist Michel Thumann said.[669]

For Albanians Dayton and Milosevic's incredible metamorphosis from enemy number one to an even temporary "partner" of the Americans and "man of peace," had special meaning, because they would cope with almost brutal realities of the power of political pragmatism and games in the service of vested interests. And, it could be said that at present, Milosevic represented a very important interest not only for what was said above, but also for the possibility of other actions related to the restructuring of the regional plan and wider not only in circumstances of disintegration of the former Yugoslavia, but also other wider developments whose direction was determined by the Americans in accordance with their interests, which were also Western interests. And, if things were to be viewed from a static perspective, the Albanians would have more reason to remain depressed and even disappointed, because by not including Kosova in the Dayton agreements reached on Bosnia and Herzegovina and between Croatia and Serbia, in which Croats restored full sovereignty of the country without being obliged to pay any price that would ever jeopardize it (eventual Serbian autonomies) it seemed as if the

---

The question of resposnibility for the war crimes that Milosevic, the "hero" of Dayton, had to face was also raised by the well-known German journalist Karl Gustav Strohm in the newspaper "Die Welt" of 23 November 1995. Strohm said on the occasion that "in politics justice was not worth, but interest."

[669] See "Der unfallendete Triumph des Nationalstates – Bosniens Weg zum Abkommen von Deyton," in Deutsche Aussenpolitik,1998, p. 28.

Balkan "peace" framework was closed, leaving their interests sideways, or as an internal issue of Serbia, as "*Die Welt*" assessed.[670]

From a dynamic standpoint – and dynamic certainly is a virtue of American politics to never be pleased with what has been achieved – there was no reason to consider the Dayton Accords as key to sealing the fate of Kosova under Serbia. Rather, the fact that the Kosova issue was not addressed in Dayton spoke in favor of the fact that Kosova's sidelining from the Dayton Conference had left the Kosova issue open with many bonds, which, as will be seen shortly, would turn to conditions moving it from a standing position to an important issue.

The professor of International Law at the University of Cologne, Georg Brunner, clarified this with professional competence in accordance with international law, noting that "not mentioning Kosova in Dayton and its absence in any of the agreements did not eliminate it as an issue. Instead, its lack of treatment made it impossible to be seen as a concluded matter. Only if it were addressed with a concrete outcome and decision, in this case in accordance with Serbia's demand to be emphasized as its integral part, then it would have the power of decision."[671]

Viktor Meier too estimated that the exclusion of Kosova in Dayton might have caused justified concerns among Albanians, but it did not represent an encumbrance to Kosova, as seen by many in those moments, as evidently the proper dealing with the resolution of the crisis of the former Yugoslavia had just begun and a lot remained to be done for it to take an outcome in accordance with its seriousness. It would have been a true impediment if it were to be addressed and defined as an inalienable part of Serbia.[672]

The author continued by saying he would like to see the issue of Kosova in Dayton and that would be possible only if Kosova had a previous status of a republic by the 1974 Constitution, but not as a relevance of "account settling" as it was intended with Knin Krajina and Slavonia, which were removed from the agenda since early August and recovered by the Croatian Army thus ceasing any need of Kosova's analogy with the Krajina Serbs in Croatia.

---

[670] "*Die Welt*," 23 November 1995.

[671] "*Ekskluzive*," 3/2000.

[672] Buxhovi, Jusuf: "Kthesa historike – shteti paralel dhe rezistenca e armatosur," Prishtina, 2009, pp. 291-299.

Horst Wesseler, political scientist and publicist, being associated with Dayton and its outcome, said that the United States of America had achieved some important results at Dayton, but that they would not stop at that. Why they made Milosevic a leader, and why they put a "peace aureole" over him did not mean anything. They used him for their own ends and would continue to do so, but now even with more pressure on getting Serbia out of Kosova.[673]

Emphasizing the issue of taking Serbia out of Kosova instead of taking Kosova out of Serbia, which Wesseler mentioned and conjured up as a hypothesis with increasingly political connotations and soon to turn by the Secretary of State Albright into a diplomatic reference after she stated that "taking Serbia out of Kosova is the main condition for peace," and into a pragmatic formula of settling the Kosova issue, which would start to be used more openly by the U.S. Administration strategy after Dayton with the slogan "Serbia out of Kosova" gaining connotations of liberation from Serbian occupation, which would not be able to hide behind the diversity of political language used in this case. Opponents of the independent state of Kosova would take note of this very well, and would rather willingly accept a syntagma of "violent secession of Kosova from Serbia," as it would be used by Belgrade, Moscow and Athens, as by doing so they would call upon the right to protection of international law and sovereignty of the state, "maintaining the right to its return" at some point in time, as something that was allegedly taken away from the Serbs by force.

But, Dayton's history, no matter what had happened there and regardless of the speculation about the exclusion of Kosova, closed one chapter, that of the behavior of Albanians in accordance with certain realities, whose main result, in addition to creating state-building infrastructure and its legitimacy in a period of two years (Constitutional Declaration of July 2, Kaçanik Assembly and declaration of the Republic of Kosova, Referendum on Independence and finally parliamentary elections of April 1992), was to avoid any conflict with Serbia, which would lead to a war with far reaching consequences for Albanians. Obviously, the option for civil resistance with the parallel state, despite its accompanying weaknesses, and the fall in the quality of life at all levels, played a very important role in maintaining the image of Kosova in all

---

[673] Conversation at *"Westdeutsche Rundfunk,"* Cologne, 21 December 1995.

areas of life, and as such, represented an unquestionable success, with countless criticism and objections, but not of a conceptual nature.

Time showed that the organization of Albanians until Dayton was of a civilized and state-building culture unprecedented for this people, of which in confrontation with similar crises had often turned to chaos orchestrated by their opponents. This time Albanians were acting in accordance with their political program implementing their declared state, regardless of the serious challenges they faced in circumstances of occupation, showing everything in a different light from that of more than a century of Belgrade and Russian-Orthodox propaganda continuing since the Eastern Crisis and beyond.

Thus, the civil-institutional resistance of Kosova Albanians with parallel state would become a new emblem marker for them, identifying them everywhere as something that connects with peace, patience and Western civilization, with its antipode of Serbian violence installed by a strong police and military apparatus acting to destroy their very being, which in turn would justify Albanians' right to self-defense by all means, including armed resistance.

CHAPTER 4
FROM DAYTON TO RAMBOUILLET

The Albanian Concern and American Pledge

Americans continue demanding Dr. Rugova follow the civil-institutional resistance, and Belgrade was receiving the first gifts from the Europeans for its cooperation with the West, while Washington conditioned the removal of the so-called outer wall of sanctions for Belgrade with "progress" in Kosova. – The U.S. Congress demanded for the first time an international protectorate for Kosova, while in March 1996, Senator Robert Dole came up again in the Senate and the House with a resolution on the Kosova issue to be resolved before sanctions were lifted from Serbia. It said that Serbia could not return to the international community before it solved the Kosova issue in accordance with the political will of the people of Kosova. The resolution also demanded the U.S. President to appoint a special envoy to deal with the issue of Kosova and its resolution. – A letter from the Secretary of State, Madeleine Albright to Dr. Rugova, among other things, stated that "genuine steps for improvements in Kosova remain the foundation of the American policy."

The Dayton conference had justly disturbed Albanians for being overlooked (even though it soon would be understood that it had focused on peace in Bosnia and Croatia), but rather because that was where the source for the change of attitude towards their adversary who had triggered the crisis in the former Yugoslavia holding hostage for years the entire region and challenging the human consciousness with crimes committed in Bosnia and Herzegovina reaching genocidal proportions, and was now turning the clock to become an American partner. At the signing ceremony in Paris, Milosevic not only was in the spotlight, but in addition he received congrats and toasts were raised in his honor from the greatest statesmen of the world, including Bill Clinton and other European leaders.

The "friendly" mood of Paris and all that had happened in the wake of the "celebrations" of peace and its "heroes," as that which happened in Belgrade on the occasion of Milosevic's return, served for spurring of a very tough campaign in Prishtina and Tirana against the civil-institutional resistance and parallel state.

Dr. Ibrahim Rugova would be targeted among the main causes of what had been called "an Albanian tragedy."

Thus, Dayton had served well the opening of inter-Albanian fronts, that rather than estimating in the best possible way what was going on and what it indeed represented within the complexity of the regional crisis and the like, followed by analyses in finding a common way on how to act in the new circumstances with a decision of whether to give up the civil resistance course and the functioning of the parallel state to be done after sounding the alarm that it all had been "lost years," and that someone had to be held accountable for it.

Thanks to Dayton profiling Kosova to one day be taken up at Rambouillet turning into a global concern – was being used more for an internal demolition than for further building around a major challenge that the Albanian world was facing demanding an approach of great responsibility.

Although Dayton had rightly brought the opening of the dilemma of civil resistance with the parallel state causing no international concern and no damage for Serbia could have been the cause for what was perceived as bypassing the Kosova issue and the like, still the parallel state would continue further as a preoccupation by most Albanians. Even though many of its supporters would seek investigating a possibility to increase its active component, this would however be required according to circumstances and developments and under the guidance and supervision of the institutions of the Republic of Kosova, which had established the Ministry of Defense and that of the Interior, whose potential had to be activated for this purpose.

The U.S. ambassador in Belgrade, Perrina, visited Dr. Rugova after he had just returned from a several-day visit to Germany, Belgium and Italy during the work of the Dayton Conference. On the occasion, he informed him on the U.S. positions, namely that nothing had changed in relation to

Kosova. The U.S. Ambassador assured President Rugova that the United States of America would further engage on the issue of Kosova and in no variation would it be forgotten or became a coin for settling accounts for other interests.

Evidently, as soon as the euphoria of the Dayton accords celebrations ended, the U.S. administration did not join in the European position to automatically reward Belgrade for its cooperation in Dayton, by lifting sanctions, to return to international institutions, credits granted and internationally recognized, as the Belgrade media had been saying out aloud, including some European media mostly French. The United States of America had been linking their *"outer wall of sanctions"* policy toward the remaining Yugoslavia "with progress in Kosova." In the UN Security Council, the USA, in principle, would agree, for a completely different behavior towards Belgrade, but their veto prevented an automatic admission of the Federal Republic of Yugoslavia in the world body, as it also prevented its admission to the OSCE, IMF, and other international mechanisms. Kosova once again turned into a condition for Belgrade's further steps on what Washington would call "progress towards its resolution."

But what, in fact, represented the American slogan of *"progress"* that was being put to Belgrade before any decision?

Was it a means for political pressure on Milosevic to move "slightly" in terms of what could be called an improvement of human rights standards? Or, was it an indication of the measured steps by Americans, under the disguise of international standards for a fundamental change of attitude towards Albanians, which included all the issues related to its status and all civilized standards, whose range was very wide and often depended on their performance, which was part of the right to self-determination and the like, which Serbia had violated a long time ago and never intended to honor for the simple reason that, as Dobrica Cosic said in Washington in April 1990 at the meeting with Robert Dole and Dr. Rugova, "they were unacceptable for Serbs, as through them the national and state identity would be lost against a biological expansion of Albanians"?[674]

---

[674] Buxhovi, Jusuf: *"Kthesa historike: Vitet e Gjermanisë dhe epoka e LDK-së,"* Prishtina, 2008, p. 274.

The American behavior and Washington's administration position from Dayton to Rambouillet would show that the "progress" condition was what raised the Kosova problem to the level of Belgrade's unsolvable issue which would grab the Milosevic regime by its neck and which would evidently and ultimately strangle it.

If attention was paid to further U.S. steps and their behavior in accordance with their *"progress"* refrain on the issue of Kosova raised to both Belgrade and the international community, especially to Europeans, who behaved as if they had lost their memory, they certainly started from the U.S. Congress (House of Representatives and Senate). Then they passed over as stances to the U.S. administration thus marking the first and full reconciliation in the relations between the U.S. administration and representatives of the House since early nineties. Thus, the problem of Kosova, occasionally, with other resolutions and amendments, would reach both the Senate and the House but they would never become legally binding, because of lack of a unique landscape of reconciliation between the legislative and executive branches.

Given the obvious American pragmatism in Dayton, Congressman Eliot Engel and others, on the eve of Dayton introduced a Congressional resolution on Kosova which was accepted by a majority vote. This resolution appeared as a package, which had to be fully implemented or else Kosova had to be placed under an international protectorate.[675]

Belgrade had to be priorly conditioned by the following:

- *A special identity for Kosova should be implemented and its citizens should have a guaranteed right to self-governance;*

- *The elected government of Kosova should be permitted to meet and exercise its legitimate mandate as elected representatives of the people of Kosova.*[676]

Following the conclusion of Dayton and history of its accords, which in the American public and politics in general were seen with a critical eye due to the fact that the logic of interim solutions prevailed while the cause of the problem and the Balkan tragedy had turned into a partner for the West, in March 1996, Senator Robert Dole appeared again in the Senate and in the House with a resolution on the Kosova issue that had to be

---

[675] House Resolution no. 1868, 7 November 1995.
[676] *Ibid.*

resolved before Serbia had its sanctions lifted. It said that Serbia could not resume its place in the international community before settling the Kosova issue in accordance with the political will of the people of Kosova. The Resolution stated the following:

- The United States should support the legitimate claims of the people of Kosova to determine their own political future;

- The President should appoint a special envoy to aid in negotiating a resolution to the crisis in Kosova

- Reaching peace in the Balkans should be conditioned by finding a solution for the Kosova status.[677]

Adding the letter of the U.S. Secretary of State Madeleine Albright sent to Dr. Rugova stating that "genuine steps for *improvements* in Kosova remains the basis of the U.S. policy,"[678] it is clear that the U.S. conditioning did not represent any kind of maneuver, but rather a substantive determination, which would be both operational and clarifying for Belgrade – that with Dayton the chapter of the crisis in the former Yugoslavia was not closed but it rather just opened – and for the European partners, who perhaps would like to forget Kosova and its issue in Serbia.

This condition was accepted by Germany, but not by some other European countries, as Paris would be the one who would ask the West to respond to Belgrade's "cooperativeness" by lifting sanctions and granting multiple loans for "Serbia to become part of Europe."[679]

The German Foreign Minister was involved in the Council of Europe to convince the Europeans to accept the American line. He proposed an amendment by which Serbia's accession was conditional upon the resolution of the Kosova issue in accordance with the democratic rights of its citizens, but did not win a majority of votes, as many European countries already had submitted to the stand of Paris supported by Rome, Athens, and also London, "to comply with the Serbs," even though it was clear that

---

[677] Senate Concurrent Resolution 50,104 Congress 2nd session, 28 March 1996.

[678] "*Kosova Daily Report,*" 1153.

[679] See articles by the German Foreign Minister Klaus Kinkel for "*Frankfurter Allgemeine Zeitung*" of 13 and 18 December 1995, where he raises the issue of the Europeans' stance towards Belgrade. Minister Kinkel warns against Milosevic's treatment as an uncontested partner, as Paris requested, as this would discredit the European politics, with Europeans still remembering his criminal past in Bosnia and Herzegovina and Croatia with the big wound of Srebrenica touching upon the human conscience.

Belgrade had not changed course, but rather hoped that through political and diplomatic makeup it could still remain an important regional factor.[680]

The German failure at the Council of Europe in accepting the American condition would have consequences in Bonn. The German government, not wanting to come to a similar situation as that of 1991 when the recognition of Croatia and Slovenia became subject to European dictates not willingly and not without difficulties, because in a cabinet meeting of Kohl's Government, it barely passed a vote of confidence. Kinkel and liberal ministers voted against and one minister from the party of Chancellor Kohl abstained.

A narrow decision to accept Belgrade affected the German Government not to remain equally loyal to Kosova's European line approaching the American one, although from the outside it did not appear so. Rather, even after accepting the Republic of Yugoslavia as a state on April 17, 1996, the German Government would not open its purse for the financial aid to Belgrade as expected. Moreover, Germany would not open its purse even when Klaus Kinkel visited Belgrade a month later and met with Milosevic, as the agreement between Milosevic and Kinkel on the return of about one hundred thousand Albanian asylum seekers who for years had taken refuge in Germany represented more than another attempt for a Serbian trick to make money before accepting Albanian refugees, who would again be expelled to Germany.

The Emergence of the Kosova Liberation Army

The assassinations against Serbian forces and the Kosova Liberation Army taking responsibility. – The beginnings of potential military activation of Kosova for resuming an armed resistance. – Presentation of the Kosova Liberation Army, based on the existing resources of the previous local resistance acting in the framework of the parallel state infuses the dynamic of Kosova's introduction into the international agenda. – The truth about the Armed Forces of the Republic of Kosova (FARK) and relations with the Kosova Liberation Army during the Dukagjin fighting in the summer of 1998 and other issues turning into

---

[680] *"Frankfurter Allgemeine Zeitung,"* 13 May 1996.

difficulties for the armed resistance. – Why there was no reconciliation of stances between the Government of Kosova and the KLA on a joint war and why the Oslo agreement failed.

The recognition of the Federal Republic of Yugoslavia by the European Union countries and the beginnings of communication with the Belgrade Government as if nothing had happened during the past five years, although not upsetting the concept of the parallel state in Kosova, it continued to function in accordance with the determination of the state of Kosova and was built from the inside despite the difficulties it faced and despite being ignored from the outside, still brought out signs of active opposition. They were reflected in guerrilla actions against Serb police and military forces in various parts of Kosova, which in "light" forms had been present earlier but without a clear "address," giving rise to different interpretations, even though they were an indivisible part of state-building capacities of the parallel state, regardless of the degree of organization and supervision over them. In January 1996, the first communiqué was sent from Geneva to the global media, in which the Kosova Liberation Army took responsibility for a guerrilla attack against Serb forces.

Soon the world media spread the alarm that the Kosova Albanians began to line up in guerrilla units. Even some actions carried out from 1992 onwards in various parts of Kosova against Serbian forces were attributed to illegal organizations, as various tracts issued by illegal organizations had been warning for a long time.

Indeed, speculations about guerrilla groups and actions from different centers and without a common "roof" and not without abhorrence of being "conducted from foreign services seeking to destabilize Kosova" and the like were responded to and blocked by the *People's Movement of Kosova* (LPK) based in Switzerland and Germany, informing about the actions of the illegal groups from a "paternalistic" perspective. Its temporary outlet *"Voice of Kosova"* informed that the Kosova Liberation Army already existed for a long time and that it was at the stage of expansion to all parts of Kosova, fighting against the Serbian invaders and occupation forces, whose goal was not only the liberation of Kosova, but also the unification of all Albanian territories.[681]

---

[681] Küntzel, Matthias: *"Der Weg in den Krieg,"* Berlin, 2000, pp. 39-59.

Under this pretense, the *People's Movement of Kosova* in Switzerland and Germany established the fund *"Fatherland is Calling,"* which although justified even though it was dedicated to funding the war in Kosova initially missed all the support, as LPK was regarded as a leftist movement with many factions and early links with the regime of Enver Hoxha, while the "three percent" fund already existed by the Government, which during its harvest mentioned a part of the fund dedicated to defense matters.

However, the money began to pour in after the first appearance of the public communiqués in January and May 1996, whereby the Kosova Liberation Army took responsibility for attacks against Serbian forces. The *People's Movement of Kosova*, which in Germany and Switzerland took over the role of a spokesman for the Kosova Liberation Army even claiming itself as its founder, attributing to itself all such actions that occurred in Kosova from 1991 onwards.[682]This position eventually was not accepted en bloc in certain zones of operation in Kosova, especially from that of Llap, whose fighters looked at the KLA as an authentic movement of armed resistance born under the concept of state building

---

[682] The establishment of the Kosovo Liberation Army, in the form it would be recognized since its public appearance in November 1997 onwards represented difficulties for the researchers of history, hampered by a lack of authentic documents and materials over organizational structures, which even today are missing in the respective archives in Prishtina, Tirana and elsewhere. Although public presentations by various persons have not been lacking, claiming to have participated in the KLA leadership structures or cells, with multiple "monographs" and editorials, often conflicting with each other, however they were insufficient to prove an objective and complete truth over the armed resistance, consisting of a wide range of activists and groups previously engaged in the overall nationwide movement led by LDK in 1989 and the formation of the Government of Kosovo in 1992, acting in its ranks, with many included in the LDK leadership structures and in the parallel state from the beginning until spring 1998, when some of them publicly joined the KLA leadership. Of this same nature was also information about the command structure from those focusing Adem Jashari as "Legendary Commander," to others "revealing" the structure of Adem Jashari's descendants after his fall in March 1998, where as commanders of the Liberation Army General Staff are mentioned: Azem Syla, Sylejman Seilimi, and lastly General Agim Ceku. The latter was recognized in relation to the international factor for war operations on the eve and during the NATO bombing from 24 March to 10 June 1999.

and the parallel state, where they had worked and had served since its establishment.[683]

All the potential of the armed resistance movement came from the parallel state and local structures that had acted similarly in the past, but its form had become controversial, i.e. activation and down streaming towards the war and its politics. These issues did not prevent the intensification of collecting funds for the war with lots of success, but simultaneously, this activity was echoed in the press and foreign media, paying great attention to the KLA factor and its role in the internationalization of the Kosova issue.[684] Thus, through public booths of the fund *"Fatherland is Calling"* and its website, KLA was propagated as a Kosova army at war with the Serbian invaders. In addition, in its media and propaganda campaign carried out through refugee clubs and the public, with the same intensity, attacks against the Democratic League of Kosova and its leaders continued,[685] whereby its founders and leaders were being condemned as Serbia's collaborators and the like, not to mention the fact that the *People's Movement of Kosova* itself, since the establishment of the LDK, had been in good cooperation terms with it being for three years part of its collective membership. In this case many of its activists had participated

---

[683] From author's conversation with *Rrustem Mustafa – "Remi,"* Commander of the Llap Zone made in Prishtina, on 2 October 2011. General "Remi" admits he had been a member of LDK from its beginning and that he and his fellow fighters, a considerable part of whom came from the local structures of the parallel state, had been fighting for the ideal of the state of Kosovo.

[684] Among foreign authors offering a more comprehensive obesrvation of the KLA, however not without flaws because of lack of authentic and deserving documents the following should be mentioned: Mattias Rüb *"Phonix aus der Ache: Die UÇK – Von der Terroroganisation zur Bodentruppe der Nato?"* (Phoenix out of Ashes: KLA – from a terrorist organization to NATO's ground troops?), 1999, Tim Judah *„Kosovo. War and Revenge,"* New Haven, 2000, Henrry H. Perry *"Ushtria Çlirimtare e Kosovës – rrëfimi prej brenda da për një kryengritje,"* "Koha," Prishtinë, 2008, James Pettifer *"Ekspresi i Kosovës,"* Prishtina 2004, Mappes-Niedek: *"Ballkan-Mafia,"* Matthias Kunzyel *"Der Weg in den Krieg,"* Stephen Schwartz: *"Prejardhja e një lufte,"* Lipius, Stefan: *"Untergrundsogranisationen im Kosovo. Ein Uberblik,"* published in "Osterreichischer Militarrische Zeitschrift," 2/1977, pp. 177-178, Lipius, Stefan: *"Zwischen Fronten: Die Befraingsarmee Kosovas (UÇK),"* published in "Schweitzer Monats-hefte" 5/1999, pp. 9-11.

[685] See articles of *"Zëri i Kosovës"* from the 1997-1999 period.

actively in the branches and sub-branches of the Democratic League of Kosova contributing a lot by setting up local governances as nucleuses of the future parallel state for which they worked with great dedication.[686]

But, even despite these divisions and rivalries as to who was "peaceful" and who was a "fighter", collecting funds upon such attributes, the situation was clear by November 28, 1997 when at the funeral of the teacher Halit Geci in Llaushë of Drenica, killed by Serb occupation forces, in front of several thousands of people, a masked trio appeared reading a proclamation to the people,[687] the Kosova Liberation Army will become a reality in Kosova, appearing day by day on the foreground of the interest of the international factor, soon to become its partner.

Indeed, after the emergence of the Kosova Liberation Army it can be said that the armed resistance turned into a powerful tool of Albanian politics, exactly in line with the well-known definition of Klausevic that war is a continuation of politics by other means and that "other means," did not come out of the blue but rather as a result of a determination supported on the basis of institutional organization, i.e. parallel state and beyond. Various sources, however, suggest that there existed a resource organization "in two lines," at almost the same time, that is, by the beginning of 1992, and that those actions were brought within the framework designed by the relations of several conversations between President Rugova and President Ramiz Alia in 1991 and 1992, which had to do with the preparation of certain military resources of Kosova to Albania, to be used in appropriate circumstances. Similar conversations about certain agreements that were to be "parallel actions" dictated by the circumstances also took place with Sali Berisha and continued with Fatos Nano and Pandeli Majko, becoming in some cases even more concrete and direct even reaching the level of war.

In these forms of action, the "first line" was followed by the Government of the Republic of Kosova, obliged by the Kaçanik Constitution to lead the defense and self-defense conducting it according to the circumstances and political positions. The "second line" was followed by the *People's Movement of Kosova* based in Switzerland and Germany, which although claiming full primate in this regard, one should not forget

---

[686] See authentic materials from the LDK Fund from the 1989-1992 period in the Archive of the Institute of History in Prishtina, Box I-VI.

[687] The KLA Trio composed of Rexhep Selimi, Daut Haradinaj and Mujë Krasniqi.

authentic illegal groups and local organizations, born in Kosova and acting outside ideological connections with Tirana or other establishments abroad, such as the *National Movement for the Liberation of Kosova (LKCK)*, and especially activities of the "Llap Group" led by Zahir Pajaziti, once a known activist of the movement involved in the state building parallel state structures of Kosova, operating in and around Prishtina in 1996-1997, a path to be followed further in the Llap Operational Zone under the command of Rrustem Mustafa – "Remi."

Although both these "lines" shared Kosova's independence as their common goal, they did not appear equally with conceptual differences (since the state of Kosova being occupied by Serbia was not being disputed and that Serbia had to be fought until liberation) of a methodological nature, as to how and when to use the means of war. The Government of the Republic of Kosova was determined for an extensive preparation of a comprehensive nature of the potential military organization, to be held on the alert and act in accordance with political decisions of state structures, harmonizing with the international factor, especially the Americans as guarantor and principal defender of Albanians, while independent groups and the *People's Movement of Kosova,* were set in the form of guerrilla action, through actions and diversions against Serbian forces, which would be occasional and intensified in early 1996, namely after Dayton.

Soon after its formation, the Government of the Republic of Kosova, along with other ministries, announced also the establishment of the Ministry of Defense. Initially it focused on the effort to prevent Albanian recruits and officers serving at that time in the People's Army of Yugoslavia, in Croatia, Bosnia and Herzegovina, and Slovenia, from being included in the war against Croatia and Slovenia, but rather to either desert from the ranks of the Yugoslav Army or surrender to Croatian or Slovenian military forces, with officers having to decide for themselves whether they would be involved in wars, or would join the army reserve units of Kosova.

Regarding this sensitive issue with great interest over the course of armed resistance in Kosova, even before the Kosova Government was formed, in the spring of 1991, a meeting was held in Zagreb between Dr. Rugova and Tudjman to discuss decisions of mutual interest to be taken. Colonel Tom Berisha, who upon insistence from the Croatian leadership was elected chairman of the Democratic League of Kosova to Croatia which was later "transformed" into the Democratic League of Albanians in Croatia, detaching itself from its base in Prishtina, was authorized to maintain regular contacts with the Croatian Government in order to attend to Albanian deserting soldiers and officers in Croatia, considering the fact that thousands of young people and hundreds of officers who were suddenly caught between two different fronts and who needed help not to become victims of confusion and indetermination.

Once the Government of the Republic of Kosova was formed, the Ministry of Defense entered into several rather vague agreements with Croats about a military organization of Albanian military officers and their involvement within the military forces of the Ministry of Defense of the Republic of Kosova, without designating any particular form of organization, as the Government of Kosova lacked political stances of the kind that would follow later.[688]

However, the preliminary data from among the Yugoslav People's Army in Croatia indicated that there were over four thousand Albanian recruits and officers of low to higher ranks. In Slovenia there were 400 Albanian soldiers and 30 officers, while in Bosnia and Herzegovina about 3,000 Albanian soldiers and 80 officers. With the resumption of fighting in Croatia and Slovenia, a considerable number of Albanian soldiers surrendered to the territorial defense units in Croatia and Slovenia. Similarly, in Bosnia and Herzegovina, Albanian soldiers and officers joined either Bosnian units or Croatian ones in the Herzegovina area. In Croatia, such as in Gospic, Djakovo, Oguljin and other counties, Albanian soldiers along with officers crossed over to the ranks of the Croatian army fighting against Yugoslav forces.[689]

Pending for clear instructions from Kosova regarding decisions on military organization, a number of Albanian officers, among them Fehmi Lladrofci, Tomor Buza, Ramë Cërvadiku, Nexhat Neziri, Bekim Berisha, and others in addition to 49 Albanian soldiers formed an Albanian unit in Gospic as part of the Croatian Army Brigade 118 fighting with great success. Besides the wounded from this unit in the fighting in Croatia, Fadil Salihu and Sami Bogujevci were killed.[690]

Dozens others were killed in Croatia and Bosnia and in unclear circumstances in Bosnia and Herzegovina, in which several thousand

---

[688] See Fehmi Pushkolli's book, *"Tomë Berisha – jeta dhe vepra,"* Prishtina, 2005.
[689] *Ibid*, p. 216.
[690] *Ibid*, p. 217.

Albanian soldiers were included, sometimes willingly and sometimes in waiting for an Albanian army to be created, and sometimes even not knowing where to turn. However, even in those confusing circumstances there was thinking about the needs for organizing that Albanian military potential, which one day would represent the nucleus of the army of Kosova.

It seemed that circumstances for doing something in that fashion in Croatia were much better, not only because the majority of Albanian recruits and officers were focused there, but also because Croatia represented a node from where the Albanian units could be included in the fighting there, but also to prepare outside fighting activities with the best opportunity to more easily coordinate with other countries, as well as with Kosova through Albania. Communication with the diaspora from Croatia could also be easily established for the soldiers and their families. However, as will be seen, from both lack of sufficient commitment and mingling of "competences" and other interests, including implications by external factors wishing to see the Albanian military organization fail or hindered as much as possible, in order not to be able to react with war, the military forms of organization in Croatia and other parts faced problems, and mostly failed. Colonel Tom Berisha accused Bukoshi's Government of lack of seriousness in this matter, while Bukoshi's military advisers would raise serious charges against Colonel Berisha for allegedly entering into separate arrangements with Tudjman, using the Albanian soldiers for the purposes of the Croatian war.[691]

Additional research (after the opening of the military archives in Croatia, Slovenia, Bosnia and Herzegovina, those in Belgrade and in Western countries directly involved in the fighting in the former Yugoslavia) certainly threw a light on this unfortunate chapter in which the Albanian soldiers in Croatia and other parts of the former Yugoslavia were involved together with those who caused the situation. However, it must be said that, despite the difficulties that the largest part of the soldiers faced at the bulk of military organization and awaiting the call for an armed resistance in Kosova, many of them, after many difficulties and pitfalls through political floundering and divisions, eventually found the

---

[691] For more see Pushkolli, Fehmi: *"Tomë Berisha – jeta dhe vepra,"* Prishtina, 2005, pp. 206-207.

way to war in Kosova in order to contribute to it professionally to be successful against a well-prepared, well-armed enemy.

Varuous sources revealed that the Government of the Republic of Kosova was engaged in some other agreements with Albania for the preparation of certain military units in Kosova. Initially there were similar verbal agreements between Ramiz Alia and Rugova to open two military training camps in Labinot, where during 1991-92 there were over one hundred persons trained.[692] Two other training camps were opened in 1993 following an agreement between Berisha and Bukoshi.[693]

According to Government sources, its attention to defense issues focused not only on military outposts scattered across the north and those who had found refuge abroad, but also on the identification and care of military and police potential in Kosova, especially the one that had been involved in the territorial defense of Kosova. As circumstances in Kosova had been specific and every action in the field of defense and security was followed with great attention by Belgrade and its intelligence services, the Government recognized that these organizations were difficult to continue and were without any concrete effect. However, there was a stand not to activate the potential, keeping it rather on hold, in accordance with political attitudes and conditions. But Serbian intelligence services would sense the organization and by the end of 1993 and in early 1994 a large number of Albanian officers from the ranks of the Ministry of Defense of the Republic of Kosova, along with the former commander of Territorial Defense of Kosova, General Hajzer Hajzeri, were arrested. Three months after the arrest of Albanian officers, over one hundred and fifty officers from the ranks of the Albanian Ministry of Interior were imprisoned, sentenced with long prison terms.[694]

---

[692] *Ibid*, pp. 206-207. Colonel Tom Berisha says that under an agreement with Ramiz Alia to open military training camps in Burrel and Selisht and sending the first cadets there, among others were mentioned the names of Adem Jashari, Zahir Pajaziti and other fighters who later represented the core of the Kosovo Liberation Army. Additional sources confirm this, however excluding certain forms of organization called KLA. So, it refers to "unspecified" activities, in which, besides the Government of Kosovo, other political entities had an influence, among which stands out the *"People's Movement of Kosovo,"* as a promoter of organizing armed resistance out of the insitutional line.

[693] See Belgrade's *"Politika,"* 24 November 1991.

[694] See "Work Report of the Government of the Republic of Kosovo 1991-1999," presented to the Assembly of Kosovo in January 2000, pp. 12-20.

Arrests and continued persecution of Kosova police and military potential, as well as efforts to deprive "pending plans" to ever be activated, shows that the concept of civil resistance with the parallel state was not simply peaceful, as one hears being said. The fact that the Government of the Republic of Kosova had its Defense Ministry and the Ministry of the Interior from the beginning indicates that the defense and self-defense were part of the state definition.[695]

Critical research, however, must present the truth and how this activity of the Government of Kosova complied with the police and military potential of Kosova. How and to what degree was it put into operation in accordance with the needs and circumstances of the politics? Since it was known that the civil-institutional resistance in Kosova and its parallel system was continuously monitored by a part of the international community, especially the Americans, who from the beginning had been its supporters and backers having the main say in each line drawn by Albanians, one can certainly find here the explanation of the dilemma of what would be called politics without war, the same as the explanation for another dilemma, that of the fact that when an armed resistance began it was a war without politics.

However, these and similar dilemmas pertaining to long-term research having as a prerequisite the consideration of all relevant archival sources, so that one day, if not fully, then partially would be answered, do not deny the fact that in addition to the institutional concept of the preparation of an armed resistance and inadequate forms even at the level of planning and "waiting" being consistent with the existing potential and its activation, also an illegal organization existed. It involved various groups and units of patriots, acting independently, as was the case with the *Albanian Resistance Front* (FNSH), active from 1991 until the arrest of some of its members in 1993 by Yugoslav organs, and as was the case with other groups from 1994 onwards, such as the *Llap Movement*, which were rather authentic and within the concept of state-building, as were also other groups directed from abroad, mainly the *People's Movement of Kosova*. To this organizational form was attributed some of the attacks and guerrilla actions against Serbian forces from late 1992 until March

---

[695] See the composition of the Government of the Republic of Kosovo, in "*Akte të Kuvendit të Republikës së Kosovës*," a publication of the Academy of Sciences and Arts of Kosovo, 2004.

1996, when the Kosova Liberation Army would take responsibility for the first time for armed actions in order to appear in public on November 28, 1997, which made the Kosova Liberation Army in the Kosova war a factor, especially since spring of 1998, reorganized with external and internal forces by a wide spectrum of a nationwide resistance, engaged in wide scale fighting with Serbian military and police forces in various parts of Kosova.

At a time of intense fighting in various parts of Kosova, alongside the Kosova Liberation Army that was largely under the aegis of the People's Movement of Kosova and the organizational structure imposed by it (its General Staff, Political Directorate, and War Operation Zones),[696] the *armed resistance* factor was joined by the formations of the *Armed Forces of the Republic of Kosova* (FARK), which were involved in fighting at Loxha and parts of Dukagjin during the summer of 1998 when after a defeat by the Yugoslav army offensive and disputes with local Kosova Liberation Army units in the Dukagjin area, were withdrawn to Albania, as were a good part of the KLA units, to return back on the eve of the NATO air campaign in March 1999 against the Yugoslav forces.[697]

However, the emergence of "parallel actions" in the 1998 fighting in Dukagjin and troubles facing the armed resistance rightly opened the dilemma as to who benefited from the mess, as it was the Albanian cause that was being harmed the most.

General Bukoshi says it was natural that in certain circumstances, after learning the lesson from Dayton, the Government of the Republic of

---

[696] According to reliable sources on the commanding core of the Kosovo Liberation Army, from its first public appearance on 28 November 1997 in Llaushë of Drenica, the General Staff Commander was initially Adem Jashari. After his fall in March 1998, the position went to Azem Syla, Sulejman Selmi and finally to General Agim Çeku and to the organizational strcutures to the following military operative zones (of Dukagjin, Pashtrik, Drenica, Llap, Shala, Nerodima, and Karadak, with commanders Ramush Haradinaj, Sami Lushtaku, Muharrem Mustafa "Remi," Rrahman Rama, Tahir Sinani, Shukri Buja and Ahmet Isufin. In the final stage, along these structures, KLA also had its Political Directorate, led by Hashim Thaci, who turned into its leading political figure. Adem Demaci was appointed the first political representative of the KLA, performing his duty until the signing of the Rambouillet agreements, to which he would not agree. The KLA spokesperson Jakup Krasniqi, a longtime collaborator of Dr. Rugova and parallel state structures which he left in February 1998, following splits at the LDK Assembly.
[697] See Bardh Hamzaj's book *"Paqja e gjeneralit,"* "Zëri," Prishtina, 2001

Kosova acted towards galvanization of the Kosova issue through "moderate" activation of armed resistance, that being its constitutional obligation,[698] while representatives of the People's Movement of Kosova assess that Rugova's and Bukoshi's calculations with their fraudulent parallel state were those that helped most the de-factorizing of the Kosova issue as to be quite ignored in Dayton, and this made engaging in the war a necessity.[699]

Although it could be said that there was something of both, time will one day respond to these actions, especially as diplomatic, political and foreign service archives involved in the overall crisis in the former Yugoslavia open. But this cannot deny the truth that even as such, the armed resistance and the war in Kosova existed and worked, despite the difficulties and other problems regardless of differences in the views and biases. Thus, Ramush Haradinaj, one of the important actors of armed resistance, Commander of the Dukagjin Operational Zone, speaks of a joint fight with units of Tahir Zemaj and good relations with his fighters, who had been mostly professional soldiers, but at the same time speaks of the difficulties that had emerged from "parallel" commands.[700]

Similarly, this would be confirmed by Tahir Zemaj as well in his memoirs about the war in his capacity as FARK Commander of the Dukagjin Zone highlighting the fact that the armed resistance of Albanians suffered internal clashes due to "different courses" between the institutional line and the one opposing it,[701] even though these "courses"

---

[698] Author's conversation with Dr. Bujar Bukoshi on 13 March 2009 in Prishtina.

[699] See "Zëri i Kosovës," June 1998.

[700] See: "Paqja e gjeneralit," Prishtina, 2001, p. 31.

[701] Mehmeti, Arbër/Krasniqi, Sefer: "Kështu foli Tahir Zemaj," Prishtina 2001. The commander of FARK troops in the Dukagjin Zone, Colonel Zemaj talked about the military operations of the Armed Forces of the Republic of Kosovo in the summer of 1998 in Dukagjin and about the joint fighting with the units of the Kosovo Liberation Army in Dukagjin. Colonel Zemaj points out the contribution of the units under his command, such as Brigade 134, in the battle of Loxha and in Koshare, able to win over being led by Albanian military officers and professionals who were able to come out victorious over the Yugoslav army stationed on the outskirts of Peja. Colonel Zemaj's claim is confirmed in the Work Report of the Republic of Kosovo1991-1999 presented to the Kosovo Assembly in January 2000, in regard to the participation of FARK units in the armed resistance against the Serb police and military forces in the 1998 summer offensive and later, especially in the Koshare Battle in May 1999, as due to the fighting of

rose from and reclined on an authentic local factor, which did not see the armed resistance as an issue of "prestige" but rather as a patriotic duty in the service of Kosova's state-building service, who had served within the system and the parallel state and had to also provide further services toward achieving this goal.

This reality, which cannot be overlooked, however, does not negate the fact that its consequence was the failure to fulfill the constitutional obligation of the Government of the Republic of Kosova and President Dr. Ibrahim Rugova, who by the Kaçanik Constitution were called to take over the organization and running of the armed resistance and the war, especially since they were for years in possession of an overall police and military potential of Kosova under the care of the Ministry of Defense and that of the Interior. Displaying Dr. Rugova as commander of the armed forces of Kosova in an operational zone, as was the request made by the Llap Operation Zone, would eliminate the difficulties, but the divisions and problems arising inside the Albanian resistance front would have serious consequences for the Kosova issue.[702]

Despite these divisions that could not have existed if the war was addressed on an institutional basis and in accordance with the Kaçanik Constitution, after the joint defeat in Dukagjin during the summer offensive by the Yugoslav military and police forces and the withdrawal of FARK military and officers to Albania, the war factor, at least until the eve of the start of the NATO air intervention against Yugoslav forces in Kosova and Serbia, though weakened, remained entirely in the hands of the Kosova Liberation Army and this would have consequences for the further consolidation of resistance. Because, after the assassination of Colonel Ahmet Krasniqi, Minister of Defense of the Republic of Kosova,

---

Brigade 131 and 134, led by commanders Rrustem Berisha, Agim Ramadani, Fadil Hadërgjonaj, Sali Çeku and other fighters, the Albanian-Kosovo border was run down. (See, Report, pp. 12-14).

[702] From author's conversation with the Commander of the Llap Operative Zone, Rrustem Mustafa -"Remi" in Prishtina, on 2 October 2011. On this occasion, Commander Remi ascertained that in the begining of 1998 he had sent a request to Dr. Ibrahim Rugova to cross over to the Operative Zone of Llap and from there led the state Presidency. Commander "Remi" said he sent the same request to Bujar Bukoshi, so that he and his ministers would be transferred to the zone enjoying the full protection of his fighters.

in Tirana, "duels" for the war and "entitlement" to its leadership were transferred on a political level. In these circumstances, as the Kosova Liberation Army would become independent of any institutional influence, claiming to remain the only determining factor not only in the military sphere but also in the political one, financial assistance would be required from Bukoshi for armaments, on the grounds that the "three percent" was a contribution for war provided by all Albanians. In Tirana and abroad several meetings between Bukoshi and representatives of the Kosova Liberation Army took place, to discuss this and other issues affecting a broad spectrum of organized armed resistance, but without success, although there were attempts for joint military action using the entire Albanian professional potential.[703] Bukoshi, on the other hand, still did not give up the idea of a combined and joint command by military professionals, although it was clear that the institutionalists, by their own fault (for failing to act in accordance with the Constitution of the Republic of Kosova and commitments arising from it), were losing "the battle for war."[704]

Many sources, however, suggest that the conflict among the Albanian military factor was actually rooted in different political concepts: on the one hand that of the LDK, on the parallel state and civil resistance, which enjoyed the support of the majority of Kosova's population, and on the other hand, that of the *People's Movement of Kosova*, which even after a "temporary accommodation" within the nationwide movement led by the Democratic League of Kosova (from 1990 to 1993 as its collective member), propagated an active opposition including armed resistance against Serbian invaders. This position continued from the beginning of war in the former Yugoslavia, but with the fall of the Berisha Government in 1987 and the arrival of the Socialists in the government led by Fatos Nano, with whom they shared ideological ties for a long time, would gain the space and support of the Albanian Government, which would take their side against Dr. Ibrahim Rugova and the parallel state.[705]

Such political delimitations would not spare the war factor, especially in the most critical phase, when the focus had to be on issues of war and armed resistance common to everyone. Obviously, the all-popular move-

---

[703] From author's conversation with Dr. Bujar Bukoshi, Prishtina, 13 March 2009.
[704] *Ibid.*
[705] Baze, Mero *"Shqipëria dhe lufta në Kosovë,"* 1999, p. 115

ment led by the Democratic League of Kosova and its concept of state building were shared by everyone and everyone was involved in it without exception supporting the concept of civil resistance in the parallel state until a part of them later committed themselves to active forms of resistance, leading to that of war. Many of them filled the ranks of the Kosova Liberation Army, managing to become leaders of Operating Zones, such as Commander "Remi" – Rrustem Mustafa in the Llap Operational Zone and Ahmet Isufi, Commander of the Karadak Operative Zone as well as numerous other pious warriors, who shed their blood for Kosova, who came from among the ranks of the Democratic League of Kosova and state-building movement, led by it and involved in the parallel state structures since their establishment.

It had already been known that the armed resistance and its manifestation represented a crucial chapter in the dynamism of the Kosova issue, carrying it onto international concern, as a matter of emergency. Likely, the direct contribution of the Kosova Liberation Army in the emergence and growth of the armed resistance even before it came into the open in Drenica had also been known. However, it must be said that this growth was mainly based on the massive resources of a past organization in the parallel state and its local structures, which even so, in many parts of the country, especially where Serbian terror was more severe, was in a stage of passing from civil resistance to an armed one. With uncertainty, however, was the joining in the resistance on this front of the Armed Forces of the Republic of Kosova (FARK), by the spring of 1998 and the fighting that took place in Dukagjin and that, jointly or separately, appeared also on the same course during the NATO air military operations from March 24 to June 10, 1999. In some documents FARK had been displayed as a "a joint factor" of the resistance, somewhere even as the "Kosova Liberation Army," especially when brigades 123, 131, and 134 were mentioned with their big role in breaking the Albania-Kosova border at Koshare in April 1999, while statements and opinions that excluded it entirely from the front of resistance, called it "an effort to disrupt the war".[706]

---

[706] See Bardh Hamzaj's book *"Paqja e Gjeneralit – dialog me Ramush Haradinaj,"* 2001, *"Kështu fliste Tahir Zemaj,"* Mero Baze *"Shqipëria dhe lufta në Kosovë,"*1999, Bedri Gashi *"Në altarin e lirisë,"* 2006, and see *"Work Report of the Government of the Republic of Kosovo 1991-1999."*

The mentioning of this fact and its disclosure is not intended to voice or reduce the size of the armed resistance on the basis of relations within its factors, which cannot be denied, or depreciated on the basis of the known divisions, that would probably have not surfaced if the Government of Kosova had activated all the internal resources in line with developments, without excluding the segment of an active resistance, which in certain circumstances, when deemed necessary, could go as far as the use of the means of war. Rather, the observation of armed resistance as a common purpose of state-building, with the participation of all patriotic layers of Albanians committed to giving their own lives on its altar, does not exclude noticing of weaknesses and flaws wherever they appear, the same as it cannot bypass highlighting of merits and successes, whenever evident as achievements in incredibly difficult circumstances. In this regard, however, the focus on a responsible factor, such as the Government of the Republic of Kosova, and its behavior in certain circumstances, is of particular importance as it had been mandated to act in accordance with the Kaçanik Constitution, where defense and self-defense were constitutional obligations, particularly given that the Government had its relevant ministries (of Defense and Interior) towards which it was supposed to exercise supervision and put them into action as necessary.

The facts, however, show that the Government of the Republic of Kosova in the field of defense and self-defense failed to perform well its constitutional obligation. Time will tell which were the factors that prevented this, but this would not alter the circumstances through which the armed resistance passed or difficulties it faced exactly as its institutional resources, both professional and patriotic, from among the ranks of the parallel state were not properly used when needed, with some of them being subject to organizations coming from different non-institutionalized clandestine clans, often ambiguous and suspicious even though the authenticity of local action was mainly preserved. What in the work reports of the Government of Kosova show as "necessary actions," such as the efforts of the great Albanian military potential from the ranks of the former Yugoslav Army was "held on the ready" abroad, mainly in Croatia, Slovenia and the West, could not justify weaknesses or delays towards the dynamics of the resistance with segments of active opposition leading to a response against Serb violence through violence, since it was known that self-defense was part of the resistance even if it were proclaimed civil.

However, evidently, after the appearance of the first proclamations of the Kosova Liberation Army, after taking the responsibility for actions against the police and military forces in Kosova in early 1996 and its public emergence in November the next year in Drenica, the Government of Kosova, which was late in this regard, moved quickly to engage in compliance with the best in armed resistance, the direction of which was already determined by the extra-institutional factor, the illegal movement headed by the *People's Movement of Kosova*, including other factors such as LKCK and other similar groups appearing as authentic in this complexity. So, on April 5, 1998, the Government of Kosova appointed as its Minister of Defense, Colonel Ahmet Krasniqi, who began gathering military officers and others to be involved in the war vortex.[707]

Here, in fact, would also appear what was called "rivalry" between the Kosova Liberation Army on one side and Kosova Armed Forces (FARK), on the other. It was transferred later to Kosova to be reflected with enough rigor in the diaspora, and especially in Albania, where the collapse of the Albanian state and the Socialists coming to power, the KLA was favored by Nano and his Socialist government. The latter had early ties with the *People's Movement of Kosova*, which declared itself openly as the founder of the Kosova Liberation Army, regardless of the fact that on its "basis" it sucked all the resources of the parallel state activists, who recently were determined to dynamize the movement through armed resistance, considering themselves constantly as its part and part of the state building and never as its opponents. In the meantime, the Government forces emerged in a "slippery" field, notably as the front space of the armed resistance seemed to be "monopolized" by the Kosova Liberation Army, and the Armed Forces of the Republic of Kosova made an effort to be part of it, either with an "institutional mandate," or with its advantage of professional military personnel and numerous tools at hand that could be materialized in its favor.

But it would soon be realized that the armed resistance would, more or less, be outlined on two parallel lines, reflected not only with separate

---

[707] See the material of the Government of the Republic of Kosovo, no. 5-4/2-98 classified "top secret" containing the Decree no. 3-98 appointing Colonel Ahmet Hajriz Krasniqi as Commander of the General Staff of the Armed Forces of the Republic of Kosovo. Komandant and General Staff FARK senior officers: First Class: Agim Ahmeti, Jahir Hyseni, Ismet Ibrahimi, Enver Basholli and Ahmet Kukolaj and Aviation Colonel Shaban Shkreli and Major Reserve Selim Rrahmanaj.

commands, but with the collection of war funds and their rivalry between the "Three Percent" of the Government of the Republic of Kosova and *"Motherland is Calling"* of the *People's Movement of Kosova,* divisions that, on a social and political plain, were likely to turn into disruption, which, with more or less vigor, continued during the war and even later with obvious consequences.

In these circumstances, it was necessary that at least some effort be made to find a common language, if not for anything, then in order to avoid the permanent threat of turning armed resistance against the invaders into an internal war among Albanians, considering certain indications in that direction, especially as Serbs wanted it to happen, including certain outside factors, having always invested in the Albanian splitting card to be used at critical moments.

Some of those who until recently had been in front of a joint civil-institutional resistance, realizing where "parallel weapons" and its consequences could lead, would agree on a joint meeting between those already profiled as factors of armed resistance. After talks between the Government of the Republic of Kosova and representatives of the Kosova Liberation Army held in Tirana, Prishtina and Germany and Switzerland, a deal was reached to organize a meeting at the highest level between representatives of the Ministry of Defense of the Republic of Kosova, headed by the Defense Minister, Colonel Ahmet Krasniqi, and Adem Demaçi as political representative of the Kosova Liberation Army. The meeting took place in May 1998 in Oslo, namely on "neutral ground" outside Albanian attention and defamation. Without going into details on what was discussed in Oslo, as it happened in such cases for the lack of written documents – and this is a big problem for historians – some kind of an agreement was reached on joint fighting, with a central leadership, composed of Albanian military experts already verified, where the officers would decide on both a general commander and command structures. Meanwhile, the financing of the armed resistance would be made from the funds of the Government of the Republic of Kosova, into which the *"Motherland is Calling"* fund would also be poured doing so in full transparency.

But, evidently, consents "in principle" in Oslo, called agreements on the main points, such as a joint command and operational plans, were not realized. Parallel actions continued, in both recruiting of volunteers to fight and during the preparation stage in Albania. However, based on various documents, it can be seen that between the Ministry of Defense of the Republic of Kosova and the General Staff of the Kosova Liberation Army, there were some points of cooperation in the field of supplying arms and dedicated war supplies. [708]

Certainly an objective drafting of the history of the armed resistance, with the crucial role of the Kosova Liberation Army, would in no way be able to bypass or minimize its "parallel lines," excreting out the real causes of such behavior and reasons as to who needed them.[709]

An Agreement on Education and the Challenge of Serbia's Democratzation

Why the decision-making international factor demanded that the Kosova Albanians should at all costs continue talks with Serbia to resolve the problems in Kosova, when they suited Milosevic and damaged the course of the Albanian civil resistance. – Was the agreement on education rather bait for Milosevic than for Rugova? – Berisha and Demaçi supported opposition protests in Serbia, while Rugova refused to take part in the so-called farce of Serbia's democratization, on which insisted the international community and especially the official Tirana.

---

[708] Based on the "Work Report of the Government of the Republic of Kosovo 1991-1999," presented to the Kosovo Assembly in January 2000, the Ministry of Defense was in possession of 22,964,000 DM and 896,890 Swiss Franks, with around 17 million DM used for purchasing weapons (with no details provided on the armament) a part of which realized through KLA. It continues that in 1999 the Ministry of Defense possessed close to 15 million DM and 100 thousand US dollars, spent on financing the war, with 3 million DM handed over to the General Staff of the Kosovo Liberation Army.

[709] On "parallel lines" of armed resistance and role of the KLA in the war, in addition to Ramush Haradinaj's stories (*"Paqja e Gjeneralit,"* a publication of "Zëri") and those of Tahir Zema (*"Kështu fliste Tahir Zemaj"*), see also the following publications: Krasniqi, Jakup: *"Kthesa e mdhe - Ushtria Çlirimtare e Kosovës,"* Prishtina, 2007; Baze, Mero: *"Shqipëria dhe lufta në Kosovë,"* Tirana, 1999; Lame, Kudisi: „*Kosova dhe Ushtria Çlirimtare e Kosovës"* 2005; Zhitia, Skënder: „*Ushtria Çlirimtare e Kosovës – Zona Operative e Llapit"* and *"Dëshmorët e UÇK-së – Zona Operative e Llapit,"* Gashi, Bahri: *"Në altarin e lirisë"* and Pushkolli, Fehmi: „*Tomë Berisha – jeta dhe vepra,"* Prishtina, 2005.

Before the Kosova Liberation Army turned into an insurmountable factor leading Kosova in the final stage developments and its crisis to an international level of an unchangeable agenda: from that of its treatment with crisis prevention means, as had been done until then, to a crisis solution through direct intervention, which would include NATO's military intervention, severing of relations at this stage between Albanians and Serbs became evident. The international factor, especially the Europeans, focused all their attention on the possibility of democratic changes in Serbia deemed possible after Dayton, since it was held that the great-Serbian hegemonic policy of Milosevic suffered a serious blow, and that this had affected Serbia towards an awakening coming forward with new realities. It was also believed that the Serbian opposition forces, despite the fact that Milosevic tried to turn his Dayton loss into a dividend for his treatment there as a partner of the West and a man of peace, would benefit, since Milosevic's tricks would not only be of no help to him, but this time rather would lower his prestige.

And, as it happened that the West set its traps against Milosevic in Bosnia and Herzegovina and Croatia before and during Dayton, regardless of the fact that they also damaged his victims, the same was done with the democratization plan for Serbia, whereby Kosova Albanians were required to participate, even without the Albanian consent. And not coincidentally, it would be Dr. Rugova, whom Dayton had badly damaged and was barely kept standing by his main supporters, Americans and Europeans, being at the same time dually challenged.

Thus, Dr. Rugova was first forced to accept the continuation of the normalization talks on education issues, although after two years of indecision in Geneva they ended without any success, possibly producing effects to suit Belgrade, while hurting the Albanians. And secondly, Dr. Rugova faced the pressure of postponing the second parliamentary elections in Kosova announced for spring 1996. Additionally, Albanians were required to participate in the Serbian elections on the grounds that "the democratization of Serbia would enable solving the Kosova issue"!

The first issue, namely education agreement to be signed on September 1 of that year between Milosevic and Dr. Rugova, first as President of Serbia and the second as an ordinary citizen of Kosova, was mediated by *Comunita di Sant Edigio* from Rome. Emphasizing Milosevic as President of Serbia and of Rugova without the designation of a President elected by the citizens of Kosova surely could have satisfied the proponents of the

Serbian President for as much as it could embolden Rugova's opponents to undertake a fresh campaign against him, as indeed happened. However, this optical trick was unable to lift the importance of truth that Serbia and the most senior representatives of the Serb state and Kosova signed for the first time an agreement that no matter how and how much it was applied bore mutual legitimacy.

It is interesting to note that the letter was not signed at the same time and in the same place by both. Milosevic signed it in Belgrade and Dr. Rugova in Prishtina without meeting at all. About the issue they had only one phone call. The Catholic community was well-known for international mediations. It had mediated in Mozambique and several other countries. As Milosevic wasn't willing to do anything to let the impression that Kosova was becoming more international, but also what was allowed there was a result of the "Serb goodwill" and humanitarian aspect, the Catholic Mission served as good cover to demonstrate humanity towards Albanian school children. In this case, the fact was being denied that discussions had been held for months with education experts from Prishtina and Belgrade attending, together with a few international consultants.

However, on a piece of paper it was written that it all was for the benefit of the Albanian students and that "it was a victory of civilization rather than of one over the other."[710] It further stated that implementation issues would be dealt with by a special working group, laying down all the details.

But, as expected, troubles appeared at the very beginning because of language differences of the text, affecting the content and opening other difficulties which made the failure appear as planned. Thus, in the Serbian language the text was about *"school children"* while in Albanian it was about *"school children and students"* and this was an important issue, because Albanians were seeking comprehensive solutions and not offline solutions or those in accordance with the minority standards. The agreement had no deadlines, so it could be a word on paper, and there were no other matters specified from those of funding teachers and professors, and no rules specifying the use of school premises, as it was known that Albanian education was attended for four years off school premises,

---

[710] Saint Ediggio's Document published by Max Weller *"The Crisis in Kosovo,"* 1999, p. 93.

which were occupied and adopted by Serbs, who led to believe they had no interest to bother themselves for Albanian children and the like.

Another difficulty, as usual, where swords mostly broke, was the curricula. There was no specification as to whether those of Kosova would be used, before 1989, i.e. before the suspension of autonomy. And, the most problematic issue of certificate seals, which had been a bone of contention during the Geneva talks three years earlier, announcing the failure of the talks, was not mentioned at all.

In all probability the deal was just a game of Milosevic tricking the international factor and nothing else, as time would tell. It took four months for only a few school buildings to be returned, and they too in an almost unusable condition. Releasing two faculty buildings, Technical and Economic, was followed by demonstrations of Serbian students and other educational personnel, who did not want their Albanian colleagues to study. With the exception of the opening of the Prishtina Institute of Albanology, other issues were hardly ever implemented. Even when the implementation agreement was signed on March 23, 1998, it was stained with blood, because in Drenica, the massacre against the Jashari family occurred and everything else in this regard represented nothing more than a fraud suiting Milosevic and Belgrade's policy alone while his war machinery was shedding blood trying, on the other hand, to leave the impression of a man of peace willing to broker a deal with those who accepted the deal, while using other means for those who did not want this.

Indeed, the education agreement, which brought Albanians anything but trouble, was very much needed by Milosevic, because by it he won the last points towards full abolition of sanctions, as soon would happen. It was also seen in the letters that Milosevic received with best wishes coming from various European centers, being praised and encouraged to continue "to follow the path of agreement with the Albanians," as "it was in the interest of peace and stability in the region"![711]

Americans were not excited by the signing of the agreement, knowing that it was its implementation that would show Milosevic's true intention and face. The U.S. administration, which repeatedly urged Dr. Rugova for dialogue with Belgrade, and as seen later, got him dipped into different

---

[711] See *"Kosova Daily Report,"* 967, 16 September 1996.

games,[712] such as his meeting with Milosevic in Belgrade on May 15, 1998, arranged at a time when the Pentagon had already initiated the procedure to have NATO prepare for possible military intervention against Serbia as a final means of pressure on Milosevic, expected concrete results from Belgrade to entirely change its position on Kosova and not through a selective problem solving strategy and in accordance with its interests, resolving the Kosova issue rather as a whole. Finally the issue of its status had to be touched, which until then was overlooked or ignored by the reasoning that "the issue in question was Serbia's internal affairs, which should be resolved by democratic means and in accordance with approved standards of human rights."

This attitude was clearly designed by Washington turning it into a determination, although for making it concrete it needed a few maneuvers in terms of both Belgrade and the European allies, who were not so interested in challenging Serbia further over Kosova, considering it could be a matter that should be left to Serbs and Albanians to settle between them, without caring that much that it was not being solved but rather kerosene being poured on the fire.

The other issue, too, that of the announced parliamentary elections in Kosova and their postponement, arguing that they should not obstruct the Serbian election announced for November of that year, turned Dr. Rugova into a victim of entrapment of democracy that the West used against Milosevic. Europeans asked Dr. Rugova to do two things at once: to postpone indefinitely the announced parliamentary elections in Kosova, the second in a row from 1992, and to participate in Serbian elections in the fall.

The latter was even urged by the Americans as well, who even though not equally assiduous as Europeans, did so on the grounds that the participation of Albanians in Serbia's elections, at least on the municipal level, would bring some benefits, such as winning over the local governance in Kosova and contributing greatly to Milosevic's loss of power and the opposition coming to power, finding it much easier to reach an agreement without excluding the possibility that peaceful democratic means could be used to realize historical aspirations.

---

[712] Rüb, Matthias "*Kosovo,*"1999, p. 64: "Rugova turned into a chess game piece that had nothing to do with Kosovo."

In accordance with this approach highlighted activities of the U.S. administration in terms of proximity with the Serbian opposition was noted, so that it could be helped as much as possible, even though Americans always had doubts on the course of the nationalist opposition leaders, Serbian from Kostunica, Djindjic, and Draskovic. This suspicion stemmed from the Vance and Owen plan for the peaceful resolution of the crisis of Bosnia and Herzegovina in 1993 when they encouraged Karadzic and Mladic to reject it, while Milosevic, even if by stealth, would do the opposite. However, in the new circumstances, first Colbroom and then Madeleine Albright received the Serbian opposition leaders in Washington (Djindjic, Kostunica, Pesic, and others), and promised U.S. support to Serbia's democratic course. Albright even reminded Serb opponents that Kosova and their position toward its solution represented the first and best test for the Serbian democracy.

Of course, Dr. Rugova categorically refused to participate in the Serbian elections on the grounds that Kosova Albanians from July 2, 1990 and September 7, 1990 had declared independence after a Referendum on Independence and had held their first elections, and that they intended to have their own independent elections that were consistent with the Kaçanik Constitution. He made it plain that those who thought that with Serbia's democratization the Serbian course towards Kosova could be changed were wrong. Rugova's statement that "the Serb opposition itself was more radical towards Kosova than Milosevic"[713]became known and quoted repeatedly by the European and world media upon the pressure exhorted on Albanians to attend Serb elections under the justification that "this represented a historic chance for them to solve their historical problems in a democratic Serbia."[714]

Analyst Matthias Rüb would go even further as to say that "it was Rugova's historic chance to topple Milosevic!"[715] even though the same author, a little later, when realizing the Serbian farce of democracy and what they produced, justified not only the refusal by Albanians of the Serbian elections, but also criticized the Western countries for their hypocritical behavior towards Rugova and his civil-institutional resistance movement with the parallel state. They praised while they needed to, but

---

[713] "*Süddeutsche Zeitung,*" 9 November 1996.

[714] "*Die Welt,*"17 March 1997.

[715] See "*Kosovo,*" 1999, p. 60.

rewarded it with nothing, while behaving with humility towards Milosevic and Serbia, ready to move on every alleged move towards alleged cooperation with the West, rewarding them for doing so with great noise.[716]

Dr. Rugova also received pressure to participate in Serbian elections from his natural ally Sali Berisha and opposition parties in Albania. Berisha was even louder to agitate that the "democratization of Serbia is in the interest of the Albanians and the entire region." Thus, between Rugova and Berisha not very cordial conversations took place, although at a rally in Tirana they came out together reading a statement welcoming any effort for democratization of Serbia.

It seemed that with the greeting of "democratization of Serbia" the extremes between Tirana and Prishtina would fade away, while the message would be twofold: that Albanians favored Serbia's democratization, but that it had to take place from inside, while the test of this democratization would be measured in relation to the Kosova issue and its resolution.

Obviously, the issue of "democratization of Serbia" continued to further divide both Rugova and Berisha, and Prishtina and Tirana in surfacing what has been called in the above as part of understandings and misunderstandings between Kosova and Albania. Berisha showed great solidarity with protests and demonstrations of the opposition bloc "Zajedno" that started in Belgrade and spread throughout Serbia against the voting fraud by Milosevic, but on the other hand would forget that Kosova had declared its own independent state, which the Albanian parliament through a statement, at least not officially, recognized, and it was pointless appealing to help the democratization of its invader in that way!

Thus, the solidarity that Tirana required from Rugova in favor of the Serbian opposition would open distrust not only in the highest political relations, but also among the wide range intellectual and social layers of the inter-Albanian spectrum, which under the circumstances, was testing the internal differences and all those romantic dreams and the visions of unification. For, in Kosova hardly anyone could agree that Serbian students and demonstrators in Belgrade should be called a "heroic youth" as Berisha had done wishing them success knowing that that "heroic youth" and those same Serbian opposition leaders, supported by Tirana,

---

[716] *Ibid*, p. 68.

continued to call on volunteers and paramilitary units to be sent in to pacify Kosova from "Albanian terrorists!"

Indeed words of support for the Serb opposition also came from Kosova through Adem Demaçi,[717] who sent a telegram of support with the wording *"Serbian people, don't give up,"* the same as Bujar Bukoshi from Bonn had done.

Serbian opposition demonstrating in Belgrade and elsewhere during the election campaign and later, not only would not distance itself from this approach, using it instead as an abomination in the new behavior, implying at least some kind of abhorrence from it, but rather at rallies Albanians were being blamed for a "pact with Milosevic" for refusing to participate in the elections in which Seselj's radicals and Arkan's paramilitaries had gained 22 mandates of the Albanians and with this they had secured a majority in the Serbian Parliament! Similar atonements were heard by some foreign media and European "reformist" politicians, who blamed the Albanians for why Milosevic continued to "democratically" stay in power, rather than posing the question to themselves from the beginning of the emergence of the Yugoslav crisis, when inaction against Milosevic had turned into support that helped him rise higher. All that recalled the allegory between the lamb and the wolf as to who was blurring the water.

The beginning of a rift of *"Zajedno"* bloc and their failure, to be best reflected with Draskovic taking Milosevic's side, reduced the international pressure against Rugova about "potential contribution" of Albanians in Serbia's democratization, realizing that the Serbian opposition was not at all that interested in the democratization of Serbia, but rather into coming to power. While, as far as Albanians, with the exception of any detached dissonance coming from some small group without political influence or human rights activist, it had been proven they were on the same wave as Milosevic (and it was natural as he had come to power thanks to a national consensus emerging from the spirit of the last Memorandum of the Serbian Academy of Sciences and Arts).

---

[717] See Bierman, Rafael *"Lehrjahre im Kosvo,"* 2004, p. 522.

The Downfall of the Albanian State and Consequences for Kosova

The 1997 spring chaos that engulfed Albania after the overthrow of the Government of Sali Berisha was a hard blow for the Kosova issue, as the Serbian and Russian propaganda was being used for spreading the thesis of Albanians as a people who did not deserve a state . – Americans demanded the postponement of the second parliamentary elections in Kosova scheduled for May, arguing that chaotic circumstances in Albania did not allow for it. – Nano's accession to power and the change in the stance towards Kosova. – At the Crete Summit, Albania eventually abandoned its support of Kosova's independence and returned to the option of cultural autonomy for Albanians within Serbia!

As the story of the temptation of Serbia's democratization through Serb opposition finally failed, Dr. Rugova again faced the Americans with their demand to give up Kosova parliamentary elections scheduled for May of that year, having been postponed a year before exactly because of a similar demand on the grounds that they coincided with Serbian elections, with the West hoping for a miracle of democracy to happen resulting in a facilitation for the resolution of the Kosova issue, as many European leaders openly declared.

This time the reason was not Serbia, but Albania and its grave situation, which continued to be of concern as in Albania the Government of Sali Berisha fell as a consequence of a pyramid system and the entire Albanian state, faced great chaos representing a risk for the region. Aware of this danger, in March 1997, Americans were the ones who asked Dr. Rugova not to have elections in Kosova arguing that the "circumstances which Albania was experiencing did not allow for that to happen!"[718]

U.S. persistence to have Kosova elections postponed on the grounds that the circumstances in Albania did not allow for them provided a special message for Kosova, at first both incomprehensible and disturbing. It gave way to thinking that for the U.S. the crisis and the collapse of the Albanian state following the pyramid affair and many other factors associated with irresponsible behavior of the position and opposition as well as the entire political class without exception, represented another major concern. It demanded focusing all attention on the Albanian state

---

[718] *Ibid*, p. 553.

and its incongruous fate coming in a position to be protected from itself by the foreigners, which in Kosova meant peace, at least temporarily, as the unrest in Albania and its exit from automatic observation gave the crisis a regional dimension, outside of which one could neither foresee a solution for the Kosova issue.

This was a dramatic twist, which would evidently affect the international factor, rather than thinking on how to find a solution to the Kosova crisis, necessarily, at a time when it was thought that Kosova's turn had come, the attention was necessarily shifted towards Albania and its collapse in order to save the Albanian state from self-contusion, which was the first such case in the history of Europe and almost without precedent until then.

Indeed, the signs of what Albania would pass during the upheavals of February and March of that year, leading to a complete collapse of the state, were seen as early as Sali Berisha won the 1996 elections with the introduction of the pyramids and their system, towards which the Albanian Government not only did not show any concern, as suggested by the outside, especially by the International Monetary Fund, warning Tirana repeatedly, with Berisha declaring out loud that what was happening in Albania with the pyramids was "clean money."[719]

Some sources indicated that soon after such statements Berisha realize all the seriousness of the problem which he was about to face, but it would be too late to do anything to prevent the downfall.[720]

The same sources estimated that faced with those developments which could not be supervised Berisha could have calculated that the radicalization of the conflict in Kosova could save Albania from an inversion. Here, one could see his efforts to excessively factorize Rugova's opponents: Demaçi, Xhaferi and others hoping that whatever "moves" in Kosova – including those not outside the grit of official Tirana and its obligations towards the international community to continue to keep Prishtina in the course of civil resistance – would relieve Albania of its turmoil coming from within.

These and similar speculations made Rugova even more skeptical of Tirana's official policy towards Kosova, which he never trusted much.[721]

---

[719] See "*Rilindja,*" 23 September 1996.
[720] See DPA, Monthly Bulletin, February 1996.

Although the events of February and March in Albania and their shift were of concern to Kosova, however, the difficulties it was going through seemed to have prevented thinking about a risk of serious proportions from Albania, more so realizing that the Americans and certain NATO structures were already there, and that Albanian riots could not get out of control. Initially, Kosova's concern for what was happening in Albania was being rightly measured in terms of the negative effects it produced in relation to the issue of Kosova being unobserved on an international plain, knowing that any mayhem in Albania would help the Serbian regime to continue its repression and at the same time to amortize support for a more comprehensive solution of the Albanian question in the Balkans, the settling of which touched upon the Serbian hegemonic interests on which it was built since the Eastern Crisis and especially after the Balkan Wars when the Albanian trunk lost about one half of its stem.

Indeed, the collapse of the Berisha Government and the overall fall of the Albanian state following an outbreak of arms with unprecedented arsenal falling into diverse hands opened the question of their uncontrolled use and penetration in different directions from Kosova to the existing fronts. That led to Albania and Albanians being labeled as trouble makers for the stability of the region in line with Serbian propaganda being consistently distributed into the world spreading bugaboo for the Albanian state as unsafe and for Albanians as undeserving of a state.

The first reports of Albanian weapons already reaching various places as well as numerous rumors about the possibility of an internal civil war in Albania could not remain without consequences and without influence over developments in Kosova towards radicalization, already stirred by unsupervised simmering in accordance with various scenarios that could trigger it unhindered being already weary of the institutional resistance in order to be able to commit a genocide in Kosova, "without excuse," as anticipated.

Similar could be said about other parts of Albanian ethnicity, particularly in Macedonia, where the situation appeared with tensions between the Macedonian state and Albanians on issues of equality, which would by no means be settled, as the first refused to recognize a constituent status to

---

[721] Buxhovi, Jusuf: *"Kthesa historike – shteti paralel dhe rezistenca e armatosur,"* Prishtina, 2009, pp. 234-258.

the latter. Certain sources began to speculate that various military formations from the ranks of the decomposed Albanian army were regrouping set to open the Kosova front without knowledge who was leading them. The surprise became even greater considering how these military formations could be of use in Kosova, as they had been when they had busted their own country or had failed to protect it accordingly.

The spread of such rumors caused great concern as it was being said that Serbia, Greece and Bulgaria had begun to take appropriate measures, in particular Belgrade and Athens, not excluding the possibility that if proven true that certain formations of the Albanian military out of command would be activated towards Kosova and Macedonia, then in turn they had to intervene directly in Albania, to prevent this, thus opening the issue of a Balkan crisis.

Thus, Albania's crisis and the chaos it involved, would once again hit Kosova hard at a very critical stage as it would be forced to adapt its own behavior to the circumstances of stabilization of the Albanian state.

Although after a while, due to American and Western supervision, the Albania crisis was kept inside its borders, with new elections that the Socialists won, things would go towards normalcy, the fear of the consequences that had caused the collapse of the state still remained open, as besides numerous weapons had fallen into the hands of insecure and suspicious actors, it was also the political climate that had already shifted relations in various directions that could produce disturbing effects.

Among these changes, however, most apparent was the loss of Dr. Rugova's importance in government levels in Albania existing during the Government of the Democratic Party and its allies, with whom Rugova had good relations, even though they had never been as cordial as it appeared in the public and presented by the veneer of mutual propaganda.

On one hand, Fatos Nano would be quick to bring Rugova's past opponents together declaring them his support, and on the other, trying to hastily woo the Belgrade regime for normalization of relations, where as noted at the Crete meeting in September 1997 between Nano and Milosevic, the solution for Kosova would be viewed as an internal issue of Serbia, at the suggestion of fulfilling the highest standards of human and cultural rights of Albanians.

This approach undoubtedly changed the layout options for resolving the issue of Kosova from an independent state, where it already stood since 1990 when the Republic of Kosova was proclaimed with its determination of implementation through the parallel state to other options of its inclusion in the Yugoslav Federation on condition it was comprised as its equal part, without excluding cultural autonomy, of which Nano was pronounced on several occasions including also other forms of which the Tirana Government had put Kosova's fate on the bargaining table by its own decision in order to have Kosova Albanians contemplate on them too.

One of these forms would also be Adem Demaçi's "*Balkania*," which was a project proposal for the federal ties with Serbia and Montenegro. "*Balkania*" provided for Serbia, Montenegro and Kosova to establish a trilateral federal-confederal connection in the spirit of federation models presented by the Comintern that were planned after World War II, envisaging Albania to take part in what would be connected with Yugoslavia and Bulgaria. However, the current federation would be much less than a Balkan one, despite being named "*Balkania*." It would be dominated by Belgrade and its well-known hegemony, which had always used similar ties since the establishment of the Serb-Croat-Slovene state in 1919, turning soon into Yugoslavia under the influence of Serbs, a model which was admitted to the Paris Peace Conference.

Demaçi's idea was supported by Mahmut Bakalli and other senior officials of the former Yugoslavia, who before and after the war found common political language with Demaçi and were greatly influenced by him.[722] Demaçi claimed that his proposal was in the spirit of the Kaçanik Constitution, namely its Article Two, leaving open the possibility of Kosova's federal-confederal ties with other units of the Federation,[723] forgetting in this case that the 1991 Referendum on Independence and 1992 elections, along with the documents passed by the Assembly in the same year, declared Kosova as an independent state, so that would be disregarding the will of the people.

At any rate, Demaçi's proposal was for certain important circumstances and deserves consideration. On one side it came from an opponent of Dr. Rugova, who had already taken over Surroi's Parliamentary Party entering into direct political rivalry with Rugova, against whom he

---

[722] See article "*Tëndosje e lartë në Kosovë*"(High Tension in Kosovo), published in "*Neue Züricher Zeitung*," 10 October 1997, with Bakalli reasoning on Demaçi's "Balkania" as an option in favor of the interests of the three nations.

[723] See the text of Kaçanik Constitution as published in "*Aktet e Kuvendit të Republikës së Kosovës*," an ASAK publication, 2005.

had not spared his criticism for years, calling his option for civil resistance with the parallel state harmful and even capitulating, while on the other hand, it was generally assumed that the one who was taken as the pioneer of the demand for national liberation and unification even by revolutionary means and had spent so many years in Yugoslav prisons, with the current demand was returning Kosova's status back to Belgrade. With this its current road to independence was being cut and the issue could come back again under a Serbian umbrella. Was this about a political maneuver by Demaçi to Belgrade and Europeans in general, who had begun to show an aversion towards Dr. Rugova's repetition on independence accusing him openly for lack of flexibility, with an Albanian position fixed in an extreme position blocking political realism, who even when appearing pragmatic opted for international protectorates "as an interim position," but always excluding any ties with Serbia? Or, was it about a new coordination between Prishtina and Tirana, after the Socialists came to power? Demaçi had quickly established contacts with them and had been greeted with great honors in Tirana, although honors had come recently from Berisha as well, who had turned into an opponent of Rugova.

Regardless of the dilemma posed by Albanians themselves, the proposal did not enthuse Milosevic, who was not interested in such solutions, in which, as the author of the recent Serbian Memorandum, Dobrica Cosic, said *"Albanians would biologically jeopardize Serbia and the Serbian people."* Belgrade's policy continued to remain preset towards Rugova, realizing that his extreme position for an independent state, as he said, "open towards both Serbia and Albania," was a variant not accepted by the international community either, so that that enabled it to continue its path of repression and violence against Albanians and blame them for being unfit for any form of talks. And, as they never gave up their determination "to destroy Serbia," Belgrade still retained the right to use all means to protect the territorial integrity without excluding the means of state violence.

The international community too, realizing that Demaçi's proposal about "Balkania" did not receive any attention from Belgrade, and much less from Albanians, did not pay much notice to Rugova's opponent, as evidently the option of independence had no alternative, no matter how difficult it was to get the support of the international community.

Rugova himself, as if he had expected this proposal to take a little breath from the anxiety created by Dayton and loss of support in Tirana, reacted very calmly saying that "Balkan alliances are on old historical models that did not interest the Albanians, although evidently there is a yearning for them."[724]

Student Demonstrations and Breaking of the *Status Quo*

Demonstrations by students of the University of Prishtina held on October 1, 1997, marked the beginning of active resistance, out of institutional structures, assessing that Albanian politics had already exhausted all the "peaceful resources," while Belgrade behaved as if the international community factor had granted it all the title-deeds over Kosova. – Europeans, however, believed in "Serbian democratic" changes that could come after the Serbian elections of September 21 – although their test had already been won by Milosevic – while the Americans, when stressing a "chance for peace" had in mind some of the Dayton Accords (about Slavonia) that Milosevic had to fulfill. – Breaking the status quo in Kosova caused the first shocks within the political scene being reflected in fractures in the Assembly of the Democratic League of Kosova, to which Rugova responded with the announcement of the second parliamentary elections for March next year. – Americans, for the first time, kept two lines of Albanian resistance open: the civil-institutional and the armed resistance, to be used in various ways.- Rugova's first meeting with Milosevic – a setup by the Americans and Europeans to get the last alibi out of Milosevic's hand.

What Demaçi's "Balkania" and major criticisms against Rugova and his course coming from all sides after signing the agreement on education failed to do, would be done by the student demonstrations at the University of Prishtina on October 1, 1997. The day in Prishtina when over twenty thousand students led by the University Rector Dr. Ejup Statovci, demonstrated with most of the faculty professors and lecturers, marked, in fact, the breaking of the status quo, which had continued from Dayton and beyond. This event also marked the beginning of an active resistance by institutional structures, such as the University and the student youth, which would soon reach as far as involvement in open war with the

---

[724] *"Rilindja,"* 22 April 1997.

Serbian military and police forces, even though some of the actors of this development preferred rather to see this expected turnaround in the circumstances (as students always belong to an avant-garde role) revealed differently, namely as detached from the complexity of the parallel state from where they came.

Therefore, not unfairly, based on the content rather than from the form of action, it can be estimated that on October 1, 1997 in Kosova once and for all the "balance of fear" was broken between the parallel state of the Albanians and the Serb occupiers to turn into a state of war, from which there would be retreat neither from Serbia nor the Albanians, an expected development unable to be stopped neither by politics nor diplomacy and other maneuvers leading to where things went, namely NATO's armed intervention in March-June 1999.

But, were student demonstrations in Prishtina a natural development produced by the circumstances that had to come out anyway, or was this something that contradicted them?

Viewed through the prism of actuality, it seemed that the student demonstrations in Prishtina were inconsistent with the views of the Albanian political forces in Kosova, the Serbs, but also with the international factor, which was focused on Albanians and Serbs to test the final options of finding a compromise solution to give politics one last chance. This, at least, was what Europeans sought, who although dissatisfied with the failure of the first test of democracy a year earlier in Serbia, however, hoped that the second test, that of the September 21 elections in Serbia and Montenegro could come a "surprise" that with the democratic favorable relations from these elections would provide the Kosova crisis with circumstances to take the direction of a peaceful settlement by agreement between the two peoples. At last, the Europeans did not want to give Milosevic a chance of victory in Kosova during the last election campaign in Serbia, knowing that he would intervene there. But, evidently, in addition to the fear of Milosevic's coming to power once again through the use of violence in Kosova, the Americans, emphasizing "the chance for peace" had some scores to settle with Milosevic related to certain Dayton agreements. This referred to a full restoration of Slavonia to Croatia, prolonged by the Serbs waiting for Milosevic to issue orders to the parallel structures that were still there representing a threat for full implementation of what was agreed upon in Dayton.

A similar opinion with the Europeans, namely that Milosevic this time would not be given any chance to win elections through Kosova, was also upheld by Fehmi Agani, Rugova's leading man for talks with Belgrade, who told the German press on the eve of the student demonstrations in Prishtina that "we are in a serious stage of significant turns which should not be swayed by anything."[725]

But what were these "serious and significant turns" that "should not be swayed by anything"?

Perhaps the German newspaper *"Frankfurter Allgemeine"* would see to it to provide an ironic response saying "if with serious and significant turns one means talks with Belgrade on a similar agreement with that on education, then students' pressure would play a positive role, as it would also push them further ahead."[726]

But it seemed that this referred rather to the fear of change in relations of the domestic scene in the Albanian politics, by which civil unorganized resistance would eventually turn into an active organized civil resistance. It came from the emergence of an active opposition against Serb violence through armed actions against Serb police forces in several parts of Kosova, in which there were persons killed from among the Serbs ranks with the KLA taking the responsibility, which continued operating clandestinely. As a result, there was fear of aggravation of the conflict with Serbia, which could take serious proportions of which the civil resistance leaders were still not interested, believing it would suit Serbian radical forces in putting their war machinery in operation into emptying Kosova to be done through the pretexts of war against Albanian "terrorists."

The "worrying" of some close associates of Rugova that the change of course in the civil resistance in favor of an active one could give rise to radical Serb forces igniting war in Kosova, which would eventually commence its ethnic cleansing of Albanians in accordance with their well-known plans, could also be a fear of losing their own domestic positions.

---

[725] See note in *"Frankfurter Allgemeine Zeitung,"* 30 September 1997, with Professor Agani speaking on an important stage of negotiations with Belgrade, as monitored by the international factor. Albin Kurti, one of the organizers of the demonstrations said the time had come for the students' supressed energy to erupt. Adem Demaçi supported the students' demonstrations accusing the LDK activists for their blockade of the students' demonstrations. He pointed out that Rugova's pacifism was beginning to produce a human with a supressed conscience, that of a permanent slave.
[726] *Ibid.*

This was also connected to the suspicion that it all could be a strategy by Bukoshi and Demaçi and supported by the left socialist government in Tirana, which had already shown that it was bothered by the internal and external authority of Dr. Rugova, in order to take over the reins of the movement in Kosova stripped of the parallel state "icon" in order to be able to easier manipulate, as it was thought, from the outside.[727]

This speculation perhaps seemed logical knowing Bukoshi's disagreements with Rugova emerging after Dayton, with the Prime Minister saying that the action required to be more active should take place, even without the consent of the Americans, who were the only key reference of the Albanians. This attitude, which also circulated through several important German newspapers, echoing increasingly the KLA factor and war in general, for which Bukoshi, although under the veil of mystery on "who was he rather working for" was seen as interconnected with some of his structures using the money that he recently poured in for the purchase of military equipment and finance preparing KLA units in Albania. In the meanwhile Rugova appeared a militant of the stance that the state of Kosova should in no way be affected nor dismantled from within with the logic of war, even if the Albanians would be forced to engage in it.[728]

Despite Rugova's moderate stance towards demonstrations and his warnings that they could be needed by Belgrade for igniting a conflict to settle scores with the parallel state, against which Milosevic evidently had no cure seeking to somehow dismantle it before it became capable by some external circumstance, such as U.S. pressure, into forcing him to accept as a partner, the demonstrators would not give up.

The fact that students were willing to appear in the political scene and do what Rugova was actually doing could be seen in the decision to postpone demonstrations scheduled for September 1 to October 1, which

---

[727] Author's conversation with analyst Viktor Meier in Zürich, in November 1997. Meier openly stressed in favor of Bujar Bukoshi taking over the steering wheel of the parallel state, by also maintaining Rugova's prestige as its representative, as he thought it to be the only way to break the status quo. He further maintained that both the students' movement and KLA had to be used to that end. He was convinced that Dr. Rugova, as an elected President of the Republic of Kosovo with the mandate of the largest part of Kosovo Albanians had to somewhat rebel himself from the Americans and their influence and, in accordance to the Kacanik Constitution, be declared KLA Commander.
[728] See article "*Lufta po i afrohet gjithnjë e më shumë Kosovës*" published in "FAZ," 18 December 1997.

was done after talks with representatives of the U.S. Embassy. So, based on a U.S. request, it was sidelined until the end of the Serbian election campaign, scheduled for September 21, and the postponement charged the students' movement with the suspicion that it too, like other moves by the Albanians was directed by the Americans, who had decided to introduce it into the game as a "tactical intermezzo" between the course of civilian resistance and armed resistance. The students' Organizing Council made every effort to be peaceful limiting their demand to the access to education in the Albanian language, which was a democratic demand, and which would also happen.

But, it was the Serb police units that would not tolerate peaceful demonstrations of thousands of Albanian students who were determined to change the situation of their lack of perspective. This was made known to both the Serbian occupation authorities and the internationals, as well as to the Albanian politicians that the time had come to end the situation of waiting, subjugation, and humiliation.

As expected, large Serb police and military forces, which had surrounded the area where students had gathered, would brutally intervene at the moment the students moved in the direction of the city to make a warning circle around the city peacefully. Tear gas and violence against demonstrators would be used to which they did not respond with violence. Multiple cameras of global-scale TV outlets recorded all the sights which would eventually break the "idyll" of the "coexistence" of the parallel authority of the Albanians and the Serb occupying power. The world witnessed the "message of peace" that the Belgrade regime was sending to Albanians and expressed its concern for the possibility of further escalation similar to that of Bosnia, which was still fresh. This was best expressed by the newspaper *"Neue Züricher Zeitung"* emphasizing "Kosova before exploding!"[729]

On the other hand, the Albanian students' peaceful and civilized manifestation displayed during the day and during two other days of demonstrations (October 29 and December 30, 1997), drew the attention

---

[729] See analysis in *"Neue Züricher Zeitung"* on 10 December 1997 warning about the fact that Belgrade did not want a peaceful agreement with Albanians, as hoped, and would not consider even the most basic demands by them, be it the most civilized ones. Belgrade wished to continue repression in Kosovo to impose the Serb dictate there. And, those who did not accept it would be driven out. Belgrade was interested in war, the newspaper says, as it thinks it the only way to realize Serb national interests.

of the international, European and U.S. diplomacy, as well as the entire international factor. The latter, after seeing that Serbia would also lose a second test of democracy within a year, and that in the last elections, the Serbian radical currents would be strengthened even more due to their anti-Albanian course that had propagated during the election campaign, began to think more seriously about the Kosova crisis and its direction, emitting all the indications of moving towards inevitable confrontations between Albanians and Serbs.[730]

And, as it happened in such cases when other factors appeared in the game, though Kosova and its problems were not unknown, but being so to say in the "vicinity" of development and "in waiting," students' leaders were in the spotlight. The world realized at once that Kosova's political landscape and scenery was different from that to which it was used for years, with Dr. Rugova turning to a single icon. The Americans invited Albin Kurti and some of his colleagues to Washington, while similar reception was made by Europeans. Of course, both the Americans and Europeans, though with slightly different attitudes about new factors and their role in the Kosova scene, agitated students to keep on the civilized course, outside political demands. Albin Kurti showed both tact and wisdom not to appear as a factor that provoked the Kosova politics to waive the course of civil-institutional resistance, where they and their university belonged, being funded by the Government and representing the pillar of national education, rather requesting to be more active and in accordance with the interests of its citizens, in order to bring about positive changes. "We demand the dignity of the ordinary citizen restored."[731]

The tolerant behavior and democratic culture of the leadership of the Kosova demonstrations won the tolerance prize recognition of the daily "Nasa Borba" in Belgrade in January of the next year.[732]

---

[730] See General Wesley K. Clark's stances in his book *"Të bësh luftë moderne"*(Waging Modern War), 2003, informing in detail, in view of American and NATO military analyses, on Milosevic's preparations to settle accounts with Albanians through the means of war. Moreover, General Clark points out Albanians' readiness to counter the Serb plans with force.

[731] Albin Kurti's statement for *"Westdeutsche Rundfunk"* of Cologne, on 22 November 1997.

[732] See Clark *"Civil Resistance,"* 2000, p. 145, cited according to Rafael Bierman *"Lehrjahre im Kosovo,"* p. 551.

This would be the first time in Serbia, at least in one independent newspaper that the civilized behavior of Albanians so convincingly reflected for years, was being appreciated rather than called hostile and separatist, as usually labeled by the press in Belgrade.

The West would have wished that this was the beginning of a significant change in the Serbian media, starting a new climate in the relationship taking place between the two hostile peoples. But, evidently, it was only a small hope, a bubble, which would soon fade away from the extreme manifestation of radical forces in the Serbian political scene, which, apparently, were in favor of aggravations in Kosova and in the Albanian political scene, where the war factor was winning over the civil-institutional resistance.[733]

This already visible shift, along with the great impact from within towards an active resistance, and its messages seemed to be very well understood outside as well. Even those who thought that with the Dayton agreements the doors of peace to everyone had been opened, would have no illusion that peace in other parts of the former Yugoslavia could be decided if an agreement between Serbs and Croats were to be reached, while neglecting the interests of others, especially the Albanians, who were showing that they were able to end the Balkan idylls to their detriment.

Student demonstrations also effected a radical change on the Kosova political scene in many directions, in which the war factor too would open doors as part of the new positions emerging. The efforts of various political parties to become its umbrella turned into an internal race, with only the Democratic League of Kosova standing aside to further state that it would maintain its current setting. Externally, it was seen as part of the strategic calculations of the Albanian political parties to share roles, with some playing the pacifist and some playing the radical, in order that it all served before the international factor for it to choose its own Albanian partners in a combination that mattered and could come into play.[734]

Thus, besides the full course of Demaçi's *Parliamentary Party of Kosova* in support of the Kosova Liberation Army, which on November 28, 1997 was displayed for the first time in Llaushë of Drenica making its presence publicly known, Rexhep Qosja also appeared in the political scene, after turning his Intellectuals Forum into a political party as the

---

[733] *Ibid*, p. 551.
[734] *"Neue Züricher Zeitung,"* 10 December 1997.

Union of Democratic Movement – (LBD), joined by a number of non-partisan intellectuals and a number of those who had been included for years in the Democratic League of Kosova, including some of the founders who had been lately disagreeing with its course.

This configuration, along with the weakening of the Democratic League of Kosova, which in its third assembly held at the end of February the following year experienced an internal thrill as several senior officials from the ranks of the 1981 students' movement and other groups of political prisoners (some of whom joined high KLA structures and others had joined Rexhep Qosja) had rightly opened the question as to whether the international factor had abandoned Dr. Rugova and his course of civil-institutional resistance.

This conjecture became even greater as the new LDK Presidency left out even Fehmi Agani, Rugova's closest associate, who for years had led various talks with Belgrade and had been involved in some secret talks with Belgrade on the status of Kosova, with other emerging options from those of the determination of the independent state of Kosova, which was in line with the Kaçanik Assembly and Referendum on Independence in 1991.

Such speculation had a conjuncture as realities too had already changed. With the new challenge increasingly undermining his power from within, but not his authority as perceived, Dr. Rugova almost demonstratively responded with the announcement of new elections for the end of March. Thus, his many opponents who were on the political scene through their regroupings in accordance to the circumstances, as happened with Rexhep Qosja's party, were offered a chance of election to test their strength and at the same time to test the loyalty of the people to the parallel state, which had been operating for years on the basis of the Referendum on Independence and the displayed will for an independent state.

Rugova therefore had mounted tremendous risk with unforeseen difficulties and risks not only for himself but also for the fate of Kosova. In circumstances when the war was already at the door, with the announcement of free elections at war, seeking a democratic test seemed to be a loss of the sense of reality or an action required from the outside, namely by Americans, who might have felt a need for a further continuation of the civil-institutional resistance to convince the world that Milosevic's only concern was war to exterminate the Albanians, and that it had to be stopped by means of war, even under humanitarian pretexts, as would really happen.

Foreign observers and powerful world media already focusing on Kosova following with great attention all the things happening in and around it, were rightly astonished by such behavior.

But, was this consequence towards a course that could resemble fanaticism regardless of the realities and the behavior accorded it? Or, was this a deal with the international factor, especially the Americans, who had already taken the reign for the resolution of the Kosova issue, so that the democratic deposition, even as a capital farce of a civil-institutional resistance among the most unparalleled ones in the world, would be used maximally and to the last moment, as the UN Security Council would demand?[735]

There seemed to be something of both and time would prove right both Dr. Rugova and his opponents. Ibrahim Rugova proved right for refusing to ruin a course from within for which he had been obliged by the Kaçanik Constitution, Referendum on Independence and free elections, a course that had become as such emblematic of a political movement with a civilized identity known and respected throughout the world, the collapse from which nothing could be gained, except for Serbia, which would be deprived of her incongruous opponent with which she could in no way manage but by turning it into part of the war. And, his opponents proved right for showing that that situation could not remain standing, and that something had to be done to change it, a change that could be fatal if it was not followed by a support from the international factor, in this case the Americans.

However, as things were seen from a time breaking point, it appeared that both Dr. Rugova's course to maintain the civil-institutional resistance and supporters of active resistance including a military one, were in accordance with the decision-making factor, especially the Americans, who in relation to the Kosova crisis and its resolution kept open two Albanian lines: that of the civil-institutional resistance of Dr. Rugova and that of the active opposition mounting up to armed resistance.

The first was encouraged not to give up at the final steps of the marathon. And, the second was taken into custody by turning it into a strong alibi even before being almost charged with the abomination of terrorism,

---

[735] See UN Security Council Resolution 1160 of 31 March 1998.

and it still remained in custody even when relieved of it. In the first case this would be used to put pressure on Belgrade to accept the resolution of Kosova before it was too late. And, in the second case to impose a resolution to Kosova through the use of ultimums against Serb forces in Kosova and in Serbia.

The U.S. policy, known for its pragmatism and determination to follow their interests to the end, was clearly planning to place the Balkans, following the recent geopolitical and geostrategic changes in the world, as part of its strategic interest, where Albanians and their space, regardless of state configurations, appeared as an important and even insurmountable factor. And since it was so, it was natural that Kosova as part of it, which had been left an open question in the complexity of the problems of the former Yugoslavia, had to play a special role in experimenting with peace and war complementing each other towards that goal.

If a comparison is made between the behavior of the Americans on the verge of Dayton (it is a time of year when they engaged in determining solution frameworks) and the American behavior toward Kosova after Dayton, they can be seen as analogies revealing a lot in common, at least in terms of making use of ultimatums for the benefit of diplomacy as a means of pressure used in the service of its movement, or through it forcing certain solutions. Thus, the imposition of a turn in Bosnia and Herzegovina in favor of Dayton, needed first an agreement between Bosnians and Croats about joining in the Bosnian-Croat Federation so that a forced merger between Bosnians and Croats followed by the formation of a common army, so that at the moment when NATO air operations began, the Bosnian-Croat forces would begin a ground offensive to retake territory in accordance with the maps presented at Dayton. Similarly, the strengthening of Croatia's military potential would proceed, which would be able to go to war with Serbian forces to return their territories occupied in the Knin Krajina and Slavonia.

Since Kosova and the West's military intervention represented another problem from that of Bosnia and Herzegovina, because the rest of the Serb-Montenegrin federation called the Federal Republic of Yugoslavia, was treated as successor to the former Yugoslavia and Kosova as part of it, a pretext was needed for it even by breaking international law and the sovereignty of the state and this could only be done under humanitarian pretexts, in accordance with Chapter Seven of the UN Charter. Approval of the UN Security Council Resolution 1160 provided such a

731

possibility, but it definitely needed two very convincing preconditions: one concerned with the proof of all peaceful means having been exhausted, and the other was concerned with clear evidence of genocide having been committed against the defenseless population, which could not help itself other than by foreign intervention from the international community.

In this context one should see further and more powerful support by the Americans and the West for the course of civil-institutional resistance of Dr. Rugova and commitment to keep it that way, even for organizing parliamentary elections in circumstances of emergency and major bloodshed of the Albanian population, such as that in Likoshan, Qirez and eventually the March 4 and 6 offensives in Prekaz when the Jashari family was massacred, a family already known for its KLA leadership. Obviously, in the meantime, as the international diplomacy and the entire political arsenal of great powers was put in motion by the first meeting of the Contact Group in March 1998 and the rest in September and finally in February of the following year, when the decision was taken on the Rambouillet Conference, with the U.S. administration using Dr. Rugova's movement to the maximum to provide further evidence of the peaceful behavior of Albanians. The most remarkable would be the one taking Rugova on May 13, 1998 to meet with Milosevic in Belgrade for allegedly talking on a peaceful settlement, with it all representing rather a farce that Americans needed, rather than Milosevic, as stated by opponents of Rugova, whose parallel state could be overcome preventing him from settling scores through war with Albanians and blaming them for it.

Although Dr. Rugova's trip in the circumstances in the eyes of the majority of Albanians seemed rather compromising knowing that nothing would come out of it but helping Milosevic to pretend that he was allegedly talking to Albanians even when Serbian military and police units were put in open action to kill and massacre everything Albanian doing so to gradually carry out a violent ethnic cleansing of Kosova Albanians, it however served the Americans and Westerners to set the final trap for Milosevic, which was the lure of Dr. Rugova's civil-institutional resistance. But, strategically, an acting democracy in the second parliamentary elections in Kosova in March 1998, the Americans and the Western alliance would need that in parallel to making decisions, such as those emerging from meetings of the Contact Group and the Holbrooke mission from September 1997 through March of the next year, preparations would begin for military intervention which would include many military and neighboring factors around Kosova. General Clark described this best, [736] revealing what seemed to be incomprehensible circumstances, of which Milosevic and his war machinery were very much aware and was desperately trying to prevent it before it happened by creating accomplished facts committed by force, among which most certainly was an accelerated ethnic cleansing.

Kosova in a War Vortex and the KLA Factor

War in Kosova as part of multiple calculations: Serbian international, and Albanian. – U.S. Representative Gelbard calling KLA a terrorist organization, while the Americans had detailed information about Serbian plans to ignite war in Kosova. – Green light issued to Belgrade by the West to settle accounts with the KLA leadership – The Drenica massacres in Qirez, Likoshan, and finally in Prekaz against the Jashari family – claiming "KLA Headquarters was liquidated" while most of those killed were children and elderly – shocked the world public opinion and highlighted Serbia's goals. – The Contact Group condemned the use of "excessive violence," but continued giving further support to the "war against terrorism." – Creation of "first liberated zones" in Dukagjin and Drenica gave Belgrade a reason to start its wide-scale military offensive in June against the Kosova Liberation Army, declaring entire Kosova a war zone. – During the summer the Serb army exercised unprecedented massacres against the defenseless population, especially in the "war zones." – In October, Milosevic declared "victory against Albanian terrorists" and allowed "humanitarian aid" for the people "terrorized by Albanian terrorists." – European Union launched humanitarian aid to help over 300 thousand Albanians displaced in various parts of Kosova.

The first public appearance of the Kosova Liberation Army, on November 28, 1997 actually marked the inclusion of Kosova in the whirlpool of war, which lasted until June 1999, when the Kumanovo technical agreement between Belgrade and NATO was signed for the withdrawal of

---

[736] See W. Clark *"Të bësh luftë moderne,"* „Zëri," Prishtina, 2003.

Serbian military and police forces from Kosova, which officially became marked as a forced extraction of Serbia from Kosova, exactly in line with the U.S. position stated by Madeleine Albright after the Rambouillet Conference.[737]

Viewed from the perspective of the dynamics, two factors affected the undeclared war in Kosova imposed by Belgrade in taking an irreversible direction despite the interaction of international mechanisms to prevent the crisis and despite the engagement of diplomacy and politics to circumvent this.

It deals on one side with Milosevic's final decision to settle accounts with the Albanians through war increasingly supposedly demonstrating his readiness for talks to do otherwise,[738] and on the other side with the determination of the Albanians to respond decisively and with all means with clear prediction that if the international community did not intervene, to do the utmost to involve both Albania and Albanians from Macedonia, Presheva Valley and Montenegro, so that the crisis totaled throughout the region. So, the time had come for this calculation too which would necessarily result in international interference.

The possibility for the Kosova conflict to include other parts of the region in the present circumstances became even more realistic and even more disturbing at the same time, following the collapse of the Albanian state in February and March 1997 with the fall of Berisha's government and the country in a chaotic situation, especially when weapon depots were broken in and large amounts of weapons had fallen into the hands of citizens and irresponsible persons from smugglers to mafia services. Although with the establishment of Bashkim Fino's Technical Govern-

---

[737] A statement by the U.S. Secretary of State Madeleine Albright to BBC on 16 March 1999. It should be pointed out that Albright and certain U.S. senior officials had been repeating in various forms statements relevant to Dr. Rugova's demand submitted to the UN Secretary General Kofi Annan in his first meeting with him in 1995 prior to Dayton. The proposal was repeated to the U.S. Administration as an interim solution by which both Albanians and Serbs would be given an opprtunity to reach a comprehensive peace agreement.

[738] Wesley K. Clark "*Të bësh luftë moderne,*" 2003. "Zëri," Prishtina, p. 187. In the meeting of General Clark accompanied by the German General, Klaus Nauman with Milosevic in Belgrade, the Serb President said the following: "*You know, General Clark, as to how one should settle accounts with Albanians, with these killers, rapists, assassinators of their own children! Before, we took care of them!... In Drenica, in 1946, we killed them all!...*"

ment, signs appeared that the country would not be included in the civil war as it had been rumored especially by those who wanted it for many reasons even working for it to happen, still circumstances in the country and free movement of arms and open trade with them opened the possibility of easy supplies in Kosova, Macedonia and other parts, giving the war even greater reasons to put into motion its interior capacities making it known that preconditions for it had already been created. Therefore, it was a message understood correctly and timely to be taken seriously by some and with concern and panic by others, however putting into action all the diplomatic, political and military potential of high-level global mechanisms from the Contact Group, UN Security Council, European Union, NATO and other organizations.

Diplomacy of crisis prevention for the first time would alert about the conflict that had already broken out, while in line with this, the Americans, as the Pentagon began preparations for the military factor to be able to be activated in time in the function of diplomacy and politics, had already opened the debate about the possibility of military intervention of the Atlantic Alliance, which in case it faced obstacles, would be taken unilaterally.[739]

It seemed that the second factor, the introduction of the option of international intervention in Kosova, which was expected and not excluded,[740] would have alerted Milosevic and his military men to use their acting of readiness to find a solution with the Albanians for deployment of additional military and police forces in Kosova, with the selective use of which two purposes would be achieved.

First – in order to break the core of the Kosova Liberation Army before it was able to become the dominating factor turning into a military partner of the North Atlantic Alliance, as it happened with the Bosnian-Croatian army in Bosnia and Herzegovina almost a year earlier, the start of NATO bombing against Serb positions around Sarajevo and other parts was being used for a ground offensive against the Serb army there and even with success.

Secondly – a selective use of military force against Kosova Liberation Army would be applied for a "careful" ethnic cleansing of Kosova, putting pressure on Europeans not to support the NATO military option, of

---

[739] Wesley K. Clark *"Të bësh luftë moderne,"* 2003, "Zëri," Prishtina, pp. 151-153.
[740] *Ibid*, p. 181.

which Serbs possessed already some information, as they would be faced with a huge wave of refugees, not only Albanians but also others from the region. In the meanwhile it was made clear to Macedonia and Albania that the great refugee crisis could bring about internal difficulties that would destabilize them, causing fresh direct trouble with Serbia, including the threat of entry into war with them. Milosevic was so determined to go through with it not hiding it at all.

But Albanians too made their purposes clear after turning to arms as a last resort convinced that it could bring about an international intervention, which war planners had envisioned as a tool that could not be understood other than a continuation of politics by other means. Thus, there was no turning back and no second way. Not even Rugova's oath of allegiance to the parallel state and civil resistance, although used by diplomacy and politics for certain purposes proving very useful as such, being so to the last moments as NATO bombs were thrown against Serbian military and police forces in Kosova and positions in Serbia.

The vortex of war, which would include Kosova appeared as a strange veil not able to hide diplomacy's face of war or war's face of diplomacy. So, this mixture helped an ongoing optical deception between the two Marches: that of 1998 and 1999 confused with the appearance of diplomacy with war and war with diplomacy, recognizing the fact that it would take Kosova from one position to another, i.e. from that of Serbian invaders and long years of violence to forcing Serbian invaders out. This seemingly unpredictable shift, however, would encompass passages of blood and multiple dead bodies, and also through diplomatic channels to reach the negotiating table at Rambouillet, when the curtain would finally be raised separating the war of diplomacy from the diplomacy of war.

Before exchanging the two, Kosova went through the trauma of neither peace nor war situation, although the latter quickly replaced the first. Events, however, followed each other with great speed, and even as it seemed that they were acting to prevent war, or to even prevent a large-size war outbreak, they actually spent the last reserves of peaceful behavior filling explosion energies instead.

This process would certainly help what might be called the chemistry of international politics, which from the very first phase of the public appearance of the Kosova Liberation Army would try to prevent the erupting war with the means of war, according to the logic that fire extinguishes fire, leaving it up to Milosevic, the one who wished it, who had started it, and who would not give it up turning it into a purposeful tool in order to finally burn in it.

This absurdity began from the Americans, who, after the students demonstrations of October 1 and conflicts in Drenica occurring after the public emergence of the Kosova Liberation Army, sent their missionaries – first Robert Gelbard, then Christopher Hill and finally Richard Holbrooke – who would be put into action, but always focused in the role of an arsonist, who had to turn into a fire-fighter!

As a representative of the U.S. President in the implementation of the Dayton accords, Gelbard was the first, who in accordance with the practice of Dayton considering partnership with Milosevic to be helpful in solving the Kosova problem, headed towards the Dedinje Palace, to work alongside his occupation with Bosnia and Croatia on testing Milosevic on "*positive arrangements*" in Kosova, by which he continued to enjoy the treatment of a "man of peace" and partner of the West. So at least thought Gelbard, whose microscope of interest included only a segment of the U.S. policy towards solving the crisis of the former Yugoslavia, as it was clear that there were more parallel channels, installed long ago on the crisis, a natural approach for a global superpower such as America, which played with many more cards in hand.

But what were the "*positive arrangements*" based on the model of Bosnia and Croatia, which the American representative would also like to see in Kosova?

And, what price was Milosevic to pay for them? And Kosova?

"*Positive arrangements*" in Bosnia, where Milosevic indeed proved to be a "skilled player," would be those that in parliamentary elections in Republika Srpska on November 23, 1997 would bring to power Milorad Dodik, an American "partner" who would remove Karadzic from power against whom the Tribunal had issued an arrest warrant. With this victory, the estimation was that Dayton was evolving towards a huge success, as Dodik in his election campaign promised to end the war and its crimes and return to genuine peace. On this occasion he declared that Bosnians would have their forcibly abducted homeland returned, and that he would also take responsibility of cooperation with the Hague Tribunal. The Americans knew that the godfather for this turning was Milosevic, who put himself openly on his side and it was enough for Bosnia to, at least formally, report overnight political changes. Dodik was invited to Washington and in his meeting with Madeleine Albright he showed even more "peace and reconciliation will" towards Bosnians and Croats. This strengthened even more the impression that Milosevic was indeed on the "right path." When at the end of January due to promises of Milosevic in Dayton, the last parts of Slavonia were finally returned to Croatia after being kept for several years by the Serb rebels living there, Washington immediately responded with promises of removing sanctions against Belgrade. During a visit with Milosevic in late January, together with his thanks from the U.S. administration for his "constructive role played in the Serbian elections in Bosnia and the implementation of agreements with Croatia," Gelbard also halted on the *Kosova Liberation Army*, qualifying it as a "terrorist group."[741]

It has been evaluated that the characterization of the KLA as a "terrorist group" was a "gift" to Milosevic for his services rendered, by which he apparently swallowed the bait which eventually choked him.

"The violence, which is apparently increasing, is very dangerous. We clearly and without hesitation condemn terrorist activities in Kosova. KLA is unequivocally a terrorist group."[742]

After these words that Milosevic would have liked immensely, Gelbard further, with a threat issued to the KLA that "it could soon be introduced in the U.S. list of terrorist organizations"[743] opened the way for Milosevic to concentrate on launching a military campaign against the KLA, which was put into operation in early March.

Gelbard's statement made in Belgrade, which for Milosevic meant a "green light" for military action in Kosova, seemed even more likely to be part of the lure for Milosevic, as the U.S. administration already had two detailed CIA reports of December and beginning of January informing that Belgrade had concentrated large forces of police and special military units in Drenica, where soon a "cleansing campaign against the head of Albanian terrorists" was anticipated to take place.[744]

There were not only American sources that possessed information on the Serbian military offensive, which would soon be launched in Drenica. Other observers too who had been able to get access to the strained areas in Kosova, spoke of staging in the north and northeast of Kosova, which

---

[741] "*Frankfurter Allgemeine Zeitung,*" 10 January 1998.

[742] Tim Judah "*Kosova, luftë dhe hakmarrje,*" 2002, p. 138 (back translation).

[743] "*Frankfurter Allgemeine Zeitung,*"10 January 1998.

[744] See Daalder/O'Honlon, "*Warning*" 2000, p. 27, cited according to Rafael Bierman "*Lehrjahre im Kosovo,*" 2004, p. 560.

created a horseshoe shape in the upper part of Drenica towards Prekaz and surrounding villages. By mid-February they reached the number of more than ten thousand military forces, mainly from special units and elite Serb army already entrenched in northern Prekaz and surrounding villages of Skenderaj. The road coming from Mitrovica was almost blocked by military vehicles, carrying war materials and heavy equipment.[745]

Troops already fortified on the above-mentioned line were added to the other four thousand special police operating units that took part in the fighting in Bosnia, but were later withdrawn, although it was being said that part of their time they spent attending Drina in flash operations in Bosnia and Herzegovina. The Serb military forces were concluded with Arkan's units, whose presence was also confirmed by the Americans.[746]

In these circumstances, however, the first "frictions" of KLA groups with Serb military police units occurred in that part of the country moving increasingly to the direction of war. On February 28 during an ambush set by the KLA guerillas, four Serbian policemen were killed with several others injured. Two Serb police vehicles were also destroyed. There were also those killed and injured from the Albanian side, who withdrew after these actions towards the Shala Mountains.[747]

In retaliation for the killing of policemen, Serb police and army units launched a punitive campaign against several villages in Drenica, where besides the burning and destruction of many houses in Qirez, they massacred 26 members of the Ahmeti family, many of them children and elderly.[748]

The Serbian military and police offensive in Drenica and the massacre of entire families aroused anger and indignation throughout Kosova. On March 2 in Prishtina over 100 thousand citizens demonstrated against violence. The police used force against the demonstrators here too. In this case over two hundred demonstrators were injured and many were imprisoned. The entire Prishtina was filled with tear gas. President Rugova declared March 3 a day of mourning in Kosova. In Likoshan and Qirez tens of thousands of citizens took part in the funeral of the massa-

---

[745] Clark, Howard *"Civil Resistance in Kosovo,"* London, 2000, p. 172.

[746] See 119th briefing at the State Department of 22 February 1998.

[747] Judah, Tim *"Kosova, luftë dhe hakmarrje,"* 2002.

[748] Schmid, Thomas *"Krieg im Kosovo,"* 1999, p. 55.

cred, burying on that very day peace and its comfort in Kosova. Because, obviously, Belgrade had already put into operation its machinery of war, which would not stop, while the answer of the Albanians was equally clear – that they would respond with all means.

During two or three days to come, despite the shocking images of Qirez and Likoshan that would flood the world, Belgrade did not receive any warning or threat to stop from going any further. Rather, Serbian propaganda continued to declare that "the situation was under supervision" and that what was happening in Drenica was just part of the "necessary and legitimate measures" that through "defensive action the environment would be cleaned of terrorist nests."[749]

And, evidently, between 4–7 of March 1998 Serbian military and police forces focused in Prekaz targeting the Jashari family, where Adem Jashari and his brother Hamza, initially activists of nationwide movement led by the Democratic League of Kosova and its members from the early days and founders of the Kosova Liberation Army, had been targeted to be exterminated under pretexts of settling accounts with "terrorist groups," which as such were originally labeled by the American administration. Surrounded by large Serbian police and military forces, the Jashari brothers (Adem – KLA commander and Hamza – his comrade at arms) stood until their last bullet, but were not able to survive facing such deadly machinery that did not even save the children of the family. Thus, on the March 5, 1998, detached and beyond any help of comrades at arms, the entire Jashari family was massacred. They were buried two days later under the care of some human rights activists and the Democratic League of Kosova.

The Prekaz massacre shocked the world, especially for the fact that Belgrade said it was fighting against "the KLA headquarters and its commander," while the footage showed that a whole family was massacred outside any broad-scale military action, as the Serb military was trumpeting. The Contact Group, however, would react two days later. However, the press release issued from the meeting appeared even more shocking than the premeditated crime committed by the Belgrade military, in which children and Jashari family members were not spared. For it would come out that Belgrade had allegedly acted in accordance with the approval it received from somewhere to "liquidate the heads of

---

[749] Clark, Howard: *"Civil Resistance in Kosovo,"* London, 2000, p. 173.

Albanian terrorism," as the Jashari brothers were already being called not only by Serbia but by its supporters as well, and that the "excessive force" used indicated that they had the approval to operate, though pouring on the occasion more bullets than needed!

Indeed at the end the press release emphasized "the use of excessive force" that "will not be tolerated," however, lacking any direct condemnation for the use of means of war by Belgrade against the citizens seeking shelter in their homes, as was the case in Likoshan and Prekaz. So, one can say that the Contact Group had condemned the Kosova Liberation Army instead!

"We condemn in particular the terrorist actions of the Kosova Liberation Army!"

Even the remarks regarding Belgrade about "its excessive use of force" would be instantly eased with the conclusion that "this should not, in any way, be misunderstood as support of terrorism"![750]

But, were children and the elderly "terrorists," people who found shelter in their own homes, who were being massacred in those days by the Serbian military in Drenica?

This question was best answered by "WDR" of Cologne with the assessment that "in Prekaz an unwarranted massacre of children and against the Jashari family took place, in which even if Belgrade – qualifying Adem and Hamza as head of the terrorist KLA – intended to arrest and try for terrorist activities, this had to be done by permitted means, in accordance with international norms, without affecting the family."[751]

The U.S. administration, feeling it had already fallen into the trap of treating and maintaining Milosevic as a "peace partner," even more so under the impression of what the U.S. envoy Gelbard days ago had said during his meeting with Milosevic, calling the KLA a "terrorist organization," would now try to at least on its own "distance itself" from the position of the Contact Group, which still continued to allow Belgrade to use "prudent force against terrorism."

Albright spoke of "grave violations against universal human rights" comparing the Drenica massacre with actions "that ignited war in the former Yugoslavia," as the world focusing on violations of human rights

---

[750] See Contact Group Communique of 9 March 1998, published in „Rilindja" on 10 March 1998.

[751] "Westdeutsche Rundfunk", Cologne, 8 March 1998.

circumvented the fact that it was all something else that would lead to war. The U.S. Secretary of State warned that the time had come to act decisively before it's too late. "Or else, we will be bearing the consequences."[752]

Even by what Albright means "disregard for standards which should not pass without consequences," Belgrade would be called to pay attention "to standards" over the use of force, but not to renounce its use being justified by the "war against terrorism."

Albright's captivation with "standards" rather than with the war that Belgrade had already started in Kosova may have had to do with the "Christmas Warning" that the Bush administration had announced in December 1992, which the Clinton Administration had accepted in 1993 seeing it as a "red line" that Milosevic should not touch, because that would be followed by a U.S. tough response.

The reality of the Drenica massacre and the deployment of police and military machinery of over 40 thousand additional troops during the last three months, which was confirmed by the CIA and other Western sources, showed that the so-called "red line" that had been the "Christmas Warning" had already been violated and stepped over. Milosevic had been testing it since the massacre of Qirez and Likoshan and getting no response from the Americans, he went further.

But there could be an American response as the U.S. administration was among the first to call KLA for its guerrilla actions a "terrorist group" threatening to include it on the U.S. terrorism list, as Gelbard warned in Belgrade in January of that year during a meeting with Milosevic.

What Gelbard made public in the form of an open threat falling on the Albanians in their most critical moments, was neither random nor an error. In August 1997, in Washington, in her meeting with Dr. Rugova, Madeleine Albright spoke of "terrorist actions of KLA" against which she asked the Albanian leader to distance himself.[753]

It must be said that these "inconsistencies" and alike would engulf the problem of Kosova and its crisis for years keeping it in a state of disarray. This would suit Milosevic well as to create the impression that he held its title-deeds and could act as he pleased. These represented the most problematic parts of international diplomacy and decision-making factor,

---

[752] See Albright's statement in Troebst Stefan: *"Conflict in Kosovo,"* 1998, p. 68.
[753] Biermann, Rafael *"Lehrjahre im Kosovo,"* 2004, p. 564.

which also affected their credibility, with their attitude towards Kosova being both controversial and largely hypocritical. Because, on one hand there was criticism and concern against violations of human rights in Kosova, and on the other hand any interference in their defense, excluding the use of force, was openly rejected. On one hand there was an expression of a desire to stop the fire of war in the Balkans from spreading, and on the other there was a display of restraint in the use of compelling tools for its termination. On one hand it was insisted upon maintaining the course of the civil resistance in Kosova with the parallel state, and on the other nothing was undertaken to stop the violence of the Serbian state in Kosova being exercised ceaselessly against Albanians. On one hand Belgrade was warned against military tightening in Kosova, and on the other, when that happened in Drenica, nothing was said. On one side clarity was demanded from the international community in making decisions, as it was required in the Contact Group, and on the other, with the introduction of Russia, an opportunity was created to undermine it by Moscow's well-known attitudes to block any solution that affected the interests of Belgrade for dominance in the region. When one adds to this the continuing disagreement between Europeans and Americans on one side, and the rest of "neutral" China and Arab and Islamic countries, those in Africa and Latin America, on the other, inclined to oppose any solution coming from the West no matter what it was, then these "inconsistencies" and contradictions posed a problem for Kosova and represented a source of its distress, which the Serbs were aware and continued playing that card. Therefore, it is not surprising why Belgrade showed such consistency in this regard and why it continued to make a mockery with the international factor until it finally met the action of force.

However, the response given to the Drenica massacre by Albanians, regardless of the fact that the Contact Group meeting on March 8 still allowed Belgrade to use "prudent actions against terrorism," permitting the means of violence, was right and inevitable. Thus, Albanians were included in an unequal war, which was imposed by Belgrade and could not be avoided any longer, and this opened a new chapter of a wider conflict, because it inevitably included other factors, something that made the international community, which until then had stood by, for the first time face the fire of a regional crisis.

Indeed, the possibility of a regional war, which had already entered the tinderbox, would cause the international factor to at once change its approach to the crisis, in order to carry it out from that of crisis prevention to crisis diplomacy.

So, after Belgrade imposed war, Albanians were necessarily united; the first half of March to early June marked what will be rightly called the "spring of war flowers." This meant an expansion and rapid spread of the ranks of the Kosova Liberation Army stretching into its border areas, through most of Drenica and approaching Prishtina, while it already appeared organized in its operational zones (seven of them: that of Dukagjin, Pashtrik, Drenica, Llap, Shale, Nerodima and Karadak), which were part of the local authentic armed resistance. They had been acting in different ways against the invaders within the parallel state, mostly as local activists or leaders, but the KLA gathered them in a common ploy of organizational war, still in the service of state building and its concept, but now also by means of war. The world media was full of pictures and stories showing fighters of the Kosova Liberation Army in war positions, exercising and even building ditches, such as those in Gllogjan and other parts of Dukagjin up to the border with Albania.[754]

The atmosphere of war already reflected in the introduction of weapons from Albania, or by sending war volunteers from abroad, reflected greatly in the global media, turned into open war as a KLA unit entered Rahovec.

And, precisely the introduction of KLA units from the "free rural zones" reining free in parts of Dukagjin and Drenica to the town of Rahovec, turned into a "trigger" for the launching of a great offensive by the Serbian police and military forces against the positions of the Kosova Liberation Army. It began first in Rahovec, and then in Dukagjin, where the resisting forces of the Kosova Liberation Army and the Armed Forces of Kosova (FARK) were, to continue in Drenica and other parts of Kosova, where the Serbian forces by mid-October were able to retake the free zones opening the roads that had been kept closed for five months (Prishtina-Peja road interrupted at the Llapushnik Gorge and the one towards Malisheva), while Milosevic would loudly declare in Belgrade in October his victory over the Kosova Liberation Army.

---

[754] Powerful world media outlets such as BBC, CNN, NTV, Euronews, ARD, ZDF, ORF, RAI and others broadcast stories from the „free zones" of Kosovo and deployments in the north of Albania. For more, they reported on the mobilization of fighters in European countries and the U.S. from the ranks of the Albanian diaspora.

General Perisic presented to the representatives of the world press and foreign diplomats his "evidence" of, as he said, "the liquidation of terrorist gangs" and even "the Yugoslav army being received as liberator in the zones of Dukagjin," which were stated as having been "liberated from the violence by Albanian terrorists!" The Belgrade media went as far as presenting "arguments" as to how Albanians had killed Albanians during the so-called "time of the free zones" in which there had been "terrorist violence and terror against the local population," which was allegedly terrorized by "Stalinist and Enverist bands," which had set in some parts "a model of an Enverist state."

But the truth was different. The Kosova Liberation Army, which admitted it had made a mistake by accepting frontal warfare rather than to preserve the way of a guerrilla war of occasional attacks,[755] had not however entirely withdrawn from the front of resistance. A tactical withdrawal towards Albania and in the direction of the distal parts of Pashtrik and Shala, and in the forest areas of the Llap Zone, had helped the guerrilla warfare strategy, particularly in the Llap Operational Zone.[756] The same was repeated with great skill even as Milosevic declared "victory" against "Albanian terrorist groups," a tactic aimed at putting into action the international community into using mechanisms of crisis diplomacy with the military factor needed to pressure Milosevic to accept Holbrooke's plan for the cessation of hostilities and acceptance of an international observers mission in Kosova, a territory that would be monitored by NATO warplanes from the air.

Furthermore, another part of the truth that came out openly after the summer offensive of the Yugoslav military and police forces in Kosova, was that not only in Kosova had there never been an "appeasement of the situation in areas terrorized by the KLA gangs," as Belgrade's propaganda

---

[755] Adem Demaçi, KLA Spokesman in Prishtina admitted that the incursion in Rahovec was but a puberty phase of the KLA and a big mistake. Because, in addition to a military defeat suffered from the police forces, it was the local population that suffered most, being forced to leave their homes annd head to the mountains or leave Kosovo. A number of analysts of the time went as far as assessing that KLA's Option for frontal war with the Yugoslav Army was intentional, as to provoke the Yugoslav Army into forntal actions against the innocent population, thus alarming the international factor to act against Belgrade. (See Erich Ratfeleders evaluation in TAZ, 12 September 1998).

[756] For more see Zhitia, Skënder: *"Ushtria Çlirimtare e Kosovës – Zona Operative e Llapit"* and *"Dëshmorët e UÇK-së – Zona Operative e Llapit."*

claimed, but it was actually where the first phase of ethnic cleansing of the Albanian border strip happened by the mountains of Decan, including Decan, Dushkaja, and Reka e Keqe, reaching as far up as Erenik of Gjakova. This area was completely cleansed of the Albanian population. Around one hundred and fifty thousand Albanians were forced to leave their ancestral homes. The Yugoslav police and army, just as the latest elaborate of Seselj and Serb Orthodox Church had envisaged and planned, had declared the north Dukagjin area with the entire part of Reka e Keqe on the border of Albania as a "border security zone," left without its inhabitants. Belgrade even began sending to the West prospects on the creation of an "ecological oasis" to become a European tourist resort with enjoyment and pleasures of hunting wild animals![757]

After the expulsion of the Albanian population of Decan, Junik and other parts of Dushkaja and Reka e Keqe, the systematic destruction of all infrastructure there belonging to the Albanian population began, destruction of homes, property and even livestock. Livestock left without care had begun to be collected by certain Serbian firms with over a hundred thousand cattle and sheep herds sent to Serbia. Systematic destruction of settlements through the use of war means after the Albanian population was forcibly removed from their lands was another crime so far unprecedented in Europe, condemned everywhere as crimes against humanity.[758]

In the meantime, faced with the size of the humanitarian crisis, but also with the consequences of a rather large-scale escalation reaching a critical stage, U.S. diplomacy, first by Hill, U.S. ambassador in Shkup, and a little later by Holbrooke, who had arranged for the Dayton agreements, would be put into action with a pace sometimes resembling panic. The concern came not only because the conversion of the conflict had already been done, but because the part of the population of Kosova, estimated to have exceeded the number of over 300 thousand displaced persons in various parts of Kosova, a part of which had found refuge in the mountains, with the approaching winter was facing a humanitarian disaster. It seemed that the humanitarian aspect would be the cause for the European politics to begin to think that the Dayton Accords had been creating their own framework of what was called "European peace," in which Belgrade had been able to restore its image of a regional factor, bringing back

---

[757] *"Rilindja,"* 30 August 1998.
[758] *"Rilindja,"* 31 August 1998.

pessimism and apathy, similar to that when faced with criminal actions of Serb militaries in Bosnia and Herzegovina as UN protected areas were being attacked one by one with the blue helmets handing them over to them without the least bit of resistance.

Indeed, Europeans would be alerted on the approaching humanitarian catastrophe, but would not begin to take any steps to pressure Belgrade. Rather, these very same European countries from among the ranks of the Contact Group, which at the meeting of March 8, 1998, after the massacres against the Jashari family and others in Drenica had been committed, issued a press release criticizing Belgrade for its "excessive force used against terrorism," namely giving their consent to proceed with "moderate means," now as if feeling an unclean conscience, declared unreserved humanitarian aid to the Albanian population!

To assist the displaced Albanian population sheltered in the mountains to survive the approaching winter, the European Union formed an emergency headquarters pouring millions of dollars for humanitarian aid into Kosova leaving it up to the humanitarian organizations to manage, such as the German humanitarian organization *Capanamur* managed by the great humanitarian Neudek, known throughout the world for its assistance. Upon his arrival in Kosova, Neudek looked at the situation of the Kosova population following the Serbian summer offensive, and alerted the international public that Kosova faced a humanitarian disaster caused by Belgrade's premeditation to force Albanians to surrender.[759]

The Failure of the Force of Diplomacy and the Beginning of the Diplomacy of Force

Hill's three drafts and the failure of the Albanian negotiating team for lack of internal consent. – Kosova Liberation Army disagreed with the composition of a second negotiating group appointed by Dr. Rugova with Adem Demaci as its spokesman dictating terms for the formation of Kosova's institutions. – After declaring military victory over KLA Milosevic forgoes negotiations with Kosova Albanians. – The emergence of the American turbo diplomat, Talbot and first ultimate demands to Belgrade for the withdrawal of police and military forces

---

[759] See interview for "*Eksluzive,*" 4/2000.

from Kosova and their replacement with a "credible" international
presence for Albanians. – NATO Summit in Vilaret, Portugal, on Sep-
tember 23 and 24 of that year and the decision to mobilize the armed
forces for possible air attack against Yugoslav forces in Kosova. – On
December 15, 1998, President Clinton issued his U.S. authorization to
NATO to take military steps against Serbia if President Milosevic con-
tinued to challenge the international community. – Under internation-
al threat, especially the ultimatum by the NATO Secretary General
Solana that Belgrade could be bombed within 68 hours if it failed to ac-
cept the catalog of the Contact Group, Milosevic accepted Holbrooke's
proposals for an international monitoring presence in Kosova and reso-
lution of the humanitarian crisis. – NATO in the ceasefire monitoring
role, while the OSCE as an international civilian mission composed of
two thousand observers, led by the American Walker.

Belgrade's police and military summer offensive against the armed
resistance in Kosova, even though allegedly intended to "liquidate Albanian terrorist groups" aimed instead at implementing the first phase of
ethnic cleansing in Kosova, the expulsion of most of Dukagjin along the
Albanian border and destruction of the Albanian armed resistance. The
latter was believed to have recovered soon, returning to the mountains of
Kosova to continue to fight using different strategies, such as the guerrilla
warfare used in its next stage.

Like years ago in Bosnia and Herzegovina, when it began to get itself
involved in resolving the conflict there, U.S. diplomacy, even in these
circumstances attempted to charge itself almost on its own in the last
minutes to reach a peaceful agreement between Albanians and Serbs.
Obviously, it did not believe in it itself but rather all had been part of the
American scenario to use even the "last policy resorts" of offers to Belgrade before opening the cards for military intervention against Serbia, to
eventually take it out of Kosova, as really happened in a year's time.

The U.S. Ambassador in Shkup, Christopher Hill was the first from
the beginning of June (i.e. after Dr. Rugova was sent without his approval
by the Americans to Belgrade to talk to Milosevic), to begin his intensive
moves on drafting an agreement according to an outline without clear
conceptual lines, however, for the first time touching on the issue of the
status of Kosova. These referred to a compromise between the demands of
the Albanians for independence and respect for the sovereignty of Serbia

over Kosova, where Albanians would be guaranteed a high degree of autonomy substantially similar to the federal unit, a task hard to achieve since attitudes between Prishtina and Belgrade were extremely opposite.

Faced with such positions and the deepening of the crisis from the beginning of the armed conflicts, as Belgrade had already started to put into action its Kosova war scenarios towards achieving its ultimate goals (ethnic cleansing), it can be said that in this respect the U.S. administration and the Contact Group as well, which began intensively to deal with the crisis in Kosova, did not have a steady line as far as a package of proposals on which to resolve the Kosova crisis. This was the biggest problem for them and it seemed as if everything was left in the hands of the American mediator Hill so that he would fail.

How could it be explained otherwise when he changed the draft three times from May to late September 1998? Changes to the drafts were many as the price was concessions made to Milosevic in order to make him accept talks. These changes went to the detriment of Albanians thus gaining the impression that it was not important at all how the Albanians would react. The important thing was to test Milosevic into seeing what his real purpose was: to finally settle accounts with the Albanians eventually peeling through the use of tools of war, that is to cleanse Kosova of them, or to bring them to such a situation as to turn them into a manipulated factor after having expelled most of them, and with the remaining few (mostly a traumatized layer of the rural population) enact an historic agreement that would none other than the Serb triumph over Kosova. According to Belgrade, this would represent a contribution to the appeasement of the region "from constant danger of the potential threat of Islamic fundamentalist terrorism existing among Albanians."

Here the situation in the battlefield played a special role, which after the great police and military summer military offensive that began by taking Rahovec and destroying one of the KLA "bases" in Dukagjin and later establishing the "free zones" in Drenica, some of which never existed except in Serbian propaganda to fan the issues in order to justify military offensives, in the circumstances of this military "triumph," Milosevic felt rather confident and accordingly presented conditions increasingly unacceptable for talks. Thus, Hill's first and second drafts seemed to have been entirely corrected by Belgrade, which caused a backlash of reactions from Albanians, demanding that they be changed.

Besides the content of drafts, which appeared as presenting difficulties for Albanians as they contained nothing but a cultural autonomy masked by a veneer of local self-government, which was not a lot in those circumstances, the problem for Hill was finding the supporting Albanian partners from the whole spectrum in the form of a negotiating team. Although Dr. Rugova and his party remained the main reference, as bearer of all the institutional civilian resistance of the time, Hill sought the participation of all the Albanian political spectrum, including the Kosova Liberation Army, though not with active participation, but rather to be consulted with and to obtain their consent, which was important for the Americans to test their ability in relation to Dr. Rugova's line of civil resistance, turning into a usable card with many opportunities.

The first fifteen-member negotiating group proposed by Dr. Rugova, left the impression of a certain unity among the Albanian political spectrum, as it also included Rugova's opponents, especially Demaçi with his *Parliamentary Party*, inherited from Surroi, considered to be the political wing of the Kosova Liberation Army.[760]

With U.S. mediation the negotiating team G-15 met with Milosevic on May 15, 1998 in Belgrade. Dr. Ibrahim Rugova was there too and this was the most sacrificial offering that the Americans would do for Milosevic to the detriment of Albanians, as Belgrade had already begun its large-scale military and police offensive in Dukagjin and other parts of Kosova, which would last throughout the summer, something that for them in the circumstances any talks with Belgrade, even if made under Washington's pressure, represented a loss of authority from within. In order to somewhat relieve Dr. Rugova of this pressure, which could undermine him and his parallel state, which both the Americans and Europeans still needed, including NATO, Washington saw to it that Rugova received an invitation from U.S. President Clinton on an official visit, which would take place on May 29, only two weeks after having met with Milosevic in Belgrade. At the White House in the meeting with Clinton, Dr. Rugova was accompanied by Fehmi Agani, Bujar Bukoshi and Veton Surroi.

---

[760] Tahiri, Edita: *"Konferenca e Rambujesë. Procesi negociator & Dokumentet,"* Prishtina, 2001, pp. 44-45. The first negotiating group G-15, appointed by Dr. Ibrahim Rugova was composed of the following: Fehmi Agani, President. Members: Edita Tahiri, Rexhep Ismaili, Veton Surroi, Adem Demaçi, Bujar Bukoshi, Mahmut Bakalli, Mehmet Hajrizi, Esat Stavileci, Bajram Kelmendi, Pajazit Nushi, Shkëlzen Maliqi, Hydajet Hyseni, Blerim Shala and Bujar Dugolli.

Even despite American encouragement for Dr. Rugova and his civil-institutional resistance being received in Washington by President Bill Clinton, in addition to the Serbian military offensive, there was also the problem of Hill's first and second drafts that the Albanians would rightly deem unacceptable and require fundamental changes. And since this did not happen, then this would be reflected in the cohesion of the Albanian negotiating team, which began to break up on this basis.

Hill's third draft, even though somewhat more balanced, as it also incorporated elements of Albanian self-administration and international supervision, would still be faced with the difficulty of establishing a transitional government to function in Kosova. The Contact Group meeting held in Bonn in July had suggested that Bukoshi's Government should not be the one to return to Prishtina, but there should be a government that would emerge out of an agreement of the local political spectrum in Kosova.[761] Furthermore, for the first time there was a demand for including representatives of the KLA in the government, foreseeing an "appeasement" of the war factor. Evidently, Belgrade did not like this at all, because it was the armed resistance and its further involvement into a spiral of conflict that enabled it to continue settling accounts with Albanians by means of war. This calculation, as would be seen after Belgrade's rejection of all the concessions offered, suited well both the Americans and NATO to use force against a Serbia that refused to show cooperation. This fulfillment of the humanitarian aspect to protect Albanians from Serbian genocide enabled the achievement of certain strategic goals in the region.

Rugova came up with a new negotiating group, but this time significantly contracted and influenced by the Democratic League of Kosova. This seemed to suggest the creation of a local government seat in Kosova that would get rid of Bukoshi, who had lost Rugova's confidence as well as the broad base of the Democratic League of Kosova, which demanded his removal because of his wooing in Albania with different forces that undermined the role of Rugova and the parallel state. On the other hand, the creation of a local government with a prime minister outside the ranks of the LDK and with KLA's consent, created circumstances for the parallel

---

[761] See "*Rilindja,*" 18 July 1998.

state for the first time to gain international legitimacy even from Belgrade, using it to become a factor for winning political capital.[762]

Rugova was in favor of this combination, which enjoyed the consent of the U.S., opting for a "moderate line," which included opponent subjects but not their leaders. Therefore, in addition to his three associates (Fehmi Agani, Fatmir Sejdiu and Edita Tahiri) from the Parliamentary Party of Kosova, came Bajram Kosumi and also Mehmet Hajrizi, who since the First Assembly of LDK in May 1991 had been elected to the Central Council and later its Presidency, holding the position until February 1998, when he together with a few others finally left the party and joined the ranks of KLA appearing as a member of its General Staff, as was the case with Rame Buja and KLA spokesman Jakup Krasniqi. So, the names of Demaçi and Qosja were missing and this posed a problem, as a result of which this negotiating group, which although mandated Mehmet Hajrizi to work in Kosova, would not win the support of the KLA. The "war wing" not only did not accept being included in such a government, but it rejected it altogether. [763]

On August 14 the Kosova Liberation Army announced Adem Demaçi as its political representative, authorized, as said, "to save the establishment of Kosova's institutions,"[764] which could be explained as an option in favor of a political solution, as he favored talks with Belgrade, but not within its dictates.

This started the final failure of Hill's mission and his drafts of major compromises to Milosevic at the expense of Albanians. It was only logical, because Belgrade on its way to concluding its military offensive against the KLA forces as "successful," even for the time being, even realizing that the war did not end with a defeat but that it would start again in spring, was not interested in a government of Kosova Albanians to be launched in Prishtina, much less that it be affected by the Kosova Liberation Army.

This would actually be the main reason for Milosevic to ignore further negotiations with the Albanians, continuing to define the frameworks of democracy through means of war, despite the fact that its reigns were

---

[762] Buxhovi, Jusuf: *"Kthesa historike – lufta e Perëndimit për Kosovën,"* Prishtina, 2009, pp. 509-514.

[763] *"Rilindja,"* 12 August 1998.

[764] *"Rilindja,"* 16 August 1998.

already being held by the Americans and its development would be determined in accordance with the interests they saw in it.

Milosevic was not impressed by a sudden movement of Holbrooke's proximity with the Kosova Liberation Army, when he suddenly in Junik met with their representatives accompanied by Fehmi Agani, Rugova's main collaborator. This gesture was also important as the Americans were thus giving a message to Albanians that the two factors (the one of civil-institutional resistance and that of armed resistance), at least for a show, were being considered alike and that they needed to find a common language. This also warned Milosevic that if he refused to be cooperative with the Americans and their regional plans, he should count on an Albanian resistance, which appeared as a medallion with two faces (civil-institutional and armed ones) that would be considered regardless of their roles.

In the beginning, Milosevic was not willing to show regard for the American messages, as he had his own option to solving the Albanian issue through means of war, which for him remained the only option in the game. Rather, the meeting of the powerful American man from Dayton with KLA representatives and conversations with them, which became a global media sensation, pushed him even more to prove unco-operative in the diplomatic plain and more severe in his military plans to step up efforts to eliminate the KLA factor militarily and eventually politically before it was too late.

Holbrooke's intervention, although based mainly on the logic of the dictate to be used against Belgrade, entirely bypassing Albanians, however, would bring out the Kosova Liberation Army as a factor in a new light, although in relation to the Yugoslav forces it had lost the battle. Because, eventually during his mission, what Milosevic celebrated as a victory against "Albanian terrorist groups" who were allegedly and finally defeated to yield to the "forces of peace and coexistence," Holbrooke turned into an American double trump: on one hand to make the point that in the name of the fight against terrorism the Albanian people were being fought with the concept of ethnic cleansing, and on the other hand, that the Albanians had created circumstances not to believe in the language of politics and peace talks but to fight back, as for years they had exhausted all the capital of a civil-institutional resistance. The humanitarian disaster that threatened about half the population of Kosova, which had been displaced across the mountains for Holbrooke could be avoided not by a triumphant military demonstration. Preventing a general uprising of armed Albanians in spring, which consequently would follow a course of the war that was imposed by Belgrade and threatened to destroy them, according to the American emissary spread the necessity of eliminating the factors that brought about the situation and of those related to the course of the war that Milosevic was pursuing.

Faced with Holbrooke, before long, Milosevic saw that the "trophies" of war with the Albanians he had thought to exploit for political purposes, and which he had taken not without the approval of the international factor, would return as a boomerang. For Holbrooke would demand that "the first signs of normalcy" in Kosova, which would precede any talks with the Albanians, should begin with the removal of police and military troops from Kosova to be done through international supervision in the form of a direct presence in Kosova to be deployed with the mandate for intervention. Albanians at this point only believed in the American presence. So, Milosevic was faced with what he was most afraid of: the international presence in Kosova, constantly demanded by Dr. Rugova as a precondition for starting talks with Belgrade.

The American turbo diplomat, unlike Hill, who wandered with drafts in his hands between Belgrade and Prishtina achieving nothing whatsoever, finally, when seeing that Milosevic was keeping his old tune, ultimately slapped his demands on the table. And they were not just intimidation cards any longer, but bore the power of a threat, similar to that which he faced four years before in Bosnia and Herzegovina as the first limited NATO combat operations began from the air against Serb forces around Sarajevo and other parts where Serbs had advanced, holding Bosnia and Herzegovina hostage pending the implementation of their plan in accordance with its division into two parts, entirely eliminating the Bosnian factor.

And, the most powerful message for Belgrade came from the NATO summit in Vilaret of Portugal on September 23 and 24 of that year with the decision to mobilize military forces from an eventual air attack against Yugoslav forces in Kosova if no agreement was signed for Kosova, as submitted by the American mediator Holbrooke and formally approved by the Contact Group.[765]

---

[765] Clark, Wesley: *"Të besh luftë moderne,"* Prishtina, 2003, p.

At the summit in Portugal the decision was followed by numerous difficulties as certain member states had requested that the Air Force mobilization that could be used against Belgrade, should be conditional upon the consent of the UN Security Council.[766] This would result in blocking the decision, as evidently Russia and China were the ones that opposed any military pressure on Belgrade. Moscow even had indicated that air bombing of NATO against Yugoslav forces would force Russia to reconsider its course of partnership with the West.

The question of issuing an ultimatum to Serbia was also accompanied by problems. Those seeking a UN Security Council resolution on any threat to Serbia would also challenge the ultimatum sent to Belgrade to accept Holbrooke's peace plan. The German Defense Minister Volker Rüe would alert that Russia's old tune not to be on the same boat with the Europeans would cost hundreds of thousands of deaths in Kosova. "Nobody dares to link Moscow's consent with the tragedy of thousands of Albanians left in the mountains. The ultimatum to Serbia, rather than NATO, was being posed by the winter."[767]

Such a warning would be provided by U.S. President Clinton for his envoy Holbrooke as he flew to Belgrade to hold final talks with Milosevic between 5 and 13 October.

> I have decided that the United States of America give NATO the authority to take military steps against Serbia if President Milosevic will continue to challenge the international community. During these days our European partners will make these kinds of decisions.[768]

U.S. president's decision about automation of the military steps against Serbian military machinery in Kosova might have further motivated Serb military and police forces (of course upon orders from above) to show what they were capable of doing if threatened by NATO. Near the village of Upper Obria, Serb military and police forces would shell the displaced in the surrounding forests massacring dozens of women and children. Milosevic was thus not only testing the Americans and NATO as to how far they were able to go, but was even provoking them.

---

[766] *Ibid.*

[767] Kuntzel, Matthias: *"Der Weg in den Krieg,"* 2000, p. 123.

[768] Kuntzel, Matthias: *"Der Weg in den Krieg,"* 2000, p. 128 (back translation).

The UN Security Council on October 2 was forced to issue a statement condemning the massacre against Albanian women and children, but failing to name the perpetrator, as Russia threatened with its veto power if there was a mention of Serb police and military forces as the perpetrator of the crime, even though the CIA and other Western military intelligence services had overwhelming evidence about the massacre carried out by Yugoslav forces. The Russians, for their part, used a statement by the Serbian deputy Milovan Bojic, who said that the massacre in Obria was a work of KLA in cooperation with the intelligence services of several countries in the West, who killed using camouflage uniforms of the Yugoslav Army in order to establish an alibi for NATO to attack Serbia![769]

On the same line of opportunism was also the next statement by Kofi Annan, the UN Secretary General, who tried to absorb the actions of Serbian militaries in Kosova, which were documented by various sources, with Serbs not hiding their intentions at all. For the absurdity to be even greater, after which the international community would finally give Americans the right to waive the World Organization during the crisis, Kofi Annan praised a Serbian government statement ostensibly about taking measures to prevent a humanitarian disaster which was threatening the population of Kosova from the summer Serbian offensives, even though the world knew for years that all Belgrade did was war and that it was trying to allegedly fix the consequences in order to carry the attention elsewhere, occasionally displacing it from one side to another.

The United States of America would not permit, as it had happened for years in Bosnia and Herzegovina, to once again be put to sleep by the United Nations, under the lullaby of the Russians, Chinese and so-called third world Islamic-Arab Africans standing on the opposite side of the West and desperately trying that when it came to the issue of Kosova, to take Serbia's side.

So, on the evening of November 8, the Contact Group in London, attended by the envoy Holbrooke and Chairman of the OSCE Bronislaw Geremek, decided to present Milosevic with a catalogue of demands that had to be fulfilled upon concrete military pressure.

The catalogue contained the following demands:

a) ceasefire,

---

[769] *Ibid*, p. 126.

b) withdrawal of security and special forces to positions prior to March 1998,

c) free access to humanitarian organizations,

d) return of all displaced persons and refugees and continuation of the dialogue with Kosova Albanians,

e) cooperation with the Hague Tribunal to prosecute war criminals from Yugoslavia and verification of these measures by the OSCE.[770]

Milosevic would not be the man he was if he did not start to play his popular games of delays in search of time "to think it over," of careful selection of points acceptable to him and others that should be discussed and so on, which would once again attempt the catalog of demands of the Contact Group to lose weight. ... Envoy Holbrooke disclosed the ultimate package to him which had to be accepted in full within forty-eight hours. So from October 11 he was issued an internal ultimatum, to which he excluded himself on the grounds that he needed some time for consultations with parliamentarians and even opposition! In the meantime even before the forty-eight hour timeframe expired, the Military Council of NATO in Brussels had given its approval for "*Activation Order.*"

But even the so-called authorization key for the use of force was not so easily achieved because it had to pass two levels: that of reconciliation without obligation and a binding consent.

As this was a serious threat, Americans succeeded in making the consent binding or otherwise it would undermine the Alliance's decision making and Milosevic would use it for other games with consequences for the Alliance itself and the international community in general. Americans would insist that as the threat remained non-binding it would be left to individual countries to decide and this meant a debacle for the Alliance at a time it was expected in April of the following year to celebrate the fiftieth jubilee. This also meant a rift for the West, which Russia could exploit, which was gradually beginning to reveal its superpower habits being camouflaged on the case pretending to be defending international

---

[770] "*Die Welt,*" 8 October 1998. Regarding the catalogue of demands submitted to Milosevic, Stefan Troebst would also be dealing in "*Südosteuropa*" 3-4, p. 181. Troebst said that Belgrade on 5 October recieved the OSCE Mission but rejected its Point F, dealing with cooperation with the Hague Tribunal.

law, although it was known that all it wanted was to restore its lost influence in the Balkans.

This forced the European allies to agree with the U.S. position and as the last European attempt to cope with the hindrances coming from some of the allies with enough perfidy, though Washington already eliminated the danger of acting on its own which would take them out of the decision-making process in facing this crisis, which then would compel the Americans to settle it in accordance with their interests, among which was mentioned the opening of the option of Albanian unification, which everyone feared, as it disturbed the region.

The NATO Secretary General Javier Solana relayed his famous decision on the next day, according to which if Milosevic failed to meet the catalog of demands as laid out by the Contact Group, then within 69 hours the NATO bombing would follow without a mandate by the UN Security Council.

Solana submitted the decision to the Supreme Commander of the armed forces of NATO, General Wesley Clark, authorizing him to commence the bombing. This forced Milosevic to accept the whole package of Holbrooke and on October 15, 1998 the Chief of the General Staff of the Yugoslav Army signed an agreement with NATO through which the U.S. and British military aircrafts were allowed a continuous surveillance over the Kosova airspace. An agreement was reached on the occasion for a significant number of British and American officers to go to Belgrade to coordinate logistical operations that this monitoring agreement provided.[771]

On October 16, 1998 Belgrade and the OSCE signed an agreement on the deployment of two thousand troops in a verification mission of the organization to be stationed in Kosova immediately. Most of them were Americans, among who was appointed chief of the OSCE Verification Mission in Kosova, William Walker, an experienced diplomat.

Walker's appointment as Head of the Verification Mission concluded one of the most important steps in the line of the Western mission in Kosova, supervised by the Americans from top to bottom. It had to do with Washington's determination at this stage when all signs led towards military intervention of NATO forces against Belgrade, to oversee all the operations in order to avoid any discrepancy occurring in the prepara-

---

[771] Holgand, Jim: *"The U.S. Role in the Balkan Expands Stealthily,"* 26 October 1998.

tions that could come as a result of the so-called "dual key" used in Bosnia and Herzegovina with a lot of damage.

Evidently Washington had informed Dr. Rugova as well on the catalog points especially about point E, *which had to do with opening the Serb-Albanian dialogue that would include an international mediated status issue.* He would also be notified about the details of the verification mission with Albanians, being asked to adhere to the agreement's provisions.[772]

Hence, for the first time the American administration met two of the main conditions that Rugova constantly sought *international mediation and an international presence in Kosova.*

In his capacity as spokesperson of the Kosova Liberation Army, Adem Demaçi was the only one from among Albanians that challenged the Holbrooke-Milosevic agreement and the West's catalog of demands. He declared that "for Albanians the agreement is unacceptable, as it eliminates the sovereignty of Kosova."[773]

Demaçi added that "only the blind can believe that Albanians would accept associating themselves with Belgrade by such an agreement, which the major powers of the West designed for their own ends."[774]

The Holbrooke-Milosevic agreement reached after the North-Atlantic Alliance used concrete pressure on Belgrade by issuing an "*Activation Order*" which opened the way to other actions necessary for the NATO air campaign which would follow in March of the next year. Everyone knew this, and so did Milosevic, who focused on doing everything to use a future conflict with the West to divide it from within and simultaneously act to put into action his entire military machinery in order to settle accounts with the Albanians. Although it would seem that by signing the agreement with Holbrooke in October signs of a relaxation would follow, in fact, under the guise of diplomatic moves, military preparations for war began from both sides. Thus, besides Belgrade, NATO also moved in the same direction.

One of these steps, representing the initiative in a somewhat camouflaged form, related to the formation of an "*Extraction Force* "composed

---

[772] *Ibid.*

[773] Matthias Kuntzel: "*Der Weg in den Krieg,*" p. 136.

[774] *Ibid*, p. 136.

759

of NATO special forces to be stationed in Macedonia to provide security for the verification mission.

It must be said that rapid action forces to be stationed in Macedonia, were somehow an option for more than a year, as the Pentagon through its major European allies, Britain, Germany and France, demanded that the core of the European countries from the ranks of the Alliance, consent to setting up a mobile body for rapid action in line with the needs and even more so with the new architecture of the North Atlantic Alliance, where the identity of the new European security within it would come out significantly. France felt very excited. It came up with the proposal for the establishment of a military elite corps of 1,500, which would be able to intervene within two hours at any point. Germans proved willing to accept the idea of a rapid intervention force in Macedonia and proposed that it be led by a French general, which would be acceptable to Americans, as for the first time Paris was taking an active role in NATO and that spoke in favor of what the jubilee summit of the Alliance in April 1999 in Washington asked for, namely that former allies demonstrate unity and readiness to continue along. The German Foreign Minister Joschka Fischer called in the French Parliament establishing a rapid response force and its deployment in Macedonia a "good starting point for the development of an indigenous European quick action force."[775]

The agreement to create a body for quick action to be stationed in Macedonia linked to the provision of the Kosova Verification Mission, moved Brussels further towards increasing its military presence in Macedonia and Albania with additional equipment as the quick action units needed military infrastructure, from mechanical to other supporting units to move, including tanks and helicopters. More in line with the preparation for rapid action forces to be more mobile, the British deployed a helicopter unit in Shkup, while the German Bundeswer, along with its monitoring mission installed long ago in the north of Albania, on its border with Kosova near Tetovo, installed intelligence equipment of the most sophisticated kind. Thus, Kosova and its space was not only monitored by all sides, but from Macedonia and Albania a semicircle military logistics infrastructure of NATO was created, to make it clear that a

---

[775] See the speech by the German Foreign Minister, Joshka Fisher in the French Parliament *"Legitimacy of European Capability and its Future"* in „Points taken on Security Policy," January 1999, p. 40.

diplomacy of force had begun force to set preconditions for the use of war against Milosevic. Therefore, an excuse was to be expected for this.

And excuses for intervention from both sides were in abundance. From Serbs who knew that the Americans were willing to intervene militarily in Kosova, realizing also that within the Atlantic Alliance, however, a political consensus of all members was needed, which, if otherwise, would require that any intervention in Kosova be "covered" with the authority of the UN Security Council, which the Russians would surely prevent. Even Albanians who knew that the cup was filled and it could spill over were really interested that it spilled but at the expense of Serbia. Thus, the Kosova Liberation Army, even though it had lost the battle front with the Yugoslav Army, which was expected and even calculated, regardless of the damage it suffered in Kosova, had sufficient potential for stirring trouble to which Yugoslav forces would be forced to react and that would suffice for the internationals to report that the agreement was not being respected. In those circumstances nobody would blame Albanian fighters, no matter how they behaved, because it was the oppressive behavior of the Belgrade regime against Kosova Albanians that they opposed for years in their commitment to the concept of parallel state and its success without violence. And, there were the images of the summer offensive and its victims, the displaced population of over 300 thousand people into the mountains, and there was the humanitarian disaster. Therefore, to expect from them a "gentleman's behavior" for the sake of an agreement was rather absurd.

In these circumstances the Kosova Liberation Army made sure that there was no agreement with Milosevic and this can be backed by some of the documents of the time and confirmed by subsequent statements by certain local commanders of the Kosova Liberation Army involved in preparation of the NATO air campaign and during its course. It was justified too as any silence between the West and the Serbs in the military plan would have fatal consequences for the Albanians and their future. On the one hand it would interrupt or hinder the international dynamics, especially for the Americans, for the Kosova crisis to be resolved with the assistance of the military, and on the other, any peace agreement with Milosevic for the Kosova Liberation Army meant an exit from the game with violent and even fatal consequences. It was obvious that for the latter, along with Albanian guerrillas, Americans and NATO too were not interested, as they had already been calculating the Kosova crisis and its solution would meet two strategic purposes of the West: taking Serbia out of Kosova and the introduction of the North Atlantic Alliance forces, as part of its important geo-strategic concept.[776]

Certainly, in accordance with this concept the guerrilla units of the Kosova Liberation Army would become significantly activated by the end of September and second half of October, at a time when agreements would be signed with Milosevic to proceed further with the "sting and run" tactics.

Various sources suggest that after the "tactical withdrawal" of most of the KLA fighters to Albania and elsewhere, the remaining formations were strengthened with Albanian military officers from the ranks of the Yugoslav Army who had fought in Croatia and Bosnia and Herzegovina against the Yugoslav Army and had a fine war experience, but there were also "disobedient" officers from the ranks of the army of Albania. Indeed, some of them showed up as volunteers in the ranks of the KLA being of Kosova origin or because they felt it their patriotic duty to help their brethren in critical moments. The KLA guerilla units were eventually joined by a large number of Albanian officers who had taken part in the ranks of the Armed Forces of the Republic of Kosova (FARK), who had left its ranks after their failure during the summer offensive in the Dukagjin fighting fronts. Aware of the new role the Albanian officers were equipped with adequate weapons for guerrilla warfare and effective action, claiming they were in possession of American "*Stingers*" used against tanks and aviation by the Mujahedeen in Afghanistan bringing the Russian army to its worst historical defeat turning into hell for the Soviet communist state.[777]

---

[776] See publications *"Der Weg in den Krieg"* by Matthias Kuntzel, *"Krieg im Kosovo"* by Thomas Shmid, *"Der Kosovo-Krieg"* co-authors Albrecht/Schefer and *"Der Kosovo-Konflikt: Wege in einern vermedidbaren Krieg,"* claiming that Kosovo crisis and its developments were maintained under full American monitoring, led by them and American intelligence services in all its phases. (Kuntzel, pp. 141-145). Furthermore, it is accentuated that the so-called Rugova's peaceful road was an American product (Albreht/Schefer, pp. 56-61) towards creating the conditions for NATO deployment in Kosovo and for a pretext for humanitarian intervention.

[777] On the regrouping of KLA guerila units and their readiness to undertake coordinated actions against the Yugoslav forces during October-December 1998 and January-February 1999 there are a number of sources. Among them the following should be mentioned: Barton Gellman *"The Path to Crisis: How the United States and its Allies*

The authoritative Swiss newspaper *"Neue Züricher Zeitung"* reflected this aspect in the following way:

> Radical forces from among the Albanians want to use what might be called an historical event to implement their national state, even though it would cost blood and victims. Albanians not unfairly say that summer comes to the door only once...[778]

Moreover, such similar and abundant writings in European media, which had rightly focused attention on the behavior of armed Albanians who in the new circumstances of monitoring and tapping by American and British aircrafts felt somewhat protected from counter attacks of the Yugoslav military, were used by several OSCE observers to load them with guilt, as did the German General Hanz Laquoi. But neither NATO nor Washington paid any attention to such charges, pointing their finger instead towards Milosevic and his army, which was still trying to sabotage the agreement to withdraw its troops from Kosova through various deception and tricks. Moreover, the U.S. administration on November 30, 1998, not only publicly renounced treating Milosevic as a partner and man of peace, as labeled after the Dayton agreements, but for the first time perceived Milosevic as being the main problem.[779]

A similar assessment came from General Clark, who blamed Serbia for the deterioration of the situation in the following statement: *"Serbs are not interested in a political solution to the Kosova crisis."*[780]

Went to War" in *"International Herald Tribune"*, on 19 April 1999; Jane Perlez: *"Kosovo Rebels"* in *"International Herald Tribune,"* on 12 November 1998.

One other source coming directly from the ranks of the verification mission is that of the German Heinz Loquoi, which would incriminate the KLA, for what he says were deliberate provocations made to entrap the Yugoslav forces. Laquoi also raised multiple charges against the head of the mission, the American Walker, saying he not only knew about these provocations, but in a way he incited them. See: „*Die OSZE-Mision im Kosovo – eine ungenutzte Friedenchance?,*" published in *"Bältter fur deutsche und internationale Politik"* 9/99, p. 1125.

[778] NZZ *"Die Macht der Mythen in Kosovo,"* 16 January 1999.

[779] See press statement by the State Department's James Rubin from *"Archiv der Gegenwart,"* 1998. Page 144 speaks of a new orientation of the U.S. policy in relation to Milosevic and other Balkan factors.

[780] *"International Herald Tribune,"* 6 January 1999.

This assessment by the U.S. general, who would later lead the NATO air campaign against the Yugoslav military and police forces in Kosova and Serbia represented in fact the core of Belgrade's policy towards Kosova, since the beginning of the crisis considering the means of war as the only one to determine the outcome in accordance with the Memorandum of Serbian academics. The international decision-making factor was aware of this. But it must have been other priorities and steps available towards the crisis of the former Yugoslavia that Kosova was left for last by reason of its complexity and the great potential for danger involved.

Also, in this respect, they had the help of the behavior by Albanians when opting for civil resistance with parallel state, in line with the concept of an independent state as announced in September 1990 trying to keep the conflict with Serbia as far away as possible although realizing that it could not be avoided forever. This suited the Americans and NATO to be posted in accordance with their scripts. Obviously, Belgrade with its own behavior, especially after Dayton, had been proving so many times not to be interested in a political solution for the Kosova problem. As early as April 1990 in Washington, in a meeting with Dr. Rugova and the powerful U.S. Senator Robert Dole and in his presence, Dobrica Cosic, author of the last Memorandum of Serbian Academy and future President of the Federal Republic of Yugoslavia, said that the Serbs did not accept democracy as that allowed Albanians to take away power from the Serbs through the ballot boxes.[781]

Indeed, Milosevic did not show any interest in a solution of the Kosova issue by political means and agreement with Albanians even as the Hague Conference after London left the doors open to determine the size of a solution treating it always as an internal matter, provided human and minority rights were respected according to the highest standards.

In the face of such circumstances, the United States of America, which took over the resolution of the Kosova crisis, had no other option than confronting Belgrade with the means of war to prevent the destruction of the Kosova Albanian factor through methods of state violence and intended ethnic cleansing. Thus, for Americans, the last year had been nothing but a political effort to use the "last resorts" of the peaceful resistance of Albanians, while using the pressure of diplomacy of force.

---

[781] Buxhovi, Jusuf: *"Kthesa historike – Vitet e Gjermanisë dhe Epoka e LDK-së,"* Prishtina, 2008, pp. 272-278.

As nonviolent resistance was losing momentum with the emergence to the stage of the Albanian war factor the scheme was also opened for it to be used in accordance with the rules of the game as set by the Americans, which had to be adhered to in full, without guarantee that it would enjoy full treatment as a war partner but never fearing to be anathemized as terrorist as had been done at the beginning at a heavy cost.

The Reçak Massacre and Crossing of the Rubicon

On 15 January 1999, in the village of Reçak, near Shtimje after a shootout with KLA fighters in retaliation for the killing of two, Serbian forces executed forty-six Albanians, many of them children and elderly. – The OSCE Observer Mission Chief Walker reported on the massacre of the civil population by the Serb police forces. – Belgrade reacted harshly calling the general a "CIA agent" declaring him non grata. – ICTY Prosecutor, Louis Arbour, was not allowed to investigate the case. – An urgent meeting of the Contact Group and the ten-point ultimatum on Belgrade to accept an International Conference for Kosova to be held in Rambouillet. – Russia prevented the authorization of the use of force by the UN Security Council.

By the end of August 1995, in the Sarajevo Markale market a grenade exploded coming from the direction of Palje, from the Serbian military fortifications holding Sarajevo under military siege and killing over thirty thousand Bosnian citizens in the city of Miljacka within more than three years.

The massacre would be the straw that broke the camel's back and as a consequence there was a decision by the West led by the U.S. to begin limited bombing against Serb positions around Sarajevo and in other parts of Bosnia and Herzegovina. With selective aerial bombing, NATO annulled in two weeks all the advantage of Serbian invasions as it managed to turn into an air umbrella for the Bosnian-Croat forces during the offensive they launched in Herzegovina and parts of the Cazin Krajina, where Bosnian forces broke the three-year old siege and headed toward Banja Luka, a once mostly Bosnian town that Karadzic and Mladic had turned into a "Serbian stronghold" after crimes committed against the local population, who was forced to vacate and and then populated by rural Serbs instead coming mainly from central Bosnia.

Serbs and the part of their supporters in the world would claim that the grenade had not been thrown by them but by someone else who "wanted an excuse" to bomb. Rather, they would claim it was all allegedly staged by NATO and the Americans, who had long planned for such an epilogue.

On the fifteenth day of January 1999, in a small village near Shtimje, called Recak, there was no grenade explosion, but a similar massacre, in which forty-six Albanian inhabitants of the village were cruelly killed. Victims were collected and taken to a hill above where they were executed at close range. Among them were the young, the elderly and even children.

The Recak massacre was preceded by a clash between Serbian police and a scattered KLA unit resulting in two Serb policemen killed. Albanian losses were not reported as they withdrew to the northeast, toward the Gorge of Carraleva. Observers of the OSCE and television companies were informed of this KLA "provocation", and allowed to approach close to the place where the shots came from.

That afternoon and evening nothing else was being reported but the fact that beneath Recak there had been sporadic fighting between Serbian forces and KLA "terrorists." This was the official Serbian version. OSCE observers needed to investigate and be sure about the two policemen killed in the clash with Albanian "terrorists." Early the next morning, Walker, the head of the verification mission, personally approached the village of Reçak and there he would not confirm "traces of the Albanian terrorist attack" as Serbian officials and their powerful machinery of propaganda Radio Television of Serbia claimed, but rather a massacre of the population of the village with many killed and bodies left on the west slope of the hill.

Following initial investigation by Walker, television cameras of the BBC, CNN, AP and others were allowed to record. He ordered a detailed filming of the entire space and even before reaching Prishtina he told the world media that a massacre had been committed in Reçak against the civilian population. From Prishtina he later officially informed his superiors as well as other factors.

Among the first to seek detailed information was the German General Klaus Neumann. Walker informed the German General, Head of the

Military Council of NATO, that in Recak, prior to that, somewhere in the siege, there had been clashes between Serbian forces and a KLA unit and that after it was over (with two Serb policemen killed), Serbian forces entered Recak and executed civilians. Walker assessed that this was revenge by Serbian police forces against the people of this "hicksville," as indeed two of the KLA members came from there.

This version can also be verified through the testimony of the local residents and other evidence on the spot. Among the evidence that conflicted with the Serb version that the killed "were terrorists killed during fighting with Serbian forces a day earlier," with certainly the most compelling being that "among the terrorists" who allegedly fought with Serb police forces there were children and the elderly. This version Walker sent in writing to the OSCE and relevant world bodies, UN, EU and other mechanisms monitoring the crisis. It was rejected by official Belgrade immediately filing charges against Walker as "a CIA terrorist disguised under the guise of a diplomat" as someone who had been staging similar mind games in Nicaragua and elsewhere, declaring him a non-grata person.

As in the case of shelling of Markalja in Sarajevo, some of the world media, fed by Serbian propaganda, began to see a U.S. and NATO "plot" against Serbia. Reçak was seen as a set up by joint special units of the KLA and agents from among U.S. and NATO, disguised as international observers, who had used the "incident" of the Serbian forces with Albani-an "terrorists" to carry out the massacre against Albanians and sell it as a work of Serbian police units![782]

A German journalist, Erich Rathfelder, who had been among the first to enter Recak and see the victims had talked with residents of Recak who had witnessed the massacre brining shocking stories bearing witnesses to the massacre, in which Serbian police units during the massacre had mortified them in unprecedented ways, including rape and torture in front of their family members! "NATO should not hesitate if it wants to

---

[782] "Le Figaro" of 1 February 1999 and the French TV channel AP-TV was particularly loud in that sense. Their assertions about a U.S.-Albanian „conspiracy" against the Serbs are mostly connected to Serbian official statements and estimates by Serbian pathologists who quickly began to "provide explanations" for the victims as being "terrorists" who were shot by Serbian forces in self-defense and in part victims deliberately by "KLA terrorists," who at the order of their fellow American agents killed them in order to create an "alibi" for NATO attacks!

save a defenseless people of killing and terrible humiliation. The introduction of ground troops is the only salvation."[783]

Reçak however had been expected as a well-planned and forewarned action by Belgrade to test the readiness of the international community on the Kosova issue in circumstances where Milosevic not only did not fulfill the obligations of the agreement, particularly regarding Article Two related to withdrawing additional forces stationed in Kosova before March, but had continued to strengthen them with others, doing more maneuvering.

NATO observers investigated this maneuver by Milosevic and this issue was brought up to the highest levels. The Military Council of NATO expressed its concern to Belgrade, but received conflicting answers in return. General Wesley Clark personally went to Belgrade on December 20, 1998 to warn Milosevic and his military personnel that the Alliance was not joking. He met with General Ojdanic, who had been recently appointed new Chief of Staff of the Yugoslav Army.[784]

General Ojdanic pretended as if there were no problems on the Yugoslav side, but that the trouble was with the "Albanian terrorists," who had been returning to their previous positions and provoked war.

General Clark responded that based on precise estimations of NATO throughout Kosova there were only 410 KLA members whose positions were known to both NATO and the Yugoslav Army and that the maps of their positions when compared between the Belgrade and Brussels monitors were almost identical.

"We saw your tanks north of Prishtina, near Podujevo. This is not an authorized position. You have been violating promises that Milosevic and your predecessor gave to NATO," General Clark told Ojdanić.[785]

An embarrassed General Ojdanic spoke of military exercises.

"And they too must be reported on time. The agreement is clear. You have not done this."[786]

Both General Clark and Solana left Belgrade for Brussels with the impression that Milosevic had started to play his notorious games and that he did not wish a political solution. There were indications that he also

---

[783] TAZ, 18 January 1999.

[784] Clark, K Wesley: *"Të bësh luftë moderne,"* Prishtina 2003, p. 192.

[785] *Ibid*, p. 192.

[786] *Ibid*, p. 192.

intended to challenge NATO to the end counting on its disunity. General Clark had informed NATO leaders on Milosevic's breach of the agreement and that this would result in fatal consequences for the Alliance itself, as it would lose credibility. It would have consequences for the people of Kosova, which according to the general's belief, stood before the blade of the sword in danger of losing their homeland forever.[787]

Various pathologists dealt with the Recak massacre by a Serbian-Belarusian and later a Finnish team, who tried to defend the Yugoslav military and police forces of guilt and this would last long. NATO demanded that the investigation of the massacre be conducted by the ICTY chief prosecutor, Luis Arbour, who was in Shkup and waiting permission to enter Kosova. However, permission for the investigation would not be granted. Upon General Clark's personal intervention, who, along with General Klaus Neumann saw Milosevic two days later to speak to him about recent aggravations, Arbour was allowed into Kosova but only as a tourist. According to General Clark this was a sufficient argument that Serbs feared the expertise of the Hague Tribunal, as they had committed the atrocity unable to hide the traces. This proved they were determined to finally settle accounts with Albanians by the use of war.[788]

However, this and others issues that would be opened in the Belgrade-Brussels relations, did not hinder the NATO Council to urgently convene on the next day upon U.S. persistence with the Americans

---

[787] *Ibid*, p. 193.

[788] See General Clark's and General Klaus Naumann's conversation with Milosevic in Belgrade on January 20 in Clark's book *"Waging Modern War,"* pp. 195-198. It includes the question of participation of the ICTY Chief Prosecutor, Ms. Arbour in the investigation, which was rejected on the grounds that Belgrade did not recognize the Tribunal, with the conversation continuing about the withdrawal of the decision to have Walker removed from Kosovo and an immediate withdrawal of all additional military and police units. An insert of the conversation between Milosevic and General Naumann is interesting with the first losing his temper:

"General Naumann strengthened me with his thoughts on similar lines. He told Milosevic that his country had been dropped by Europe.

- You will end up in ruins, if not convinced.

Milosevic erupted. With a red face he began spitting his words out. This was the same man I had seen threatening Holbrooke in Dayton.

- Who are you to accuse us? These are lies. Serbia is democracy itself ... You are threatening! ... You are war criminals! ..."

demanding an approval decision for air strikes against Yugoslav forces in Kosova, which had to be punished for the massacre. The U.S. proposal for immediate bombardment however was not accepted. The justification was that "bombing could turn into a sky umbrella for the KLA."[789]

The German side came up with the proposal regarding the political aims that the air intervention had to follow.

This dilemma was justified as bombing without a political solution would give cause for new tensions in the region and open up the possibility of involving other factors in the crisis, particularly considering the risk of things getting out of control. Former Foreign Minister Klaus Kinkel, in accordance with this fear, suggested that in Kosova joint ground troops of NATO and Russia be deployed, after discussions and consent from both sides.[790]

Although Kinkel's proposal was quickly brushed away, introducing such an opinion was not accidental nor outside the political concept which the West, especially its European part, needed, so that the Kosova crisis and its solution would not get "out of control" being kept instead tied to a particular concept, which would maintain the balance between the American interests for maximalist solutions, namely for Kosova to gain independence without consideration for Serbia and those of the Europeans who were interested to find a compromise between the demands of the Albanians for independence and Serbia's rejection. In a way it brought to its temporary placement under international supervision, as a protectorate or otherwise, leaving the settlement for later under more appropriate circumstances. Evidently, the European position within the North Atlantic Alliance prevailed turning into a political concept that preceded the preparations for the Rambouillet conference call on February 6.

Before connecting the airstrikes with the political concept of solving the Kosova crisis, two meetings of the NATO Council were held on January 20 and 22 respectively. In both the first and second meetings of the Council, a U.S. request for punitive actions against Serbia from the air was rejected. The refusal of immediate punishment, evidently planned by the Americans to be used as a counterbalance to win Europeans' support for an ultimatum to Belgrade, would, however, set the first contours of the

---

[789] "Le Figaro," 20 February 1999.
[790] Kuntzel, Matthias: "*Der weg in den Krieg,*" 2000, p. 160.

proposal for a political settlement, which needed an ultimatum considering it was high time to hinder Serbia from realizing its goals by means of war in the meantime offering Albanians something concrete that would keep them from entering into direct conflict with Belgrade.

It was clear that the past road of civil-institutional resistance and endurance that the Albanians pursued would be accompanied by armed resistance as well as a necessary response to an imposed war. This was already known and obvious to everyone. Even the Europeans, who by both the remnants of old interests and the fear that Kosova and its crisis could set in motion a whole avalanche in South-Eastern Europe, opening many issues, demanded that a diplomacy of force had its say, however with a necessary political approach and solution framework, which would be in line with Western interests in the region.

This should have been the American goal too, succeeding to "punish Serb forces for the Recak massacre, even acting on their own" – that the Europeans did not want in any way for fear that it would exclude them from the whole process – to replace it with an ultimatum to Belgrade, which was sent to Milosevic to accept a political solution for the Kosova crisis without the right to modify anything but to either to accept or reject it. A rejection would bring about military intervention by NATO.

The German support by giving assurances that they would go along with the Americans in all eventual actions of the Alliance would somehow be conditioned by becoming leading bearers of the concept of peaceful settlement of the Kosova problem. Chancellor Schroeder, Foreign Minister Fischer, and Minister of Defense Scharping, enforced their rhetoric for the U.S. support in fostering a political solution for Kosova, something that would build support for them among the political ranks, and even the public, as Germans still suffered from an inferiority complex that existed from the end of World War II.

In addition, the German politics had a reason to seek "primacy" over political concepts for solving the Kosova crisis, being the Chair of the European Union, while another German General Klaus Neumann was in charge of the NATO Military Council. These two positions allowed it, at least formally, to spearhead the initiative, in which a united Germany would emerge as an important factor in the new global circumstances engaged so that the new concept of European security identity would not be built on the basis of "a special road," which would unavoidably include

Russia, as part of it, but rather within an overall Western one with the Americans as carriers of the new security doctrine.

Obviously the Contact Group, which was responsible for the political settlement of the Kosova crisis, accepted Germany's role in this regard. Even Russia, which was not part of the orchestrating West was keen to see Germany maintain a balance between the West and Russia, as between the two countries there were specific economic interests.

It should be said that the interest of Germany for an international conference on Kosova, conceived as Dayton II, dated from a long time ago. Even before coming to power the left (Social Democrats and the Greens) emphasized the necessity of holding such a conference, since all roads led toward an inevitable conflict of Albanians and Serbs. The left did not like this in any way, but its occurrence would put the Germans automatically into a position to support American options, which compared with European ones, appeared more radical as there were warnings that Washington did not rule out from the settlement of the Kosova issue the package for a total solution for the Albanian question in the region, a view that Europeans disliked. Joschka Fischer, the leader of the Greens, approached the idea as soon as he came to power, but the Recak massacre and the hardening of Belgrade's course postponed its inclusion on the agenda for the German engagement.[791]

During his first telephone conversation with U.S. Secretary of State Albright, after the massacre at Recak, the German Foreign Minister proposed holding a conference for Kosova, which would be prepared by the Contact Group. Albright, who had good experience with the Contact Group for the Balkans during Kinkel's chairmanship, was somewhat reluctant to put on the first plan an ultimatum for Belgrade and its

---

[791] See Joshka Fischer's book *Die rot-grune Jahre"* 2007 translated in Albanian as „Vitet kuq-gjelbër" and published in 2008. The former German Foreign Minister was one among the German politicians engaged in finding a solution for the Kosovo crisis. Though from the ranks of the Greens, a pacisfist party, he stated that one could not allow genocide to happen, as was happening in Kosovo, on the grounds of pacifist principles. His saying in the German Parliament became well known: "We will not tolerate another Auschwitz in Europe" giving the green light to plans for NATO's air intervention. Fischer was one of those who prepared documents for the Rambouillet Conference and the principles on which it relied. Also, he helped to include Russia in the approval of the Security Council Resolution 1244 of 10 June 1999 placing Kosovo under international supervision.

punishment as a precondition to future talks, as no agreement could be reached then since Moscow was ordinarily against it and other Europeans stood undecided.[792]

However, after Albright visited Moscow and got the agreement of her colleague Ivanov to hold a conference for Kosova (as informing Fischer in advance) while pressure would be mentioned but not military threat, the U.S. Secretary of State announced that Fischer could begin preparations for a Conference on Kosova.

Upon Ficsher's initiative the Contact Group held two meetings: in Brussels on January 22 and in London on January 29. In the second, Germany was already promoted as its sponsor and came up with the final ten-point concept which after a ten-hour debate, together with the invitation to Rambouillet, in the form of an ultimatum, was sent on the same day to both Belgrade and Prishtina.

The ten points were the following:

1. An immediate end of violence and ceasefire holding,

2. The solution should be sought within an autonomy and through dialogue,

3. A transitional period of three years, which would serve to find a permanent solution,

4. Unilateral enforcement of transitional status until a final settlement is reached,

5. Territorial integrity of Yugoslavia,

6. Protection of the rights of ethnic groups,

7. Holding of free elections under the supervision and organization of the OSCE,

8. Wavering of judicial prosecution of persons involved in conflicts over holding of talks

9. Amnesty and release of all political prisoners and

10. Cooperation of the two parties in conflict with the participation of internationals.[793]

The next day the NATO Council met supporting the ultimatum of the Contact Group. Negotiating parties, Serbs and Albanians were threat-

---

[792] Fisher, Joshka: "Vitet kuq-gjelber," Prishtina, 2007, p. 123
[793] "Le Monde Diplomatique," February 1999, p. 18.

ened that if a settlement was not reached and the conference failed, then they would be bombed.

In this case, it turned out that achieving consent on the ultimatum by the Contact Group had not been an easy job. Representatives of the six countries (U.S., Russia, Germany, Great Britain, France and Italy) were divided. The U.S., supported by Germany, as usual guarded a stance of a tough course towards Belgrade demanding NATO start bombing after the expiration of the ultimatum. The UK required a slightly softer language, but maintained the line of force. Russia demanded that the issue be discussed at the UN Security Council for getting a mandated use of force if achieved on this deal, which was known in advance that it was not possible. Italy and France demanded that the issue of the authorization of force, if the conference failed, be once again presented to the Contact Group in order to seek other solutions as well, not excluding UN involvement as only with its participation could one ensure eventual mandates for the use of force. Americans, as usual, demanded the setting of triggered steps, namely a fixed time set for action and bombings.

Both the Europeans and Russia, who knew what might follow after the use of force – and the most likely option was that the capitulation of Serbia, opening Albanian Pandora's box – however submitted to U.S. pressure, but as compensation for the ultimatum, which could enter into force without UN approval, required that the Rambouillet document and the conference rested on two non-negotiable principles:

- Autonomy for Kosova (no matter what it would be) and
- The preservation of the territorial integrity of the remaining Yugoslavia.

The Americans desired to save the spirit of the conference and the agreement of the Albanians by accepting a three-year interim proposal by the Germans, under the auspices of the United Nations.

With this proposal the United States of America, although not openly, paved the way to what Albright called *"getting Serbia out of Kosova,"* which broken down in political language meant liberation of Kosova from Serbian occupation. But, at the same time they would make "concessions" to Russia, which as Serb defender was in need of them, with emphasis on preserving the integrity of Yugoslavia and the incorporation of UN in the process of implementation of agreements to maintain face, which in a political language meant *"getting Serbia out of Kosova with it remaining in Yugoslavia."*

Without entering into the U.S. formula of extraction of Serbia from Kosova or Kosova's extraction from Serbia, both Washington and Moscow had already begun to manipulate the German Defense Minister Rudolf Scharping, as one of the proponents of West's tough course against Milosevic, urging both Russia and the UN to be held close by, as without them there could hardly be anything and with them much could be achieved.[794]

In addition the compromise would also please other countries therefore it could be said that the ultimatum of the Contact Group on Belgrade and Prishtina somehow had the approval of the entire international community.

So, Kosova and its problem was already in the process of getting Serbia out or getting it out of Serbia, formulations upon which its future was being decided by already drawing the option of an independent state, if Serbia was taken out of Kosova, as Albright said, or if Kosova was taken out of Serbia, as Moscow sought, to be transferred within the Yugoslav Federation. This bidirectional development, which, regardless of its direction, was separating Kosova from Serbia and could not stop now, as it was Serbia itself, which by opting to solve the Kosova issue by means of war, had lost all of the alibis for its further possession. It was left to diplomacy of force to create the necessary frameworks and those were sought at Rambouillet.

---

[794] See the publication *"Wir dürfen nicht wegsehen – der Kosovo Krieg und Europa"* by the German Defense Minister, Rudolf Scharping, published in 1999. Scharping, among others things, provides colorful details about the Serbian plan *"Horseshoe,"* in which the ethnic cleansing of Kosovo was planned during the NATO bombing. According to Scharping, the Bulgarian Intelligence Service had come up with reliable information that the Serbs would begin intensive preparations during the Rambouillet talks in order to avoid the investigation of military preparations. And, the operation would start as soon as the second round of Rambouillet talks started in Paris on March 15. The German Minister of Defense defended his thesis that Serbia had been prepared for an ethnic cleansing of Kosovo in connection with NATO's air campaign in order to throw the blame on the North Atlantic Alliance.

The Rambouillet Conference – Albanians' First Pact with NATO

In Rambouillet Albanians faced limits set by the politics as the art of the possible with rejection excluded from the game and acceptance contrasting with waiver requests. – A refusal to sign the Rambouillet documents by Serbia would release Albanians of the judgment of history, but not of the weight of political responsibility over a document which contradicted the determination of the people of Kosova as an independent state, as expressed in the Referendum for Independence in May 1991. – Faced with American pressure, Albanians would agree to a withdrawal from maximalist position such as the independent state of Kosova to transform it instead into a transitional autonomous status, which would be conditional to determining a date for a referendum, to be held in three years' time, which would in its turn be conditioned on a deployment of NATO troops as guarantor of transition. – Serbia was willing to accept the political platform but not the referendum and the stationing of troops of the North Atlantic Alliance. – The Albanian delegation, in principle agreed with the signing of the agreement, but it demanded two weeks' time "to review it with the base" from where signs of dissent came from local commanders, a postponement that suited Belgrade to increase its troops stationed in Kosova for ethnic cleansing Kosova, which commenced before the start of the NATO air campaign.

The Rambouillet Conference was scheduled as the last event of saving peace to be done through a binding agreement, with Serbs and Albanians abandoning "extreme positions" in favor of an agreement, even if temporary, which opened doors to other issues that were perceived as needing more relaxation from both sides.

Although there was much doubt and skepticism from all sides and rightly so, it was still believed that it was the American involvement and open pressure to use force by NATO that brought about the first step towards further agreement between Albanians and Serbs, enabled by the recognition of what was considered an "interim solution," with which no one could claim complete victory.

However, the very fact that the Albanian and Serbian delegations were represented at Rambouillet said something, despite the fact that in this case the first appeared as an extra-institutional representation (although they declared their state in 1992 that functioned as a parallel power in Kosova not recognized from the outside), and the latter as a state (although reduced in Kosova in the role of an occupier). Despite this approach of the political realities discriminated against by those of state sovereignty, for the Albanians, a Rambouillet-like conference was of particular importance, because the issue of Kosova, regardless of the limits facing its status, had reached its highest level of internationalization. Meanwhile, it was clear to Belgrade as well that the time had come when it had to decide on dealing with Albanians, regardless of how painful "losing Kosova" would be, or opting to fight, not with Albanians, but the Americans and NATO with no chance of winning. Reaching at this point, for Belgrade the loss of Kosova meant loss either by peace or by war. The diplomacy force imposed itself and it was expected it either be converted into a force of diplomacy giving politics a chance to turn policy issues into agreement, or the opposite, with diplomacy finally yielding to the use of force.

So Rambouillet appeared as a Rubicon for both sides.

Based on the ultimate ten points of the Contact Group, Albanians were unlikely to cross the Rubicon, as they had to agree to autonomy within Yugoslavia (despite the fact that the Americans promised after three years "considering the will of the people" – which was political support without international guarantees).

In their first confrontation of a similar nature with the international community, especially the Americans, Albanians had managed to entirely submit to international dictates, as they realized that their case was undergoing a move of internationalization to which it had been working for a long time, but that it too had its limits as to how far it could go and what consequences they could face if they opposed.

Before doing this, they had to agree to appear in Rambouillet as a joint delegation. And secondly, they had to agree on the concept of the conference, by which they could in no way turn into rejectionists, as that hindered NATO's intervention against Serbian military and police forces in Kosova.

Although the agreement for a joint delegation was viewed from the outside like a technical issue, since Albanians had no other option that, too, had its troubles because this referred to diametrically opposite positions between the line defending a political solution and the one opting for a solution with radical means that went against the international factor encountering a "red line," where both the parallel state and civil resistance and armed resistance turned to the same point so as to be in compliance with U.S. and Western interests. It certainly brought the "war side" to a much more difficult position than the "institutionalists" who were constantly linking Kosova's independence and its implementation with the decision-making international factor and with different areas of interest, seeing it as a political issue that could be achieved step by step, with the "transitional period" and various compromises and agreements with the goal justifying the means.[795]

On the eve of and during Rambouillet, representatives of the Kosova Liberation Army would be aware of this, and the Conference approached the logic of the politics, i.e. reaching of the possible and this would bring them together with "institutionalists," although obviously some of the KLA representatives (Krasniqi and Rame Buja) found it easy as only until a few months before had they been in the LDK Presidency with Dr. Rugova and other leadership positions in the parallel state, from where at the Third Assembly they left the party along with several others (Hydajet Hyseni, Rugova's Vice President and Mehmet Hajrizi, member of the Presidency), who were also in Rambouillet with Qosja's LBD but leaving and joining the "war wing" instead.

The possible for Albanians in Rambouillet passed through an absurd trial of not being measured by consequences rather than by results, where the goal went through the trigger turning into the final goal because both the rejection and acceptance of documents depended on consequences being measured by the extent to which they risked turning into a goal purpose. Thus, the positioning in favor of "consequences" required a feeling of political perfidy and behavior consistent with it that generally seemed very difficult for the Albanian delegation, because it all went

---

[795] On the preparations of the delegation of Kosovo Albanians for the Rambouillet see Edita Tahiri: "*Konferenca e Rambujesë. Procesi negociues & Dokumentet,*" Prishtina, 2001. According to E.Tahiri, the Kosovo delegation in Rambouillet consisted of four components: LDK and institutions of the Republic of Kosovo represented by Ibrahim Rugova, Fehmi Agani, Edita Tahiri, Bujar Bukoshi and Dr. Idriz Ajeti, KLA represented by Hashim Thaçi, Jakup Krasniqi, Ramë Buja, Azem Syla and Xhavit Haliti, LBD by Rexhep Qosja, Mehmet Hajrizi, Hydajet Hyseni and Bajram Kosumi and Veton Surroi and Blerim Shala as non-party representatives. The delegation elected a three-member presidency: Dr. Ibrahim Rugova, Hashim Thaçi and Rexhep Qosja.

through a certain psychology, which only special circumstances can create to be called historic.

Evidently, *focusing on the consequences* rather than *current results* changed the character of the conference, turning it into a "political ward of psychiatric therapy," unseen until then, which often seemed to confuse the boundary between the "patient" and the "therapist."

In this atmosphere, the conference started work on February 6 with great pomp in the medieval castle of Rambouillet, known for stirs and events related to the history of France during the last two centuries. At one time various political opponents were kept confined there mostly for "processing" but not for liquidation, as it would befall the time of the French Revolution onwards.

The "processing" component was not just a metaphor, but a reality, as both Albanians and Serbs were being subject to pressure from the international factor, especially the Americans, who had presented letters before them with deadlines set of several days for having to agree or not agree. They had no other way out, even though both agreeing and disagreeing was part of the loss in order for it to turn into an investment for peace or war.

The French President Jacques Chirac in his greeting speech commemorated the symbolism of Rambouillet linking it to a start that could be historic not only for Serbs and Albanians, but also for the region in general and in this spirit he wished for things to proceed. The co-chairs of the Conference, the American Hill, Austrian Petritsch and Russian Boris Majorski "promoted" the basic document of the conference before the press as a *"Temporary Framework Agreement for Peace and Self-Governance in Kosova"* prepared by the Contact Group.

The agreement represented a systematic framework of ideas that had emerged in recent months. In several chapters general principles were included, while others dealt with security issues, institutions of self-governance in Kosova of both the legislative and executive branches. The project envisaged international forces to be deployed in Kosova as guarantee for the execution of the agreement. It also stressed that the agreement would be reviewed after three years. Matters of Kosova's status were mentioned with more sensitivity or intentionally concealed with rather perfidious formulations.[796]

---

[796] *"Rilindja,"* 7 February 1999.

In fact the most controversial points were those on which the Albanians insisted that the *transitional time* be determined to be followed with a referendum and the stationing of an international force, which over time would also appear in the role of a guarantor of peace and as a factor that would enable the return of confidence, which then would be linked to the return of the displaced population from Serb violence in recent years.

Here direct consequences of accepting the Rambouillet agreement in opposite directions were being projected because the Albanian project moving toward independence depended on their performance and that of Serbs in order to impede it. Therefore, the focus of all attention inside and outside the castle of Rambouillet on these two key points on which peace or war depended was understandable because they were the only prerequisite for the consequences, which the Albanians saw in favor of taking Serbia out of Kosova, while Serbia wanted to see Kosova remain within Serbia.

Initially, Albanians focused on the referendum after three years and the stationing of NATO troops in Kosova, a strategy that would not be waived being in line with the American concept known to have been lobbied among the Albanians for a long time and, in various ways, investing in it from Dayton and on, especially during the last year, focusing on the Kosova issues and its solution by means of pressure on the Milosevic regime, counting also on an Albanian armed resistance, using it rather as a means of intent rather than in the function of the intent.

This, however, was firmly opposed by Serbs from the beginning, even though at Rambouillet they showed up with a 14-member delegation, headed by Serbian President Milutinovic, who spent most of the time walking around Paris making political noise, rather than in the castle where they belonged.

Even before arriving at Rambouillet, the Serbs were determined not to accept the issue of the referendum even if they agreed to the wording of the "interim solution" and also not to accept the stationing of NATO troops. It would be seen that they would still try all their political and diplomatic means to use and exploit these issues. If they evaded others while trying to prove cooperative, on these issues they were entirely categorical. Thus, the status issue passed on to a second plain being replaced by the stationing of international troops emerging as a guarantor of the transition time.

This "political mutation," introduced into the game by the Americans even out of the agreement and the spirit of the Contact Group, certainly suited the Albanians, as it saved them from the blight of the status, which viewed offline, featured a much narrower autonomy from what the violent Serb constitution of 1989 foresaw. This would simultaneously release them of the pressure coming from the Albanian public and its expectation, which since the beginning, measured the results of Rambouillet rather on whether NATO troops would be stationed in Kosova than with any Serb "concession" that could go as far as accepting Kosova as a third republic within the Yugoslav Federation.

For Albanians the presence of NATO troops in Kosova, even with an autonomous definition, was more important than a republic within the Yugoslav federation with the presence of the Yugoslav army and police. Bitter experience had shown that only the presence of NATO forces posed security for Albanians. Their appearance alone could represent a temporary remedy for independence. Only it could represent an interconnection agreement between those in the Albanian political scene who had recently turned extreme: of politics without war and war without politics in which both "lines" could be holding onto something.

The German Foreign Minister Joschka Fischer, who was one of the originators of what he would call Dayton II and had done much to prepare the basic documents of the Conference, noted that the Albanians "had a well-processed strategy" transforming their maximalist demands, such as the independence of Kosova, an oath they could never depart from, into that of a transitional autonomous status, conditional upon the determination of a date for referendum and upon deployment of NATO troops to guarantee the transition. As for the Serbs, the German Foreign Minister said they had been obsessively positioned against the presence of any international force in Kosova, as they were convinced that, as happened in Bosnia, it would cost them the final loss of Kosova.[797]

Joschka Fischer, however, estimated that the very presence of NATO in Kosova through an agreement would help Belgrade at least formally to retain sovereignty over Kosova, though it would lose all supervision over it, would rather help Serbs to remain there with NATO protecting them from any pressure coming from Albanians:

---

[797] Fischer, Joschka: *"Vitet kuq-gjelbër,"* Prishtina, 2007, p. 137.

Serbia found itself faced with an alternative, that by accepting the Rambouillet agreement maintain its presence in Kosova and Serbs in it. Or, rejecting it, which meant war, loss of Kosova and with Serbs losing their place of birth.[798]

Joschka Fischer, nevertheless, admitted that in the first stage of the Conference, namely from 6 to 14 February, 1999, the issue of the presence of NATO troops in Kosova, which expectedly emerged as an Albanian proposal turned into "confusion" for the Contact Group, as U.S. representative Hill, on his own, traveled to Belgrade to meet with Milosevic. He traveled there without the presence of Petritsch and Majorski and without informing the Contact Group, at least formally.[799]

Americans, therefore, as they had done in Dayton, were trying to turn Milosevic into a "hero" of peace, keeping him as their major partner. Was there something similar here to Dayton and its curves, or was it a last warning to Milosevic before it was too late?

However the Germans, and not only them, felt somewhat alienated and confused and this opened the way for them and others to take actions on their own. Also, according to the German diplomat, there was a suspicion that Milosevic could have invented something to drive Europeans out of the game and it would be unacceptable to them even if that "something" would be in line with U.S. interests, which could not be other than Western interests in general.

Against these circumstances, the Germans soon tried "to counter" Hill by opening the Kosova theme with Russians, outside the protocol and rules of the Contact Group. And, this happened on May 18, 1999 in Moscow, as the delegation headed by German Chancellor Gerhard Schroeder and Foreign Minister Fischer, in the Kremlin and off protocol, discussed the Kosova issue with the Russian President Boris Yeltsin more than other issues listed related to G-8 Summit, which was to be held in June in Cologne representing a great event for the Russians with Yeltsin believing the summit would ease internal tensions caused by economic difficulties.[800]

Although there is no denying that the Germans in Moscow were able to open any issue that would be off the western setting, however, it can be

---

[798] *Ibid*, p. 138

[799] *Ibid*, p. 139.

[800] *Ibid*, p. 140.

understood that the German political leader focused on the Kosova issue during talks with Yeltsin and top Russian officials to have Moscow show greater cooperation on the issue, while poaching Russia's involvement in the concept of a new identity for European security called the "third way" to which Americans showed certain reservations and even opposition.

The Germans played the Russian card later, this time in agreement with the Americans, especially during the preparations for the G-8 summit, when Russian President Yeltsin would be tempted to consent to the 1244 Resolution. But as to the final stage of negotiations with Milosevic, he appointed the Russian envoy Chernomyrdin to attend together with Ahtisaari the talks on the signing of the Kumanovo Agreement on June 10, 1999, when Serbia would eventually be taken out of Kosova.

Prior to the outcome of Rambouillet, it is noteworthy that the first phase of the Rambouillet talks scheduled for two weeks and extended for one more, would risk complete failure, as planned by Milosevic, if Albanians refused to sign the agreement thus being held responsible for it, which would save Belgrade from NATO's military intervention. According to the German Foreign Minister Fischer, who was Chairman of the Contact Group and at the same time chair of the Ministerial Council of the European Union, the Contact Group met in Paris on February 20, 1999 and to the surprise of those present, Madeleine Albright spoke about the difficulties she had with Albanians, who according to her, refused to sign the agreement without a referendum set after the time specified as transitional, and without the presence of NATO forces and their deployment in Kosova.

Albright explained that the "the problem was the fear that KLA leaders and more specifically Hashim Thaci had, feeling threatened by Adem Demaçi and his supporters, who had refused Rambouillet, calling it treason."[801]

The German Foreign Minister Joschka Fischer, in conversation with Madeleine Albright would lay the dilemma before the American authority over the KLA before the fact that Americans were overseeing it.[802] The demand was to exert full pressure on the Albanians to overcome the fear of becoming victims of international diplomacy.

---

[801] *Ibid*, p. 142.
[802] *Ibid*, p. 134.

Minister Fischer feared that the failure to sign the agreement in time by the Albanians would jeopardize the entire Conference strategy for maximum pressure on Belgrade. He also reiterated that "in addition, even the continuation of the Conference was a wrong signal, as it gave Belgrade the impression that the West was not so serious in its threats."[803]

Despite encouraging signs sent to Milosevic by the reluctance of the Albanian delegation to sign the agreement, the conference was, however, saved at the last moment due to American intervention, indicating that perhaps Americans too needed some kind of "reluctance" by the Albanians to show that they, like the Russians with the Serbs, did not find it easy with Albanians.

Some sources even speculated that the two weeks were needed for the NATO military men to prepare for military intervention.

Joschka Fischer said that this was done "as Hashim Thaci was maneuvered aside and the Kosova Albanian delegation consented to the document. Among other things, the Kosovars *were promised a referendum, which was not a binding policy in accordance with international law.*"[804]

The consent by the Albanians to the Rambouillet document and the warning that it would be signed in Paris after two weeks, would have its good and also its bad side. The two week delay somewhat relieved Albanians of external pressure, but the bad side of it was that the Rambouillet agreement was opposed by the "base," i.e. from the ranks of local commanders, who had great influence, especially as they placed Adem Damaci on the forefront as a political spokesman for the KLA acting publicly and in downtown Prishtina.

But, rather the way of intoning the dispute than its self-maintaining appeared as a problem, which put to the test the credibility of the Kosova Liberation Army and its national unity, having been noted so many times even turning into unnecessary "primacy" rhetoric in relation to the recent difficulties that Rugova's civil-institutional resistance movement was facing, largely speculated with "loss" of his authority. If this was added the fact that the Kosova Liberation Army Staff, through its spokesperson, two days before the Rambouillet Conference, had announced the participation of the KLA delegates to Rambouillet even though it was known that the

---

[803] *Ibid*, p. 142
[804] *Ibid*, p. 142.

basic points were not going to be negotiated there. Therefore, what was often being said in the foreign press would prove to be right in pointing out "many centers" within the armed resistance, where the main authority was played by the local commanders. They appeared as part of the "mentality" of the parallel state and its structures in which they were involved and had acted with success for many years, from where they really came, connected to the concept and logic of the state building, where, nevertheless, a hierarchy existed with common and legal decision-making.

For the power of local commanders and "independent paths," related to authentic local resistance associated with the parallel state and its structures, both Hill and Holbrooke would speak during the meetings with several representatives of the KLA on the ground during July and August of 1998, however, not believing that the situation was such as to keeping trapped those appearing as "key leaders."

This relation, which came "suddenly," on one side, cast out the impact of the Tirana line leading off the KLA, coming from the "resources" of the People's Movement of Kosova, headquartered in Switzerland and Germany, unknown to local structures, which were largely seated in Tirana, especially after the coming to power of Fatos Nano and the Socialists following the fall of Berisha's government two years earlier. On the other side, this spoke to the true power of local commanders, in zones where armed resistance appeared authentic (especially in the Llap and Karadak Zones), closely related to the parallel state structures, where many of its commanders and leaders of its units came directly from the ranks of local government led by the Democratic League of Kosova, as most of the fighters came from, which was only natural for them to appear as insurmountable local authorities, who demanded to be heard.

Although after the fall of the Berisha government it would seem that the KLA had won the internal "battle" with the Armed Forces of the Republic of Kosova (FARK) – and after losses suffered during the Serbian offensive of summer 1998 it had absorbed all of its military arsenal (high ranking officers from the former Yugoslav Army ranks, who had fought in Croatia and Bosnia and Herzegovina) – however Rambouillet would bring out the differences between the leaders of the war, where the "local" authority, i.e. of commanders coming from the authentic armed resistance associated with the parallel state was greater than the authority of Tirana.

However, the KLA leaders who had participated at Rambouillet, upon return to base, would carry the burden of turning war pathetic which they had used quite often into political language and its reasoning, something that was done with great concern among the ranks of the command body. This can also be explained by Adem Demaçi's resignation from the post of KLA political representative, who still continued to call the signing of the Rambouillet agreement a mistake. The consent in principle to the Rambouillet agreement was granted by many local commanders who led the armed resistance on the basis of the authenticity of its inseparable links with the parallel state and the concept of state-building, with the exception of Ahmet Isufi, Commander of the Operative Zone of Karadak,[805] but it would not close the gaps in the ranks of the armed resistance, which were defined on this basis.

The two-week postponement of the Conference did not go without consequences for Kosova and events to come, because as it is known, Milosevic, and his military used it for the preparation of war and its purpose, namely for the cleansing operation of Kosova's ethnic Albanians, before NATO was able to react in the way it did from March 24, 1999 onwards. It is estimated that this would have a double cost for Kosova Albanians, with thousands more victims, with about two hundred thousand more refugees and the standing of the Yugoslav Army for more than two months before giving up.

The consent of the Albanians to the Rambouillet document to be signed in Paris on March 18, would, however, mean for Serbia a definite turn to war as a last resort to achieve its goals, ethnic cleansing of Kosova Albanians. So, the time had come for Belgrade and for a Serbian oath as expressed in the last Memorandum of the Serbian Academy of Sciences and Arts. Joschka Fischer, Foreign Minister of Germany, who in the context of the Contact Group on March 8 started a Balkan tour to Belgrade, Prishtina, Shkup, and Tirana, in his visit to Belgrade smelled a Serbian decision for war in Kosova. Here's how the German Foreign Minister describes his meeting and conversation with Milosevic, after which the history of the Serbs and Albanians would change:

> ... I tried to clarify to Milosevic the seriousness of the situation and the various options, but before long the conversation began to move in a circle. Af-

---

[805] From author's conversation with Ahmet Isufi, Commander of the Operative Zone of Karadak, in Prishtina on 3 October 2011.

ter that, I asked the Yugoslav president for an eye to eye conversation. We withdrew to a side room of the house and continued talking eye to eye, without an interpreter, in English.

In clear words I began to show him the seriousness of the situation and also the way out, i.e. the Rambouillet agreement.

Was it clear to him, I asked, that he was about to face war against the United States, a war, which Yugoslavia would never win? His Russian friends would not jeopardize Russia's strategic opening to the West for his sake, nor would China stand by it. He could not take Europeans and Germans seriously, which I consider a big mistake, but entering war with the U.S., the only global superpower, is simply a distraction. In the end there would be a nonsensical destruction of Serbia and its loss of Kosova. In this confrontation he could never win.

Milosevic was of the opinion that the U.S. as early as in Vietnam had to understand the limits of their power and that their experience would be repeated in Yugoslavia, if they really intended to attack the country.

I could not believe that the President of Serbia, given the threatening war with NATO (and thus the U.S.), relied primarily on the Vietnam War. Neither Russia nor China would support him massively with weapons and would not be threatening a global political confrontation in case of an invasion, as they did during the Vietnam War. Serbia was not Vietnam, and Milosevic was no Ho Chi Minh.

Milosevic consistently returned to KLA and wanted to know why the West was joining it. The KLA people, he said, were murderers, thugs and offenders with whom he would finish work in two weeks...

The conversation was again brought into a circle and flowed without producing anything. Milosevic did not signal any openness of his position and simply rejected the presence of NATO units in Kosova. In the context of this conversation, I had the impression that the Serbian Presidency had taken the decision for war against Albanians...[806]

---

[806] Fischer, Joschka: *"Vitet kuq-gjelbër,"* Prishtina, 2007, pp. 144-145.

The continuation of the Conference in Paris on March 15 did not bring anything new. Albanians confirmed the signing, which they had coveted before leaving Paris for Kosova,[807] although the use of internal and external "convincing" for signatures, continued to be tested including various personalities involved such as Robert Dole, who arrived in Shkup to convince Albanian fighters personally to sign, indicating that this was an issue of to be or not be.

On March 18, 1999, in the Kleber center in Paris, at a ceremony without expected pomp, Hashim Thaçi, Rexhep Qosja, Ibrahim Rugova, and Veton Surroi on behalf of the Kosova Albanian delegation signed the agreement. Serbs would not sign it while the co-chair of the Conference, the Russian Majorski, did not attend.

So this was the first NATO "pact" with Albanians of historical importance, which would open the way to all developments leading to what years later emerged as the epilogue of the Kosova issue.

After two days, a large number of military and police forces began their offensive in Kosova, planned and prepared in advance with accuracy. It could not be stopped even by Holbrooke's last trip to Belgrade on March 23 when he met with Milosevic offering him once again an opportunity to avoid the worst, even making some concessions, which would later be known, that were not in line with the concept of the Rambouillet agreement and what Albanians had signed. Thereafter, the Secretary General of NATO, Javier Solana, forwarded an order to the Supreme

---

[807] *"Rilindja,"* 24 February 1999. This was the only newspaper to report on the consent of the Kosovo Albanian delegation and its covertion to the Conference chairs, while the Albanian public at large was being informed that "a part of the delegation did not concede and was about to reject the deal unless it met the demands of the Albanians." This was confirmed two years later by Edita Tahiri, part of the Albanian delegation at Rambouillet in her book *"Konferenca e Rambujesë. Procesi u negociua & Documentet,"* Prishtina 2001, p. 226. Years later this was also admitted by Mark Weller in his book *"Shtetësia e kontestuar"* (Contested Statehood), Prishtina, 2009, p. 230. Weller, who had served as a legal adviser to the delegation of Kosovo Albanians at Rambouillet even revealed certain details on the drama during the signing of documents at Rambouillet saying that the signing "blockade" was broken by Dr. Ibrahim Rugova "who until then had not been active in the negotiation process, daringly offering himself to sign the agreement not as member of the presiding delegation but rather in the capacity of an elected President of Kosovo..." Weller further states that "all of this left the mediators in a state of absolute awe."

Commander of the North Atlantic Alliance forces, Gen. Wesley Clark, to launch air strikes against Serbia, which commenced the next day.

Thus, the West was entering war against Serbia for Kosova and this was being done on humanitarian grounds, and evidently for its own ends, which agreed with the interests of Albanians.

This was the *cause* that the Rambouillet Conference produced, which would never happen without the signing of the Albanians while the Serbs signing it would cancel it. A different viewing of the conference and its documentation based on this fact would burden the signatories of Rambouillet with heavy historical guilt.

CHAPTER 5
RAISING KOSOVA AS AN INTERNATIONAL ISSUE

The First NATO War for Kosova

The resolution of the Kosova crisis even with ultimatum tools appeared to be in the interest of Albanians, in NATO's immediate interest, and also an interest of the US and Europe. – The first military intervention of NATO against a sovereign state on humanitarian pretense changed the new world order, which protected dictators and oppression by international law, thus putting the Alliance in a new role.- Kosova and its crisis played a special role, as almost forcefully it politically emancipated Europeans to a leading role of the West, as well as its challenge on a geopolitical and geostrategic plain, where they, along with the Americans, had to participate in accordance with their economic power, even at a time when it seemed that the new behavior contradicted some of the traditional definitions. – The aspect of Kosova's geostrategic importance, associated with Albania and Macedonia, gained its true dimension, creating a key area in the region and beyond. – Russians, realizing they were unable to prevent Western intervention in favor of Kosova, fearing that this would immediately be followed by its independence, played the card of placing Kosova under an imposed international supervision.

The first NATO bombs, which would be dropped on March 24, 1999 by U.S. warships stationed in the Adriatic against Yugoslav military positions in Kosova and Serbia, as well as the Alliance military aircraft flights that flew from Aviano in Italy and other bases in the Mediterranean from that day on for seventy-six days in a row, represented the first NATO intervention against a sovereign country, even without the mandate of the World Organization, which was in violation of international law over state sovereignty derived from the UN Charter.

Both these issues are of particular importance. The first changed the character of the North Atlantic Alliance, along with the role it had before being transformed into a mechanism for the protection of democracy and human rights outside its radius of action. And, secondly, it also broke the convention of the right of state sovereignty as international law, being used for the benefit of the protection of human rights and democracy when threatened by the state after attaining proportions of a humanitarian disaster that could result in genocide. Therefore, the right question is whether the Kosova case marked a precedence, which needed that kind of attitude to prevent a humanitarian catastrophe, or was it a change that the new world order needed in the new circumstances, and that this crisis was very appropriate in order to promote these changes?

It may be said without hesitation that the first issue – that is, the new role of NATO in the circumstances of the fall of bipolarity of the blocs, as well as the second issue, namely – touching upon the right of state sovereignty as an international norm, in favor of protection of human rights and humanitarian law, Kosova and its profound crisis served as an excuse for them (Albanians) to gain international legitimacy, no matter how it would be received, and how much it would be challenged then and later. This applies especially to the first issue, which draws upon the latter not only at the level of principles, but also factoring, since NATO as an organized military force remains the only one that is able to act not only in preventing regional crisis, but also in engaging in the role of a peace-maker.

But if Kosova and its problem appeared as the first and very important test for the North Atlantic Alliance, which, however, passed successfully, as it also appeared as a "provocation" to the defenders of the state sovereignty right (Russia, China and many other countries that face minority problems), no matter what the violations are – blocking also the UN Security Council in favor of the preservation of this convention – then its settlement emerged inevitably as an interest of the main stake-holders of the Atlantic Alliance itself – the United States of America and Great Britain, which constitute the backbone of NATO and the West in general, as a force that must determine the political and legal frameworks of the new world order dominated by them.

Here, too, Kosova and its crisis played a special role, because almost necessarily it politically emancipated Europeans to track the extractor role of the West as well as its challenge in the geopolitical and geostrategic plan, where they, along with the Americans, had to participate in line with their economic power, even as it seemed that the new behavior contradicted some of the traditional definitions.

Following the order of the factors, displaying the Kosova crisis as a challenge in circumstances when the new world order was changing, it inevitably played a role in relation to Russia as well, regardless of Moscow's traditional stance benefiting their ally in the Balkans, Serbia. Not to be out of the game, the Russians were included in the final phase of its resolution, not as much to gain accentuation of its interest in the region, as to prevent it in as far as a) keeping it entirely under the jurisdiction of the U.S. and NATO, and b) taking it upon itself the opening of the whole question of the Albanian crisis, turning it into a motif of a global approach of its treatment and resolution.

In accordance with this outline, the resolution of the Kosova crisis, even with the use of *ultima ratio*, as would be those of limited air intervention by NATO from March 24 to June 10, 1999 against Serb military and police forces in Kosova and in Serbia and Serbian military positions emerged as follows:

1. as an immediate NATO interest,

2. as a geostrategic interest of the United States of America,

3. as a European interest, at least in as much as limiting itself within its own shell, that is, preventing it from becoming an initiator of opening the whole Albanian question, and, finally,

4. It appeared also as a Russian interest, which, although unable to prevent American primacy over it, would do their utmost to ensure international supervision, considering it important for the circumstances and developments which were to take place later.

1) The resolution of the Kosova crisis as NATO's interest had to do primarily with the very existence of the Atlantic Alliance in the post-communist circumstances and fall of the bloc bipolarity. Whether its rise to the level of a global crisis was part of its interest or not, it does not matter for treatment in terms of its resolution, as the observation is concerned only with the recent focus and not of plotting the problem. In any case, the North Atlantic Alliance, which came out a winner in the long race of the blocs, could not feed itself enough on the past in order to survive. On the contrary, it needed the future, too, in which it would provide the proof it deserved. And, it could only be secured in the new role as guardian of the peace, and if necessary, even as its creator. Military variations needed also a political framework, which would help the Alliance to change its concept of mere military force as it was until then, returning to a broader mechanism of social and political nature, which was concerned with a democratic aspect as well.

That NATO had previously shown interest in a new role in terms of creating the circumstances for the imposition of peace, it was also seen during the crisis of Bosnia and Herzegovina, as it engaged in limited military action against the breach of the blockade over Sarajevo, committed by Serb forces. From that time on, NATO and its new role more and more would be mentioned related to the power diplomacy at a time when the power of diplomacy did not work. Deepening of the Kosova crisis and the concentration of Milosevic to respond to it only by means of war, on which he leaned from the beginning of 1998, when the Kosova Liberation Army appeared on stage carrying out an armed resistance in Kosova, NATO was provided with opportunities to be involved in the process of creating the preconditions for political negotiations over Kosova in terms of external pressure that the power of diplomacy needed in order to move the parties toward a compromise that led to a solution.

External pressure that came to Milosevic through "brandishing" of NATO military leaders through various political debates did not make an impression, as he knew very well that they could carry weight only if the Alliance achieved domestic political consensus for action, which needed a long procedure of agreements and accords in order to gain full legitimacy.[808]

In order to overcome this obstacle, which, as will be seen, in some circumstances played an important role serving Milosevic to continue his games with the international community, this would be ensured by the United States of America, which by the summer offensive of the Serbian military and police forces of 1998 against the Kosova Liberation Army, turned against Milosevic and his military, after having come to the

---

[808] On the internal political concensus of NATO in reaching a decision, such as the one issuing a warning to Belgrade, see for more Wesley K. Clark: *"Të bësh luftë moderne,"* Prishtina, 2003.

position that Belgrade was not fighting "Albanian terrorism" in the KLA ranks, but rather that this was an excuse for it to finally settle scores with Albanians to ethnically cleanse Kosova once and for all, without excluding the use of genocide as a last resort in order to achieve this goal.

This conviction struck General Clark too, during his last conversation with Milosevic in Belgrade shortly before NATO started bombing Yugoslav Army positions in Kosova, upon which he unequivocally said: "*You know, General Clark, that we know how to settle accounts with Albanians, with these killers, these offenders, these assassins of their own children.*" [809] He illustrated his words with the following: "*In Drenica, in 1946* (in fact 1945 – note J. B.), *we killed them. We killed them all!*"[810]

To eliminate even the last possibility of a consensus used for such purposes, with Milosevic using the delay to carry out new violence, as it had done for years in Croatia and in Bosnia and Herzegovina, the Americans, in the wake of the Lisbon Summit, on September 23, 1998, threatened with early intervention of their own against Belgrade, by which then the resolution of the Kosova crisis could take a different direction from the one that the Europeans wanted, something that had an impact on the countries reluctant to give consent to NATO's threat against Belgrade (ACWARN – or Activation Warning – *compliance of members of North Atlantic Alliance countries to make available their military forces for the implementation of military operations against Yugoslavia*), were able to do so thus creating conditions which combined diplomatic force with military threat. As would be seen, ACWARN would turn to a last resort to resolve the Kosova crisis, from March 24, 1999 until June 10 of that year, when NATO conducted aerial military operations against Yugoslav military and police forces in Kosova and other parts of Serbia.

In this interval it became apparent what Milosevic and his military had as their main objective, namely the ethnic cleansing of Kosova, as designed in the "Horseshoe" plan,[811] which they began to implement four

---

[809] Wesley K. Clark: "*Të bësh luftë moderne,*" Prishtina 2003, p. 187.

[810] *Ibid*, p.187.

[811] The first to inform about the Serbian military plan "Horseshoe" which planned an ethnic cleansing of Kosovo, moments before the start of NATO bombing in Kosovo, was the German Defense Minister Rudolf Scharping. He notified the German public and the world about the details with which the final fight of the Yugoslav military and police forces in Kosovo to implement this plan had begun. Scharping announced that the plan had been received by the Bulgarian intelligence service, the authenticity of which would

days before the start of NATO air strikes, to continue successfully afterwards, when within a few days towards Macedonia and Albania over one million Albanians were deported, by which Serbia virtually for the first time, even for a little while, succeeded in its historic goal to cleanse Kosova of Albanians.

However, it was the North Atlantic Alliance, which with its fight to protect the Albanians, not only saved them from Serbian genocide, but at the same time it established opportunities for their return to their lands, after having forced the withdrawal of Serbian forces from Kosova.

2) The resolution of the Kosova crisis as an interest of the United States of America should be seen in terms of the American commitment to freedom, democracy and protection of human rights, which is consistent with the moral concept of this state to protect human values , and also in terms of a geostrategic interest, related to the complexity of the spheres of interest in the new circumstances in the region and beyond, where Kosova in particular, and Albanian space in general, play a role in American plans of this nature. In this context, the resolution of the Kosova crisis, no matter what the given answer would be, automatically affected the Albanian issue as an open question, as it also affected the regional realignment, which as such it inevitably touched upon other issues by shaking them in different forms.

Seen from this point of view, from the very onset it was clear to the Americans that the issue of Kosova cannot be solved without separating it and treating it apart from its relation to Serbia, so that it remains, as the American President Woodrow Wilson saw in the twenties the case of Albania, demanding from the Paris Peace Conference to separate it from that of the Adriatic, where it was included and risked become a coin of settling of Italian-Greek-Yugoslav accounts about territories.

Although never said openly, even since the Hague Conference and onwards, at least nominally, its independence was not supported by Washington's political moves – from that of the "*Christmas Warning*" in

---

be confirmed in its entirety during the time air bombing operations against Serbian military positions in Kosovo began, as reflected by the eviction from Kosovo, when within a few days, over a million Kosovo Albanians were deported in the direction of Macedonia and Albania. (See Scharping, Rudolf: "*Wir dürften nicht wegsehen* – We could not look the other way," Berlin 1999.)

December of 1992, when President George Bush drew a red line to Belgrade in relation to transferring the war to Kosova to the prelude of the Rambouillet agreement – it had been clear to Serbia that the outcome of the Kosova problem depended on the U.S. position, and that ultimately Washington would be the one that would determine the outline of a solution, of course, in accordance with their own interests, which cannot be other than that of a geostrategic nature.

Although, besides the *"Christmas Warning,"* the diplomatic language of Washington maintained the flexibility needed in a process to be put into action, Milosevic knew that the Kosova card would be what fate would determine to the Balkan poker, keeping it as a war card implicating other facts as well.

A careful study of the Rambouillet agreement, regardless of what appeared as great "concessions" to Belgrade and at first glance they did appear as such – especially by the fact that the transitional period of three years legitimized Yugoslav sovereignty over Kosova raising the question if during those three years everything would go according to the American anticipation – everything forewarned a separation process between Albanians and Serbs under international supervision, which enabled it by its presence (in this case stationing of about 30 thousand NATO troops in Kosova was envisaged). Of course, for Europeans, who would fear for many reasons such cuts, the language to be used in the Rambouillet accords would be satisfactory and even acceptable, because there, at least in principle, they saw the possibility of an agreement between Serbs and Albanians, which offered *transitional Government time,* where circumstances and developments could play a role in order to avoid "extreme" positions (that of independence of Albanians and that of keeping Kosova in Serbia by Belgrade).

Even based on European reservations for the opening of the Kosova issue and the possibility of a domino-effect for the region, Americans even considered putting diplomatic Aesopism in use.

So, despite all this, one may say that in Rambouillet, the Americans aimed to initiate the process of solving the Kosova crisis in line with the concept that the end should lead to its secession from Serbia in agreement, but if they failed because of Belgrade cementation, as would actually happen, then other tools may be used, including those of compulsion.

After all, the whole concept of the Rambouillet conference and its accords were built on the same methodology. Furthermore, in addition to the content dealing with aspects of an interim period defined as self-governance and emerging as ultimate, sanctioning of rejection with the means of war, determined in advance the process of separation between the two nations and by no means of agreements, which were impossible.

To this end, the Americans took all measures that NATO be put on alert and for the first time in its history, put into action its military infrastructure on full alert turning it into a meaningful threat, as happened with ACWARNIN as approved at the Lisbon summit, on September 23, 1998.

The issue, even in terms of geostrategic importance of Kosova, was a decisive point that created good opportunities for supervising the region from almost all views to which the Americans were able to foist the means of war game, as they would do. Perhaps this component did not quite clearly emerge in itself. Associated with Albania and Macedonia, it gained virtual dimension, creating a critical space in the region.

3) *The resolution of the Kosova crisis as a European interest*, even by means of *ultima ratios*, as used, dealt not only with the extinction of a great crisis in the region, which threatened to become a disruptive factor of large proportions, it also threatened the very concept of the European edifice extending towards the East, including in it the countries of the former communist regimes, with vital importance to the European Union.

The first aspect, i.e. that of disruption in the region, which the crisis implied, was duly understood by the Europeans, and it was even quite clear, as there were the traditional circumstances themselves of spheres of interest that had created it since the Eastern Crisis, when the Albanian question, by admission of Albania as a country at the London Conference in 1913, and later its confirmation at the Peace Conference in Paris in 1919, was given an incomplete answer (since over half of Albanian ethnic space remained offline as part of Yugoslavia and Greece), while even after the collapse of the first Yugoslavia, in 1941 and the breakup of the second Yugoslavia in 1991, Kosova always presented a crisis factor, as it was not allowed union with Albania, which would be only natural, although its violent amputations in favor of Yugoslavia never worked either. This was quite clear particularly following the dismantling of the second Yugoslavia, as the Zabljak creature[812] of 1992, self-declared by Serbia and Monte-

---

[812] Zabljak, a small settlement on the border between Serbia and Montenegro, in which Milosevic, by the end of April 1992, i.e. before the London Conference, gathered the

negro, called the Federal Republic of Yugoslavia, Kosova was left fairing on behalf of the recognition of the heritage of the second Yugoslavia, which was a rather arbitrary attitude of the international decision-making factor, especially of the Europeans, who ignored the political will of the Albanians stated clearly as early as 1990 with the Constitutional Declaration of July 2, declaring the Republic of Kosova at the Kaçanik Assembly and Referendum on Independence of 1991. Even the slightest sense of democracy and respect to its own values on which the European edifice stands would have sufficed that the Kosova issue be granted a different answer from what was violently imposed by Belgrade.

Over time, as the real goals of Serbia became clear and as it also became clear that neither would the Albanians give up their determination to protect their road toward independence that they had declared, and that this determination could lead to a fresh austerity of regional dimensions because they inevitably would also include Albania and in its aftermath even other neighboring countries, the Europeans would begin to show a different approach to the solution of the Kosova issue, at least in order to strip it of its potential neighborhood reflection, opening up the

---

"representatives" of the two republics, without asking the Montenegrin ones, presenting to them the draft of the Serb-Montenegrin "agreement" to unite in a common state, called the Federal Republic of Yugoslavia, which announced itself as the legitimate successor of the former Yugoslavia. As such, it was not subject to the criteria of the Badinter Commission, established by the Hague Conference of 1991, when the decision to terminate the existence of AVNOJ Yugoslavia, according to which members of the former Federal Yugoslavia had to enter a bid for international recognition, as Croatia, Slovenia, Macedonia, Bosnia and Herzegovina and recently Kosovo did after it declared independence from Serbia with the Constitutional Declaration of 2 July 1990 and the proclamation of the Republic of Kosovo in the Assembly of Kacanik on 7 September 1990. Although the London Conference recognized the Zabljak creation, with some of the countries of the European Union accepting it as the legitimate heir of the second Yugoslavia, due to the U.S. rejection stance towards it, it was not admitted to the UN. Kosovo President, Dr. Rugova, considered the declaration of this artificial creature that would not stand the test of time, as illegitimate for Kosovo, while calling the presence of military and police forces with violent administrative apparatus as the third reoccupation of Kosovo by Serbia. This argument was constantly used by Kosovo to show itself as occupied by Serbia.

option of an interim solution, where an international protectorate seemed most proper in order to "roast the meat without burning the skewer."

The option of placing Kosova under an interim international supervision initially concerned both the Germans and the French with the foreign ministers of Bonn and Paris, Kinkel and Juppe, elaborating it somehow as one of the possible interim solutions, but afraid that the initiative could mean taking the side of the Albanians, they were unable to properly animate it, even though Belgrade rejected it on the same grounds. Along with Paris and Bonn, the idea also preoccupied some other European countries, especially London. But the English too, known for their diplomatic and political finesse, were not be able to dispose of it because the countries of the region, particularly Greece and Italy, and Spain as well, would not accept raising the issue from the fear that it, especially by Athens, prejudged Kosova's independence followed by paving the way for unification with Albania, an ancient abomination with which it is charged, and the Greeks have always seen as a thorn in the eye. This logic led to the blocking of the resolution of the Kosova issue with this being in Belgrade's favor not to accept any compromises, while the Albanians, after six years of civil resistance with a parallel state, never renouncing it, were drawn into an armed resistance option as a last resort, to realize political goals by other means, namely those of war.

The emergence of this option, occurring from 1996 onwards, when Albanian guerrilla armed actions commenced, gaining full legitimacy after a year, with the public emergence of the Kosova Liberation Army – would move the international community, and especially the Europeans cemented around their position of Kosova as part of Serbia whose solution should be sought within its borders, away from the barricade not that the issue needed to be given a fair solution, but out of the fear that it might turn into a major Balkan conflict, which ultimately would gain the option of resolving the Albanian issue through war, which meant Albanian union, to which Americans and NATO were not in disfavor, calculating it in the long-run as part of their spheres of interest. Therefore, even when the Europeans moved towards a solution, they always sought to find a common language with Belgrade, even though it was clear that Serbia did not accept it, was aware as to where that would lead.

Americans would be the ones who would solve the European node through enforcement of the solution, as dealt with the concept of Rambouillet: an agreement on interim self-government supervised by the international factor and guaranteed by the presence of NATO troops in Kosova.

The Europeans were forced to accept this, because the Americans were warning about potential escalation of the conflict between Serbs and Albanians, which would also include Albania and other Balkan countries to follow, turning it all into a major regional and world crisis, which in turn would definitely need a large-scale military intervention, which would ultimately have to end with the defeat of the Serbs as the main instigators of the crisis, a result of which Albanians would come out victorious and this victory would not mean an independent Kosova, but rather an Albanian unification.

The option of Albanian unification and an almost pathological fear of it pushed the Europeans to accept finding a compromise solution, even if temporary, such as the one that followed the sixty-seven-day NATO bombing on targets of the Yugoslav military and police forces in Kosova and Serbia when Kosova was placed under an international protectorate, just as Albanians had been asking since the London Conference of 1992, when President Rugova, as a compromise to Albanians demand for independence and offering the international community an opportunity to quietly solve other problems in the former Yugoslavia, (the war in Bosnia and Herzegovina, the Serbian-Croatian conflict and other issues), had proposed an interim international protectorate, which would create the conditions for free declaration of Albanians about their future. This request by Rugova was repeated to Kofi Annan in 1995 in the wake of the Dayton Conference, and the same request was sent to President Clinton, to have as a backup option in Dayton, although falling against the independent state of Kosova, which came out of a referendum on independence in 1991 and the Kaçanik Constitution of Kacanik.[813]

4) The solution of the Kosova issue as a Russian interest – albeit with a different looking-glass – became apparent at the moment when it took the proportions of an armed resistance and the emergence of the Kosova Liberation Army as its carrier showing that there would be no going back, as the war factor, appearing as a continuation of politics by other means, which is fraught with a parallel state where Albanians for years and

---

[813] For more see Buxhovi, Jusuf: *"Kthesa historike - Shteti paralel dhe rezistenca e armatosur,"* Prishtina, 2009, pp. 282-291.

through their patience, had offered peace a chance, which Serbs and the international community, especially the Europeans, did not use.

Until then more cemented after clamping of the right of sovereignty of the state under the UN Charter and its protection for its own reasons (in the case of Chechnya and separatist movements in the Caucasus), in support of Belgrade by traditional ties on the basis of orthodoxy and Slavism, from the beginning of 1998, Russia began to move towards solving the problems of the Kosova issue, following the start of direct U.S. involvement, especially as things were taken over by the turbo-diplomat Richard Holbrooke, known as the architect of the Dayton accords.

This time the radius of his focus was not Serb-Croat "reconciliation" about Bosnia and Herzegovina as an artificial creature – with which they should agree temporarily, having a share price in the area of their interest, with the prospect of direct supervision over them, in order that one day they would be able to swallow as such – but rather the option of Serb-Albanian historical separation emerged, as an inevitable development, which would be in the interest of the two peoples, and the region in general, no matter that through myth Serbs had turned it into their spiritual and historical center.

Faced with a situation where on the one hand could stand aside in re-sponding to one of the biggest crises of the time, and on the other side fearing that it would take its own direction as determined entirely by Americans, whose aims where thought to be going towards a maximalist solution, opening up the option of Albanian unification, Russia joined the international decision-making group (the Contact Group) thus satisfying Europeans, primarily Germans and French, who repeatedly demanded for Russia to be on their boat.

Of course Russia demonstrated compliance towards the option of a peaceful resolution of the Kosova problem, as the United States put in custody all international mechanisms, having the main say running a risk of determining a solution outcome according to its measure, which for the Russians meant, besides external marginalization, loss of prestige from the inside, which they feared even more.

But, it should be noted that Russia joined the concept of decision-making powers by setting two clear goals:

a) To strengthen the so-called "line of European identity," intended to minimize the U.S. role in Europe and in the world, and

b) To simultaneously affect the resolution of the Kosova issue if it were to take an "extreme direction" towards independence, in lacking international legitimacy. The latter depended on Moscow, which had the opportunity of the use of veto at the UN Security Council.

Americans, who realized the Russian goal, proved satisfied with their participation asking Yeltsin for constructive behavior, which would be reflected primarily in their impact on Milosevic, in order to "diminish" him before he was faced with force. Because, according to U.S. assessments, and not only, it would be the very Russian attitude that encouraged Milosevic to behave with arrogance and cunning at the same time through the security given by the Russian policy in the World Organization that would prevent approval of any resolution that would be to their own detriment.

This was the first trap that Americans set for Russia, so that along with the political and diplomatic aspects, Moscow, backed against the wall, had to accept, being in its interests to strengthen its position in the G-8, whose summit was to be held in June 1999 in Germany, expecting Western economic aid to open. Although Russia was aware of what the present trap of this role was, trying to avoid it in different ways, it bit the first bait exactly at the UN Security Council, at its meeting of September 24, 1998, when the American side put to a vote Resolution 1199, which, in accordance with the Charter of the Organization in preventing a humanitarian disaster, provides the *means of compliance*. In this case, as the situation in Kosova was assessed as standing on edge of a humanitarian disaster caused by summer-autumn offensive military and police forces in Kosova on the grounds of "liquidating KLA terrorist gangs" (not that it lacked the approval of Westerners and even Americans) – while it was apparent that for the Serbs it had been all along a well calculated campaign for ethnic cleansing in Kosova – it opened the door to NATO intervention on this basis, even without any special resolution, as it would actually happen. The Russian Foreign Minister Ivanov accepted this a little later, however, contesting that this represented a cover for NATO air intervention that would follow from March 24 to June 10 of the following year against the Yugoslav military and police forces in Kosova and other military targets in Serbia.[814]

---

[814] An interview by Ivanov to the Germnan ARD TV program, 22 June 1999, aired on "*Tagestemen*" at 22:30.

The joining of Russia in the decision-making "common boat" had opened opportunities to close down Milosevic maneuver roads, increasing the chances for a common position of the international community, which would be built on a minimum of several criteria of a political nature, which would open the way for resolving the Kosova crisis, at least putting it on tracks of any option acceptable to both parties, or, if this proved to be impossible, would then use compliance. And, the criteria would be the well-known ten points, which Germany, on behalf of the Contact Group, conceived in three emergency meetings in Brussels, Moscow, and finally in London on January 29, held after the Reçak massacre on January 15, when the final decision to call the Rambouillet Conference, on February 6, was taken.

It is worth noting that Russia's cooperation with the Contact Group was achieved after the meeting of the U.S. Secretary of State, Albright, with the Russian Foreign Minister Ivanov in Moscow. In this long meeting, the Russian got "guarantees" from the Americans that Rambouillet would use equal pressure on the Serbs to accept the agreement and the KLA. Furthermore, the meeting announced that Russia demanded from Albright that the Americans do not authorize the ACTWARN threat code with the Secretary General of NATO, which could issue an order to the Atlantic Alliance for attacks against the military forces of the Federal Republic of Yugoslavia, as this would be considered by Moscow as unilateral pressure on Belgrade and encouragement for the KLA to continue provocations against the Yugoslav forces in Kosova, upon which grounds for intervention would be created.

As would be seen, Americans did not comply with the second demand, because on January 29, 1999 the Yugoslav military and police forces carried out another massacre in Rugova Has killing over 20 Albanians on the grounds that they had been dealing with "terrorist forces" that had provoked them. The OSCE Verification Mission, however, assessed that this had been no case involving "terrorists" but rather a massacre of civilians. Its reports spoke of members of two families, killed after a siege, which represented another bloody provocation after the one that happened on January 15 in Recak. Found in an unpleasant situation, as the threat of NATO had already taken shape and could be activated at any time, Russia continued to stay "in the common boat," although in despair because of the fact that the dynamics of events was moving towards Serbia's conflict with NATO, and that it could be stopped only through a

Rambouillet miracle, which according to the Russians was not the signing by the Serbs, but rather not signing by the Albanians.

A War between Law and Ethics

The stance of the German philosopher Jorgen Habermas regarding humanitarian intervention in Kosova and the necessity for the right to state sovereignty lost its importance in favor of human and democratic rights. – The case of NATO intervention in Kosova would be evaluated by the German philosopher as a moral act establishing a policy to indemnify a great injustice and violence done for years against Albanians by the Belgrade regime, committed in the name of state sovereignty, even when they, with their civil-institutional resistance and parallel state, offered the most dignified evidence that Europe ever witnessed. – According to Professor Georg Brunner, an expert on international law, the international community by treating Kosova as an internal part of Serbial made two errors simultaneously: a) why would it ignore the fact that it, in the first place was part of the Yugoslav Federation and that according to the positive right was most deserving of its legal status (in this case the federative in relation to the republican), and b) because it did not respect the will of self-determination for Albanians expressed in a free and democratic Constitutional Declaration of July 2, 1990, the decision of Kosova's declaration of a republic in Kacanik Assembly on September 7 of that year and the Referendum on Independence in 1991 when the Albanians opted unanimously for independence, as deserving in the circumstances when autonomy was ruined through violence. – Justifications of the Secretary General of the North Atlantic Alliance, Solana, that NATO's intervention in Kosova as humanitarian intervention found support in Resolutions 1160 and 1199 of the UN Security Council.

In Paris, on March 18, 1999, Albanians signed the Rambouillet Accords document, while the Serbs refused to do so. At the signing ceremony, along with international representatives from among the G-8, the Russian Boris Mayorski failed to show up, after having participated in the trio that had led the talks in Rambouillet and Paris (with the U.S.), and boycotted the ceremony signature on the grounds that the agreement without Belgrade's signature had no international validity. However, this was no question of the validity of a document inasmuch as a decision for war. Because Russia knew to where that was leading, which inevitably led towards the first NATO intervention against a sovereign country, which with such murderous actions against the Albanians had lost this "right" a long time ago, by which the relations, until then good, between Americans and Russians, and also the West and Moscow were placed before a first trial of a serious crisis.

It would be exactly the NATO intervention against a sovereign country on humanitarian grounds, which was already a matter of hours far from commencing without UN authorization, i.e., without the mandate of the Security Council, that which opened discussions and disagreements not only among the international factors, but also among different countries, who felt threatened by the creation of such a precedence, and above all, the issue sparked a public debate among jurists, intellectuals, philosophers of various profiles concentrating on *international law* and *morality*, controversies and polemics that would inevitably raise the issue of state sovereignty in accordance with the UN Charter and its vulnerability when this right is abused for human and collective rights violations of an ethnic group or a nation, as was the case of Serbia against Albanians, the dimensions of which were so large-scale and so brutal that in addition to massive repression, application of methods of apartheid and other forms of severe discrimination were applied, as concluded for years by humanitarian organizations and those dealing with the protection of human rights, which lately threatened with ethnic cleansing and committing genocide, for which Belgrade had started to put into action the means of war to achieve its goal.

The focus on the *legitimacy of an intervention*, because it lacked *UN authorization mandate*, which was on the brink and any wavering had its cost in numerous innocent lives, who for years had become defenseless victims of Serb violence, in a way that over a quarter of a million Bosnians who experienced the same fate before the commencing of an American intervention against the Serb-Yugoslav positions around Sarajevo and other Serb military forces in this country that massacred in the eyes of the world and which included the entire UN "protected zones," where the world had a legitimacy to intervene but did not, revealed *the political morality crisis of the international factor rather than that of international law*, as things were reaching a point in which the international policy and its mechanisms were suffering full moral bust because Kosova had come to that situation, therefore as far as Belgrade was a culprit with its hegemonic and chauvinistic policy towards Albanians, even more so was the international factor, especially the one from among the Europeans, which, since its emergence had been treating it as if it were a prey of Serbia, which can act as it wished in the name of its right of state sovereignty and its inviolability!

Here were the beginnings of what the famous German philosopher, Jürgen Habermas, saw as a *crisis of the law* and *moral crisis*, so that the issue of Kosova and international intervention, which he saw to be inevitable, was called a *war between law and morality*.[815]

Unlike treatments focusing on theoretical or political issues, which produced confusion rather than helped theoretical enlightening, philosopher Habermas examined precisely the relationship between politics and international law, not in terms of their misunderstandings, as the philosopher says that in Kosova there was no confusion, especially as it was evident that Yugoslavia was dismembered and Belgrade's unitarian policy was responsible for it, but uncertainties lay in the attitudes and political

---

[815] For more on this see Jürgen Habermas: *"Bestialität und Humanitet"* (Cruelty and Humanity), published in the book *"Kosovo Krieg und das Völkerrecht,"* Frankfurt, 2000, pp. 52-56. Also on the issue of legitimacy of Kosovo war and its contest see the following analyses published in the book by Dieter S. Lutz *"Der kosovo-Krieg: rechliche und rechtsetische Aspekte"* (Kosovo War – Aspects of Law and Ethics), Baden-Baden, 2000: Jost Delbrück: *"Effektivität des UN-Gewaltverbotes,"* Christian Tamuschat: „*Völkerrechliche Aspekte des Kosovo-Konflikts*, Ulrich K Preuß: „*Zwieschen Legalität und Gerechtigkeit,"* Dieter Senghaas: „*Der Grenzfall: Weltrechtsordnung vs.Rowdiestaaten,"* Herman Kühner: „*Humaniträre NATO-Einsätze ohne Mandat,"* Knut Ipsen: „*Der Kosovo-Einsatz – Ilegal? Gerechtfertigt? Entschuldbar?,"* Michael Köhler: „*Zum völkerrechtlichen Begriff der humanitären Intervention,"* Daniel Thürer: „*Die NATO-Einsätze in Kosovo und das Völkerrecht,"* August Pradetto: „*Die NATO, humanitäre Intervention und Völkerrecht,"* Henning Vorscherau: „*Krieg al Mittel der Politik,"* Dieter S. Lutz: „*Angriff und Verteidigung sind Sigerdefinitionen, oder: War der Kosovo-Krieg wierklich unabwendbar?,"* Sibylle Tönnies: „*Die gute Ansicht allein ist suspekt,"* Herman Scheer: „*Von der Selbstbeschränkun im Krieg,"* Heinz-gerhard Justenhoven: „*Selbstbestimmungsrecht der Völker und Nichteinmischung in inneren Anglelegenheiten im Wiederstretit,"* Hauke Brunkhorst: *"Menschenrechte und Interevention,"* Reinchard Merkel: „*Das Elend der Beschützten,"* Gerhard Bestermöller: „*Abschid von der UNO?,"* Olaf Asbach: „*Das Recht, die Politik und der Krieg."*

decisions that produced the next crisis. The German philosopher, who in his political essay supported the NATO intervention in Kosova stripping the German leftist policy, which was in power (coalition between Schroeder's Social Democrats and Fisher's Greens) of its ability to respond through leftist intellectuals, who were very loud in public and had a tendency to turn a blind eye towards such evil, *raised the level of discussion to reconsidering the issue of the right of the myth of state sovereignty in favor of respect for human rights, ethnic and democratic rights in general, which had to be imposed on those of state sovereignty.* Habermas concluded that it was not only unfair but also immoral to impede human rights standards and democratic rights through the right of state sovereignty even fighting them by all means on the basis of this right, turning automatically into another even greater injustice, which may not be valid any longer in the context of major global changes.[816]

Thus, the German philosopher used the case of Kosova to promote universal human and ethnic rights in the world and take precedence over the right of state sovereignty. He rightly criticized the discrepancy between globalization and the conventional practice of international law, demanding that the new world order radically change the approach to human and ethnic rights, not only to handle them on the basis of universality, but also to create mechanisms to protect them at all times and in all circumstances. He assessed the case of NATO's intervention in Kosova as a moral act for the decision making to indemnify a great injustice that had been done for years against Albanians by the Belgrade regime exhorting to violence in the name of state sovereignty, despite the fact that they gave the most dignified evidence of civil resistance that Europe ever saw, and that this case, which should not create a precedence, should immediately instigate changes so that human, collective and democratic rights stand over those of national sovereignty.

So, it was viewed from a point of deliberate errors made to its approach by the Hague Conference of 1991 and beyond, when the Badinter Commission, after having come to the position that the second Yugoslavia was in the process of dissolution, treated Kosova as Serbia's internal affair. In this case the constitutional situation of 1974 was not considered, when Kosova was a constituent part of the Yugoslav Federation, with the same consensus right like other federal entities, considering instead the 1989

---

[816] *Ibid*, p. 53.

constitutional position, after Serbia's violent destruction of the autonomy of Kosova in March of that year. This starting point was not the legal nature of international law, but simply of a political conjectural nature, which was consistent with the political stance of the European Union and other world factors so that the Kosova issue would not be touched at that stage in accordance to the right it had, as it divided Europeans, especially Albanian neighbors, rather than the actors themselves of the Yugoslav crisis.

According to Professor Georg Brunner, an expert on international law, professor at the University of Cologne, author of several books on international law, the international community, treating Kosova as an internal part of Serbia, made two errors at once:

a) by ignoring the fact that Kosova, in the first place, was part of the Yugoslav Federation, and based on international law, the higher rank, the Federal Yugoslavia find Kosova deserving of a legal status (in this case the federal in relation to the republican) rather than remaining under Serbia, and

b) by not respecting the will of self-determination for the Albanians as expressed in a free and democratic Constitutional Declaration of July 2, 1990, the Decision of Kosova's Declaration of the Republic in Kacanik Assembly on September 7 of that year, and the Independence Referendum of 1990, when the Albanians opted unanimously for independence, which they deserved in circumstances when their autonomy was suspended through violence.[817]

Professor Bruner, though not only he, assessed that the grounds of a humanitarian nature to be used for intervening in Kosova, may pose a "conscience scruple" feeling guilty for Albanians for what they experienced, but the humanitarian veneer served as an internal "compromise," silent on the one hand, between the Americans and Europeans, to draw Kosova out of Serbia (despite the status that would follow later, as if that did not occur immediately there was a risk to attain regional dimensions and destabilize the entire region, which then could result in an Albanian unification as well). On the other hand, the situation could mean a similar agreement between the Americans and the Russians, so that the

---

[817] See author's long conversation with Professor G. Bruner on *"Ekskluzive"* 3/2001. For more on the issue see also Viktor Meier: *"Jugoslawiens Erben – Die neuen Staaten und die Politik des Westens,"* München, 2001.

case of Kosova would not create precedent, since as such it would disrupt the Russian Federation, in particular by encouraging separatist movements in the Caucasus, which could seem reasonable as the Americans too would not have any significant interest for Russia to be destabilized at a most strategic point, but also seeing no interest in the Kosova crisis becoming a regional crisis that could open other issues with a domino effect as well. This even explains the case of Chechnya and its crisis too, which, despite an open genocide that Russians exercised there, and despite the fact that this place was once independent and for some time during the Lenin era, it even enjoyed some kind of a special status in the Soviet Federation, destroyed by Stalin turning it violently as part of the Russian Federation, unfortunately, was left at the mercy of a ruthless Russia.

The West, pushed by the United States of America, reasoning on humanitarian intervention in Kosova, did not admit that this was outside the UN mandate, or that it represented "aggression against a sovereign country," as Belgrade evaluated it,[818] backed later by the Russian Duma but not by official Moscow. That everything was aligned with the UN terms for more than a year, and that the eventual intervention would have a cover, was clarified by Javier Solana, Secretary General of NATO, at a press conference in Brussels on October 9, 1998, when all the issues of the legitimacy of the intervention were justified in the following summarized terms:

1. *The FRY has not yet complied with the urgent demands of the International Community, despite UNSC Resolution 1160 of March 31, 1998 followed by UNSC Resolution 1199 of September 23, 1998, both acting under Chapter VII of the UN Charter.*

2. *The very stringent report of the Secretary General of the United Nations pursuant to both resolutions, warned of the danger of a humanitarian disaster in Kosova.*

3. *The humanitarian catastrophe continued because no concrete measures towards a peaceful solution of the crisis have been taken by the FRY.*

---

[818] See the letter sent by Belgrade to the UN Security Council on 1 February 1999, following NATO's authorization of 29 January for its Secretary General to commence the bombing.

4. *The deterioration of the situation in Kosova and its magnitude constitute a serious threat to peace and security in the region as explicitly referred to in the UNSC Resolution 1199.*

5. *On the basis of this discussion, I conclude that the Allies believe in the particular circumstances with respect to the present crisis in Kosova as described in UNSC Resolution 1199, there are legitimate grounds for the Alliance to threaten, and if necessary, to use force.*[819]

The mentioned resolutions (1160 and 1199), which are based on Chapter VII of the UN Charter, which were voted in favor by both Russia and China, were not the only ones regarding the legitimacy of NATO intervention in Kosova. There were several other arguments as well to be passed by the UN Security Council indicating that NATO's intervention in Kosova was becoming inevitable as Belgrade had already calculated to achieve its goals by exhorting to ethnic cleansing of Kosova, as revealed in its plan the "Horseshoe," which was to coincide with the start of the NATO air bombing campaign. On October 24, 1998 the UN Security Council's resolution 1203 supported Holbrooke's agreement with Milosevic reached in Belgrade on October 15 and 16, based on Resolution 1199, under which the Federal Republic of Yugoslavia and all others in Kosova, should act in accordance with the above Holbrooke-Milosevic agreement. The Resolution also noted that the unresolved situation in Kosova continued to pose a threat to peace and stability in the region.[820]

In addition, in line with preparations for the legitimacy of NATO's intervention in Kosova there was a statement of the UN Secretary General, Kofi Annan, in a conversation he had with representatives of the North Atlantic Alliance Council. Among other things he said:

> We need to have the excellent cooperation with UN and SFOR in Bosnia extended and continued and on its basis, combining and adopting military means and diplomacy, act everywhere in the Balkans for the benefit of ensuring peace.[821]

---

[819] Javier Solana's letter sent to permanent members of the Council of North Atlantic Alliance on 9 October 1998, cited according to the Reinhard Merkel: *"Der Kosovo Krieg und das Völkerrecht,"* Frankfurt, 2000, p. 20.

[820] Merkel, Reinhard (Publisher): *"Der Kosovo Krieg und das Völkerrcht,"* Frankfurt, 2000, p. 21.

[821] *Ibid*, p. 22.

In order to round up the NATO military threat against the FRY, the Secretary General of the North Atlantic Alliance fully supported the initiative of the Contact Group meeting of January 29, which decided to call the Rambouillet Conference, which began on February 6 and ended after a two-week break in Paris on March 18 with the signing of the agreement by the Albanian side only, so that the first serious attempt of the decision-making international community failed, a failure that brought about the start of the North Atlantic Alliance air campaign against the Yugoslav military and police forces in Kosova and its military bases and infrastructure in Serbia.

Bombing Starts: Troubles among the Allies and the Refugee Crisis

On the evening of March 24, at exactly 7 pm, from the military bases in the south of Italy towards the positions of the Yugoslav military forces in Kosova and several military bases in Serbia, the first NATO missiles were launched. – That same evening, President Bill Clinton addressed the American public with the message that the North Atlantic Alliance had begun a campaign of limited military intervention from the air against Yugoslav military forces in Kosova to end the violence that the Milosevic regime had applyied for years against the Albanian population, which was in a difficult situation and facing a humanitarian catastrophe.- The German Chancellor Gerhard Schroeder, on an 8 o'clock ARD television news edition, addressed the country with a dramatic message, announcing that Germany was not going to war with the Serbian people or the Federal Republic of Yugoslavia, but was joining the international community's efforts to end the violence in Kosova in a manner as to give peace a chance, which was lost in Rambouillet. Belgrade used the first NATO bombs to continue settling accounts with Albanians and blaming the West for it. Serbian police and paramilitary forces began their operations for an organized ethnic cleansing of Kosova, starting with Prishtina and vicinity and continuing to other areas. From the eighth to the eleventh day of bombings about 150 thousand people were deported from Prishtina and vicinity to Macedonia and Albania, and the number increased day by day to reach as high as over 800 thousand within two months. – The background of efforts to end the bombing through various initiatives, such as the Italian one, and the destructive role of certain diplomacies, particularly Italian and Greek to draw NATO out of its bombing dynamics, which benefited Belgrade. – Bllaca and the emergence of an American option for land intervention. – On May 25, 1999 the International Court Tribunal on Yugoslavia (ICTY) raised charges of crimes against humanity committed in Kosova against President Milosevic and his associates from the state and military leadership of the Yugoslav state, establishing legal support for the military intervention.

On the evening of March 24, at exactly 7 pm, from the military bases in the south of Italy towards the positions of the Yugoslav military forces in Kosova and several military bases in Serbia the first NATO missiles were launched. After 10 pm the first aircraft of NATO's air fleet penetrated the Yugoslav space, bringing down three Russian Mig-29 aircrafts belonging to the Yugoslav army, considered among the best fighter aircrafts in the world.

This was the first NATO intervention in its fifty-year old history outside of its activity range, undertaken in defense of Kosova Albanians, marking the West's first war for Kosova.

That same evening, President Bill Clinton addressed the American public with the message that the North Atlantic Alliance had begun a campaign of limited military intervention from the air against Yugoslav military forces in Kosova to end the violence that the Milosevic regime had applied for years against the Albanian population, which was in a difficult situation and facing a humanitarian catastrophe. The U.S. President also mentioned the determination of the Albanians for Peace and Democracy, which they had manifested in continuity, and which was not enough for the Belgrade regime to renounce his state violence against them.

The German Chancellor Gerhard Schroeder, on an 8 o'clock ARD television news edition, addressed the country with a dramatic message, announcing that Germany was not going to war with the Serbian people or the Federal Republic of Yugoslavia, but was joining the international community's efforts to end the violence in Kosova in a manner as to give peace a chance, which was lost in Rambouillet.

The next day at noon in Mons, NATO Headquarters near Brussels, in an extraordinary press conference, one of the most attended ones so far in the fifty-year old history of the Alliance, the Secretary General Javier

Solana appeared accompanied by some of the senior military leaders conducting the campaign, among them General Klaus Neumann, Chief of NATO's Military Council. They said they regarded the first bombs as a "warning" to Belgrade to bear in mind what it could expect, stating that they would intensify the attacks within the next two or three days in accordance with the first phase of military operations, which included the decommissioning of radar, missile systems and other infrastructure related to Yugoslav military logistics.

Evidently, Belgrade not only rejected the "warning" received that same evening from NATO bombs, but its political leadership kept a completely deaf ear towards the bids that remained open, while its military continued to operate in Kosova and its surrounding under disguise, responding by starting on that same night, massacres in several important centers in Kosova, such as the burning of the Old Bazaar in Gjakova and massacres carried out by its mobile paramilitary units in the city against its elite, and in some other parts of the country (Krushë e Madhe, Shirokë, Rahovec), making it clear to the Kosova Albanians that the air campaign and other NATO attacks on the Yugoslav army positions would be accompanied by Serbian countermeasures, as part of a long time Serbian scenario.

"They will be the lords of the sky, and we of the land, and let us see who will be stronger," General Ojdanic stated,[822] indicating that Belgrade would use its military campaign to carry out ethnic cleansing and other atrocities to finally settle scores with Albanians and even blaming the intervention of the North Atlantic Alliance for it.

The next two nights, NATO continued to send more "warnings", rather than seriously attacking the Yugoslav military infrastructure in and around Kosova. Only after the third night its missiles hit some of the radars in Kosova and parts of Serbia as well as strategic parts of the Yugoslav Army commanding infrastructure. NATO reconnaissance planes and satellites revealed that many of the significant military targets in Kosova had been disguised by the Yugoslav Army in populated areas, while the main radar systems and anti-aircraft defenses remained inactive in order not to be exposed to the bombings.[823]

---

[822] See Vlajković Vladan: *"Vojna Tajna,"* Part One, Beograd, 2004, p. 87.

[823] For more see Wesley K. Clark: *"Të bësh luftë moderne,"* Prishtina, 2003.

The Yugoslav military and police forces stationed in Kosova compensated the "passivity" towards NATO aircrafts by increasing violence against the defenseless Albanian population, which grew more and more in line with intensified NATO bombings.

Thus, on the seventh day, the Serbian police and paramilitary forces began organized operations of ethnic cleansing of Kosova, beginning with Prishtina and vicinity and continuing to other parts. From the eighth to the eleventh day of bombings, about 150 thousand people were deported from Prishtina and vicinity to Macedonia and Albania, mainly women, children and elderly, not counting those who had already left Kosova on their own, whose number was just as great.

Dozens of trains ran daily between Prishtina-Fushë-Kosovë and Han i Elezit (near Macedonian border) full of Albanians, who were forcibly evicted from their homes and disembarked near the border with Macedonia, walking for a few hundred meters over the railways before reaching Bllaca. Big worldwide television companies were broadcasting live the long lines of Albanians walking through the railways into Macedonia chased by Serbian paramilitary units.

These were awe-inspiring scenes recalling the deportation of Jews in Nazi camps during World War II, from where many of them would never return. The world public was alarmed and saddened and at the same time expressed doubt if the NATO air campaign undertaken with the humanitarian pretext would ever succeed not only in stopping the crime but also preventing the risk of intensifying it even more.

The Serbs had been expecting all along not only the opening of this dilemma but also its impact on a growing mood against NATO intervention, which already had been fed by certain neo-leftist circles, ecologists and pacifists of various breeds, to begin protests and demonstrations in the streets and squares of European cities, joined by Islamist fundamentalists of anti-American orientation.

The intensifying humanitarian catastrophe on the one hand, reflected in large-scale proportions of ethnic cleansing and intensification of violence against people who had already remained hostage to the police and paramilitary forces operating under disguise with a high efficiency of organized crime, and on the other, the failure of the initial stage of operations as selected bombing was not able to even closely harm the Yugoslav military infrastructure in Kosova and less so destroy it, was being reconsidered by NATO military experts as to how the intervention would result in success. At this point, there arose differences, but also disagreements within the Atlantic Alliance, as skipping from one stage to the next action in expanding the bombing range (a total of four of them had been envisaged) was subject to political consensus of the nineteen countries. This presented major difficulties, as some member countries, after ten days, not only were not interested to shift to the second stage of operations, which foresaw the collapse of the Yugoslav Army's military infrastructure in the interior of Serbia (bombing military factories, demolishing roads and traffic bridges leading to Kosova, bringing down television relays used by the army for military purposes and the like), but, in some ways, demanded a halt for several days, with the reasoning that peace needed a chance.

Greeks and Italians suggested that Easter Day (April 4) be used for this purpose, as according to the first, there were indications from Belgrade to continue talks in Rambouillet, while the latter demanded it as the Vatican and the Pope were interested that the messages of peace, at least during the Easter, should not be accompanied by bombs and increasing human misery, such as the massive influx of refugees.[824]

The question of the cessation of the bombing, sometimes called a "pause" and sometimes a "new chance for peace," etc., was not only an expression of revolt of the pacifists, neo-leftists, opponents of NATO and numerous supporters of Serbia, which was being reflected in various public protests, not a matter of public debate increasingly used for political purposes, but would begin to include the governments of some of the countries participating in the Alliance's air campaign, such as Italy, Spain, Portugal, and some others. Besides Greece, as its representative to the Council of North Atlantic Alliance – although not taking part in the campaign – on behalf of the Greek Foreign Ministry, on April 6, demanded an immediate cessation of the military campaign on the grounds that Athens[825] received a threat from a senior American military officer, Italy too, would demand it, repeatedly finding "humanitarian" or political grounds for it.[826]

One of these initiatives of the highest level was that of May 16 when the Italian Prime Minister Massimo D'Alema, asked the Council of the

---

[824] Wesley K. Clark: *"Të bësh luftë moderne,"* Prishtina, 2003, p. 248.

[825] *Ibid*, p. 248.

[826] Massimo D'Alema: *"Kosova, italianët dhe lufta,"* Tirana, 2004, p. 60.

North Atlantic Alliance, and also the European Union, for a temporary cessation of the bombing with two possible directions to follow: in the direction of Moscow and Beijing with them joining in an interim solution of the Kosova issue by adopting a new UN Security Council Resolution, and also in the direction of Belgrade so that it would accept international conditions by offering a more "acceptable" option of the international presence in Kosova, which, apart from the NATO contingent would also include Russian, Chinese, and third world countries troops under a blue-helmet command. D'Alema proposed that if Serbia rejected the "peace package" then ground deployment had to begin.[827]

D'Alema's proposal was quickly rejected, with the British reacting quite harshly, calling it an irresponsible behavior that would encourage Belgrade to play the card of dividing the Alliance. Even Germans were not at all thrilled with D'Alema's proposal as it provided as a last resort ground deployment of troops, something to which the Germans stood firmly against.[828]

The Italian Prime Minister was counting on Albania for help with the initiative to influence the temporary cessation of the bombing, regardless of the fact that the Albanian Government and Albanians in general were in solidarity with the NATO campaign, and any diplomatic initiative that would have to grant Milosevic even the slightest chance for manipulation was rejected. However, the Italian efforts to raise the issue through the Albanian Foreign Ministry to be addressed in the Tirana Government cabinet had failed, not only because the Albanian Government had been duly warned by Brussels not to fall into the trap of such initiatives, but also because Albania too was aware that that was a dangerous adventure that would suit Belgrade.

Before some countries of the Alliance showed the first signs of internal rifts, reflected in demands for cessation of bombing, either in allegedly granting another chance to political initiatives, or on humanitarian and even religious grounds (as was the Easter break), the first Russian attempt came from the highest level, in order to divide the Alliance on the basis of the cessation of bombing in the name of "returning" Belgrade to the negotiating process "under Russian guarantees."

---

[827] "*Republika*," 16 April 1999.

[828] Massimo D'Alema: "*Kosova, italianët dhe lufta,*" Tirana, 2004, p. 61.

Russian Prime Minister Primakov, known for his pro-Serbian stance during his tenure as the Russian Foreign Minister, caused big trouble for the Contact Group (seemingly Yeltsin removed him from the post in mid-May replacing him with Stepasin), officially informing Bonn of his intentions to travel to Belgrade to talk to Milosevic and from there visit the German capital to meet Chancellor Gerhard Schroeder, who was also chairing the European Union. Earlier, the Russian Foreign Minister Ivanov addressed the German Foreign Minister Joschka Fischer, to announce the Russian initiative and Moscow's mediating role in relation to Milosevic. The Russian proposal consisted of three points:
- *Wide autonomy for Kosova,*
- *A reduced presence of Serb forces in Kosova, and*
- *A return of humanitarian organizations and continuation of negotiations on all other issues.*

As a condition for Belgrade to accept these points, Russia demanded an immediate cessation of air strikes.[829]

On March 30, Russian Prime Minister Primakov arrived in Bonn from Belgrade, where he declared that he had long talks with Milosevic. Primakov met with German Chancellor Schroeder laying before him the three points from Belgrade:

1. Cessation of air strikes followed by the start of negotiations,

2. Political talks, but not in the context of the Contact Group (i.e. rejection of the Rambouillet formula), and

3. Reduction of police forces in Kosova to the pre-war level. [830]

Russian initiatives were rejected without any hesitation by Europeans. It seems that the Russians themselves were convinced that this was unlikely to cause any changes, and that the initiative was made rather for internal and external use. For internal use – because it needed to somehow offset the effects of severe public reactions on the outlook for Russian passivity while NATO was bombing "Serbian Orthodox brothers," and externally it needed to test the internal unity of the Alliance on the sensitivity of the issue, which as would be seen, continued to be a controversial topic even as the NATO summit in Washington on April 23 and

---

[829] See Joshka, Fischer: *"Vitet kuq-gjelbër,"* Prishtina, 2007, p. 172.
[830] *Ibid*, p. 174.

24, 1999, on the occasion of the 50th Anniversary, at least in terms of Alliance's first intervention in a country outside the range of its action, demonstrated unity with the commitment that the bombing from the air, without excluding the option of a ground invasion, would be intensified to the extent that would bring Belgrade to its knees.

The question of the cessation of the bombing, temporary suspension, pause and various proposals emerging during the NATO bombing campaign against Yugoslav military and police forces in Kosova and the "hope" that they help to achieve something would be one of the cards that Serbia had calculated for long by hoping on one hand to split the Atlantic Alliance from within and on the other to divide the West politically and to cause a rift in the decision-making international community of the highest levels, such as the UN Security Council. Within this strategy Belgrade put into play several factors exhorting to pressure in reaching multifaceted rifts: from the intensification of ethnic cleansing to the transfer of crisis to neighboring countries (Macedonia and Albania), and efforts to spread the armed conflict to Macedonia and Albania, with the crisis gaining the scale of a regional crisis.

Belgrade used the first factor in a more efficient way, as within just ten days, with the deportation of about 150 thousand Albanians to Macedonia and Albania it was able to create a refugee crisis. It started çausing concerns in Macedonia, as that of Bllaca, when the official Shkup, in order to protect itself from an "invasion" of Albanian refugees, closed the border, while in no man's land in Bllaca, almost "spontaneously" the first large-scale refugee camp was established. The latter terrified European and world public as CNN, BBC, NTV and other powerful worldwide media outlets were bringing live horrific images of deportation of Albanians stuck in a dump hole under appalling conditions, vulnerable to bad weather and lack of outside assistance.

Although after four days, thanks to American intervention and UNHCR, as well as European countries to accept refugees remaining in Bllaca, the temporary concentration camp of Bllaca was removed from the agenda,[831] at least in its existing extreme form, although refugees contin-

---

[831] Bllaca closed on April 4. Thanks to the mediation of UNHCR, European countries and the U.S. and Canada, within a few days about 100 thousand refugees were taken out of Skopje. Germany received 14 thousand refugees, U.S. 10 thousand, Canada 6 thousand. Other European countries: Austria, Sweden, Denmark, the Netherlands and Norway w received several thousand refugees each.

ued to pass through it. However, the issue of refugees continued to be a burden to the overall situation attaining proportions of a crisis that would aggravate the continuation of NATO air intervention against the Yugoslav military and police positions in Kosova.

In this respect, Belgrade won the first "battle" with NATO, although, on the other hand, this affected the NATO army leaders to get rid of the dilemmas and "reservations" prevailing among politicians to intensify the bombing in the second and third stage. The Yugoslav military and Milosevic soon realized that the North Atlantic Alliance air intervention, even though being in the service of politics, could not accept an end as determined by politics (withdrawal from the bombing or similar), but only by military determination, meaning to come out as a winner and in no other way.

Belgrade further continued to abuse with the refugee crisis, which was increasingly growing with the number of refugees reaching as many as 300 thousand, exploiting it to weaken the cohesion of NATO from within. The aim was to deprive politics of its arguments of military pressure while removing the influence of politics over the military. In this way, by eliminating the military option from politics and politics free of the illusion of military pressure as the only means of diplomacy of force, Belgrade also conveniently used the time factor to produce the first rifts among Westerners.

It was therefore a very clear account that Belgrade made misusing Albanian refugees to further gather "points" against the bombing, because as that was being staged it not only yielded no results by being unable to break the Serbian military force in Kosova and around it, but it seemed that the campaign would not be able to cause any harm to the Yugoslav military arsenal in Kosova, except those referred to as collateral, in which Kosovars and their property suffered.

The latter being so frequent and usually accompanied by tragedy was being used by Belgrade propaganda against NATO intervention displaying the destruction of civilian facilities and casualties (bridges, roads, drainage and water systems, train and bus stations, and others), with multiple victims and fleeing refugees being hit while missing military convoys, showing tractors and vehicles with displaced people wandering through the streets of Kosova.

Faced with these developments the Atlantic Alliance reconsidered targets to include military targets, which, for the first time would make clear the following two things to the politicians:

First – to stop any calculation concerning the cessation or temporary suspension of bombing, and

Second – to consider the option of an invasion with ground troops, which would be initiated by the British at the NATO Council in early May, an option that would be discussed three days later in Washington by the top military at the Pentagon, in a meeting attended by President Clinton, in which a green light would be issued for such plans but without taking any particular position.[832]

The first issue, that of renouncing any calculation for the termination or temporary suspension of bombing under various excuses coming from many sides to "give peace a chance" and the like, started diminishing hopes for Belgrade to continue believing in the likelihood of causing a rift within the Alliance. Bringing an end to this issue also affected that of refugees and ethnic cleansing, which Belgrade had set in motion and greatly exploited for this purpose. The latter was not any longer seen in terms of prevention and dealing with it from a position of the consequences, but rather as an emergency in order to provide them with temporary care mainly in Macedonia and Albania (with the construction of large capacity refugee camps) without letting difficulties being built up for these countries, as was the case in Macedonia when the presence of refugees also raised political issues.

The West, therefore, accepted the challenge of refugees, turning it into a counter-reaction to Belgrade, on the one hand, by intensified air bombardment from the first to the third phase, which included the bombing of strategic facilities in Serbia (power plants, bridges, communications systems crippling Serbia quickly) and, on the other hand, recognizing as a possible option military ground invasion in two directions: towards the South – from Albania and Macedonia and towards the North – from Hungary towards Belgrade, something that was related to the second issue as well.

It should be noted in this case that the West won a crucial battle against Belgrade and its double strategy of using ethnic cleansing for

---

[832] For more on the issue see Wesley K. Clark: *"Të bësh luftë moderne,"* Prishtina, 2003, pp. 274, 311.

strategic purposes and gains when the Hague Tribunal on May 25, 1999 raised charges of crimes against humanity committed in Kosova against President Milosevic and his military and state leadership.[833]

So, with this, the NATO air campaign gained both moral and legal support.

ICTY indictment effects on both the progress of the air campaign and of the political process to follow were multifaceted, with the main ones being the following:

1) the real cause of ethnic cleansing and all that was accelerated from the beginning of the air campaign by the military and police forces in Kosova, which Belgrade propaganda, supported by different neo-leftist groups, pacifists and others tried to exploit and blame on NATO, was now clear – Milosevic, who could now be held responsible and liable to respond before the International Tribunal for Crimes Against Humanity at the Hague;

2) raising charges on crimes committed against humanity against the President of the Federal Republic of Yugoslavia by ICTY, not only the president of the country was indicted but Belgrade's entire policy against Albanians as well, admitting also that serious errors of the decision-making international community starting from the Hague Conference of 1991 and onwards, when it decided to ignore the legitimate demands of the Albanians to secede from such a murderous policy allowing to leave them as its hostage;

3) The ICTY issuing of an indictment against Milosevic on suspicion that he had committed crimes against humanity in Kosova and Albanians removed the theoretical possibility for him of returning as a "partner" for the West in the way it happened with the signing of the Dayton accords. It also eliminated the possibility of any effort that the Serbian politics could undertake in its last moments, after having carried out the ethnic cleansing of Kosova, in order to show itself as cooperating with the West to conclude a similar peace agreement;

---

[833] Besides Slobodan Milosevic, President of the Federal Republic of Yugoslavia from 1997, the ICTY took action against the following persons: Milan Milutinovic, President of Serbia since 1997, Nikola Sainovic, Deputy Prime Minister of the FRY from 1998, General Lieutenant-Colonel Dragoljub Ojdanic - chief of General Staff of the Armed Forces of Yugoslavia (AJ) and Vlajko Stoilkovic – Serbia's Interior Minister since 1998.

4) With ICTY issuing the indictment against Milosevic, the West had created internal circumstances in Serbia to remove him from the political scene, even forcefully, as it had no need for him any longer because he would turn into an obstacle for the Serb politics and state itself, as it would be excluded from any state jurisdiction in relation to the international community.

The "Apache" and the Ground Intervention Option

Why were the American "Apache" helicopters not allowed to join the military actions in Kosova, since they were stationed in Albania preparing for rapid intervention? – The bombing of the Kosova Liberation Army units in Koshare by French "Mirage" fighters was not a mistake, as stated, but rather a warning to the Albanian guerrillas not to penetrate further into Kosova, as the West had come to a bargain that NATO military intervention should not result in a classic winner/loser situation, in line with the political stance to have Serbia pull out of Kosova with Kosova remaining under Yugoslav sovereignty. – At the NATO jubilee summit in Washington held on March 23 and 24, the Alliance demonstrated internal unity, supporting intensified air bombing to the final victory and at the same time opened the possibility of ground deployment in Yugoslavia. In addition, the Washington summit prepared a five-point package of demands to be sent to Milosevic, included in the final platform policy ending the war. It was these decisions that determined not only the fate of NATO victory during this intervention, but also political developments pulling Serbia out of Kosova and placing the latter under international protectorate.

Introducing the option of ground deployment that preoccupied the Atlantic Alliance for the first two weeks of May was preceded by considerations at the highest military levels on possible use of "Apache" helicopters in the air campaign against Yugoslav military and police forces in Kosova. The need for their involvement in the war was initiated by the Commander of NATO's southern wing, U.S. General, Wesley K. Clark, by the end of the first phase of the Alliance's operations against the Yugoslav military forces positions in Kosova.[834] These operations had barely been able to yield the expected results, although NATO spokesman in Brussels, Jamie Shea, had been "bombing" the public day by day on Yugoslav army targets destroyed, repeating the same day after day indicating a game of words whose aim was to conceal the failures of the first stage, a truth that the military was keeping to itself convinced that things could change before they went public.

In order to make a change one of the two following things had to be done: signing up the use of "Apache" helicopters or intensifying the bombing from the air passing immediately from stage one to stage three, and prepare for the fourth, the most severe one without excluding plan B.

General Clark was personally convinced that the introduction of the "Apache" would be the best way to break the "guard" of military and police forces in Kosova along with other military infrastructure, no matter how long and how it would continue to be disguised by the Yugoslav defense, showing great versatility. "Apache" helicopters were the most powerful and sophisticated weapon for such purposes.

Introducing helicopters in the war had to pass through two simultaneous procedures: get both permissions from Pentagon and Military Council of the Alliance, as "special parts of war operations" connecting air and ground forces and thus subject to special tactical treatment, sometimes preparatory and sometimes unintelligible to those who confused political with military reasoning or vice versa. General Clark raised the issue immediately asking the Pentagon for permission to deploy two squadrons from Germany to Albania, standing at alert just in case, as their deployment and readiness to join in the operation required a period of two to three weeks under any circumstance.

Also, the place of deployment played a role, especially realizing that the helicopters had to stand away of the reach of Yugoslav missiles being relatively mobile and ready to be used for surprise action. Therefore, the stationing of the "Apache" in Albania rather than Macedonia, as proposed earlier was linked to greater security provided by the Albanian territory as compared to Macedonia, with the Shkup airport located within the reach of the Yugoslav medium-range radius of action, stationed in the vicinity of Nis, which could easily bring down "Apache" squadrons. Besides security, Albania also provided other conditions appropriate to join the

---

[834] See Wesley K. Clark: *"Të bësh luftë moderne,"* Prishtina, 2003, pp. 442-349.

action, especially in the northern part of the country, on the border with Kosova, where Yugoslav military forces were located along with covert missile systems, which the "Apache" could eliminate without any major difficulty.

Subsequently this very strength of these helicopters turned into an obstacle for their use, first on grounds that there were some technical issues (their transportation and logistics in Albania could not meet the proper requirements and this could have consequences for their efficacy and safety). Secondly, there was the overall concept of air operations, which changed with the introduction of the "Apache," and this could jeopardize the success of the mission, planned as warfare from the sky excluding direct involvement in the operations. Introducing the "Apache" would set forth such conditions.

General Clark was very surprised by such excuses, especially as they came from the Pentagon, which was able to assess the situation according-ly, though this time it seemed not to be interested in doing so because the high command and the Pentagon in general had to retain "sovereignty" over NATO command, even though it was led by U.S. generals. This was a result of an internal rivalry hardly comprehensible from the outside. The U.S. general described these later in details in his memoires about the war in Kosova.[835]

However, even in those incomprehensible squirms between the American military wing within the military command structure of NATO and the Pentagon, the issue reached up to the highest levels of the U.S. military command where the "Apache" did nevertheless get the green light to be sent to Albania and begin preparations. But their engagement in operations needed a special decision by the U.S. President after receiv-ing the recommendation of the Pentagon and specifically Secretary Cohen. Two "Apache" squads were transferred from U.S. military bases in Germany to Albania, where they resumed preparations in the north, on the border with Kosova, quite intense but with no consequences except for a threatening effect for Yugoslav forces positioned near the border with Albania. Furthermore, during the exercises, two of the "Apache" helicopters went down opening speculation that the Yugoslav defense

---

[835] On the difficulties of this nature, for more see Wesley K. Clark's book "Waging Modern War," Prishtina, 2003, describing among other things the fierce "rivalry" between the Pentagon and NATO and the U.S. administration on several military issues, which had consequences for the progress of the mission in Kosovo.

missile system aided by Russian protection was involved. This could have affected the decision to be taken on later by President Clinton, by the end of May, to not involve the "Apache" in combat.

The decision not to engage the "Apache" was of a rather political nature than of a military one. Although, the latter too did not seem unlikely in the circumstances of "rivalries" between internal war strategists and animosities the schemers of the air strikes shared against this weapon's planners, who were now able to stand against it on grounds that it set the stage for ground intervention, which meant loss of lives, which the American public was not able to accept, especially when dealing with confusing civil wars such as those in the Balkans where the toll could run high.

In addition to military reasons, which General Clark explained in detail, there were, however, the political ones that prevented the "Apache" from being engaged in the war. Because, the use of this very effective weapon for ground combat changed the concept of military intervention in Yugoslavia, which stood on the West's political stand not aiming a complete military defeat of the Yugoslav army forcing its capitulation, but rather compelling its withdrawal, as actually happened after the signing of the Kumanovo military-technical agreement on June 10, 1999 between NATO's top military and the Yugoslav Army General Staff.

The attitude not to inflict a military defeat to the Yugoslav Army fraught another most important issue, that in this war, despite the fact that "below" there should be neither a classic loser or winner, which could be the Kosova Liberation Army, as its victory could upset the military and political character of the entire matter, for which no one was interested, much less the West, which had entered the war to save Kosova from the worst, namely humanitarian reasons, and not turn Albanians into a winner. On the contrary, if Serbs were to emerge as a loser, then the loser had to accept capitulation, and capitulation then implied punishment, and punishment meant also that Kosova had to gain full independence, and this independence by the international community could not be accepted in such circumstances, as it opened other issues for the region, arguing that the removal of one straw drew so many others behind.

The issue of not resulting in Albanians as winners in this war was removed from the agenda long ago. Furthermore, since the Kosova Liberation Army went public for the first time in November 1997 and competent informative services of western countries knew everything that was hiding behind it (who constituted it, what goals were pursued in a political plain and others) – Albanian armed resistance factor would receive tasks and services, but never military partnership, or much less victory. Furthermore, every time that various spokespersons of Kosova Liberation Army began to reveal the "strategy" of their liberation war for "national unification" to the world (although they were part of marketing rather than any piece of real engagement they could get into in those circumstances), specific political and military circles in the West used the Albanian "threat" for a national liberation war, which according to them had already started, to be exploited for establishing an internal unity in order to find a modus for the solution of the Kosova crisis that would exclude the component of an Albanian unification.

There were numerous indications that the deal between NATO and French, and some other partners within the North Atlantic Alliance for joint military action was done in terms of a preliminary agreement with the Americans as to not accept as partners both the Kosova Liberation Army (KLA) and the Government Defense Force of the Republic of Kosova (FARK), emerging during fighting in some parts of Dukagjin in 1998, although during the air campaign they would accept a number of their various services in the field. The reason was that this, on the one hand, presumed independence, which in the circumstances, with the exception of the Americans and British who might have had it in their plans as "reserve options," nobody else supported, and on the other hand, it meant placing the West on the Albanian side against the Serbs, which was also unacceptable.

That the Europeans remained faithful to this approach is best seen in the Koshare case when some of the Kosova Liberation Army units tore down the border that had separated Albanians on both sides for more than seven decades. It was the French "Mirage" fighter planes that bombed the Kosova Liberation Army fighters causing them great harm, making it clear that the fate of the war and unintended winners or losers were not decided from "below" but rather that the issue remained to be decided from "above," according to an undeclared agreement that the Atlantic Alliance partners knew and had to abide by.

Shortly after the end of the war, it would be exactly General Wesley Clark, who in his memoirs and press statements in the Western media, released some of the "seasonings" of secret agreements explaining that the action of the French "Mirage: fighter planes against the Kosova Liberation

Army forces in Koshare was not a mistake, as an official NATO statement said, but rather a deliberate action of the French, who, in accordance with the unwritten deal that disallowed KLA to come out a winner of the war and much less liberator of Kosova, had bombed Albanian fighters positions, telling them what they dared and dared not do.[836] This underscored the limits to which the overall Albanian movement of *politics without war* and *war without politics* were subjected.

Removing the "Apache" from the agenda by President Clinton's decision on May 19, as a concession to be made to *war planners from above* and Europeans to whom the use of those weapons nourished fears that following their use in Kosova the Kosova Liberation Army marching would follow, bombing intensified in accordance with the prescribed stages from one to four dropping the concern for shared political consensus powers leaving it to the planners of the war and the military to decide upon them. In the meantime, for the first time the option of terrestrial intervention was brought out as plan B, which until then was discussed in closed circles, but excluded en bloc by most of the member countries of the North Atlantic Alliance. Germany and some other countries had, even, requested that the matter be dropped from the agenda entirely, because of fear that even a limited intervention by air would not receive adequate support.

---

[836] See Wesley K. Clark: *"Të bësh luftë moderne,"* Prishtina, 2003 and see also the long conversation of General Clark on a BBC broadcast on German ARD program of October 20, 1999. An opinion contrary to this, with the Kosovo Liberation Army, by the Americans, NATO, and partly by the German Bundeswehr being prepared for a long time "to turn it into a right hand of the Atlantic Alliance" to destroy the Federal Republic of Yugoslavia is expressed by some German authors with the most vocal among them being Mattias Küntzel's book *"Der Weg tissue den Krieg - Deutshland, Die Nato und das Kosovo"* (Road to War - Germany, NATO and Kosovo), Berlin, 2000, which protects views that certain military and intelligence services of NATO, the U.S. and Germany, worked very hard to highlight the Kosovo Liberation Army, in order to use it politically and militarily, of course for their goals and interests, to destroy the Federal Republic of Yugoslavia, but without allowing it to turn into a military virtual factor, because, according to the author, neither the Americans nor the Germans were interested, who, after having used the KLA for their own purposes to enter in the Balkans, would quickly demilitarize it, turning it into the Kosovo Protection Corps (KPC) held under strict supervision.

Over time, realizing that airstrikes were not yielding wanted results and there was a danger that as long as it lasted it could disrupt the Alliance from within, the British opened the issue of land troop deployment. Initially this was done by the U.S. military, who already introduced plan B, as a last option, but here too the last word belonged to politics. After having consulted with the country's military leadership, President Clinton would agree that the issue of opting for ground intervention was a possible option but only as a last resort. As such, the issue was raised in the meeting of the Council of the North Atlantic Alliance in the wake of Washington's jubilee summit held on March 23 and 24, 1999. There too the ground troop deployment was given the green light in principle, but as a preparation and after all the necessary details had been provided.

The military leadership demanded from politics that an eventual deployment was followed by political clarity. According to NATO military experts, ground military deployment planning required at least 45 days of intensive preparations, so if a decision was made on the military deployment option, it had to be taken no later than June 1, in order to begin operation in early September. Postponing the eventual deployment for October would be equivalent to defeat, as that would impede the continental autumn and winter to develop successfully. "NATO cannot risk remaining trapped by storms and Balkan slush to become a target of Milosevic's partisans," General Clark declared.[837]

Also part of the plan had to be the place of landing and the number of soldiers with military infrastructure as part of a special operation, since, in addition to weapons a lot of supplementary material had to be transported. According to General Clark, the bulk of the military asserted that the landing should be made by Albania and Macedonia, as these countries had much better conditions for a successful penetration through land. However, a landing plan from the north was also not excluded, i.e. from Hungary, assessing that within two or three days NATO forces would take Belgrade inflicting the last blow to the Yugoslav Army and the Milosevic regime.

In any case, at the NATO jubilee summit in Washington, held on March 23 and 24, 1999, the Alliance proved internal unity, supporting an intensification of airstrikes until final victory opening the way for land deployment in Yugoslavia. In addition, in the Washington summit a five-

---

[837] *Ibid.*

point package of applications was developed that would be sent to Milosevic included in the final platform policy to end the war. These were decisions to determine not only the fate of NATO victory during the intervention, but political developments that would bring Serbia out of Kosova, commencing an inevitable process of Kosova's final secession from Serbia to follow after placing Kosova under international supervision.

The American Formula for Pulling Serbia out of Kosova

With the establishment of a political platform for the peaceful resolution of the Kosova crisis and dilemmas about the attitude that the Rambouillet accords had to follow, Germany came up with a triangle proposal: Serbia out, NATO in, and the return of refugees, a proposal finding the support of the Western countries. – Passing from the Contact Group over to the Group-8.8 and agreements in principle between the Americans and the Russians about a new framework of solving the Kosova crisis through temporary international protectorate. – The jubilee Summit of NATO in Bonn and the five-point conditions to Belgrade. – The first meeting of the Group-8 in Bonn and seven-point proposal. – Ahtisaari, Talbot and Chernomyrdin assume the role of the mediators aimed at reaching an agreement with Milosevic designed in accordance with the formula of losing the war without capitulation, which would open the doors for an international protectorate in Kosova, as a compromise necessary for a transitional solution before coming to a final solution.

After the visit of March 31, 1999 of the Russian Prime Minister Primakov in Belgrade, where he met with Milosevic and thence continued to Bonn he presented his three-point demands, which brought nothing new, but that would confirm the Russian-Serb efforts to cause a rift among the North Atlantic Alliance through well-known trickery, as had been tried for years with the international community, it was time for the Western countries to emerge with political options to resolve the crisis. U.S. Secretary of State Albright, rejecting three Russian points of Primakov, conditioning an immediate cessation of the bombing, associated it with a request from the West to begin negotiations for a comprehensive political initiative to bring about the solution of the Kosova crisis. During her talks with German Foreign Minister Fischer, whose country chaired the European Union, she demanded that the Contact Group, as soon as possible be presented with a project, which would revolve around the triangle *"Serbia out, NATO in, and the return of refugees."*[838]

The triangle of demands as mentioned by the U.S. Secretary of State in her first telephone conversation with German Foreign Minister Fischer, meant as support for endorsement by the Contact Group, turned into a Western concept aimed at getting Serbia out of Kosova and getting NATO in. The plan was gradually clarified during the time of deliberations about the response to the entire matter before the adoption of UN Security Council Resolution 1244 of June 10, 1999. The sidelines of the five-point plan that began to appear in daily conversations of the "Quint" (the four consisting of foreign ministers of the U.S., UK, France, and Germany) had to explain the two main issues: the stance regarding the Rambouillet documents and the role of the Contact Group, both of them being already overwhelmed by the circumstances. The French Foreign Minister said that the Rambouillet accords had been invalidated by now with the military intervention bringing it out of the game, while the British foreign minister Cook noted that the issues should be oriented based on the UN Charter on which military intervention was supported, adding that the term "genocide against Albanians" should be introduced in the Western terminology. Meanwhile, the U.S. Secretary of State, Albright raised the issue of an international protectorate for Kosova as a compromise solution for an interim period of time, meaning that the Rambouillet accords remained the main reference despite the fact that it was not signed by Serbia nor supported by Russia because of Serb rejection. But, in the new circumstances, according to U.S. Secretary of State and the disposition of the majority of Western countries, the slogan *"Serbia out, NATO in, and the return of refugees,"* meant focusing on the international protectorate and NATO entry into Kosova.

Finding support on the Rambouillet accords and the return of its political nomenclature more than expected, however, did not mean automatic support of the Contact Group at any cost, which in the new circumstances would appear outdated. Here too the "Quint" reached the position that a different solution had to be found and for the moment it would be

---

[838] Fischer, Joschka: *"Vitet kuq-gjelbër,"* Prishtina, 2008, p. 178.

Group-8, with a place for Russia, provided it accepted beneficial cooperation and also the concept upon which would stand a political solution to the Kosova crisis, pursuant to the initial position – namely that it should be placed under international supervision with the presence of an international security force with a NATO nucleus.

At the meeting of political directors of the Contact Group, on April 7 in Brussels, it would be the Russians who would have the last blow by rejecting such a forum from discussing the circumstances while bombing was going on. [839]

Russian Foreign Minister, Andreyev, known as a proponent of the conservative line, was the first to ignore the warning of the Contact Group meeting of April 8, 1999, which would be the last, on the grounds that the "hot" issues should be discussed with Deputy Secretary of State, Talbot. This implied that Russians in such circumstances aimed at skipping the Europeans, and this could be part of their strategy to cause new rifts among the ranks of Western politics by demanding that issues be transferred to the level of the "two great ones," which, at least on the home front were acting without letting others know what they wanted to achieve. Apparently the Americans would like this, accepting the Russian game, but without hurting at all relations with the Europeans, as impenetrable partners linked strongly in their air campaign in Kosova, as on this relationship relied not only the survival of NATO in the new circumstances, but also the expansion of the Western sphere of interest in a crucial geostrategic space.

U.S. Secretary of State Albright, two days following the meeting in Oslo, got approval for the inclusion of the Russians in the G-8 and also received approval that the issue of an interim protectorate for Kosova should get passage through the UN Security Council. While harmonizing attitudes with the Russians, an agreement was reached on the role of Europeans for the implementation of peace in Kosova, as already anticipated to share the burden of funding that fell on the European Union.

Establishing direct links between Americans and Russians, as Moscow had demanded, led to agreements on main principles: placing Kosova under international supervision, international presence – in charge of security, and the withdrawal of the Yugoslav military and police forces, without touching upon formal sovereignty of Yugoslavia. This principled

---

[839] *Ibid*, p.191.

agreement left open the issue of the modalities which should be clarified and defined, in particular the issue of the international security presence in Kosova and its character, knowing the West's position about the role of NATO and other issues to clarify the political and security aspects, although there were also humanitarian issues, the return of refugees and IDPs, which were not only technical but also closely linked to political solutions.

Here, however, the position that had to be taken against Milosevic was also of significance. How should they handle him when he rejected the Rambouillet opting for a final account settling with the Albanians? What would be the address that the international community had to call if needed and so on? If Vedrin said that Rambouillet should be forgotten, along with past negotiations (even though this would not happen remaining the only reference), one could not say the same about the inevitable man with whom one had to keep ties, without excluding the possibility of having to sign a deal with him one day.

U.S. Secretary of State Albright, using political eloquence shifted this dilemma "for a later time" meaning that for the moment there was no dealing with Milosevic, but minding one's own issues. This "let's wait and see,"[840] would soon receive a response on April 27 when ICTY chief prosecutor, Arbour, raised charges of committing crimes against humanity against Milosevic and political and military leaders of the Federal Republic of Yugoslavia and Serbia. This meant removing Milosevic once and for all from the partnership role with the West, as it also reduced the likelihood that the formula for the final settlement of the Kosova crisis would be found tied to Serbia, even though it still remained in the political vocabulary, but rather as a matter of compromise to move forward in order to avoid blocking the process through radical demands, which were inevitable. For out of this context, i.e. the removal of Serb administrative right and its replacement with the international one, there was no moral or political credibility to any claims about coexistence between Serbs and Albanians in circumstances with blood and serious crimes that the Serbian authorities had committed against them by means of war, not only during the war, but in a historical continuity since the beginning of the Eastern Crisis, supported by memoranda drafted by Serbian intellec-

---

[840] *Ibid*, p. 179.

tuals, turning into political concepts with tasks issued to the military to carry out accordingly "in defense of the fatherland!"

That the Tribunal's decision to bring charges against Milosevic and Belgrade military and state leadership for serious crimes against humanity committed in Kosova, not only seemed like a matter of "marketing" to remove from the game the most dangerous and unpredictable player who had been dragging for years the international community while his military machine and police had committed serious crimes against humanity, first in Croatia, then in Bosnia and Herzegovina and finally in Kosova – crimes committed in a continuity by Belgrade as part of a continued hegemonic and chauvinist program – in the next day of the indictment, the German public was presented with the 1937 Memorandum of Vasa Cubrilovic.[841] The Memorandum was accompanied by an opening remark providing similar points of the Cubrilovic program with that of Milosevic on the chauvinist policy against Albanians and elaborates to settle accounts with them including by means of warfare, as was being done now.

The complexity of anti-Albanian morbid policies of Belgrade and its continuity in those days was revealed in an even more bizarre way, in the book published by the German Defense Minister Rudolf Scharping, "*Wir dürfen nicht wegsehen*" ("We could not look the other way").[842] For the

---

[841] "*Frankfurter Rundschau,*" 28-30 April 1999.

[842] The book of the German Defense Minister Rudolf Scharping: "Wir dürfen nicht wegsehen," Berlin, 1999 represents a "mix" between a journal and political assessment of the Kosovo crisis in the most critical time, on the eve of and during Kosovo bombing as experienced from the perspective of those who saw the political side of it, but also the invisible – the military one, related to the crimes and atrocities committed by the Yugoslav Army and paramilitary units in Kosovo by the secret plan "Horseshoe." Scharping was the sturdiest German politician to openly confront Serb chauvinist policy demanding for Kosovo to secede from Serbia, while its state apparatus and military be indicted for crimes against humanity in The Hague, which actually happened. The German left, from whence Scharping was coming, that never agreed with neither NATO's intervention against the Yugoslav Army in Kosovo nor the German Bundeswer participation in this mission, would not forget his "bias" in favor of Albanians. Three years later he would fall victim to several stagings of scandals that cost him the loss of his position as the highest leader of the Social Democratic Party (SPD). Later on they would again gain momentum by attacking him in his private domain, compelling him to leave the party and politics to end up as Chairman of the Association of German Cyclists!

first time the book brought details about the secret plan "Horseshoe," prepared by the Yugoslavs for a final settling of accounts with Albanians on the eve of and during the continuation of NATO's air campaign against Yugoslav military and police targets in Kosova.

According to NATO, the plan "Horseshoe," of which the Germans were informed by the Bulgarians, was authentic and had begun to be implemented on March 20, four days before the NATO air campaign began against Yugoslav forces in Kosova, while its intensive preparations for its implementation had been carried out by the Yugoslav Army exactly at the duration of the break of the Rambouillet conference, when Albanians asked for "more time" to convince their base about signing the document. In any case, the German public, which had quite a dilemma as to whether or not it should join the NATO campaign based on their history, would have the opportunity to be convinced that the German commitment, this time, was not of a military nature for aggressive neo-imperialist American purposes, as stated by the neo-leftists, pacifists and other anti-American movements in Germany and in several streets and leftist-oriented media outlets, but rather to save a people from genocide to which it was already exposed and without help would vanish.

Of the same nature, in order to rid Kosovar Albanians once and for all of Serb genocide and free them of the physical shadow of their perpetrators, were also the clear-cut five-point demands that NATO addressed to Belgrade on the occasion of the jubilee summit in Washington, on April 23 and 24, 1999,[843] which in turn helped to further clarify the political aspects related to what was already foreseen as a transitional solution under the international protectorate.

---

[843] See Statement of North Atlantic Council on Kosovo of 23 April 1999. The five demands to Milosevic were:
1. *Ensure a verifiable stop to all military action and the immediate ending of violence and repression in Kosovo;*
2. *Withdraw from Kosovo his military, police and para-military forces;*
3. *Agree to the stationing in Kosovo of an international military presence;*
4. *Agree to the unconditional and safe return of all refugees and displaced persons, and unhindered access to them by humanitarian aid organisations; and*
5. *Provide credible assurance of his willingness to work for the establishment of a political framework agreement based on the Rambouillet accords.*

The agreement in principle between Albright and Ivanov in Oslo about the main frameworks of the agreement, which were in line with those that had already received the epithet of the "Fischer Plan" enjoying the European support, needed a G-8 meeting on a ministerial level in order to clarify all the details and dilemmas before the UN Security Council and before the entire issue was handed over for the adoption as a special resolution to gain full legitimacy.

In this respect positive signs were already coming, as Russia had accepted principles and was in favor of G-8 involvement, not only to restore the lost reputation it suffered from Rambouillet, but also because the Russian government in order to survive in circumstances where the country was threatened by financial collapse needed to show its cooperation with the West in order to be able to receive an economic support package. To see to it, Yeltsin proved his serious approach to the issue by appointing his envoy, former Prime Minister Viktor Chernomyrdin as his special envoy to Yugoslavia. As the Americans had already done so by appointing Deputy Secretary of State, Strobe Talbot, it was left to the EU and UN to appoint their representatives to round up a trio that would take over the key intermediary tasks. Europeans nominated the former Finnish president Martti Ahtisaari and this was requested by the World Organization. But initially the UN did not show much interest in this proposal, because it felt overlooked on the issue of Kosova. However, realizing that in the future it could only be present in Kosova in the civil package and in no way in a military or any other security issue – it sought to stay somewhat neutral with the promise that depending on developments, it would engage itself in the work of intermediaries.

The European Union, however, was determined to give Martti Ahtisaari, former Finn President, well-known for his useful international services, the role of the European envoy in this mission, leaving open for him also the position as UN mediator in certain circumstances. Furthermore, with this UN linking role Ahtisaari was accepted by Kofi Annan on the occasion of their meeting in Finland, where they discussed the role the UN should play in a second stage, that of the implementation of peace in Kosova in civil matters, for which it had greater resources for such a job.

The first ministerial summit of G-8 was held at Petersberg, near Bonn, on May 6. Germans proved good and committed organizers to act for a joint working atmosphere, while the Americans asserted themselves as the first violin. After a work that was called constructive, ministers adopted a plan of action on resolving through political principles, confirming certain preconditions confirmed earlier by the NATO jubilee summit in Washington regarding the conditions that the Atlantic Alliance had announced to stop the bombing. Here, it is worth mentioning the principles, because, based on them, the agreement with Yugoslavia and the Security Council's decision to organize the activities after the bombing were later engendered:

1. An immediate and verifiable stop to violence and repression in Kosova;

2. Withdrawal of military, police and paramilitary forces from Kosova;

3. Stationing of efficient civil and military international body in Kosova to be decided by the UN.

4. Building an interim administration in Kosova based on UN Security Council decision.

5. Safe and free return of all refugees and displaced persons and unhindered access to them by humanitarian aid organizations.

6. Beginning of a political process to work for the establishment of bases for an autonomous Kosova, based on the Rambouillet accords, considering Yugoslavia's demand for territorial integrity.

7. Overall decision-making on economy and stability of the entire region.[844]

In addition to these principles, the G-8 decided to begin drafting a UN resolution and the program planning for achieving a solution. Germany, as head of the group, had a duty to inform the government of China on the decisions of the meeting.

The first document of the G-8 from Petersberg, however, at least in two points, was subject to Russian "dictate," aimed at gaining something for their willingness to join the G-8 and at the same time to ensure that the proposed solution at the UN Security Council gained legitimacy. Item 5, stating that the establishment of the Interim Administration in Kosova was the decision of the UN Security Council, and Item 6, stating that the foundations for an autonomous Kosova were made on the basis of the Rambouillet accords- renouncing the planned meeting for three years later to decide on the status of Kosova, i.e., for independence – implied

---

[844] Ahtisaari, Martti: *"Detyra në Beograd,"* Prishtina, 2008, p. 49

that draft resolution to be presented to the UN Security Council, not only needed a lot of work, but that the West, led by the United States of America, in order to win the battle for Kosova in accordance with Albright's catchphrase "*Serbia out of Kosova, NATO in Kosova*" was facing a tough match with the Russians.

Staged Mediation and the Role of the Mediating Troika

> *The American political fixation "Serbia out of Kosova and NATO in Kosova," was turning the Kosova issue into a political battle between the United State of America and the West in general with Russia, the latter supported by China, India, most of the Islamic and Arab countries, would inflict the first defeat to the right of state sovereignty in its battle with civilization values and protection of human and democratic rights. – The political battle of the United States of America and the West for Kosova against Russia and its supporters, consisting of these two items (the dominance of NATO as a security force in Kosova and complete removal of Serb military and police forces from Kosova) would not be an easy one as that was the breaking point for the Convention of International Law and of victory for the new world order and globalization formula.- Ahtisaari first considered Chernomyrdin to be a Milosevic advocate, although he found Talbot to be a calm, patient and very dedicated diplomat to achieve his goals. – Ahtisaari asserted that Yugoslavia had lost the right to negotiate for peace and that Milosevic should be contacted only for presenting ultimatums and in no way other than that.*

The agreement in principle between the Americans and the Russians on the approach to the Kosova crisis and the definition of frames within which it would be set created the conditions for a move towards its conclusion, although it failed in removing all the obstacles and prejudices emerging from the past. This was especially true for the Russians, who even when stating that they wished to accept the new realities that the changes brought about after the fall of the bloc bipolarity and the Cold War, tried to behave in accordance with the threat of introducing a "cold peace" game, which the Europeans feared, as this could hamper reform processes for which they had major interests. For the Americans, it was important that the Russians get involved in the whole process and abide by it, as this would create opportunities for NATO intervention to gain international legitimacy regardless of whether it would lead to the fulfillment of all the provisions with which it had begun. As both the Americans and the West generally needed success in the campaign, on condition that it was achieved quickly and without witnessing initial internal cracks, with the Russians wanting to close the Kosova snag without having Belgrade militarily capitulated, as this would have a chain effect for the region opening up other issues, it was expected that Washington and Moscow, albeit from different positions, would turn to each other, and this approach implied a positional agreement on Kosova's interim international administration, formally maintaining the sovereignty of the Federal Republic of Yugoslavia, and about the fact that security would be taken over by a UN-mandated international security force, with NATO as its main force, in which Russia and other countries ought to take part. These positions were now non-negotiable. But even as such they left too much room for disagreement, friction and even unforeseen difficulties, because the limits imposed did not simplify matters. Rather, they created huge possibilities for complications, especially in view of hidden goals related to specific aims, such as those of Milosevic and Russian radical forces from the communist-nationalist bloc, which although aware that they could not turn the wheel of history back, however, demanded that Russia maintain hegemony and even use them as a threat. Kosova and its crisis for both sides showed a very good opportunity for various tests.

In these circumstances, and based on these premises, mediators started their mission: Martti Ahtisaari, Strobe Talbot and Victor Chernomyrdin. The first was representing the European Union, the second the United States of America and the third Russia. Thus, between Washington and Moscow, as opposite poles with their mutual interests finding common language even in those circumstances, there was the European "catalyst," which in fact, was part of the West, regardless that the Finn would try to appear as a "peacemaker" of both edges and demand compromises, which, in fact, were not in West's disfavor but less so in Russia's favor. However, despite the common framework established by the Americans and Russians, the scope of action for the missionaries remained largely not so much a matter of their skills in dealing with bringing closer the opposites than of posturing dictates coming from the countries represented. Indeed, Ahtisaari's preliminary meetings of an "intermediate pole" for so long as he got full authorization by the European Union, would reveal at that very early stage both the differences over the settlement of the Kosova crisis in U.S.A. – Russia relations and those between the U.S. and Europeans as the Americans required complete removal of Serbia from Kosova, the Russians wanted the rest of Kosova in Serbia, while Europeans sought a temporary international protectorate, which would preserve sovereignty of the Federal Republic of Yugoslavia. On Martti Ahtisaari's part, keeping his place in the middle being a representative of Europeans and knowing what kind of trouble would arise if the issues were to begin with the status and not with others that could destroy it in the future, he admitted that during his meetings with key Western partners (U.S., UK, France and Germany) he was confronted with different views, with the American one considering the five points of the NATO summit in Washington and seven points of the first G-8 summit in Petersberg as "minimum requirements," which should be strengthened even more and the move towards a more complete exclusion of Serbia from Kosova and strengthening the NATO role, on the other hand, and the other position of the European Union for an international protectorate to be achieved with Russia's consent and with NATO's five points and G-8 points remaining as the main limits.

Differences among the Westerners were not only seen in EU-US relations, but also within them. Thus, on one side were the French, who did not rule out autonomous links between Kosova and Serbia, and on the other, the British, who also wanted to treat the transitional phase as time for creating circumstances for an agreed separation of Albanians and Serbs and in no way as a communion circumstance.[845]

The only thing where there were no differences whatsoever was the stance in regard to the Kosova Liberation Army, as both the Americans and Europeans had already reached an agreement that it should be demilitarized and turned into a limited defense force supervised by NATO. But if the further fate of the KLA in the context of peace was already seen as sealed, however, its presence, even as temporary and its role before and after the NATO's air campaign against Yugoslav military and police forces in Kosova was important. As would be seen, on the Kosova Liberation Army factor, during the course of negotiations with the Russians, two of the main stands of the United States of America and the

---

[845] For more see Ahtisaari, Martti: *Detyra në Beograd*," Prishtina, 2008, pp. 32-61.

West in general were built: the international security presence in Kosova under the supervision of NATO and the complete removal of the Yugoslav military and police forces from Kosova. NATO's presence would be justified in that that they were the only ones to be able to influence the KLA in agreement with the Americans and the West to disarm, as the Albanians considered the American presence and NATO army in Kosova as a prerequisite for the removal of Serbian occupation.

Faced with these currents, Ahtisaari initially retained the conviction that Kosova should remain part of Serbia with a wide autonomy because, according to him, *"independence would undermine the balance of the entire Balkan changes."*[846]

On this issue Ahtisaari argued that the "will of the people," which was defined in the Rambouillet accords had to find a solution.[847] He even asserted that it was necessary, because Yugoslavia, since the violent destruction of Kosova's autonomy in 1989 and the refusal to respect legitimate determinations of Albanians from both July 1990 Constitutional Declaration, the declaration of the Republic of Kosova in September of the same year, and organizing of their own parallel state – which according to the Finnish former President represented one of the most civilized depositions of Albanians, which Belgrade ought to consider, something it had not done, failing to comply with the will of the Albanians behaving in a most brutal way, going as far as attempting genocide against them – had lost the right to be treated as an equal state, as it lost the right to talk and much less to decide on behalf of Albanians in the name of state sovereignty.[848]

Ahtisaari, who knew very well within the five points of the NATO jubilee summit of Washington, pointing out autonomy and Yugoslav sovereignty as well as the positions of G-8 of the first summit of Petersberg of May 6,which also mentioned the autonomy and its Yugoslav frameworks – would deliberately release to the public the "Yugoslav failed state theory," so that, even when its attributes of a sovereignty state were being highlighted upon Russia's persistence conditioning by it its participation in the efforts for a peaceful solution – it automatically would be deprived of decision-making, as would indeed happen. *"Yugoslavia should*

---

[846] *Ibid*, p. 35.

[847] *Ibid*, p.35.

[848] *Ibid*, p.204.

not talk about peace and much less be asked about it. She should be pre-sented the positions and told to choose between: 'yes' or 'no', accepting or rejecting it."[849]

Here trouble began between him and Russian envoy Chernomyrdin, the latter trying all the time to play the state sovereignty and the UN charter cards on this issue to keep constantly in hand in order to prevent Kosova from going out of the framework of the Yugoslav state, even when giving consent to an interim international administration in Kosova and the presence of the security forces, by which the Yugoslav Army and police forces had to leave Kosova, thus virtually beginning the demolition of the sovereignty of Yugoslavia over Kosova, knowing that this interna-tional supervision would bring about conditions of its breaking away from it, as would happen, in fact, eight years later, so elegantly allowing for no way to restore it back.

In Ahtisaari's mission Russians tried to continue, to the extent possi-ble, exploiting the gaps between Westerners, especially those, who for various reasons were not in favor of the air campaign nor had agreed to participate in it (Greece), in order to exclude North Atlantic Alliance affiliation and its loyalty to the United States of America from being the only power carrier of the new world order with a new European identity, but also to show proximity to Russia and its presence that could be achieved on the basis of new cooperation and trust, where geo-economic interests should have priority over geostrategic ones. Of course, Ahtisaari would be spared in time from this challenge as it would be the American Talbot, who with five points of NATO's jubilee summit and seven G-8 points, approved at the summit of Petersberg, would embrace, but also rule out any possibility for the Russian side to manipulate with the "different opinions" of Europeans, whether Greek, Spanish, or Italian, trying to cause the Troika mission a dissonance such as those about the cessation of the bombing, "neutrality" or similar proposals, but to no avail. Talbot appeared very cold, but also a diplomat, shunning away the Greek proposals to stop the bombing, expecting to be made on behalf of a European-Russian peace initiative gaining legitimacy in the UN, as well as an Italian initiative[850] in the UN Security Council introduced as a joint resolution of the European Union, Russia and China for a peaceful

---

[849] *Ibid*, p.204.

[850] See Massimo D'Alema: *"Kosova, italianët dhe lufta,"* Tirana, 2004, pp. 60, 61.

solution in Kosova, provided that the bombing stopped, evaded it by believing that barren peace initiatives already had their chance so frequently in the past but used mostly by Milosevic to establish the facts through violence.

The American mediator, Talbot, concurred by Ahtisaari, removed out of any discussion the following two issues: the cessation of bombing, "giving peace a chance," and stopping any effort to negotiate with Belgrade, or namely Milosevic.

With these categorical positions, Talbot helped the intermediary work of Troika: on the one hand to make Russia understand that it was the West, namely the United States of America, which imposed rules of the game, and that those who enter it should behave in accordance with them, and on the other, to let Belgrade know that there was no negotiation, that it had lost the right over Kosova, and had to accept the dictate if it was to avoid complete destruction and be compelled to accept even more difficult conditions.

Ahtisaari accepted Talbot's clarity, diplomacy and his demonstrated toughness, which, according to him, could rather be taken as a victory of American diplomacy over Russia to accept the new role based on the U.S. conditions when dealing with Belgrade, subject to the conditions of peace, which were presented on behalf of the international community, without the right to negotiate.[851] Thus, the Finnish mediator had noticed the harsh language and clarity of Talbot during the first meeting of the mediating Troika in Helsinki, on May 20, as the platform about a package that would ensure Belgrade's surrender was being made, based on five items of NATO and G-8 summit held in Petersberg, when the harmonized seven points of the peaceful framework for Kosova were accepted as mandatory for everyone. In this regard, Talbot forced Chernomyrdin to divest all that appeared as Russian special interests, which reflected in two main points: (a) Accept in its entirety the crucial role of NATO as a security force in Kosova; and (b) Full departure of the Yugoslav military and police forces from Kosova, regardless of whether or not their presence was related to the national sovereignty.

The very support on Chapter VII of the UN Charter as well as the issuing of the ICTY indictment against Slobodan Milosevic and political and military leadership of Yugoslavia and Serbia, was reinforcement for

---

[851] Martti Ahtisaari: *"Detyra në Beograd,"* Prishtina, 2008, p. 128.

the conditions, which turned the American political fixation "Serbia out of Kosova and NATO in Kosova" into a political battle between the United States of America and the West in general with Russia, supported by China, India, most of the Arab and Islamic countries globally, inflicting the right of state sovereignty the first defeat in its war with civilized values as were those for the protection of human and democratic rights.

The political battle of the United States of America and the West for Kosova against Russia and its supporters, which accounted for more than half of the world, consisting in the above-mentioned two points (domination of NATO as a security force in Kosova and complete removal of Serb military and police forces from Kosova), would not be easy as that was the breaking point of the conventions of international law and victory for the new world order and globalization formula.

This configuration, supported on the formula for finding the solution of the Kosova crisis, during the first three weeks of May, needed three marathon meetings of the mediating Troika consultations in Washington-Moscow relations and many more "local battles" between NATO military with Russian and Yugoslav ones, for things to go as far as reaching "common formulations," which were rather American impositions with cosmetic concessions to the Russians than as a matter of understanding to achieve a peace agreement, as the G-8 Summit would state at a meeting in Cologne, on June 7 and 8 attended by the world's most developed economic countries plus Russia (7 +1).

The Struggle for NATO's Entry in Kosova and Two Faces of Russia

The return of refugees and demilitarization of the Kosova Liberation Army: two of the factors that opened the doors to NATO entry in Kosova. – Russians tried all the time to operate with an international civil presence in Kosova supervised by the UN, but realizing that was not going to happen, as neither the establishment of international administration, nor the return of refugees could be achieved without a credible military and armed presence, which would be primarily accepted by the Albanians who were victims of the Serbian state, they modified their attitudes towards acceptance of an international security force, consisting first by a multiethnic force and then by excluding countries participating in the bombing campaign on grounds that it

was unacceptable for Belgrade. – U.S. mediator Talbot left no maneu-
vering space to Russian Envoy Chernomyrdin, who tried to keep NATO
as far away from the presence of the international security force in
Kosova as possible. – In the final phase of negotiations over the final
text that would be accepted as part of the UN Security Council resolu-
tion, the Americans succeeded to fully meet both of their goals: full le-
gitimization of the international security force presence and complete
removal of the Yugoslav military and police forces from Kosova.

NATO's war in Kosova would make sense only if it would enter Kosova so it would be perceived as victory if it would be able to settle in Kosova under the mandate of an international security force, legitimized by the United Nations Security Council. With this the contest of the air campaign would also be legitimized.

But NATO's struggle to enter the country began even before the launch of its air bombing campaign as it featured the vital military and political interest of the West.

The emergence of the Yugoslav crisis and its dramatic deepening in the new conditions after the fall of bloc bipolarity leading to the end of the Cold War, and especially those emerging after the collapse of the red Soviet empire, however, suggested that a lasting peace and time of world harmony was more than an illusion, and that the cold war was likely to be replaced by cold peace. Perennial continuation of the crisis and clear signs that it could become a catalyst of reincarnation of traditional European spheres of interest, finally, affected the United States of America and European countries to come up with a conclusion that the Kosova crisis should come to an end through *ultimatum* enforcement, not for its temporary appeasement and in favor of the Belgrade regime granting it the "title-deeds," but rather in order for it to be taken out of it once and forever, and do so by camouflaging its alleged maintenance with the Yugoslav state sovereignty as mentioned in the five points of the NATO jubilee summit in Washington on April 23 and 24 and accepted with the additional requirements of the G-8 ministerial meeting in Petersberg near Bonn, thus setting the platform that would later turn into the internation-al administration in Kosova, on which Kosova's independence could be based.

That the mention of the Yugoslav state sovereignty in the documents in order to create legitimacy over the issue of getting Kosova out of Serbia, placing it under an interim international protectorate, was only a camouflage known by everyone. Furthermore, this was also known by Russia which accepted the formula of Kosova's international administration, by not preventing the process, but rather incorporating her own Russian interests which at that time were of a political and economic nature. Those of a political nature implied returning at the first international dining table, not on an equal right, as it could not even claim in circumstances when Russia was in a process of internal consolidation with many unexpected and unknowns, but in order to be there. And, those of an economic nature had to do precisely with the first issue, as the economic consolidation could not be done without great financial help from outside, i.e. from the West, whose political position was better unopposed because of the pending demands for economic support. The billions that Russia received from Germany after allowing for German unification had been digested very quickly, becoming prey to government oligarchy, which was not well fed. Kosova and its crisis appeared to be welcomed in this regard. Thus, Moscow tried as much as possible to increase the cost of political cooperation with the West without excluding the introduction to the game of pastime "habits."

In this regard, it can be said that neither mediator Chernomyrdin, nor Milosevic as "tamed" by the presence of Russia, would help Moscow much, as the entire mediation process of one month yielded little more than the first bargain made between U.S. Secretary of State Albright and Russian Prime Minister Primakov, at their meeting in Oslo in late April where the draft framework of what would be called the peace agreement would be prepared to be formally accepted on June 10 with the Security Council adopting Resolution 1244, declaring the crisis closed and beginning the process of NATO entering Kosova and of Yugoslav military forces leaving Kosova.

However, during the mediation phase, the problems of Americans were not of a substantial nature, as Russia did not oppose NATO's role in what would emerge as the international presence in Kosova, but rather of a formal nature beginning from reducing its role in the entire mission to the possibility of having it kept under the UN supervision. Thus, swords initially broke from the formal definition of the character of the mission and its name according to aspects of the general command and zoning in Kosova. During all this time the Russians tried to operate with an international civil presence in Kosova supervised by the World Organization, but upon realizing that this was of no effect at all, since neither the establishment of international administration, nor the return of refugees could take place without a credible and armed military presence, which in the first place would be acceptable to the Albanians who were victims of the Serbian state, they would modify their attitudes towards acceptance of an international security force, consisting first of a multiethnic force and then by excluding countries that participated in the bombing campaign on the grounds that it was unacceptable for Belgrade. But as the request was rejected categorically by the Americans, then Moscow appeared "somewhat more flexible" embracing a wide participation of NATO countries, but that this ratio, compared with Russia would be two to one in NATO's favor, with a command connected to the UN, on a zone-based hierarchy of stationing of troops, which meant practical division of Kosova in accordance with their scope, in the north with the Russians- in the Serbian part, and in the south with NATO – in the Albanian part. As this proposal would also be rejected, the Russians put into play a "parallel command," i.e., NATO leading its own sectors, and Russia leading its own (the north), which also meant separation of Kosova into two parts, as Belgrade had proposed on several occasions, keeping for itself along with the north other parts where Orthodox medieval monasteries existed. Americans accepted neither of these proposals and, in the last phase of mediation, realizing that the Russians were trying to benefit in time and even suspecting that the postponement of talks aimed at other scenarios as well to emerge a little later, threatened with a continuation of the bombing until complete destruction of the Yugoslav military potential, not excluding even ground landing, which could open other issues that would cost even more dearly to Belgrade and Russia. That cost would include not only the loss of Kosova, but also of other parts inhabited by Albanians, such as the Presheva Valley with great strategic importance. Obviously, they would succeed, because the Russians would see that their behavior had come to the limits of having to accept the U.S. dictate, which was in accordance with the agreement in principle between Albright and Primakov in Oslo a month before or leave the whole process to be marginalized even more, something they did not want to happen as it meant total defeat.

Thus, in the final stage of negotiations over the final text that was accepted by the UN Security Council resolution, the Americans succeeded in fully meeting both of their goals: full legitimacy for an international security force, and full departure of Yugoslav military and police forces.

Item 3 of Annex 2 of Resolution 1244 says:

> Deployment in Kosova under United Nations auspices of effective international civil and security presences, acting as may be decided under Chapter VII of the Charter, capable of guaranteeing the achievement of common objectives.

In the following item this international force is sanctioned in a clear cut formulation:

> The international security presence with substantial North Atlantic Treaty Organization participation must be deployed under unified command and control and authorized to establish a safe environment for all people in Kosova...[852]

Accomplishing this goal related to achieving the stance on complete removal of the Yugoslav military and police forces, which was considered as a cause of the crisis, as they actively participated in achieving hegemonic goals laid out by Belgrade's official policy of the recent years, and were also be charged with hindering the peace agreement, because neither would Albanians accept returning to an environment where their killers were present even symbolically and also the Kosova Liberation Army would not agree to give up arms before those against whom they had fought to defend their own people would give up theirs.

In the contest with the Russians for and against the presence of Yugoslav forces, even symbolically in Kosova, the Americans had managed through tactical avoidance to get the consent of the Russians for complete removal of Yugoslav and Serb military and police forces allowing for the formulation that *"an agreed number of Yugoslav and Serbian personnel will be permitted to return to perform particular functions if considered necessary by the international security force in Kosova."*

The issue at hand was the demining of the territory and non-combat units that were to be subordinated to the international security forces, NATO, which would evidently not be happening as KFOR would reject

---

[852] See UN Security Council Resolution of 10 June 1999, cited according to Jusuf Buxhovi: *"Kthesa historike - Shteti paralel dhe rezistenca e armatosur,"* Prishtina, 2009, p. 600.

any request from Belgrade to return its forces to Kosova in accordance with the Kumanovo agreement.

Another challenge made to the Americans by the Russians was the issue of the presence of the Yugoslav police force. Americans had a definite answer to that as well in their stance that the entire police service should leave along with military forces, as the Serbian police forces were engaged all the time as part of the violence and reprisals against Albanians. Indeed, in the last phase, special police units had committed serious crimes, ranging from leading ethnic cleansing to mass killings of the Albanian population.

The American mediator, Talbot, had ruled out any possibility that some police units would remain, including those of public order and police civil services remaining in Kosova, even under international police commands. Here, too, the reason prevailing was that the presence of Serbian police forces was unacceptable to the Albanians and the West, who had to intervene militarily in Kosova to prevent the action of this police service against the Albanians. In the resolution, along with a request for the removal of all verifiable Serbian police units from Kosova, a formulation was introduced on the creation of the new Kosova police, assisted by the international community and consistent with its population. Here too the American mediator, Talbot, was uncompromising. All of Chernomyrdin's efforts to keep something of the military and police apparatus in Kosova failed in accordance with Chapter VII of the UN Charter, upon which the NATO air campaign against Yugoslav military and police forces in Kosova and to its bases in Serbia had taken place. This was the bait that Moscow would bite from the beginning to prevent further consequences by which Serbia could be declared guilty and punishable with an immediate loss of Kosova.

The Americans tried saving the Russians' face by recognizing modifications of formal and unsubstantial nature which found a place in the Security Council Resolution 1244 of June 10, legitimizing the entire peace process while in a skillful way transferring military issues to the NATO military-technical agreement to be signed with Yugoslav military leadership.

This had been the most difficult and painful issue for Milosevic, but also for the Yugoslav military, who despite the war with NATO did not come out as declared loser or in a classic military capitulation, they nonetheless had to leave Kosova with their equipment and all military infrastructure, which for the Yugoslav army from a strategic point of view was of great importance. In addition to this loss, the Yugoslav Army was forced to accept other serious conditions, such as those of security zones in the Yugoslav territory in an air distance of 25 kilometers, and 5 km of land distance, which were called neutral safety zones. In these zones, no Yugoslav military presence was allowed, including the simplest forms of military activities.

In the G-8 summit in Cologne, held 18-20 June 1999, Russian President Boris Yeltsin, together with U.S. President Clinton were the focus of European and world opinion. They had not met for a long time. The Kosova crisis had cast aside their telephone conversations which were frequent and often without humor. In Cologne they spoke openly that disagreements over Kosova were over, which turned US-Russian relations back on a normal track.

Leaders of the world's most powerful countries had reasons to be cheerful. Clinton – by closing the Kosova crisis in accordance with the American concept and in the interests of the West, had managed to bring together into the solution NATO, the European Union and lastly, to give legitimacy to all the action that had been able to bring the UN into the forefront. And, Yeltsin – because of being involved in the resolution of the Kosova crisis, despite the fact that he played to the tune of the Americans, was back on the world political scene succeeding to get from the G-8 summit preconditions for good financial support so necessary to strengthen the economy of his country as it was facing difficulties. Yeltsin had also harvested a domestic victory against permanent opponents from the ranks of the Communists and nationalists of all colors, who, along with the military, behind his back, aimed at exploiting Kosova in order to change the Kremlin's course towards the cold war, as expressed the best in the Prishtina airport crisis, at a moment before the signing of the peace agreement considering that the world had left behind a great distress.

But, to what extent and in what manner had the Kosova crisis challenged Yeltsin to say that his position on this issue was not identical to that of the general Russian political spectrum, as it was not the same as the position of Yeltsin towards Milosevic and support, which was given to him, which brought to the conclusion that Yeltsin in Kosova was not fighting for the interests of Serbia, but for those of a modern Russia, to be in step with the time? Did actually Russia have two "faces" towards the

Kosova crisis and its resolution or simply one and the same revealing itself as varying accordingly?

Initially it can be said that Yeltsin might have had a few hegemonic illusions remaining from the mists of ancient times, but in time he would realize that they could turn into a real burden for Russia's modernization and its return among the important countries of the world. Thus, the former leader of the Communist Russian embellishments which would join Gorbachev's "Perestroika," the Soviet Union with ideological baggage saw it as a burden to be removed as soon as possible. This, therefore, meant a detachment from the entire czarist hegemony views and what had been inherited from her failed Soviet empire, which had turned into a new ideology of imperialism although it had crashed against it as a boomerang.

Viewed from this aspect, the crisis in the former Yugoslavia would not encourage Yeltsin all that much as he knew that he would meet both the same factors (the czarist and ideological), which had historically caused more harm than help. Indeed, the power of the latter for the worse would be tested as early as 1991 with Jesuit's military coup attempts, when he along with Moscow's Red generals tried to restore Soviet Bolshevism to power. It would be Yeltsin who would break the last efforts of communist plotters, whose only support came from Milosevic who congratulated their victory even in moments when they were trapped in the Russian Parliament building and being bombed by tanks commanded by Yeltsin. This alone would be enough for Yeltsin to have no "friendly and brotherly" attitude towards Milosevic and his policies, even though Belgrade would always try to put in the card for such a game with Russia, calling without wavering on Orthodoxy and other issues, which were fading away. However, the ideological and personal animosity against Milosevic and his course without any historical perspective did not turn Yeltsin into an open opponent, but neither as seeming supportive. Rather, with the crisis in the former Yugoslavia, Yeltsin tried to maintain partnerships with European countries, much more though since they shared the same views about this crisis, seeing it as an internal issue of Serbia, which had to be solved in a democratic way as autonomy and nothing more. Although the opposite was happening, with efforts under way to settle scores with an entire population for ethnic reasons, Yeltsin had no reason to bother with all of that as the Russian military were behaving in the same fashion in Chechnya, warning other Caucasian provinces as well that responding by means of war against "separatist" movements was not only a Russian but also a European "specialty."

Even in terms of spheres of interest, which, since Dayton, the Americans were evidently extending into the former Yugoslavia for their own benefit, it did not bother Yeltsin that much, who, unlike the communist-nationalist forces of Russian Orthodox mixture had given up the Balkans for the benefit of strengthening Russia from within, a strengthening that was closely related to cooperation with the Europeans, but also with the United States of America, where the former arms race would be replaced by a broad economic cooperation in all areas, especially those involving exploitation of large Russian resources.

If Yeltsin and his government reform wing, including modern Russian politics, looked at the Yugoslav crisis and the problems that it would bring as rather a European problem, to which they had to provide a solution (of course in the case of Kosova while maintaining the right of state sovereignty frames) would be Russian-hegemonic nationalist forces from the ranks of former Communists, nationalists, and fanatic clergy, using the breakup of Yugoslavia and the Kosova issue as welcome nourishment to fight on one side against Yeltsin's course for a modern Russia outside hegemonic appetites, and on the other to restore once again the great Russia dreams. This course was upheld by Russia's domestic difficulties during its transitional phase, highlighting not only the expected weaknesses but also the phenomenon of disintegration of general social and moral values, which paved the way for a great social crisis in this country with among the world's richest natural resources. In these circumstances, the failed powers, among other things, used the crisis in the former Yugoslavia for internal fights, to which the pan-Slavic nostalgia on the basis of orthodoxy always gave great impetus. Of course, Milosevic also used this, finding his allies among Yeltsin's opponents, the national-chauvinists Zhirinovsky and Communist fanatics, who played an important role in the Duma (Russian Parliament), sending Belgrade support messages and exhorting constant pressure to Yeltsin compelling him willingly or not, at least nominally, to show support for Milosevic and his regime. In the last stage, with the beginning of NATO threats against Belgrade to accept the dictate of the Rambouillet Accords, and with the start of the bombing, the end of which could very well be anticipated, Yeltsin found himself in the trap of Russian national hegemony of all kinds in a united Duma, passing extremely tough and belligerent resolutions, severed even more by sending Russian volunteers into Kosova including notorious paramilitary units who committed serious crimes against humanity and the defenseless population.

Even within this pressure, Yeltsin behaved realistically when after realizing that things had reached the point for NATO air intervention threatening to really declare Kosova independent and at the same time have the remaining rest of Yugoslavia fragmented. He accepted the American offer to be involved in resolving the Kosova crisis on the following formula: Serbia out of Kosova, NATO in Kosova, meaning nothing other than opening the way for its secession from Belgrade. During a pragmatic meeting between M. Albright and Prime Minister Primakov in Oslo at the end of April following the Washington NATO Summit, which issued clear messages that the Alliance would not stop, but rather it would continue to pound Serbia until it accepted the peace conditions, Yeltsin fully accepted the American offer. What would occur during the Troika mediation mission (Talbot, Chernomyrdin and Ahtisaari) would only be US-Russian agreement modalities of Oslo, where on one side Russian realism would emerge, or rather the face of Russia's real politics led by Yeltsin, trying through the Kosova crisis to protect Russia and not Serbia, and on the other hand, the other Russian face was reflected – the nationalistic and hegemonic one that defended Serbia on behalf of yesterday's Russia.

"It is in Russia's interest to connect with the global multipolar concept flows and not to harden for the relics of the past," said Boris Yeltsin in his memoirs published after the war. He noted further that:

> Russia could only have two choices: to accept the fact that in the present circumstances, it could only have a peripheral role on important decisions or that under my leadership it joined global modernity. The solution to the Kosova crisis provided a good opportunity for the latter which presented our own national interest.[853]

---

[853] See Yeltsin, Boris: *"Meine Jahre in Kremlin"* (*My Years in Kremlin*), Berlin, 2000. The Russian President provides more details about his troubles with the right-wing Russian nationalists and ultra-Communists, who, regarding the issue of Kosovo constituted one and the same bloc seeing its solution in accordance with the national programs that the Milosevic regime followed. In this book, Yeltsin pointed out an interesting fact contrary to most analysts. It regards NATO's project of ground invasion if aerial bombardment were to fail. Yeltsin said that Milosevic and Seselj's radicals were more interested in

Matches between these Russian "faces" towards Kosova during the high level negotiations, when Yeltsin's Russia was trying to return through this crisis to the world political scene and to take advantage of it, as it would benefit, would not only be of a position-opposition nature or of different views, but they also turned into tough clashes, which could have serious consequences not only for the resolution of the Kosova crisis, but also for the West-East relations if Yeltsin were to lose power at that very time.

Therefore, it was not accidental though that during the intensive negotiations of international intermediaries Ahtisaari, Talbot and Chernomyrdin about the final drafting of the peace accords, the other Russian nationalistic hegemonic "face" would emerge as very aggressive exhorting to double pressure: on the negotiating Troika and down to the military levels, dealing with issues related to the termination of NATO's air campaign against Yugoslav military and police forces in Kosova and their bases in Serbia without sparing overall military infrastructure in the country. Thus, in Moscow, during talks with the Russians, envoys Ahtisaari and Talbot faced both public and military pressure, concealed and caught during the talks between the military about the drafting of the final text of the military technical agreement between NATO and the Yugoslav military in Kumanovo.

The public nature pressure had to do with the emergence of the "*Russian Memorandum*," an analysis of intellectuals and politicians called nationalists, which was handed over to mediators Ahtisaari and Talbot while negotiating with Chernomyrdin in Moscow that did not appear as

---

ground landing, as according to them, they saw in it a genuine opportunity to split NATO or even inflict a loss! "Milosevic would tell Russian generals that he was very interested in ground landing. As they replied that he was unlikely to win that war, even if he could cause losses to the invading ground forces, as they would follow with the policy of the scorched land, he said that Westerners are sensitive when they see their soldiers being killed. This led to reactions against the war and the military failed before the politicians fighting for power." Yeltsin admitted that there were Russian generals who felt the same as Milosevic and wished for ground war because it would give an opportunity to them to restore the power they once had. Even despite Milosevic's adventurous tendencies, Yeltsin said that "Russia did not allow Milosevic to lose the war, the way he deserved it and asked for, because this would upset regional balances, which would be detrimental to Moscow."

pressure addressed against Yeltsin not to concede in resolving the issue of Kosova in accordance with the concept of making it an international protectorate, as the G-8 requested, together with the European Union, and to which Russia had also agreed, but rather to give up all that was called an alleged "plot against Russia."[854]

The authors of the "*Russian Memorandum*" assumed that NATO (the United States of America), in fact, aimed at the liquidation of Yugoslavia as a political factor in Europe. According to them,

> Yugoslavia was the only country in Europe which did not seek NATO affiliation and did not participate in the Partnership for Peace program. This country is skewed towards Russia and is a very strong state. NATO wants to have a bridge-crossing in the Balkans. It has already been positioned in Bosnia and Croatia and is strengthening its presence in Macedonia. Only Serbia and Montenegro prevent NATO's aims, not interested for a just solution of the crisis, but rather wants to prove that it is the only effective force.[855]

The "*Russian Memorandum*" concluded that the West, through Kosova, after having eliminated Yugoslavia, intended to finally attack against Russia. "*The ultimate goal is the removal of Russia as a global factor.*"[856]

According to the authors of the "*Russian Memorandum,*" Russia must strengthen its position which was weakened during Kozyeriev's time. The creation of a world where one single country has the lead must be prevented. Russia should strengthen its political and military readiness and should strengthen its anti-American propaganda."[857]

The attitude of the "Russian Memorandum" cannot be seen as separate from the strengthening of Russian nationalism tinged with the spirit of pan-Orthodoxy, appearing as an intellectual and social movement to save Russia from the humiliation and destruction it was experiencing. The platform for the salvation of Russia on the basis of nationalism and Orthodoxy had already been declared by the renowned Russian writer Alexander Solzhenitsyn, the Nobel Prize winner for literature, a dissident

---

[854] Ahtisaari, Martti: "*Detyra në Beograd,*" Prishtina, 2008, p. 122.

[855] *Ibid*, p.122.

[856] *Ibid*, p.122.

[857] *Ibid*, p.122.

writer of anti-communist convictions, who, after the dissolution of the Soviet empire returned to Russia not in a spirit of democratic reform and definitions, as expected, but as a proponent of new Russian chauvinism that would nurture all-Russian chauvinist national platforms, where the West and democracy for Russians appeared as harmful as it stripped them of an "inborn right" to be a superpower!

That the other Russian "face" in regard to the Kosova crisis was not "in the shadow" as perceived by a marketing part of communist and nationalist forces in the Duma, but that it rather required its space in the official part in order to turn into a strong hand state politics, was seen in another article written by the Russian broker in the peace process Chernomyrdin, published in the American popular newspaper "*Washington Post*" of May 27, 1999, on the very day when Ahtisaari and Talbot flew to Moscow to provide the final version of the draft to be submitted to Belgrade. Using a particularly harsh tone in the article and contradicting completely his role as a high level missionary appointed by Yeltsin, Chernomyrdin was blaming the United States and NATO for the Kosova crisis. Chernomyrdin insisted that the NATO attack against Yugoslavia was an event similar to the engagement of Soviet forces in Prague, in 1968. Clinton's thoughts that Russia was engaged in looking for a way as to how Belgrade could accept peace, and that NATO's strategy over time would strengthen relations with Russia, were wrong. Chernomyrdin stressed that Russia would not accept a mediator to intentionally help NATO to achieve its strategic goals, among which, according to him, were handing over Milosevic and the establishment of a NATO protectorate in Kosova. These were against the Russian policy, which aimed at the deployment of UN troops in Kosova and strengthening the integrity and territorial sovereignty of Yugoslavia.

Chernomyrdin asserted that the bombing had hardly achieved anything other than unnecessary destruction. He went back to history mentioning examples from World War II, Vietnam and Chechnya. He also noted that the policy of the United States would lead to the extent that even small countries would like to have nuclear weapons and missiles against possible U.S. attacks: "*NATO's victory would be a Pyrrhic victory, because, first, it would destroy Kosova and then be forced to rebuild it again.*"[858]

Clearly, these Chernomyrdin's assessments about KLA appear identical to those of Milosevic, as he expressed them during the last meeting with General Clark in Belgrade in October 1998,[859] as well as those about the bugaboo of a Greater Albania used as the one-hundred-year speculation by Belgrade and Moscow. In it Albanian fighters are called *"terrorists, who get their money from drug trafficking,"* and that, *"by helping them, the West would help drug trafficking. In addition, these terrorists' dreams of a Greater Albania will enhance the volatile situation in the Balkans, will expand military operations and would result constantly with new border conflicts."*[860]

The article ended with the threat that if they did not stop the bombing, Yeltsin would be advised that Russia should not participate in the peace talks, should end its military-technical cooperation with the United States of America and the West, not ratify START II agreement and prevent with its veto the adoption of the UN resolution on Kosova.[861]

The American mediator, Talbot responded against the duality of Russian "faces" towards Kosova on the same day he arrived in Moscow to begin crucial rounds of talks with Moscow. When at a press conference he was asked what he thought about Chernomyrdin's article in the *"Washington Post,"* he said he was dealing with Chernomyrdin the diplomat and not Chernomyrdin the journalist, much less with the analyst who satisfied the tastes of nationalist circles.[862]

Diplomat Chernomyrdin, despite these trivialities and despite the initial impression that he was there to play the role of Milosevic's advocate, in the concluding part of the mission, had not only been conciliatory with the Western intermediaries, Talbot and Ahtisaari on what he would call in the American newspaper as *"a life-or-death struggle between NATO and Russia that took place in Kosova,"* but had also accepted to personally hand over to Milosevic in Belgrade the ultimatum demands, which he would finally accept. This said a lot about Russian behavior in the circum-

---

[858] *"Washington Post,"* 17 April 1999, cited according to Ahtisaari, Martti: *"Tasks in Belgrade,"* pp. 128/29.

[859] See Wesley K. Clark: *"Të bësh luftë moderne,"* Prishtina, 2003, p. 219.

[860] *Ibid*, p.129.

[861] *Ibid*, p.129.

[862] *Ibid*, p.131.

stances and the Russian position ranging between political realism and Byzantinism.

The End of the Air Campaign and the Role of the KLA

Moments that would affect the end of the Kosova crisis: the unity of the NATO jubilee summit, deciding on the land troop deployment option and the Kosova Liberation Army's role as a factor in the war.- Kosova Liberation Army combat operations in Pashtrik, Koshare and Llap were of great importance, as they kept several Yugoslav forces battalions engaged, which were forced to counteract against ceaseless attacks of Albanian fighters, especially as they became offensive, as was the case with the Koshare battle where KLA units had penetrated the border with the assumption that two of the three battalions were getting ready to penetrate deeper towards Dukagjin. For Gen. Clark, the war that KLA was waging in Pashtrik and vicinity was of great importance, as through continued military actions in addition to forcing of Yugoslav forces out of their hiding positions becoming quickly NATO targets and eliminated, that front line was intended as a possible point of ground invasion of the allies in terms of Kosova. – NATO Generals Clark and Mike Short recognized and emphasized the importance and great commitment of Albanian fighters, saying that without their willingness to wash in blood every inch of their land this success could not have been achieved.

Three moments were crucial leading to the end of the Kosova crisis on June 10, 1999, a day when the UN Security Council adopted Resolution 1244, preceded with the signing of the Kumanovo agreement between NATO and Yugoslav Army generals.

First – is related to unity in the NATO jubilee summit in Washington when Milosevic was demonstratively presented with the 5-point conditions which could end the bombing.

Second – is related to the position of North Atlantic Alliance, reached at the summit, that in addition to the continued bombing with increased intensity, one does not exclude the possibility for land troop deployment.

Third – has to do with Kosova Liberation Army as a fast growing factor and useful partner on the ground during NATO operations from the air, which, with its success achieved during the bombing campaign was becoming part of all the military combinations to its final phase in which Yugoslav forces would be given a final blow through a combination of air and land operations with the use of the "Apache" to be considered as a special ground force, which would be armed with the best American weapons for offensive action on the ground, as vanguard to the introduction of American ground forces if deemed necessary.

The first and second moments are, however, of particular importance, as they, on one hand, closed the way to all the speculation about divisions within the Atlantic Alliance on which Belgrade counted hoping they would quickly emerge bringing about NATO's failure, and on the other hand, that introducing into the game the option of ground military intervention changed the concept of resolving the Kosova crisis from that of the alternative of a compromise agreement to maximalist options, namely Kosova's secession from Serbia but also of the Presheva Valley and other matters that would be fatal to Serbia. European politicians repeatedly suggested the issue to Milosevic. The last postings of these messages were carried to him through General Clark during their last meeting in October 1998.[863]

In this regard, the Kosova Liberation Army, which throughout the NATO air operations along with restricted movements inside Kosova and permanent actions from Podujeva to the border with Serbia, rather provoking the Yugoslav military forces in the area around Prishtina to leave their positions, there were an additional three important extensions of positional war: Pashtrik, the northern part of Koshare, and the Operative Zone of Llap, thus proving to be an increasingly useful and unavoidable ally. It was gaining strategic weight not only because it succeeded to pull the grounded Yugoslav forces out of their hideouts thus turning them into detected targets for NATO aircrafts who were watching for any such moves to destroy from the air. In addition, the KLA, thanks to its military and combat readiness, which it had been demonstrating, was becoming a significant partner with which NATO military strategists began to calculate both in terms of its use on the ground to be combined well for galvanizing ground and air forces, which could be done with the introduction of the "Apache" into action after being stationed in Albania waiting for the order to be issued, in the sense that they served as vanguard for the

---

[863] Wesley K. Clark: *"Të bësh luftë moderne,"* Prishtina, 2003, p. 181.

ground forces at the moment the decision was taken for the deployment of allied forces to enter Kosova.

General Clark assessed that the Kosova Liberation Army combat operations in Pashtrik, Koshare and Llap were of great importance, as they kept engaged several Yugoslav forces battalions, which were forced to counteract against ceaseless attacks of Albanian fighters, especially as they became offensive, as was the case with the Koshare battle where KLA units had penetrated the border with the assumption that two of the three battalions were getting ready to penetrate deeper towards Dukagjin. But, for Gen. Clark, the war that KLA was waging in Pashtrik and vicinity was of great importance, as through continued military actions in addition to the forcing of Yugoslav forces out of their hiding positions becoming quickly NATO targets and eliminated, that front line was intended as a possible point of ground invasion of the Allies towards Kosova. Therefore, because of this the Allies were interested in keeping KLA on the line and having it progress as deep as possible.[864]

When on May 26 the Kosova Liberation Army launched an offensive from the top of Pashtrik Mountain against Yugoslav forces deployed on its slopes, General Clark asked Washington to allow for the introduction of the "Apache" into military action in order to back KLA incursions which could break the most powerful "guard" positions of the Yugoslav forces. In conversation with General Hugh Shelton, Head of Staff of U.S. Armed Forces, Gen. Clark disclosed the importance of the KLA battle of Pashtrik as being of double significance. General Shelton accepted Clark's suggestions for quick deployment of the "Apache" but declared he too needed Washington's approval. This never came because, as General Clark says, there were some of the top military men who thought politically about the war, and one of the political attitudes of this kind was the one that had to do with the fact that there were other allies from among the Europeans who wanted victory in the war, but that in no case the Kosova Liberation Army should turn into a sole winner as this would change the concept of a political settlement option, which had to be completed with an interim international protectorate in Kosova, maintaining the frames of the Yugoslav state sovereignty as a compromise so that NATO's intervention would not end in a classical defeat or capitulation for the Yugoslav forces but rather in a technical military agreement

---

[864] *Ibid*, p.327.

for their full withdrawal from Kosova, which for those circumstances was in fact the main purpose of the West.

No matter that politics decided on the main course of the war it should be pointed out that the participation and commitment of the Kosova Liberation Army marked a significant chapter in its strategy in both the combat and strategic-tactical terms. In military terms, the Kosova Liberation Army rose to the level of a NATO partner and ally, although this was often admitted but unspoken, it was ignored completely in the agreements with Yugoslavs. In tactical-strategic terms, it became an important part of planning eventual ground troop deployment of Western Allies in Kosova.

Both these aspects are of great importance, because firstly, the West's war for Kosova, Albanians too participated to the extent they were allowed, and it was the spilled blood of hundreds and thousands of fighters in the fronts of Pashtrik, Koshare, Llap, Karadak and other parts of Kosova, as well as their willingness to fight to the end, no matter how big the price, that sealed the destiny of war and its ending with the departure of the Yugoslav military and police forces from Kosova.

General Clark was most sincere and grateful in this regard when he talked about the great role of Albanian fighters alongside the Western Allies. Although he did not succeed to engage the "Apache" in the Pashtrik front in order to break the first line of defense of the Yugoslav military forces in the direction of Prizren with the success rightly attributed to the Albanian guerrillas who had already shed so much blood in that area throughout the air campaign, however, for the Kosova Liberation Army, war was crucial that the Yugoslav military forces suffer one of the worst and perhaps decisive defeats between 2 and 6 of June.

Thanks to the dedication of the KLA war to withstand the offensive of Yugoslav forces in that part, B-52 and B-1 planes were put into action for the first time with cassette bombs used against positions of Yugoslav forces, consequently with an immediate disbanding of a Yugoslav battalion and destruction of defense infrastructure in a large zone creating conditions for land deployment.

Even if the ground war option would be held as a threat in the air, it would be enough to use all the potential of the Kosova Liberation Army followed with adequate weaponry and logistics by air and background (especially that of "Apache" action) for the Yugoslav forces to suffer losses in this part of the front and generally in Kosova, provided that NATO did not allow their repackaging and reinforcements from Serbia. This was admitted by both General Clark and General Mike Short alike emphasizing the importance and great commitment of fighters adding that without their willingness to wash in blood every inch of their land this achievement could not have been possible.[865]

Therefore, it is of great importance to say that the involvement and participation of KLA in the Pashtrik battle, that of Koshare and other parts of Kosova, particularly in the Llap and Shalë of Bajgora, helped directly in the "taming" of Belgrade in order for it to accept the peaceful bid to resolve the issue of Kosova, because with or without ground landing it would be Albanian fighters who would give the ongoing war its direction and end, as liberators, whose military victory would change the concept of resolving it.

As the aureole of victory for the Kosova Liberation Army in this war was not wanted by both Serbs and Moscow, and not wanted by the Europeans as well, then what was left was to accept the option of the United States of America and the West for accepting NATO and G-8 conditions, appearing also as conditions of the international community and UN, with the latter giving the agreement proper legitimacy through a resolution, which would be in accordance with the terms of NATO and G-8, modified and moderated by the mediating Troika (Ahtisaari, Talbot and Chernomyrdin).

The end of the air campaign was closely linked to documents binding Belgrade with accepting conditions imposed by the international community, which in this case from top to bottom had the authorship of the United States of America, in which Russia was also included with its interest to accommodate itself in it rather than seek any extreme solution. Thus, Belgrade accepted both of them on June 2, but as will be seen, it would take another seven days wandering to and from Moscow to "clarify" all the details. However, at the same time certain other "circumstances" were created, connected to a behind-the-scene meeting between the Russian military and Milosevic to split Kosova thus providing for the Russian presence in the North.

---

[865] More broadly about KLA involvement in the Pashtrik war and the great contribution of Albanian fighters in pushing the Yugoslav forces out of their positions and forcing them to attack, see Wesley K. Clark: *"Të bësh luftë moderne,"* Prishtina, 2003, pp. 370-388.

So that the issue would not look like a war defeat and as a precursor of the loss of Kosova, but rather to have it all appear "as a victory of peace," Milosevic hosted a "parliamentary reality show" to "deal" with the international community, in which the dictate of the West would get a verdict from the parliamentarians celebrating it as a victory of "keeping Kosova," while in Kumanovo NATO and Yugoslav Army military leaders would conclude the military-technical agreement for complete withdrawal of all military and police forces from Kosova within seven days. In addition, the entire military equipment and logistics infrastructure in Kosova and around it was to withdraw as well, thus practically and formally ending the third occupation of Kosova by Serb-Yugoslav forces (first in 1912, second in 1917, and third in 1944).

The departure of the Yugoslav military and police forces, which was called the "withdrawal," was in need of a resolution of the UN Security Council and a military-technical agreement between NATO and Belgrade. So that it would not turn into a game, which could have consequences for the entire mission, the U.S. and NATO showed vigilance, rigor and determination at the same time knowing Milosevic was a master of fraud. General Clark constantly advised the Pentagon, but also Talbot, who was involved in the final negotiations not to yield to the Serbian and Russian gimmicks about the cessation of bombing. Instead, General Clark, who knew full well what Milosevic was able to do in order to trick even NATO itself into the game, explicitly warned that NATO air operations would not stop even if the signing of agreements was not verifiable in advance. This affected the creation of a so-called default between the signing of the Kumanovo military-technical agreement with the approval of the UN Security - Council Resolution 1244 on June 10, 1999, just one hour after the Kumanovo military technical agreement had been signed for a verifiable withdrawal of all military and police forces from Kosova within a period of one week. NATO agreed to suspend bombing from the deadline of the beginning of the verifiable withdrawal of Yugoslav forces in accordance with the Kumanovo agreement, but not to end the operation. This default would be more efficient, as it would eliminate all possibilities of Milosevic's gimmicks. But this did not prevent him from entering into a secret scenario game for a partition of Kosova through the introduction of Russian forces ahead of those of NATO, by which the crisis would gain a new dimension of international dimensions, just as its architects had anticipated as early as the nineties emphasizing that the partitioning of Kosova would bring war between the U.S. and Russia.

Before the UN Security Council approved Resolution 1244, on June 10, it would be the foreign ministers of the seven most industrialized countries in the world and that of Russia, who in the Cologne Summit on June 8, 1999, would decide on the final draft of the resolution. There the ten famous points were approved to be part of the concept of a preceding summit held on May 6 at Petersberg near Bonn, where the G-8 ministerial-level summit complied with the five points of the NATO jubilee summit in Washington on April 23 and 24, 1999, to be included in Annex 1 of Resolution 1244. In the Cologne ministerial summit everything went according to schedule. Albright and Ivanov tried on behalf of the two world "poles" to exploit harmonizing the draft resolution on Kosova as a new phase to overcome the chills introduced between them by unauthorized NATO bombing and emphasizing the willingness of both countries to contribute to the implementation of the peace accords in Kosova which would enable both nations, enemies of yesterday, to decide on the common future in democratic circumstances and by democratic means.

The Cologne Summit, in addition to the final draft text of the UN resolution also passed a decision to have the peace process in Kosova and generally in the former Yugoslavia to be assisted with an economic development package similar to the Marshall Plan after World War II, in which emerging European countries devastated by World War II were assisted by the U.S.. This program was called the "Balkan Stability Pact" and Kosova was given special attention. It became clear that European countries would organize a donor conference to give more support to the Stability Pact.

An accompanying item of G-8 Ministerial Summit was a scheduled meeting of U.S. Secretary of State, Madeleine Albright, with the top leaders of Kosova, signatories of the Rambouillet Accords: *Ibrahim Rugova, Hashim Thaci* and *Rexhep Qosja*. Albright's meeting with Kosovar leaders was planned to be held during the afternoon of June 7, in Petersberg near Bonn. However, as talks with the Russian minister had lasted much more than anticipated, the meeting with Albright and the press conference were postponed for the next day. Albanian leaders were brought to Bonn to be informed about the content of the text to be sent to the UN Security Council for approval as soon as the Kumanovo agreement was signed between the NATO delegation, headed by General

Michael Jackson and the Yugoslav Army delegation, headed by General Svetozar Marojevic.

The meeting with Albanian leaders lasted for about an hour, in the form of a joint breakfast, in which Albright informed about the main points of the text of the resolution as well as the concept of the international administration in Kosova, accompanied by a Defense Security Force KFOR, the core of which would be represented by NATO. By the Kosovar leaders side there was no remark made other than the question as to why the formulation regarding a three-year transitional period and the expression of the will of the people had been excluded.[866]

In the brief press conference, appearing alongside Albanian leaders and in a good mood, Albright declared that *"she felt well that the international community and Albanian leaders were of one mind about the peace agreement for Kosova, which was a good guarantee for its success."*[867]

Thus, Kosovar leaders, Ibrahim Rugova, Hashim Thaçi and Rexhep Qosja, signatories of the Rambouillet Accords, were in a situation that within six months would give their verbal consent about another historical document, UN Security Council Resolution 1244 placing Kosova under an interim international protectorate, taken out of Serbia where it was forcefully placed, but not out of the formal sovereignty of the Yugoslav state. The departure of the Yugoslav army and police forces from Kosova and NATO's entry, however, represented a crucial step towards placing Kosova under UN international protectorate, which opened the way to a process that led to the independence of Kosova.

---

[866] *"Rilindja,"* 9 June 1999.
[867] *Ibid.*

CHAPTER 6
NATO IN KOSOVA

The "Surprise" Advent of Russian Troops and Attempts to Divide Kosova

Dragging the Kumanovo agreement for two days – part of the plan for the penetration of Russian military forces in Kosova which would impose its division. – General Clark sought to stop the advancement of Russian forces in Kosova by military means, and he was rejected. – Kosova Liberation Army prepared to be involved in operations to stop the entry of Russian troops in Kosova, but it was barred by General Jackson. – Washington kept its temper and would not concede to Russian provocations. – Yeltsin admitted behind-the-scene scenarios made by certain military circles that wanted to use the Kosova crisis to restore to power communists and nationalists.

On June 10, 1999 the world waited with great interest and relief for the events that followed from the New York – Kumanovo – Brussels triangle. Now a peaceful resolution of the Kosova issue appeared as a related package, in which the signing of the military technical agreement between the NATO generals and the Yugoslav Army on the one hand, and Security Council Resolution 1244, on the other, had to have an impact on the NATO Supreme Command and Secretary General to suspend the air campaign. During the long and arduous negotiations among international mediators (Ahtisaari, Talbot and Chernomyrdin) and Milosevic it was agreed that the UN Security Council Resolution could be approved at the moment the news of the signing of the Kumanovo agreement was issued to be followed by NATO's response to the temporary suspension of the air campaign, in order to create the conditions for a verifiable withdrawal of all Yugoslav military and police forces from Kosova along with overall equipment and weaponry in a time interval of seven days.

After a long delay and "explanations" for details, which measured the credibility of the agreement, on the evening of June 9, exactly at 23:45 (11:45 pm) in Kumanovo an agreement was signed between NATO and Yugoslav generals so that after twenty minutes, exactly at 5 minutes after midnight of June 10, the UN Security Council adopted Resolution 1244, which defined all the details of placing Kosova under an interim UN administration to be provided by the International Security Force, details of which were defined in Annex II of the Kumanovo Agreement, which would be recognized as an official part of the document.

Half an hour later, the NATO Secretary General, Javier Solana, enacted the decision to temporarily suspend the air campaign, not including the supervisory mission that would verify the withdrawal of Yugoslav forces under the Kumanovo agreement. With the Kumanovo agreement, NATO and the Yugoslav Army had formed a joint supervision and verification body for the entire operation, which functioned as a whole in accordance with the agreement even without the slightest incident.

Raising the toast for a peaceful agreement of resolution for the Kosova crisis, occurring all around, would quickly fade away and even stop by the news coming from large TV companies such as BBC, CNN, NTV, Euronews, and others, suggesting that a Russian battalion unit of SFOR mission in Bosnia and Herzegovina had just crossed the Drina bridge at Bijelina, and was headed for Kosova without the knowledge of NATO and the international community that dealt with the Kosova issue. Furthermore, the Russian unit had not even received prior permission from the SFOR command in Bosnia and Herzegovina (for each movement it needed a four-month advance notice), except announcing that *"it was being deployed in Kosova by order of the Minister of Defense, Sergeyev, to join the International Security Force."*[868]

It seems that the news might have surprised even the NATO leadership including General Clark himself, who was notified about the movement of Russian troops to Kosova, although he admits that in recent conversations that his envoy in Moscow, General Foglesong, had with Colonel General Ivasov, who insisted that Russians should have a special section under their supervision – including the North – they made their

---

[868] Ahtisaari, Martti: *"Detyra në Beograd,"* Prishtina, 2008, p. 180.

appetites known, although from the information he had from the U.S. military and NATO who had been negotiating with the Russians, he was not under the impression that this claim, which was being rejected by the Americans, would begin to unilaterally or forcefully be implemented.[869] Thus, the issue was alarming from both a military and also political point of view. General Clark contacted General Jackson, Commander of the European Command of the Alliance for Rapid Reaction Corps, demanding that all measures were taken to prevent the Russians from entering Kosova. According to him, there could be no contemplation of the Russians occupying the Prishtina airport. General Jackson would say, *"I want to make sure that KFOR reaches there first. I do not want to be greeted by a Russian battalion, claiming he dominated the airport, and then be forced to negotiate its use with them."* [870]

What General Ivasov had arrogantly stated on that same evening that *"Russia had decided to board on its own train,"* suggesting that Russia through Russian soldiers deployed to Kosova, had begun to fight for its own sector in the North and not only that. Furthermore, he stated that the UN Security Council Resolution 1244 did not define or mandate who would be responsible for each respective sector, so that gave Russia the right that in case NATO sent in Kosova 50 thousand soldiers, to have a contingent of 10 thousand soldiers of its own.[871]

About the Russian intentions to move into Kosova within six hours, namely before NATO and to settle in the North, General Clark was notified shortly by a phone call from General George Casey from Moscow, when he revealed to him the contents of a conversation he had an hour before with Russian Deputy Foreign Minister, Andreyev, which had confirmed General Ivasov's words, *"Russians will take the sector they wish in Kosova."*[872]

News coming from Moscow about NATO and the West, the latter following with concern what was happening, would be controversial reflecting what would a little later be explained as an attempt to realize a secret military scenario of Russian military leadership with Milosevic to divide Kosova, a plan that had probably been operating outside of Yelt-

---

[869] Clark, Wesley K.: *"Të bësh luftë moderne,"* Prishtina, 2003, p. 420.
[870] *Ibid*, p.421.
[871] *Ibid*, p.421.
[872] *Ibid*, p.421.

sin's knowledge, although there were some who believed that he had been notified but posed in waiting for a response from the Americans. What can be understood from General Clark, U.S. mediator Talbot, and NATO generals, who held talks with Russian generals in Moscow and from Chernomyrdin and Ivanov, is that it was the Nationalist-Communist military line, beyond the supervision of Stepasin's Government who had prepared a hidden script with Milosevic and his military on their own to divide Kosova into two parts: in the Serb north and the Albanian south. Indeed, this option had been acceptable to Serbs and they from the time of Cosic onwards, had occasionally sent signals to Albanians on being ready to enter such a game.[873]

Mediator Martti Ahtisaari, after all he had the opportunity to experience during meetings with the Russians, had the impression that the Russian generals were destructive, and that they were working under and above cover. *"Chernomyrdin and Ivanov were often not sharing a common language with Sergeyev's military and this led to trouble,"* said the Finnish diplomat, seeing the showcase with the Russian soldiers and occupation of Prishtina airport from three o'clock in the evening of June 11, 1999 as part of the scenario for the division of Kosova. He noted that:

> Yugoslav military had deliberately stalled Kumanovo talks preparing to infiltrate the Russians in Kosova before NATO. Between the Russian and Yugoslav military a plan existed according to which as soon as the military-technical agreement was signed and a UN Security Council Resolution approved, Russian soldiers would march on to invade northern Kosova on behalf of the right to participate in the International Security Force. Prishtina Airport was chosen, not by chance, as it posed a military logistics infrastructure node from where Russian troops had to disembark and simultaneously prevent NATO to have an airport for air deployment.[874]

What would be presented by Ahtisaari as open suspicion about the Russian secret scenario for the occupation of Prishtina airport and Russian sector in the North, which would divide Kosova into two parts, is confirmed by General Clark and some additional sources referring to the

---

[873] For more on this see Buxhovi, Jusuf: *"Kthesa historike - Shteti paralel dhe rezistenca e armatosur,"* Book Two, Prishtina, 2009, pp. 14-15.

[874] For more on this see Ahtisaari, Martti: *"Detyra në Beograd,"* Prishtina, 2008, pp. 180-187.

dramatic developments of those days, which, however, would have a satisfactory outcome during the highest level US-Russian summit of June 18,1999 in Helsinki between Clinton and Yeltsin, when the two presidents would agree about partnership in the resolution of Kosova rather than confrontation, regardless of the differences between the two countries.

Before the summit took place, and before the Washington-Moscow relations defused tensions that kept the world for full forty-eight hours in a state similar to that of the cold war era, it is worth mentioning first the tensions among the NATO structure itself (as its supreme command would be blocked by lack of national political consensus), then between the Atlantic Alliance and Washington and among the Americans themselves. General Clark, as NATO General Commander, demanded clarity and action in order to prevent the Russians from entering Kosova even through military confrontation. For this very reason General Jackson, who was Commander of the Alliance's European Rapid Reaction Corps, had demanded that the Russians should be stopped through an air blockade. As he had been informed that he could not operate with helicopter units because it conflicted with the Kumanovo military-technical agreement, signed a few days before, Clark demanded that the Russians be stopped at the entrance to Kosova. But even this was not possible because such an operation by NATO troops needed over ten hours to get through to the North. Furthermore, this insight was not without problems, because even if Yugoslavs had to be informed, who had begun the withdrawal of their forces and had blocked all the roads from Ferizaj and Prishtina towards Podujeva, this could be used by them as an alibi to slow their withdrawal. Therefore, it remained for NATO to arrive at the Prishtina airport before the Russians did and block all access. Even this option could technically hardly be realized, as the allied troops needed two hours to reach there before the Russians. General Clark asked General Jackson for the use of helicopters flying from Shkup to Prishtina and to disembark units to be deployed at Prishtina airport. However, on this too, Jackson presented a mandate that had to come from the NATO Military Council, as this represented a mission outside their mandate. Jackson also disclosed that he was in contact with Britain's defense minister and for him the British recommendation was valid, which seemed that NATO's mission was not only entering a command crisis, but also a conceptual crisis in most critical moments when the seventy-six-day investment of air operations could go to waste if the Russians would be able to define the concept of security protective force that had to be stationed in Kosova as part of the international mission as set forth by the UN Security Council Resolution that had just been approved.

This was followed by harsh tones, as General Clark noted that General Jackson, who by military and command positions was subordinated to his orders, tried to ignore them. In a moment, Jackson would go as far as saying the following:

Sir, I am not about to start a Third World War by your order![875]

General Clark would later admit that he had acted as a soldier rather than as a politician. But it was the weight of the mission and its importance that made him think as a soldier considering it as the right way. On this occasion he had forgotten that first of all it was an issue demanding political solutions. For, the confrontation with the Russians, even at a dimension of an "excess" for the moment meant more than a military prestige issue. Therefore, the command authority, no matter what it might be, was subject to political authority. This General Clark would understand in those extremely difficult two days, which he called as the tensest ones he faced in his career as a four-star general. It even cost him his post, as it would be the Pentagon, with which he had a lot of troubles precisely because he wanted to settle the NATO military operation in Kosova by military means, which sent him to retirement three months prematurely.

During the next forty-eight hours, the world political scene had seemingly gone through a phase of cold war revival of the past, combined with the cold peace policy of the present, bringing an end to the hidden scenario of Russian military division of Kosova using precisely its own tools. Washington and London or Clinton and Blair respectively immediately fell in contact with Yeltsin, as Albright had done with Ivanov, getting informed first hand that it was not he who had ordered the deployment of Russian soldiers in Kosova, but it was the military leaders led by Ivasov and others, who had acted behind his back.

Whether this was one hundred per cent so, was not that important for Clinton and Blair. The important thing was to act calmly so that, on the one hand, Yeltsin got the support to take over the work, if it really was "the military that had gone out of hand," and, on the other hand, to offset the Russian military leaders if they really had gone out of Yeltsin's hand,

---

[875] Clark, Wesley K: *"Të bësh luftë moderne,"* Prishtina, 2003, p. 438.

so that without being given the opportunity for confrontation with the West to have their teeth broken from inside as it had happened eight years before when Yeltsin had won the war with Iazov and his coup.

After having learned further details of plans of the Russian military invasion in Kosova with 10 thousand soldiers already waiting in St. Petersburg to fly to Prishtina, Washington immediately took measures to block the air space for the Russian aircrafts. Thus, Hungary, Romania and Bulgaria closed their airspaces for Russian planes. These three countries that already had partnership relations with NATO immediately helped with the closure of airspace and this made it technically impossible for the Russians to deploy thousands of soldiers to Prishtina.

Judging from the nervous reactions of Milosevic and his military in Belgrade pending the deployment of thousands of Russian soldiers in Prishtina, it can be said that the Russian generals, outside of official channels, might have received tacit approval for flying from Romanian or Bulgarian generals that could be disguised as a request for civil flights and the like, but with no guarantee that the air space of these two countries would be able to remain open if they would follow military intervention with the political one to close it as did happen.[876]

From what they agreed a little later, the situation, however, was dramatic and with high tensions between Washington and Moscow, as it seemed that the Russian generals, at least for a few hours, were out of Yeltsin's oversight. They, despite notification from Hungary, Romania and Bulgaria that they were not allowed to fly, had launched two military "Antonov" aircrafts with over four hundred troops towards Kosova. From St. Petersburg after two and a half hours they reached the territory of Ukraine, and after flying over it for about an hour, they landed on Sochi of Crimea. It remains unclear if the suspension of Russian aircraft flights towards Kosova was made as they had been forced to do so by the threat that they would be prevented from flying over the airspace of Hungary, Romania and Bulgaria even through the use of force or because finally

---

[876] Extensively on this issue, see Vlajkovic, Vladan: "Vojna tajna," Belgrade, 2004, which describes extremely furious reactions of Milosevic when he found out that the Russian landing in Prishtina was not about to happen because Romanians and Bulgarians had closed the air space for Russian military aircrafts: "How is it possible that a great Russia be hampered by Bulgarian and Romanian scabies?" In one moment Milosevic claimed that Russia had cheated him.

Yeltsin had turned the situation into his own hands and the military conspirators were convinced that NATO was not joking but was ready to use force. The West itself, namely the U.S. and NATO, did not give any details about why and how Russian planes had returned from the flight, as no one was going to sever the tensions. The important thing was that Washington and Moscow had passed the first difficult test since the Cuban crisis.

Since the option of Russian air deployment was prevented, while land deployment too was impossible, the Russian soldiers who had penetrated into Kosova, while passing through Serbia, being hailed and celebrated by the Serbian Orthodox clergy as saviors – and that night as they were greeted in Prishtina as liberators by thousands of frenzied Serbs, shooting and killing several residents of Prishtina and terrorizing many others, happy to set their homes on fire - had no choice but to get to the Prishtina airport the next morning and there disconnected, closed and surrounded by NATO forces, remain without water and food.

However, the departure of the Russians for Kosova and their penetration in Prishtina on the evening of June 11, 1999, and then their positioning in the Prishtina airport in Sllatina on the next morning, was not only a concern for NATO and the West, but also for Albanians, especially the Kosova Liberation Army units from the Llap Operating Area, which oversaw the roads through which the Russians were to cross. Although on the same day the Llap Operating Zone was notified about the Russian march, upon which the British officer near the area had indicated that the KLA should not undertake any military action as it was a matter of NATO's operational units, the Llap Zone, stationed in Koliq, disregarding the order of the NATO liaison officer, came down to Prishtina entering the city a few hours ahead of the Russian troops. ...On this occasion, in a state of full combat readiness, the movement of the Russians was followed, ready to act in case they would leave the routes determined by NATO, thus reaching the airport, passing through the center of Prishtina, with Russian troops entering Prishtina welcomed by thousands of enthusiastic Serbs who had committed several crimes in the center of Prishtina, killing several Albanians, and leaving two hours later towards the airport, getting there before NATO forces and taking positions there. KLA was prevented from reacting on this occasion,[877] but that would not be repeated the next day when there would be "friction" with a KLA unit from the Drenica Zone, which was quickly discontinued after an intervention from General Jackson.[878]

During those three critical days, in which the inability of the Russian military to threaten the world and dictate terms, as had happened once was put into test- the Russian government policy through Ivanov and Deputy Minister Andreyev, but also through an inexperienced Prime Minister Stepasin, who Yeltsin had replaced for the nationalistic Andropov – would quickly correct that, which supposedly was to be destroyed by Sergeyev's militaries headed by General Ivasov.

From the beginning of the onset of the crisis of Russian soldiers Ivanov declared that the issue in question was "a mistake," and that the Russians would not enter Kosova without an agreement with NATO and prematurely. Rather, he called twice on the U.S. Secretary of State, Albright that the Russians had no purposes other than those that were already aligned with the West over Kosova, while the issue of the Russian sector and their presence in the mission should be regulated jointly and agreed upon. Even despite this promise, after midnight the Russian troops were entering Kosova and reaching Prishtina. Their penetration in Serbia

---

[877] From the author's conversation with Rrustem Mustafa, "Remi," Commander of the Operative Zone of Llap, in Prishtina, on 2 October 2011. Commander "Remi" admits that during all the time he had followed with concern the deployment of Russians in Kosovo. General Jackson had personally told him by phone not to take any military action against the Russians on the grounds that it was a NATO issue to be resolved in Washington-Moscow relations. Commander "Remi" also admits that he was obliged to abide by the order of General Jackson, but he ordered some units first to enter Prishtina "illegally," which occurred on the same evening, while two operative units were ordered to follow Russian movements from Prishtina to the airport.

[878] From the author's conversation with Rustem Mustafa, "Remi," Commander of the Operative Zone of Llap, made in Prishtina, on 2 October 2011. Commander "Remi" says that on the morning of June 12, upon his order, a unit of the Operative Zone of Llap had attacked the Russians near Prishtina Airport, upon which the main command of NATO troops of Skopje had intervened to end any military action against the Russians, as it could upset negotiations among Washington, Brussels and Moscow on the issue. Commander "Remi" acknowledges that the allied forces command in Skopje told them this was a "spontaneous" act from a unit of the Drenica Zone, which was not familiar with the instructions received from General Jackson for non-engagement.

and entry into Kosova, which returned the bloodshed in the streets of Prishtina, watching offline and out of what politics was moving through its hidden circles, seemed to be warning a severity of the Kosova crisis, exactly when it was expected that after the agreements and UN Security Council Resolution that the opposite would happen. But, evidently the crisis as anticipated and premeditated by somewhere, even if for small calculations, (let alone that it could not be excluded as goals for the division of Kosova) would not happen.

The West led by the United States of America, which had successfully led the air campaign against Serbian military and police forces in Kosova, succeeded with enough composure to manage the *first crisis* of the Kosova crisis before it was concluded in peace agreements and gained legitimacy in the world's highest forum. In Helsinki the American and Russian Foreign and Interior ministers, Albright, Cohen, Ivanov, and Sergeyev, signed agreements on the modalities of involvement of Russian troops in the international mission in Kosova, which the official Washington and Moscow hailed as an important step towards restoring trust between the two countries, leaving behind disputes over Kosova and its crisis. The US-Russian agreement on designing a security structure that would assume responsibility for the transition time, namely that of placing Kosova under international protection, indicated the importance of the Kosova problem worldwide and the importance of its proportions. It therefore rendered the West's war for Kosova even more complex.

KFOR and the Issue of the North of Kosova

The American-Russian Ministerial Summit in Helsinki on June 16 and 17, 1999 and the agreement on the shape of KFOR in the North commanded by the French, the South by the Germans, the West by the Italians, the Center by Americans and the East by the British.- Russians are left without a sector of their own distributed in three parts: in the American, French and German sectors. – KFOR maintained its command model, similar to that of SFOR in Bosnia and Herzegovina. – In Kosova, NATO was not only being tested as an enforcer of peace but also as a peace builder, which needed full professional competence and command under its supervision. – However, the public emergence of the sector schemes awakened interest in both the military and political

aspects, as the division of sectors seemed to be warning of specific polit-
ical, strategic, and economic interests of certain western countries to-
wards Kosova.

The battle for military sector sharing in Kosova was a struggle to protect NATO and its concept as a safety mechanism that must withstand the
new challenges of the world. This battle could not be won if NATO would
lose the joint control over the International Security Force, no matter
what would be the options for a political solution to the Kosova crisis. In
Kosova, NATO was not only being tested as a binder of peace, as had
happened with the seventy-six-day air campaign, which had been undertaken against the Yugoslav military and police forces – and, despite
internal difficulties, had been successfully overcome – but it was also
being tested as a peace builder, which needed full professional competence and command under its supervision.

If it can be said that between Americans and Russians, from the Al-
bright-Andreyev meeting of Oslo in April there had been an agreement in
principle on the concept as to how the Kosova crisis should be resolved
(without a NATO declared victory and without an accepted defeat of
Yugoslav forces, which would result in the entry of international forces in
Kosova and departure of the Yugoslav forces creating space for an interim
international protectorate), however, details appeared leaving opportunities for maneuver and manipulation, as occurred with the last ones at
Prishtina airport, which challenged the peace process in Kosova, not only
during the start-up phase, but also for later and even to the end. And, one
of the issues expected to cause trouble, one over which swords would be
broken, was the issue of military sectors and command over the International Security Force mission stationed in Kosova. As would be seen, over
these issues the strategy of protecting the integrity of Kosova was built,
but also put to test. The political process and final solution to the Kosova
crisis were then supported on these issues.

Since evidently the Kosova crisis, however resolved, would need a
prelude of international intervention, i.e. coming from NATO, it was also
clear that the implementation of the peace would need a presence of a
security force, the core of which would be represented by NATO, which
had initiated the power of diplomacy and the diplomacy of force as a last
resort. Of course this also envisaged a Russian presence for the issue to
gain international legitimacy (adoption of a UN Security Council Resolu-

tion), but providing it would not undermine the basic concept of this presence, such as the joint command led by NATO and military sectors in Kosova, which should be divided among the main countries of NATO, which would include the Russians involved in one of the key sectors that would be done through agreement and this would suffice.

From what was known about the North-Atlantic Alliance in the summit in Lisbon on September 23, 1998, approving ACTWARN (order of a 96-hour threat), which the Council of North Atlantic Alliance at the meeting of October 12, 1998 authorized as ACTORD (authorization of NATO air strikes), one could conclude that Kosova would be divided into five military sectors: the South, North, East, West and Central. The Southern sector would be taken by the Germans, the North by the French, the West by Italians, the East by Americans, and the Central by the British. The Southern Sector, commanded by Germans, included a part of Dukagjin from Suhareka, Prizren to the border of Albania going towards Gjakova and reaching as far as the Ura e Shenjte (Holy Bridge). From the Holy Bridge of Drin towards Gjakova met with the Italian Sector, which following the border line with Albania through Rekë e Keqe, reached Peja and Klina to stop at the vicinity of Mitrovica with the French sector in the North, which captured Mitrovica and went as far as Leposavic, i.e. at the border with Serbia. The Northern Sector separated from the Central one at the Ibar River and proceeded towards Prishtina extending in Drenica and including Ferizaj. This sector was under the British command and regarded as the most important, because it linked the North and East, as bordering points with Serbia, which also linked Albanian and Serb ethnicities. The Eastern Sector with Gjilan, Vitia and Anamorava and up to the border with Serbia would be commanded by the Americans, and it was important that U.S. and British troops were "neighbors" as they created together the eastern arch of Kosova from Macedonia to Serbia with a special strategic importance.

A public presentation of the sector schemes awakened interest in both the military and political aspects, as the division of sectors seemed to forewarn political, strategic and economic interests of certain western countries towards Kosova. Thus, it was rumored that the Southern Sector was of economic importance for the Germans, as the area from Prizren to the Albanian border, linking a wide layer of certain resources to be found on both sides of the Albanian border (chrome and iron ores, and water reserves) for which Germany was very much interested. The same went for the Italian Sector with Gjakova and Peja and most of Dukagjin and Drin, where Italians traditionally had their own interests in this part, especially for the Decan Gorge, that of Peja, and the road to Rozhaje and Kollashin. For the most problematic sector, that of the North, from Mitrovica to Leposavic, its French command awoke associations of the French close military and political ties with the Serbs during the last two wars, when they were key allies of the Serbs and "Godfather" to their state, which by the Albanians was viewed with suspicion of being behind a secret background that would serve for the partition of Kosova, or at least, holding it as part of Serbia, which would hinder its integral functioning and create similar dilemmas that would be brought into reality. The American and British sectors would be linked with the strategic aspects of the sphere of interest of a higher conjuncture. These and other speculations that circulated not only through political circles of the West but also in the military, did not raise the political, diplomatic and strategic ratings of the Kosova crisis, as assessed during and after the NATO campaign,[879] but would rather reveal the entire weight and importance it had for a long time, being either deliberately ignored or overlooked by the fear that it automatically opened the unresolved Albanian issue as a stirring factor in the region.

In any case, the military sectors and their division, even without certain prejudices, offered the opportunity to open the issue of the practical configuration of the security protection factor in Kosova and their competences in the context of the transitional international administration of Kosova, as it was also associated with the creation of the police force and other segments, especially knowing that this factor had a duty to demilitarize the Kosova Liberation Army, using the latter as the basis of what would become the Kosova Protection Corps and the Kosova Police Service.

Viewed from this aspect, the composition of the Protection and Security Force, its internal organization across sectors and virtually its command system turned into political issues, as they carried the main burden of establishing circumstances for normality and prosperity in Kosova. The United States of America, leading the Western campaign, were the only ones to have had the concept about NATO as the foundation of this

---

[879] See Küntzel, Matthias: „Der Weg in den Krieg: Deitschland, Die NATO und das Kosovo," Berlin, 2000.

mission and command structure, similar to that of SFOR in Bosnia and Herzegovina, able to protect it in the way they protected it, but other companions, with the exception of the British, in addition to joining this concept did not have any certain attitude about the real size of this military mission and much less a clear-cut position on the internal organization beyond thick lines. This caused the Russians, who, although in principle agreed with the mission, to seek to engage at least in rivalry with NATO, no matter what size it could be. Evidently, in the negotiation process of the mediating trio (Ahtisaari, Talbot, and Chernomyrdin) the Russians would claim an independent sector, including that of the north, because according to them that would calm down both the Serbs and Russian opposition, which saw the issue of Russian involvement in the international mission to be rather in the service of Russian interests than resolving it as a crisis of great importance. Americans rejected categorically a Russian sector on the grounds that it would break the concept of a unique command of NATO mission in Kosova as carrier of Protection and Security Force in Kosova. During the mediation talks, General Clark disclosed to the Pentagon that a Russian sector should not be allowed at any cost, because the Bosnian experience had shown that Russians never gave up their secret links with the Serbs, which, in the case of Kosova would have serious consequences and could lead to its division, if they were to be allowed in the north, as demanded, and would act in that direction.[880] However, evidently, the Americans at this stage needed to "keep the Russians on the common boat," so even Talbot and Cohen during negotiations with the Russians would not be very assiduous on the issue. They took into account the UN Security Council Resolution, as necessary for the Kosova crisis to close and gain international legitimacy with some compromises to the Russians, which did not affect the essence of the American concept that was based on two points: pulling Serbia out of Kosova and NATO's entry in Kosova. In fact, that is what actually happened. During the mediators conversations starting from the beginning of May and continuing until June 10, and later in Helsinki between the Americans and the Russians, on June 17 and 18, 1999, completed with the highest level meeting Clinton-Yeltsin at the G-8 summit in Cologne, on June 20, the Americans aligned more and more Russians to themselves with promises of economic and financial assistance, which were very

---

[880] Clark, Wesley K: *"Të bësh luftë moderne,"* Prishtina, 2003, p. 421.

important to the Russians being clear that through cooperativeness in resolving the Kosova crisis they could boost the bargaining agreements with the Americans. Certainly in this direction things would follow a more normal course if it were not for the secret scenario of the Russian generals with Milosevic about a Russian sector in the North, which meant nothing more than a division of Kosova, as a satisfaction of joint Serbian and Russian nationalists and communists, while undermining the American concept of including Kosova in the western sphere of interest.

However, it should be pointed out that the crisis of the Prishtina airport and all that happened from June 11 to 13, when the Russians entered Kosova and occupied the Prishtina airport, was not without a suitable space for such actions. What General Ivasov would tell the Americans sporadically about the Russians protecting the Serbs, scrubbing now with a statement issued from Moscow on that day stating that "the Russians had no reason to cooperate with NATO,"[881] had the formal support of Security Council Resolution 1244, approved a few days earlier by the highest world forum. Because, the resolution, besides stating that the International Security Force would take over Kosova guided by a joint command as defined by the UN did not save an exclusive place for NATO and did not exclude a place for the Russians and others. In Annex II of the Resolution, speaking of an authorized international force, which had to constitute the core of the mission pointing out to the North Atlantic Alliance, did not exempt a Russian presence. The Annex too did not speak of sectors or way of internal distribution of the force, as everything was left to the jurisdiction of further agreements between the members of the force constituting KFOR. The Russians would try to use the "gaps" in the documents, which were inevitable at that stage of negotiations when trying to keep the Russians aboard at all costs. These tactics would even repeat themselves with the startup alarm spreading and the penetration of Russian forces in Kosova, when both London and Washington were forced to ease down General Clark, indicating to him that there should be no military conflict with the Russians, no matter how badly and widely he was being provoked by them, and that a solution had to be found through political and diplomatic means. At this point, the internal solidarity of NATO and the command hierarchy failed the test, at a time when instead of showing resolve fell subject to the logic of national interests, which for

---

[881] *Ibid*, p.434.

General Clark represented a disappointment as well as disambiguation in understanding that there are political interests those that set the limits of military action even at such a level as NATO.[882]

The politics managing one of the first crises between the West and the Russians at that time, coming out after eight years of cessation of the cold war and its atmosphere that kept the world captivated for half a century, again displayed the major superiority of the Americans over the Russians. Because in the US-Russian talks in Helsinki on June 17 and 18, 1999 between Albright-Cohen and Ivanov-Sergeyev, with little concessions the American line came out a winner. Americans and Russians signed an agreement about the shape of the International Security Force in Kosova, KFOR, where Russia was left without a sector of its own (distributed in the U.S., French, Italian and German sectors) and the command structure was resolved in a way analogous to that in Bosnia, namely, the Russian forces were not subject to NATO command, but KFOR Command was coordinated by an American general, who was also not subject to the NATO Command. It was decided also that the total number of the Russian contingents in Kosova could not exceed the number of 2,600 soldiers.

US-Russian agreement in Helsinki removed the dilemma of the Russian sector and fears that it could turn into a cause for the partitioning of Kosova. But granting the northern sector to the French North at the same time added to suspicions that what was not allowed to the Russians could be tolerated by the French, so that the Kosova crisis would continue to remain open in an extremely vulnerable segment that exceeded Serbian-Albanian relations to be carried to geostrategic ones, which could grant the international presence in Kosova and crisis mechanisms an alibi for an unlimited stay.

There were not only Albanians who were rightly suspicious of the role of the French in recent history, at least from the Balkan wars and later, in favor of the Serbs and against the Albanians. Mistrust appeared also from among the ranks of the West, particularly the United States of America, which had many objections on the conduct of French troops in Bosnia and Herzegovina from the SFOR ranks, not only because there in many cases they failed to be impartial, demonstrating open support for Serbs at the expense of others, but also because occasionally their officers

---

[882] *Ibid*, p. 446.

were the ones who provided Karadzic and Mladic with confidential information on how to escape prosecution by SFOR special forces, which were acting to capture them. The International Mission in Bosnia and Herzegovina, at times, demanded that the French military be held responsible and this overloaded the NATO-France military relations. Official Paris would bring criminal charges only against one of its officers who provided the Serbs with secret documents from SFOR headquarters, and he too escaped punishment as he was found mentally unfit, while several other officers received "disciplinary warnings" and were withdrawn from the mission.

The problem with the French soldiers would also be pointed out by the NATO command in Brussels during preparations for air strikes, when a French liaison officer with NATO headquarters had provided Belgrade with plans for air strikes causing great disarray. The French officer was sentenced to six months in prison, but the damage caused to NATO was overwhelming.[883]

It is likely that the very such pro-Serbian "mortgages" must have affected the Americans, concurring with the British and the Germans, to be determined to leave the northern sector to the French. And, this could have both military and political reasons, but not in terms of restoring overall confidence in Kosova between Albanians and Serbs in line with the statements given.

Military reasons were associated with the fact that the Americans and the West in general, after the confrontation with the Russians about the North as well as their elimination, needed to send someone who was acceptable to Belgrade, Moscow, as well as Kosova Serbs, without considering that the French could have among their ranks officers and soldiers who still maintained sympathies for the Serbs and could even share information with them that went to the detriment of the mission. The NATO military presence in the North with the French, at least for the

---

[883] Extensively on this issue, see Clark, Wesley: *"Waging Modern War,"* Prishtina, 2003. Besides French officers espionage cases in favor of Belgrade and Moscow, General Clark also spoke with great distrust about the behavior of the French during the air campaign when it had bombed the Kosovo Liberation Army positions in Koshare on its own, in May killing 17 soldiers and wounding many others. He also raised similar charges on the French military refusal of any potential action by NATO forces to prevent the penetration of Russian troops at Prishtina airport on 11 of May.

beginning, would not be met with rejection as it could happen with the Americans and others.

Political reasons too, when the issues were regarded only from the Serbian perspective, which prejudiced the general trust, as the presence of French troops in the North created an impression for the Serbs that Kosova had not been lost to them, as they repeatedly heard from the radical propaganda of other powers that were against the international presence in Kosova and by Albanian nationalists, and that it still remained as their hearth, as the state sovereignty of the FRY over Kosova was confirmed by the UNSC Resolution 1244. This would have practical effects as well, because from other sectors, the majority of the Serb population left together with Yugoslav military and police forces, while the North not only stayed, but a great number of Serbs coming from southern and central Kosova would stop across the northern part of the town.

Indicatively, in the north there was no military presence or activity of the Kosova Liberation Army, even before, during, or after the NATO intervention.

Therefore, it was estimated that the implementation of peace with the French troops in the North and the appointment of Frenchman Bernard Kushner to the task of the international "governor" of Kosova would play the role of "softening" of the Serbs to accept and join governance structures created by the international administration and this would be a prerequisite to a good start in Kosova.

Evidently, neither the presence of French troops in the North, nor the international administration that allowed the preservation of the entire Great Serbian iconography in the North along with the presence of masked paramilitary troops and other security forces from the ranks of the Yugoslav police, not only did not succeed to encourage the Serbs to become part of a multiethnic Kosova, as stated in UN Security Council Resolution 1244 and loudly propagated everywhere, but the Serbs were allowed a division to turn it as part of the rejection of the presence of the international administration of Kosova and its unique governance concept, which also included Serbs with many privileges of a positive nature from local administration to the central representation level.

It would be a biased judgment to say that the north of Kosova would enter a state that would be in favor of creation of partitioning circumstances, if not with external, then with internal political consequences, due to the Serb refusal to accept the new realities. The Kosova Serbs unequivocally appeared as instrumental, but behind this one could not say that different scenarios were hiding there, from that of an internal division of Kosova into two ethnic groups: the Albanian south and the Serbian north, to the projects for full division of Kosova.

The history of the international conjunctures, at least those from the Eastern crisis and on, speaks of keeping this area in a "special therapy" oversight because it represented one of the most strategic corridors, a contiguity point of East and West, since the Middle Ages. At the same time, Mitrovica and the area reaching to Kopaonik in the North and West to the Drina, from antiquity onwards, were known for lead, silver and gold ores, among the largest reserves in Southeastern Europe, had begun to be exploited since the Roman period. Thus, it is not by accident that at the Congress of Berlin in 1878, the part connecting Kosova, Sanxhak, and Bosnia and Herzegovina to Mitrovica, was placed under a special status by Austria-Hungary, namely to be overseen by the West.[884] The annexation of this area with that of Bosnia and Herzegovina by Austria-Hungary, in 1908, would not coincidentally turn into a trigger of war between Vienna and Serbia, causing the First World War. It was France and its aims to create the "Small Entente" with Serbia, or Serb-Croat-Slovene Kingdom respectively, and later Yugoslavia, as a main regional center providing Belgrade with the so-called "green transversal" routes connecting the East with the West through the middle of the Balkans controlled by Serbs, France's allies. In 1941, following the capitulation of Versailles Yugoslavia and after Croatia was created out of its remnants, while a good part of Kosova and Western Macedonia united with Albania under the umbrella of Mussolini's fascist Italy, Mitrovica with Trepca and Vushtrri remained as a German zone. So, Hitler, who knew the strategic importance of the Ibar valley and large resources of Trepca, kept this part for himself installing local quisling governance. Communist Yugoslavia too made every effort to upset as much as possible the ethnic Albanian element of the north that existed always changing its borders in the north with attaching Leposavic and surrounding villages of Kopaonik to Mitrovica, and by ceding other Albanian-inhabited parts in favor of Serbia, Montenegro, and Macedonia. With this administrative "adjustment" the north of Kosova added some 30 thousand Serbs, while almost silently a decision

---

[884] For more on this see Buxhovi, Jusuf: *"Kongresi i Berlinit 1878,"* Prishtina, 2008, pp. 143-150.

was taken to have the Presheva Valley, with over 150 thousand Albanians, with the municipalities of Presheva, Bujanovc and Medvexha, within the Leskovac district as a regional center, detach from Kosova and join Serbia.[885]

Silently a unilateral change of border of Kosova with Montenegro happened at Rozhaje, going down to Kuçishtë, just thirty miles away from Peja. Under a federal law on forests, Montenegro absorbed most of the Hajla forests up to the Cursed Mountains, upon which thousands of hectares of forests among the richest in the region were taken away from Kosova, with twenty villages with about 30 thousand Albanians. Even in terms of Macedonia, at this time, some parts of Kosova, such as Dragash Gora and slopes of the Sharri Mountains up to Mavrovo were off to join Macedonia instead. Several thousand Albanians allegedly declaring themselves as "Gorani" and Torbesh separated forever from Kosova.

Subsequent developments generated suspicion that the deployment of French soldiers in the North and the stance not to allow Albanians to return to their homes on the grounds that it frustrated the Serbs, spoke about an internal division of Kosova, if not through an active scenario, than a "passive" one, which in certain circumstances could come into play.

The Installation of the International Protectorate

Inclusion of Rugova, Thaci and Qosja in Kosova Transitional Council marked the end of parallel power structures, derived from the first parliamentary elections in Kosova in 1992, which had operated for seven

---

[885] Leposavic's unilateral joining with Mitrovica district and the Presevo Valley secession from Kosovo and its union with Serbia took place in 1953 in the framework of spatial reforms in Serbia, in line with the Serbian Parliament law passed in April 1953 for the administrative reorganization of the Republic in the new districts. The Province (Oblast) of Kosovo was not consulted at all, so this measure significantly changed its demographic structure at the expense of the Albanians and to the benefit of the Serbs, as by this 30 thousand Serbs were added in the north and 250 thousand Albanians were out of the East. This affected the total number of the population changing significantly at the expense of the Albanians, from 81% as it was down to 63%. For more see: Radonić, M: "*Oblast Kosova i Metohije,*" Beograd, 1957.

years, as well as the end of the parallel state of Kosova as Kosova's statehood foundation.

Regardless of what happened with the "sudden" incursion of Russian soldiers in Kosova on the evening of June 11, 1999 and the invasion of Prishtina airport the next day, which got a response one week later with the American-Russian agreement in Helsinki – where the Russians gave up their claim to the northern sector and their units were distributed in three zones (German, French, and American) – the withdrawal of the Yugoslav military and police forces was done under the Kumanovo military-technical agreement, without any significant difficulty, while the introduction of NATO troops from two directions would preclude the emergence of any security vacuum. The Kosova Liberation Army formations too, with a small exception, adhered to the agreements with the allies.

In accordance with the dynamics of approved agreements and UN Security Council Resolution 1244, of June 10 and 13, 1999, the UN Secretary General Kofi Annan appointed Vieira de Mello as a UN envoy to open the UNMIK office to assume the establishment of the Interim Administration in Kosova responsible for the implementation of peace agreements. Thus began one of the most important stages of international administration, which took responsibility for creating the circumstances for internal self-government in Kosova. With Resolution 1244 and its annexes determining the entire fundamental points of interim administration, as well as the principles for solving the general political crisis, the appointment of the envoy represented an important prerequisite for the entire deployment of the civilian and military mission in Kosova under UN auspices, although the military presence, as was being stated, "established by the Member States and relevant international organizations" was not subject to the authority of the UN Secretary General.[886]

But even without supervision over KFOR, the work of the UNMIK chief appeared of great relevance, as the civil presence had the mandate pending to a final settlement, the creation of a substantial self-governing autonomy in Kosova, taking full account of Annex 2 and the Rambouillet Accords (S/19999/648).

The Head of UNMIK was charged with the following duties:

---

[886] See UN SC Resolution 1244 of 10 June 1999, the documents part.

- *Performing basic civilian administrative functions where and as long as required;*
- *Organizing and overseeing the development of provisional institutions for democratic and autonomous self-government pending a political settlement, including the holding of elections;*
- *Transferring, as these institutions are established, its administrative responsibilities while overseeing and supporting the consolidation of Kosova's local provisional institutions and other peace building activities;*
- *Facilitating a political process designed to determine Kosova's future status, taking into account the Rambouillet accords (S/19999/648);*
- *In a final stage, overseeing the transfer of authority from Kosova's provisional institutions to institutions established under a political settlement;*
- *Supporting the reconstruction of key infrastructure and other economic reconstruction;*
- *Supporting, in coordination with international humanitarian organizations, humanitarian and disaster relief aid;*
- *Maintaining civil law and order, including establishing local police forces and meanwhile through the deployment of international police personnel to serve in Kosova;*
- *Protecting and promoting human rights;*
- *Assuring the safe and unimpeded return of all refugees and displaced persons to their homes in Kosova.*

Secretary General of the UN on July 15 appointed the Frenchman Bernard Kushner as Special Envoy, replacing Vieira de Mello and confirming UNMIK structure with four pillars. On July 16, Kushner established the Kosova Transitional Council, allowing Kosovar leaders informal participation in policy review.

The Kosova Transitional Council was joined by three of the signatories of the Rambouillet Accords: Ibrahim Rugova, Hashim Thaci, Rexhep Qosja, and from the Serb side, Rada Trajkovic.

The inclusion of Kosovar leaders in the Transitional Council marked the beginning of an important phase of partnership between the local leaders and an international interim government of Kosova bringing to an end all the structures of the time that had been part of the Albanian parallel state for eight years as well as those of the armed resistance led by the Kosova Liberation Army, which, although came out of the war as a NATO ally, pursuant to Resolution 1244 of the UN Security Council was to be demilitarized as envisaged by the agreement reached on June 21, 1999 between General Jackson, on behalf of KFOR and Hashim Thaci on behalf of the KLA, under which the guerrillas, within 90 days, were subject to restructuring in what emerged as the Kosova Protection Corps (KPC) or within the Kosova Police Service.

The engagement of Ibrahim Rugova and Hashim Thaci in *Kosova Transitional Council* was important, on the one hand, because the international administration of Kosova included main stakeholders of former parallel state structures and armed resistance of Kosova: Rugova as President-elect of the Kosova Albanians and Thaci as Political Director of the Kosova Liberation Army, and on the other, because through that a lid was put over internal political frictions that had been boiling since the end of the Rambouillet Conference, when a verbal agreement between Rugova and Thaci had been reached for the establishment of the Provisional Government of Kosova. The latter had taken place in the presence of the American Secretary of State, Albright, who suggested in Paris the creation of a Provisional Government of Kosova by means of which the Albanian military and political factor, until then in an internal inconsistency, would unite around common governance, but that was not met.

The German Foreign Minister Joschka Fischer linked Albright's commitment on reaching a consent on the establishment of the Provisional Government of Kosova with the fact that the representatives of the KLA and more specifically Hashim Thaci, along with the demand for a referendum after three years, had also presented a request for the establishment of the Provisional Government of Kosova to be led by him.[887] Albright asked Rugova for his "concession" on this, which he accepted but not implemented, as he would be marginalized by that.[888]

Evidently, the Provisional Government, in accordance with the oral agreement, and with the joint participation of three subjects (LDK, KLA and LBD), was not formed because of the commencement of NATO bombing and the Paris pledgers displayed different views, whether of a

---

[887] For more on this see Fischer, Joschka: "*Vitet kuq-gjelbër*," Prishtina, 2008, p. 142.

[888] The author possesses written statements of Ibrahim Rugova about an eye to eye conversation with U.S. Secretary of State Albright about this issue and other details associated with the agreement in principle about the formation of the Provisional Government of Kosovo.

"principled" nature – which as justified by the Democratic League of Kosova had to do with the creation of basic circumstances and party membership consultation, whether of "dividing" nature, as representatives of Kosova Liberation Army complained – and with this abhorrence Rugova was personally charged for refusing to fulfill the promises because he would "lose his fictitious power he had exercised for years."[889]

Indeed, in Tirana, during the NATO bombing, although the Bukoshi government discussed also the prospects for a Provisional Government of Kosova, without LDK, with the latter having appointed ministers and distributed various short-term "positions" that could not have legitimacy without the party despite the fact that some authority was exerted and the Albanian Parliament with a statement released by the end of May "recognized it."

Nevertheless, the inclusion of the Kosova trio in the Kosova Transitional Council turned into taxonomy all that was said about the Provisional Government of Kosova and other existing and non-existing structures which had emerged from it. But one could not deny the great value and merits of a decade organization of Albanians, starting in December 1989 with the establishment of the Democratic League of Kosova, as the carrier of all-popular and state-building movement, which sponsored the Constitutional Declaration of July 2, 1990, Constitutional Assembly of Kaçanik of September 7 when Kosova was declared a republic and the holding of a referendum on independence in 1991, granting the state of Kosova legitimacy in accordance with its will.

The Albanian parallel state, with or without difficulties, along with armed resistance led by the Kosova Liberation Army functioned to the day NATO bombing started remaining one of the most important chapters of Kosova's statehood whose structures included an entire people, determined to reach their historical aspirations for freedom and independence. The final decision to be released by the Government of the Republic of Kosova was the decision of the Ministry of Education, dated March 23, ordering an indefinite suspension of the learning process in all schools in Kosova during the NATO air bombing campaign.[890]

---

[889] "*Koha jonë*," 25 May 1999.

[890] See decision of Ministry of Education of the Republic of Kosova dated 23 March 1999 in a circular letter form addressed to Kosovo schools.

The three-month vacuum of NATO air campaign against Serb armed forces in Kosova, despite the parallel emergence of two governments of Kosova in rivalry with each other mostly in Tirana, ended more quickly following the Decree No. 1999/1 of July 25, 1999, when the international administration authority was established, stating as follows:

> The entire legislative and executive power in regard to Kosova, including administration of legal bodies, is attributed to UNMIK and exercised by the UN Special Representative.

During the first phase of the international rule of UN Special Representative (SRSG), Bernard Kushner, Kosovar actors carried mainly consultative powers. However, relatively quickly, a second phase started, beginning in 2000 with the establishment of the *"Joint Interim Administrative Structure"* – (JIAS). It consisted of twenty departments with responsibility for civil administration. These departments were chaired jointly by a foreign and a local official. In addition, municipal elections and the establishment of local self-government structures occurred by the end of 2000. The third phase envisaged conditioned self-governance complying with the terms of the Constitutional Framework adopted in 2001.[891]

---

[891] Weller, Marc: *"Shtetësia e kontestuar,"* Prishtina, 2009, p. 301.

CONCLUSION

As U.S. Secretary of State Madeleine Albright concluded the Contact Group meeting in Bonn on June 9, she had an historic announcement to deliver: the Yugoslav army and police force would withdraw from Kosova. The following day, NATO general and Milošević's representatives reaffirmed the end of the conflict with the Kumanovo Treaty, while the United Nations Security Council passed Resolution 1244 to provide for the international administration of Kosova. The events had a clear political epilogue, pulling Serbia out of Kosova and ending the occupation.

This arrangement, which ultimately affected the Albanian-Serbian relations, had long provoked Russia's attention. On numerous occasions, notably in the adoption of the Security Council resolution, Moscow took care to prevent the pulling of Kosova out of Serbia. The UN body's document established an international protectorate over Kosova, but made no change to existing interstate borders. In political terms, Serbia retained its "moral right" to refuse any territorial cessions, while depicting the international administration as a violent takeover of Kosova.

Albright's announcement and the Russian involvement presented two competing views and interests over the Kosova war. In essence, the one view held the Serbs as aggressors against Kosova, while the other vilified the Albanians as invaders of a "Serb Kosova." As the United States and the Russian Federation careened into a diplomatic battle on the Serbian withdrawal, the two powers reconciled by keeping Kosova under Yugoslav sovereignty. While Milošević would pull out his forces, Kosova would remain a nominal part of federal Yugoslavia, which had by then been reduced to two states, Serbia and Montenegro. To the Albanians, the decision was unacceptable, for they were left to live in the same state that had twice suppressed their political will by force (in 1945 and in 1989), and whose recent genocide campaign had prompted NATO's intervention.

The outcome of the UNSC resolution was nonetheless important. By permitting Kosova to separate from Serbia through the imposition of the

Yugoslav sovereignty, the UN document resembled the model by which the Balkan country had obtained its autonomy decades earlier. Constitutional reform in Yugoslavia in 1967 and 1971 gradually elevated Kosova to the status of a constituent unit of the federation.

The series of changes echoed the calls for a Republic of Kosova, which first appeared in the summer of 1968 at the public forum for constitutional amendments. Activists and intellectuals also raised the right to self-determination, the very principle that the Bujan Conference had adopted in early 1944 to resolve the political status at the end of World War II. The decision, however, was sidelined by the Yugoslav partisans, who occupied Kosova in summer 1945, and incorporated it into the federal state of Serbia. To formalize the move, the partisans organized a sham assembly in Prizren that "freely expressed [its] will" in favor of the takeover.

Kosova's annexation was again "legitimized" in 1946 by the first constitutions of both Socialist Yugoslavia and Serbia. The documents defined Kosova as an oblast, an administrative unit with a very low level of self-government. In 1953, the province was wholly effaced from the federal constitution and kept solely under Serbia's tutelage. It was not until 1967, with the ratification of the Seventh Amendment to the Yugoslav Constitution, that Kosova became again a federal subject. In 1971, the autonomous province consolidated its position as a new federal constitution came into effect. Three years later, Kosova adopted its own provincial constitution. The new political arrangement in Yugoslavia practically raised Kosova to the same level with other units of the federation, although the formal relationship with Serbia remained.

The demands for a republic took widespread dimensions in October 1968. All-popular demonstrations broke out in many towns and continued for several weeks, ending on November 27 in Prishtina. The events marked a change not only in the political activism of the Albanians, but also in their social and political conscience. Equality appeared as a cornerstone of a process of liberation from Serbia. Kosova sought to become a federal unit on par with other members of the Yugoslav federation, a status that would also guarantee the right to self-determination, which could be exercised in accordance with the political circumstances of the time.

From inception, the struggle for the Republic of Kosova presented an existential challenge to the Yugoslav federation. After another series of demonstrations in 1981, in particular, the pro-republic activists became increasingly critical of Yugoslavia, which they viewed as "counterrevolutionary." This label then served as a pretext for Serbia as it sought to impose its control over the entire federation, thereby turning Kosova into a factor of crisis and marking the beginning of Yugoslavia's demise.

The dissolution of the federation began on March 23, 1989, when Belgrade resorted to violence to revoke Kosova's autonomy. As Serbian troops poured into Kosovar territory, the Albanian population witnessed what it viewed as the fourth Serbian occupation of Kosova in the century. The situation prompted an immediate response, and intellectuals conscientious of their historical responsibility assumed the leading role. On December 23, 1989, they formed the Democratic League of Kosova, the political party and mass organization that oversaw the popular effort for statehood. The movement consolidated rapidly, and on July 2, 1990, the provincial assembly passed a constitutional document declaring Kosova a republic separate from Serbia. The assembly also succeeded in adopting a new constitution within a few months. The Referendum for Independence of September 26, 1991, and the first parliamentary elections in April 1992 also marked the beginning of the parallel state as part of the civil and institutional resistance against the Serbian occupation. The peaceful movement was followed by the armed struggle, the embodiment of which became the Kosova Liberation Army (KLA).

The efforts of the parallel Kosovar state to exercise government powers suffered from the limitations that the occupation imposed. Despite the difficulties, activities at the grass-roots level proved effective. As the Democratic League of Kosova formed its regional and local offices throughout the country, the Serbian regime garnered no acceptance from the population, which embraced the parallel structures. This form of organization became remarkably successful, for it was directed by an authentic leadership that, for the first time, was not appointed by Belgrade or another foreign power, but gained a popular mandate from the Albanians.

In addition to the Serbian occupation, the Albanians faced another two challenges that weighed on Kosova's future at once. The dissolution of Yugoslavia took a violent turn, when the federal army launched its aggression against Slovenia in May 1991; war ensued shortly after in Croatia, too. In the meantime, the international factor did not appear concerned about the situation in Kosova, when annual conferences held at The Hague and London treated the Albanians as a minority in Serbia.

The Badinter Commission, formed to address Yugoslavia's dissolution, also failed to pay any heed to Kosova. The international body conditioned independence on the right of self-determination that the Yugoslav republics enjoyed. However, Kosova's dual status, as a federal unit yet as part of Serbia, was ignored! Even after the government of the Republic of Kosova timely submitted its application for review by the Badinter group, the international decision-makers refused to change their position.

The lack of apparent support from abroad also highlighted internal difficulties for the parallel state of Kosova. To Albanians, it appeared as if they had chosen a wrong and entirely useless path, for they would be branded as a minority with a status more unfavorable than any of their prior experiences.

Kosovar Albanians, nonetheless, did not lose their courage, let alone give up. The parallel state continued, inspiring hope that path of peaceful resistance and patience was the only way to save the people from war, which under the circumstances would bring a fatal end. "War through patience" became the motto of Dr. Ibrahim Rugova, elected as first President of the Republic of Kosova in 1992. His vision worked, despite its difficulties, and determined the direction of the resistance movement, sparing it from desperation and lack of perspective. Ultimately, the peaceful approach helped raise awareness about Kosova in the West, and created the circumstances for the international factor to intervene in the matter, as most notably during the NATO campaign in 1999.

One must note that a constant and powerful source of encouragement for the Albanian civil disobedience was the American support. In December 1992, U.S. President George H.W. Bush sent his "Christmas Warnings" to Belgrade that the United States would respond by military intervention, if the Serb leadership were to expand the Yugoslav wars to Kosova. This message was to become a sort of talisman that prevented the collapse of Albanians under the Serbian state violence and limited the exodus of the population that—as the terror in Croatia and Bosnia and Herzegovina ensued—had reason to fear and flee persecution.

Washington protected the Albanians and encouraged them to continue their civil disobedience. In the meantime, the American advice also called for cooperation through peaceful initiatives and dialogue with Belgrade, as Kosova accepted an unequal negotiating position in several instances, including The Hague Conference, the meetings of the Special Group for Kosova in Geneva, and other open and secret talks with the Serbian leadership. Noticeably, however, the Kosovar negotiators consistently pursued the country's independence, albeit considering a transitional period under international supervision or an interim protectorate. This flexibility served as a powerful tool the Albanians used to keep the possibilities open, while refusing to submit to Serbia's rule.

Kosova's negotiating strategy did not uproot the international stereotypes that treated the Albanians as a minority. However, owing to their parallel state and the civil resistance, the people earned great sympathy as well as support in the world opinion. The democratic movement succeeded in removing the stigma that the Serbian propaganda had foisted on the Albanians for over a century, and erected a new image of a civilized and peace-loving people, which had chosen non-violent means to achieve its aspirations and historical rights.

In addition to the U.S. support for the Kosovar movement, a great help also came from Germany. The newly united German state was among the first nations to open its doors to those fleeing the Serbian violence. Soon, over 100,000 Albanian refugees found shelter in the country, and within five years the number reached 300,000. Besides the humanitarian aid, Germany also assumed a political role, siding with the United States in decisive moments to prevent Belgrade's plans for ethnic cleansing.

Following the Geneva process, no major negotiations took place until three years later. During this period, the parallel state pursued remarkable institution-building efforts, which greatly consolidated the concept of peaceful resistance as a virtue of civilization. Defying the occupation, the popular movement succeeded in establishing an independent system of education, with schools ranging from the elementary level to the university—albeit some 300,000 students attended classes in private homes and other inadequate buildings. This impacted the quality of learning and teaching standards, but there was no other way; for if the schools were to cease altogether, then the parallel system and struggle for an independent state would fail, too. Accordingly, the government of the Republic of Kosova, then in exile, began to effectively collect solidarity contributions. Revenue increased particularly owing to a three-percent income tax payment by Kosovars holding a job. Considerable amounts collected, especially from expats, were then dedicated primarily to education, but occasionally also to research and scientific work, which survived in spite of the circumstances.

Along the efforts for practical progress, the school system endeavored to make political contributions to the state of Kosova, too. During the Geneva discussions of the Special Group, the Kosovar delegation focused much of its attention on education, hoping to raise awareness and earn greater support from the international community. In fact, the very failure in 1993 of the Geneva talks shed positive light on the educational system and elevated the Kosova issue to levels of international importance, as Belgrade not only demonstrated its unwillingness to resolve the crisis, but that the war on Albanian schools was the pivotal segment of the Serbian strategy. The violent regime had targeted Kosova's cultural and intellectual identity, as it was the collapse of this identity that would provide Serbia with a political victory over the Albanians and the Kosovar state.

Preoccupied with the increasingly devastating war in Bosnia and Herzegovina, the international decision-makers had great stakes in preventing a conflict in Kosova. The world powers wished to confine the Yugoslav wars, fearing that the crisis could spill over across the region. Therefore, the Albanian determination for the parallel state would earn praises, and the West would make great efforts to improve the conditions for education, hoping that this would help, at the very least, self-restraint among the people.

Under the circumstances, it appeared as if the progress of the parallel state was becoming a handicap. Since no armed conflict had broken out and the Albanians had created an absurd "coexistence" with the Serbian regime, Kosova did not present a pressing concern on the international agenda. Decision-makers hoped that Prishtina and Belgrade would ultimately find grounds for reconciliation after both sides had realized their maximum goals were not feasible: Serbia could not force the Albanians to accept its regime, while Kosova could not secede because of restrictions under international law. In the meantime, there was also hope among foreign powers that Serbia and Kosova could "reconcile" even at the insistence of the international factor, which would find the "golden milieu" of reconciliation.

Nonetheless, the Dayton Conference in November 1995 sent a clear message to Kosovar Albanians that peaceful resistance was unlikely to be awarded. Following air strikes against Serb forces in Bosnia and Herzegovina, the United States was able to bring the belligerent parties to the negotiating table. While the conference concluded with peace, the Serbs succeeded in imposing the state's internal division into ethnic entities and *confederal units, creating the impression that the perpetrators of war crimes rather than proponents of peace earned the blessings of the West.*

U.S. President Bill Clinton wrote to Dr. Rugova to explain why Kosova was not on the agenda at Dayton, but promised that a future conference would address the issue. But the Albanians had been rightly disappointed with the international factor, including the United States, which had been the main supporters and mentors of the civil resistance movement.

To Kosova, the Dayton Accords were both a misfortune but also a lesson. The Albanians knew that, after the Bosnian war had come to an end, conflict in Kosova was imminent. The Yugoslav crisis hence was to return to where it had begun in 1989. And all forecasts warned of violence. Serbia was not interested in resolving disputes with the Albanians by peaceful means, but planned on using violence to settle the issue once and for all by ethnically cleansing Kosova. Belgrade now had another reason to rid Kosova of Albanians: after the defeat in Croatia and parts of Bosnia and Herzegovina, over half a million ethnic Serb refugees poured into Serbia. Ethnic cleansing would hence provide Belgrade with the living room needed to accommodate the refugees and prevent a domestic crisis that could lead to a civil war.

While the Albanians maintained their commitment to the parallel state and civil disobedience, the situation inevitably compelled them to contemplate active resistance, including such means that could lead to an armed uprising against the occupying regime and its police and military apparatus stationed in Kosova. The masses as the backbone of the peaceful movement began to demand a more active approach. After the Dayton Accords, popular discontent led to increasing defiance against the Serbian regime and gradually mounted to an armed resistance, an inalienable right and last resort of a people that had exhausted all means of defending themselves from the violence of an occupying regime.

The shift to arms reached its first milestone with the emergence of the Kosova Liberation Army. Relying of the overall infrastructure of the parallel state and the resources accumulated over the years, the KLA became an insurmountable factor that transformed the international community's focus on the Kosova question. This was no longer an issue of minority rights, but a crisis requiring a prompt response to prevent diffusion of violence into other parts of the region.

The armed resistance was neither coincidental nor unexpected. While Dayton concluded the war in Bosnia and Herzegovina and Croatia, it was the conference that set off the crisis in Kosova, precisely by keeping it off the agenda. President Clinton's promise of a future forum that would treat Kosova as a special issue provided great reassurance, but at the same, it served as a call for action. For the international community to pay heed to Kosova, the country needed to present a "special issue," and the Albanians needed to shift their course to gain the world's attention.

Three months after the Dayton Conference, several attacks were carried out against the Serbian police force in Kosova. The Liberation Army assumed responsibility, while still a covert organization. Over a year later, on November 28, 1997, KLA soldiers appeared among citizens, making a live announcement at a public event. The KLA's emergence as a continuation of the popular resistance by other means permanently changed the way the international community approached the Kosova question. After six years of Belgrade's violence against the institutional movement, it was the expected and legitimate moment for the Albanians to resort to armed resistance.

The KLA grew in size and power, despite the challenges the army faced in its early days. The United States initially listed the KLA as a terrorist organization. Encouraged by the label, Belgrade launched expansive police and military operations in pursuing KLA leaders in early 1998. Serb forces attacked several villages in the central region of Drenica, killing a handful of civilians in the Qirez and Llausha villages and massacring nearly fifty members of an extended family in Prekaz.

After the KLA appeared in public, Albanian leaders took additional steps in favor of the armed resistance. The government-in-exile of the Republic of Kosova became actively involved in the movement, by providing recruits, assisting with logistics, and conducting military operations. Albanian officers and soldiers, many of whom had been enlisted as reserve troops for years and had participated in the Croatian and Bosnian wars, were called to duty. As members of the Armed Forces of the Republic of Kosova (FARK), government soldiers fought alongside the KLA, notably during the Serb offensive in the western region of Dukagjin in 1998. In the meantime, the exiled state officials also took care to ensure that the KLA received adequate supplies of armament and logistics.

The Liberation Army had gained the upper hand in the armed resistance, but the Kosovar government was keen in providing institutional support, despite the uneasy relationship with the KLA's General Staff and the unnecessary internal rivalries that continued throughout the war. The

900

involvement of the parallel state ensured that the resistance front was united and comprehensive, for the aim of all participants was the country's independence. In fact, the KLA and the republic were one party when the international community began its efforts for a political solution of the crisis. A single delegation consisting of KLA and government members represented Kosova at the Rambouillet Conference in February and March 1999. The delegation remained united as it signed the proposed agreement, whose ultimate rejection by the Serbs led to NATO's intervention weeks later.

The active resistance marked a sharp turn in the approach of both the Albanians and the international community. Often times, many zealous advocates of action had called for a rush to arms and a renouncement of what they viewed as the failed platform of the parallel state and civil movement. However, the prevailing opinion was to preserve the political struggle by other means, while incorporating military power as a factor in service of the institutional efforts.

The balanced approach was of historic importance as it earned the support of the majority of Albanians, but also raised a question about the role and responsibilities of President Rugova and Prime Minister Bujar Bukoshi. Why did they not organize the armed resistance promptly and in accordance with the duties they held under the Kaçanik Constitution? The government of the republic had its own ministries of defense and internal affairs, which should have overseen the armed resistance, while President Rugova was Commander-in-Chief of the Armed Forces with the responsibility of leading the war.

On the other hand, it is noteworthy that the United States and other Western powers contributed to the balanced approach of armed and civil resistance. The international community ensured to prevent any internal strife or friction between the republic and the KLA, by treating them as parallel lines of the same movement.

The United States relied on both "lines" equally when it worked on raising Kosova's importance on the international agenda. And to give the issue an adequate response, Washington then went as far as redefining international law, especially in regards to the protection of minorities. The United States led the NATO campaign against Yugoslavia, justifying the action on humanitarian grounds, which also created the conditions to expel the Serbian regime from Kosova.

Serbia's withdrawal was a historic achievement that would have been impossible had the Albanians pursued their statehood in disaccord with principles of civility and democratic notions of the Western world. To the contrary, the popular struggle for independence in the late 1980s and 1990s, demonstrated once again that they belonged in the West. Drawing inspiration from the political concept of the Albanian movement since the 1800s, the Kosovar resistence reclaimed the place in the European family from where the Albanians had been forcibly removed centuries ago.

Therefore, even the seventy-six days of the North Atlantic alliance was the fruit of the Albanian adherence in the West and the Western civilization. While the NATO strikes ousted the Serbian-Yugoslavian military after eighty-seven years of its presence in Kosova, the issue of the final status and the Yugoslav state's sovereignty remained open. Nonetheless, the establishment of an interim international administration and the Kosova Force (KFOR) peacekeeping mission marked the final capitulation of the disintegrating Yugoslav federation.

The transitional period was not without its challenges. As soon as the UN Security Council approved Resolution 1244 on June 10, Russian troops from a peacekeeping mission in Bosnia hurriedly took off to reclaim parts of Kosova. As they sought to assume control of northern Kosova, the Russians threatened a move that would divide the country into a Serb part in the north and an Albanian part in the south, similar to the way Germany was partitioned after World War II.

The Russian military rebellion held the world in awe for three consecutive days. Eventually, no changes to Kosova's borders occurred, but an international division became apparent once French troops of the KFOR arrived in the northern section. This event not only highlighted the unwillingness of Belgrade and Serbs to accept historical realities as they are, but also revealed the anathema of foreign influence. Subjected to certain spheres of influence, such international conjunctures have often been inclined to keep the northern part of Kosova "under supervision" or occupation. As early as 1878, the Berlin Congress assigned Austria-Hungary oversight of the region, which the dual monarchy controlled until the 1912 Balkan Wars, when Serbia occupied Kosova. Then again, when World War I broke out, Vienna restored its authority for the last three years of the conflict. Similarly, Nazi Germany was in charge of the area between 1941 and 1944.

Although unable to repudiate the sigma about the north, the Western powers responsible for security played an instrumental role in Kosova's path to statehood. The principal NATO members with the United States as the leading force supported the country's independence, despite the issue of the northern region. On February 17, 2008, the representatives of the people declared Kosova an independent state, concluding with historic success a century-long process, in which generations had invested their blood, brains, sweat, and tears.

NOTES AND BIBLIOGRAPHY

Acronyms

ACTORD	Action order for NATO air attacks within 96 hours
ACTWARN	Action Warning
EU	European Union
G-8	Cooperation body among the G7 countries, world's richest countries, and Russia
KFOR	International forces in Kosova authorized by the UN Security Council
NAC	North Atlantic Council
SC	Security Council
KVM	Kosova Verification Mission
JIAS	Joint Interim Administration Structure
ISGK	Interim Self-Governing Institutions in Kosova
LDK	Democratic League of Kosova
NATO	North Atlantic Treaty Organization
OSCE	Organization of Security and Cooperation in Europe
UN	United Nations Organization
FRY	Federal Republic of Yugoslavia
YA	Yugoslav Army
WEU	West European Union
UNMIK	United Nations Mission in Kosova
SFOR	International force in Bosnia and Herzegovina

Books

Academy of Sciences and Arts of Kosova, group of authors: *"Akte të Kuvendit të Republikës së Kosovës 1990-1992,"* Prishtina, 2005.

Abrashi, Aziz/Kavaja, Burhan: *"Epopeja e minatorëve,"* Prishtina, 1966.

Academy of Sciences of Albania: *"Historia e Popullit Shqiptar"* I,II,III, Tirana, 2002-2007.

Ahtisaari, Martti: *"Detyra në Beograd,"* Prishtina, 2008.

Ahrens, Gert-Heinrich: *"Containing Ethnic Conflict,"* Washington, 2005.

Albriht, Madeline: *"Zonja Sekretare,"* Tirana, 2004.

Altmann, Franz-Lothar: *"Kosovo 2005/06:Unabhängigkeit auf raten?,"* Berlin 2006.

Armstrong Hearton:*"Gjashtë muaj mbretëri 1914,"* Tirana, 2001.

Albrecht, Ulricht/Schefer, Paul: *"Der Kosovo-Krieg. Fakten, Hintergrunde, Alternative,"* Köln, 1999.

Baker, James: *"Drei Jahre, die die Welt verenderteretn: Erinnerungen,"* Berlin 1996.

Bajrami, Hakif dr: "Rrethanat politike-shoqërore në Kosovë më 1918-1941," Prishtina, 1981.

Bajrami, Hakif: *"Dosja Demaçi,"* Prishtina, 2004.

Boekh, Katrin: *"Von den Balkankriegen zum Ersten Weltkrieg. Kleinstaatenpolitik und ethnische Selbestimmung auf dem Balkan,"* München, 1996.

Brunner, Georg: *"Der Transformationsprozess in Mittel-und Osteuropa. Wachsende Problene mit den Ethnien,"* München, 1999.

Brunner, Georg: *"Völkerrrecht und Selbststimungsrecht in Kosovo,"* published in *"Der Kosovo Konflikt. Ursachen. Verlafu, Perspektiven,"* Klagenfurt, Wien, Ljubljana, 2005.

Brzezinski, Zbigniew: *"Die enzige Weltmacht. Amerika Strategie der Vorherrschaft,"* Weinhemim 1997.

Buckley, William J: *"Kosovo: Contending Voices on Balkan Intereventions,"* Grand Rapids, 2000.

Butka, Uran: *"Mukja – shans i bashkimit, peng i tradhtisë,"* Tirana, 1998.

Buxhovi, Jusuf: *"Kthesa historike – Vitet e Gjermanisë dhe Epoka e LDK-së,"* Prishtina, 2008.

Buxhovi, Jusuf: *"Kthesa historike – Shteti paralel dhe rezistenca e armatosur,"* Book Two, Prishtina, 2009.

Buxhovi, Jusuf: *"Kongresi i Berlinit 1878,"* Prishtina, 2008.

Buxhovi, Jusuf: *"Nga Shqipëria Osmane te Shqipëria Evropiane,"* Prishtina, 2010.

Cana, Zekeria: *"Lëvizja kombëtare Shqiptare në Kosovë 1908-1912,"* Prishtina, 1979.

Cana, Zekeria: *"Socialdemokracia serbe dhe çështja Shqiptare 1903-1914,"* Prishtina, 1986.

Cana, Zekeria: *"Apeli 215 i intelektualëve shqiptarë,"* Prishtina, 2001.

Cana, Zekeria: *"Shpalime historike,"* Prishtina, 1982.

Carrinton, Lord: *"A Soldier's Peace,"* 1994.

Coloc, Marie-Janine: *"Vor dem Frieden im Kosovo?,"* 1999.

Clinton, Bill: *"My Life,"* New York, 2005.

Clark, Howard: *"Civil Resisitanc in Kosovo,"* London, 2000.

Clark, Wesley: *"Të bësh luftë moderne,"* Prishtina, 2007.

Clewing, Konrad/Reuter, Ernst: *"Der Kosovo-Konflikt. Ursachen, Akteure, Verlauf,"* München, 2000.

Cenčić, Vjećeslav: *"Titova posljednja ispovjest,"* Zagreb, 1984.

Čubrilović, Vasa: *"Iseljavanje Arnauta."* Vojno Istorijski Institut JNA. No. 3, F. 4. Box 69.

Čosić, Dobrica: *"Stvarno i moguce,"* Ljubljana-Zagreb, 1988.

Čosić, Dobrica: *"Srpsko pitanje – demokratsko pitanje,"* Beograd 1992.

Čosić, Dobrica: „*Kosovo 1965-1999,"* Beograd, 2004.

Črikanović, Fedro: *"Jugoslavija između dva rata,"* Zagreb, 1968.

Çeku, Ethem: *"Kosova në sfondin e diplomacisë së Jugosllavisë dhe të Shqipërisë 1945-1981,"* Prishtina, 2009.

Çeku, Ethem: *"Shekulli i ilegalës,"* Prishtina, 2004.

Chlumetzky,Leoplod Frh:*"Östereich-Ungarn und Italien,"* Wien, 1904.

Daadler, Ivo: *" Getting to Dayton. The Making of America's Bosnia Policy."* Washington, 2000.

Duizings, Gerlachus: *"Religion and the pilitics of identity in Kosovo,"* London, 2000.

Dukovski, Darko: *"Makedonien und Jugoslawien Konflikt,"*1999.

Dedijer, Vladimir: *"Novi prilozi za noviju biografiju Josipa Borza Tita,"* Volume III, Beograd, 1984.

Dedijer, Vladimir:*"Jugoslovensko – albanski odnosi,"* Beograd 1949

Dermaku, Ismet: *"Gjon Serreçi dhe NDSH-ja,"* Prishtina, 2002.

Drnovšek, Janez: *"Meine Warheit,"* Zürich, 1998.

Djaković, Spasoje: *"Sukobi na Kosovu,"* Beograd, 1984.

Dosja Sekrete e UDB-së *"Emigracioni Shqiptar 1944-1953,"* Prishtina, Tirana, 2004.

Djordjević,Vladan:" *"Albanien und das Großmähte,"* Leipzig, 1913.

Dode, Luan: *"Kosova në qëndrimet e Enver Hoxhës,"* Tirana 2006.

Frashëri, Mehdi:*"Historia e lashtë e Shqipërisë,"*Tirana, 2000.

Fischer, Joschka: *"Vitet kuq-gjelbër,"* Prishtina 2007.

Gadin, Marie Amelia von: *"Aus de neuen Albanien,"*Win, 1914.

Gashi, Dardan: *"Kosovo: Der gordische Knoten des Balkans,"* Frankfurt 1998.

Gashi, Bahri: *"Në Altarin e lirisë,"* Prishtina, 2006.

Glenny ,Misha: *"Der Krieg, der nach Europa kam,"* München 1993.

Glenny, Misha: *"Historia e Ballkanit 1804-1999,"* Tirana,

Genscher, Hans-Didetrich: *"Erinnerungen,"* Berlin, 1995.

Gorbatchow, Michail: *"Erinnerungen,"* Berlin, 1995.

Grow, James: *"Triumph of the Lack of Will: International Diplomacy and the Yugoslav War,"* London, 1997

Gucia, Ismet: *"Burimet natyrore si faktor i zhvillimit ekonomik të Kosovës,"* Prishtina, 1982.

Guzina, Ružica: *"Opštine u Srbiji 1913-1918,"* Beograd, 1976.

Hadri, Ali dr: *"Lëvizja nacionalçlirimtare në Kosovë 1941-1945,"* Prishtina, 1971.

Hadri, Ali dr: *"Këshillat Nacionalçlirimtarë të Kosovës 1941-1945,"* Prishtina, 1974.

Haxhiu, Ajet: *"Hasan Prishtina dhe lëvizja politike e Kosovës,"* Tirana, 1964.

Hasani, Sinan: *"Kosova – të vërtetat dhe mashtrimet,"* Prishtina, 1986.

Hoxha, Fadil: *"Kako smo se pripremili za Bujan,"* "Borba" 20-25 June.

Hoxha, Fadil: *"Kur pranvera vonohet,"* Prishtina, 1971.

Hajrizi, Mehmet: *"Historia e një organizate politike dhe demonstrata e vitit 1981,"* Tirana, 2008.

Hoxha, Enver: *"Titistët,"* Tirana, 1982.

Hoxha, Enver: *"Rreziku anglo-amerikan për Shqipërinë,"* Tirana, 1982.

Holbrooke, Richad: *"Meine Mission,"* München, 1998.

Hoti, Izber: *"Forcat e armatosura në Kosovë gjatë Luftës së Dytë Botërore,"* Prishtina, 1998.

Henitze, Hans-Joachim: *"Selbstbestimmungsrecht und Minderheitenrechte im Völkerrecht,"* Baden-Baden, 1994.

Hamzaj, Bardh: *"Paqja e gjeneralit – dialog me Ramush Haradinajn,"* Prishtina, 2001

Hofbauer, Hannes: *"Balkankrieg. Der Zerstorüng Jugoslawiens,"* Vienna,1999.

Horvat, Branko: *"Kosovsko pitanje,"* Zagreb, 1987.

Hockenos, Paul: *"Homeland calling – elite patriotism and Balkan wars,"* London, 2003.

Hrabak, Bogumil: *"Albanija od Julske krize do proljeća 1916, na osnovu ruske diplomatike građe,"* „Obeležja," Prishtina, 1973.

Hrabak, Bogumil – Janković, Dragoslav: „Srbija 1918," Beograd, 1968.

Hrabak, Bogumil: „*Reokupacija oblasti srpske i crnogorske države s arbanaškom većinom stanovništva u jesen 1918. Godine i držanje Arbanasa prema uspostavljenoj vlasti,"* „Gjurmime Albanologjike," Prishtina, 1969, no. 1.

Islami, Hivzi: *"Spastrimet etnike, politika gjenocidiale serbe ndaj Shqiptarëve,"* Peja, 2003.

Izzet Pascha, Ahmet: *"Denkwüdigkeiten des Marschalls Izzet Pascha,"* Leipzig,1927.

"I izoluari – rrugëtimet e tunelit të tmerrit," Prishtina, 2009.

Joetze, Gunter: *"Der letzte Krieg in Europa? Das Kosovo und die deutsche Politik,"* München, 2001.

Judah, Tim: *"Kosova, luftë dhe hakmarrje,"* Prishtina, 2002.

Kola, Harilla: *"Gjenocidi serb ndaj Shqiptarëve në viset e tyre etnike në Jugosllavi, 1941-1967,"* Tirana, 2000.

Kohl, Christine von: *"Albanien,"* München 1998.

Kramer, Helmut/Đihić ,Vedran: *"Die Kosovo-Bilanz. Scheitert die internacionale Gemeinschaft?,"* Münster 2005.

Krizman, Bogadan:*"Elaborat dr Ive Andrica o Albaniji iz 1939 godine."* "Casopis za suvremenu povijets "1977, nr 2, f. 77-99.

Krasniqi, Jakup: *"Kthesa e madhe – Ushtria Çlirimtare e Kosovës,"* Prishtina, 2007.

Krsitć, Đorđe: *"Kolonizacija južne Srbije,"* Shkup, 1928.

Kuntzel, Matthias: *"Der Weg in den Krieg: Deutschland, die NATO und das Kosovo,"* Berlin 2000.

Libald, Michael: *"Balkan,"* München, 1987.

Libald, Wolfgang: *"Das Ende Jugoslawiens. Selbstzestorüng, Krieg und Onhmacht der Welt,"*Vienna, 1993.

Laquoi, Heinz: *"Der Kosovo-Konflikt: Wege in einen vermeidbaren Krieg,"* Baden-Baden, 2000.

Lukas, Hans-Dieter: *"Genscher, Deutschland und Europa,"* Baden-Baden, 2002.

Lutz, Dieter: *"Der Kosovo-Krieg. Rechtliche und rechtsethische Aspekte,"* Baden-Baden, 2000.

Lory, Bernard: *"Europa ballkanike nga 1945 deri në ditët tona,"* Tirana, 2007.

Lose, I: *"Die wölkerrechtlichen u politischen Bezihungen Albaniens zu Italien,"* Würzburg, 1930.

Nasi, Lefter: *"Ripushtimi i Kosovës,"* Tirana, 1994.

Novosella, Selatin: *"Demonstratat e gjashtëdhjetetetës"* 1,2,3, Prishtina, 2009.

Novaković, Kosta: *"Nacionalizacija i srbizacija,"* Wien, 1913.

Matković, Hrvoje: *"Povijesti Jugoslavije 1918-1991-2003,"* Zagreb, 2003.

Neziri, Zymer: *"Isa Demaj – jeta dhe veprimtaria atdhetare,"* Prishtina, 2000.

Mehmeti, Arbër/Krasniqi Sefedin: *"Kështu foli Tahir Zemaj,"* Prishtina, 2001.

Marko, Joseph: *"Der Mindeheitenschütz ind den jugoslawischen Nachfolgenstaaten,"* Bonn, 1996.

Meier, Viktor: *"Wie Jugoslawien verspielt wurde,"* München, 1995.

Meier, Viktor: *"Jugoslawiens Erben: Die neuen Staaten und die Politik des Westens,"* Munich, 2001.

Milo, Paskal: *"Shqipëria dhe Jugosllavia 1918-1927,"* Tirana, 1991.

Melćic, Dunja: *"Der Jugoslawien-Konflikt. Handbuch zu Vorgeschihten, verlauf und Konsequenzen,"* Wiesbaden, 1999.

Mirić, Jovan: *"Sistem u krizi,"* Zagreb, 1984.

Merkel, Reinhard: *"Der Kosovo-Krieg und das Völkerrecht,"* Frankfurt, 2000.

M.Schmid-Neke:*"Entschtehung und Ausbau der Königsdikatur in Albanine 1912-1939"*, München, 1987.

Mišović, Miloš: *"Ko je tražio republiku,"* Beograd, 1987.

Mugosa, Dusan: *"Shënime nga puna në Shqipëri 1941-1944,"* Tirana, 2002.

Oschlie, Wolf: *"Gros-Staaten auf dem Balkan, Urspunge, Formen und Folgen des etnischen Imperlialismus,"* in *"Südosteuropa,"* Berlin, 2002.

Obradović, Milovan: *"Agrarna reforma i kolonizacija na Kosovu 1918-1941,"* Instituti i Historisë së Kosovës, Prishtina, 1981.

Owen, David: *"Balkan-Odyse,"* London, 1995.

Prishtina, Hasan: *"Nji shkurtim kujtimesh mbi kryengritjen Shqiptare 1912,"* Bari, 1925.

Perrit Jr, Henry H: *"Ushtria Çlirimtare e Kosovës – Rrëfimi prej brenda për një kryengritje,"* Prishtina, 2008.

Petranović, Branko: *"Istorija Jugoslavije 1918-1978,"* Beograd, 1980.

Pettifer, James: *"Ekspresi i Kosovës,"* Prishtina, 2004.

Petric,Wolfgang/Pihler Robert: *"Rruga e gjatë në luftë. Kosova dhe bashkësia ndërkombëtare,"* Prishtina, 2002.

Perunović, Branko: *"Istorija Jugoslavie 1918-1980,"* Beograd, 1980.

Pireva, Adil: *„Gjashtëdhjeteteta shqiptare,"* Prishtina, 2002.

Pushkolli, Fehmi: *"Mbrojtja Kombëtare Shqiptare e Kosovës 1878-1990,"* Prishtina, 1991.

Paulsen, Thomas: *"Die Jugoslawienpolitik der USA 1989-1994,"* Baden-Baden, 1995.

Placzek, Norbert: *"Der Kosovo-Konflikt. Genese und Perspektive,"* Hamburg, 1996.

Pirraku, Muhamet: *"Mulla Idriz Gjilani dhe Mbrojtja Kombëtare e Kosovës Lindore,"* Prishtina, 1995

Pipa, Arshi: *"Stalinizmi Shqiptar,"* Tirana, 2007.

Popović, Milorad: *"Vidovdan i casni krst,"* Beograd, 1976.

Popović, Janićije: *"Kosovo u ropstvo pod bugarima 1915-1918,"* Leskovac, 1921.

Popović, Janićije: *„Toplički ustanak,"* Beograd, 1956.

Rakić, Milan: *"Konsulska pisma 1905-1911,"* Prosveta, Beograd, 1985.

Rajovic, Radoshin: *"Autonomia e Kosovës,"* Prishtina, 1987.

Reissmuller,Johann Georg: *"Jugoslawien. Vielvölkerstat zwieschen Ost und West,"* Köln, 1971

Reiter, Erich: *"Der Krieg um das Kosovo 1998/99,"* Mainz, 2000.

Reuters, Jens: *"Die Albaner in Jugoslawien,"* München, 1982.

Rushiti, Liman: *"Lëvizja kaçake në Kosovë 1918-1928,"* Rilindja, Prishtina, 1981.

Rushiti, Limon: *"Rrethanat politiko-shoqërore në Kosovë 1912-1918,"* Prishtina, 1986.

Rieger, Henriette: *"Einmal Daytonn und zurück.Perspektiven einer Nachkriegsordnung im ehemaligen Jugoslawien,"* Wien, 1999.

Reiter, Erich (Hrsg): *"Der Krieg um das Kosovo"* 1998/99, München, 2000.

Rüb, Matthias: *"Balkan Transit. Das Erbe Jugoslawiens,"* Vienna, 1998.

Rüb, Matthias. *"Kosovo. Ursachen und Folgen eines Krieges in Europa,"* Munich, 1999.

Universiteti i Tiranas (group of authors): *"Historia e popullit Shqiptar I, II,"* Prishtina, 1969.

San Guliamo, A: *"Briefe über Albanien,"* Leipzig,1913.

Salihu, Kurtesh: *"Lindja, zhvillimi, pozita dhe aspektet e autonomitetit te Krahinës Socialiste Autonome të Kosovës në Jugosllavinë Socialiste,"* Prishtina, 1984.

Šišić, E: *„Dokumenti o postanku kraljevine SHS 1914-1918,"* Zagreb, 1928.

Sufflay, Milan: *"Srbi i Arbabasi. Njihova simbioza u srednjem veku,"* Beograd, 1925.

Sufflay, Milan: *"Histori e Shqiptarëve të veriut,"* Prishtina, 2009.

Scharping, Rudolf: *"Wier dürfen nicht wegsehen. Der Kosovo-Krieg und Europa,"* Berlin, 1999.

Schubert,Peter: *"Die Albanische Frage und ihr Einfluss auf Siherheitslage des Balkans,"* Eberhausen, 1996.

Schubert,Peter: *"Zündstoff im Konflikfeld des Balkans: Die Albanische Frage,"* Baden-Baden, 1997.

Schmid, Thomas: *"Krieg im Kosovo,"* Hamburg 1999.

Schuman, Hass Gerhard: *"Anatomi des Agression – Neue Documents zu den Kiriegzielen der faschistisschen Imperialismus zu Zweiten Weltkrieg,"* Ost-Berlin, 1972.

Sundhaussen, Holm: *"Experiment Jugoslawien.Von der Staatsgrundung bis zum Staatszerfall,"* Manhaim/Laipzig/Wien/Zurich, 1993.

Sopjani, Enver: *"Përmbledhje aktesh ndërkombëtare për Kosovën 1999-2004,"* Prishtina, 2005.

Schwartz, Stephen: *"Kosova – Prejardhja e një lufte,"* Prishtina, 2006.

Schwartz, Stephen: *"Islami tjetër – sofizmi dhe rrëfimi për respektin,"* Prishtina, 2009.

Schmidt-Eendboom, Erich: *"Der Schattenkrieger – Klasus Kinkel und der BND,"* Düsseldorf, 1995.

Schmidt-Eendboom, Erich: *"Kosovo-Krieg und Interesse – einseitige Anmerkungen zur Geopolitk,"* Weilheim, 1999.

Tahiri, Edita: *"Konferenca e Rambujesë. Procesi negociator & Documentst,"* Prishtina, 2001.

Tahiri, Abdyl dr: *"Hasan Prishinta,"* Prishtina, 2003.

Trotsky, Leon: *"The Balkans Wars,"* New York, 1980.

Troebst, Stefan: *"Conflict in Kosovo: Failure of Preventions? An Analytic Documentation 1992-1998,"* Flensburg, 1998.

Thopia, Karl: *"Das Fürstentum Albanien, eine zeitgeschihtliche Studie,"* Budapest, 1916.

Vlora, Qemal Ismali: *"Kujtime,"* Tirana, 1997.

Vlora, Eqrem bej: *"Kujtime,"* vol. I, 1885-1912, Tirana, 2001.

Vlora, Eqrem bej: *"Kujtime,"* vol. II, 1912-1925, Tirana, 2001.

Vickers, Miranda/Pettifer, James: *"Albania:from anarchy to a Balkan identity,"* New York, 2000.

Vickers, Miranda: *"Between Serb and Albanian. A History of Kosovo."* London, 1998.

Verli, Marenglen: *"Kosova sfida Shqiptare në historinë e një shekulli,"* Tirana, 2007.

Vukmanović, Svetozar Tempo: "Memoari I, II 1966-1969," Beograd-Zagreb, 1985.

Xhemaili, Mustafë: *"Hysen Tërpeza – një legjendë Kosove,"* publicistikë, Prishtina.

Welfens, Paul J: *"Der Kosvo-Krieg und die Zukunft Europas. Dieplomatieversagen,Kriegseskalation, Wideraufbau, Euroland,"* Munih, 1999.

Weller, Marc: *"The Kosovo Cobflikt:Conduct and Termination of Hostiltetes and the Renewed Search for a Sattelment,"* Londër, 1999.

Weller, Marc: "Shtetësia e kontestuar," Prishtina, 2009.

Wied, W:*"Denkschrift über Alabanien,"* manuscript, 1917.

Wilede, Zommy: "Von der Untergrundtruppe zur Ordnungsmacht," 1999.

Woorwards, Susan: *"Balkan Tragedy: Chaos and Dissolution after tge Cold War,"* Washington, 1995.

Wolf, Winfried: *"Bombengeschäfte. Zur Okonömie des Kosovo-Krieges,"* Hamburg, 1996.

Zhitia, Skënder: *"Ushtria Çlirimtare e Kosovës – Zona operative e Llapit,"* Prishtina, 2008.

Scholarly Articles

Altman, Franz Lotar: *"Die Balkanpolitik der EU,"* në Südosteuropa 10-11, pp. 503-515.

Bartel, Petr: *"Historische Ursachen eines aktuellen Konflikts,"* botuar në "Die Friedens Warte," pp. 351-360.

Clark, Howard: *"Das Ende des gewaltfreien Widerstandes im Kosovo. Fur eine civile Politik im Kosovo."* Viereteljaresshefte für Friden und Gerechtigkeit, pp. 179-186.

Clewing, Konrad: *"Amerikanische und französische Kosovopolitik vor Dayton,"* Südosteuropa 1996, pp. 4-24.

-*"Die radikale Kosovopolitik der politischen Opposition in Serbien: Noch ein Grund fur eine Internationalisierung des serbisch-Albanischen Dialogs,"* Südosteuropa, 1996, pp. 179-186.

Kraft, Ekkerard:*" Der Balkan nach Dayton. Auf dem Weg zu einer trugerischen Stabiliat?,"* from "Aspekte deutscher Sicherheitspolitik," Baden-Baden 1997, pp. 33-55.

Elsie, Robert: *"The Albanian Media in Kosovo and the Spectre of Ethnik Cleasing."* Südosteuropa, 1995, pp. 614-619.

Eiff, Hansjörg: *"Die deutsh-jugoslawieschen Beziehungen,"* published in "Internationael Politik," 988, p. 4.

Elsassr, Jürgen: *"Die Falle von Ramboulliet,"* Kokret 5/1999.

Moore, Patrick:*" Der Kosovo-Konflikt un seine sicherheitspolitische Implikationetn"* in "Südosteuropa Mitteilugnen," 1968, no. 4.

Naumam, Klaus: *"Der nachste Konflikt wird kommen. Erfarungen aus dem Kosovo-Einsatz.,"* published in "Europaische Sicherheit" 11/1999, pp. 8-22.

Oschlies, Wolf: *"Slawiesche Bruder und russishe Balkan-Politik,"* në "Osteuropa," no. 6/1999.

Reuter, Jens/Katsaropoulu,Meppomeni: *"Die Konfrenz von Ramboulliet und die Folgen."* "Südosteuropa" 48, pp. 3-4, 1999.

Lange, Klaus: *"Die UÇK – Anmerkungen zu geschihte, Struktur und Zielen,"* in "Associated Press," 34/1999, pp. 33-39.

Lenddvai, Paul: *"Jugoslawien ohne Jugoslawien. Die Würtzlen der Staatkriese,"* published in "Associated Press," 45/1990, pp. 375-580.

Lipius, Stefan: *"Politische Fürung zerstriten,"* published in "Südosteuropa" 8/1999, pp. 359-372.

Lipius, Stefan: *"Untergrundsogranisationen im Kosvo. Ein Uberblik,"* published in "Osterreichischer Militarrische Zeitschrift," 2/1977, pp. 177-178.

Lipius, Stefan: *"Zwischen Fronten: Die Befraingsarmee Kosovas (UÇK),"* published in "Schweitzer Monats-hefte" , 5/1999, pp. 9-11.

Maliqi, Shkëlzen: *"Der gewakfreie Widerstand i Kosovo,"* published in "Komune." "Forum für Poltik, Okonomie, Kultur." 1995, pp. 15-21.

Oeter, Stefan:" *Selbstbestimmungsrecht im Wandel,"* published in "Zeitschrift fur ausländisches offentliches Recht und Völkerrecht" 52/1992, pp. 741-780.

Raffone, Paolo: *"Der Weg nach Dayton. Diplomatische Stationen enies Fridensprozesses,"* published in "Blätter für deutsche und internacionale Politik," 1996, pp. 231-240.

Reuter, Jens: *"Die Albanische Intelligenz in Kosovo,"* published in "Südosteuropa" 1990, pp. 309-317.

Reuter, Jens: *"Die Enstehung des Kosovo-Problems,"* published in "Associated Press," 34/1999, pp. 3-10.

Reuter, Jens: *"Die 'isolatinon' der Albanischen Intelligenz. Südamerikanische methoden in Kosovo. Dokumentation,"* published in "Südosteuropa,"1989, pp. 1-15.

Reuter, Jens: *"Wer ist die UÇK?,"* published in "Blätter fur deutsche und internacionale Politik," 3/1999, pp. 281-284.

Troenst, Stefan: *"Chronologie einer gescheiterten Pravention. Vom Konflikt zum Krieg im Kosovo 1989-1999,"* published in "Osteuropa," 8/1999, pp. 35-54.

Documents

"Diplomatische Aktenstücke betrefend die Eereingnise auf dem Balkan," herausgegeben von Österreichisch-Ungarischen Ministerium des Äußen 1914 (*„Aktet diplomatike rreth ngjarjeve ballkanike,"* published by Foreign Ministry of Austria-Hungary – 1914).

HHStA – Haus-Hof-und Staatsarchiv, Politisches Archiv, Wien. Albanien, III –XXXVIII (1871-1918); Türkei, IV (1879-1882).

Die grosse Politik der Europäischen Kabinette 1871-1914, Berlin.

Political Archive of German Foreign Ministry, Bonn.

Materials of German Government in Bonn for the period 1990-1998.

Reports analyzed in the German Bundestag in Bonn in the period 1991-1998. Among them an SPD Request in the meeting of 18 March 1992 on the topic *"Violence in Kosovo and return of autonomy."* Documentation of Germn Ministry of Defense, Bonn, May-July, 1999. Süd-Ostinstitut, München

Auerswald, Philip E/Auerswald, David: *"The Kosovo Conflict. A Diplomatic History Through Documentes,* Cambridge/Den Haag, 2000.

Auswartiges Amt: *"Deutsche Aussenpolitik 1995. Telgramme asu Dayton. Eine Dokumentation,"* Bonn, 1998.

Bundesmisterium der Verteidigung: *"Der Kosovo-Konflikt. Eine Dokumnetation,"* Stand: 10 May, 1999.

- *"Der Kosovo-Konflikt. Eine Dokumentation,"* Stand: 28 May, 1999.

- *"Der Kosovo-Konflikt. Eine Dokumentation,"* Stand: 11 June, 1999.

Bundesminister des Innern: *"Verfassungschutz"* (annual report of German Intellegence Service) 1977-1999.

Documents: Arkivi i Kosovës, Prishtina.

Documents: AQSH, Tirana.

Documents: Arhiv Jugoslavije, Beograd.

Documents: Državni Arhiv Jugoslavije , Beograd.

Documents: Arhiv Vojng Instituta Jugoslavije, Beograd.

Documents: Arhiv CK, SKJ, Beograd.

Jusuf Buxhovi

KOSOVA
Volume 3

Printed by
"PROGRAF"
Prishtina, Kosova

Buxhovi, Jusuf
    Kosova: (From Occupation to
International Protectorate)
Jalifat Publishing, 2013
Houston, Texas
www.jalifatpublishing.com

Volume 3

ISBN 978-0-9767140-7-1
ISBN 978-0-9767140-8-8